The

Bessie Parmet Kannerstein '32

𝔐emorial 𝔉und

Established by

MR. JOSEPH PARMET

for the purchase of

REFERENCE BOOKS

for the

CEDAR CREST COLLEGE

LIBRARY

PSYCHOANALYSIS, PSYCHOLOGY, AND LITERATURE █ █ A BIBLIOGRAPHY

Second Edition

Edited by NORMAN KIELL

Volume 1

THE SCARECROW PRESS, INC.
Metuchen, N.J., & London █ 1982

821466

Library of Congress Cataloging in Publication Data

Kiell, Norman.
    Psychoanalysis, psychology, and literature, a
bibliography.

    Includes index.
    1. Psychology and literature--Indexes.
I. Title.
Z6514. P78K53   1981   [PN56. P93] 016. 801'92   81-2475
ISBN 0-8108-1421-8   AACR2

FOR MATTHEW

CONTENTS

INTRODUCTION

When the first edition of this bibliography was published in 1963 by the University of Wisconsin Press, it contained 4460 items. In its Introduction, I wrote that the proliferation of psychological writing about literature had reached a point that led me to compile in "one volume a listing of material which is now scattered and difficult to track down." In the 17 years intervening between the two editions, the listing has burgeoned to approximately five times the number of items, i. e. , about 20, 000.

I have incorporated the first edition into the present volume. Thus the reader will find most of the original entries sprinkled among the now swollen quintuple figure. Two sections have been eliminated entirely (Comics and Journalism) and two have been substituted (Therapy and Technical Studies). The astonishing increase in the number of critical scholarly articles and books is reflected in the unparalleled multiplication of journals which have appeared on the scene. Many of these journals are devoted to a single author, including Anaïs Nin, Flannery O'Connor, Schnitzler, Twain, Conrad, Thoreau, Pound, Yeats, Woolf, and Joyce.

The usefulness of a bibliography is in its accuracy and comprehensiveness. I have tried for both, but agree wholeheartedly with Norman Holland that "Perfection in matters bibliographical ... is to be hoped for rather than achieved" (Psychoanalysis and Shakespeare). Similarly, there is no contest with Bernice Slote's cogent comment, "One salutary thing for scholars to observe is that most bibliographies remain unfinished" (American Literary Scholarship, 1973).

While a bibliography is never completed, it does not necessarily mean it is out of date. I have made every effort to check the original entries of the first edition and bring

them up to date when articles have been reprinted in collections or anthologies and when books have gone into a new or
revised edition. For example, Edmund Wilson's Freudian interpretation of "The Turn of the Screw" has only one listing
in the original bibliography, but subsequent printings of his
article bring the number of reprints to five. They will be
found herein. I have tried to avoid duplicate entries. Thus,
where a book or article is concerned with multiple interests,
it has generally been placed under the rubric of Criticism.

The oldest traceable entry which I located is McKenzie's
"Criticism on the Character and Tragedy of Hamlet," dated
1790. The listings which foreshadow contemporary psychological modalities follow 50 and 60 years later, such as Webb's
"An Essay on the Influence of Poetry on the Mind" (1839), and
Amariah Brigham's "Insanity, Illustrated by Histories of Distinguished Men and by the Writings of Poets and Novelists,"
which appeared in the American Journal of Insanity in 1844.

Bibliographic material was gathered from a variety of
sources. In addition to the references listed below, I checked
all of the psychological and psychoanalytic journals published
in English, primarily from 1900 to 1980. There are a thousand or more entries published prior to 1900 but the vast cor-
pus of material is to be found in the past half-century.

Titles in the original French, German, Italian and
Spanish have generally been retained. Wherever possible,
the translations for the more esoteric languages, such as Dan-
ish, East European, Russian, Hebrew, Arabic, and Japanese
are rendered into English.

It is hoped that the Subject Index at the end of the
Bibliography will be used extensively. No one could be ex-
pected to read all of the 20,000 items in this bibliography,
and I haven't. What I have done is to rely heavily on the
abstracts and reviews in the following journals: Literature
and Psychology, Psychological Abstracts, MLA Abstracts,
Abstracts of English Studies, Annual Survey of Psychoanalysis,
and American Literary Scholarship; An Annual, The Modern
Language Review, and Modern Fiction Studies. And I have
skimmed through as many psychoanalytic and psychological
journals as I could, as well as every issue of the Hartford
Studies in Literature, American Imago, Literature and Psychology, and the Psychoanalytic Review.

Secondary sources include the following:

Abstracts of the Collected Works of Carl G. Jung.
Abstracts of English Studies, Vols. 1-20, 1957-1977.
Abstracts of Folklore Studies, Vols. 1-9, 1963-1971.
American Literary Scholarship; An Annual, 1963-1980.
Annual Bibliography of English Language and Literature. Cam-
      bridge: Bowes & Bowes, Cambridge University Press,
      Vols. 1-32; London: Modern Humanities Research Associa-
      tion, Vols. 37-51, 1964-1980.
Annual Survey of Psychoanalysis, Vols. 1-8, 1961-1968.
Bibliographie de la littérature française du Moyen Age à nos
      jours. Paris: Colin, 1967-1979.
Bibliography of the History of Medicine.
Cumulative Index Medicus, Vols. 1-211, 1960-1980.
Education Index, Vols. 1-29, 1929-1979.
Essay and General Literary Index, Vols. 1-13, 1900-1979.
French Bibliography, Vols. 1-4, 1940-1967; French XIX Bib-
      liography; French XX Bibliography.
Humanities Index, Vols. 1-6, 1974-1979.
Index Medicus (N. S.), Vols. 1-2. 1960-1961.
International Index of Periodicals, Vols. 1-18, 1907-1965.
Journal of Aesthetics and Art Criticism, Vols. 1-37, 1941-
      1979.
MLA Abstracts in Scholarly Journals, 1970-1975.
PMLA International Bibliography. Publications of the Modern
      Language Association, Vols. 63-95, 1958-1979.
Psychological Index, Vols. 1-42, 1900-1942.
The Romantic Movement Bibliography, Vols. 1-6, 1936-1970.
Social Science Index, Vols. 1-6, 1974-1979.
Social Science and Humanities Index, Vols. 19-27, 1965-1974.
Year's Work in English Studies, Vols. 1-40, 1919-1959. Lon-
      don: Oxford University Press.
The Year's Work in Modern Language Studies, Vols. 1-25,
      1932-1964. Cambridge: Cambridge University Press.
The Year's Work in Modern Language Studies, Vols. 25-41,
      1964-1980. London: Modern Humanities Research Asso-
      ciation.

*   *   *

Baldensperger, Fernand, & Friedrich, Werner P. (eds).
      Bibliography of Comparative Literature. NY: Russell &
      Russell, 1960, 705p.
Berlin, Jeffrey B. Arthur Schnitzler Bibliography. Modern
      Austrian Literature, Vols. 4-10, 1971-1977.
Bullough, Vern L. , Legg, W. Dorr, Elcano, Barrett W. , &
      Kepner James (eds). An Annotated Bibliography of Homo-
      sexuality, 2 Vols. NY: Garland, 1976.

Caldwell, Richard S.   Selected bibliography on psychoanalysis and classical studies.   Arethusa, 1974, 7:115-134.

Carpenter, Charles A.   Modern drama studies: an annual bibliography.   In Modern Drama, 1974-1980, Vols. 17-23.

Chanover, E. Pierre.   Walt Whitman: a psychological and psychoanalytical bibliography.   Psychoanalytic Review, 1972, 59:467-474.

Chanover, E. Pierre.   Marcel Proust: a medical and psychological bibliography.   Psychoanalytic Review, 1969-70, 56:638-641.

Chanover, E. Pierre.   A psychological bibliography of Jean Racine.   American Imago, 1971, 28:84-90.

Chanover, E. Pierre.   Jean-Jacques Rousseau: a psychoanalytic and psychological bibliography.   American Imago, 1974, 31:95-100.

Deming, Robert H. (ed).   A Bibliography of James Joyce Studies.   2nd Edition, Revised and Enlarged.   Boston: Hall, 1977.

Dewhurst, Kenneth, & Reeves, Nigel.   Friedrich Schiller. Medicine, Psychology and Literature.   Berkeley: Univ. California Press, 1978.

Drevet, Marguerite L. (ed).   Bibliographie de la Littérature Française 1940-1949.   Geneva: Libraire E. Droz, 1954, 644p.

Edmunds, L., & Ingber, R.   Psychoanalytic Writings on the Oedipus legend: a bibliography.   American Imago, 1977, 34:374-386.

Gerlach, John C., & Gerlach, Lana (eds).   The Critical Index.   A Bibliography of Articles on Film in English, 1946, 1973, Arranged by Name and Topics.   NY: Teachers College Press, 1974.

Greenberg, Bette.   Fedor Mikhailovich Dostoevsky (1821-1881).   Medico-psychological and psychoanalytic studies on his life and writings: a bibliography.   Psychoanalytic Review, 1975, 62:509-513.

Greenberg, Bette, & Rothenberg, Albert.   William Shakespeare (1564-1616):   medico-psychological and psychoanalytic studies on his life and works: a bibliography.   International Review of Psychoanalysis, 1974, 1:245-256.

Greig, J. Y. T.   The Psychology of Laughter and Comedy. NY: Cooper Square Publishers, 1969, pp. 280-298.

Grinstein, Alexander (ed).   Index of Psychoanalytic Writings, 14 Vols. NY: International Universities Press, 1956-1975.

Hammond, W. A.   A Bibliography of Aesthetics and of the Philosophy of Fine Arts from 1900 to 1932.   Revised Ed. NY: Longmanns, Green, 1934.

Holland, Norman N.   Psychoanalysis and Shakespeare.   NY: McGraw-Hill, 1966.

Kearney, E. I. , & Fitzgerald, L. S. (eds). The Continental Novel: A Checklist of Criticism in English, 1900-1966. Metuchen, NJ: Scarecrow Press, 1968.

Litto, Frederic M. (ed). American Dissertations on the Drama and the Theatre. A Bibliography. Kent, Ohio: Kent State University Press, 1969.

Perloff, Evelyn (ed). A selected bibliography on psychology and literature: Psychological Abstracts, 1960-1969. Catalog of Selected Documents in Psychology, 1974, 4:68-69. MS. 661.

Roback, Abraham A. (ed). A Bibliography of Character and Personality. Cambridge, Mass: Sci-Art Publishers, 1927.

Rothgeb, Carrie Lee, Clemens, Siegfried M. , & Lloyd, Edith M. (eds). Abstracts of The Psychoanalytic Study of the Child, Vols. 1-25. Rockville, Md: U. S. Department of Health Education & Welfare. National Institute of Mental Health, 1972.

Rothgeb, Carrie Lee (ed). Abstract of the Standard Edition of the Complete Psychological Works of Sigmund Freud. Washington, D. C. : Department of Health, Education & Welfare, 1971, 1972; NY: International Universities Press, 1973.

Sackatt, Theodore A. (ed). Pérez Galdós. An Annotated Bibliography. Albuquerque: University of New Mexico Press, 1968.

Smith, Gordon R. (ed). A Classified Shakespeare Bibliography, 1936-1958. University Park: Penn State University Press, 1958, 1963.

Stein, Morris, & Heinze, Shirley J. (eds). Creativity and the Individual. Summaries of Selected Literature. Chicago: Free Press, 1960.

Templeman, William D. (ed). Bibliographies of Studies in Victorian Literature for the Thirteen Years 1932-1944. Urbana: University of Illinois Press, 1945.

Vowles, Richard B. Psychology and drama: a selected checklist. Wisconsin Studies in Contemporary Literature, 1962, 3:35-48.

Willbern, David. William Shakespeare: a bibliography of psychoanalytic and psychological criticism, 1964-1975. International Review of Psychoanalysis, 1978, 5:361-372.

Wright, Austin (ed). Bibliographies of Studies in Victorian Literature for the Ten Years 1943-1954. Urbana: University of Illinois Press, 1956.

It is a pleasure for me to acknowledge my indebtedness to Mr. Irving Adelman, Chief Reference Librarian at the East Meadow Public Library, for his generous help and cooperation. His assistance helped ease many difficulties inevitable in a bibliographic venture. I owe particular thanks to Norman N. Holland, Jeffrey B. Berlin and Leonard F. Manheim for their encouragement, suggestions and graciousness during the early stages of preparation of this bibliography. I am also very, very grateful for the contributions my wife, Adele, has made, in more ways than I can enumerate.

January 6, 1981
Long Beach, New York

KEY TO ABBREVIATIONS

General

Amer	American
Anal	Analysis, Analytic
Assn	Association
Int	International, Internationale
J	Journal
Lit	Literature, Literary
Psychiat	Psychiatry, Psychiatric
Psychoanal	Psychoanalysis, Psychoanalytic
Psychol	Psychology, Psychological
Q	Quarterly
Rev	Review
Univ	University

Journals and Books

Almanach	Almanach der Psycho-Analyse
DA, DAI	Dissertation Abstracts; Dissertation Abstracts International
ETC	ETC: A Review of General Semantics
IUP	International Universities Press
Int J Psycho-Anal	International Journal of Psycho-Analysis
JAAC	Journal of Arts and Aesthetic Criticism
JAMA	Journal of the American Medical Association

JAPA	Journal of the American Psychoanalytic Association
JNMD	Journal of Nervous and Mental Disease
JPNP	Journal de Psychologie Normale et Pathologique
MAHS	Medical Aspects of Human Sexuality
PMLA	Publications of the Modern Language Association
Samiksa	Samiksa: Journal of the Indian Psycho-Analytic Society
Standard Edition	The Standard Edition of the Complete Psychological Works of Sigmund Freud. Ed: James Strachey. London: Hogarth Press, 1966; NY: Basic Books.

AUTOBIOGRAPHY, BIOGRAPHY, DIARIES, LETTERS

1. Abel, Theodora. Yukio Mishima: a psychoanalytic interpretation. J Amer Academy Psychoanal, 1978, 6:403-424.
2. Abellán, M. Manuel de Unamuno. Madrid: 1964.
3. Abely, Paul. En relisant Balzac psychiatrie occasionnel. Annales Médico-Psychologiques, 1958, 2:751-761.
4. Abrahamsen, David. The Mind and Death of a Genius. NY: Columbia Univ. Press, 1946.
5. Achelis, Werner. Die Deutung Augustins. Analyse eines geistigen Schaffens. Chiemsee: Kampann u Schnabel, 1921.
6. Adam, Antoine. Le Vrai Verlaine: Essai Psychanalytique. Paris: Droz, 1936.
7. Adams, James Truslow. New modes in biography. Current History, 1929, 31:257-264; In The Tempo of Modern Life. NY: Boni, 1931, 171-186.
8. Adams, Mauiranne. Family disintegration and creative disintegration: the case of Charlotte Brontë and Jane Eyre. In Wohl, A. S. (ed), The Victorian Family; Structure and Stresses. NY: St. Martin's. 1978, 148-179.
9. Adler, Alfred. Dostoievsky. In The Practice and Theory of Individual Psychology. Paterson, NJ: Littlefield, Adams, 1959, 1963 (1927), 280-290.
10. Adolf, E. Knut Hamsun's Veranlagung und Weltbild. In Beth, K., & Braunmüller, W. (eds). Religionspsychologie, Vol. III. Vienna u Leipzig, 22-28.
11. Adorno, Theodor. Versuch über Wagner. Munich: Droemer-Knaur, 1964.
12. Agamit, S. Shaul Tchernichovsky, 1875-1943. Hebrew Medical J, 1964, 1:250-300.
13. Agris, J. Walt Whitman: poet, philosopher, male nurse. J Dermatologic Surgery & Oncology, 1979, 5(11):917.
14. Aigrisse, Gilberte. Psychanalyse de Paul Valéry. Paris: Edit. Universitaires, 1964.
15. _____. Vers une psychanalyse de Mallarmé. Action et Pensée, 1950
16. Aiken, Conrad. John Keats. Dial, 1925, 27:476-490.
17. _____. Poet of creative dissolution. Wake, 1952, 11:102.
18. _____. Ushant: An Essay. NY: Duell, Sloan & Pearce, 1952.
19. Alajouanine, Th. Alphasia and artistic realization. Brain, 1948, 71:229-241.
20. Albérès, R. M. Jean-Paul Sartre. London: Merlin, 1961.

21. Albrecht, Milton C.   A study of Julien Green.   J Abnormal
    Social Psychol, 1946.
22. Albright, Daniel.   Personality and Impersonality: Lawrence,
    Woolf and Mann.   Chicago: Univ. Chicago Press, 1978.
23. Aldridge, A. O.   Form and substance in Franklin's Autobiog-
    raphy.   In Gohdes, C.   (ed), Essays on American Literature.
    Durham, N. C. : Duke Univ. Press, 1967, 47-62.
24. Aldridge, John W.   The anatomy of passion in the consummate
    Henry James.   Saturday Rev, 12 Feb. 1972, 65-68.
25. Alexander, Doris M.   The Tempering of Eugene O'Neill.   NY:
    Harcourt, Brace & World, 1962.
26. Alexander, Theodor W.   From the scientific to the supernatural
    in Schnitzler.   South Central Bulletin, 1971, 31:164-167.
27. _____. Olga Waissnix: the model for the character of the
    married woman in the early works of Arthur Schnitzler.
    Modern Austrian Lit, 1974, 7(1-2):99-107.
28. Allen, Clifford.   Homosexuality and Oscar Wilde: a psycholog-
    ical study.   Int J Sexology, 1949, 2:2-5, 215; In Ruitenbeek,
    H. M. (ed), Homosexuality and Creative Genius.   NY: Ob-
    olensky, 1967, 60-83.
29. _____. The personality of Radclyffe Hall.   Int J Sexology,
    1950, 4:95-98; In Ruitenbeek, H. M. (ed), Homosexuality and
    Creative Genius.   NY: Obolensky, 1967, 183-188.
30. _____. The problem of John Ruskin: a psycho-sexological
    analysis.   Int J Sexology, 1950, 4:7-14.
31. Allen, D. C.   The genesis of Donne's dreams.   Modern Lan-
    guage Notes, 1960, 75:293-295.
32. Allen, Gay Wilson.   The Solitary Singer, A Critical Biography
    of Walt Whitman.   NY: Macmillan, 1955; NY: New York
    Univ. Press, 1967.
33. Allen, Hervey.   Israfel: The Life and Times of Edgar Allan
    Poe.   NY: Farrar & Rinehart, 1934.
34. Allen, Louis.   Letters of Huysmans and Zola to Raffalovich.
    Forum for Modern Language Studies, 1966, 2:214-221.
35. Allen, Walker M.   Paul Laurence Dunbar: a study in genius.
    Psychoanal Rev, 1938, 25:53-82.
36. Allentuch, Harriet M. R.   A Descriptive Analysis of the Per-
    sonality of Madame de Sévigné.   DAI, 1974, 34:4238A-39A.
37. Allport, Gordon W.   The study of personality by the intuitive
    method.   An experiment in teaching from The Locomotive-
    God.   J Abnormal Social Psychol, 1929, 24:14-27.
38. _____. The Use of Personal Documents in Psychological
    Science.   NY: Social Science Research Council, 1945.
39. Alonso del Campo, U.   Processo psicológico de la conversion
    religiosa de S. Augustin.   Rome: S. Pio X, 1972.
40. Alston, Edwin Frederick.   James Barrie's M'Connachie--his
    'writing half. '   Amer Imago, 1972, 29:257-277.
41. Alter, Robert, & Cosman Carol.   A Lion for Love.   A Critical
    Biography of Stendhal.   NY: Basic Books, 1979.
42. Altick, Richard D.   The Oath.   In Lives and Letters; A History
    of Literary Biography in England and America.   NY: Knopf,
    1965, 301-343.
43. Alvarez, Alfred.   In the gloomy country of Graham Greene's
    heart.   Saturday Rev, 25 Sept. 1971, 33-35.

44. _____. The Savage God, A Study of Suicide. NY: Random House, 1972; London: Weidenfeld & Nicolson, 1972.
45. _____. Sylvia Plath: a memoir. In The New American Review. NY: Simon & Schuster, 1971, 9-40.
46. _____. The wretched poet who lived in the house of bedlam. Saturday Rev, 1970, 53:27-29.
47. Alvarez, Walter C. Minds That Came Back. Philadelphia: Lippincott, 1961.
48. Amador Sánchez, Luis. La personalidad de Pío Baroja. La Nueva Democracia, 1958, 38:60-63.
49. Amar, Robert. Trois homosexuels mariés. Arcadie, 1962, 100:225-232; 1962, 102:386-392; 1962, 103-104; 427-428; 1964, 132:549-558.
50. Amo, Javier del. Litetratura y psicología. La neurosis del escritor español. Madrid: Edicusa, 1976.
51. Amster, J. Dream Keepers: The Young Brontës. NY: William Frederick, 1973.
52. Anastasi, Anne, & Schaefer, C. E. Biographical correlates of artistic and literary creativity in adolescent girls. J Applied Psychol, 1969, 53:267-273.
53. Anderson, Camilla M. Saints, Sinners and Psychiatry. Philadelphia: Lippincott, 1950.
54. Anderson, E. W. Strindberg's illness. Psychol Medicine, 1971, 1:104-117.
55. Anderson, James William. An interview with Leon Edel on the James family. Psychohistory Rev, 1979, 8(1-2):15-22.
56. Anderson, M. The neurological illness of Sir Walter Scott. Practitioner, 1976, 217:968-974.
57. Andreasen, Nancy J. C. Ariel's flight. The death of Sylvia Plath. JAMA, 1974, 228-595-599.
58. _____. James Joyce: a portrait of the artist as a schizoid. JAMA, 1973, 224:67-71.
59. Andreas-Salomé, Louise. The Freud Journal of Lou Andreas-Salomé. NY: Basic Books, 1973, 1965.
60. Angrisani, D. Saggio su William Somerset Maugham, medico-scrittore. Ospedale Psichiatria, 1966, 34:198-211.
61. Annan, Noël. Love and friendship. New Statesman. 26 Oct 1973, 601-602.
62. Annis, Arthur P. The autobiography: its uses and value in professional psychology. J Counseling Psychol, 1967, 14: 9-17.
63. Anon. At the end of the line. Times Lit Supplement, 26 Nov 1970, 1479-1480.
64. _____. The case of Oscar Wilde. Lancet, 1948, 2:440.
65. _____. Death of a poet. New Republic, 11 May 1932.
66. _____. Les Homosexuels. Le Crapouillot, 1955, No. 30.
67. _____. Idaho iconoclast. The indomitable individuality of Vardis Fisher. M. D. Medical Newsmagazine, 1961, 5:143-146.
68. _____. Introducing the reader to Anaïs Nin. J Otto Rank Assn, 1966, 1(1):30-31.
69. _____. Magna est veritas. Psychiat Q, 1946, 20:150-156.
70. _____. Marcel Proust as data for psychology. Internationale Zeitschrift für Individual-Psychologie, 1929, 1:57-59.

71. _____. The matter of the master. Times Lit Supplement, 18 Aug 1972, 957-959.
72. _____. In memoriam D. A. Levy (1942-1968). Serif, 1971, 8(4):2-28.
73. _____. Multisided servant. Life and thought of Sir Francis Bacon. M. D. Medical Newsmagazine, 1961, 5:195-198.
74. _____. The mythopoetics of mescal. Times Lit Supplement, 19 Apr 1974, 417-418.
75. _____. The personality of Gide. Times Lit Supplement, 14 Dec 1951.
76. _____. Psychoanalyzing great poets and novelists. Current Opinion, 1919, 47:51-52.
77. Anshin, Roman. Creativity, mid-life crisis, and Herman Hesse. J Amer Academy Psychoanal, 1976, 4:215-226.
78. Anthony, Katherine Susan. The Lambs. A Story of Pre-Victorian England. NY: Knopf, 1945; London: Hammond, 1949.
79. _____. Margaret Fuller: A Psychological Biography. NY: Harcourt, Brace, 1920.
80. Antonini, G. Psicopatologia di Vittorio Alfieri. Archivio di Psichiatria, Antropologia Criminale, 1898, 19:177-252.
81. _____, & Cognetti di Martiis, L. Vittorio Alfieri. Studi Psicopatologici. Turin: Bocca, 1898.
82. Apter, T. E. Bert Lawrence and Lady Jane. In Smith, A. (ed), Lawrence and Women. NY: Barnes & Noble, 1978, 178-188.
83. Araki, James T. The Mishima incident. Yukio Mishima (1925-1970). Hartford Studies in Lit, 1978, 10:182-199.
84. Archambault, Paul. Humanité d'André Gide; Essai de Biographie et Psychologiques. Paris: Bloud et Gay, 1946.
85. Archer, W. Jean Jacques Rousseau, écrivain de l'amitié. Paris: Nizet, 1971.
86. Archibald, Douglas N. Father and son: John Butler and William Butler Yeats. Massachusetts Rev, 1974, 15:481-501.
87. Aring, C. D. Case becomes less strange. Amer Scholar, 1960, 30:67-78.
88. Armaingaud, (?). Montaigue était-il hypocondrique? Chronique Médicale, 1908, 15:177-184.
89. Arms, George, & Wasserstrom, William. That psychological stain and rejoinder. New England Q, 1960, 33:243-245.
90. Arner, Robert D. Westover and the wilderness: William Byrd's images of Virginia. Southern Lit J, 1975, 7(2):105-123.
91. Arnold, A. James, & Piriou, Jean-Pierre. Genèse et critique d'une autobiographie: Les Mots de Jean-Paul Sartre. Paris: Archives des Lettres Modernes, 1973.
92. Arvin, Newton. Hawthorne. Boston: Little, Brown, 1929.
93. Ashe, T. (ed). Miscellanies, Aesthetic and Literary. London: Bell, 1885, 163-168.
94. Asselineau, Roger. Edgar Allan Poe. Minneapolis: Univ. Minnesota Pamphlets on American Writers 89, 1970.
95. _____. The Evolution of Walt Whitman. The Creation of a Personality, Vol. 1. Cambridge: Harvard Univ. Press,

1960; Reviews: Gay Wilson Allen, Walt Whitman Rev, 1963, 9:19-20; F. Stovall, Amer Lit, 1963, 35:96-97.

96. _____. Un Narcisse puritain: Quelques réflexions sur la personnalité de Thoreau. Europe, 1967, No. 459-460, 149-157.

97. Atlas, James. Delmore Schwartz: The Life of an American Poet. NY: Farrar, Straus & Cudahy, 1977.

98. Aubin, H. Le Cas Rimbaud. Evolution Psychiatrique, 1955, 2:329-347.

99. Augustin, H. Adelbert Stifters Krankheit und Tod. Eine biographische Quellenstudie. Basle-Stuttgart: Schwabe, 1964.

100. Austarheim, Kristen. Henrik Wergeland. En psykiatrisk studie. Bind II. Fra gratialet og giftermålet til hans død. Oslo: Oslo Universitat Press, 1974.

101. _____. Wergelands Digte. Første Ring. Forsøk på en biografisk-psykolgist analyse. Edda, 1967, 67.

102. Axberger, Gunnar. Diktarfantasi och eld, del I. Stockholm: Natur och Kultur, 1967.

103. Axtell, Bryan. Symbolic representation of an unresolved Oedipal conflict: Gulliver in Lilliput. Psychology, 1967, 4:22-23.

104. Aznar, Blas. Personalidad biológica de Azorin. Salamanca: Institut de Historia de la Medecina Española, 1973.

105. Bachelard, Gaston. Lautréamont. Paris: Corti, 1964.

106. Bachler, Karl. Alfred Kubin und die Flucht ins Traumreich. Psychoanalytische Bewegung, 1933, 5:53-65.

107. _____. August Strindberg. Eine psychoanalytische Studie. Psychoanalytische Bewegung, 1930, 2:365-381, 555-579.

108. Baetzhold, Howard G. Found: Mark Twain's 'Lost Sweet-heart.' Amer Lit, 1972, 44:414-429.

109. Baillie, J. B. The mind of John Bunyan. Hibbert J, 1929, 27:385-405.

110. Bain, Read. Man is the measure; writing, neurotic and normal. Sociometry, 1944, 7:332-337.

111. _____. Spencer's love for George Eliot. Psychoan Rev, 1926, 14:37-55.

112. Baines, Jocelyn. Joseph Conrad: A Critical Biography. NY: McGraw-Hill, 1960.

113. Bajenoff, N. Guy de Maupassant et Dostoevsky; un studie comparative et psychopathologique. Archive d'Anthropologie Criminelle, 1904, 19:1-39.

114. Bakan, David. Some thoughts on reading Augustine's Confessions. J Scientific Study Religion, 1965, 5:149-152.

115. Baker, Carlos. Ernest Hemingway: A Life Story. NY: Avon/Discus, 1980.

116. Balaban, N. I. [The pathological in the personality of Leo Tolstoy.] Sovet Psikhonevrol, 1933, 3:108-112.

117. Balakian, Anna. André Breton: Magus of Surrealism. NY: Oxford Univ. Press, 1971.

118. _____. André Breton and psychiatry. In Peschel, E. R. (ed), Medicine and Literature. NY: Watson, 1980, 160-170.

119. _____. Breton and drugs. Yale French Studies, 1974, 50:96-107.

120. _____. Literary Origins of Surrealism. NY: New York Univ. Press, 1966.

121. Balcom, Lis. The Value of a Comparative Analysis of an Author's Autobiographical and Fictional Writings for Interpretation of Aspects of His Personality: A Study Based on Selected Works of William Dean Howells. DA, 1956, 16:373.

122. Bald, M. A. Shelley's mental progress. Essays & Studies, 1928, 13:112-137.

123. Balderston, Katherine C. Johnson's vile melancholy. In The Age of Johnson: Essays Presented to Chauncey Brewster Tinker. New Haven, Conn: Yale Univ. Press, 1949, 3-14.

124. Balmas, E. [The relevance of Oedipe to Gide.] Rev d'Histoire Litteraire de la France, 1970, 70.

125. Balta, François. Freud et Céline. In Céline: Actes du colloque international de Paris. Paris: Société d'études céliniennes, 1978, 247-258.

126. Banerjee, M. Dr Samuel Johnson: a study in psycho-somatic symptoms. Samiksa, 1976, 30:20-26.

127. Baranger, W. Depresión, introyección y creación literaria en Marcel Proust. Revista de Psicoanálisis, 1952, 9:143-171.

128. Barine, A. Névroses: Hoffmann; Quincey; Edgar Poë; G. de Nerval. Paris: Hachette, 1898.

129. Barker, Warren J. The nonsense of Edward Lear. Psychoanal Q, 1966, 35:568-586.

130. Barnshaw, H. D. Walt Whitman's physicians in Camden. Transactions & Studies College Physicians of Philadelphia, 1964, 31:227-230.

131. Barrett, William. Delmore: a 30's friendship and beyond. Commentary, 1974, 58:41-54.

132. Barrett, William G. Mark Twain's osteopathic cure. Psychoanal Q, 1953, 22:539-547.

133. Baruch, Franklin R. Milton's blindness: the conscious and unconscious patterns of autobiography. J English Lit History, 1975, 42:26-37.

134. Baruch, Grace K. Anne Frank on adolescence. Adolescence, 1968-69, 3:425-434.

135. Barvine, Arvède. Essais de littérature pathologique: l'alcohol: Edgar Poe. Rev de Deux Mondes, 1897, 142:336-373.

136. Barza, Steven. About John Berryman. Colorado Q, 1977, 26(3):51-72.

137. Barzun, Jacques. Biography and criticism: a misalliance disputed. Critical Inquiry, 1975, 1:479-496.

138. Bataille, Georges. La Litterature et le mal. Emily Brontë --Baudelaire--Michelet--Blake--Sade--Proust--Kafka-- Genet. Paris: Gallimard, 1967, 1957.

139. Bate, Walker Jackson. The Achievement of Samuel Johnson. NY: Oxford Univ. Press, 1955.

140. _____. Samuel Johnson. NY: Harcourt Brace Jovanovich, 1977.
141. Bateson, Frederick Wilse. Wordsworth: A Re-interpretation. London: Longmans, 1956, 1954.
142. Baudoin, Charles. Anatole France. Genèse d'un scepticism. Psyché, 1947, 2:1075-1082.
143. _____. Jean Baptiste Racine, l'enfant du désert. Paris: Plon, 1964.
144. _____. Petite suite pascalienne. Action et Pensée, 1941, 17:33-39.
145. _____. Psychanalyse de Victor Hugo. Geneva: Mont Blanc, 1943; Paris: Colin, 1972.
146. _____. Sous le signe du feu: la crise de Racine. Action et Pensée, 1942, 3:68-79.
147. _____. La Sublimation des images chez Huysmans lors sa conversion. Psyché, 1950, 5:378-385.
148. Baumgärtel, Knut. Die Jugend Stendhals. Int Zeitschrift für Individual-Psychologie, 1949, 18:130-133.
149. Baumgarten, Franziska. Character traits derived from biographies. Character & Personality, 1937, 6:147-149.
150. Baylen, Joseph O. Sleep and some late Victorian men of letters. English Lit in Transition 1880-1920, 1967, 10: 201-203.
151. Baym, Nancy Topping. Virginia Woolf's quest for equilibrium. Modern Language Q, 1971, 32:305-319.
152. Bazin, Nancy Topping. Virginia Woolf and the Androgynous Vision. New Brunswick, NJ: Rutgers Univ. Press, 1973.
153. Beauvoir, Simone de. Must we burn Sade? In Dinnage, P. (ed), The Marquis de Sade; an Essay. NY: Grove, 1953, 9-82.
154. Beck, Evelyn Torton. Franz Kafka and Else Lasker-Schüler: alienation and exile: a psychocultural comparison. Perspectives on Contemporary Lit, 1975, 1(2):31-47.
155. Beck, Walter. Die biographische Methode in der Sozial-Psychologie. Psychologische Rundschau, 1952, 3:203-213.
156. Bédé, Jean-Albert. Madame de Staël, Rousseau et le suicide. Rev d'histoire Littéraire de la France, 1966, 66(1):52-70.
157. Beebe, Maurice. The masks of Conrad. Bucknell Rev, 1963, 11:35-53, In Garvin, H.R. (ed), Makers of the Twentieth-Century Novel. Lewisburg, Pa.: Bucknell Univ. Press, 1977, 70-83.
158. Behariell, Frederick J. Freud's double: Arthur Schnitzler. JAPA, 1962, 10:722-730; Schnitzler: Freuds Doppelgänger. Literatur und Kritik, 1967, 2:546-555.
159. Behn, Siegfried. Biographie und Psychoanalyse. Psychologische Beiträge, 1956, 2:375-389.
160. Beirnaert, Louis. St. Ignatius's Diario espiritual. Rev Historique de la Spiritualité, 1975, 51:43-72.
161. Beker, Miroslav. [Human personality in literary work.] Forum (Zagreb), 1975, 29:784-802.
162. Bell, Millicent. Henry James: the man who lived. Massachusetts Rev, 1973, 14:391-414.
163. _____. Virginia Woolf now. Massachusetts Rev, 1973, 14:655-687.

164. Bell, Quentin. Virginia Woolf: A Biography. NY: Harcourt Brace Jovanovich, 1972; London: Hogarth, 1972; Reviews: Suzanne Henig, Virginia Woolf Q, 1973, 1(2):55-69; Cynthia Ozick, Commentary, 1973, 56(2):33-44.

165. Beltran, Juan R. El complejo psicologico de Lope de Vega. Anales del Instituto de Psicologia B. Aires, 1941, 3:81-93.

166. Bem, A. L. Dostoevskij Psichoanalitceskie Etjudy. Berlin: Petropolis, 1938.

167. _____. [The Secret Personality of Dostoevsky.] Prague: Otto, 1928.

168. Benoit, J. C. [Lautréamont. Genius or mental disease?] Presse Médicale, 1965, 73:2175-2177.

169. Benon, R. La Folie de J. -J. Rousseau. Progrés Médicale, 1950, 78:465-470.

170. Benrekassa, G. L'Individual et le sexe: In discourse de l'Emile au texte des Confessions. Rev des Sciences Humaines, 1976, 161:45-61.

171. Benson, Arthur Christopher. Ruskin. A Study in Personality. NY: Putnam, 1911; London: Smith, Elder, 1911.

172. Bensoussan, D. La Maladie de Rousseau. Paris: Klincksieck, 1974.

173. Benton, John F. The personality of Guibert of Nogent. Psychoanal Rev, 1970, 57:563-586.

174. Berendsohn, W. A. Knut Hamsun und die Psychoanalyse. Psychoanalytische Bewegung, 1930, 2:60-68.

175. Beres, David. The contribution of psychoanalysis to the biography of the artist: a commentary on methodology. Int J Psycho-Anal, 1959, 40:26-37.

176. Bergler, Edmund. Die Biographik macht der Psychoanalyse Konzessionen. Psychoanalytische Bewegung, 1933, 5:501-512.

177. Bergler, Edmund. John Ruskin's marital secret and J. E. Millais' painting 'The Order of Release.' Amer Imago, 1948, 5:182-201.

178. _____. Proust and the 'torture theory' of love. Amer Imago, 1953, 10:265-288.

179. _____. The relation of the artist to society: a psychoanalyst's comment on the exchange of letters among V. S. Pritchett, Elizabeth Bowen and Graham Greene. Amer Imago, 1948, 5:247-258.

180. _____. Samuel Johnson's Life of the Poet Richard Savage --a paradigm for a type. Amer Imago, 1947, 4:42-63.

181. _____. Talleyrand--Napoleon--Stendhal--Goethe. Vienna: Int Psychoanalytischer Verlag, 1934.

182. _____. Victor Hugo's identifications. Amer Imago, 1958, 15:433-436.

183. Bergmann, M. S. Limitations of method in psychoanalytic biography: a historical inquiry. JAPA, 1973, 21:833-850.

184. Berlin, Jeffrey B., & Levy, Elizabeth J. On the letters of Theodore Reik to Arthur Schnitzler. Psychoanal Rev, 1978, 65:109-130; In Sherman, M. H. (ed), Psychoanalysis and Old Vienna. NY: Human Sciences Press, 1978.

185. Berman, L. E. Gilbert's first night anxiety. Psychoanal Q, 1976, 45:110-127.
186. Berman, Jeffrey. Sylvia Plath and the art of dying: Sylvia Plath (1932-1963). Hartford Studies in Lit, 1978, 10:137-155.
187. Bernabei, M. Maria Baskirtsewa. L'Eroina dell'io. Milan: Soc ed Dante Alighieri, 1932.
188. Bernfeld, Siegfried. Trieb und Tradition im Jugendalter: Kulturpsychologische Studien an Tagebüchern. Schweizerischen Zeitschrift für Psychologie, 1931, 54:1-181.
189. Bernhard, Rudolf K. Stifter's personality as a factor in the reevaluation of his literary works. Papers Michigan Academy of Science, Arts & Letters, 1951, 37:415-422.
190. Berryman, John. Stephen Crane. NY: Sloane, 1950; London: Methuen, 1950.
191. Bersani, Leo A. Marcel Proust; The Fictions of Life and of Art. London: Oxford Univ. Press, 1965.
192. Berteaux, J. Un Pervers degénie Jean-Jacques Rousseau: Essai de Synthèse médico-psychologique. Thèse, Lille, 1939.
193. Berthier, Philippe. Barbey d'Aurevilly et l'imagination. Geneva: Droz, 1978.
194. Bertz, E. Walt Whitman, ein Charakterbild. Jahrbuch für Sexuelle Zwischenstufen, 1905.
195. Besdine, Matthew. Jocasta and Oedipus: another look. In Pathways in Child Guidance. NY: Bureau of Child Guidance, Board of Education of the City of New York, 1968, 1-4; Psychoanal Rev, 1968-69, 259-277, 574-600.
196. _____. The Jocasta complex, mothering and woman geniuses. Psychoanal Rev, 1971, 58:51-74.
197. _____. Mrs. Oedipus. Psychol Today, 1969, 2(8):40-47, 67.
198. _____. George Sand: psychosexual life of a woman genius. MAHS, 1972, 6(2):1-8.
199. _____. Shakespeare: the homosexual element in the life of a genius. MAHS, 1971, 5(2):158, 160, 164, 168-169, 176-177, 183.
200. Bett, Walter R. The Infirmities of Genius. NY: Philosophical Library, 1952.
201. Bettelheim, Bruno. The ignored lesson of Anne Frank. In Surviving, and Other Essays. NY: Knopf, 1979, 246-257.
202. Bettinson, C. D. Gide and religious conversion: the case of Les Caves du Vatican. Forum Modern Language Studies, 1976, 12:105-117.
203. Bhat, Vishnu. D. H. Lawrence's sexual ideal. Lit Half-Yearly, 1969, 10:68-73.
204. Biéder, J. [The polymorphous perverse: a reading of Freud and the Bible.] Annales Médico-Psychologiques, 1973, 1:274-281.
205. Billy, Andre. Jules Verne psychanalyse. Le Figaro, 30 Mars 1960.
206. Bilsland, John W. DeQuincey's opium experiences. Dalhousie Rev, 1975, 55:419-430.

207. Binet, A. La Création littéraire. Portrait psychologique de M. Paul Hervieu. Année Psychologique, 1904, 10:1-62.

208. _____. The paradox of Diderot. Popular Science Monthly, 1897, 51:539-543.

209. Binet-Sanglé, C. Association de la religiosité et du génie poétique. L'Hiérosyncrotème Racine. Chronique médicale, 1905, 385-391, 417-430.

210. _____. La Malade de Blaise Pascal. Annales Médico-Psychologiques, 1898, 9:177-199.

211. Binion, Rudolph. Frau Lou. Nietzsche's Wayward Disciple. Princeton: Princeton Univ. Press, 1968, 1974.

212. Binswanger, Ludwig. Henrik Ibsen und das Problem der Selbst-realisation in der Kunst. Heidelberg: Schneider, 1949, 1952.

213. _____. Studien zum Schizophrenieproblem: der Fall Suzanne Urban: der Fall Jean Jacques Rousseau. Schweizer Archiv für Neurologie und Psychiatrie, 1952, 70:1-32.

214. Birenbaum, Harvey. The personality of Sir Thomas Wyatt. Essays in Criticism, 1964, 14:43-64.

215. Birkin, Andrew. J. M. Barrie and the Lost Boys: The Love Story That Gave Birth to Peter Pan. NY: Potter/Crown, 1979.

216. Bisanz, A. J. Die Ursprünge der Seelenkrankheit bei K. P. Moritz. Heidelberg: Winter, 1970.

217. Bittner, C. Frédéric Schiller. Tribune Médicale, 5 May 1955.

218. Bittner, William. Poe and the 'invisible demon.' Georgia Rev, 1963, 17:134-138.

219. Black, Isabella. Was it [Thomas] Arnold's doing? A psychological study of Arthur Hugh Clough. Psychoanal Rev, 1961, 48:104-110.

220. Blackshear, Helen F. Mama Sayre, Scott Fitzgerald's mother-in-law. Georgia Rev, 1965, 19:465-470.

221. Blake, Kathleen. Plays, Games, and Sport. The Literary Works of Lewis Carroll. Ithaca, NY: Cornell Univ. Press, 1974.

222. Blampignon, E. A. Le Génie et la démence chez Jean-Jacques Rousseau. Annales Philosophiques Chrétiennes, 1902-03, 145:534-555; 1903, 146:287-305; 1903-04, 147:150-169; 1904, 148:259-277; 1904-05, 149:481-504.

223. Blanchard, William H. Psychodynamic aspects of the peak experience. Psychoanal Rev, 1969, 56:87-42.

224. _____. Rousseau and the Spirit of Revolt: A Psychological Study. Ann Arbor: Univ. Michigan Press, 1967.

225. Blanck, Karl. Heine und die Frau. Münich: Müller, 1913.

226. Bleich, David. Symbolmaking and suicide. Hart Crane (1899-1932). Hartford Studies in Lit, 1978, 10:70-102.

227. Blin, Georges. Le Sadism de Baudelaire. Paris: Corti, 1948.

228. Bliven, Naomi. Home James. New Yorker, 29 Apr 1972, 137-140.

229. Bloch, Iwan. Marquis de Sade; the Man and His Age. Newark, NJ: Julian, 1931.

230. Bloom, Lynn Z. Heritages: dimensions of mother-daughter relationships in women's autobiographies. In Davidson, C. N., & Broner, E. M. (eds), The Lost Tradition. NY: Ungar, 1980, 291-303.

231. Blum, C. Diderot and the problem of virtue. Studies on Voltaire & the 18th Century, 1972, 87:167-179.

232. Bockel, Pierre. Malraux and death. In Dorenlot, F., & Tison-Braun, M. (eds), André Malraux; Metamorphosis and Imagination. NY: Literary Forum, 1979, 75-82.

233. Bocquillon, E. Jean-Jacques Rousseau ce méconnu. Paris: Dervy, 1962.

234. Boehm, Felix. Bemerkungen zu Balzacs Liebesleben. Almanach, 1928, 154-163.

235. Bollème, Geneviève. Gustave Flaubert: rêve du 3 mars 1856. Mercure de France, 1964, 1203.

236. Bolitho, Hector. The doctor and the biographer. Texas Q, 1968, 11:52-60.

237. Bollettiere, Rosa M. B. The importance of Trieste in Joyce's work, with reference to his knowledge of psycho-analyses. James Joyce Q, 1970, 7:177-185.

238. Bonaparte, Marie. A defense of biography. Int J Psycho-Anal, 1939, 20:231-240.

239. _____. Deuil, nécrophilie et sadisme à propos d'Edgar Poe. Rev Française de Psychanalyse, 1930-31, 4:716-734; Paris: Denoël et Steele, 1932.

240. _____. De l'élaboration et de la fonction de l'oeuvre littéraire. Rev Français de Psychanalyse, 1932, 5:649-683.

241. _____. L'Epilepsie et le sado-masochisme dans la vie et l'oeuvre de Dostoïevski. Rev Française de Psychanalyse, 1962, 26:715-730.

242. _____. The Life and Works of Edgar Allan Poe. A Psychoanalytic Interpretation, 2 Vols. London: Imago, 1949; Paris: Denoël et Steele, 1933; Vienna: Int Psychoanalytischer Verlag, 1934. Review: Abram Kardiner, Psychoanal Q, 1934, 3:143-145.

243. _____. La Structure psychique d'Edgar Poe. Hygiène Mentale, 1933, 28:193-201.

244. Booth, Marcella. Through the smoke hole: Ezra Pound's last year at St. Elizabeths. Paideuma, 1974, 3:329-334.

245. Bopp, Léon. Amiel et les femmes. Nouvelle Rev Française, 1954, 17:947-960.

246. _____. Psychologie des 'Fleurs du Mal.' Geneva: Droz, 1964, 1966, 4 Vols.

247. Bordeaux, André. La Personalité d'Hilaire Belloc et sa réputation d'écrivain. Etudes anglaises, 1958, 11:331-337.

248. Borel, Jacques. Genié et folie de Jean-Jacques Rousseau. Paris: Corti, 1966.

249. Boros, Marie-D. La Métaphore du crabe dans l'oeuvre littéraire de Jean-Paul Sartre. PMLA, 1966, 81:446-450.

250. Boschi, Gaetano. Non follia ma nevrosi quella de Torquato Tasso. Neuropsichiatria, 1962, 1:1-17.

251. Bosha, Francis J. Faulkner, Pound and the P. P. P. Paideuma, 1979, 8:249-256.

252. Bottome, Phyllis. Is neurosis a handicap to genius? Lit &
     Psychol, 1955, 5(2):20-25.
253. Boulanger, J. B. Un Cas d'inversion coupable: Marcel
     Proust. Union Médicale du Canada, 1951, 80:483-493.
254. Boulenger, M. Racine et les dames. Opinion, 1908, 1:23-
     25.
255. Boulger, James D. Personality and existence in Yeats.
     Thought, 1964, 39:591-612.
256. Bourbon Busset, J. de. Valéry, ou le mystique sans Dieu.
     Paris: Plon, 1964.
257. Boven, W. Edmond Crisinel: poète de la mélancolie.
     Schweiz Archiv Neurologie und Psychiatrie, 1967, 99:155-
     157.
258. Bowerman, George F. The new biography. Wilson Library
     Bulletin, 1929, 4:153-158.
259. Bowman, Frank Paul. Suffering, madness, and literary cre-
     ation in 17th-century spiritual autobiography. French
     Forum, 1976, 1:24-48.
260. Boyd, Ernest. Sex in biography. Harper's, 1932, 165:752-
     759.
261. Boyer, Selwyn L. George Orwell: the pursuit of decency.
     Social Work, 1967, 12:96-100.
262. Brachfeld, O. André Gides Werdegang. Int Zeitschrift für
     Individual-Psychologie, 1930, 8:376-388.
263. Braddy, Haldeen. Poe's flight from reality. Texas Studies
     in Lit & Language, 1959, 1:394-400.
264. Bragman, Louis J. The case of Algernon Charles Swinburne:
     a study in sadism. Psychoanal Rev, 1934, 21:51-74.
265. _____. The case of Arthur Symons. The psychopathology
     of a man of letters. British J Medical Psychol, 1932,
     12:346-362.
266. _____. The case of Dante Gabriel Rossetti. Amer J
     Psychiat, 1936, 92:1111-1122.
267. _____. The case of Floyd Dell: a study in the psychol-
     ogy of adolescence. Amer J Psychiat, 1937, 93:1401-
     1411.
268. _____. The case of John Aldington Symonds. A study in
     aesthetic homosexuality. Amer J Psychiat, 1936, 93:375-
     398; In Ruitenbeek, H. M. (ed), Homosexuality and Creative
     Genius. NY: Obolensky, 1967, 86-111.
269. _____. The case of Ludwig Lewisohn. Amer J Psychiat,
     1931, 11:319-331.
270. _____. The case of John Ruskin. A study in cyclothymia.
     Amer J Psychiat, 1935, 91:1137-1159.
271. Brain, Walter Russell. Authors and psychopaths. British
     Medical J, 1949, 2.
272. _____. The illness of Dean Swift. Irish J Medical Sci-
     ence, Ser. 6, 1952, 337-345; Reprinted as: Jonathan
     Swift: l'enfant terrible. In Some Reflections on Genius
     and Other Essays. Philadelphia: Lippincott, 1960, 23-33.
273. _____. A post-mortem on Dr. Johnson. London Hospital
     Gazette, 1934, 37:225-230, 288-289.
274. _____. Some Reflections on Genius and Other Essays.
     Philadelphia: Lippincott, 1961.

275. Brand, Howard. Kafka's creative crisis. J Amer Academy Psychoanal, 1976, 4:249-260.
276. Brandell, Gunnar. Freud--A Man of His Century. NY: Humanities Press, 1979.
277. _____. Revolt i dikt och andra studier. Stockholm: Alba, 1977.
278. Brann, Henry Walter. Nietzsche und die Frauen. Bonn: Bouvier, 1978 (1931).
279. Brasher, T. L. Whitman's conversion to phrenology. Walt Whitman Newsletter, 1958, 4:95-97.
280. Breathnach, C. S. Francis Thompson--student, addict, poet. J Irish Medical Assn, 1959, 45:98-103.
281. Brecco, Stephen B. High hopes: Eugene O'Neill and alcohol. Yale French Studies, 1974, 142-149.
282. Brèdif, L. Du Caractère Intellectuel et Moral de J. J. Rousseau. Paris: Hachette, 1906.
283. Breen, J. Wilfred Owen (1893-1918) his recovery from shellshock. Notes & Queries, 1976, 23:301-305.
284. Breitwieser, Mitchell Robert. Cotton Mather's crazed wife. Glyph, 1979, 5:88-113.
285. Breslin, James E. Allen Ginsberg: the origins of 'Howl' and 'Kaddish.' Iowa Rev, 1977, 8:82-108.
286. Brett, Judith M. Hugo von Hofmannsthal: 'Letter of Lord Chandos'--the writer's relationship to his language. Amer Imago, 1978, 35:228-258.
287. Brian-Chaninov, N. [Two Russian epileptics: Dostoevsky and Tolstoy.] Psiquiatria y Criminologia, 1936, 1:210-214.
288. Briand, C. Maladie et sommeil chez Proust. Les Temps Modernes, 1951, 51:169-187.
289. _____. Le Secret de Marcel Proust. Paris: Lefebvre, 1950.
290. Briggs, Charles F. The personality of Poe. Independent, 1877, 29:1-2.
291. Brigham, Amariah. Insanity, illustrated by histories of distinguished men and by the writings of poets and novelists. Amer J Insanity, 1844, 1:9-46.
292. Bringmann, Wolfgang G., Krichev, Alan, & Balence, William. Goethe as behavior therapist. J History Behavioral Sciences, 1970, 6:151-159.
293. Brink, Andrew. Loss and Symbolic Repair: A Psychological Study of Some English Poets. Hamilton, Ontario: Cromlech, 1977.
294. Brink, Louise, & Jelliffe, Smith Ely. Emil Kraepelin, psychiatrist and poet. JNMD, 1933, 77:134-152, 274-282.
295. Brisson, P. A. E. Les Deux visages de Racine. Paris: Gallimard, 1944.
296. Brod, Max. Franz Kafka: A Biography. NY: Schocken, 1947, 1937; Review: René Wellek, Scrutiny, 1938, 7:86-89.
297. _____. Kafka: father and son. In Ruitenbeek, H. M. (ed), The Literary Imagination. Chicago: Quadrangle, 1965, 81-96; Partisan Rev, 1938, 4:21-28.
298. Brooks, Michael. Love and possession in a Victorian household: the example of the Ruskins. In Wohl, A. S. (ed),

The Victorian Family; Structure and Stresses. NY: St. Martin's, 1978, 82-100.

299. Brooks, Van Wyck. The Ordeal of Mark Twain. NY: Dutton, 1920, 1932.

300. Brower, Judith F. Personal documents. In Brower, Daniel, & Abt, Lawrence (eds), Progress in Clinical Psychology, Vol. 1. NY: Grune & Stratton, 1952, 63-66.

301. Brown, D. F. Veil of Tanit: the personal significance of a woman's adornment to Gustave Flaubert. Romanic Rev, 1943, 34:196-210.

302. Brown, Ivor. The bard and the body. Medical World, 1959, 91:60-64.

303. Brown, Terence. MacNeice: father and son. In Brown, T., & Reid, Alec (eds), Time Was Away: The World of Louis MacNeice. Dublin: Dolmen, 1974, 21-34.

304. Browne, D. The problem of Byron's lameness. Proceedings Royal Society Medicine, 1960, 53:440-442.

305. Brownell, William Crary. American Prose Masters: Cooper, Hawthorne, Emerson, Poe, Lowell, Henry James. NY: Scribner, 1892, 1909.

306. Brownley, Martine W. Gibbon: the formation of mind and character. In Bowersock, G.W., et al. (eds), Edward Gibbon and the Decline and Fall of the Roman Empire. Cambridge: Howard Univ. Press, 1977, 13-25.

307. Brückner, Peter. Sigmund Freuds Privatlektüre. Psyche, 1962, 15:881-902; 16:721-743.

308. Brunetière, F. La Folie de Jean-Jacques Rousseau. Paris: Presses Universitaires de France, 1952.

309. Brunot, Henriette. Balzac et les femmes. Psyche, 1951, 6:206-223.

310. Bruss, Elizabeth W. Autobiographical Acts, The Changing Situation of a Literary Genre. Baltimore: Johns Hopkins Univ. Press, 1976.

311. Brussell, James A. M.D. (Master of dice). Psychiat Q Supplement, 1948, 22:102-110.

312. Bryden, Ronald. Shams and penances. New Statesman, 25 Jan 1974, 115-116.

313. Buchet, E. E. Marcel Proust ou la puissance de l'anormal. In Ecrivains intelligents du XXe siècle. Paris: Corréa, 1945, 37-86.

314. Buchloh, Paul G. Gesellschaft, Individuum und Gemeinschaft bei Tennessee Williams. Studium Generale, 1968, 21:49-73.

315. Buddeberg, Elsa. Rainer Maria Rilke: Eine innerl Biographie. Stuttgart: 1954.

316. Bühler, Charlotte. The curve of life as studied in biographies. J Applied Psychol, 1935, 19:405-409.

317. _____. [The Human Course of Life as a Psychological Problem.] Leipzig: 1933.

318. _____, & Goldenberg, H. Structural aspects of the individual's history. In Bühler, C., & Massarik, F. (eds), The Course of Human Life: A Study of Goals in the Humanistic Perspective. NY: 1968, 54-63.

319. _____, & Rubinov, O. The course of man's life--a psychological problem. J Abnormal Social Psychol, 1933, 28:207-215.

320. Buisine, A. [Maupassant's necrophilia.] Rev des Sciences Humaines, 1975, 160:539-551.

321. Burchell, Samuel C. Marcel Proust, an interpretation of his life. Psychoanal Rev, 1928, 15:300-303.

322. Burg, B. R. Richard Mather of Dorchester. Lexington: Univ. Press Kentucky, 1976.

323. Burgelin, P. La Philosophie de l'existence de Jean-Jacques Rousseau. Paris: Presses Universitaires de France, 1952.

324. Burgess, Anthony. Nothing Like the Sun: A Story of Shakespeare's Love-Life. NY: Norton, 1964; London: Heinemann, 1964; Ontario: Collins, 1964.

325. Burke, E. C. Chekhov, the physician. Minnesota Medicine, 1972, 55:681-684.

326. Burnham, Donald L. The need-fear dilemma in August Strindberg's object relations. [Abstract.] Bulletin Los Angeles Psychoanal Society Institute, 1969, 6(1).

327. _____. Restitutional functions of symbol and myth in Strindberg's Inferno. Psychiatry, 1973, 36:229-243.

328. _____. Strindberg's Inferno and Sullivan's 'extravasation of meaning.' Contemporary Psychoanal, 1973, 9:190-208.

329. _____. Strindbergs kontaktdilemma studerat i hans förhållande till Harriet Bosse. In Meddelanden från Strindbergssällskapet, 1971, 50:8-26.

330. _____, & Bergmann, Sven A. August Strindberg's need-fear dilemma, as seen in his relationship with Harriet Bosse. In Smith, J. H. (ed), Psychiatry and the Humanities, Vol. 1. New Haven: Yale Univ. Press, 1976, 73-97.

331. Burns, Wayne. His mother's son: the emotional development of Charles Reade. Lit & Psychol, 1954, 4(3):31-47.

332. Burroughs, William S. Points of distinction between sedative and consciousness-expanding drugs. In Solomon, D. (ed), Marihuana Papers. NY: Signet, 1966, 440-446.

333. Burrow, Trigant. Psychoanalytic improvisations and the personal equation. Psychoanal Rev, 1926, 13:173-186.

334. _____. A Search for Man's Sanity. NY: Oxford Univ. Press, 1958.

335. Burt, Forrest D. William Somerset Maugham: an Adlerian interpretation. J Individual Psychol, 1970, 26:64-82.

336. _____. A New Methodology for Psychological Criticism of Literature: A Case Study of William Somerset Maugham. DA, 1967, 28:2202A.

337. Busi, Frederick. Sartre on Flaubert. Research Studies, 1973, 41:9-17.

338. Butler, Lord. The prevalence of indirect biography. Essays by Divers Hands, 1972, 37:17-30.

339. Butler, R. N. The destiny of creativity in later life: studies of creative people and the creative process. In Levin, S., & Kahana, R. J. (eds), Psychodynamic Studies on Aging. NY: IUP, 1967.

340. Butscher, Edward. Sylvia Plath: Method and Madness. NY:
      Seabury/Continuum, 1976.
341. _____. Whitman's attitudes toward death: the essential
      paradox. Walt Whitman Rev, 1971, 17(1):16-19.
342. Bychowski, Gustav. Das Drama Winckelmanns. In Cremeri-
      us, J. (ed), Neurose und Genialität. Psychoanalytische
      Biographien. Frankfort: Fischer, 1971, 215-233.
343. _____. Marcel Proust and his mother. Amer Imago,
      1973, 30:8-25.
344. _____. Platonic love and the quest for beauty. The
      drama of J. J. Winckelmann. Amer Imago, 1964, 21:80-
      94; Platonische Liebe und die Suche nach der Schonheit.
      Das Drama Winckelmanns. Psyche, 1966, 20:700-714.
345. _____. Struggle against the introjects. Int J Psycho-Anal,
      1958, 39:182-187.
346. Byram, R. S. John Donne (1572-1631). The case history of
      a poet. Nursing Times, 1970, 66:1306-1307.
347. Byrom, Thomas. A sketch of Edward Lear's Life. In Non-
      sense and Wonder. The Poems and Cartoons of Edward
      Lear. NY: Dutton, 1977, 1-47.

348. Cabaleiro Goãs, M. Personajes literarios, psicologia y psi-
      copatologia. Actas Luso-Espanolas de Neurologica y Psi-
      quiatria, 1965, 24:181-192.
349. Cabanes, A. Le Cabinet secret de l'histoire III. Jean-
      Jacques Rousseau, ses infirmités physique et leur influ-
      ence sur son caractère et son talent. Paris: Charles,
      1898.
350. _____. Epilepsie et genie: Dostoevsky. Rev Mondiale,
      1922, 149:235-246, 344-353.
351. _____. Grands névropathes malades immortels. Paris:
      Michel, 1930-1935, 3 Vols.
352. Cady, Edwin H. The neuroticism of William Dean Howells.
      PMLA, 1946, 61:229-238; In Eble, K. (ed), Howells: A
      Century of Criticism. Dallas: Southern Methodist Univ.
      Press, 1962, 138-150.
353. Calero Hervas, J. Azorín y Proust, ante el complejo de
      Edipo. Cuadernos Hispano-Americanos, 1974, 288:563-577.
354. Callow, Philip. Son and Lover: The Young Lawrence. Lon-
      don: Bodley Head, 1975.
355. Calo, Jeanne. La Création de la femme chez Michelet.
      Paris: Nizet, 1975.
356. Calot, F. Les Portraits de Racine; vrais et faux visages.
      Paris: Glameau, 1941.
357. Campbell, C. Macfie. Psychology and biography. Amer J
      Psychiat, 1931, 77:708-722.
358. Campbell, Killis. The Mind of Poe and Other Studies. Cam-
      bridge: Harvard Univ. Press, 1933.
359. Campbell, Oscar J. The biographical approach to literature.
      English J, 1936, 25:292-307.
360. Canby, Henry Seidel. Problem child of American literature.
      Saturday Rev Lit, 1943, 26:6-8.

361. _____. Thoreau. Boston: Houghton Mifflin, 1939.
362. _____. Walt Whitman, an American: A Study in Biogra-
     phy. Boston: Houghton Mifflin, 1943.
363. Canetti, Elias. The Tongue Set Free: Remembrance of a
     European Childhood. NY: Seabury, 1979.
364. Carabba, Claudio. Tozzi. Florence: La Nuova Italia, 1970.
365. Cardinal, Clive H. Einiges über die Pathologie des Genies
     bei Rainer Maria Rilke. In Baldner, R.W. (ed), Proceed-
     ings, Pacific Northwest Conference on Foreign Languages,
     Vol. 18. Victoria, B.C.: Univ. Victoria Press, 1967,
     79-84.
366. Cardozo, Nancy. Lucky Eyes and a High Heart: The Life
     of Maud Gonne. Indianapolis: Bobbs-Merrill, 1978.
367. Carduner, Jean René. Metamorphosis and biography. In
     Dorenlot, F., & Tison-Braun, M. (eds), André Malraux;
     Metamorphosis and Imagination. NY: Literary Forum,
     1979, 37-54.
368. Carile, Paolo. Céline, un allucinato di genio. In Olschki,
     L. S. (ed), Studi di letteratura, storia e filosofia. Flor-
     ence: Archivium Romanicum, 1965, 135-154.
369. _____. Louis Ferdinand Céline: un allucinato di genio.
     Bologna: Pàtron, 1969.
370. Carlisle, E. Fred. The Uncertain Self: Whitman's Drama
     of Identity. E. Lansing: Michigan State Univ. Press,
     1973.
371. _____. Walt Whitman: the drama of identity. Criticism,
     1968, 10:259-276.
372. Carpenter, Andrew (ed). Place, Personality and the Irish
     Writer. NY: Barnes & Noble, 1977.
373. Carpenter, Edward. Some Friends of Walt Whitman: A
     Study in Sex-Psychology. London: British Society for
     Study of Sex Psychology, 1924.
374. _____, & Barnefield, G. The Psychology of the Poet Shel-
     ley. London: Allen & Unwin, 1925.
375. Carr, Virginia Spencer. The Lonely Hunter: A Biography of
     Carson McCullers. NY: Doubleday, 1975.
376. Carrère, J. Degeneration in the Great French Masters:
     Rousseau, Chateaubriand, Balzac, Stendhal, Sand, Musset,
     Baudelaire, Flaubert, Verlaine, Zola. NY: Brentano,
     1922.
377. Carroll, Paul. John Logan: was Frau Heine a monster? or
     yung and easily freudened in Düsseldorf and Hamburg and
     Berlin and Paris and New York City. Minnesota Rev,
     1968, 8:67-84.
378. Carton, P. Le Faux naturisme de Jean-Jacques Rousseau.
     Paris: 1931.
379. Cassirer, Ernst. The Question of Jean-Jacques Rousseau.
     NY: Columbia Univ. Press, 1954 (1932).
380. Cassity, John H. Psychopathological glimpses of Lord Byron.
     Psychoanal Rev, 1925, 12:397-413.
381. Castellani, Jean-Pierre. La Vraie personnalité de Vicente
     Aleixandre. Langues Modernes, 1978, 72:604-611.
382. Castiglioni, A. Visita medica a Giacomo Leopardi. Rivista
     di Psicologia Normale e Patologica, 1938, 34:26-39.

383. Castiglioni, T. R. La personalità religiosa di Ernesto Bon-aiuti. Cenobio, 1966, 15:334-341.
384. Castilla del Pino, C. Ganivet. Insula, 1965, 228-229(5).
385. Cattavi, G. Proust perdu et retrouvé. Paris: Plon, 1964.
386. Cawthorne, T. The fatal illness of Oscar Wilde. Annals of Otology, 1966, 75:657-666.
387. Cellerino, A. [Benvenuto Cellini in the guise of patient. Points from his Vita.] Minerva Medica, 1960, 51:1567-1570.
388. Chaliff, Cynthia. Emily Dickinson Against the World: An Interpretation of the Poet's Life and Work. DAI, 1967, 28:1070 A.
389. _____. Emily Dickinson as the deprived child. Emily Dickinson Bulletin, 1970, 13:34-43.
390. Chambers, Ross. Gautier et le complexe de Pygmalion. Rev d'Histoire Littéraire de la France, 1972, 72(4):641-658.
391. Château, Jean. Montaigne, psychologue et pédagogue. Paris: Vrin, 1964.
392. Chatelain, A. La Folie de Jean-Jacques Rousseau. Paris: Fischbacher, 1890.
393. Cheney, Anne. Millay in Greenwich Village. University: University Alabama Press, 1975.
394. Cherkovski, Neeli. Ferlinghetti: A Biography. Garden City, NY: Doubleday, 1979.
395. Chernowitz, Maurice E. Proust and Painting. NY: IUP, 1945.
396. Chesler, Phyllis. Women and Madness. NY: Avon, 1972.
397. Chesneau, Albert. Essai de psychocritique de Louis-Ferdinand Céline. Paris: Minard, 1971.
398. Chesser, Eustace. Shelley and Zastrozzi: Self-Revelation of a Neurotic. London: Gregg & Archive, 1965.
399. Chicoteau, M. La Personnalité mystique de Racine è travers son oeuvre. Cahiers raciniens, 1961, 9:632-661.
400. Chitty, Susan. The Beast and the Monk. A Life of Charles Kingsley. NY: Mason/Charter, 1975.
401. Choron, Jacques. Concerning suicide in Soviet Russia. Bulletin of Suicidology, 1968, 31-36.
402. Christ, Jack M. History and Personality in Autobiography. DAI, 1971, 31:5392A.
403. Christian, Diane. Inversion and the erotic: the case of William Blake. In Babcock, B. A. (ed), The Reversible World; Symbolic Inversion in Art and Society. Ithaca: Cornell Univ. Press, 1978, 117-128.
404. Claparède, E. J. -J. Rousseau et la signification de l'enfance. Annales Suisses d'Hygiene Scolaire, 1912, 13:525-553.
405. Clark, C. E. Frazer, Jr. (ed). The Love Letters of Nathaniel Hawthorne. Washington, D. C.: NCR/Microcard, 1972.
406. Clark, L. Pierce. A study of the epilepsy of Dostojewsky. Boston Medical & Surgical J, 1915, 172:46-51.
407. _____. A psycho-historical study of the epileptic personality in genius. Psychoanal Rev, 1922, 9:367-401.

408.   Clarke, E. L.   American Men of Letters: Their Nature and
       Nurture.   NY: Columbia Univ.   Press, 1916.
409.   Clément, Pierre-Paul.   Jean-Jacques Rousseau.   De l'éros
       coupable à l'éros glorieux.   Neuchâtel: Baconnière, 1976.
410.   Cleugh, James.   The First Masochist; A Biography of Leopold
       von Sacher-Masoch.   NY: Stein & Day, 1967.
411.   _____.   The Marquis and the Chevalier: A Study in the
       Psychology of Sex as Illustrated by the Lives and Person-
       alities of the Marquis de Sade (1740-1814) and the Cheva-
       lier von Sacher-Masoch (1836-1905).   NY: Duell, Sloan
       & Pearce, 1952.
412.   Clifford, James L.   Dictionary Johnson: Samuel Johnson's
       Middle Years.   NY: McGraw-Hill, 1979.
413.   Clubbe, John.   Victorian Forerunner, the Later Career of
       Thomas Hood.   Durham, NC: Duke Univ.   Press, 1968;
       Review: Thomas L. Ashton, Hartford Studies in Lit,
       1969, 1:223-229.
414.   Clurman, Harold.   Defense of the artist as neurotic.   In
       The Naked Image; Observations on the Modern Theatre.
       NY: Macmillan, 1966, 264-269.
415.   Coale, Samuel.   Whitman's war: the march of a poet.   Walt
       Whitman Rev, 1975, 21:85-101.
416.   Cobb, Edith.   The Ecology of Imagination in Childhood.   NY:
       Columbia Univ.   Press, 1978.
417.   Cochet, M. A.   L'Ame proustienne.   Brussels: Collignon,
       1929.
418.   Cocks, G.   A. A.   Milne: sources of his creativity.   Amer
       Imago, 1977, 34:313-326.
419.   Cocteau, Jean.   Lettres à Milorad.   Paris: St. Germain-des-
       Pres, 1975.
420.   _____.   Opium: Journal d'une Désintoxication.   Paris:
       Stock, 1930; Opium.   London: Owen, 1957.
421.   Cody, John.   After Great Pain; The Inner Life of Emily Dick-
       inson.   Cambridge: Belknap Press, 1971; Reviews: Cyn-
       thia Chaliff, Lit & Psychol, 1972, 22:45-47; Eleanor Lyons,
       Hartford Studies in Lit, 1972, 4:174-179.
422.   _____.   Emily Dickinson and nature's dining room: an
       unusual poet's essential hunger.   Michigan Q Rev, 1968,
       7:249-254.
423.   _____.   Metamorphosis of a malady: summary of a psy-
       choanalytic study of Emily Dickinson.   Hartford Studies in
       Lit, 1970, 2:113-132.
424.   _____.   Mourner among the children: I.   Psychiat Q,
       1967, 41:12-37.
425.   _____.   Mourner among the children.   II.   The psycho-
       logical crisis of Emily Dickinson.   Psychiat Q, 1967,
       41:233-263.
426.   _____.   Watchers upon the east.   The ocular complaints
       of Emily Dickinson.   Psychiat Q, 1968, 42:548-576.
427.   Cogny, P.   Dix-neuf lettres inédites de Guy de Maupassant
       au docteur Grancher.   Rev d'Histoire Littéraire, 1974,
       74:265-277.
428.   _____.   A propos d'une psychanalyse de J-K Huysmans.
       Cahiers Psychiatrie, 1950, No. 4.

429. Cole, Hunter McKelva. Walter B. C. Watkins and the 'Tiger' melancholia. Notes on Mississippi Writers, 1975, 8(1): 3-12.
430. Coleman, Elliott. A note on Joyce and Jung. James Joyce Q, 1963, 1(1):11-16.
431. Coleman, Stanley M. August Strindberg: the autobiographies. Psychoanal Rev, 1936, 23:248-273.
432. Coleridge, E. H. Anema Poetae. London: Heineman, 1895, 242-245, 277-278.
433. Coleridge, Samuel Taylor. Biographia Literaria. London: Dent, 1956; London: Everyman's, 1906.
434. Collins, Joseph. The Doctor Looks at Biography. Psychological Studies of Life and Letters. NY: Doran, 1925.
435. _____. The Doctor Looks at Literature. Psychological Studies of Life and Letters. NY: Doran, 1923.
436. Colloms, Brenda. Charles Kingsley: The Lion of Eversley. NY: Harper & Row, 1975.
437. Cololian, Paul. Psychopathologie. Gustave Flaubert et la psychoanalyse. Hippocrate, 1937, 5:488-495.
438. Coltrera, Joseph T. Lives, events, and other players: directions in psychobiography. In Lives, Events, and Other Players: Studies in Psychobiography. NY: Aronson, 1980.
439. Concha, J. Los orígenes. Revista Iberoamericana, 1971, 75:325-348.
440. Conde Gargollo, E. [Personality of Ganivet.] Cuadernos Hispano-Americanos, 1964, 58:51-71.
441. Conroy, Stephen S. Emerson and phrenology. American Q, 1964, 16:215-217.
442. Cook, David A. The Autobiography of John Cowper Powys: a portrait of the artist as other. Modern Philology, 1974, 72:30-45.
443. _____. The Quest for Identity in John Cowper Powys: A Reading of the 'Autobiography' and His Wessex Series. DAI, 1972, 32:4606A.
444. Cooke, Michael Gerard. DeQuincey, Coleridge, and the formal use of intoxication. Yale French Studies, 1974, 50: 26-41.
445. Cope, Zachary. Jane Austen's last illness. In Sorsby, A. (ed), Tenements of Clay. London: Friedmann, 1974, 174-179.
446. Coplin, Keith. John and Sam Clemens: a father's influence. Mark Twain J, 1970, 15:1-6.
447. Corganian, C. Influence de l'asthme sur l'oeuvre de Marcel Proust. Paris: Nouvelle Edition, 1945.
448. Cormican, John D. Samuel Johnson's struggle with his personality as revealed in his prayers. Ball State Univ. Forum, 1974, 15(3):19-25.
449. Corrêa, Paulo Dias. Atirar objetos e ... Goethe. Rev Braseileros Medicin, 1950, 7:114.
450. Courcel, Martine Hallade de (ed). Malraux; Life and Work. NY: Harcourt Brace Jovanovich, 1976.
451. Courtney, J. F. Addiction and Edgar Allan Poe. Medical Times, 1972, 100:162-163 passim.

452. Couser, G. Thomas. Epilogue: prophetic autobiography and prophetic behavior. In American Autobiography. Amherst: Univ. Massachusetts Press, 1979, 197-201.

453. _____. Of time and identity: Walt Whitman and Gertrude Stein as autobiographers. Texas Studies in Lit & Language, 1976, 17:787-804.

454. Cowley, Malcolm. Remembering Hart Crane. New Republic, 14 Apr 1941; excerpt in The Exile's Return.

455. Cox, C. B. Joseph Conrad and the question of suicide. Bulletin John Rylands Library, 1973, 55:285-299.

456. _____. The two Conrads. Books & Bookmen, 1974, 19(11):22-23.

457. Cox, James M. The muse of Samuel Clemens. Massachusetts Rev, 1963, 5:127-141.

458. Crandall, Norma. Charlotte, Emily, and Bramwell Brontë. Amer Book College, 1963, 13:21-22.

459. _____. Emily Brontë. A Psychological Portrait. Rindge, NH: Smith, 1957.

460. Cremerius, J. [Arnold Zweig--Sigmund Freud. The fate of an acted-out transference love.] Psyche (Stuttgart), 1973, 27:658-668.

461. _____. (ed). Neurose und Genialität. Psychoanalytische Biographien. Frankfort: Fischer, 1971.

462. Criado Miguel, Isabel. Personalidad de Pío Baroja, trasfondo psicológico de un mundo litteraria. Barcelona: Planeta, 1974.

463. Critchley, M. Four illustrious neuroluetics (Heinrich Heine, Jules de Goncourt, Alphonse Daudet, Guy de Maupassant). Proceedings Royal Society Medicine, 1969, 62:669-673.

464. Crocker, L. G. Rousseau and the common people. In Pappas, J. (ed), Essays on Diderot and the Enlightenment. Geneva: Droz, 1974, 89-111.

465. Croisé, J. Ivan Bunin, 1870-1953. Russian Rev, 1954, 13: 146-151.

466. Crompton, Margaret. Shelley's Dream Women. NY: A. S. Barnes, 1967.

467. Cruickshank, John. Romain Rolland: the psychological basis of political belief. Hermathena, 1954, 83:30-47. In Ruitenbeek, H. M. (ed), Psychoanalysis and Literature. NY: Dutton, 1964, 169-185.

468. Cruttwell, Patrick. Alexander Pope in the Augustan world. Centennial Rev, 1966, 10:13-36.

469. _____. Eminent Edwardians. Hudson Rev, 1968-69, 21: 726-736.

470. Curtin, J. C. Autobiography and the dialectic of consciousness. Int Philosophical Q, 1974, 14:343-346.

471. Daemmrich, Horst S. The Shattered Self. E. T. A. Hoffmann's Tragic Vision. Detroit: Wayne State Univ. Press, 1973.

472. _____. Thomas Mann's perception of self-insight. Papers on Language & Lit, 1977, 13:270-282.

473. d'Aguiar, Asdrubal. Soror Marianne. Estudo sobre a Religiosa Portugeza. Lisbon: 1924.
474. Daleski, Herman M. The Forked Flame: A Study of D. H. Lawrence. Evanston, Ill.: Northwestern Univ. Press, 1965.
475. D'Alfonso, N. R. Guglielmo Shakespeare attore et autore. Milan, 1917.
476. Daly, C. D. The mother complex in literature. Samiksa, 1947, 1:157-190.
477. Dandieu, Arnaud. Marcel Proust: Sa revelation psychologique. Paris: Firmin-Didot, 1936.
478. d'Andlau, B. La Jeuness de Mme de Staël (de 1766 à 1786). Geneva: Droz, 1970.
479. Dasgupta, J. C. A study of a Don Juan; a psychological essay on Byron. Indian J Psychol, 1944, 19:165-176.
480. Davenport, Guy. Ezra Pound 1885-1972. Arion, 1973, 1: 188-196.
481. Davis, Derek Russel. The death of the artist's father: Henrik Ibsen. British J Medical Psychol, 1973, 46:135-141.
482. Davis, Frederick B. Three letters from Sigmund Freud to André Breton. JAPA, 1973, 21:127-134.
483. Day, Douglas. Malcolm Lowry. NY: Oxford Univ. Press, 1973.
484. Debray-Ritzen, P. Le Docteur Tchékhov. Seminar des Hôpitaux de Paris, 1972, 48:3491-3497.
485. Décaudin, M. [Apollinaire's melancholy.] Cahiers du Sud, 1966, 386, 3-36.
486. Decurtius, F. Beiträge zur Kenntnis der Personlichkeit Franz Grillparzers (1791-1872). Allgemeine Zeitschrift für Psychiatrie, 1934, 102:313 ff.
487. Delaney, Paul W. Fragments of the Self: Mark Twain and the Problem of Identity. DAI, 1972, 33:2888A.
488. Delanne, René. Le Problème psychopathologique de Marcel Proust: quelques jugements de Marcel Proust sur le médicine; les médicins dans l'oeuvre de Proust. Rev Belge de Médicine et Pharmacie, 1950.
489. Delay, Jean. Meeting with Oscar Wilde. In Ruitenbeek, H. M. (ed), Homosexuality and Creative Genius. NY: Obolensky, 1967, 239-248.
490. _____. The Youth of André Gide. Chicago: Univ. Chicago Press, 1963; La Jeunesse d'André Gide, 2 Vols. Paris: Gallimard, 1956-57; Review: Eleanor B. Manheim, Lit & Psychol, 1966, 16:117-119.
491. Del Greco, Francesco. Sulle anormalite di carettere di alcuni grandi intelletuali. Archivio Generale di Neurologie. Psichiatria e Psicoanalisti, 1929, 10:182-189.
492. Dell, Floyd. An autobiographical critique. Psychoanal Q, 1932, 1:715-730.
493. _____. A literary self-analysis. Modern Q, 1927, 4:149-160.
494. dell'Orto, V. J. K. P. Moritz in England: a psychological study of the traveller. Modern Language Notes, 1976, 91:453-466.

495. Dembo, L. S. Norman Holmes Pearson on H. D.: an interview. Contemporary Lit, 1969, 10:431-677.
496. Demetrakopolous, Stephanie A. Archetypal constellations of feminine consciousness in Nin's first diary. Mosaic, 1978, 11(2):121-137.
497. Demetz, Peter. Rainer Rilkes Prager Jahre. Düsseldorf: Dietrichs, 1954.
498. De Mijolla, Alain. The desertion of Captain Rimbaud. Revue Française de Psychanalyse, 1975, 39:427-458.
499. Demole, Victor. Analyse psychiatrique des Confessions de Rousseau. Schweizer Archiv für Neurologie und Psychiatrie, 1913, 2:272-307.
500. Derré, Françoise. Schnitzler, man of science. In L'Oeuvre d'Arthur Schnitzler. Paris: 1966, 196-215.
501. Deutsch, Felix. Artistic expression and neurotic illness. I. The respiratory neurosis of Charles Kingsley. The Water Babies and Anton Locke's dream. Amer Imago, 1947, 4: 64-102; In The Yearbook of Psychoanalysis, 4:140-171. NY: IUP, 1948.
502. Deutsch, Helene. Ein Frauenschicksal. Imago, 1928, 14: 344-357; Almanach, 1929, 150-177.
503. Devereux, George. The nature of Sappho's seizure in fr. 31 LP as evidence of her inversion. Classical Q, 1970, 20: 17-31.
504. De Voto, Bernard. Mark Twain at Work. Cambridge: Harvard Univ. Press, 1942.
505. _____. The skeptical biographer. Harper's, 1933, 166: 181-192.
506. Dickson, Lovat. Radclyffe Hall at the 'Well of Loneliness': A Sapphic Chronicle. NY: Scribner, 1976; London: Collins, 1975.
507. Didier, Béatrice. Femme/Identité/Ecriture: A propos de L'Histoire de ma vie de George Sand. Rev des Sciences Humaines, 1977, 168:561-576.
508. Dieckhöfer, K. Die Epilepsie im Zitat der römanischen Schriftsteller Plautus, Seneca und Apuleius. Confinia Psychiatrica, 1972, 15:212-219.
509. Dieckmann, A. Die Einstellung Rainer Maria Rilkes zu den Elternimagines. Zeitschrift für Psychosomatische Medizin, 1957, 4:51-57.
510. Dietz, H. Goethes morphologische Sicht, seine Persönlichkeit und sein personaler Werdegang in der deutschen Gegenwarts-psychologie. Studies in Germanics, 1970, 2:18-32.
511. Dilthey, Wilhelm. Das Erlebnis und die Dichtung. Lessing, Goethe, Novalis, Hölderlin. Leipzig: Teubner, 1910.
512. Dingle, Herbert. The Mind of Emily Brontë. London: Brian & O'Keeffe, 1974.
513. Dinnage, P. (ed). The Marquis de Sade. NY: Grove, 1953.
514. Disertori, B. Una trauma di Federico Garcia Lorca. Annale Ospedale Maria Vittoria Torino, 1977, 20:91-92.
515. Dittmeyer, Hannelore. Gerardo Diego: Dichtung und Welthaltung; Manuel de Espumas als Ausdruck einer Dichterpersönalichkeit. Romantisches Jahrbuch, 1959, 9:331-353.

516. Dobinson, David. The personality of the writer. London Rev, 1976-77, 9:11-19.
517. Dobrinsky, Joseph. La Jeunesse de Somerset Maugham (1874-1903). Paris: Didier, 1976.
518. Dombroski, Robert S. Introduzione allo studio di Carlo E. Gadda. Florence: Vallechi, 1974.
519. Dooley, Lucile. Psychoanalysis of the character of Emily Brontë. Psychoanal Rev, 1930, 17:208-239; In Ruitenbeek, H. M. (ed), The Literary Imagination. Chicago: Quadrangle, 1965, 43-79.
520. _____. Psychoanalysis of Charlotte Brontë as a type of the woman genius. Amer J Psychol, 1920, 31:221-272.
521. _____. Psychoanalytic studies of genius. Amer J Psychol, 1916, 27:363-416.
522. Doolittle, Hilda [H. D.]. End to Torment, A Memoir of Ezra Pound by H. D. Edited by N. H. Pearson & M. King. NY: New Directions, 1979.
523. _____. 'Hur som helst, Er tillgivne....' In Sjöback, H., & Westerlundh, B. (eds), Sigmund Freud. Liv och personlighet. Ögonvittnen berättar. Malmö, Sweden: Bo Cavefors, 1977, 338-346.
524. _____. Tribute to Freud; with Unpublished Letters by Freud to the Author. NY: Pantheon, 1956; Boston: Godine, 1974.
525. Dorgelès, R. Utrillo, Drieu la Rochelle. Rev des Deux Mondes, 1975, 11:282-289.
526. Douglas, Norman. Edgar Allan Poe from an English point of view. Putnam's Monthly, 1909, 5:436.
527. Downing, Christine. Re-visioning autobiography: the bequest of Freud and Jung. Soundings, 1977, 60:210-228.
528. Downing, David. Myth and sexuality in Edward Dahlberg's Because I Was Flesh. Lit & Psychol, 1977, 27:148-155.
529. Drabble, Margaret. Arnold Bennett. London: Weidenfeld & Nicolson, 1974.
530. Dracoulidès, N. N. Profil psychanalytique de Charles Baudelaire. Psyché, 1953, 8:461-485.
531. Drake, William. Sara Teasdale. Woman and Poet. NY: Harper & Row, 1979.
532. Dreiser, Vera. My Uncle Theodore. NY: Nash, 1976.
533. Drevdahl, John E., & Cattell, Raymond B. Personality and creativity in artists and writers. J Clinical Psychol, 1958, 14:107-111.
534. Dubois, C. -G. Les Grands hommes de l'Antiquité et l'humanisme français. In Association Guillaume Budé: Actes du IXᵉ congrès Rome, 13-18 avril, 1973, Vol. II. Paris: Les Belles Lettres, 1975, 619-628.
535. Dubovsky, H. Anton Chekhov (1860-1904). Writer, physician and tuberculosis patient. South Africa Medical J, 1979, 55:682-686.
536. Dubro, James R. The third sex: Lord Hervey and his coterie. Eighteenth-Century Life, 1976, 2:89-95.
537. Dubu, J. Racine et le rituel d'Aleth; meditation devant un acte de baptême. In Studi in onore di Vittorio Lugli e Diego Valeri, 1961, 347-362.

538.   Dubujadoux, G.   Les Lettres françaises et l'inconscient.
        Mercure de France, 1924, 169:577-611.
539.   Du Cann, C. G. L.   Gide and homosexuality.   Lit Guide, 1955,
        70(9):7-8.
540.   Dudek, S. Z.   The artist as person; generalizations based on
        Rorschach records of writers and painters.   JNMD, 1970,
        150:232-241.
541.   _____.   Regression and creativity.   A comparison of the
        Rorschach records of successful vs.   unsuccessful painters
        and writers.   JNMD, 1968, 147:535-546.
542.   Dufar, Pierre.   Celui dont on ne parle pas: Eugène Hugo, sa
        vie, sa folie, ses oeuvres.   Paris: Fort, 1924.
543.   Duff, I. F.   Grant.   A one-sided sketch of Jonathan Swift.
        Psychoanal Q, 1937, 6:238-259.
544.   Dufrenoy, M. L.   La Psychopathologie de Jean-Jacques Rous-
        seau.   Rev de Pathologie comparée et de Médecine expéri-
        mentale, 1967, 67:245-254.
545.   Dugonjić, A.   Epilepsija u zivotu i literarnom opusu F. M.
        Dostojevskog.   Neuropsihijatrija, 1975, 23:185-190.
546.   Dunn, Douglas.   Gaiety and lamentation: the defeat of John
        Berryman.   Encounter, 1974, 43:72-77.
547.   Dupouy, R.   Charles Baudelaire toxicomane et opiomane.
        Annales Médico-Psychologiques, 1911, 11:353.
548.   _____.   Coleridge.   Opiumisme et psychose periodique.
        JPNP, 1910, 7:226-247.
549.   _____.   L'Opiumisme d'Edgar Poe.   Annales Médico-
        Psychologiques, 1911, 13:5-19.
550.   Durham, John.   The influence of John Stuart Mill's mental
        crisis on his thoughts.   Amer Imago, 1963, 20:369-384.
551.   Durling, R. M.   The ascent of Mt. Ventoux and the crisis of
        allegory.   Italian Q, 1974, 18 no. 69:7-28.
552.   Durozoi, Gérard.   Artaud: l'alienation et la folie.   Paris:
        Larousse, 1972.
553.   Dussinger, John A.   Style and intention in Johnson's Life of
        Savage.   J English Lit History, 1970, 37:564-580.
554.   Duyckaerts, F.   De Quelques mécanismes psychiques de la
        fugue chez Jean-Jacques Rousseau.   Acta Psychiatrica Bel-
        gica, 1970, 70:78-102.

555.   Earnest, Ernest.   S. Weir Mitchell: Novelist and Physician.
        Philadelphia: Univ. Pennsylvania Press, 1950.
556.   East, E. M.   Insanity and genius.   J Heredity, 1938, 29:275-
        279.
557.   Eastman, Max.   Heroes I Have Known.   NY: Simon &
        Schuster, 1942.
558.   Eberhart, Richard.   Robert Frost: his personality.   In Of
        Poetry and Poets.   Urbana: Univ. Illinois Press, 1979,
        179-201; Southern Rev, 1967, 2:762-788.
559.   Ebin, David (ed).   The Drug Experience.   NY: Orion, 1961.
560.   Ebon, Martin.   The psychic world of Aldous Huxley.   Psychic,
        1971, 2(4):26-30.
561.   Ebstein, E.   [Dostoevsky's illness and his art].   Medizinische
        Welt, 1928, 2:1623-1625.

562. Edel, Leon. The biographer and psycho-analysis. Int J Psycho-Anal, 1961, 13:458-466; New World Writing, 1961, 18:50-64.

563. _____. Bloomsbury: A House of Lions. Philadelphia: Lippincott, 1979; NY: Avon, 1980.

564. _____. Henry James. The Conquest of London: 1870-1881. Philadelphia: Lippincott, 1962; NY: Avon, 1978; Reviews: Robert M. Adams, Hudson Rev, 1963, 16:150-157; Frederick J. Hoffman, Virginia Q Rev, 1963, 39:518-528.

565. _____. Henry James. The Master: 1901-1916. Philadelphia: Lippincott, 1972; NY: Avon, 1978; Reviews: Quentin Anderson, Virginia Q Rev, 1972, 48:621-630; Oscar Cargill, Amer Lit, 1972, 44:330-332; Joseph Wisenfarth, Commonweal, 1972, 96(2):44-45.

566. _____. Henry James. The Middle Years: 1882-1895. Philadelphia: Lippincott, 1962; NY: Avon, 1978; Reviews: Robert M. Adams, Hudson Rev, 1963, 16:150-157; Frederick J. Hoffman, Virginia Q Rev, 1963, 39:518-528; Herbert Read, Listener, 1963, 69:761-762.

567. _____. Henry James. The Treacherous Years: 1895-1901. Philadelphia: Lippincott, 1969; NY: Avon, 1978.

568. _____. Henry James. The Untried Years: 1843-1870. Philadelphia: Lippincott, 1953; NY: Avon, 1978.

569. _____. Hugh Walpole and Henry James: the fantasy of the Killer and the Slain. Amer Imago, 1951, 8:351-369.

570. _____. Literary Biography. Garden City, NY: Doubleday Anchor, 1959, 1975.

571. _____. Literature and biography. In Thorpe, J. (ed), Relations of Literary Study. NY: Modern Language Assn, 1967, 57-72.

572. _____. The poetics of biography. In Schiff, H. (ed), Contemporary Approaches to English Studies. NY: Barnes & Noble, 1977, 38-58.

573. _____. Revision of a chapter from the Life of Henry James. Psychohistory Rev, 1979, 8(1-2):47-52.

574. _____, et al. Telling Lives: The Biographer's Art. NY: New Republic, 1979.

575. Ehrenpreis, Irvin. The pattern of Swift's women. PMLA, 1955, 70:706-716.

576. _____. The Personality of Jonathan Swift. Cambridge: Harvard Univ. Press; London: Methuen, 1958.

577. Ehrenstein, A. Das Martyrium des Edgar Allan Poe. Int Zeitschrift für Individual-Psychologie, 1930, 8:389-400.

578. Ehrentiel, O. F. The almost forgotten Feuchtersleben: poet, essayist, popular philosopher and psychiatrist, J History Behavioural Sciences, 1975, 11(1):82-86.

579. Ehrlich, G. E. Shakespeare's rheumatology. Annals of the Rheumatic Diseases, 1967, 26:562-563.

580. Ehrmann, Jacques. Rameu's nephew: an existential psychoanalysis of Diderot by himself. J Existential Psychiat, 1963-64, 4:59-68.

581. Eigeldinger, M. Jean-Jacques Rousseau et la réalité de l'imaginaire. Neuchâtel: La Baconnière, 1962.

582. Eisenberg, D. Textos y documentes lorquianos. Gainesville: Florida State Univ. Press, 1975.
583. Eisenbud, Jules. Descartes and Shaw: some spatial aspects of object loss. Int Rev Psycho-Anal, 1978, 5:285-296.
584. Eissler, Kurt R. A clinical note on moral masochism: Eckermann's relationship to Goethe. In Loewenstein, R. M. (ed), Drives, Affects, Behaviour. NY: IUP, 1953, 285-326.
585. _____. Goethe. A Psychoanalytic Study, 1775-1786. Detroit: Wayne State Univ. Press, 1963. Reviews: N. F. Ellenberger, Dialogue, 1965-66, 4:540-545; David Beres, Psychoanal Q, 1965, 34:447-450; Joseph T. Coltrera, JAPA, 1965, 13:634-703.
586. _____. Goethe and science: a contribution to the psychology of Goethe's psychosis. In Psychoanalysis and the Social Sciences, Vol. 5. NY: IUP, 1958, 51-98; Abstract in Annual Survey of Psychoanalysis, Vol. 9. NY: IUP, 1958, 472-479.
587. _____. Notes on the environment of a genius. In The Psychoanalytic Study of the Child, Vol. 14. NY: IUP, 1959, 267-313; In Ruitenbeek, H. M. (ed), The Literary Imagination. Chicago: Quadrangle, 1965, 275-327.
588. _____. Psychopathology and creativity. Amer Imago, 1967, 24:35-81.
589. _____. An unknown autobiographical letter by Freud and a short comment. Int J Psycho-Anal, 1951, 32:319-324.
590. Ek, S. R. Verklighet och vision. En studie i Bergmans romankonst. Stockholm: Bonniers, 1964.
591. Eklund, Torsten. Tjänstekoinnans son: en psykologisk Strindbergsstudie. Stockholm: Bonnier, 1948.
592. Ellerman, Carl P. Nietzsche's madness: tragic wisdom. Amer Imago, 1970, 27:338-357.
593. Elliott, Leota W. Benito Pérez Galdós and Abnormal Psychology. Univ. New Mexico Abstracts of Thesis, 1933-37, 1946, 29-30.
594. Ellis, Havelock. From Rousseau to Proust. Boston: Houghton Mifflin, 1953.
595. Ellmann, Richard. How Wallace Stevens saw himself. In Doggett, F., & Buttel, R. (eds), Wallace Stevens. Princeton: Princeton Univ. Press, 1980, 149-170.
596. _____. James Joyce. NY: Oxford Univ. Press, 1959.
597. Emery, L. Rousseau l'annonciateur. Lyon: Audin, 1954.
598. Emmanuel, Pierre. Notes sur la création poetique. JPNP, 1951, 44:261-268.
599. Endore, Guy. The Heart and the Mind: The Story of Rousseau and Voltaire. London: Allen, 1962.
600. Eng, Erling. Cellini's two childhood memories. Amer Imago, 1956, 13:189-203.
601. Epstein, J. What makes Vidal run. Commentary, 1977, 63: 72-75.
602. Epstein, Perle S. The Private Labyrinth of Malcolm Lowry. Under the Volcano of the Cabbala. NY: Holt, Rinehart & Winston, 1969.

603. Erikson, Erik H. The legend of Maxim Gorky's Youth. In Childhood and Society. NY: Norton, 1950, 316-358.
604. Ernest, J. M., Jr. Whittier and Whitman: uncongenial personalities. Bulletin Friends of History Assn, 1953, 42:21.
605. Escoffier Lambiotte (?). Marcel Proust et la médicine psychosomatique. Le Monde, edition hebomadaire du 25 avril au 1er mai 1957.
606. Esselbrugge, Kurt. Zur Psychologie des Unbewussten in Hebbels Tagebüchern und Briefen. Hebbel-Jahrbuch, 1960, 117-142.
607. Esswein, H. August Strindberg. Ein psychologischer Versuch. Munich: Bergmann, 1907.
608. Estève, P. L. Marcel Proust. Psychologie et vie, 1928, 2: 21-25.
609. Etiemble, René. Le Style de Marcel Proust, est-il celui d'un asthmatique? Temps Modernes, 1947, 20:1489-1496.
610. Euziere, J. [The Balzac mystery as seen by a physician.] Montpellier Médecine, 1959, 56:105-119.
611. Evans, William N. Notes on the conversion of John Bunyan: a study in English Puritanism. Int J Psycho-Anal, 1943, 24:176-185.
612. Eyesenck, H. J. Biography in the service of science: a look at astrology. Biography, 1979, 1.

613. Faber, M. D. Psychoanalytic remarks on a poem by Emily Dickinson. Psychoanal Rev, 1969, 56:246-264.
614. _____. The son-father kills the father-son. Lucius Annaeus Seneca (4 B.C.?-65 A.D.). Hartford Studies in Lit, 1978, 10:14-30.
615. Fabricant, Noah D. Thirteen Famous Patients. Philadelphia: Chilton, 1960.
616. Fairchild, Francis G. A mad man of letters. Scribner's Monthly, 1875, 10:690-699.
617. Falk, Doris V. That paradox O'Neill. Modern Drama, 1963, 6:221-238.
618. Falke, Rita. Biographisch-literarische Hintergründe von Kafkas 'Urteil.' Germanisch-Romanische Monatsschrift, 1960, 10:164-180.
619. Fanthan, H. B. Charles Dickens: a biological study of his personality. Character & Personality, 1934, 2:222-230.
620. Farber, Ada. Freud's love letters. Intimations of psychoanalytic theory. Psychoanal Rev, 1978, 65:166-189.
621. Febvre, L. Sensibility and history: how to reconstitute the emotional life of the past. Annales d'Histoire Sociale, 1941, 3; In Combats pour l'Histoire. Paris: 1953; in Burke, P. (ed), A New Kind of History: From the Writings of Febvre. London: Routledge & Kegan Paul, 1973, 12-26.
622. Fedorov, I. V. [The curator's registration card of the student Chekhov (from archival material).] Klinischesksia Meditsina, 1960, 41:148-153.
623. Fehr, Karl. Leben und Tod bei G. Keller. Speech Monographs, 1950, 30:565-580.

624. Feinberg, Charles E. Walt Whitman and his doctors. Archives Internal Medicine, 1964, 114:834-842.
625. Feinstein, Howard M. The double in The Autobiography of the elder Henry James. Amer Imago, 1974, 31:93-315.
626. _____. The use and abuse of illness in the James family circle: a view of neurasthenia as a social phenomenon. Psychohistory Rev, 1979, 8(1-2):6-14.
627. Feldman, A. Bronson. The confessions of William Shakespeare. Amer Imago, 1953, 10:113-165.
628. _____. The imperial dreams of Disraeli. Psychoanal Rev, 1966-67, 53:609-641.
629. Feldman, Eugene S. Sherwood Anderson's search. Psychoanalysis, 1955, 3(3):44-51.
630. Fellman, Michael. Sexual longing in Richard Henry Dana Jr.'s American Victorian diary. Canadian Rev of Amer Studies, 1972, 3:96-105.
631. Ferdière, Gaston. Folie et littérature: l'expérience vécue de Leonora Carrington. Psyché, 1948, 3:690-697.
632. Ferenczi, Sándor. Anatole France als Analytiker. Zentralblatt für Psychoanalyse, 1911, 1:460-471.
633. _____. The kite as a symbol of erection. In Further Contributions to the Problems and Methods of Psychoanalysis. NY: Basic Books, 1955, 359-360; Int Zeitschrift für Psychoanalyse, 1913, 1:379.
634. _____. To whom does one relate one's dreams? In Further Contributions to the Theory and Technique of Psychoanalysis. NY: Basic Books, 1952, 349; Int Zeitschrift für Psychoanalyse, 1913, 3:258.
635. Fernandez, Diane. John Cowper Powys ou la persistance oedipienne. Preuves, 1967, 196:63-68.
636. _____. Powys et l'eau de l'inconscient maternel. Nouvelle Rev Française, 1972, 20:34-45.
637. Fernández, P. H. El problema de la personalidad en Unamuno. Madrid: Mayfe, 1966.
638. Fernandez, Ramon. La Vie de Molière. Paris: Gallimard, 1929; Review: W. Küchler, Neueren Sprachen, 1930, 38:209-218.
639. Ferrand, Michel. Marcel Proust asthmatique. Paris: Arnette, 1939.
640. Ferrière, A. Marcel Proust et l'asthme. Rev Medical Liege, 1967, 22:287-291.
641. Ferval, C. Jean-Jacques Rousseau et les femmes. Paris: Fayard, 1934.
642. Festa-McCormick, Diana. Proust's asthma: a malady begets a melody. In Peschel, E. R. (ed), Medicine and Literature. NY: Watson, 1980, 120-127.
643. Feustle, Joseph A. Mario Vargas Llosa: a labyrinth of solitude. In Rossman, C. R., & Friedman, A. W. (eds), Mario Vargas Llosa. Austin: Univ. Texas Press, 1978, 128-135; Texas Studies in Lit & Language, 1977, 19:522-529.
644. Field, Leslie. Thomas Wolfe on the couch and in symposium. Southern Lit J, 1972, 5(1):163-176.

645. Fields, Beverly. Reality's Dark Dream: Dejection in Coleridge. Kent, Ohio: Kent State Univ. Press, 1967; DA,
1965, 26:3333-34; Review: Mary Jane Lupton, Lit &
Psychol, 1968, 18:238-241.
646. Fields, Madeleine. De la critique de la raison dialectique
aux Séquestrés D'Altona. PMLA, 1963, 78:623-630.
647. Fifield, William. Joyce's brother, Lawrence's wife, Wolfe's
mother, Twain's daughter. Texas Q, 1967, 10:69-87.
648. Finch, Bernard. The sexual power of drugs. In Passport
to Paradise. NY: Philosophical Library, 1960, 25, 28-
37, 55-56.
649. Fishbein, Leslie. Floyd Dell: the impact of Freud and
Marx on a radical mind. Psychoanal Rev, 1976, 63:267-
280.
650. Fisher, David J. Sigmund Freud and Romain Rolland: the
terrestrial animal and his great oceanic friend. Amer
Imago, 1976, 33:1-59.
651. Fitzgerald, J. A. Death of elderly primigravida in early
pregnancy. Charlotte Brontë. New York State J Medicine, 1979, 79(5):796-799.
652. Flak, Micheline. L'Homme de Concord. Europe 1967, No.
459-460, 158-162.
653. Flanders, Jane. Katherine Anne Porter and the ordeal of
Southern womanhood. Southern Lit J, 1976, 9:47-60.
654. Fleming, Robert E. Hemingway's treatment of suicide:
'fathers and sons' and For Whom the Bell Tolls. Arizona
Q, 1977, 33:121-132.
655. Flood, Jean. Synge's ecstatic dance and the myth of the un-
dying father. Amer Imago, 1976, 133:174-196.
656. Flugel, J. C. Men and Their Motives; Psycho-Analytical
Studies. NY: IUP, 1947; London: Kegan Paul, 1934.
657. Fodéré, René [Jean-Maurienne]. Maupassant est-il mort fou?
Considerations médicales et littéraires sur la vie et la
mort de Guy de Maupassant. Paris: Gründ, 1947.
658. Folman, M. Les Impuissants de genie. Paris: 1957.
659. Fonsny, J. Balzac et sa mère. Études Classiques, 1948,
16(3):221-238.
660. Forclaz, Roger. Le Monde d'Edgar Poe. Bern: Herbert
Lang, 1974; Frankfort: Peter Lang, 1974.
661. Forestier, Louis. G. Nouveau. Paris: Seghers, 1971.
662. Forssberger, Annalisa. Herman Bang. Ekko og Spejling.
Copenhagen: Nordisk Bogforlag, 1975.
663. Fossi, P. La Conversione di Alessandro Manzoni. Bari:
Laterza, 1933.
664. Foster, W. D. Edward Gibbon's health. British Medical J,
1979, 22-29(6205):1633-1655.
665. Foulkes, S. H. Some remarks on a chapter of Helen Keller's
book, The World I Live In. Psychoanal Rev, 1941, 28:
512-519.
666. Fowlie, Wallace. Rimbaud. Chicago: Univ. Chicago Press,
1965; originally 2 Vols.: Rimbaud: The Myth of Childhood. London: Dobson, 1946, and Rimbaud's Illuminations: A Study in Angelism. London: Harvill, 1953;
NY: Grove, 1953.

667. Foy, J. L., et al. Dostoevsky and suicide. Confinia Psychiatrica, 1979, 22(2):65-80.
668. Frade Correia, João. Dinamene ou o Drama Psicológico de Camões. Oporto: Castelo Branco, 1946.
669. Fraiberg, Louis B. Discussion of M. L. Miller's 'Manic depressive cycles of the poet Shelley.' Psychoanal Forum, 1966, 1:196-197.
670. _____. Poe's intimations of mortality. Hartford Studies in Lit, 1973, 5:106-125.
671. Frank, Eduard. Parapsychologisches im Leben und Werk der A. von Droste-Hülshoff. Natur und Kultur, 1954, 46:24-31.
672. Frank, H. R. E. T. A. Hoffmans Todeskrankheit. Deutsches Ärzteblatt, 1967, 64.
673. Frank, Joseph. Freud's case-history of Dostoevsky. Times Lit Supplement, 18 July 1975, 807-808.
674. Franz, Marie-Louise von. Der Traum des Descartes. In Zeitlose Dokumente der Seele. Zürich: Rascher, 1952, 49-119.
675. Franzosa, John. 'The Custom House, ' The Scarlet Letter, and Hawthorne's separation from Salem. Esq: J Amer Renaissance, 1978, 24:57-71.
676. Frederickson, Hélène. Baudelaire: héros et fils. Dualité et problèmes du travail dans les lettres à sa mère. Saratoga, Cal.: Anma Libre, 1977.
677. Frederiksen, Elke P. Grillparzers Tagebücher als Suche nach Selbstverständmis. DAI, 1974, 34:7751A-52A.
678. Fredeman, William E. Prelude to the last decade: Dante Gabriel Rossetti in the summer of 1872. Bulletin John Rylands Library, 1970, 53:75-121.
679. Freedman, Burrill, & Freedman, Sumner. The psychology of Casanova. Psychoanal Rev, 1933, 20:73-78.
680. Freeman, Erika. Insights. Conversations with Theodor Reik. Englewood Cliffs, NJ: Prentice-Hall, 1971.
681. Freeman, Frank R. Oscar Wilde: poet, novelist, playwright, homosexual. MAHS, 1971, 5(6):112-124, passim.
682. Freimark, H. Tolstoj als Charakter. Eine Studie auf Grund seiner Shriften. Wiesbaden: Bergmann, 1909.
683. French, R. S. From Homer to Helen Keller: A Social and Educational Study of the Blind. NY: Amer Foundation for the Blind, 1932.
684. Frenkel, E. Studies in biographical psychology. Character & Personality, 1936, 5:1-34.
685. Fretet, J. Flaubert: l'épilepsie et le style. Evolution Psychiatrique, 1939, 3:3-32.
686. Freud, Sigmund. A childhood recollection from Dichtung und Wahrheit. In Collected Papers, Vol. 4. NY: Basic Books, 1959, 357-367; In Standard Edition, Vol. 17. London: Hogarth, 1955 (1917), 146-156; In Obras Completas, Vol. 18. Buenos Aires, 169-183.
687. _____. A disturbance of memory on the Acropolis. In Standard Edition, Vol. 22. London: Hogarth, 1936, 239-248.

688. _____. Dostoevsky and parricide. Realist, 1929, 2:18-33; Almanach, 1930, 9-31; Int J Psycho-Anal, 1945, 26:1-8; In Collected Papers, Vol. 5. NY: Basic Books, 1959, 222-242; In Standard Edition, Vol. 21. London: Hogarth, 1961; NY: Basic Books, 1961, 177-194; in Wellek, R. (ed), Dostoevsky. A Collection of Critical Essays. Englewood Cliffs, NJ: Prentice-Hall, 1962, 98-111; In Ruitenbeek, H. M. (ed), Literary Imagination. Chicago: Quadrangle, 1965, 329-348.

689. _____. Letters. London: Hogarth, 1961, 261, 344.

690. _____. Preface to Marie Bonaparte's Edgar Poe, Etude Psychanalytique. Paris: Denoël et Steele, 1933; London: Imago, 1949, XI; In Standard Edition, Vol. 22. London: Hogarth, 1961.

691. Fricke, Hermann. Zur Pathographie des Dichters Theodor Fontane. In Theodor-Fontane-Archiv (ed), Theodor Fontanes Werk in unserer Zeit. Potsdam: Brandenburgische Landes- und Hochschulbibliothek, 1966, 95-112.

692. Friedlander, Kate. Charlotte Brontë: a study of a masochistic character. Int J Psycho-Anal, 1943, 24:45-54; Int Zeitschrift für Psychoanalyse, 1941, 26:32-49; In Ruitenbeek, H. M. (ed), The Literary Imagination. Chicago: Quadrangle, 1965, 187-209.

693. Friedman, Michael H. The princely and contracted Wordsworth: a study of Wordsworth's personality in terms of psychoanalytic ego psychology. Wordsworth Circle, 1978, 9:406-412.

694. Friedrich, Otto. Clover. NY: Simon & Schuster, 1979.

695. Frijling-Schreuder, Elisabeth C. M. Honoré de Balzac--a disturbed boy who did not get treatment. Int J Psycho-Anal, 1964, 45:426-430; Psyche, 1965, 18:608-615; In Ruitenbeek, H. M. (ed), The Literary Imagination. Chicago: Quadrangle, 1965, 379-390.

696. Fromm, Harold. Virginia Woolf: art and sexuality. Virginia Q Rev, 1979, 55:441-459.

697. Fruhock, W. M. Thomas Wolfe: of time and neurosis. Southwest Rev, 1948, 33:349-360; In Ruitenbeek, H. M. (ed), The Literary Imagination. Chicago: Quadrangle, 1965, 211-231.

698. Fruman, Norman. Coleridge, the Damaged Archangel. NY: Braziller, 1971.

699. _____. Coleridge and the opium mystique. [Review article.] Queens Q, 1975, 440-444.

700. Fülop-Miller, R. Dostojewski's 'heilige krankheit.' Neue Schweizer Rundschau, 1924, 17:1184-1201.

701. Fujimura, Thomas H. The personal element in Dryden's poetry. PMLA, 1974, 89:1007-1023.

702. Funck-Bretano, T. Jean-Jacques Rousseau. Etude historique et médicale sur la folie et ses conséquences philosophiques. Annales Philosophiques Chrétiennes, 1895, 131:56-579.

703. Furbank, P. N. E. M. Forster: A Life. NY: Harcourt Brace Jovanovich, 1978.

704. Futrell, Michael. Dostoyevsky and Islam (and Chokan Valikhanov). Slavonic & East European Rev, 1979, 57:16-31.

705. Gabel, Joseph. Génie et folie chez Guy de Maupassant.
       These médicine. Paris: Jouve, 1940.
706. _____. Swift et le schizophrénie. Le Point de vue du
       psychiatrie. Psyché, 1949, 4:253-258.
707. Galand, René. La Vision de l'inconscient chez Baudelaire.
       Symposium, 1972, 26:15-23.
708. Galant, I. B. [The psychopathological figure of L. Andreyev.]
       Klinischeski Arkiv Genialnosti i Odarennosti, 1927, 2:147-
       165.
709. Galant, Johann S. Die prägenitale Sexualität nach einem Kind-
       heitserlebnis Leonid Andrejews. Archivo für Kinderheil-
       kunde, 1927, 81:262-280.
710. _____. Zur Psychopathologie des Traumlebens Maxim
       Gorkis. Über zwei Träume Maxim Gorkis, ihre Deutung
       durch Leo Nikolajewitsch Tolstoi und ihre richtige Psy-
       choanalyse. Zentralblatt für Psychotherapie, 1928, 1:528-
       536.
711. Galdston, Iago. Descartes and modern psychiatric thought.
       Isis, 1944, 35:118-128.
712. Gallati, Ernst. Neues zur Persönlichkeit des alten Goethe
       (nach bisher unbekannten Briefen von Frédéric Soret). In
       Arnold, A., et al. (eds), Analecta Helvetica et Germanica:
       Eine Festschrift zu Ehren von Hermann Boeschenstein.
       Bonn: Bouvier, 1979.
713. Gallot, H. M. Psychoanalyse de Huysmans. Evolution Psy-
       chiatrique, 1948, 4:53-72.
714. Gandelman, Claude. Proust's draft copy-books: sketches of
       his dreams. Amer Imago, 1977, 34:297-312.
715. Garde, Noel I. Jonathan to Gide. The Homosexual in His-
       tory. NY: Vantage, 1964.
716. Gardner, Joseph H. Mark Twain and Dickens. PMLA, 1969,
       84:90-101.
717. Gardner, Thomas. Vladimir Nabokov. Studium Generale,
       1968, 21:94-110.
718. Garma, Angel. Essai de psychanalyse d'Arthur Rimbaud.
       Rev Française de Psychoanalyse, 1938, 10:383-420; Rev
       de Psiquiatria y Criminalia, 1940, 5:167-200; In Ruiten-
       beek, H. M. (ed), Homosexuality and Creative Genius.
       NY: Obolensky, 1967, 205-236.
719. Garraty, John A. The application of content analysis to
       biography and history. In Pool, I. de S. (ed), Trends
       in Content Analysis. Urbana: Univ. Illinois Press,
       1959.
720. _____. The interrelations of psychology and biography.
       Psychol Bulletin, 1954, 51:569-582.
721. _____. The Nature of Biography. NY: Knopf, 1957;
       London: Cape, 1958; NY: Random House, 1964.
722. Garrett, Marvin P. Early recollections and structural irony
       in The Autobiography of an Ex-Colored Man. Criticism,
       1971, 13(2):5-14.
723. Gass, William H. The anatomy of mind. In The World
       Within the Word. NY: Knopf, 1978, 208-252; New York
       Rev of Books, 17 Apr 1975, 1 May 1975, 15 May 1975.

724. Gastaut, H. Fyodor Mikhailovitch Dostoevsky's involuntary contribution to the symptomology and prognosis of epilepsy. Epilepsia, 1978, 19:186-201.

725. Gatti, Guglielmo. Le case di D'Annunzio. Osservatore Politico Letterario, 1965, 11(7):57-68.

726. Gaudot, H. Tableaux généalogiques. Les Ascendants paternels et maternels de Jean Racine. Cahiers Raciniens, 1965, 18:87-95.

727. Gautier, Théophile. The hashish club. In Solomon, D. (ed), The Marihuana Papers. NY: Signet, 1966, 163-178; In Pichois, C. (ed), Le Club des hachichins. Paris: Gallimard, 1977 (1846).

728. Gay, Carol. The fettered tongue: a study of the speech defect of Cotton Mather. Amer Lit, 1975, 46:451-464.

729. _____. The philosopher and his daughter: Amos Bronson Alcott and Louisa. Essays in Lit, 1975, 2:181-191.

730. Gazarian, Maria-Lise. The Prose of Gabriela Mistral: An Expression of Her Life and Personality. DAI, 1971, 31: 4769A.

731. Gedo, John E. The method of psychoanalytic biography. JAPA, 1972, 20:638-649.

732. _____, & Wolf, Ernest S. Freud's novelas ejemplares. In Gedo, J. E., & Pollock, G. H. (eds), Freud: The Fusion of Science and Humanism. NY: IUP, Psychological Issues, 9(2-3), Monograph 34-35, 1976, 87-111; In Annual of Psychoanalysis, Vol. 1. NY: Quadrangle, 1973, 299-317.

733. Geha, Richard. Albert Camus: another will for death. Psychoanal Rev, 1967, 54:662-678.

734. _____. Richard Crashaw: (1613?-1650?): the ego's soft fall. Amer Imago, 1966, 23:158-168.

735. Gelma, E. La Dépression mélancolique du poète Ovide pendant son exil. Médicine d'Alsace et de Lorraine, 1935, 28p.

736. _____. A propos d'une psychanalyse de Joris-Karl Huysmans. Cahiers Psychiatrie, 1949, 3.

737. Gerber, John C. Mark Twain's search for identity. In Schultz, M. F., et al. (eds), Essays in American and English Literature. Athens: Ohio Univ. Press, 1967, 27-47.

738. _____. Mark Twain's use of the comic pose. PMLA, 1962, 77:297-304.

739. Gérin, Winifred. The Brontës. I. The formative years. Writers & Their Work, No. 232, 1973, 1-68.

740. Gerle, B. Elden i brott och skapande fantasi. Svensk Litteraturtidskrift, 1970, 33, No. 3.

741. Gerrard, Charlotte F. Montherlant and Suicide. Madrid: Turanzas, 1978; Washington, DC: Catholic Univ. of America, 1977.

742. Gidley, Mick. Another psychologist, a physiologist and William Faulkner. Ariel: Rev Int English Lit, 1971, 2(4): 78-86.

743. Giese, Hans. Casanova und Don Juan. Philosophische Jahrbuch, 1949.

744. Giles, James K., & Giles, Wanda. An interview with Jim Rechy. Chicago Rev, 1973, 25:19-31.
745. Gille-Maisani, J.-C. Écritures de poètes de Byron à Baudelaire. Paris: Dervy-Livres, 1977.
746. Gilmore, Myron P. An Italian personality. Belfagor, 1967, 22:314-316.
747. Girard, N. Superman in the underground: strategies of madness. Nietzsche, Wagner and Dostoyevsky. Modern Language Notes, 1976, 91:1161-1185.
748. Giordan, H. [Eroticism in Bernanos.] Rev des Lettres Modernes, 1971, Nos. 254-259.
749. _____. Romain Rolland à la découverte de l'italianité. Rev de Littérature Comparée, 1966, 40:258-270.
750. Giraud, R. Rousseau's happiness--triumph or tragedy. Yale French Studies, 1961-62, 28:75-82.
751. Gittleman, Edwin. Jones Very: The Effective Years 1833-1840. NY: Columbia Univ. Press, 1967.
752. Glaser, R. Goethes Vater. Sein Leben nach Tagebüchern und Zeitberichten. Leipzig, 1929.
753. Glenn, Jules. Narcissistic aspect of Freud and his doubles. In Kanzer, M., & Glenn, J. (eds), Freud and His Self Analysis. NY: Aronson, 1980.
754. Goad, Mary E. The image and the woman in the life and writings of Mark Twain. Emporia State Research Studies, 1971, 19(3):5-70.
755. Gobled, R. A la recherche de L.-F. Céline. Archives Médico-Chirugicales de Normandie, 1964, 365-368.
756. Godlewski, G. Balzac ou la fureur de se d'etruire. Seminar des Hopitaux de Paris, 1975, 51:3041-3054.
757. Goertzel, Victor. So They Had Problems Too. Boston: Little Brown, 1961.
758. Golan, Shmuel (ed). Introduction to Yoman (A Diary). Ofakim, 1954, 8:258-288.
759. Gold, Maxwell. Swift's Marriage to Stella. Cambridge: Harvard Univ. Press, 1937, 126-146.
760. Goldman, Arnold. The vanity of personality: the development of Eugene O'Neill. In Brown, J.R., & Harris, B. (eds), American Theatre. London: Arnold, 1967, 28-51.
761. Goldstein, Jan Ellen. The Woolfs' response to Freud; water-spiders, singing canaries, and the second apple. Psychoanal Q, 1974, 43:438-476.
762. Gonchar, Ruth M. Rhetorical Biography. DAI, 1976, 37:1871A.
763. Goodwin, Donald W. The alcoholism of Eugene O'Neill. JAMA, 1971, 216:99-104.
764. _____. The alcoholism of F. Scott Fitzgerald. JAMA, 1970, 212:86-90.
765. Gorceix, Simone, & Gorceix, Antoine. Thomas Chatterton: 'Un suicide d'adolescent à Londres en 1770.' Annales Médico-Psychologiques, 1971, 1:161-184.
766. Gordon, Lois, & Gordon, Alan. Say goodbye to Randall Jarrell (1914-1965). Hartford Studies in Lit, 1978, 10:122-136.

767. Gordon, William Alexander. Autobiography and identity: Wordsworth's The Borderers. Tulane Studies in English, 1972, 20:71-86.

768. Gorer, Geoffrey. The Life and Ideas of the Marquis de Sade. NY: Norton, 1963; London: Owen, 1953.

769. _____. The myth in Jane Austen. Amer Imago, 1941, 2:197-204; In Phillips, W. (ed), Art and Psychoanalysis. NY: Criterion, 1957, 218-225.

770. Gottleib, M. Pablo Neruda, poeta de amor. Cuadernos Americanos, 1966, 25:211-222.

771. Gougeon, Leonard G. The Forgotten God: A Study of Ralph Waldo Emerson as Man and Myth. DAI, 1974, 35:2940A-41A.

772. Gould, G. M. A biographic clinic on Gustav Flaubert. Medical Record, 1906, 69:569-578.

773. _____. Biographic Clinics. The Origin of the Ill-Health of DeQuincey, Carlyle, Darwin, Huxley and Browning. Philadelphia: Blakiston, 1903.

774. _____. Lafcadio Hearn. A study of his personality and art. Fortnightly Rev, 1906, 86:685-695, 881-892.

775. Gozzi, Raymond D. Mother-Nature. In Harding, W. (ed), Henry David Thoreau: A Profile. NY: Hill & Wang, 1973, 172-187.

776. _____. Some aspects of Thoreau's personality. In Harding, W. (ed), Henry David Thoreau: A Profile. NY: Hill & Wang, 1973, 150-172.

777. _____. Tropes and Figures: A Psychological Study of Henry David Thoreau. Doctoral dissertation, New York Univ., 1957; Ann Arbor: Univ. Microfilms No. 21, 762, 1957.

778. Gracie, William J., Jr. Father-Son Conflict in Selected Victorian Autobiographies and Autobiographical Novels. DAI, 1970, 30:4411A.

779. Graf, Max. Methodology of the psychology of poets. In Nunberg, H., & Federn, E. (eds), Minutes of the Vienna Psychoanalytic Society, Vol. 1: 1906-1908. NY: IUP, 1962, 259-269.

780. Graham, V. E. Water imagery and symbolism in Proust. Romanic Rev, 1959, 50:118-128.

781. Grandgeorges, Pierre. Rimbaud ou l'adolescence. La Grive, 1954, 80:2-10.

782. Grant, Richard B. Théophile Gautier. Boston: Twayne, 1975.

783. Grant, Vernon W. Edgar Allan Poe: a psychosexual biography. MAHS, 1971, 5(9):172-185 passim.

784. _____. Great Abnormals: The Pathological Genius of Kafka, van Gogh, Strindberg and Poe. NY: Hawthorn, 1968.

785. _____. Paranoid dynamics: a case study. Amer J Psychiat, 1956, 113:143-148.

786. Grattan, Clinton Hartley. The Three Jameses: A Family of Minds. NY: Longmans, Green, 1932.

787. Graucob, K. Hans Carossas Selbstdarstellung seiner Kindheit
und Jugend in ihrer Entwicklungs-und typenspsychologischen
Bedeutung. Zeitschrift für angewandte Psychologie, 1933,
44:217-244.

788. Graves, Richard Perceval. A. E. Housman. The Scholar-
Poet. NY: Scribner's, 1980.

789. Gray, Charlotte Schlander. From opposition to identification:
social and psychological structure behind Henrik Pontop-
pidan's literary development. Scandinavian Studies, 1979,
51:273-284.

790. Grebanier, Bernard D. The Uninhibited Byron: An Account
of His Sexual Confusion. NY: Crown, 1971.

791. Greco, Francesco del. Sulle anormalita di caracttere di alcuni grandi intellecttuali. Archivio Generale di Neurologie, Psichiatria e Psicoanalisti, 1929, 10:182-189.

792. Grecco, Stephen R. High hopes: Eugene O'Neill and alcohol.
Yale French Studies, 1974, 50:142-149.

793. Green, Frederick C. Jean-Jacques Rousseau. Cambridge:
Cambridge Univ. Press, 1955.

794. _____. The Mind of Proust. Cambridge, Eng.: Cambridge Univ. Press, 1949.

795. Greenacre, Phyllis. Charles Lutwidge Dodgson and Lewis
Carroll: Reconstitution et interprétation d'une évolution.
[Excerpt from Swift and Carroll.] In Parisot, H. (ed),
Lewis Carroll. Paris: l'Herne, 1971, 187-210.

796. _____. The childhood of the artist: libidinal phase development and giftedness. In The Psychoanalytic Study of
the Child, Vol. 12. NY: IUP, 1957, 47-72; In Emotional
Growth: Psychoanalytic Studies of the Gifted, Vol. 2.
NY: IUP, 1971, 479-504; In Ruitenbeek, H. M. (ed), The
Creative Imagination. Chicago: Quadrangle, 1965, 161-
191.

797. _____. Emotional Growth: Psychoanalytic Studies of the
Gifted and a Great Variety of Other Individuals. NY:
IUP, 1971, 399-618.

798. _____. The family romance of the artist. In The Psychoanalytic Study of the Child, Vol. 13. NY: IUP, 1958, 9-
43; In Emotional Growth: Psychoanalytic Studies of the
Gifted, Vol. 2. NY: IUP, 1971, 505-532.

799. _____. The imposter. Psychoanalytic Q, 1958, 27:359-
382; In Emotional Growth: Psychoanalytic Studies of the
Gifted, Vol. 1. NY: IUP, 1971, 93-112.

800. _____. 'It's my own invention': a special screen memory
of Mr. Lewis Carroll, its form and its history. Psychoanal Q, 1955; 24:200-244; In Emotional Growth: Psychoanalytic Studies of the Gifted, Vol. 2. NY: IUP, 1971,
438-478.

801. _____. On nonsense. In Emotional Growth: Psychoanalytic Studies of the Gifted, Vol. 2. NY: IUP, 1971,
(1966), 592-615.

802. _____. Notes on plagiarism: the Henley-Stevenson quarrel. JAPA, 1978, 26:507-539.

803. _____. Swift and Carroll: A Psychoanalytic Study of Two Lives. NY: IUP, 1955; Review: Frederick Wyatt, Contemporary Psychol, 1956, 1:105-107.

804. _____. Woman as artist. Psychoanalytic Q, 1960, 29: 208-227; In Emotional Growth: Psychoanalytic Studies of the Gifted, Vol. 2. NY: IUP, 1971, 575-591.

805. Greenblatt, Howard Bruce. Studies in Self-Portraiture: Essays on Rousseau, Joyce, Proust, Miller, Céline. DAI, 1976, 37:963A.

806. Greensberger, Evelyn B. The Phoenix on the wall: consciousness in Emerson's early and late journals. Amer Transcendental Q, 1974, 21:45-56.

807. Greenwood, A. John Milton. Int Zeitschrift für Individual-Psychologie, 1930, 8:401-416.

808. Gregory, Hoosag K. Cowper's love of subhuman nature: a psychoanalytic approach. Philological Q, 1967, 46:42-57.

809. _____. Lord Byron and Thomas Wolfe, A Comparison of Their Philosophical and Personal Problems. Master's Thesis, Univ. Illinois, 1940.

810. _____. The Prisoner and His Crimes: A Psychological Approach to William Cowper's Life and Writings. Doctoral dissertation. Harvard Univ., 1951.

811. _____. The prisoner and his crimes: summary comments on a longer study of the mind of William Cowper. Lit & Psychol, 1956, 6(2):53-59.

812. Gribben, Alan. Mark Twain, phrenology and the 'temperament': a study of pseudoscientific influence. Amer Q, 1972, 24:45-68.

813. Gribble, F. H. Rousseau and the Women He Loved. NY: Scribner's, 1908.

814. Grier, Edward F. Whitman's sexuality. Walt Whitman Rev, 1976, 22:163-166.

815. Griffith, John. Franklin's sanity and the man behind the mask. In Lemay, J. A. L. (ed), The Oldest Revolutionary: Essays on Benjamin Franklin. Philadelphia: Univ. Pennsylvania Press, 1976, 123-138.

816. Griggs, E. L. (ed). Collected Letters of Samuel Taylor Coleridge. 4 Vols. London: Clarendon, 1956, 1959. Vol. 1, 246, 277.

817. _____. Samuel Taylor Coleridge and opium. Huntington Library Q, 1954, 357-378.

818. Grigson, Geoffrey. Lou Andreas-Salomé. In The Contrary View. Totowa, N. J.: Rowman & Littlefield, 1974, 44-47.

819. Grimsley, Ronald R. Jean-Jacques Rousseau: A Study in Self-Awareness. Cardiff: Univ. Wales Press, 1961.

820. Grinstein, Alexander. On Oscar Wilde. In The Annual of Psychoanalysis, Vol. 1. NY: Quadrangle, 1973, 345-362.

821. _____. Oscar Wilde. Amer Imago, 1980, 37:125-179.

822. _____. On Sigmund Freud's Dreams. Detroit: Wayne State Univ. Press, 1975; NY: IUP, 1979.

823. Grolnick, Simon A. Emily and the psychobiographer, Lit & Psychol, 1973, 23:68-81.

\. Gross, Gloria Sybil. Samuel Johnson's case history of Richard Savage. Hartford Studies in Lit, 1980, 12:39-47.

825. Gross, Rebecca H. Voltaire: Nonconformist. NY: Philosophical Library, 1965.

826. Grosskurth, Phyllis. Havelock Ellis, A Biography. NY: Knopf, 1980.

827. _____. The problem. In John Addington Symonds, A Biography. London: Longmans, 1964, 262-294.

828. Grotjahn, Martin. The defenses against creative anxiety in the life and work of James Barrie: commentary to John Skinner's research of 'The boy who wouldn't grow up.' Amer Imago, 1957, 14:143-148.

829. _____. Sigmund Freud and the art of letter writing. JAMA, 1967, 200(1):13-18.

830. _____. Sigmund Freud as dreamer, writer and friend. Voices, 1969, 5(2):70-73.

831. Groves, B. Cowan. The death of Poe: the case for hypoglycemia. RE: Artes Liberales, 1979, 5:7-19.

832. Gruhle, H. W. Selbstbiographie und Personlichkeitsforschung. Berliner Kongress für experimentalle Psychologie, 1924, 8:165-167.

833. Guéhnno, J. Jean-Jacques: Histoire d'une conscience. Paris: Gallimard, 1962.

834. Guerard, Albert J. André Gide. Cambridge: Harvard Univ. Press, 1969.

835. _____. Thomas Hardy. Norfolk, Conn.: New Directions, 1964.

836. Guerin, J. G. E. Pathologie de Honoré de Balzac. Paris: Thèse Médicine, 1938.

837. Guggenheim, M. Des Essais aux Confessions: Deux écrivains devant leur moi. French Rev, 1961, 34:517-524.

838. Guillaume, L., & Dubreuil-Chambardel, (?). Le Cerveau d'Anatole France. Bulletin de l'Academie de Médicine, 1927, 91:328-336.

839. Guillemain, Bernard. Sade était masochiste. Psyché, 1953, 8:486-497.

840. Guillemin, H. Un homme, deux ombres (Jean-Jacques, Julie, Sophie). Geneva: du Milieu du Monde, 1943.

841. Guimarães, Vicente. Joãozito. Infância de João Guimarães Rosa. Rio de Janeiro: Olympio, 1973.

842. Gurrier, P. Etude médico-psychologique sur Thomas de Quincey. Lyon: Rey, 1908.

843. Gustafsson, B. Karin Boyes okända förklaring. Svensk Litteraturtidskrift, 1973, 36(4):31-34.

844. Gutheil, Emil A. The exhibitionism of Jean Jacques Rousseau: an abstract of Stekel's analysis. Amer J Psychotherapy, 1962, 16:266-277.

845. _____. Sexual dysfunctions in men. In Arieti, S. (ed), American Handbook of Psychiatry, Vol. I. NY: Basic Books, 1959, 708-726.

846. Guthke, K. S. (ed). Remarks on the Conduct of Jean-Jacques Rousseau (1767). Los Angeles: Univ. California Los Angeles, 1960.

847. Gutwirth, Madelyn. Madame de Staël, Novelist: The Emergence of the Artist as Woman. Urbana: Univ. Illinois Press, 1978.

848. Haas, R. Eugene O'Neill. Studium Generale, 1968, 21:19-35.

849. Haffenden, John. Beginning of the end: John Berryman, December 1970 to January 1971. Critical Q, 1976, 18: 81-90.

850. _____. Drink as disease: John Berryman. Partisan Rev, 1977, 44:565-583.

851. Hagenbüchle, Roland. Whitman's unfinished quest for an American identity. J English Lit History, 1973, 40:428-478.

852. Hahn, L. Psycho-pathologie de Goethe. Chronique Médicale, 1904, 11:10.

853. Hahn, Otto. Portrait d'Antonin Artaud. Paris: Soleil Noir, 1968.

854. Haight, Gordon S. George Eliot: A Biography. NY: Oxford Univ. Press, 1968.

855. _____. Virginia Woolf. Yale Rev, 1973, 62:426-431.

856. Haimovici, J. Amiel ou l'introspection morbide en littérature. Paris Médicine: La Semaine du Clinician, 1929, 19:3-7.

857. Hakim, Eleanor. Jean-Paul Sartre: the dialectics of myth. Rev Existential Psychol & Psychiat, 1974, 13:1-29.

858. Haldane, Charlotte. Alfred: The Passionate Life of Alfred de Musset. NY: Roy, 1961.

859. Hall, Calvin S., & Lind, Richard E. Dreams, Life, and Literature--A Study of Franz Kafka. Chapel Hill: Univ. North Carolina Press, 1970; Review: Robert N. Wilson, Contemporary Psychology, 1970, 15:596-597.

860. Hall, G. Stanley. Adolescence in literature, biography and history. In Adolescence: Its Psychology, Vol. 1. NY: Appleton, 1904, 513-589.

861. Halliday, James L. Mr. Carlyle, My Patient: A Psychosomatic Biography. NY: Grune & Stratton, 1950.

862. Halpert, Eugene. Lermontov and the Wolf Man. Amer Imago, 1975, 32:315-328.

863. Haltresht, Michael. Sadomasochism in John Osborne's 'A Letter to My Fellow Countrymen.' Notes on Contemporary Lit, 1974, 4(3):10-12.

864. Hamburger, Käte. Leo Tolstoi: Gestalt und Problem. Bern: Francke, 1950.

865. Hamilton, Alice. Loneliness and alienation: the life and work of Carson McCullers. Dalhousie Rev, 1970, 50: 215-229.

866. Hamilton, James W. Internal consistency and the scope of interpretation in psychobiography. Psychohistory Rev, 1980, 8(4):37-45.

867. _____. Joseph Conrad: his development as an artist, 1889-1910. In The Psychoanalytic Study of Society, Vol. 8. New Haven: Yale Univ. Press, 1979, 277-330.

868. _____. The significance of depersonalization in the life and writings of Joseph Conrad. Psychoanal Q, 1975, 44:612-630.

869. Hamilton, Kenneth. Mr. Albee's dream. Queen's Q, 1963, 60:393-399.

870. Hamilton, L. Beiträge zu Oscar Wildes Biographie. Zeit-
     schrift für Sexualwissenschaft, 1918, 4:321-332.
871. Hampshire, Stuart N. Freud and Lou Andreas-Salomé. In
     Modern Writers and Other Essays. NY: Knopf, 1970,
     88-95.
872. Hannay, Margaret P. C. S. Lewis and homosexuality. Bul-
     letin New York C. S. Lewis Society, 1973, 5(1):2-5.
873. Hansen, Alb. Hans Christian Andersen. Beweis seiner Homo-
     sexualität. Jahrbuch für Sexuelle Zwischenstufen, 1901,
     3:203-230.
874. Harding, Gösta. Psykoanalytiskt intermezzo. Horisont, 1968,
     15(1-2):52-56.
875. _____. Sin egen psykiater. Bonniers Litterära Magasin,
     1963, 32:556-558.
876. Hardy, Evelyn. The Conjured Spirit: A Study in the Rela-
     tionship of Swift, Stella and Vanessa. London: Hogarth,
     1949.
877. Hardy, Richard E., & Cull, John G. Hemingway: A Psycho-
     logical Portrait. Birmingham, Ala.: Banner, 1977.
878. Harms, Ernest. Die psychologische Bedeutung des Tages-
     buches. Psyche, 1934, 9.
879. Harris, Irving D. Tendencies in literature. In The Promised
     Seed. A Comparative Study of Eminent First and Later
     Sons. NY: Free Press, 1964, 171-196.
880. Harris, Kathryn Gibbs. Two difficult biographies of Robert
     Frost. Lit & Psychol, 1979, 29:19-24.
881. Hartsock, Mildred E. Biography: the treacherous art. J
     Modern Lit, 1970, 1(1):116-119.
882. _____. The most valuable thing: James on death. Mod-
     ern Fiction Studies, 1977, 22:507-524.
883. Hassan, Ihab Habib. Sade: prisoner of consciousness.
     Triquarterly, 1969, 15:23-41.
884. Hassoun, Jacques. Variations psychoanalytiques sur un thème
     généalogique de Heinrich von Kleist. Romantisme, 1974,
     8.
885. Hatcher, Harlan H. Sherwood Anderson. In Creating the
     Modern American Novel. NY: Russell & Russell, 1965
     (1935) 155-172.
886. Hatten, J. [Bernanos' use of key words.] Rev des Lettres
     Modernes, 1971, Nos. 254-259.
887. Hausner, Henry H. Die Beziehungen zwischen Arthur Schnitz-
     ler und Sigmund Freud. Modern Austrian Lit, 1970, 3(2):
     48-61.
888. Häutler, Adolph. Nietzsche's Ecce Homo. In Nunberg, H., &
     Federn, E. (eds), Minutes of the Vienna Psychoanalytic
     Society, Vol. 2: 1908-1910, NY: IUP, 1967, 25-33.
889. Havenstein, Martin. Thomas Mann, der Dichter und Schrift-
     steller. Berlin: Wiegand & Grieben, 1927.
890. Hawthorne, Manning. Parental and family influences on Haw-
     thorne. Essex Institute Historical Collections, 1940.
891. Hayman, Ronald. Artaud and After. NY: Oxford Univ.
     Press, 1977.
892. _____. De Sade: A Critical Biography. NY: Crowell,
     1978.

893. Haynes, Jean. Keats's paternal relatives. Keats-Shelley
     Memorial Bulletin, 1964, No. 15, 27-28.
894. Hedenberg, Sven. August Strindberg: opinions of German
     psychiatrists; criticism of studies by Jaspers, Rahmer
     and Storch. Acta Psychiatrica et Neurologica Scandina-
     vica, 1954, 34:325-339.
895. _____. Strindberg's fear of dogs. Acta Psychiatrica
     Scandinavia, 1964, 40: (Suppl 180):111-113.
896. _____. Strindberg i skärselden. En psykiatrisk studie.
     Göteborg: Akademiförlaget-Gumperts, 1961.
897. Hedges, William L. Irving, Hawthorne, and the image of the
     wife. Amer Transcendental Q, 1970, 5:22-26.
898. Heidenhain, Adolf. J. J. Rousseau, Persönlichkeit, Philo-
     sophie, und Psychose. Munich: Bergmann, 1924.
899. _____. Über den Menschenhass. Eine pathographische
     Untersuchung über Jonathan Swift. Stuttgart: 1934.
900. Heider, Fritz. The description of the psychological environ-
     ment of Marcel Proust. Character & Personality, 1941,
     9:295-314; Psychol Issues, 1959, 1:85-107.
901. Heidler, H. B., & Lehman, H. C. Chronological age and
     productivity. English J, 1937, 294-304.
902. Heilbrunn, E. Stendhal. Jahrbuch für Charakterologie, 1929,
     6:155-177.
903. Heimann, J. Die Heilung der Elisabeth Browning in ihrer
     Sonetten. Imago, 1935, 21:227-254.
904. Helein, Suzanne. Une Etude caracterologique de la person-
     nalité d'André Gide. DA, 1960, 20:4659-4660.
905. Heller, Erich. Autobiography and literature. Introduction to
     Thomas Mann's Death in Venice. NY: Modern Library,
     1970.
906. Heller, Peter. The liberal radical as a suicide: notes on
     Ernst Toller. Modernist Studies: Lit & Culture 1920-
     1940, 1976, 2(1):3-13.
907. Helweg, H. Hans Christian Andersen: masturbator and
     hetero rather than homosexual. Zeitschrift für Neurologie
     und Psychiatrie, 1929, 118:777-788.
908. Hendel, C. W. Jean-Jacques Rousseau, Moralist. NY: Ox-
     ford Univ. Press, 1934; Philadelphia: Bobbs Merrill,
     1962.
909. Henderson, Archibald. Coriolanus and the grief of Shake-
     speare. In Stafford, T. J. (ed), Shakespeare in the South-
     west. Some New Directions. Austin: Univ. Texas
     Press, 1969, 71-79.
910. Henighan, T. J. Mr. Bransdon: a Ford lampoon of Conrad?
     Amer Notes & Queries, 1969, 8:3-4; 20-22.
911. Henmark, K. Fran Delphi till Det heliga landet. Bonniers
     Litterära Magasin, 1965, 34(4).
912. Hennessey, J. P. Robert Louis Stevenson. NY: Simon &
     Schuster, 1975.
913. Henriot, E. Les Secrets du coeur de Racine. Courrier lit-
     téraire du XVIIe siècle, 1959, 11:136-141, 182-186.
914. Henseler, Donna L. The psychic world of James Joyce.
     Psychic, 1972, 3(4):27-31.

915. Hermann, Imré. Gustav Theodor Fechner. Eine psycho-analytische Studie über individuelle Bedingtheiten wissen-schaftlicher Ideen. Vienna: Int Psychoanalytischer Ver-lag, 1925.

916. _____. Die Regression zum zeichnerischen Ausdruck bei Goethe. Imago, 1924, 10:424-430.

917. _____. Zwei Überlieferungen aus Pascals Kinderjahren. Imago, 1925, 11:346-351.

918. Herring, Maben D. The Defined Self in Black Autobiography. DAI, 1974, 35:404A.

919. Hess, E. Dostojewsky über seine epileptischen Anfälle. Zentralblatt für Psychiatrie, 1898, 55:117-119.

920. Hesse, Hermann. Autobiographical Writings. NY: Farrar, Straus & Giroux, 1972.

921. _____. Hesse and Jung. Two letters. Psychoanal Rev, 1963, 50:16.

922. Hesse, Ninon, & Kirschhoff, Gerhard (eds). Kindheit und Jugend vor Neunzehnhundert: Hermann Hesse in Briefen und Lebensgeugnissen. II. 1895-1900. Frankfort: Suhrkamp, 1978.

923. Highet, Gilbert. The personality of Joyce. In Explorations. NY: Oxford Univ. Press, 1971, 135-146.

924. Hijiya, James. New England women and madness: an essay review. Essex Institute Historical Collections, 1975, 111:228-239.

925. Hildebrand, J. Jean-Jacques Rousseau vom Standpunkt der Psychiatrie. Clèves: 1884.

926. Hilles, F. W. Dr. Johnson on Swift's last years: some mis-conceptions and distortions. Phililogical Q, 1975, 54:370-379.

927. Hillway, Tyrus. The personality of H. D. Thoreau. College English, 1945, 6:328-330.

928. Himmelfarb, Gertrude. Clio and Oedipus. Times Lit Sup-plement, 23 May 1975, 565-566.

929. Hirth, G. Er pathologisch? Ein Beitrag zur Feier von Goethes 150. Geburstag. Munich: Hirth, 1899.

930. Hitschmann, Edward. Die Bedeutung der Psychoanalyse für die Biographik. Psychoanalytische Bewegung, 1930, 2:305-313.

931. _____. Die Bindung Eckermanns an Goethe demonstriert an zwei Träumen Eckermanns. Psychoanalytische Bewe-gung, 1933, 5:520-528.

932. _____. Boswell: the biographer's character; a psycho-analytic interpretation. Psychoanal Q, 1948, 17:212-225; In The Yearbook of Psychoanalysis, Vol. 5. NY: IUP, 1949, 294-305.

933. _____. Ein Dichter und sein Vater--Dauthendy. Imago, 1916, 4:337-345.

934. _____. Ein Gespent aus der Kindhert Knut Hamsuns. Imago, 1926, 12:336-360; Vienna: Int Psychoanalytischer Verlag, 1926.

935. _____. Franz Werfel als Erzieher--der Vater. Psycho-analytische Bewegung, 1932, 4:57-61; Almanach, 1933, 243-248.

936. _____. Gottfried Keller. Psychoanalyse des Dichters, seine Gestalten und Motive. Vienna: Int Psychoanalytischer Verlag, 1919.

937. _____. Great Men: Psychoanalytic Studies. NY: IUP, 1956.

938. _____. Johann Peter Eckermann. Psychoanalytische Bewegung, 1933, 5:392-414.

939. _____. Knut Hamsun und die Psychoanalyse. Psychoanalytische Bewegung, 1929, 1:318-324.

940. _____. Psychoanalytic comments on the personality of Goethe. In Ruitenbeek, H. M. (ed), The Literary Imagination. Chicago: Quadrangle, 1965, 115-141.

941. _____. Psychoanalytisches zur Persönlichkeit Goethes. In Cremerius, J. (ed), Neurose und Genialität. Psychoanalytische Biographien. Frankfurt: Fischer, 1971, 151-181; Imago, 1932, 18:42-66.

942. _____. Samuel Johnson's character: a psychoanalytic interpretation. Psychoanal Rev, 1945, 32:207-218.

943. _____. Selma Lagerlöf ihr Wesen und ihr Werk. Imago, 1939, 24:304-332.

944. _____. Some psycho-analytic aspects of biography. Int J Psycho-Anal, 1956, 37:265-269.

945. _____. Über Träume Gottfried Kellers. Int Zeitschrift für Psychoanalyse, 1914, 2:41-43.

946. _____. Von, um und über Knut Hamsun. Imago, 1928, 14:358-363.

947. _____. Zum Werden eines Romandichters. Imago, 1912, 1:49.

948. Hobsbaum, Philip. The temptation of giant despair. Hudson Rev, 1972-73, 25:596-612.

949. Hoeltje, Hubert H. Inward Sky: The Mind and Heart of Nathaniel Hawthorne. Durham, NC: Duke Univ. Press, 1962.

950. Hoffman, Frederick J. Conrad Aiken. NY: Twayne, 1962.

951. Hoffman, Nancy. Franz Kafka--his father's son. A study in literary sexuality. JAMA, 1974, 229:1623-1626.

952. Hoffmann, P. Le Désir et la loi. Saggi e ricerche di letteratura francese, 1977, 16:277-297.

953. Hohenstein, Lily. Adalbert Stifter: Lebensgeschichte eines Überwinders. Bonn: 1952.

954. Holbrook, David. Sylvia Plath, Poetry and Existence. London: Athlone, 1976; Atlantic Highlands, NJ: Humanities Press, 1976.

955. Holland, Norman N. The art of scientific biography. Kenyon Rev, 1968, 30:702-707.

956. _____. Freud and H. D. Int J Psycho-Anal, 1969, 50:309-351; In Ruitenbeek, H. M. (ed), Freud As We Knew Him. Detroit: Wayne State Univ. Press, 1969, 449-462.

957. _____. H. D. and the 'blameless physician.' Contemporary Lit, 1969, 10:474-506. In Ruitenbeek, H. M. (ed), Freud As We Knew Him. Detroit: Wayne State Univ. Press, 1969, 464-494.

958. _____. H. D. et Freud. Etudes freudiennes, 1970, 3-4: 143-156.

959. _____. Is Shakespeare our contemporary. Report of pa-
     per. Shakespeare Newsletter, 1973, 23:30.
960. Hollis, Charles Carroll. The 'mad poet' McDonald Clarke.
     In Petit, H. H. (ed), Essays and Studies in Language and
     Literature. Pittsburgh: Duquesne Univ. Press, 1964,
     176-206.
961. Holloway, Emory. Free and Lonesome Hearts: The Secret
     of Walt Whitman. NY: Vantage, 1960.
962. _____. Walt Whitman's love affairs. Dial, 1920, 49:473-
     483.
963. _____. Whitman, An Interpretation in Narrative. NY:
     Knopf, 1926.
964. Holmes, John Clellon. The last cause: Gershon Legman.
     Evergreen Rev, 1966, 10(44):28-32.
965. _____. Revolution below the belt. In Robinson, F., &
     Lehrman, N. (eds), Sex American Style. Chicago: Play-
     boy Press, 1971.
966. Holmgren, O. Resan till Eklandet. Bonniers Litterära
     Magasin, 1972, 42(1):13-20.
967. Holroyd, Michael. Lytton Strachey: A Study in English
     Character and Eccentricity. London: Heinemann, 1968;
     Lytton Strachey; A Critical Biography. NY: Holt, Rine-
     hart & Winston, 1967; Review: Murray H. Sherman,
     Psychoanal Rev, 1969, 56:597-608.
968. Homan, John. Henry David Thoreau as Self-Actualizer.
     DAI, 1978, 39:2273-74A.
969. Homans, Peter. The uses and limits of psychobiography as
     an approach to popular culture: the case of the 'West-
     erns.' In Reynolds, F. E., & Capps, D. (eds), The Bio-
     graphical Process. The Hague: Mouton, 1976, 297-316.
970. Hoover, Suzanne R. Coleridge, Humphrey Davy, and some
     early experiments with a consciousness-altering drug.
     Bulletin Research in Humanities, 1978, 81:9-27.
971. Hopkins, Vivian C. Emerson and the world of dreams. In
     Carlson, E. W., & Dameron, J. L. (eds), Emerson's
     Relevance Today: A Symposium. Hartford: Transcen-
     dental Books, 1971, 56-69.
972. Hoppe, A. Psychopathologische bei Schiller und Ibsen. Zen-
     tralblatt für Nervenheilkunde und Psychiatrie, 1907, 18:
     223-228.
973. Hopper, Stanley Romaine. Kafka and Kierkegaard: the func-
     tion of ambiguity. Amer Imago, 1978, 35:92-105.
974. Horowitz, I. L. Autobiography as the presentation of self for
     social immortality. New Literary History, 1977, 9:173-
     179.
975. Horton, Philip. Hart Crane: The Life of an American Poet.
     NY: Norton, 1937.
976. Horvat, A. Lord Byrons Charakter. Int Zeitschrift für In-
     dividual-Psychologie, 1936, 14:37-49.
977. Hotchner, A. E. Papa Hemingway: A Personal Memoir.
     NY: Random House, 1966.
978. Howard, William Lee. Poe and his misunderstood personal-
     ity. Arena, 1904, 31:76-80.

979. Howe, Irving. The literature of suicide. In The Critical Point; On Literature and Culture. NY: Horizon, 1973, 170-180.

980. _____. Sherwood Anderson. NY: Sloane, 1951; London: Methuen, 1952.

981. Hubble, D. Lord Moran and James Boswell: the two diarists compared and contrasted. Medical History, 1969, 13:1-10.

982. Hughes, C. H. A neurologist's plea for Lord Byron. Alienist & Neurologist, 1902, 23:349-351.

983. Huige, Frida F. L. Nerval's Aurélia: schizophrenia and art. Amer Imago, 1965, 22:255-274.

984. Hungerford, E. Walt Whitman and his chart of bumps. Amer Lit, 1931, 2:350-384.

985. Hunt, Nancy. Mirror Image. NY: Holt, Rinehart & Winston, 1978.

986. Hutch, Richard A. Emerson and incest. Psychoanal Rev, 1975, 62:320-332.

987. Hutter, Albert D. Psychoanalysis and biography. Dickens' experience at Warren's Blacking. Hartford Studies in Lit, 1976, 8:23-37.

988. _____. Reconstructive autobiography: the experience of Warren's Blacking. Dickens Studies Annual, 1977, 6:1-14.

989. Hyslop, T. B. The Great Abnormals. London: Allen, 1925.

990. Hytier, Jean. André Gide et l'esthétique de la personnalité. Rev d'Histoire Littéraire de la France, 1970, 70(2):230-243.

991. Iga, Mamoru. Further reflections on the suicide of Kawabata Yasunari. Suicide & Life-Threatening Behavior, 1978, 8:32-40.

992. _____. Personal situation as a factor in suicide, with reference to Yashunari Kawabata and Yukio Mishima. In Wolman, B. B. (ed), Between Survival and Suicide. NY: Halsted, 1976, 103-128.

993. Igirosianu, Josef. La Personnalité humaine de Molière. Rev d'Histoire du Théâtre, 1974, 26:156-159.

994. Ignoffo, Matthew F. What the War Did to Whitman: A Brief Study of the Effects of the Civil War on the Mind of Walt Whitman. NY: Vantage, 1975.

995. Ilan, E. [Analysis of a conflict in family education and its influence.] Ofakim, 1953, 7:242-250.

996. Illingworth, R. S., & Illingworth, C. M. Lessons from Childhood. Some Aspects of the Early Life of Unusual Men and Women. Edinburgh: Livingston, 1969.

997. Ireland, Patricia Daly. A Rage Against the Dying of the Light: Antonin Artaud's Struggles to Convey His Schizophrenic Experience, 1920-1926. DAI, 1977, 37(10):6477A.

998. Irish, Carol. The myth of success in Fitzgerald's boyhood. Studies in Amer Fiction, 1973, 1:176-187.

999. Irwin, George. Samuel Johnson: A Personality in Conflict. Auckland, NZ: Auckland Univ. Press, 1971; NY: Oxford Univ. Press, 1971.

1000. Ishida, Kenji. Hawthorne's aloofness and melancholy. Rising Generation, (Japan), 1947, 93, No. 12.
1001. Isou, Isidore. Antonin Artaud torturé par les psychiatres; les ignobles erreurs d'André Breton, Tristan Tzara, Robert Desnos et Claude Bourdet dans l'affaire de l'internement d'Antonin Artaud. Paris: Centre de Créative-Edition Littéraire, 1977.
1002. Iyengar, K. R. Srinivasa. Lytton Strachey: A Critical Study. London: Chatto & Windus, 1939.

1003. Jackson, Paul R. Henry Miller, Emerson, and the divided self. Amer Lit, 1971, 43:231-241.
1004. Jacobson, Arthur C. Literary genius and manic-depressive insanity: with special reference to the alleged case of Dean Swift. Scientific Amer Supplement, 1913, 75:2-8; In Ruitenbeek, H. M. (ed), The Literary Imagination. Chicago: Quadrangle, 1965, 433-443; Medical Record, 1912, 82:937-939.
1005. Jacquette, A. R. P. Arnaud's Ann Radcliffe et le fantastique: essay de psychobiographie. Eighteenth Century Studies, 1977-78, 11:280-283.
1006. James, William. [Tolstoy.] In The Varieties of Religious Experience. NY: Longmans, Green, 1902, 151-157.
1007. Jannaco, C. Personalità e poetica di Alessandro Tassoni. Studi Secenteschi, 1966, 56-64.
1008. Jason, Philip K. Doubles/Don Juans: Anaïs Nin and Otto Rank. Mosaic, 1978, 11(2):81-94.
1009. Jaspers, Karl. Patografia de Strindberg en los años que escribo La Señorita Julia. Primer Acto, 1973, 154:30-34.
1010. _____. Strindberg und van Gogh: Versuch einer pathographischen Analyse unter vergleichender Heranziehung von Swedenborg und Hölderlin. Leipzig: Bircher, 1922; Berlin: Springer, 1926.
1011. Jastrow, Joseph. Helen Keller: a psychological autobiography. Popular Science Monthly, 1903, 43:71-83.
1012. Jean, Raymond. Le Suicide de Gérard de Nerval. PMLA, 1955, 70:78.
1013. Jeanneau, A. Henri Michaux et la recherche psychopathologique. Evolution Psychiatrique, 1972, 37:407-433.
1014. Jeffares, A. Norman. Place, space, and personality and the Irish writer. In Carpenter, A. (ed), Place, Personality, and the Irish Writer. NY: Barnes & Noble, 1977, 11-40.
1015. Jelinek, Estelle C. (ed). Women's Autobiography: Essays in Criticism. Bloomington: Indiana State Univ. Press, 1980.
1016. Jelliffe, Smith Ely. A consideration of Julian Green. NY: 1936.
1017. _____. Ibsen. In The Apostle of the Psychopath. London: Lewis, 1929, 239-251.
1018. Jenkins, Logan Burris. The Literature of Addiction: Confessions 1821-1960. DAI, 1977, 38:237A.

1019.   Jespers, Henri-Floris.   Oscar Wilde en Lord Alfred Douglas:
        Deel 1:   Een Relaas (1891-1897).   Nieuw Vlaams Tijd-
        schrift, 1970, 23:378-402.
1020.   Jofen, Jean.   Das letzte Geheimnis: Eine psychologische
        Studie über die Brüder Gerhart und Carl Hauptmann.
        Bern: Francke, 1972.
1021.   Johnson, H. K.   Thomas Lovell Beddoes.   Psychiat Q, 1943,
        17:447-469.
1022.   Johnson, J.   Literary and historical aspects of disorders of
        sexual potency.   In Disorders of Sexual Potency in the
        Male.   NY: Pergamon, 1968, 1-9.
1023.   Johnson, Niel M.   Pro-Freud and pro-nazi: the paradox of
        George S. Viereck.   Psychoanal Rev, 1971-72, 58:553-
        562.
1024.   Johnson, Pamela Hansford.   The fascination of the paranoid
        personality: Baron Corvo.   Essays & Studies, 1963, 16:
        12-15.
1025.   Johnson, Wallace H.   MacKenzie and Goethe: two 'men of
        feeling' on suicide.   Studies in Scottish Lit, 1967, 4:228-
        229.
1026.   Johnston, Dillon.   The recreation of self in Wells's Experi-
        ment in Autobiography.   Criticism, 1972, 14:345-360.
1027.   Johnston, George A.   The new biography.   Atlantic, 1929,
        143:336-339.
1028.   Johnston, James C.   Biography: The Literature of Personal-
        ity.   NY: Century, 1927.
1029.   Jolas, Eugene.   My friend James Joyce.   Partisan Rev, 1941,
        8:82-93.
1030.   Jolles, Charlotte.   Theodor Fontane.   Metzler: 1972.
1031.   Jones, Ernest.   On 'dying together,' with special reference
        to Heinrich von Kleist's suicide.   In Essays in Applied
        Psycho-Analysis.   London: Hogarth, 1923, 99-105; 1951,
        Vol. 1, 9-15; Int Zeitschrift für Psychoanalyse, 1911,
        1:563-567.
1032.   _____.   Strindberg über Geburt und Tod.   Int Zeitschrift
        für Psychoanalyse, 1912, 3:55.
1033.   Jones, Harry L.   The Very madness: a new manuscript.
        College Language Assn J, 1967, 10:196-200.
1034.   Jones, Lucy.   A propos de Lewis Carroll.   Rev Française
        de Psychoanalyse, 1950, 14:511-522.
1035.   Jones, Stanley.   A further note on Keats's morbidity of
        temperament.   Notes & Queries, 1977, 24:329.
1036.   Jong, M. J. G. de.   Nogmaals inzake Achterberg.   The Hague:
        Nijgh & Van Ditmar, 1972; Bruges: Sonneville, 1972.
1037.   Jordan, Thornton Flournoy.   Dependence and Initiative: The
        Psychological Framework in Emerson's Life and Works.
        DAI, 1977, 38:2790A-91A.
1038.   Jordan, Winthrop D.   Familial politics: Thomas Paine and
        the killing of the King, 1776.   J Amer History, 1973,
        60:294-308.
1039.   Joseph, Robert J.   John Ruskin: radical and psychotic
        genius.   Psychoanal Rev, 1969, 56:425-441.
1040.   Josephson, Matthew.   Stendhal, or the Pursuit of Happiness.
        NY: Doubleday, Doran, 1947; Reviews: A. J. Liebling,

New Yorker, 19 Oct 1947, 126, 129-132; Harry Levin,
New Republic, 4 Nov 1947, 595-597.
1041. Joset, J. El bestiario de Garcia G. Márquez. Nueva Revista de Filologia, 1974, 23:65-87.
1042. Jost, F. Rousseau suisse: Etude sur sa personnalité et sa
pensée. Fribourg: Editions Universitaires, 1962.
1043. Jourdain, Louis. Le Concept psychique de Mallarmé. Cahiers du Sud, 1964, 51:9-28.
1044. Juergensen, Jans, Jr. The Use of the Symbol in the Prose
Works of Conrad Ferdinand Meyer. Doctoral dissertation, Johns Hopkins Univ., 1951.
1045. Jung, E. J. J. Rousseau als Psychoanalytiker. Int Zeitschrift für Psychoanalyse, 1912-13, 3:52.
1046. Jury, Paul. Déscartes, psychoanalyste avant la lettre.
Psyché, 1950, 5:150-164.
1047. _____. La Fessée de Jean-Jacques Rousseau. Psyché,
1947, 2:159-182.
1048. _____. George Sand et Musset. Psyché, 1949, 4:229-
252, 626-636.
1049. _____. Une nuit de Racine. Psyché, 1947, 13-14:1480-1500.

1050. Kästner, A. Goethes Bild der Kindheit. Zeitschrift für
pädagogische Psychologie, 1939, 40:100-107.
1051. Kafka, Franz. Two letters. Chicago Rev, 1977, 29:49-55.
1052. Kafka, John S., & Bolgar, Hedda. Notes on the clinical use
of autobiographies. Rorschach Research Exchange, 1949,
13:341-346.
1053. Kahl, Konrad. Adelbert Stifter in seinen Briefen. Olten:
Oltener Liebhaber Drucker, 1967.
1054. Kahn, Sy. Hart Crane and Harry Crosby: a transit of poets.
J Modern Lit, 1970, 1:45-56.
1055. Kallich, Martin. Psychoanalysis, sexuality, and Lytton
Strachey's theory of biography. Amer Imago, 1958, 15:
331-370.
1056. _____. The Psychological Milieu of Lytton Strachey. NY:
Bookman, 1961; New Haven: College & Univ. Press,
1963.
1057. Kaltenback, Michèle. Wilfred Owen's personality as revealed
by his letters. Caliban, 1973, 10:43-54.
1058. Kamiya, Mieko. Virginia Woolf. An outline of a study on
her personality, illness and work. Confinia Psychiatrica,
1965, 8:189-205.
1059. Kanngriesser, F. Zur Krankheit Lenaus und Byrons. Acta
Psychiatrica et Neurologica, 1917, 57(3).
1060. Kanzer, Mark. Autobiographical aspects of the writer's
imagery. Int J Psycho-Anal, 1959, 40:52-58.
1061. _____. Dostoevsky's matricidal impulses. Psychoanal
Rev, 1948, 35:115-125; In Coltrera, J. T. (ed), Lives,
Events, and Other Players: Studies in Psychobiography.
NY: Aronson, 1980.
1062. _____. Dostoevsky's Peasant Mary. Amer Imago, 1947,
4:78-88; In Coltrera, J. T. (ed), Lives, Events, and Other

Players: Studies in Psychobiography. NY: Aronson, 1980.

1063. _____. Freud and the demon. J Hillside Hospital, 1961, 10:190-202.

1064. _____. Freud and his literary doubles. Amer Imago, 1976, 33:231-243; In Kanzer, M., & Glenn, J. (eds), Freud and His Self Analysis. NY: Aronson, 1980.

1065. _____. The self-analytic literature of Robert Louis Stevenson. In Psychoanalysis and Culture. NY: IUP, 1951, 425-435.

1066. _____. Sigmund and Alexander Freud on the Acropolis. Amer Imago, 1969, 26:324-354; In Kanzer, M., & Glenn, J. (eds), Freud and His Self-Analysis. NY: Aronson, 1980.

1067. _____. Victor Tausk--the creativity and suicide of a psychoanalyst. Psychoanal Q, 1972, 41:556-584.

1068. _____. Writers and the early loss of parents. J Hillside Hospital, 1953, 2:148-153.

1069. Kaplan, Justin. Mr. Clemens and Mark Twain: A Biography. NY: Simon & Schuster, 1966.

1070. _____. On Mark Twain: 'never quite sane in the night.' Psychoanal Rev, 1968-69, 56:113-127.

1071. _____. Walt Whitman, A Life. NY: Simon & Schuster, 1980.

1072. Kapp, Frederic T. Ezra Pound's creativity and treason: clues from his life and work. Comprehensive Psychiat, 1968, 9:414-427.

1073. Karl, Frederick Robert. The Brontës: the self defined, redefined, and refined. In Levine, Richard A. (ed), The Victorian Experience: The Novelists. Athens: Ohio Univ. Press, 1976, 121-150.

1074. Karl, L. J. Jean Racine: Eine psychologische Charakterstudie. Vienna: Leo, 1937.

1075. Karlinger, F., & Pinto Novais, J. (eds). Antero de Quental [by K. Rumbucher]. Munich: Hueber, 1968.

1076. Karlinsky, Simon. The Sexual Labyrinth of Nikolai Gogol. Cambridge: Harvard Univ. Press, 1976.

1077. Kassel-Muhlfelder, Martha. Wedekinds Erotik. Sexualprobleme, 9 Feb. 1913.

1078. Katz, Jonathan. Gay American History: Lesbians and Gay Men in the U.S.A.: A Documentary. NY: Crowell, 1976.

1079. Katz, Joseph. Balzac and Wolfe: a study of self-destructive overproductivity. Psychoanalysis, 1957, 5:3-20.

1080. Kaus, Otto. Der Fall Gogol. Munich: Reinhardt, 1912.

1081. Kavka, Jerome. Ezra Pound's sanity: the agony of public disclosure. Paideuma, 1975, 4:527-529.

1082. _____. Oscar Wilde's narcissism. In The Annual of Psychoanalysis, Vol. 3. NY: IUP, 1975, 397-408.

1083. Kayy, W. H. The Gay Geniuses: Psychiatric and Literary Studies of Famous Homosexuals. Glendale, CA: Miller, 1965.

1084. Kazin, Alfred. The conquistador: Freud in his letters. Griffin, 1960, 9:2-8.

1085. _____. 'The giant killer': drink and the American writer. Commentary, 1976, 63:44-50.
1086. Kearney, J. F. The psychological biography. Catholic World, 1929, 96-98.
1087. Keating, Jerome Francis. Personal Identity in Jonathan Edwards, Ralph Waldo Emerson, and Alfred North Whitehead. DAI, 1972, 33:5682A.
1088. Keene, Donald. The death of Mishima. In Dillon, W. S. (ed), The Cultural Drama; Modern Identities and Social Ferment. Washington, DC: Smithsonian Institution Press, 1974, 271-287.
1089. Keischwitz, Otto. O'Neill. Berlin: Junker und Dünnhaupt, 1938.
1090. Keith, Arthur. Shakespeare's skull and brain. In Sorsby, A. (ed), Tenements of Clay. London: Friedmann, 1974, 70-84.
1091. Keller, Evelyn Fox. Lewis Carroll: a study of mathematical inhibition. JAPA, 1980, 28:133-160.
1092. Kelley, D. M. The autobiographical study as an aid to psychotherapy. Amer J Psychiat, 1945, 102:375-377.
1093. Kelly, Erna Emmighausen. Whitman and Wordsworth: childhood experiences and the future poet. Walt Whitman Rev, 1977, 23:59-68.
1094. Kennedy, Richard S. Dreams in the Mirror. A Biography of E. E. Cummings. NY: Liveright, 1980.
1095. Kenner, Hugh. Ezra Pound und das Geld. Neue Deutsche Hefte, 1967, 14:22-40.
1096. Kenney, S. M. Two endings: Virginia Woolf's suicide and Between the Acts. Univ. Toronto Q, 1975, 44:265-289.
1097. Kenney, William D. Dr. Johnson and the psychiatrists. J Psychiat, 1945, 102:375-377.
1098. Kiefer, Otto. Sokrates und die Homosexualität. Jahrbuch für Sexuelle Zwischenstufen, 1908, 9:197-212.
1099. Kiell, Norman. The Universal Experience of Adolescence. NY: IUP, 1964, 1969; Boston: Beacon, 1967, 1968; London: Univ. London Press, 1967. Reviews: Peter Blos, Psychoanal Q, 1965, 34(2): 296-297; Margaret Mead, Teachers College Record, Oct 1964; Eugene B. Brody, JNMD, 1965, 140(3); Lawrence S. Wrightman, Contemporary Psychol, 1965, 10(10):476-477; Herbert R. Strean, Psychoanal Rev, 1964-65, 679-681.
1100. Kierulf, H. Dostojevskij og epilepsien. Tidsskrift for den Norske Laegeforening, 1972, 92:1303-1307.
1101. Kihn, B. Uber E. T. A. Hoffmann. In Speer, E. (ed), Lindauer Psychotherapiewoche, 1950. Stuttgart: Hippokrates, 1951, 110-121.
1102. Kimball, Jean. Freud, Leonardo, and Joyce: the dimensions of a childhood memory. James Joyce Q, 1980, 17.
1103. King, J. K. Lenz viewed sane. Germanic Rev, 1974, 49: 146-153.
1104. Kirchhoff, Frederick A. Love is enough: a crisis in William Morris' poetic development. Victorian Poetry, 1977, 15:297-306.

1105. Kitayama, R. Psychoanalytische Studien über den Roman-schreiber, Soseki Natume. Zeitschrift für Psychoanalyse, 1938, 6(2).

1106. Kizer, Helen. Amy Lowell: a personality. North Amer Rev, 1918, 207:736-747.

1107. Klein, Mia. Sherwood Anderson: the artist's struggle for self-respect. Twentieth Century Lit, 1977, 23:40-52.

1108. Kleinschmidt, Hans J. The angry act: the role of aggression in creativity. Amer Imago, 1967, 24:98-128.

1109. Klibbe, Hélène Foustanos. Alfred de Musset: Etude de caractérologie. DA, 1965, 25:6595-96.

1110. Kligerman, Charles. The character of Jean Jacques Rousseau. Psychoanal Q, 1951, 20:237-252; In The Yearbook of Psychoanalysis, Vol. 8. NY: IUP, 1952, 361-373; In Ruitenbeek, H. M. (ed), Psychoanalysis and the Genius of the Writer. Chicago: Quadrangle, 1965, 247-264.

1111. _____. The dream of Charles Dickens. JAPA, 1970, 18: 783-799.

1112. _____. Notes on Benvenuto Cellini. In The Annual of Psychoanalysis, Vol. 3. NY: IUP, 1975, 409-422.

1113. _____. A psychoanalytic study of the Confessions of St. Augustine. JAPA, 1957, 5:469-484.

1114. _____. Psychology of Herman Melville. Psychoanal Rev, 1953, 40:125-143.

1115. Klof, Frank S. 'Night Song': Nietzsche's poetic insight into the psychotic process. Psychoanal Rev, 1959, 46:80-84.

1116. Kloss, Robert J. An ancient and famous capital: Delmore Schwartz's dream. Psychoanal Rev, 1978, 65:475-490.

1117. Klossowski, P. Eléments d'une étude psychoanalytique sur le Marquis de Sade. Rev Française de Psychoanalytique, 1933, 6:458-474.

1118. Kluckhohn, Clyde. Needed refinements in the biographical approach. In Sargent, S. S., & Smith, M. W. (eds), Culture and Personality. NY: Viking Fund, 1949, 75-92.

1119. Knapp, Bettina L. Anaïs Nin. NY: Ungar, 1979.

1120. _____. Antonin Artaud, Man of Vision. NY: Lewis, 1969.

1121. _____. From hero to horror. Louis-Ferdinand Céline, M. D. In Peschel, E. R. (ed), Medicine and Literature. NY: Watson, 1980, 18-27.

1122. Knickerbocker, James Harris. Swift Expires: Johnson's Life of Swift as Moral Exemplum and Psychological Study. DAI, 1976, 36:4512A.

1123. Knight, George Wilson. Lord Byron's Marriage: The Evidence of Asterisks. London: Routledge & Kegan Paul, 1957; NY: Macmillan, 1957.

1124. Knott, John. The last illness of Byron; a study in the borderland of genius and madness. St Paul Medical J, 1912, 14:1-43.

1125. Kobylinski, M. [Dostoevsky's illness.] Vrachetnoye Dielo, 1927, 10:505-508; Illustrazione Medicina Italiana, 1926, 8:75-77.

1126. Koch, Max. Theodor Reik's Arthur Schnitzler als Psycholog. Die schöne Literatur, 1914, 15:185-186.
1127. Koekebakker, J. [Role conflict in André Gide.] Nederlandsch Tijdsschrift voor de Psychologie, 1962, 17:317-333.
1128. Kofman, Sarah. Baubô: perversion théologique et fétichisme chez Nietzsche. Nuova Corrente, 1975, 68-69:648-680.
1129. Kolb, Philip. Proust ve-Freud. Keshet, 1975, 66:59-62.
1130. Kolb-Seletski, Nathalia M. Gastronomy, Gogol, and his fiction. Slavic Rev, 1970, 29:35-57.
1131. Körner, Josef. Theodor Reik's Arthur Schnitzler als Psycholog. Das Literarische Echo, 1917, 19:802-805.
1132. Korges, James. Gide and Mishima: homosexuality as metaphor. Critique, 1970, 12:127-137.
1133. Kotsovsky, D. Dostoevskii, Tolstoi i Bol'shevizm. NY: All-Slavic Publishing, 1955; Munich: 1960.
1134. Kouretas, Demetrios. [The unconscious significance of 'Letter to Father' by Kafka.] Educational Hygiene, 1963, 211; Epoches, 1963, 5.
1135. Kozlov, A. S. [Psychoanalytical and biographical research in American criticism of the 1920s.] Voprosy Filologii, 1972, 2:116-124.
1136. Kraft, Werner. Sigmund Freud-Preis: Uberlegungen zum Thema Biographie und Autobiographie. Deutsche Akademie für Sprache und Dichtung, 1971(1972):70-79.
1137. Kramer, Hilton. Henry James. New York Times Book Rev, 6 Feb 1972, 1, 32-33.
1138. Kréa, Henri. La Génération de la mescaline. Nouvel Observateur, 1965, n. s., no. 12, 21.
1139. Krenis, Lee. Authority and rebellion in Victorian autobiography. J British Studies, 1978, 18:107-130.
1140. Kress-Rosen, N. Réalité du souvenir et vérité du discours-étude de l'énonciation dans un texte des Confessions. Littérature, 1973, 10:20-30.
1141. Kring, Walter D., & Carey, Jonathan S. Two discoveries concerning Herman Melville. Proceedings Massachusetts Historical Society, 1975, 87:137-141.
1142. Krippendorf, Ilse. Rainer Maria Rilke, Psyche und Werk. I. Die Personlichkeit und ihre Wandlungen. Zeitschrift für Psychotherapie und medizinische Psychologie, 1952, 2:61-76.
1143. Kris, Ernst. The personal myth; a problem in psychoanalytic technique. The autobiography as screen. JAPA, 1956, 4:653-681.
1144. _____. Zur Psychologie der älteren Biographik. Imago, 1933, 21.
1145. Krook, Dorothea. Recollections of Sylvia Plath. Critical Q, 1976, 18:5-14.
1146. Krutch, Joseph Wood. Edgar Allan Poe: A Study in Genius. NY: Knopf, 1926.
1147. _____. Genius and neuroticism. In And Even If You Do; Essays on Man, Manners and Machines. NY: Morrow, 1967, 145-152; Saturday Rev, 1963, 45:12-14; In Nunoka-

wa, W. D. (ed), Readings in Abnormal Psychology. Chicago: Scott, Foresman, 1965, 116-120.

1148. _____. The strange case of Poe. Amer Mercury, 1925, 6:349-356.

1149. Krupnick, Mark L. Henry James: the artist as emperor-- on Henry James, The Master, 1901-1916. Novel: A Forum on Fiction, 1973, 6:257-265.

1150. Kucera, Otakar. Stephane Mallarmé. Revista de Psicoanálisis, 1949, 7:249-294.

1151. Kuiper, Pieter C. Die psychoanalytische Biographie der schöpferischen Persönlichkeit. Psyche, 1966, 20:104-127.

1152. Kunemann, G. E. T. A. Hoffmann. Etudes médico-psychologiques. Paris: 1911.

1153. Kupper, Herbert I., & Rollman-Branch, Hilda S. Freud and Schnitzler-Doppelgänger. JAPA, 1959, 7:109-126. In Ruitenbeek, H. M. (ed), Freud As We Knew Him. Detroit: Wayne State Univ. Press, 1973, 412-427.

1154. Kurz, E. [The diseases and death of Adalbert Stifter. Did this poet in fact commit suicide?] Munchener Medizinische Wochenschrift, 1966, 108:1177-1182.

1155. Kushen, Betty. Benjamin Franklin, Oedipus, and the price of submission. Lit & Psychol, 1975, 25:147-157.

1156. Kushwaha, M. S. Byron: a search for identity. In New Light on Byron. Salzburg: Univ. Salzburg Press, 1978, 5-20.

1157. Labor, Earle. Jack London. NY: Twayne, 1974.

1158. Lacan, Jacques. L'Ego de Joyce. Seminar on Le Sinthome: 1975-1976 (May 11, 1976). Ornicar, 1976, 11.

1159. La Charité, Virginia A. The poet as patient: Henri Michaux. In Peschel, E. R. (ed), Medicine and Literature. NY: Watson, 1980, 140-146.

1160. Ladame, Charles. Guy de Maupassant. Une Brochure. Lausanne: Romande, 1919.

1161. Ladell, R. G. M. The neurosis of Dr. Samuel Johnson. British J Medical Psychol, 1929, 9:314-323.

1162. Laforgue, René. Baudelaire et sa pensée. Psyché, 1955, 10:185-204.

1163. _____. The Defeat of Baudelaire: A Psycho-Analytic Study of the Neurosis of Charles Baudelaire. London: Hogarth, 1932; Paris: Denoël et Steele, 1931; Vienna: Int Psychoanalytischer Verlag, 1932; Geneva: Edit. du Mont-Blanc, 1964.

1164. _____. Devant la barrière de la nevrose. Etude psychoanalyse sur le nevrose du Charles Baudelaire. Rev Française de Psychanalyse, 1930-31, 4:274-406.

1165. _____. Etude sur Jean-Jacques Rousseau. Rev Française de Psychanalyse, 1927, 1:370-402; In Psychopathologie de l'Echec. Geneva: Mont-Blanc, 1963, 117-144.

1166. _____. Jean-Jacques Rousseau. Eine psychoanalytische Untersuchung. Imago, 1930, 16:145-172.

1167. _____. Masochismus und Selbstbestrafungstandensen bei Charles Baudelaire. Almanach, 1934, 106-116.

1168. _____. Ein Traum Baudelaires. Psychoanalytische Bewegung, 1930, 2:394-400.
1169. Lagerlöf, K. E. Den unge Karl Vennberg. Stockholm: Bonniers, 1967.
1170. Lagriffe, Lucien. Guy de Maupassant. Etude de psychologie pathologique. Annales Médico-Psychologiques, 1908, 8: 203-238, 353-372; 1909, 9:5-14, 177-193.
1171. _____. Un problème psychologique. --Les Deux aspects d'Arthur Rimbaud. JPNP, 1910, 7:499-523.
1172. _____. La Psychologie d'August Strindberg. JPNP, 1912, 9:481-500.
1173. Lahr, John. Prick Up Your Ears. The Biography of Joe Orton. NY: Knopf, 1979.
1174. Lamb, Charles. On the sanity of true genius. In Hutchinson, T. (ed), The Works of Charles Lamb. London: Milford, 1924.
1175. Lamblin, M. Le 'Laocoon' de Lessing. Bulletin de Psychologie, 1967, 20(18-19), 1054-1060.
1176. Lamm, M. Strindberg. Zeitschrift für Aesthetik und Allgemeine Kunstwissenschaft, 1926, 20:141-156.
1177. Lamoine, Georges. La Pensée religieuse et le suicide de Thomas Chatterton. Etudes Anglaises, 1970, 23:369-379.
1178. Landa, Louis A. Jonathan Swift: the critical significance of biographical evidence. In English Institute Essays, 1946. NY: Columbia Univ. Press, 1947.
1179. Landa, R. La personalidad de Giner de los Rios. Cuadernos Americanos, 1965, 24(2):89-101.
1180. Langbaum, Robert Woodrow. Max and dandyism. Victorian Poetry, 1966, 4:121-126.
1181. Lange, W. Die Psychose Maupassants. Ein kritischer Versuch. Leipzig: Barth, 1909.
1182. Lange-Eichbaum, W. Genie-Irrsinn und Ruhm. Munich: Reinhardt, 1928.
1183. _____. The Problem of Genius. NY: Macmillan, 1932.
1184. Langner, E. Form- und Farbbeachtung und psychophysische Konstitution bei zeitgenössischen Dichtern. Zeitschrift für menschliche Vererbungs- und Konstitutionslehre, 1936, 20:93-147.
1185. Laplanche, Jean. Hölderlin et la question du père. Paris: Presses Universitaires de France, 1969, 1961; Review: M. C. Boons-Grafé, Rev Française Psychoanalyse, 1964, 28:280-283.
1186. Lapp, J. C. Watcher betrayed and the fatal woman: some recurring patterns in Zola. PMLA, 1959, 74:276-284.
1187. Lash, John S. Baldwin beside himself: a study in modern phallicism. College Language Assn J, 1964, 8:132-140.
1188. Launay, M. Jean Jacques Rousseau, écrivain politique. Grenoble: Acer, 1971.
1189. Lauter, Paul. Walt Whitman: lover and comrade. Amer Imago, 1959, 16:407-435; In Ruitenbeek, H. M. (ed), The Literary Imagination. Chicago: Quadrangle, 1965, 349-378.
1190. Lauvrière, Emile. Edgar Poe et le Freudisme. Grande Rev, 1933.

1191. _____. Le Génie morbide d'Edgar Poe. Paris: Desclés de Brouwen, 1935; Paris: Alcan, 1904.

1192. Lay, Wilfred. John Barleycorn under psychoanalysis. Bookman, 1917, 45:47-54.

1193. Lease, Benjamin. The chemistry of genius: Herman Melville and Anton Bruckner. Personalist, 1967, 48:224-241.

1194. Lebeaux, Richard Mark. Young Man Thoreau. Amherst: Univ. Massachusetts Press, 1977; NY: Harper Colophon, 1977; Reviews: Lawrence Buell, New England Q, 1977, 50:684-688; Bennett Simon, Psychoanal Q, 1978, 47:458-464.

1195. _____. 'Young Man Thoreau': A Psychological Study of Henry David Thoreau's pre-Walden Life and Writings. DAI, 1975, 36:1505A.

1196. Leben, Breda Cigoj. Ernest Renan et sa soeur Henriette. Contribution à une meilleure intelligence de la personnalité morale de Renan. Ljubljana: Chez l'auteur-éditeur, 1971.

1197. LeBost, B. 'The way it is': something else on Hemingway. J Existentialism, 1965-66, 6:175-180.

1198. Lebra, Joyce C. Mishima's last act. Lit East & West, 1971, 15:279-298.

1199. Lebrun, Y., Hasquin-Deleval, J., & Brihaye, J. L'Aphasie de Charles Baudelaire. Rev Neurologie, 1971, 125:310-316.

1200. Le Comte, Edward S. Milton and Sex. NY: Columbia Univ. Press, 1978.

1201. _____, & Shawcross, John T. An exchange of letters: by sex obsessed. Milton Q, 1974, 8:55-57.

1202. Lefebure, Molly. Samuel Taylor Coleridge: A Bondage to Opium. Briarcliff Manor, NY: Stein & Day, 1974.

1203. Leftwich, Ralph W. The evidence of disease in Shakespeare's handwriting. In Sorsby, A. (ed), Tenements of Clay. London: Friedmann, 1974, 86-96.

1204. _____. Shakespeare's handwriting. British Medical J, 1918, 1:542-543.

1205. Legewie, B. Augustinus, eine Psychographie. Bonn: Marcus u Weber, 1925.

1206. Leggett, John. Two American Tragedies. NY: Simon & Schuster, 1974.

1207. Legman, Gershon. Introduction to The Mammoth Cod and Address to the Stomach Club. Milwaukee: Maledicta Press, 1976.

1208. Lehmann, Herbert. Freud, Zweig, and biography. Psychoanal Q, 1963, 32:94-97.

1209. _____. Sigmund Freud and Thomas Mann. Psychoanal Q, 1970, 39:198-214; In Ruitenbeek, H.M. (ed), Freud As We Knew Him. Detroit: Wayne State Univ. Press, 1973, 504-517.

1210. Lehner, Fritz. Zum Thema Biographik und Psychoanalyse. Psychoanalytische Bewegung, 1933, 5:201-202.

1211. Lehnert, Herbert H. Fictional orientations in Thomas Mann's biography. PMLA, 1973, 88:1146-1161.

1212.   Leibman, Mary C.   Dr.   Maudsley, forgotten Poe diagnosti-
        cian.   Poe Studies, 1972, 5(2):55.
1213.   Leibowitz, Herbert.   Stoking the Oedipal furnace: Edward
        Dahlberg's Because I Was Flesh.   Amer Scholar, 1975,
        44:473-483.
1214.   Lejeune, Philippe.   Le 'dangereux supplément':   lecture d'un
        aveu de Rousseau.   Annales.   Economies--Sociétés--
        Civilisations, 1974, 29:1009-1022.
1215.   _____.   Exercices d'ambiguïté.   Lectures de 'Si le grain
        ne meurt' d'Andre Gide.   Paris: Minard, 1974.
1216.   _____.   Lire Leiris.   Autobiographie et langage.   Paris:
        Klincksieck, 1975.
1217.   _____.   La Punition des enfants: lecture d'un aveu de
        Rousseau.   Littérature, 1973, 10:31-56.
1218.   Lejins, Hamilkars.   Suicide in Garsin's life and stories.
        South Central Bulletin, 1967, 27(4):34-44.
1219.   Lély, Gilbert.   Esquisse d'une psychopathologie de Jean Ra-
        cine.   Mercure de France, 1940, 296:481-485.
1220.   _____.   The Marquis de Sade.   A Biography.   London:
        Elek, 1961.
1221.   Lennon, Florence Becker.   Life of Lewis Carroll.   NY:
        Dover, 1971.
1222.   Leonard, William Ellery.   The Locomotive-God.   NY: Cen-
        tury, 1927.
1223.   Leonhard, Karl.   [Masochism in Rousseau's life and litera-
        ture.]   Zeitschrift für klinische Psychologie und Psycho-
        therapie, 1974, 22:324-339.
1224.   Lerner, M.   E.   Rod (1857-1910), A Portrait of the Novelist
        and His Times.   The Hague: Mouton, 1975.
1225.   LeRoy, Gaylord C.   John Ruskin: an interpretation of his
        'daily maddening rage.'   Modern Language Q, 1949, 10:
        81-88.
1226.   Leroy, Maxime.   Descartes, le philosophe au masque.
        Paris: Rieder, 1929.
1227.   Lesser, Simon O.   Creativity versus death.   Virginia Woolf
        (1882-1941).   Hartford Studies in Lit, 1978, 10:49-69.
1228.   L'Etang, H.   James Joyce.   J Alcohol, 1969, 4:223-225.
1229.   Leux, I.   Hermann Sudermann (1857-1928).   Eine individual-
        analytische und schaffens-psychologische Studie.   J für
        Psychologie und Neurologie, 1931, 42:231-413; Leipzig:
        Barth, 1931.
1230.   Levi, A.W.   The 'mental crisis' of John Stuart Mill.   Psy-
        choanal Rev, 1945, 32:86-101.
1231.   Levi-Bianchini, M.   [Psychoanalytic essay on the unfamiliar
        anagapic childhood neuroses of Dostoevsky and Baude-
        laire.]   Annali di Neuropsichiatria e Psicoanalisi, 1957,
        4:5-12.
1232.   Levin, David.   Baldwin's autobiographical essays: the prob-
        lem of Negro identity.   Massachusetts Rev, 1964, 5:239-
        247.
1233.   Levin, Harry.   James Joyce.   NY: New Directions, 1960.
1234.   _____.   Proust, Gide, and the sexes.   PMLA, 1950, 65:
        648-653.

Norman Kiell 58

1235. Levitt, Morton P. Shalt be accurst? The martyr in James
Joyce. James Joyce Q, 1968, 5:285-296.
1236. Levowitz-Treu, Micheline. L'Amour et la mort chez Stendhal. Métamorphoses d'un apprentissage affectif. Aran,
Switzerland: Grand Cheney, 1978.
1237. Lewis, Hanna B. Hofmannsthal and America. Rice Univ.
Studies, 1969, 55(3):131-141.
1238. Lewis, Richard W. B. Edith Wharton: A Biography. NY:
Harper & Row, 1975.
1239. Lewis, Thomas S. W. Hart Crane and his mother: a correspondence. Salmagundi, 1969, 9:61-87.
1240. Lewis, Wyndham. Ezra: the portrait of a personality.
Quart Rev Lit, 1949, 5:136-144.
1241. Lhermitte, Jean. De l'Angoisse au genié. De l'anxieté de
Lucréce, l'angoisse de Pascal. Encéphale (et Hygiène
Mentale). J de Psychiatrie, 1946-47, 36:60-64.
1242. Libhart, B. R. Julien Green's troubled American: a fiction-
alized self-portrait. PMLA, 1974, 89:341-352.
1243. Lichtenberg, Joseph D. Psychoanalysis and biography. In
The Annual of Psychoanalysis, Vol. 6/1978. NY: IUP,
1979.
1244. _____, & Lichtenberg, C. Eugene O'Neill and falling in
love. Psychoanal Q, 1972, 41:63-89.
1245. Lichtenstein, Heinz. The malignant no: a hypothesis concerning the interdependence of the sense of self and the
instinctual drives. In Kanzer, M. (ed), The Unconscious
Today. NY: IUP, 1971, 147-176.
1246. Lidz, Theodore. August Strindberg: a study of the relationship between his creativity and schizophrenia. Int J Psycho-Anal, 1964, 45:399-406; Psyche, 1965, 18:591-605;
In Ruitenbeek, H. M. (ed), The Literary Imagination.
Chicago: Quadrangle, 1965, 97-113.
1247. _____. Strindbergs skapande och schizofreni. Bonniers
Litterära Magasin, 1962, 32:548-556.
1248. Lifton, Robert J., Kato, Shuichi, & Reich, Michael R.
Yukio Mishima. In Six Lives Six Deaths. New Haven:
Yale Univ. Press, 1980.
1249. Lind, Sidney E. Poe and mesmerism. PMLA, 1947, 57:
1077-1094.
1250. Lindenau, Heinrich. Eine Tagebucheintragung Goethes über
Fehlleistungen. Psychoanalytische Bewegung, 1933, 4:86.
1251. Linder, E. Hj. Kärleks och faderhus farväl. Hj. Bergmans liv och diktning från Markurells i Wadköping till
Farmor och Vår Herre. Stockholm: Bonnier, 1973.
1252. Linder, Lyle Dean. MLA Seminar-new perspectives on the
gilded age--applications from social science to literary
biography: the family world of Stephen Crane. Amer
Lit Realism, 1974, 7:280-282.
1253. Lindsay, Jack. Charles Dickens. A Biographical and Critical Study. NY: Philosophical Library, 1950, 192-193;
London: Dakers, 1950.
1254. Lindsay, Philip. The Haunted Man: A Portrait of Edgar
Allan Poe. London: Hutchinson, 1953.

1255. Lisi, L. de. Analisis di un personnaggio di Stendhal. La
       Serpe, Revista letterarie dell' Associaztione dei medici
       d' Italia, 1958, 8.
1256. Lloyd, J. H. The case of William Cowper, the English poet.
       Archives Neurology & Psychiat, 1930, 24:682-689.
1257. Lobet, Marcel. Du mal de Sade à l'ennui de Benjamin Con-
       stant. Rev Générale Belge, 1964, 9:21-33.
1258. Locklin, Gerald. The man behind the novels. In Madden, D.
       (ed), Nathanael West: The Cheaters and the Cheated.
       De Land, Fla.: Everett/Edwards, 1973, 1-15.
1259. Loesch, R. Burckhardt, Persönlichkeit, Werke und Wirkun-
       gen. Europa-Archiv, 1948, 3:1293-1297.
1260. Lo Gatto, E. Il problema religioso in Dostojeoskij. Bilych-
       nis, 1927, 16:333-346.
1261. Logre, J. B. L'Anxiété de Lucrèce. Paris: Janin, 1946;
       Review: L. Hermann, Latomus, 1949, 8:177-178.
1262. _____. L'Anxiété de Lucrèce. Psyché, 1949, 4:50-63.
1263. Lombard, A. Guy de Maupassant, sa vie, son oeuvre, sa
       maladie, sa mort. Les tentatives de suicide de G. de
       Maupassant. Chronique Médica, 1908, 15:34-40.
1264. Lombroso, Cesare. Emile Zola in the light of researches
       by Dr. Toulouse and recent theories of genius. Medical
       Weekly, 1897, 5:25-29.
1265. _____. Genio e degenerazione. Milan: Sandron, 1907.
1266. _____. Le Neurosi in Dante e Michaelangelo. Archivio di
       Psichiatria Scienza Penale e Antropologia Criminale, 1894.
1267. Long, E. H. Twain's ordeal in retrospect. Southwest Rev,
       1963, 338-348.
1268. Longaker, Mark. Contemporary Biography. Philadelphia:
       Univ. Pennsylvania Press, 1934.
1269. Lorenz, Emil F. Leo N. Tolstoi. Kindheit. Imago, 1913,
       2:93-96.
1270. Loughman, Celeste. The experience of old age in contempo-
       rary autobiography. Hartford Studies in Lit, 1980, 12:18-
       28.
1271. Love, Jean O. Virginia Woolf: Sources of Madness and Art.
       Berkeley: Univ. California Press, 1978; Review: J L'En-
       fant, Southern Rev, 1979, 15:688-695.
1272. Lovering, Joseph P. S. Weir Mitchell. NY: Twayne, 1971.
1273. Loving, Jerome M. Walt Whitman: is he persecuted. Walt
       Whitman Rev, 1976, 22:25-26; In White, W. (ed), The Bi-
       centennial Walt Whitman: Essays from The Long Island-
       er, 24 June, 1976 Supplement to Walt Whitman Rev, 22.
1274. Lowenfels, W. Whitman's many loves. Olympia, 1963, 4:
       23-32.
1275. Lowery, Bruce. Marcel Proust et Henry James. Rev de
       Paris, 1964, 71:74-82.
1276. _____. Marcel Proust et Henry James. Paris: Plon,
       1964.
1277. Loygue, P. G. Etude médico-psychologique sur Dostoiewsky;
       considerations sur les états morbides liés au génie.
       Thèse, Lyon, 1903.
1278. Lozano, Rafael. Paul Valéry y el narcisismo. Rev National
       de Cultura, 1954, 16:65-71.

1279. Lucid, Robert F. Norman Mailer: the artist as fantasy figure. Massachusetts Rev, 1974, 15:581-595.

1280. Ludington, Townsend. The hotel childhood of John Dos Passos. Virginia Q Rev, 1978, 54:297-313.

1281. Lund, M. Dosztojevskij és höseinek epilepsziája. Orvosi Hetalap, 1973, 114:817-818.

1282. Lupton, Mary Jane. The dark dream of 'dejection.' Lit & Psychol, 1968, 18:39-47.

1283. Lynch, David. Yeats: The Poetics of Self. Chicago: Univ. Chicago Press, 1979.

1284. Lyons, John B. James Joyce and medicine. JAMA, 1973, 225:313-314.

1285. _____. James Joyce and Medicine. NY: Oxford Univ. Press, 1973.

1286. Lyons, Judson S. Thomas De Quincey. NY: Twayne, 1969.

1287. McAdams, Laura J. H. Taine: The Neurotic. DA, 1958, 18:665-666.

1288. McClatchy, J. D. John Berryman: the impediments to salvation. Modern Poetry Studies, 1975, 6:246-277.

1289. McCormack, Jerusha. Masks without faces: the personalities of Oscar Wilde. English Lit in Transition, 1979, 22:253-269.

1290. McCormick, Jane L. William Butler Yeats and psychic phenomena. Psychic, 1970, 1(6):19-23.

1291. McCurdy, Harold G. The childhood patterns of genius. In Smithsonian Report for 1958. Washington, DC: Smithsonian Institution, 1959, 527-542.

1292. _____. Literature and personality. Character & Personality, 1939, 7:300-308.

1293. _____. Literature as a resource in personality study: theory and methods. JAAC, 1949, 8:42-46.

1294. _____. The Personality of Shakespeare. A Venture in Psychological Method. New Haven: Yale Univ. Press, 1953; Port Washington, NY: Kennikat, 1973.

1295. _____. Shakespeare: king of infinite space. Psychol Today, 1968, 1(11):38-41, 66-68.

1296. McDonald, Marcia. The function of the person in Ransom's critical prose. Mississippi Q, 1977, 30:87-100.

1297. McFarland, Thomas. Coleridge's anxiety. In Beer, J. (ed), Coleridge's Variety: Bicentenary Studies. Pittsburgh: Univ. Pittsburgh Press, 1975, 134-165, 249-251.

1298. McGarrity, G. J. Letter: Franz Kafka--his father's son. JAMA, 1975, 231:571.

1299. McGovern, James R. David Graham Phillips and the virility impulse of progressives. New England Q, 1966, 39:334-355.

1300. Mack, John E. A Prince of Our Disorder: The Life of T. E. Lawrence. Boston: Little, Brown, 1976.

1301. _____. T. E. Lawrence: charlatan or tragic hero. Amer J Psychiat, 1969, 125:1604-1607.

1302. _____. T. E. Lawrence: a study of heroism and conflict. Amer J Psychiat, 1969, 125:1083-1092.

1303. Mackey, Agnes E. The Universal Self. A Study of Paul Valéry. Toronto: Univ. Toronto Press, 1961; London: Routledge & Kegan Paul, 1961.

1304. McLaughlin, John J., & Ansbacher, Rowena R. Sane Ben Franklin: an Adlerian view of his autobiography. J Individual Psychol, 1971, 27:189-207.

1305. McLaughlin, Sigrid. Some aspects of Tolstoy's intellectual development: Tolstoy and Schopenhauer. California Slavic Studies, 1973, 5:187-245.

1306. MacShane, Frank. The Life of Raymond Chandler. NY: Dutton, 1976.

1307. Macy, John Albert. Swift's relations with women. New Republic, 1921, 27:354-355; In The Critical Game. NY: Boni & Liveright, 1922, 163-172.

1308. Madenheim, Helmuth. Kindheitserinnerungen französischer Dichter. Neueren Sprachen, 1966, 1:30-37.

1309. Mainland, W. F. The literary personality of Gerhart Hauptmann. In Knight, K. G., & Norman, F. (eds), Hauptmann Centenary Lectures. London: Univ. London Press, 1964, 9-30.

1310. Malkin, Edward E., & Malkin, Michael D. J.-J. Rousseau: hints of a repressed episode. Int Rev Psycho-Anal, 1976, 3:331-340.

1311. Mallac, Guy de. Selbstmord des Schreibers. In Pelters, W., Schimmelpfennig, P., & Menges, K. (eds), Wahrheit und Sprache. Göppingen: Kümmerle, 1972, 217-225.

1312. Maller, J. B. Studies in character and personality in German psychological literature. Psychol Bulletin, 1953, 30:209-232.

1313. Manheim, Eleanor B. Labrunie's quest. Gérard de Nerval (1808-1855). Hartford Studies in Lit, 1978, 10:31-48.

1314. Manheim, Leonard F. An author wrecked by success: Ross Lockridge, Jr. (1914-1948). Hartford Studies in Lit, 1978, 10:103-121.

1315. Mankowitz, Wolf. The Extraordinary Mr. Poe: A Biography of Edgar Allan Poe. Sydney, Australia: Summit Book, 1978.

1316. Mann, M. (ed). Das Thomas Mann-Buch. Eine innere Biographie in Selbstzeugnissen. Frankfurt: Fischer, 1965.

1317. Mann, Phyllis G. Keats's maternal relations. Keats-Shelley Memorial Bulletin, 1964, No. 15, 32-34.

1318. Mannoni, O. Vertu et culpabilité. Psyché, 1948, 3:496-505.

1319. Marañon, G. Amiel. Un Estudio de la Timidiez. Madrid: Espasa-Calpe, 1932.

1320. Marchand, Max. Du Marquis de Sade à André Gide. Essai de critique psychopathologique et psychosexuelle. Oran: 1956.

1321. Marcus, Steven. Dickens: From Pickwick to Dombey. NY: Basic Books, 1965; London: Chatto & Windus, 1965; NY: Touchstone-Clarion, 1968.

1322. Marcuse, Ludwig. Heine: A Life Between Love and Hate. NY: Farrar, 1933.

1323. _____. Sigmund Freud. Sein Bild von Menschen. Hamburg: 1956.

1324. Marcuse, M. Lenz, Vater und Sohn. Zeitschrift für Sexual-
       wissenschaft, 1928, 14:395-397.
1325. Mare, Margaret. Annette von Droste-Hülshoff. London:
       Methuen, 1965.
1326. Margis, Paul. E. T. A. Hoffmann. Eine psychographische
       Individualyse. Leipzig: Barth, 1911.
1327. Mariani, C. E. Appunti per uno studio sulla psicosi del genio
       in Tolstoi. Archivio de Psichiatria, Antropologia Crim-
       inale, 1901, 22.
1328. _____. L. N. Tolstoi. Studio Psicologico. Torino: Boc-
       ca, 1903.
1329. Marks, Jeanette Augusta. Genius and Disaster: Studies in
       Drugs and Genius. NY: Greenberg, 1925.
1330. Marovitz, Sanford E. Testament of a patriot: The Virginian,
       the tenderfoot, and Owen Wister. Texas Studies in Lit &
       Language, 1973, 15:551-575.
1331. Martin, Jay. Conrad Aiken: A Life of His Art. Princeton:
       Princeton Univ. Press, 1962.
1332. Martins, Wilson. O suicídio de Lúcio Cardoso. O Estado
       de São Paulo, Suplemento Literário, 4 Aug 1974, 3.
1333. Massis, H. Le Drame de Marcel Proust. Paris: Grasset,
       1957.
1334. Masson, Raoul. La Psycho-physiologie du jeune Schiller.
       Etudes Germaniques, 1959, 14:363-373.
1335. Matlack, Richard E. Wordsworth's Lucy poems in psycho-
       biographical context. PMLA, 1978, 93:46-65.
1336. Maudsley, Henry. Edgar Allan Poe. Amer J Insanity, 1860,
       17:167.
1337. _____. Shakespeare. In Heredity, Variations and Genius.
       London: Bales & Danielson, 1908, 110-189.
1338. Mauerhoder, Hugo. Die Introversion, mit spezieller Berück-
       sichtung des Dichters Hermann Hesse. Berne: 1929.
1339. Maurois, André. The modern biographer. Yale Rev, 1928,
       17:231-236.
1340. _____. Proust: Portrait of a Genius. NY: Harper,
       1950.
1341. Mauron, Charles. Le Dernier Baudelaire. Paris: Corti,
       1966.
1342. _____. L'Inconscient dans l'oeuvre et la vie de Racine.
       Paris: Corti, 1969.
1343. _____. Introduction a la psychanalyse de Mallarmé.
       Temps Modernes, 1948, 4:455-478.
1344. _____. Introduction à la Psychanalyse de Mallarmé.
       Neuchâtel: La Baconnière, 1950.
1345. _____. Mallarmé l'obscur. Paris: Corti, 1968.
1346. _____. Mallarmé par lui-même. Paris: Seuil, 1964.
1347. _____. Une nouvelle explication de Mallarmé. La Mort
       de sa jeune soeur Maria. Figaro Littéraire, 1948.
1348. _____. La Personnalité affective de Baudelaire. Orbis
       Litterarum, 1957, 12(3-4):203-221.
1349. Mayer, W. Zum Problem des Dichters Lenz. Archiv für
       Psychiatrie und Nervankrankheiten, 1921, 63:889-890.
1350. Mays, Milton A. Henry James or the beast in the palace of
       art. Amer Lit, 1968, 39:467-487.

1351. Mazlish, Bruce. Autobiography and psycho-analysis: between truth and self-deception. Encounter, 1970, 35:28-37.

1352. _____. James and John Stuart Mill. NY: Basic Books, 1975; Reviews: Mill News Letter, 1976, 11(2):27-31; R. Skidelsky, Spectator, 6 Sept 1975, 313.

1353. _____. The Mills: father and son. In Lifton, R.J., & Olson, E. (eds), Explanations in Psychohistory. NY: Simon & Schuster, 1974, 136-148.

1354. Meehan, James. Seed of destruction: the death of Thomas Wolfe. South Atlantic Q, 1974, 73:173-183.

1355. Meer, J. Grundlagen einer psychopathologischen Beurteilung der Persönlichkeit und der Typen Dostojewskijs. Psychologie und Medizin, 1930, 4:110-199.

1356. Meeüs, M.A. De. La Double vie de Jean Racine. Cahiers Raciniens, 1966, 19:25-81; 1966, 20:2-110.

1357. Mégroz, Rodolphe L. Joseph Conrad's Mind and Method: A Study of Personality in Art. London: Faber & Faber, 1931.

1358. Mehlman, Jeffrey. A Structural Study of Autobiography. Proust, Leiris, Sartre, Lévi-Strauss. Ithaca: Cornell Univ. Press, 1974.

1359. Mehrotra, R.R. The little secret: Wordsworth's relationship with Dorothy. Samiksa, 1975, 29(2):62-79.

1360. Mélou R. de Gordejuela, S. Moratín por dentro. Oviedo: Univ. Oviedo Press, 1964.

1361. Menasce, Jean de. Du suicide de Montherlant. In La Porte sur le jardin. Paris: Cerf, 1975, 256-258.

1362. Menéndez Pidal, R. Observaciones críticas sobre las biografías de Fray Bartolomé de las Casas. In Actas del primer congreso internacional de hispanistas, 1965, 13-24.

1363. Merle, R. Oscar Wilde, ou la 'destinée' de l'homosexuel. Paris: Gallimard, 1955.

1364. Mesnard, Pierre. L'Analyse caractérologique des journaux intimes. Psyché, 1953, 8:535-550.

1365. Mette, Alexander. Schillers Krankenbericht aus dem Jahre 1780 und seine theoretischen Grundlagen. Psychiatrie, Neurologie und medizinische Psychologie, 1957, Heft 9, 276-280.

1366. Meyer, Bernard C. Conrad's duel. Polish Rev, 1963, 8:46.

1367. _____. Joseph Conrad: A Psychoanalytic Biography. Princeton: Princeton Univ. Press, 1967; Reviews: Betty J. Kronsky, Lit & Psychol, 1970, 20:37-41; Lennart Peterson, Samlaren, 1973, 93:280-281.

1368. _____. The last written words of Joseph Conrad. Amer Imago, 1979, 36:275-286.

1369. _____. The little prince: speculations on the disappearance of Antoine de Saint-Exupéry. JAPA, 1974, 22:142-159.

1370. _____. Psychoanalytic studies on Joseph Conrad III: Aspects of orality. JAPA, 1964, 12:562-586.

1371. _____. I: The family romance. JAPA, 1964, 12:32-58.

1372. _____. _____. II: Fetishism. JAPA, 1964, 12:357-391.

1373. _____. _____. IV: The flow and ebb of artistry. JAPA, 1964, 12:802-825.

1374. _____. Some reflections on the contribution of psychoanalysis to biography. In Holt, R.R., & Peterfreund, E. (eds), Psychoanalysis and Contemporary Science, Vol. I. NY: Macmillan, 1972, 373-392.

1375. Meyers, Jeffrey. Married to Genius. NY: Barnes & Noble, 1977.

1376. _____. Orwell's painful childhood. Ariel, 1972, 3(1):54-61.

1377. Meyers, Joyce. The revisions of Seven Pillars of Wisdom. PMLA, 1973, 88:1066-1082.

1378. Michaels, Karin. Edgar Poe--im Lichte der Psychoanalyse. Politiken, 27 Jan 1935; Almanach, 1936, 155-167.

1379. Michaud, Guy. Comme un guettier mélancolique: Essai sur la personnalité d'Apollinaire. Rev des Lettres Modernes, 1971, 276-79:7-34.

1380. _____. La Personnalité de Mallarmé. Synthèses, 1968, 23:71-75.

1381. Middendorf, John Harlan. Johnson on the couch. Review, 1979, 1:1-12.

1382. Migliorino, G. Profilo psicologico di Goethe. Rivista di Psicologia Normale e Patologica, 1943, 39:162-165.

1383. Mijolla, Alain de. The desertion of Captain Rimbaud. Rev Française de Psychoanalyse, 1975, 39:427-458.

1384. Mikriammos, Philippe. William S. Burroughs. Paris: Seghers, 1974.

1385. Mileck, Joseph. Hermann Hesse: Biography and Bibliography. 2 vols. Berkeley: Univ. California Press, 1977.

1386. _____. Hermann Hesse: Life and Art. Berkeley: Univ. California Press, 1978.

1387. Miles, Peter. Bibliography and insanity: Smollett and the mad-business. Library (London), 1976, 31:205-222.

1388. Milford, Nancy. Zelda, A Biography. NY: Harper & Row, 1970.

1389. Milhaud, Gérard. Psychopathologie de Musset. Europe, 1977, 583-584:5-16.

1390. Miller, Betty Spiro. Robert Browning: A Portrait. NY: Scribner, 1953; London: Murray, 1952.

1391. Miller, Edwin Haviland. Melville: A Biography. NY: Braziller, 1975; Reviews: R. Milden, Emerson Society Q, 1976, 22:169-182; Donald Yannella, Studies in the Novel, 1976, 8:214-222.

1392. Miller, James E., Jr. The several selves of Whitman. Prairie Schooner, 1962, 36:280-282.

1393. _____. T.S. Eliot's Personal Waste Land: Exorcism of the Demons. University Park: Penn State Univ. Press, 1977.

1394. Miller, Milton L. Manic depressive cycles of the poet Shelley. Psychoanal Forum, 1966, 1:188-195, 202-203, 418-419.

1395. _____. Mirrors and insight. Psychiat Forum, 1978,
7(2):1.
1396. _____. Nostalgia: A Psychoanalytic Study of Marcel
Proust. Boston: Houghton Mifflin, 1956.
1397. _____. Psychanalyse de Proust. Paris: Fayard, 1977.
Review: P. Bertheier, Bulletin des Lettres, 1977, no.
389, 321-322.
1398. Millet, L. La Pensée de Rousseau. Paris: Bordas, 1966.
1399. Millgate, Michael. The emotional commitment of William
Dean Howells. Neophilologus, 1960, 44:48-54.
1400. Millhauser, Milton. Poet and burger: a comic variation on
a serious theme. Victorian Poetry, 1969, 7:163-168.
1401. _____. The two boyhoods. Hartford Studies in Lit, 1972,
4:36-50.
1402. Miner, Earl. Literary diaries and the boundaries of literature. Yearbook Comparative & General Lit, 1972, No.
21, 46-51.
1403. Minissi, Nullo. La personalità di Lermontov. Richerche
slavistiche, 1957, 5:225-242.
1404. Minkowski, E., & Fusswerk, J. [The Dostoevsky problem
and the structure of epilepsy: a formal psychological
essay.] Annales Médico-Psychologiques, 1955, 113:369-
409.
1405. Minn, Jay P. The Primary Personality Traits of Rimbaud.
DA, 1959, 19:2616.
1406. Mirek, Roman. [The personality of William Shakespeare.]
Przeglad Lekarski, 1969, 25:556-558.
1407. Misch, Georg. A History of Autobiography in Antiquity, 2
Vols. Cambridge: Harvard Univ. Press, 1951.
1408. Mitchell, John D. André Gide, rebel and conformist. Amer
Imago, 1959, 16:148-153; In Ruitenbeek, H. M. (ed), The
Liberal Imagination. Chicago: Quadrangle, 1965, 265-
274.
1409. Mitscherlich-Nielsen, Margarete. Psychoanalytic notes on
Franz Kafka. Psychocultural Rev, 1979, 3:1-24; Psyche,
1977, 31:60-83.
1410. Mitzman, Arthur. Gustav Flaubert und Max Weber. Psyche
(Stuttgart), 1978, 32:441-462.
1411. _____. The unstrung Orpheus: Flaubert's youth and the
psycho-social origins of art for art's sake. Psychohistory Rev, 1977, 6(1):27-44.
1412. Miws, Kimitada. In the shadow of leaves and Mishima's
death. In Takayanagi, S., & Miwa, K. (eds), Postwar
Trends in Japan. Tokyo: Univ. Tokyo Press, 1975,
229-249.
1413. Möbius, P. J. Über J. J. Rousseau's Jugend. Langenzalza:
Beyer, 1899.
1414. Moers, Ellen. Two Dreisers. NY: Viking, 1969.
1415. Moglen, Helene S. Charlotte Brontë: The Self-Conceived.
NY: Norton, 1976.
1416. Molino, Corrado. La personalità del D'Annunzio. Idea,
1968, 24:166-169.
1417. Mondolfo, R. Rousseau e la conscienza moderna. Florence:
Nuova Italia-Biblioteca di cultura, 1954.

1418. Monférier, Jacques. Le Livre posthume, memoires d'un
       suicide, de Maxime DuCamp. Rev d'Histoire Littéraire
       de la France, 1966, 66:439-450.
1419. Montal, Robert. L'Adolescent Rimbaud. Lyon: Les Ecri-
       vains Reunis, Armand Henneuse, 1954.
1420. Moon, Samuel. The springs of action: a psychological por-
       trait of Robert Creeley (Part I: The Whip). Boundary,
       1978, 6(3) 7(1):247-262.
1421. Moore, Hastings. Emily Dickinson and orthothanasia. Emily
       Dickinson Bulletin, 1977, 32:110-118.
1422. Moore, Jack B. Maxwell Bodenheim. NY: Twayne, 1970.
1423. Moore, Rayburn S. The full light of a higher criticism:
       Edel's biography and other recent studies of Henry
       James. South Atlantic Q, 1964, 63:104-114.
1424. _____. Henry James, Ltd., and the chairman of the
       board: Leon Edel's biography. South Atlantic Q, 1974,
       73:261-269.
1425. Moore, Thomas V. Percy Bysshe Shelley: an introduction
       to the study of character. Psychol Monographs, 1922,
       31:1-62.
1426. _____. A study in sadism: the life of Algernon Charles
       Swinburne. Character & Personality, 1937, 6:1-15.
1427. Moorman, Mary. William and Dorothy Wordsworth. Essays
       by Divers Hands, 1972, 37:75-94.
1428. Mora, G. One hundred years from Lombroso's first essay.
       'Genius and Insanity.' Amer J Psychiat, 1964, 121:562-
       571.
1429. Moraitis, George, & Pletsch, Carl. Psychoanalytic contri-
       bution to method in biography. Psychohistory Rev, 1979,
       8(1-2):72-74.
1430. Morcos, Mona Louis. Elements of the autobiographical in
       The Alexandria Quartet. Modern Fiction Studies, 1968,
       13:343-359.
1431. Moré, M. Le Tres Curieux Jules Verne. Paris: Galli-
       mard, 1960.
1432. Moreux, Françoise. Thomas de Quincey, la Vie, l'Homme,
       l'Oeuvre. Paris: Presses Universitaires de Paris, 1964.
1433. Morgan, Ted. Maugham: A Biography. NY: Simon &
       Schuster, 1980.
1434. Morin, G. H. Essai sur la vie et le caractère de Jean-
       Jacques Rousseau. Geneva: Slatkine, 1970 (1851).
1435. Morizot, Carol A. Just This Side of Madness: Creativity
       and the Drive to Create. Houston, Texas: Harold House,
       1978.
1436. Morley, S. G. The detection of personality in literature.
       PMLA, 1905, 20:305-321.
1437. Morris, John N. Versions of the Self: Studies in English
       Autobiography from John Bunyan to John Stuart Mill.
       NY: Basic Books, 1966; Review: Richard W. Noland,
       Lit & Psychol, 1967, 17:239-241.
1438. Morse, J. I. T. S. Eliot in 1921: toward dissociation of
       sensibility. Western Humanities Rev, 1976, 30:31-40.

1439. Moser, Thomas C. From Olive Garnett's diary: impressions of Ford Madox Ford and his friends, 1890-1906. Texas Studies in Lit & Language, 1974, 16:511-533.
1440. Moss, Sidney. Hawthorne and Melville: an inquiry into their art and the mystery of their friendship. Lit Monographs, 1975, 7:47-84.
1441. Mossberg, Barbara A. C. When a Writer Is a Daughter: Aesthetics of Identity in the Life and Art of Emily Dickinson. DAI, 1978, 38:6729A.
1442. Motola, Gabriel. Hemingway's code: literature and life. Modern Fiction Studies, 1964-65, 10:319-329.
1443. Mounier, Guy-Fernand. Etude psychopathologique sur l'écrivain Kafka. Bordeaux: Samie, 1951.
1444. Mucchielli, Roger. [A. Hesnard: searcher and humanist.] Evolution Psychiatrique, 1971, 36:363-374.
1445. Muensterberger, Warner & Axelrad, Sidney. Psychobiography. In Psychoanalysis and the Social Sciences, Vol. 5. NY: IUP, 1959.
1446. Muller, M. Sodome I ou la naturalisation de Charles. Poétique, 1971, 8:470-478.
1447. Müller-Braunschweig, Hans. Psychopathology and creativity. In The Psychoanalytic Study of Society, Vol. 6. NY: IUP, 1975, 71-99.
1448. Mumford, Lewis. Herman Melville. NY: Harcourt, 1929.
1449. Munro, John M. Arthur Symon's mental breakdown: Bologna, 1908. Notes & Queries, 1967, 14:250.
1450. Munson, G. Hart Crane: young titan in the sacred wood. In Destinations; A Canvas of American Literature Since 1900. NY: Sears, 1928, 1925.
1451. Muntéano, B. La Solitude de Rousseau. Annales Jean-Jacques Rousseau, 1946-49, 31:79-168.
1452. Murphy, B. W. Creation and destruction: notes on Dylan Thomas. British J Medical Psychol, 1968, 41:149-167.
1453. Murphy, William M. Psychic daughter, mythic son, sceptic father. In Harper, G. M. (ed), Yeats and the Occult. Toronto: Macmillan, 1975, 11-26.
1454. Murray, Henry A. Dead to the world: the passions of Herman Melville. In Schneidman, E. S. (ed), Essays in Self-Destruction. NY: Science House, 1967, 7-29.
1455. _____. Personality and creative imagination. English Institute Essays 1942. NY: Columbia Univ. Press, 1943, 139-162.
1456. Murry, John Middleton. Jonathan Swift. A Critical Biography. London: Cape, 1954.
1457. _____. The Son of Woman: The Story of D. H. Lawrence. NY: Smith, 1931; London: Cape, 1931.
1458. Myers, J. A. Fedor Dostoevsky. In Fighters of Fate. Baltimore: Williams & Wilkins, 1927, 140-150.
1459. Myers, William. George Eliot: politics and personality. In Lucas, W. J. (ed), Literature and Politics in the Nineteenth Century. NY: Barnes & Noble, 1971, 105-129.

1460. Nabokov, Vladimir. Nikolai Gogol. London: Nicholson & Watson, 1947, 9-10.

1461. Näcke, Paul. War Mörike homosexuell? Jahrbuch für Sexuelle Zwischenstufen, 1909-1910, 10:416-426.

1462. Naesgaard, Sigurd. Le Complex de Sartre. Psyché, 1948, 3:655-664.

1463. Nagel, Bert. Der Arme Heinrich Hartmanns von Aue. Tübingen: Niemeyer, 1952.

1464. Nathan, John. Mishima. Boston: Little, Brown, 1974.

1465. Nehring, Wolfgang. Schnitzler, Freud's alter ego? Modern Austrian Lit, 1977, 10:179-194.

1466. Neill, T. P. Mother Nature's bad boy. Catholic World, 1946, 164:240-247.

1467. Nelson, Benjamin F. Hesse and Jung; two newly recovered letters. Psychoanal Rev, 1963, 50:361-366.

1468. Nelson, Hilda. Théophile Gautier: the invisible and impalpable world: à demi-conviction. French Rev, 1972, 45: 819-830.

1469. Nelson, L. A. Why John Ruskin never learned how to live. Mental Hygiene, 1928, 12:673-705.

1470. Neraut-Sutterman, T. [Parricide and epilepsy: apropos of an article by Freud on Dostoevsky.] Rev Française de Psychanalyse, 1970, 34:635-652.

1471. Nethercot, Arthur H. Bernard Shaw and psychoanalysis. Modern Drama, 1969, 11:356-375.

1472. _____. The psychoanalyzing of Eugene O'Neill: postscript. Modern Drama, 1965, 8:150-155.

1473. _____. The psychoanalyzing of Eugene O'Neill: P. P. S. Modern Drama, 1973, 16:35-48.

1474. Nett, Paul Edward. A Closer Look at the Mind and Art of Edgar Allan Poe. DAI, 1975, 36:1507A.

1475. Neufeld, Johan. Dostojewski; Skizze zu seiner Psychoanalyse. Leipzig: Int Psychoanalytischer Verlag, 1923.

1476. Neumann, Erich. Georg Trakl: the person and the myth. In Creative Man: Five Essays. Princeton: Princeton Univ. Press, 1980, 138-231.

1477. Newlin, Margaret. 'Unhelpful Hymen': Marianne Moore and Hilda Doolittle. Essays in Criticism, 1977, 27:216-230.

1478. Niall, Brenda. The double alienation of Martin Boyd. Twentieth Century (Australia), 1963, 17:197-206.

1479. Nicola, Pietre de. Sulla presunta psicopatia ossessiva w dissociativa del poeta R. M. Rilke. Archivio di Psicologia, Neurolgia y Psichiatria, 1948, 9:363-374.

1480. Nicolson, Harold George. The health of authors. In The English Sense of Humour, and Other Essays. NY: Funk & Wagnalls, 1968, 63-88.

1481. Nicolson, Nigel. Portrait of a Marriage. London: Weidenfeld & Nicolson, 1973.

1482. Niederland, William G. Conrad Ferdinand Meyer: Eine tiefenpsychologische Studie. In Mitscherlich, A. (ed), Psycho-Pathographien, I: Schriftsteller und Psychoanalyse. Frankfurt: Suhrkamp, 1972, 128-141.

1483. Niess, Robert J. Autobiographical symbolism in Maupassant's last works. Symposium, 1960, 14:218-220.

1484. Nietzsche, Friedrich. My Sister and I. London: Boar's
       Head, 1953.
1485. Nin, Anaïs. The Diary of Anaïs Nin, Vol. 1, 1931-34; Vol.
       2, 1934-1939; Vol. 3, 1939-1944; Vol. 4, 1944-1947; Vol.
       5, 1947-1955; Vol. 6, 1955-1966; Vol. 7, 1966-1974.
       NY: Harcourt Brace Jovanovich, 1966-1980.
1486. Ninck, Martin. Die Jugendschrift Conrad Ferdinand Meyers.
       Schweizerischen Zeitschrift für Psychologie und ihre An-
       wendungen, 1953, 20:74-79.
1487. Nisbet, J. F. Neuropathic aspects of Shakespeare's life, etc.
       In The Insanity of Genius. London: Ward & Downey,
       1891, 146-162.
1488. Nissen, Ingjald. Sjelelige Kriser i Menneskets Liv. Henrik
       Ibsen og den Moderne Psykologi. Oslo: Aschehoug, 1931.
1489. Noad, K. B. Young laurels: the brief lives of John Irvine
       Hunter, Rene Laennec and John Keats. Medical J Aus-
       tralia, 1960, 47:521-527.
1490. Noble, C. A. M. Erkenntnisekel und Erkenntnisfreude:
       Über Thomas Manns Verhältnis zu Sigmund Freud. Rev
       des Langues Vivantes, 1972, 38:154-163.
1491. Noland, Richard W. Psychobiography: case history or life
       history? Midwest Q, 1978, 20:7-17.
1492. Nomura, Akichika. [Edgar Allan Poe: Art and Pathology.]
       Tokyo: Kongosha, 1969, 1973.
1493. Nordlicht, Stephen. Franz Kafka. Struggle to survive. New
       York State J Medicine, 1978, 78:110-114.
1494. _____. Yukio Mishima; twentieth century samurai. New
       York State J Medicine, 1979, 79:1950-1953.
1495. Nordon, P. Conan Doyle: A Biography. NY: Holt, Rine-
       hart & Winston, 1967.
1496. Normand, Jean. Anaïs Nin ou le labyrinth radieux. Etudes
       Anglaises, 1976, 29:478-486.
1497. _____. Les Ironies de la solitude. Europe, 1967, No.
       459-460, 162-169.
1498. Nötzel, Karl. Das Gatten- und Elternerlebnis in Dostojewski.
       Vivos Voco I, 1921, 2:207-210.
1499. Novak, Jane. The Razor Edge of Balance: A Study of Vir-
       ginia Woolf. Coral Gables, Fla.: Univ. Miami Press,
       1974.
1500. Novak, Maximillian E. Defoe and the Nature of Man. Lon-
       don: Oxford Univ. Press, 1963.
1501. Nuñez, Antonio. La personalidad humana y creadora de
       Lauro Olmo. Insula, 1963, 18(197):5.
1502. Nussbaum, Felicity A. Father and son in Boswell's London
       journal. Philological Q, 1978, 57:383-397.
1503. Nyirö, C. Kötözseni és pszichiátria. Magyar Pszichologia
       Szemle, 1933, 6:63-86.

1504. Oakeshott, Edna. Childhood Experience in Autobiography.
       London: Cambridge Univ. Press, 1960.
1505. Ober, William B. Boswell's clap. JAMA, 1970, 212:91-
       95.

1506. _____. Boswell's Clap and Other Essays; Medical Analyses of Literary Men's Afflictions. Carbondale: Southern Illinois Univ. Press, 1979.

1507. _____. Boswell's gonorrhea. Bulletin New York Academy Medicine, 1969, 45:587-636.

1508. _____. Drowsed with the fume of poppies; opium and John Keats. Bulletin New York Academy Medicine, 1968, 44: 862-881.

1509. _____. A few kind words about W. Somerset Maugham. New York State J Medicine, 1969, 69:2692-2701.

1510. _____. Madness and poetry: a note on Collins, Cowper and Smart. Bulletin New York Academy Medicine, 1970, 46:203-266.

1511. _____. Oliver St. John Gogarty, M. D. (1878-1957). Buck Mulligan of Irish renaissance. New York State J Medicine, 1969, 69:469-480.

1512. _____. Swinburne's masochism: neuropathology and psychopathology. Bulletin Menninger Clinic, 1975, 39:500-555.

1513. _____. William Carlos Williams, M. D. (1883-1963). Physician as poet. New York State J Medicine, 1969, 69:1084-1098.

1514. O'Brien, Sharon. The limits of passion: Willa Cather's review of The Awakening. Women & Lit, 1975, 3(2):10-20.

1515. O'Connor, Richard. Jack London: A Biography. Boston: Little, Brown, 1964.

1516. O'Connor, William V., & Stone, Edward. A Casebook on Ezra Pound. NY: Crowell, 1960.

1517. Odinot, R. Etude médico-psychologique sur Alfred de Musset. Lyon: Storck, 1908.

1518. O'Donnell, Thomas J. The Confessions of T. E. Lawrence: The Romantic Hero's Presentation of Self. Columbus: Ohio State Univ. Press, 1979.

1519. _____. The confessions of T. E. Lawrence: the sadomasochistic hero. Amer Imago, 1977, 34:115-132.

1520. Odoul, P. Le Drame intime d'Alfred de Musset: étude psychoanalytique de l'oeuvre et de la vie d'Alfred de Musset. Paris: 1976.

1521. O'Higgins, Harvey, & Reede, E. H. The American Mind in Action. NY: Harper, 1920, 1923, 1924.

1522. Ojo-Ade, Femi. Social and psychological alienation of the black writer: a study of René Maran (1887-1960). Manna (Toronto), 1972, 3:6-12.

1523. Olney, James Leslie (ed). Autobiography. Essays Theoretical and Critical. Princeton: Princeton Univ. Press, 1980.

1524. _____. Metaphors of Self; The Meaning of Autobiography. Princeton: Princeton Univ. Press, 1972.

1525. Olson, Charles. Encounter with Ezra Pound. Antaeus, 1975, 17:73-92.

1526. Olsson, H. Vinlövsranka och hagtornskrans. En bok om Fröding. Stockholm: Norstedt, 1970.

1527. Ong, Walter J. Swift on the mind: the myth of asepsis. Modern Language Q, 1954, 15:208-221.

1528.   Onimus, Jean.   Peur et poésie, l'angoisse de vivre chez
        Henri Michaux.   Etudes, 1957, 292:217-237.
1529.   Onorato, Richard C.   The Character of the Poet: Words-
        worth in 'The Prelude.'   Princeton: Princeton Univ.
        Press, 1971.
1530.   Oppeln-Bronikowski, Friedrich.   Eros als Schicksal bei
        Friedrich dem Grossen und bei Stendhal.   Psychoanaly-
        tische Bewegung, 1930, 2:314-325.
1531.   Orgel, Shelley.   Sylvia Plath: fusion with the victim and
        suicide.   Psychoanal Q, 1974, 43:262-287; In Coltrera,
        J. T. (ed), Lives, Events and Other Players: Studies in
        Psychobiography.   NY: Aronson, 1980.
1532.   Orlando, Francesco.   La Découverte du souvenir d'enfance
        au premier livre des Confessions.   Annales de la Société
        Jean-Jacques Rousseau, 1971, 37:149-173.
1533.   Orvell, Miles D.   'The Raven' and the chair.   Poe Studies,
        1972, 5(2):54.
1534.   Ossipow, N.   Tolstois Kindheitserinnerungen.   Ein Beitrag zu
        Freuds Libidotheorie.   Vienna: Int Psychoanalytischer
        Verlag, 1923.
1535.   ____. Über Leo Tolstois Seelenleiden.   Imago, 1923, 9:
        495-498.
1536.   Ostenfeld, Ib.   Søren Kierkegaard's Psykologi.   Undersøgelse
        og Indlevelse.   Copenhagen: Rhodos, 1972.
1537.   Ott, Marie Laure.   Patrick Hamilton.   Etudes Anglaises,
        1975, 28:420-428.
1538.   Ozick, Cynthia.   Forster as homosexual.   Commentary, 1971,
        52(6):81-85.

1539.   Pacaly, Josette.   Biographies et autobiographies sartriennes:
        Essai de critique psychoanalytique.   L'Information Littér-
        aire, 1978, 30:212-214.
1540.   Page, Christopher.   Dylan and the scissormen.   Anglo-Welsh
        Rev, 1974, 24:76-81.
1541.   Paglia, Camille Ann.   Lord Hervey and Pope.   Eighteenth-
        Century Studies, 1973, 6:348-371.
1542.   Painter, George Duncan.   Marcel Proust: A Biography, 2
        Vols.   NY: Random House, 1978.
1543.   ____. The personality of Gide.   Times Lit Supplement,
        14 Dec 1951, no. 2602, 805.
1544.   Panken, Shirley.   Some psychodynamics in Sons and Lovers:
        a new look at the Oedipal theme.   Psychoanal Rev, 1974-
        75, 61:571-589.
1545.   Pannenborg, W. A.   Een vergelijkend biografisch onderzoek
        naar eenige psychische eigenschappen van de tragedian
        comedieschrijvers.   Algemeen Nederlands Tijdschrift voor
        Wijsbegeerte en Psychologie, 1943, 36:107-123.
1546.   Papu, Edgar.   A multilateral personality.   Romanian Rev,
        1970, 24(4):52-53.
1547.   Parkinson, Thomas.   Yeats and the love lyric.   James Joyce
        Q, 1965, 3:109-123.
1548.   Parsons, C. O.   The devil and Samuel Clemens.   Virginia Q
        Rev, 1947.

1549. Partridge, G. E. Psychopathological study of Jean-Nicolas-Arthur Rimbaud. Psychoanal Rev, 1930, 17:401-425.

1550. Pascal, Roy. Autobiography as an art form. In Proceedings of the 1957 Conference of FLLM. Böckmann, 1959.

1551. _____. Design and Truth in Autobiography. Cambridge: Harvard Univ. Press, 1960.

1552. Patterson, Rebecca. Emily Dickinson's 'double' Tim: masculine identification. Amer Imago, 1971, 28:330-362.

1553. _____. The Riddle of Emily Dickinson. Boston: Houghton Mifflin, 1951.

1554. Paul, Sherman. The Shores of America: Thoreau's Inward Exploration. Urbana: Univ. Illinois Press, 1958.

1555. Paulhan, F. Herbert Spencer d'après son autobiographie. Rev Philosophique de la France, 1907, 64:145-148.

1556. Paulsen, Wolfgang. Christoph Martin Wieland: Der Mensch und Sein Werk in psychologischen Perspektiven. Bern: Francke, 1975.

1557. Paulson, A. Probing Strindberg's psyche. Amer Scandinavian Rev, 1965, 53.

1558. Paulson, Arthur Barry. The Transparent Eyeball: Identity and Young Man Emerson. A Psychoanalytic Study. DAI, 1975, 35:6728A.

1559. Paulus, Jean. Les Deux visages de Stendhal. In Miscellanea Psychologica Albert Michotte. Paris: Libraire Philosophique, 1947, 429-439.

1560. Pauly, Robert. L'Epilepsie de Dostoiëvsky: réalité de l'épilepsie: épilepsie et travail intellectuel; épilepsie et mysticisme. Médical Bordeaux, 1948, 125:337-345.

1561. Pavilionis, Rolandas. [Thoreau and self-determination of personality.] Problemos (Vilnius), 1973, 2:40-49.

1562- Pazi, M. Max Brod. Werk und Persönlichkeit. Bonn: Bou-
3.   vier, 1970.

1564. Peñuelas, Marcelino C. Personalidad y obra de Forner. Hispanófila, 1966, No. 26, 23-31.

1565. Perazzi, Francesco. La malattia di Torquato Tasso in una sua lettera a Gerolamo Mercuriale. Vita ospedaliera, 1962, 1:9-11.

1566. Perkins, J. A. Justification and excuses in Rousseau. Studies on Voltaire and the 18th Century, 1972, 89:1277-1292.

1567. Perkus, Gerald H. Meredith's unhappy love life: worthy of the muse. Cithara, 1970, 9(2):32-46.

1568. Pernicone, Vincenzo. Il messaggio della personalità e della poesia di Dante. In Miscellanea di studi danteschi. Genoa: Bozzi, 1966, 103-132.

1569. Perry, R. Henry James' sexuality and his obscure hurt. Int J Social Psychiat, 1978, 24:33-37.

1570. Peters, Heinz Frederick. My Sister, My Spouse; A Biography of Lou Andreas-Salomé. NY: Norton, 1974.

1571. _____. Zarathustra's Sister: The Case of Elisabeth and Friedrich Nietzsche. NY: Crown, 1977.

1572. Peterson, Dale Alfred. The Literature of Madness: Autobiographical Writings by Mad People and Mental Patients in England and America from 1436 to 1975. DAI, 1977, 38:1369A.

1573. Petesch, Donald A. Faulkner on Negroes: the conflict between the public man and the private art. Southern Humanities Rev, 1976, 10:55-63.
1574. Petit, Jacques. Claudel et l'usurpateur. Paris: Desclée de Brouwer, 1971.
1575. Petrocchi, M., & Calcagni, C. Studio caratteriologico dei personaggi del Tolstoj e anticpazione die problemi medicosociali ne' la Sonata a Kreutzer. Rivista Storia Medica, 1966, 10:79-93.
1576. Peyrouton, N. C. Boz and the American phrenomesmerists. Dickens Studies, 1967, 3:38-50.
1577. Phillips, Elizabeth. Edgar Allan Poe: An American Imagination. Port Washington, NY: Kennikat, 1979.
1578. Phillips, Steven R. Hemingway and the bullfight: the archetypes of tragedy. Arizona Q, 1973, 29:37-56.
1579. Phillips, William. Artistic truth and warped vision. In Howe, I. (ed), The Idea of the Modern in Literature and the Arts. NY: Horizon, 1968, 97-108.
1580. Phillipson, J. S. Swift's half-way house. Medical History, 1969, 13:297-298.
1581. Phillipson, Nicholas. Intuitions and interactions. Times Lit Supplement, 24 Jan 1975, 90.
1582. Philonenko, Alexis. Mélancolie et consolation chez Nietzsche. Rev de Métaphysique et de Morale, 1971, 76:77-98.
1583. Picchi, Fernando. La droga in due esperienze parallele: Baudelaire e De Quincey. Bologna: Cappelli, 1974.
1584. Piccini, L. Epicrisi nella tragedia di Casa Carducci. Osservatore Politico Letterario, 1967, 13:11-17.
1585. Pichois, Claude, & Kopp, Robert. Baudelaire et l'opium: une enquête à reprendre. Europe, 1967, 456-57:61-79.
1586. Pichon-Riviere, Arminda A. de. Balzac, un caracter oral. Revista de Psicoanálisis, 1947, 4:705-717.
1587. Pickering, George. Creative Malady: Illness in the Lives and Minds of Charles Darwin, Florence Nightingale, Mary Baker Eddy, Sigmund Freud, Marcel Proust and Elizabeth Barrett Browning. London: Allen & Unwin; Toronto: Methuen, 1974; NY: Oxford Univ. Press, 1974.
1588. Pickering, William C. A Personality Study of Aldous Huxley, Using Fictional and Non-Fictional Materials within the Theoretical Structure of Gordon Allport's Personology. DAI, 1973, 34:1283.
1589. Piechowski, Michael M. Self-actualization as a development structure: a profile of Antoine de Saint-Exupéry. Genetic Psychol Monographs, 1978, 97 (Second Half):181-242.
1590. Piegnot, Jerome. Maine de Biran le Malheureux. Mercure de France, 1960, 338:660-682.
1591. Pine, Richard. The personality of Wilde. Dublin Magazine, 1971-72, 9(2):52-59.
1592. Pinney, Thomas (ed). Letters of Thomas Babington Macaulay. Cambridge: Cambridge Univ. Press, 1974.

1593. Plank, Emma N. Memories of early childhood in autobiographies. In The Psychoanalytic Study of the Child, Vol. 8. NY: IUP, 1953, 381-393.

1594. Plank, Robert. On 'Seeing the Salamander.' In The Psychoanalytic Study of the Child, Vol. 12. NY: IUP, 1957, 379-398.

1595. Plesso, G. I. [Concerning the psychopathy of I. S. Turgenev.] Klinicheski Arkhiv Genialnosti i Odarennosti, 1928, 4:54-68.

1596. Plewa, F. Zur frage der psychischen Kompensation der Augenmindervertigkeit. Int Zeitschrift für Individual-Psychologie, 1931, 6:455-456.

1597. Polak, E. Individualpsychologische Betrachtungen über Tolstoi. Int Zeitschrift für Individual-Psychologie, 1928, 6:456-481.

1598. Polansky, Norman A. How shall a life-history be written? Character & Personality, 1941, 9:188-207.

1599. Politzer, Heinz. Auf der Suche nach Idendität: zu Heinrich von Kleists Würzburger Reise. Euphorion, 1967, 61:383-399.

1600. Pollin, Burton R. Fanny Godwin's suicide re-examined. Etudes Anglaises, 1965, 18:258-268.

1601. _____. Nicholson's lost portrait of William Godwin: a study in phrenology. Keats-Shelley J, 1967, 16:51-60.

1602. _____. Poe's invention to the 'psychological autobiographists.' Poe Studies, 1978, 11:15-16.

1603. Pollock, G. On mourning, immortality and utopia. JAPA, 1975, 23:334-362.

1604. Pollock, George H. Glückel von Hameln: Bertha Pappenheim's idealized ancestor. Amer Imago, 1971, 28:216-227.

1605. Pomeau, R. Foi et raison de Jean-Jacques. Europe, 1961, 391-392:57-65.

1606. Pomeau, René. Candide entre Marx et Freud. Studies on Voltaire the 18th Century, 1972, 89:1305-1323.

1607. Poole, Roger. The Unknown Virginia Woolf. Cambridge: Cambridge Univ. Press, 1978.

1608. Pope Hennessy, James. Robert Louis Stevenson. NY: Simon & Schuster, 1975.

1609. Popper-Lynkeus, J. Voltaire, eine Charakteranalyse. Vienna: Löwit, 1925.

1610. Porché, F. Portrait psychologique de Tolstoy. Paris: 1935.

1611. Potts, Margaret L. The genesis and evolution of the creative personality: a Rankian analysis of The Diary of Anaïs Nin. J Otto Rank Assn, 1974-75, 9(2):1-37.

1612. _____. The Genesis and Evolution of the Creative Personality: A Rankian Analysis of The Diary of Anaïs Nin, Volumes I-V. DAI, 1974, 34:4279A-80A.

1613. Poulet, Robert. L'Homosexualité dans les lettres contemporaines. In Les Homosexuelles. Le Crapouillot, No. 30, 1955, 55-62.

1614. Prätorius, Numa. The dispute about Walt Whitman's homosexuality in Mercure de France. In Ruitenbeek, H. M.

(ed), Homosexuality and Creative Genius. NY: Obolensky, 1967, 121-139; Der Streit um Walt Whitmans Homosexualität im Mercure de France und im l'Archives d'anthropologie criminelle, von Jahre 1913-14. Zeitschrift für
Sexuelwissenschaft, 1916-17, 3:326-339, 364-374.

1615.   . Oskar Wilde, eine Bericht. Jahrbuch für Sexuelle
Zwischenstufen, 1901, 3:265-274.

1616.   . A seventeenth-century homosexual poet Saint-
Pavin, the 'King of Sodom, ' a psychological study. Zeitschrift für Sexual-Wissenschaft, 1918, 5:261-271; In
Ruitenbeek, H. M. (ed), Homosexuality and Creative Genius. NY: Obolensky, 1967, 191-202.

1617.   . Voltaire und die Homosexualität. Zeitschrift für
Sexuellwissenschaft, 1928-1929, 15:571-579.

1618.   . Zur Homosexualität von Walt Whitman. Jahrbuch
für Sexuelle Zwischenstufen, 1915-1917, 15:68-75.

1619. Pratt, Audrey E. Franz Kafka und sein Vater: des Verhältnis der beiden und dessen Einwirkung auf Kafkas Werk.
Doctoral dissertation, McGill Univ., 1949.

1620. Pratt, Branwen Bailey. Dickens and father: notes on the
family romance. Hartford Studies in Lit, 1976, 8:4-22.

1621. Praz, Mario. Joyce e l'ossessione di Dublino. In Cronache
letterarie anglosassoni. Rome: Storia e Letteratura,
1966, 64-69.

1622.   . Poe and psychoanalysis. Sewanee Rev, 1960, 68:
375-389.

1623. Proal, L. La Psychologie de Jean-Jacques Rousseau. Les
Larmes et la bile. Correspondant, 1912, 247:1099-1117.

1624.   . La Psychologie de J. J. Rousseau. Paris: Alcan,
1923, 1930.

1625. Prochnik, Leon. Endings. Death, Glorious and Otherwise,
as Faced by Ten Outstanding Figures of Our Time. NY:
Crown, 1979.

1626. Promis Ojeda, José. Infancia y adolescencia de Gabriela
Mistral (1889-1910): Años de formación y aprendizaje.
Revista Signos de Valparaiso, 1971, 5(1):27-47.

1627. Proudfit, I. The big round world. A psychiatric study of
Louis Stevenson. Psychoanal Rev, 1936, 23:121-148.

1628. Pruette, Lorine. A psychoanalytic study of Edgar Allan Poe.
Amer J Psychol, 1920, 31:370-402; In Ruitenbeek, H. M.
(ed), The Literary Imagination. Chicago: Quadrangle,
1965, 391-432.

1629. Pruitt, Virginia D. Yeats and the Steinach operation. Amer
Imago, 1977, 34:287-296.

1630. Quinn, Arthur Hobson. Edgar Allan Poe: A Critical Biography. NY: Appleton-Century, 1941.

1631. Quinn, Patrick Frank. Four views of Edgar Poe. Jahrbuch
für Amerikastudien, 1960, 5:138-146.

1632. Quinn, Vincent. H. D. 's 'Hermetic Definition': the poet as
archetypal mother. Contemporary Lit, 1977, 18:51-61.

1633. Quirk, Eugene F. Mr. Dickens & Dr. Elliotson. Review:
Fred Kaplan's Dickens and Mesmerism. Hartford Studies
in Lit, 1976, 8:50-59.

1634. Raabe, Paul. Die Briefe Hölderlins: Studien zur Entwicklung und Persönlichkeit des Dichters. Stuttgart: Metzler, 1963.

1635. Radin, Paul. Report on the mescaline experience of Crash-
ing Thunder; excerpts from The Autobiography of a Winnebago Indian. Edited by Paul Radin, 1920. In Aaronson, B. S., & Osmond, H. (eds), Psychedelics. NY:
Anchor, 1970, 86-90.

1636. Rahmer, S. August Strindberg. Ein pathologische Studie.
Munich: Bergmann, 1907.

1637. _____. Nicolaus Lenau, als Mensch und Dichter. Ein
Beitrag zur Sexualpathologie. Berlin: Curtius, 1910.

1638. Railton, Stephen. Fenimore Cooper: A Study of His Life
and Imagination. Princeton: Princeton Univ. Press,
1978.

1639. Rakowsky, Christine H. To Inhabit Eternity: Virginia
Woolf's Coming to Terms with Death. DAI, 1978, 38:
7315A.

1640. Ralli, A. Emily Brontë: the problem of personality. North
Amer Rev, 1925, 221:495-507.

1641. Randal, Fred V. Eating and drinking in Lamb's Elia Essays. J English Lit History, 1970, 37:57-76.

1642. Rank, Otto. Ein Selbstbekenntnis Wilhelm Buschs. Int Zeitschrift für Psychoanalyse, 1911, 1:523.

1643. _____. Zu Baudelaires Inzest-komplex. Int Zeitschrift
für Psychoanalyse, 1911, 1:275.

1644. Rankin, Anne V. Odi et amo: Gaius Valerius Catullus and
Freud's essay on 'A special type of choice of object made
by men.' Amer Imago, 1962, 19:437-448.

1645. Rantavaara, Irma. On Lytton Strachey's personality and
style. Neuphilologische Mitteilungen, 1972, 73(1-2):326-
339.

1646. Raskin, Evelyn. Comparison of scientific and literary ability: a biographical study of eminent scientists and men
of letters of the nineteenth century. J Abnormal & Social Psychol, 1936, 32:20-35.

1647. Ratchford, Fannie E. The Brontës Web of Childhood. NY:
Columbia Univ. Press, 1941.

1648. Rathlef, E. Goethe Pathologisch. Riga: Jonck u Poliewsky,
1904.

1649. Rattner, Josef. Kafka und das Vater-Problem: Ein Beitrag
zum tiefenpsychologischen Problem der Kindererziehung:
Interpretation von Kafkas 'Brief an den Vater.' Munich:
Reinhardt, 1964.

1650. Raviart, G. Le Génie de Balzac. Annales Médico-Psychologiques, 1954, 4:481-503.

1651. Ravn, J. [The psychic constitution of Selma Lagerlöf.]
Acta Psychiatria et Neurologica Scandinavica, 1959, 34:
321-324.

1652. Rawson, Wyatt. William Blake--psychic, visionary and
       prophet. Light, 1970, 90:3483:188-194.
1653. Ray, Gordon N. The Buried Life. A Study of the Relation
       Between Thackeray's Fiction and His Personal History.
       Cambridge: Harvard Univ. Press, 1952.
1654. Raymond, M. Deux aspects de la vie intérieure de Rous-
       seau. Annales Jean-Jacques Rousseau, 1941-42, 29.
1655. _____. Jean-Jacques Rousseau, de quête de soi et la
       rêverie. Paris: Corti, 1963.
1656. Read, Herbert. Charlotte and Emily Brontë. In Reason and
       Romanticism. London: Faber & Gwyer, 1926, 161-188.
1657. _____. In defence of Shelley. In In Defence of Shelley
       and Other Essays. London: Heinemann, 1936, 1-86.
1658. _____. The personality of the poet; excerpt from Form
       in Modern Poetry. In Selected Writings: Poetry and
       Criticism. NY: Horizon, 1964, 81-97; In his Collected
       Essays in Literary Criticism. London: Faber, 1938,
       1951, 21-40.
1659. Reed, H. B. The Heraclitan obsession of Whitman. Per-
       sonalist, 1934, 15:125-138.
1660. Rees, Helen E. A Psychology of Artistic Creation as Evi-
       denced in Autobiographical Statements of Artists. NY:
       Teachers College, 1942.
1661. Régis, E. La Dramomanie de J. J. Rousseau. Chronique
       Médicale, 1909, 16.
1662. _____. Étude médicale sur J. J. Rousseau. Chronique
       Médicale, 1900, 7:65-76, 132-140, 173-178, 194-206.
1663. Reid, Eva C. Literary genius and manic-depressive insan-
       ity; with special reference to the alleged case of Dean
       Swift. Medical Record, 1913, 83.
1664. _____. Manifestations of manic-depressive insanity in
       literary genius. Amer J Insanity, 1912.
1665. Reid, Stephen. The Apology of Socrates. Psychoanal Rev,
       1975, 62:97-106.
1666. Reik, Theodor. Aus den Denkwürdigkeiten der Glückel von
       Hameln. Int Zeitschrift für Psychoanalyse, 1915, 3:235-
       239.
1667. _____. Eugene Chrikov. In Thirty Years with Freud.
       NY: Farrar & Rinehart, 1940, 185-196.
1668. _____. Flaubert und seine 'Versuchung des heiligen An-
       tonius.' Ein Beitrag zur Künstlerpsychologie. Bruns:
       1912.
1669. _____. Flauberts Jugendregungen. Der liebende Flau-
       bert. Pan (Berlin), 2 Nov 1911; Int Zeitschrift für Psy-
       choanalyse, 1912, 2:356.
1670. _____. Fragment of a Great Confession. NY: Farrar,
       Straus, 1949.
1671. _____. Ein Kindheitserringerung Alexandre Dumas.
       Imago, 1917, 5:128-129.
1672. _____. Aus dem Leben Guy de Maupassants. Imago,
       1913, 2:519-521.
1673. _____. On the effect of unconscious death wishes.
       Psychoanal Rev, 1978, 65:38-67.

1674. _____. Richard Beer-Hofmann. Leipzig: Eichler, 1912.
1675. _____. The Secret Self: Psychoanalytic Experiences in Life and Literature. NY: Farrar, Straus & Young, 1952.
1676. _____. The study on Dostoevsky. In Thirty Years with Freud. NY: Farrar & Rinehart, 1940, 158-176; Imago, 1929, 15:232-242; Almanach, 1930, 32-44.
1677. _____. From Thirty Years with Freud. NY: Farrar & Rinehart, 1940; London: Hogarth, 1940; Toronto: Macmillan, 1940.
1678. _____. Der Tod und die Liebe (In memoriam Arthur Schnitzler). Almanach, 1934, 78-84.
1679. _____. Warum verliess Goethe Friederike? Ein psychoanalytische Monographie. Imago, 1929, 15:400-537; Vienna: Int Psychoanalytischer Verlag, 1930.
1680. _____. Zwei Träume Flauberts. Int Zeitschrift für Psychoanalyse, 1913, 3:222-224.
1681. Reilly, E. Sylvia Plath: talented poet, tortured woman. Perspectives in Psychiat Care, 1978, 16:129-136.
1682. Rein, David M. Edgar A. Poe: The Inner Pattern. NY: Philosophical Library, 1960.
1683. _____. Poe's dreams. Amer Q, 1958, 10:367-371; London Magazine, 1962, 2:42-58.
1684. _____. S. Weir Mitchell As a Psychiatric Novelist. NY: IUP, 1952.
1685. Reinert, R. E. The confessions of a 19th century opium eater: Thomas De Quincey. Bullinger Menninger Clinic, 1972, 36:455-459.
1686. Reinhard, F. Schiller als Psychotherapeut. Münchener Medizinische Wochenschrift, 1928, 74:441.
1687. Reits, G. V. [August Strindberg's life and work.] Sbornik, posoyashennyi V. M. Bekhterevu k 40-letnyu professorskoi deyatalelnosti, 1926, 691-710.
1688. Remus Araico, José. Edipo, Lutero y Kafka y la crisis de idendidad. Cuadernos de Psicoanálisis, 1965, 1:343-348.
1689. Rens, I. El suicidio de Arguedas. Cuadernos Americanos, 1976, 35(4):97-127.
1690. Reus, Robert. Portrait-Morphopsychologique de Maxence Van der Meersch. Paris: Clairac, 1952.
1691. Révész-Alexander, M. Portret en Zelfportret als Menselijk Document. Nederlandsch Tijdschrift voor de Psychologie, 1954, 9:372-384.
1692. Rhodes, Philip. A medical appraisal of the Brontës. Brontë Society Transactions, 1972, 16(2):101-109.
1693. Ribnikov, N. A. [Autobiographies as psychological documents.] Psikhologiya, 1930, 3:440-458.
1694. _____. [Psychology and the study of biography.] Psikhologiya, 1929, 2:215-225.
1695. Ribon, J. F. Dostoevsky ou le déicide à la recherche du Christ. Evolution Psychiatrique, 1972, 37:205-223.
1696. Rich, Adrienne Cecile. Of Woman Born, Motherhood as Experience and Institution. NY: Norton, 1976.
1697. _____. Vesuvius at home: the power of Emily Dickinson. Parnassus, 1976, 5(1):49-74.

1698. Richardson, H. Edward. William Faulkner: The Journey to Self-Discovery. Columbia: Univ. Missouri Press, 1969.

1699. Richmond, Hugh M. Personal identity and literary personae: a study in historical psychology. PMLA, 1975, 90:209-221.

1700. Rico-Avello, Carlos. Lope de Vega (Flaquezas y Dolencias). Madrid: Aguilar, 1973.

1701. Rico Verdú, José. Un Azorín desconocido. Estudio psicológico de su obra. Alicante: Institut de Estudios Alicantos, 1973.

1702. Riely, John C. The pattern of imagery in Johnson's periodical essays. Eighteenth-Century Studies, 1970, 3:384-397.

1703. Riley, M. M. Persona and theme in George Moore's Confessions of a Young Man. English Lit in Transition, 1976, 19:87-95.

1704. Rimanelli, Giose. Pavese's Diario: why suicide? why not? in Rimanelli, G., & Atchity, K. J. (ed), Italian Literature: Roots and Branches. New Haven: Yale Univ. Press, 1976, 383-405.

1705. Rinaker, Clarissa. A psychoanalytic note on Jane Austen. Psychoanal Q, 1936, 5:108-115.

1706. Rivero, Luis L. La orfandad de Bécquer como explicación de su actitud en la vida. Cuadernos Hispanoamericanos, 1970, 421-435.

1707. Rivers, W. C. L'Inversion de Walt Whitman: évidence nouvelle. Archivio di Anthropologia, Criminale, Psichiatria e Medici Legale, 1914, 4:41-50.

1708. _____. Walt Whitman's Anomaly. London: Allen & Unwin, 1913.

1709. Roazen, Paul. A curious triangle: Freud, Lou Andreas-Salomé, and Victor Tausk. Encounter, 1969, 33(4):3-8.

1710. Roback, Abraham A. O. L. Peretz. Psychologist of Literature. Cambridge: Sci-Art, 1935.

1711. Roberts, Donald R. The death wish of John Donne. PMLA, 1957, 42:958-976.

1712. _____. A Freudian view of Jonathan Swift. Lit & Psychol, 1956, 6:8-17.

1713. Robertson, John W. Edgar A. Poe: A Psychopathic Study. NY: Putnam, 1922; San Francisco: Newbegin, 1921.

1714. Robinson, Virginia P. The double soul: Mark Twain and Otto Rank. J Otto Rank Assn, 1972, 6:32-53.

1715. Robitscher, Jonas. Accepting the psychiatrist's authority: the cases of Virginia Woolf and Janet Gothin. In The Powers of Psychiatry. Boston: Houghton Mifflin, 1980, 10-18.

1716. Rocchietta, S. [Friederich Hölderlin, 1770-1843, the mad poet.] Minerva Medica, 1963, 54: Supplement: 1504-1511.

1717. Rochefoucault, E. de la. L'Angoisse et les écrivains. Paris: Grasset, 1974.

1718. Roderick, Colin. The personality of Henry Handel Richardson. Australian Q, 1948, 20:44-55.

1719. Rof Carballo, Juan. Poesía y delincuencia. Acta Psiquiatrica y Psicológica de America Latina, 1965, 11:223-237.

1720. Rogawski, A. Young Freud as a poet. In Celebration of Laughter. Los Angeles: Mara, 1970.

1721. Rogoff, Gordon. The restless intellect of Tennessee Williams. Tulane Drama Rev, 1966, 10: 78-92.

1722. Rohrs, H. Jean-Jacques Rousseau: Vision und Wirklichkeit. Heidelberg: Duelle und Meyer, 1957.

1723. Rolland, P. H. Etude psycho-pathologique sur le mysticisme de J. K. Huysmans. Thèse de Médicin de Paris, 1930.

1724. Rolleston, Humphrey. Samuel Johnson's medical experiences. In Sorsby, A. (ed), Tenements of Clay. London: Friedmann, 1974, 132-147.

1725. Rolleston, J. D. Venereal disease in Pepy's diary. British J Venereal Diseases, 1943, 19:169-173.

1726. Rollman-Branch, Hilda S. The first-born child, male: vicissitudes of preoedipal problems. Int J Psycho-Anal, 1966, 47:404-415.

1727. Rom, Paul. Adler and Goethe. Individual Psychol, 1963, 1(2):2-4.

1728. _____. Goethe's earliest recollection. J Individual Psychol, 1965, 21:189-193.

1729. Rose, Harriet. Towards the pleasure principle: character revelation in Benjamin Franklin's To the Royal Academy. Paunch, 1972, 35:16-25.

1730. Rose, Phyllis. Portrait of a woman of letters. Partisan Rev, 1978, 45(3):446-457.

1731. _____. A Woman of Letters: A Life of Virginia Woolf. NY: Oxford Univ. Press, 1978.

1732. Rosebury, T. VD in the famous and the infamous. MAHS, 1973, 7(3):137, passim.

1733. Rosenberg, John D. The Darkening Glass: A Portrait of Ruskin's Genius. NY: Columbia Univ. Press, 1961.

1734. Rosenberg, Samuel. Why Freud Fainted. Indianapolis: Bobbs-Merrill, 1978.

1735. Rosenheim, F. Flight from home: some episodes in the life of Herman Melville. Amer Imago, 1940, 1:1-30.

1736. Rosenthal, A. Mérimée and the supernatural: diversion or obsession? Nineteenth-Century French Studies, 1973, 1:138-154.

1737. Rosenthal, David. Was Thomas Wolfe a borderline? Schizophrenia Bulletin, 1979, 5:87-94.

1738. Rosenthal, M. L. Randall Jarrell. Univ. Minnesota Pamphlets on American Writers, 1972, 103:1-48.

1739. Rosenthal, Peggy. Feminism and life in feminist biography. College English, 1974, 36:180-184.

1740. Rosenthal, Tatjana. [On Dostoevsky.] In Bericht über die Fortschritte der Psychoanalyse, 1914-1919. Vienna: Int Psychoanalytischer Verlag, 1921.

1741. Rosenwald, George C. Personality description from the viewpoint of adaptation. Psychiatry, 1968, 31:16-31.

1742. Rosenzweig, Saul. The ghost of Henry James: a study in thematic apperception. Character & Personality, 1943, 12:79-100.

1743. Ross, W. O. Concerning Dreiser's mind. Amer Lit, 1946, 18:233-243.

1744. Roth, Nathan. The porphyria of Heinrich Heine. Comprehensive Psychiatry, 1969, 10:90-106.
1745. Roubicek, J. Franz Kafka. Confinia Psychiatrica, 1975, 18:73-94.
1746. Rovit, Earl. Ernest Hemingway. NY: Twayne, 1963.
1747. Rowlette, Robert. 'Howells as his head makes him': a phrenologist's report. Amer Notes & Queries, 1973, 11:115-116.
1748. Rowse, Alfred Leslie. The personality of Shakespeare. Huntington Library Q, 1964, 27:193-209.
1749. _____. Sex and Society in Shakespeare's Age: Simon Forman the Astrologer. London: Weidenfeld, 1974.
1750. Roy, David. Lytton Strachey and the masochistic basis of homosexuality. Psychoanal Rev, 1972-73, 59:579-584.
1751. Roy, J. Passion et mort de Saint-Exupéry. Paris: Julliard, 1964.
1752. Rozelaar, M. Seneca--a new approach to his personality. Psychiatry, 1973, 36:82-92.
1753. Rubenstein, Jill. The curse of subjectivity: De Quincey's Confessions of an English Opium Eater and Baudelaire's Paradis Artificiels. Romance Notes, 1973, 15:68-73.
1754. Rubin, Louis D., Jr. Thomas Wolfe. The Weather of His Youth. Baton Rouge: Louisiana State Univ. Press, 1955.
1755. _____. William Faulkner: the discovery of a man's vocation. In Wolfe, G. H. (ed), Fifty Years After the Marble Faun. Tuscaloosa: Univ. Alabama Press, 1976.
1756. Ruitenbeek, Hendrik M. (ed). Homosexuality and Creative Genius. NY: Astor-Honor, 1967.
1757. Rule, Jane V. Lesbian Images. Garden City, NY: Doubleday, 1975.
1758. Rusch, Frederic E. Dreiser's other tragedy. Modern Fiction Studies, 1977, 23:449-456.
1759. Russell, D., & McIntire, D. In paths untrodden: a study of Walt Whitman. One: The Homosexual Magazine, 1954, 2:4-15.
1760. Russell, Stanley C. Self-destroying love in Keats. Keats-Shelley J, 1967, 16:78-91.
1761. Russell, Walter Sanders, Jr. Stravinsky and Eliot: Personality, Poetics, and Cultural Politics. DAI, 1976, 37:2485A-86A.
1762. Rusu, L. Goethe. Cluj: Tipografia Vista, 1932.
1763. Ryan, Michael. Narcissus autobiographer: Marius the Epicurean. ELH, 1976, 43:184-208.
1764. _____. Self-de(con)struction. Diacritics, 1975, 6:34-41.
1765. Ryers, Catherene J. M. Hostility and aggression in American and German Autobiographers. DAI, 1971, 32:930A-31A.

1766. Sabourin, P. Lewis Carroll et Ses Fantasmes: Psychopathologie. Thèse, 1968, No. 298.
1767. Sachs, Hanns. Baudelaire, der Verfluchte. Almanach, 1922, 191-194.

1768. _____. Benvenuto Cellini. Int Zeitschrift für Psychoanalyse, 1913, 1:518.

1769. _____. Edgar Allan Poe. [Review.] Psychoanal Q, 1935,
4:294-306.

1770. _____. Theodor Reik's Arthur Schnitzler als Psycholog.
Imago, 1914, 3:302-304.

1771. _____. Spittelers Erdenfahrt. Imago, 1935, 21:92-96.

1772. _____. Swift. In Nunberg, H., & Federn, E. (eds),
Minutes of the Vienna Psychoanalytic Society, Vol. 4:
1912-1918. NY: IUP, 1975, 183-184.

1773. _____. What would have happened if.... Amer Imago,
1946, 3:61-66.

1774. Sachs, Lisbeth J., & Stern, Bernard H. Bernard Shaw and
his women. British J Medical Psychol, 1964, 37:343-
350.

1775. _____, & Stern, Bernard H. The little preoedipal boy in
Papa Hemingway and how he created his artistry. In
Costerus, Essays in English & Amer Language & Lit,
1972, 1:221-240.

1776. Sacristan, J. M. [Dostoevsky's epilepsy.] Siglo Médico,
1947, 115:547-548.

1777. _____. [Fedor Dostoevsky.] In Genialidad y Psicopatologia. Madrid: Biblioteca Nueva, 1960, 73-78.

1778. Sackville-West, Edward. The personality of Henry James.
In Inclinations. Port Washington, NY: Kennikat, 1967
(1949), 42-71.

1779. Sadger, Isador. August von Platen. Eine pathologische
studie. Nord und Sud, 1905.

1780. _____. From Hebbel's boyhood. In Nunberg, H., &
Federn, E. (eds), Minutes of the Vienna Psychoanalytic
Society, Vol. 4: 1912-1918. NY: IUP, 1975, 13-19.

1781. _____. Heinrich von Kleist. In Nunberg, H., & Federn,
E. (eds), Minutes of the Vienna Psychoanalytic Society,
Vol. 2: 1908-1910. NY: IUP, 1967, 220-226.

1782. _____. Heinrich von Kleist. Eine Pathographic-Psycho-
logische Studie. Wiesbaden: Bergmann, 1910.

1783. _____. Konrad Ferdinand Meyer. Eine pathographisch-
psychogische Studie. In Grenzfragen des Nerven- und
Seelenlebens, Heft 59. Wiesbaden: Bergmann, 1908.

1784. _____. Aus dem Liebesleben Nicolaus Lenaus. Leipzig:
Deuticke, 1909; Sammlungen zur angewandten Seelenkunde, 1925, 6.

1785. _____. Von der Pathographie zur Psychographie. Imago,
1912, 1:158-175.

1786. St. Armand, Barton Levi. Hawthorne's 'haunted mind': a
subterranean drama of the self. Criticism, 1971, 13:1-
25.

1787. Sakamoto, Masayuki. [Hawthorne: A Descent into the Blackness of Despair.] Tokyo: Tohjusha, 1977.

1788. Salcedo, E. Vida de don Miguel. Madrid: Salamanca, 1964.

1789. Salem, E. D. Autobiography of a lesbian. Humanist, 1965,
80(2):50-52.

1790. Salem, Gerard. [The book of Prince Korab: analysis of the writing of a paranoid.] Schweizer Archiv für Neurologie, Neurochirgie und Psychiatrie, 1978, 123:107-139.

1791. Salgado, M. A. [J. R. Jiménez.] Hispanōfila, 1970, 38:49-58.

1792. Salomon, Louis B. Hawthorne and his father: a conjecture. Lit & Psychol, 1963, 13:12-17.

1793. Salomon, M. I. Arthur Schnitzler--physician, novelist and playwright. New England J Medicine, 1971, 285:1061-1063.

1794. Sanborn, K. The Vanity and Insanity of Genius. NY: 1886.

1795. Sánchez-Rivera Peiro, J. M. La última metáfora de Yukio Mishima. Razón y Fe, 1971, 183:87-95.

1796. Sanders, Charles Richard. Carlyle's Friendships, and Other Studies. Durham, NC: Duke Univ. Press, 1977.

1797. _____. Lytton Strachey's conception of biography. PMLA, 1951, 66:295-315.

1798. Sanders-Clark, Robin. Sir Arthur Conan Doyle: a portrait. Psychic, 1972, 4(2):48-55.

1799. Sanford, C. Edgar Allan Poe: a blight upon the landscape. Amer Q, 1968, 20:54-66; Rives, 1962, No. 18.

1800. Santiago, Luciano P. R. The Children of Oedipus: Brother-Sister Incest in Psychiatry, Literature, History and Mythology. Roslyn Heights, NY: Libra, 1973.

1801. Sarker, Sarasi Lal. A conversion phenomenon in the life of dramatist Girish Chandra Ghose. Int J Psycho-Anal, 1930, 11:228-231.

1802. Sartre, Jean-Paul. The creator of Our Lady of the Flowers. Psychoanal Rev, 1963, 50:172-176.

1803. _____. Saint Genet: Actor and Martyr. NY: Braziller, 1964.

1804. Satto, Tokio. Kindheit und Charakter Bashios, der Dichter. Tokyo Zeitschrift für Psychoanalyse, 1937, 5.

1805. Saugstad, Per. J. S. Welhaven. En idealenes vokter. Copenhagen: Gyldendal, 1967.

1806. Savage, D. S. Christopher Isherwood: the novelist as homosexualist. Lit & Psychol, 1979, 29:71-88.

1807. _____. The mind of Virginia Woolf. South Atlantic Q, 1947, 46:556-573.

1808. _____. Swift. Western Rev, 1950, 15:25-36.

1809. Saxton, Martha. Louisa May: A Modern Biography of Louisa May Alcott. Boston: Houghton Mifflin, 1977.

1810. Sborowitz, Arie. Ludwig Binswanger's 'Henrik Ibsen und das Problem der Selbstrealisation in der Kunst.' [Review.] Psyche, 1950, 4:50-52.

1811. Scarlett, George. Adolescent thinking and the diary of Anne Frank. Psychoanal Rev, 1971, 58:265-278.

1812. Schachter, M. Certainties and doubts concerning the personality and disease of the poet Heinrich Heine (1797-1856). In Riese, H. (ed), Historical Explorations in Medicine and Psychiatry. NY: Springer, 1978, 99-108.

1813. _____. Etude psychopathographique d'Oscar Wilde (1854-1900). J Médicale Lyon, 1977, 58:613-621.

1814. Schadner, H.   Die Handschrift Adelbert Stifter.   Ein Weg-
      weiser zu seiner Persönlichkeit.   In Schriftenreihe des
      A. Stifter-Instituts des Landes Oberösterreich, Folge 19.
      Graz: 1963.
1815. Schaefer, P.   Das Schuldbewusstsein in den Confessiones des
      heligen Augustinus.   Würzberg: Becker, 1930.
1816. Schechner, Mark.   The song of the wandering Aengus: James
      Joyce and his mother.   James Joyce Q, 1972, 10:72-89;
      In Staley, T. F. (ed), Ulysses: Fifty Years.   Blooming-
      ton: Indiana Univ. Press, 1974, 72-89.
1817. Scherr, Arthur.   Albert Camus: revolt against the mother.
      Amer Imago, 1977, 24:170-178.
1818. Schifano, Jean-Noel.   Esquisse pour une psychobiographie
      d'Italo Svevo.   Italica, 1971, 48:425-445.
1819. Schiller, F.   Thomas de Quincey's lifelong addiction.   Per-
      spectives in Biology & Medicine, 1976, 20:131-141.
1820. Schlack, Beverly Ann.   Portrait of the artist as young wom-
      an: The Letters of Virginia Woolf.   Lit & Psychol, 1976,
      26:118-123.
1821. Schlaf, Johannes.   Walt Whitman Homosexueller?   Kritische
      Revision Einer Whitman-Abhandlung von Dr. Bertz.
      Minden: Brun, 1906.
1822. Schloss, Carol.   John Berryman on Stephen Crane: the nature
      of speculation in biography.   Lit & Psychol, 1979, 39:
      169-175.
1823. Schlumberger, Jean.   André Gide--Persönlichkeit und Werk.
      Antares, 1957, 5:16-24.
1824. Schmid, Hans R.   Hermann Hesse.   Zurich: Frauenfeld,
      1928.
1825. Schmidl, Fritz.   Problems and method in applied psychoanaly-
      sis.   Psychoanal Q, 1972, 41:402-419.
1826. Schmidt, G. [The death instinct of Heinrich von Kleist.]
      Munchener Medizinische Wochenschrift, 1970, 112:758-
      763.
1827. _____.   Die Krankheit zum Tode.   Stuttgart: Enke, 1968.
1828. Schmidt, Pierre.   Quelques aspects des états crépusculaires
      et épileptiques dans le vie et l'oeuvre de Dostoïewski.
      Encéphale (et Hygiène Mentale).   J de Psychiatrie, 1951,
      40:312-340.
1829. Schmitt, F.   Krankheit und Schaffen bei Friedrich Schiller.
      Allgemeine Zeitschrift für Psychiatrie, 1937, 105, Heft 1,
      1-34.
1830. Schneider, Duane.   Anaïs Nin in the Diary: the creation and
      development of a persona.   Mosaic, 1978, 11(2):9-19.
1831. Schneider, Elisabeth.   Coleridge, Opium, and Kubla Khan.
      Chicago: Univ. Chicago Press, 1953; Cambridge: Cam-
      bridge Univ. Press, 1954.
1832. Schneiderman, Leo.   Hemingway: a psychological study.
      Connecticut Rev, 1973, 6(2):34-49.
1833. Schneidman, Edwin S.   The deaths of Herman Melville.   In
      Schneidman, E. S. , Farberow, N. L. , & Litman, R. E.
      (eds), Deaths of Man.   NY: Quadrangle, 1973, 161-178;
      In The Psychology of Suicide.   NY: Science House, 1970,

587-613; In Vincent, H. P. (ed), Melville and Hawthorne in the Berkshires. Kent, Ohio: Kent State Univ. Press, 1968, 118-143.

1834. _____. Some psychological reflections on the death of Malcolm Melville. Suicide and Life-Threatening Behavior, 1976, 6:231-242; Extracts, 1976, 25:4.

1835. Schnitzler, Arthur. Jugend in Wien. Eine Autobiographie. Munich: Dtv-Taschenbuch, 1971.

1836. Scholtens, Marguerite. Antoine Menjot, docteur en médecine, ami de Pascal, réforme au temps des persécutions: Etudes historiques et psychologiques. Assen: Van Gorcum, 1968.

1837. Scholtens, Murjke. Etudes médico-psychologiques sur Pascal. Haarlem: Enschéde, 1958; Assen: Royal Van Gorcum, 1968; Paris: Librairie de Varenne, 1968.

1838. Schou, Lene. A propos L'Age d'homme: Note sur le rapport 'critique litteraire' et psychoanalyse. Prépub, 1976, 24: 25-44.

1839. Schramm, W. von. Die Bedeutung der Träume und Traumdichtungen im Werk und Leben Jean Pauls. Jean-Paul Blätter, 1927, 2:17-24.

1840. Schueller, Herbert M., & Peters, Robert L. (eds). The Letters of John Addington Symonds, 3 Vols. Detroit: Wayne State Univ. Press, 1967-8-9.

1841. Schuh, O. F. 'Die Kunst ist das Gewissen der Menschheit.' In Koopmann, L. (ed), Hebbel Jahrbuch 1964. Heide in Holstein: Westholsteinische Verlagsanstalt Boyens, 1964.

1842. Schulhof, H. Zur Psychologie Strindbergs. Int Zeitschrift für Individual-Psychologie, 1924, 2:20-25.

1843. Schultz, M. G. The 'strange case' of Robert Louis Stevenson. JAMA, 1971, 216:90-94.

1844. Schulz, G. (ed). Beiträge zu Werk und Persönlichkeit F. von Hardenbergs. Darmstadt: Wissenschaftliche Buchgesellschaft, 1971.

1845. Schulz, Max F. Coleridge agonistes. J English Germanic Philology, 1962, 61:268-277.

1846. Schur, Max. Marie Bonaparte (1882-1962). Psychoanal Q, 1963, 32:98-100.

1847. Schütte, E. Jean-Jacques Rousseau, seine Persönlichkeit und sein Stil. Leipzig: Xenien, 1910.

1848. Schwaber, Paul. On reading Poe. Lit & Psychol, 1971, 21: 81-99.

1849. Schwartz, Delmore. In dreams begin responsibilities. Partisan Rev, 1937, 4:5-11; In Altenbernd, L., & Lewis, L. L. (eds), Introduction to Literature: Stories. NY: Macmillan, 1969, 468-472.

1850. Schweishheimer, W. Die Krankheit Dostojewskis. Wissen und Leben, 1921, 15:176-182.

1851. Schweitzer, Albert. Goethe: his personality and his work. In Bergstrasser, A. (ed), Goethe and the Modern Age. Chicago: Regnery, 1950.

1852. Schwelling, O. P. Faust und Faustine. Eine psychographische Studie um Goethe's Eros. Cologne-Graz: Böhlau, 1964.

1853. Schwyn, W. La Musique comme catalyseur de l'émotion stendhalienne. Paris: Grand Cliêne, 1968.
1854. Scott-Stokes, Henry. The Life and Death of Yukio Mishima. NY: Farrar Straus & Giroux, 1974.
1855. Scrivano, R. Pietro Fortini. La Rassegna della Letteratura Italiana, 1964, 68(1).
1856. Sears, Robert R. Mark Twain's separation anxiety. Psychol Today, 1979, 13:100+.
1857. _____, & Lapidus, Deborah. Episodic analysis of novels. J Psychol, 1973, 85:267-276.
1858. _____, Lapidus, Deborah, and Cozzens, Christine. Content analysis of Mark Twain's novels and letters as a biographical method. Poetics, 78, 7:155-175.
1859. Seelye, Catherine (ed). Charles Olson and Ezra Pound: An Encounter at Saint Elizabeths. NY: Grossman/Viking, 1975.
1860. Segaloff, T. Die Krankheit Dostojewskys. Eine ärztlich- psychologische Studie mit einem Bildnis Dostojewskys. Munich: Reinhardt, 1907.
1861. Seillière, E. A. L'Egotisme pathologique chez Stendhal. Rev de deux Mondes, 1906, 3:334-361, 650-679.
1862. _____. Marcel Proust. Paris: Editions de la Nouvelle Revue Critique, 1931.
1863. Sell, F. Jean Pauls 'Dualismus. ' Bonn: Eisele, 1919.
1864. Sero, Os. Der Fall Wilde und das Problem der Homosexual- ität. Ein Prozess und ein Interview. Leipzig: Spohr, 1896.
1865. Serrahima, Maurici. Proust como asmático. Insula, 1954, año ix, No. 97.
1866. Serrano, Miguel. C. G. Jung and Hermann Hesse, A Record of Two Friendships. NY: Schocken, 1966; London: Routledge & Kegan Paul, 1966; Santiago, Chile: Zig-Zag, 1965.
1867. Severgnini, L. La polemica sul dramma di Casa Carducci. Osservatore Politico Letterario, 1967, 13:1-10.
1868. Sewell, Elizabeth. Poe for the sixth time. Parnassus, 1976, 5:9-19.
1869. Shafar, J. Sir James Kay-Shuttleworth and the Brontë inter- lude. J Royal College Physicians London, 1979, 13:224- 226.
1870. Shapiro, Karl J. The death of Randall Jarrell. In The Po- etry Wreck; Selected Essays: 1950-1970. NY: Random House, 1975, 268-299.
1871. Shapiro, Stephen A. The dark continent of literature. Com- parative Lit Studies, 1968, 5:421-454.
1872. Sharp, Robert L. Stevenson's and James's childhood. Nine- teenth Century Fiction, 1953, 8:236-237.
1873. Sharpe, Ella Freeman. Francis Thompson: a psychoanalytic study. British J Medical Psychol, 1925, 5:329-344.
1874. Sheaffer, Louis. O'Neill. Son and Artist. Boston: Little, Brown, 1973.
1875. _____. O'Neill. Son and Playwright. Boston: Little, Brown, 1968.

1876. Shengold, Leonard. An attempt at soul murder: Rudyard
Kipling's early life and work. In The Psychoanalytic
Study of the Child, Vol. 30. New Haven: Yale Univ.
Press, 1975, 683-724; In Coltrera, J. T. (ed), Lives,
Events, and Other Players: Studies in Psychobiography.
NY: Aronson, 1980.

1877. _____. Chekhov and Schreber: vicissitudes of a certain
kind of father-son relationship. Int J Psycho-Anal, 1961,
42:431-438.

1878. _____. Freud and Joseph. In Kanzer, M. (ed), The Unconscious Today: Essays in Memory of Max Schur. NY:
IUP, 1971, 473-494.

1879. _____. Freud's dreams revisited. Amer Imago, 1969,
26:242-250.

1880. _____. The metaphor of the journey in The Interpretation
of Dreams. Amer Imago, 1966, 23:316-331.

1881. Sherman, Murray H. Introduction: Theodor Reik's Of Lust
and Love: On the Psychoanalysis of Romantic and Sexual
Emotions. NY: Aronson, 1974.

1882. _____. Lytton Strachey: a study in English character and
eccentricity. Psychoanal Rev, 1969-70, 56:597-608.

1883. _____. Prefatory notes: Arthur Schnitzler and Karl
Kraus. Psychoanal Rev, 1978, 65:5-13.

1884. _____. Reik, Schnitzler, Freud, and The Murderer: The
limits of insight in psychoanalysis. Psychoanal Rev,
1978, 65:68-108; Modern Austrian Lit, 1977, 10:195-216.

1885. Shivers, Alfred S. Jack London: not a suicide. Dalhousie
Rev, 1970, 49:43-57.

1886. Shoemaker, W. ¿Cómo era Galdós? Anales Galdosianos,
1973(1974), 8.

1887. Shulman, Arthur D. Exploratory literary analysis of inter-
racial behaviors. J Social Psychol, 1974, 92:127-132.

1888. Shuman, Robert Baird. William Inge. NY: Twayne, 1966.

1889. Sigman, Joseph, & Slobodin, Richard. Stammering in the
Dodgson family; an unpublished letter by Lewis Carroll.
Victorian Newsletter, 1976, 49:26-27.

1890. Simenauer, Erich. Rainer Maria Rilke, Legende und Mythos.
Berne: Haupt, 1954.

1891. _____. Rilkes Bezichungen zum Fallen und zur Fallsucht.
Psychologie (Bern), 1955, 7:310-314, 373-378.

1892. Simenon, Georges. Letter to My Mother. NY: Harcourt
Brace Jovanovich, 1976.

1893. Simmons, Ernest J. Dostoievski: The Making of a Novelist.
London: Oxford Univ. Press, 1940.

1894. Simon, Louis. Charles Baudouin 1893-1963. Cahiers des
Amis de Han Ryner, 1963, n. s., no. 70, 3-5.

1895. Simone, Francesco, Felici, Fiorelli, Valerio, Paolo, & Mon-
tella, Patrizia. Suicide in the literary work of Cesare
Pavese. Suicide & Life-Threatening Behavior, 1977,
7:183-188.

1896. Simonsen, Peter. Om Hedda Gabler, Lille Eyolf og Lord
Byron. Edda, 1962, 62:176-184.

1897. Simpson, Allen. Knut Hamsun's anti-semitism. Edda, 1977,
273-293.

1898. Sinán, Rogelio. Psychobiografia de Dostoiewski. Archivos Panameños de Psicologia, 1965, 1(2):170-175.
1899. Singer, D. Ludwig Lewisohn and Freud: the Zionist therapeutic. Psychoanal Rev, 1971, 58:169-182.
1900. Siyavisgil, Sabri Esat. Le Problème psychologique de la personalité litteraire. In Baumgarten, F. (ed), La Psychotechnique dans le monde moderne. Paris: Presses Universitaires de France, 1952, 111-117.
1901. Skerrett, Joseph Taylor, Jr. Take My Burden Up: Three Studies in Psychobiographical Criticism and Afro-American Fiction. DAI, 1975, 36:3719A.
1902. Skinner, B. F. Has Gertrude Stein a secret? Atlantic Monthly, 1934, 153:50.
1903. _____. Particulars of My Life. NY: Knopf, 1976.
1904. Skinner, John. James M. Barrie or the boy who wouldn't grow up. Amer Imago, 1957, 14:111-141.
1905. _____. Lewis Carroll's adventures in wonderland. Amer Imago, 1947, 4:3-31; In The Yearbook of Psychoanalysis, Vol. 4. NY: IUP, 1948, 330-354.
1906. Sklar, Dusty. Hawthorne and the supernatural. Psychic, 1973, 4(3):39-42.
1907. Slater, J. F. Self-concealment and self-revelation in Shelley's 'Epipsychidion.' Papers in Language & Lit, 1975, 11: 279-292.
1908. Slochower, Harry. Eissler's Goethe: a preliminary comment. Amer Imago, 1965, 22:275-280.
1909. _____. Freud's Gradiva: mater nuda rediviva. A wish-fulfillment of the 'memory' on the Acropolis. Psychoanal Q, 1971, 40:646-662.
1910. Smeed, John W. Jean Paul's dreams. In Norman, F. (ed), Essays in German Literature, I. London: Institute for Germanic Studies, 1965.
1911. Smidt, Kristian. Psykologiska problemer i Swifts liv og diktning. Edda, 1952, 52:329-344.
1912. Smith, Anne. A new Adam and a new Eve--Lawrence and women: a biographical overview. In Lawrence and Women. NY: Barnes & Noble, 1978, 9-48.
1913. Smith, Bradford. Mark Twain and the mystery of identity. College English, 1963, 24:425-430.
1914. Smith, David. William Byrd surveys America. Early Amer Lit, 1976, 11:296-310.
1915. Smith, I. H. Gide's narcissism. J Australian Univs Language & Lit Assn, 1955, 3:12-13.
1916. Smith, Michael A. The Personality of the Essayist: Virginia Woolf and Thomas Mann. DAI, 1974, 35:3772A.
1917. Smith, Samuel S., & Isotoff, A. The abnormal from within: Dostoevsky. Psychoanal Rev, 1935, 22:361-391; Univ. Oregon Publications Studies in Psychol, Vol. 1, 1935.
1918. Smuts, Jan Christian. Walt Whitman: A Study in the Evolution of Personality. Detroit: Wayne Univ. Press, 1973 (1894-95).
1919. Snyder, William U. Thomas Wolfe: Ulysses and Narcissus. Athens: Ohio Univ. Press, 1971; Review: Stanley Wertheim, Lit & Psychol, 1973, 23:82-85.

1920. Soleh, A. [The social-psychological basis in Doestoevsky's writings.] Ofakim, 1956, 10:295-300.
1921. Solomon, Eric. The crucible of childhood; excerpt from 'Stephen Crane.' In Bassan, M. (ed), Stephen Crane; A Collection of Critical Essays. Englewood-Cliffs, NJ: Prentice-Hall, 1967, 165-176.
1922. Solomon, Maynard. Freud's father on the Acropolis. Amer Imago, 1973, 30:142-156.
1923. Sorrell, Walter. Three Women: Lives of Sex and Genius. Indianapolis: Bobbs-Merrill, 1975.
1924. Sorsby, Arnold (ed). Tenements of Clay. An Anthology of Medical Biographical Essays. London: Friedmann, 1974.
1925. Soulier, Jean-Pierre. Lautréamont, génie ou maladie mentale? Nouveau bilan psychopathologique. Paris: Minard, 1978; Geneva: Dros, 1964.
1926. Soupault, Robert. Considérations, surtout médicales, à propos de la vie et des écrits de Proust. Europe, 1971, 508-09:200-210.
1927. _____. Marcel Proust du coté de la médecine. Paris: Plon, 1967.
1928. _____. Marcel Proust et les médecins. Lyon Médicale, 1971, 225:1109-1116.
1929. _____. Stendhal intime, suivi d'une étude graphologique par Mme J. Monnot. Paris: Sept Couleurs, 1975.
1930. Southall, Raymond. The personality of Sir Thomas Wyatt. Essays in Criticism, 1964, 14:43-64.
1931. Spacks, Patricia Ann Meyer. Imagining a Self: Autobiography and Novel in Eighteenth-Century England. Cambridge: Harvard Univ. Press, 1976; Review: K. Stewart, English Language Notes, 1979, 16:336-339.
1932. Spater, George, & Parsons, Ian. A Marriage of True Minds: An Intimate Portrait of Leonard and Virginia Woolf. NY: Harcourt Brace Jovanovich, 1977; Reviews: D. Doner, Modern Fiction Studies, 1978-79, 24:575-578; Sewanee Rev, 1979, 87:325-332.
1933. Spencer, Sharon. Collage of Dreams: The Writings of Anaïs Nin. Chicago: Swallow, 1977.
1934. _____. A novel triangle: Anaïs Nin--Henry Miller--Otto Rank. Par Rapport, 1978, 1:139-144.
1935. Spender, Natasha. Chandler's own long goodbye: a memoir. Partisan Rev, 1978, 45:38-65; New Rev (London), 1976, 3(27):15-28.
1936. Spender, Stephen (ed). D. H. Lawrence: Novelist, Poet, Playwright. NY: Harper & Row, 1973.
1937. _____. How much should a biographer tell? Saturday Rev, 1964, 47:16-19.
1938. Sperber, Alice. Von Dantes unbewussten Seelenleben. Imago, 1914, 3:205-249.
1939. Sperber, M. Knut Hamsun. Int Zeitschrift für Individual-Psychologie, 1929, 7:447-449.
1940. Spilka, Mark. Henry James and Walter Besant: 'The Art of Fiction' controversy. Novel: A Forum on Fiction, 1973, 6:100-119.

1941. Spire, Andrew. [Proust and his Jewish identity.] Keshet, 1975, 66:165-171.
1942. Spitzer, Michael. Hawthorne's Women: Female Influences on the Life and Fiction of Nathaniel Hawthorne. DAI, 1975, 35:4561A.
1943. Sprinchorn, Evert. Strindberg and the wit to go mad. Scandinavian Studies, 1976, 48:247-255.
1944. _____. Zola of the occult: Strindberg's experimental method. Modern Drama, 1974, 17:251-266.
1945. Sprinker, John Michael. Fictions of the self: the end of autobiography. In Olney, J. (ed), Autobiography: Essays Theoretical and Critical. Princeton: Princeton Univ. Press, 1980, 321-342.
1946. Squires, Paul C. The case of Dickens as viewed by biology and psychology. A nearer approach to the explanation of the rift between the novelist and his wife. J Abnormal Social Psychol, 1936, 30:468-473.
1947. _____. The clairpsychism of Strindberg. Psychoanal Rev, 1942, 29:50-70.
1948. _____. Fyodor Dostoevsky; a psychopathological sketch. Psychoanal Rev, 1937, 24:365-388.
1949. _____. Jean Paul Friedrich Richter: a psychoanalytic portraiture. Psychoanal Rev, 1939, 26:191-218.
1950. Srabian de Fabry, A. Amours et mathématiques: Rousseau et les femmes. Rice Univ. Studies, 1973, 59(3):27-36.
1951. Stallman, R. W. Stephen Crane: A Biography. NY: Braziller, 1968.
1952. Stanford, Derek. Coleridge: the psychological sage. Month, 1962, 214:276-280.
1953. Stanley, H. M. The Browning-Barrett love letters and the psychology of love. Open Court, 1899, 13:731-741.
1954. Starkie, E. Baudelaire. NY: Putnam, 1933; London: Faber, 1957; NY: New Directions, 1958.
1955. Starobinski, Jean. Rousseau's Anklage der Gesellschaft. Universitätsverlag Konstanz, 1977.
1956. _____. The style of autobiography. In Chatman, S. (ed), Literary Style. NY: Oxford Univ. Press, 1971, 285-296.
1957. Stasz, Clarice. The social construction of biography: the case of Jack London. Modern Fiction Studies, 1976, 22: 595-599.
1958. Stäuble, Michele, & Wulf, Lippman. De Quincey, Baudelaire e i Paradisi artificiali. Nuova Antologia, 1972, 514:245-254.
1959. Stavola, Thomas John. Crisis in American Identity: An Application of Erik Erikson's Psychoanalytic Theories to the Life and Fiction of F. Scott Fitzgerald. DAI, 1977, 38 (4-A), 2130.
1960. _____. Scott Fitzgerald: Crisis in an American Identity. NY: Barnes & Noble, 1979.
1961. Steegmuller, Francis (ed). Flaubert on syphilis. In The Letters of Gustave Flaubert, 1830-1857. Cambridge: Harvard Univ. Press, 1979.
1962. Steel, David. Gide et Freud. Rev d'Histoire Littéraire de la France, 1977, 77:48-74.

1963. Steele, Richard. Thomas Wolfe: An Applied Psychoanalytic Investigation. DAI, 1974, 34:4059A.

1964. Stein, M. H. A psychoanalytic view of mental health. Samuel Pepys and his diary. Psychoanal Q, 1977, 46:82-115.

1965. Stekel, Wilhelm. Aus Gerhart Hauptmanns Diarum. Int Zeitschrift für Psychoanal, 1912, 2:365-366.

1966. _____. Goethe äussert sich über die Macht infantiler Eindrücke. Int Zeitschrift für Psychoanalyse, 1912, 2:106.

1967. _____. Poetry and neurosis. In Nunberg, H., & Federn, E. (eds), Minutes of the Vienna Psychoanalytic Society, Vol. 2:1908-1910. NY: IUP, 1967, 101-105.

1968. _____. Ein Traumbild des Benvenuto Cellini. Int Zeitschrift für Psychoanalyse, 1914, 4:322-323.

1969. _____. Zur Psychologie der Inzest-liebe. Auf Baudelaires Briefen, 1841-1866. Int Zeitschrift für Psychoanalyse, 1910, 1:72.

1970. Stephanos, S., et al. [Elaboration of the psychosomatic phenomenon: observations on the biography of Blaise Pascal.] Confinia Psychiatrica, 1977, 20(2-3):168-179.

1971. Stephen, Leslie. On psychology in biography. National Rev, 1893, 22:181.

1972. Sterba, Richard F. The psychoanalyst in a world of change. Psychoanal Q, 1969, 38:432-454.

1973. Sterlin, H. Liberation and self-destruction in the creative process. In Psychiatry and the Humanities, Vol. 1. New Haven: Yale Univ. Press, 1976.

1974. Stern, Madeline B. Mark Twain had his head examined. Amer Lit, 1969, 41:207-218.

1975. _____. Poe: 'the mental temperament' for phrenologists. Amer Lit, 1968, 40:155-163.

1976. _____. Walt Whitman, care of Fowler and Wells. In Heads and Headlines: The Phrenological Fowlers. Norman: Univ. Oklahoma Press, 1971, 99-123.

1977. Stewart, H. L. Tolstoy as a problem in psychoanalysis. Proceedings & Transactions Royal Society of Canada, 1923, 17:29-39.

1978. Stierlin, Helm. Hölderlins dichterische Schaffen im Lichte seiner schizophrenen Psychose. Psyche, 1972, 26:530-548.

1979. _____. Lyrical creativity and schizophrenic psychosis as reflected in Friedrich Hölderlin's fate. In George, E. E. (ed), Friedrich Hölderlin: An Early Modern. Ann Arbor: Univ. Michigan Press, 1972, 192-215.

1980. Stillinger, J. (ed). The Early Draft of John Stuart Mill's Autobiography. Urbana: Univ. Illinois Press, 1961.

1981. Stillman, Claudia Ruth. Swift in Wonderland: the language of dream in the Journal to Stella. Lit & Psychol, 1975, 25:108-116.

1982. Stimpson, Catharine R. Mind, body, and Gertrude Stein. Critical Inquiry, 1977, 3:489-506.

1983. Stock, Jerold Howard. Suggestions of Death-Anxiety in the Life of William Faulkner. DAI, 1977, 38:2130-31A.

1984. Stocker, A. L'Amour Interdit: Trois Anges sur la Route de Sodome. Genève: Collection Action et Pensee, n. d.

1985. _____. Benjamin Constant ou la Névrose Compensée. Geneva, 1940.

1986. _____. Le Pain de Paul Claudel. Psychologie de l'Homme Ecartelé. Geneva, 1941.

1987. Stoddard, R. H. Edgar Allan Poe. National Magazine, 1853, 2: 200-204.

1988. Stoltzfus, Ben F. The neurotic love of Frédéric Moreau. French Rev, 1958, 31: 509-511.

1989. Stone, Albert E. Autobiography and American culture. Amer Studies, 1972, 11(2): 22-36.

1990. Stone, M. H. Middle-class childhood between 1500 and 1800: examples of the lives of artists, musicians and writers. J Amer Academy Psychoanal, 1976, 4: 545-574.

1991. Storch, Alfred. August Strindberg im Lichte seiner Selbstbiographie. Eine psychopathologische Persönlichkeitanalyse. Wiesbaden: Bergmann, 1921.

1992. Storfer, Adolf J. Thomas Mann 'entlarvt.' Psychoanalytische Bewegung, 1929, 1: 174-175.

1993. Storm, Ole. Mark Twain og Mr Samuel L. Clemens. Copenhagen: Lademann, 1978.

1994. Stovall, F. Walt Whitman: the man and the myth. South Atlantic Q, 1955, 54: 538-551.

1995. Strandberg, Victor. Festering lilies: on surveying the secret life of William Shakespeare. Four Quarters, 1975, 24(2): 3-15.

1996. Strauch, Carl F. Hatred's swift repulsion: Emerson, Margaret Fuller, and others. Studies in Romanticism, 1968, 7: 65-103.

1997. Straus, B. Illness, creativity and Marcel Proust. Mt Sinai J Medicine, 1979, 46: 175-180.

1998. Strickland, Charles. A transcendental father: the childrearing practices of Bronson Alcott. Perspectives in Amer History, 1969, 3: 5-73.

1999. Strouse, Jean. A Biography of Alice James. Boston: Houghton Mifflin, 1980; Rev: J. Rossner, Saturday Rev, 1980, 7 (15): 64-65.

2000. Strunsky, Simeon. The scandal of Euclid: a Freudian analysis. Atlantic Monthly, 1919, 124: 332-337.

2001. Stümcke, Heinrich. Strindberg und die Frauen. Zeitschrift für Sexualwissenschaft, 1919, 5: 367-375.

2002. Styron, William. The shade of Thomas Wolfe. Harper's, 1968, 236(4): 96-104.

2003. Sullivan, J. P. 'Castas odisse puellas': a reconsideration of Propertius I.1. Wiener Studien, 1961, 74: 96-110.

2004. Sulzberger, Carl F. Two new documents on Freud. Psychoanalysis, 1955-56, 4(2): 9-21.

2005. Supprian, U. Schizophrenie und Sprache bei Hölderlin. Eine psycholinguistische Untersuchung zum Problem der präschizophrenen Psychopathie. Fortschrift der Neurologie und Psychiatrie, 1974, 42: 615-634.

2006. Susmann-Galant, J. Leo Tolstoi und seine Beziehungen zur Psychiatrie. Psychiatrisch-neurologische Wochenschrift, 1929, 31: 31-34.

2007. Sutherland, John. Blake: a crisis of love and jealousy.
       PMLA, 1972, 87:424-431.
2008. Sutton, William A. Exit to Elsinore. Ball State Monograph
       No. 7; In Sherwood Anderson's Formative Years (1876-
       1913). Doctoral dissertation, Ohio State Univ., 1943.
2009. _____. Sherwood Anderson's second wife. Ball State
       Univ. Forum, 1966, 7:39-46.
2010. Sveino, Per. Orestes A. Brownson's Road to Catholicism.
       Oslo: Universitetsforlaget, 1970; Atlantic Highlands, NJ:
       Humanities Press, 1971.
2011. Swift, T. G. Swift's personality and death-masks. Rev Eng-
       lish Lit, 1962, 3:39-68.
2012. Swisher, Walter S. A psychoanalysis of Browning's 'Pauline. '
       Psychoanal Rev, 1920, 7:115-133.
2013. Symons, Arthur. Confessions, a Study in Pathology. NY:
       Fountain, 1930.
2014. Szasz, Thomas. Karl Kraus and the Soul-Doctors: A Pioneer
       Critic and His Criticism of Psychiatry and Psychoanalysis.
       Baton Rouge: Louisiana State Univ. Press, 1976.

2015. Talbert, E. L. On the enigmatic personality of Amiel. J
       Abnormal Social Psychol, 1939, 34:129-132.
2016. Talbot, Serge. L'Homosexualité latent d'Edgar Poe. Ar-
       cadie, 1971, 213:374-381.
2017. Tavernier-Courbin, Jacqueline. Striving for power: Hem-
       ingway's neurosis. J General Education, 1978, 30:137-
       153.
2018. Taylor, Donald S. Chatterton: insults and gifts to the Rev.
       Mr. Catcott. Lit & Psychol, 1972, 22:35-44.
2019. _____. Chatterton's suicide. Philological Q, 1952, 31:63-
       69.
2020. Taylor, James Bentley. The case of William Blake: crea-
       tion, regression and pathology. Psychoanal Rev, 1963,
       50:489-504.
2021. Taylor, William S., & Culler, E. The problem of The Loco-
       motive-God. J Abnormal Social Psychol, 1929, 24:342-
       399.
2022. T., E. [Jessie Chambers]. D. H. Lawrence: A Personal
       Record. London, 1935.
2023. Teensma, B. N. [Pessoa.] Aufsätze zur portugiesichen Kul-
       turgeschichte, Görres-Gesellschaft, 1969 (1972), 9:65-96.
2024. Tellenbach, I., et al. Epileptiker-Gestalten Dostojewskijs.
       Jahrbuch für Psychologie, Psychotherapie und medizinische
       Anthrolpologie, 1966, 14:1-68.
2025. Teller, F. Die Wechselbeziehungen von psychischen Konflict
       und körperlichem Leiden bei Schiller. Imago, 1921, 7:95-
       126.
2026. Theilhaber, F. A. Goethe, Sexus und Eros. Grunewald:
       Horen, 1929.
2027. Therrien, Madeleine B. Rousseau: lucidité et sincérité.
       Studies on Voltaire & the 18th Century, 1976, 155:2071-
       2082.

2028. Thimme, W. Augustin's Selbstbildnis in den Konfessionen. Eine religion-psychologische Studie. Guetersloh: Bertelsmann, 1929.

2029. Thomae, Hans. Biographie und psychologie. Sammlung, 1951, 6:443-455.

2030. Thompson, Frederick Stephen. Order Out of Chaos: Purpose and Design in Autobiography. DAI, 1975, 36:3665A-66A.

2031. Thrift, Inez E. Religion and madness. The case of William Cowper. Psychoanal Rev, 1926, 13:312-317.

2032. Thurin, Erik Ingvar. The Universal Autobiography of Ralph Waldo Emerson. Lund: Gleerup, 1974.

2033. Tiefenbrun, R. Moment of Torment. Carbondale: Southern Illinois Univ. Press, 1973.

2034. Tison-Braun, Micheline. La Crise de l'humanisme: le conflit de l'individu et de la société dans la littérature française moderne, II: 1914-1939. Paris: Nizet, 1967.

2035. Tissi, Silvio. Au Microscope Psychoanalytique: Pirandello, Shakespeare, Tolstoi, Shaw, Bourget, Gide. Milan: Ulrico Hoepli, 1932.

2036. Todd, J. Drug addiction and artistic genius. Practitioner, 1968, 201:513-523.

2037. Todd, John, & Dewhurst, K. The periodic depression of Charlotte Brontë. Perspectives in Biology & Medicine, 1968, 11:208-216.

2038. Towne, Jackson E. Carlyle and Oedipus. Psychoanal Rev, 1935, 22:297-305.

2039. Trämer, M. Geistige Reigung-probleme. III: Die Entwicklung Hans Christian Andersens, 1805-1875. Zeitschrift für Kinderpsychiatrie, 1956, 23:33-47.

2040. Trent, J.C. Walt Whitman--a case history. A diagnostic study of Whitman's thirty years of ill health and the causes of his death. Surgery, Gynecology, Obstetrics, 1948, 87:113-121.

2041. Trilling, Lionel. W.H. Auden: in memory of Sigmund Freud (d. Sept. 1939). In Prefaces to the Experience of Literature. NY: Harcourt Brace Jovanovich, 1979, 291-297.

2042. Trimble, John R. The Psychological Landscape of Pope's Life and Art. DAI, 1972, 32:3968A.

2043. Trinquet, Roger. Le Ménage de Montaigne. Bulletin de la Société des Amis de Montaigne, 1973, 7-8:7-26.

2044. Tripathi, S.N. Neurosis and creativity: A study of two Indian writers. Samiksa, 1976, 30(3-4):86-92.

2045. Trosman, Harry. After The Waste Land: psychological factors in the religious conversion of T.S. Eliot. Int Rev Psycho-Anal, 1977, 4:295-304.

2046. _____. Freud's cultural background. In The Annual of Psychoanalysis, Vol. 1. NY: Quadrangle, 1973, 318-335.

2047. _____. T.S. Eliot and The Waste Land. Psychopathological antecedents and transformations. Archives General Psychiat, 1974, 30:709-717.

2048. Trousson, R. Jean-Jacques et les biographes. In Mortier, R., & Hasquin, H. (eds). Etudes sur le dix-huitième siècle. Brussels: Univ. de Bruxelles, 1974, 49-58.

2049. Troy, William. Stendhal. In quest of Henri Beyle. Partisan Rev, 1942, 9:3-10.
2050. Trueblood, A. S. The histrionic element in Lope's life and work. Hispanic Rev, 1964, 32(4).
2051. Turnbull, Andrew. Scott Fitzgerald. NY: Scribner, 1962.
2052. Tyler, Parker. Dostoievsky's personal Devil. In Every Artist His Own Scandal: A Study of Real and Fictive Heroes. NY: Horizon, 1964, 53-69.
2053. Tytell, John. Naked Angels: The Lives and Literature of the Beat Generation. NY: McGraw-Hill, 1976.

2054. Ubben, John H. Heredity and alcoholism in the life and works of Theodor Storm. German Q, 1955, 28:231-236.
2055. Uchinuma, Y. [A pathographic study of Yukio Mishima, a Japanese novelist.] Psychiatria et Neurologia Japonica, 1972, 74:413-429.
2056. Uijterwaal, J. Julien Green: personnalité et création littér- aire. Assen: Van Gorcum, 1968; Paris: Vareune, 1968.
2057. Ullmann, Stephen. Style and personality. Rev English Lit, 1965, 6:21-31.
2058. Umbral, F. Larra. Anatomia de un dandy. Madrid: Alfa- guara, 1965.
2059. _____. Lorca, poeta maldito. Madrid: Biblioteca Nueva, 1968.
2060. Unali, Lina. Proiezione dell'io e concetto di virtù nella let- teratura americana del '700: Benjamin Franklin e John Woolman. Trimestre, 1976, 9:17-43.
2061. Unterecker, John. Voyager: A Life of Hart Crane. NY: Farrar, Straus & Giroux, 1969.
2062. Updike, John. Bruno Schulz, hidden genius. New York Times Book Review, 9 Sept. 1979, 1, 36-39.
2063. Uppvall, Axel Johan. August Strindberg. A Psychoanalytic Study with Special Reference to the Oedipus Complex. Doctoral dissertation, Clark Univ., 1920; Boston, Badger, 1920; NY: Haskell, 1970.
2064. Urban, Bernd. Schnitzler and Freud as doubles: poetic in- tuition and early research on hysteria. In Sherman, M. H. (ed), Psychoanalysis and Old Vienna. NY: Human Sciences Press, 1978; Psychoanal Rev, 1978, 65:131-165.
2065. _____. Vier unveröffentlichte Briefe Arthur Schnitzler an den Psychoanalytiker Theodor Reik. Modern Austrian Lit, 1975, 8:236-247.

2066. Valbuena Prat, A. El artista del detalle y la melancolía. Letras de Deusto, 1973, 6.
2067. Vallery-Radot, Pierre. [Epilepsy and genius: twenty years of the life of Dostoevsky (1837-1857).] Presse Médicale, 1956, 64:2065-2066.
2068. _____. La Maladie de Maupassant. Le Fureteur Médical, 1964, 3-7.

2069. Van Alphen, Albert W. A Study of the Effects of Inferiority Feelings on the Life and Works of Kafka. DAI, 1970, 30:3028A.

2070. Van der Tuin, Henri. L'Evolution psychologique esthétique et littéraire de Théophile Gautier: étude de caractérologie littéraire. Paris: Nizet, 1933.

2071. Van Doren, Carl. The lion and the uniform. In The Roving Critic. NY: Knopf, 1923, 49-56.

2072. Varenne, Georges. Les Trois 'visions' de Benvenuto Cellini. Archiv Internationales de Neurologie, 1913, Jan.

2073. Various. Self-confrontation and social vision. [Special issue.] New Lit History, 1977, 9:1.

2074. Vennberg, Karl. I marginalin till en avhandling. Bonniers Litterära Magasin, 1967, 36:6.

2075. Verbeek, Ernst. Arthur Rimbaud, een Pathografie. Amsterdam: Swets en Zeitlinger, 1957.

2076. _____. Le Cercueil prématuré d'Arthur Rimbaud. Acta Psychiatrica Belgique, 1971, 71:513-531.

2077. _____. The Measure and the Choice; A Pathographic Essay on Samuel Johnson. Ghent: Story Scientia, 1971.

2078. Veylon, R. Oscar Fingal O'Flahertie Wills Wilde (1854-1900). A propos d'un essai de pathobiographie du célèbre Dady. Presse Médicale, 1969, 77:1361-1364.

2079. Vinberg, O. August Strindberg och Hans Kvinnohat. Stockholm: Chelius, 1929.

2080. Vivas, Eliseo. The two Lawrences. Bucknell Rev, 1958, 7(3):113-132; In D.H. Lawrence: The Failure and the Triumph of Art. Evanston: Northwestern Univ. Press, Ch. 1; In Garvin, H.R. (ed), Makers of the Twentieth-Century Novel. Lewisburg: Bucknell Univ. Press, 1977, 103-117.

2081. Vogel, Paul. Von der Selbstwahrnehmung der Epilepsie der Fall Dostojewski. Jahrbuch für Psychologie, Psychotherapie, und medizinische Anthropologie, 1966, 14:30-37.

2082. Voizard, F. Sainte-Beuve, l'homme et l'oeuvre. Etude médico-psychologique. Lyon: 1912.

2083. Volckmann-Delabesse, Thelma. [On Proust's asthma.] Bulletin de la Societé des Amis de Proust, 1967, 17.

2084. Von Abele, Rudolph Radama. Death of the Artist; A Study of Hawthorne's Disintegration. The Hague: Nijhoff, 1955.

2085. Vonalt, Larry P. Marianne Moore's medicines. Sewanee Rev, 1970, 78:669-678.

2086. Vorberg, Gaston. Der Fall Jean-Jacques Rousseau. Zeitschrift für Sexualwissenschaft, 1923, 10:37-40.

2087. Vorwahl, H. Zu Goethes Liebesleben. Zeitschrift für Sexualwissenschaft, 1932, 18:503-507.

2088. Vranich, Stanko B. Sigmund Freud and the 'Case History of Berganza': Freud's psychoanalytic beginnings. Psychoanal Rev, 1976, 63:73-82.

2089. Wagatsuma, Hiroshi, & DeVos, George. A Kōan of sincerity. Osamu Dazai (1909-1947). Hartford Studies in Lit, 1978, 10:156-181.

2090. Wagenaar, D. , & Iwamoto, J. Yukio Mishima: the dialectics of mind and body. Contemporary Lit, 1975, 16:41-60.
2091. Wagenknecht, Edward Charles. Gamaliel Bradford, psychographer. In Langford, R. E. , & Taylor, W. E. (eds), The Twenties; Poetry and Prose; 20 Critical Essays. De Land, Fla: Everett Edwards, 1966, 53-58.
2092. _____. James Russell Lowell: Portrait of a Many-Sided Man. NY: Oxford Univ. Press, 1971.
2093. _____. John Greenleaf Whittier, A Portrait in Paradox. NY: Oxford Univ. Press, 1967.
2094. _____. The Personality of Chaucer. Norman: Univ. Oklahoma Press, 1968.
2095. _____. The Personality of Milton. Norman: Univ. Oklahoma Press, 1970.
2096. _____. The Personality of Shakespeare. Norman: Univ. Oklahoma Press, 1972.
2097. _____. Ralph Waldo Emerson: Portrait of a Balanced Soul. NY: Oxford Univ. Press, 1974.
2098. _____. William Dean Howells: The Friendly Eye. NY: Oxford Univ. Press, 1969.
2099. Wagner, Lydia E. Coleridge's use of laudanum and opium, as connected with his interest in contemporary investigations concerning stimulation and sensation. Psychoanal Rev, 1938, 25:309-334.
2100. Wahl, Jean. La Bipolarité de Rousseau. Annales Jean-Jacques Rousseau, 1953-1955.
2101. Waldron, Philip. T. S. Eliot, Mr. Whiteside and 'the psychobiographical approach. ' Southern Rev: Australian J Lit Studies, 1973, 6:138-147.
2102. Wand, Martin, & Sewall, Richard B. 'Eyes be blind, heart be still': a new perspective on Emily Dickinson's eye problem. New England Q, 1979, 52:400-406.
2103. Wang Gunguri (ed). Self and Biography: Essays on the Individual and Society in Asia. Sidney: Sidney Univ. Press, 1975.
2104. Wangh, Martin. The scope of the contribution of psychoanalysis to the biography of the artist. JAPA, 1957, 5:564-575.
2105. Ward, Aileen. John Keats: The Making of a Poet. NY: Viking, 1963.
2106. Ward, Theodora. The Capsule of the Mind. Cambridge: Harvard Univ. Press, 1961.
2107. _____. The finest secret: emotional currents in the life of Emily Dickinson after 1865. Harvard Library Bulletin, 1960, 14:82-106.
2108. Walther, Luann. The invention of childhood in Victorian autobiography. In Landow, G. P. (ed), Approaches to Victorian Autobiography. Athens: Ohio Univ. Press, 1979, 64-83.
2109. Wasserstrom, William. The goad of guilt: Henry Adams, Scott and Zelda. J Modern Lit, 1977, 6:289-310.
2110. Watkins, Walter B. C. Perilous Balance. The Tragic Genius of Swift, Johnson and Sterne. Princeton: Princeton Univ. Press, 1959.

2111. Watson, George I. A. E. Housman: A Divided Life. London: Hart-Davis, 1957; Boston: Beacon, 1958.
2112. Watson, Sarah Ruth. Robert Louis Stevenson and his family of engineers. English Lit in Transition: 1880-1920, 1967, 10:181-193.
2113. Waugaman, Richard. The intellectual relationship between Nietzsche and Freud. Psychiatry, 1973, 36:458-467.
2114. Waugh, Dorothy. Emily Dickinson's Beloved: A Surmise. NY: Vantage, 1976.
2115. Webb, Donald A. The Life and Works of Dostoevsky: A Theological and Depth-Psychological Study. DA, 1966, 66-14, 1756.
2116. Webster, Brenda S. Yeats: A Psychoanalytic Study. Stanford, CA: Stanford Univ. Press, 1973.
2117. Wegelin, Christof. Jamesian biography. [Review article.] Nineteenth-Century Fiction, 1963, 18:283-287.
2118. Wegrocki, H. J. Masochistic motives in the literary and graphic art of Bruno Schultz. Psychoanal Rev, 1946, 33:154-164.
2119. Weichbrodt, R. Der Dichter Lenz. Eine Pathographie. Archiv für Psychiatrie und Nervenkrankheiten, 1920, 62:153-187.
2120. Weiersheuser, William J. The Mother in the Life and Works of Hebbel. DA, 1955, 15:2220.
2121. Weightman, John. Gide and sexual liberation. In The Concept of the Avant-Garde. La Salle, Ill: Library Press, 1973, 98-112.
2122. Weinapple, Martin. Torquato Tasso: a psychodynamic case study. Research Communications in Psychol, Psychiat & Behavior, 1978, 3:177-211.
2123. Weiss, Karl. Strindberg über Fehlleistungen. Int Zeitschrift für Psychoanalyse, 1913, 1:268-269.
2124. Weissman, Philip. The childhood and legacy of Stanislavski. In The Psychoanalytic Study of the Child, Vol. 12. NY: IUP, 1957, 399-417.
2125. _____. Conscious and unconscious autobiographical dramas of Eugene O'Neill. JAPA, 1957, 5:432-460.
2126. _____. Shaw's Childhood and Pygmalion. In The Psychoanalytic Study of the Child, Vol. 13. NY: IUP, 1958, 541-561.
2127. Wellek, Albert. Goethe und die Psychologie. Schweizerischen Zeitschrift für Psychologie, 1950, 9:1-24.
2128. Wells, Anna M. Was Emily Dickinson psychotic? Amer Imago, 1962, 19:309-321.
2129. Wells, F. L. Hölderlin: greatest of schizophrenics. J Abnormal Social Psychol, 1946, 41:199-206; In Ruitenbeek, H. M. (ed), The Literary Imagination. Chicago: Quadrangle, 1965, 233-246.
2130. Wells, Henry W. Poet and Psychiatrist: Merrill Moore, M. D. NY: Twayne, 1955.
2131. Wells, Walter A. A Doctor's Life of Keats. NY: Vantage, 1959.
2132. Wendlinger, Robert M. Psychoanalysis in the creation of biography. [Review.] Hudson Rev, 1950, 3:303-312.

2133. Wenghöfer, W. Das Problem der Persönlichkeit bei Jean Paul. Jena: Neuenhahn, 1907.
2134. Werman, David S. Letter: Rolland et Freud. French Rev, 1971, 45:416-417.
2135. _____. Sigmund Freud and Romain Rolland. Int Rev Psycho-Anal, 1977, 4:225-242.
2136. Werner, W.L. The psychology of Marcel Proust. Sewanee Rev, 1931, 39:276-281; In Ruitenbeek, H.M. (ed), Homosexuality and Creative Genius. NY: Obolensky, 1967, 284-289.
2137. Wertham, Frederic. The road to Rapallo: a psychiatric study. Amer J Psychol, 1949, 3:585-600.
2138. Westbury, Barry. His allegorical way of expressing it: civil war and psychic conflict in Oliver Twist and A Child's History. Studies in the Novel, 1974, 6:27-37.
2139. Whitaker, P.K. The inferiority complex of Hermann Sudermann's life and works. Monatshefte, 1948, 40:73-76.
2140. Whitaker, Virgil K. Shakespeare's Use of Learning. An Inquiry into the Growth of His Mind and Art. San Marino, CA: Huntington Library, 1964.
2141. White, G.A. Clinical approaches to biography: the high price of mixed truth. Sewanee Rev, 1977, 85:326-327.
2142. White, Gertrude M. Critics key: poem or personality? English Lit in Transition, 1880-1920, 1968, 11:174-179.
2143. White, John S. Georg Buechner or the suffering through the father. Amer Imago, 1952, 9:365-427.
2144. _____. Psyche and tuberculosis: the libido organization of Franz Kafka. In The Psychoanalytic Study of Society, Vol. 4. NY: IUP, 1967; 85-251.
2145. White, Ralph K. Black Boy: a value analysis. J Abnormal Social Psychol, 1947, 42:440-461.
2146. _____. The versatility of genius. J Social Psychol, 1931, 2:460-489.
2147. White, Robert W. (ed). The Study of Lives. Englewood Cliffs, NJ: Prentice-Hall, 1964; London: Atherton, 1963.
2148. White, William. Ernest Hemingway: violence, blood, death. Orient/West, 1961, 7(11):11-23.
2149. _____. Father and son: some comments on Hemingway's psychology. Dalhousie Rev, 1952, 31:276-284.
2150. White, William M. Dickinson's biography and criticism of her art. Emily Dickinson Bulletin, 1976, 30:66-76.
2151. Whiteside, George. T.S. Eliot: the psychobiographical approach. Southern Rev: Australian J Lit Studies, 1973, 6:3-27; 253-256.
2152. Whitfield, E. Hemingway: the man. Why, 1953, 1:10-19.
2153. Whitlock, Baird D. The heredity and childhood of John Donne. Notes & Queries, 1959, 6:257-262, 348-353.
2154. Wijsenbeek-Franken, Caroline. Marcel Proust. Amer Imago, 1941, 2:323-346; In Ruitenbeek, H.M. (ed), The Literary Imagination. Chicago: Quadrangle, 1965, 143-168.
2155. Wilde, Meta Carpenter, & Bornsten, Orin. A Loving Gentleman: The Love Story of William Faulkner and Meta Carpenter. NY: Simon & Schuster, 1976.

2156. Wilde, W. R. The closing years of Dean Swift's life. Dublin Quart J Medical Science, 1847, 1849, 70-76.

2157. Williams, Irene. Asylum of the Mind: Emerson's Self-Reliance as a Retreat from Men, Women and Society. DAI, 1975, 36:1512A-13A.

2158. Williams, Mentor. Mark Twain's Joan of Arc. Michigan Alumnus Q Rev, 1948.

2159. Williams, Tennessee. Memoirs. Garden City, NY: Doubleday, 1975.

2160. Williamson, Jack. H. G. Wells--critic of progress. The ideas of H. G. Wells. Riverside Q, 1967, 3:6-31.

2161. Wilson, Edmund. The all-star literary vaudeville. In The Shores of Light. NY: Farrar, Straus & Young, 1952, 238, 652.

2162. _____. The personality of Marcel Proust. New Republic, 1930, 61:316-321.

2163. Wilson, Elizabeth G. Thomas Wolfe, His Life and Personality. Master's thesis, Cornell Univ., 1944.

2164. Wilson, F. A. C. Fabrication and fact in Swinburne's The Sisters. Victorian Poetry, 1971, 9:237-248.

2165. Wilson, James S. The personality of Poe. Virginia Magazine of History & Biography, 1959, 67:131-142.

2166. Wilson, Robert N. F. Scott Fitzgerald: personality and culture. In The Arts in Society. Englewood Cliffs, NJ: Prentice-Hall, 1964, 271-298.

2167. Wilson, T. G. Swift's deafness and his last illness. Irish J Medical Science, Ser 6, No. 162, 1939, 241-256; Annals Medical History, 1940, 2:291-305.

2168. _____. Swift's deafness and his last illness. In Sorsby, A. (ed), Tenements of Clay. London: Friedmann, 1974, 115-131.

2169. Winivar, Frances. Jean-Jacques Rousseau: Conscience of an Era. NY: Random House, 1961.

2170. Winters, Warrington. Unusual Mental Phenomena in the Life and Works of Charles Dickens. Doctoral dissertation, Univ. Minnesota, 1942.

2171. Winterstein, Alfred R. F. Rousseaus Bekenntnisse. Int Zeitschrift für Psychoanalyse, 1912, 2:225.

2172. Wispelaere, Paul de. Het dagboek van Anaïs Nin. De Vlaamse Gids, 1967, 130, v:350-353.

2173. Witcutt, W. P. Blake: A Psychological Study. London: Hollis & Carter, 1947.

2174. Withim, Philip M. Joseph Conrad: his character and genius. Psychoanal Rev, 1969, 56:242-246.

2175. Wittels, Fritz. Le Grand amour. Psychoanalytische Bewegung, 1929, 1:242.

2176. _____. Heinrich von Kleist--Prussian Junker and creative genius: a study in bisexuality. J Criminal Psychopathology, 1940, 1:363-365; Amer Imago, 1954, 11:11-31; In Phillips, W. (ed), Art and Psychoanalysis. NY: Criterion, 1957, 165-182; NY: Meridian, 1963; In Ruitenbeek, H. M. (ed), The Literary Imagination. Chicago: Quadrangle, 1965, 23-42.

2177.   . Revision of a biography. Amer J Psychol, 1933,
          45:745-749.
2178. Wittenberg, Judith Bryant. Faulkner: The Transfiguration
          of Biography. Lincoln: Univ. Nebraska Press, 1979.
2179. Wittkopp-Ménardeau, Gabrielle von. E. T. A. Hoffmann in
          Selbstzeugnissen und Bilddokumenten. Reinbeck bei Ham-
          burg: Rowholt, 1966.
2180.   . E. T. A. Hoffmans Leben und Werk in Daten und
          Bilden. Frankfort: Insel, 1968.
2181. Wittkower, Rudolf, & Wittkower, Margot. Born under Saturn:
          The Character and Conduct of Artists; A Documented His-
          tory from Antiquity to the French Revolution. NY: Ran-
          dom House, 1963.
2182. Wiznitzer, H. Sur la rapports entre Sigmund Freud et Arnold
          Zweig. Etudes Germaniques, 1973, 28:205-208.
2183. Wohlfarth, P. Die psychologische Entwicklung von Dostojew-
          skis Jüngling. Int Zeitschrift für Individual-Psychologie,
          1935, 13:104-115.
2184.   . Die verbrecherische Persönlichkeit bei Dostojewski
          und Joseph Conrad. Monatsschrift für Kriminal-Psychol-
          ogie und Strafrechtsreform, 1935, 26:349-357.
2185. Wolberg, Lewis R. The Divine Comedy of Dante. Psycho-
          anal Rev, 1943, 30:33-46.
2186. Wolf, Ernest S., & Gedo, John E. The last introspective
          psychologist before Freud: Michel de Montaigne. In
          The Annual of Psychoanalysis, Vol. 3. NY: IUP, 1975,
          297-310.
2187. Wolf, E. Arthur Rimbaud fut-il schizophrène? Annales
          Médico-Psychologiques, 1956, 2:429-444.
2188. Wolfenstein, Martha. The image of the lost parent. In The
          Psychoanalytic Study of the Child, Vol. 28. New Haven:
          Yale Univ. Press, 1973, 433-456.
2189. Wolff, Cynthia Griffin. A Feast of Words. The Triumph of
          Edith Wharton. NY: Oxford Univ. Press, 1977.
2190.   . Samuel Richardson and the Eighteenth-Century
          Puritan Character. Hamden, Conn.: Shoe String Press,
          1972.
2191. Wollheim, Richard. Freud and the understanding of art. In
          On Art and the Mind. Cambridge: Harvard Univ. Press,
          1974, 202-219.
2192. Wood, Clement. Amy Lovell. NY: Vinal, 1926.
2193. Woodward, A. G. The emergence of the self: James Boswell
          in his journals. English Studies in Africa, 1976, 19:57-
          63.
2194. Woolf, Leonard. Génie et folie de Virginia Woolf. Rev de
          Paris, 1965, 72:91-111.
2195.   . Virginia Woolf: writer and personality. Listener,
          1965, 73:327-328.
2196. Woolf, Virginia. The art of biography. In The Death of the
          Moth. NY: Harcourt, Brace, 1942.
2197. Woollam, P. H. Donne, disease and doctors. Medical allu-
          sions in the works of the seventeenth-century poet and
          divine. Medical History, 1961, 5:144-153.

2198. Workman, Denise S. Anatole France, étude sur sa personnalité dans sa critique et dans ses oeuvres. DAI, 1971,
31:4185A.

2199. Wright, A. D. Venereal diseases and the great. British J
Venereal Diseases, 1971, 47:295-306.

2200. Wright, George Thaddeus. T. S. Eliot: the transformation
of a personality. In Mazzaro, J. (ed), Modern American
Poetry; Essays in Criticism. NY: McKay, 1970, 222-
248.

2201. Wrobel, Arthur. A poet's self-esteem: Whitman alters his
'bumps.' Walt Whitman Rev, 1971, 17:129-135.

2202. _____. Whitman and the phrenologists: the divine body
and the sensuous soul. PMLA, 1974, 89:17-23.

2203. Wuertz, H. Goethes Wesen und Umwelt im Spiegel der
Krüppelpsychologie. Leipzig: 1932.

2204. Wunberg, G. Der frühe Hofmannsthal. Schizophrenie als
dichterische Struktur. Stuttgart: Kohlhammer, 1965.

2205. Wyatt, Frederick. Psychoanalytic biography: a review of
Phyllis Greenacre's Swift and Carroll. Contemporary
Psychol, 1956, 1:105-107.

2206. Wylie, Harold A. Breton, schizophrenia and Nadja. French
Rev, 1970, 43(1):100-106.

2207. Yake, J. Stanley. Mill's mental crisis revisited. Mill Newsletter, 1973, 9(1):2-12.

2208. Yamamoto, Joe, & Iga, Mamoru. Japanese suicide: Yasunari Kawabata and Yuokio Mishima. J Amer Academy
Psychoanal, 1975, 3:179-186.

2209. Yamanouchi, Hisaaki. The Mind's Abyss: A Study of Melancholy and Associated States in Some Late Eighteenth-Century Writers, and in Wordsworth and Coleridge. Doctoral dissertation, Univ. Cambridge, 1975.

2210. Yaron, Mark S. The War Games of James Joyce: A Study
of an Aspect of the Personality, Life, and Works of a
Great Artist. DAI, 1973, 33:6380A.

2211. Yoda, A. [A psychological study of diaries.] Report 6th
Congress Japanese Psychol Assn, 1938, 268-279.

2212. Yoder, Jonathan A. Jack London as wolf barleycorn. Western Amer Lit, 1976, 11:103-119.

2213. _____. Pound as Odysseus, the prisoner psychotic.
Rendezvous, 1973, 8:1-11.

2214. Young, A. C. Comptes rendus critiques. Rev de Littérature
Comparée, 1967, 41:313-315.

2215. Young, Philip. Ernest Hemingway. NY: Rinehart, 1953,
1963.

2216. _____. Ernest Hemingway: A Reconsideration. University Park: Penn State Univ. Press, 1966 (1952); NY:
Harcourt, Brace, & World, 1967.

2217. _____. Hemingway and me. Kenyon Rev, 1966, 28:15-35.

2218. _____. Our Hemingway man. Kenyon Rev, 1964, 26:676-
707.

2219. Yurman, N. [The illness of Dostoevsky.] Klinicheskii Arkhiv Genial'nosti i Odarennosti, 1928, 4(1).

2220. Zabludovskii, P. E. , et al. [L. N. Tolstoi and medicine.]
Klinicheskaia Meditsina (Moscow), 1978, 56(10):140-142.
2221. Zanalda, A. Psicobiografia di un suicido. Minerva Medicin,
1968, 59:4905-4099.
2222. Zangwill, O. L. A case of paramnesia in Nathaniel Hawthorne. Character & Personality, 1945, 13:246-260.
2223. Zaniboni, Maria R. La Rivincita delle vedove nel capolavoro
manzoniano. Fiera letteraria, 1967, 42:9.
2224. Zegger, Hrisey D. May Sinclair. Boston: Twayne, 1976.
2225. Zeldin, T. Biographie et psychologie sous le Second Empire.
Rev d'Histoire Moderne et Contemporaine, 1974, 21:58-74.
2226. Zicino, G. Shakespeare un psicopata sessuale? Archivio
delle Psicopatie Sessuali, Nov 1896.
2227. Ziemer, M. Schillers Charakter. Breslau: Brieg, 1934.
2228. Ziino, Giuseppe. [Was Shakespeare a sexual psychopath?]
Archivio delle Psicopatie Sessuali, 1896, 1:307-309.
2229. Zilboory, Gregory. Psychology of the creative personality.
In Smith, P. (ed), Creativity: An Examination of the
Creative Process. NY: Hastings, 1959, 21-32.
2230. Zimmerman, Michael. Stephen's mother in Ulysses: some
notes for the autobiography of James Joyce. Pacific
Coast Philology, 1975, 10:59-68.
2231. Zitarosa, G. R. Personalità di Gabriele D'Annunzio. Aspetti
Letterari, 1965, No. 3-4, 24-34, No. 6, 27-76.
2232. _____. Personalità di Gabriele D'Annunzio. Naples:
Lupi, 1966.
2233. Zmigrodzka, Maria. [Personality and author's life in liter-
ary-historical monographs.] Pamietnik Literacki, 1975,
66(4):5-23.
2234. Zohar, Zvi. [Dostoyevski in the eyes of the father of psychoanalysis.] Ofakim, 1956, 10:290-294.
2235. Zohn, H. Karl Kraus. NY: Twayne, 1971.
2236. _____. A Karl Kraus chronology. In Kraus, K. , In
These Great Times. Montreal: Engendra, 1976.
2237. Zweig, Stefan. Three Masters: Balzac--Dickens--Dostoeff-
sky. NY: Viking, 1930; Leipzig: Inselverlag, 1920.

2238. Aarbakke, J. H. Høyt på en vinget hest. En studie i drømmer og syner i A. Sandemoses forfatterskap. Oslo: Aschehoug, 1976.
2239. Aaronson, Bernard S. Lilliput and Brobdignag--self and world. Amer J Clinical Hypnosis, 1968, 10:160-166.
2240. Abadi, E. Le Monde extérieur selon l'intuition artistique et l'observation psychologique. Psychologie et Vie, 1930, 4:175-178.
2241. Abadi, M. [The chorus and the hero.] Revista de Psicoanálisis, 1959, 16:322-332.
2242. Abell, Walter. The Collective Dream in Art. A PsychoHistorical Theory of Culture Based on Relations between the Arts, Psychology, and the Social Sciences. Cambridge: Harvard Univ. Press, 1957.
2243. Abraham, Nicolas, & Torok, Maria. L'Encore et le noyau. Paris: Aubier-Flammarion, 1978.
2244. Abraham, P. Figures. Récherches sur la création intellectuelle. Paris: Gallimard, 1929.
2245. Abrams, Meyer Howard. Behaviorism and deconstruction: a comment on Morse Peckham's 'The Infinitude of Pluralism.' Critical Inquiry, 1977, 4:181-193.
2246. _____. Mechanical and organic psychologies of literary invention. In Rosenbaum, S. P. (ed), English Literature and British Philosophy. Chicago: Univ. Chicago Press, 1971, 136-167.
2247. _____. The Milk of Paradise: The Effect of Opium Visions on the Works of De Quincey, Crabbe, Francis Thompson and Coleridge. Cambridge: Harvard Univ. Press, 1934.
2248. _____. The Mirror and the Lamp. NY: Oxford Univ. Press, 1953; Review: René Wellek, Comparative Lit, 1954, 6:178-181.
2249. _____. A note on Wittgenstein and literary criticism. In Paulston, R., & Stein, A. (eds), ELH Essays for Earl R. Wasserman. Baltimore: Johns Hopkins Univ. Press, 1976, 248-261.
2250. Abutille, Mario C. Angst und Zynismus bei Georg Büchner. Bern: Francke, 1969.
2251. Adamowski, Thomas H. Character and consciousness: D. H. Lawrence, Wilhelm Reich and Jean-Paul Sartre. Univ. Toronto Q, 1974, 43:311-334.

2252. Adams, Grace. The rise and fall of psychology. Atlantic Monthly, 1934, 153:82-92.

2253. Adams, Robert M. Literature and psychology: a question of significant form. Lit & Psychol, 1955, 5(4):67-72.

2254. Adelson, Joseph. Creativity and the dream. Merrill-Palmer Q, 1960, 6:92-97.

2255. Adorno, Theodor W. Noten zur Literatur, 4 Vols. Berlin: Suhrkamp, 1958-1974.

2256. Afassishew (Afasizev), M. Kritik des Biologismus in Kunsttheorie und Ästhetik. Kunst und Literatur, 1972, 20:373-382; Iskusstvo, 1971, 10.

2257. Agnew, L. R. Of grasshoppers, figs, and death. British Medical J, 1979, 16:1053-1055.

2258. Aguirre, J. M. Apostellas a 'El sonambulismo de Féderico Garcia Lorca.' Bulletin Hispanic Studies, 1976, 53:127-132.

2259. Aigrisse, Gilberte. La Notion de symbole dans la psychologie moderne. Cahiers Internationaux de Symbolisme, 1963, 3:3-18.

2260. Aiken, Conrad. The analysis of poetry. New Republic, 1922, 31:222-223.

2261. _____. Answer to inquiry about the influence of Freud. New Verse, 1934, 11:13.

2262. _____. A basis for criticism. New Republic, 1923, 34, Pt. II, 1-6.

2263. _____. Forslin and Freud. Reedy's Mirror, 1917, 26:273.

2264. _____. A Reviewer's ABC: Collected Criticism. Ed. Rufus A. Blanshard. NY: Meridian, 1958.

2265. _____. Skepticisms: Notes on Contemporary Poetry. NY: Knopf, 1919.

2266. _____. Sludgery. New Republic, 1922, 32:340-341.

2267. Akasofu, Tetsuji. [The fate of Logos: A Study of Contemporary American Literature.] Tokyo: Eichosha, 1974.

2268. Akmakjian, H. Psychoanalysis and the future of literary criticism. Psychoanal Rev, 1962, 51:3-28.

2269. Aldington, Hilda Doolittle. Tribute to Freud. Oxford: Carcanet, 1971.

2270. Alexander, Charlotte A. The Emancipation of Lambert Strether: A Study of the Relationship Between the Ideas of William and Henry James. DA, 1967, 28:661A-662A.

2271. Alexander, I. W. Maine de Biran and phenomenology. J British Society for Phenomenology, 1970, 1:24-37.

2272. _____. The phenomenological philosophy in France: an analysis of its themes, significance and implications. In Currents of Thought in French Literature. Oxford: Blackwell, 1965.

2273. Alexander, Theodor W. The author's debt to the physician: aphonia in the works of Arthur Schnitzler. J Int Arthur Schnitzler Research Assn, 1965, 4(4):3-10.

2274. Alexandrian, Sarane. Le Surrealisme et le rêve. Paris: Gallimard, 1974.

2275. Allen, D. C. Genesis of Donne's dreams. Modern Language Notes, 1960, 75:293-295.

2276. Allen, Frederick Lewis. Analyzing the psychoanalysts. Rev of Reviews, 1927, 76:322-323.
2277. Allen, Gay Wilson. Emerson and the unconscious. Amer Transcendental Q, 1973, 19:26-30.
2278. _____. James's Varieties of Religious Experience as introduction to American Transcendentalism. Emerson Society Q, 1965, 39:81-85.
2279. Allen, James Sloan. Self-consciousness and the modernist temper. Georgia Rev, 1979, 33:601-620.
2280. Allen, Jeffner. Madness and the poet. Rev Existential Psychol & Psychiat, 1978-79, 16.
2281. Allen, Richard E. El amor y lo fantástico como temas en dos libros de Adolfo Bioy Casares. Boletin Cultural y Bibliográfico, 1968, 11:149-157.
2282. Allen, Richard O. Hysteria and heroism: tragic dissociation and the two tragedies. College English, 1971, 32:399-417.
2283. Allport, Gordon W. Personality: a problem for science or a problem for art? Rev de Psihologie, 1938, 1:488-502.
2284. Allsop, Kenneth. The technicolor wasteland. On drugs and literature. Encounter, 1969, 32(3):64-72.
2285. Almeras, H. d'. La Femme amoureuse dans la vie et dans la littérature. Paris: Michel, 1921.
2286. Alpert, Barry. Fielding Dawson: not as Jung as he used to be. Open Letter, 1974, 2d Series, No. 7:72-83.
2287. Altenhofer, Norbert. Harzreise in die Zeit. Zum Funktionszusammenhang von Traum, Witz und Zensur in Heine's frühem Prosa. Düsseldorf: H. H. -Gesellschaft, 1972.
2288. Alter, Robert. Literary lives. Commentary, 1979, 67:56-62.
2289. Altieri, Charles. Wittgenstein on consciousness and language: a challenge to Derridean literary theory. MLN, 1976, 91:1397-1423.
2290. Alvarez, Alfred. The art of suicide. Partisan Rev, 1970, 37:339-358.
2291. _____. Beyond All This Fiddle: Essays 1955-67. Baltimore: Penguin, 1968; Random House, 1969.
2292. _____. Literature [and suicide] in the nineteenth and twentieth centuries. In Perlin, S. (ed), A Handbook for the Study of Suicide. NY: Oxford Univ. Press, 1975, 31-60.
2293. Alvès, José. Essai de caractérologie d'Antero de Quental. Sillages, 1973, 3:77-127.
2294. Amano, T. A point of view on productive process in literature. Japanese J Psychol, 1929, 4, No. 3.
2295. Amo, Javier del. Litteratura y neuroses. Madrid: Escalada, 1974.
2296. Amrith, M. V. Influence of Freud on modern literature. All-India Weekly, (Bombay) 23 Sept 1944; Indian J Psychol, 1940 (Freud Memorial No.).
2297. Anandamurthy, U. R. The search for an identity: a Kannada writer's viewpoint. Vagartha, 1976, 15:1-16.
2298. Anastasia, Anne, & Foley, John P., Jr. A survey of the literature on artistic behavior in the abnormal: ap-

proaches to interrelationships. Annual New York Academy Science, 1941, 42:1-112.
2299. Anderson, Chester G. On the sublime and its anal origins in Pope, Eliot, and Joyce. In Porter, R. J., & Brophy, J. D. (eds), Modern Irish Literature: A Festschrift for William York Tindall. NY: Iowa College Press/Twayne, 1972, 235-249.
2300. Anderson, Harold H. (ed). Creativity and Its Cultivation. NY: Harper, 1959.
2301. Anderson, Sherwood. Man and his imagination. In The Intent of the Artist. Princeton: Princeton Univ. Press, 1941.
2302. Andrews, Michael F. (ed). Creativity and Psychological Health. Syracuse: Syracuse Univ. Press, 1961.
2303. Anghinetti, Paul W. Alienation, Rebellion, and Myth: A Study of the Works of Nietzsche, Jung, Yeats, Camus, and Joyce. DAI, 1969, 30:1974-75.
2304. Anon. Arthur Schnitzler und die Psychoanalyse. Psychoanalytische Bewegung, 1932, 4:62-63.
2305. _____. Freud und die moderne Literatur. Psychoanalytische Bewegung, 1931, 3:186-188.
2306. _____. Gadda's La meccanica. Times Lit Supplement, 25 Sept 1970.
2307. _____. Literature and sexual inversion. Urologic & Cutaneous Rev, 1933, 37:920-921.
2308. _____. M. H. R. Lenormand: literature of the subconscious. The Times (London), 19 Feb 1951, no. 51, 929, 8.
2309. _____. Psychoanalyse und Literaturwissenschaft. Psychoanalytische Bewegung, 1930, 2:68-69.
2310. _____. Psychoanalysis viewed as detrimental to our literature. Current Opinion, 1922, 73:257-258.
2311. _____. Psychoanalyzing great poets and novelists. Current Opinion, 1919, 67:51.
2312. Ansart-Dourlen, Michèle. Dénaturation et violence dans la pensée de J. -J. Rousseau. Paris: Klincksieck, 1975; Review: Beatrice C. Fink, French Rev, 1976, 50:344-345.
2313. Anthi, P. Kriminalforfatteren Sandemose. Samtiden, 1972, 81:397-400.
2314. Anz, Thomas. Literatur der Existenz. Literarische Psychographie und ihre soziale Bedeutung im Frühexpressionismus. Stuttgart: Metzler, 1977.
2315. Anzieu, Annie. Des mots et des femmes: L'économie libidinale feminine et l'écriture. Nouvelle Rev de Psychanalyse, 1977, 16.
2316. Anzieu, Didier. L'Image, le texte et la pensée: a propos du peintre Francis Bacon et de l'écrivain Samuel Beckett. Nouvelle Rev de Psychanalyse, 1977, 16.
2317. _____. Naissance du concept du vide chez Pascal. Nouvelle Rev de Psychanalyse, 1975, 11.
2318. _____, et al. Psychanalyse du genie créateur. Paris: Dunod, 1974.

2319. _____. La Structure nécéssairement narcissique de l'oeuvre. Bulletin de Psychologie, 1978, 31:12-17.
2320. Appel, Alfred, Jr. An interview with Vladimir Nabokov. Wisconsin Studies in Contemporary Lit, 1967, 8:127-152.
2321. Arias, Ricardo. El hospital de locos, de Valdivielso, interpretación dramática de la metáfora locurapecado. In Finke, W. H. (ed), Estudios de historia, literatura y arte hispanicos ofrecidos a Rodrigo A. Molina. Madrid: Insula, 1977, 25-37.
2322. Arias de la Canal, Fredo. Intento de psicoanálisis de Cervantes. Mexico: Norte, 1970. [Pamphlet.]
2323. _____. El mamífero hipócrita. Norte: Revista Hispano Americano, 1976, 270:43-63; 276:43-53; 277:43-65.
2324. Arieti, Silvano. From primary process to creativity. J Creative Behavior, 1978, 12:225-246.
2325. Ariotti, Piero E., & Bronowski, Rita (eds). Jacob Bronowski. The Visionary Eye: Essays in the Arts, Literature and Science. Cambridge: MIT Press, 1978.
2326. Armatage, Elizabeth Kay. The Mother of Us All: The Woman in the Writings of Gertrude Stein. DAI, 1978, 38: 6116A.
2327. Arnheim, Rudolf. Entropy and Art: An Essay on Disorder and Order. Berkeley: Univ. California Press, 1971.
2328. _____. Toward a Psychology of Art: Collected Essays. Berkeley: Univ. California Press, 1966.
2329. Arnold, Aerol. What the new criticism cannot do. California English J, 1966, 2:47-55.
2330. Arnold, Armin (ed). D. H. Lawrence. The Symbolic Meaning. The Uncollected Versions of Studies in Classic American Literature. NY: Viking, 1964.
2331. Arnold, H. L. (ed). Karl Kraus. Munich: Text und Kritik, 1975.
2332. Arrivé, Michel. Un Aspect de l'isotopie sexuelle dans le texte de Jarry: sadisme et masochisme. Romanic Rev, 1975, 66:58-75.
2333. _____. Lire Jarry. Paris: Coll Dialectiques, 1976.
2334. Arrowsmith, William. Literature and the uses of anxiety. Western Humanities Rev, 1956, 10:325-335.
2335. Artaud, Antonin. L'Aive et l'aume, tentative antigrammaticale contre Lewis Carroll. L'Arbalète, 1947, 12.
2336. Ashmun, M. A study of temperaments as illustrated in literature. J Abnormal Social Psychol, 1908, 19:519-535.
2337. Askew, Melvin W. Courtly love: neuroses as institution. Psychoanal Rev, 1965, 52:19-29; 1967, 54:36-50.
2338. _____. Psychoanalysis and literary criticism. Psychoanal Rev, 1964, 51:211-218.
2339. Aswell, Mary Louise (ed). The World Within. NY: McGraw-Hill, 1947.
2340. Atkins, John. Sex in Literature. The Erotic Impulse in Literature. NY: Grove, 1970.
2341. Auden, W. H. The Enchafèd Flood; Or, the Romantic Iconography of the Sea. NY: Random House, 1949; London: Faber, 1951.

2342. _____. In memory of Sigmund Freud (d. Sept 1949), In Trilling, L. (ed), Prefaces to the Experience of Litera- ture. NY: Harcourt Brace Jovanovich, 1979, 291-297.

2343. _____. Psychology and art today. In Grigson, G. (ed), The Arts Today. London: Lane, 1935, 1-21.

2344. _____. The quest hero. Texas Q, 1961, 6; In Grebstein, S. N. (ed), Perspectives in Contemporary Criticism. NY: Harper & Row, 1968, 370-381.

2345. _____. Talent, genius and unhappiness. New Yorker, 30 Nov 1957, 221-237.

2346. Audiat, P. La Critique littéraire devant la psychologie con- temporaine. J de Psychologie, 1924, 21:461-474.

2347. Audry, J. La Folie dans l'art. Lyon: Médical, 1924.

2348. Auerbach, E. Mimesis: The Representation of Reality in Western Literature. Princeton: Princeton Univ. Press, 1953.

2349. Aulagne, Louis J. Sade ou l'apologétique à l'envers. Psy- ché, 1948, 3:1245-1264.

2350. Austarheim, Kristen. Henrik Wergeland: 'Skabelsen, Men- nesket og Messias. ' En undersøkelse fra psykiatrisk synsvinkel. Arbok for Universitetet i Bergen. Human- istisk serie, 1965. Bergen: Universitetsforlaget, 1967.

2351. Austin, Allen. T. S. Eliot's theory of personal expression. PMLA, 1966, 81:301-307.

2352. Austin, M. Sex in American literature. Bookman, 1923, 57:385-393.

2353. Avendaño, Fausto. Jung, la figure del Anima y la narrativa latinoamericana. DAI, 1973, 34:2604A-05A.

2354. Ayer, A. J. Jean-Paul Sartre. Encounter, 1961, 16:75-77.

2355. Ayerbe-Chaux, R. Aspectos de la temática de H. A. Murena. Symposium, 1973, 27:293-302.

2356. Aymore, Renato. Saba e la psicoanalisi. Naples: Guida, 1971.

2357. Babb, Lawrence. The Elizabethan Malady: A Study of Mel- ancholia in English Literature from 1580 to 1640. East Lansing: Michigan State Univ. Press, 1951.

2358. _____. Melancholy and the Elizabethan man of letters. Huntington Library Q, 1941, 4:247-261.

2359. _____. Sanity in Bedlam: A Study of Robert Burton's Anatomy of Melancholy. East Lansing: Michigan State Univ. Press, 1959.

2360. Babcock, Barbara Allen (ed). The Reversible World; Sym- bolic Inversion in Art and Society. Ithaca: Cornell Univ. Press, 1978.

2361. Bacchiega, Franca. Femminismo e letteratura. Paragone, 1972, 264:110-126.

2362. Bach, David. Jean Paul. In Nunberg, H. , & Federn, E. (eds), Minutes of the Vienna Psychoanalytic Society, Vol. 1: 1906-1908. NY: IUP, 1962, 166-174.

2363. Bachelard, Gaston. L'Air et les songes. Paris: Corti, 1943; Air and Songs, in On Poetic Imagination and Rev- erie. Indianapolis: Bobbs-Merrill, 1971.

2364. _____. L'Eau and les rêves. Paris: Corti, 1942; Water
and Dreams, in On Poetic Imagination and Reverie. Indianapolis: Bobbs-Merrill, 1971.
2365. _____. On Poetic Imagination and Reverie: Selections
from the Works of Gaston Bachelard. Indianapolis:
Bobbs-Merrill, 1971.
2366. _____. The Poetics of Reverie, Childhood, Language, and
the Cosmos. Boston: Beacon, 1969; La Poétique de la
reverie. Paris: Presses Universitaires de France,
1960.
2367. _____. The Poetics of Space. Boston: Beacon, 1969.
2368. _____. The Psychoanalysis of Fire. Boston: Beacon,
1964 (1937); Review: Tony Tanner, London Magazine,
1965, 5:80-87.
2369. _____. Une psychologie du langage littéraire. Jean Paulhan. Les fleurs de Tarbes. Revue Philosophique de la
France, 1942-43, 4-6, 150-156.
2370. Bachler, Karl. Alfred Kubin und die Flucht ins Traumreich;
ein Beitrag zur Deutung des künsterlischen Schaffens.
Psychoanalytische Bewegung, 1933, 5:53-65.
2371. Backscheider, Paul R. (ed). Probability, Time, and Space
in Eighteenth-Century Literature. NY: AMS Press,
1979; Review: G. S. Rousseau, Isis, 1980, 71:348-349.
2372. Baczko, B. Lumière et utopie. Problèmes de recherche.
Annales. Economies--Sociétés--Civilisations, 1971, 26:
355-386.
2373. Baeumer, Max L. Zur Psychologie des Dionysischen in der
Literaturwissenschaft. In Paulsen, W. (ed), Psychologie
in der Literaturwissenschaft. Heidelberg: Stiehm, 1971,
79-111.
2374. Bagenoff, N. Eléments psychopathologiques de l'imagination
créatrice. Archive de Neurologie, 1914, 5.
2375. Baggesen, Søren. Steen Steensen Blicher's tragiske livssyn.
Almanak, 1967, 2(1)(2).
2376. Bahia, A. B. El contenido y la defense en la creación artis-
tica. Revista de Psicoanálisis, 1952, 9:311-341.
2377. Bain, Read. Man is the measure: writing, neurotic and
normal. Sociometry, 1944, 7:332-337.
2378. Baird, James. Jungian psychology in criticism. In Strelka,
J. P. (ed), Literary Criticism and Psychology. University
Park: Penn State Univ. Press, 1976, 3-30.
2379. Baker, Christopher P. Comments on the relationship between psychoanalysis and literary criticism. Lamar J
Humanities, 1977, 3(1):41-44.
2380. Balakian, Anna. Freud and the surrealist mind. Lit &
Psychol, 1953, 3.
2381. Baldensperger, Fernand. Le Part de la Russie dans l'ac-
ceptance française du subconscient en littèrature. PMLA,
1946, 61:293-308.
2382. Ball, Esther Hudson. Emotional Life in Schnitzler's Early
Works. Master's thesis, Duke Univ., 1937.
2383. Ballew, Hal L. Rubén Dario's literary personality. South
Central Bulletin, 1967, 27(4):58-63.

2384. Bamborough, J. B. The Little World of Man. London: Longmans, 1952.
2385. Bandera, Cesáreo. Literature and desire: poetic frenzy and the love potion. Mosaic, 1975, 8(2):33-52.
2386. Banta, Martha A. American apocalypses: excrement and ennui. Studies in the Lit Imagination, 1974, 7:1-30.
2387. _____. Failure and Success in America: A Literary Debate. Princeton: Princeton Univ. Press, 1978.
2388. Barach, Alvan L. Promethean anxieties. Columbia Forum, 1966, 9:22-26.
2389. Baratta, E. A. Surrealistische Züge im Werke Jean Pauls. Bonn: Bouvier, 1972.
2390. Barbeau, Anne T. The disembodied rebels: psychic origins of rebellion in Absalom and Achitophel. In Studies in Eighteenth-Century Culture, Vol. 9. Madison: Univ. Wisconsin Press, 1979.
2391. Barchilon, Jacques. Development of artistic stylization. In The Psychoanalytic Study of the Child, Vol. 19. NY: IUP, 1964, 256-274.
2392. Barfield, Owen. Coleridge collected. Encounter, 1970, 35(5):74-83.
2393. Barilli, Renato. La linea Svevo-Pirandello. Milan: Mursia, 1972.
2394. Barnard, Guy Christian. Samuel Beckett: A New Approach: A Study of the Novels and Plays. NY: Dodd, Mead, 1970; London: Dent, 1970.
2395. Barnes, Annette. Female criticism: a prologue. In Diamond, A., & Edwards, L. R. (eds), The Authority of Experience. Essays in Feminine Criticism. Amherst: Univ. Massachusetts Press, 1977, 1-15.
2396. Barnes, Hazel F. The Literature of Possibility: A Study in Human Existentialism. Lincoln: Univ. Nebraska Press, 1959.
2397. Barney, Richard Johnston. The Evolution of Self: The Concept of Death in the Works of Arthur Schnitzler. Doctoral dissertation, Princeton Univ., 1971.
2398. Barrett, William. Writers and madness. Partisan Rev, 1947, 14:5-22.
2399. Barron, Frank X. Bisociates: artist and scientist in the act of creation. In Harris, H. A. (ed), Astride the Two Cultures; Arthur Koestler at 70. NY: Random House, 1976, 37-49.
2400. _____. The psychology of the creative writer. In Monney, R. L., & Razik, T. A. (eds), Explorations in Creativity. NY: Harper & Row, 1967.
2401. Barrows, Susanna Isabel. Crowd Psychology in the Late Nineteenth-Century France: The Riddle of the Sphinx. DAI, 1977, 38(6):3663-64A.
2402. Barrucand, D., & Barrucand, M. Psychopathologie de l'expression chez A. Kubin. Annales Médico-Psychologiques, 1967, 125(2):389-405.
2403. Barthes, Roland. L'Eros racinien. Esprit, 1959, 11:471-482.

2404. _____. L'Homme racinien. Paris: Club Français du livre, 1960.
2405. _____. An introduction to the structural analysis of narrative. New Lit History, 1975, 6(2):256-260.
2406. _____. Masculin, féminin, neutre. In Pouillon, J., & Maranda, P. (eds). Echanges et communications: Mélanges offerts à Claude Lévi-Strauss, Vol. 2. The Hague: Mouton, 1970, 893-907.
2407. _____. S/Z. Paris: Seuil, 1970.
2408. Bartlett, Francis H. The limitations of Freud. Science & Society, 1939, 3:64-105.
2409. Bartlett, Irving H., & Cambor, C. Glenn. The history and psychodynamics of Southern womanhood. Women's Studies, 1974, 2:9-24.
2410. Bartolomei, G. Psicoanalisi di Carolina Invernizio. Belfagor, 1973, 28:109-115.
2411. Basny, Lionel. Samuel Johnson and the psychology of war. Midwest Q, 1974, 16:12-24.
2412. Bassett, Sharon. Tristes critiques: Harold Bloom and the sorrows of secular art. Lit & Psychol, 1977, 27:106-112.
2413. _____. Women's words and works: the idiom of psychoanalytic sexism. Lit & Psychol, 1979, 29:64-70.
2414. Bataille, Georges. Death and Sensuality: A Study of Eroticism and Taboo. NY: Walker, 1962; NY: Ballantine, 1969.
2415. _____. Eroticism. London: Calder, 1962; Paris: Editions de Minuit, 1957.
2416. _____. L'Expérience Intérieure. Paris: 1943.
2417. Baudouin, Charles. Petite suite pascalienne. Action et Pensée, 1941, 17:33-39.
2418. _____. Psychoanalyse de l'art. Paris: Alcan, 1929.
2419. _____. La Sublimation des images chez Huysmans, lors de sa conversion. Psyché, 1950, 43:378-385.
2420. _____. Von Pestalozzi zu Tolstoi. Zeitschrift für psychoanalytische Pädagogik, 1926-27, 1:143-149.
2421. Baudry, Jean-Louis. Freud et la création littéraire. Tel Quel, 1968, 32:63-85; In Foucault, J., Barthes, R., & Derrida, J. (eds), Théorie d'ensemble. Paris: Seuil, 1968, 149-174.
2422. Bauman, Marianne. Der Traum im Werk von J. Gotthelf. Doctoral dissertation, Bern, 1945.
2423. Bayley, John. The Characters of Love: A Study in the Literature of Personality. NY: Basic Books, 1960.
2424. Bazin, Nancy T., & Freeman, Alma. The androgynous vision. Women's Studies, 1974, 2:185-215.
2425. Beardsley, Monroe C. Aesthetic intentions and fictive illocutions. In Hernadi, P. (ed), What Is Literature? Bloomington: Indiana Univ. Press, 1978, 161-177.
2426. Beaty, Frederick L. Light from Heaven; Love in British Romantic Literature. DeKalb, Ill: Northern Illinois Univ. Press, 1971.

2427. Beaujean, M.   Der Trivialroman in der zweiten Hälfte des 18. Jhs. Die Ursprünge des modernen Unterhaltungs- roman. Bonn: Bouvier, 1964.
2428. Beaumont, Ernest. Claudel and Sophia. In Griffiths (ed), Claudel: A Reappraisal. Chester Springs, Pa: Dufour, 1970.
2429. Beauvoir, Simone de. Brigitte Bardot and the Lolita Syn- drome. NY: Arno, 1972 (1960).
2430. _____. The Second Sex. NY: Knopf, 1951; NY: Ban- tam, 1961, 1970; Paris: Gallimard, 1949; Review: Patrick Mullahy, Psychiatry, 1952, 15:221-224.
2431. Beaver, Harold. A monument to muse power. Times Lit Supplement, 7 July 1978, no. 3979:754.
2432. Beck, M. et al. (eds). The Analysis of Hispanic Texts: Current Trends in Methodology. NY: Bilingual Press, 1976.
2433. Beguelin, M. Henri Michaux esclâve et démiurge. Laus- anne: L'Age d'homme, 1974.
2434. Béguin, Albert. L'Ame romantique et le rêve. Paris: 1963.
2435. _____. The night-side of life. Transition, 1938, 28:197- 218.
2436. Beharriel, Frederic J. C. F. Meyer and the origin of psy- choanalysis. Monatshefte für deutschen Unterricht, deutsche Sprache und Literatur, 1955, 47:140-148.
2437. _____. Freud and literature. Queens Q, 1958, 65:118- 125.
2438. _____. Freud's debt to literature. Psychoanalysis, 1956, 4:18-28.
2439. _____. Schnitzler's anticipation of Freud's dream theory. Monatshefte für Unterricht, deutsche Sprache und Litera- tur, 1953, 45:81-89.
2440. Beinlich, Alexander. Kindheit und Kinderseele in der deutsch- en Dichtung um 1900. Breslau, 1900.
2441. Beirnaert, Louis. Une Lecture psychanalytique du Journal spirituel d'Ignace de Loyola. Rev d'Histoire de la Spirit- ualité, 1975, 51:99-112.
2442. Belaja, Galina. Zur psychologischen Darstellung in der Sow- jetliteratur. Kunst und Literatur, 1972, 20:183-187; Voprosy Literatury, 1971, 7.
2443. Belaval, Yvon. Psychanalyse et critique littéraire en France. La Nouvelle Rev Française, 1970, 214.
2444. Bell, Clive. Dr. Freud on art. Nation & Athenaeum, 1924, 35:690-691; Dial, 1925, 78:280-284; Lit Digest, 1924, 83:32.
2445. Bellak, Leopold. Creativity. Some random notes to a sys- tematic consideration. J Projective Techniques, 1958, 22:363-380.
2446. Belleli, Maria L. Armonia di struttura e coerenze psico- logica in 'Sylvie' di Gérard de Nerval. Turin: Grap- pichelli, 1970.
2447. Bellemin-Noel, Jean. Psychanalyse et littérature. Paris: Presses Universitaires, 1978.
2448. Benda, Julien. Psychologie des gens de lettres. Fontaine, 1947, 59:163-165; Ordre, 8 Dec 1946.

2449. Benedict, Ruth.   Mary Wollstonecraft.   In Mead, M. (ed),
       An Anthropologist at Work.   Writings of Ruth Benedict.
       Boston: Houghton Mifflin, 1959, 491-519.
2450. Benesch, A.   Friedrich Schillers psychologische Ansichten.
       In Wellek, A. (ed), Bericht über den 21.   Kongress der
       deutschen Gesellschaft für Psychologie (1957).   Göttingen:
       1958, 124-128.
2451. Bensimon, Marc.   The significance of eye imagery in the
       Renaissance from Bosch to Montaigne.   Yale French
       Studies, 1972, 47:266-290.
2452. Bercovitch, Sacvan.   Literature and the repetition compul-
       sion.   College English, 1968, 29:607-615.
2453. Beres, David.   Certainty: a failed quest?   Psychoanal Q,
       1980, 49:1-26.
2454. _____.   Communication in psychoanalysis and in the crea-
       tive process: a parallel.   JAPA, 1957, 5:408-423.
2455. _____.   The psychoanalytic psychology of imagination.
       JAPA, 1960, 8:252-269.
2456. _____, & Arlow, Jacob A.   Fantasy and identification in
       empathy.   Psychoanal Q, 1974, 43:26-50.
2457. Berg, Karin Westman.   Looking at women in literature.
       Scandinavian Rev, 1975, 63(2):48-55.
2458. Berger, A. von.   Die Dichter hat sie für sich.   Psychoanaly-
       tische Bewegung, 1923, 4:73-76.
2459. Bergler, Edmund.   Can the writer 'resign' from his calling?
       Int J Psycho-Anal, 1953, 34:40-42.
2460. _____.   Forward to A. Wormhoudt's The Demon Lover,
       A Psychoanalytic Approach to Literature.   NY: Exposi-
       tion, 1949.
2461. _____.   Further contributions to the psychoanalysis of
       writers.   Psychoanal Rev, 1947, 34:449-468; 1948, 35:
       33-50.
2462. _____.   Literary critics who can spell but cannot read;
       contribution to the occupational hazard of reviewers--
       'emotional reading block.'   Amer Imago, 1951, 8:189-
       218.
2463. _____.   Malcolm Cowley's literary hatchet turns into a
       boomerang.   Amer Imago, 1954, 11:375-384.
2464. _____.   Myth, merit and mirage in literary style.   Amer
       Imago, 1950, 7:279-287.
2465. _____.   A new misconception in literary criticism.
       Amer Imago, 1949, 6:275-279.
2466. _____.   On a clinical approach to the psychoanalysis of
       writers.   Psychoanal Rev, 1944, 31:40-70.
2467. _____.   Psychoanalysis of writers and literary productiv-
       ity.   In The Psychoanalytic Study of Society, Vol. 5.
       NY: IUP, 1947, 247-296.
2468. _____.   The relation of writers to literary criticism.
       Amer Imago, 1955, 12:337-341.
2469. _____.   The second book and the second play.   Psychoanal
       Rev, 1955, 42:293-297.
2470. _____.   Story-tellers and story-writers.   Amer Imago,
       1949, 6:51-56.

2471. _____. Symposium. Psychoanalysis and Literature. Transcript, Study Guide. NY: Queens College, 1950.

2472. _____. This typewriter to hire: psychology of the 'hack-writer.' Psychiat Q Supplement, 1948, 22:290-299.

2473. _____. True feelings and 'tear-jerkers' in literary work. Amer Imago, 1953, 10:83-86.

2474. _____. The Writer and Psychoanalysis. Garden City, NY: Doubleday, 1950; NY: Brunner, 1954.

2475. _____. Writers and ulcers. Amer Imago, 1953, 10:87-92.

2476. _____. Zur Problematik des 'oralen' Pessimisten, demonstriert an Christian Friedrich Grabbe. Imago, 1934, 20:330-376.

2477. Bergmann, G. Zur analytischen Theorie literarischer Wertmasstabe (mit einer Bemerkung zur Grundlagendiskussion). Imago, 1935, 21:498-504.

2478. Berlin, Jeffrey Bennett. An Annotated Arthur Schnitzler Bibliography 1965-1977. With an Essay on the Meaning of the Schnitzler-Renaissance. Munich: Fink, 1978.

2479. _____. Arthur Schnitzler's Attitude Toward Betrayal and Deception. Master's Thesis, Temple Univ., 1971.

2480. _____. Some images of the betrayer in Arthur Schnitzler's work. German Life & Letters, 1972, 26:20-24.

2481. Berlyne, D. E. (ed). Studies in the New Experimental Aesthetics: Steps Toward an Objective Psychology of Aesthetic Appreciation. NY: Halsted, 1974.

2482. Bernay, Jérome. Les Homosexuels dans l'oeuvre de Juvénal. Arcadie, 1975, 259-260:356-364.

2483. Berninghaus, Ursula. Der Traum in der Dichtung des Biedermeier. Doctoral dissertation, Munich, 1933.

2484. Berry, Nicole. L'Experience d'écriture. Nouvelle Rev de Psychanalyse, 1977, 16.

2485. Berry, Ralph. The frontier of metaphor and symbol. British J Aesthetics, 1967, 7:76-83.

2486. Bersani, Leo. From Bachelard to Barthes. In Plimpton, G., & Ardery, P. (eds). The American Literary Anthology, Vol. 2. NY: Random House, 1969, 3-22.

2487. _____. A Future for Astyanax: Character and Desire in Literature. Boston: Little, Brown, 1976; Review: U. Weisstein, Sewanee Rev, 1978, 86:309-316.

2488. _____. The other Freud. Humanities in Society, 1978, 1(1):35-49.

2489. Bertelli, Italo. I fondamenti psicologici e letterari del Dolce stil novo. In Cultura e paese. Milan: Bignami, 1968, 81-93.

2490. Berthier, Philippe. Barbey d'Aurevilly et l'imagination. Geneva: Droz, 1978; Review: Joyce O. Lowrie, French Rev, 1979, 53:296-297.

2491. Berthoff, Ann E. Recalling another Freudian model--a consumer caveat. CEA Critic, 1973, 35(4):12-14.

2492. Bertocci, Peter A. Susan K. Langer's theory of feeling and mind. Rev Metaphysics, 1970, 23:527-551.

2493. Bessette, Gérard. La Psychocritique. Voix et Images, 1975, 1:72-79.

2494. Bettelheim, Bruno. Violence: a neglected mode of behavior. Annals Amer Academy, 1966, 364:50-59.

2495. Beutin, Wolfgang (ed). Literatur und Psychoanalyse: Ansätze zu einer Psychoanalytischen Textinterpretation: 13 Aufsätze. Munich: Nymphenburger, 1972; Review: Frederick J. Beharriell, Modern Austrian Lit, 1974, 7:203-205.

2496. Bévand, Richard. L'Oeuvre psychologique de Charles Baudouin. Rev de Théologie et de Philosophie, 1964, 97: 151-154.

2497. Beyerle, D. Marie de France und die Witwe von Ephesus. Romanistisches Jahrbuch, 1971, 22:84-100.

2498. Bianquis, G. Le Temps dans l'oeuvre de Thomas Mann. JPNP, 1951, 44:352-370.

2499. Biasin, Gian-Paolo. Disease as language: the case of the writer and the madman. In Peschel, E.R. (ed), Medicine and Literature. NY: Watson, 1980, 171-177.

2500. _____. Strategies of the anti-hero: Svevo, Pirandello, and Montale. In Rimanelli, G., & Atchity, K.J. (eds), Italian Literature: Roots and Branches. New Haven: Yale Univ. Press, 1976, 363-381.

2501. Bieber, H. Dichtung und Psychoanalyse. In Prinzhorn, H., Auswirkungen der Psychoanalyse in Wissenschaft und Leben. Leipzig: Die Neue Geist Verlag, 1928, 400-412.

2502. Biéder, J. Bergson et les rêves. Annales Médico-Psychologiques, 1973, 1:125-131.

2503. Bigeard, M. La Folie et les fous litteraires en Espagne (1500-1650). Paris: Centre de Recherches de l'Institut d'Etudes Hispaniques, 1972.

2504. Bigelow, Gordon E. Thoreau's melting sandbag: birth of a symbol. Int J Symbology, 1971, 2(3):7-13.

2505. Bilan, R.P. The basic concepts and criteria of F.R. Leavis's novel criticism. In Spilka, M. (ed), Towards a Poetics of Fiction. Bloomington: Indiana Univ. Press, 1977, 157-176.

2506. Binkley, Robert C. Of Freud and the future. Virginia Q Rev, 1937, 12:612-615.

2507. Binswanger, Ludwig. Haraklitus Auffassung des Menschen. Die Antike, 1935, 11:1-38.

2508. _____. Über den Satz von Hofmannsthal: 'Was Geist ist, erfasst nur der Bedrängte.' Studia Philosophica, 1948, 8:1-11.

2509. Bishop, Lloyd. The banquet scene in Moderato Cantabile: a stylistic analysis. Romance Rev, 1978, 69:222-235.

2510. Bizzicari, A. Stile e personalità di S. Caterina da Siena. Acme, 1966, 19:243-268.

2511. Björck, Staffan. Sångaren och plågan: Ett litteratur-psykologiskt motiv och ett diktkomplex hos Birger Sjöberg. Birger Sjöberg Sällskapet, 1966, 34-52.

2512. Björnsson, Sigurjon. Leiðin til Skaldskapar. [The Road to Poetry.] Menningarspour, Reykjavik, 1964.

2513. _____. [Psychological theories on literature.] Lesbók Morgunblaðsins, n.d., 41(4):5-6, 12-15; n.d., 41(5):5-7, 12-13.

2514. Black, S. On reading psychoanalytically. College English, 1977, 39:267-275; Reply with rejoinder, College English, 1978, 40:223-228.

2515. Blackman, Maurice John. Gérard de Nerval et la littérature anglaise: Etude psychocritique de l'influence littéraire. DAI, 1976, 36:6079A.

2516. Blackwell, Fritz (ed). Feminine sensibility and characterization in South Asian literature. [Special issue.] J South Asian Lit, 1977, 12(3-4).

2517. _____. Misogyny and philogyny: the bifurcation and ambivalence of the stereotypes of the courtesan and the mother in literary tradition. J South Asian Lit, 1977, 12(3-4):37-43.

2518. Bleich, David. More's Utopia: confessional modes. Amer Imago, 1971, 28:24-52.

2519. _____. Motives and truth in classroom communication. College Composition & Communication, 1975, 26:371-378.

2520. _____. Pedagogical directions in subjective criticism. College English, 1976, 37:454-467. Reply with rejoinder: N.N. Holland, 1976, 38:298-301.

2521. _____. Readings and Feelings: An Introduction to Subjective Criticism. Urbana, Ill: National Council Teachers English, 1975.

2522. _____. Subjective Criticism. Baltimore: Johns Hopkins Univ. Press, 1978.

2523. _____. The subjective paradigm in science, psychology, and criticism. College English, 1976, 37:454-467.

2524. Blesch, Edwin J., Jr. 'A species hardly a degree above a monkey': Jonathan Swift's concept of woman. Nassau Rev, 1977, 3(3):74-84.

2525. Blöcker, Günter. Mythos plus Psychologie. Athena, 1946-47, 1(4):29-33.

2526. Bloede, Barbara Royle. James Hogg's Private Memoirs and Confessions of a Justified Sinner: the genesis of the double. Etudes Anglaises, 1973, 26:174-186.

2527. Bloom, Harold. A compass for the labyrinth. Yale Rev, 1969, 59:109-111.

2528. _____. Figures of Capable Imagination. NY: Seabury, 1976.

2529. _____. Freud's concepts of defense and the poetic will. In Smith, J.H. (ed), The Literary Freud. New Haven: Yale Univ. Press, 1980, 1-28.

2530. _____. Kabbalah and Criticism. NY: Seabury, 1975; Review: Joseph N. Riddel, Georgia Rev, 1976, 30:989-1006.

2531. _____. A Map of Misreading. NY: Oxford Univ. Press, 1975.

2532. _____. Poetic crossing: rhetoric and psychology. Georgia Rev, 1976, 30:495-524, 772-796.

2533. _____. Ringers in the Tower. Chicago: Univ. Chicago Press, 1971.

2534. _____. Walter Pater: the intoxication of belatedness. Yale French Studies, 1974, 50:163-190.

2535. Blue, Rose. Reading and emotional response. Teacher, 1975, 92:52-54+.

2536. Blum, Ernst. Zur Symbolik des Raben. Psychoanalytische Bewegung, 1931, 3:359-368.

2537. Blum, W. C. Improbable purity. Dial, 1925, 78:318-323.

2538. Blumenthal, Walter Hart. Alcove for alienists. In Bookmen's Bedlam of Literary Oddities. New Brunswick, NJ: Rutgers Univ. Press, 1955, 191-207.

2539. Bode, Carl. The half-hidden Thoreau. Massachusetts Rev, 1962, 4:68-80.

2540. Bodkin, Maude. Literary criticism and the study of the unconscious. Monist, 1927, 37:445-469.

2541. _____. Literature and the individual reader. Lit & Psychol, 1960, 10:39-46.

2542. _____. The relevance of psychoanalysis to art criticism. British J Psychol, 1924, 15:174-183.

2543. Boeschenstein, Hermann. Psychoanalysis in modern literature. In Smith, H. (ed), Columbia Dictionary of Modern Literature, NY: Columbia Univ. Press, 1947, 651-657.

2544. Boethcher Joeres, R. E. The triumph of the woman: J. Kinkel's Hans Ibeles in London (1860). Euphorion, 1976, 70:187-197.

2545. Boisdeffre, Pierre de. Barrès Parmi Nous; Essai de Psychologie Littéraire et Politique Suivi de Témoignages Inédits. Paris: Amiot-Dumont, 1952.

2546. Bologa, L. Lectura Tinerstului. Cluj, Rumania: Institut de Psichologi Universiti Cluj, 1933.

2547. Bolsterli, Margaret. Studies in context: the homosexual ambience of twentieth-century literary culture. D. H. Lawrence Rev, 1973, 6:71-85.

2548. Bonaparte, Marie. De l'Elaboration et de la fonction de l'oeuvre littéraire. Rev Française de Psychanalyse, 1932, 5:649-683.

2549. _____. L'Inquiétant etrangeté essais de psychanalyse appliquée. Paris: Gallimard, 1971.

2550. Bond, D. F. The neo-classic psychology of the imagination. ELH, 1937, 4:245-264.

2551. Bonime, Florence & Eckhardt, Marianne H. On psychoanalyzing literary characters. J Amer Academy Psychoanal, 1977, 5:159-174.

2552. Bonnet, H. Le Monde, l'amour et l'amitié, Vol. 1; L'Eudémonisme esthetique de Proust, Vol. 2. The 2 Vols. titled: Le Progrès spirituel dans l'oeuvre de Marcel Proust. Paris: Vrin, 1946-1949.

2553. Bonnet, Jean-Claude. Le Systeme de la cuisine et du repas chez Rousseau. Poétique, 1975, 24:244-267.

2554. Bonnycastle, S. Robertson Davies and the ethics of monologue. J Canadian Studies, 1977, 12:2040.

2555. Boone, William F. Into the Labyrinth: The Daydream Mode in Literature. DAI, 1972, 32:5219A-20A.

2556. Booth, Wayne C. Distance and point-of-view: an essay in classification. Essays in Criticism, 1961, 11; In Stevick, P. (ed), The Theory of the Novel. NY: Free Press, 1967, 87-107.

2557. Boring, Edwin G. The book review. Amer J Psychol, 1951, 64:281-283.

2558. Bornecque, J. -H. Les Méchanismes et les antagonismes psychologiques de la création littéraire. AULLA Proceedings, 1964, (2), 10a-10b.

2559. Boros, Marie-D. Un Séquestré, l'homme sartrien. Paris: Nizet, 1968.

2560. Borreli, Guy. Barrès et la psychologie de l'art. In Maurice Barrès. Actes du colloque organisé par la Faculté de l'Université de Nancy. Nancy: Univ. de Nancy, 1963, 85-94.

2561. Borup Jensen, Thorkild. Laesevaner og laeserforudsaettninger: Litteratursociologishe og litteraturpsykologiske perspektiver. In Litteraturpaedogogik. Copenhagen: Reitzel, 1978, 127-152.

2562. Bosch, Raimundo. Temperamento y amor. Rev de Medical Legale de Colombia, 1946, 8:44-65.

2563. Bougard, Roger Gilbert. Erotisme et amour physique dans la littérature française du XVIIe siècle. DAI, 1975, 36:300A.

2564. Bourget, Paul. Essais de psychologie contemporaine. Paris: Lemerre, 1886; Paris: Plon, 1924.

2565. Bousquet, Jacques. Les Thèmes du rêve dans la littérature romantique. Paris: Didier, 1964.

2566. Bouyssou, Roland. L'Angoisse existentielle de C. Day Lewis. Caliban, 1970, 7:59-65.

2567. Bowden, James H. Exlit: external literature. College English, 1976, 38 287-291; Reply with rejoinder: D. P. Nelson, College English, 1978, 39:636-638.

2568. Bowman, Frank Paul. Roland Barthes par Roland Barthes et Charles Fourier. Romanic Rev, 1978, 69:236-241.

2569. Boyer, Alain-Michel. Michel Leiris. Paris: Editions Universitaires, 1974.

2570. Boyers, Peggy. After Freud: sacrificial crisis and the origins of culture. Salmagundi, 1978, 41:128-138.

2571. Boyers, Robert. Ideology in the steam-bath [rev. article]. Times Lit Supplement, 30 May 1980, no. 4027, 603-604.

2572. _____, & Wees, Dustin. Art and technology: a dialogue between Harold Rosenberg and Benjamin Nelson. Salmagundi, 1974, 27:40-56.

2573. Bradley, Noel. Primal scene experience in human evolution and its phantasy derivatives in art, proto-science, and philosophy. In The Psychoanalytic Study of Society, Vol. 4, NY: IUP, 1967, 34-82.

2574. Braet, M. [Dream motif in medieval literature.] In Cormier, R. J. (ed), Voices of Conscience. Essays on Medieval and Modern French Literature. Philadelphia: Temple Univ. Press, 1977, 107-118.

2575. Bragman, Louis J. Ambrose Bierce, purveyor of morbidities. Welfare Magazine, 1928, 19:780-782.

2576. _____. Ludwig Lewisohn on The Creative Eros. Psychoanal Rev, 1933, 20:5-9.

2577. _____. Ludwig Lewisohn: psychoanalyst of literature. Psychoanal Rev, 1934, 21:300-315.

2578. Brahimi, Denise. Restif féministe? Etude de quelques Con-
       temporaines'. In Mortier, R., & Hasquin, H. (eds),
       Etudes sur le XVIIIe siècle. III. Les Préoccupations
       économiques et sociales des philosophes, littérateurs et
       artistes au XVIIIe siècle. Brussels: Univ. de Bruxelles,
       1976, 77-92.
2579. Brain, Walter Russell. Diagnosis of genius. British J Aes-
       thetics, 1963, 3:114-128.
2580. Brambila, Antonio. Melancolia por el suicidio. Revista
       Chicano-Riqueña. Abside, 1974, 38:279-284.
2581. Branch, W. G. Darl Bundren's cubistic vision. Texas Studies
       in Lit & Language, 1977, 19:42-59.
2582. Branfman, Theodore, & Bergler, Edmund. The psychology of
       'perfectionism.' Amer Imago, 1955, 12:9-15.
2583. Brater, Enoch. The I in Beckett's not I. Twentieth Century
       Lit, 1974, 20:189-200.
2584. Braybrooke, P. Character and the author. Ethological J,
       1928, 13:17-26.
2585. Brée, Germaine. Literary analysis: today's mandarins. In
       Davis, Lisa E., & Tarán, Isabel C. (eds), The Analysis
       of Hispanic Texts: Current Trends in Methodology.
       Jamaica: Bilingual Press, 1976, 1-10.
2586. Brenkman, John. The other and the one: psychoanalysis,
       reading, the Symposium. Yale French Studies, 1977,
       55-56:396-456.
2587. Brenman-Gibson, Margaret. Notes on the study of the crea-
       tive process. In Psychology Versus Metapsychology:
       Psychoanalytic Essays in Memory of George Klein. NY:
       IUP, 1976, 326-357.
2588. Breuer, Horst. Samuel Beckett: Lernpsychologie und lieb-
       liche Determination. Munich: Fink, 1972.
2589. Breugelmans, Rene. Jacques Perk. NY: Twayne, 1974.
2590. Brians, Paul. Sexuality and the opposite sex: variations on
       a theme by Théophile Gautier and Anaïs Nin. Essays in
       Lit, 1977, 4:122-137.
2591. Bricke, John. Hume on self-identity, memory and causal-
       ity. In Morice, G. P. (ed), David Hume: Bicentenary
       Papers. Austin: Univ. Texas Press, 1977, 167-
       174.
2592. Bridgwater, Patric. English writers and Nietzsche. In Pal-
       sey, M. (ed), Nietzsche: Imagery and Thought. Berke-
       ley: Univ. California, 1978, 220-258.
2593. _____. Kafke and Nietzsche. Bonn: Bouvier, 1979.
2594. _____. Nietzsche in Anglosaxony. NY: Humanities
       Press, 1972.
2595. Brightenback, K. Review: A. Knapton's Mythe et psychologie
       chez Marie de France dans Guigemar. Romance Philol-
       ogy, 1977, 31:443-445.
2596. Brink, Andrew. Aggression in the psychology of art. Sphinx,
       1975, 3:41-50.
2597. _____. Bunyan's Pilgrims Progress and the secular read-
       er: a psychological approach. English Studies in Canada,
       1975, 1:386-405.

2598. _____. Depression and loss: a theme in Robert Burton's Anatomy of Melancholy. Canadian J Psychiat, 1979, 24: 767-772.

2599. _____. On the psychological sources of creative imagination. Queens Q, 1974, 81:1-19.

2600. Brisman, Susan Hawk, & Brisman, Leslie. Lies against solitude: symbolic, imaginary, and real. In Smith, J.H. (ed), The Literary Freud. New Haven: Yale Univ. Press, 1980, 29-65.

2601. Brodeur, L.A. Le Corps-sphère, clef de la symbolique claudélienne. Montreal: Cosmos, 1970.

2602. Brombert, Victor. The Romantic Prison; the French Tradition. Princeton: Princeton Univ. Press, 1978.

2603. _____. The will to ecstasy: the example of Baudelaire's 'La Chevelure.' Yale French Studies, 1974, 50:55-64.

2604. Bromley, J. F. The literature of madness. Central Lit Magazine, 1964, 41:4.

2605. Brøndsted, Mogens. [Applicability of depth psychology to literature.] Kritik, 1968, 5.

2606. Bronson, Bertrand H. The retreat from reason. In Pagliaro, H. (ed), Studies in Eighteenth-Century Culture, Vol. II. Cleveland: Case Western Reserve Univ. Press, 1972, 225-238.

2607. Brooks, Peter. Freud's masterplot: questions of narrative. Yale French Studies, 1977, 280-300.

2608. Brooks, Van Wyck. The Writer in America. NY: Dutton, 1953.

2609. Broom, M.E. A study of literary appreciation. J Applied Psychol, 1934, 18:357-363.

2610. Brophy, Brigid. The rococo seducer. London Magazine, 1962, 2:54-71.

2611. Brown, Ashley. An interview with Conrad Aiken. Shenandoah, 1963, 15(1):18-40.

2612. Brown, Daniel Russell. A look at archetypal criticism. JAAC, 1969-70, 28:465-472.

2613. Brown, Helen W. A literary forerunner of Freud. Psychoanal Rev, 1917, 4:64-69.

2614. Brown, J.W. El hermano asno from Fioretti through Freud. Symposium, 1971, 25:321-332.

2615. Brown, Kenneth. Los Buendías de Antaño. Cuadernos Hispano-Americanos, 1976, 311:440-450.

2616. Brown, Norman O. Life Against Death. The Psychoanalytic Meaning of History. Middletown: Wesleyan Univ. Press, 1959; NY: Vintage, 1959.

2617. _____. Love's Body. NY: Random House, 1966.

2618. _____. Psychoanalysis and classics. Classical J, 1957, 52:241-245.

2619. Brown, Sterling. Negro character as seen by white authors. J Negro Education, 1933, 2:179-203.

2620. Brown, W.L. The psychology of modernism in literature. JAMA, 1935, 104:401-402.

2621. Brown, William Richard. William James and the language of personal literature. Style, 1971, 5:151-163.

2622. Browne, F. W. Stella.   Der weiblische Typus Inversus in der neuren Literatur.   Neue Generation, 1922, 18:90-96.

2623. Bruckner, Ferdinand.   Freud und die Schriftsteller.   Literature, 1930, Feb.

2624. Brückl, O.   Psychology and myth in twentieth-century German literature and criticism.   English Studies in Africa, 1967, 10:47-66.

2625. Bruner, Jerome S.   Freud and the image of man.   Partisan Rev, 1956, 23:340-347.

2626. _____.   On Knowing.   Essays for the Left Hand.   Cambridge: Harvard Univ. Press, 1962.

2627. Buchen, Irving H. (ed).   The Perverse Imagination: Sexuality and Literary Culture.   NY: New York Univ. Press, 1970.

2628. Bühler, Charlotte.   Erfindung und Entdeckung: Zwei Grundbegriffe der Literaturpsychologie.   Zeitschrift für Aesthetik, 1921, 15:43-87.

2629. Bullough, Edward.   'Psychical distance' as a factor in art and aesthetic principle.   British J Psychol, 1912, 5:87-118;   In Weitz, M. (ed), Problems in Aesthetics.   NY: Macmillan, 1959, 646-656.

2630. _____.   The relation of aesthetics to psychology.   British J Psychol, 1919-20, 10:43-50.

2631. Bundy, M. W.   The theory of imagination in classical and mediaeval thought.   Univ. Illinois Studies in Language & Lit, 1927, Nos. 2-3.

2632. Büren, E. von.   Zur Bedeutung der Psychologie im Werk Robert Musils.   Zurich: Atlantis, 1970.

2633. Burgess, C. F.   The seeds of art: Henry James's 'donnée.'   Lit & Psychol, 1963, 13:67-73.

2634. Burgum, Edwin Berry.   Marxism, psychoanalysis and artistic creativity.   Studies on the Left, 1961, 1:114-119.

2635. _____.   The neoclassical period in English literature: a psychological definition.   Sewanee Rev, 1944, 52:247-265.

2636. Burke, Kenneth.   On catharsis, or resolution.   Kenyon Rev, 1959, 21:337-375.

2637. _____.   Catharsis: second view.   Centennial Rev, 1961, 5;   In Grebstein, S. N. (ed), Perspectives in Contemporary Criticism.   NY: Harper & Row, 1968, 268-283.

2638. _____.   Freud and the analysis of poetry.   Amer J Sociology, 1939, 45:391-417;   In The Philosophy of Literary Form: Studies in Symbolic Action.   Baton Rouge: Louisiana State Univ. Press, 1941, 1967, 258-292;   NY: Vintage, 1957;   In Ruitenbeek, H. M. (ed), Psychoanalysis and Literature.   NY: Dutton, 1964, 114-141.

2639. _____.   A Grammar of Motives.   Englewood Cliffs, NJ: Prentice-Hall, 1945.

2640. _____.   Language as Symbolic Action.   Essays on Life, Literature, and Method.   Berkeley: Univ. California Press, 1968;   London: Cambridge Univ. Press, 1968.

2641. _____.   The poetic process.   In Scott, W. (ed), Five Approaches to Literary Criticism.   NY: Macmillan, 1962, 75-90.

2642. _____.   Psychology and form.   Dial, 1925, 79:30-46;   In Counter-Statement.   NY: Harcourt, Brace, 1931, 38-56;

In Zabel, M. D. (ed), Literary Opinion in America, Vol. 2. Gloucester, Mass: Smith, 1968, 667-676, and NY: Harper, 1962, 667-676; In Handy, W. J., & Westbrook, M. (eds), Twentieth Century. NY: Free Press, 1974, 267-276.

2643. _____. A Rhetoric of Motives. Englewood Cliffs, NJ: Prentice-Hall, 1950.

2644. _____. The thinking of the body. Comments on the image-ry of catharsis in literature. Psychoanal Rev, 1963, 50: 375-413; In Language as Symbolic Action. Berkeley: Univ. California Press, 1966, 308-343; In Phillips, R. S. (ed), Aspects of Alice. NY: Vanguard, 1971, 340-343.

2645. Burnshaw, Stanley (ed). Varieties of Literary Experience: Eighteen Essays in World Literature. NY: New York Univ. Press, 1962.

2646. Burrow, Trigant. Psychoanalytic improvisations and the personal equation. Psychoanal Rev, 1926, 13:173-186.

2647. Burton, J. Sexuality and the mythic dimension in Pedro Páramo. Symposium, 1974, 28:228-247.

2648. Bush, Marshall. The problem of form in the psychoanalytic theory of art. Psychoanal Rev, 1967, 54:5-35.

2649. Buss, Hannelore Krannich. Goethe und Freud: Eine Unter-suchung anhand der Goethe--Zitate im Werke Sigmund Freud. DAI, 1975, 36:302A-03A.

2650. Busst, A. J. L. The image of the androgyne in the nineteenth century. In Fletcher, I. (ed), Romantic Mythologies. London: Routledge & Kegan Paul, 1967; NY: Barnes & Noble, 1967, 1-96.

2651. Butcher, Samuel Henry. Aristotle's Theory of Poetry and Fine Arts. NY: Dover, 1951.

2652. Butler, Christopher. The self in dissolution. Times Lit Sup-plement, 18 Aug 1978, no. 3985:927.

2653. Butler, Colin. Psychology and faith in Arnim's Der tolle In-valide. Studies in Romanticism, 1978, 17:149-162.

2654. Butler, Francelia, & Brockman, Bennett A. (eds). Children's Literature: The Great Excluded, Vol. 3. Storrs, Conn: Children's Lit Assn, 1974.

2655. Büttner, Ludwig. Michael Kohlhaas--eine paranoische oder heroische Gestalt. Seminar: A Journal Germanic Stud-ies, 1968, 4:26-41.

2656. Bychowski, Gustav. From catharsis to work of art: the making of an artist. In Psychoanalysis and Culture. NY: IUP, 1951, 390-409.

2657. _____. The metapsychology of artistic creation. Psycho-anal Q, 1951, 20:592-602.

2658. _____. The nature of talent. Bulletin Amer Psychoanal Assn, 1950, 6:58-63.

2659. Byrd, Max. Visits to Bedlam: Madmen and Literature in the Eighteenth Century. Columbia: Univ. South Carolina Press, 1974.

2660. Cadot, Michel, Dimić, Milan V., Malone, David, & Sza-
       bolcsi, Miklós (eds). Actes du VIe Congrès de l'Associ-
       tion Internationale de Littérature Comparée. Stuttgart:
       Bieber, 1975.

2661. Cain, J., & Naville, P. [Sade as forerunner of modern psy-
       chology.] In Le Marquis de Sade. Paris: Colin, 1968.

2662. Calhoun, R. C. Recent literary criticism. South Atlantic
       Bulletin, 1961, 27:1-6.

2663. Calhoun, Richard James. Existentialism, phenomenology, and
       literary theory. South Atlantic Bulletin, 1963, 28(4):4-8.

2664. Callan, Richard J. The archetype of psychic renewal in La
       vorágine. Hispania, 1971, 54:470-476.

2665. Calverton, V. F. Sex Expression in Literature. NY: Boni
       & Liveright, 1926.

2666. Campbell, Oscar J., Van Gundy, Justine, & Shrodes, Caro-
       line (eds). Patterns for Living. NY: Macmillan, 1947.

2667. Canetti, Elias. The Conscience of Words. NY: Continuum:
       Seabury, 1979.

2668. Cantril, Hadley, & Bumstead, Charles H. Reflections on the
       Human Venture. NY: New York Univ. Press, 1960.

2669. Capek, Milic. Stream of consciousness and 'durée réele.'
       Philosophy & Phenomenological Research, 1950, 10:331-
       353.

2670. Capone, G. [Dynamics of the unconscious in art.] Archivio
       Patologia Clinica Medica, 1961, 38:79-130.

2671. Cargill, Oscar. Intellectual America: Ideas on the March.
       NY: Macmillan, 1941.

2672. Carlsen, George Robert. Literature and emotional maturity.
       English J, 1949, 38:138-140.

2673. Carlsen, James W. Persona, personality, and performance.
       In Doyle, E. M., & Floyd, V. H. (eds), Studies in Inter-
       pretation, Vol. 2. Amsterdam: Rodopi, 1977, 221-232.

2674. Carpenter, Frederic I. American Literature and the Dreams.
       NY: Philosophical Library, 1955.

2675. Carter, Angela. The Sadeian Woman. NY: Pantheon, 1979.

2676. Carvalho, Nídia Corrêa da C. O Complexo de Edipo na Obra
       de Josué Montello. Minas Gerais, Suplemento Literário,
       28 Feb 1976, 8-9.

2677. Carver, Larry D. Domineering Phantom: A Study in the
       Representations of the Father in Restoration Literature.
       DAI, 1973, 34:2550A.

2678. Cary, Richard. Poe and the literary ladies. Texas Studies
       in Lit & Language, 1967, 9:91-101.

2679. Casebier, Allan. The concept of aesthetic distance. Per-
       sonalist, 1971, 52:70-91.

2680. Castelli, E. Il Demoniaco nell'arte. Milan: Electa Milano,
       1952.

2681. Cautela, Joseph R. Use of psychoanalysis in the study of the
       classics. Psychoanal Rev, 1960, 47:117-119.

2682. Cawelti, John G. Myth, symbol, and formula. J Popular
       Culture, 1974, 8:1-9.

2683. Cazamian, Louis. Etudes de psychologie littéraire. Paris:
       Payot, 1913.

2684. _____. L'Evolution psychologique et la littérature en Angleterre, 1600-1914. Paris: 1920.

2685. _____. La Psychanalyse et la critique littéraire. In Essai en deux langues. Paris: Didier, 1938; Rev de Littérature Comparée, 1924, 4:449-475.

2686. _____. Psycho-analysis and literary criticism. Rice Institute Pamphlets, 1924, 11:139-153.

2687. Cazaux, Jean. Surréalisme et psychologie: endophasie et écriture automatique. Lyon: José Corti, 1938.

2688. Ceccaroni, Arnaldo. Le figure e i contenuti: Sulla teoria freudiana di Francesco Orlando. Lingua e Stile, 1975, 10:493-519.

2689. Celli, John Paul. The Uses of the Term 'Archetype' in Contemporary Literary Criticism. DAI, 1975, 36:304A-05A.

2690. Cerio, Miguel Diaz de. Neurosis, religión y cultura. Indice, 1964, 17, num. 189, 25.

2691. Chabot, J. [J. Giono's Jean le Bleu.] Rev des Lettres Modernes, 1976.

2692. Chandler, Albert R. Beauty and Human Nature: Elements of Psychological Aesthetics. NY: 1934.

2693. Chapman, M. Female archetypes in Fifth Business. Canadian Lit, 1979, 80:131-136+.

2694. Charreton, P. Montherlant feministe? ou une clef pour Le Songe. Travaux III de Linguistique et de Littérature, 1972, 93-101.

2695. Chasseguet-Smirgel, Janine. Pour une psychanalyse de l'art et de la créativité. Paris: Payot, 1971; Review: Francis D. Baudry, Psychoanal Q, 1977, 46:339-341.

2696. _____. Reflexions sur le concept de réparation et la hiérarchie des actes créateurs. Rev Française de Psychanalyse, 1965, 39(1).

2697. _____. Le Tsarévitch immolé par Alain Besancon. Paris: Plon, 1967.

2698. Châtelet, Francois. L'Homme de Marx et l'homme de Freud. Nouvel Observateur, 1965, no. 26, 20-21.

2699. Chazaud, J. Psychanalyse et créativité culturelle. Toulouse: Privat, 1971.

2700. Chemain-Degrange, Arlette. Emancipation féminine et littérature négro-africaine (poésie et roman). Annales de l'Université de Brazzaville, 1973, 9:3-21.

2701. Chen Chong-Keng. Some psychopathological thoughts in the Book of Tso Chuen. Acta Psychologica Sinica, 1963, 23: 156-164.

2702. Chernush, A. Madness file. Columbia Forum, 1974, 3:40-42.

2703. Cheskis, J. I. The problem of eternal punishment in Jean-Jacques Rousseau. Open Court, 1921, 35:167-171.

2704. Chesterton, Gilbert K. The game of psychoanalysis. Century, 1923, 106:34-43.

2705. Chicoteau, M. Les Attributs de l'éphectisme grec et leur survivance dans une cosmologie racinienne. Cardiff, 1943, 8:1-14.

2706. Choisy, Maryse. Le Fils d'l'amazone. Psyché, 1957, 11: 337-340.

2707. _____. Liberté ou engagement. Niéme meditation sur la littérature. Psyché, 1949, 4:194-221.

2708. Charon, Jacques. Discussion of L. J. Friedman, 'From Gradiva to the death instinct?' Psychoanal Forum, 1966, 1:59.

2709. Chouinard, Timothy. The symbol and the archetype in analytical psychology and literary criticism. J Analytical Psychol, 1970, 15(2):155-164.

2710. Christensen, Erik M. Den blicherske tolkning. Kritik, 1967, 4.

2711. Chu, K. T. [The Psychology of Literature and Arts.] Shanghai: Kai Ming, 1937.

2712. Cinca, Stelian. Posibilitati de interpretare psihoanalitica a operei lui Gib, I. Mihaescu. Philologica, 1970, 1:143-150.

2713. Cioran, Samuel David. A prism for the absolute: the symbolic colors of Andre Bely. In Janecek, G. (ed), Andre Bely; A Critical Review. Lexington: Univ. Kentucky Press, 1978, 103-114.

2714. Cismaru, Alfred, & Klein, Theodore. The concept of suicide in Camus and Beckett. Renascence, 1976, 28:105-110.

2715. Clancier, Georges-Emmanuel. Psychanalyse, littérature et critique. La Nef: Cahier Trimestriel, 1967, 24:101-110.

2716. Clancier-Gravelat, Anne. Psychanalyse et critique littéraire. Information Psychologique, 1970, 10:28-39.

2717. _____. Psychanalyse et critique littéraire. Toulouse: Privat, 1973.

2718. Clark, Arthur. Studies in Literary Modes. London: Oliver, 1958.

2719. Clark, William Bedford. The serpent of lust in the southern garden. Southern Rev, 1974, 10:805-822.

2720. Clasen, H. Über Schillers psychologische Anschauungen. In Oberreal- und Landwirtschaftsschule in Flensburg; Jahresbericht 1906-07. Flensburg, 1907.

2721. Clayborough, Arthur. The Grotesque in English Literature. Oxford: Clarendon, 1965; Review: Michael Steig, Lit & Psychol, 1967, 17:60-63.

2722. Cleckley, Hervey. The Caricature of Love: A Discussion of Social, Psychiatric and Literary Manifestations of Pathologic Sexuality. NY: Ronald Press, 1957.

2723. Clément, Pierre-Paul. Jean-Jacques Rousseau: de l'éros coupable à l'éros glorieux. Neuchâtel: Baconnière, 1976.

2724. Closs, A. Dichter und Dichtung im Wandel der gegenwart Welthldes. Antaios, 1964-65, 6:527-536.

2725. Clough, Wilson O. Psychology and the art of literature. Educational Forum, 1967, 31:173-179.

2726. Cloutier, Cécile. Le Symbole en littérature et en psychanalyse. Rev de l'Université d'Ottawa, 1965, 35:207-212.

2727. Coburn, Kathleen (ed). The Notebooks of Samuel Taylor Coleridge, 2 Vols. London: Routledge & Kegan Paul, 1957, 1962; Vol. 1, 1078, 1620, 1726; Vol. 2, 2064, 2073, 2080, 2559.

2728. Cockerham, Harry. Gautier: from hallucination to supernatural vision. Yale French Studies, 1974, 50:42-54.

2729. Cocking, John M. La Nouvelle critique. Southern Rev, 1969, 5:1069-1090.

2730. Coggins, K. Introversion and the appreciation of literature. Amer J Psychol, 1943, 55:560-561.

2731. Cohen, Gustave. Montaigne et la psychanalyse. Psyché, 1951, 6:224-232.

2732. Cohen, Larry L. Freudian symbol-hunting: for men only? CEA Critic, 1971, 34:1.

2733. Cohen, Miriam Myra. Arthur Schnitzler: with Special Reference to the Characterization of Women in the 'Erzählende Schriften.' Master's thesis, Univ. Birmingham, 1935.

2734. Cohn, Alice. The Concept of Death in the Works of Arthur Schnitzler. Master's Thesis, Columbia Univ., 1947.

2735. Cohn, Jan, & Miles, Thomas H. The sublime in alchemy, aesthetics and psychoanalysis. Modern Philology, 1977, 74:289-304.

2736. Coimbra Martins, A. [Queirós' treatment of sexual relationships.] Bulletin des Etudes Portugaises, 1967-68, 28-29: 287-325; In Ensaios Queirosianos. Lisbon: Europa-América, 1967.

2737. Coleridge, Samuel T. Lectures and Notes on Shakespeare and Other English Poets. London: Bell, 1884.

2738. Colletti, Giovanni. Psicologia o filosofia in Bergson? Sophia, 1964, 320-331.

2739. Collins, Joseph. Idling in Italy: Studies of Literature and of Life. NY: Scribner, 1920.

2740. _____. Taking the Literary Pulse; Psychological Studies of Life and Literature. NY: Doran, 1934.

2741. Collins, Margery L., & Pierce, Christine. Holes and slime: sexism in Sartre's psychoanalysis. In Gould, C.C., & Wartofsky, M.W. (eds), Women and Philosophy; Toward a Theory of Liberation. NY: Putnam, 1976, 112-127.

2742. Collins, Terence George. A Psychoanalytic Introduction to Reader Response to Racial Literature. DAI, 1976, 37: 3611A.

2743. Coltrera, Joseph T. On the creation of beauty and thought: the unique as vicissitude. JAPA, 1965, 13:634-703.

2744. Comes, Salvatore. Interpretazione dell'adolescenza. Quaderni Dannunziani, 1965, 30-31:101-117.

2745. Comfort, Alex. Darwin and the Naked Lady: Discursive Essays on Biology and Art. NY: Braziller, 1962.

2746. Comoth, René. Psychanalyse et critique littéraire: Le cas Pavese. Marche Romane, 1969, 19:88-90.

2747. Conchon, Georges. Psychanalyse et création romanesque. Table Ronde, 1956, 108:150-156.

2748. Connolly, Francis X. Literary consciousness and literary conscience. Thought, 1950, 25:663-680.

2749. Conty, J.M. Artistes, économie et culpabilité. Psyché, 1948, 506-513.

2750. Copelman, L., Cantacuzene, J., & Zamfiresco, I. [The reflections of psychiatry in the mirror of world literature.] Annales Médico-Psychologiques, 1961, 119:316-322.

2751. Corbière-Gille, Gisèle. Les Bas-bleus et le féminisme. Rev des Lettres Modernes, 1973, nos. 351-354, 119-124.
2752. Corção, Gustavo. O Desconcêrto do Mundo. Rio de Janeiro: Agir, 1965.
2753. Cornford, F. M. The unconscious element in literature and philosophy. Proceedings Classical Assn, 1922.
2754. Cornwell, Ethel F. Decreasing aesthetic distance: the problem of universality. West Virginia Univ. Bulletin: Philological Papers, 1973, 20:47-55.
2755. Corrêa, Paulo Dias. O mistério da criação literária. Acaiaca, 1948, 1:11.
2756. Corrigan, Matthew. Phenomenology and Literary Criticism: A Definition and an Application. DAI, 1971, 31:4761A.
2757. Costa, S. A., & Mavaro, G. Rassegna analitica dei motivi e dei personaggi. In Problemi di critica verghiana. Florence: Le Monnier, 1971, 513-546.
2758. Cournut, Jean. De l'Ecriture à l'inscription ou le scribe de l'inconscient. Rev Française de Psychanalyse, 1974, 38(1):57-73.
2759. _____. La Machine à écrire. Etudes freudiennes, 1970, 3-4.
2760. _____. Les Trois recommandations. Etudes freudiennes, 1975, 9-10.
2761. _____. Si je n'était que moi. Etudes freudiennes, 1976, 11-12.
2762. Court, Franklin E. Pater and the subject of duality. English Lit in Transition (1880-1920), 1972, 15:21-35.
2763. Coveney, Peter. Poor Monkey. The Child in Literature. London: Rockliff, 1957.
2764. Cowley, Malcolm. The Literary Situation. NY: Viking, 1954.
2765. _____. Marginalia. New Republic, 1952, 126:17-18.
2766. _____. Psychoanalysis and writers. Harper's Magazine, 1954, 209:87-93.
2767. _____. Rebels, artists, and scoundrels. In And I Worked at the Writer's Trade; Chapters in Literary History, 1918-1978. NY: Viking, 1978, 249-266.
2768. _____. Young Mr. Elkins. Broom, 1922, 4:55.
2769. Cox, Stephen D. 'The Stranger within Thee': The Self in British Literature of the Later Eighteenth Century. DAI, 1976, 37:2193A-94A.
2770. Craig, George. Reading: who is doing what to whom? In Josipovici, G. (ed), The Modern English Novel: The Reader, the Writer and the Work. NY: Barnes & Noble, 1976.
2771. Craig, Hardin. The Enchanted Glass. The Elizabethan Mind in Literature. NY: Oxford Univ. Press, 1936, 233-237.
2772. Crämer, Rudolf. Thomas Manns Reaktion und Psychoanalyse. Heidelberg Student, 1929, 15:36.
2773. Crane, R. S. The Languages of Criticism and the Structure of Poetry. Toronto: Univ. Toronto Press, 1953, 128-138.
2774. Cranston, M. Jean-Paul Sartre. Encounter, 1962, 18:34-45.

2775. Craven, T. J. The Freudian incubus. Dial, 1922, 73:104-105.

2776. Crawford, N. A. Literature and the psychopathic. Psychoanal Rev, 1923, 10:441.

2777. Crawshaw, William H. Literary Interpretations of Life. NY: Macmillan, 1900.

2778. Creeley, Robert. Sparrow 6. Los Angeles: Black Sparrow Press, 1973.

2779. Cremerius, Johannes, & Urban, Bernd. Die Literaten und Sigmund Freud. Die Rezeption der Psychoanalyse durch deutschsprachige Dichter und Schriftsteller in der ersten Jahrhünderthälfte. Frankfurt: Fischer, 1979.

2780. Cretulescu, Ioana. Psihanaliza si literatura sau seductie si risc. Virittajä: Rev de Kotikielen Seura, 1971, 23(6): 92-96.

2781. Crew, Louie, & Norton, Rictor. The homophobic imagination: an editorial. College English, 1974, 36:272-290.

2782. Crews, Frederick C. Can literature be psychoanalyzed. In Out of My System: Psychoanalysis, Ideology and Critical Method. NY: Oxford Univ. Press, 1975, 1966.

2783. _____. Literature and psychology. In Thorpe, J. (ed), Relations of Literary Study. NY: Modern Language Assn, 1967, 73-87.

2784. _____. Love in the western world. Partisan Rev, 1967, 34:272-287.

2785. _____. Out of My System: Psychoanalysis, Ideology and Critical Method. NY: Oxford Univ. Press, 1975.

2786. _____. The Pooh Perplex. NY: Dutton, 1965, 124-137.

2787. _____. Psychoanalysis and Literary Process. Cambridge, Mass: Winthrop, 1970; Reviews: Leonard F. Manheim, Criticism, 1971, 13:209-213; S. Smith, Contemporary Psychol, 1971, 16:207-210.

2788. _____. Reductionism and its discontents. Critical Inquiry, 1975, 1:543-558.

2789. Cronin, M. Hawthorne on romantic love and the status of women. PMLA, 1954, 69:89-98.

2790. Crouzet, Michel. Psychanalyse et culture littéraire. Revue d'histoire littéraire de la France, 1970, 884-917.

2791. Cruickshank, John. Psychocriticism and literary judgement. British J Aesthetics, 1964, 4:155-159.

2792. Cruttwell, Patrick. Physiology and psychology in Shakespeare's age. J Historical Ideas, 1951, 12:75-80.

2793. Cuenat, P. Littérature et sexualité. Documents et recherches-lettres, 1973, 2:25-27.

2794. Cunliffe, W. G. Existentialist elements in Frisch's work. Monatshefte, 1970, 62:113-123.

2795. Curatorium of the C. G. Jung Institute (ed). Evil. Evanston, Ill: Northwestern Univ. Press, 1967.

2796. Currie, R. Hector. The energies of tragedy: cosmic and psychic. Centennial Rev, 1967, 11:220-236.

2797. Currier, Barbara. The Gift of Personality: An Appraisal of 'Impressionist Criticism.' DAI, 1973, 33:5673A.

2798. Da Cal, Ernesto Guerra. Da ambiguidade psicológica em
       Lusco-Frisco. Colóquio/Letras, 1974, 20:47-53.
2799. Daemmrich, Horst S. Lituraturkritik in Theorie und Praxis.
       Munich: Francke, 1974.
2800. D'Agostino, V. Locuzioni cesarians relative al mondo dello
       spirito. Archivio Italiano di Psicologia, 1935, 13:39-56.
2801. Dahlberg, Edward. The Carnal Myth: A Search into Classi-
       cal Sensuality. NY: Weybright & Talley, 1968.
2802. Daiches, David. Criticism and psychology. In Critical Ap-
       proaches to Literature. Englewood Cliffs, NJ: Prentice-
       Hall, 1956, 340-357.
2803. _____. Shakespearean criticism and scholarship. In
       Critical Approaches to Literature. London: Longmans,
       1956, 336-338.
2804. Daly, Claude D. The mother complex in literature. Samik-
       sa, 1947, 1:157-190; In The Yearbook of Psychoanalysis,
       Vol. 4. NY: IUP, 1948, 172-210; In Ruitenbeek, H. M.
       (ed), Homosexuality and Creative Genius. NY: Astor-
       Honor, 1967.
2805. Danks, K. B. The bibliographical and psychological fallacies
       in Pollard's second proposition. Notes & Queries, 1959,
       6:439-440.
2806. Da Ponte, Durant. James Agee: the quest for identity.
       Tennessee Studies in Lit, 1963, 8:25-37.
2807. d'Arch Smith, Timothy (ed). Love in Earnest. London:
       Routledge & Kegan Paul, 1971.
2808. David, Christian. Ecriture, sexe, bisexualité. Nouvelle
       Rev de Psychanalyse, 1977, 16.
2809. _____. Une Littérature sans écrivain ni textes. Rev
       Française de Psychanalyse, 1974, 38(1):131-135.
2810. David, E. Literature and psychology. In Eysenck, H. J.,
       et al. (eds), Encyclopedia of Psychology. NY: Seabury,
       1979, 602-607.
2811. David, Michel. La critica psicoanalitica. In Corti, M., &
       Segre, C. (eds), I metodi attuali della critica in Italia.
       Turin: ERT, 1970.
2812. _____. Letteratura e psicoanalisi. Milan: Mursia, 1967.
2813. _____. La psicoanalisi nella cultura italiana. Turin:
       Boringhieri, 1966.
2814. _____. Psychoanalytic criticism in Italy. Gradiva, 1976,
       1(1):65-75.
2815. David-Schwarz, H. Der Typus der 'weissen Frau' im Werk
       Eduard von Keyserlings. Psychologische Rundschau, 1931,
       1:367-370.
2816. Davidson, Cathy N., & Broner, E. M. (eds). The Lost Tra-
       dition: Mothers and Daughters in Literature. NY: Un-
       gar, 1980.
2817. Davis, David Brion. Violence in American literature. An-
       nals Amer Academy, 1966, 364:28-36.
2818. Davis, Robert Gorham. Art and anxiety. Partisan Rev,
       1945, 12:310-321; In Phillips, W. (ed), Art and Psycho-
       analysis. Cleveland: World, 1963.
2819. _____. The perilous balance. Hudson Rev, 1963, 16:280-
       289.

2820. Davis, Robin R. Literature and woman's body. Paunch, 1978, 52:55-66.

2821. Dease, Barbara C. 'Negritude' and the Mythopoeic Quest in Black Literature of French Expression. DAI, 1977, 37: 7741-7742.

2822. Debidour, V. -H. Le Rêve dans la littérature française. Bulletin des Lettres, 1951, 126:263-270.

2823. DeBoer, John James. Literature and human behavior. English J, 1950, 39:76-82; Education Digest, 1950, 39:76-82;

2824. De Busscher, Jacques. L'Influence de la doctrine psychanalytique en littérature. J Belge de Neurologie et de Psychiatrie, 1929, 29:619-629.

2825. De Gain, Philippe. Voltaire et les femmes. DAI, 1973, 34: 1900A-01A.

2826. Delacroix, Henri. Psychologie de l'art. Paris: Alcan, 1907.

2827. Delage, Yves. La Rêve dans la littérature moderne. Rev Philosophique, 1916, 81:209-274.

2828. Delbouille, Paul. Carl-Gustav Jung et la psychanalyse littéraire. Cahiers d'Analyse Textuelle, 1964, 6:7-22.

2829. Deleito y Piñuela, José. El sentimento de tristeza en la literatura contemporánea. Barcelona: Minerva, 1922.

2830. Deleuze, Gilles. Le Schizophrène et le mot. Critique (Paris), 1968, 24:255-256, 731-746.

2831. _____, & Guattari, Felix. Psychoanalysis and ethnology. Sub-stance, 1975, 11-12:170-197.

2832. De Lutri, J. R. Rimbaud and Fournier: the end of the quest. Romance Notes, 1977, 18:153-156.

2833. De Man, Paul. Blindness and Insight: Essays in the Rhetoric of Contemporary Criticism. NY: Oxford Univ. Press, 1971.

2834. Dembo, L. S. Dissent and dissent: a look at Fiedler and Trilling. In Malin, I. (ed), Contemporary American-Jewish Literature. Bloomington: Indiana Univ. Press, 1973, 134-155.

2835. Demel, Helmut. Der Traum bei Gottfried Keller. Doctoral dissertation, Innsbruck, 1954.

2836. Demetrakopoulos, Stephanie. Anaïs Nin and the feminine quest for consciousness: the quelling of the devouring mother and ascension of Sophia. Bucknell Rev, 1978, 24:119-136.

2837. Demole, V. Rôle du tempérament et des idées délirantes de Rousseau dans la genèse de ses principales théories. Annales Médico-Psychologiques, 1922, 1:12-34.

2838. DeMott, Benjamin. 'But he's a homosexual....' In Supergrow; Essays and Reports on Imagination in America. NY: Dutton, 1969, 17-34.

2839. Denis, Anne-Marie. Psychanalyse de la raison chez Gaston Bachelard. Rev Philosophique de Louvain, 1963, 61:644-663.

2840. Derla, Luigi. Joseph de Maistre e l'irrazionalismo. Studi Francesi, 1971, 15:238-253.

2841. Derrida, Jacques. Coming into one's own. In Hartman, G. H. (ed), Psychoanalysis and the Question of the Text. Baltimore: Johns Hopkins Univ. Press, 1978, 114-148.

2842. _____. Le Facteur de la verité. Poétique, 1975, 21:96-
147; Yale French Studies, 1975, 52:31-113.
2843. _____. Freud and the scene of writing. In Writing and
Difference. Chicago: Univ. Chicago Press, 1978, 196-
231; In L'Ecriture et la différence. Paris: Seuil, 1967,
293-340; Yale French Studies, 1972, 48:74-117.
2844. Dervin, Daniel A. D. H. Lawrence and Freud. Amer Imago,
1979, 36:95-117.
2845. _____. Michael Balint's contributions to the psychoanalysis of literature. Psychoanal Rev, 1979-80, 66:553-570.
2846. DeSalvo, Louise. Literature and sexuality. Education Digest,
1979, 45:48-60.
2847. Deshaeis, Gabriel. Psychologie d'une simulation. L'Hygiène
Mentale, 1948, 37(6):80-92.
2848. Desideri, Gionavanella (ed). Psicoanalisis e critica letteraria. Rome: Riunit, 1975.
2849. Desroches, Richard H. Pre-Romantic melancholy and the
philosophic mind: an unusual rationalization of suicide.
Pacific Coast Philology, 1968, 3:24-30.
2850. Dessoir, Max. Das Doppel-Ich. Leipzig: Gunthers, 1890,
1896.
2851. Dettmering, Peter. Dichtung und Psychoanalyse. I. Thomas
Mann, Rainer Maria Rilke, Richard Wagner. Munich:
Nymphenburger, 1969.
2852. _____. Dichtung und Psychoanalyse. II. Shakespeare--
Goethe--Jean Paul--Doderer. Munich: Nymphenburger,
1974.
2853. _____. [Psychoanalysis as a tool in the study of literature.] Psyche, 1973, 27:601-613.
2854. Deutelbaum, Wendy. Epistemology and Fantasmatics in the
Psychoanalytic Criticism of Charles Mauron and Norman
Holland. DAI, 1978, 39:2234A.
2855. Deutsch, Helene. The Psychology of Women, 2 Vols. NY:
Grune & Stratton, 1944.
2856. Devereux, George. Art and mythology: a general theory.
In Kaplan, B. (ed), Studying Personality Cross-Culturally.
Evanston, Ill: Row, Peterson, 1961, 361-386.
2857. _____. The structure of tragedy and the structure of
psyche in Aristotle's Poetics. In Hanly, C., & Lazero-
witz, M. (eds), Psychoanalysis and Philosophy. NY:
IUP, 1971, 46-75.
2858. De Voto, Bernard. Freud in American literature. Psychoanal Q, 1940, 9:236-245.
2859. _____. Freud's influence on literature. Saturday Rev,
1939, 20:10-11.
2860. _____. Wanted: an umpire; a psychoanalytic study of
literature. Harper's Magazine, 1950, 200:60-63.
2861. DeWaelhens, Alphonse. Inconscient, sujet, vérité. Rev
Philosophique de Louvain, 1974, 72:268-283.
2862. Diamond, Arlyn, and Edwards, Lee R. (eds). The Authority
of Experience. Essays in Feminist Criticism. Amherst:
Univ. Massachusetts Press, 1977.

2863. Díaz, Janet Winecroff. The Major Themes of Existentialism in the Work of Ortega y Gasset. Chapel Hill: Univ. North Carolina Press, 1970.

2864. Di Candia, Severino. Presenza della psicoanalisi nella letteratura americana. Parrucca, 1962, 7(1):312-313.

2865. Dickie, George. Bullough and Casebier: disappearing in the distance. Personalist, 1972, 53:127-131.

2866. _____. I. A. Richards's phantom double. British J Aesthetics, 1968, 8:54-59.

2867. Didier, Béatrice. Le Journal intime. Paris: Presses Universitaire de France, 1976.

2868. _____. Sade dramaturge de ses carceri. Nouvelle Rev Française, 1970, 216:72-80.

2869. Dieckhöfer, K. Die Epilepsie im Zitat der römanischen Schriftsteller Plautus, Seneca und Apuleius. Confinia Psychiatria, 1972, 15:212-219.

2870. Diéguez, Manuel de. Brief biography of an idea: the existential psychoanalysis of style. A letter to an American friend. In Strelka, J. P. (ed), Patterns of Literary Style. University Park: Penn State Univ. Press, 1971, 15-41.

2871. Diehl, Joanne Feit. Emerson, Dickinson, and the abyss. J English Lit History, 1977, 44:683-700.

2872. Diener, Gottfried. Goethe's Lila. Heilung eines 'Wahsinns' durch 'psychische Kur.' Vergleichende Interpretation der drei Fassungen. Frankfurt: Athenäum, 1971.

2873. Dierick, Augustine P. Epiphany shared: an interpretation of Hofmannsthal's Raoul Richter, 1896. Modern Language Rev, 1979, 74:349-360.

2874. Diersch, Manfred. Empiriokritizismus und Impressionismus. Über Beziehungen zwischen Philosophie, Asthetik und Literatur um 1900 in Wien. Berlin: Rütten & Loening, 1973.

2875. Dietrichson, Jan W. The literary criticism of Richard Chase. Edda, 1973, 6:345-360.

2876. Diéz, Luis A. Three conversations and one monologue on human failure. World Lit Today, 1978, 52:63-67.

2877. Dijkstra, Bram. Androgyne in nineteenth-century art and literature. Comparative Lit, 1974, 26:62-73.

2878. Dillingham, Louise B. The Creative Imagination of Théophile Gautier: A Study in Literary Psychology. Princeton: Princeton Univ. Press, 1927; Psychol Monographs, 1927, 37:1-355.

2879. Dillman, Richard H. The psychological rhetoric of Walden. Emerson Society Q, 1979, 25:79-91.

2880. Dimitroff, Michaïl. [Psychoanalytic interpretation of artistic creativity.] Annals Univ. Sofia, 1933.

2881. Diserens, C. M., & Wood, T. W. Psychophysiological behavior under various types of literature. J Abnormal Social Psychol, 1936, 30:484-501.

2882. Di Tommaso, Andrea. Insania and Furor: a diagnostic note on Orlando's malady. Romance Notes, 1973, 14:583-588.

2883. Dobiásová, L. Literárne psychologická studie o strachu ze smrti--I. cást. Ceskoslovenska Psychiatrie, 1977, 73:344-352.

2884. Doederlein, Sue W.   A Compendium of Wit: The Psychologi-
       cal Vocabulary of John Dryden's Literary Criticism.
       DAI, 1971, 31:3542A.
2885. Donadio, Stephen.   Nietzsche, Henry James, and the Artistic
       Will.   NY: Oxford Univ. Press, 1978.
2886. Donaldson, Scott, & Massa, Ann.   Dreams and nightmares.
       In American Literature: Nineteenth and Early Twentieth
       Centuries.   NY: Barnes & Noble, 1978, 81-119.
2887. Donato, Eugenio.   Ruins of memory: archaeological frag-
       ments and textual artifacts.   MLN, 1978, 93:575-596.
2888. Donnelly, Mabel Collins.   Freud and literary criticisms.
       College English, 1953, 15:155-158.
2889. Donop, W.R.   Archetypal vision in Hofmannsthal's Reiter-
       geschichte.   German Life & Letters, 1969, 22:126-133.
2890. Doob, P.B.   Nebuchadnezzar's Children: Conventions of Mad-
       ness in Middle English Literature.   New Haven: Yale
       Univ. Press, 1974; Doctoral dissertation, Stanford Univ.,
       1969.
2891. Dooley, D.J.   Freudian critics.   Triumph, 1974, 9(2):34-39.
2892. Dorfman, A.   Imaginación y violencia en América.   Santiago:
       Universitaria, 1970.
2893. Downey, June E.   Creative Imagination.   Studies in the Psy-
       chology of Literature.   NY: Harcourt, Brace, 1929.
2894. _____.   Literary self-projections.   Psychol Rev, 1912,
       19:299-311.
2895. _____.   Literary synesthesia.   J Philosophy, 1912, 9:490-
       498.
2896. _____.   A program for a psychology of literature.   J Ap-
       plied Psychol, 1918, 2:366-377.
2897. Downing, Christine.   Towards an erotics of the psyche.
       Amer Academy of Religion J, 1976, 44:629-638.
2898. Doyle, L.F.   Hounds of Freud.   America, 1946, 75:501-502.
2899. Dracoulidès, N.N.   Créativité de l'artiste psychanalyse.
       Acta Psychotherapeutica et Psychosomatica, 1964, 12:391-
       401.
2900. _____.   Interpretation psychanalytique de pseudonyme.
       Nea Estia, 1943, Mar. 1.
2901. _____.   La Littérature paresthetique.   Proïa, 25-26 Sept
       1943.
2902. _____.   Psychanalyse de l'artiste et son oeuvre.   Gen-
       eva: Action et Pensée, 1952.
2903. _____.   Regression infantile et littérature moderne.   Bul-
       letin de l'APB, 1951, No. 13, 19.
2904. Drake, Patricia.   Grillparzer and the dream.   Modern Lan-
       guage Q, 1951, 12:72-85.
2905. Dreaney, Kent Edward.   Language of Dream/Dream of Lan-
       guage: A Study of the Logic of the Subjective Experience
       in the Works of Charles Nodier.   DAI, 1977, 38:2160A.
2906. Drevdah, J.E., & Cattell, R.B.   Personality and creativity
       in artists and writers.   J Clinical Psychol, 1958, 14:
       107-111.
2907. Dreyfus, Dina.   De Freud à Sartre.   Anhembi, 1951, 1:190-
       198.

2908.   Dubouchet, Jeanne. Le Monde physique symbole du psychis-
        me individuel. Cahiers Internationaux de Symbolisme,
        1967, 13:19-31.
2909.   Dubujadoux, G. Les Lettres françaises et l'inconscient.
        Mercure de France, 1924, 159:577-611.
2910.   Dudek, Louis. The psychology of literature. Canadian Lit,
        1977, 72:5-20.
2911.   Dufort, Robert H. A suggested approach to the study of
        utopian writings by the psychologist. J Psychol, 1965,
        60:25-30.
2912.   Dufrenne, Mikel. Critique littéraire et phénoménologie.
        Rev Internationale de Philosophie, 1964, 18:193-308.
2913.   Dugas, L. Les Timides dans la littérature. Paris: 1925.
2914.   Dumesnil, G. Psychologie des poètes. Nouvelle Nouvelle
        Rev Française, 1899, 119:609-626.
2915.   Duncan, Catherine, & Peraldi, François. Discourse of the
        erotic--the erotic in the discourse. Meanjin Q, 1974,
        33:62-71.
2916.   Durán, Gloria. ¿Baroja, antifeminista? Insula, 1972, 308-
        309.
2917.   Durr, R. A. Poetic Vision and the Psychedelic Experience.
        Syracuse: Syracuse Univ. Press, 1970.

2918.   Eastman, Max. The Literary Mind: Its Place in an Age of
        Science. NY: Scribner's, 1931.
2919.   Eben, E. Karl Kraus und die Psychiatrie. Ein Essay.
        Confinia Psychiatria, 1979, 22:9-18.
2920.   Echeruo, Michael J. C. The Conditioned Imagination from
        Shakespeare to Conrad. NY: Holmes & Meier, 1978.
2921.   Echeverri Mejía. Porfirio Barba Jacob: Cabellero de la
        angustia. La Estafeta Literaria, 1967, 364.
2922.   Eck, Marcel. L'Homme et l'angoisse. Paris: Fayard,
        1964.
2923.   Eckhert, Mary Ellen. Astrology and Humors in the Theory
        of Man: The Works of Marin Cureau de la Chambre and
        Their Importance in the Cultural Evolution of the Seven-
        teenth Century. DAI, 1975, 36:923A.
2924.   Eco, Umberto. The Role of the Reader: Explorations in the
        Semiotics of Texts. Bloomington: Indiana Univ. Press,
        1979.
2925.   Edel, Leon. Criticism and psychoanalysis: notes on the two
        disciplines. Chicago Rev, 1961, 15:100-109.
2926.   _____. Literary criticism and psychoanalysis. Contempo-
        rary Psychol, 1965, 1:51-63.
2927.   _____. Literature and psychiatry. In Arieti, S. (ed),
        American Handbook of Psychiatry, I: The Foundations of
        Psychiatry. NY: Basic Books, 1974, 1024-1033.
2928.   _____. Literature and psychology. In Stallknecht, N. P.,
        & Frenz, H. (eds), Comparative Literature. Method and
        Perspective. Carbondale: Southern Illinois Univ. Press,
        1961, 1971, 122-144; London: Feffer & Simons, 1971,
        122-144.

2929.　　　　　. The madness of art. Amer J Psychiat, 1975, 32:1005-1012.
2930.　　　　　. Notes on the use of psychological tools in literary scholarship. Lit & Psychol, 1951, 1(4):1-3.
2931.　　　　　. Portrait of the artist as an old man. Amer Scholar, 1977-78, 47(1):52-68.
2932.　　　　　. Psychoanalysis and the 'creative' arts. In Marmor, J. (ed), Modern Psychoanalysis. New Directions and Perspectives. NY: Basic Books, 1968, 626-641.
2933.　　　　　. Walden: the myth and the mystery. Amer Scholar, 1975, 44:272-281.
2934. Edelheit, Henry. Mythopoiesis and the primal scene. In The Psychoanalytic Study of Society, Vol. 5. NY: IUP, 1972, 212-233.
2935. Edie, James M. Sartre as phenomenologist and as existential psychoanalyst. In Lee, E. N., & Mandebaum, M. H. (eds), Phenomenology and Existentialism. Baltimore: Johns Hopkins Univ. Press, 1967, 139-178.
2936. Editorial. Literature and psychiatry. Canadian Medical Assn J, 1962, 87:1290.
2937.　　　　　. Literature and sexual inversion. Urology & Cutaneous Rev, 1933, 37:920-921.
2938. Edwards, A. S. G. Lydgate's attitudes to women. English Studies, 1971, 51:436-437.
2939. Edwards, G. Grimeses. Essays in Criticism, 1977, 27:122-140.
2940. Eger, Barbara Frame. Supernatural and Apparently Supernatural Elements in the Works of Arthur Schnitzler. DAI, 1971, 32:2682A.
2941. Ehrenpreis, Irvin. Meaning: implicit and explicit. In Harth, J. P. (ed), New Approaches to Eighteenth-Century Literature. NY: Columbia Univ. Press, 1974, 117-155.
2942. Ehrenreich, Alfred. T. E. Lawrence, The Mint--ein psychologischen Problem. Neueren Sprachen, 1956, 348-352.
2943. Ehrenstein, W. Der Dichterpsycholog und der Fachpsycholog. Zeitschrift für pädagogische Psychologie, 1930, 31:305-318.
2944. Ehrenzweig, Anton. The Hidden Order of Art. A Study in the Psychology of Artistic Imagination. Berkeley: Univ. California Press, 1967, 1979.
2945.　　　　　. The Psycho-Analysis of Artistic Vision and Hearing: An Introduction to a Theory of Unconscious Perception. NY: Braziller, 1965; NY: Julian, 1953.
2946.　　　　　. Unconscious form-creation in art. British J Medical Psychol, 1948, 21:88-109; 1949, 22:185-214.
2947.　　　　　. The undifferentiated matrix of artistic imagination. In Muensterberger, W., & Axelrad, S. (eds), The Psychoanalytic Study of Society, Vol. 3. NY: IUP, 1972, 373-398.
2948. Ehrlich, Victor. Reading conscious and unconscious. College English, 1975, 36:766-775.
2949. Ehrmann, Jacques. Introduction to Gaston Bachelard. Modern Language Notes, 1966, 81:572-578.

2950. Eiseley, Loren. Darwin, Coleridge and the theory of unconscious creation. Library Chronicle, 1965, 31:7-22; Daedalus, 1965, 94:588-602.

2951. Eisler, R. Der Fisch als Sexualsymbol. Imago, 1914, 3:
165-196.

2952. Eissler, Kurt R. The relation of explaining and understand-
ing in psychoanalysis: demonstrated by one aspect of
Freud's approach to literature. In The Psychoanalytic
Study of the Child, Vol. 23. NY: IUP, 1968, 141-177.

2953. _____. Remarks on an aspect of creativity. Amer Imago,
1978, 35:59-76.

2954. Ekelund, L. Rabbe Enckell, Modernism och klassicism.
Stockholm: Wahlström & Widstrand, 1974.

2955. Ekman, Tore. Die Psychoanalyse als literarische Forschungs-
methode. Zeitschrift Fronten, 1932.

2956. Eldridge, G. The 'mind distrest': literary allusions in Benjamin Rush's Diseases of the Mind. Lit & Psychol, 1966,
16:93-102.

2957. El Koli, A. [Psychology and literature.] Egyptian J Psychol, 1945, 1:36-51.

2958. Elliott, George P. The enemies of intimacy. Harper's,
1980, 261:50-56.

2959. Elliott, Susan M. A new critical epistemology. Hartford
Studies in Lit, 1975, 7:170-189.

2960. Ellis, Havelock. The Colour-Sense in Literature. London:
Ulysses Book Shop, 1931.

2961. _____. The Genius of Europe. London: Williams & Norgate, 1950.

2962. Ellman, Richard (ed). The Artist as Critic: Critical Writings of Oscar Wilde. NY: Vintage, 1970; Review:
Robert Keefe, Hartford Studies in Lit, 1972, 4:81-86.

2963. _____, & Feidelson, Charles, Jr. (eds). The unconscious.
In The Modern Tradition. Backgrounds of Modern Literature. NY: Oxford Univ. Press, 1965, 539-613.

2964. Ellmann, Mary. Thinking about Women. NY: Harcourt
Brace Jovanovich, 1968.

2965. Embeita, M. Personajes femeninos en la obra de Baroja.
La Estafeta Literaria.

2966. Emden, Cecil Stuart. Dr. Johnson's attitude to women.
Quarterly Rev, 1966, 304:419-430.

2967. Emerson, L. E. Emerson and Freud: a study in contrasts.
Psychoanal Rev, 1933, 20:208-214.

2968. Emery, L. Rousseau and the foundations of human regener-
acy. Yale French Studies, 1961-62, 28:3-12.

2969. Empson, William. Emotions in words again. Kenyon Rev,
1948, 10:579-601.

2970. _____. Seven Types of Ambiguity. NY: Meridian, 1953;
NY: Noonday, 1955 (1931).

2971. _____. Some Versions of Pastoral. London: Chatto &
Windus, 1935.

2972. Emrich, Wilhelm. Kritisches und mythisch dirigiertes Bewusstsein. Neue Deutsche Hefte, 1964, 98:5-22.

2973. _____. The Literary Revolution and Modern Society and
Other Essays. NY: Ungar, 1971, 1-27.

2974.   . Die Literaturrevolution und die moderne Gesell-
              schaft. In Protest und Verheissung. Frankfurt: Athen-
              äum.
2975.   Enachescu, Constantin. [Some psychopathologic aspects of
              the plastic arts and literature.] Neurologia, Psihiatria,
              Neurochirurgia, 1972, 17:97-108.
2976.   Engel, E. Psychologie der französichen Literatur. Berlin:
              Simeon, 1904.
2977.   Entin-Bates, Lee Robert. Montaigne's remarks on impotence.
              Modern Language Notes, 1976, 91:640-654.
2978.   . Sexuality in the Essais of Montaigne. DAI, 1977,
              38:823A-24A.
2979.   Ephron, Beulah K. The reader and the writer. In Lindner,
              R. (ed), Explorations in Psychoanalysis. NY: Julian,
              1953, 116-127.
2980.   Ephron, Henry D. The cult of the omnipresent mother-god-
              dess. Proceedings of the Pacific Northwest Conference
              on Foreign Languages, 1964, 15:82-92.
2981.   Epstein, Edna S. The entanglement of sexuality and aesthetics
              in Gautier and Mallarmé. Nineteenth-Century French
              Studies, 1972, 1(1):5-20.
2982.   Erlich, Victor. Georgics of the mind: the experience of
              Bacon's essays. In Fish, S. E. (ed), Seventeenth Century
              Prose. NY: Oxford Univ. Press, 1971, 254-262.
2983.   . Reading conscious and unconscious. College Eng-
              lish, 1975, 36:766-775.
2984.   Espiau de la Maëstre, A. Le Rêve dans la pensée et l'oeu-
              vre de Paul Claudel. Archives Paul Claudel 10. Ar-
              chives des Lettres Modernes, 1973, 148, 64p.
2985.   Etiemble, René. De la psychiatrie en critique littéraire.
              Temps Modernes, 1952, 78:1845-1857.
2986.   Evans, Bergen. The Psychiatry of Robert Burton. NY:
              Columbia Univ. Press, 1944.
2987.   Evans, Oliver. Anaïs Nin and the discovery of inner space.
              Prairie Schooner, 1962, 36:217-230.
2988.   Evans, William N. Two kinds of romantic love. Psychoanal
              Q, 1953, 22:75-85.

2989.   Faber, M. D. Analytic prolegomena to the study of western
              tragedy. Hartford Studies in Lit, 1973, 5:31-60.
2990.   . Don Juan and Castaneda: the psychology of altered
              awareness. Psychoanal Rev, 1977, 64:323-379.
2991.   Fabre, J. Lumières et romantisme: Energie et nostalgie de
              Rousseau à Mickiewicz. Paris: Klincksieck, 1963.
2992.   Fabrizio, Richard. The Complex Oedipus: The Oedipus
              Figure in European Literature. DAI, 1974, 34:4258A-59A.
2993.   Faester, Hans. Vär stutte tid blir her: Psykologi og buds-
              kap has Tarjei Vesaas. Norsk Litteraer Arbok, 1972,
              71-98.
2994.   Fairbairn, W. R. D. Prolegomena to a psychology of art.
              British J Psychol, 1938, 28:288-290.
2995.   . The ultimate basis of aesthetic experience. Brit-
              ish J Psychol, 1938, 29:167-181.

2996. Fairchild, Susan L.   Les Personnages de femmes dans huit
       pièces de Musset.   Nineteenth-Century French Studies,
       1976, 4:213-219.
2997. Falvey, John.   Psychological analysis and moral ambiguity in
       the narrative processes of Challes, Prévost and Mari-
       vaux.   Studies on Voltaire & the 18th Century, 1972, 94:
       141-158.
2998. _____.   Women and sexuality in the thought of La Mettrie.
       In Jacobs, E., et al. (eds), Women and Society in Eight-
       eenth-Century France.   London: Athlone, 1979, 55-68.
2999. Fandal, Carolos D.   The Concept of 'Self' in the 'Essais' of
       Michel de Montaigne.   DA, 1968, 29:567A.
3000. Farnell, F.J.   Eroticism as portrayed in literature.   Int J
       Psycho-Anal, 1920, 1:396-413; In Ruitenbeek, H.M. (ed),
       Homosexuality and Creative Genius.   NY: Obolensky,
       1967, 3-20.
3001. Farrell, Edith Rogers.   'Water and Dreams' by Gaston
       Bachelard: An Annotated Translation.   DA, 1965, 26:
       1645.
3002. Fásquez, F.   Ortega, Dalí y Freud.   Arbor, 1972, 321-2.
3003. Feal Deibe, Carlos.   Eros y Lorca.   Barcelona: EDHASA,
       1973.
3004. _____.   Nada de C. Laforet: la iniciación de una ado-
       lescente.   In Beck, M., et al. (eds), The Analysis of
       Hispanic Texts: Current Trends in Methodology.   NY:
       Bilingual Press, 1976, 221-241.
3005. _____.   Psychoanalysis.   In Beck, M.A., et al. (eds),
       The Analysis of Hispanic Texts.   Current Trends in
       Methodology.   NY: Bilingual Press, 1976.
3006. Fearing, F.   The interpretive process.   In Writers Con-
       gress, Proceedings.   Berkeley: Univ. California Press,
       1944, 508-524.
3007. Fearn, Liliane.   Sur un rêve dans Pléiade II, 760.   Bulletin
       de la Société des Amis de Proust, 1967, 17.
3008. Feder, Lillian.   Madness in Literature.   Princeton: Prince-
       ton Univ. Press, 1980.
3009. _____.   Myth as self-revealing instrument.   Books
       Abroad, 1974, 48:7-14.
3010. Federn, Paul.   The neurotic style.   Psychiat Q, 1957, 31:
       681-689.
3011. Fédida, P.   La Table d'écriture.   Nouvelle Rev de Psych-
       analyse, 1977, 16.
3012. Fein, P.L.M.   Crébillon fils and eroticism.   Studies in Vol-
       taire & the 18th Century, 1976, 152:723-728.
3013. Fein, Richard J.   Walden and the village of the mind.   Ball
       State Univ. Forum, 1967, 8:55-61.
3014. Feldman, A. Bronson.   Fifty years of the psychoanalysis of
       literature: 1900-1950.   Lit & Psychol, 1955, 5:40-42,
       54-64.
3015. _____.   Reik and the interpretation of literature.   In Lind-
       ner, R. (ed), Explorations in Psychoanalysis.   NY:
       Julian, 1953, 97-115.
3016. _____.   Stages in the development of love.   Amer Imago,
       1964, 21:64-79.

3017. Feldman, Sandor S. Crying at the happy ending. JAPA, 1956, 4:477-485.
3018. Fell, Joseph P. Emotion in the Thought of Sartre. NY: Columbia Univ. Press, 1965.
3019. Fellows, Jay F. John Ruskin and the Topography of Consciousness: A Study of the Antithetical Architecture of Ruskin's Mind. DAI, 1974, 34:7748A-49A.
3020. Felman, Shoshana. La Folie et la chose littéraire. Paris: Seuil, 1978.
3021. _____. Literature and psychoanalysis: the question of reading otherwise. [Special issue.] Yale French Studies, 1977, 55-56.
3022. _____. Madness and philosophy or literature's reason. Yale French Studies, 1975, 52:206-228.
3023. _____. La Méprise et sa chance. L'Arc, 1974, 58:40-48.
3024. _____. On reading poetry: reflections on the limits and possibilities of psychoanalytical approaches. In Smith, J.H. (ed), The Literary Freud. New Haven: Yale Univ. Press, 1980, 119-148.
3025. Ferenczi, Sándor. Further Considerations to the Problems and Methods of Psychoanalysis. NY: Basic Books, 1952; London: Hogarth, 1950.
3026. _____. Goethe on the reality value of the poet's fantasy. In Final Contributions to the Problems and Methods of Psychoanalysis. NY: Basic Books, 1955, 324; Goethe über den Realitätswert der Phantasie beim Dichter. Int Zeitschrift für Psychoanalyse, 1912, 2:679.
3027. _____. Goethe über Verdrängung und Abreagieren. Int Zeitschrift für Psychoanalyse, 1939, 3:26-44.
3028. _____. Thalassa. NY: Norton, 1968.
3029. Ferguson, Margaret W. Border territories of defense: Freud and defenses of poetry. In Smith, J.H. (ed), The Literary Freud. New Haven: Yale Univ. Press, 1980, 149-180.
3030. Ferguson, Mary Anne. Images of Women in Literature. Boston: Houghton, Mifflin, 1977.
3031. Fernandez, Dominique. L'Arbre jusqu'aux racines: psychanalyse et creation. Paris: Grasset, 1972.
3032. _____. Culture réaliste et psychanalyse. Nouvelle Nouvelle Rev Française, 1957, 51:513-519.
3033. Ferrante, Joan M. Woman as Image in Medieval Literature. From the Twelfth Century to Dante. NY: Columbia Univ. Press, 1975.
3034. Feuerwerker, Yi-tsi M. The changing relationship between literature and life: aspects of the writer's role in Ding Ling. In Goldman, M. (ed), Modern Chinese Literature in the May Fourth Era. Cambridge: Harvard Univ. Press, 1977, 281-307.
3035. Fiedler, Leslie A. Archetype and signature. In Phillips, W. (ed), Art and Psychoanalysis. Cleveland: World, 1963; Sewanee Rev, 1952, 60(2).
3036. _____. An End to Innocence. Boston: Beacon, 1955.
3037. _____. Eros and Thanatos: or, the mythic aetiology of the dirty old man. Salmagundi, 1977, 38-39:3-19.

3038. _____. Freaks and the literary imagination. In Freaks: Myths & Images of the Secret Self. NY: Simon & Schuster, 1978.

3039. _____. No! in Thunder. Essays on Myth and Literature. Boston: Beacon, 1960.

3040. Filippov, L. I. [The existential psychoanalysis of J. P. Sartre: conception and consequence.] Voprosy Filosofii, 1968, 22(7):77-88.

3041. Filloux, Jean-Claude. L'Inconscient. Paris: Presses Universitaires de France, 1965.

3042. Fischer, Ottokar. Über Verbidnung von Farbe und Klang. Eine literar-psychologische Untersuchung. Zeitschrift für Ästhetik und allgemeine Kunstwissenschaft, 1907, 2:501-534.

3043. Fish, Stanley Eugene. Literature in the reader: affective stylistics. New Lit History, 1970, 2:123-162; In Primeau, R. (ed), Influx: Essays on Literary Influence. Port Washington, NY: Kennikat, 1977, 154-179.

3044. Flavell, K. Goethe, Rousseau and the 'hyp.' Oxford German Studies, 1973, 7:5-23.

3045. Fleissner, Robert F. 'Pot luck': drugs and romanticism. English Assn of Ohio Bulletin, 1970, 11(4):9-11.

3046. Fletcher, Angus. Allegory: The Theory of a Symbolic Mode. Ithaca: Cornell Univ. Press, 1964.

3047. Fliess, Robert. Erogeneity and Libido. NY: IUP, 1957.

3048. Florence, Jean. Psychanalyse-littérature. Rev de Psychologie et des Sciences de l'Education, 1974, 9:209-229.

3049. Flores, R. Psichedelismo e letteratura. In Atti del Io, congresso nazionale, Accademia ambrosiana medici umanisti e scrittori. Rome: Arti Grafiche e Cossidente, 1968, 15-33.

3050. Fogle, Richard Harter. The Idea of Coleridge's Criticism. Berkeley: Univ. California Press, 1962.

3051. Fong, Anne Curtiss. Exis and Praxis: Woman's Dilemma in the Works of Simone de Beauvoir. DAI, 1975, 35:5401A.

3052. Forclay, Roger. Edgar Poe et la psychanalyse, I, II. Rev des Langues Vivantes, 1970, 36:272-288, 375-389.

3053. Ford, Jane M. The Father/Daughter/Suitor Triangle in Shakespeare, Dickens, James, Conrad, and Joyce. DAI, 1976, 36:4507A.

3054. Forest, L. Psychologie des dedicaces littéraires. Revue des Revues, 1899, 29:66-75.

3055. Forest, Louise C. Turner. Caveat for critics against evoking Elizabethan psychology. PMLA, 1946, 61:651-672.

3056. Forsberg, J. Hjalmar. Invelse och Objecktwering i frage om Diktverk. Nordisk Psykologi, 1953, 5:184.

3057. Forster, E. M. What I believe. In Two Cheers for Democracy. London: Arnold, 1951; NY: Harcourt, Brace, 1951; NY: Harvest Books, 1962.

3058. Förster, Max von. The psychological basis of literary periods. In Caffee, N. M., & Kirby, T. A. (eds), Studies for William A. Read. Baton Rouge: Louisiana State Univ. Press, 1940, 254-268.

3059. Forsythe, Neil.   Gaston Bachelard's theory of the poetic
       imagination: psychoanalysis to phenomenology.   In Hardi-
       son, D. B. , Jr. (ed), The Quest for Imagination.   Cleve-
       land: Case Western Reserve Univ. Press, 1971, 225-
       253.
3060. Fort, Keith.   The psychopathology of everyday language of the
       profession of literary studies.   College English, 1979,
       40: 751-763.
3061. Fournier, C.   Les Thèmes édéniques dans l'oeuvre de S. -J.
       Perse.   Archives des Lettres Modernes, 1976, 167.
3062. Fowler, A.   Rousseau and Sade: freedom unlimited.   South-
       west Rev, 1958, 43: 205-211.
3063. Fox, R. A.   The Tangled Chain: The Structure of Disorder
       in the Anatomy of Melancholy.   Doctoral dissertation,
       Ohio State Univ. , 1971.
3064. Fraiberg, Louis B.   Freud's writing in art.   Int J Psycho-
       Anal, 1956, 37:82-96; Lit & Psychol, 1956, 6:116-130;
       In Psychoanalysis and American Literary Criticism.   De-
       troit: Wayne State Univ. Press, 1960, 1-46.
3065. _____.   New views of art and the creative process in psy-
       choanalytic ego psychology.   In Ruitenbeek, H. M. (ed),
       The Creative Imagination; Psychoanalysis and the Genius
       of Inspiration.   Chicago: Quadrangle, 1965, 223-243; Lit
       & Psychol, 1961, 11:45-55.
3066. _____.   Psychoanalysis and American Literary Criticism.
       Detroit: Wayne State Univ. Press, 1960; Review: Mark
       Kanzer, Lit & Psychol, 1960, 10:56-58.
3067. _____.   Psychology and the writer: the creative process.
       Lit & Psychol, 1955, 5(4):72-77.
3068. _____.   The Use of Psychoanalytic Ideas by Literary
       Critics.   DA, 1957, 17:1336-1337.
3069. Francastel, Pierre.   Art et psychologie.   Explorations et
       théories de demi-siècle.   JPNP, 1954, 47-51(1-2):91-108.
3070. Frank, Armin Paul.   Neuere Entwicklungen in der amerikan-
       ischen Literaturtheorie und Literaturkritik.   In Die amer-
       ikanische Literatur der Gegenwart.   Berlin: de Gruyter,
       1977, 271-310.
3071. Frank, Joseph.   Spatial form in modern literature.   In
       Schorer, M. , et al. , (eds), Criticism, The Foundation
       of Modern Literary Judgment.   NY: Harcourt, Brace,
       1948.
3072. Frank, Waldo.   Joyful wisdom.   In Time Exposures; By
       Search Light....   NY: Boni & Liveright, 1926, 97-98.
3073. _____.   Sigmund Freud.   Virginia Q Rev, 1934, 10:536;
       In In the American Jungle.   NY: Farrar & Rinehart,
       1937, 81-90.
3074. Frankau, Gilbert.   Man's unconscious and his published words.
       In Bax, C. (ed), Essays by Divers Hands, Vol. 24.
       London: Cumberlege, 1948, 21-39.
3075. Franke, Victor E.   Was sagt der Psychiater zur modernen
       Kunst?   In Lebend. Stadt, 1955, 2:101-107.
3076. Franklin, H. Bruce.   The Victim as Criminal and Artist.
       NY: Oxford Univ. Press, 1978; Review: John V.
       Crangle, Lit & Psychol, 1979, 29:137-140.

3077. Franzosa, J. C., Jr. Criticism and the uses of psychoanalysis. College English, 1973, 34:927-933.

3078. Frappier, Jean. Sur Lucien Fèbvre et son interprétation psychologique du XVIᵉ siècle. In Mélanges d'histoire littéraire (XVIᵉ-XVIIᵉ siècle). Paris: Nizet, 1969, 19-31.

3079. Fraser, John. Violence in the Arts. London: Cambridge Univ. Press, 1974.

3080. Frautschi, R. Narrative voice in Les Angoisses doulour-euses. French Forum, 1976, 2:209-216.

3081. Freeman, D. I. Literature and homosexuality. One, 1955, 3:13-15.

3082. Freilach, Joan S. An introduction to new techniques of literary analysis. Teaching Language Through Lit, 1974, 14:12-22.

3083. Freud, Sigmund. Creative writers and daydreaming. In Standard Edition, Vol. 9. London: Hogarth, 1959 (1908), 142-153; In Hardison, O. B. (ed), Modern Continental Literary Criticism. NY: Appleton-Century-Crofts, 1962, 240-249.

3084. _____. On Creativity and the Unconscious. Papers on the Psychology of Art, Literature, Love, Religion. NY: Harper, 1958.

3085. _____. The Origins of Psychoanalysis. NY: Basic Books, 1954, 256-257.

3086. Frey, Lina. Der Eros und die Kunst. Leipzig: Huber, 1932.

3087. Friedman, Eva M. The child in German literature: from marionette through symbol to reality. Univ. Dayton Rev, 1969, 6(3):17-27.

3088. Friedman, Lawrence. Psychoanalysis, existentialism, and the esthetic universe. J Philosophy, 1958, 55:617-631.

3089. Friedman, Melvin J. The achievement of Frederick Hoffman. Massachusetts Rev, 1965, 6:862-867.

3090. Friedman, Norman. Psychology and literary form. Psychocultural Rev, 1978, 2(2):75-95.

3091. Friedman, Paul. The bridge: a study in symbolism. Psychoanal Q, 1952, 31:49-80; In The Yearbook of Psychoanalysis, Vol. 9. NY: IUP, 1953, 257-282.

3092. Friedreich, J. B. Versuch einer Literärgeschichte der Pathologie und Therapie der psychischen Krankheiten. Würzburg, 1930.

3093. Friedrich, Hugo. S. Freuds Anweisungen für Patient und Arzt in Vergleich mit M. Montaignes Essais. Schweizerischen Zeitschrift für Psychologie, 1951, 10:163-164.

3094. Friedrich, Otto. Going Crazy: An Inquiry into Madness in Our Time. NY: Simon & Schuster, 1976; Review: R. Lasson, Book Week, 22 Feb 1976, 3.

3095. Fries, Thomas. The impossible object: the feminine, the narrative (Laclos's Les Liaisons dangereuses and Kleist's Marquise von O...). Modern Language Notes, 1976, 91: 1296-1326.

3096. Fritche, W. Freudism and art. Lit of the World Revolution, 1931, No. 5, 80-92.

3097. Fritsche, Alfred. Dekadenz im Werk Arthur Schnitzlers.
       Bern: Lang, 1974.
3098. Fromm, Erich. The Forgotten Language. An Introduction to
       the Understanding of Dreams, Fairy Tales and Myths.
       NY: Rinehart, 1951; NY: Evergreen, 1959; London:
       Gollancz, 1952; Review: R. Nace, Psychiatry, 1952, 15:
       482-484.
3099. Fruman, Norman. Coleridge and the opium mystique.
       Queen's Q, 1975, 82:440-444.
3100. Fry, Roger. The Artist and Psychoanalysis. London:
       Hogarth, 1924. Review: Herbert Read, Criterion,
       1925, 3:471.
3101. _____ . The artist and psycho-analysis. In Burgum, E. B.
       (ed), The New Criticism: An Anthology of Modern Aes-
       thetics and Literary Criticism. NY: Prentice-Hall, 1930.
3102. Frye, Northrop. Anatomy of Criticism. Princeton: Prince-
       ton Univ. Press, 1957.
3103. _____ . The archetypes of literature. Kenyon Rev, 1951,
       13:92-110; In Handy, W. J. , & Westbrook, M. (eds),
       Twentieth Century Criticism. NY: Free Press, 1974,
       233-243; In his Fables of Identity. NY: Harcourt, Brace
       & World, 1963, 1961; in Vickery, J. B. (ed), Myth and
       Literature. Lincoln: Univ. Nebraska Press, 1966, 87-
       97.
3104. _____ . The Educated Imagination. Bloomington: Indiana
       Univ. Press, 1964.
3105. _____ . Northrop Frye on Culture and Literature; A Col-
       lection of Review Articles. Chicago: Univ. Chicago
       Press, 1978.
3106. _____ . The Secular Scripture. A Study of the Structure
       of Romance. Cambridge: Harvard Univ. Press, 1976.
3107. Furness, R. The androgynous ideal: its significance in Ger-
       man literature. Modern Language Rev, 1965, 60:58-64.

3108. Gabel, P. Freud's death instinct and Sartre's fundamental
       project. Psychoanal Rev, 1974, 61:217-227.
3109. Galdenzi, A. L'Allucinazione nella documentazione letteraria
       da Aristotele a Cechov. Pagine di Storia della Medicina,
       1970, 14:64-83.
3110. Galenbeck, Susan. Higher innocence: David Bleich, the
       Geneva school, and reader criticism. College English,
       1979, 40:788-801.
3111. Gallop, David. Dreaming and waking in Plato. In Anton,
       J. P. (ed), Essays in Ancient Greek Philosophy. Albany:
       State Univ. New York Press, 1971, 187-201.
3112. Garcia, Daniel Peter. Theories of Catharsis in Modern Lit-
       erary Criticism: The Influence of Psychoanalysis, Anthro-
       pology, and the New Criticism. DAI, 1962, 23:2134-35.
3113. Garcin, Philippe. Parti-Pres. NY: Payot, 1977, 179-216.
3114. Gardiner, Judith Kegan. Elizabethan psychology and Burton's
       Anatomy of Melancholy. J History Ideas, 1977, 38:373-388.

3115. _____. Psychoanalytic criticism and the female reader. Lit & Psychol, 1976, 26:100-107.

3116. Gartner, Paul. Literarische Komplexreis. Psychoanalytische Praxis, 1933, 3:83-86.

3117. Garzilli, Enrico F. Circles without Center: Paths to the Discovery and Creation of Self in Modern Literature. Cambridge: Harvard Univ. Press, 1972; DAI, 1971, 6604.

3118. Gascar, Pierre. L'Ecrivain devant les troubles de l'esprit. Hygiène Mentale, 1961, 50:289-309.

3119. Gasiorowska, Xenia. Solzhenitsyn's women. In Dunlop, J. B., Haugh, R., & Klimoff, A. (eds), Aleksandr Solzhenitsyn: Critical Essays and Documentary Materials. NY: Collier, 1975, 117-128.

3120. Gass, William H. The World Within the Word. NY: Knopf, 1978.

3121. Gaudin, Colette. L'Imagination et la reverie: remarques sur la poétique de Gaston Bachelard. Symposium, 1966, 20: 207-225.

3122. Gaulke, J. Die Homosexualität in der Weltliteratur. Der Eigene, 1903.

3123. Gaupp, Robert. Das Pathologische in Kunst und Literatur. Deutsche Rundschau, 1911, 36.

3124. Gauthier, Xavière. Surréalisme et sexualité. Paris: Gallimard, 1971.

3125. Gay, Peter. Victorian sexuality: old texts and new insights [rev. article]. Amer Scholar, 1980, 49:372-377.

3126. Gaylin, Willard M. Psychoanaliterature: the hazards of a hybrid. Columbia Univ. Forum, 1963, 6(2):11-16.

3127. Gebser, J. Über das Weden des Dichterischen. Schweizerischen Zeitschrift für Psychologie, 1944, 3:216-231.

3128. Gedo, John E. The psychoanalyst and the literary hero: an interpretation. Comprehensive Psychiat, 1970, 11:174-181.

3129. _____. The psychology of genius revisited. In The Annual of Psychoanalysis, Vol. VII/1979. NY: IUP, 1980.

3130. Geduld, Carolyn. Bernard Wolfe. NY: Twayne, 1972.

3131. Geers, G. J. Towards the solution of the baroque problem. Neophilologus, 1960, 44:299-307.

3132. Gelderman, C. W. The male nature of tragedy. Prairie Schooner, 1975, 49:220-227.

3133. Gellert, B. J. Three Literary Treatments of Melancholy: Marston, Shakespeare and Burton. Doctoral dissertation, Columbia Univ., 1967.

3134. Gendre, André. Gaston Bachelard et les Aventures d'Arthur Gordon Pym d'Edgar Poe. LR, 1972, 26:169-180.

3135. _____. Humanisme et folie chez Sébastien Brant, Erasme et Rabelais. Basel/Stuttgart: Helbing & Lichtenhahn, 1978.

3136. Gennari, Geneviève. Spécial: la femme. Ecriture et défoulement. Les Nouvelles Littéraires, 1966, 2022, 6.

3137. George, E. (ed). Friedrich Hölderlin: An Early Modern. Ann Arbor: Univ. Michigan Press, 1972.

3138. Gérard, A.   Pour une phénomenologie du baroque littéraire.
Essai sur la tragédie européenne au XVIIe siècle. Publication de l'Univ. de l'Etat à Elisabethville, 1963, No. 5, 25-65.

3139. Germino, Dante.   Machiavelli's thoughts on the psyche and
society. In Parei, A. (ed), The Political Calculus: Essays on Machiavelli's Philosophy. Toronto: Univ. Toronto Press, 1972, 59-82.

3140. Gershman, H.   Homosexuality and some aspects of creativity.
Amer J Psychoanal, 1964, 24:29-38.

3141. Gerstinger, Heinz.   Traum und Trauer als Tradition: Anmerkungen zu Österreichs neuer Literatur. Welt und
Wort, 1970, 25:203-204.

3142. Geyer, Harold.   Dichter der Wahnsinns; eine Untersuchung
über die dichterische Darstellbarkeit seelischer Ausnahmezustände. Göttingen: Musterschmidt, 1955.

3143. Ghiselin, Brewster (ed).   The Creative Process, A Symposium. NY: New American Library, 1955; NY: Mentor,
1965.

3144. _____. Literary and psychological insight. Western Humanities Rev, 1977, 31:31-42.

3145. Ghosal, Hironmoy.   Jean-Paul Sartre. Samiksa, 1967, 21(4):
169.

3146. Giannelli, Maria Teresa.   Simone de Beauvoir eretica dell'
esistenzialismo. Pensiero Critico, 1962, 4:20-32.

3147. Gibbons, Mark L.   Identity as Literary Device: Self-Pre-
sentation in Five Eighteenth-Century Writers. DAI, 1972,
33:2373A-74A.

3148. Gibbons, Tom.   The new Hellenism: Havelock Ellis as a literary critic. Renaissance & Modern Studies, 1973, 17:
122-140.

3149. Gibbs, M. E.   Wîpllîchez Wîbes Reht. A Study of the Women
Characters in the Works of Wolfram von Eschenbach.
Duquesne: Duquesne Univ. Press, 1972.

3150. Gide, André.   Corydon. NY: Farrar, Straus, 1950 (1911).

3151. Giersing, Morten.   Kaerlighedsoprørets patologi. Anal kort-
prosa, 1971, 1:159-179.

3152. Gil-Albert, J.   'Heracles': Sobre una manera de ser. Madrid: Taller, 1975.

3153. Gilbert, Claire P.   The Theme of the Double in the Works
of Gérard de Nerval. DAI, 1972, 32:6974A-75A.

3154. Gilbert, Sandra M., & Gubar, Susan.   The Madwoman in the
Attic. The Woman Writer and the Nineteenth-Century
Literary Imagination. New Haven: Yale Univ. Press,
1979, 1980.

3155. Gillibert, Jean.   La Création littéraire. La Nef, 1967, 31.

3156. Gilman, L.   Literature unveiled. North Amer Rev, 1919,
209:557-558.

3157. Gilman, Sander L.   On the use and abuse of the history of
psychiatry for literary studies. Deutsche Vierteljahrsschrift für Literaturwissenschaft und Geistegeschichte,
1978, 52:381-399.

3158. _____. Seeing the insane: MacKenzie, Kleist, William
James. MLN, 1978, 93:871-887.

3159. _____. The uncontrollable steed. A study of the meta-morphosis of a literary image. Euphorion, 1972, 66(1).
3160. Ginferrer, P. El testimonio de O. Paz. Insula, 1966, 239.
3161. Ginzburg, L. O psixologiceskoj proze. Leningrad: Sovetskij pisatel', 1971, 1977.
3162. Girard, René. Existentialism and literary criticism. In Foray through Existentialism. Yale French Studies No. 16. New Haven: Yale Univ. Press, 1955-56, 45-52.
3163. _____. Lévi-Strauss, Frye, Derrida and Shakespearean criticism. Diacritics, 1973, 3(3):34-38.
3164. _____. Système du délire. Critique, 1972, 28:957-999.
3165. _____. The underground critic. In 'To Double Business Bound.' Baltimore: Johns Hopkins Univ. Press, 1978, 36-60.
3166. _____. Violence and the Sacred. Baltimore: Johns Hopkins Univ. Press, 1977.
3167. Girault, C. Le Thème du feu dans l'oeuvre de H. Bosco. Table Ronde, 1964, 203.
3168. Glaser, Horst. Arthur Schnitzler und Frank Wedekind--Der doppelköpfige Sexus. In Wollüstige Phantasie. Sexualästhetik der Literatur. Munich: Hanser, 1974, 148-184.
3169. _____. Wollüstige Phantasie. Sexualästhetik der Literatur. Munich: Hanser, 1974.
3170. Glenn, Jules (NMI). Psychoanalytic writings on Greek and Latin authors, 1911-1960. Classical World, 1972, 66: 129-145.
3171. Glenn, Michael L., & Forrest, David V. Psychological criticism: essence or extract? Archives General Psychiat, 1969, 20:38-47.
3172. Glicksberg, Charles I. Forms of madness in literature. Arizona Q, 1961, 17:42-53.
3173. _____. Literature and Freudianism. Prairie Schooner, 1949, 23:359-373.
3174. _____. The Literature of Commitment. Lewisburg: Bucknell Univ. Press, 1977.
3175. _____. Marxism, Freudianism, and modern writings. Queen's Q, 1947, 54:297-310.
3176. _____. Nihilism and suicide. In The Literature of Nihilism. Lewisburg, Pa: Bucknell Univ. Press, 1975, 95-115.
3177. _____. Psychoanalytic aesthetics. Prairie Schooner, 1955, 39:13-23.
3178. _____. The psychology of surrealism. Polemic, 1947, 8:46-55.
3179. _____. Sex in contemporary literature. Colorado Q, 1961, 9:277-287.
3180. _____. Sons of Freud. South Atlantic Q, 1945, 44:406-414.
3181. _____. To be or not to be: the literature of suicide. Queen's Q, 1960, 68:384-395.
3182. Godin, J.C. H. Bosco: une poétique du mystère. Montreal: Montreal Univ. Press, 1968.
3183. Goerppert, S. [The use of psychoanalysis in literary interpretation.] Confinia Psychiatrica, 1977, 20:95-107.

3184. Goetz, William R. Criticism and autobiography in James's
      prefaces. Amer Lit, 1979, 51:333-348.
3185. Goitein, Lionel. Art and the Unconscious. NY: United Book
      Guild, 1948.
3186. Golann, S. E. Psychological studies of creativity. Psychol
      Bulletin, 1963, 60:548-565.
3187. Goldberg, Gerald J., & Goldberg, Nancy M. (eds). The
      Modern Critical Spectrum. Englewood Cliffs, NJ: Pren-
      tice-Hall, 1962.
3188. Goldenweiser, A. History, Psychology and Culture. NY:
      Knopf, 1933.
3189. Goldiamond, Israel. Literary behavior analysis. J Applied
      Behavior Analysis, 1977, 10:527-529.
3190. Goldings, Carmen R. Some new trends in children's litera-
      ture from the perspective of the child psychiatrist. J
      Amer Academy Child Psychiat, 1968, 7:377-397.
3191. Goldman, Suzy. John Donovan: sexuality, stereotypes, and
      self. Lion & Unicorn, 1978, 2(2):27-36.
3192. Goldstein, Melvin. Literature and psychology, 1948-1968.
      A commentary. Lit & Psychol, 1967, 17:159-176.
3193. _____. La verità non è stata ancora inventata: Anglo-
      American literary criticism and psychology. In Strelka,
      J. (ed), Literary Criticism and Psychology. University
      Park: Penn State Univ. Press, 1976, 260-293.
3194. Gom, L. M. Laurence and the use of memory. Canadian Lit,
      1976, 71:48-58.
3195. Gomes, Martin. A Creaçõa Esthetica e a Psychanalyse.
      Porto Alegre: Livraria do Globo, 1929.
3196. Goodheart, Eugene. The Cult of the Ego; The Self in Modern
      Literature. Chicago: Univ. Chicago Press, 1968.
3197. Goodman, Paul. The psychological revolution and the writer's
      life-view. Psychoanal Rev, 1963, 50:367-374.
3198. Gor, G. Die Selbstbeobachtung des Schriftstellers als Mate-
      rial zur Psychologie des künstlerischen Schaffens. Kunst
      und Literatur, 1971, 19:14-25; Iskusstvo (Moscow), 1968.
3199. Gordon, David J. Literary Art and the Unconscious. Baton
      Rouge: Louisiana State Univ. Press, 1976.
3200. _____. Two anti-Puritan Puritans: Bernard Shaw and
      D. H. Lawrence. Yale Rev, 1966, 56:76-90.
3201. Gordon, Kate. Imagination: a psychological study. J Gen-
      eral Psychol, 1935, 12:194-207.
3202. _____. Imagination and emotion. J Psychol, 1937, 4:121-
      138.
3203. _____. Memory viewed as imagination. J General Psy-
      chol, 1937, 17:113-124.
3204. Gordon, S. Stewart. Reading and personality. School Rev,
      1950, 58:197-198.
3205. Gordon, Walter M. Suicide in Thomas More's Dialogue of
      Comfort. Amer Benedictine Rev, 1978, 29:358-370.
3206. Gorlin, Lalla. The Problem of Loneliness in the Works of
      Arthur Schnitzler. NY: Columbia Univ. Press, 1968;
      DAI, 1971, 32:1511A.
3207. Gornick, Vivian. Twice-told tales. Nation, 1978, 227:278-
      281.

3208. Govaart, Th. Adam voor de psychologen geworpen: of het
       scheppende kunstwerk. Streven, 1962, 16:38-52.
3209. Gove, A. F. The feminine stereotype and beyond: role con-
       flict and resolution in the poetics of Marina Tsvetaeva.
       Slavic Rev, 1977, 36:231-255.
3210. Graf, Claude. Sottise et folie dans la Satire des trois états.
       Recherches Anglaises et Américaines, 1974, 3:5-27.
3211. Graff, Gerald E. What was new criticism? Literary inter-
       pretation and scientific objectivity. Salmagundi, 1974,
       27:72-93.
3212. Graham, R. Rousseau's sexism revolutionized. In Fritz,
       P., & Morton, R. (ed), Women in the 18th Century and
       Other Essays. Toronto: Stevens, Hakkert, 1976, 127-
       139.
3213. Graham, Robert J. Concepts of Women in American Litera-
       ture, 1813-1871. DAI, 1973, 34:1867A.
3214. Graumann, Carl-Friedrich. Zur Psychologie des kritischen
       Verhaltens. Studium Generale, 1959, 12:694-716.
3215. Graves, Robert. Poetic Unreason and Other Studies. Lon-
       don: Palmer, 1925, 108, 126-132, 141.
3216. Gray, Bennison. The lesson of Leo Spitzer. Modern Lan-
       guage Rev, 1966, 61:547-555.
3217. Grebstein, Sheldon Norman. The psychological critic; the
       mythopoeic critic. In Perspectives in Contemporary Crit-
       icism. A Collection of Recent Essays by American, Eng-
       lish, and European Literary Critics. NY: Harper &
       Row, 1968, 237-247, 311-321.
3218. Green, André. La déliaison. Littérature, 1971, 3.
3219. _____. The double and the absent. In Roland, A. (ed),
       Psychoanalysis, Creativity, and Literature. NY: Colum-
       bia Univ. Press, 1978, 271-291; Critique, 1973.
3220. _____. Idealization and catharsis. Times Lit Supplement,
       29 Sept 1972, 1159-1161; In The Psychoanalytic Study of
       Society, Vol. 3. NY: IUP, 1975, 11-19.
3221. _____. L'Illusoir ou la Dame en Jeu. Nouvelle Rev de
       Psychanalyse, 1971, 4.
3222. Greene, Theodore M. Anxiety and the search for meaning.
       Texas Q, 1958, 1:172-191.
3223. Greene, Vivian Yvonne. The Artistic Value of Emotional
       Disorder for Goethe. DAI, 1977, 37:6521A.
3224. Greenfield, Jerome. Wilhelm Reich: a new approach to art.
       Paunch, 1975, 42-43:43-58.
3225. Greer, Germaine. Women and literature--II: Flying pigs and
       double standards. Times Lit Supplement, 26 July 1974,
       784-785.
3226. Gregg, Richard A. Brackish Hippocrene: Nekrasov, Panae-
       va, and the prose in love. Slavic Rev, 1975, 34:731-751.
3227. _____. The nature of nature and the nature of Eugene in
       The Bronze Horseman. Slavic & East European J, 1977,
       21:167-179.
3228. Gribble, James. Logical and psychological considerations in
       the criticism of F. R. Leavis. British J Aesthetics, 1970,
       10:39-57.

3229. Grieder, J. [Baculard D'Arnaud.] French Studies, 1970, 24:
       113-124.
3230. Griffin, William J. (ed). Literature in the Modern World.
       Nashville: Peabody Bureau Publications, 1954.
3231. _____. The use and abuse of psychoanalysis in the study
       of literature. Lit & Psychol, 1951, 1(4):3-20; In Man-
       heim, L. & Manheim, E. (eds), Hidden Patterns. NY:
       Macmillan, 1966, 19-36.
3232. Griffith, Paul. The 'Jewels' of Anaïs Nin. J Otto Rank
       Assn, 1970, 5(2):82-91.
3233. Griffiths, D. C. The Psychology of Literary Appreciation.
       Melbourne: Melbourne Univ. Press, 1932.
3234. Grimaud, Michel Robert. Critical notes: systems theory,
       semiotics, psychoanalysis, literature. Sub-stance, 1978,
       20:115-118.
3235. _____. Hermeneutics, onomastics and poetics in English
       and French literature. MLN, 1977, 92:888-921.
3236. _____. Psychoanalysis, contemporary science and the
       quandaries of psychocriticism. Lit & Psychol, 1977, 27:
       183-189.
3237. _____. Recent trends in psychoanalysis: a survey with
       emphasis on psychological criticism in English literature
       and related areas. Sub-Stance, 1976, 13:136-161.
3238. Grimsley, Ronald R. Psychoanalysis and literary criticism
       in historical perspective. In Wolman, B. B. (ed), The
       Psychoanalytic Interpretation of History. NY: Basic
       Books, 1971, 50-78.
3239. _____. Rousseau and Allen Ramsey, or psychology versus
       art. Rev du Pacifique, 1975, 1:54-61.
3240. _____. Two philosophical views of the literary imagina-
       tion: Sartre and Bachelard. Comparative Lit Studies,
       1971, 8:42-57.
3241. Grisi, F. Smarrimenti e speranze del personaggio nella nar-
       rativa contemporanea. Nuova Antologia, 1963, 491.
3242. Groddeck, Georg Walter. Psychoanalytische Schriften zur
       Literatur und Kunst. Wiesbaden: Limes, 1964.
3243. Groeben, Norbert. Literaturpsychologie. In Arnold, H. L.,
       & Sinemus, V. (eds), Grundzüge der Literatur- und
       Sprachwissenschaft. Bd. I: Literaturwissenschaft. Mun-
       ich: Deutscher Taschenbuch, 1973, 388-397.
3244. _____. Psihologia literarii. Bucharest: Univers, 1978.
3245. _____. Wissenpsychologische Dimension der Rezeptions-
       forschung: Zur Präzierung der kommunikationswissen-
       schaftlichen Funktion einer empirischen Literaturwissen-
       schaft. Zeitschrift für Literaturwissenschaft und Linguis-
       tik, 1974, 15:61-79.
3246. Grosclaude, P. Le Moi, l'instant présent et le sentiment de
       l'existence chez Jean Jacques Rousseau. Europe, 1962,
       No. 391-392, 52-56.
3247. Grossman, J. D. Genius and madness: the return of the
       romantic concept of the poet in Russia at the end of the
       19th century. In Terras, V. (ed), Literature and Folk-
       lore. The Hague: Mouton, 1973, 247-260.

3248. Grossvogel, David I. Perception as a form of phenomenological criticism. Hartford Studies in Lit, 1969, 1:83-88.

3249. Grotjahn, Martin. About the representation of death in the art of antiquity and in the unconscious of modern men. In Wilbur, G.W., & Muensterberger, W. (eds), Psychoanalysis and Culture. NY: IUP, 1951, 410-424.

3250. _____. The Voice of the Symbol. Los Angeles: Mara, 1971.

3251. Gruen, Arno. The discontinuity in the ontogeny of self: possibilities for integration or destructiveness. Psychoanal Rev, 1974-75, 61:557-570.

3252. Guerin, Wilfred L., Labor, Earle G., Morgan, Lee, & Willingham, John R. (eds). A Handbook of Critical Approaches to Literature. NY: Harper & Row, 1966.

3253. Guibert, R. [O. Paz on amor y erotismo.] Revista Iberoamericana, 1971, 76-77:507-515.

3254. Guild, Susan Savran. Les Couleurs chez Gérard de Nerval. DAI, 1976, 36:7462A-63A.

3255. Guillory, Daniel L. The mystique of childhood in American literature. Tulane Studies in English, 1978, 23:229-247.

3256. Guiraud, Pierre. Semiology. London: Routledge & Kegan Paul, 1975.

3257. Gullischen, Harald. Kort møter med Don Juan: noen hovedtrekk av Don Juanskikkelsens historie og psikologi. Edda, 1955, 55:305-327.

3258. Gundlach, Ralph H. Psychology and aesthetics. In Marcuse, F. L. (ed), Areas of Psychology. NY: Harper, 1954, 478-524.

3259. Gupta, Marianne Heinicke. The Doppelgänger in Selected Works of Diderot and Goethe. DAI, 1977, 37:6475A.

3260. Gustin, John C. The psychoanalyst-writer affair. Psychoanalysis, 1960, 47:106-115.

3261. Gutwirth, Marcel M. Mme de Staël, Rousseau and the woman question. PMLA, 1971, 86:100-109.

3262. Gyertyán, Ervin. Marx, Freud, József Attila: Két új József Attila könyv tanulságai. Irodalomtörténet, 1977, 59:139-185.

3263. Hacker, Frederick J. On artistic production. In Lindner, R. (ed), Explorations in Psychoanalysis. NY: Julian, 1953, 128-138.

3264. Hädecke, Wolfgang. Der taube Lärm unterhalb der Geschichte. Das Thema Wahnsinn in der neuesten Literatur. Neue Rundschau, 1978, 89:120-130.

3265. Hagan, William H., Jr. The Metaphysical Implications of Incest in Romantic Literature. DAI, 1974, 35:2222A.

3266. Hagopian, John V. Literary criticism as a science. Topic, 1966, 6(12):50-57.

3267. Hagstrum, Jean H. Sex and Sensibility. Ideal and Erotic Love from Milton to Mozart. Chicago: Univ. Chicago Press, 1980.

3268. Haidu, P. Realism, convention, fictionality and a theory of genres in Le Bel Inconnu. L'Esprit créateur, 1972, 12: 37-60.

3269. Hairston, Maxine. Carl Roger's alternative to traditional rhetoric. College Composition & Communication, 1976, 27:372-377.

3270. Halász, László. [Comparative examination of literary creativity.] Pszichológiai Tanulmányok, 1966, 9:367-382.

3271. _____. [Examination of some of the psychological features of literary talent.] Pszichológiai Tanulmányok, 1967, No. 10, 485-495.

3272. _____. Irodalompszichológiai vizsgálatok. Budapest: Tankönyvkiadó, 1971.

3273. Hale, William Harlan. Memorandum from Sigmund Freud. Horizon, 1962, 4:54-55.

3274. Hall, Vernon, Jr. Freudianism and literature. In A Short History of Literary Criticism. NY: New York Univ. Press, 1963, 156-162; Review: Leonard Manheim, Lit & Psychol, 1965, 15:256-257.

3275. Hallamore, J. The reflected self in Annette von Droste-Hülshoff's work: a challenge to self-discovery. Monatshefte, 1968, 61:58-74.

3276. Hallman, Ralph J. Psychology of Literature: A Study of Alienation and Tragedy. NY: Philosophical Library, 1961.

3277. Halsey, Brian. Freud on the nature of art. Amer J Art Therapy, 1977, 16:99-103.

3278. Haltresht, Michael. Interpreting dreams and visions in literature. J English Teaching Techniques, 1973, 6(2):1-8.

3279. _____. The meaning of De Quincey's 'Dream-Fugue on ... Sudden Death.' Lit & Psychol, 1976, 26:31-36.

3280. Halverson, John. Amour and Eros in the Middle Ages. Psychoanal Rev, 1970, 57:245-258.

3281. Hamburger, Käte. The Logic of Literature. Bloomington: Indiana Univ. Press, 1973.

3282. Hamburger, Michael. Existential psycho-analysis. In Art as Second Nature. Chester Springs, Pa: Dufour, 1975.

3283. Hamecher, Peter. Zwischen den Geschlectern. Zurich: Schmidt, 1901.

3284. Hamilton, James W. Transitional fantasies and the creative process. In The Psychoanalytic Study of Society, Vol. 6. NY: IUP, 1975, 53-70.

3285. Hammer, Jean-Pierre. Lenaus Faust und Don Juan im Lichte der Psychokritik. Lenau Forum, 1972, 4(1-2):17-36.

3286. Hamsun, Knut. Psychologie und Dichtung. Stuttgart: Kohlhammer, 1964 (1890-91).

3287. Handy, William J., & Westbrook, Max (eds). Twentieth Century Criticism. The Major Statements. NY: Free Press, 1974.

3288. Hankiss, Elemér. Az irodalomtudomány és a pszichológia. In Nyiro, L. (ed), Irodalomtudomány: Tanulmányok a XX. századi irodalomtudomány irányzatairól. Budapest: Akad. Kiadó, 1970, 413-468.

3289. Hankiss, M. J.   Les Genres littéraires et leur base psycho-
       logique. Helicon, 1940, 2.
3290. _____. Les Périodes littéraires et la psychologie collec-
       tive. Bulletin Int Committee History Sciences, 1937, 9:
       280-286.
3291. Hanneborg, Knut. The Study of Literature. A Contribution
       to the Phenomenology of the Human Sciences. Oslo: Uni-
       versitäts-forlaget, 1967.
3292. Hans, James S. Gaston Bachelard and the phenomenology of
       the reading consciousness. JAAC, 1977, 35:315-327.
3293. Hansen, Hans-Sievert. Neuere deutsche Beiträge zur psycho-
       analytischen Literaturbetrachtung (1971-1976). Literatur
       in Wissenschaft und Unterricht, 1978, 11:97-117.
3294. Harari, Joshué V. Changing the object of criticism: 1965-
       1978. MLN, 1979, 94:784-796.
3295. _____. Exogamy and incest: de Sade's structure of kin-
       ship. MLN, 1973, 88:1212-1237.
3296. _____. Textual Strategies; Perspectives in Post-Structur-
       alist Criticism. Ithaca, NY: Cornell Univ. Press, 1979.
3297. Harding, Denys W. The hinterland of thought. In Experi-
       ence into Words. NY: Horizon, 1964, 175-197; London:
       Chatto & Windus, 1963, 175-197.
3298. _____. Reading and author. In Experience into Words.
       London: Chatto & Windus, 1963, 163-174; NY: Horizon,
       1964, 163-174.
3299. Hardison, Osborne Bennett (ed). The Quest for Imagination;
       Essays in Twentieth-Century Aesthetic Criticism. Cleve-
       land: Case Western Reserve Univ., 1971.
3300. Hardwick, Elizabeth. Seduction and Betrayal. Women and
       Literature. NY: Random House, 1974.
3301. Hardy, Barbara N. Memory and memories. In Tellers and
       Listeners; The Narrative Imagination. London: Athlone,
       1975, 56-101.
3302. Hargreaves, H. L. The 'faculty' of imagination. British J
       Psychol, Monograph Suppl III, 1927.
3303. Harlow, Barbara. Sur la lecture. MLN, 1975, 90:849-871.
3304. Hárnik, J. Nachtrag zur Kenntnis der Rettungsphantasie bei
       Goethe. Int Zeitschrift für Psychoanalyse, 1919, 5:120-
       129.
3305. _____. Psychoanalytisches aus und über Goethes Wahlver-
       wandtschaften. Imago, 1912, 1:507-518.
3306. Harrington, Henry R. Charles Kingsley's fallen athlete.
       Victorian Studies, 1977, 21:73-86.
3307. Harris, Daniel A. Androgyny: the sexist myth in disguise.
       Women's Studies, 1974, 2:171-184.
3308. Harrison, Charles T. Santayana's literary psychology.
       Sewanee Rev, 1953, 61:206-220.
3309. Hart, W. A. Over een mogelikj heuristische betekenis van
       het literaire Kunstwerk voor de methodiek der psychologie.
       Nederlandsch Týdschrift voor de Psychologie, 1949, 4:57-
       69.
3310. Hartl, Robert. Versuch einer psychologischen Grundlegung
       der Dichtungsgattungen. Vienna: Oesterreichischer, 1924.

3311. Hartman, Geoffrey H.   Centaur: remarks on the psychology
       of the critic. Salmagundi, 1979, 43:130-139.
3312. _____. The dream of communication. In Brower, R.,
       Vendler, H., & Hollander, J. (eds), I.A. Richards: Es-
       says in His Honor. NY: Oxford Univ. Press, 1973.
3313. _____. The interpreter: a self-analysis. New Lit His-
       tory, 1973, 4:213-228.
3314. _____. Monsieur Texte: on Jacques Derrida, his Glas.
       Georgia Rev, 1975, 29:759-797.
3315. _____. Psychoanalysis and the Question of the Text.
       Baltimore: Johns Hopkins Univ. Press, 1978.
3316. _____. Structuralism: the Anglo-American adventure.
       Yale French Studies, 1966, 36-37:148-168.
3317. _____. Words and wounds. In Peschel, E.R. (ed),
       Medicine and Literature. NY: Watson, 1980, 178-188.
3318. Hartungen, Christian von. Die Psychoanalyse in der mod-
       ernen Literatur. Int Zeitschrift Psychoanalyse, 1911,
       1:499-501.
3319. Hasenfus, Nancy A.   Cross-media style: a psychological ap-
       proach. Poetics: Int Rev for Theory of Lit, 1978, 7(2):
       207-216.
3320. Hassan, Ihat Habib.   The daydream and nightmare of nar-
       cissus. Wisconsin Studies in Contemporary Lit, 1960, 1:
       5-21.
3321. Hatch, Mary Gies.   'Krankheitzum Tode': Goethe's concept
       of suicide. South Atlantic Bulletin, 1978, 43(4):67-73.
3322. Hauptman, Robert.   The Pathological Vision--Three Studies:
       Jean Genet, Louis-Ferdinand Céline, Tennessee Williams.
       DAI, 1972, 32:5229A.
3323. Häutler, A. Religiöse Menschlichkeit. Int Zeitschrift für
       Individual-Psychologie, 1932, 10:127-136.
3324. Havelka, Jaroslav.   The Nature of the Creative Process in
       Art: A Psychological Study. The Hague: Nykoff, 1965,
       1968.
3325. Hayashi, Nobuyuki.   [Studies in American Literature: Liter-
       ature of Symbolism, Irony, and Search for Identity.]
       Tokyo: Hokuseido, 1977.
3326. Hayes, Francis.   The great dismal swamp of amateur Freud-
       ian literary criticism. Modern Language J, 1974, 58:339-
       342.
3327. Hayman, R.   The art of being someone else. Encounter,
       1977, 49:77-80+.
3328. Hayter, Alethea.   Opium and the Romantic Imagination.
       Berkeley: Univ. California Press, 1968; London: Faber
       & Faber, 1968.
3329. _____. Victorian brothers and sisters. Times Lit Sup-
       plement, 9 Aug 1974, 859.
3330. Hechler, Jacob.   Accent on Form and other works by Lance-
       lot Law Whyte. J Otto Rank Assn, 1968, 3(2):98-111.
3331. Heffernan, James A.W.   Wordsworth on imagination: the
       emblemizing power. PMLA, 1966, 81:389-399.
3332. Heger, H.   Die Melancholie bei den französischen Lyriken
       des Spätmittelalters. Bonn: Romanisches Seminar der
       Universität, 1967.

3333. Heilbrun, Carolyn G. Axiothea's grief: the disability of the
      female imagination. In Weiner, D. B. , & Keylor, W. R.
      (eds), From Parnassus: Essays in Honor of Jacques
      Barzun. NY: Harper & Row, 1976, 227-236.

3334. _____ . Further notes toward a recognition of androgyny.
      Women's Studies, 1974, 2:143-149.

3335. _____ . Toward a Recognition of Androgyny. NY: Knopf,
      1973.

3336. Heilman, Robert Bechtold. The cult of personality. In The
      Ghost on the Ramparts, and Other Essays in the Humani-
      ties. Athens: Univ. Georgia Press, 1973, 19-31.

3337. _____ . History and criticism--psychological and pedagogi-
      cal notes. College English, 1965, 27:32-38.

3338. Heinemann, F. Goethe's phenomenological method. Philos-
      ophy, 1934, 9:67-81.

3339. Heiner, Hans-Joachim. Das 'goldene Zeitalter' in der
      deutschen Romantik: Zur sozialpsychologischen Funktion
      eines Topos. Zeitschrift für Deutsche Philologie, 1972,
      91:206-234.

3340. Helein, S. La Caractérologie et ses applications littéraires.
      French Rev, 1962, 36:146-151.

3341. Hélein-Koss, Suzanne. Gaston Bachelard: vers une nouvelle
      méthodologie de l'image littéraire? French Rev, 1971,
      45:353-364.

3342. Heller, Erich. The dismantling of a marionette theatre; or,
      psychology and the misinterpretation of literature. Critical
      Inquiry, 1978, 4:417-432.

3343. _____ . Man guilty and man ashamed. Psychiatry, 1974,
      37:10-21, 99-103.

3344. _____ . Observations on psychoanalysis and modern liter-
      ature. Salmagundi, 1975, 31-32:17-28; In Smith, J. H.
      (ed), Psychiatry and the Humanities, Vol. 1. New Haven:
      Yale Univ. Press, 1976, 35-50.

3345. _____ . The Poet's Self and the Poem; Essays on Goethe,
      Nietzsche, Rilke and Thomas Mann. London: Athlone,
      1976.

3346. _____ . Psychoanalyse und Literatur. Bemerkungen zum
      hundertsten Geburstag Sigmund Freud. Jahresring, 1956-
      57, 74-83.

3347. _____ . 'Yet there is method in it': psychology and the
      misinterpretation of literature. In Sokel, W. H. , et al.
      (eds), Probleme der Komparatistik und Interpretation.
      Bonn: Bouvier, 1978, 280-295.

3348. Heller, Peter. Nietzsches Kampf mit dem romantischen
      Pessimismus. Nietzsche Studien, 1978, 7:27-58.

3349. _____ . The Writer's Image of the Writer: A Study in
      the Ideologies of Six German Authors, 1918-1933. Doc-
      toral dissertation, Univ. Microfilms, 1952.

3350. Hellman, Geoffrey T. Leon Edel. New Yorker, 1971, 47:
      322-332.

3351. Helms, Randel. Orc: the id in Blake and Tolkien. Lit &
      Psychol, 1970, 20:31-35.

3352. Helson, J. The heroic, the comic, and the tender: patterns of literary fantasy and their authors. J Personality, 1973, 41:163-184.
3353. Helson, Ravenna. Inner reality of women. Arts in Society, 1974, 11:25-36.
3354. _____. The psychological origins of fantasy for children in mid-Victorian England. In Butler, F., & Brockman, B.A. (eds), Children's Literature: The Great Excluded, Vol. III. Storrs, Conn: Children's Lit Assn, 1974, 66-76.
3355. Henriksen, Aage. [Applicability of depth psychology to literature.] Kritik, 1967, 4.
3356. Hepburn, James G. Deeper chaos and larger order: psychoanalysis confronting art. Lit & Psychol, 1961, 11:101-111.
3357. Heptner, Elisabeth Maria. Two Nineteenth-Century Conceptions of Womanhood: A Comparison of the Attitudes of Kleist and Hebbel. DAI, 1975, 36:2196A-97A.
3358. Herbert, S. The Unconscious in Life and Art. Essays of a Psychoanalyst. London: Allen & Unwin, 1932.
3359. Hérenger, Alexander. Goethe und Freud. Psychoanalytische Bewegung, 1931, 3:19-31.
3360. Hermann, Imre. [Dream in the Old Hungarian literature.] Magyar Pszichológiai Szemle, 1969, 24:459-461.
3361. Hernadi, Paul (ed). What Is Literature? Bloomington: Indiana Univ. Press, 1978.
3362. Herrera, José Luís. Freud y Sartre: supuestos antropológicos de sus teorias psicoanalíticas. Cuadernos Hispanoamericanos, 1965, núm. 182, 259-290.
3363. Herrero, Jesús. Freud y Ortega frente al conflicto de generaciones: (Estudio teórico-comparativo). Arbor, 1976, 366:7-36.
3364. _____. Ortega, Freud, y Piaget a la hisqueda del ser humano. Arbor, 1973, 226:43-70.
3365. Hertling, Gunter H. Conrad Ferdinand Meyers Epik: Traumbeseelung, Traumbesinnung und Traumbesitz. Bern: Francke, 1973.
3366. Hertz, Neil. The notion of blockage in the literature of the sublime. In Hartman, G.H. (ed), Psychoanalysis and the Question of the Text. Baltimore: Johns Hopkins Univ. Press, 1978, 62-85.
3367. Hertzman, Max. Psychology, literature, and the life situation. Psychoanalysis, 1955, 3:2-9.
3368. Herz, Mary E. The monomyth in 'The Great Good Place.' College English, 1963, 24:439-443.
3369. Herzfeld, Marianne von. Goethe's images of children. German Life & Letters, 1972, 25:219-231.
3370. Herzog, U. Literatur in Isolation und Eisamkeit. Catharina von Greiffenberg und ihr literarischer Freundeskreis. Deutsches Vierteljahrsschrift für Literaturwissenschaft und Geistesgeschichte, 1971, 45:515-546.
3371. Hespen, Richard C. Ludwig Lewisohn as Literary Critic. DA, 1967, 66-14, 528.

3372. Hesse, Hermann. Artist and psychoanalyst. Psychoanal Rev, 1962, 50:6-10; Frankfurter Zeitung, 16 July, 1918, No. 195; Almanach des Internationalen Psychoanalytischen Verlags, 1926, 34-38.

3373. _____. C. G. Jung. In My Belief. Essays on Life and Art. NY: Farrar, Straus & Giroux, 1974 (1931, 1934), 358-360.

3374. _____. Sigmund Freud. In My Belief. Essays on Life and Art. NY: Farrar, Straus & Giroux, 1974 (1919, 1925), 355-357.

3375. Hessen, H., & Green, A. Sur l'héautoscopie. Encephale, 1957, 46:581-594.

3376. Hibbett, Howard S. Akutagawa Ryūnosuke and the negative ideal. In Craig, A. M., & Shively, D. H. (eds), Personality in Japanese History. Berkeley: Univ. California Press, 1970, 425-451.

3377. Hibler, David J. Sexual Rhetoric in Seventeenth-Century American Literature. DAI, 1971, 31:4121A.

3378. Hicks, John. Exploration of value: Warren's criticism. South Atlantic Q, 1963, 62:508-515.

3379. Hiddleston, J. A. L'Univers de Sartre. Paris: Corti, 1965.

3380. Highsmith, P. The glint of madness. Times Lit Supplement, 24 Dec 1976, 3902:1601.

3381. Hill, James L. Defensive strategies in nineteenth and twentieth-century criticism. JAAC, 1969, 28:177-185.

3382. Hilpert, Constantin. Eine stilpsychologische Untersuchung an Hugo von Hofmannsthal. Zeitschrift für Asthetik und allgemeine Kunstwissenschaft, 1908, 3:361-393.

3383. Hine, E. McN. The woman question in early 18th century French literature: the influence of François Poulain de la Barre. Studies on Voltaire & the 18th Century, 1973, 116:65-79.

3384. Hinrichson, Otto. Depression und Produktivität. Zentralblatt für die gesante Neurologie und Psychiatrie, 1933, 144(3-4).

3385. _____. Produktion und Neurose. Zentralblatt für die gesamte Neurologie und Psychiatrie, 1932, 142:712-719.

3386. _____. Zur Psychologie und Psychopathologie des Dichters. In Loewenfeld, L. (ed), Grenzfragen des Nerven- und Seelenlebens, Vol. 12. Wiesbaden: 1912.

3387. Hinton, N. Anagogue and archetype: the phenomenology of medieval literature. Annuale Mediaevale, 1966, 7.

3388. Hinz, Evelyn J. The beginning and the end: D. H. Lawrence's Psychoanalysis and Fantasia. Dalhousie Rev, 1972, 52:251-265.

3389. _____. The Mirror and the Garden: Realism and Reality in the Writings of Anaïs Nin. Columbus: Ohio State Univ. Libraries, 1971.

3390. _____. A Woman Speaks. The Lectures, Seminars and Interviews of Anaïs Nin. Chicago: Swallow, 1975.

3391. Hirsch, B. The want of that true theory: Julian and Maddalo as dramatic monologue. Studies in Romanticism, 1978, 17:13-34.

3392. Hirsch, Eric Donald. Validity in Interpretation. New Haven: Yale Univ. Press, 1967.

3393. Hitschmann, Edward.   Eckermann über Goethe und Träume.
       Int Zeitschrift für Psychoanalyse, 1911, 1:273.
3394. _____. Goethe als Vatersymbol.   Int Zeitschrift für Psy-
       choanalyse, 1913, 1:569-570.
3395. _____. Goethe über die Psychoanalyse.   Psychoanalytische
       Bewegung, 1932, 4:386-392, 498-504.
3396. _____. Eine literarische verwertung des Vatermordes.
       Int Zeitschrift für Psychoanalyse, 1919, 5:309.
3397. Hoche, A. E.   Die geisteskranken in der Dichtung.   Munich,
       1939.
3398. Hock, Richard A.   Henry James and Pragmatistic Thought:
       A Study in the Relationship Between the Philosophy of Wil-
       liam James and the Literary Art of Henry James.   Chapel
       Hill: Univ. North Carolina Press, 1974.
3399. Hodgart, Matthew.   Psychology and literary criticism.   Lis-
       tener, 11 Sept 1952, 420-421.
3400. Hofmann, F. M.   Dichter--Schrifsteller--Journalist.   Eine
       Gegenüberstellung auf psychologische Basis.   Doctoral dis-
       sertation, Univ. Innsbruck, 1955.
3401. Hoffman, Frederick J.   The elusive ego: Beckett's M's.   In
       Friedman, M. J. (ed), Samuel Beckett Now: Critical Ap-
       proaches to His Novels, Poetry and Plays.   Chicago:
       Univ. Chicago, 1970, 31-58.
3402. _____. Freudianism and the Literary Mind.   Baton Rouge:
       Louisiana State Univ. Press, 1945, 1957, 1967; Westport,
       Conn: Greenwood, 1977; Review: Ernst Kris, Psychoanal
       Q, 1946, 15:226-234.
3403. _____. _____. [Excerpt.]   In White, R. L. (ed), The
       Achievement of Sherwood Anderson.   Chapel Hill: Univ.
       North Carolina Press, 1966, 174-192.
3404. _____. Gertrude Stein.   In Wright, G. T. (ed), Seven
       American Stylists from Poe to Mailer: An Introduction.
       Minneapolis: Univ. Minnesota Press, 1973, 124-161.
3405. _____. Gertrude Stein in the psychology lab.   Amer Q,
       1965, 17:127-132.
3406. _____. Grace, violence, and self: death and modern lit-
       erature.   Virginia Q Rev, 1958, 34:439-454.
3407. _____. Lawrence's quarrel with Freud.   [Excerpt from
       Freudianism and the Literary Mind.]   In Hoffman, F. J.,
       & Moore, H. T., The Achievement of D. H. Lawrence.
       Norman: Univ. Oklahoma Press, 1953.
3408. _____. Literary form and psychic tension.   In Manheim,
       L., & Manheim, E. (eds), Hidden Patterns.   NY: Mac-
       millan, 1966, 50-65; Original title, Psychology and litera-
       ture.   Lit & Psychol, 1956, 6:111-115; and Kenyon Rev,
       1957, 19:605-619.
3409. _____. The Mortal No: Death and the Modern Imagina-
       tion.   Princeton: Princeton Univ. Press, 1964.
3410. _____. Mortality and modern literature.   In Feifel, H.
       (ed), The Meaning of Death.   NY: McGraw-Hill, 1959.
3411. _____. Psychoanalysis and literary criticism.   Amer Q,
       1950, 2:144-154.

3412. _____. 'Pure psychic automation': some extremities of improvisation. In The Twenties; American Writing in the Postwar Decade. NY: Viking, 1955, 206-216.

3413. _____. The Reception and Use of Freudian Psychology in England and America, 1920-1935. Doctoral dissertation, Ohio State Univ., 1942.

3414. _____. Samuel Beckett: The Language of Self. Carbondale: Southern Illinois Univ. Press, 1962.

3415. _____. William James and the modern literary consciousness. Criticism, 1962, 4:1-13.

3416. Hoffman, Michael J. Gertrude Stein in the psychological laboratory. Amer Q, 1965, 17:127-132.

3417. Hoffmann, P. Marivaux féministe. Travaux de Linguistique et de Littérature, 1977, 15(2):91-100.

3418. _____. Significations de l'état de nature dans la pensée de Jean Jacques Rousseau. Travaux de Linguistique et de Littérature, 1972, 2:97-107.

3419. Hofling, Charles K. Percival Lowell and the canals of Mars. British J Medical Psychol, 1964, 37:33-42.

3420. Hoheisel, Peter. Coleridge on Shakespeare: method amid the rhetoric. Studies in Romanticism, 1974, 13:15-23.

3421. Holbrook, David. Pornography and death. Critical Q, 1972, 14:29-40.

3422. Holdsworth, R.V. Ben Jonson's use of pimp. Notes & Queries, 1979, 26:147-148.

3423. Holland, Norman N. Clinical, yes. Healthy, no. Lit & Psychol, 1964, 14:121-125.

3424. _____. A colloquy with Norman N. Holland. Gypsy Scholar, 1978, 5:57-68.

3425. _____. Defense, displacement and the ego's algebra. Int J Psycho-Anal, 1973, 54:247-257.

3426. _____. The Dynamics of Literary Response. London: Oxford Univ. Press; NY: Norton, 1975. Reviews: Norman D. Weiner, Bulletin Philadelphia Assn Psychoanal, 1969, 19:91-94; Jules Gelernt, Lit & Psychol, 1970, 20: 129-134; D. Carmichael, Contemporary Psychol, 1970, 15:242-244.

3427. _____. Dynamics revisited. Lit & Psychol, 1971, 21:57-60.

3428. _____. English and identities. CEA Critic, 1973, 35:4-11.

3429. _____. Freud and the poet's eye. Lit & Psychol, 1961, 11:36-45; In Manheim, L., & Manheim, E. (eds), Hidden Patterns: Studies in Psychoanalytic Criticism. NY: Macmillan, 1966, 155-170.

3430. _____. Human identity. Critical Inquiry, 1978, 4:451-469.

3431. _____. Identity: an interrogation at the border of psychology. Language & Style, 1977, 10:199-209.

3432. _____. A letter to Leonard [Manheim]. Hartford Studies in Lit, 1973, 5:9-30.

3433. _____. A literary critic's view of Heinz Hartmann's concept of adaptation. Bulletin Philadelphia Assn Psychoanal, 1965, 15:4-9.

3434. _____. Literary suicide: a question of style. Psycho-cultural Rev, 1977, 1:285-303.

3435. _____. Literature as transaction. In Hernadi, P. (ed), What Is Literature? Bloomington: Indiana Univ. Press, 1978, 206-218; In Primeau, R. (ed), Influx: Essays on Literary Influence. Port Washington, NY: Kennikat, 1977, 137-153.

3436. _____. Literature, the irrational, and Professor Shumaker. Lit & Psychol, 1962, 12:51-54.

3437. _____. The new paradigm: subjective or transactive? New Lit History, 1976, 7:335-346.

3438. _____. The next new criticism. Nation, 1961, 192:339-341.

3439. _____. Poem opening: an invitation to transactive criticism. College English, 1978, 40:2-16.

3440. _____. Poems in persons. Research Teaching English, 1974, 8:12-14.

3441. _____. Preface to The Whispered Meanings: Selected Essays of Simon O. Lesser. Amherst: Univ. Massachusetts Press, 1977, vii-viii.

3442. _____. Prose and minds: a psychoanalytic approach to non-fiction. In Levine, G., & Madden, W. (eds), The Art of Victorian Prose. NY: Oxford Univ. Press, 1968, 314-337.

3443. _____. Psychanalyse et critique psychanalytique: la phase d'identité. Rev Française d'Etude Américaine, 1977, 3:29-45.

3444. _____. Psychanalyse et lecture. Etudes Littéraires, 1978, 11:491-518.

3445. _____. Psychoanalytic criticism and perceptual psychology. Lit & Psychol, 1966, 16:81-92.

3446. _____. Reading and identity: a psychoanalytic revolution. Academy Forum, 1979, 23:7-9.

3447. _____. Realism and the psychological critic. Lit & Psychol, 1960, 10:5-8.

3448. _____. Toward a psychoanalysis of poetic form: some mixed metaphors unmixed. Lit & Psychol, 1965, 15:79-91.

3449. _____. Transacting my 'good-morrow' or bring back the vanished critic. Studies in Lit Imagination, 1979, 12:61-79.

3450. _____. A transactive account of transactive criticism. Poetics, 1978, 7:177-189.

3451. _____. Transactive criticism: recreation through identity. Criticism, 1976, 18:334-352.

3452. _____. The 'unconscious' of literature: the psychoanalytic approach. In Bradbury, M., & Palmer, D. (eds), Contemporary Criticism. London: Arnold, 1970, 130-153.

3453. _____. Unity identity text self. PMLA, 1975, 90:813-822; Gradiva, 1976, 1:5-20; Psyche (Stuttgart), 1979, 33: 1127-1148.

3454. _____. Why organic unity? College English, 1968, 30: 19-30.

3455. _____. The 'willing suspension of disbelief' revisited. Centennial Rev, 1967, 11:1-23.

3456. Holmberg, Arthur Carl. Louis Lambert and Maximiliano Rubin: the inner vision and the outer man. Hispanic Rev, 1978, 46:119-136.

3457. Holman, C. Hugh. The defense of art: criticism since 1930. In Stovall, F. (ed), The Development of American Literary Criticism. Chapel Hill: Univ. North Carolina Press, 1955, 216-225.

3458. _____. Narcissistic criticism. Sewanee Rev, 1980, 88: 278-282.

3459. Holzhausen, P. Dichter und Psychopathan. Kölnische Zeitung, 16 June 1923.

3460. Honsza, Norbert. [Identity and the motif of the mask in the works of Max Frisch.] Kwartalnik Neofilologiczny, 1975, 22:219-229.

3461. Hoops, Reinald. Der Einfluss der Psychoanalyse auf die englische Literatur. Heidelberg: Winter, 1934; Anglistische Forschungen, 77.

3462. Horney, Karen. The dread of woman. Int J Psycho-Anal, 1932, 13:348-360.

3463. Horowitz, Ellen. The rebirth of the artist. In Kostelanetz, R. (ed), On Contemporary Literature. NY: Avon, 1964, 330-346.

3464. Horst, K.A. Der Schrifsteller und seine Offentlichkeit. Studium Generale, 1970, 23:698-709.

3465. Horst-Witt, (?). Arthur Symons Buch: The Symbolist Movement in Literature. Int Zeitschrift für Psychoanalyse, 1914, 4:512.

3466. Hospers, John. Literature and human nature. JAAC, 1958, 17:45-57.

3467. Hough, Graham. Psychoanalysis and literary interpretation. In Image and Experience; Studies in Literary Revolution. NY: Greenwood, 1968 (1960).

3468. Hourecade, P. La Représentation de la femme dans 'La Precieuse.' Rev d'Histoire Littéraire de la France, 1977, 77:470-477.

3469. House, Samuel D. The concept of realization in literature and life. Psychoanal Rev, 1926, 13:461-469.

3470. Houston, Robert W. Coleridge's psychometaphysics. Thoth, 1968, 9:14-24.

3471. Hovey, Richard N. Dr. Samuel Johnson, psychiatrist. Modern Language Q, 1954, 15:321-325.

3472. _____. Mythopoesis: a satire. CEA Critic, 1961, 23.

3473. Howe, Irving. Literature on the couch. New Republic, 1960, 143:17-19.

3474. Howells, Christina M. Sartre and the language of literature. Modern Language Rev, 1979, 74:572-579.

3475. Huang, Chin-Lung. The literature of Chuang Tzǔ: an emotional intellectual, scientific synthesis. Tamkang Rev, 1976, 7(2):123-135.

3476. Hudde, Hinrich. Ödipus als Detektive: Die Urszene als Geheimnis des geschlossenen Raums. Zeitschrift für Französischer Sprache und Literatur, 1976, 86:1-25.

3477. Hughes, David Y. Mood of a modern utopia. Extrapolation, 1977, 19:59-67.

3478. Hughes, Judith. Self-suppression and attachment: mid-Vic-
       torian emotional life. Massachusetts Rev, 1978, 19:541-
       555.

3479. Hughes, J. M. The Dialectic of Death in Poe, Dickinson,
       Emerson, and Whitman. Doctoral dissertation, Univ.
       Pennsylvania, 1969.

3480. Huguet, Louis. Conflit des générations, lutte des sexes:
       Essai psychocritique structurelle. Annales de l'Université
       d'Abidjan, 1976, 9D:117-205.

3481. Hulbeck, Charles R. The creative personality. Psychoanaly-
       sis, 1945, 5:49-58.

3482. Hume, Kathryn. Romance: a perdurable pattern. College
       English, 1974, 36:129-146; Reply with rejoinder: F. W.
       Ramey. College English, 1977, 38:516-517.

3483. Hunter, R. A., & Macalpine, L. Smollett's reading in psy-
       chiatry. Modern Language Rev, 1956, 51:409-411.

3484. Hutchens, John K. One thing and another. Saturday Rev,
       20 Dec 1969, 24-25.

3485. Hutcheon, L. Modes et formes du narcissisme littéraire.
       Poétique, 1977, 29:90-106.

3486. Hutchinson, E. D. Materials for the study of creative think-
       ing. Psychol Bulletin, 1931, 28:392-409.

3487. Hux, Samuel. On American literary existentialism. Forum,
       1969, 7(1):37-42.

3488. Huxley, Aldous. Our contemporary hocus-pocus. Forum,
       1925, 73:313-320.

3489. Hyde, H. Montgomery. Sexual deviants. Books & Bookman,
       1971, 16(6):41, 58-59.

3490. Hyman, Stanley Edgar. The critical achievement of Carolyn
       Spurgeon. Kenyon Rev, 1948, 10:92-108.

3491. _____ . A critical look at psychology. In The Promised
       End. NY: World, 1963; Amer Scholar, 1959, 29:21-29.

3492. _____ . Images of Sigmund Freud. In The Critic's Cre-
       dentials. Essays and Reviews. NY: Atheneum, 1978
       (1962), 279-283.

3493. _____ . Introduction to William Troy: Selected Essays.
       New Brunswick, NJ: Rutgers Univ. Press, 1967.

3494. _____ . Maud Bodkin and psychological criticism. In The
       Armed Vision: A Study in the Methods of Modern Literary
       Criticism. NY: Knopf, 1958; In Phillips, W. (ed), Art
       and Psychoanalysis. Cleveland: Meridian, 1963; NY:
       Criterion, 1957.

3495. _____ . Psychoanalysis and the climate of tragedy. In
       The Promised End. NY: World, 1963, 102-120; In Nel-
       son, B. (ed), Freud and the Twentieth Century. NY:
       Meridian, 1957, 167-185; Original title: Freud and the
       climate of tragedy. Partisan Rev, 1956, 23:198-214.

3496. _____ . The psychoanalytic criticism of literature. West-
       ern Rev, 1948, 12:106-115.

3497. _____ . The Tangled Bank: Darwin, Marx, Frazer and
       Freud as Imaginative Writers. NY: Atheneum, 1962.

3498. _____ . William Troy's work. Kenyon Rev, 1966, 28:
       326-338.

3499. Imada, Junzo. [Psychoanalysis of English and American Literature.] Tokyo: Kaibunsha, 1977.

3500. Inagaki, Sadahiro. 'La Psychanalyse du feu' de Gaston Bachelard. In Annual Reports of Studies, Vol. 22. Kyoto: Doshisha Women's College, 1971, 22-33.

3501. Ingarden, Roman. Das literarische Kunstwerk. Halle, 1931.

3502. _____. Psychologism and psychology in literary scholarship. New Lit History, 1974, 5:213-223.

3503. Ingenieros, José. La psicopatología en el arte. Nosotros, 1920, 14:145-162.

3504. Ingler, James B. Woman as Myth in the Works of Gérard de Nerval. DA, 1966, 27:1824A.

3505. Insdorf, Cecile. Montaigne and Feminism. Chapel Hill: North Carolina Studies in Romance Languages and Literatures, 1977; Review: E. B. Turk, French Rev, 1978, 52: 342-343.

3506. Isaacs, Harold R. Bringing up the father question. Daedalus, 1978, 107(4):189-203.

3507. Isaacs, Neil D. The autoerotic metaphor in Joyce, Sterne, Lawrence, Stevens and Whitman. Lit & Psychol, 1965, 15:92-106.

3508. Isnenghi, Mario. Materiali per la psicanalisi della guerra (1914-18). Belfagor, 1967, 22:474-478.

3509. Israel, Moshe. [Brother and sister as motive and first symbol in literature.] Ofakim, 1960, 14:226-236.

3510. Ivasheva, Valentina. How the mind of man is treated by modern writers. Soviet Lit, 1979, No. 5: 150-158.

3511. Jackson, J.R. De J. Coleridge on Shakespeare's preparation. Rev English Lit, 1966, 7:53-63.

3512. _____. Method and Imagination in Coleridge's Criticism. London: Routledge, 1969.

3513. Jackson, Rosemary. Women of doubtful gender. Encounter, 1977, 49:67-68+.

3514. Jacobi, Jolande. Complex/Archetype/Symbol, in the Psychology of C. G. Jung. NY: Pantheon, 1959; London: Routledge, 1959; Review: Paul Bergman, Psychiatry, 1962, 25:83-95.

3515. Jacobs, Edward C. Thoreau and modern psychology. Thoreau Society Bulletin, 1974, 127:4-5.

3516. Jacobs, Robert D. Poe: Journalist and Critic. Baton Rouge: Louisiana State Univ. Press, 1969.

3517. Jacobson, J.W. The culpable male: Grimmelshausen on women. German Q, 1966, 39(2):149-161.

3518. Jacobson, Sheldon A. Pathology and the classics. Improving College & Univ. Teaching, 1971, 19:7-11.

3519. Jaffe, Aniela (ed). C.G. Jung. Word and Image. Princeton: Princeton Univ. Press, 1979.

3520. Jagunkova, V. P. Individualno psichologitscheskoje osobienosti akolnikov, sposobnich k literaturomu tvor cestvu. In Kruteski, V.A. (ed), Voprosi psichologii sposobnostei skolnikov. Moscow; 1964.

3521. Jaloux, Edmond. Observations sur la psychologie du féerique.
J de Psychologie, 1926, 23:123-132.

3522. James, William. The stream of consciousness. In The
Principles of Psychology, Vol. I. NY: Holt, 1890, 224-
290; excerpt in Ellmann, R., & Feidelson, C., Jr. (eds),
The Modern Tradition. NY: Oxford Univ. Press, 1965,
715-723.

3523. Jameson, Fredric. The ideology of form: partial systems
in La Vieille Fille. Sub-stance, 1976, 15:29-49.

3524. _____. The imaginary and symbolic in Lacan: Marxism,
psychoanalytic criticism, and the problem of the subject.
Yale French Studies, 1977, 55-56:338-395.

3525. Janeway, Elizabeth. Images of women. Arts in Society,
1974, 11:9-18.

3526. Janssens, Marcel. Het sadistische universum. Dietsche
Warande en Belfort, 1965, 110:763-764.

3527. Jarrett, James L. On psychical distance. Personalist,
1971, 52:61-69.

3528. Jarry, André. Au-delà de la psychocritique mauronienne.
Mondes [des Livres], 28 Oct 1977, no. 10185, 22.

3529. Jason, Philip K. (ed). Anaïs Nin Reader. Chicago: Swallow, 1973.

3530. Jastrow, Joseph. Psychology and literature. Saturday Rev,
1931, 7:969-970.

3531. Jayne, Edward. Affective Criticism: Theories of Emotion
and Synaethesis in the Experience of Literature. DAI,
1971, 31:6612A-13A.

3532. _____. The dialectics of paranoid form. Genre, 1978,
11:131-157.

3533. Jean, Raymond. Mauron et la méthode psychocritique. La
Quinzaine Littéraire, 1967, 19(10).

3534. Jeanneau, A. Henri Michaux et la recherche psychopathologique. Evolution Psychiatrique, 1972, 37:407-433.

3535. Jeanneret, Michel. La Lettre perdue: écriture et folie dans
l'oeuvre de Nerval. Paris: Flammarion, 1978.

3536. Jekels, Ludwig. The problem of duplicated expression of
psychic themes. Int J Psycho-Anal, 1933, 14:300-309.

3537. _____. Selected Papers. NY: IUP, 1952.

3538. Jenkins, I. Plato and the dilemma of literary criticism.
Psychol Bulletin, 1939, 36:610.

3539. Jennermann, Donald. The Literary Criticism and Theory of
Kenneth Burke in Light of Aristotle, Freud, and Marx.
DAI, 1975, 35:6668A.

3540. Jennings, Lee Bryson. Der aufgespiesste Schmetterling, J.
Kerner und die Frage der psychischen Entwicklung.
Antaios (Stuttgart), 1968, 10.

3541. _____. Geister und Germanisten: Literarisch-parapsycho-
logische Betrachtungen zum Fall K.-Morike. In Bauer, E.
(ed), Psi und Psyche. Neue Forschungen zur Parapsychologie. Stuttgart: Deutsche Verlaganstalt, 1974.

3542. Johansen, Jørgen Dines. Om fortolkningssituationen. Copenhagen: Munksgaard, 1972.

3543. _____. Psykoanalyse, litteratur tekst-teori I: Tradionen og perspektiver; II: Psykoanalytiske begreber, kommentar, bibliografi. Copenhagen: Borgen/Basis, 1977.

3544. _____. Psychoanalyse, litteratur, tekstteori. Psychoanalytiske begreber, kommentar, bibliografi, Vol. 2. Copenhagen: Borgen/Basis, 1977.

3545. Johnsen, William A. Toward a redefinition of modernism. Boundary 2, 1974, 2:539-556.

3546. Johnson, Charlotte F. Leonardo and Dante. Amer Imago, 1972, 29:177-185.

3547. Johnson, Dorothy M. Psychology vs literature. Harper Books & Authors, 1961, 12:1-4.

3548. Johnson, Ellwood. Emerson's psychology of power. Rendezvous, 1970, 5(1):13-25.

3549. Jolas, Eugene. The dream. Transition, 1930, 19-20:46-47.

3550. _____. Inquiry into the spirit and language of night. Transition, 1938, 27:233-245.

3551. _____. Literature and the new man. Transition, 1930, 19-20:13-22.

3552. Joly, R. Deux Etudes sur la préhistoire du réalisme: Diderot, Restif de la Bretonne. Quebec: Laval Univ. Presses, 1969.

3553. Jonas, Klaus M. Richard Beer-Hofmann. Modern Austrian Lit, 1975, 8:43-73.

3554. Jones, David G. Butterfly on the Rock: A Study of Themes and Images in Canadian Literature. Toronto: Univ. Toronto Press, 1970. Review: Peter C. Noel-Bentley, Mosaic, 1970, 4:127-133.

3555. Jones, Edward T. Literature and homosexuality: notes toward a critical study. Illinois Q, 1974, 37(2):24-34.

3556. Jones, Ernest. Literature. In The Life and Work of Sigmund Freud, Vol. 3. NY: Basic Books, 1957, 417-431.

3557. _____. Psychoanalysis and the artist. Psyche, 1928, 8: 73-88.

3558. Jones, Judith P., & Seibel, Sherianne S. Thomas More's feminism: to reform or re-form. In Moore, M.J. (ed), Quincentennial Essays on St. Thomas More. Boone, North Carolina: Albion, 1978, 67-77.

3559. Jones, Louisa. La Femme dans la littérature française du dix-neuvième siècle: ange et diable. Orbis Litterarum, 1975, 30:51-17.

3560. Jørgensen, John Christian. Litteraer metodelaere. Metoder i dansk lit.-forskning efter 1870. Copenhagen: Borgen, 1971.

3561. Josephs, Herbert. Sade and women: exorcising the awe of the sacred. Studies in Burke & His Time, 1977, 18:99-113.

3562. Josephson, Matthew. Instant note on Waldo Frank. Broom, 1922, 4:57.

3563. Jost, François. Le Je à la recherche de son identité. Poétique, 1975, 24:479-487.

3564. Jouvenel, B. de. Rousseau the pessimistic evolutionist. Yale French Studies, 1961-62, 28:83-96.

3565. Jovanović, Radmilo. [Psychological-existential aspects of literature.] Izraz, 1976, 40:385-407.
3566. Juhász, A. Avilágirodalom élettöténete. Budapest: Révay, 1927.
3567. Jung, Carl Gustav. Is there a Freudian type of poetry? In Collected Works of C. G. Jung, Vol. 18. Princeton: Princeton Univ. Press, 1976, 765-766.
3568. _____. Psychology and literature. In Modern Man in Search of His Soul. NY: Harcourt, Brace, 1934, 1956, 175-179; In Collected Works of C. G. Jung, Vol. 15. Princeton: Princeton Univ. Press, 1966, 84-105; In Schorer, M., et al. (eds), Criticism. NY: Harcourt Brace & World, 1948, 1958, 116-121; In Rader, M. (ed), A Modern Book of Aesthetics. NY: Holt, Rinehart & Winston, 1960, 140-154; In Gross, L. (ed), An Introduction to Literary Criticism. NY: Capricorn, 1972, 275-283.
3569. _____. Psychology and poetry. Transition, 1930, 19-20: 23-45.
3570. _____. On the relation of analytical psychology to poetry. British J Medical Psychol, 1923, 3:213-231; In Collected Works of C. G. Jung, Vol. 15. Princeton: Princeton Univ. Press, 1966, 65-83; Zurich, 1922, 23 p; Paris: Stock, 1931; In Hardison, O. B. (ed), Modern Continental Literary Criticism. NY: Appleton-Century-Crofts, 1962, 267-288; In Contributions to Analytical Psychology. NY: Harcourt, Brace, 1928.
3571. _____. Symbols of Transformation. In Collected Works, Vol. 5. Princeton: Princeton Univ. Press, 1968.
3572. Jung, Emma. J.J. Rousseau als Psychoanalytiker. Int Zeitschrift für Psychoanalyse, 1911-13, 3:52.
3573. Justman, Stuart. The strange case of Dostoevsky and Freud: a lesson in the necessity of imagination. Gypsy Scholar, 1975, 2:94-101.

3574. Kadir, Djelal. Intimations of terror in Borges' metaphysics. Symposium, 1977, 31:196-211.
3575. Kadrnoska, Franz. 'Der Waldgänger': Ein Versuch zur schaffenpsychologischen Erfassung der dichterischen Struktur. Adelbert Stifter Institut des Landes Oberösterreich, 1970, 19:129-140.
3576. Kafka, Franz. Meditations. In Slochower, H. et al. (eds), A Franz Kafka Miscellany. NY: Twice a Year Press, 1940.
3577. Kahane, Claire. Artificial niggers. Massachusetts Rev, 1978, 19:183-198.
3578. Kahler, Erich. The forms of form. Centennial Rev, 1963, 7:131-143.
3579. _____. The nature of the symbol. In May, R. (ed), Symbolism in Religion and Literature. NY: Braziller, 1960, 50-74.

3580. Kainz, Friedrich. Das Steigerungsphänomen als künstlerische Gestaltungsprinzip. Eine literaturpsychologische Untersuchung. Zeitschrift für angewandte Psychologie, 1924, 33:45.

3581. _____. Zur Psychologie der aesthetischen Grundgestalten bei Goethe. Archiv für die gesamte Psychologie, 1934, 90: 427-494.

3582. Kallich, Martin. The Association of Ideas and Critical Theory in Eighteenth-Century England: A History of Psychological Method in English Criticism. The Hague: Mouton, 1970.

3583. _____. The associationist psychology in Samuel Johnson's criticism. Modern Language Notes, 1954, 69:17-76.

3584. _____. On Paul Obler's 'Psychology and criticism.' Lit & Psychol, 1959, 9:4-5.

3585. Kanters, Robert. Psychanalyse et littérature. Rev de Paris, 1967, 74:123-131.

3586. Kantorowitz, Arnie. Homosexuals and literature. College English, 1974, 36:324-331.

3587. Kanzer, Mark. Applied psychoanalysis. I. Arts and aesthetics. In Annual Survey of Psychoanalysis, Vol. 2. NY: IUP, 1951, 438-475.

3588. _____. _____. III. Arts and aesthetics. In Annual Survey of Psychoanalysis, Vol. 3. NY: IUP, 1952, 511-546.

3589. _____. _____. III. Literature, art and aesthetics. In Annual Survey of Psychoanalysis, Vol. 4. NY: IUP, 1953, 355-389.

3590. _____. _____. III. Literature, arts, and aesthetics. In Annual Survey of Psychoanalysis, Vol. 5. NY: IUP, 1954, 457-473.

3591. _____. _____. III. Literature, arts, and aesthetics. In Annual Survey of Psychoanalysis, Vol. 6. NY: IUP, 1955, 444-465.

3592. _____. Contemporary psychoanalytic views of aesthetics. JAPA, 1957, 5:515-524.

3593. _____. Pioneers of applied analysis: Vol. III of the Minutes. Amer Imago, 1975, 32:59-76.

3594. _____. Review: Robert Jay Lifton, Shuichi Kato and Michael R. Reich's Six Lives. Six Deaths. Lit & Psychol, 1979, 29:89-92.

3595. Kapidzić-Osmanagić, Hanifa. Psihoanaliza--nadrealizam--marksizam. In Lukić, S., & Palavestra, P. (eds), Marksizam i knjizevna kritika u Jugoslaviji 1918-1941. Belgrade: Inst. za knjizevnost i umetnost, 1978, 171-186.

3596. Kaplan, Leo. The psychology of literary invention. Psyche & Eros, 1921, 2:65-80.

3597. Kaplan, Morton. The American Imago in retrospect: an article-review. Lit & Psychol, 1963, 13:112-116.

3598. _____, & Kloss, Robert J. The Unspoken Motive. A Guide to Psychoanalytic Literary Criticism. NY: Free Press, 1973; Reviews: Virginia R. Mollenkott, Christianity & Lit, 1975, 25:57-62; Richard W. Noland, Hartford Studies in Lit, 1975, 7:48-58.

3599. Karier, Clarence J. Art in a therapeutic age. J Aesthetic
       Education, 1979, 13:51-66.
3600. Karnani, Chetan. Criticism Aesthetics and Psychology: A
       Study of the Writings of I. A. Richards. New Delhi, India:
       Arnold Heinemann, 1977; Livingston, NJ: Orient Book,
       1980.
3601. _____. Criticism and Gestalt: a study of I. A. Richards'
       poetics. Banasthali Patrika, 1967, 9:45-48.
3602. Karriker, Alexander H. Double vision: Sasha Sakolov's
       School for Fools. World Lit Today, 1979, 33:610-613.
3603. Katzenelson, Boje. Psykologi og litteratur: Et meta-psyko-
       logisk essay for psykologer. Nordisk Psykologi, 1971,
       23(1):1-142.
3604. Kaufman, Pamela. Burke, Freud, and the Gothic. Studies
       in Burke & His Time, 1972, 13:2178-2192.
3605. Kaufmann, Walter. From Shakespeare to Existentialism.
       Boston: Beacon, 1959; Garden City, NY: Doubleday An-
       chor, 1960.
3606. Kaul, R. K. Dr. Johnson on the emotional effect of tragedy.
       Cairo Studies in English, 1963-66, 203-211.
3607. Kaviraj, Sudipta. Alienation and literature: a provisional
       paradigm. In Bhatti, A. (ed), Language and Literature in
       Society. New Delhi: Jawaharlal Nehru Univ., 1974, 1-27.
3608. Kayser, Wolfgang. The Grotesque in Art and Literature.
       Bloomington: Indiana Univ. Press, 1963.
3609. Kazin, Alfred. The language of pundits. In Contemporaries.
       Boston: Little, Brown, 1962, 382-393; In Manheim, L. F.,
       & Manheim, E. (eds), Hidden Patterns. NY: Macmillan,
       1966, 37-49.
3610. _____. Psychoanalysis and literary culture today. Parti-
       san Rev, 1959, 16:45-55; In Ruitenbeek, H. M. (ed), Psy-
       choanalysis and Literature. NY: Dutton, 1964, 3-13.
3611. Kearney, J. F. Psychology in the New Literature. Chicago:
       Loyola Univ. Press, 1931.
3612. Keesey, Donald. On some recent interpretations of catharsis.
       Classical World, 1978, 72:193-205.
3613. Keller, Karl. The Rev. Mr. Edward Taylor's bawdry. New
       England Q, 1970, 43:382-406.
3614. Kermode, Frank. Fighting Freud. New York Rev Books,
       29 Apr 1976, 39-41.
3615. Kern, Edith. Existential Thought and Fictional Technique:
       Kierkegaard, Sartre, Beckett. New Haven: Yale Univ.
       Press, 1970.
3616. Kernan, Alvin Bernard. Aggression and satire: art consid-
       ered as a forum of biological adaptation. In Brady, F.,
       Palmer, J., & Price, M. (eds), Literary Theory and
       Structure. New Haven: Yale Univ. Press, 1973, 115-129.
3617. Kerrigan, William. The articulation of the ego in the English
       Renaissance. In Smith, J. H. (ed), The Literary Freud.
       New Haven: Yale Univ. Press, 1980, 261-308.
3618. Khan, Asif Iqbal. Psychological criticism and the English
       literary tradition. Explorations, 1977, 4(2):26-32.
3619. King, Richard H. The Cultural Awakening of the American
       South, 1930-1955. NY: Oxford Univ. Press, 1980.

3620. Kinghorn, A. M. Literary aesthetics and the sympathetic emotions--a main trend in eighteenth century Scottish criticism. Studies in Scottish Lit, 1963, 1:35-47.

3621. Kirk, Russell. Literature, anxiety, and norms. Western Humanities Rev, 1957, 11:79-84.

3622. Kirkpatrick, Hope. Lewis contra Freud. Bulletin New York C. S. Lewis Society, 1973, 4(4):2-6.

3623. Kirkpatrick, Joanna. Women in Indian-English literature: the question of individuation. J South Asian Lit, 1977, 12(3-4):121-129.

3624. Kirsch, Hilde (ed). The Well-Tended Tree; Essays into the Spirit of Our Time. The C. G. Jung Foundation for Analytical Psychology. NY: Putnam, 1971.

3625. Kirschbaum, Gisela. Studien zur Psychologie Mörikes. Doctoral dissertation, Cologne, 1948.

3626. Kirsner, Douglas. The Schizoid World of Jean-Paul Sartre and R. D. Laing. Atlantic Highlands, NJ: Humanities Press, 1977.

3627. Kittler, F. A. Der Traum und die Rede. Eine Analyse der Kommunikationssituation. Conrad Ferdinand Meyer. Bern: Francke, 1977.

3628. Kjørup, Søren. Aesthetiske problemer. En indføring i kunstens filosofi. Copenhagen: Munksgaard, 1971.

3629. Klages, Ludwig. Goethe als Seelenforscher. Leipzig: Barth, 1933, 1940.

3630. Klein, Viola. The Feminine Character: History of an Ideology. NY: International University, 1948.

3631. Kligerman, Charles. Review: A. Ehrenzweig's The Psychoanalysis of Artistic Vision and Hearing. In Frosch, J., & Ross, N. (eds), The Annual Survey of Psychoanalysis, Vol. 4. NY: IUP, 1957, 578-590.

3632. Klineberg, Otto. Emotional expression in Chinese literature. J Abnormal Social Psychol, 1938, 33:517-520.

3633. Klinger, Eric. The flow of thought and its implications for a literary communication. Poetics: Int Rev for Theory of Lit, 1978, 7(2).

3634. Knapp, Bettina L. Anaïs Nin. NY: Ungar, 1978.

3635. _____. Archetypes: dissolution as a creation. In Dorenlot, F., & Tison-Braun, M. (eds), André Malraux; Metamorphosis and Imagination. NY: Literary Forum, 1979, 149-154.

3636. _____. Dream and Image. Troy, NY: Whitson, 1977.

3637. Knauer, Irmgard. Frauenzeichnung und Frauenpsychologie bei Franz Grillparzer. Doctoral dissertation, Munich, 1947.

3638. Knight, A. E. The farce wife: myth, parody and caricature. In Lacy, N. J. (ed), A Medieval French Miscellany. Lawrence: Univ. Kansas Publications, 1972.

3639. Knight, Isabel F. Utopian dream as psychic reality. Studies in Eighteenth-Century Culture, 1977, 6:427-438.

3640. Kockelmans, Joseph J. On suicide: reflections upon Camus' view of the problem. Psychoanal Rev, 1967, 54:31-48.

3641. Koenigsburg, Richard A.   Culture and unconscious fantasy:
      observations on courtly love. Psychoanal Rev, 1967, 54:
      36-50.
3642. Kofman, Sarah.   L'Enfance de l'art: une interprétation de
      l'esthétique freudienne. Paris: Payot, 1970.
3643. Kohlberg, Lawrence.   Moral psychology and the study of
      tragedy. In Weintraub, S., & Young, P. (eds), Directions
      in Literary Criticism: Contemporary Approaches to Liter-
      ature. University Park: Penn State Univ. Press, 1973,
      24-52.
3644. Kohut, Heinz.   Psychoanalysis and the interpretation of liter-
      ature: a correspondence with Erich Heller. Critical In-
      quiry, 1978, 4:433-450.
3645. Kolodny, Annette.   The land-as-woman: literary convention
      and latent psychological content. Women's Studies, 1973,
      1:167-182.
3646. Konda, Junzo. [Psychoanalytic Criticism of English and
      American Literature.] Kobe: Rokko Shuppan-Insatsu, 1970.
3647. Koppes, Phyllis Bixler.   The Child in Pastoral Myth: A
      Study in Rousseau and Wordsworth, Children's Literature
      and Literary Fantasy. DAI, 1978, 38:4141A.
3648. Kopposch, Michael S.   The dynamics of jealousy in the work
      of Madame de Lafayette. MLN, 1979, 94:757-773.
3649. Korner, J. Die Psychoanalyse des Stils. Literarische Echo,
      1919.
3650. Korpan, B.D.   Transcending the limitations of new criticism
      and later literary theory. Romance Philology, 1969, 22:
      300-313.
3651. Kostyleff, Nicolas.   La Psychanalyse appliquée a l'étude ob-
      jective de l'imagination. Rev Philosophique, 1912, 72:367-
      396.
3652. Kothari, Ujamlal C.   On the bullfight. Psychoanal Rev,
      1962, 49:123-127.
3653. Kozicki, Henry.   Critical methods in the literary evaluation
      of Sir Degare. Modern Language Q, 1968, 29:3-14.
3654. Krause, Sydney Joseph (ed). Essays on Determinism in
      American Literature. Kent, Ohio: Kent State Univ.
      Press, 1965.
3655. Krause-Jensen, Esbern.   Eksistentialistisk og faenomenologisk
      orienteret kritik. In Egebak, N. (ed), Aspekter af nyere fransk
      litteraturkritik. Copenhagen: Munksgaard, 1972, 11-44.
3656. Kreibig, J.   Beiträge zur Psychologie des Kuntschaffens.
      Zeitschrift für Ästhetik, 1909, 4:532-558.
3657. Kreitler, Hans, & Kreitler, Shulamith. Psychology of the
      Arts. Durham, NC: Duke Univ. Press, 1972.
3658. Krickel, Edward.   Narcissus in North Carolina: Harold Gri-
      er McCurdy. Georgia Rev, 1972, 26:71-77.
3659. Krieger, Murray.   The critic as person and persona. In
      Strekla, J. (ed), The Personality of the Critic. University
      Park: Penn State Univ. Press, 1973.
3660. _____. Northrop Frye in Modern Criticism. Selected Pa-
      pers from the English Institute. NY: Columbia Univ.
      Press, 1966.

3661. _____, & Dembo, L. S. (eds). Directions for Criticism: Structuralism and Its Alternatives. Madison: Univ. Wisconsin Press, 1977.

3662. Kris, Ernst. Psychoanalysis and the study of creative imagination. Bulletin New York Academy Medicine, 1953, 29: 334-351; In Ruitenbeek, H. M. (ed), The Creative Imagination: Psychoanalysis and the Genius of Inspiration. Chicago: Quadrangle, 1965, 23-45.

3663. _____. Psychoanalytic Explorations in Art. NY: IUP, 1952; São Paulo, Brazil: Editoria Brasilieuse, n. d.; Belgrade: Misav i Dileme, 1970.

3664. Krogmann, W. Motivanalyse. Zeitschrift für angewandte Psychologie, 1932, 42:264-272.

3665. _____. Neuere Schriften zur Literatur-psychologie. Zeitschrift für angewandte Psychologie, 1933, 44:142-151.

3666. Kronhausen, Eberhard, & Kronhausen, Phyllis. Pornography and the Law. The Psychology of Erotic Realism and 'Hard Core' Pornography. NY: Ballantine, 1959.

3667. Kruithof, Jacques. Literatuur en psychoanalyse. [Review: Hendrik M. Ruitenbeek's Psychoanalyse en literatuur.] Raam, 1970, 69:48-61.

3668. Krutch, Joseph Wood. Poe's idea of beauty. Nation, 1926, 122:285-287.

3669. Krutz-Ahlring, Ingrid. Literatur als Kommunikation: Zur Frage der historischen und psychosozialen Vermittlung positivistischer Denkweisen in Literatur und Literaturkritik. Giessen: Focus, 1976.

3670. Kubal, David. Lionel Trilling: the mind and its discontents. Hudson Rev, 1978, 31:279-295.

3671. Kubie, Lawrence S. Neurotic Distortion of the Creative Process. Lawrence: Univ. Kansas Press, 1958; Toronto: Noonday, 1958.

3672. Kuczkowski, Richard J. Lawrence's 'Esoteric' Psychology: Psychoanalysis and the Unconscious and Fantasia of the Unconscious. DAI, 1974, 35:1107A.

3673. Kudszus, Winfried G. Literatur und Schizophrenie. Forschungslage und Forschungsaufgaben. Confinia Psychiatria, 1979, 22:160-175.

3674. _____. Literatur und Schizophrenie. Theorie und Interpretation eines Grenzgebiets. Berlin: DTV & Niemeyer, 1977.

3675. _____. Reflections on the double bind of literature and psychopathology. Sub-stance, 1978, 20:19-36.

3676. Kuhn, Ortwin. Mythos-Neuplatonismus-Mystik: Studien zur Gestaltung des Alkestisstoffes. Munich: Goldmann, 1972.

3677. Kuhn, Reinhard. The Demon of Noontide: Ennui in Western Literature. Princeton: Princeton Univ. Press, 1976.

3678. Kuhr, V. Aesthetik Oplevn og Kunstnerisk Skaben. Copenhagen: Gyldenalske, 1927.

3679. Kunene, Daniel P. Problems in creating creative writing: the example of southern Africa. Rev National Lit, 1971, 2(2):81-103.

3680. Kunkel, Francis L. Passion and the Passion. Sex and Religion in Modern Literature. Philadelphia: Westminster Press, 1975.

3681. Kuntz, Paul Grimley. Art as public dream: the practice and theory of Anaïs Nin. JAAC, 1974, 32:525-537; In Zaller, R. (ed), A Casebook on Anaïs Nin. NY: New American Library, 1974, 77-99.

3682. Kurth, W. Das Traumbuch des Artemidoros in Lichte der Freudschen Traumlehre. Psyche, 1951, 4:488-512.

3683. Kussel, Peter B. From the anus to the mouth to the eye. Semiotexte, 1976, 2(2):105-119.

3684. Kuttner, A. B. The artist. Seven Arts, 1917, 1:409-412, 549-551.

3685. Kuznets, Lois R. Games of dark: psychofantasy in children's literature. Lion and Unicorn, 1977, 1(2):17-24.

3686. Laborde, A. M. La Notion de l'isolisme et ses implications lyriques dans l'oeuvre du marquis de Sade. Studies on Voltaire & the 18th Century, 1972, 88:871-880.

3687. Lacan, Jacques. Ecrits. Le Camp freudien. Paris: Seuil, 1966; Ecrits. A Selection. NY: Norton, 1977; Reviews: Richard H. King, Georgia Rev, 1978, 32:926-930; Stuart Allen Schneiderman, New Republic, 1977, 177(20):34-35.

3688. _____. La Fonction de l'écrit. In Le Séminaire XX: Encore. Paris: Seuil, 1975 (1972).

3689. _____. Homage fait à Marguerite Duras du ravissement de Lol. V. Stein. Cahiers Renaud-Barrault, 1965, 52.

3690. _____. L'Instance de la lettre dans l'inconscient ou la raison depuis Freud. La Psychanalyse, 1957, 3:47-81.

3691. _____. The insistence of the letter in the unconscious. Yale French Studies, 1966, 36-37:112-148; In Ehrmann, J. (ed), Structuralism. Garden City, NY: Doubleday, 1970, 103-136.

3692. _____. Kant avec Sade. Critique, 1963, No. 191, 2:93-313.

3693. _____. The Language of the Self. The Function of Language in Psychoanalysis. Translated with notes and commentary by Anthony Wilden. Baltimore: Johns Hopkins Univ. Press, 1968.

3694. _____. Lituraterre. Littérature, 1971, 3:2-5.

3695. _____. Le Myth individuel du nevrosé ou 'Poesie et Verité' dans la névrose. Paris: Editions des Grandes-Têtes-Molles de notre epoque, n. d.

3696. _____. Retour à Freud. La Quinzaine Littéraire, 1966, 15:4-5.

3697. _____. Of structure as an inmixing of an otherness prerequisite to any subject whatever. In Macksey, R., & Donato, E. U. (eds), The Languages of Criticism and the Sciences of Man; The Structuralist Controversy. Baltimore: Johns Hopkins Univ. Press, 1970, 186-195.

3698. Lacaux, André, & Pachet, Pierre. L'Apport de la psychanalyse à l'études des oeuvres littéraires. Dossiers pédagogiques de la RT scolaire, 1971-72, no. 1, 14-17.

3699. Lacey, Stephen W. Structure for Awareness in Dante and Shakespeare. DAI, 1973, 33:4421-A.

3700. Lacombe, P. La Psychologie de Taine appliquée à l'histoire littéraire. Rev Philosophique, 1905, 40:173-190.

3701. Lacroix, Jean. Les Ecrits de Lacan ou retour à Freud. Le Monde, 24 Dec 1966, no. 6827, 11.

3702. Laden, Richard A. Terror, nature, and the sacrifice in the Comtesse de Ségur's Les Petites filles modèles. MLN, 1979, 94:742-756.

3703. Laere, F. van. Jean-Jacques Rousseau: du phantasme à l'ecriture. Les Révélations du 'Lévite d'Ephraim.' Archives des Lettres Modernes, 1967, 81.

3704. Lafitte, Maryse. L'Image de la femme chez Breton: contradictions et virtualités. Rev Romane, 1976, 11:286-305.

3705. Lagache, Elisabeth. Medicine mentale et expression théatrale. Jeune Afrique, 1974, 22:40-41.

3706. La Galliot, Jean. Psychanalyse et langages littéraires: théorie et pratique. Paris: Nathan, 1977.

3707. LaGuardia, Eric. Lacan's full and empty words, and literary discourse. In Cadot, M. et al., (eds), Actes du VIe Congrès de l'Association Internationale de Littérature Comparée. Stuttgart: Bieber, 1975, 57-61.

3708. Lamb, Charles. 'Sanity of True Genius.' In The Last Essays of Elia. London: Newnes, 253-254.

3709. Landau, Jacob. Loneliness and creativity. In Hartog, J., Audy, J.R., & Cohen, Y.A. (eds). The Anatomy of Loneliness. NY: IUP, 1980.

3710. Lane, Lauriat, Jr. The literary archetype: some reconsiderations. JAAC, 1954, 13:226-232.

3711. Langbaum, Robert Woodrow. The mysteries of identity: a theme in modern literature. Amer Scholar, 1965, 34:569-586; In his The Modern Spirit; Essays on the Continuity of Nineteenth- and Twentieth-Century Literature. NY: Oxford Univ. Press, 1970, 164-184.

3712. _____. _____. NY: Oxford Univ. Press, 1977; Reviews: T. Parkinson, Southern Rev, 1979, 15:742-752; R. Schleifer, MLN, 1978, 1052-1059.

3713. Lange, Victor. Goethe in psychologischer und ästhetischer Sicht. In Paulsen, W. (ed), Psychologie in der Literaturwissenschaft. Heidelberg: Stiehm, 1971, 140-156.

3714. Langenbucher, W. Der aktuelle Unterhaltungsroman. Beitrage zur Geschichte und Theorie der massenhaft verbreitete Literatur. Bonn: Bouvier, 1964.

3715. Langer, Lawrence L. Time, space, and dreams in the holocaust universe. Centerpoint, 1977, 2(3):65-68.

3716. Langer, Suzanne K. On artistic sensibility. Daedalus, 1960, 89:242-244.

3717. _____. Feeling and Form. NY: Scribner's, 1953.

3718. _____. Mind: An Essay on Human Feeling, Vol. I. Baltimore: Johns Hopkins, 1967.

3719. Languth, William. The world and life of the dreams. Yale French Studies, 1965, No. 34, 117-130.

3720. Laplanche, Jean, & Leclaire, Serge. The unconscious: a psychoanalytic study. Yale French Rev, 1972, 48:118-175.

3721.   Lapouge, Gilles.   Jacques Lacan veut que la psychanalyse
        'redevienne la peste.'   Le Figaro Littéraire, 1 Dec 1966,
        no. 1076, 11.
3722.   _____.   Sartre contra Lacan, bataille absurde, mais....
        Figaro Littéraire, 29 Dec 1966, 4.
3723.   Larulle, François.   Le Style di-phallique de Jacques Der-
        rida.   Critique (Paris): 1975, 31:320-339.
3724.   Laskowsky, Henry I.   The rhetoric of sex.   Colorado Q,
        1974, 23:149-157.
3725.   Lauren, Mary.   Psychological approaches to literary criti-
        cism.   Catholic School J, 1968, 68:57-59.
3726.   Lavers, Annette.   L'Usurpateur et le prétendant, essai.   Le
        Psychologue dans la littérature contemporaine.   Paris:
        Minard, 1964.
3727.   Lawall, Sally N.   Review: Joseph P. Strelka (ed), Problems
        of Literary Evaluation.   Hartford Studies in Lit, 1970, 2:
        256-262.
3728.   Lawall, Sarah.   Critics of Consciousness.   The Existential
        Structures of Literature.   Cambridge: Harvard Univ.
        Press, 1968.
3729.   Lawrence, D. H.   A new theory of neuroses.   Bookman, 1927,
        66:314; In Phoenix: The Posthumous Papers of D. H. Law-
        rence.   NY: Viking, 1936, 377, 378; London: Heinem-
        mann, 1936, 377, 378.
3730.   _____.   Psychoanalysis and the Unconscious; Fantasia of
        the Unconscious.   NY: Viking, 1960; NY: Seltzer,
        1921.
3731.   _____.   Sex, Literature and Censorship.   NY: Twayne,
        1953; NY: Viking, 1959.
3732.   Lawson, Richard H., & Stamon, Peggy.   Love-death struc-
        tures in the works of Arthur Schnitzler.   Modern Austrian
        Lit, 1975, 8(3-4):266-281.
3733.   Lawton, R. A.   Almeida Garrett, l'intime contrainte.   Paris:
        Didier, 1966; Review: J. Roche, Caravelle, 1968, 11:
        231-233.
3734.   Lazzeroni, Virgilio.   La psicologia di Henri Bergson.
        Sophia, 1942, 10:275-289, 424-440.
3735.   Lease, Benjamin.   Hawthorne and the archaeology of the
        cinema.   Nathaniel Hawthorne J, 1977, 6:133-171.
3736.   Leavy, Stanley A.   L'Ecole freudienne.   New York Times
        Book Rev, 2 Oct 1977, 10, 38-39.
3737.   _____.   Psychoanalytic interpretation.   In The Psycho-
        analytic Study of the Child, Vol. 28.   New Haven: Yale
        Univ. Press, 1973, 305-330.
3738.   _____.   The significance of Jacques Lacan.   In Smith,
        J. H. (ed), Psychoanalysis and Language.   New Haven:
        Yale Univ. Press, 1978, 271-292.
3739.   Lebel, Maurice.   Etudes littéraires.   Tome II.   De René
        Bazin à Antoine de Saint-Exupéry.   Montréal: Centre de
        Psychologie et de Pédagogie, 1964.
3740.   _____.   _____.   Tome I.   De Saint François de Sales
        à Alphonse Daudet.   Montréal: Centre de Psychologie et
        de Pédagogie, 1964.

3741. Lebois, André. Amitié, amour et inceste dans Cleveland. In Fabre, J. (ed), L'Abbé Prévost. Actes du Colloque d'Aix-en-Provence. Aix-en-Provence: Ophrys, 1965, 125-137.

3742. Lechner, Emil T. Experience of the Numinous in Yeats, Jung, and Bonhoeffer. DAI, 1974, 35:2280A-81A.

3743. Leclaire, Serge. Démasquer le réel: Un essai sur l'object en psychanalyse. Paris: Seuil, 1971.

3744. _____. Psychanalyser: Un essai sur l'ordre de l'inconscient et la pratique de la lettre. Paris: Seuil, 1968.

3745. _____. Le Réel dans le texte. Littérature, 1971, 3:30-32.

3746. Leclercq, Jean. Modern psychology and the interpretation of medieval texts. Speculum, 1973, 48:476-490.

3747. _____. Psicologia moderna e interpretazione di testi medievali. Nuova Rivista Storica, 1976, 40:150-168.

3748. Ledru, P. Un Aspect de la névrose dans la littérature décandente. In Mélanges Pierre Lambert consacrés à Huysmans. Paris: Nizet, 1975, 291-316.

3749. Leduc-Fayette, D. Jean-Jacques Rousseau et le mythe de l'antiquité. Paris: Vrin, 1974.

3750. Lee, Brian. Theory and Personality: The Significance of T.S. Eliot's Criticism. London: Athlone, 1980; Atlantic Highlands, NJ: Humanities, 1979.

3751. Lee, Harry B. The creative imagination as a psychoanalytic problem. Psychoanal Q, 1949, 18:351-360.

3752. _____. A theory concerning free creation in the inventive arts. Psychiatry, 1940, 3:229-294.

3753. Lee, Vernon (Violet Paget). The Handling of Words and Other Studies in Literary Psychology. London: Lane, 1927.

3754. _____. Studies in literary psychology: III. Carlyle and the present tense. Contemporary Rev, 1904, 85:386-392.

3755. _____. _____. I. The syntax of DeQuincey. Contemporary Rev, 1903, 84:713-723, 856-864.

3756. Lefcowitz, Barbara F., & Lefcowitz, Allan B. Old age and the modern literary imagination: an overview. Soundings, 1976, 59:447-466.

3757. Lefebvre, J. Les Fols et la folie. Etude sur les genres du comique et la création littéraire en Allemagne pendant la Renaissance. Paris: Klincksieck, 1968.

3758. Lefebve, Maurice-Jean. L'Image, la psychanalyse et l'explication littéraire. Rev de l'université de Bruxelles, 1965, 15:199-214.

3759. LeGalliot, Jean. Psychanalyse et langage littéraires. Paris: Nathan, 1977; Review: Larry W. Riggs, French Rev, 1979, 53:117.

3760. Le Gates, M. The cult of womanhood in eighteenth-century thought. Eighteenth Century Studies, 1976, 10:21-39.

3761. Lehmann, Günther K. Phantasie und künstlerische Arbeit: Betrachtungen zur poetischen Phantasie. Berlin: Aufbau, 1966.

3762. _____. Die Theorie der literarischen Rezeption aus soziologischer und psychologischer Sicht. Weimarer Beiträge, 1974, 20(8):49-70.

3763. Lehner, Fritz. Der Einbruch der Psychoanalyse in de fran-
       zösische Literatur. Almanach, 1929, 202-210.

3764. Leigh, James Anthony. Reading the Text: A Study of Se-
       lected Writings of Michel Leiris, Claude Simon, Alain
       Robbe-Grillet, Samuel Beckett and Maurice Roche within
       the Context of Contemporary Critical Thought. DAI, 1976,
       37:3613A.

3765. Leighton, Jean U. The Concept of Woman in the Works of
       Simone de Beauvoir. DAI, 1970, 30:3947A.

3766. _____. Simone de Beauvoir on Women. Cranbury, NJ:
       Fairleigh Dickinson Univ. Press, 1975.

3767. Leitch, Vincent B. Primer of recent critical theories: re-
       ception aesthetics, Geneva criticism, and Buffalo criticism.
       College English, 1977, 39:138-152.

3768. Leite, Dante Moreira. Psicologia e Literatura. São Paulo:
       Conselho Estadual de Cultura, 1965; São Paulo: Nacional,
       1967.

3769. Lejeune, R. La Femme dans les littératures française et
       occitane du XIe au XIIIe siècle. Cahiers de Civilisation
       Médiévale, 1977, 20:201-217.

3770. Le Maire, Louis. L'Importance de la littérature comme
       facteur criminologéne. Acta Psychiatrica et Neurologica,
       1946, 21:585-593.

3771. LeMettrie, Julien Offray de. Discours sur le bonheur.
       Edited by John Falvey. Oxford: Voltaire Foundation,
       1975.

3772. Lemon, Lee T. Beyond alienation. Aegis, 1973, 2:5-12.

3773. _____. The Partial Critics. NY: Oxford Univ. Press,
       1965, 91-95.

3774. Lerner, Laurence. Literature and money. In Ellrodt, R.
       (comp.), English Association. Essays and Studies, Vol.
       28. NY: Humanities Press, 1975, 106-122.

3775. _____. Psychology in criticism. In Strelka, J. P. (ed),
       Literary Criticism and Psychology. University Park:
       Penn State Univ. Press, 1976.

3776. Le Sage, Laurent. Charles Mauron in retrospect. L'Esprit
       créateur, 1974, 14:265-276.

3777. Lesort, Paul-André. J'en avais assez de la psychologie.
       Monde [des Livres], 25 Mar 1977, no. 10,000, 19.

3778. Lessa, Luis C. Psicanálise, sociologia e critica literária.
       Ocidente, 1972, 82:270-274.

3779. Lesser, Simon O. The function of form in narrative art.
       Psychiatry, 1955, 18:51-63.

3780. _____. The nature of psychoanalytic criticism. Lit &
       Psychol, 1962, 12:5-9.

3781. _____. The Whispered Meanings; Selected Essays. Edited
       by Sprich, R., & Noland, R.W. Amherst: Univ. Massa-
       chusetts Press, 1977.

3782. Lessner, Johanna W. Melpomene and Psyche: The Synergy
       of Literature and Psychology. DAI, 1974, 34:1259.

3783. LeUnes, Arnold. Readings in abnormal behavior: another
       visit with an old friend. Psychol Reports, 1976, 39:696-
       698.

3784. Leverenz, David. The Language of Puritan Feeling: An Exploration in Literature, Psychology, and Social History. New Brunswick, NJ: Rutgers Univ. Press, 1980.

3785. Levi Bianchini, Marco. La psicoanalisi della fantasia creatrice e il pensiere autistico nell'arte e nelle psicosi. Archivio Generale di Neurologie, Psichiatria e Psicoanalisti, 1922, 3:19-39, 73-76.

3786. Levin, Harry. Contexts of Criticism. Cambridge: Harvard Univ. Press, 1957.

3787. _____. From obsession to imagination: the psychology of the writer. Michigan Q Rev, 1974, 13:183-202.

3788. Levin, Meyer. A new fear in writers. Psychoanalysis, 1953, 2(1):34-38.

3789. Levinson, R. B. Gertrude Stein, William James and grammar. Amer J Psychol, 1941, 54:124-128.

3790. Levitt, H. N. Psychoanalyst, artist and critic. Contemporary Psychoanal, 1976, 12:140-143.

3791. Levy, Elizabeth J. The Concept of Jealousy in Selected Works of Arthur Schnitzler. Master's thesis, Temple Univ., 1974.

3792. Lewandowski, Herbert. Das Sexualproblem in der modernen Literatur und Kunst ... Seit 1800. Dresden: Arets, 1927.

3793. Lewin, K. K. The value of psychoanalytic literary criticism. Psychiat Communications, 1962, 5:103-106.

3794. Lewinter, Roger. Diderot, ou les mots de l'absence. Essai sur la forme de l'oeuvre. Paris: Champ Libre, 1976.

3795. Lewis, Clive S. Psycho-analysis and literary criticism. In Hooper, W. (ed), Selected Literary Criticism. Cambridge: University Press, 1969, 282-291; Essays & Studies, 1942, 27:7-21.

3796. Lewis, T. (ed). Symbols and Sentiments: Cross-cultural Studies in Symbolism. NY: Academic, 1977.

3797. Lewisohn, Ludwig. Expression in America. NY: Harper, 1932; The Story of American Literature. [Reissue.] NY: Modern Library, 1939.

3798. Lhermitte, Jean. De l'Angoisse au génie. De l'anxieté de Lucrèce, l'angoisse de Pascal. Encéphale (et Hygiène Mentale). J de Psychiatrie, 1946-47, 36:60-64.

3799. Lhoté, Andre. The unconscious in art. Transition, 1937, 26:82-96.

3800. Lifton, Robert Jay. From analysis to form: towards a shift in psychological paradigm. Salmagundi, 1975, 28:43-78.

3801. Linck, Alice E. Meyer. The Psychological Basis of Hazlitt's Criticism. Doctoral dissertation, Univ. Kansas, 1961.

3802. Lindauer, Martin S. Pleasant and unpleasant emotions in literature: a comparison with the affective tone of psychology. J Psychol, 1968, 70:55-67.

3803. _____. The Psychological Study of Literature. Limitations, Possibilities, and Accomplishments. Chicago: Nelson-Hall, 1973, Review: John V. Knapp, Modern Fiction Studies, 1975, 21:669-672.

3804. Lindgren, Sören. Den psykologiska genren och Solveig von Schoultz. Nya Argus, 1965, 58:299-301.

3805. Lindner, Robert (ed). Explorations in Psychoanalysis. NY: Julian, 1953.

3806. Lindskoog, Kathryn. Getting it together: C. S. Lewis and the two hemispheres of knowing. J Psychol & Theology, 1975, 3:290-293.

3807. Linebargar, Paul M. STASM: psychological warfare and literary criticism. South Atlantic Q, 1947, 46:344-348.

3808. Linnér, Sven. Om den psykologiska argumentationem: studier i litteraturhistorisk metodpraxis II. Samlaren, 1962, 83:92-124.

3809. Lira, O. Ortega y Gasset en su espiritu, Vol. 2. Santiago: Univ. Chile Press, 1967.

3810. Littlewood, A. R. The symbolism of the apple in Greek and Roman literature. Harvard Studies Classical Philology, 1968, 72:147-181.

3811. Litwinski, Leon. La Psychologie et la littérature. Lisbon: Grafica de Coimbra, 1944.

3812. Litz, Arthur Walton. Literary criticism. In Hoffman, D. (ed), Harvard Guide to Contemporary American Writing. Cambridge: Harvard Univ. Press, 1979.

3813. Livingstone, Leon. The law of nature and women's liberation in Tristana. Anales Galdosianos, 1972, 7.

3814. Ljungdal, Arnold. Avantgardism och alienation hos Lukács. Bonniers Litterära Magasin, 1967, 36:114-125.

3815. ———. Lukács, alienationem och konsten. Bonniers Litterära Magasin, 1967, 36:35-43.

3816. Lloyd, Danuta E. A Woman Looks at Man: The Male Psyche as Depicted in the Works of Marie von Ebner-Eschenbach. DA, 1969, 30:2535A.

3817. Lobb, Edward. Armah's Fragments and the vision of the whole. Ariel, 1979, 10:25-38.

3818. Lobsiger, Ernst. Die Funktion des Psychiaters in der deutschen Literatur zwischen 1917 und 1966. DAI, 1974, 34:5110A.

3819. Lo Cicero, Vincent. A study of persona in selected works of Arthur Schnitzler. Modern Austrian Lit, 1969, 2(4): 7-29.

3820. Loganbill, Dean. Literature as initiation. Proceedings Society for New Language Study, 1972, 1(1):19-24.

3821. Loof, B. H. Inzicht in en kennis van literatuur. Levende Talen, 1972, 287:216-221.

3822. Lopes, Oscar. A infância e a adolescência na ficção portuguesa. Seara Nova, 1963, 42:222-226, 235.

3823. Lotz, Steven D. Symbols of cosmic sexuality: archetypes of divine generation. Int J Symbology, 1973, 4(1):12-30.

3824. Lucas, Frank L. Literature and Psychology. Ann Arbor: Ann Arbor Books, 1957; London: Cassell, 1951.

3825. Lucka, Emil. Verdoppelunger des Ich. Preussische Jahrbücher, 1904, 115:54-83.

3826. Lukianowicz, N. [Autoscopic phenomena.] Archives Neurologica Psychiatria, 1958, 80:199-200.

3827. Lüking, Bernd. Introducing Theodor W. Adorno: the use of aesthetic theory for literature and criticism. Unisa English Studies, 1978, 16(2):59-63.

3828. Lund, Mary Graham.   The androgynous mind: Woolf and
      Eliot.   Renascence, 1960, 12(2):74-78.
3829. Luppé, R.   Délivrance par la littérature.   Paris: Aubier,
      1946.
3830. Luquet, Pierre.   Art et fantasmes.   Rev Française de Psy-
      chanalyse, 1964, 28(4).
3831. _____.   La Fonction esthétique de la personnalité et son
      rôle structurant.   In Entretiens sur l'art et la psych-
      analyse.   The Hague: Mouton, 1968.
3832. _____.   Ouverture sur l'artiste et le psychanalyste: la
      fonction esthétique du moi.   Rev Française de Psych-
      analyse, 1963, 27(6).
3833. Lusser-Mertelsmann, G.   Max Frisch.   Die Identitätsprob-
      lematik in seinem Werk aus psychoanalytischer Sicht.
      Stuttgart: Heinz, 1976.
3834. Lussheimer, Paul.   The growth of artistic creativity through
      the psychoanalytic process.   In Ruitenbeek, H. M. (ed),
      The Creative Imagination.   Chicago: Quadrangle, 1965,
      161-191.
3835. Lyman, Mead, Margaret, Arnheim, Rudolf, & Nahm, Milton.
      The conditions for creativity.   In Summerfield, J. D., &
      Thatcher, L. (eds), The Creative Mind and Method: Ex-
      ploring the Nature of Creativeness in American Arts, Sci-
      ences, and Professions.   Austin: Univ. Texas Press,
      1960.
3836. Lynch, W. F.   The task of enlargement.   Thought, 1976, 51:
      345-355.
3837. Lyon, Melvin.   Symbol and Idea in Henry Adams.   Lincoln:
      Univ. Nebraska Press, 1970.
3838. Lyons, Bridget Gellert.   Voices of Melancholy: Studies in
      Literary Treatments of Melancholy in Renaissance Eng-
      land.   NY: Barnes & Noble, 1971.
3839. Lyons, John O.   The Invention of the Self: The Hinge of
      Consciousness in the Eighteenth Century.   Carbondale:
      Southern Illinois Univ. Press, 1978.
3840. Lyotard, Jean-François.   Oedipe Juif.   Critique: Rev Gén-
      érale des Publications Françaises et Etrangères, 1970,
      26(277):530-545; Jewish Oedipus, Genre, 1977, 10:395-411.
3841. _____.   Principales tendances actuelles de l'étude psych-
      analytique des expressions artistiques et littéraires.
      Dérive à partir de Marx et Freud.   Paris: 10/18, 1973.

3842. MacAdam, Alfred J.   Machado de Assis: satire and mad-
      ness.   In Modern Latin American Narratives: the
      Dreams of Reason.   Chicago: Univ. Chicago Press,
      1977, 11-28.
3843. _____.   Origins and narratives.   MLN, 1980, 95:424-435.
3844. McAleer, John J.   The therapeutic vituperations of Thoreau.
      Amer Transcendental Q, 1971, 11:81-87.
3845. McAllister, H. S.   Be a man, be a woman: androgyny in
      House Made of Dawn.   Amer Indian Q, 1975, 2:14-22.
3846. McAuley, James.   Sex and love in literature.   Quadrant: An
      Australian Bi-Monthly, 1972, 78:15-23.

3847. McCurdy, Harold G.   Psychological Analysis of Literary Pro-
        ductivity as a Revelation of Personality.   Doctoral dis-
        sertation, Duke Univ., 1938.

3848. _____.   The psychology of literature.   In Sills, D. L. (ed),
        International Encyclopedia of the Social Sciences, Vol. 9.
        NY: Macmillan, 1968.

3849. McDowell, Frederick P. W.   E. M. Forster's theory of litera-
        ture.   Criticism, 1966, 8:19-43.

3850. McElroy, David Dunbar.   Existentialism and Modern Litera-
        ture: An Essay in Existential Criticism.   NY: Citadel,
        1963.

3851. _____.   The Study of Literature: An Existential Appraisal.
        NY: Philosophical Library, 1965.

3852. McFarland, Thomas.   The origin and significance of Coler-
        idge's theory of secondary imagination.   In Hartman, G.
        H. (ed), New Perspectives on Coleridge and Wordsworth.
        NY: Columbia Univ. Press, 1972, 195-246.

3853. McIntosh, James.   Emerson's unmoored self.   Yale Rev,
        1976, 65:232-240.

3854. Mackay, A. T.   The religious significance of animal magnet-
        ism in the later works of Jean Paul.   German Life &
        Letters, 1970, 23:216-225.

3855. McKay, Llewelyn R.   The Problem of Death in the Viennese
        School as Represented by Schnitzler, Rilke, and Hofmanns-
        thal.   Palo Alto, Cal: Stanford Univ. Press, 1939.

3856. McKellar, P.   Imagination and Thinking: A Psychological
        Analysis.   NY: Basic Books, 1957.

3857. McKenzie, Gordon.   Critical Responsiveness.   A Study of the
        Psychological Current in Later Eighteenth-Century Criti-
        cism.   Berkeley: Univ. California Press, 1949.

3858. McKinney, F.   Psychology in relation to literature.   In Psy-
        chology in Action: Basic Readings.   NY: Macmillan,
        1967.

3859. McLean, Helen V.   Freud and literature.   Saturday Rev,
        1948, 3:18-19.

3860. Maclean, Robert Michael.   Narcissus and the Voyeur:
        Some Aspects of Empirical Description.   DAI, 1978,
        38:4159A.

3861. McMaster, R. D.   Dickens, Jung, and Coleridge.   Dalhousie
        Rev, 1959, 38.

3862. McMunn, Meradith T.   Children and literature in medieval
        France.   Children's Lit, 1975, 4:51-58.

3863. McSweeney, Kerry.   Melville, Dickinson, Whitman and psy-
        choanalytic criticism.   Critical Q, 1977, 19(1):71-82.

3864. Maddaloni, Arnold.   The meaning of empathy.   Amer Imago,
        1961, 18:21-33.

3865. Madden, Deanna Kay.   Laboratory of the Soul: The Influence
        of Psychoanalysis in the Work of Anaïs Nin.   DAI, 1976,
        36:6138A-39A.

3866. Madden, William A.   Matthew Arnold: A Study of the Aes-
        thetic Temperament in Victorian England.   Bloomington:
        Indiana Univ. Press, 1967.

3867. Maeland, Odd M. Psykiatri og/eller litteraturforskning?
       Edda, 1968, 55:264-274.

3868- Magat, J. A. Emerson's aesthetics of fiction. Emerson So-
9.   ciety Q, 1977, 23:139-155.

3870. Magliola, Robert R. The phenomenological approach to liter-
       ature: its theory and methodology. Language & Style,
       1972, 5:79-99.

3871. _____. Phenomenology and Literature. West Lafayette,
       Ind: Purdue Univ. Press, 1977; Review: D. H. Hirsch,
       Sewanee Rev, 1979, 87:628-638; D. G. Marshall, Philo-
       logical Q, 1978, 57:273-274.

3872. Magny, C. E. Existentialisme et littérature. Poésie, 1946,
       29:58-67.

3873. Mahoney, John L. Addison and Akenside: the impact of
       psychological criticism on early English poetry. British
       J Aesthetics, 1966, 6:365-374.

3874. Maier, Norman R. F., & Reninger, H. Willard. A Psycho-
       logical Approach to Literary Criticism. NY: Appleton,
       1933; Darby, Pa: Arden, 1980.

3875. Maini, Darshan Singh. Psychoanalysis and modern American
       criticism. In Chandir, J., & Pradhan, N. S. (eds),
       Studies in American Literature. Delhi: Oxford Univ.
       Press, 1976, 1-16.

3876. Maire, Gilbert. Une Régression mentale d'Henri Bergson à
       Jean-Paul Sartre. Paris: Grasset, 1962.

3877. Majewski, H. Genius and poetry in the Pre-Romantic imagi-
       nation of L. S. Mercier. Romanic Rev, 1966, 57:177-
       187.

3878. Major, Jean-Louis. Le Philosophe comme critique littéraire.
       Dialogue, 1965-66, 4:230-242.

3879. Major, René. L'Agonie du jour: Francis Bacon. L'Arc,
       1978, 73.

3880. Malek, James S. The influence of empirical psychology on
       aesthetic discourse: two eighteenth century theories of
       art. Enlightenment Essays, 1970, 1(1):1-16.

3881. Malone, David H. (ed). The Frontiers of Literary Criticism.
       Los Angeles: Hennessey & Ingalls, 1974.

3882. Malpique, Cruz. Psicologia literária do homem do Porto:
       De como o portuense se divertia noutros tempos e o que
       mais se verá. Boletim Cultural, Câmara Municipal do
       Porto, 1961, 24:283-316.

3883. Manganyi, N. Chabani. The violent reverie: the unconscious
       in literature and society. In Mashangu's Reveries and
       Other Essays. Johannesburg: Ravan, 1977, 53-71.

3884. Manheim, Leonard F. The Buffalo school of psychoanalytic
       critics. Hartford Studies in Lit, 1971, 3:213-218.

3885. _____. New dimensions in psychoanalytic criticism.
       CEA Chapbook, 1972, 35:29-34.

3886. _____. The problem of the normative fallacy. In Strelka,
       J. P. (ed), Yearbook of Comparative Criticism, Vol. 2.
       University Park: Penn State Univ. Press, 1969, 129-
       139.

3887. _____. Psychopathia literaria: a commentary. In Paje, J. D. (ed), Approaches to Psychopathology. NY: Columbia Univ. Press, 1966, 116-138.

3888. _____. Recent developments in psychoanalytic literary criticism. CEA Chapbook, Supplement, CEA Critic, 1972, 34:29-34; Peabody J Education, 1972, 59:29-32.

3889. _____. Toward a psychoanalytic theory of literature. Shenandoah, 1966, 17:61-68; Lit & Psychol, 1966, 16:192-197; Introduction to Hidden Patterns. NY: Macmillan, 1966.

3890. _____, Faber, M. D., & Resnik, Harvey, L. P. (eds). A new anatomy of melancholy. Patterns of self-aggression among authors. [Speech issue.] Hartford Studies in Lit, 1978, 10:1-199.

3891. Mann, Thomas. Freud and the future. Int J Psycho-Anal, 1956, 37:106-115; Daedalus, 1959, 88:374-378; In Essays of Three Decades. NY: Knopf, 1937, 1947 (1936), 311-323; In Ellmann, R., & Feidelson, C., Jr. (eds), The Modern Tradition: Backgrounds of Modern Literature. NY: Oxford Univ. Press, 1965, 672-679.

3892. _____. Freud, Goethe, Wagner. NY: Knopf, 1937.

3893. _____. Mein Verhältnis zur Psychoanalyse. Die Psychoanalyse und die Dichter. Almanach, 1926, 32-33.

3894. _____. Thomas Mann über Psychoanalyse. Frankfurter Zeitung, 11 Sept 1925.

3895. Mannoni, Octave. Clefs pour l'Imaginaire ou l'Autre Scène. Paris: Seuil, 1969.

3896. Mansuy, Michel. Bachelard et Lautréamont: I. La psychanalyse de la bête humaine. Etudes Françaises, 1965, 1:26-51.

3897. Manuel, Frank Edward. Toward a psychological history of utopias. Daedalus, 1965, 293-322; In Utopias and Utopian Thought. Boston: Houghton Mifflin, 1966, 69-98; In Freedom from History. NY: New York Univ. Press, 1971, 115-148.

3898. _____, & Manuel, Fritzie P. Utopian Thought in the Western World. Cambridge: Belknap Press of Harvard Univ. Press, 1979.

3899. March, Richard. Psychology and criticism. Scrutiny, 1936, 5:32-43; Comment by Harding, D. W., 44-47.

3900. Marcus, Leah S. Childhood and Cultural Despair: A Theme and Variations in Seventeenth-Century Literature. Pittsburgh: Univ. Pittsburgh Press, 1978.

3901. Marcus, Steven. The American Negro in search of identity. Commentary, 1953, 16:456-463.

3902. _____. The faces of Freud. Partisan Rev, 1977, 44:528-538.

3903. _____. Madness, literature, and society. In Representations; Essays on Literature and Society. NY: Random House, 1975, 137-160.

3904. _____. The Other Victorians. A Study of Sexuality and Pornography in Mid-Nineteenth-Century England. NY: Basic Books, 1966; NY: Bantam, 1967.

3905. _____. Representations: Essays on Literature and Society. NY: Random House, 1976.

3906. _____. Three obsessed critics. Partisan Rev, 1958, 25: 591-620.

3907. Marcuse, Herbert. Eros and Civilization; A Philosophical Inquiry into Freud. Boston: Beacon, 1955; London: Routledge & Kegan Paul, 1956.

3908. Marcuse, Ludwig. Freuds aesthetik. PMLA, 1957, 72:444-463; JAAC, 1958, 17:1-21.

3909. _____. Obscene. The History of an Indignation. NY: Fernhill, 1965; Munich: 1962.

3910. _____. The oldest younger generation. Partisan Rev, 1952, 19:211-216.

3911. Margolin, Uri. Harold Bloom. The Anxiety of Influence: A Theory of Poetry. Canadian Rev Comparative Lit, 1977, 4:103-109.

3912. Marin, Gladys C. Psicocritica e investigación literari. In Maturo, G. (ed), Hacia una crítica literaria latinoamericana. Buenos Aires: Cambeiro, 1976, 197-212.

3913. Markham, John W. Writing out and through. Amer Imago, 1966, 23:235-243.

3914. Markiewicz, Susanna. The Question of Feminine Liberty in the Writings of Denis Diderot. DAI, 1973, 33:6921A.

3915. Marotti, Arthur Francis. Countertransference, the communication process, and the dimensions of psychoanalytic criticism. Critical Inquiry, 1978, 4:471-489.

3916. Marquard, Odo. On the importance of the theory of the unconscious for a theory of no longer fine art. In Amacher, R.E., & Lange, V. (eds), New Perspectives in German Literary Criticism. Princeton: Princeton Univ. Press, 1979, 260-278.

3917. Marti-Ibanez, F. Casanova, then and now. Int Record Medicine, 1960, 173:458-462.

3918. Martin, Alexander R. Nostalgia. Psychoanalysis, 1954, 14: 93-104.

3919. _____, Trilling, Lionel, & Vivas, E. The legacy of Sigmund Freud: an appraisal. Kenyon Rev, 1940, 2:135-185.

3920. Martin, Claude. Gide, Cocteau, Oedipe: le mythe ou le complex. Rev des Lettres Modernes, 1972, 298-303:143-165.

3921. Martin, Del, & Mariah, Paul. Homosexual love--woman to woman, man to man. In Otto, H.A. (ed), Love Today; A New Exploration. NY: Association Press, 1972, 120-134.

3922. Martin, F. David. The imperative of stylistic development: psychological and formal. Bucknell Rev, 1963, 11(2):53-70.

3923. Martin, Louis C. A note on Hazlitt. Int J Psycho-Anal, 1920, 1:414-419.

3924. Martin, Percival William. Experiment in Depth. A Study of the Work of Jung, Eliot and Toynbee. London: Routledge & Kegan Paul, 1955; NY: Pantheon, 1955.

3925. Martin, Wallace. Freud and imagism. Notes & Queries, 1961, 8:407-471, 474.

3926. _____. The sources of the imagistic aesthetic. PMLA, 1970, 85:196-204.

3927. Martindale, Colin. Psychological contributions to poetics. Poetics: Int Rev for Theory of Lit, 1978, 7(2):121-133.

3928. _____. The Psychology of Literary Change. Doctoral dissertation, Harvard Univ., 1969.

3929. _____. Romantic Progression: The Psychology of Literary History. Washington, DC: Hemisphere, 1975; Reviews: Morse Peckham, Amer Lit, 1976, 48:249-251; Ravenna Helson, Computers & J Humanities, 1976, 10:354-356.

3930. Martini, F. Der Tod Neros-Suetonius, Anton Ulrich von Braunschweig, Sigmund von Birken oder: Erzählerische Fiktion und Stil der frühen Aufklärung. In Probleme des Erzählens in der Weltliteratur. Stuttgart: Klett, 1971, 22-86.

3931. Martz, Louis L., & Williams, Aubrey L. (eds). The Author in His Work; Essays on a Problem in Criticism. New Haven: Yale Univ. Press, 1978.

3932. Marvin, Valerie Scott. Explorations: Samuel Johnson as a Moral Psychologist. DAI, 1975, 36:1529A.

3933. Maslow, Abraham H. Emotional blocks to creativity. Humanist, 1958, 18:325-332.

3934. Masson, Raoul. Un ancêtre de Franz Moor. Etudes Germaniques, 1970, 25:1-6.

3935. Masson-Oursel, Paul. Intérêt psychanalytique et valeur humaine de Montaigne. Psyché, 1947, 2:1109-1111.

3936. _____. La Rochefoucauld devant l'inconscient. Psyché, 1947, 2:143-149.

3937. Mathieu, Michel. L'Art et la psychanalyse. Critique (Paris), 1971, 26:1044-1045.

3938. Mathis, Paul. Ecriture et psychanalyse. Recueil de comptes rendus des travaux de la section II: psychanalyse appliquée. Congrès du 30 octobre-1er novembre 1966. Paris: Publication Ecole Freudienne de Paris, 1966.

3939. Matt, P. von. Die gemalte Geliebte. Zur Problematik von Einbildungskraft und Selbsterkenntnis im erzählenden Werk E. T. A. Hoffmanns. Germanisch-Romanische Monatsschrift, 1971, 21, 4.

3940. Matthews, J. H. Le Désir qui ne se refuse rien--Les Vases communicants d'Andre Breton. Symposium, 1977, 31:212-230.

3941. Maulnier, Thierry. Jean-Paul Sartre et le suicide de la littérature. La Table Ronde, 1948, 1(2):195-210.

3942. Mauron, Charles. L'Art et la psychanalyse. Psyché, 1952, 63:24-36.

3943. _____. Des Métaphors obsédantes au mythe personnel. Introduction à la psychocritique. Paris: Corti, 1963.

3944. _____. Nerval et la psycho-critique. Cahiers du Sud, 1949, 29:76-98.

3945. _____. La Psychocritique et sa méthode. Orbis litterarum. Supplement 2, 1958, 104-116.

3946. _____. Le Rire baudelairien. Europe, 1967, 456-57:54-61.

3947. May, Charles E.   Explorers in the realm of sex. In Mars-
       den, M. T. (comp), Proceedings of the Fifth National Con-
       vention of the Popular Culture Association. Bowling
       Green, Ohio: Bowling Green State Univ. Popular Press,
       1975, 1156-1174.
3948. May, G.   Préromantisme rousseauiste et égotisme stendhali-
       en: convergences et divergences. L'Esprit créateur,
       1966, 6:97-107.
3949. May, Rollo.   Power and Innocence: A Search for the Sources
       of Violence.   NY: Norton, 1972; Psychol Today, 1972,
       6:53-58.
3950. Mayo, Elton.   Some Notes on the Psychology of Pierre Janet.
       Cambridge: Harvard Univ. Press, 1948.
3951. Mead, Gerald.   Language and the unconscious in Surrealism.
       Centennial Rev, 1976, 20:278-289.
3952. Meares, Russell.   Beckett, Sarraute, and the perceptual ex-
       perience of schizophrenia. Psychiatry, 1973, 36:61-69.
3953. Meerloo, Joost A.   Creativity and Eternization. Assen, Hol-
       land: Royal Van Gorcum, 1967.
3954. Meeus, Adrien de.   Le Romantisme. Paris: Fayard, 1947.
3955. Mehlman, Jeffrey.   Entre Psychanalyse et psychocritique.
       Poétique, 1970, 3:365-385.
3956. _____. The 'floating signifier': from Lévi-Strauss to
       Lacan. Yale French Rev, 1972, 48:10-37.
3957. _____. French Freud. Yale French Rev, 1972, 48:5-9.
3958. Mehnert, Henning.   Melancholie und Inspiration: Begriffs-und
       wissenschaftsgeschichtliche Untersuchungen zur poetischen
       'Psychologie' Baudelaires, Flauberts und Mallarmes: Mit
       einer Studie über Rabelais. Heidelberg: Winter, 1978.
3959. Mehrotra, R. R.   Coleridge's hobby-horse: psychology. In-
       dian J English Studies, 1971, 12:22-32.
3960. Meissner, W. W.   Some notes on the psychology of the liter-
       ary character: a psychoanalytic perspective. Seminars
       in Psychiat, 1973, 5:261-274.
3961. Memel-Fote, Harris.   Les Conditions sociales et psycho-
       logiques de la création. Annales de l'Université d'Abid-
       jan, 1970, 3D:11-18.
3962. Menaker, Esther.   Creativity as the central concept in the
       psychology of Otto Rank. In Roland, A. (ed), Psycho-
       analysis, Creativity, and Literature. NY: Columbia
       Univ. Press, 1976, 162-177; J Otto Rank Assn, 1976-77,
       11.
3963. Mendel, Sidney.   Hamletian man. Arizona Q, 1960, 16:223-
       236.
3964. Mendes, João.   Garrett e a sua expressao. [Review.]
       Brotéria, 1968, 87:623-643.
3965. _____. A máscara de Garrett. [Review.] Brotéria,
       1968, 87:349-354.
3966. _____. Máscara, luz e chama en Garrett. [Review.]
       Brotéria, 1968, 87:493-511.
3967. Menninger-Lerchenthal, E.   Der eigene Doppelgänger. Psycho-
       therapeutische Praxis, 1937, 3:143-194; Schweizer Zeit-
       schrift für Psychologie, Supplement 11, 96pp, 1946.

3968. Mercier, Roger. L'Esprit et le coeur: aux origines d'un débat psychologique et littérature. In Hepp, N., Mauzi, R., & Pichois, C. (eds), Mélanges de littérature française. Paris: Klincksieck, 1975, 339-350.

3969. Mérei, Ferenc. [The social psychological premises of evaluative analysis.] Helikon, 1978, 24:264-275.

3970. Merian-Genast, Christine. Die Gestalt des Künstlers im werk Conrad Ferdinand Meyers. Bern: Lang, 1973.

3971. Mérigot, Bernard. Freud et la critique littéraire: le lien du texte. Europe, 1974, 539:189-199.

3972. _____. La Psychanalyse doit-elle être enseignée à l'université? Littérature, 1971, 3:117-120.

3973. Mermall, T. O. Paz, el laberinto de la soledad y el sicoanalisis de la historia. Cuadernos Americanos, 1968, 156, No. 1, 97-115.

3974. _____. O. Paz y las máscaras. Cuadernos Americanos, 1972, 31(1):195-207.

3975. Merrifield, D. F. Das Bild der Frau bei Max Frisch. Freiburg: Becksmann, 1971.

3976. Meschonnic, Henri. Le Signe et le poème. Paris: Gallimard, 1975.

3977. Mesnard, Pierre. Les Principaux courants de la psychologie française contemporaine. Rev Mediterranée, 1947, 4(6): 676-693, 1948, 5(1):36-49.

3978. Metcalf, J. T. Psychological studies of literary form. Psychol Bulletin, 1938, 35:337-357.

3979. Meyer, Victoria Junco. The images of women in contemporary Mexican literature. In Roberts, J. I. (ed), Beyond Intellectual Criticism; A New Woman, A New Reality. NY: McKay, 1976, 210-228.

3980. Michaut, Gustave. Pascal, Molière, Musset. Essais de critique et de psychologie. Paris: Alsatia, 1942.

3981. Mickel, Emanuel John. Gautier's use of opium and hashish as a structural device. Studi Francesi, 1972, 15:491-495.

3982. _____. The poetic image of the 'noire idole.' In Cargo, R. T. (ed), Studies in Honor of Alfred G. Engstrom. Chapel Hill: Univ. North Carolina Press, 1972, 87-98.

3983. Miel, Jan. Jacques Lacan and the structure of the unconscious. Yale French Studies, 1966, 36-37:104-111.

3984. Mikhailov, Alexandre. Character and personality in seventeenth-century German literature. Diogenes, 1974, 86: 73-93.

3985. Mileck, Joseph. Freud and Jung, psychoanalysis and literature, art and disease. Seminar, 1978, 14:105-116.

3986. Miles, Josephine. Pathetic Fallacy in the Nineteenth Century; A Study of a Changing Relation Between Object and Emotion. Berkeley: Univ. California Press, 1942.

3987. Milic, Louis Tonko. The metaphor of time as space. In Backscheider, P. R. (ed), Probability, Time, and Space in Eighteenth-Century Literature. NY: AMS Press, 1979, 249-258.

3988. Millar, Kenneth (Ross Macdonald). The Inward Eye. A Revaluation of Coleridge's Psychological Criticism. Doctoral dissertation, Univ. Michigan Press, 1952.

3989. Miller, C. A. Nietzsches 'Soteriopsychologie' im Spiegel von
       Dostoevskijs Auseinander-setzung mit dem europäischen
       Nihilismus. Nietzsche Studien, 1978, 7:130-157.
3990. Miller, Henry. Psychoanalysis: a clinical perspective. In
       Miller, J. (ed), Freud: The Man, His World, His Influ-
       ence. Boston: Little, Brown, 1972, 111-123.
3991. Miller, James E., Jr. Unchartered interiors: the American
       romantics revisited. Emerson Society Q, 1964, 34:34-39.
3992. Miller, Jay Hillis. Geneva or Paris? The recent work of
       Georges Poulet. Univ. Toronto Q, 1970, 39:212-228.
3993. _____. The Geneva school: the criticism of Marcel Ray-
       mond, Albert Beguin, Georges Poulet, Jean Rousset,
       Jean-Pierre Richard, and Jean Starobinski. Critical Q,
       1966, 8:305-321.
3994. Miller, J. L. Burton's Anatomy of Melancholy. Annals Medi-
       cal History, 1936, 8:14-53.
3995. Millet, Kate. The balance of power. Partisan Rev, 1970,
       37:199-218.
3996. Mindess, Veronica P. Unconscious Motivation of Main Char-
       acters in Arthur Schnitzler's Plays and Narratives. Mas-
       ter's thesis, Univ. California, Los Angeles, 1952.
3997. Minkowski, Eugene. Création-expression-psychologie form-
       elle. In Alazard, J., et al. (eds), Mélanges Georges
       Jamati: Création et vie intérieur. Recherches sur les
       sciences et les arts. Paris: Centre National de la Re-
       cherche scientifique, 1956, 225-231.
3998. Minor, Nata. Freud, Schnitzler et la Reine de la Nuit.
       Etudes freudiennes, 1972, 5-6.
3999. Mitchell, Juliet. Psychoanalysis and Feminism. NY: Ran-
       dom House, 1975.
4000. Mitchell, Ruth. The Critical Relationship: A Theory of
       Reader Response. DAI, 1977, 37:5845A-55A.
4001. Mitchell-Caron, Marie-Anne. Eros et l'aveu féminin dans
       la littérature française (entre 1550 et 1630). DAI, 1974,
       34:4225A.
4002. Mitra, Suhrit Chandra. Psychology and literature. Indian J
       Psychol, 1938, 13:161-175.
4003. Mitscherlich-Nielsen, Margarete. Sittlichkeit und Kriminali-
       tät: Psychoanalytische Bewerkungen zu Karl Kraus. In
       Arnold, H. L. (ed), Karl Kraus. Munich: Text & Kritik,
       1977, 21-38.
4004. Mittenzwei, Ingrid. Die Sprache als Thema. Frankfurt:
       Gehlen, 1970.
4005. Mog, Paul. Ratio und Gefühlskultur: Studien zu Psychogenese
       und Literatur im 18. Jahrhundert. Tübingen: Niemeyer,
       1977.
4006. Möller, Karin. The Theme of Identity in the Essays of
       James Baldwin: An Interpretation. Gothenburg Studies
       in English, 32. Gothenburg: Univ. Gothenburg, 1975.
4007. Moller, Mary Elkins. Thoreau, womankind, and sexuality.
       ESQ: J Amer Renaissance, 1976, 22:123-148.
4008. Mollinger, Robert N. Psychoanalytic Approach to Literature.
       Chicago: Nelson-Hall, 1976.

4009. Monteiro, George. Poetry and madness: Melville's redis-
       covery of Camões in 1867. New England Q, 1978, 51:
       561-565.
4010. Montgomery, Robert Langford. The Reader's Eye; Studies in
       Didactic Literary Theory from Dante to Tasso. Berkeley:
       Univ. California Press, 1979.
4011. Moog, Willy. Probleme einer Psychology der Literatur.
       Zeitschrift für Psychologie und Physiologie, 1932, 124:
       129-146.
4012. Moore, F. C. T. The Psychology of Main de Biran. Oxford:
       Clarendon, 1969.
4013. Moore, Kathleen B. Bernanos and the Dream. DA, 1967,
       27:3464A.
4014. Moore, Merrill. Concerning the creative process in litera-
       ture. In Hoch, P., & Zubin, J. (eds), Experimental
       Psychopathology. NY: Grune & Stratton, 1957, 120-128.
4015. _____. Some psychiatric considerations concerning writing
       and criticism. Amer J Psychiat, 1955, 112:423-429.
4016. Moragues, J. Condiciones psicologiques de la literatura per
       a infants. Rev de Psicologia y Pedagogia, 1953, 3:251-
       263.
4017. Moran, J. C. Conducta humana y coherencia y existencial en
       Un guapo del 900 de S. Eichelbaum. In Estudios litera-
       tura e interdisciplinarias. Buenos Aires: Univ. Nacional
       de la Plata, 1968, 63-88.
4018. Moravia, Alberto. Psychoanalysis. In Man As an End. NY:
       Farrar, Straus & Giroux, 1966, 87-88.
4019. Morby, E. S. Franz Titelmans in Lope's 'Arcadia. ' Modern
       Language Notes, 1967, 82:185-197.
4020. Mordell, Albert. The Erotic Motive in Literature. NY:
       Boni & Liveright, 1919; London: Kegan Paul, 1920; NY:
       Collier, 1962.
4021. _____. The Literature of Ecstacy. NY: Boni & Liver-
       ight, 1921.
4022. Moreau, P. Les Moralités légendaires de J. Laforgue.
       Egotisme et symbolisme. In Studi in onore di Italo
       Siciliano. Biblioteca dell'Archivum Romanicum, 1966,
       86.
4023. Moreira Andres, N. El psicoanálisis en la literatura españ-
       ola. Un estudio sobre Las adelfas de los hermanos Mach-
       ado. Asclepo, 1971, 23:337-350.
4024. Morgan, Douglas W. Creativity today: a constructive analy-
       tic review of certain philosophical and psychological
       work. JAAC, 1953, 12:1-24.
4025. _____. Psychology and art today: a summary and cri-
       tique. J Aesthetics, 1950, 10:81-96; In Vivas, E., &
       Krieger, M. (eds), The Problems of Aesthetics. NY:
       Rinehart, 1953, 30-47.
4026. Morgan, M. Gwyn. Catullus 112: a pathicus in politics.
       Amer J Philology, 1979, 100:377-380.
4027. Morier, Henri. La Psychologie des styles. Geneva: Georg,
       1959.

4028. Morizot, Carol Ann. Just This Side of Madness: Creativity
      and the Drive to Create. Houston: Harold, 1978; Review:
      Sharon Spencer, Motheroot J, 1979, 1(27):6.
4029. Mornin, Edward. Art and alienation in Tieck's Franz Stern-
      balds Wanderlungen. Modern Language Notes, 1979, 94:
      510-523.
4030. Morrell, Roy. The psychology of tragic pleasure. Essays
      in Criticism, 1956, 6:22-37.
4031. Morris, Bertram. The legacy of Freud in art criticism.
      Colorado Q, 1960, 9:165-174.
4032. Morris, Humphrey. The need to connect: representations of
      Freud's psychical apparatus. In Smith, J. H. (ed), The
      Literary Freud. New Haven: Yale Univ. Press, 1980,
      309-344.
4033. Morrison, Claudia C. Depth Psychology in American Liter-
      ary Criticism, 1900-1926. DA, 1965, 26:652-53.
4034. _____. Freud and the Critic: The Early Use of Depth
      Psychology in Literary Criticism. Chapel Hill: Univ.
      North Carolina Press, 1968.
4035. Morros, Lucy M. S. Women in the Expository Works of
      Madame de Stael. DAI, 1976, 36:6139A-40A.
4036. Mortara, B. Note sui Ritratti di Daniello Bartoli. Lettere
      Italiene, 1965, 129-140.
4037. _____. Osservazioni sul discorso indiretto in Daniello
      Bartoli. AIL, 1963, 526-532.
4038. _____. Un uso particolare dell'infinito in Daniello Bartoli.
      AIL, 1962, 486-495.
4039. Mortier, R. Libertinage littéraire et tensions sociales dans
      la littérature de l'ancien régime: de la 'Picara' à la
      'Fille de joie.' Rev de Littérature Comparée, 1972, 46:
      35-45.
4040. Morton, B. N. Beaumarchais et le prospectus de l'édition de
      Kehl. Studies on Voltaire & the 18th Century, 1971, 81:
      133-147.
4041. Mosse, E. P. Psychological mechanisms in art production.
      Psychoanal Rev, 1951, 38:66-74.
4042. Mossner, E. C. Rousseau's hero-worship, an unpublished in-
      timate record of 1766. Modern Language Notes, 1940,
      55:399-451.
4043. Mott, F. W. A study of character by the dramatists and
      novelists. J Mental Science, 1915, 61.
4044. Moustakas, Clark. Creativity and Conformity. Princeton:
      Van Nostrand, 1967.
4045. Muller, Armand. L'Art et la psychanalyse. Rev Fran-
      çaise de Psychanalyse, 1953, 17:297-319.
4046. Muller, M., & Martínez Moreno, C. Psicoanálisis y litera-
      tura en 'Cien anõs de soledad.' Montivideo: Cuadernos
      de Literatura, 1975.
4047. Mühler, Robert. Dichtung der Krise: Mythos und Psycho-
      logie in der Dichtung des 19. und 20. Jahrhunderts. Vi-
      enna, 1951.
4048. Muller-Braunschweig, H. Psychopathology and creativity.
      Psyche, 1974, 28:600-634.

4049. Müller-Freienfels, Richard. Die Aufgaben einer Literatur-
       psychologie. Das literarische Echo, 1913-14, 16:805-811.
4050. _____. Psychologie und Literaturforschung. Das liter-
       arische Echo, 1922, 25(2).
4051. Müller-Hegemann, D. Über die Beziehungen der Psychopath-
       ologie zur Literatur. Psychiatrie, Neurologie und medi-
       zinische Psychologie, 1953, 5:341-346.
4052. Müller-Hegemann, I. Psychopathologie und Literatur. Neue
       Deutsche Literatur, 1954, 9:112-122.
4053. Müller-Volmer, Kurt. Towards a Phenomenological Theory
       of Literature: A Study of Wilhelm Dilthey's 'Poetik.'
       The Hague: Mouton, 1963.
4054. Munro, James S. Studies in sub-conscious motivation in Lac-
       los and Marivaux. Studies in Voltaire & the Eighteenth
       Century, 1972, 89:1153-1168.
4055. Muntéano, B. Les 'Contradictions' de Jean-Jacques Rousseau.
       In Rousseau et son oeuvre. Problèmes et Recherches.
       Paris: Klincksieck 1964.
4056. Murray, Henry A. Vicissitudes of creativity. In Anderson,
       H. H. (ed), Creativity and Its Cultivation. NY: Harper,
       1959, 96-118.
4057. Murry, John Middleton. C. G. Jung's psychological types.
       In Poets, Critics, Mystics; A Selection of Criticism Writ-
       ten Between 1919 and 1955. Carbondale: Southern Illinois
       Univ. Press, 1970, 112-116.
4058. Muschg, Walter. Psychoanalyse und Literaturwissenschaft.
       Berlin: Junker und Dünnhaupt, 1930; Psychoanalitsche
       Bewegung, 1930, 2:68-69.
4059. _____. Die Psychoanalyse als Rivalin der Literaturwissen-
       schaft. Psychoanalytische Bewegung, 1930, 2:178-185.
4060. _____. Tragische Literaturgeschichte. Bern: Franke,
       1948.
4061. Musurillo, H. Dream symbolism in Petronius. Classical
       Philology, 1958, 53:108-110.
4062. Mutiso, G. C. M. Women in African literature. East Africa
       J, 1971, 8(3):4-13.
4063. Mutterle, Anco Marzio. [Debenedetti.] Belfagor, 1970, 3:
       288-321.
4064. M'Uzan, Michel de. Aperçus psychanalytiques sur le proc-
       essus de la création littéraire. Tel Quel, 1964, no. 19,
       27-39; Rev Française de Psychanalyse, 1965, 29:43-77.
4065. _____, & Pontalis, J. -B. Ecrire, Psychanalyser, Ecrire:
       Echange de vues. Nouvelle Rev de Psychanalyse, 1977,
       16.
4066. Myer, John C. The Romantic response. Psychology, 1969,
       6(2):40-47.
4067. Myers, Henry A. Tragedy--A View of Life. Ithaca: Cor-
       nell Univ. Press, 1956.
4068. Myerson, Ignace. Les Fonctions psychologiques et les
       oeuvres. Paris: Vrin, 1948.
4069. Myerson, Paul G. How the psychiatrist might relate to the
       writer. Seminars in Psychiat, 1973, 5:301-312.

4070. Nadel, Barbara S., & Altrocchi, John. Attribution of hostile intent in literature. Psychol Reports, 1969, 25:747-763.

4071. Nägele, Rainer. Freud und die Topologie des Textes. MLN, 1978, 93:416-429.

4072. Nahas, Hélène. Etude de la femme dans la littérature existentielle française: Jean-Paul Sartre et Simone de Beauvoir. DA, 1954, 14:1220.

4073. _____. La Femme dans la littérature existentielle. Paris: Presses Universitaires de France, 1957.

4074. Namjoshi, S. Double landscape. Canadian Lit, 1976, 67:21-30.

4075. Narducci, Emanuele. Il lapsus da Freud alla critica testuale. Il Ponte, 1975, 31:553-557.

4076. Natov, N. Daily life and individual psychology in Soviet-Russian prose of the 1970s. Russian Rev, 1974, 33:357-371.

4077. Naville, Pierre. Psychologie, marxisme, matérialisme. Essais critiques. Paris: Rivière, 1946, 1948.

4078. Neboit-Mombet, Janine. Un Logicien de la déraison. Europe, 1972, 522:48-53.

4079. Nedelin, V. V sumerkax psixonaliza. Invstrannaja literatura, 1963, 9(10):196-216.

4080. Nelson, Benjamin N. Freud and the Twentieth Century. Gloucester, Mass: Smith, 1958; NY: Meridian, 1960.

4081. Nelson, Cary. The psychology of criticism, or what can be said. In Hartman, G.H. (ed), Psychoanalysis and the Question of the Text. Baltimore: Johns Hopkins Univ. Press, 1978, 45-61.

4082. Nelson, Lowry, Jr. Mens insana in corpore insano. Yale Rev, 1974, 64:93-102.

4083. Nerman, B. Den skapande processen. En studie i Walter Ljs diktarmetod. Stockholm: Gebers, 1976.

4084. Nesbit, Louis. Freudian influence in Schnitzler's works. Medical Life, 1935, 40:10.

4085. _____. The Medical Approach to Literature with Particular Reference to Arthur Schnitzler. Master's thesis, Cornell Univ., 1934.

4086. Neubert, Werner. Zur Ideologie und Psychologie des Werkes von Franz Fühmann. In Jarmatz, K., & Berger, C. (eds), Weggenossen: Fünfzehn Schriftsteller der DDR. Frankfurt: Röderberg, 1975, 267-298.

4087. Neumann, Erich. Creative Man: Five Essays. Princeton: Princeton Univ. Press, 1980.

4088. Neumarkt, Paul. Amos Tutuola: emerging African literature. Amer Imago, 1971, 28:129-145.

4089. Newbigin, Nerida. Canzone nella morte d'una civetta: some notes on a sixteenth-century text. Studies in Philology, 1979, 76:109-126.

4090. Newman, Paul B. Vers une phénoménologie de la littérature: L'exemplarisme français. DAI, 1972, 32:4626A.

4091. Niederland, William G. Freud's literary style: some observations. Amer Imago, 1971, 28:17-23.

4092. _____. On Hesperian depression. Digest Neurology & Psychiat, 1972.

4093. _____. Psychoanalytic approaches to creativity. Psychoanal Q, 1976, 185-211.

4094. Nikiforova, O. I. Psixologija vospryatija xudozestvennoj literatury. Moscow: Kniga, 1972.

4095. Nin, Anaïs. On feminism and creation. Michigan Q Rev, 1974, 13(1):4-13.

4096. Noland, Richard W. Contemporary psychoanalytic criticism. Hartford Studies in Lit, 1971, 3:132-148.

4097. _____. The future of psychological criticism. Hartford Studies in Lit, 1973, 5:92-105.

4098. _____. Psychoanalytic criticism: past and present. Hartford Studies in Lit, 1975, 7:48-58.

4099. _____. The psychological criticism of Norman N. Holland. Hartford Studies in Lit, 1974, 6:72-79.

4100. Nordmeyer, Henry W. An existentialist approach to literature. Modern Language J, 1949, 33:583-593.

4101. Norton, G. Montaigne and the Introspective Mind. The Hague: Mouton, 1975.

4102. Norton, Rictor Carl. The Homosexual Literary Tradition: An Interpretation. NY: Revisionist Press, 1974.

4103. _____. Studies of the Union of Love and Death: I. Heracles and Hylas: The Homosexual Archetype. II. The Pursuit of Ganymede in Renaissance Pastoral Literature. III. Folklore and Myth in Who's Afraid of Virginia Woolf? IV. 'The Turn of the Screw': Coincidents Oppositorium. DAI, 1973, 33:5190A-91A.

4104. Notcutt, B. Some relations between psychology and literature. Theoria: Natal Univ. College Pietermaritzburg, 1947, 111-127.

4105. Nott, Kathleen. The Trojan horses: Koestler and the behaviourists. In Harris, H. (ed), Astride the Two Cultures: Arthur Koestler at 70. London: Hutchinson, 1975; NY: Random House, 1976, 162-174.

4106. Nougué, A. [Galateo.] Erasmus, 1969, 21:150-154.

4107. Noy, Pinchas. About art and artistic talent. Int J Psycho-Anal, 1972, 53:243-249.

4108. _____. Insight and creativity. JAPA, 1978, 26:717-748.

4109. _____. On the development of artistic talent. Israel Annals Psychiat, 1966, 4:211-218.

4110. _____. Symbolism and mental representation. The Annual of Psychoanal, Vol. I. NY: Quadrangle, 1973, 125-158.

4111. _____. A theory of art and esthetic experience. Psychoanal Rev, 1968, 55:623-645.

4112. Nuebert, Werner. Franz Fühmann: Zur Ideologie und Psychologie eines Werkes. In Kowalski, E. (ed), Verteidigung der Menschheit. Berlin: Akademie, 1975, 478-492.

4113. Nyang, Sulayman S. Literature and the cosmic schizophrenic tendencies of man. Black Orpheus: J African & Afro-Amer Lit, 1976, 3(4):38-43.

4114. Ober, William B.   Thomas Shadwell: his exitus revis'd.
Annals Internal Medicine, 1971, 74:126-130.

4115. Oberndorf, Clarence P.   The literary and historical contributions of Dr. Smith Ely Jellife.   JNMD, 1947, 106:228-
232.

4116. _____.   Oliver Wendell Holmes--a precursor of Freud.
JNMD, 1941, 93:759-764; Bulletin New York Academy
Medicine, 1941, 17(5).

4117. _____.   The psychic determinism of Holmes and Freud.
JNMD, 1943, 98:184-188.

4118. Obler, Paul C.   Psychology and literary criticism: a summary and a critique.   Lit & Psychol, 1958, 8:50-59.

4119. O'Brien-Moore, Ainsworth.   Madness in Ancient Literature.
NY: Steckert, 1933; Weimar, 1924.

4120. O'Connor, William Van.   An Age of Criticism.   Chicago:
Regnery, 1952, 151-155.

4121. O'Flaherty, James C.   Eros and creativity in Nietzsche's
Birth of Tragedy.   In Mews, S. (ed), Studies in German
Literature of the 19th and 20th Centuries.   Chapel Hill:
Univ. North Carolina Press, 1970, 83-104.

4122. Okazaki, Y.   Das 'Aware' als eine geistige Grundlage der
japanischen Literatur.   Tohoku psychologica folia, 1940,
8:99-106.

4123. Olivaux, Robert.   Le Symbolisme sexuel de l'act d'écrire.
Cahiers Internationaux de Symbolisme, 1967-68, 15-16:
61-70.

4124. Ong, Walter J.   Beyond objectivity: the reader-writer transaction as an altered state of consciousness.   CEA Critic,
1977, 40(1):6-13.

4125. _____.   Interfaces of the Words: Studies in the Evolution
of Consciousness and Culture.   Ithaca: Cornell Univ.
Press, 1977.

4126. _____.   Psyche and the geometers: associationist critical
theory.   In Rhetoric, Romance and Technology; Studies
in the Interaction of Expression and Culture.   Ithaca,
NY: Cornell Univ. Press, 1971, 213-236; Modern Philology, 1951, 49:16-27.

4127. _____.   Psychiatry and literature: a report with reflections.   In Institute on Human Values in Medicine: Proceedings of the First Session.   Philadelphia: Society of
Health & Human Values, 1972, 23-46.

4128. Openchaim, M.   La Psychologie et l'imagination chez J-P
Sartre et chez F. Schneerson.   Paris, 56, Rue de Clichy,
1957, 5p.

4129. Oppenheim, J.   Editorial [on the artist and neuroses].   Seven
Arts, 1917, 1:392-394.

4130. Orlando, Francesco.   Per una teoria freudiana della letteratura.   Torino: Einaudi, 1973.

4131. _____.   Psicanalisi e letteratura.   Yearbook of Italian
Studies, 1973-75, 201-218.

4132. Orloff, Kossia.   The trap of 'androgyny.'   Regionalism &
Female Imagination, 1978, 4(2):1-3.

4133. Ormsby-Lennon, Hugh.   Metaphor and madness.   ETC, 1976,
33:307-318.

4134. Örnkloo, U. Kärlekens marodörer. Bonniers Litterära
       Magasin, 1972, 41(1):17-25.
4135. Ortigues, Edmond. Le Discours et le symbole. Paris:
       Aubier, 1962.
4136. Osborne, Harold. Emotion et attitudes dans l'art littéraire.
       In Philosophie et littéraire. Deuxieme colloque de la
       société britannique de philosophie de langue français.
       Hull: Fretwell, 1963, 13-20.
4137. Osmont, R. Contributions à l'étude psychologique des 'Rev-
       eries' du promeneur solitaire. Annales Jean-Jacques
       Rousseau, 1934, 23:7-135.
4138. Ossola, C. Métaphor et inventaire de la folie dans la lit-
       térature italienne du XVIe siècle. In Folie et déraison à
       la Renaissance. Brussels: Univ. Bruxelles Press, 1976,
       171-196.
4139. Ostenfeld, Ib. 'Hosekraemmeren' and 'Fjorten Dage i Jyl-
       land': Blicher-Studier. In Livsfangen og andre Mennes-
       kildringer fra Fantasi og Virkelighed. Copenhagen: Nyt
       Nordisk, 1968, 173-194.
4140. O'Sullivan, Deborah H. Janus and Narcissus: Woman's Situ-
       ation as Depicted in The Second Sex, the Works of Fic-
       tion and the Autobiography of Simone de Beauvoir. DAI,
       1972, 32:4628A.
4141. Oxenhandler, Neal. Retrieving the self: the critic as exis-
       tentialist psychoanalyst. Boundary, 1975, 4:299-302.

4142. Pacifici, Sergio J. Existentialism and Italian literature.
       Yale French Studies, 1955-56, 16:79-88.
4143. _____. From engagement to alienation: a view of con-
       temporary Italian literature. Italica, 1963, 40:236-258.
4144. Padmanabha, Jayanta. Women and literature. Times Lit
       Supplement, 30 Aug 1974, 930-931.
4145. Paivio, Allan. Psychological processes in the comprehension
       of metaphor. In Ortony, A. (ed), Metaphor and Thought.
       Cambridge: Cambridge Univ. Press, 1979, 150-171.
4146. Paletta, Coletta. The behavior of configurations. Art Psy-
       chotherapy, 1977, 4:225-226.
4147. Palls, B. P. [La fénix de Salamanca.] Hispanófila, 1973,
       47:59-71.
4148. Palmer, Donald D. Unamuno, Freud and the case of Alonso
       Quijano; Vida de Don Quijote. Hispania, 1971, 54:243-
       249.
4149. Pandit, Sneh. In defence of psychical distance. British J
       Aesthetics, 1976, 16:56-60.
4150. Paolini, Gilbert. La psicopatologia en la literature italo-
       española: D'Annunzio y Palacio Valdés. In Bugliani,
       A. (ed), The Two Hesperias. Madrid: Porrúa, 1977,
       275-289.
4151. Papanoutsos, E. P. L'Emotion esthétique. Rev d'esthetique,
       1960, 13:178-184.
4152. Papst, Edmund. Grillparzers Theorie des psychologischen
       Realismus (mit einen Exkura über den Armen Spellmann.)
       Grillparzer Forum Forchtenstein, 1973, 7-23.

4153. Paraíso de Leal, J. J. R. Jiménez. Vivencia y palabra.
Madrid: Alhambra, 1976.

4154. Parc, Pierre. Le Sens de la complexité psychologique chez
Montaigne. Humanities Assn Rev, 1977, 28:307-313.

4155. Paris, Bernard J. Horney's theory and the study of literature. Amer J Psychoanal, 1978, 38:343-353.

4156. Paris, Jean. The mortal sign: psychological implications
of linguistic elements in literature. In Strelka, J. (ed),
Literary Criticism and Psychology. University Park:
Penn State Univ. Press, 1976, 174-197.

4157. Parrella, Gilda C. Projection and adoption: toward a clari-
fication of the concept of empathy. Quart J Speech,
1971, 57:204-213.

4158. Pascal, Blaise. Das sexuelle Problem in der modernen Literatur. Berlin: Berg, 1890.

4159. Pastor, José Francisco. Zur Problematik der Anwendung
der psychoanalytischen Methode auf literarhistorischen
Gebiet. Neophilologus, 1937, 22:205-209.

4160. Patri, Aime. A propos de Lautréamont et la psychanalyse.
Psyché, 1948, 20:665-673.

4161. Patrides, C. A. Psychopannychism in Renaissance Europe.
Studies in Philology, 1963, 60:227-229.

4162. Pattison, Robert. Child Figure in English Literature.
Athens: Univ. Georgia Press, 1978; Review: A. E.
Haas, Ariel, 1978, 9:98-101.

4163. Pattison, W. T. [J. Rivas.] Symposium, 1967, 31:67-81.

4164. Paulsen, Wolfgang (ed). Psychologie in der Literaturwissenschaft: Viertes Amherster Kolloquium zur modernen
deutschen Literatur 1970. Heidelberg: Stiehm, 1971.

4165. Pauly, T. H. The literary sketch in nineteenth-century
America. Texas Studies in Lit & Language, 1975, 17:
489-503.

4166. Payne, Michael. La Critique engagée: literature and politics. CEA Critic, 1973, 35(2):4-8.

4167. _____. Do psychologists and critics speak the same language? J General Education, 1972, 24:179-183.

4168. _____. Origins and prospects of myth criticism. J
General Education, 1974, 26:37-44.

4169. Pear, H. T. Mental imagery and style in writing. Univ.
Toronto Q, 1935, 4:453-467.

4170. Peckham, Morse. Art and disorder. Lit & Psychol, 1966,
16:62-80.

4171. _____. On the historical interpretation of literature. In
The Triumph of Romanticism. Columbia: Univ. South
Carolina Press, 1970, 445-450; In Elledge, W. P., &
Hoffman, R. L. (eds), Romantic and Victorian. Teaneck,
NJ: Fairleigh Dickinson Univ. Press, 1971, 21-25.

4172. _____. The infinitude of pluralism. Critical Inquiry,
1977, 3:803-816.

4173. _____. Man's Rage for Chaos; Biology, Behavior, and
the Arts. Philadelphia: Chilton, 1965.

4174. _____. Perceptual and semiotic discontinuity in art. Int
Rev for Theory of Lit, 1978, 7(2).

4175. _____. Psychology and literature. In Strelka, J. P.
       (ed), Literary Criticism and Psychology. University
       Park: Penn State Univ. Press, 1976, 48-68.
4176. _____. Romanticism and Behavior. Columbia: Univ.
       South Carolina Press, 1976.
4177. _____. Victorian counterculture. Victorian Studies, 1975,
       18:257-276.
4178. Peddie, Richard L. The relation of haptic perception to lit-
       erary creative work. Q Bulletin British Psychol Society,
       1952, 3:19-21.
4179. Pederson-Krag, Giraldine. Report on panel: psychoanalysis
       of the creative imagination. Bulletin Amer Psychoanal
       Assn, 1948, 4:39-44.
4180. Peltz, Richard. Ontology and the work of art. JAAC, 1965,
       24:487-499.
4181. Peña, Aniano. La 'volkerpsychologie' y la visión de España
       en la generación del noventa y ocho. Cuadernos Hispano-
       americanos, 1978, 331:83-112.
4182. Penna Aařao Reis, S. O homossexualismo na literatura. In
       Congresso brasileiro de Sociedade Brasileiro de Escrit-
       ores médicos, 3d, 1970. São Paulo: Anais, 1970, 164-
       165.
4183. Penny, Bernard. Vsevolod Mikhailovich Garshin: A Study
       of the Dynamics of Guilt. DAI, 1977, 38:835-36A.
4184. Pensa, Mario. C. F. Meyer. Saggio psicologico-estetico.
       Bari: Univ. Bari, 1950.
4185. Penuel, Arnold M. Galdós, Freud, and humanistic psychol-
       ogy. Hispania, 1972, 55:66-75.
4186. Perella, Nicholas James. The Kiss Sacred and Profane:
       An Interpretative History of Kiss Symbolism and Related
       Religio-Erotic Themes. Berkeley: Univ. California
       Press, 1969.
4187. Pérez, L. A. El método paranoico-critico de El otoño del
       Patriarca. Caribe, 1976, 1(2):109-117.
4188. Periñan, Blanca. Lenguaje agudo entre Gracián y Freud.
       Studi Ispanici (Pisa), 1977, 69-94.
4189. Perky, C. W. An experimental study of imagination. Amer
       J Psychol, 1910, 21:422-452.
4190. Perls, Laura. The psychoanalyst and the critic. Complex,
       1950, 2:41-47.
4191. Peters, Diana S. The dream as bridge in the works of
       E. T. A. Hoffmann. Oxford German Studies, 1973, 8:60-
       85.
4192. Petersen, Margarethe. Ein Ausspruch Diderots. Int Zeit-
       schrift für Psychoanalyse, 1912, 2:473.
4193. Peterson, B. G. Life maladjustment through children's lit-
       erature. Elementary English, 1963, 40:716-718.
4194. Petit, Jacques. Essais de lectures des 'Diaboliques' de Bar-
       bey D'Aurevilly. Paris: Lettres modernes, 1974.
4195. _____. La Femme dominatrice. Rev des Lettres Mod-
       ernes, 1973, 351-354:125-130.
4196. Peyre, Henri. Existential humanism: reflections in litera-
       ture. In Greening, T. C. (ed), Existential Humanistic

Psychology. Belmont, Cal: Brooks/Cole, 1971, 135-150.

4197. Peyre, Yvonne David. Le Personnage du médecin et la re-lation médecin-malade dans la littérature ibérique--XVIe et XVIIe siècles. Paris: Eds Hispano-Americanos, 1971.

4198. Pfanner, Helmut F. Zur Psychologie des Exils: Eine Deut-ung der Gestalt Dantes bei C. F. Meyer. Schweizer Monatshefte, 1976, 65:789-795.

4199. Phillips, Daniel Edward. The Human Element in Literature. NY: Fortuny, 1940.

4200. Phillips, William (ed). Art and Psychoanalysis. NY: Me-ridian, 1963; NY: Criterion, 1957.

4201. _____. Writing about sex. Partisan Rev, 1967, 34:552-563.

4202. Piatier, Jacqueline. En Marge du débat sur la critique. Un entretien avec Jean Pommier: 'L'Etude de la créa-tion littéraire débouche sur la psychologie et la tech-nique. ' Le Monde, 3-4 May 1964, no. 6002, 11.

4203. Pickens, Rupert T. The concept of woman in Villon's Testa-ment. In Dutton, B. , Hassell, J.W. , & Keller, J. E. (eds), Medieval Studies. Valencia: Castalia, 1973, 163-176.

4204. Picoche, Jacqueline. Le Vocabulaire psychologique dans les 'Chroniques' de Froissart. Paris: Klincksieck, 1976.

4205. Pierce, F. W. Amadís de Gaula. NY: Twayne, 1976.

4206. Pierssens, Michel. Questions sur le signifiant en littéra-ture. Sub-stance, 1972, 3.

4207. Pigeon, Gerard G. Dynamics of alienation in French black literature. J Black Studies, 1977, 8:169-188.

4208. Pimentel, Osmar. A Lâmpada e o Passado. (Estudos de Literatura e Psicologia.) São Paulo: Conselho Estadual de Cultura, 1968.

4209. Pincherle, Albert (pseud Alberto Moravia). Psychoanalysis. In Man As an End, a Defense of Humanism: Literary, Social and Political Essays. NY: Farrar, Straus, 1965, 87-88; London: Secker & Warburg, 1965, 87-88.

4210. Pingaud, Bernard. L'Oeuvre et l'analyste. Temps Mod-ernes, 1965, 21, 638-646.

4211. _____. Le Romanesque comme fantasme. Rev Fran-çaise de Psychoanalyse, 1974, 38(1).

4212. Pinkava, Jindrich. Psychoanalýza a literatura. Ceska Lit-eratura, 1967, 15:342-359.

4213. Pinto, Eveline. La Névrose objective chez Sartre (L'Idiot de la famille, tome III): Sartre historien. Temps Mod-ernes, 1974, 30:35-76.

4214. Placzwk, Siegfried. Erotik und Schaffen. Berlin: Marcus u Weber, 1934.

4215. Plank, Robert. Can Lewis and Freud be reconciled? Bul-letin New York C. S. Lewis Society, 1973, 4(5):5-7.

4216. _____. Freud, Michelangelo's Moses and Conrad Ferdi-nand Meyer. Amer Imago, 1977, 34:109-114.

4217. Podro, Michael. Art and Freud's displacement of aesthetics.
In Miller, J. (ed), Freud: The Man, His World, His
Influence. Boston: Little, Brown, 1972, 125-135.

4218. Poels, Fr. Jacques J. Zéphir: Psychologie de Salavin de
Georges Duhamel. Lettres Romanes, 1977, 31:81-82.

4219. Poggioli, Renato. Pascal's classicism: psychological, aesthetic, and scriptural. Harvard Library Bulletin, 1960,
14:366-391.

4220. _____. The Phoenix and the Spider: A Book of Essays
about Some Russian Writers and Their View of the Self.
Cambridge: Harvard Univ. Press, 1957.

4221. Politzer, Georges. La Crise de la psychologie contemporaine. Paris: Sociales, 1947.

4222. Politzer, Heinz. Diagnose und Dichtung. Zum Werk Arthur
Schnitzlers. In Das Schweizigen der Sirenen. Stuttgart:
1968.

4223. _____. Franz Grillparzer oder das abgründige Biedermeier. Vienna: Molden, 1972.

4224. _____. Hatte Ödipus einen Ödipus-Komplex? Munich:
Piper, 1974.

4225. Pollard, Richard N., & Pollard, H. M. B. From Human
Sentience to Drama. Athens: Ohio Univ. Press, 1974.

4226. Pollmann, Leo. Sartre und Camus: Literatur der Existenz.
Stuttgart: Kohlhammer, 1967.

4227. Pontalis, J. -B. Entre le rêve et la douleur. Paris: Gallimard, 1977.

4228. _____. La Question de la psychanalyse. Nouvelle Rev
de Psychanalyse, 1970, 1.

4229. Poore, Charles. Freud, Goethe, Wagner. New York Times,
4 Aug 1937, p. 14.

4230. Poortere, José de. De dichter en de psychiater. Dietsche
Warande en Belfort, 1976, 121:626-628.

4231. Pope, Randolph D. (ed). The Analysis of Literary Texts.
Ypsilanti, Mich: Bilingual Press, 1980.

4232. Pörksen, Uwe. Zur Metaphorik der naturwissenschaftlichen
Sprache: dargestellt am Beispiel Goethes, Darwins und
Freuds. Neue Rundschau, 1978, 89:64-82.

4233. Porte, Joel. Thoreau on love: a lexicon of hate. Univ.
Rev, 1964, 30:111-116.

4234. Porter, Laurence M. Do literary dreams have a 'latent
content?' The Jungian view. J Altered States Consciousness, 1978-79, 4:37-42.

4235. _____. Literary structure and the concept of decadence:
Huysmans, D'Annunzio, and Wilde. Centennial Rev,
1978, 22:188-200.

4236. Portnoy, Julius. Is the creative process similar in the
arts? JAAC, 1960, 19:191-195.

4237. _____. Poetry, drama, and the novel. In A Psychology
of Art Creation. Chapel Hill: Univ. North Carolina,
1942, 47-68.

4238. Pouillon, J. Le Dieu caché, ou l'homme visible. Temps
Modernes, 1957-58, 13:890-918.

4239. Poulet, Georges. Bachelard et la critique contemporaine.
        In Ireson, J. C. (ed), Currents of Thought in French Lit-
        erature. Oxford: Blackwell, 1965; NY: Barnes & Noble,
        1966, 353-357.

4240. _____. La Conscience critique. Paris: Corti, 1971.

4241. _____. Expansion et concentration chez Rousseau. Temps
        Modernes, 1961, 16:949-973.

4242. _____. The Interior Distance. Studies in Human Time.
        Baltimore: Johns Hopkins Univ. Press, 1959; Oxford:
        Burns & MacEachern, 1952.

4243. _____. The Metamorphoses of the Circle. Baltimore:
        Johns Hopkins Univ. Press, 1966; Paris: 1961.

4244. _____. Le Point de Départ. Paris: 1964.

4245. _____. Poulet on Poulet: the self and the other in criti-
        cal consciousness. Diacritics: A Rev of Contemporary
        Criticism, 1972, 2(1):46-50.

4246. _____. Le Volontarisme de R. Fernandez. MLN, 1972,
        87(6):53-57.

4247. Powers, R. H. Rousseau's 'useless science': dilemma or
        paradox. French Historical Studies, 1962, 2:430-449.

4248. Powys, John Cowper. Psychoanalysis and Morality. San
        Francisco: Colbert, 1923.

4249. Poyatos, M. B. La muralia de Calvo Sotelo, auto de psi-
        cologia Freudiana. Hispania, 1974, 57:31-39.

4250. Pratt, Annis. Archetypal approaches to the new feminist
        criticism. Bucknell Rev, 1973, 21:3-14.

4251. Praz, Mario. Erotismo in arte e in lettertura. Ulisse,
        1970, 89-104.

4252. _____. La figura del neurotico nella letteratura. Cultura
        e Scuola, 1966, 4:46-59.

4253. _____. The Neurotic in Literature. Victoria: Melbourne
        Univ. Press, 1965; NY: Cambridge Univ. Press, 1966.

4254. _____. The Romantic Agony. NY: Meridian, 1933,
        1956, 1960; NY: Oxford Univ. Press, 1951, 1971; NY:
        Meridian, 1956.

4255. Preminger, Alex (ed). Encyclopedia of Poetry and Poetics.
        Princeton: Princeton Univ. Press, 1965, 158-174.

4256. Prescott, Frederick C. The Poetic Mind. NY: Macmillan,
        1922; Review: Mark Van Doren, Lit Rev, 1922, 700.

4257. _____. Poetry and Dreams. Boston: Four Seas, 1912.

4258. Proal, L. L'Esprit satirique de Jean-Jacques Rousseau.
        Grande Revue, 1923, 3:425-448.

4259. Proffitt, Edward. Science and romanticism. Georgia Rev,
        1980, 34:55-80.

4260. Prosetskii, V. A. Primer literaturnogo geroia kak faktor
        formirovaniia lichnosti. Voprosi Psikhologii, 1958, 4:
        100-108.

4261. Pullen, Charles. Eighteenth-century madness: Swift and A
        Modest Proposal. Dalhousie Rev, 1978, 58:53-62.

4262. Raaphorst, M. Voltaire et le féminisme: un examen du thé-
        âtre et des contes. Studies on Voltaire & the 18th Cen-
        tury, 1972, 89:1325-1335.

4263.   Ragland-Sullivan, Ellie.   Explicating Jacques Lacan: an
        overview.   Hartford Studies in Lit, 1979, 11:140-156.
4264.   Ragussis, Michael.   The Subterfuge of Art, Language and the
        Romantic Tradition.   Baltimore: Johns Hopkins Univ.
        Press, 1978, 5-16.
4265.   Rahv, Philip.   Freud and the literary mind.   In Literature
        and the Sixth Sense.   Boston: Houghton Mifflin, 1970
        (1949),   150-167.
4266.   _____.   Image and Idea.   Norwalk, Conn: New Directions,
        1957.
4267.   _____.   Literature and the Sixth Sense.   Boston: Hough-
        ton   Mifflin, 1969.
4268.   Ramos, Maria Luiza.   Fenomenologia da otra literária.   Rio
        de Janeiro: Forense, 1969.
4269.   Ramos Calles, R.   Los personajes de Gallegos a través del
        psicoanálisis.   Caracas: Monte Avila, 1969 (1947).
4270.   Ramsay, A.W.   Psychology and literary criticism.   Criterion,
        1936, 15:627-643.
4271.   Ranald, Josef.   Pens and Personalities.   London: Vision,
        1959.
4272.   Ranis, Gustav.   The tale and the artist.   Yale Rev, 1972,
        62:161-186.
4273.   Rank, Otto.   Art and Artist: Creative Urge and Personality
        Development.   NY: Knopf, 1932.
4274.   _____.   Der Doppelgänger: eine psychoanalytische Studie.
        Imago, 1914, 3:97-164; Vienna: Int Psychoanalytische
        Verlag, 1924; Review: Erich Stern, Die Literatur, 1926,
        1927, 29:555-558.
4275.   _____.   The Double: A Psychoanalytic Study.   Chapel
        Hill: Univ. North Carolina Press, 1971.
4276.   _____.   The double as immortal self.   In Beyond Psychol-
        ogy.   Camden, NJ: Haddon, 1941, 62-101; NY: Dover,
        1958,   62-101.
4277.   _____.   The incest drama and its complications.   In Nun-
        berg, H., & Federn, E. (eds), Minutes of the Vienna
        Psychoanalytic Society, Vol. 1:   1906-1908.   NY: IUP,
        1962,   7-29.
4278.   _____.   Das Inzestmotiv in Dichtung und Sage.   Vienna:
        Deuticke, 1926.
4279.   _____.   Die Inzestphantasie bei Schiller: Zur Psychologie
        der Entwürfe und Fragmente.   In Beutin, W. (ed), Liter-
        atur und Psychoanalyse.   Munich: Nymphenburger, 1972,
        205-261.
4280.   _____.   Der Künstler, und andere Beiträge zur Psycho-
        analyse des dichterischen Schaffens.   Leipzig: Int Psycho-
        analytischer Verlag, 1925.
4281.   _____.   Der Künstler: Ansätze zu einer Sexualpsychologie.
        Vienna: Heller, 1907.
4282.   _____.   Life and creation.   In Ruitenbeek, H.M. (ed),
        The Creative Imagination.   Chicago: Quadrangle, 1965,
        69-96.
4283.   _____.   Das Unbewusste und seine Ausdrucksformen.   In
        Beutin, W. (ed), Literatur und Psychoanalyse.   Munich:
        Nymphenburger, 1972,   49-64.

4284. _____, & Sachs, Hanns. The significance of psychoanaly-
sis for the humanities. Amer Imago, 1964, 21:6-133; In
Psychoanalysis As an Art and a Science. Detroit: Wayne
State Univ. Press, 1968, 7-133.

4285. Ransom, John Crowe. Freud and literature. Saturday Rev
Lit, 1924, 1:161-162.

4286. _____. I. A. Richards: the psychological critic and William Empson, his pupil. In The New Criticism. NY:
New Directions, 1941.

4287. Rao, Adapa Ramakrishna. Emerson and the feminists. Indian J Amer Studies, 1974, 4(1-2):13-20.

4288. Rapaport, Elizabeth. On the future of love: Rousseau and
the radical feminists. In Gould, C. C., & Wartofsky,
M. W. (eds), Women and Philosophy. NY: Putnam, 1976,
185-205.

4289. Rastier, François. Un Concept dans le discours des études
littéraires. In Essais de sémiotique discursive. Paris:
Mame, 1973, 185-206.

4290. Rauber, Christian. Le Thème de l'enfance dans la littérature
actuelle. Thèse, Univ. de Zürich, 1971. Zurich: Juris,
1972.

4291. Ravier, A. Jean-Jacques Rousseau ou 'l'insecte ou milieu
de sa toile. ' Etudes, 1962, 314:49-62.

4292. Ray, Paul C. The anti-surrealism of Christopher Caudwell.
Comparative Lit Studies, 1969, 6:61-67.

4293. Read, Herbert. Art and Alienation: The Role of the Artist
in Society. NY: Horizon, 1967; London: Thames, 1967.

4294. _____. Collected Essays in Literary Criticism. London:
Faber, 1938.

4295. _____. The Forms of Things Unknown. NY: Horizon,
1963.

4296. _____. Lost leader; or the psychopathology of reaction in
the arts. Sewanee Rev, 1955, 63:551-566.

4297. _____. The Nature of Literature. NY: Grove, 1958.

4298. _____. Poetic Consciousness and Creative Experience.
Zurich: Eranos Yearbook, 1956.

4299. _____. Psychoanalysis and the critic. Criterion, 1925,
3:214-230. In Reason and Romanticism. London: Faber
& Gwyer, 1926, 83-106; In Goldberg, G. J., & Goldberg,
N. M. (eds), The Modern Critical Spectrum. Englewood
Cliffs, NJ: Prentice-Hall, 1962, 251-261; In Handy, W.
J., & Westbrook, M. (eds), Twentieth Century Criticism.
NY: Free Press, 1974, 419-429.

4300. _____. Psycho-analysis and literary criticism. In Selected Writings; Poetry and Criticism. NY: Horizon,
1964, 98-116.

4301. _____. Psychoanalysis and the problem of aesthetic value.
In The Yearbook of Psychoanalysis, Vol. 8. NY: IUP,
1952, 344-360.

4302. _____. The True Voice of Feeling. NY: Pantheon, 1947;
London: Faber & Faber, 1947.

4303. _____. The Tenth Muse: Essays in Criticism. NY:
Horizon, 1958.

4304. Reaver, J. Russell. Emerson on the psychic potential.
      Amer Transcendental Q, 1971, 9:52-55.
4305. Redde, Brian (ed). Sexual Heretics. London: Routledge &
      Kegan Paul, 1971.
4306. Redding, Mary Edrich. Emerson's 'Instant Eternity': an
      existential approach. In Carlson, E. W., & Dameron, J.
      L. (eds), Emerson's Relevance Today: A Symposium.
      Hartford: Transcendental Books, 1971, 43-52.
4307. Reed, Raoul. Psychoanalysis in literature. Freeman, 1922,
      5:490-491.
4308. Rehder, Helmut (ed). Literary Symbolism. Austin: Univ.
      Texas Press, 1965.
4309. Reich, K. Stattsrecht und Ethik bei Rousseau. Romanische
      Forschungen, 1947, 60:719-734.
4310. Reichert, Herbert. Schnitzler's egoistische Künstlergestalten.
      J Int Arthur Schnitzler Research Assn, 1965, 4(2):20-27.
4311. Reicke, Ilse. Das Dichtern in psychologischen Betrachtung.
      Zeitschrift für Ästhetik, 1915, 10:290-345; 1906, 1:613-
      614.
4312. Reid, L. A. Artistic experience. Mind, 1926, 35:181-203.
4313. Reik, Theodor. Aesthetik, Literatur, Kunst. Jahrbuch der
      Psychoanalyse, 1914, 6:387-392.
4314. _____. Die 'Almacht der Gedanken' bei Arthur Schnitzler.
      Imago, 1913, 2:319-335.
4315. _____. Arthur Schnitzler als Psycholog. Minden: Bruns,
      1913.
4316. _____. Arthur Schnitzler und der Krieg. Berliner Tage-
      blatt, Nr. 36, 7 Sept 1914.
4317. _____. Freud als Kulturkritik. 1930.
4318. _____. Das Geschlechtsverhältnis bei Schnitzler. Die
      neue Generation, 1913, 9:128-135.
4319. _____. Der kleine Anti-Schnitzler. Pan, 1912, 2(40),
      1118.
4320. _____. Listening with the Third Ear. NY: Farrar,
      Straus, 1948.
4321. _____. The Need to Be Loved. NY: Farrar, Straus,
      1963, passim.
4322. _____. On death and sexuality. In Nunberg, H., & Fed-
      ern, E. (eds), Minutes of the Vienna Psychoanalytic Soci-
      ety, Vol. 3. NY: IUP, 1974, 310-319.
4323. _____. Psychoanalytic experience in life, literature, and
      music. In The Search Within. NY: Farrar, Straus &
      Cudahy, 1956, 331-472.
4324. _____. Psychoanalytic remarks on Schnitzler's poetic
      works. In Nunberg, H., & Federn, E. (eds), Minutes of
      the Vienna Psychoanalytic Society, Vol. 4, 1912-1918.
      NY: IUP, 172-175.
4325. _____. A Psychologist Looks at Love. NY: Farrar &
      Rinehart, 1944, passim.
4326. _____. Psychology of Sex Relations. NY: Farrar &
      Rinehart, 1945, passim.
4327. _____. Review: Arthur Schnitzler's Frau Beate und ihr
      Sohn. Imago, 1914, 3:537-539.

4328. _____. The Secret Self. Psychoanalytic Experiences in
        Life and Literature. NY: Farrar, Straus & Young,
        1952; NY: Greenwood, 1973, passim.
4329. _____. Voices from the Inaudible. NY: Farrar, Straus,
        1964, passim.
4330. _____. Das Werk Richard Beer-Hofmanns. Vienna:
        Loewit, 1919.
4331. Réja, M. L'Art chez les fous: le dessin, la prose, la po-
        ésie. Paris: Mercure de France, 1908.
4332. Rella, Franco. Descrivere, rappresentare, figurare: Lo
        stile di Freud. Nuova Corrente, 1975, 67:244-261.
4333. Renoir, Alain. The inept lover and the reluctant mistress:
        remarks on sexual inefficiency in medieval literature.
        In Vasra, E., & Thundy, Z. P. (eds), Chaucerian Prob-
        lems and Perspectives. South Bend, Ind: Univ. Notre
        Dame Press, 1979, 180-206.
4334. Rey, Jean-Michel. Freud's writing on writing. Yale French
        Studies, 1977, 55-56:301-328.
4335. Rich, Adrienne Cecile. 'It is the lesbian in us....' In On
        Lies, Secrets, and Silence; Selected Prose, 1966-1978.
        NY: Norton, 1979, 199-202.
4336. Richard, Kenneth L. Fantasy in a literature of transition:
        projection and withdrawal. In Ota, S., & Fukuda, R.
        (eds), Studies in Japanese Culture, Vols. 1&2. Tokyo:
        Japan P. E. N. Club, 1973, 114-122.
4337. Richards, Ivor Armstrong. Coleridge on Imagination. NY:
        Harcourt, Brace, 1935.
4338. _____. Emotion and art. In Complementarities. Cam-
        bridge: Harvard Univ. Press, 1976, 7-11.
4339. _____. Practical Criticism: A Study in Literary Judg-
        ment. NY: Harcourt, 1929; NY: Harcourt, Brace, 1952;
        NY: Harvest, 1958.
4340. _____. The Principles of Literary Criticism. London:
        Kegan Paul, 1924, 1925; NY: Harvest, 1959.
4341. Richardson, John Adkins, & Ades, John I. D. H. Lawrence
        on Cézanne: A study in the psychology of criticial in-
        tuition. JAAC, 1970, 28:441-453.
4342. Richer, J. Nerval et ses fantômes. Mercure de France,
        1951, 312:282-301.
4343. Richetti, John J. The portrayal of women in Restoration and
        eighteenth-century English literature. In Springer, M.
        (ed), What Manner of Woman: Essays on English and
        American Life and Literature. NY: New York Univ.
        Press, 1977, 65-97.
4344. Rickett, Adele A. The personality of the Chinese critic. In
        Strelka, Joseph P. (ed), The Personality of the Critic.
        University Park: Penn State Univ. Press, 1973, 111-134.
4345. Rider, Frederick. The Dialectic of Selfhood in Montaigne.
        Stanford, Cal: Stanford Univ. Press, 1973.
4346. _____. Psychological Development in the Essays of Michel
        de Montaigne. DAI, 1973, 33:5745A.
4347. Rieff, Philip. Freud: The Mind of the Moralist. NY: Vik-
        ing, 1959, 118-147; Garden City, NY: Doubleday Anchor,
        1961.

4348. _____. Introduction to D. H. Lawrence's Psychoanalysis and the Unconscious and Fantasia of the Unconscious. NY: Viking, 1960.

4349. Rieger, Dietmar. Le Rideau cramoisi von Barbey d'Aurevilly: Versuch einer tiefen-psychogischen Interpretation. Germanisch-Romanische Monatsschrift, 1972, 22:176-192.

4350. Riep, Albert R. Krankheit, Medizin und Arzt in den Werken Grimmelshausen. DAI, 1967, 27:3061A.

4351. Rieser, Max. Analyse der poetischen Denkens. Vienna: Sexl, 1954.

4352. Rifflet-Lemaire, Anika. Jacques Lacan. Brussels: Dessart, 1970.

4353. Ritzen, Quentin. Les Nervures de l'être. Elements d'une psychologie de la littérature. Lausanne: Rencontre, 1967.

4354. Riviere, Jacques. The Ideal Reader. NY: Meridian, 1960.

4355. Riviere, Joan. The unconscious phantasy of an inner world reflected in examples from English literature. Int J Psycho-Anal, 1952, 33:160-172.

4356. Roazen, Deborah H. George Eliot and Wordsworth: 'The Natural History of German Life' and peasant psychology. Research Studies, 1973, 41:166-178.

4357. Roback, Abraham A. Psikhologie und literatur. Literatur und Lebn, 1915, 1.

4358. _____. The psychology of literature. In Present-Day Psychology. NY: Greenwood, 1968, 867-896; NY: Philosophical Library, 1955, 867-896.

4359. _____. Psychology Through Yiddish Literature: Apologia pro Vita Yiddicia. Cambridge, Mass: Sci-Art, 1942.

4360. _____. The Story of Yiddish Literature. Cambridge, Mass: Sci-Art Press, 1939; Review: William V. Silverberg, Psychiatry, 1940, 3:569-571.

4361. _____, & Baskin, W. Psychology of post-Freudian literature. In Powers, G. P., & Baskin, W. (eds), New Outlooks in Psychology. NY: Philosophical Library, 1968, 405-437.

4362. Robert, Bernard-Paul. Le Surréalisme désocculté. Ottawa: Editions de l'Université d'Ottowa, 1975.

4363. Roberts, Jeanne A. Literary criticism as dream analysis. CEA Critic, 1970, 33:14-16.

4364. Robertz, Egon. Feuer und Traum. Studien zur Literaturkritik Gaston Bachelards. Frankfurt: Lang, 1978; Bern: Lang, 1978.

4365. Robichon, Jacques. Un Virtuose du sadisme: James Hadley Chase. Nouvelles Littéraires, 11 March 1965, 1, 11.

4366. Robinson, Christopher. The idealist revolt. In French Literature in the Nineteenth Century. NY: Barnes & Noble, 1978, 13-49.

4367. Robinson, Judith. Valéry's view of mental creativity. Yale French Studies, 1970, 44:3-18.

4368. Rocamora, P. R. de Maeztu y la generacíon del 98. Arbor, 1974, 341:7-22.

4369. Rocchietta, S. [The literary and scientific work of Jean Rostand.] Minerva Medica, 1960, 51:12.

4370. Roditi, Edouard. [Literary personality of Pessoa.] Ocidente (Lisbon), 1964, 66:205-215.

4371. Rof Carballo, Juan. La emoción del paisaje en el hombre gallego. Grial, 1966, No. 11, 14-34.

4372. Rogers, Carmen. English Renaissance melancholy: a prologue of men and manners. Florida State Univ. Studies, 1952, 5:45-66.

4373. Rogers, H. L. The crypto-psychological character of the oral formula. English Studies, 1966, 47:89-102.

4374. Rogers, Katherine M. The Troublesome Helpmate: A History of Misogyny in Literature. Seattle: Univ. Washington Press, 1966, 1968.

4375. Rogers, Robert. The dynamics of metaphor: modes of mentation in poetry. Hartford Studies in Lit, 171, 3:157-190.

4376. _____. Literary value and the clinical fallacy. Lit & Psychol, 1964, 14:116-121.

4377. _____. Metaphor and the Unconscious: A Revised View. Berkeley: Univ. California Press, 1978; Review: Strother Purdy, Lit & Psychol, 1979, 29:141-144.

4378. _____. On the metapsychology of poetic language: modal ambiguity. Int J Psycho-Anal, 1973, 54:61-74.

4379. _____. A Psychoanalytic Study of the Double in Literature. Detroit: Wayne State Univ. Press, 1970.

4380. Roiphe, Anne. A writer looks at the void. Amer J Psychoanal, 1975, 35:55-61.

4381. Roland, Alan. Imagery and symbolic expression in dreams and art. Int J Psycho-Anal, 1972, 53:531-539.

4382. _____ (ed). Psychoanalysis, Creativity, and Literature: A French-American Inquiry. NY: Columbia Univ. Press, 1978.

4383. _____. Psychoanalytic literary criticism--promise and problems. Book Forum, 1974, 1:275-284.

4384. _____. Toward a reorientation of psychoanalytic literary criticism. Psychoanal Rev, 1978, 65:391-414; In Psychoanalysis, Creativity, and Literature: A French-American Inquiry. NY: Columbia Univ. Press, 1978, 248-270.

4385. Rolfs, Daniel J. The portrayal of suicide in Italian literature of the Counter-Reformation era. Forum Italicum, 1975, 9:37-59.

4386. Rom, Paul. Goethe as an interpreter of dreams. Lit & Psychol, 1962, 12:37-38.

4387. Romains, Jules. A sketch of psychoanalysis. In O'Brien, J. (ed), From the NRF. NY: Meridian, 1959, 240-255.

4388. Romano, John. Beckett without angst. Amer Scholar, 1977-78, 47:95-102.

4389. Rombouts, Jos. Schrijven als alchimie: een analyse van Mulisch'. Voer voor Psychologen. Restant, 1978, 7(1):67-79.

4390. Romera Castillo, José. Surrealismo y psicocrítica. Insula, 1974, 337:18.

4391. Romero Márquez, A. 'Heracles': Gil-Albert nos pone a prueba. Insula, 1976, 356-7:18.

4392. Ronda, Bruce Allen. The Transcendental Child: Images and
       Concepts of the Child in American Transcendentalism.
       DAI, 1976, 36:8063A.
4393. Rorty, Amélie O. (ed). A literary postscript: characters,
       persons, selves, individuals. In The Identities of Per-
       sons. Berkeley: Univ. California Press, 1976, 301-323.
4394. Rosanoff, Aaron J. Plato and Dostoyevski anticipating Freud.
       Psychoanal Rev, 1922, 9:90-91.
4395. Rosasco, J. Aux sources de la Vivonne. Poétique, 1976, 7:
       72-84.
4396. Rose, Gilbert J. Narcissistic fusion states and creativity.
       In Kanzer, M. (ed), The Unconscious Today. NY: IUP,
       1971, 495-505.
4397. Rose, William John. The psychological approach to the study
       of literature. In German Studies. Chester Springs, Pa:
       Dufour, 1962, 171-190; Oxford: Blackwell, 1952, 171-190.
4398. Rosen, George. Forms of irrationality in the eighteenth cen-
       tury. In Pagliaro, H. (ed), Studies in Eighteenth Century
       Literature, Vol. II. Cleveland: Case Western Reserve
       Univ. Press, 1972, 255-288.
4399. Rosenbaum, C. Peter, & Rossi, Romolo. Herodotus: ob-
       server of sexual psychopathology. Amer Imago, 1971,
       28:71-78.
4400. Rosenberg, Harold. The psychoanalyst and the writer; moth-
       er's milk and inspiration. Commentary, 1950, 10:272-
       275.
4401. Rosenberg, Marvin. The mind of the critic. Amer Scholar,
       1962, 31:551-563.
4402. _____. A sceptical look at sceptical criticism. Philologi-
       cal Q, 1954, 33:66-77.
4403. Rosenblatt, Louise M. Literature as Exploration. NY: Ap-
       pleton-Century, 1938; NY: Barnes & Noble, 1968.
4404. _____. The Reader, the Text, and the Poem: The Trans-
       actional Theory of the Literary Work. Carbondale: South-
       ern Illinois Univ. Press, 1978; London: Feffer, 1978.
4405. _____. Towards a transactional theory of reading. In
       Primeau, R. (ed), Influx; Essays on Literary Influence.
       Port Washington, NY: Kennikat, 1977, 121-136.
4406. Rosenfeld, Alvin. Armed for war: notes on the antithetical
       criticism of Harold Bloom. Southern Rev, 1977, 13:554-
       566.
4407. Rosenfels, Paul. Homosexuality: The Psychology of the Cre-
       ative Process. Roslyn Heights, NY: Libra, 1971.
4408. Rosenzweig, Saul. William James et le courant de conscience.
       Bulletin de Psychologie, 1969-1970, 23(17-19):1001-1009.
4409. Rosmarin, Leonard A. The unsublimated libido: Saint-
       Evremond's conception of love. French Rev, 1972, 46:
       263-270.
4410. Rosolato, Guy. Essais sur le symbolique. Paris: Galli-
       mard, 1969.
4411. _____. Psicoanalisi del simbolico. Verri, 1968, 28:44-
       51.

4412. Ross, Carol Jean.   Schiller and Hebbel: Characters and
       Ideas and the Portrayal of Women.   DAI, 1977, 37:7738A.
4413. Ross, Donald, Jr.   Verbal wit and Walden.   Amer Trans-
       cendental Q, 1971, 11:38-44.
4414. Ross, Frank. 'Once more unto the breach, dear friends....'
       Paunch, 1965, 23:36-45.
4415. Ross, W. A. Carpentier o sobre la metamorfosis del ti-
       empo.   In Actas del Tercer Congreso Internacional de
       Hispanistas.   Mexico: 1970, 753-764.
4416. Rossky, William.   Imagination in the English Renaissance:
       psychology and poetic.   Studies in the Renaissance, 1958,
       5:49-73.
4417. _____.   The Theory of Imagination in Elizabethan Litera-
       ture: Psychology, Rhetoric and Poetic.   Doctoral dis-
       sertation, New York Univ., 1953.
4418. Rosso, Jeannette G.   Montesquieu et la féminité.   Pisa:
       Goliardica, 1977.
4419. Rothenberg, Albert.   The defense of psychoanalysis in litera-
       ture.   Comparative Drama, 1973, 7:51-67.
4420. _____.   The Emerging Goddess.   The Creative Process in
       Art, Science, and Other Fields.   Chicago: Univ. Chicago
       Press, 1979.
4421. _____.   The flesh-and-blood face on the commemorative
       stamp.   Saturday Rev, 1971, 11:174-181.
4422. _____.   Homospatial thinking in creativity.   Archives Gen-
       eral Psychiat, 1976, 33:17-26.
4423. _____.   Opposite responding as a measure of creativity.
       Psychol Reports, 1973, 33:15-18.
4424. _____.   The process of Janusian thinking in creativity.
       Archives General Psychiat, 1971, 24:195-205.
4425. _____.   The unconscious and creativity.   In Roland, A.
       (ed), Psychoanalysis, Creativity, and Literature.   NY:
       Columbia Univ. Press, 1976, 144-161.
4426. _____.   Word association and creativity.   Psychol Reports,
       1973, 33:3-12.
4427. Rouch, J.   Le Thème de l'amour dans Racine.   Bulletin geo-
       graphique, 1949-50, 63:29-48.
4428. Roudiez, Leon S.   Characters and personality: the novelist's
       dilemma.   French Rev, 1962, 35:553-563.
4429. _____.   La Condition humaine: an awareness of the other.
       Twentieth Century Lit, 1978, 24:303-313.
4430. _____.   Les Tendances actuelles de l'écriture.   French
       Rev, 1971, 45:321-332.
4431. Rousseau, G. S.   Literature and science: the state of the
       field.   Isis, 1978, 69(249):583-591.
4432. Rovit, Earl.   The American literary ego: an essay in psycho-
       history.   Southern Rev, 1978, 14:409-427.
4433. Rowley, Brian A.   Psychology and literary criticism.   In
       Psychoanalysis and the Social Sciences, Vol. 5.   NY:
       IUP, 1959, 200-220.
4434. Rowse, Alfred Leslie.   Homosexuals in History: A Study of
       Ambivalence in Society, Literature and the Arts.   NY:
       Macmillan, 1977.

4435. Roy, Jean-Pierre.   Bachelard ou le concept contre l'image.
       Montreal: Presse de l'Univ. de Montréal, 1977.
4436. Roy-Katz, Ginette.   Conscient ou inconscient?   Réponse à
       l'article de Judith Stora-Sandor sur 'Littérature et psych-
       analyse. '   Les Langues Modernes, 1978, 72:53-57.
4437. Rubin, Abba.   The Jew in English Literature: 1660-1830.
       DAI, 1975, 35:5360A-61A.
4438. Rudnick, Hans H.   Kant and the personality of the critic.   In
       Strelka, J. P. (ed), The Personality of the Critic.   Uni-
       versity Park: Penn State Univ. Press, 1973, 135-154.
4439. Rueckert, William H.   Kenneth Burke and the Drama of Hu-
       man Relations.   Minneapolis: Univ. Minnesota Press,
       1963; London: Oxford Univ. Press, 1963.
4440. _____.   Kenneth Burke and structuralism.   Shenandoah,
       1969, 21:19-28.
4441. Ruitenbeek, Hendrik M. (ed).   The Creative Imagination:
       Psychoanalysis and the Genius of Inspiration.   Chicago:
       Quadrangle, 1965; Review: Riva Novey, Psychoanal Q,
       1967, 36:463-466.
4442. _____.   Psychoanalysis and Literature.   NY: Dutton,
       1964.
4443. Rümke, H. C.   Les Doublures névrotique de la souffrance hu-
       maine.   Evolution Psychiatrique, 1956, 1:331-337.
4444. Russell, David H.   Psychology and literature.   College Eng-
       lish, 1964, 25:551-553; Elementary English, 1964, 41:420-
       422+; English J, 1964, 53:289-291.
4445. Ryan, Steven T.   The importance of Thomas S. Kuhn's sci-
       entific paradigm theory to literary criticism.   Midwest
       Q, 1978, 19:151-159.
4446. Rycroft, Charles.   Freud and the imagination.   New York
       Rev Books, 1975, April, 26-30.
4447. _____.   Imagination and Reality: Psychoanalytic Essays
       1951-1961.   London: Hogarth, 1968.
4448. Ryner, Han.   La Psychanalyse.   Rev de l'Epoque, 5 Feb
       1920, no. 5, 5 Mar 1920, no. 7; Cahiers des Amis de
       Han Ryner, n. s., 1964, no. 74, 9-12.

4449. Saagpakk, Paul L.   A survey of psychopathology in British
       literature from Shakespeare to Hardy.   Lit & Psychol,
       1967, 18, 135-165.
4450. Sabik, Vincent.   Lev S. Vygotskij e jeho psychologická kone-
       cepcia kritiky.   Slovenské Pohl'ady, 1967, 83(9):111-116.
4451. Sabin, Margery.   Imagination in Rousseau and Wordsworth.
       Comparative Lit, 1970, 32:328-345.
4452. Saccone, Eduardo.   Alleg (o) ria di novembre: la sublimation
       imperfetta di Aldo Palazzeschi.   MLN, 1977, 92:79-116.
4453. Sachs, Hanns.   Aesthetics and psychology of the artist.   Int
       J Psycho-Anal, 1921, 2:94-100; In Ruitenbeek, H. M. (ed),
       The Creative Imagination.   Chicago: Quadrangle, 1965,
       47-53.
4454. _____.   On the applicability of psychoanalysis to poetic
       works.   In Nunberg, H. , & Federn, E. (eds), Minutes of

the Vienna Psychoanalytic Society, Vol. 3, 1910-1911.
NY: IUP, 1974, 159-167.

4455. _____. Bericht über die Fortschritte der Psychoanalyse
in den Jahren 1914-1919. Leipzig: Internationaler Psychoanalytischer Verlag, 1921.

4456. _____. The Creative Unconscious. Studies in the Psychoanalysis of Art. Cambridge: Sci-Art, 1951.

4457. _____. The delay of the machine age. [Excerpt from
The Creative Unconscious, 100-131.] Arion, 1965, 4:
496-511.

4458. _____. Die Motivgestaltung bei Arthur Schnitzler. Imago,
1913, 2:302.

4459. _____. Strindberg über Eifersucht und Homosexualität.
Int Zeitschrift für Psychoanalyse, 1916, 4:210-211.

4460. Sachs, Vida (ed). Le Blanc et le noir caez. Melville et
Faulkner. Paris: Mouton, 1974.

4461. Sachs, Wulf. Psychoanalysis: Its Meaning and Applications.
London: Cassell, 1934.

4462. Sacks, S. The psychologic implications of generic distinc-
tions. Genre, 1968, 1:87-123.

4463. Sadger, Isador. Konrad F. Meyer. In Nunberg, H., &
Federn, E. (eds), Minutes of the Vienna Psychoanalytic
Society, Vol. 1: 1906-1908. NY: IUP, 1962, 254-258.

4464. _____. Psychiatrisch-Neurologisches in psychoanalytischer
Beleuchtung. Zeitschrift für den Gesamtgeb der Medizin,
1908, 7-8.

4465. _____. Sleep Walking and Moon Walking: A Medico-Lit-
erary Study. NY: Nervous & Mental Disease Publishers,
1920; Psychoanal Rev, 1918, 6:158-193, 309-342, 424-449;
1920, 7:43-70, 163-180; Über Nachwandeln und Mond-
sucht; Eine medizinisch-literarische Studie. Leipzig:
Deuticke, 1914.

4466. Saez, Richard. James Merrill's Oedipal fire. Parnassus,
1974, 3:159-184.

4467. Sage, Lorna. Women and literature--III. The case of the
active victim. Times Lit Supplement, 26 July 1974, 26:
803-804.

4468. Sahlberg, Oskar. Gottfried Benns Phantasiewelt. 'Wo Lust
und Leiche winkt. ' Munich: Kritik, 1977.

4469. _____. Die psychologische Wirkung des Faschismus am
Beispiel von Gottfried Benns. Kürbiskern, 1977, 1:72-88.

4470. Sakharoff, M. Des G: un cas de double identité. Rev des
Sciences Humaines, 1971, 36:357-364.

4471. Salber, Wilhelm. Literaturpsychologie: Gelebte und erlebte
Literatur. Bonn: Bouvier, 1975.

4472. Salem, G. [The work by Prince Korab. Analysis of the
writings of a paranoiac.] Schweitzer Archiv für Neurologie und Psychiatrie, 1978, 123:107-139.

4473. Salières, François. Pathologie et littérature. Presse Médicale, 1949, 37:516-517.

4474. Salinas, Judy. The image of woman in Chicano literature.
Revista Chicano-Riqueña, 1976, 4(4):139-148.

4475. Salinas, Oscar. Emerson's Nature: oral merger fantasy.
Amer Imago, 1978, 35:397-406.

4476.   Sallenave, Danièle. A propos du 'monologue intérieur. '
        Lecture d'une théorie. Littérature, 1972, 5:69-87.
4477.   Salm, Peter. Faust, Eros and knowledge. German Q, 1966,
        3:329-339.
4478.   Sammons, Jeffrey L. Fate and psychology: another look at
        Mörike's Maler Nolten. In Sammons, J. L., & Schürer,
        E. (eds), Lebendige Form. Interpretationen zur deutsch-
        en Literatur. Munich: Fink, 1970, 211-227.
4479.   Sampurnanand, ?. Notes on soma. Psychedelic Rev, 1967,
        9:67-70.
4480.   Sánchez, P. Eros y Thanatos en Al filo del Agua. Cuader-
        nos Americanos, 1969, 163, No. 3, 252-262.
4481.   Sant'Anna, Dionisio. Dois contra-sensos de psicologia liter-
        ária: Fradique e Jacinto. Palaestra, 1968, 32:15-20.
4482.   Santayana, George. Literary psychology. In Essays in Lit-
        erary Criticism. NY: Scribner, 1956, 394-401.
4483.   Santiago, Luciano P. R. The Children of Oedipus: Brother-
        Sister Incest in Psychiatry, Literature, History and
        Mythology. Roslyn Heights, NY: Libra, 1973.
4484.   _____. The Ulysses complex. Amer Imago, 1971, 28:
        158-186.
4485.   Sartre, Jean-Paul. The Psychology of Imagination. NY:
        Philosophical Library, 1948; London: Rider, 1949;
        L'Imaginaire: Psychologie phénoménologique de l'imagi-
        nation. Paris: Gallimard, 1940, 1948.
4486.   Sasayama, Takashi. [The task of psychoanalytical criticism.]
        Eigo Seinen, 1978, 124:312-314.
4487.   Schaarschmidt, C. Interior monologue and Soviet literary
        criticism. Canadian Slavonic Papers, 1966, 8:143-152.
4488.   Schärer, Kurt. The singularity of the double. Diacritics,
        1972, 2(1):29-35.
4489.   Schechner, Mark. Psychoanalysis and liberalism: the case
        of Lionel Trilling. Salmagundi, 1978, 41:3-32.
4490.   Scheick, William J. Nonsense from a lisping child: Edward
        Taylor on the word as piety. Texas Studies in Lit & Lan-
        guage, 1971, 13:39-54.
4491.   Scherer, J. Le Cardinal et l'orang-outang. Essai sur les
        inversions et les distances dans la pensée de Diderot.
        Paris: Société d'Editions d'Enseignement Supérieur,
        1972.
4492.   Scherf, Walter. Handling og spaending: Om aestetisk og
        psykologisk kritik af børnelitteratur. Copenhagen: Gyl-
        dendal, 1978.
4493.   Schertel, E. Der erotische Komplex: Untersuchung zum
        Problem der paranomalen Erotik in Leben, Literatur und
        Bilderei. Berlin: Pergamon, 1932.
4494.   _____. Der Flagellantismus als literarische Motiv. Leip-
        zig: 1930.
4495.   Schiff, Paul. A propos de l'imagination de Sartre. Destin
        de l'image de Ludovic-Antoine Muratori à Jean-Paul
        Sartre. Evolution Psychiatrique, 1947, 1:319-331.
4496.   Schlüter, H. Das Pygmalion-Symbol bei Rousseau, Hermann,
        Schiller: Drei Studien zur Geistesgeschichte der Goethe-
        zeit. Zurich: Juris, 1968.

4497.   Schmidt, Willa.   The Changing Role of Women in the Works
        of Arthur Schnitzler.   DAI, 1974, 35:474A.
4498.   Schmidtbonn, Wilhelm.   Der Doppelgänger.   Berlin: Deutsche
        Buch-Gemeinschaft, 1928.
4499.   Schmitz, Oskar A. H.   Don Juan, Casanova, und andere ero-
        tische Charaktere: ein Versuch.   Stuttgart: Juncker,
        1913.
4500.   _____.   Die Triebfeder des künstlerischen Schaffens.
        Osterreich Rundschau, 1921, 17, 1 & 1.
4501.   Schneider, Daniel E.   The Psychoanalyst and the Artist.   NY:
        Farrar, Straus, 1950.
4502.   Schneider, Daniel John.   Symbolism: The Manichean Vision;
        a Study in the Art of James, Conrad, Woolf and Stevens.
        Lincoln: Univ. Nebraska Press, 1975.
4503.   Schneider, Gerd Klaus.   Arthur Schnitzler und die Psychologie
        seiner Zeit, unter besonderer Berücksichtigung der Phi-
        losophie Friedrich Nietzsches.   DA, 1968, 29(7):2281-82A.
4504.   Schneider, Manfred.   Die Angst und das Paradies des Nörg-
        lers.   Versuch über Karl Kraus.   Frankfurt: Syndikat,
        1977.
4505.   Schnitzler, Arthur.   Über Psychoanalyse.   Protokolle, 1976,
        2:277-286.
4506.   Schönau, Walter.   Literanalyse und Psychoanalyse: Ein
        Plädoyer für die Verbesserung ihrer Beziehungen.   In
        Handelingen van bet tweeëndertigste Nederlands Filologen-
        congres.   Amsterdam: Holland Univ. Press, 1974, 267-
        274.
4507.   _____.   Sigmund Freuds Prosa.   Literarische Elemente
        Seines Stils.   Stuttgart: Metzlersche, 1968.
4508.   Scholes, Robert E.   Toward a semiotics of literature.   In
        Hernadi, P. (ed), What Is Literature?   Bloomington:
        Indiana Univ. Press, 1978, 231-250.
4509.   Schrecker, Paul.   Goethe über das Verhältnis der Geshlech-
        ter.   Int Zeitschrift für Psychoanalyse, 1913, 3:643.
4510.   Schrey, Gisela.   Literatur-Asthetik der Psychoanalyse und
        ihre Rezeption in der deutschen Germantik vor 1933.
        Frankfurt: Athenaion, 1975.
4511.   Schulhof, H.   Goethes Weg vom Ich zum Wir.   Int Zeit-
        schrift für Individual-Psychologie, 1934, 12:184-193.
4512.   Schulman, G.   To create the self.   Twentieth Century Lit,
        1977, 23:299-313.
4513.   Schultz, J.   Psychologie des Wortspiels.   Zeitschrift für
        Aesthetic und allgemeine Kunstwissenschaft, 1927, 21:16-
        37.
4514.   Schwartz, Delmore.   The grapes of crisis.   Partisan Rev,
        1951, 18:7-15.
4515.   Schwartz, Murray M.   The space of psychological criticism.
        Hartford Studies in Lit, 1973, 5:xiv.
4516.   Schwartz, Paul.   Perspectives in psychology: IX. Literature
        as art and as knowledge.   Psychol Record, 1959, 9:7-10.
4517.   Schwelling, Otto Peter.   Faust und Faustine.   Eine psycho-
        grafische Studie von Goethes Eros.   Cologne: Boehlau,
        1965.

4518. Scott, Nathan A. The broken center: a definition of the cri-
       sis of values in modern literature. In May, R. (ed),
       Symbolism in Religion and Literature. NY: Braziller,
       1960, 178-202.
4519. Scott, Wilbur (ed). Five Approaches to Literary Criticism.
       NY: Macmillan, 1962.
4520. Scott-James, R. A. Personality in Literature, 1913-1931.
       London: Secker & Warburg, 1931; NY: Holt, 1932.
4521. Scruton, R. Incantations of the self. Times Lit Supplement,
       11 Aug 1978, 3984:909.
4522. Secher, Claus. Kunsten og den forvaltede verden. En analyse
       af Theodor W. Adornos aestetiske teori og literatur-kri-
       tiske praksis. Poetik (Copenhagen), 1972, 5:133-173.
4523. Secor, Cynthia. Androgyny: an early reappraisal. Women's
       Studies, 1974, 2:161-169.
4524. _____. The androgyny papers. Women's Studies, 1974,
       2:139-141.
4525. Seefeldt, Carol, Galper, Alice, Serock, Kathy, & Jantz,
       Richard K. The coming of age in children's literature.
       Childhood Education, 1978, 54(3):123-127.
4526. Seem, Mark. To Oedipalize or not to Oedipalize, that is the
       question.... Sub-stance, 1975, 11-12:166-169.
4527. Segal, Hanna. A psychoanalytic approach to aesthetics. In
       Klein, M., Heimann, P., & Mony-Kyrle, R. E. (eds),
       New Directions in Psychoanalysis. NY: Basic Books,
       1957; Int J Psycho-Anal, 1952, 33:196-207.
4528. Segal, H. P. Young West: the psyche of technological utopi-
       anism. Extrapolation, 1977, 19:50-58.
4529. Seidenberg, Robert. Fidelity and jealousy: socio-cultural
       considerations. Psychoanal Rev, 1967, 54:27-52.
4530. _____. Marriage in Life and Literature. NY: Philosophi-
       cal Library, 1970.
4531. Seidl, J. Im Maquis von Dichtung und Psyche. Akzente,
       1966, 13:580-591.
4532. Seillère, E. A. La Psychologie naturiste dans l'oeuvre de
       Diderot. In Various (eds), Mélanges Pierre Janet.
       Paris: d'Artrey, 1939, 243-252.
4533. Selander, S. The influence of psycho-analysis in modern lit-
       erature. Dagens Nyheter, 5 Dec 1931, 6.
4534. Selinger, Bernie. The nature and function of the double.
       Sphinx, 1977, 8:37-51.
4535. Sena, John F. Melancholic madness and the Puritans. Har-
       vard Theological Rev, 1973, 66:293-309.
4536. _____. Swift as moral physician: scatology and the tradi-
       tion of love melancholy. J English Germanic Philology,
       1977, 76:346-362.
4537. Senior, John. The Way Down and Out. Westport, Conn:
       Greenwood, 1968.
4538. Servadio, Emilio. Crítica y psicoanálisis. Archivos Pana-
       meños de Psicología, 1965, 1(2):164-169.
4539. _____. Le Mangeur de rêves. Psyché, 1953, 8:455-460.
4540. _____. Problemi psicologici dello scrittore. Bolletin Sin-
       dacato Naz Scrittori, 1963, 14:3-6.

4541. _____ . Psicoanalisi e letterature. Rivista di Psicologia, 1936, 32:226-233.

4542. Sevin, Dieter. Arthur Schnitzlers Gestalt des erotischen Abenteurers. Univ. Dayton Rev, 1973, 10(1):59-65.

4543. Sgard, J. L'Espérance chez Prévost et Voltaire. In Macary, J. (ed), Essays on the Age of Enlightenment. Geneva: Droz, 1977, 271-279.

4544. Shainess, Natalie. Images of woman: past and present, overt and obscured. Amer J Psychotherapy, 1969, 23:77-97; Miller, J. B. (ed), Psychoanalysis and Women. NY: Brunner/Mazel, 1973, 261-286.

4545. Shapiro, Theodore. The symbolic process: a colloquium. Amer Imago, 1971, 28:195-215.

4546. Shattuck, Roger. The Banquet Years. The Origins of the Avant-Garde in France, 1885 to World War One. NY: Arno, 1978; London: Cape, 1969; NY: Vintage, 1968; NY: Harcourt, Brace, 1958.

4547. Shaw, D. L'Esthétique de la structure dans Psyché de La Fontaine. Studi Francesi, 1973, 17:15-28.

4548. Shawcross, John T. Some literary uses of numerology. Hartford Studies in Lit, 1969, 1:50-62.

4549. Sherman, Sandra E. A Portrait of Woman Through the Eyes of Denis Diderot. DAI, 1971, 32:400A.

4550. Shervil, R. W. Lope's ways with women. Bulletin of the Comediantes, 1963, 15(1):10-13.

4551. Shin, Oh-Hyun. Sartre's Concept of the Self. DAI, 1975, 36:3774A-75A.

4552. Shklovski, V. O teorii prozy. Moscow: 1929; Excerpt: L'Art comme procédé. In Todorov, T. (ed), Théorie de la littérature: textes des formalistes russes. Paris: 1966, 76-97.

4553. Shores, D. L. Psychoanalysis in literary study. Peabody J Education, 1966, 43:293-298.

4554. Showalter, Elaine. The Double Standard: Criticism of Women Writers in England, 1845-1880. DAI, 1971, 31:4795A.

4555. _____ . Victorian women and menstruation. In Vicinus, M. (ed), Suffer and Be Still: Women in the Victorian Age. Bloomington: Indiana Univ. Press, 1972, 38-44; Victorian Studies, 1970, 14:83-89.

4556. Shrodes, Caroline, Van Gundy, Justine, & Husband, Richard (eds). Psychology Through Literature: An Anthology. NY: Oxford Univ. Press, 1943.

4557. Shupe, Donald R. Representation versus detection as a model for psychological criticism. JAAC, 1976, 34:431-440.

4558. Siboney, Daniel. L'Autre incastrable: psychanalyse-écritures. Paris: Seuil, 1978.

4559. Siegert, Michael. De Sade und wir: Zur Sexualökonom. Pathologie des Imperialismus. Frankfurt: Makol, 1971.

4560. Silbert, Miriam. In Search of Self: A Typology of Deviant Identities from a Literary Perspective. DA, 1969, 29:3222.

4561. Simms, Edna N. The antifeminist element in the works of Alfonso Martinez and Juan Luis Vives. College Language Assn J, 1974, 18:52-68.

4562. Simon, Bennett. Mind and Madness in Ancient Greece; The Classical Roots of Modern Psychiatry. Ithaca: Cornell Univ. Press, 1978.

4563. Simon, Pierre-Henri. Dimensions de l'héroisme racinien. Rev de l'Université Laval, 1961, 16:14-21.

4564. _____. De la psychocritique de Charles Mauron à la critique transcendantale de Georges Poulet. In Diagnostic des lettres françaises contemporaines. Brussels: La Renaissance du Livre, 1966, 406-413.

4565. Simon-Miller, Françoise L. Ambivalence and identification: Freud on literature. Lit & Psychol, 1978, 28:23-40, 52-68, 151-167.

4566. Simonton, Dean K. Time series analysis of literary creativity: a potential paradigm. Poetics: Int Rev for Theory of Lit, 1978, 7(2).

4567. Simpson, Catherine R. The mind, the body, and Gertrude Stein. Critical Inquiry, 1977, 3:489-506.

4568. Simpson, Lewis P. Sex and history: origins of Faulkner's apocrypha. In Harrington, E., & Abadie, A. J. (eds), The Maker and the Myth. Jackson: Univ. Mississippi Press, 1977, 43-70.

4569. Sinanoglou, Leah Powell. For of Such Is the Kingdom of Heaven: Childhood in Seventeenth-Century English Literature. DAI, 1975, 35:4558A.

4570. Singer, Armand E. Don Juan among the psychiatrists. Laurel Rev, 1968, 8(1):27-35.

4571. Singer, Irving (ed). Literary psychology. In Essays in Literary Criticism of George Santayana. NY: Scribner's, 1956, 394-401.

4572. Sito Alba, Manuel. Vida o sueño en Montherlant: El 'daydream' como elemento constitutivo de la obra literaria. Cuadernos Hispanoamericanos, 1978, 340:148-154.

4573. Sitwell, Edith. Foreword to Lancelot L. Whyte's The Unconscious Before Freud. London: Tavistock, 1962.

4574. Skard, Sigmund. Use of Color in Literature. A Survey of Research. Philadelphia: American Philosophical Society, 1946 [Vol. 90, 3:162-249]; Review: René Wellek, Amer Lit, 1947, 19, 342-343.

4575. Skorna, H. J. Dichtung als Lebenshilfe. Psychologische Rundschau, 1963, 17:30-36.

4576. Skura, Meredith Anne. Creativity: transgressing the limits of consciousness. Daedalus, 1980, 109:127-146.

4577. _____. Revisions and rereadings in dreams and allegories. In Smith, J. H. (ed), The Literary Freud. New Haven: Yale Univ. Press, 1980, 345-379.

4578. Skurbe, Astrida. Psihologiskās prozas socialitate. In Vienotā daudzveidiba. Riga: Zinātne, 1978, 159-179.

4579. Skyum-Nielsen, Erik. [Literature and psychology demonstrated by certain critical terms.] Kritik, 1973, 26:94-123.

4580. Slaby, Andrew E., & Tancredi, Laurence R. Literary insights and theories of person. In Peschel, E. R. (ed), Medicine and Literature. NY: Watson, 1980, 113-119.

4581. Slobodnik, Dusan. Psychoanalýza a literárna kritika. Kultúrny Zivot, 1967, 22(8):1, 4.

4582. Slochower, Harry. Contemporary psychoanalytic theories on creativity in the arts. In Strelka, J. P. (ed), Literary Criticism and Psychology. University Park: Penn State Univ. Press, 1967, 207-222.

4583. _____. Eros and the trauma of death. Amer Imago, 1964, 21:11-22.

4584. _____. Freud and Marx in contemporary literature. Sewanee Rev, 1941, 49:315-324.

4585. _____. Genius, psychopathology and creativity. Amer Imago, 1967, 24:3-5.

4586. _____. Literature and Philosophy Between Two World Wars. The Problem of Alienation in a War Culture. NY: Citadel, 1964; Original title: No Voice Is Wholly Lost. NY: Farrar, Straus & Giroux, 1945; NY: Octagon, 1973.

4587. _____. Psychoanalysis and creativity. In Rosner, S., & Abt, L. E. (eds), Essays on Creativity. Croton-on-Hudson, NY: North River Press, 1974, 151-190.

4588. _____. Psychoanalysis and literature. In Abt, L. E., & Riess, B. (eds), Progress in Clinical Psychology, Vol. 4. NY: Grune & Stratton, 1960, 169-178.

4589. _____. The psychoanalytic approach to literature: some pitfalls and promises. Lit & Psychol, 1971, 21:107-111; Rev Française de Psychanalyse, 1972.

4590. _____. Symbolism and the creative process of art. Amer Imago, 1965, 22:112-127.

4591. Slosson, E. E. Jonathan Edwards as a Freudian. Science, 1920, 52:600.

4592. Smarr, Janet Levarie. Masuccio and the irrational. Roman Philology, 1979, 32:315-320.

4593. Smeed, John W. Jean Paul's Dreams. London: Oxford Univ. Press, 1966.

4594. Smirnoff, Victor N. L'Oeuvre lue. Nouvelle Rev de Psychanalyse, 1970, 1.

4595. Smith, Hilda Lee. Feminism in Seventeenth-Century England. DAI, 1975, 36:2382A-83A.

4596. Smith, Joseph H., & Parloff, Gloria H. (eds). The Literary Freud: Mechanisms of Defense and the Poetic Will. Psychiatry and the Humanities, Vol. 4. New Haven: Yale Univ. Press, 1980.

4597. Smith, Llewellyn Hillyer. Psychoanalysis and Literary History: A New Synthesis. DAI, 1975, 36:2184A.

4598. Smith, Marilynn J. Condemned to survival: the comic unsuccessful suicide. Comparative Lit Studies, 1980, 17: 26-32.

4599. Smith, Timothy d'Asch. Love in Earnest. London: Routledge & Kegan Paul, 1970.

4600. Smolenaars, A. J. Psychologie en literatuurbeschouwing: Hernieuwd liason. Levende Talen, 1963, No. 219, 181-196.

4601. Snider, Clifton. C. G. Jung's analytical psychology and literary criticism: I. Psychocultural Rev, 1977, 1(1):96-108.

4602. Snipes, Katherine. Robert Graves. NY: Ungar, 1979.
4603. Snodgrass, William DeWitt. In Radical Pursuit; Critical Essays and Lectures. NY: Harper & Row, 1975.
4604. Snyder, A.D. Coleridge on Logic and Learning. New Haven: Yale Univ. Press, 1929.
4605. Snyder-Ott, Joelynn. Women and Creativity. Milbrae, Cal: Les Femmes, 1978.
4606. Søholm, Ejgil. Goldschmidt's to jyske fortaellinger. Danske Studier, 1968, 63.
4607. Sollers, Philippe. Freud's hand. Yale French Studies, 1977, 55-56:329-337.
4608. Somolinos Palencia, Juan. Psico surrealismo. Norte, 1976, 271:48-51.
4609. Soucy, Robert. Psycho-sexual aspects of the fascism of Drieu La Rochelle. J Psychohistory, 1976, 4:71-92.
4610. Spector, Jack G. [Freud and the artist.[Keshet, 1976, 70: 130-147.
4611. _____. The Aesthetics of Freud: A Study in Psychoanalysis and Art. NY: Praeger, 1972; London: Lane, 1972.
4612. Spencer, Sharon. The dream of twinship in the writings of Anaïs Nin. J Otto Rank Assn, 1974-75, 9(2):81-90.
4613. Spiegel, Leo A. The new jargon: psychology in literature. Sewanee Rev, 1932, 40:476-491.
4614. Spielrein, Sabina. Russische Literatur. Bericht über die Fortschritte der Psychoanalyse, 1914-19, 356-365.
4615. Spilka, Mark. Ian Watt on intrusive authors, or the future of an illusion. Hebrew Univ. Studies in Lit, 1973, 1(1):1-24; In Durzak, M., Reichmann, E., & Weisstein, U. (eds), Texte und Kontexte: Studien zur deutschen und vergleichenden Litteraturwissenschaft. Bern: Francke, 1973, 249-266.
4616. Spiller, Robert E. Milestones in American Literary History. Westport, Conn: Greenwood, 1977.
4617. Spingler, M.K. The Roles of Perception and Imagination in the Written Work of Henri Michaux. DAI, 1967, 28:694-A.
4618. Spires, R. Técnica y tema en La familia de Pascual Duarte. Tres incidentes claves. Insula, 1971, 26, no. 298:1, 13.
4619. Spithill, A.C. Valuable allies. Personnel & Guidance J, 1968, 46:879-883.
4620. Spitzer, Juraj. Marxismus, strukturalizmus, freudizmus. Slovenská Literatúra, 1970, 17:306-320.
4621. Spitzer, Leo. Studien zu Henri Barbusse. Bonn: Cohen, 1920.
4622. Spivak, Gayatri C. The letter as cutting edge. Yale French Studies, 1977, 55-56:208-226.
4623. Sprich, Robert. Pressed flowers/fresh flowers: new directions in psychoanalytic criticism. Colby Library Q, 1977, 13:67-72.
4624. _____, & Noland, Richard W. (eds). The Whispered Meanings: Selected Essays of Simon O. Lesser. Amherst: Univ. Massachusetts Press, 1977.

4625. Springer, Marlene A. (ed). What Manner of Woman; Essays
       on English and American Life and Literature. NY: New
       York Univ. Press, 1977.
4626. Stade, George. Robert Graves. Columbia Essays on Modern
       Writers, 1967, No. 25, 1-48.
4627. Stafford, William T. William James as critic of his brother
       Henry. Personalist, 1959, 40:341-353.
4628. Stallknecht, Newton P., & Frenz, Horst (eds). Comparative
       Literature: Method and Perspective. Carbondale: South-
       ern Illinois Univ. Press, 1961, 1971.
4629. Stambolian, George, & Marks, Elaine (eds). Homosexualities
       and French Literature: Cultural Contexts/Critical Texts.
       Ithaca, NY: Cornell Univ. Press, 1979.
4630. Stamm, Julian L. Creativity and sublimination. Amer
       Imago, 1967, 24:82-97.
4631. Stamon, Peggy, & Lawson, Richard H. Love-death struc-
       tures in the works of Arthur Schnitzler. Modern Austrian
       Lit, 1975, 8:266-283.
4632. Stanford, Derek. Sex and style in the literature of the '90s.
       Contemporary Rev, 1970, 216:95-100.
4633. Starobinski, Jean. [Attitude of Breton to Freud.] In Eigel-
       dinger, M. (ed), André Breton, essais. Neuchâtel: La
       Baconnière, 1970, 1950.
4634. _____. Consideraciones sobre el estado actual de la
       crítica literaria. Revista de Occidente, 1970, 30:1-19.
4635. _____. Freud, Breton, Meyers. Verri, 1968, 28:5-19.
4636. _____. Imagination. In Jost, F. (ed), Proceedings of the
       IVth Congress of the International Comparative Language
       Association, Vol. 2. The Hague: Mouton, 1966, 952-
       963.
4637. _____. Jean-Jacques Rousseau et les pouvoirs de l'imag-
       inaire. Rev Internationale de Philosophie, 1960, 14:43-
       67.
4638. _____. Jean-Jacques Rousseau, La transparence et l'ob-
       stacle. Paris: Plon, 1958.
4639. _____. La Littérature et l'irrationnel. Cahiers Roumains
       d'Etudes Littéraires, 1974, 2:4-15.
4640. _____. L'Oeil vivant. Paris: Gallimard, 1961.
4641. _____. L'Oeil vivant, 2: La Relation critique. Paris:
       Gallimard, 1970.
4642. _____. Psychanalyse et critique littéraire. Preuves,
       1966, 16:21-32.
4643. _____. [Rousseau and Bouffon.] Gesnerus, 1964, 21:83-
       94.
4644. _____. Rousseau and the longing for transference. Amer
       Society Legion of Honor Magazine, 1958, 27:148-158.
4645. _____. Suicide et mélancolie chez Mme de Staël.
       Preuves, 1966, 190:41-48.
4646. _____. Tout le mal vient de l'inégalité. Europe, 1961,
       391-392:135-149.
4647. Stearns, M. W. Robert Henryson and the Aristotelian tradi-
       tion of psychology. Studies in Philology, 1944, 41:492-
       500.

4648. Steel, Eric M. Diderot's Imagery: A Study of a Literary Personality. NY: Haskell, 1968.

4649. Steeves, Edna L. The girl that I marry: feminine stereotypes in literature. CEA Critic, 1975, 37(4):22-24.

4650. Stegmann, I. Die Wirklichkeit des Traumes bei E. T. A. Hoffmann. Zeitschrift für Deutsche Philologie, 1976.

4651. Steig, Michael. The challenge of subjectivism. West Coast Rev, 1976, 10:15-23.

4652. _____. A chapter of noses: George Cruikshank's psychonography of the nose. Criticism, 1975, 17:308-325.

4653. _____. Defining the grotesque: an attempt at synthesis. JAAC, 1970, 29:253-260.

4654. Stein, Martin. The cliché: a phenomenon of resistance. JAPA, 1958, 6:263-277.

4655. Stein, Morris I. Creativity and culture. J Psychol, 1953, 36:311-322.

4656. Stein, Richard L. The private themes of Pater's Renaissance. In Crews, F. C. (ed), Psychoanalysis and Literary Process. Cambridge, Mass: Winthrop, 1970, 163-218.

4657. Stekel, Wilhelm. Ein anderes treffendes Wort Goethes. Int Zeitschrift für Psychoanalyse, 1912, 2:105-106.

4658. _____. Goethe äussert sich über die Macht infantiler Eindrücke. Int Zeitschrift für Psychoanalyse, 1912, 2:106.

4659. _____. Goethe über einen Fall von Konversion. Int Zeitschrift für Psychoanalyse, 1912, 2:105.

4660. Stepankova, Julie. Premyslení a snení o poesii. (G. Bachelarda cesta od psychoanalyzy k fenomenologii). Comparative Lit, 1966, 14:128-133.

4661. Sterba, Richard F. The problem of art in Freud's writings. Psychoanal Q, 1940, 9:256-268.

4662. Stern, J. P. On Realism. London: Routledge & Kegan Paul, 1973.

4663. Stern, Leopold. Sacher-Masoch ou l'amour de la souffrance. Paris: Grasset, 1933.

4664. Sterrenburg, Lee. Psychoanalysis and the iconography of revolution. Victorian Studies, 1975, 19:241-264.

4665. Stewart, Allegra. Gertrude Stein and the Present. Cambridge: Harvard Univ. Press, 1967.

4666. Stimpson, Catharine R. The androgyne and the homosexual. Women's Studies, 1974, 2:237-248.

4667. Stockinger, Jacob. Toward a gay criticism. College English, 1974, 36:303-310.

4668. Stokes, Adrian Durham. Form in art: a psycho-analytic interpretation. In A Game That Must Be Lost. Chester Springs, Pa: Dufour, 1973, 109-115.

4669. Stolte, Heinz. Moderne Weltdeutung im dichterischen Werk Friedrich Hebbels. In Koopmann, L. (ed), Hebbel Jahrbuch 1965. Heide in Holstein: Westholsteinische Verlagsanstalt Boyens, 1966.

4670. Stone, Albert E. Psychoanalysis and American literary culture. Amer Q, 1976, 28:309-323.

4671. Stora-Sandor, Judith. Littérature et psychanalyse: Propositions pour une méthodologie. Les Langues Modernes, 1977, 71:391-417.

4672. Storr, Anthony. The Dynamics of Creation. NY: Atheneum, 1972.

4673. Storz, Gerhard. Laudatio auf Harald Weinrich. Deutsche Akademie für Sprach und Dichtung, 1977, 82-86.

4674. Stragnell, S. A study in sublimations. Psychoanal Rev, 1923, 10:209-213.

4675. Straub-Fischer, Esther. Die Farben und ihre Bedeutung im dichterischen Werk Gottfried Kellers. Berlin: Laufhütte, 1973.

4676. Streatfield, D. Persephone: A Study of Two Worlds. NY: Messner, 1959; London: Routledge, 1959.

4677. Strelka, Joseph P. (ed). Literary Criticism and Psychology. Yearbook of Comparative Criticism, Vol. 8. University Park: Penn State Univ. Press, 1967; Review: John V. Knapp, Modern Fiction Studies, 1978-79, 24:654-658.

4678. _____. The Personality of the Critic. University Park: Penn State Univ. Press, 1973.

4679. _____. Perspectives in Literary Symbolism. University Park: Penn State Univ. Press, 1968.

4680. _____. Psychoanalyse und Mythenforschung in der Literaturwissenschaft. In Zmegac, V., & Skeb, Z. (eds), Zur Kritik literaturwissenschaftlicher Methodologie. Frankfurt: Athenäum, 1973, 199-215.

4681. _____. Auf der Suche nach dem verloren Selbst. Zu deutscher Erzählprosa des 20. Jahrhunderts. Bern: Francke, 1977.

4682. _____. Werk, Werkverständnis, Wertung: Grundproblem vergleichender Literaturkritik. Bern: Francke, 1978.

4683. Strikovíc, J. [Psychological and philosophical aspects of time phenomena in the works of Njegos.] Srpski Arhiv za Celokupno Lekarstvo, 1979, 107(7-8):673-768.

4684. Strong, L. A. G. The Sacred River: An Approach to James Joyce. NY: Pellegrini & Cudahy, 1951.

4685. Strozier, Robert M. Dynamic patterns: a psychoanalytic theory of plot. Southern Rev, 1974, 7:254-263.

4686. Stuart, Simon. New Phoenix Wings: Reparation in Literature. London: Routledge & Kegan Paul, 1979.

4687. Suchkov, B. Individualism and personality. In Gierow, K. R. (ed). Problems of International Literary Understanding. Stockholm: Almqvist & Wiksell, 1968; NY: Interscience, 1968, 83-91.

4688. Sucre, G. The body of language and the language of the body. In Seven Voices. NY: Knopf, 1972.

4689. Suleiman, Susan, & Crosman, Inge (eds). The Reader and the Text: Essays on Audience and Interpretation. Princeton: Princeton Univ. Press, 1980.

4690. Sullivan, Friedrun Auguste. 'Je jette le plus souvent la plume au vent': Montaigne and Interior Monologue. DAI, 1976, 36:4459A.

4691. Summerhayes, D. Joyce's Ulysses and Whitman's 'self': a query. Wisconsin Studies in Contemporary Lit, 1963, 4:216-224.

4692. Supprian, U. [Schizophrenia and language in Hölderlin.]
       Fortschritte der Neurologie, Psychiatrie und ihrer Gren-
       zegebeite, 1974, 42:615-634.
4693. Sussman, Herbert L. Victorians and the Machine: The Lit-
       erary Response to Technology. Cambridge: Harvard Univ.
       Press, 1968.
4694. Sutton, Walter. Modern American Criticism. Englewood
       Cliffs, NJ: Prentice-Hall, 1963.
4695. Swanson, Don R. Toward a psychology of metaphor. Criti-
       cal Inquiry, 1978, 5:163-166.
4696. Swanton, Michael. Heroes, heroism and heroic literature.
       English Assn Essays & Studies, 1977, 30:1-21.
4697. Swartz, Paul. Perspectives in psychology: IX. literature
       as art and as knowledge. Psychol Record, 1959, 9:7-10.
4698. Swinnerton, Frank. Post-Freud. In The Georgian Scene.
       NY: Farrar & Rinehart, 1934, 415-419; London: Radius
       Book-Hutchinson, 1969, 324-327.
4699. Sylvestre, Guy. Existentialisme et littérature. Rev de l'uni-
       versité Laval, 1947, 1:423-433.
4700. Symons, Arthur. The Symbolist Movement in Literature.
       NY: Dutton, 1958.
4701. Szasz, Thomas. Karl Kraus and the Soul-Doctors: A Pio-
       neer Critic and His Criticism of Psychiatry and Psycho-
       analysis. Baton Rouge: Louisiana State Univ. Press,
       1976.
4702. Szilágyi, Géza. Magyar szerzök az ujabb freudista irodalom-
       ban. Pesti Napló, 1922.

4703. Tanaka, Yukio. [Herbert Read's criticism and psychoanaly-
       sis.] Eigo Seinen (Tokyo), 1968, 114:650-651.
4704. Tanksley, William R. Frederick J. Hoffman as Literary
       Scholar and Critic. DAI, 1970, 31:769A.
4705. Tap, Pierre. Pour une psychologie personnaliste. In Prés-
       ence de Mounier. Bordeaux: Frères du Monde, 1964,
       61-64.
4706. Tarizzo, Domenico. Forma e simbolismo dopo Freud.
       Degrès, 1973, 4:h-h5.
4707. Tausk, Victor. Two contributions to the psychoanalysis of
       the inhibition of artistic productivity. In Nunberg, H.,
       & Federn, E. (eds), Minutes of the Vienna Psychoanalytic
       Society, Vol. 4, 1912-1918. NY: IUP, 1975, 126-127.
4708. Taylor, R. Music and mystery: thoughts on the unity of the
       work of E. T. A. Hoffmann. J English Germanic Philol-
       ogy, 1976, 75:477-491.
4709. Teagarden, F. M. Some psychological trends in modern lit-
       erature. Kadelpian Rev, 1930, 4:309-322.
4710. Teller, Frida. Die Wechselbeziehungen vom psychischen Kon-
       flict und körperlichem Leiden bei Schiller. Imago, 1921,
       7:95-126.
4711. Tennenhouse, Leonard (ed). The Practice of Psychoanalytic
       Criticism. Detroit: Wayne State Univ. Press, 1976;

Review: C. Walhout, Papers in Language & Lit, 1978, 14:361-362.

4712.   Terrasse, J.   Public fictif et public réel: Les Rêveries du promenuer solitaire. Rev Belge de Philologie et d'Histoire, 1966, 44:925-935.

4713.   Terwiel, J.   Rousseaus Ansichten über die geistige Entwicklung des Kindes und die hentige Kinderpsychologie. Thesis, Münster, 1907.

4714.   Tetel, Marcel (ed).   Symbolism and Modern Literature; Studies in Honor of Wallace Fowlie. Durham: Duke Univ. Press, 1978.

4715.   Thibaudet, Albert.   Psychanalyse et littérature. Nouvelle Rev Française, 1921, Apr.

4716.   _____.   Réflexions sur la littérature: psychanalyse et littérature. Nouvelle Rev Française, Apr 1921, 467-481.

4717.   Thoma-Herterich, Christa.   Zur Kritik der Psychokritik. Frankfurt A/M: Lang Bern, 1976.

4718.   Thomalla, Ariane.   Die 'Femme fragile': Ein literarischer Frauentyp der Jahrhundertwende. Düsseldorf: Bertelsmann, 1973.

4719.   Thomas, Dylan.   Answer to inquiry about Freud's influence. New Verse, 1934, 11:9.

4720.   Thomas, J. -F.   Le Pélagianisme de Jean-Jacques Rousseau. Paris: Nizet, 1956.

4721.   Thorburn, J. M.   Art and the unconscious. Monist, 1921, 31:589-595.

4722.   _____.   Art and the Unconscious: A Psychological Approach to a Problem of Philosophy. London: Kegan Paul, 1925.

4723.   Thorp, C. D.   Some notices of empathy before Lipps. Papers Michigan Academy Science, Arts & Letters, 1938, 23:525-533.

4724.   Thorp, Willard.   The literary scholar as chameleon. In Camden, C. (ed), Literary Views: Critical and Historical Essays. Chicago: Univ. Chicago Press, 1964, 166-171.

4725.   Thorpe, C. De W.   The Aesthetic Theory of Thomas Hobbes. With Special Reference to His Contribution to the Psychological Approach in Literary Criticism. Ann Arbor: Univ. Michigan Press, 1940; London: Milford, Oxford Univ. Press, 1940.

4726.   Thorpe, James (ed).   Relations of Literary Study: Essays on Interdisciplinary Contributions. NY: Modern Language Assn, 1967; Review: Eleanor B. Manheim & Leonard F. Manheim, Hartford Studies in Lit, 1969, 1: 146-155.

4727.   Thorslev, Peter L., Jr.   Existentialism and literature. Graduate Student English, 1960, 3:31-34.

4728.   _____.   Incest as romantic symbol. Comparative Lit Studies, 1965, 2:41-58.

4729.   _____.   Romanticism and the literary consciousness. J History Ideas, 1975, 36:563-572.

4730. Thumb, A. Satzrhythmus und Satzmelodie in der altgriesch-
       ischen Prose. Fortschritte der Psychologie und ihrer
       Andwendung, 1913, 1:137-168.
4731. Tierney, Lani. People in crisis. English J, 1977, 66:64-
       65.
4732. Tillotson, G. Dreams in English literature. London Mer-
       cury, 1933, 27:516-523.
4733. Timpanaro, Sebastiano. The Freudian Slip: Psychoanalysis
       and Textual Criticism. NY: Schocken, 1976.
4734. Tindall, William York. D. H. Lawrence and Susan His Cow.
       NY: Columbia Univ. Press, 1939; London: Oxford Univ.
       Press, 1940.
4735. Tissi, S. Al Microscopio Psicanalitico. Milan: Hoepli, 1946.
4736. Tlili, M. L'Idée de nature chez Rousseau. Les Cahiers de
       Tunisie, 1975, 23:247-270.
4737. Todorov, Tzvetan. The notion of literature. New Literary
       History, 1973, 5:5-16.
4738. _____. Poétique de la prose. Paris: Seuil, 1971; Ithaca,
       NY: Cornell Univ. Press, 1977.
4739. _____. Recherches sur le symbolisme linguistique. Le
       Mot d'esprit et ses rapport avec le symbolique. Poét-
       ique, 1974, 18:215-245.
4740. _____. Théories du symbole. Paris: Seuil, 1977.
4741. Toliver, Harold. Animate Illusions: Explorations of Narra-
       tive Structure. Lincoln: Univ. Nebraska Press, 1974.
4742. Tolstoi, Leo N. Emotionalism: excerpts from 'What Is
       Art?' In Weitz, M. (ed), Problems in Aesthetics. NY:
       Macmillan, 1959, 612-621.
4743. Tompkins, Jane P. Criticism and feeling. College English,
       1977, 39:169-178.
4744. Torres, M. Psicoanálisis del Escritor. Mexico: Editorial
       Pax-Mexico, 1969.
4745. Toth, Emily. The independent woman and 'free love.'
       Massachusetts Rev, 1975, 16:647-664.
4746. Tournadre, C. (ed). Les Critiques de notre temps et Apol-
       linaire. Paris: Garmer, 1971.
4747. Towers, Bernard. Jung and Teilhard. In Braybrooke, N.
       (ed), The Wind and the Rain. London: Secker & War-
       burg, 1962, 79-87.
4748. Tranouez, Pierre. L'Esthénique, l'amazone et l'androgyne.
       Rev des Lettres Modernes, 1977, nos. 491-497: 87-113.
4749. Trienens, Roger. The Green-eyed Monster: A Study of Sex-
       ual Jealousy in the Literature of the English Renaissance.
       Doctoral dissertation, Evanston, Ill: Northwestern Univ.,
       1951.
4750. Trilling, Diana. Our uncomplaining homosexuals. Harpers,
       Aug 1969, 90-95; In We Must March My Darlings; A
       Critical Decade. NY: Harcourt Brace Jovanovich, 1977,
       157-171.
4751. Trilling, Lionel. Aggression and utopia. A note on William
       Morris's News from Nowhere. Psychoanal Q, 1973, 42:
       214-233.

4752. _____. Art and neurosis. [Excerpt from The Liberal
        Imagination.] Books and Bookmen, 1971, 16(5):18-24; In
        Howe, I. (ed), Modern Literary Criticism. Boston:
        1958, 94-111; In Glicksberg, Charles I. (ed), American
        Literary Criticism 1900-1950. NY: Hendricks, 1951,
        550-566.

4753. _____. Freud and the Crisis of our Culture. Boston:
        Beacon, 1955.

4754. _____. The Freud/Jung letters. In The Last Decade;
        Essays and Reviews, 1965-75. NY: Harcourt Brace
        Jovanovich, 1979, 177-184.

4755. _____. Freud and literature. Horizon, 1947, 16:182-200;
        In The Liberal Imagination. NY: Viking, 1950, 34-57;
        In Schorer, M., et al. (eds), Criticism, The Foundation
        of Modern Literary Judgment. NY: Harcourt Brace,
        1948, 172-182; In Levitt, M. (ed), Readings in Psycho-
        analytic Psychology. NY: Appleton-Century-Crofts,
        1959; In Zabel, M. D. (ed), Literary Opinion in America,
        Vol. 2. Gloucester, Mass: Smith, 1968, 677-692; In
        Ruitenbeek, H. M. (ed), Psychoanalysis and Literature.
        NY: Dutton, 1964, 251-271.

4756. _____. A Gathering of Fugitives. Boston: Beacon, 1956;
        NY: Harcourt Brace Jovanovich, 1978.

4757. _____. The Last Decade: Essays and Reviews, 1965-75.
        NY: Harcourt Brace Jovanovich, 1979.

4758. _____. The legacy of Sigmund Freud; II. Literary and
        aesthetic. Kenyon Rev, 1940, 2:162-168.

4759. _____. The Liberal Imagination. NY: Macmillan, 1948;
        NY: Viking, 1953; NY: Harcourt Brace Jovanovich,
        1978.

4760. _____. A note on art and neurosis. Partisan Rev, 1945,
        12:41-48; In Phillips, W. (ed), Art and Psychoanalysis.
        NY: Stratford, 1957.

4761. _____. The Opposing Self. NY: Viking, 1955; NY: Har-
        court Brace Jovanovich, 1978.

4762. _____. Prefaces to the Experience of Literature. NY:
        Harcourt Brace Jovanovich, 1979.

4763. _____. Psychoanalysis and literature. Monatshefte für
        deutschen Unterricht, 1951, 35:477-489.

4764. _____. What is criticism? In Literary Criticisms. An
        Introductory Reader. NY: Holt, Rinehart & Winston,
        1970, 1-28.

4765. Trinquet, Roger. La Curiosité psychologique chez Montaigne
        des ses premiers essais (I, II, De la tristesse). Bulletin
        de la Société des Amis de Montaigne, 1974, 9:21-28.

4766. Trollope, L. Freud and literature. Horizons, 1947.

4767. Trousson, R. La Conscience en face du mythe. Socrate
        devant Voltaire, Diderot, Rousseau. Paris: Minard,
        1967.

4768. Trowbridge, Frederick Hoyt. Perception, imagination, and
        feeling in Dryden's criticism. In From Dryden to Jane
        Austen. Albuquerque: Univ. New Mexico Press, 1977,
        32-77.

4769. Trueblood, C. K. Saint-Beuve and the psychology of personality. Character & Personality, 1939, 8:120-143.
4770. Tsanoff, Radoslav A. The Ways of Genius. NY: Harper, 1949.
4771. Tsur, Reuven. Two critical attitudes: quest for certitude and negative capability. College English, 1975, 36:776-788.
4772. Tubach, F. C. 'Perfectibilite': Der zweite Diskurs Rousseau und die deutsche Aufklarung. Etudes Germaniques, 1960, 15:144-151.
4773. Tucker, Harry. The importance of Otto Rank's theory of the double. J Otto Rank Assn, 1977-78, 12(2):59-65.
4774. Tuerk, Richard. Thoreau's early versions of a myth. Amer Transcendental Q, 1971, 10:32-38.
4775. Tuin, H. van der. L'Evolution psychologique; esthetique et littéraire de Theophile Gautier. Amsterdam: Holdert, 1933; Paris: Nizet, 1933.
4776. Twomey, John H., Jr. Human Relations: The Problem of Enseada Amena. DAI, 1974, 35:3015A.
4777. Tytell, Pamela V. The French Psychoanalytic Culture. French Psychoanalysts and Their Relationship to the Literary Text. Doctoral dissertation, Columbia Univ., 1979.

4778. Ulivi, Ferruccio. Manzoni e la psicanalisi. Rassegna di Cultura e Vita Scolastica, 1971, 25(1):1-3.
4779. Ulivi, Lucia Urbani. La psicologia di Abelardo e il Tractatus de Intellectibus. Rome: Ed. di Storia e Leteratura, 1976.
4780. Ullmann, Stephen. Psychologie et stylistique. JPNP, 1953, 46(2):133-156.
4781. Ulmer, Gregory L. Fetishism in Roland Barthe's Nietzschean phase. Papers in Language & Lit, 1978, 14:334-355.
4782. Umbral, F. [Sex and death in García Lorca.] La Estafeta Literaria, 1968, 387.
4783. Urbach, Reinhard. Arthur Schnitzler. NY: Ungar, 1973.
4784. Urban, Bernd. Arthur Schnitzler und Sigmund Freud. Aus den Anfängen des 'Doppelgängers.' Zur Differenzierung dichterischer Intuition und frühen Umgebung der Hysterieforschung. Germanisch-Romanische Monatsschrift, 1974, 24:193-223.
4785. _____. Hofmannsthal, Freud und die Psychoanalyse: Quellenkundliche Untersuchungen. Frankfort: Lang, 1978.
4786. _____. Psychoanalyse und Literaturwissenschaft; Texte zur Geschichte ihrer Beziehungen; mit einer weiterführenden Bibliographie. Tübingen: Niemeyer, 1973.
4787. Urzidil, J. From Goethe to Freud. Life & Letters, 1948, 58:5-21.
4788. Ushida, Ichigure. [A review of psychological studies on Edgar Allan Poe, 1860-1967.] In Collected Essays by Members of Faculty, Kyoritsu Women's Junior College, no. 13. Kyoritsu, Japan, 1970, 120-139.

4789. Vaget, H. R. Schach von Wuthenow: 'Psychographie' und 'Spiegelung' im 14. Kapitel von Fontanes Schach von Wuthenow. Monatshefte, 1969, 61:1-14.

4790. Valentine, Robert Y. Cortazar's rhetoric of reader participation. In Pope, R. D. (ed), The Analysis of Literary Texts. Ypsilanti, Mich: Bilingual Press, 1980, 212-223.

4791. Van Bark, Bella S. The alienated person in literature. Amer J Psychol, 1961, 21:198-206.

4792. Van Kaam, Adrian. Personality, personal unfolding and the aesthetic experience of literature. Humanities, 1968, 4:223-236.

4793. _____, & Healy, Kathleen. The Demon and the Dove: Personality Growth Through Literature. Pittsburgh: Duquesne Univ. Press, 1967.

4794. Varin, René. L'Erotisme dans la littérature française. Paris: Champs Fleuris, 1951.

4795. Various. Comment l'interprétation vient au psychanalyste: Journées Confrontation 1976. Paris: Aubier-Montaigne, 1977.

4796. _____. Comments on 'The Homosexual Imagination' in College English, November 1974. College English, 1975, 37:62-85.

4797. _____. Creativity. [Charles Kligerman, reporter.] Int J Psycho-Anal, 1972, 53:21-30.

4798. _____. Ecriture, feminité, féminisme. [Special number.] Rev des Sciences Humaines, 1977, 44, no. 168.

4799. _____. French Freud: Structural Studies in Psychoanalysis. [Entire Issue.] Yale French Studies, 1972, 48:1-202.

4800. _____. The homosexual imagination. [Special issue.] College English, 1974, 36.

4801. _____. Intoxication and literature. [Entire issue.] Yale French Studies, 1974, 50:5-205.

4802. _____. Literature and psychoanalysis. The question of reading: otherwise. [Entire issue.] Yale French Studies, 1977, 55-56:2-507.

4803. _____. Men portray women; women portray men. [Special issue.] Ploughshares, 1978, 4(2).

4804. _____. New critical practices I. [Entire issue.] L'Esprit créateur, 1974, 14(3).

4805. _____. Poetics and psychology. [Entire issue.] Poetics: Int Rev for Theory of Lit, 1978, 7(2).

4806. _____. Psicoanalisi e poesia. [Entire issue.] Verri, 1968, 28:5-95.

4807. _____. The reader's experience; symposium. English J, 1977, 66:32-51.

4808. _____. Research in response to literature; a symposium. Research in the Teaching of English, 1976, 10:203-276.

4809. _____. Women in literature and criticism. [Special issue.] CEA Critic, 1975, 37(4).

4810. _____. Women, literature, criticism. [Special issue.] Bucknell Rev, 1978, 24(1).

4811. Vartanian, Aram. Diderot and the phenomenology of the dream. Diderot Studies, 1966, 8:217-253.

4812. Veenstra, F. Dromen zonder Freud. Spektator, 1975, 4: 582-616.

4813. Veley, Charles R. Literature and the Emotions: A Psychology of Literary Response. DAI, 1971, 32:935A-36A.

4814. Verhoeff, Han. Psychoanalyse en literatuurbeschouwing. Forum der Letteren, 1977, 252-269.

4815. Vernière, P. Un Aspect de l'irrationalisme au 18e siècle: la démonologie et son exploitation littéraire. In Pagliaro, H. E. (ed), Irrationalism in the Eighteenth Century. Cleveland: Case Western Reserve Univ. Press, 1972, 289-302.

4816. Vernon, John. The Garden and the Map: Schizophrenia in Twentieth Century Literature and Culture. Urbana: Univ. Illinois Press, 1973; Review: Campbell Tatham, Boundary, 1975, 2:305-322.

4817. Verstraeten, Pierre. L'Homme du plaisir chez Hegel et l'homme du désir chez Lacan. Rev de l'Université de Bruxelles, 1976, 3-4:351-394.

4818. Vetrano, A. J. La problemática psico-social en Icaza. Miami: Universal, 1974.

4819. Vickery, John B. The scapegoat in literature: some kinds and uses. In McCune, M. W., Orbison, T., & Withim, P. M. (eds), The Binding of Proteus: Perspectives on Myth and the Literary Process. Lewisburg, Pa: Bucknell Univ. Press, 1980, 264-278.

4820. Viderman, Serge. Le Céleste et le sublunaire. Paris: Presses Universitaires de France, 1977.

4821. Vietta, S., & Kemper, H. -G. Expressionismus. Munich: Fink, 1975.

4822. Viglieno, Lawrence. Richardson et Rousseau devant la loi du père: Tentative de psychocritique comparée. In Etudes et recherches de littérature générale et comparée. Paris: Belles Lettres, 1979, 167-179.

4823. Vigolo, Giorgio. Per una psicologia dell'anti-romanticismo contemporaneo. In Chiarini, P., et al. (eds), Miscellanea di studi in onore di Bonaventura Tecchi, 2 Vols. Rome: dell'Ateneo, 1969, 723-737.

4824. Villena, L. A. de. Heracles invoca a Hylas (un tratado sobre la homosexualidad). Papeles de Son Armadans, 1976, 241:101-110.

4825. Vinge, Louise. The Narcissus Theme in Western European Literature up to the Early Nineteenth Century. Lund, Sweden: Gleerup, 1967.

4826. Vivante, L. The misleading comparison between art and dreams. Criterion, 1926, 4:436-454.

4827. Vivas, Eliseo. Creation and Discovery: Essays in Criticism and Aesthetics. NY: Noonday Press, 1955.

4828. _____. Literature and knowledge. Sewanee Rev, 1952, 60:561-592.

4829. Volhand, E. Literaturwissenschaft und Psychoanalyse. In Prinzhorn, H. (ed), Auswirkungen der Psychoanalyse in

Wissenschaft und Leben. Leipzig: Der neue Geist, 1928, 134-152.

4830. Volkmann, K. Psychologie der Zauberkunst. Archiv für die gesamte Psychologie, 1933, 87:541-567.

4831. Voster, S. A. Lope de Vega y Titelmans. Revista de Literatura, 1962, 21:5-33.

4832. Voutsinas, D. Un Auteur de psychologie en profondeur: Maine de Biran. Bulletin de psychologie, 5 Nov 1960.

4833. _____. La Psychologie de Maine de Biran, 1766-1824. Thèse, Univ. Strasbourg, 1963; Paris: Société d'Imprimerie Periodique, 1964.

4834. Waelder, Robert. Psychoanalytic Avenues to Art. NY: IUP, 1965.

4835. Wagener, Elaine H. Does literature affect self-concept? Peabody J Education, 1976, 53:299-302.

4836. Wagner, W. Die Gestalt der jungen Isolde in Goethe's Tristan. Euphorion, 1973, 67:52-59.

4837. Wahl, Jean. L'Angoisse et l'instant. Nouvelle Rev Française, 1932, 38.

4838. Wais, Kurt K. T. Das Vater-Sohn Motiv in der Dichtung bis 1880. Berlin: De Gruyter, 1931.

4839. Waldberg, Patrick. Eros in La Belle Epoque. NY: Grove, 1969.

4840. Waldeck, Peter B. Anxiety and the biopsychology of literature. Susquehanna Univ. Studies, 1976, 10:69-84.

4841. _____. Hermann Broch und Freud. Colloquia Germanica (Berne), 1970, 4:62-76.

4842. _____. Die Kindheitsproblematik bei Hermann Broch. Munich: Fink, 1968.

4843. Ward, J. P. T-group; absurdity and the consequences. Encounter, 1974, 42:30-40.

4844. Wasiolek, Edward. The future of psychoanalytic criticism. In Malone, D. H. (ed), The Frontiers of Literary Criticism. Los Angeles: Hennessey & Ingalls, 1974, 149-168.

4845. Wasserman, E. R. The pleasures of tragedy. J English Lit History, 1947, 14:283-307.

4846. Wasserstrom, William J. Abandoned in Providence. Hartford Studies in Lit, 1973, 5:77-87.

4847. Wasson, Richard. The Green Child: Herbert Read's ironic fantasy. PMLA, 1962, 77:645-651.

4848. Watanabe, Nancy Ann. Creative Destruction: The Irony of Self-Betrayal in the Psychosymbolic Monologue: Browning, Poe, Eliot, Kafka, and Camus. DAI, 1976, 36: 5289A-90A.

4849. Waterman, Arthur. Conrad Aiken as critic: the consistent view. Mississippi Q, 1971, 24:91-110.

4850. Watt, I. Literature and society. In Wilson, R. N. (ed), The Arts in Society. Englewood Cliffs, NJ: Prentice-Hall, 1964, 299-314.

4851. Wax, Rosalie H. Les Notions de l'ego et de l'id dans la veille littérature scandinave. Rev de Psychologie des Peuples, 1957, 12:317-332.

4852. Weathers, Winston. The Archetype and the Psyche: Essays in World Literature. Tulsa, Oklahoma: Univ. Tulsa Press, 1968.

4853. Weber, Joseph G. The personal in the style of La Rochefoucauld's Maximes. PMLA, 1974, 89:250-255.

4854. _____. The poetics of memory. Symposium, 1979, 33: 293-298.

4855. Weber, S. M. The aesthetics of Rousseau's Pygmalion. Modern Language Notes, 1968, 83:900-918.

4856. Webster, William B. Meaning and Significance: The Limits of Archetypal Interpretation. DAI, 1973, 33:4370A.

4857. Wegner, P. C. Melancholie in Ludwig Tiecks 'William Lovell.' Medizinhistorie J, 1974, 9(3-4):201-206.

4858. Weidhorn, Manfred. Dreams in Seventeenth-Century Literature. The Hague: Mouton, 1970; DA, 1965, 26:1638.

4859. Weidling, Friedrich. Drei deutsche Psyche-Dichtungen. Jauer, 1903.

4860. Weigand, Hermann J. Surveys and Soundings in European Literature. Leslie A. Willson (ed). Princeton: Princeton Univ. Press, 1966.

4861. Weigand, P. Psychological types in Friedrich Schiller and William James. J History Ideas, 1952, 13:376-383.

4862. Weigel, John A. Confessions of a verbal behaviorist. College Composition & Communication, 1968, 187-191.

4863. Weinberg, Albert K. Nephew and maternal uncle: a motive of early literature in the light of the Freudian psychology. Psychoanal Rev, 1918, 5:392-397.

4864. Weinstein, Norman. Gertrude Stein and the Literature of the Modern Consciousness. NY: Ungar, 1970.

4865. Weisinger, Herbert. The hard vision of Freud. In The Agony and the Triumph; Papers on the Use and Abuse of Myth. East Lansing: Michigan State Univ. Press, 1964, 134-145; Lit & Psychol, 1957, 7:5-8.

4866. _____. Tragedy and the Paradox of the Fortunate Fall. East Lansing: Michigan State College Press, 1953; London: Routledge & Kegan Paul, 1953.

4867. Weiss, Eduardo. Su alcune critiche di autori italiani in tema di psicoanalisi. Archivio Generale di Neurologie, Psichiatria e Psicoanalisi, 1923-24, 4-5:129-139.

4868. Weiss, Karl. Von Reim und Refrain: Ein Beitrag zur Psychogenese dichterischer Ausdrucksmittel. In Beutin, W. (ed), Literatur und Psychoanalyse, 1972, 137-158.

4869. Weiss, Robert O. Death in the Works of Arthur Schnitzler. Master's thesis, Univ. Missouri, 1951.

4870. _____. The human element in Arthur Schnitzler's social criticism. Modern Austrian Lit, 1972, 5:30-44.

4871. _____. Introduction: Arthur Schnitzler's Some Day Peace Will Return. NY: Ungar, 1972.

4872. _____. The psychoses in the works of Arthur Schnitzler. German Q, 1968, 41:377-400.

4873. _____. Schnitzler's ideas on Schmutzliteratur and the marriage contract. Modern Austrian Lit, 1976, 2:50-54.

4874. _____. A Study of Arthur Schnitzler with Special Consideration of the Problem of Psychosis in Flight into Darkness. DA, 1956, 16:124.

4875. Weissfeld, M. Goethe über Verdrängung und Abreagieren. Int Zeitschrift für Psychoanalyse, 1913, 1:606-607.

4876. Weissman, Philip. The psychology of the critic and psychological criticism. JAPA, 1962, 10:745-761.

4877. Weliky, Deirdre Gail Berlin. The Study of Interhuman Relationships in the Work of Simone de Beauvoir. DAI, 1977, 37(11):7125-A.

4878. Wellek, Albert. Goethe und die Psychologie. In Witz. Lyrik. Sprache. Beiträge zur Literatur- und Sprachtheorie. Bern: Francke, 1970, 68-94.

4879. _____. [Literature--psychology.] Archiv für Psychologie, 1972, 124:158-173.

4880. Wellek, René. Kenneth Burke and literary criticism. Sewanee Rev, 1971, 79:171-188.

4881. _____, & Warren, Austin. Literature and psychology. In Theory of Literature. NY: Harvest, 1956, 81-93; NY: Harcourt, Brace, 1949; Madrid: Gredos, 1959; Tokyo: Chi-kuma, 1954; Bologna: Il Mulino, 1956; Bad Homburg: Gentner, 1959; Seoul: Shinku Moonhwa, 1959; London: Cape, 1966.

4882. Wells, Charles V. Psychoanalysis in French literary criticism, 1920-1939. Lit & Psychol, 1960, 10:67-68.

4883. Wells, H. G. Suppressions and symbolism in dreamland. In The Happy Turning. NY: Didier, 1946, 4-7; London: Heinemann, 1945, 4-7.

4884. Wellwarth, G. E. Fritz Hochwälder: the drama within the self. Quart J Speech, 1963, 49:274-281.

4885. Welter, Barbara. Dimity Convictions: The American Woman in the Nineteenth Century. Athens: Ohio Univ. Press, 1976.

4886. Wentzel, Knud. Litteratur og psykologi. Kritik, 1972, 24: 31-46.

4887. Wertime, Richard A. Leslie Farber and the nature of will. Lit & Psychol, 1977, 27:16-20.

4888. Wescott, Roger W. The Divine Animal. NY: Funk & Wagnalls, 1969.

4889. West, Rebecca. The Strange Necessity. Garden City, NY: Doubleday, 1928.

4890. Westland, Gordon. The psychologist's search for scientific objectivity in aesthetics. British J Aesthetics, 1967, 7: 350-357.

4891. Westman-Berg, K. Looking at women in literature. Scandinavian Rev, 1975, 63(2):48-55.

4892. Weston, Jessie L. From Ritual to Romance. Garden City, NY: Doubleday, 1957.

4893. Wexler, V. G. 'Made for man's delight': Rousseau as antifeminist. Amer Historical Rev, 1976, 81:266-291.

4894. Whatley, J. L'Age équivoque: Marivaux and the middle-aged woman. Univ. Toronto Q, 1976, 46:68-82.

4895. Wheeler, O. A. An analysis of literary appreciation. British
      J Psychol, 1923, 13:229-242.
4896. Wheelwright, Philip Ellis. The archetypal symbol. In Strel-
      ka, J. (ed), Perspectives in Literary Symbolism. Uni-
      versity Park: Penn State Univ. Press, 1968, 214-243.
4897. _____. Metaphor and Reality. Bloomington: Indiana
      Univ. Press, 1962.
4898. _____. Mimesis and katharsis: an archetypal considera-
      tion. In Wimsatt, W. K. (ed), Literary Criticism: Idea
      and Act. Berkeley: Univ. California Press, 1974, 110-
      127.
4899. White, Victor. Soul and Psyche. NY: Harper & Row, 1960.
4900. Whitehead, G. Psychoanalysis and Art. London: Bale &
      Danielsson, 1930.
4901. Whitehouse, P. G. 'The meaning of emotion' in Dewey's Art
      as Experience. JAAC, 1978, 37:149-156.
4902. Whiton, John N. The Problem of Marriage in the Works of
      Arthur Schnitzler. DA, 1967, 28(7):2701A.
4903. Whitrow, G. J. Reflections on the history of the concept of
      time. Studium Generale, 1970, 23:498-508.
4904. Wiggins, Clarence Albin. The Concept of Death in the Work
      of Arthur Schnitzler. Master's thesis, New York Univ.,
      1954.
4905. Wijsen, Louis M. P. T. From text to symbol: the cognitive
      and affective response to literature. Psychocultural Rev,
      1978, 2(3).
4906. _____. Psychoanalysis and the Literary Symbol: A Struc-
      tural Approach to Imagery, Language and Thought in Lit-
      erature. DAI, 1978, 38:4860A.
4907. Wilbanks, Evelyn R. The Changing Images of Women in the
      Works of Petrarch, Boccaccio, Alberti, and Castiglione.
      DAI, 1978, 38:7483A.
4908. Wilbur, George B., & Muensterberger, Warner (eds). Psy-
      choanalysis and Culture. NY: IUP, 1951.
4909. Wilden, Anthony G. Freud, Signorelli, and Lacan: the re-
      pression of the signifier. Amer Imago, 1966, 23:332-
      366.
4910. _____. The Language of the Self. Baltimore: Johns Hop-
      kins Univ. Press, 1968.
4911. Will, Frederic. Psychoanalysis and the study of ancient
      Greek literature. In Literature Inside Out. Cleveland:
      Western Reserve Univ. Press, 1966, 39-53.
4912. Willenberg, Heiner. Die Darstellung des Bewusstseins in
      der Literatur. Vergleichende Studien zu Philosophie,
      Psychologie und deutscher Literatur von Schnitzler bis
      Broch. Frankfurt: Akademische, 1974.
4913. Williams, David Anthony. Condorcet, feminism and the
      egalitarian principle. Studies Eighteenth-Century Culture,
      1976, 5:151-163.
4914. Wilner, Eleanor. Gathering the Winds: Visionary Imagina-
      tion and Radical Transformation of Self and Society.
      Baltimore: Johns Hopkins Univ. Press, 1975.
4915. Wilson, Edmund. Axel's Castle: A Study in the Imaginative
      Literature of 1870-1930. NY: Scribner's, 1947.

4916. _____. Philoctetes: the wound and the bow in art and
       psychoanalysis. In The Wound and the Bow. NY: Ox-
       ford Univ. Press, 1929; In Phillips, W. (ed), Art and
       Psychoanalysis. NY: Criterion, 1957.

4917. _____. Sophocles, Babbitt and Freud. New Republic,
       1930, 45.

4918. _____. The Wound and the Bow. Seven Studies in Liter-
       ature. NY: Oxford Univ. Press, 1929, 1937; Boston:
       Houghton Mifflin, 1941; London: Secker & Warburg,
       1942.

4919. Wilson, Robert N. (ed). The Arts in Society. Englewood
       Cliffs, NJ: Prentice-Hall, 1964.

4920. _____. Literary experience and personality. JAAC, 1952,
       10:297-309.

4921. _____. Literature, society, and personality. JAAC,
       1952, 10:297-309.

4922. Wilson, T. G. The iconography of Swift. J Royal College
       Surgeons Edinborough, 1968, 13:174-188.

4923. Wimsatt, William K. , Jr. , & Beardsley, M. C. The inten-
       tional fallacy. Sewanee Rev, 1946, 59:468-488.

4924. _____, & Brooks, Cleanth. Literary Criticism: A Short
       History. NY: Knopf, 1957; London: Routledge & Kegan
       Paul, 1958.

4925. Windt, Judith H. Not Cast in Other Women's Mold: Strong
       Women Characters in Shakespeare's Henry VI Trilogy,
       Drayton's Englands Heroicall Epistles and Jonson's Poems
       to Ladies. DAI, 1974, 35:3777A-78A.

4926. Winterstein, Alfred R. F. Zum thema: Künsterlischer Schaf-
       fen und Kunstgenuss. Int Zeitschrift für Psychoanalyse,
       1911, 2:291.

4927. _____, & Bergler, Edmund. Zur Psychologie des Pathos.
       In Beutin, W. (ed), Literatur und Psychoanalyse. Munich:
       Nymphenberger, 1972, 159-168; The psychology of pathos.
       Int J Psycho-Anal, 1935, 16:414-424.

4928. Winthrop, Henry. Alienation and existentialism in relation
       to literature and youth. J General Education, 1967, 18:
       289-298.

4929. _____. Disalienation, decadence, and pathology in art.
       Dalhousie Rev, 1969, 49:331-345.

4930. Withim, Philip M. From symptom to process: the move-
       ment of psychoanalytic criticism. J General Education,
       1973, 25:173-183.

4931. _____. The psychodynamics of literature. Psychoanal
       Rev, 1969-70:56:556-585.

4932. Wittels, Fritz. Art. In Freud and His Time. NY: Gros-
       set & Dunlap, 1931, 398-421.

4933. _____. A contribution to a symposium on religious art
       and literature. J Hillside Hospital, 1952, 1:3-6.

4934. _____. The 'Fackel' neurosis. In Nunberg, H. , & Fed-
       ern, E. (eds), Minutes of the Vienna Psychoanalytic Soci-
       ety, Vol. 2. NY: IUP, 1967, 382-393.

4935. _____. Goethe und Freud. Psychoanalytische Bewegung,
       1930, 5:431-466.

4936.   . The Lilith neurosis. Psychoanal Rev, 1932, 19:
       241-256; Psychoanalytische Bewegung, 1932, 4:197-211.
4937.   . Psychoanalysis and literature. In Lorand, S. (ed),
       Psychoanalysis Today. NY: Covici-Friede, 1933, 338-
       348; NY: IUP, 1944, 371-380.
4938. Witzleben, Henry von. Goethe und Freud. Studium Generale,
       1966, 19:606-627.
4939. Wolf, Ernest S. Saxa Loguuntur: artistic aspects of Freud's
       The Aetiology of Hysteria. In The Psychoanalytic Study
       of the Child, Vol. 26. Chicago: Quadrangle, 1971, 535-
       534.
4940. Wolff, Cynthia Griffin. A mirror for men: stereotypes of
       women in literature. Massachusetts Rev, 1972, 13:205-
       218.
4941. Wolff, Reinhold. Zur Ästhetisierung der aufklärerischen
       Tabukritik bei Montesquieu und Rousseau. Munich: Fink,
       1972.
4942. Wollenberg, F. W. Brentanos Jugendlyrik. Studien zur Struk-
       tur seiner dichterischen Persönlichkeit. Doctoral dis-
       sertation, Univ. Hamburg, 1964.
4943. Wollenberg, Robert. Die Stellung der Psychiatrie in der Uni-
       versitas Literarum. Breslau: Hirt, 1928.
4944. Wolman, Benjamin B. Creative art and psychopathology.
       Amer Imago, 1967, 24:140-150.
4945. Wood, Margaret W. Paths of Loneliness. NY: Columbia
       Univ. Press, 1953.
4946. Woodard, Charles R. The archetype of the fall. College
       English, 1966, 28:576-580.
4947. Worby, Diana Zacharia. The death of the child in literature.
       Mid-Hudson Language Studies, 1978, 1:125-140.
4948. Wormhoudt, Arthur. The five layer structure of sublimation
       in literary analysis. Amer Imago, 1956, 13:205-219.
4949.   . Freud and literary theory. Amer Imago, 1949,
       6:217-225.
4950.   . The unconscious bird symbol in literature. Amer
       Imago, 1950, 7:173-182.
4951. Worren, Arne. Ein psykologisk analyse av hovudpersonen og
       temaet 'indre liv.' In Boyson, E. (ed), Vandring mot
       havet: en prosadiktming. Oslo: Gyldendal, 1974, 119-
       126.
4952. Worthington, Mabel P. Don Juan: Theme and Development
       in the Nineteenth Century. Doctoral dissertation, Colum-
       bia Univ., 1952.
4953. Wunberg, Gotthart. Hofmannsthal im Urteil seiner Kritiker:
       Dokumente zur Wirkunsgeschichte Hugo von Hofmannsthals
       in Deutschland. Frankfurt: Athenäum, 1972.
4954. Wyatt, David. Prodigal Sons; A Study of Authorship and Au-
       thority. Baltimore: Johns Hopkins Univ. Press, 1980.
4955. Wyatt, Frederick. Das psychologische in der Literatur. In
       Paulsen, W. (ed), Psychologie in der Literaturwissen-
       schaft. Heidelberg: Stiehm, 1971, 15-33.
4956. Wyrsch, Jakob. [Don Juan and psychopathology.] Confinia
       Psychiatrica, 1962, 5:61-95.

4957. Wysor, B. Lesbianism in literature. In The Lesbian Myth. NY: Random House, 1974, 190-256.

4958. Yamanouchi, Hisaaki. Abe Kōbō, and Oe Kenzaburō: the search for identity in contemporary Japanese literature. in Beasley, W. G. (ed), Modern Japan; Aspects of History, Literature and Society. Berkeley: Univ. California Press, 1975, 166-186.

4959. Yglesias, L. E. Alienation and the Poetic Word: A Study of the Poetics of Miguel de Unamuno and Antonio Machado. Doctoral dissertation, Harvard Univ., 1968.

4960. Young, Douglas. Ermakov and psychoanalytic criticism in Russia. Slavic & East European J, 1979, 23:72-86.

4961. Young, Ian. The Male Homosexual in Literature. Metuchen, NJ: Scarecrow, 1975.

4962. Young, L. A. Modern American scientific approach to criticism: psychological and sociological. Letters, 1929, 3: 8-18.

4963. Zagari, Luciano. Gusto psicologico e stile simbolico nelle Affinita Elettive. Annali Istituto Universitario Orientale, Napoli, Sezione Germanica, 1962, 5:183-212.

4964. Zaller, Robert M. Anaïs Nin and the truth of feeling. Arts in Society, 1973, 10:308-312.

4965. _____. A Casebook on Anaïs Nin. NY: New American Library, 1975.

4966. Zambrano, María. Dreams and literary creation. In Grunebaum, G. E. von, & Caillois, R. (eds), The Dream and Human Societies. Berkeley: Univ. California Press, 1966.

4967. Zanco, Aurelio. Temi e psicologia di Thomas de Quincey. Rev di Letterature Moderne e Comparate, 1956, 9:200-210.

4968. Zapparoli, Gian Carlo. La vocazione e l'attitudine psicanalitica. Verri, 1968, 28:52-57.

4969. Zarev, P. Narodnaja psixologija i sovremmenyj process. Voprosy Literatury, 1974, 18(9):111-134.

4970. Zatlin, Linda. 'You Are Old, Father William': the problem of aging in 20th century literature. In Marsden, M. T. (comp), Proceedings of the Fifth National Convention of the Popular Cultural Assn. Bowling Green, Ohio: Bowling Green State Univ. Popular Press, 1975, 1448-1456.

4971. Zdenek, Joseph W. Psychical conflicts in Benavente's La malquerida. Romance Notes, 1978, 19:183-189.

4972. Zee, Nancy S. Anaïs Nin: Beyond the Mask. DAI, 1974, 34:6671A.

4973. Zéphir, Jacques J. Psychologie de Salavin de Georges Duhamel. Paris: Éditions Université, 1970.

4974. Zesmer, David Mordecai. Love and Marriage in The Anatomy of Melancholy. DA, 1964, 25:490.

4975.   Zinn, G.A., Jr.   Mandala symbolism and use in the mysti-
        cism of Hugh of St. Victor.   History of Religion, 1973,
        12:317-341.
4976.   Zinnes, Harriet.   Anaïs Nin.   Book Abroad, 1963, 37:283-
        286.
4977.   Ziolkowski, Theodore.   Disenchanted Images: A Literary
        Iconology.   Princeton: Princeton Univ. Press, 1977.
4978.   Ziomek, H.   [Dream states in Pessoa.]   Kentucky Romance
        Q, 1973, 20:483-493.
4979.   Zlotchew, Clark M.   Galdós and mass psychology.   Anales
        Galdosianos, 1977, 12:5-19.
4980.   Zurabashvili, A.D.   [Shota Rustaveli, Nikoloz Baratashvili,
        Vazha Pshavela: A Psychological Essay.]   Tbilisi,
        USSR: Merani, 1970.

4981. Aarons, Z. Alexander. Normality and abnormality: with a digression on Prince Hal--'the sowing of wild oats.' In The Psychoanalytic Study of the Child, Vol. 25. NY: IUP, 324-339.

4982. Abastado, Cl. Eugene Ionesco, étude suivi d'un Entretien. Paris: Bordas, 1971.

4983. Abbe, Jessica. Anne Bogart's journeys. Drama Rev, 1980, 24:85-100.

4984. Abel, Lionel. Metatheatre: A New View of Dramatic Form. NY: Hill & Wang, 1963.

4985. _____. So who's not mad: on Marat/Sade and nihilism. Dissent, 1966, 13:166-171.

4986. Abenheimer, Karl M. On narcissism--including an analysis of Shakespeare's King Lear. British J Medical Psychol, 1945, 20:322-329.

4987. _____. Shakespeare's Tempest: a psychological analysis. Psychoanal Rev, 1946, 33:399-415; In Faber, M. D. (ed), The Design Within. NY: Science House, 1970, 502-519.

4988. Abirached, Robert. Ionesco et l'obsession de la mort. Etudes, 1963, 317:88-91.

4989. Abood, Edward F., & Harris, Phyllis. The splintered personality in Euripides. Psychol Perspectives, 1977, 8:60-75.

4990. Abrams, Samuel, & Shengold, Leonard. The meaning of 'nothing': I. A note on 'nothing'; II. More about the meaning of 'nothing.' Psychoanal Q, 1974, 43:115-119.

4991. Adamowski, Thomas H. The aesthetic attitude and narcissism in Othello. Lit & Psychol, 1968, 18:73-81.

4992. Adams, Elsie. Feminism and female stereotypes in Shaw. Shaw Rev, 1974, 17:17-22.

4993. Adams, George R. Black militant drama. Amer Imago, 1971, 28:107-128.

4994. Adams, J. F. All's Well That Ends Well: the paradox of procreation. Shakespeare Q, 1960, 12:261-270.

4995. Addington, D. W. Varieties of audience research: some prospects for the future. Educational Theatre J, 1974, 26:482-487.

4996. Adelman, Janet. The Common Liar: An Essay on Antony and Cleopatra. New Haven: Yale Univ. Press, 1973.

4997. Adler, Charles A. Richard III--his significance as a study in criminal life-style. Int J Individual Psychol, 1936, 2:55-60.

4998. Adler, Gerhard. Foreword to Kirsch, J.: Shakespeare's Royal Self. NY: Putnam, 1966.

4999. Adler, Meinhard. Brecht im Spiel der technischen Zeit. Naturwissenschaftliche, psychologische und wissenschaftliche Kategorien im Werk Bertolt Brechts. Ein Beitrag zur Literaturpsychologie. Berlin: Nolte, 1976.

5000. _____. [Some common categories in the language of Bert Brecht and the speech of schizophrenics.] Confinia Psychiatrica, 1975, 18:95-111.

5001. Adler, Thomas P. Robert Anderson: playwright of middle-aged loneliness. Ball State Univ. Forum, 1975, 16(2):58-64.

5002. Adnès, André. Shakespeare et la folie; étude médico-psychologique. Paris: Maloine, 1936.

5003. _____. Shakespeare et la pathologie mentale. Thèse, Paris, 1935; Paris: Maloine, 1935; Review: W. Keller, Shakespeare Jahrbuch, 1935, 71:113-114.

5004. Agnihotrri, S. M. Child-symbol and imagery in Edward Albee's Who's Afraid of Virginia Woolf? Punjab Univ. Research Bulletin, 1972, 3:107-111.

5005. Aguirre, A. M. El personaje femenino en el teatro de Manuel y Antonio Machado. DAI, 1969, 29:3996-A.

5006. Ahrends, Günter. Traumwelt und Wirklichkeit im Spätwerk Eugene O'Neills. Heidelberg: Winter, 1978.

5007. Alberich, J. El erotismo femenino en el teatro de García Lorca. Papeles de Son Armadans, 1965, 39:9-36.

5008. Albert, Sidney P. Reflections on Shaw and psychoanalysis. Modern Drama, 1971, 14:169-195.

5009. Albrecht, H. Frauencharaktere in Ibsens Dramen. Leipzig: Wigand, 1907.

5010. Albrecht, W. P. Hazlitt, passion, and King Lear. Studies in English Lit, 1978, 18:611-624.

5011. Alexander, Doris M. Psychological fate in Mourning Becomes Electra. PMLA, 1953, 68:923-934.

5012. _____. Strange Interlude and Schopenhauer. Amer Lit, 1953, 25:213-228.

5013. Alexander, Franz. A note on Falstaff. Psychoanal Q, 1933, 2:592-606; Almanach, 1935, 161-179; Revista de Psicoanálisis, 1948, 6:497-510.

5014. Alexander, Nigel. Critical disagreement about Oedipus and Hamlet. Shakespeare Survey, 1967, 20:33-40.

5015. Alexander, Rose. Hamlet the classical malingerer. Medical J & Record, 1929, 130:287-290.

5016. Alexander, Theodor W. Arthur Schnitzler's Die Frau mit dem Dolche: déjà vu experience or hypnotic trance? Modern Austrian Lit, 1974, 7(1-2):108-112.

5017. Allen, Glen O. The aesthetic paradox in Hamlet. JAAC, 1969, 27:303-315.

5018. Allen, J. C. Was Hamlet insane? Open Court, 1904, 18:434-437.

5019. Allen, L. H. Repression in Hamlet. Australasian J Psychol & Philosophy, 1925, 3:53-56.

5020. _____. The hypnosis scene in The Tempest. Australasian J Psychol & Philosophy, 1926, 4:110-118.

5021. Allen, Rupert C. 'Psyche and Symbol' in the Theatre of
       Federico García Lorca. Austin: Univ. Texas Press,
       1974.
5022. Allentuch, Harriet M. R. Pauline and the Princesse de
       Cleves. Modern Language Q, 1969, 30:171-182.
5023. _____. Reflections on women in the theatre of Corneille.
       Kentucky Romance Q, 1974, 21:97-111.
5024. Alter, Maria P. The technique of alienation in Bertolt
       Brecht's The Caucasian Chalk Circle. College Language
       Assn J, 1964, 8:60-65.
5025. Alvarez-Altman, G. Nihilismo sexual en La casa de B. A.:
       consideraciones onomásticas. García Lorca Rev, 1975,
       67-69.
5026. Amat, C. Le Thème de la vision dans l'Andromaque de
       Racine. Rev des Sciences Humaines, 1973, 38:645-654.
5027. Ambrose, Mary Jo. An Examination of the Independent Role
       of Women in Friedrich Hebbel's Major Dramas. DAI,
       1977, 38:6752A-53A.
5028. Amikura, Sumie. [Desire Under the Elms by Eugene
       O'Neill.] English Lit (Waseda Univ.), 1962, No. 21, 66-
       80.
5029. Anderson, F. M. B. The insanity of the hero, an intrinsic
       detail of the Orestes vendetta. Transactions Amer Philo-
       logical Assn, 1927.
5030. Anderson, Mary Castiglie. Staging the unconscious: Edward
       Albee's Tiny Alice. Renascence, 1980, 32:178-192.
5031. Anderson, Michael. From epic to alienation. New Theatre
       Magazine, 1967, 7(2):19-25, 7(3):25-34.
5032. Anderson, Peter S. Shakespeare's Caesar: the language of
       sacrifice. Comparative Drama, 1969, 3:3-26.
5033. Anderson, Ruth Leila. Elizabethan Psychology and Shake-
       speare's Plays. NY: Russell & Russell, 1966; Ames:
       Univ. Iowa Humanistic Studies, 1928; Doctoral disserta-
       tion, Univ. Iowa, 1927.
5034. Andreas-Salomé, Lou. Henrik Ibsens Frauengestalten.
       Jena: 1910.
5035. Andreasen, Nancy J. C. The artist as scientist. Psychiatric
       diagnosis in Shakespeare's tragedies. JAMA, 1976, 235:
       1868-1872.
5036. André-Carraz, Danièle. L'Expérience intérieure d'Antonin
       Artaud. Paris: Librairie St. -Germain-des-Prés, 1973.
5037. Angress, Ruth K. 'Dreams that were more than dreams' in
       Lessing's Nathan. Lessing Yearbook, 1971, 3:108-127.
5038. Annenkov, I. P. Merry sanatorium. Drama Rev, 1975, 19:
       110-112.
5039. Anon. After the Fall. Psychology, 1965, 12:215-217.
5040. _____. Commentary. [Freud and Shakespeare.] Times
       Lit Supplement, 30 Jan. 1969.
5041. _____. Macbeth: a psychological study. J Mental Sci-
       ence, 1858, 4:477-507.
5042. _____. Psychanalyse en Shakespeare. Rev Générale de
       Clinique et de Thérapeutique, 1935, 49:773.
5043. Anthonisen, Niels L. The ghost in Hamlet. Amer Imago,
       1965, 22:232-249.

5044. Antoni, Nils. Hamlet: En psykologisk studie. Bonniers Litterära Magasin, 1960, 29:405-408.

5045. Appelbaum, S. A. Jesus Christ Superstar. The rock opera's contribution to the psychology of fame and success. Bulletin Menninger Clinic, 1972, 36:352-356.

5046. Appelbaum Graham, Ilse. Die Struktur der Persönlichkeit in Schillers dramatischer Dichtung. Jahrbuch der deutschen Schillergesellschaft, 1960, 4:270-303.

5047. Archer, William. Character and psychology. In Play-Making. A Manual of Craftsmanship. NY: Dover, 1960, 245-251.

5048. Arieti, Silvano. The Will to Be Human. NY: Quadrangle, 1972.

5049. Arjona, J. Modern psychology in Lope de Vega. Bulletin of the Comediantes, 1956, 8:5-6.

5050. Armand-Laroche, Jean-Louis. Antonin Artaud et son double. Avec huit portraits et deux dessin in édits. Périgueux: Fanlac, 1964.

5051. _____ . _____ . Essai d'analyse psychopathologique. Bergerac: Générale du Sud-Ouest, 1963.

5052. Armato, Philip Michele. Tennessee Williams' meditations on life and death in Suddenly Last Summer, The Night of the Iguana, and The Milk Train Doesn't Stop Here Anymore. In Tharpe, J. (ed) Tennessee Williams: A Tribute. Hattiesburg: Univ. Mississippi Press, 1977, 558-570.

5053. Armstrong, Edward A. Shakespeare's Imagination. A Study of the Psychology of Imagination and Inspiration. London: Drummond, 1946; Lincoln: Univ. Nebraska Press, 1963.

5054. Arnold, A. Recapitulation dream in Richard III and Macbeth. Shakespeare Q, 1955, 6:51-62.

5055. Arnold, Paul. Elements de l'art dramatique. JPNP, 1951, 44:371-387.

5056. _____ . From the dream in Aeschylus to the surrealist theater. JAAC, 1949, 7:349-354.

5057. Aronsohn, Oscar. Das Problem in Baumeister Solness. Halle: Marhold, 1911.

5058. Aronson, Alexander. Psyche and Symbol in Shakespeare. Bloomington: Indiana Univ. Press, 1972.

5059. _____ . Sakonnet point. Drama Rev, 1975, 19:27-35.

5060. Aronson, Harry. Identitetsproblemet hos Max Frisch. Vär Lösen: Kristen Kulturtidskrift, 1966, 57:508-513.

5061. Arrivé, Michel. Un Aspect de l'isotopie sexuelle dans le texte de Jarry: sadisme et masochisme. Romanic Rev, 1975, 66:57-75.

5062. Artaud, Antonin. Le Théâtre et son double. Paris: Gallimard, 1962 (1938).

5063. Arthos, John. Naive imagination and the destruction of Macbeth. J English Lit History, 1947, 14:114-126.

5064. _____ . Shakespeare's Use of Dream and Vision. Totowa, NJ: Rowman & Littlefield, 1977. Review: A. D. Nuttall, Shakespeare Q, 30:421-423.

5065. Ashley, Franklin B. The Theme of Guilt and Responsibility in the Plays of Arthur Miller. DAI, 1971, 31:5349A.

5066. Askew, Melvin W. Catharsis and modern tragedy. Psychoanalysis, 1961, 48(3):81-88.

5067. _____. Classical tragedy and psychotherapeutic catharsis. Psychoanalysis, 1960, 47(3):116-123.
5068. Athanassakis, A. Some thoughts on double-entendres in Seneca and Apocolocyntosis. Classical Philology, 1973, 68: 292-294.
5069. Atkins, Frances. The social meaning of the Oedipus myth. J Individual Psychol, 1966, 22:173-184.
5070. Aubouin, Elie. Technique et psychologie du comique. Marseille: 1948.
5071. Auden, W. H. The alienated city: reflections on Othello. Encounter, 1961, 3-14.
5072. Auerbach, L. Racine und die Leidenschaften. Germanisch-Romanische Monatsschrift, 1926, 14:371-380.
5073. Aufhauser, Marcia C. On the guilt of Oedipus. Psychoanal Rev, 1977, 64:135-145.
5074. Auld, L. Note sur Hippolyte amoureux. Cahiers raciniens, 1964, 16:93-114.
5075. Ault, H. C. The tragic protagonist and the tragic subject in Britannicus. French Studies, 1955, 9:18-29.
5076. Avery, L. G. A proposal concerning the study of early American drama. Educational Theatre J, 1977, 29:243-250.
5077. Avery, Nicholas C. The exorcism of the tabooed wish: an analysis of Who's Afraid of Virginia Woolf? Seminars in Psychiat, 1973, 5:347-357.
5078. Axel, Johan Uppvall. August Strindberg. A Psychoanalytic Study. Doctoral dissertation, Clark Univ., 1919.
5079. Ayda, A. Racine et l'inconscient. Analyse d'une scène de Phèdre. Dialogus, 1949, 1:43-53; 1951, 2:134-149.

5080. Babb, Lawrence. Abnormal psychology in John Ford's Perkin Warbeck. Modern Language Notes, 1936, 51:234-237.
5081. _____. Hamlet, melancholy, and the devil. Modern Language Notes, 1944, 59:120-122.
5082. _____. John Ford and Seventeenth Century Drama. Doctoral dissertation. Yale Univ., 1934.
5083. _____. Love melancholy in the Elizabethan and early Stuart drama. Bulletin History Medicine, 1943, 13:117-132.
5084. _____. Physiological conception of love in the Elizabethan and early Stuart drama. PMLA, 1941, 56:1020-1035.
5085. _____. Scientific theories of grief in some Elizabethan plays. Studies in Philology, 1943, 40:502-519.
5086. _____. Sorrow and love on the Elizabethan stage. Shakespeare Assn Bulletin, 1943, 18:137-142.
5087. Babcock, Weston. Hamlet: A Tragedy of Errors. Lafayette, Ind: Purdue Univ. Studies, 1961.
5088. Babula, William. Three sisters, time, and the audience. Modern Drama, 1975, 18:365-369.
5089. Bachler, Karl. Das Theater als Abwehr und Wunscherfüllung. Psychoanalytischer Bewegung, 1932, 4:359-364.
5090. Bachmann, Susan. 'Daggers in men's smiles': the 'trust issue' in Macbeth. Int Rev Psycho-Anal, 1978, 5:97-104.

5091- Bacon, Helen H. Woman's two faces: Sophocles' view of the
2.   tragedy of Oedipus and his family. In Masserman, J. H.
            (ed), Science and Psychoanalysis, Vol. 10. NY: Grune
            & Stratton, 1966, 10-24.

5093. Bailey, N. Le Mythe de la féminité dans le théâtre de Sartre.
            French Studies, 1977, 31:294-306.

5094. Baiwir, Albert. Alas, poor Hamlet. Rev des Langues Viv-
            ante, 1971, 37:373-387.

5095. Bajomée, Danielle. Lumière, ténèbres et chaos dans l'In-
            nommable de Samuel Beckett. Lettres Romanes, 1969,
            23:139-158.

5096. Baker, Anthony. Mistress Quickley's bawdy. Notes & Que-
            ries, N. S., 1966, 13:132.

5097. Baker, Sidney J. Shakespeare and sex. Int J Sexology,
            1950, 4:35-39.

5098. Baldensperger, Fernand. Encore la 'Cabale' de Phèdre:
            Leibnitz du mauvais côté? Modern Language Notes, 1943,
            58:523-526.

5099. Balinkin, Ausma. The Central Women Figures in Carl Zuck-
            mayer's Dramas. DAI, 1976, 37:2907A.

5100. Bancroft, D. The poetic wonderland of Cocteau's Thomas
            l'Imposteur. Australian J French Studies, 1966,
            3:36-50.

5101. Banzinger, George. Intergenerational communication in
            prominent western drama. Gerontologist, 1979, 19:471-
            480.

5102. Baranger, M. S. Ibsen's Peer Gynt. Explicator, 1970, 29.
5103. Baranger, Willy. El personaje de Edipo en la obra de Sofo-
            cles. Revista de Psicoanálisis, 1948, 5:861-873.

5104. Barber, C. L. The death of Zenocrate: 'conceiving and sub-
            duing both' in Marlowe's Tamburlaine. Lit & Psych,
            1966, 16:15-24.

5105. _____. The form of Faustus' fortunes good or bad.
            Tulane Drama Rev, 1964, 8:92-119.

5106. _____. Shakespearian comedy: The Comedy of Errors.
            College English, 1964, 25:493-497.

5107. _____. 'Thou that beget'st him that did thee beget':
            transformation in Pericles and The Winter's Tale.
            Shakespeare Survey, 1969, 22:59-67.

5108- Barchilon, Jacques. Le Cid: une interprétation psychanaly-
9.   tique. Studi Francescani, 1975, 57:475-480.

5110. Barker, C. Image in show business. Theatre Q, 1978, 8:7-
            11.

5111. Barko, I. La Symbolique de Racine: Essai d'interprétations
            des images de lumière et de ténèbres dans la vision
            tragique de Racine. Rev des Sciences Humaines, 1964,
            115:353-377.

5112. _____. Symbolism in Racine: light and darkness.
            AULLA Proceedings, 1964, 2:12-13.

5113. Barnard, Guy Christian. Samuel Beckett, a New Approach:
            A Study of the Novels and Plays. NY: Dodd, Mead,
            1970; London: Dent, 1970.

5114. Barnett, Joseph. Hamlet and the family ideology. J Amer
      Academy Psychoanal, 1975, 3:405-417.
5115. Barnstone, Willis. Lope's Leonido: an existential hero.
      Tulane Drama Rev, 1962, 7:56-57.
5116. Barranger, M. S. Lady from the Sea: Ibsen in transition.
      Modern Drama, 1978, 21:393-403.
5117. Barratt, Harold S. 'The Rose Distilled': Virginity,
      Fertility and Marriage in Shakespeare. DAI, 1976,
      36:5309A.
5118. Barricelli, Jean-Pierre. 'Sogno' and 'Sueno': Dante and
      Calderón. Comparative Lit Studies, 1972, 10:130-140.
5119. Barroll, John Leeds. Artificial Persons: The Formation of
      Character in the Tragedies of Shakespeare. Columbia:
      Univ. South Carolina Press, 1974; Review: M. D. Faber,
      Psychoanal Rev, 1975, 62:181-183.
5120. Barron, David B. The babe that milks: an organic study of
      Macbeth. Amer Imago, 1960, 17:133-161; In Faber, M. D.
      (ed), The Design Within. NY: Science House, 1970,
      253-279.
5121. _____. Coriolanus: portrait of the artist as infant.
      Amer Imago, 1962, 19:171-193.
5122. Barron, Frank, & Rosenberg, Marvin. King Lear and his
      fool: a study of the conception and enactment of dramatic
      role in relation to self-conception. Educational Theatre
      J, 1970, 22:276-283.
5123. Barsness, John A. Ken Kesey: the hero in modern dress.
      Rocky Mountain Modern Language Assn Bulletin, 1969,
      23:27-33.
5124. Barthes, Roland. On Racine. NY: Hill & Wang, 1964;
      Paris: Seuil, 1963.
5125. Batchelor, Jean. Montherlant: un théâtre psychologique et
      métaphysique. Nouvelles Littéraires, 15 Jan 1970, 13.
5126. Batchelor, J. W. Existence and Imagination, the Theatre of
      Henry de Montherlant. Queensland, Australia: Queens-
      land Univ. Press, 1968.
5127. Bauer, Robert V. The Use of Humors in Comedy by Ben
      Jonson and His Contemporaries. Doctoral dissertation.
      Univ. Illinois, 1947.
5128. Bayr, Rudolf. Delphischer Apollon: Ein Theaterbuch. Salz-
      burg: 1966.
5129. Bayuk, Milla. The submissive wife stereotype in Anton Chek-
      hov's Darling. College Language Assn J, 1977, 20:533-
      538.
5130. Bean, S. C. Moliere and medicine. North Carolina Medical
      J, 1970, 31:229-231 passim.
5131. Beardsell, Peter R. Insanity and poetic justice in Usigli's
      Corona se sombra. Latin American Theatre Rev, 1976,
      10:5-14.
5132. Beaudin, M. Le Visage humain dans la tragédie de la Cal-
      prenède. Modern Language Notes, 1930, 45:114-119.
5133. Beck, A. Die Krisis des Menschen im Dramen des jungen
      Schiller. Euphorion, 1955, 49:163-202.

5134. Becker, Lucille. Henry de Montherlant and suicide. Romance Notes, 1975, 16:254-257.

5135. Beckerath, Thea von. Ausdruck und Darstellung, vergegenwärtigt an der Schauspielkunst. Psychologische Rundschau, 1965, 16:79-97.

5136. Beckerman, Bernard. Theatrical perception. Theatre Research Int, 1979, 4:157-171.

5137. Béguin, Albert. Phèdre nocturne. Labyrinthe, No. 7, 15 April 1945.

5138. Bell, Gerda. Windows: a study of a symbol in Georg Büchner's work. Germanic Rev, 1972, 47:95-108.

5139. Bella, C. Ricerca della motivazione 'agente' nell'opera tragica di Vittorio Alfieri. Paragone, 1976, 27, no. 232:69-101.

5140. Bellsort, A. Le Mystère de Racine. Correspondant, 1913, 253:1096-1124.

5141. Belsey, Catherine. The case of Hamlet's conscience. Studies in Philology, 1979, 76:127-148.

5142. Bentley, Eric Russell. Father's day. Drama Rev, 1968, 13(1):57-72.

5143. _____. The homosexual question. Canadian Theatre Rev, 1976, 12:15-23.

5144. _____. The psychology of farce. New Republic, 6 Jan 1958, 138:17-19, 13 Jan 1958, 138:17-19. Introduction to Let's Get a Divorce! and Other Plays. NY: Hill & Wang, 1958, viii-xx.

5145. Bercovitch, Sacvan. Love and strife in Kyd's Spanish Tragedy. Studies in English Lit: 1500-1900, 1969, 9:215-229.

5146. Berger, Harry, Jr. Miraculous harp: a reading of Shakespeare's Tempest. Shakespeare Studies, 1970, 5:253-283.

5147. _____. Theater, drama, and the second world: a prologue to Shakespeare. Comparative Drama, 1968, 2:3-20.

5148. _____. Troilus and Cressida: the observer as basilisk. Comparative Drama, 1968, 2:122-136.

5149. Berghlolz, Harry. Autopsy on Solness. Lit & Psychol, 1958, 8:3-5.

5150. Bergler, Edmund. Anxiety, Feet of Clay, and comedy. Amer Imago, 1949, 6:97-109.

5151. _____. Homosexuality, Shakespeare's Hamlet, and D. H. Lawrence's The Fox. In One Thousand Homosexuals. Paterson, NJ: Pageant, 1959, 217-241.

5152. _____. Psychoanalyse im modernen Drama. Psychoanalytische Bewegung, 1932, 4:562-563.

5153. _____. Salome, the turning point in the life of Oscar Wilde. Psychoanal Rev, 1956, 43:97-103.

5154. _____. The seven paradoxes in Shakespeare's Hamlet. Amer Imago, 1959, 16:379-405; In Selected Papers. NY: Greene & Stratton, 1969, 445-464.

5155. Beringer, Edmund. The psychology of Lady Macbeth. Ethological J, 1929, 14:1-17.

5156. Berk, Philip R. The therapy of art in Le Malade imaginaire. French Rev, 1972, 45(4):39-48.

5157. Berkowitz, Gerald M. The destruction of identity in Pinter's early plays. Ariel, 1978, 9:83-92.

5158.   Berlin, Jeffrey B.   Arthur Schnitzler's Die Frau mit dem
        Dolche: déjà vu experience or hypnotic trance.   Modern
        Austrian Lit, 1974, 7:108-112.

5159.   _____.   The Treatment of Truth in the Dramatic Work of
        Henrik Ibsen and Arthur Schnitzler.   DAI, 1976, 37:
        1576A.

5160.   Berman, Ronald S.   Fathers and sons in the Henry VI plays.
        Shakespeare Q, 1962, 13:487-497.

5161.   _____.   The nature of guilt in the Henry IV plays.   Shake-
        speare Studies, 1965, 1:18-28.

5162.   _____.   Shakespearean comedy and the uses of reason.
        South Atlantic Q, 1964, 63:1-9.

5163.   Berne, Eric.   Notes on games and theatre.   Tulane Drama
        Rev, 1966, 11:89-91.

5164.   Berry, Edward I.   Prospero's brave spirit.   Studies in Phi-
        lology, 1979, 76:36-48.

5165.   Berry, Ralph.   Sexual imagery in Coriolanus.   Studies in
        English Lit, 1500-1900, 1973, 13:301-316.

5166.   _____.   'To say one': an essay on Hamlet.   Shakespeare
        Survey, 1975, 28:107-115.

5167.   Bersani, Leo.   Artaud, birth, and defecation.   Partisan Rev,
        1976, 43:439-452.

5168.   Berst, Charles A.   The devil and Major Barbara.   PMLA,
        1968, 83:71-79.

5169.   Best, Otto F.   Peter Weiss.   NY: Ungar, 1976; Bern:
        Francke, 1971.

5170.   Bettelheim, Bruno.   A Home for the Heart.   NY: Knopf,
        1973.

5171.   Bettencourt-Ferreira, J.   La Folie au théâtre.   Quelques
        considérations sur l'état morbide représénté dans Hamlet.
        Rev de Psychologie Clinique et Thérapeutique, 1900, 4:
        108-114.

5172.   Béttica-Giovannini, R.   Divagazioni mediche sulla vita e sull'
        opera di Gabriele D'Annunzio.   Pagine di Storia della
        Medicina, 1973, 17:71-116.

5173.   Bettina, M.   Willy Loman's brother Ben: tragic insight in
        Death of a Salesman.   Modern Drama, 1962, 4:409-412.

5174.   Betto, Saverio.   A Psychological Aesthetical Analysis of
        Christopher Marlowe's Works.   Master's thesis.   Ca Fos-
        cari (Italy), 1928.

5175.   Bevington, David M.   The domineering female in Henry VI.
        Shakespeare Studies, 1966, 2:51-58.

5176.   Beyer, H.   Symbolene i Brand.   In Various (eds), Festskrift
        til Anathon Aall.   Oslo: Aschenbourg, 1937, 257-267.

5177.   Biaute, Alcée.   Etude médico-psychologique sur Shakespeare
        et ses oeuvres, sur Hamlet en particulier.   Nantes, 1889;
        Echo Médical, 1899, 3, 52, 65, 76, 87, 99.

5178.   Bicknell, Catherine.   The Poetry of Pain: Neurosis in the
        Works of Adamov.   DAI, 1978, 39:910A-11A.

5179.   Bieber, Gustav A.   Der Melancholikertypus Shakespeares und
        sein Ursprung.   Heidelberg: Winter, 1913.

5180.   Bigelow, H. R.   Hamlet's insanity.   Chicago Medical J, 1873,
        30:513-519.

5181. Biggins, Dennis. Sexuality, witchcraft, and violence in Macbeth. Shakespeare Studies, 1975, 8:255-277.

5182. Biggs, Murray. A neurotic Portia. Shakespeare Survey, 1972, 25:153-159.

5183. Biggs, P. The disease theme in Sophocles' Ajax, Philoctetes, and Trachiniae. Classical Philology, 1966, 61:224-227.

5184. Bigsby, C. W. The strategy of madness: an analysis of Edward Albee's A Delicate Balance. Wisconsin Studies Contemporary Lit, 1968, 9:223-235.

5185. Binet, A., & Passy, J. Notes psychologiques sur les auteurs dramatiques. Année Psychologique, 1895, 1:60-118.

5186. Binns, J. W. Women or transvestites on the Elizabethan stage? An Oxford controversy. Sixteenth-Century J, 1974, 5(2):95-120.

5187. Binswanger, Ludwig. Heinrich Ibsen und das Problem der Selbstrealisation in der Kunst. Heidelberg: Schneider, 1949.

5188. Bird, Christine M. Games courtiers play in Love's Labor's Lost. Hartford Studies in Lit, 1979, 11:41-48.

5189. Birstein, J. Edmond Rostand über die Entstehung des Cyrano. Int Zeitschrift für Psychoanalyse, 1913, 3:557.

5190. Bishop, Sharon. Another look at Desdemona, heroine of dry dreams. Paunch, 1965, 23:5-9.

5191. Black, Michael. Othello: a study of the self. In The Literature of Fidelity. NY: Harper & Row, 1975, 16-42.

5192. Blackwell, Louise. Tennessee Williams and the predicament of women. South Atlantic Bulletin, 1970, 35(2):9-14.

5193. Blake, E. V. The impediment of adipose: a celebrated case. Popular Science Monthly, 1880, 17:60-71.

5194. Blamires, D. Sexual comedy in the Mären of Hans Rosenplüt. Trivium, 1976, 11:90-113.

5195. Blanchet, A. Phèdre entre le soleil et la nuit. Etudes, 1958, 299:55-74.

5196. Blasi, Augusto. On becoming responsible: Orestes in Aeschylus and in Sartre. Rev Existential Psychol & Psychiat, 1974, 13:70-87.

5197. Blau, H. Seeming, seeming: the disappearing act. Drama Rev, 1976, 20:7-24.

5198. Blaya, Marcelo. El uso de fensas maniacas en una obra teatral: O Pagador de Promeasus. Revista Uruguayan Psicoanálisis, 1966, 8:281-287.

5199. Bleich, David. Emotional origins of literary meaning. College English, 1969, 31:30-40.

5200. _____. The psychological bases of learning from literature. College English, 1971, 33:32-45.

5201. Bligh, John. The women in the Hamlet story. Dalhousie Rev, 1973, 53:275-285.

5202. Blin, M. La Fonction de la répétition dans Le Professeur Taranne: essai d'approche sémio-analytique d'une pièce d'Adamov. Rev du Pacifique, 1976, 11:61-80.

5203. Blum, E. Faust und die 'Sorge.' Schweizer Archiv für Neurologie und Psychiatrie, 1951, 67:5-14.

5204. Blum, Harold. A psychoanalytic view of Who's Afraid of Virginia Woolf? JAPA, 1969, 17:883-903; In Coltrera, J. T. (ed), Lives, Events, and Other Players: Studies in Psychobiography. NY: Aronson, 1980.

5205. Blum, M. I. Thème symbolique dans le théâtre de Racine. II. Le divin préparé par les thèmes de la famille, de la raison d'état, de la diplomatie. Paris: Nizet, 1962, 1965.

5206. Bock, Hedwig, & Schütt, Edda. Edward Albee, The Zoo Story: Versuch einer formalästhetischen und psychoanalytischen Interpretation. Jahrbuch der Psychoanalyse, 1975, 8:91-119.

5207. Bodamer, J. Über eine psychiatrische Beobachtung des jungen Schiller. Deutsche medizinische Wochenschrift, 1952, 77(23):754-756.

5208. Bodkin, Maude. The Quest for Salvation in an Ancient and a Modern Play. London: Oxford Univ. Press, 1941.

5209. Bodros, Paul. Théâtre et psychiatrie. Presse Médicale, 1949, 48:699-700.

5210. Body, Jacques. Intermezzo, Faust et Freud. Cahiers Jean Giraudoux, 1975, 4:81-89.

5211. Böckmann, P. Die innere Form in Schillers Jugenddramen. Euphorion, 1934, 35:439-480.

5212. Boëthius, U. Strindberg och kvinnofrågan till och med 'Giftas I.' Stockholm: Prisma, 1969.

5213. Bofinger, A. Das psychologische Problem in Paul Lindaus Schauspiel, Der Andere. Der Irrenfreund, 1894, 36:50-56.

5214. Boggs, W. Oedipus and All My Sons. Personalist, 1961, 42:555-558.

5215. Bongiorno, Dominick. Hamlet's Oedipus complex: a query. Shakespeare Newsletter, 1967, 17:15.

5216. _____, Grebanier, Bernard, Slochower, Harry, Fleissner, R. F., & Cheney, David. Remarks on the Freud-Jones theory of Hamlet. Shakespeare Newsletter, 1967, 17:15, 36, 58.

5217. Bonnet, P. Les Diverses manières d'appeler Néron dans Britannicus. Bulletin de liaison racinienne, Uzès, 1958.

5218. Boose, Lynda Elizabeth. 'Lust in Action': Othello as Shakepeare's Tragedy of Human Sexuality. DAI, 1977, 37: 7136A-37A.

5219. _____. Othello's handkerchief: the recognizance and pledge of love. English Lit Renaissance, 1975, 5:360-374.

5220. Boring, Phyllis Z. Arrabals' mother image. Kentucky Romance Q, 1968, 15:285-292.

5221. _____. Fantasy and lunacy in the contemporary Spanish theatre. Kentucky Romance Q, 1967, 13 (Suppl):41-51.

5222. _____. Feminine roles and attitudes toward marriage in the comedies of Miguel Mihura. Romance Notes, 1973, 14:445-449.

5223. Bosselaers, R. Le Remords de Phèdre. Levende Talen, 1956, 316-318.

5224. Bouffard, D. Un Révolté classique: Néron de Britannicus. Culture, 1960, 21:229-245.

5225. Bouissounouse, Janine. Montherlant et les femmes. Contrepoint-Trimentriel, 1978, 27:79-87.

5226. Bour, Pierre. Le Psychodrame et la vie. Paris/Bruges: Desclée de Brouwer, 1968.

5227. Bourciez, J. Psychologie amoureuse d'Aubanel. Cahiers du Sud, 1942, 249:252-258.

5228. Bowden, William R. The mind of Brutus. Shakespeare Q, 1966, 27:57-67.

5229. Bowen, Barbara C. Metaphorical obscenity in French farce, 1460-1560. Comparative Drama, 1977-78, 11:331-344.

5230. Bowers, Fredson. Hamlet's 'sullied' or 'solid' flesh: a biographical case-history. Shakespeare Survey, 1956, 9:44-48.

5231. Boyers, Robert. On the sanity of Marat/Sade: in defense of the young leftist. Dissent, 1966, 13:421-424.

5232. Boyette, Purvis Elton. Wanton humor and wanton poets: homosexuality in Marlowe's Edward II. Tulane Studies in English, 1977, 22:33-50.

5233. B-r., V. M. [Shakespeare's Hamlet from a medico-psychological point of view; a history of his mental state.] Archiv Psichiatrii, 1897, 30(2):39-107.

5234. Brachfield, O. Andre Gide's Oedipus. Zeitschrift für Sexualwissenschaft, 1931, 28:236-242.

5235. Braendel, Doris Brenan. The limits of clarity: Lyly's Endymion, Bronzino's Allegory of Venus and Cupid, Webster's White Devil, and Botticelli's Primavera. Hartford Studies in Lit, 1972, 4:197-215.

5236. Braga, Thomas J. Madness in the theater of Tristan l'Hermite. French Rev, 1975, 48:539-547.

5237. Brandell, Gunnar. Strindbergs Infernokris. Stockholm: Bonnier, 1950.

5238. Branson, J. S. The Tragedy of King Lear. Oxford: Blackwell, 1934.

5239. Brashear, William R. Nietzsche and Spengler on Hamlet: an elaboration and synthesis. Comparative Drama, 1971, 5:106-116.

5240. Brathwaite, Elise. Children in Elizabethan and Jacobean Drama. DAI, 1978, 38:6738A-39A.

5241. Brée, Germaine. Le Thème de la violence dans le monde tragique de Racine. Romanic Rev, 1947, 38:216-225.

5242. Breithart, Sara. Hedda Gabler: a critical analysis. Amer J Psychoanal, 1948, 5:55-58.

5243. Bremond, H. Notes sur Racine. Les Criminels de Racine et la délicatesse morale du XVIIe siècle. Vie Intellectuelle, 1930, 8:292-313.

5244. Brenman-Gibson, Margaret. The creation of plays: with a specimen analysis. In Roland, A. (ed), Psychoanalysis, Creativity, and Literature. NY: Columbia Univ. Press, 1978, 178-230; Psychoanal Rev, 1977, 64:237-288.

5245. Brennan, Elizabeth. The relationship between brother and sister in the plays of John Webster. Modern Language Rev, 1963, 58:488-494.

5246. Brenner, Arthur B. The fantasies of W. S. Gilbert. Psychoanal Q, 1952, 21:373-401.
5247. Breuer, Horst. Zur Methodik der Hamlet--Deutung von Ernest Jones. Shakespeare Jahrbuch, 1973, 144-171.
5248. _____. Samuel Beckett: Lernpsychologie und lieblische Determination. Munich: Fink, 1972.
5249. Brierre de Boismont, Alexandre. [Psychological studies on celebrated personnages. Shakespeare, his acquaintance with insanity. I. Hamlet, melancholy, pretended insanity.] Annales Médico-Psychologiques, 1868, 12:329-345; Union Médicale, 1868, 6:165-173.
5250. _____. [Psychological studies on celebrated personnages. Shakespeare, his acquaintance with insanity. II. Lear, mania.] Annales Médico-Psychologiques, 1869, 1:11-19; Union Médicale, 1869, 7:493-496.
5251. Brivic, Sheldon R. Structure and meaning in Joyce's Exiles. James Joyce Q, 1968, 6:29-52.
5252. Brock, J. H. E. Iago and Some Shakespearean Villains. Cambridge, Eng: Heffer, 1937.
5253. Brody, J. Les Yeux de César: the language of vision in Britannicus. Studies in Seventeenth Century French Lit, 1962, 33:185-201; In Demorest, J. J. (ed). Garden City, NY: Doubleday Anchor, 1966, 185-200.
5254. Brody, Paula. Shylock's omophagia: a ritual approach to The Merchant of Venice. Lit & Psychol, 1967, 17:229-234.
5255. Bronsen, David. Consuming struggle vs. killing time: preludes to dying in the dramas of Ibsen and Beckett. In Spicker, B. F., Woodward, K. M., & Van Tassel, D. D. (eds), Aging and the Elderly, Humanistic Perspectives in Gerontology. Atlantic Highlands: Humanities, 1978, 261-281.
5256. Brookbank, Charles D. The Theme of Boredom in Selected Modern Dramas. DAI, 1972, 32:5929A.
5257. Brooks, Cleanth. In pursuit of the self: the actor and society. Yale Theatre, 1977, 8:95-103.
5258. Brophy, Brigid. Mozart the Dramatist: a Psychological and Historical Study of Genius. NY: Harcourt, Brace & World, 1964.
5259. Brown, Kenneth. The significance of insanity in four plays by Antonio Buero Vallejo. Revista de Estudios Hispánicos, 1974, 8:247-260.
5260. Brown, Susan Rand. 'Mothers' and 'Sons': The Development of Autobiographical Themes in the Plays of Eugene O'Neill. DAI, 1976, 36:4481A-2A.
5261. Bruehl, William J. Polus Naufrangia: a key symbol in The Ascent of F6. Modern Drama, 1967, 10:161-164.
5262. Brundrett, Ralph B., Jr. The role of the ego in Grillparzer's Sappho and Schiller's Jungfrau. German Q, 1958, 31:16-23.
5263. Brunn Walter, L. von. [Georg Büchner.] Deutsch medizinische Wochenschrift, 1964, 89:1356-1360.
5264. Brunot, Henriette. Faut-il pleurer au spectacle? Psyché, 1947, 2:935-939.

5265. _____. Hamlet de Shakespeare, traduction d'André Gide. Psyché, 1946, 1:229-232.

5266. Brustein, Robert Sanford. The men-taming women of William Inge: The Dark at the Top of the Stairs. In Kernan, A. B. (ed), The Modern American Theater. Englewood Cliffs, NJ: Prentice-Hall, 1967, 70-79.

5267. Bryan, Margaret B. Food symbolism in A Woman Killed with Kindness. Renaissance Papers, 1974, 9-17.

5268. Bucknill, John Charles. King Lear: a psychological study. J Mental Science, 1859, 5:301, 348.

5269. _____. The Mad Folk of Shakespeare: Psychological Essays. Philadelphia: West, 1978; London: Macmillan, 1867.

5270. _____. The Psychology of Shakespeare. London: Longmans, Brown, 1858; London: Macmillan, 1960.

5271. Buell, John. The evil imagery in Tennessee Williams. Thought, 1963, 38:167-189.

5272. Bugliani, Ann. Women and the Feminine Principle in the Works of Paul Claudel. Madrid: Turanzas, 1977; Review: Ralph Tarica, French Rev, 1980, 53:944-945.

5273. Bukala, C. R. Sartre's 'Kean': the drama of consciousness. Rev Existential Psychol & Psychiat, 1974, 13:57-69.

5274. Bundy, Murray W. Shakespeare and Elizabethan psychology. J English & Germanic Philology, 1924, 23:516-549.

5275. Bünnings, E. Die Frau im Drama Ibsens. Leipzig: Xenienverlag, 1910.

5276. Burge, Barbara J. Hamlet: the search for identity. Rev English Lit, 1964, 5:58-71.

5277. _____. 'Nature Erring from Itself,' Identity in Shakespeare's Tragedies: A Study of the Use of 'I Am Not What I Am' and Its Related Variations in the Delineation of Character. DA, 1967, 27:4216A-17A.

5278. Burgess, J. Roger Planchon's Gilles de Rais at Villeurbanne. Theatre Q, 1976, 6:3-24.

5279. Burghardt, Lorraine H. Game playing in three by Pinter. Modern Drama, 1974, 17:377-388.

5280. Burkart, Veronika. Befreiung durch Aktionem: Die Analyse der gemeinsamen Elemente in Psychodrama und Theater. Vienna: Böhlau, 1972.

5281. Burke, Kenneth. Coriolanus--and the delights of faction. In Language as Symbolic Action. Berkeley: Univ. California Press, 1966, 81-97.

5282. _____. King Lear: its form and psychosis. Shenandoah, 1969, 21:3-18.

5283. _____. Othello: an essay to illustrate a method. Hudson Rev, 1951-52, 4:186-198.

5284. _____. Shakespearean persuasion: Antony and Cleopatra. In Language as Symbolic Action. Berkeley: Univ. California Press, 1966, 101-114.

5285. _____. Timon of Athens and misanthropic gold. In Language as Symbolic Action. Berkeley: Univ. California Press, 1966, 115-124.

5286. Burland, J. Alexis. Discussion of papers on Equus. Int J Psychoanal Psychotherapy, 1976, 5:501-505.

5287. Burnett, A. P. Catastrophe Survived. Oxford: Oxford Univ.
      Press, 1971.
5288. Burnham, D. L. Restitutional functions of symbol and myth
      in Strindberg's inferno. Psychiatry, 1973, 36:229-243.
5289. Burton, J. Earth, air, fire, and water: imagery and sym-
      bols in the tragedies of Federico García Lorca. García
      Lorca Rev, 1975, 99-120.
5290. Byles, Joan Mary. A Basic Pattern of Psychological Conflict
      in Shakespearean Tragic Drama. DAI, 1978, 39(6-A),
      3592.
5291. _____. The basic pattern of psychological conflict in
      Shakespearean tragic drama. Hartford Studies in Lit,
      1979, 11:58-71.
5292. _____. The Winter's Tale, Othello, and Troilus and Cres-
      sida: narcissism and sexual betrayal. Amer Imago,
      1979, 36:80-93.
5293. Byrd, S. Panerotism: a progressive concept in the final
      trilogy of García Lorcas. García Lorcas Rev, 1975,
      53-56.

5294. Calderwood, James L. Styles of knowing in All's Well.
      Modern Language Q, 1964, 25:272-294.
5295. Caldwell, Richard S. The blindness of Oedipus. Int Rev
      Psychoanal, 1974, 1:207-218.
5296. _____. The misogyny of Eteocles. Arethusa, 1973, 6:
      197-231.
5297. _____. The pattern of Aeschylean tragedy. Transactions
      Amer Philological Assn, 1970, 101:77-94.
5298. _____. The psychology of Aeschylus' Supplices. Are-
      thusa, 1974, 7:45-70.
5299. Calef, Victor. Lady Macbeth and infanticide or 'How many
      children had Lady Macbeth' murdered? JAPA, 1969, 17:
      528-548.
5300. Callahan, Robert D. Shakespeare's Troilus and Cressida:
      lechery as warfare. Paunch, 1965, 23:57-67.
5301. _____. The theme of 'government' in Measure for Meas-
      ure. Paunch, 1965, 25:31-52.
5302. Callan, Edward. W. H. Auden's first dramatization of Jung:
      the charade of loving and terrible mothers. Comparative
      Drama, 1977-78, 11:287-302.
5303. Camden, Carroll. Marlowe and Elizabethan psychology.
      Philological Q, 1929, 8:69-78.
5304. _____. On Ophelia's madness. Shakespeare Q, 1964, 15:
      247-255.
5305. _____. Shakespeare on sleep and dreams. Rice Institute
      Pamphlets, 1936, 23:106-133.
5306. Campbell, Ellen Mary. A Concept of Comic Catharsis as
      Applied to the Comedies of Thomas Middleton. DAI,
      1978, 39:892A.
5307. Campbell, John Libby, Jr. Timon of Athens: An Existential
      and Psychological Approach. DAI, 1976, 37:1560A-61A.
5308. Campbell, Lily Bess. Shakespeare's Tragic Heroes: Slaves
      of Passion. NY: Barnes & Noble, 1952.

5309. Campbell, Oscar J. What's the matter with Hamlet? Yale Rev, 1942, 32:309-322.

5310. Cantarella, Raffaele. Elementi Psicanalitic nella Tragadie Greca. Dioniso, Bolletino dell Instituto Nazionale del Dramma Antico, 1933, 3:321-335; 1934, 4:120-141, 211-229; Almanach, 1936, 128-149; In Scritti Minori sul Teatro Greco. Brescia: 1970, 59-112.

5311. Cantrell, Carol Helmstter. The Metamorphosis: Kafka's story of a family. Modern Fiction Studies, 1977-78, 23: 578-585.

5312. Carbonnell Basset, Delfín. Tres dramas existenciales de F. García Lorca. Cuadernos Hispanoamericanos, 1965, 64: 118-130.

5313. Carlisky, Mario. De Hamlet a Fausto. Buenos Aires: Ayacucho, 1947.

5314. _____. The Oedipus legend and Oedipus Rex. Amer Imago, 1958, 15:91-95.

5315. _____. Primal scene, procreation and the number 13. Amer Imago, 1962, 19:19-20.

5316. Carpenter, T. Freudian elements in the plays of Lenormand. Asides, 1942, 3:31-40.

5317. Carr, Joan. 'The Forest's Revenge': subconscious motivation in The Wild Duck. Modern Language Rev, 1977, 72, 845-856.

5318. Carré, M-R. Phèdre: Le Monde réel et les mondes imaginaires dans le théâtre de Racine. PMLA, 1967, 81:369-376.

5319. Carson, Neil. Elizabethan soliloquy--direct address or monologue? Theatre Notebook, 1976, 30:12-18.

5320. _____. Sexuality and identity in Fortune and Men's Eyes. Twentieth Century Lit, 1972, 18:207-218.

5321. Carstens, Erik. Fra en psykoanalytikers arbejdsvaerelse. Copenhagen: Dansk Psykoterapeutforening, 1970.

5322. Carter, A. E. Racine, poet of destruction. Univ. Toronto Q, 1946, 16:231-238.

5323. Castelli, Ferdinando. Le ossessioni di Eugène Ionesco. Civiltà Cattolica, 1975, 126(3):125-139.

5324. Castro, Ginette. Les Femmes dans le théâtre de O'Neill: essai d'interprétation féministe. Annales, 2:131-158.

5325. Casty, Alan. Tennessee Williams and the small hands of the rain. Mad River Rev, 1965, 1(3):27-43.

5326. Cavell, Stanley. The avoidance of love: a reading of King Lear. In Must We Mean What We Say? NY: Scribner's, 1969, 267-353.

5327. Cazalbou, J., & Sevely, D. Molière, précurseur de la comédie sérieuse et du drame bourgeois. Europe, 1972, 78-91.

5328. Cerf, Walter. Psychoanalysis and the realistic drama. JAAC, 1958, 16:328-336.

5329. Cetta, Lewis T. Profane Play, Ritual and Jean Genet: A Study of his Drama. University: Univ. Alabama Press, 1974.

5330. Chabrow, Leonard. Ritual and Pathos: The Theater of O'Neill. Lewisburg, Pa: Bucknell Univ. Press, 1976.

5331. Chadbrowe, Leonard. Dionysus in The Iceman Cometh. Modern Drama, 1962, 4:377-388.

5332. Chandler, Albert R. Tragic Effect in Sophocles Analyzed According to the Freudian Method. Cambridge: Harvard Univ. Press, 1912; Monist, 1913, 23:59-89.

5333. Chaplin, William H. Aeschylus, the Oresteian, and Psychoanalysis: Experience into Myth. DAI, 1973, 33(9-A), 5115-16.

5334. _____. Form and psychology in King Lear. Lit & Psychol, 1969, 19:31-46.

5335. Chapman, J. The effacement of the racinian image. French Studies, 1961, 15:122-133.

5336. Charpentier, F. La Vie psychologique dans le théâtre de Racine. Rev de l'Université d'Ottawa, 1940, 10:277-294.

5337. Chastel, G. L'Ame de Racine. Etudes: Rev catholique, 1939, 241:653-666.

5338. Chateaubriant, Alphonse de. La Psychologie et le drame des temps présents. Cercle europeen, Sceaux, Charaire, 1943.

5339. Cheney, David R. Hamlet--complex Oedipus complex continued. Shakespeare Newsletter, 1967, 17:58.

5340. Chesler, S. A. Orpheus descending. Players Magazine, 1977, 52:10-13.

5341. Chesterton, G. K. Hamlet and the psychoanalyst. In Fancies Versus Fads. NY: Dodd, 1923, 24-41; London: Methuen, 1923, 24-41.

5342. Childres, Clare Fooshee. Feminine Character and Sexual Roles in the Plays of Thomas Middleton (1580-1627). DAI, 1976, 36:4503A.

5343. Choisy, Maryse. Complexes de théâtre. Psyché, 1951, 6: 126-128.

5344. Christin, (?). Hamlet. Seminaire littéraire, 7 May 1921.

5345. Church, D. M. Structure and dramatic technique in Gide's Saul and Le Roi Candaule. PMLA, 1969, 84:1639-1644.

5346. Circeo, Ermanno. D'Annunzio e la psicocritica. Cultura e Scuola, 1972, 43:32-40.

5347. Cismaru, Alfred, & Klein, Theodore. The concept of suicide in Camus and Beckett. Renascence, 1976, 28:105-110.

5348. Cixous, Hélène. Jules César: un repas sacré. Discours autour d'un meurtre ritual. Les Langues Modernes, 1967, 61:53-55.

5349. Clark, Cumberland. Shakespeare and Psychology. Philadelphia: West, 1978; London: Williams & Norgate, 1936.

5350. Clark, M. J. , & Rockelein, L. A new interpretation of Hamlet. Int J Psycho-Anal, 1949, 30:92-107.

5351. Clark, W. Hoover. Existentialism and Pirandello's Sei personaggi. Italica, 1966, 43:3.

5352. Clasen, H. Uber Schillers psychologische Auschauungen. In Oberreal- und Landwirtschaftsschule in Flensburg. Flensburg: 1907.

5353. Clay, Charlotte N. The Role of Anxiety in English Tragedy: 1580-1642. Salzburg: Univ. Salzburg, 1974.

5354. Clemens, W. H. The Development of Shakespeare's Imagery. Washington, D. C.: Howard Univ. Press, 1951.

5355. Clevenger, Theodore, Jr. Behavioral research in theatre. Educational Theatre J, 1965, 17:118-121.

5356. Cloonan, William J. Father and son in Mithridate. French Rev, 1976, 49:514-521.

5357. _____. Love and gloire in Bérénice: a Freudian perspective. Kentucky Romance Q, 1975, 22:517-526.

5358. _____. Racine's Theatre: The Politics of Love. Romance Monograph Series, 28. Jackson: University Mississippi Press, 1977.

5359. Clum, J. M. Letter: Shakespeare and psychiatry. JAMA, 1976, 236:1239.

5360. Cluny, C. M. 'Oui a peur de Jean Racine?' Nouvelle Rev Française, 1964, 12:321-330.

5361. Clutton-Brock, Arthur. Shakespeare's Hamlet. London: Methuen, 1922; Review: Ernest Jones, Int J Psycho-Anal, 1922, 3:495-497.

5362. Coe, R. M. Beyond absurdity: Albee's awareness of audience in Tiny Alice. Modern Drama, 1975, 18:371-383.

5363. _____. Logic, paradox, and Pinter's Homecoming. Educational Theatre J, 1975, 27:488-497.

5364. Coffey, Warren. Tennessee Williams: the playwright as analysand. Ramparts, 1962, 1:48-57.

5365. Cohen, I. R. Answers to questions. Drama Rev, 1975, 19-111-116.

5366. Cohn, E. J. Shakespeare, the psychiatrist; an alienist shows that Shakespeare knew intuitively much that science today considers new. Welfare Magazine, 1928, 19:1124-1127.

5367. Colby, R. A. The sorcery of Medea. Univ. Kansas City Rev, 1959, 25:249-255.

5368. Colley, John Scott. Disguise and new guise in Cymbeline. Shakespeare Studies, 1974, 7:233-252.

5369. Collinge, N. Medical terms and clinical attitudes in the tragedians. London Institute Classical Studies Bulletin, 1962, 9:50-52.

5370. Collmer, Robert G. An existentialist approach to Macbeth. Personalist, 1960, 41:484-491.

5371. Colman, E. A. M. The Dramatic Use of Bawdy in Shakespeare. NY: Longman, 1976 (1964).

5372. Colvin, Clare. Feminism in the theatre. Contemporary Rev, 1977, 230:316-317.

5373. Conner, Maurice W. An Investigation of Three Themes Pertaining to Life and Death in the Works of Arthur Schnitzler, with Particular Emphasis on the Drama Der Ruf des Lebens. DAI, 1974, 34:4250A.

5374. Connolly, John. A Study of Hamlet. London: Moxon, 1893.

5375. Connolly, Thomas F. Shakespeare and the double man. Shakespeare Q, 1950, 1:30-35.

5376. Cook, Albert S. Language and action in drama. College English, 1966, 28:15-25.

5377. Cooperman, Stanley. Shakespeare's anti-hero: Hamlet and the underground man. Shakespeare Studies, 1965, 1:37-63.

5378. Corbin, John. O'Neill and Aeschylus. Saturday Rev Lit, 1932, 8:693-695.

5379. Coriat, Isadore H.   Anal-erotic character traits in Shylock.
Int J Psycho-Anal, 1921, 2:354-360.

5380. _____. The Hysteria of Lady Macbeth.   NY: Moffat,
Yard, 1912; Boston: Four Seas, 1920.

5381. _____. Die Psychoanalyse der Lady Macbeth.   Int Zeitschrift für Psychoanalyse, 1914, 4:384-400; Wiesbaden:
Bergmann, 1914.

5382. _____. The sadism in Oscar Wilde's Salome.   Psychoanal
Rev, 1914, 1:257-259.

5383. Cornelison, Gayle Lynn.   Death and Childhood: Attitudes and
Approaches in Society, Children's Literature and Children's Theatre and Drama.   DAI, 1976, 37:37A.

5384. Corrao, Francero.   Psicanalisi ed arte.   Rivista di Psicoanalisi, 1965, 11:235-245.

5385. Corrigan, M. A.   Realism and theatricalism in A Streetcar
Named Desire.   Modern Drama, 1976, 19:385-396.

5386. Corrigan, Robert W.   The achievement of Arthur Miller.
Contemporary Drama, 1968, 3:141-160.

5387. _____. Comedy: Meaning and Form.   San Francisco:
Chandler, 1966.

5388. _____. Theatre in the Twentieth Century.   NY: Grove,
1965; Review: Robert Seidenberg, Psychoanal Q, 1967,
36:121-122.

5389. Couch, Lotte S.   Der Reigen: Schnitzler und Sigmund Freud.
Österreich in Geschichte und Literatur, 1972, 16(6):217-
227.

5390. Coulet, H.   L'Innamoramento dans les tragédies de Racine.
Bulletin liaison racienne, 1958, 6:8-15.

5391. Cousin, J.   Phèdre est incestueuse.   Rev d'Histoire Littéraire de France, 1932, 39.

5392. Cowen, Roy.   Identity and conscience in Büchner's works.
Germanic Rev, 1968, 43:258-266.

5393. Cox, Marjorie K.   Adolescent processes in Romeo and Juliet.
Psychoanal Rev, 1976, 63:379-392.

5394. Cox, Sergeant.   The psychology of Hamlet.   Proceedings
Psychol Society Great Britain, 1875-1879, 1880, 263-275.

5395. Cozzi, Emilie Ann.   Self-Actualization in Selected Plays of
Ugo Betti.   DAI, 1978, 38:5799A-800A.

5396. Crackel, Robert James.   A Behavioral Analysis of A. Artaud's Theater: Theory and Practice.   DAI, 1978, 39:
2966A.

5397. Craddock, George Edward.   The Concept of Identity in the
Theatre of Ionesco.   DA, 1966, 27:199A.

5398. Craig, David.   Shakespeare, Lawrence, and sexual freedom.
In The Real Foundations; Literature and Social Change.
NY: Oxford Univ. Press, 1974, 17-38.

5399. Craig, Hardin.   Motivation in Shakespeare's choice of materials.   Shakespeare Survey, 1951, 4:26-34.

5400. _____. Shakespeare and Elizabethan psychology: status
of the subject.   In Shakespeare-Studien Festschrift für
Heinrich Mutschmann.   Marburg: Elivert, 1951, 48-55.

5401. Craig, Virginia W.   The Brother-Sister Theme in Lope de
Vega's Plays.   DAI, 1969, 29:3607A.

5402. Crane, Gladys M. Shaw and women's lib. Shaw Rev, 1974, 17:23-31.

5403. Crass, E. Das liebesproblem in der tragödie des französischen Klassizmus. Leipzig: 1921.

5404. Cremerius, Johannes. [Gerhart Hauptmann and psychoanalysis.] Zeitschrift für Psychotherapie und medizinische Psychologie, 1973, 23:156-165.

5405. Crosby, Donald H. Psychological realism in the works of Kleist: Penthesilea and Die Marquise von O.... Lit & Psychol, 1969, 19:3-16.

5406. Crossley, R. Education and fantasy. College English, 1975, 37:281-293.

5407. Crowson, L. Cocteau and Le numero Barbette. Modern Drama, 1976, 19:79-87.

5408. Cruickshank, D. W. 'Pongo mi mano en sangre bañada a la puerta': adultery in El médico de su honra. In Jones, R. O. (ed), Studies in Spanish Literature of the Golden Age. London: Támesis, 1973, 45-62.

5409. Cunningham, James V. Woe or Wonder: The Emotional Effect of Shakespearean Tragedy. Denver: Univ. Denver Press, 1951.

5410. Curry, Ryder Hector, & Porte, Michael. The surprising unconscious of Edward Albee. Drama Survey, 1968-69, 7: 59-68.

5411. Dace, Edwin Wallace. Psychological Melodrama in Modern Opera with Translations of Two Representative Works, Erwartung and Wozzeck, and an Original Libretto, Captain Mark. Doctoral dissertation, Univ. Denver, 1952.

5412. Dachslager, E. L. Frye, Jung, and the structure of Shakespearean comedy. Abstract, in Proceedings of Conference of College Teachers of English at Texas, 1976, 41:65.

5413. Daemmrich, Horst S. The incest motif in Lessing's Nathan der Weise and Schiller's Braut von Messina. Germanic Rev, 1967, 42:184-196.

5414. Daiches, David. Guilt and justice in Shakespeare. In Literary Essays. NY: Philosophical Library, 1958.

5415. _____. Psychoanalytic study of the characters in a literary work. In Critical Approaches to Literature. London: Longman, 1956, 348-355.

5416. Dale, Leona. Jonson's sick society. Rocky Mountain MLA Bulletin, 1970, 24(2):66-74.

5417. D'Alfonso, N. R. La Follia di Ofelia. Rome: 1896.

5418. _____. Note psicologische al Macbeth di Shakespeare. Rome: Paravia, 1899.

5419. _____. Filosofi e psicologi nell' Amleto. Nuova antologia, 1925, 239:183-194.

5420. _____. Note psicologische, estetiche e criminali al drammi di G. Shakespeare: Macbeth, Amleto, Re Lear, Otello. Macerata: S. Tip, 1914.

5421. _____. La Personalita di Amleto. Note psicologische. Torino: 1894.

5422. _____. [The philosophy and psychology of Hamlet.] Nuova Antologia, 1925, 239:183-194.

5423. _____. Il Re Lear. Rome: Alighieri, 1900.

5424. _____. Le Spettro dell' Amelto. Note psychologische. Rome: 1893.

5425. Dalma, Giovanni. La figlia di Jorio di Gabriele d'Annunzio; sagio d'interpretazione psicoanalitica. Archivio Generale di Neurologie, Psichiatria e Psicoanalisi, 1929, 10:383-395.

5426. Dammers, Richard H. Female Characters and Feminine Morality in the Tragedies of Nicholas Rowe. DAI, 1971, 32:2635A.

5427. Daniels, M. Marivaux, precursor of the Théâtre de l'inexprime. Modern Language Rev, 1950, 45:465-472.

5428. Danks, K. B. The bibliographical and psychological fallacies in Pollard's second proposition. Notes & Queries, 1959, 6:439-440.

5429. DaPonte, Durant. Tennessee Williams' gallery of feminine characters. Tennessee Studies in Lit, 1965, 10:7-26.

5430. Darst, D. H. The Comic Art of Tirso de Molina. Chapel Hill: Univ. North Carolina Press, 1974.

5431. Darwin, L. Nature and nurture in Shakespeare's plays and elsewhere. Eugenics Rev, 1927, 19:181-191.

5432. d'Arx, P. La Femme dans le théâtre de Henry de Montherlant. Paris: Nizet, 1973.

5433. Daubenton, Annie. Clins d'oeil psychanalytiques sur le Théâtre de Boulevard. Entretien avec de Dr Hachette. Nouvelle Littéraires, 1977, No. 2616.

5434. D'Avanzo, Mario L. He mildews the white wheat: King Lear, III. iv. 120-124. Shakespeare Q, 1977, 28:88-89.

5435. David, Christian. La Fascination de l'illimité: antagonisme sexuel et oppositions pulsionelles dans la Penthésilée de Kleist. Rev Française de Psychanalyse, 1970, 34:653-684.

5436. David-Peyre, Y. Un Cas d'observation clinique chez Tirso de Molina. Les Langues Néo-Latines, 1971, 65:9-22.

5437. David-Schwarz, H. Zur Psychologie und Pathologie von Gerhardt Hauptmanns College Crampton. Psychologische Rundschau, 1930, 2:41-45.

5438. Davidson, S. E. 'Stream-of-consciousness' drama; an introduction to the To Damascus trilogy of Strindberg. Poet Lore, 1933, 42:71-80.

5439. Davie, T. M. Hamlet's 'madness.' J Mental Science, 1942, 88:449-450.

5440. Davis, D. Russell. A re-appraisal of Ibsen's Ghosts. Family Process, 1963, 2:81-94.

5441. Davison, Darlyn D. The Role of Women in Miguel Mihura's Plays. DAI, 1975, 36:307A.

5442. Davison, Ned J. Psychological Values in the Works of Eduardo Barrios. Doctoral dissertation, Univ. California, 1957.

5443. Dean, Leonard F. A Casebook on Othello. NY: Crowell, 1961.

5444. De Caprariis, E. Considerazioni e spunti psico-somatici nelle tragedie di Seneca. Minerva Medicine, 1971, 62: 1136-1144.

5445. Decina, Paolo. Henry IV by Luigi Pirandello--a psychiatric comment. J Amer Academy Psychoanal, 1978, 6:79-87.

5446. De Cort, J. Method in madness. Die Motivik in Thomas Bernhards epischem Werk. Archiv für das Studium der Neueren Sprachen, 1977, 214:281-293.

5447. Dees, (?). Timon von Athen's Drama von Shakespeare, nach psychopathologischen Gesichtspunkten erklärt. Zeitschrift für die gesamte Neurologie und Psychiatrie, 1915, 28:50-64.

5448. Defrenne, M. Absence et présence chez Racine. Rev de l'Université de Bruxelles, 1962, 40:192-203.

5449. deFuria, Richard. At the intersection of Freud and Ionesco. MLN, 1972, 87:971-976.

5450. Delbouille, Paul. Les Tragédies de Racine, reflets de l'inconscient ou chronique du siècle? French Studies, 1961, 15:103-120.

5451. Delbrück, Anton. [On Hamlet's madness.] Sammlung Gemeinverständlicher Wissenschaftlicher Vorträger, Neue Folge, No. 172, 117-148.

5452. Delcroix, Maurice. La Tragedie de Racine est-elle psychologique? In Venesoen, C. (ed), Racine, Mythes et Réalités. Paris: Société de L'Etude du XVIIe Siècle, 1976, 103-119.

5453. Deleo, J. V. A Jungian Perspective of the Drama and the Writings of Tennessee Williams. DAI, 1978, 38:4448.

5454. Delgado, Honorio F. El enigma psicológico de Hamlet. Crónica Médica, 1920, 37:158-162.

5455. Del Greco, Francesco. [Emotion and insanity in the heroic of William Shakespeare.] Manicomio, 1914, 31:203-214.

5456. _____. [Insanity in the women of Shakespeare and female psychology.] Manicomio, 1914, 29:1-16.

5457. Dellevaux, Raumond. L'Existentialism et le théâtre de Jean-Paul Sartre. Brussels: Edit la Lecture au Foyer, 1953.

5458. Delort-Ciardi, Janine. La Folle de Chaillot: une folie sans illusions. In Mélanges du littérature: du moyen âge au XXe siècle. Paris: Ecole Normale Supérieure de Jeunes Filles, 1978, 815-822.

5459. Denker, Henry. Preliminary journey to a far country. Theatre Arts, 1962, 46:26-27.

5460. Derrida, Jacques. The theater of cruelty and the closure of representation. Theater, 1978, 9(3):7-19.

5461. Dervin, Daniel A. Bernard Shaw: A Psychological Study. Lewisburg: Bucknell Univ. Press, 1975.

5462. Desai, R. W. Freudian undertones in the Isabella-Angelo relationship of Measure for Measure. Psychoanal Rev, 1977, 64:487-494.

5463. Desmonde, William H. The ritual origin of Shakespeare's Titus Andronicus. Int J Psycho-Anal, 1955, 36:61-65; In Faber, M. D. (ed), The Design Within. NY: Science House, 1970, 21-31.

5464. Dessoir, Max. Types caracterologiques. JPNP, 1935, 32: 100-108.

5465. Desvignes, L. L'Adolescence et la découverte de l'amour sur la scène du XVIIIe siècle. Rev des Sciences Humaines, 1970, 35:369-382.

5466. Dettmering, Peter. [Reflections on Kleist's Marionette Theater.] Praxis der Psychotherapy, 1974, 19:233-236.

5467. Deutschbein, Max. Die Bedeutung von 'Mind' im 16. Jahrhundert. Eine Vorstudie zu Shakespeares Hamlet. Anglia, 1942, 66:169-222.

5468. Devereux, George. Dreams in Greek Tragedy: An Ethnopsychoanalytical Study. Berkeley: Univ. California Press, 1976.

5469. _____. L'Etat dépressif et le rêve de Ménélas. Rev des Etudes grecques, 1968, 81:12-15.

5470. _____. Why Oedipus killed Laius; a note on the complementary Oedipus complex in Greek drama. Int J Psycho-Anal, 1953, 34:132-141; In The Yearbook of Psychoanalysis, Vol. 10. NY: IUP, 1954, 258-274; In Ruitenbeek, H.M. (ed), Psychoanalysis and Literature. NY: Dutton, 1964, 168-186.

5471. deWit-Tak, T. The function of obscenity in Aristophanes. Mnemosyne, 1968, 2:357-368.

5472. D'Heurle, A., et al. Lost children: the role of the child in the psychological plays of Henrik Ibsen. Psychoanal Rev, 1976, 63:27-47.

5473. Dickerson, Harold D., Jr. Arthur Schnitzler's Die Frau des Richters: a statement of futility. German Q, 1970, 43: 223-236.

5474. Dickes, Robert. Desdemona: an innocent victim. Amer Imago, 1970, 27:279-297.

5475. Dickinson, Hugh. Eugene Ionesco: the existential Oedipus. In Lamonte, R.C. (ed), Ionesco: A Collection of Critical Essays. Englewood Cliffs, NJ: Prentice-Hall, 1973, 99-119.

5476. _____. Myth on the Modern Stage. Urbana: Univ. Illinois Press, 1969.

5477. Dickson, R. Archetypal symbolism in Lorca's Bodas de Sangre. Lit & Psychol, 1960, 10(2):76-79.

5478. Dieckhöfer, K. Lope de Vegas Komödie Los Locos de Valencia--ein kulturhistorischer Einblick in eine psychiatrische Anhalt des 15. Jahrhunderts. Schweizer Archiv für Neurologie und Psychiatrie, 1975, 116:343-351.

5479. Dieckman, Suzanne. Levels of commitment: an approach to the role of Weiss's Marat. Educational Theatre J, 1978, 30:54-62.

5480. Dietrich, Margret. Die Kollekrivseele und die psychologische Soziometrie im Drama. In Das Moderne Drama. Stuttgart: Kröner, 1961, 231-242.

5481. Dietz, P.A. De Psychologie van de Misdaad bij Shakespeare. Haagsch Maandblad, 1938, 1:260-268.

5482. Digeon, A. Racine dramaturge de la jalousie. Rev Hongrie, 1914, 13:306-314.

5483. Diggle, J. Review: George Devereux's Dreams in Greek Tragedy: An Ethno-Psycho-Analytic Study. Classical Rev, 1978, NS. 28(2):226-228.

5484. Dillingham, William B. Arthur Miller and the loss of conscience. Emory Univ. Q, 1960, 16:40-50.

5485. Dillon, George L. The Art How to Know Men: A Study of Rationalist Psychology and Neo-Classical Dramatic Theory. DAI, 1970, 31(2-A), 727.

5486. DiMaio, Carlo. Antifeminism in Selected Works of Enrique Jardiel Poncela. DAI, 1974, 35:2987A.

5487. Dirks, Mary D. The Tragic Heroine in the Mythological Drama, 1800 to 1960. DA, 1964, 24(7):2908.

5488. Dizac, J. -C. , & Gorceix, A. [Oedipal gout.] Annales Médico-Psychologiques, 1976, 2:481-485.

5489. DiZenzo, S. Miti ed archetipi nell'Ottavia dell'Alfieri. Naples: Liguori, 1975.

5490. Doat, Jan. Entrée du public; la psychologie collective et la contagion mentale dans l'art dramatique. Paris: Flore, 1947.

5491. Dodds, Eric R. The Greeks and the Irrational. Berkeley: Univ. California Press, 1951; Boston: Beacon, 1957.

5492. Doherty, Lois G. The Women of Musset's Theater. DAI, 1978, 38:6157A.

5493. Dollard, John. The hidden meaning of Who's Afraid...? Connecticut Rev, 1973, 7:24-48.

5494. Donaldson, Ian. Double meanings: IV. Shakespeare's serious indecency. Essays in Criticism, 1974, 24:363-367.

5495. Donnelly, John. Incest, ingratitude, and insanity: aspects of the psychopathology of King Lear. Psychoanal Rev, 1953, 40:149-155; In Bonheim, H. (ed), The King Lear Perplex. Belmont, Cal: Wadsworth, 1960.

5496. Dooley, J. A. The re-emergence of the male tan in the Chinese theatre. Theatre Q, 1979, 9:42-47.

5497. Doolittle, J. Heroism and passion in Polyeucte. Symposium, 1955, 8:217-241.

5498. Doubrovsky, Serge. Corneille et la dialectique du héros. Paris: Gallimard, 1964.

5499. Douthit, Dorothy. The Concept of Women in Ernst Barlach's Dramas. DAI, 1968, 28:4169A.

5500. Dowden, Edward. Elizabethan psychology. In Essays, Modern and Elizabethan. NY: Dutton, 1910, 308-333.

5501. Dozier, R. J. Adultery and disappointment in Who's Afraid of Virginia Woolf? Modern Drama, 1969, 11:432-436.

5502. Dracoulidès, N. N. Aristophanes: The Clouds and The Wasps: Foreshadowing of psychoanalysis and psychodrama. Amer Imago, 1966, 23:48-62.

5503. _____. La Génealogie des Atrides et l'adventure d'Oreste. Psyché, 1952, 7:805-817; 1953, 8:32-34.

5504. _____. Origine de la psychanalyse et du psychodrame dans mes 'muées' et les 'guêpes' d'Aristophane. Historia Scientia Medica (Colombia), 1967, 1:101-112.

5505. _____. Psychanalyse d'Aristophane; de sa vie et de ses oeuvres. Paris: Editions Universitaires, 1967.

5506. _____. [Psychoanalytic interpretation of Euripides' Bac-
       chantes.] Acta Psychotherapeutica et Psychosomatica,
       1963, 11:14-27.
5507. _____. Psychoanalytical investigation of Shakespeare's
       Hamlet. Transactional Mental Health Research Newslet-
       ter, 1977, 19:2-9.
5508. _____. [Psychoanalytic sketch of Shakespeare's Hamlet:
       misogyny and arrhenophily.] Psyché, 1959, 14:4-11.
5509. _____. Tracé psychanalytique sur Hamlet de Shakespeare.
       Psyché, 1956, 11:129-155.
5510. Draper, John W. The character of Richard II. Psychiat Q,
       1942, 21:228-236.
5511. _____. Coriolanus: a study in Renaissance psychology.
       West Virginia Univ. Bulletin, 1939, 3:22-36.
5512. _____. The Humors and Shakespeare's Characters. Dur-
       ham, NC: Duke Univ. Press, 1945.
5513. _____. The humors: some psychological aspects of Shake-
       speare's tragedies. JAMA, 1964, 188:259-262.
5514. _____. 'Kate the curst.' JNMD, 1939, 89:757-764.
5515. _____. Lady Macbeth. Psychoanal Rev, 1941, 28:479-
       486.
5516. _____. Shakespeare's attitude toward old age. J Geron-
       tology, 1946, 1:118-126.
5517. _____. Shattered personality in Shakespeare's Antony.
       Psychiat Q, 39:448-456.
5518. _____. Subjective conflict in Shakespearean tragedy.
       Neuphilologische Mitteilungen, 1960, 61:214-221.
5519. Dreyfuss, Cecilia Ann S. Femina Sapiens in Drama: Aeschy-
       lus to Grillparzer. DAI, 1975, 36:3676A.
5520. Driscoll, James P. Aspects of Identity in Shakespearean
       Drama. DAI, 1972, 33:2323-A.
5521. Driver, Tom F. 'Psychologism': roadblock to religious
       drama. Religion in Life, 1959-60, 29(1):59-60.
5522. Drost, Carla Lowrey. The Major Female Characters in
       Georg Büchner's Dramas. DAI, 1975, 36:308A.
5523. Dubu, J. De quelque raisons esthétiques du silence de Racine
       après Phèdre. XVIIe Siècle, No. 20, 1953.
5524. Du Cann, C. G. L. Bernard Shaw et les femmes. Paris: La
       Palatine, 1965.
5525. Duckworth, Ingrid O. The Family in the Works of Gerhart
       Hauptmann. DAI, 1972, 33:1165A.
5526. Dugas, A. Néron-monstre naissant. Le Bayou, 1958, 73:
       25-32.
5527. Dührssen, Annemarie. Lebenproblem und Daseinkrise bei
       Hamlet und Ophelia. Zeitschrift für psycho-somatische
       Medizin, 1956, 2:220-235, 295-311.
5528. Dukore, Bernard F. The cat has nine lives. Tulane Drama
       Rev, 1963, 8:95-100.
5529. _____. The Fabian and the Freudian. Shavian, 1961,
       2:8-11.
5530. Duncan, Bruce. Ich platze! Gerstenberg's Ugolino and the
       mid-life crisis. Germanic Rev, 1978, 53:13-19.

5531. Dunham, Theodore C. The Psychological Motivation in Grill-
       parzer's Tragedies. Doctoral dissertation, Univ. Wiscon-
       sin, 1935.

5532. _____. Symbolism in Grillparzer's Das goldene Vliess.
       PMLA, 1959, 74:75-82.

5533. Dunn, Hough-Lewis. Shakespeare's Cymbeline, II, v, 15-17.
       Explicator, 1972, 30:Item 57.

5534. Dupee, F.W. Adjusting Hamlet. Partisan Rev, 1948, 15:
       1136-1139.

5535. Duque, Aquilino. Repressión y conformismo. Revista de Oc-
       cidente, 1970, 28:309-318.

5536. Durbach, Errol. Form and vision in erotic tragedy. Modern
       Language Rev, 1968, 1:35-52.

5537. _____. The temptation to err: the dénouement of Ros-
       mersholm. Educational Theatre J, 1977, 29:477-485.

5538. Durham, Mildred. Drama of the dying god in Julius Caesar.
       Hartford Studies in Lit, 1979, 11:49-57.

5539. Dusenberg, Winifred L. The Theme of Loneliness in Modern
       American Drama. Gainesville: Univ. Florida Press,
       1960.

5540. Dusinberre, Juliet. Shakespeare and the Nature of Women.
       NY: Barnes & Noble, 1976; Review: J.B. Holm, Shake-
       speare Q, 1978, 29:110-112.

5541. Duve, Arne. Ibsen--bak kulissene. Copenhagen: Gyldendal,
       1971. [Revised ed. of Symbolikken i Hendrik Ibsens
       skuespill, 1945.]

5542. _____, & Ree, K. Ibsens legeskikkelser. Tidsskrift
       Norge Laegeforen, 1975, 95:1872-1874.

5543. Duvignaud, Jean. Une Expérience d'apparition du sentiment
       esthétique. JPNP, 1956, 53:81-85.

5544. Eaker, J. Gordon. Varieties of tragic catharsis. Rendez-
       vous, 1971, 6(2):15-20.

5545. Eastman, Richard M. Drama as psychological argument.
       College English, 1958, 19:327-332.

5546. Ebel, Henry. Caesar's wounds: a study of William Shake-
       speare. Psychoanal Rev, 1975, 62:107-130.

5547. Eckstein, Rudolph. Psychoanalytic precursors in Greek
       antiquity. Bulletin Menninger Clinic, 1975, 39:246-267.

5548. Eco, Umberto. Semiotics of theatrical performance. Drama
       Rev, 1977, 21:107-117.

5549. Edgar, Irving I. Amariah Brigham, Isaac Ray and Shake-
       speare. Psychiat Q, 1961, 35:666-674.

5550. _____. Humoral physiology-psychology and Shakespeare's
       dramas. J Michigan State Medical Society, 1956, 55:701-
       704.

5551. _____. The psychoanalytic approach to Shakespeare's
       Hamlet. Canadian Psychiat Assn J, 1961, 6:353-355.

5552. _____. Shakespeare, Medicine and Psychiatry. An His-
       torical Study in Criticism and Interpretation. NY: Phi-
       losophical Library, 1970; Review: David P. Willbern,
       Psychiat in Medicine, 1973, 4:117-121.

5553. _____. Shakespeare's Hamlet: the great modern Oedipus tragedy. Psychiat Q Supplement, 1963, 37:1-22.

5554. _____. Shakespeare's medical knowledge with particular reference to his delineation of madness; preliminary survey of critical opinion. Annals Medical History, n. s., 1934, 6:150-168.

5555. _____. Shakespeare's psychopathological knowledge: a study of criticism and interpretation. J Abnormal Social Psychol, 1935, 30:70-83.

5556. Editorial. The theater and the homosexual. JAMA, 1966, 198:1027-1028.

5557. Eggers, Herm. [Shakespeare, Hamlet, and alcohol.] Internationale Monatsschrift zur Erforschung des Alkoholismus, 1905, 15:271-275.

5558. Egri, Péter. The social and psychological aspects of the conflict in Eugene O'Neill's Mourning Becomes Electra. In Perényi, E., & Frank, T. (eds), Studies in English and American, Vol. II. Budapest: L. Eötöös Univ., 1975, 171-214.

5559. Ehrl, C. Sprachstil und Charakter bei Shakespeare. Heidelberg: Quelle und Meyer, 1957.

5560. Eissler, Kurt R. Discourse on Hamlet and 'Hamlet.' A Psychoanalytic Inquiry. NY: IUP, 1970.

5561. _____. The function of details in the interpretation of works of literature. Psychoanal Q, 1959, 28:1-20.

5562. _____. Fortinbras and Hamlet. Amer Imago, 1968, 25:199-223.

5563. _____. On Hamlet. Samiksa, 1953, 7:85-132, 155-202.

5564. Elam, Keir. Language in the theater. Sub-stance, 1977, 18-19:139-161.

5565. Eliasberg, W. The stage thriller: sociometric interpretation of the relationships between the stage, the play, and the audience. J Social Psychol, 1944, 19:229-239.

5566. Elledge, W. Paul. Imagery and theme in Byron's Cain. Keats-Shelley J, 1966, 15:49-57.

5567. Elliott, George P. Nihilism and Marat/Sade. Dissent, 1966, 13:333-335.

5568. Elliott, Susan M. Fantasy Behind Play: A Study of Emotional Responses to Harold Pinter's The Birthday Party, The Caretaker, and The Homecoming. DAI, 1974, 34:5963A-64A.

5569. Ellis, John. Rooted affection: the genesis of jealousy in The Winter's Tale. College English, 1964, 25:545-547.

5570. Ellmann, Richard. Overtures to Wilde's Salomé. Triquarterly, 1969, 15:45-63.

5571. Ellrodt, R. Self-consciousness in Montaigne and Shakespeare. Shakespeare Survey, 1975, 28:37-50.

5572. Elsom, John. Erotic Theatre. NY: Taplinger, 1973.

5573. Embrey, Glenn Thomas. Sexual Confusion in the Major Plays of Tennessee Williams. DAI, 1975, 36:309A.

5574. Emden, Cecil Stuart. Shakespeare and the eye. Shakespeare Survey, 1973, 26:129-137.

5575. Emery, John P. Othello's epilepsy. Psychoanalysis, 1959, 44(4):30-32.

5576. Emmett, V. J. Jr. 1 Henry IV: structure, Platonic psychol-
       ogy, and politics. Midwest Q, 1978, 19:355-369.
5577. Empson, William. Kyd's Spanish Tragedy. Nimbus, 1956,
       3:16-19; In Kaufmann, R. J. (ed), Elizabethan Drama:
       Modern Essays in Criticism. NY: 1961, 60-80.
5578. Engel, Edwin A. The Haunted Heroes of Eugene O'Neill.
       Cambridge: Harvard Univ. Press, 1953.
5579. _____. Ideas in the plays of O'Neill. In Gassner, J.
       (ed), Ideas in the Drama. NY: Columbia Univ. Press,
       1964.
5580. Engel, J. [Shakespeare's delinquency from a psychophysio-
       logical point of view.] Preussische Jahrbücher, 1909,
       137:61-79.
5581. Erdös, L. Felsöbbrendü tévedéseink Ibsen drámáiban. Buda-
       pest: Az Egyetemi Nyomda Konyvesboltja, 1938.
5582. Erikson, Erik Homburg. Youth: fidelity and diversity.
       Daedalus, 1962, 91:5-27.
5583. Erlich, Avi. Hamlet's Absent Father. Princeton: Princeton
       Univ. Press, 1977; Review: W. Thomas MacCary, Lit &
       Psychol, 1979, 29:93-96.
5584. Ernst, Earle. The Kabuki Theatre. NY: Grove, 1956.
5585. Esslin, Martin. Alienation in Brecht, Beckett and Pinter.
       Perspectives on Contemporary Lit, 1975, 1:3-21.
5586. _____. 'The neurosis of neutrals': Friedrich Dürren-
       matt. In Reflections; Essays on Modern Theatre. NY:
       Doubleday, 1969, 107-114.
5587. _____. The People Wound: The Work of Harold Pinter.
       Garden City, NY: Doubleday, 1970.
5588. Estang, Luc. Jean Giradoux analyste. Confluences, 1944,
       4:89-93.
5589. Evans, B. Ifor. The Language of Shakespeare's Plays.
       London: Methuen, 1952.
5590. Evans, Richard J. Psychology and Arthur Miller. NY:
       Dutton, 1969; Review: Harvey Mindess, Contemporary
       Psychol, 1970, 15:428-429.
5591. Ewbank, Inga-Stina. Shakespeare's portrayal of women: a
       1970s view. In Bevington, D. , & Halio, J. L. (eds),
       Shakespeare, Pattern of Excelling Nature. Newark:
       Univ. Delaware Press, 1978, 222-229; London: Associ-
       ated Univ. Press, 1978, 222-229.
5592. Ewing, Fayette C. Hamlet: An Analytic and Psychological
       Study. Boston: Stratford, 1934.
5593. Ewing, S. Blaine. Burtonian Melancholy in the Plays of John
       Ford. Princeton: Princeton Univ. Press, 1940.
5594. Ey, Henn. Pirandello, les personnages et la réalité (ou le
       moi n'est pas l'autre). Evolution Psychiatrique, 1971,
       36:429-444.

5595. Faber, M. D. The adolescent suicides of Romeo and Juliet.
       Psychoanal Rev, 1972, 59:169-181.
5596. _____. The character of Jimmy Porter: an approach to
       Look Back in Anger. Modern Drama, 1970, 13:67-77.

5597.   _____. The Design Within: Psychoanalytic Approaches to Shakespeare. NY: Science House, 1970; Reviews: Harold G. McCurdy, Contemporary Psychol, 1971, 16:115-117; Robert D. Callahan, West Coast Rev, 1971, 6:54-56; Stephen Reid, Psychoanal Rev, 1972, 59:148-149.

5598.   _____. Falstaff behind the arras. Amer Imago, 1970, 27:197-225.

5599.   _____. Freud and Shakespeare's mobs. Lit & Psychol, 1965, 15:238-255.

5600.   _____. Hamlet, sarcasm and psychoanalysis. Psychoanal Rev, 1968, 55:79-90.

5601.   _____. Hermia's dream: royal road to A Midsummer Night's Dream. Lit & Psychol, 1972, 22:179-190.

5602.   _____. Lord Brutus' wife: a modern view. Psychoanal Rev, 1965-66, 52:109-115.

5603.   _____. Lady Macbeth's suicide. Amer Notes Queries, 1966, 5:19.

5604.   _____. Oedipal patterns in Henry IV. Psychoanal Q, 1967, 36:426-434; In The Design Within. NY: Science House, 1970, 430-438.

5605.   _____. Oedipus Rex: a psychoanalytic interpretation. Psychoanal Rev, 1975, 62:239-268.

5606.   _____. On Jacques: psychological remarks. Univ. Rev, 1970, 36:89-96, 179-182.

5607.   _____. Ophelia's doubtful death. Lit & Psychol, 1966, 16:103-108.

5608.   _____. Othello: symbolic action, ritual, and myth. Amer Imago, 1974, 31:159-205.

5609.   _____. Othello: the justice of it pleases. Amer Imago, 1971, 28:228-246.

5610.   _____. Self-destruction in Oedipus Rex. Amer Imago, 1970, 27:41-51.

5611.   _____. Shakespeare's ghosts. Notes & Queries, 1967, 9:131-132.

5612.   _____. Shakespeare's suicides. In Schneidman, E. (ed), Essays in Self-Destruction. NY: Aronson, 1967, 30-58.

5613.   _____. Some remarks on the suicide of King Lear's eldest daughter. Univ. Rev, 1967, 33:313-317.

5614.   _____. Suicide and the Ajax of Sophocles. Psychoanal Rev, 1967, 54:49-60.

5615.   _____. Suicide and Greek Tragedy. NY: Sphinx, 1970.

5616.   _____. Suicide in Shakespeare. DA, 1964, 24:4697-98.

5617.   _____. Two studies in self-aggression in Shakespearean tragedy. I. The conscience of the King: a preliminary investigation of Claudius' self-destructive urges. II. Suicidal patterns in Othello. Lit & Psychol, 1964, 14:80-96.

5618.   _____. The victims and the victimizers. Amer Imago, 1972, 29:338-352.

5619.   _____, & Dilnot, Alan F. On a line of Iago's. Amer Imago, 1968, 25:86-90.

5620.   Fackler, Herbert V. William Sharp's House of Usna (1900): a one-act psychic drama. South Central Bulletin, 1970, 30:87-89.

5621. Fagin, N. Bryllion. 'Freud' on Broadway. Educational Theatre J, 1950, 2(4):298-300.
5622. Faigel, H. C. The Barrie syndrome. Peter Pan as the
dramatization of emotional retardation. Clinical Pediat-
rics, 1965, 4:342-347.
5623. Falk, Doris V. Eugene O'Neill and the Tragic Tension: An
Interpretive Study of the Plays. New Brunswick, NJ:
Rutgers Univ. Press, 1974, 1958.
5624. Fanchette, Jean. Hamlet: au coeur de la catharsis Shake-
spearienne. Annales Médico-Psychologiques, 1969, 1:369-
374.
5625. _____. Pirandello ou le jeu dangereux des miroirs. Annales Médico-Psychologiques, 1971, 2:185-191.
5626. _____. Psychodrame et théatre moderne. Paris: Union
Générale, 1977.
5627. Feal, Gisèle. La Magnificence du Roi Candaule: comparison
d'une pièce de Gide et d'une pièce de Crommelynck. Romance Notes, 1971, 13:197-203.
5628. _____. Le Théâtre de Crommelynck--érotisme et spiritualité. Paris: Minard, 1976; Review: C. Toloudis,
French Rev, 1978, 51:614-615.
5629. _____, & Feal Deibe, Carlos. Calderón's Life Is a
Dream: from psychology to myth. Hartford Studies in
Lit, 1974, 6:1-28.
5630. Feal Deibe, Carlos. La anunciación a Bonis: análisis de
Su único hijo. Bulletin Hispanic Studies, 1974, 41:255-
271.
5631. _____. El Burlador de Tirso y la mujer. Symposium,
1975, 29:300-313.
5632. _____. Consideraciones psicoanáliticas sobre Tiempo de
silencio de Luis Martín-Santos. Revista Hispánica Moderna, 1970-7, 36:117-127.
5633. _____. Fedra en la obra de Unamuno. Rev Littérature
Comparee, 1975, 49:19-27.
5634. _____. García Lorca y el psicoanálisis. Apostillas a
unas apostillas. Bulletin Hispanic Studies, 1977, 56:311-
314.
5635. _____. El hermano Juan. Symposium, 1972, 26:293-313.
5636. _____. Lorca's two farces: Don Perlimplin and Don
Cristobal. Amer Imago, 1970, 27:358-377.
5637. _____. Los Machado y el psicoanálisis (en torno a Las
adelfas). Insula, 1974, 29:1, 14.
5638. Fedder, N. J. The influence of D. H. Lawrence on Tennessee
Williams. Studies in American Lit, 1966, 5.
5639. Federico, Joseph Anthony. Metatheater: Self-Consciousness
and Role-Playing in the Dramas of Max Frisch, Friedrich Dürrenmatt, and Peter Handke. DAI, 1977, 37:
7148A-49A.
5640. Fedor, Joan Roberta. The Importance of the Female in the
Plays of Samuel Beckett, Harold Pinter and Edward Albee. DAI, 1977, 38(3):1378-A.
5641. Feiner, Arthur H. A note on Ravich's 'Shakespeare and
psychiatry. ' Lit & Psychol, 1965, 15:125-128.

5642. Feinstein, Howard. Hamlet's Horatio and the therapeutic mode. Amer J Psychiat, 1967, 123:803-809.
5643. Feldhaus, Eugene A. A Treatment of Moral and Psychological Values in the Plays of Philip Barry. Doctoral dissertation, St. John's Univ., 1958.
5644. Feldman, A. Bronson. Freud's allusion to Gilbert's Mikado. Notes & Queries, 1958, 5:469-470.
5645. _____. Imaginary incest: a study of Shakespeare's Pericles. Amer Imago, 1955, 12:117-155.
5646. _____. Othello in reality. Amer Imago, 1954, 11:147-179.
5647. _____. Othello's obsessions. Amer Imago, 1952, 9:147-163.
5648. _____. The pattern of promiscuity seen in Schnitzler's Round Dance. Psychoanalysis, 1960, 47(1):24-34.
5649. _____. Portals of discovery. Amer Imago, 1959, 16:77-107.
5650. _____. Shakespeare's early errors. Int J Psycho-Anal, 1955, 36:114-133.
5651. _____. Shakespeare worship. Psychoanalysis, 1955, 2:57-72.
5652. _____. The yellow malady; short studies of five tragedies of jealousy. Lit & Psychol, 1956, 6(2):38-52.
5653. Feldman, Harold. Unconscious envy in Brutus. Amer Imago, 1952, 9:307-335.
5654. Feldman, Robert L. Tragedy and the common man: existential analysis and Arthur Miller. Family Therapy, 1980, 7(1):71p.
5655. Fenichel, Otto. On acting. Psychoanal Q, 1946, 15:144-160.
5656. Fergusson, Francis. After paranoia, what next? Tulane Drama Rev, 1962, 7(4):22-26.
5657. _____. Edipo según Freud, Sófocles y Cocteau. Asomante, 1965, 21(3):29-36.
5658. _____. The Human Image in Dramatic Literature. Gloucester, Mass: Smith, 1957; Garden City, NY: Doubleday Anchor, 1957.
5659. _____. The Idea of a Theater. Princeton: Princeton Univ. Press, 1949; Garden City, NY: Doubleday Anchor, 1953.
5660. _____. Oedipus according to Freud, Sophocles, and Cocteau. In Literary Landmarks: Essays on the Theory and Practice of Literature. New Brunswick, NJ: Rutgers Univ. Press, 1975, 101-113.
5661. _____. Oedipus Rex: the tragic rhythm of action. [Excerpt from The Idea of a Theater.] In Schorer, M., et al. (eds), Criticism. NY: Harcourt Brace & World, 1948, 1958, 121-134.
5662. _____. Poetry and drama. In Tetel, M. (ed), Symbolism and Modern Literature. Durham: Duke Univ. Press, 1978, 13-25.
5663. Ferris, Lesley K. TA and drama. Transactional Analysis J, 1975, 5:158-160.
5664. Feynman, Alberta E. The fetal quality of 'character' in plays of the absurd. Modern Drama, 1966, 9:18-25.

5665. _____. The Infernal Machine, Hamlet, and Ernest Jones. Modern Drama, 1963, 6:72-83.

5666. Fiedler, Leslie A. The defense of the illusion and the creation of the myth; device and symbol in the plays of Shakespeare. In Wimsatt, W. K. (ed), Literary Criticism: Idea and Act. Berkeley: Univ. California Press, 1974, 97-109.

5667. _____. The Stranger in Shakespeare. NY: Stein & Day, 1972.

5668. Field, B. S., Jr. Hamartia in Death of a Salesman. Twentieth Century Lit, 1972, 18:19-24.

5669. Fierz, H. E. Uber die psychologischen Grenzen der dramatischen Gestaltung. In Die kulturelle Bedeutung den komplexen Psychologie. Berlin: Springer, 1935, 434-461.

5670. Fineman, Joel. Fratricide and cuckoldry: Shakespeare's doubles. Psychoanal Rev, 1977, 64:409-413.

5671. _____. Hamlet and Fratricidal Difference: Violence of Doubles in Shakespeare. DAI, 1975, 35:6664A-65A.

5672. Firges, Jean. Anouilhs Antigone: ein Exempel der Pathologie oder der Metaphysik? Die Neueren Sprachen, 1973, 72:595-607.

5673. Fischer, Eileen. Discourse of the other in Not I: a confluence of Beckett and Lacan. Theater, 1979, 10:101-103.

5674. Fischer, Ernst. Samuel Beckett: play and film. Mosaic, 1969, 2:96-116.

5675. Fischer, Susan L. Psychological and Esthetic Implications of Role-Change in Selected Plays by Calderón. DAI, 1974, 34:4197.

5676. _____. The art of role-change in Calderonian drama. Bulletin of the Comediantes, 1975, 27:73-79.

5677. Fitz, L. T. Egyptian queens and male reviewers: sexist attitudes in Antony and Cleopatra criticism. Shakespeare Q, 1977, 28:297-316.

5678. Fitzgerald, Geraldine. Another neurotic Electra: a new look at Mary Tyrone. In Floyd, V. (ed), Eugene O'Neill; A World View. NY: Ungar, 1980, 290-292.

5679. Fitzgerald, John. Guilt and redemption in O'Neill's last play: a study of The Moon for the Misbegotten. Texas Q, 1966, 9(1):146-158.

5680. Fjelde, Rolf. Peer Gynt, naturalism and the dissolving self. Drama Rev, 1968, 13(2):28-43.

5681. Flasch, Joy. Games people play in Who's Afraid of Virginia Woolf? Modern Drama, 1967, 10:280-288.

5682. Flatter, Richard. Hamlet's Father. New Haven: Yale Univ. Press, 1949.

5683. _____. Shakespeare's Producing Hand: A Study of His Marks of Expression to Be Found in the First Folio. NY: Norton, 1948.

5684. _____. Sigmund Freud on Shakespeare. Shakespeare Q, 1951, 2:368-369.

5685. _____. 'Solid' or 'sullied,' and another query. Shakespeare Q, 1960, 11:490-493.

5686. Flaumenhaft, Mera J. Begetting and belonging in Shakespeare's Othello. Interpretation, 1975, 4:197-216.

5687. Fleit, Muriel. The Application of Interaction Process Analysis to Selected Plays of Tennessee Williams. DAI, 1978, 39:1931A.

5688. Fleming, R. Of contrast between tragedy and comedy. J Philosophy, 1939, 36:543-553.

5689. Fletcher, John. 'A psychology based on antagonism': Ionesco, Pinter, Albee, and others. In Lamont, R. C., & Friedman, M. J. (eds), The Two Faces of Ionesco. Troy, NY: Whitston, 1979, 175-195.

5690. Fliess, Elenore S., & Fliess, Robert. Shakespeare's Juliet and her nurse. Amer Imago, 1976, 33:244-260.

5691. Flint, Austin. Cases of insanity in Shakespeare. Open Court, 1904, 18:257-273.

5692. Florence, Jean-Felix. Théâtre et psychanalyse ou la psychologie jouée. Marche Romane, 1971, 20(3):53-58.

5693. _____. Théâtre et psychologie. Cahiers-Théâtre Louvain, 1968-69, 6:5-14.

5694. Flügel, J. C. A note on the phallic significance of the tongue and speech. Int J Psycho-Anal, 1925, 6:209-215.

5695. Flynn, John T. The problem of the Prince. In Identification and Individuality. NY: Beekman, 1970, 52-60.

5696. Flynn, Susan Kingston. The Alienated Hero in Contemporary Spanish American Drama. DAI, 1977, 38:299A.

5697. Foakes, R. A. The player's passion: some notes on Elizabethan psychology and acting. Essays & Studies, 1954, 7:62-77.

5698. _____. What's new in Shakespeare criticism. English, 1974, 23:5-10.

5699. Fodor, A. Shakespeare's Portia. Amer Imago, 1959, 16:49-64.

5700- Forest, George C. The 'Cosmonaught's Song' in Dürren-
1. matt's Physicists. Hartford Studies in Lit, 1970, 2:229-237.

5702. Fornoff, F. H. Symbolic action in Tirso's El vergonzoso en palacio. Revista Hispánica Moderna, 1977, 39:38-48.

5703. Forrest, L. C. T. Caveat for critics against invoking Elizabethan psychology. PMLA, 1946, 61:651-672.

5704. Forrest, Tess. The family dynamics of the Oedipus drama. Contemporary Psychoanal, 1968, 4:138-160.

5705. Forsberg, J. Hjalmar. Intevelse och objectivering i fraga om diktverk. Nordisk psykologi, 1953, 5:184.

5706. Fortin, René E. Twelfth Night: Shakespeare's drama of initiation. Papers on Language & Lit, 1972, 8:135-146.

5707. Foster, Verna Ann. The deed's creature: the tragedy of Bianca in Women Beware Women. J English & Germanic Philology, 1979, 78:508-521.

5708. Foulds, Elizabeth. Enter Ophelia, distracted. Life & Letters Today, 1943, 36:36-41.

5709. Francastel, Pierre. Imagination plastique, vision théâtrale et signification humaine. JPNP, 1953, 46:157-187.

5710. François, C. Phèdre et les dieux. French Rev, 1962, 35:269-278.

5711. Frank, A. De Racine et des solitaires. Cahiers de la Com-
       pagnie Madeleine. Renaud--Jean Louis Barault, 1962,
       40:121-123.
5712. Frank, Henry. The Tragedy of Hamlet; A Psychological
       Study. Boston: Sherman, French, 1910.
5713. Frank, Luanne T. 'The Strangest Love Scene in World Lit-
       erature' (the dismemberment of Achilles in Kleist's Pen-
       thesilea) reassessed. In Kraft, W. C. (ed), Proceedings:
       Pacific Northwest Conference on Foreign Languages, Vol.
       25, Part 1. Corvallis: Oregon State Univ. Press, 1974,
       236-241.
5714. Frank, Mike. Shakespeare's existential comedy. In Tobias,
       R. C., & Zolbrod, P. G. (eds), Shakespeare's Late Plays.
       Athens: Ohio Univ. Press, 1974, 142-165.
5715. Franzblau, Abraham Norman. A psychiatrist looks at The
       Birthday Party. Saturday Rev, 1967, 50:46-47.
5716. _____. A psychiatrist looks at The Homecoming. Satur-
       day Rev, 1967, 50:58.
5717. _____. A psychiatrist looks at Tiny Alice. Saturday Rev,
       1965, 48:39.
5718. Frazer, Winifred L. King Lear and Hickey: bridegroom and
       iceman. Modern Drama, 1972, 15:267-278.
5719. Freed, Donald. Freud and Stanislavsky. New Directions in
       the Performing Arts. NY: Vantage, 1964; Review:
       Robert Seidenberg, Psychoanal Q, 1966, 35:141-142.
5720. Freedman, Burrill. H. R. Lenormand: a psychoanalytic
       dramatist. Psychoanal Rev, 1932, 19:64-71.
5721. Freedman, William. Impotence and self-destruction in The
       Country Wife. English Studies, 1972, 53:421-431.
5722. Freidson, Eliot. Adult discount: an aspect of children's
       changing taste. Child Development, 1953, 24:39-49.
5723. Freilach, Joan S. Paul Claudel's 'Le Soulier de satin'; A
       Stylistic, Structuralist, and Psychoanalytic Interpretation.
       Toronto: Univ. Toronto Press, 1973.
5724. _____. Le Soulier de satin: four levels through imagery.
       Claudel Studies, 1972, 1(1):44-55.
5725. Freiman, Gwenne. Hamlet as theatre and as a play. Amer
       Imago, 1972, 29:377-383.
5726. Freud, Anna. Rostand's Cyrano de Bergerac. In The Ego
       and the Mechanisms of Defense. London: Hogarth, 1954,
       143-146.
5727. Freud, Sigmund. Briefe an Arthur Schnitzler. Die neue
       Rundschau, 1955, 67:97.
5728. _____. On Hamlet and Oedipus. In The Interpretation of
       Dreams. In Standard Edition, Vol. 4. London: Hogarth,
       1961, 264-266; NY: Basic Books, 1961, 264-266; In Fab-
       er, M. D. (ed), The Design Within. NY: Science House,
       1970, 81-86.
5729. _____. Henry VIII. In The Interpretation of Dreams.
       NY: Basic Books, 1958, 212-213.
5730. _____. Julius Caesar. In The Interpretation of Dreams.
       NY: Basic Books, 1958, 483-484.
5731. _____. Psychopathic characters on the stage. Psychoanal
       Q, 1942, 11:459-464; In Standard Edition, 7:305-310 (1905).

5732. _____. [On Richard III.] In Standard Edition, Vol. 14.
London: Hogarth, 1958, 314-315; In Faber, M. D. (ed),
The Design Within. NY: Science House, 1970, 343-346.

5733. _____. Some character-types met with in psycho-analytic
work. In Collected Papers, Vol. 4. London: Hogarth,
1925, 318-334; NY: Basic Books, 1959, 318-334; In
Hardison, O. B. (ed), Modern Continental Literary Criticism. NY: Appleton-Century-Crofts, 1962, 249-265.

5734. _____. The taboo of virginity. In Collected Papers, Vol.
4. London: Hogarth, 1925, 217-235; New York: Basic
Books, 1959, 217-235.

5735. _____. The theme of the three caskets. In Collected Papers, Vol. 4. London: Hogarth, 1925, 244-256; NY:
Basic Books, 1959, 244-256; Imago, 1913, 2:257-267; Rev
Française de Psychanalyse, 1927, 1:549-561; In Manheim,
L., & Manheim, E. (eds), Hidden Patterns. NY: Macmillan, 1966, 79-92. In Standard Edition, Vol. 12. London: Hogarth, 1955, 290-301 (1913).

5736. Friedlander, M. A Psychoanalytic approach to Wagner's
Ring. Connotation, 1963, 25-53.

5737. Friedman, B. H. R. Lenormand: a psychoanalytic dramatist.
Psychoanal Rev, 1932, 19:64-71.

5738. Friedman, Joel, & Gassel, Sylvia. The chorus in Sophocles'
Oedipus Tyrannus: a psychoanalytic approach to dramatic
criticism. Psychoanal Q, 1950, 19:213-216.

5739. _____, & Gassel, Sylvia. Orestes: a psychoanalytic approach to dramatic criticism II. Psychoanal Q, 1951,
20:423-433.

5740. Friedman, Neil, & Jones, Richard M. On the mutuality of
the Oedipus complex. Notes on the Hamlet case. Amer
Imago, 1963, 20:107-129; In Faber, M. D. (ed), The Design Within. NY: Science House, 1970, 123-146.

5741. Friedman, Simon. Some Shakespearian Characterizations of
Women and Their Traditions. DAI, 1973, 34:312A.

5742. Friedrich, Gustav. Hamlet und seine Gemuthskrankheit.
Heidelberg: Weiss, 1899.

5743. Frost, W. Shakespeare his own granpaw. College English,
1956, 17:219-222.

5744. _____. Shakespeare's rituals and the opening of King
Lear. Hudson Rev, 1957-58, 10:577-585.

5745. Frumkes, George. The Oedipus theme in the stories of the
opera. J Hillside Hospital, 1955, 4:14-24.

5746. Frye, Northrop. The argument of comedy. In English Institute Essays. NY: Columbia Univ. Press, 1948.

5747. _____. Old and new comedy. Shakespeare Survey, 1969,
22:1-5.

5748. Fuchs, H. Die Homosexualität im Drama der Gegenwart und
Zukunft. Kritik, 1902.

5749. Fuegi, John. The alienated woman: Brecht's The Good Person of Setzuan. In Mews, S., & Knust, H. (eds), Essays
on Brecht; Theater and Politics. Chapel Hill: Univ.
North Carolina Press, 1974, 190-196.

5750. Füller, F. Das psychologische Problem der Frau in Kleists
Dramen und Novellen. Leipzig: Hässel, 1924.

5751. Funt, Dorothy. Arthur Schnitzler's Attitude Toward the Ethical Problems of Love and Marriage, as Shown in His Dramatic Works. Master's Thesis, New York Univ., 1933.

5752. Furtmüller, Carl. Iphigenie auf Tauris. Zeitschrift für Individual Psychologie, 1932, 10:328-329.

5753. _____. Schnitzlers Tragikömodie Das weite Land. Int Zeitschrift für Psychoanalyse, 1913, 4:28-40.

5754. Fuzellier, Etienne. Le Drame du pére et du fils chez Montherlant. L'Anneau d'Or, 1961, no. 101, 388-397.

5755. Fuzier, Jean. Shakespeare et la médecine mentale de son temps d'apres La Comédie des erreurs. Etudes Anglaises, 1964, 17:412-433.

5756. Fyler, Anson C., Jr. Self-unification: an archetypal analysis of Prospero in The Tempest. Hartford Studies in Lit, 1971, 3:45-50.

5757. Gabbard, Lucina Pacquet. The Dream Structure of Pinter's Plays: A Psychoanalytic Approach. Rutherford: Fairleigh Dickinson Univ. Press, 1976; DAI, 1975, 35:4518A; Reviews: Modern Drama, 1979, 22:89-92; J. E. Dearlove, South Atlantic Q, 1978, 77:126-122.

5758. Gajdusek, R. E. Death, incest, and the triple bond in the later plays of Shakespeare. Amer Imago, 1974, 31:109-158.

5759. Gallagher, Kent G. Emotion in tragedy and melodrama. Educational Theatre J, 1965, 17:215-219.

5760. Gallarati, Paolo. Psicologia e mito nel Flauto magico. Belfagor, 1976, 31:217-224.

5761. Gallart Capdevila, J. M. Estudio psicológico comparado de los teatros inglés y Español en el siglo de Cervantes. In Congrès International d'Història de la Medicine Catalana, 1st, Barcelona-Montpellier, 1970, Vol. 3. Barcelona: Libre d'actes, 1971, 229-243.

5762. Galler, Dieter. The different spheres of sequestration in Jean-Paul Sartre's play Les Séquestrés d'Altona. South Central Bulletin, 1971, 31:179-182.

5763. _____. Jean-Paul Sartre's drama Les Séquestrés d'Altona: two more examples of the schizophrenic syndrome. Language Q, 1970, 8(3-4):55-60.

5764. _____. Jean-Paul Sartre's Les Séquestrés d'Altona: old Von Gerlach--portrait of a schizophrenic. Language Q, 1969, 8(1-2):33-38.

5765. _____. The phases of schizophrenia in Jean-Paul Sartre's Les Séquestrés d'Altona. Language Q, 1973, 11(3-4):5-10, 16.

5766. _____. Le Portrait d'une schizophrène dans la pièce de Jean-Paul Sartre Les Séquestrés d'Altona. South Central Bulletin, 1969, 29:136-138.

5767. _____. The relationship between soma and psyche in Jean-Paul Sartre's drama Les Séquestrés d'Altona. Language Q, 1967, 6(1-2):35-38.

5768. Ganim, Carole. The divided self: Caliban from Shakespeare to Auden. Kentucky Philological Assn Bulletin, 1975, 9-15.

5769. Garber, Marjorie Beth. Coming of age in Shakespeare; sexual maturation. Yale Rev, 1977, 66:517-533.

5770. _____. Dream in Shakespeare: From Metaphor to Metamorphosis. New Haven: Yale Univ. Press, 1974; DAI, 1970, 31:1227A.

5771. Garcia, Angelina M. A critique on Wilfrido Ma. Guerriero's play, Close-Up. Diliman Rev, 1972, 20(1):137-143.

5772. García Reinoso, Diego. Notas sobre la obesidad a través del estudio de Falstaff. Revista de Psicoanálisis, 1956, 13: 170-177.

5773. Gardiner, Judith Kegan. Infantile sexuality, adult critics, and Bartholomew Fair. Lit & Psychol, 1974, 24:124-131.

5774. Gassenmeier, Michael. 'Odi et amo': Das Dilemma von Shakespeares Coriolan. Anglia, 1975, 93:70-110.

5775. Gassner, John. Review: H. Denker's The Far Country. Educational Theatre J, 1961, 13:214-217.

5776. Gaster, Theodor. Thespis: Ritual, Myth and Drama in the Ancient Near East. Garden City, NY: Doubleday, 1950.

5777. Gearey, John. Heinrich von Kleist: A Study in Tragedy and Anxiety. Philadelphia: Univ. Pennsylvania Press, 1968.

5778. Gedo, John E., Weinberg, Richard, & Faber, M. D. Review: K. R. Eissler's Discourse on 'Hamlet' and Hamlet. Amer Imago, 1977, 29:293-352.

5779. Gehlen, A. Die Struktur der Tragödie. Neue psychologische Studien, 1934, 12:47-58.

5780. Gellé, L. La Psychologie d'Hamlet. Rev de monde catholique, 1897, Dec.

5781. Gellert, B. J. The iconography of melancholy in the graveyard scene of Hamlet. Studies in Philology, 1970, 67:57-66.

5782. _____. Three Literary Treatments of Melancholy: Marston, Shakespeare and Burton. Doctoral dissertation, Columbia Univ., 1967.

5783. Gellert, Roger. A survey of the treatment of the homosexual in some plays. Encore, 1961, 8:29-39.

5784. Gerber, Richard. Elizabethan convention and psychological realism in the dream and last soliloquy of Richard III. English Studies, 1959, 40:294-300.

5785. Gerenday, Lynn de. Play, ritualization, and ambivalence in Julius Caesar. Lit & Psychol, 1974, 24:24-33.

5786. Gerrard, Charlotte F. Montherlant and Suicide. Madrid: Porrúa, 1977.

5787. Geyer, Horst. Ein psychogener Dämmerzustand. Shakespeares Ophelia. In Eine Untersuchung über die dichterische Darstellbarkeit seelischer Ausnahmezustände. Göttingen: Musterschmidt, 1955, 73-94, 269-282.

5788. Geyer-Kordesch, Johanna Maria. Die Psychologie des moralischen Handelns: Psychologie, Medizin und Dramentheorie bei Lessing, Mendelssohn und Friedrich Nicolai. DAI, 1977, 38:2151A.

5789. Giacoman, Helmy F. El caballero de Olmedo. Hispanófila, 1967, 10:1.
5790. Giauque, Gerald S. The psycho-structure of Britannicus: Neron's artistic Duperie. Rocky Mountain Rev Language & Lit, 1977, 31:39-46.
5791. Gifford, G. H. L'Inceste dans Phédre. Rev d'Histoire Littéraire de France, 1932, 39:560-562.
5792. Gifford, Sanford. 'Pop' psychoanalysis, kitsch, and the 'as if' theater: further notes on Peter Shaffer's Equus. Int J Psychoanal Psychotherapy, 1976, 5:466-472.
5793. Gilbert, Sandra M. All the dead voices. Drama Survey, 1968, 6:244-257.
5794. Gilborn, Steven N. The Family Plight in the Plays of Emily Augler: A Psychoanalytic Study. DAI, 1969, 30:1264.
5795. Gild, David C. Psychodrama on Broadway: three plays of psychodrama by Philip Barry. Markham Rev, 1970, 2(4): 65-74.
5796. Gill, Margaret Jones. Review: Lillian Hellman's The Children's Hour. JNMD, 1935, 82:587-588.
5797. Gill, Stephen M. Shaw, the suffragist. Lit Half-Yearly, 1973, 14(2):153-156.
5798. Gillibert, Jean. L'Oedipe maniaque. Paris: Payot, 1978.
5799. Gilmartin, Andrina. Mr. Shaw's many mothers. In Weintraub, R. (ed), Fabian Feminist: Bernard Shaw and Women. University Park: Pennsylvania State Univ. Press, 1977, 143-155; Shaw Rev, 1965, 8:93-103.
5800. Gilot, M. La Vocation comique de Marivaux. Saggi e ricerche di letteratura francese, 1971, 11:59-86.
5801. Ginn, Robert M. Psychodrama: a theatre for our time. Group Psychotherapy & Psychodrama, 1974, 27:123-146.
5802. Girard, René. Myth and identity crisis in A Midsummer Night's Dream. In Malone, D. H. (ed), The Frontiers of Literary Criticism. Los Angeles: Univ. Southern California Press, 1974, 121-148.
5803. _____. Racine, poète de la Gloire. Critique, 1964, 20: 483-506.
5804. Giuliano, W. A defense of Buero Vallejo. Modern Drama, 1977, 20:223-233.
5805. Glassman, Susan Flora. The Emancipated Woman in John Dryden's Comedies. DAI, 1978, 39:2953A.
5806. Glaz, A. Andre. Hamlet, or the tragedy of Shakespeare. Amer Imago, 1961, 18:129-158.
5807. _____. Iago or moral sadism. Amer Imago, 1962, 19: 323-348.
5808. Glenn, Jules. The adoption theme in Edward Albee's Tiny Alice and The American Dream. In Coltrera, J. T. (ed), Lives, Events, and Other Players: Studies in Psychobiography. NY: Aronson, 1980; in The Psychoanalytic Study of the Child, Vol. 29. New Haven: Yale Univ. Press, 1974, 413-429.
5809. _____. Alan Strang as an adolescent: a discussion of Peter Shaffer's Equus. Int J Psychoanal & Psychotherapy, 1976, 5:473-488.

5810. _____. Anthony and Peter Shaffer's plays: the influence of twinship on creativity. Amer Imago, 1974, 31:270-293.

5811. _____. Twins in disguise. I: A psychoanalytic essay on Sleuth and The Royal Hunt of the Sun. Psychoanal Q, 1974, 43:288-302.

5812. _____. _____. II: Content, style and form in plays by Anthony and Peter Shaffer. Int Rev Psychoanal, 1974, 1:373-381.

5813. Glenn, Richard F. The loss of identity: towards a definition of the dialectic in Lope's early drama. Hispanic Rev, 1973, 41:609-626.

5814. Glicksberg, Charles I. Depersonalization in the modern drama. Personalist, 1958, 39:158-169.

5815. _____. Psychoanalysis and the tragic vision. In The Tragic Vision in Twentieth-Century Literature. Carbondale: Southern Illinois Univ. Press, 1963, 85-96.

5816. Gobin, Pierre. Le Fou et ses doubles: figures de la dramaturgie québécois Montreal: Montreal Univ. Press, 1978.

5817. Godlewski, G. Les Médecins de Molière et leur modéles. Therapeutique, 1971, 47:297-307.

5818. Goeppert, H. C., et al. [Understanding language and transference in Beckett's Endgame.] Confinia Psychiatrica, 1979, 22(3):145-159.

5819. Goitein, P. Lionel. The Lady from the Sea. Psychoanal Rev, 1927, 14:375-419.

5820. _____. A new approach to an analysis of Mary Rose. British J Medical Psychol, 1926, 6:178-208.

5821. _____. The phantasy of the naked truth. Psychoanal Rev, 1929, 16:121-142.

5822. Golden, Leon. Aristotle and the audience for tragedy. Mnemosyne, 1976, 29(4):351-359.

5823. Goldhamer, Allen D. Everyman: a dramatization of death. Quart J Speech, 1973, 59:87-98.

5824. Goldstein, Malcolm. Pathos and personality in the tragedies of Nicholas Rowe. In Middendorf, J. H. (ed), English Writers of the Eighteenth Century. NY: Columbia Univ. Press, 1971, 172-185.

5825. Goldstein, Melvin. Body and soul on Broadway. Modern Drama, 1965, 7:411-421.

5826. _____. Identity crises in a mid-summer nightmare: comedy as terror in disguise. Psychoanal Rev, 1973, 60:169-204.

5827. _____. Multiple psychoanalytic approaches. Review: M. D. Faber (ed), The Design Within. Hartford Studies in Lit, 1971, 3:55-58.

5828. Goldstone, Herbert. Not so puzzling Pinter: The Homecoming. Theatre Annual, 1969, 25:20-27.

5829. Gomis, Juan. Sucedio en el Liceo. El correo catalán, 1978, 8(1).

5830. Goode, Bill. How little the lady knew her lord: a note on Macbeth. Amer Imago, 1963, 20:349-356.

5831. Goodhand, Robert. Psychological development in Jean Giradoux's Eglantine. French Rev, 1964, 38:173-179.

5832. Gordon, David J. Literature and repression: the case of Shavian drama. In Smith, J. H. (ed), The Literary Freud. New Haven: Yale Univ. Press, 1980, 198-203.

5833. Gorowara, Krishna. The fire symbol in Tennessee Williams. Literary Half-Yearly, 1967, 8:57-73.

5834. Gossman, L. Signs of the theatre. Theatre Research Int, 1976, 2:1-15.

5835. Gottschalk, Paul A. The Meaning of Hamlet: Modes of Literary Interpretation Since Bradley. Albuquerque: Univ. New Mexico Press, 1972.

5836. _____. The universe of madness in King Lear. Bucknell Rev, 1971, 19(3):51-68.

5837. Gougenheim, G. La Valeur psychologique des temps dans le monologue de Figaro. JPNP, 1951, 44:472-477.

5838. Gouhier, H. Categories esthetiques et categories dramatiques. JPNP, 1937, 34:626-631.

5839. Grabe, Herbert. Das amerikanische Drama nach O'Neill. In Die Amerikanische Literatur der Gegenwart. Berlin: de Gruyter, 1977, 28-48.

5840. Graf, Max. Problem des dramatischen Schaffens. Österreichische Rundschau, 1907, 10:326-337.

5841. Graham, Lindsay A. Wagner and Lohengrin, a psychoanalytic study. Psychiat J Univ. Ottawa, 1978, 3:39-49.

5842. Graham-White, Anthony. Jean Genet and the psychology of colonialism. Comparative Drama, 1970, 4:208-216.

5843. Grain, Frances. The interpersonal psychology of some of Ibsen's later plays. Ibsenforbundet: Arbok, 1974, 127-147.

5844. Granville-Barker, Harley. Freudianism in literature. In Study in Drama. Cambridge: Cambridge Univ. Press, 1934, 53-56.

5845. Gratz, David Kenneth. Emotion, Modes of Expression, and Effects on Plot, in Selected Comedies: 1670-1780. DAI, 1976, 36:702A-03A.

5846. Grayson, Patricia J. Fathers and Daughters in German Drama: 1740-1784. DAI, 1977, 37:4383A-84A.

5847. Grecco, Stephen R. A physician healing himself: Chekhov's treatment of doctors in the major plays. In Peschel, E. R. (ed), Medicine and Literature. NY: Watson, 1980, 3-10.

5848. Green, André. Lear ou les voi(es)x de la nature. Critique, 1971, 284.

5849. _____. Shakespeare, Freud, et le parricide. La Nef, 1967, 31:64-82.

5850. Gregg, Nancy P. Variations on a theme. Int J Psycho-Anal, 1953, 34:142-145.

5851. Gregory, J. W. Madness in the 'Heracles,' 'Orestes,' and 'Bacchae': A Study in Euripidean Drama. Doctoral dissertation, Harvard Univ., 1974.

5852. Grene, David. Reality and the Heroic Pattern: Last Plays of Ibsen, Shakespeare, and Sophocles. Chicago: Univ. Chicago Press, 1967.

5853. Grimm, Reinhold. Notizen zu Brecht, Freud and Nietzsche. Brecht J, 1974, 34-52.

5854. Grinstein, Alexander. The dramatic device: a play within a play. JAPA, 1956, 4:49-52; In Faber, M.D. (ed), The Design Within. NY: Science House, 1970, 149-153.

5855. _____. King Lear's impending death. Amer Imago, 1973, 30:121-141.

5856. Grivelet, Michel. Shakespeare, Molière, and the comedy of ambiguity. Shakespeare Survey, 1969, 22:15-26.

5857. Gross, George C. Mary Cowden Clarke: 'The Girlhood of Shakespeare's Heroines, ' and the sex education of Victorian women. Victorian Studies, 1972, 16:37-58.

5858. Gross, N. Conceit and metaphor in Racine's Les Plaideurs. Symposium, 1967, 20:226-236.

5859. Gross, R. The play as dramatic action. Players Magazine, 1974, 49:32-35.

5860. Grotjahn, Martin. The recognition of the Oedipus complex in Greek antiquity. Samiksa, 1955, 9:28-34.

5861. Gruenberg, Sidonie M. The Lady from the Sea. Psyche, 1929, 9:84-92.

5862. Guéguen, Pierre. Poésie de Racine, les tragédies nautiques, les passions. Paris: Editions du Rond-point, 1946.

5863. _____. Situation de l'art dramatique dans une psychologie de l'ennui. Psyché, 1949, 37-38:1033-1045.

5864. Gui, Weston A. Bottom's dream. Amer Imago, 1952, 9:251-305.

5865. Guiliano, William. The role of man and of woman in Buero Vallejo's plays. Hispanofila, 1970, 39:21-28.

5866. Gumpertz, Karl. Der Judith-Komplex. Versuch einer Analyse von Hebbels Judith und Flauberts Salammbô. Zeitschrift für Sexualwissenschaft, 1927, 14:289-301.

5867. Gurewitch, Morton. Comedy: The Irrational Vision. Ithaca, NY: Cornell Univ. Press, 1975.

5868. Gutheil, Emil A. Eine grossartige psychoanalytische Tragödie. Bericht über eine amerikanische Aufführung. Psychoanalytische Praxis, 1933, 3:144-146.

5869. Guthke, Karl S. Hauptmann und Freud: eine Arabeske über die Logik des Kuriosen. Neue Deutsche Hefte, 1979, 26(1):21-44.

5870. Guthmann, A. Hamlet als Neurastheniker. Medizet Berliner Wochenschrift, 1927, 3:60.

5871. Gutierrez, Donald. Coming of age in Mayo: Synge's Playboy of the Western World. Hartford Studies in Lit, 1974, 6:159-166.

5872. Gutteling, J.F.C. Modern Hamlet criticism. Neophilologus, 1941, 25:276-286.

5873. Gutwirth, Marcel M. La Problématique de l'innocence dans le théâtre de Racine. Rev des Sciences Humaines, 1962, 106:183-202.

5874. Haefner, Gerhard. Die Rede des Brutus--Psychologie der Masse und ihrer Führer. Ein Beitrag zur politischen Rede. Praxis des Neuesprachlichen, 1971, 18:266-269.

5875. Hagopian, John V. Psychology and the coherent form of
       Shakespeare's Othello. Proceedings Michigan Academy
       Science, Arts, & Letters, 1960, 45:373-380.
5876. Hahn, Vera T. The Plays of Eugene O'Neill. A Psychologi-
       cal Analysis. Doctoral dissertation, Louisiana State
       Univ., 1939.
5877. Haines, K. J. Lorenzo in Wonderland: a short play based
       upon the death of D. H. Lawrence. Suicide & Life-
       Threatening Behavior, 1978, 8:250-256.
5878. Haley, M. P. Peripetia and recognition in Racine. PMLA,
       1940, 55:426-439.
5879. Halio, Jay L. Anxiety in Othello. Costerus, 1972, 1:123-
       131.
5880. Hall, R. The psychological motivation of Wagner's Gotter-
       dämmerung. German Q, 1963, 34:245-257.
5881. Halleck, Reuben P. Shakespeare. In Education of the Cen-
       tral Nervous System. NY: 1902.
5882. Hallett, Charles A. Andrea, Andrugiv and King Hamlet: the
       ghost as spirit of revenge. Philological Q, 1977, 56:43-
       64.
5883. _____. Middleton's Cynics: A Study of Middleton's Insight
       into the Moral Psychology of the Mediocre Mind. Salz-
       burg: Univ. Salzburg, 1978; Review: Richard Levin,
       Modern Language Rev, 1978, 73:396-398.
5884. _____. Penitent brothel, the succubus and parson's Reso-
       lution: a reappraisal of penitent's position in Middleton's
       canon. Studies in Philology, 1972, 69:72-86.
5885. _____. The psychological drama of Women Beware Wom-
       en. Studies in English Lit, 1500-1900, 1972, 12:375-389.
5886. _____. Volpone as the source of the sickroom scheme in
       Middleton's Mad World. Notes & Queries, 1971, 18:24-
       25.
5887. Halliday, F. E. The Cult of Shakespeare. NY: Yoseloff,
       1960.
5888. Hallman, Ralph J. Psychology of Literature: A Study of
       Alienation and Tragedy. NY: Philosophical Library,
       1961.
5889. Hallstead, R. N. Idolatrous love: a new approach to Othello.
       Shakespeare Q, 1968, 19:107-124.
5890. Halpern, S. Free association in 432 B. C.: Socrates in The
       Clouds. Psychoanal Rev, 1963, 50:419-436.
5891. Haltresht, Michael. Guilt and expiation in John Osborne's
       plays. Cithara, 1976, 16(1):33-39.
5892. Hamilton, James W. Early trauma, dreaming and creativity:
       the works of Eugene O'Neill. Int Rev Psycho-Anal, 1976,
       3:341-364.
5893. Hammerström, Eckart. Narzisstiche Figuren in elisabethan-
       ischen Tragödien. Salzburg: Univ. Salzburg Press,
       1976; Thèse, Univ. Münster, 1975.
5894. Handelman, Susan. Timon of Athens: the rage of disillusion.
       Amer Imago, 1979, 36:45-68.
5895. Hankins, John Erskine. Hamlet and Oedipus reconsidered.
       Shakespeare Newsletter, 1956, 6:11.

5896. Hannah, Barbara. All's Well That Ends Well. In Studien
       zur analytische Psychologie C. G. Jung, Vol. 2. Zurich:
       Rascher, 1955, 344-363.
5897. Hannemann, Bruno. Satirisches Psychogramm der Mäch-
       tigen: zur Kunst der Provokation in Thomas Bernhards
       Der Präsident. Maske und Kothurn. Int Beiträge zur
       Theaterwissenschaft, 1977, 23:147-158.
5898. Hanse, J. Regards sur Racine. Les Lettres Romanes, 1961,
       15:111-133.
5899. Hansen, Carol Louise. Woman as Individual in English Ren-
       aissance Drama: A Defiance of the Masculine Code.
       DAI, 1975, 35:7867A.
5900. Harding, Denys W. Shakespeare's final view of women.
       Times Lit Supplement, 30 Nov 1979, No. 4002:59-61.
5901. _____. Women's fantasy of manhood. A Shakespearian
       theme. Shakespeare Q, 1969, 20:245-253.
5902. Harding, F. J. W. Fantasy, imagination and Shakespeare.
       British J Aesthetics, 1964, 4:305-320.
5903. Harmon, Maurice. Richard Rowan, his own scapegoat.
       James Joyce Q, 1965, 3:35-40.
5904. Hárnik, J. Eine infantile Sexualtheorie bei Gerhart Haupt-
       mann. Int Zeitschrift für Psychoanalyse, 1912, 2:363-
       364.
5905. Harshbarger, Karl. The Burning Jungle: An Analysis of
       Arthur Miller's 'Death of a Salesman. ' Washington, DC:
       University Press of America, 1978.
5906. _____. The report of the bedroom scene in Sophocles'
       Oedipus. Hartford Studies in Lit, 1974, 6:197-220.
5907. Hartl, Edwin. Karl Kraus und die Psychoanalyse. Merkur,
       1976, 31:144-146.
5908. Hartle, R. Racine's hidden metaphors. Modern Language
       Notes, 1961, 76:132-139.
5909. Hartman, Murray. The skeletons in O'Neill's Mansions.
       Drama Survey, 1967, 5:276-279.
5910. Hartsock, Mildred E. The complexity of Julius Caesar.
       PMLA, 1966, 81:56-62.
5911. Hartweg, Norman. Homosexuality. Tulane Drama Rev, 1965,
       10:208-213.
5912. Hartwig, Theodor. Hamlets Hemmungen. Psychologische
       Studie. Vienna: Cerny, 1952.
5913. Hatfield, Henry Caraway. Cave matrem: the battle of the
       sexes in Ernst Barlach's Der tote Tag. In Crosby,
       D. H. , & Schoolfield, G. C. (eds), Studies in the German
       Drama. Chapel Hill: Univ. North Carolina Press, 1974,
       225-234.
5914. Hathaway, B. Lucretian 'return upon ourselves' in eight-
       eenth-century theories of tragedy. PMLA, 1947, 62:672-
       689.
5915. Hayles, Nancy K. Sexual disguise in As You Like It and
       Twelfth Night. Shakespeare Survey, 1979, 32:63-72.
5916. Hayse, Joseph M. Madness on Stage: The History of the
       Tragedy in Drama. DAI, 1976, 37:3602A.
5917. Hazard, Forrest E. The Ascent of F6: a new interpretation.
       Tennessee Studies in Lit, 1970, 15:165-175.

5918.   . The Father Christmas passage in Auden's Paid on
          Both Sides. Modern Drama, 1969, 12:155-164.
5919. Head, F. H. Shakespeare's Insomnia and the Causes Thereof.
          Chicago: Maxwell, 1886; Boston: Houghton Mifflin, 1899.
5920. Hécaen, H. Review: Jean-Louis Armand-Laroche. --Antonin
          Artaud et son double. Essai d'analyse psychopathologique,
          JPNP, 1964, 61:115-116.
5921. Hedrick, Carlyle P. Shakespeare's Changing Use of Psycho-
          logical Reference in His Comedies. DAI, 1978, 39:896A-
          97A.
5922. Heilbron, Carolyn. The character of Hamlet's mother.
          Shakespeare Q, 1957, 8:201-206.
5923. Heilman, Robert B. The criminal as tragic hero: dramatic
          methods. Shakespeare Survey, 1966, 19:12-24.
5924.   . Magic in the Web. Action and Language in Othel-
          lo. Lexington: Univ. Kentucky Press, 1956.
5925.   . The Taming untamed, or the return of the shrew.
          Modern Language Q, 1966, 27:147-161.
5926.   . This Great Stage: Image and Structure in King
          Lear. Seattle: Univ. Washington Press, 1963.
5927.   . Wit and witchcraft: an approach to Othello. In
          Dean, L. F. (ed), Shakespeare: Modern Essays in Criti-
          cism. NY: Oxford Univ. Press, 1957.
5928. Heiman, Nanette. Oedipus at Colonus: a study of old age
          and death. Amer Imago, 1962, 19:91-98.
5929. Heims, Neil Stephen. Fathers and Daughters in the Plays
          of Shakespeare. DAI, 1978, 39:2954A.
5930. Heindl, Brigitta. Die Gestalt der Arztes im Drama Arthur
          Schnitzlers und Karl Schönherrs. Vienna: Universität
          Wien, 1973.
5931. Heisdsieck, Arnold. Psychologische Strukturen im Werk
          Bertolt Brechts bis 1932. In Ideologiekritische Studien
          zur Literatur: Essays II. Bern: Lang, 1975, 31-71.
5932. Heitmann, Klaus. Marivaux: Le Jeu de l'amour et du hasard.
          In Das französiche Theater vom Barock bis zur Gegen-
          wart. Düsseldorf: Bagel, 1968, 34-54.
5933. Hélein-Koss, Suzanne. Rêve et fantasmes dans Les Enfants
          terribles de Jean Cocteau. French Rev, 1974, 6:151-161.
5934. Heller, Erich. Die Demolierung eines Marionettentheaters
          oder Psychoanalyse und der Missbrauch der Literatur.
          Merkur, 1977, 31:1071-1085.
5935. Heller, Lora, & Heller, Abraham. Hamlet's parents: the
          dynamic formulation of a tragedy. Amer Imago, 1960,
          17:413-421.
5936. Helmreich-Marsilian, A. L'Ironie tragique de Racine. J
          Australasian Universities Language Lit Assn, 1966, 23:
          49-70.
5937. Henderson, Jeffrey. The Maculate Muse: Obscene Language
          in Attic Poetry. New Haven: Yale Univ. Press, 1975.
5938. Henderson, Joseph L. Stages of psychological development
          exemplified in the poetical works of T. S. Eliot. J Analy-
          tical Psychol, 1957, 2(1):34-49.

5939. _____. Symbolism of the unconscious in two plays of
        Shakespeare. In Kirsch, H. (ed), The Well-Tended Tree.
        NY: Putnam, 1971, 284-299.

5940. Hendrick, Ives. Facts and Theories of Psychoanalysis. NY:
        Knopf, 1941, 298-299.

5941. Henke, Frederick Goodrich. The Psychology of Ritual. Doc-
        toral dissertation, Univ. Chicago, 1910.

5942. Henke, James T. He shot her with great stones: prominent
        sexual metaphors in the non-Shakespearean drama of Ren-
        aissance England. Maledicta, 1977, 1(1):49-62.

5943. Hennings, Elsa. Literarische Kritik contra Psychiatrie. In
        Hamlet: Shakespeares 'Faust'-Tragödie. Bonn: Bouvier,
        1954, 106-123.

5944. Hense, C. C. Die Darstellung der Seelenkrank-Leiten in
        Shakespeares Dramen. Jahrbuch der deutschen Shake-
        speare-Gesellschaft, 1878, 13:212-247.

5945. Hepburn, James G. A dream that hath no bottom. Com-
        ment on Mr. Holland's paper. Lit & Psychol, 1964,
        14:3-6.

5946. Herbert, Edward T. Myth and archetype in Julius Caesar.
        Psychoanal Rev, 1970, 57:303-308.

5947. Hernadi, Paul. Berthold Brecht. In Strelka, J. P. (ed),
        Literary Criticism and Psychology. University Park:
        Penn State Univ. Press, 1976.

5948. Hershey, Jane. Female playwrights of the eighteenth century:
        shaping the market place of love. Amer J Psychoanal,
        1975, 35:69-74.

5949. Hertrich, Charles. Maurice Maeterlinck, poète, dramaturge,
        philosophe du subconscient. St. Etienne: Flambeaux,
        1946.

5950. Herzel, R. W. Anagnorisis and peripeteis in comedy. Educa-
        tional Theatre J, 1974, 26:495-505.

5951. Hesse, Everett W. Análisis e interpretación de la comedia.
        Madrid: Castalia, 1968.

5952. _____. El Caballero de Olmedo. Symposium, 1965,
        19(1).

5953. _____. Eco y Narciso. Boletin de la Biblioteca Menéndez
        y Pelayo, 1963, 39(1-3).

5954. _____. Estructura e interpretación de una comedia de
        Calderón: Eco y Narciso. Filología, 1961 [1963], 7:61-
        76.

5955. _____. Guiterre's personality in El médico de su honra.
        Bulletin of the 'Comediantes,' 1976, 28:11-16.

5956. _____. Honor and behavioral patterns in El médico de su
        honra. Romanische Forschungen, 1976, 88:1-15.

5957. _____. The incest motif in Tirso's La venganza de Tam-
        ar. Hispania, 1964, 47:268-276.

5958. _____. El motivo del sueño. Segismundo, 1967, 3:55-62.

5959. _____. Psychic phenomena in La vida es sueño. In Sola-
        Solé, J. M., Crisfulli, A., & Damiani, B. (eds), Estudios
        literarios de hispanistas norteamericanos. Barcelona:
        Hispan, 1975, 275-286.

5960- _____. The terrible mother image in Calderon's Eco y
1. Narciso. Romance Notes, 1960, 1:133-136.
5962. Heuermann, Hartmut. Die Psychomachie in Tennessee Williams The Milktrain Doesn't Stop Here Anymore. Amerikastudien, 1979, 19:266-279.
5963. Hewes, Henry. Freud and the theatre. Saturday Rev, 1956,
39:10.
5964. _____. Frothy Shakespeare; obsessed O'Neill. Saturday
Rev, 1973, 55:72.
5965. Heyn, Gisa. Der junge Schiller als Psychologe. Zurich:
Juris, 1966.
5966. Higgins, Michael H. Chapman's Senecal man: a study in
Elizabethan psychology. Rev English Studies, 1945,
47(83):186-191.
5967. Hilgar, M. F. La Folie dans le théatre du XVIIe siècle en
France. Romance Notes, 1975, 16:383-389.
5968. Hill, Linda Marjenna. Language as Agression: Studies in
the Postwar Drama. Bonn: Bouvier, 1976; DAI, 1975,
35:4524A.
5969. Hill, Roger Cleveland. Psychoanalysis and Shakespearean
Production. DA, 1963, 24:1748; Speech Monographs,
1965, 31:275-276.
5970. Hillach, Ansgar. Das Volksstück also Kosmologie der Ge-
walt: Psychologie und Marxismus in Ödön von Harvaths
Revolte auf Côte 3018. Germanisch-Romanische Monatsschrift, 1974, 24:223-243.
5971. Hillman, Richard W. Meaning and morality in some Renaissance revenge plays. Univ. Toronto Q, 1979, 49:1-17.
5972. Hinchliffe, Arnold P. (ed). Drama Criticism: Developments
Since Ibsen; a Casebook. London: Macmillan, 1979.
5973. Hinden, Michael. The Birth of Tragedy and The Great God
Brown. Modern Drama, 1973, 16:129-141.
5974. Hindjosa, Armando. La tragedia de Edipo. Revista de Psicoanálisis, Psiquiatría y Psicología, 1968, No. 10, 32-43.
5975. Hinrichsen, Otto. Das Hamlet-Problem gelost? Psychia-
trische-Neurologische-Wochenschrift, 1937, 39:36-40.
5976. _____. Der verständliche-unwerstandene Hamlet. Schweizer Archiv für Neurologie und Psychiatrie, 1933, 31:261-
283; 1934, 32:33-43.
5977. Hirsch, Foster. Sexual imagery in Tennessee Williams'
Kingdom of Earth. Notes on Contemporary Lit, 1971,
1(2):10-13.
5978. Hirschbach, Frank Donald. Black milk: the treatment of
guilt in German post war literature. Minnesota Rev,
1963, 3:250-253.
5979. Hirschfeld, Jacob. Ophelia, ein poetisches Lebensbild von
Shakespeare, zum ersten Mal im Lichte ärztlicher Wissenschaft. Danzig: 1881.
5980. _____. Shakespeare as a psychologist of crime. Ethological J, 1929, 14:8-10.
5981. Hitschmann, Edward. Zur Psychoanalyse des Misanthropen
von Molière. Imago, 1928, 14:88-99; Almanach, 1929,
138-150.

5982.   H. K.   Hamlet psycho-analysed.   Punch, 1948, 214:128-129.
5983.   Hobday, C. H.   Imagery and irony in Henry V.   Shakespeare
        Survey, 1968, 21:107-114.
5984.   Hoch, Alfred E.   Geisteskranke bei Shakespeare.   Kölnische
        Zeitung, 1939, 407-408.
5985.   Hoche, Alfred E.   Shakespeare und die Psychiatrie.   In Aus
        der Werkstatt.   Munich: Lehmanns, 1935, 25-37.
5986.   Hodess, Kenneth M.   In Search of the Divided Self: A Psy-
        choanalytic Inquiry into Selected Plays of Luigi Pirandello.
        DAI, 1978, 39:1191A.
5987.   Hoey, Thomas F.   On the theme of introversion in Oedipus
        Rex.   Classical J, 1969, 64:296-299.
5988.   Hofling, Charles K.   An interpretation of Shakespeare's Cori-
        olanus.   Amer Imago, 1957, 14:407-437; In Faber, M. D.
        (ed), The Design Within.   NY: Science House, 1970, 289-
        305.
5989.   _____.   Notes on Shakespeare's Cymbeline.   Shakespeare
        Studies, 1965, 1:118-136.
5990.   Hofling, Charles K.   Notes on Shakespeare's Winter's Tale.
        Psychoanal Rev, 1971, 58:90-110.
5991.   _____.   Psychoanalytic aspects of Shakespeare's Tempest.
        Psychoanal Rev, 1974, 61:375-395.
5992.   Hogan, A. P.   'Tis Pity She's a Whore: the overall design.
        Studies in English Lit, 1977, 17:303-316.
5993.   Hogan, Patrick Colm.   King Lear: splitting and its epistemic
        Agon.   Amer Imago, 1974, 36:32-44.
5994.   Holland, Joyce M.   Human relations in Eliot's drama.   Ren-
        ascence, 1970, 22:151-161.
5995.   Holland, Norman N.   Caliban's dream.   Psychoanal Q, 1968,
        37:114-125; In Faber, M. D. (ed), The Design Within.
        NY: Science House, 1970, 522-533.
5996.   _____.   Comment on 'The death of Zenocrate.'   Lit &
        Psychol, 1966, 16:25-26.
5997.   _____.   Freud on Shakespeare.   PMLA, 1960, 65:163-173;
        Show, 1964, 4:86, 108; Publications in Humanities No.
        47.   Cambridge: MIT Press, 1961.
5998.   _____.   Hamlet--my greatest creation.   J Amer Academy
        Psychoanal, 1975, 3:419-427.
5999.   _____.   Hermia's dream.   In The Annual of Psychoanalysis
        Vol. VII/1979.   NY: IUP, 1980; In Schwartz, M. M., &
        Kahn, C. (eds), Representing Shakespeare.   Baltimore:
        Johns Hopkins Univ. Press.
6000.   _____.   How can Dr. Johnson's remarks on the death of
        Cordelia add to my own response? In Hartman, G. H.
        (ed), Psychoanalysis and the Question of the Text.   Balti-
        more: Johns Hopkins Univ. Press, 1978, 18-44.
6001.   _____.   Introduction to Henry IV, Part 2.   NY: New
        American Library, 1965; In Faber, M. D. (ed), The De-
        sign Within.   NY: Science House, 1970, 411-429.
6002.   _____.   Macbeth as hibernal giant.   Lit & Psychol, 1960,
        10:37-38.
6003.   _____.   Mercutio, mine own son the dentist.   In Smith,
        G. R. (ed), Essays on Shakespeare.   University Park:
        Penn State Univ. Press, 1965, 3-14.

6004. _____. Psychoanalysis and Shakespeare. NY: McGraw-Hill, 1966; NY: Octagon, 1968; Reviews: Maurice Charney, Shakespeare Q, 1968, 19:401-403; Robert Plank, Lit & Psychol, 1966, 16:200-203; Denis Donoghue, Hudson Rev, 1966, 19:503-506; Norbert D. Weiner, Bulletin Philadelphia Assn Psychoanal, 1967, 17:169-172.

6005. _____. Psychology in Shakespeare, 1897-2064. Shakespeare Newsletter, 1964, 14:2-3, 27.

6006. _____. Realism and the psychological critic; or how many complexes has Lady Macbeth? Lit & Psychol, 1960, 10: 5-8.

6007. _____. Romeo's dream and the paradox of literary realism. Lit & Psychol, 1963, 13:97-103; In Faber, M. D. (ed), The Design Within. NY: Science House, 1970, 43-54.

6008. _____. The Shakespearean Imagination. NY: Macmillan, 1964; Bloomington: Indiana Univ. Press, 1968.

6009. _____. Shakespearean tragedy and the three ways of psychoanalytic criticism. Hudson Rev, 1962, 15:217-222; In Ruitenbeek, H. M. (ed), Psychoanalysis and Literature. NY: Dutton, 1964, 207-217.

6010. _____. Shakespeare's Mercutio and ours. Michigan Q Rev, 1966, 5:115-123.

6011. _____. Transactive teaching: Cordelia's death. College English, 1977, 39:276-285.

6012. _____. Words and psychoanalysis: Hamlet again. Contemporary Psychol, 1972, 17:331-332.

6013. Hollingworth, H. L. The Psychology of the Audience. NY: American Book, 1927.

6014. Holtz, Jutta. Abnorme Charakters bei Shakespeare: Othello, Richard III, Macbeth. Tübingen Medical Dissertation, 1933.

6015. Holzapfel, Tamara. The theater of René Marqués: in search of identity and form. In Lyday, L. F., & Woodyard, G. W. (eds), Dramatists in Revolt: The New Latin American Theater. Austin: Univ. Texas Press, 1976, 146-166.

6016. Holzhausen, P. Irrsinn und psychologische Grenzzustände im Spiegel der dramatischen Dichtung. Kölnische Zeitung, 1923, 717-747.

6017. Homan, Sidney R. The single world of A Midsummer Night's Dream. Bucknell Rev, 1969, 17:72-84.

6018. Honig, Edwin. Sejanus and Coriolanus: a study in alienation. Modern Language Q, 1951, 12:408-421.

6019. Hoppe, A. Psychopathologisches bei Schiller und Ibsen. Zentralblatt für Nervenkeilhunde, 1907, 18:223-228.

6020. Horne, R. H. Madness as treated by Shakespeare: a psychological essay. J Psychol Medicine, 1849, 2:589-607.

6021. Host, Else. Henrik Ibsens Vildanden. Oslo: Aschehoug, 1967; Review: Harry Bergholz, Lit & Psychol, 1967, 17: 150-154.

6022. Hovey, Richard P. Psychiatrist and saint in The Cocktail Party. Lit & Psychol, 1959, 9:51-55; In Manheim, L. F.,

& Manheim, E. (eds), Hidden Patterns. NY: Macmillan, 1966, 230-242.

6023. Howarth, W. D. La Notion de la catharsis dans la comédie française classique. Rev des Sciences Humaines, 1973, 38:521-539.

6024. Howe, T. Taboo in the Oedipus theme. Transactions & Proceedings American Philological Assn, 1962, 93:124-143.

6025. Hoy, Cyrus. Fathers and daughters in Shakespeare's romances. In Kay, C. M., & Jacobs, H. E. (eds), Shakespeare's Romances Reconsidered. Lincoln: Univ. Nebraska Press, 1978, 77-90.

6026. Hubbs, V. C. Heinrich von Kleist and the symbol of the wise man. Symposium, 1959, 16:165-179.

6027. Hubert, J. D. Essai d'exégèse racinienne--Les Secrets témoins. Paris: Nizet, 1956.

6028. _____. The timeless temple in Athalie. French Studies, 1956, 10:140-153.

6029. _____. Le Triomphe symbolique d'Hector. French Rev, 1954, 27:446-452.

6030. Huebert, Ronald. An artificial way to grieve: the forsaken woman in Beaumont and Fletcher, Massinger and Ford. J English Lit History, 1977, 44:601-624.

6031. Huhner, Max. Shakespeare's Hamlet. Studies in Psychology and Sanity. NY: Farrar, 1950.

6032. Hull, Elizabeth Anne. A Transactional Analysis of the Plays of Edward Albee. DAI, 1975, 36:313A-314A.

6033. _____. A popular psychology illuminates an 'elite' art medium: a look at Albee's A Delicate Balance through transactional analysis. In Marsden, M. T. (comp), Proceedings of the 6th National Convention of the Popular Culture Assn. Bowling Green, Ohio: Bowling Green State Univ. Popular Press, 1976, 1071-1086.

6034. Hunt, Joseph A. Interaction Process Analysis of Harold Pinter's The Homecoming: Toward a Phenomenological Criticism of Drama. DAI, 1972, 32:4159A.

6035. Hurrell, John D. Romersholm, the existentialist drama, and the dilemma of modern tragedy. Educational Theatre J, 1963, 15:118-124.

6036. Huss, Roy. Kirche, Kuchen und Kinder by Tennessee Williams. A review. Psychoanal Rev, 1980, 67:777-781.

6037. Huston, J. Dennis. 'When I come to man's estate': Twelfth Night and problems of identity. Modern Language Q, 1972, 33:274-288.

6038. Hutter, Albert D. The language of Hamlet. J Amer Academy Psychoanal, 1975, 3:429-438.

6039. Hyman, Stanley Edgar. Iago psychologically motivated. Centennial Rev, 1970, 14:369-384.

6040. _____. Iago: Some Approaches to the Illusion of His Motivation. NY: Atheneum, 1970.

6041. _____. Portraits of the artist: Iago and Prospero. Shenandoah, 1970, 21:18-42.

6042. _____. Untuning the Othello music: Iago as stage villain. In Cheuse, A. , & Koffler, R. (eds), The Rarer Action. New Brunswick, NJ: Rutgers Univ. Press, 1970, 55-67.
6043. Hytier, J. L'Esthetique du drame. J de Psychologie, 1932, 29:74-104.

6044. Ide, Richard S. The theatre of the mind: an essay on Macbeth. J English Lit History, 1975, 42:338-361.
6045. Inge, William Motter. The schizophrenic wonder. In Frenz, H. (ed), American Playwrights on Drama. NY: Hill & Wang, 1965, 89-93.
6046. Ingen, Ferdinand van. Faust--homo melancholicus. In Bormann, A. von, et al. (eds), Wissen und Erfahrungen. Tübingen: Niemeyer, 1976, 256-281.
6047. Irgat, Mina. Disease imagery in the plays of John Webster. Litera, 1955, 2:22-24.

6048. Jaarsma, Richard J. The 'Lear complex' in The Two Gentlemen of Verona. Lit & Psychol, 1972, 22:199-202.
6049. _____. The tragedy of Banquo. Lit & Psychol, 1967, 17: 87-94.
6050. Jacerme, Pierre. La 'Folie' de Sophocle à l'antipsychiatrie. Paris: Bordas, 1974.
6051. Jacobi, Walter. Falstaff, eine psychologisch-ästhetische Studie. Shakespeare-Jahrbuch, 1941, 77:2-48.
6052. Jacobs, Richard. Sex and money: a note on Hamlet I, iii, 108-109. Shakespeare Q, 1980, 31:88-90.
6053. Jacobson, G. F. A note on Shakespeare's Midsummer Night's Dream. Amer Imago, 1962, 19:21-26.
6054. Jacobson, Irving F. The Fallen Family: A Study in the Work of Arthur Miller. DAI, 1974, 35:2271A-72A.
6055. Jacoubet, H. L'Inceste dans Phèdre. Rev d'Histoire Littéraire de France, 1931, 38:397-399.
6056. Jaeger, William M. The Application of the Psycho-Analytical Theories of Karen Horney to the Stanislavski System of Acting. Doctoral dissertation, New York Univ. , 1964.
6057. Jaffe, Sidney. Parents and Children on the French Stage, 1850-1914. Doctoral dissertation, Harvard Univ. , 1938.
6058. Jago, David. School and theater: polarities of homosexual writing in England. College English, 1974, 36:360-368.
6059. Janet, Pierre M. F. La Psychologie dans les tragédies de Racine. Rev des Deux Mondes, 1875, 5:263-294.
6060. Jankelevitch, S. Le Délire onirique dans les drames de Shakespeare. Psyché, 1950, 5:305-328.
6061. Janton, Pierre. Othello's 'weak function. ' Cahiers Elisabéthains, 1975, 7:43-50.
6062. Jantz, Harold. Goethe, Faust, alchemy, and Jung. German Q, 1962, 35:129-141.
6063. _____. The place of the 'eternal-womanly' in Goethe's Faust drama. PMLA, 1953, 48:791-805.
6064. Jarxo, V. [A psychoanalytic interpretation of Sophocles' Oedipus Rex.] Voprosy Literatury, 1978, 10:189-213.

6065.   Jasenas, E.   Le Thème de la chasse au monstre dans la
        Phèdre de Racine.   Symposium, 1968, 21:118-131.
6066.   Jasinski, R.   Les Héros racinien.   Cahiers raciniens, 1962,
        11:9-17.
6067.   Jeffreys, Harold.   Ibsen's Peer Gynt: a psychoanalytic study.
        Psychoanal Rev, 1924, 11:361-402.
6068.   Jekels, Ludwig.   On the psychology of comedy.   In Selected
        Papers.   NY: IUP, 1952, 97-104; Imago, 1926, 12:328-
        335; Almanach, 1927, 190-198; Tulane Drama Rev, 1958,
        2:55-61.
6069.   _____.   The problem of the duplicated expression of psy-
        chic themes.   Int J Psycho-Anal, 1933, 14:300-309; In
        Selected Papers.   NY: IUP, 1952, 131-141.
6070.   _____.   The riddle of Shakespeare's Macbeth.   Psychoanal
        Rev, 1943, 30:361-385; Imago, 1917, 5:170-195; In Selected
        Papers.   NY: IUP, 1952, 105-130; London: Hogarth,
        1952, 105-130; In Ruitenbeek, H. M. (ed), Psychoanalysis
        and Literature.   NY: Dutton, 1964, 142-167; In Faber,
        M. D.   (ed), The Design Within.   NY: Science House,
        1970, 235-249.
6071.   _____.   Shakespeare's Macbeth.   Imago, 1917-19, 5:170-
        195.
6072.   Jelliffe, Smith Ely.   Dear Brutus: the dramatist's use of the
        dream.   New York Medical J, 1919, 109:577-583; Medical
        Woman's J, 1920, 27:195-204.
6073.   _____.   Psychotherapy and the drama: the therapeutic
        message of Peter Ibbetson.   New York Medical J, 1917,
        106:442-447.
6074.   _____, & Brink, Louise.   The Jest: the destruction
        wrought by hate.   New York Medical J, 1919, 110:573-
        577.
6075.   _____.   Psychoanalysis and the Drama.   NY: Nervous &
        Mental Disease Publ., 1922.
6076.   _____.   The Wild Duck.   Psychoanal Rev, 1919, 6:357-378.
6077.   Jennings, Lee Bryson.   Hoffmann's hauntings: notes toward
        a parapsychological approach to literature.   J English &
        Germanic Philology, 1976, 75:559-567.
6078.   Jerotić, Vladeta.   Luidji Pirandelo i savremena psihologija.
        Književnost, 1975, 60:118-135.
6079.   Jeske, Jeffrey M.   Macbeth, Ahab, and the unconscious.
        Amer Transcendental Q, 1976, 31:8-12.
6080.   Jiji, Vera M.   Pinter's four dimensional house: The Home-
        coming.   Modern Drama, 1974, 17:433-442.
6081.   _____.   Portia revisited: the influence of unconscious fac-
        tors upon theme and characterization in The Merchant of
        Venice.   Lit & Psychol, 1976, 26:5-16.
6082.   Jofen, Jean B.   Two mad heroines: a study of the mental
        disorders of Ophelia in Hamlet and Margarete in Faust.
        Lit & Psychol, 1961, 11:70-77.
6083.   John, S. B.   Obsession and technique in the plays of Jean
        Anouilh.   In Bogard, T., & Oliver, W. I. (eds), Modern
        Drama: Essays in Criticism.   NY: Oxford Univ. Press,
        1966, 20-42.

6084.   Johns, Marilyne E.   Strindberg's Folkungasagen and Berg-
        man's Det sjunde inseglet: medieval epic and psychologi-
        cal drama.   Scandinavica, 1979, 18:21-34.
6085.   Johnson, Francis R.   Elizabethan drama and the Elizabethan
        science of psychology.   In Wrenn, C. L., & Bullough, G.
        (eds), English Studies Today.   London: Oxford Univ.
        Press, 1951, 1952, 111-119.
6086.   Johnson, Marilyn L.   Images of Women in the Works of
        Thomas Heywood.   Salzburg: Institut für Englische
        Sprache und Literatur, 1974; DAI, 1974, 35:3685A-86A.
6087.   Jonard, M.   L'Amour, la femme et la société dans la narra-
        tive de Pirandello.   Rev des Etudes Italiennes, 1966, 12:
        19-60.
6088.   Jones, A. David, Stewart, Abigail J., & Winter, David G.
        Socialization and themes in popular drama: an analysis
        of the content of child-rearing manuals and Don Juan
        plays in sixteenth to twentieth centuries.   European J So-
        cial Psychol, 1974, 4:65-84.
6089.   Jones, Ernest.   The death of Hamlet's father.   Int J Psych-
        Anal, 1948, 29:174-176; In Phillips, W. (ed), Art and
        Psychoanalysis.   NY: Criterion, 1957, 146-150; In The
        Yearbook of Psychoanalysis, Vol. 6.   NY: IUP, 1950,
        276-280; In Essays in Applied Psycho-Analysis, Vol. 1.
        London: Hogarth, 1951, 323-328; In Ruitenbeek, H. M.
        (ed), Psychoanalysis and Literature.   NY: Dutton, 1964,
        14-18.
6090.   _____.   Hamlet and Oedipus.   A Classic Study in the Psy-
        choanalysis of Literature.   NY: Doubleday Anchor, 1954;
        NY: Norton, 1949; London: Gollancz, 1910, 1949; Paris:
        Gallimard, 1967.   Excerpt: Hamlet: the psycho-analyti-
        cal solution.   In Handy, W. J., & Westbrook, M. (eds),
        Twentieth Century Criticism.   NY: Free Press, 1974,
        484-499; Review: Harry Slochower, Complex, 1951, 3:46-
        49.
6091.   _____.   Hamlet: the psycho-analytic solution.   [Excerpt
        from Hamlet and Oedipus.]   In Handy, W. J., & West-
        brook, M. (eds), Twentieth Century Criticism.   NY:
        Free Press, 1974, 484-499.
6092.   _____.   The Oedipus complex as an explanation of Ham-
        let's mystery: a study in motive.   Amer J Psychol,
        1910, 21:72-113; Revised: A psycho-analytic study of
        Hamlet.   In Essays in Applied Psycho-Analysis.   London:
        Hogarth, 1923, 1-98.   Introduction to Hamlet, with title,
        The problem of Hamlet and the Oedipus-complex.   Lon-
        don: Vision, 1947; NY: Funk & Wagnalls, 1947, 7-42;
        Leipzig: Deuticke, 1911.
6093.   _____.   On Julius Caesar.   In Faber, M. D. (ed), The
        Design Within.   NY: Science House, 1970, 57-61.
6094.   _____.   Das Problem des Hamlet und der Oedipus-Kom-
        plex.   In Schriften zur Angewandten Seelenkunde, Heft 10.
        1911.
6095.   _____.   A psycho-analytic study of Hamlet.   In Essays in
        Applied Psycho-Analysis.   London: Hogarth, 1923, 1-98.

6096. _____. Strindberg über und Tod. Int Zeitschrift für Psy-
       choanalyse, 1912, 3:55.
6097. Jones, R. E. The Alienated Hero in Modern French Drama.
       Athens: Univ. Georgia Monographs, 1962.
6098. Jones, Robert Emmet. Sexual roles in the works of Tennes-
       see Williams. In Tharpe, J. (ed), Tennessee Williams:
       A Tribute. Hattiesburg: Univ. Mississippi Press, 1977,
       545-557.
6099. Jordan, John O. The sweet face of mothers: psychological
       patterns in Atalanta in Calydon. Victorian Poetry, 1973,
       11:101-114.
6100. Jordan, Robert. Myth and psychology in The Changeling.
       Renaissance Drama, 1970, 3:157-165.
6101. Jorgensen, Paul A. Lear's Self-Discovery. Berkeley: Univ.
       California Press, 1967; London: Cambridge Univ. Press,
       1967.
6102. Josephs, Lois S. The Women of Eugene O'Neill: sex role
       stereotypes. Ball State Univ. Forum, 1973, 14(3):3-8.
6103. Judd, Arnold. How do we judge King Lear? Criticism,
       1972, 14:207-226.
6104. Juliusberger, Otto. Shakespeares Hamlet ein Sexualproblem.
       Neue Generation, 1913, 9:636-641.
6105. Jung, Carl Gustav. Aspects du Drame Contemporain. Gen-
       eva: Georg, 1928; Paris: Colonne Vendôme, 1948.
6106. _____. Foreword to Gilli: The Dark Brother. In Col-
       lected Works of C. G. Jung, Vol. 18. Princeton: Prince-
       ton Univ. Press, 1976, 776-778.
6107. Juretschke, Hans. La estética del emocionalismo y su reper-
       cusión en las teorías sobre el carácter de la tragedia en
       la Alemania del siglo XVIII. Filología Moderna, 1970,
       10:205-224.
6108. Jutrin, M. Le Théâtre de Marivaux: 'une phénoménologie
       du coeur?' Dix-huitième Siècle, 1975, 7:157-179.

6109. Kaester, Otto. Über die Schuld des König Oedipus. In
       Beiträge zur geistigen, Überlieferung. Godesburg: 1947.
6110. Kahn, Coppélia. The Taming of the Shrew: Shakespeare's
       mirror of marriage. Modern Language Studies, 1975,
       5(1); In Diamond, A., & Edwards, L. R. (eds), The Au-
       thority of Experience. Essays in Feminist Criticism.
       Amherst: Univ. Massachusetts Press, 1977, 84-100.
6111. Kahn, Sholom J. Enter Lear mad. Shakespeare Q, 1957,
       8:311-329.
6112. Kahn, Sy. Through a glass menagerie darkly: the world of
       Tennessee Williams. In Taylor, W. E. (ed), Modern
       American Drama, 1968, 71-89.
6113. Kainz, Friedrich. Arthur Schnitzler und Karl Schönherr.
       In Nagl, J., Zeidler, J., & Castle, E. (eds), Deutsch-
       Österreichische Literaturgeschichte. Vienna: 1937.
6114. Kaiser, Hellmuth. Kleist's Prinz von Homburg. Imago,
       1930, 16:119-137.
6115. Kaiser, J. W. Einführung in die Interpretation des Dramas.
       Int Zeitschrift für Individual-Psychologie, 1929, 7:112-124.

6116. Kalkschmidt, Eugen. Hamlet, ein Mutterproblem. März, 1913, 7:573-575.

6117. Kallich, Martin. Oedipus: from man to archetype. Comparative Lit Studies, 1966, 3:33-46.

6118. Kalson, Albert E. Insanity and the rational man in the plays of David Storey. Modern Drama, 1976, 19:111-128.

6119. Kanner, L. A psychiatric study of Ibsen's Peer Gynt. J Abnormal Psychol, 1925, 19:381-386.

6120. Kanter, Victor B. Freud and Shakespeare. Reply to TLS 'Commentary.' Times Lit Supplement, 27 Feb 1969, 210-211.

6121. _____. Freud's reading of Shakespeare. Bulletin British Psychol Soc, 1969, 22(76):225-226.

6122. Kanters, Robert. Théâtre et psychanalyse. Table Ronde, 1956, 108:160-164.

6123. Kanzer, Mark. The central theme in Shakespeare's works. Psychoanal Rev, 1951, 38:1-16.

6124. _____. Imagery in King Lear. Amer Imago, 1965, 22:3-13; In Faber, M. D. (ed), The Design Within. NY: Science House, 1970, 221-231.

6125. _____. The Oedipus trilogy. Psychoanal Q, 1950, 19:561-572; In The Yearbook of Psychoanalysis, Vol. 7. NY: IUP, 1951, 244-253; In Manheim, L., & Manheim, E. (eds), Hidden Patterns, NY: Macmillan, 1966, 66-78.

6126. _____. On interpreting the Oedipus plays. In Muensterberger, W., & Axelrad, S. (eds), The Psychoanalytic Study of Society, Vol. 3. NY: IUP, 1964, 26-38.

6127. _____. The 'passing of the Oedipus complex' in Greek drama. Int J Psycho-Anal, 1948, 29:131-134; In The Yearbook of Psychoanalysis, Vol. 5. NY: IUP, 1949, 306-313; In Ruitenbeek, H. M. (ed), Psychoanalysis and Literature. NY: Dutton, 1964, 243-250.

6128. _____. Shakespeare's dog images--hidden keys to Julius Caesar. Amer Imago, 1979, 36:2-30.

6129. _____. Victor Tausk: analyst and dramatic critic. Amer Imago, 1973, 30:371-379.

6130. Kaplan, Bert. On 'reason in madness' in King Lear. In Bugental, J. F. T. (ed), Challenge of Humanistic Psychology. NY: McGraw-Hill, 1967, 313-318.

6131. Kaplan, Donald M. Character and theatre: psychoanalytic notes on modern realism. Tulane Drama Rev, 1966, 10:93-108.

6132. _____. Homosexuality and the American theater: a psychoanalytic comment. Tulane Drama Rev, 1965, 9(3):25-55.

6133. _____. K. R. Eissler's Discourse on Hamlet. A symposium. Reflections on Eissler's doxaletheic function. Amer Imago, 1972, 29:353-376.

6134. Kaplan, Leo. Zur Psychologie des Tragischen. Imago, 1912, 1:132-157.

6135. _____. Strindberg's The Father analyzed. Psyche & Eros, 1921, 2:215-221.

6136. _____. Der tragische Held und der Verbrecher. Imago, 1915, 4:96-124.

6137. Kaplan, M. B. Equus--a psychiatrist questions his priestly powers. Hastings Center Report, 1975, 5:9-10.

6138. Kaplan, Morton. Dream at Thebes. Lit & Psychol, 1961, 11:12-19.

6139. _____. Fantasy of the 'family romance': Shakespeare's The Tempest. In Kaplan, M., & Kloss, R. J. (eds), The Unspoken Motive. NY: Free Press, 1973, 88-104.

6140. Kapur, Jit L. An Experimental Study of Audience Responses to a Play Rehearsed with and without a Play Analysis by a Professional Psychoanalyst. DA, 1960: 21:265-266.

6141. Karadaghi, Mohamad R. The Theme of Alienation in Eugene O'Neill's Plays. DAI, 1972, 32:5232A.

6142. Karpe, Marietta. The meaning of Barrie's Mary Rose. Int J Psycho-Anal, 1957, 38:408-411.

6143. _____. The origins of Peter Pan. Psychoanal Rev, 1956, 43:104-110.

6144. Katz, Joseph. Faith, reason and art. Amer Scholar, 1952, 21:151-160.

6145. Kaufman, Anthony. Idealization, disillusion and narcissistic rage in Wycherley's The Plain Dealer. Criticism, 1979, 21:119-133.

6146. _____. 'This hard condition of woman's fate': Southerne's The Wives' Excuse. Modern Language Q, 1973, 34:36-47.

6147. _____. Wycherley's The Country Wife and the Don Juan character. Eighteenth-Centuries Studies, 1975-76, 9:216-231.

6148. Kaufman, M. W. Strindberg's historical imagination: Erik XIV. Comparative Drama, 1975-76, 9:318-331.

6149. Kaufman, R. J. Ford's Waste Land: the broken heart. Renaissance Drama, 1970, 3:167-187.

6150. Kauffmann, Stanley. Homosexual drama and its disguises. In Persons of the Drama; Theater Criticism and Comment. NY: Harper & Row, 1976.

6151. Kay, W. B. The Theatre of Jean Mairet: The Metamorphosis of Sensuality. DA, 1966, 26:3955.

6152. Keene, Donald. Dramatic elements in Japanese literature. Comparative Drama, 1976-77, 10:275-297.

6153. Keller, A. C. Death and passion in Racine's Phèdre. Symposium, 1962, 16:190-192.

6154. _____. Error and invention in Racine: Phèdre, IV, 2. Romanic Rev, 1959, 50:99-106.

6155. Kellogg, A. O. The Hamlet of Edwin Booth: a psychological study. Quart J Psychol, 1872, 6:209-220.

6156. _____. Shakespeare's Delineations of Insanity, Imbecility and Suicide. NY: Hurd & Houghton, 1866.

6157. _____. Shakespeare's delineations of mental imbecility as exhibited in his fools and clowns. Amer J Insanity, 1861-62, 18:98-111, 224-236; 1862-63, 19:176-185, 322-332.

6158. _____. Shakespeare's psychological delineations. Amer J Insanity, 1863-64, 20:1-10, 257-270; 1864, 21:1-21.

6159. Kelly, Justin J. Identity and Time: Hamlet, Macbeth, and King Lear. DAI, 1974, 35:2943A.

6160. Kempf, Edward J. The psychology of The Yellow Jacket. Psychoanal Rev, 1917, 4:393-423.

6161. Kennedy, Carroll E. After the Fall: one man's look at his human nature. J Counseling Psychol, 1965, 12:215-216.

6162. Kennedy, H. A. The melancholy of Hamlet. Notes & Queries, 1875, 4:305.

6163. Kern, O. Schiller un seinen Beziehungen zur Psychiatrie. Psychiatrisch-Neurologische Wochenschrift, 1905-06, 7:41-46.

6164. Kernberg, O. F. Adolescent sexuality in the light of group processes. Psychoan Q, 1980, 49:27-47.

6165. Kerr, Walter F. Today's play can't afford to be without a psychiatrist. Los Angeles Times, 13 June 1954, Sec IV, 2.

6166. Keyssar, Helen. Theatre games, language games and Endgame. Theatre J, 1979, 31:221-238.

6167. Kiehl, Bruno. Wiederkehrende Begetenheiten und Verhältnisse in Shakespeares Dramen. Ein Beitrag zur Shakepeare-Psychologie. Berlin: Mayer und Müller, 1904.

6168. Kielholz, Arthur. Tell und Parricida. Psychoanalytische Bewegung, 1931, 3:292-306.

6169. Kimball, Sue L. Games people play in Congreve's The Way of the World. In Kay, D. (ed), A Provision of Human Nature. University: University Alabama Press, 1977, 191-207.

6170. King, S. Carl. Symbolic use of color in Casona's La sirena varada. Romance Notes, 1973, 15:226-229.

6171- Kirby, E. T. Paranoid pseudo community in Pinter's The
2.   Birthday Party. Educational Theatre J, 1978, 30:157-164.

6173. Kirby, Michael. Manifesto of structuralism. Drama Rev, 1975, 19:82-83.

6174. _____. Richard Foreman's ontological-hysteric theatre. Tulane Drama Rev, 1973, 17(2):5-32.

6175. Kirsch, Arthur. The polarization of erotic love in Othello. Modern Language Rev, 1978, 73:721-740.

6176. Kirsch, James. Shakespeare's Royal Self. NY: Putnam, 1966.

6177. Kirschbaum, Leo. Banquo and Edgar. Essays in Criticism, 1957, 7:1-21.

6178. _____. Character and Characterization in Shakespeare. Detroit: Wayne State Univ. Press, 1962.

6179. _____. Hamlet and Ophelia. Philological Q, 1956, 35: 376-393; In Character and Characterization. Detroit: Wayne State Univ. Press, 1962, Ch. 4.

6180. _____. The modern Othello. English Lit History, 1944, 2:283-296.

6181. Kistner, A. L., & Kistner, M. K. Will, fate, and the social order in Women Beware Women. Essays in Lit, 1976, 3:17-31.

6182. Kittang, Atle. The Pretenders: historical vision or psychological tragedy? In Various, Contemporary Approaches to Ibsen. Oslo: Universitetsforlaget, 1977, 78-88.

6183. Klarman, A. Psychological motivation in Grillparzer's Sappho. Monatshefte, 1948, 40:271-278.

6184. Klein, Dennis A. Asi que pasen cinco años: a search for
       sexual identity. J Spanish Studies: Twentieth Century,
       1975, 3:115-123.
6185. Kligerman, Charles. A psychoanalytic study of Pirandello's
       Six Characters in Search of an Author. JAPA, 1962,
       10:731-744.
6186. Kloepfel, Fritz. [Shakespeare, the psychiatrist.] Velhagen
       und Klasings Monatshefte, 1897, 12:111-120.
6187. Klof, Frank S. Strindberg: The Origin of Psychology in
       Modern Drama. NY: Citadel, 1963.
6188. Kluth, Lynn Frederick. The Alienation Motif in Nineteenth
       Century Continental Drama. DA, 1965, 25(8):4863-4.
6189. Knapp, Bettina L. Alchemical brew: from separatio to co-
       agulatio in Yeats's The Only Jealousy of Emer. Educa-
       tional Theatre J, 1978, 30:447-465.
6190. _____. The Dybbuk: the spagyric marriage. J Altered
       States of Consciousness, 1978-79, 4:253-276.
6191. _____. Iphigenia ... a cruelty. Modern Drama, 1969,
       12:260-269.
6192. _____. Jean Racine: Mythos and Renewal in Modern The-
       ater. University: Univ. Alabama Press, 1971.
6193. _____. Maeterlinck's The Blind; or the dying complex.
       Yale Theatre, 1974, 5:79-86.
6194. Knight, George Wilson. The eroticism of Julius Caesar. In
       The Imperial Theme. Further Interpretations of Shake-
       speare's Tragedies Including the Roman Plays. NY:
       Barnes & Noble, 1963, 63-95; London: Methuen, 1954.
6195. _____. Hamlet's melancholia. In The Wheel of Fire.
       London: Oxford Univ. Press, 1930, 19-33; London:
       Methuen, 1949.
6196. _____. The Shakespearean Tempest. London: Methuen,
       1953.
6197. Knights, L. C. Integration in The Winter's Tale. Sewanee
       Rev, 1976, 84:595-613.
6198. _____. Personality and politics in Julius Caesar. Anglica
       (Osaka), 1964, 5:1-24.
6199. _____. Primal scenes of Elsinore. Times Lit Supplement,
       21 Apr 1978, 3968:443.
6200. Knox, Bernard. Clytemnestra on the couch. Times Lit Sup-
       plement, 10 Dec 1976, no. 3900:1534-5.
6201. Knutson, Harold C. Molière: An Archetypal Approach. Tor-
       onto: Univ. Toronto Press, 1976.
6202. _____. Molière, Mauron and myth. L'Esprit Créateur,
       1976, 16:138-148.
6203. Koch, P. Innocent Hippolyte. French Rev, 1970, 43:775-782.
6204. Kocher, Paul. Lady Macbeth and the doctor. Southwestern
       Q, 1954, 5:341-349.
6205. Köhler, Klaus. Psychodiagnose und Gesellschaftsanalyse im
       Bühnenwerk von Tennessee Williams. In Brüning, E.,
       Kohler, K., & Scheller, B. (eds), Studien zum amerikan-
       ischen Drama nach dem zweiten Weltkrieg. Berlin: Rüt-
       ten und Loening, 1977, 54-104.

6206. Kohler, P. Racine et les passions. Etudes de Lettres,
      1939, 139:63-70.
6207. Kolb, Cynthia L. The war in Antony and Cleopatra. Lit &
      Psychol, 1963, 13:63-66.
6208. Kolbe, Frederick C. Shakespeare's Way: A Psychological
      Study. London: Sheed, 1930.
6209. Kommerell, M. Schiller als Psychologe. In Geist und Buch-
      stabe der Dichtung. Frankfurt: 1944, 175-242; In Dame
      Dichterin und andere Essays. Munich: 1967, 65-115.
6210. Konan, Jean. La Foi, comme phénomène psychologique dans
      El condenado por desconfiado. Annales de l'Université
      d'Abidjan, 1974, 7D:139-147.
6211. Konstantinovic, Zoran. Die Schuld und der Frau: Ein Beit-
      rag zur Thematologie der Werke von Max Frisch. In
      Jurgensen, M. (ed), Frisch: Kritik-Thesen-Analysen.
      Bern: Francke, 1977, 145-155.
6212. Koplik, Irwin J. Jung's Psychology in the Plays of O'Neill.
      DA, 1967, 27:3872A.
6213. Kornfield, Lawrence. Conflict and change: the theatre of
      Gertrude Stein. Amer J Psychoanal, 1977, 37:73-82.
6214. Kott, Jan. Hamlet and Orestes. PMLA, 1967, 82:303-313.
6215. _____. Head for maidenhead, maidenhead for head: the
      structure of exchange in Measure for Measure. Theatre
      Q, 1978, 8:18-24.
6216. _____. The vertical axis: the ambiguities of Prometheus.
      Mosaic, 1970, 3:1-26.
6217. Kotte, M. Schillers Malteser--eine homosexuellen Dramen-
      fragment. Zeitschrift für Sexuellwissenschaft, July
      1909.
6218. Kourétas, Demetrios. [Abnormal Characters in the Ancient
      Greek Drama. A Psychoanalytical and Psychological
      Study.] Athens, 1951.
6219. _____. [Abnormal characters in the ancient drama.]
      Athens: 1951; Review: G. Lyketsos, Psychoanal Q,
      1953, 22:110-112.
6220. _____. [Io's Oedipal complex in The Suppliants and the
      Prometheus Bound of Aeschylus.] Rev Française de Psy-
      chanalyse, 1949, 13:445; In Ancient Greek Dramas.
      Athens, 1930.
6221. _____. [The meaning of the Euripides Bacchantes from
      the psychoanalytical point of view.] Aixoni, 1951, July.
6222. _____. La Névrose sexuelle des Danaïdes d'apres les
      Suppliantes d'Eschyle. Rev Français de Psychanalyse,
      1957, 21:597-602.
6223. _____. A psychiatrist looks at Shakespeare's King Lear.
      Paraskenia J, 1938.
6224. _____. [The psychosis in literature.] In [Ancient Greek
      Dramas.] Athens, 1930.
6225. Kovel, Joel. Othello. Amer Imago, 1978, 35:113-119.
6226. Kowzan, Tadeusz. The sign in the theater: an introduction
      to the semiology of the art of the spectacle. Diogenes,
      1968, 61:52-80.

6227. Kozintsev, Grigoril M. Shakespeare: Time and Conscience.
NY: Hill & Wang, 1966.

6228. Kraker, Lester G. La Correspondance de Diderot. Son In-
teret Documentaire, Psychologique, et Littéraire. Doctoral dissertation, Univ. California, 1937.

6229. Kramer, Melinda Gamble. The Suburbs of Hell: Madness,
Cruelty, and Violence in Six Jacobean Tragedies. DAI,
1976, 36:6705A-6A.

6230. Krapf, E. Eduardo. El judío de Shakespeare: una contribucion a la psychología del anti-semitismo. Revista de Psicoanálisis, 1951, 8:173-202.

6231. _____. Shylock and Antonio: a psychoanalytic study of
Shakespeare and antisemitism. Psychoanal Rev, 1955,
42:113-130.

6232. Kreider, Paul V. Elizabethan Comic Character Conventions
as Revealed in the Comedies of George Chapman. Ann
Arbor: Univ. Michigan, 1935.

6233. Krieger, Murray. The dark generations of Richard III.
Criticism, 1959, 1:32-48; In Faber, M. D. (ed), The Design Within. NY: Science House, 1970, 349-366.

6234. Kris, Ernst. Prince Hal's conflict. Psychoanal Q, 1948,
17:487-506; In Psychoanalytic Explorations in Art. NY:
IUP, 1952, 273-290; In Goldberg, G. J., & Goldberg,
N. M. (eds), The Modern Critical Spectrum. Englewood
Cliffs, NJ: Prentice-Hall, 1962, 262-274; In Faber,
M. D. (ed), The Design Within. NY: Science House,
1970, 389-407.

6235. Krutch, Joseph Wood. The American Drama Since 1918.
An Informal History. NY: Braziller, 1939, 1957, 1967,
111-112.

6236. _____. Comedy and Conscience After the Restoration.
NY: Columbia Univ. Press, 1949.

6237. _____. Pirandello and the dissolution of the ego. In
Caputi, A. F. (ed), Modern Drama: Annotated Texts.
NY: Norton, 1966, 1960, 471-492.

6238. Kuehne, A. de. El egoísmo, la frustración y el castigo de
la mujer mexicana en los dramas de Gonzáles Cabellero.
Revista Iberoamericana, 1966, 62:281-288.

6239. Kühne, W. Venus, Amor and Bacchus in Shakespeares Dramen. Eine medizinisch-poetische Studie. Braunschweig:
1902.

6240. Kuritz, Paul Thomas. Transactional Analysis of Character
in Drama for the Actor. DAI, 1978, 38:5130A-31A.

6241. Kuriyama, Constance Brown. Hammer or Anvil. Psychological Patterns in Christopher Marlowe's Plays. New
Brunswick, NJ: Rutgers Univ. Press, 1979; DAI, 1974,
34:7710A.

6242- _____. The Mother of the world: a psychoanalytic inter-
3. pretation of Shakespeare's Antony and Cleopatra. English
Lit Renaissance, 1977, 7:324-351.

6244. Kustow, M. More things in heaven and earth. Plays &
Players, 1976, 23:14-17.

6245. Kwal, Teri Susan. An Experimental Study of Sex as a Factor Influencing Audience Evaluation of Performer Effectiveness and Audience Comprehension of Performance for Selected Dramatic Monologues. DAI, 1977, 37:5443A.

6246. La Belle, Maurice M. Dionysus and despair: the influence of Nietzsche upon O'Neill's drama. Educational Theatre J, 1973, 25:436-442.

6247. Labinger, Andrea G. Time, space and the refracted self in Gorostiza's El nuevo paraíso. Latin American Theatre Rev, 1979, 12:37-41.

6248. Lacan, Jacques. Desire and the interpretation of desire in Hamlet. Yale French Studies, 1977, 55-56:11-52.

6249. Lacant, Jacques. Marivaux en Allemagne: Reflets de son théâtre dans le miroir allemand, Vol. I, L'Accuel. Paris: Klincksieck, 1975.

6250- Lacoue-Labarthe, Philippe. Theatrum analyticum. Glyph,
1. 1977, 2:122-143.

6252. La Forgue, René. Au dela du materialisme du XIX siècle. Psyché, 1952, 7:321-342.

6253. _____. A propos de la pièce de J. P. Sartre Les Main Sales. Psyché, 1948, 3:652-654.

6254. Lähr, H. Die Darstellung krankhafter Geisteszustände in Shakespeares Dramen. Mit ausfürlichen Verzeichnis der einschlägigen Literatur. Stuttgart: Neff, 1898.

6255. Lahr, John. Cracking the Pinter puzzle. Evergreen Rev, 1971, 15(86):74-76.

6256. Laignel-Lavasting, Maxime. Shakespeare psychiatrie. Semaine des Hopitaux de Paris, 1949, 25:1007-1014.

6257. Lambert, P. Réalité et ironie: les jeux de l'illusion dans le théâtre de Marivaux. Fribourg: Université de Fribourg, 1973.

6258. Landmann, S. [On the psychiatric diagnosis process, with particular reference to Hamlet's mental state.] Zeitschrift für Psychologie, 1896, 11:134-152.

6259. Langbaum, Robert Woodrow. Beckett: the self at zero. Georgia Rev, 1976, 30:884-905.

6260. Lantz, K. A. Čexov and the scenka. Slavic & East European J, 1975, 19:377-387.

6261. Lapp, John C. Athalie's dream. Studies in Philosophy, 1954, 51:461-469.

6262. _____. Racine's symbolism. Yale French Studies, 1952, 9:40-45.

6263. _____. Symbolism and Character in Racine. Oberlin: Oberlin College Press, 1949.

6264. _____. Time, space, and symbol in Iphigénie. PMLA, 1951, 66:1023-1032.

6265. _____. The 'traite des passions' and Racine. Modern Language Q, 1942, 111:611-619.

6266. Larimer, Cynthia D. M. A Study of Female Characters in the Eight Plays of Lillian Hellman. DAI, 1971, 31:5410A.

6267.   Laroque, Pierre.   Essai sur l'évolution du 'moi.'   Paris:
        Vigot, 1934.
6268.   Larraya, F. P.   [The maka theater of the Gran Chaco Gual-
        ambra.   Research in transcultural psychiatry.]   Acta
        Physiologica Latinoamericana, 1978, 24:171-200.
6269.   La Rue, Jene A.   Prurience uncovered: the psychology of
        Euripides' Pentheus.   Classical J, 1968, 63:209-214.
6270.   Lasher-Schlitt, Dorothy.   Grillparzers Hero und Leander:
        Eine psychologische Untersuchung.   Jahrbuch der Grill-
        parzer--Gesellschaft, 1960, 3:106-114.
6271.   Lasso de la Vega, José S.   El dolor y la condición humana
        en el teatro de Sófocles.   Asclepio, 1968, 20:3-65.
6272.   _____.   Una interpretación psicológica del mito de Orfeo,
        Eurydice de Anouilh.   Cuadernos Hispanoamericanos,
        1974, no. 284, 267-312.
6273.   Latham, Jacqueline E. M.   Unconscious self-revelation by Gon-
        eril and Regan.   Shakespeare-Jahrbuch, 1977, 113:164-167.
6274.   Laumont, Bernard.   Psychologie d'un évasion: A propos de
        la représentation du Voyageur sans bagages.   Verger,
        1947, no. 3, 29-32.
6275.   Lawinter, Roger.   Diderot et son théâtre: pour une psycho-
        critique formelle.   Temps Modernes, 1968, 23:698-721.
6276.   Lawrence, W. W.   Ophelia's heritage; the influence of the
        sources on Shakespeare.   Modern Language Rev, 1947,
        42:409-416.
6277.   _____.   The phallus on the early English stage.   Psyche
        & Eros, 1921, 2:161-165.
6278.   Lawson, John H.   Modern U. S. dramaturgy.   Inostrannaya
        Literatura, 1962, 1:186-196.
6279.   Lazarsfeld, S.   Did Oedipus have an Oedipus complex?
        Amer J Orthopsychiatry, 1944, 14:226-229.
6280.   Leavis, F. R.   Diabolic intellect and the noble hero: a note
        on Othello.   Scrutiny, 1937, 6:259-283.
6281.   Lebel, Maurice.   Jean Giraudoux et les myths grecs dans le
        théâtre contemporain.   Mosaic, 1969, 2:62-68.
6282.   LeBidois, G.   La Délicatesse dans la tragédie de Racine.
        L'Honneur au miroir de nos lettres, 1919, 210-240.
6283.   Lederer, Herbert.   Die Dramen Lotte Ingrischs.   Modern
        Austrian Lit, 1974, 7(1&2):132-140.
6284.   Lederer, Wolfgang.   Handke's ride.   Chicago Rev, 1974, 26:
        171-176.
6285.   Lederman, Marie Jean.   The Myth of the Dead and Resur-
        rected God in Seven Plays of W. B. Yeats: A Psycho-
        analytic Interpretation.   DA, 1969, 27:1059A.
6286.   Ledgerwood, R.   Measurement of the appeal of performance
        in the theater.   J Applied Psychology, 1932, 16:403-405.
6287.   Lee, Ronald J.   Jungian approach to theater: Shaffer's
        Equus.   Psychol Perspectives, 1977, 8:10-21.
6288.   Leech, Clifford.   The Freudians.   Shakespeare Survey, 1956,
        9:12-13.
6289.   Lefcowitz, Barbara.   The inviolable grove (metamorphosis of
        a symbol in Oedipus at Colonus).   Lit & Psychol, 1967,
        17:78-86.

6290. Legouis, Emile. La Psychologie dans le songe d'une nuit d'été. Etudes Anglaises, 1939, 3:113-117.

6291. Legouis, P. Presentation de la Tempête de Shakespeare. Etudes Anglaises, 1960, 13:260-263.

6292. Le Hir, J. Ombres et reflets temporel dans Iphigénie de Racine. Etudes Classiques, 1967, 34:39-50.

6293. Lehman, Margaret. Eine Interpretation von Ernst Barlachs Dramen Gestutzt auf die Psychologie von C. G. Jung. Doctoral dissertation, New York Univ., 1965.

6294. Leighton, Charles. Alejandro Casona and suicide. Hispania, 1972, 55:436-445.

6295. Leighton, William. The Subjection of Hamlet: An Essay Toward an Explanation of the Motives of Thought and Action of Shakespeare's Prince of Denmark. Philadelphia: Lippincott, 1882.

6296. Leite, Dante Moreira. Hamlet visto por Freud. Occidente, 1964, 127-131.

6297. Le Moigne, M-C. Racine et le bonheur. Annales de Bretagne, 1965, 72:457-461.

6298. Lenormand, Henri Rose. Das Unbewusste im Drama. Almanach, 1926, 39-43.

6299. Leon, Ferdinand. Time, fantasy, and reality in Night of the Iguana. Modern Drama, 1968, 11:87-96.

6300. Lesser, Simon O. Act one, scene one, of Lear. College English, 1970, 32:155-171.

6301. _____. Freud and Hamlet again. Amer Imago, 1955, 12: 207-220.

6302. _____. Macbeth. In Strelka, J. P. (ed), Literary Criticism and Psychology. University Park: Penn State Univ. Press, 1976.

6303. _____. Oedipus the King: the two dramas, the two conflicts. College English, 1967, 29:175-197; College English, 1968, 29:564-569.

6304. _____. Reflections on Pinter's The Birthday Party. Contemporary Lit, 1972, 13:34-43.

6305. _____. Tragedy, comedy and the esthetic experience. Lit & Psychol, 1956, 6:131-139.

6306. Lester, David. Comment on Faber's analysis of Jocasta's suicide in Oedipus Rex. Psychol Reports, 1974, 34:182.

6307. _____. Suicide in Ibsen's plays. Life-Threatening Behavior, 1972, 2:35-41.

6308. Lev, I. D. [The creative legacy of A. P. Chekhov.] Arkhiv Anatomii, Histologii, i Embriologii, 1960, 38:117-122.

6309. Leverenz, David. The woman in Hamlet: an interpersonal view. Signs, 1978, 4:291-308.

6310. Levin, Richard. Mistress Quickly's case. Notes & Queries, n. s., 1966, 13:293.

6311. _____. Sexual equations in the Elizabethan double plot. Lit & Psychol, 1966, 16:2-14.

6312. Levy, Maurice. Albee: un théâtre qui fait peur. Caliban, 1971, 8:151-164.

6313. Lewis, Allan. A Midsummer Night's Dream: fairy fantasy or erotic nightmare? Educational Theater Forum, 1969, 21: 251-258.

6314. Lewis, Theophilus. Freud and the split-level drama. Catholic World, 1958, 187:99-103.
6315. Libby, M. F. Shakespeare and adolescence. Pedagogical Seminary, 1901, 8:163-205.
6316. Libby, Walter. [Shakespeare as a psychologist.] Archeion: Archivio di Storia della Scienza, 1930, 12:282-295.
6317. Libellule, M., fils. Pour une lecture homo/sexuelle de Racine. French Rev, 1976, 49:653-660.
6318. Lichtenberg, Joseph D., & Lichtenberg, Charlotte. Prince Hal's conflict: adolescent idealism and buffoonery. JAPA, 1969, 17:873-887.
6319. Lickorish, John R. The casket scenes from The Merchant of Venice: symbolism or life style. J Individual Psychol, 1969, 25:202-212.
6320. Lidz, Theodore. Hamlet's Enemy. Madness and Myth in Hamlet. NY: Basic Books, 1975; Review: David Willbern, Psychoanal Q, 1978, 47:643-645.
6321. Liemke, Renate. Doppelbödigkeit der Charaktere im Werk Pierre Corneilles. Bern: Lang, 1973.
6322. Lindauer, Martin S. Quantitative analyses of psychoanalytic studies of Shakespeare. J Psychol, 1969, 72:3-9.
6323. Lindbäck, Erland. Hamlet i psykoanalytisk belysning. Skrifter utgivna av Svenska literaturs-allskapet (Studier tillagnade Anton Blanck), 1946, 30:61-79.
6324. Lindemann, Valeska. Raum und Zeit in ihrer Beziehung zur sozialen und psychologischen Thematik in Arnold Weskers Werk. Literatur in Wissenschaft und Unterricht, 1978, 11:161-177.
6325. Lindenbaum, Peter. Time, sexual love, and the uses of pastoral in The Winter's Tale. Modern Language Q, 1972, 33:3-22.
6326. Lindken, Hans-Ulrich. Die Rolle die Kindes in Hofmannsthals Lustpiel Der Unbestechliche. Österreich in Geschichte und Literatur, 1971, 15:32-44.
6327. Lindner, Robert M. The equivalent of matricide. Psychoanal Q, 1948, 17:453-470.
6328. Lindsay, F. W. Néron and Narcisse: a duality resolved. Modern Language Q, 1950, 11:169-179.
6329. Lindsay, Jack. Shakespeare and Tom Thumb. Life & Letters, 1948, 58:119-127.
6330. Lindström, Hans. Hjärnornas kamp. Psykologiska idéer och motiv i Strindbergs attiolalsdiktning. Stockholm: Natur och kultur, 1952.
6331. Lion, F. Les Rêves de Racine. Paris: Laffont, 1948.
6332. Lipscomb, A. A. Psychological study of Hamlet. Methodist Q Rev, 1885, 44:665.
6333. Litowitz, Norman S., & Newman, Kenneth M. Borderline personality and the theatre of the absurd. Archives General Psychiat, 1967, 16:268-280.
6334. Little, M. J. Notes on Ibsen's Peer Gynt. Int J Psychoanal Psychotherapy, 1977, 6:403-414.
6335. Llorca, Raymond L. Macbeth and the use of appetite in tragedy. Silliman J, 1968, 15:151-189.

6336.   Lloyd, James Hendrie.   The so-called Oedipus-complex in
        Hamlet.   JAMA, 1911, 56:1377-1379.
6337.   LoCicero, Vincent.   Schnitzler, O'Neill and reality.   J Int
        Arthur Schnitzler Research Assn, 1965, 4(3):4-26.
6338.   Loeffler, Donald L.   An Analysis of the Treatment of the
        Homosexual Character in Dramas Produced in the New
        York Theatre from 1950 to 1968.   DAI, 1970, 29:4599A;
        NY: Arno, 1975..
6339.   Loening, Richard.   Über die physiologischen Grundlagen der
        Shakespeareschen Psychologie.   Jahrbuch der deutschen
        Shakespeare-Gesellschaft, 1895, 31:1-37.
6340.   Lolli, Giorgio.   Alcoholism and homosexuality in Tennessee
        Williams' Cat on a Hot Tin Roof.   Quart J Studies Al-
        cohol, 1956, 17:543-553.
6341.   Lombroso, Caesare.   Il delinquente e il pazzo nel dramma e
        nel romanzo moderno.   Nuova antologia, 1899, 163:665-
        681.
6342.   Longe, R.   Pirandello tra realismo e mistificazione.   Naples:
        Guida, 1972.
6343.   Lorenz, Emil F.   Oedipus auf Kolonos.   Imago, 1915, 4:22-
        40.
6344.   Lozano, Luis.   Recursos psicológicos de El si de las niñas.
        Explicación de Textos Literarios, 1974, 3:77-83.
6345.   Lundeluis, Ruth.   Tirso's view of women in El burlador de
        Sevilla.   Bulletin of the 'Comediantes, ' 1975, 27:5-14.
6346-   Lundholm, H.   Antony's speech and the psychology of per-
7.   suasion.   Character & Personality, 1938, 6:293-305.
6348.   Lupini, G. M.   Shakespeare e l'Amleto.   Studio critico-psy-
        chologico.   Torino: Roux, Frassati, 1895.
6349.   Lyday, L. F.   Egon Woolf's Los invasores, a play within a
        dream.   Latin-American Theatre Rev, 1973, 6(1):19-26.
6350.   Lynch, William.   The imagination of the drama.   Rev Exis-
        tential Psychol & Psychiat, 1975-76, 14:1-10.
6351.   Lyons, Bridget Gellert.   Iconography of Ophelia.   J English
        Lit Hist, 1977, 44:60-74.
6352.   Lyons, Charles.   The archetypal action of male submission
        in Strindberg's The Father.   Scandinavian Studies, 1964,
        36(3):218-232.
6353.   _____.   The function of dream and reality in John Gabriel
        Borkman.   Scandinavian Studies, 1973, 45:293-309.
6354.   _____.   Henry Ibsen.   The Divided Consciousness.   Car-
        bondale: Southern Illinois Univ. Press, 1972.
6355.   _____.   The psychological base of Arrabal's L'Architecte
        et l'Empereur d'Assyrie.   French Rev, 1972, 45:123-
        136.
6356.   _____.   Some analogies between the epic Brecht and the
        absurdist Beckett.   Comparative Drama, 1967-68, 1:297-
        304.
6357.   _____.   Some variations of Kindermord as dramatic arche-
        type.   Comparative Drama, 1967, 1:56-70.
6358.   Lyons, Clifford.   The complex Oedipus complex of Shake-
        speare's plays.   Shakespeare Newsletter, 1968, 18:40-41.

6359. Lyons, John D. Artaud: intoxication and its double. Yale French Studies, 1974, 50:120-129.

6360. MacBride, R. Quelques réflexiones sur le héros cornélien. XVIIe Siècle, 1974, 104:45-60.

6361. McCauley, Janie Caves. The Function of Child Characters in Shakespeare's Plays. DAI, 1978, 39:2294A-95A.

6362. Maccoby, H. Z. Difficulties in the plot of The Family Reunion. Notes & Queries, 1968, 15:296-302.

6363. McCollom, William G. Tragedy. NY: Macmillan, 1957.

6364. McConaghy, N. Drama and psychiatry: some insights of Euripides. Australian/New Zealand J Psychiat, 1970, 4:109-112.

6365. McCullen, Joseph T., Jr. Brother hate and fratricide in Shakespeare. Shakespeare Q, 1952, 3:335-340.

6366. _____. The function of songs aroused by madness in Elizabethan drama. In Williams, A. (ed), A Tribute to George Coffin Taylor. Durham: Univ. North Carolina, 1952, 185-196; London: Oxford Univ. Press, 1952, 185-196.

6367. _____. The Functions or Uses of Madness in Elizabethan Drama Between 1590 and 1638. Doctoral dissertation, Univ. North Carolina, 1948.

6368. _____. Madness and isolation of character in Elizabethan and early Stuart drama. Studies in Philology, 1951, 48: 206-218.

6369. _____. The Use of Madness in Shakespearean Tragedy for Characterization and for Protection in Satire. Master's thesis, Univ. North Carolina, 1939.

6370. MacCurdy, J. T. Concerning Hamlet and Orestes. J Abnormal Psychol, 1919, 13:250-260.

6371. McDonald, David. The face of absence: a Derridean analysis of Oedipus Rex. Theatre J, 1979, 31:147-161.

6372. _____. Phenomenology of the glance in Long Day's Journey into Night. Theatre J, 1979, 31:343-356.

6373. McDonald, June. The Roles of the Hero: Isolation in Shakespeare's Tragedies of 1600-1606. DA, 1966, 26:5415.

6374. McDonald, Margaret Lamb. The Independent Woman in the Restoration Comedy of Manners. Salzburg: Univ. Salzburg, 1976.

6375. McDonald, Russ. Othello, Thorello, and the problem of the foolish hero. Shakespeare Q, 1979, 30:51-67.

6376. McDonnell, Thomas P. O'Neill's drama of the psyche. Catholic World, 1963, 197:120-125.

6377. McDougal, H. C. Is Hamlet insane? Amer J Surgery & Gynaecology, 1894-95, 5:121-128; Kansas City Medical Index, 1895, 16:69-76.

6378. McFadden, Karen D. George Bernard Shaw and the Woman Question. DAI, 1978, 39:2230A.

6379. McGee, Arthur R. Macbeth and the Furies. Shakespeare Studies, 1966, 19:55-67.

6380. McGeoch, A. Shakespeare the syphilologist. Medical J Australia, 1960, 47:348-350.

6381. McGinnis, Robert M. The image of 'La Belle Dame sans
       Merci' in Wilde's plays. Lit & Psychol, 1968, 18:123-
       134.
6382. McGlinn, Jeanne M. Tennessee Williams' women: illusion
       and reality, sexuality and love. In Tharpe, J. (ed),
       Tennessee Williams: A Tribute. Jackson: Univ. Press
       Mississippi, 1977, 510-524.
6383. McGranahan, Donald V., & Wayne, Ivor. German and Amer-
       ican traits reflected in popular drama. Human Relations,
       1948, 1:429-455.
6384. Macht, David I. A physical and pharmacological appreciation
       of Hamlet, Act I, scene 5, lines 59-73. Bulletin History
       Medicine, 1949, 23:189-194.
6385. Machts, Walter. Das Menschenbild in den Dramen Tennessee
       Williams. Neueren Sprachen, 1962, 10:445-455.
6386. MacInnes, Colin. Hamlet and the ghetto. Encounter, 1960,
       14(5):62-64.
6387. McInness, Edward. Psychological insight and moral aware-
       ness in Grillparzer's Das goldene Vliess. Modern Lan-
       guage Rev, 1980, 75:575-582.
6388. _____. Social insight and tragic feeling in Wagner's Die
       Kindermörderin. New German Studies, 1976, 4:27-38.
6389. _____. The Sturm und Drang and the development of the
       social drama. Deutsche Vierteljahrsschrift für Literatur-
       wissenschaft und Geistesgeschichte, 1972, 46:61-81.
6390. McKendrick, M. La mujer esquiva. Hispanic Rev, 1972,
       40:162-197.
6391. Mackenzie, A. M. The Women in Shakespeare's Plays. NY:
       Doubleday, Page, 1924.
6392. Mackenzie, Henry. Criticism on the character and tragedy
       of Hamlet. Mirror, 18 & 20 Apr 1790, Nos. 99-100,
       397-400.
6393. McKewin, Carole. Shakespeare liberata: Shakespeare, the
       nature of women, and the new feminist criticism. Mo-
       saic, 1977, 10(3):157-164.
6394. McLaughlin, Ann L. The journeys in King Lear. Amer
       Imago, 1972, 29:384-399.
6395. McLaughlin, John J. Cruelty in the Comic: A Study of Ag-
       gression in Drama. DA, 1967, 66-9318.
6396. _____. The dynamics of power in King Lear: an Adlerian
       interpretation. Shakespeare Q, 1978, 29:37-43.
6397. McLees, A. A. Elements of Sartrian philosophy in Electra
       Garrigó. Latin-American Theatre Rev, 1973, 7(1):5-11.
6398. McLenden, Will L. Giradoux and the split personality.
       PMLA, 1958, 73:573-584.
6399. McLeod, Ralph O. The Theater of René Marqués: A Search
       for Identity in Life and in Literature. DAI, 1976, 36:
       6730A.
6400. McLeod, Robert Randall. Thanatos and Eros: An Analysis
       of the Dialectic of Sex and Death in Shakespeare. DAI,
       1978, 39:1553A-54A.
6401. McLeod, Susan H. Duality in The White Devil. Studies in
       English Lit, 1980, 20:271-285.

6402. McMahon, Carol E. Psychosomatic concepts in the works of Shakespeare. J History Behavioral Sciences, 1976, 12: 275-282.

6403. McNamara, L. F. Dramatic convention and the psychological study of character in Othello. Michigan Academy Science, Arts, & Letters, 1962, 47:649-658.

6404. McPeek, James A. S. Richard II and his shadow world. Amer Imago, 1958, 15:195-212; In Faber, M. D. (ed), The Design Within. NY: Science House, 1970, 369-386.

6405. Madsen, Børge Gedsp. The Impact of French Naturalists and Psychologists on August Strindberg's Plays of the 1880's and Early 1890's. DA, 1959, 19:140.

6406. Magakis, George. Greek Tragedies Without Gods: A Psychological Analysis of Character Interaction in Three Modern Plays. DAI, 1974, 35:2409.

6407. Magid, Marion. The innocence of Tennessee Williams. Commentary, 1963, 35:34-43.

6408. Mahlendorf, Ursula R. The wounded self: Kleist's Penthesilea. German Q, 1979, 52:252-272.

6409. Mairet, Philippe. Hamlet, der Neurotiker. Int Zeitschrift für Individual-Psychologie, 1931, 6:424-437.

6410. _____. Hamlet as a study in individual psychology. J Individual Psychol, 1969, 25:71-88.

6411. Maitra, Sitansu. Psychological Realism and Archetypes: The Trickster in Shakespeare. Calcutta: 1967.

6412. Malicet, Michel. L'Image de la femme dans le théâtre de Claudel. Thèse lettres, Univ. Paris, 1977.

6413. _____. La Lecture psychanalytique de l'oeuvre de Claudel: le monde imaginaire. Paris: Les Belles Lettres, 1978.

6414. _____. Lecture psychanalytique de l'oeuvre Claudel. Le Premier théâtre ou le théâtre de l'interdiction. Les Belles Lettres, 1979.

6415. _____. Lecture psychanalytique de l'oeuvre de Claudel. Les Structures dramatiques ou les fantasmes du fils. Paris: Les Belles Lettres, 1979.

6416. _____. La Peur de la femme dans Le Soulier de satin. Rev des Lettres Modernes, 1974, nos. 391-397.

6417. _____. [Le Repos du septième jour.] Rev des Lettres Modernes, 1973, nos. 366-9.

6418. _____. [Trance scenes in Paul Claudel.] Rev des Lettres Modernes, 1971, nos. 217-275.

6419. Malkin, Michael R. Hypnosis, a New View: Implications for Dramatic Theory and Practice. DAI, 1972, 33:3061A.

6420. Mallinckrodt, Frieda. Zur Psychoanalyse der Lady Macbeth. Int Zeitschrift für Psychoanalyse, 1914, 4:612-613.

6421. Mandel, Jerome. Dream and imagination in Shakespeare. Shakespeare Q, 1973, 24:61-68.

6422. Mandelbaum, Bernard. A Comparative Analysis of the Symbolic Structures of Selected Dramatic Renditions of the 'Myth of the Hero.' Doctoral dissertation, New York Univ., 1962.

6423. Manheim, Eleanor B. Pandora's box: persistent fantasies in themes in the plays of Jean Anouilh. Lit & Psychol, 1958, 8:6-10.

6424.   Manheim, Leonard F.   The mythical joys of Shakespeare: or
        what you will.   In Paolucci, A. (ed), Shakespeare En-
        comium.   NY: City College, 1964; In Faber, M. D. (ed),
        The Design Within.   NY: Science House, 1970, 465-478.
6425.   Mann, M.   Zur Charakterologie in Schillers Wallenstein.
        Euphorion, 1969, 63:329-339.
6426.   Mannoni, Octave.   L'Illusion comique ou le théâtre du point de
        vue de l'imaginaire.   In Clefs pour l'Imaginaire ou l'Autre
        Scène.   Paris: Seuil, 1969.
6427.   _____.   Prospero and Caliban.   NY: Praeger, 1956, 97-
        108.
6428.   Maranini, L.   Malheur et sentiments di Andromaque et di
        Pyrrhus.   Rivista di letterature moderne e comparate,
        1957, 10:56-83.
6429.   Marcondes, Durval.   Commentário sôbre a peça Edipo Rei.
        Revista Brasilia de Psicanálisis, 1967, 1:222-223.
6430.   Marder, Louis.   Hamlet: the complex Oedipus complex.
        Shakespeare Newsletter, 1967, 17:36.
6431.   Margitic, M. R.   Essai sur la mythologie du 'Cid. '   Jackson:
        Univ. Mississippi Press, 1976.
6432.   Margoshes, Adam, & Litt, S.   Projective imagery in Shake-
        speare.   J Projective Techniques, 1966, 30:290-292.
6433.   Marie, D.   Paul Claudel 6:   La Première version de La
        Ville.   Rev des Lettres Modernes, 1969, Nos. 209-211.
6434.   Markson, John W.   Tiny Alice; Edward Albee's negative
        Oedipal enigma.   Amer Imago, 1966, 23:3-21.
6435.   Markus, Thomas B.   The psychological universe of Genet.
        Drama Survey, 1964, 3:386-392.
6436.   Marshall, William G.   Madness and Divinity: Wycherley's
        Reflexive Drama.   DAI, 1978, 38:4848A.
6437.   Martin, Graham Dunstan.   Racism in Genet's Les Nègres.
        Modern Language Rev, 1975, 70:517-525.
6438.   Martin, Peter A.   A psychoanalytic study of the Marchallin
        theme from Der Rosenkavalier.   JAPA, 1966, 14:760-
        774.
6439.   Martin, Terence S.   The Protestant Concern with Parent-
        Child Relationships and with the Education of Youth as
        Shown in the Extant Drama of the Period 1532-1576.
        DAI, 1973, 33:5131A-32A.
6440.   Martucci-Vento, M.   Racine et les femmes de son théâtre.
        Palermo: 1911.
6441.   Masson, Raoul.   La Psycho-physiologie du jeune Schiller.
        Etudes germaniques, 1959, 14:363-373.
6442.   Matlaw, Myron.   Eliot the dramatist.   College Language Assn
        J, 1968, 12:116-122.
6443.   Matturro, Richard C.   Shakespeare and Sex: A Comprehen-
        sive Study of Shakespeare's Attitude Toward Sex as Re-
        flected in His Works.   DAI, 1973, 34:1863A-64A.
6444.   Maurens, J.   Noblesse et passion dans le théâtre de Racine.
        Cahiers raciniens, 1957, 1:72-79.
6445.   Mauriac, François.   Le Labyrinthe de Jean Racine.   Figaro
        Littéraire, 2 Jan 1958, 1, 9.
6446.   Maurin, Mario.   D'Oedipe à Anatole France.   Modern Lan-
        guage Notes, 1968, 83:565-576.

6447. Maurois, André. Un psychiatre pour Hamlet. Nouvelle Lit-
       téraires, No. 1838, 22 Nov 1962, 1, 10.
6448. Mauron, Charles. Des Métaphores obsédantes au mythe per-
       sonnel. Introduction à la psychocritique. Paris: Corti,
       1964; L'Information littéraire, 1964, 16:1-8.
6449. _____. Phèdre. Paris: Corti, 1968.
6450. _____. Le Théâtre de Gide: Etude psychocritique. Paris:
       Corti, 1971.
6451. Mauser, Wolfram. Hugo von Hofmannsthal. Konfliktbewälti-
       gung und Werkstruktur. Eine psychosoziologische Inter-
       pretation. Munich: Fink, 1977.
6452. Maxwell, Baldwin. Hamlet's mother. Shakespeare Q, 1914,
       15:247-255.
6453. Mazzaro, Jerome. National and individual psychohistory in
       Robert Lowell's Endecott and the Red Time. Univ. Wind-
       sor Rev, 1972, 8:99-113.
6454. _____. Robert Lowell's The Old Glory: cycle and epi-
       cycle. Western Humanities Rev, 1970, 24:347-358.
6455. Meadows, Arthur. Hamlet, an Essay. Edinburgh: Macla-
       chalan & Stewart, 1871.
6456. Medlicott, R. W. Oedipus. Australian/New Zealand J Psy-
       chiat, 1976, 10:229-236.
6457. Mehnert, Henning. Pirandellos Enrico IV und das Problem
       der multiplen Persönlichkeit. Germanisch-Romanische
       Monatsschrift, 1978, 28:325-335.
6458. Meissner, B. Mythisches und Rationales in der Psychologie
       der Euripideuschen Tragödie. Doctoral dissertation,
       Univ. Göttingen, 1951.
6459. Meister, R. Society and guilt: some ignored aspects of the
       Eichmann case and the Deputy. J Existential Psychiat,
       1964, 4:275-282.
6460. Melián Lafinur, Luis. El 'humour, ' la fantasia, la pasión,
       el crimen y la virtud en Shakespeare. Revista nacional,
       1952, 56:128-145.
6461. Mellamphy, Ninian. Macbeth's visionary dagger: hallucina-
       tion or revelation. English Studies in Canada, 1978, 4:
       379-392.
6462. Melon, J. [A study of the psychopathology of inter-racial
       marriage.] Feuillets Psychiatriques de Liège, 1972, 5:5-
       14.
6463. Meltzer, J. Some psycho-analytical angles on aspects of
       Shakespearean drama. Discussion, (South Africa), 1952,
       1(6):47-50.
6464. Melzer, A. N. Louis Aragon's L'Armoire à glace un beau
       soir: a play of the surrealist époque de sommeil. Com-
       parative Drama, 1977, 11:45-62.
6465. Mendel, Sidney. Hamletian man. Arizona Q, 1960, 16:223-
       236.
6466. _____. The revolt against the father: the adolescent hero
       in Hamlet and The Wild Duck. Essays in Criticism,
       1964, 14:171-178.
6467. Mendes, J. [The plays of Gil Vincente.] Broteria, 1968,
       86:456-475.

6468. Mennen, R. Jerzy Grotowski's paratheatrical projects. Drama Rev, 1975, 19:58-60.
6469. Menninger, C. F. The insanity of Hamlet. Menninger Q, 1952, 6:1-8; J Kansas Medical Society, 1934, 35:334-338.
6470. Mertens, C. J. Alidor, bon ami, mauvant amant. Rev d'Histoire Littéraire de la France, 1972, 72:400-405.
6471. Messenger, Ann P. Blindness and the problem of identity in Pinter's plays. Neueren Sprachen, 1972, 21:481-490.
6472. Metman, Eva. Reflections on Samuel Beckett's plays. J Analytical Psychol, 1960, 5:55-63; In Esslin, M. (ed), Samuel Beckett. Englewood Cliffs, NJ: Prentice-Hall, 1965, 117-139.
6473. Mette, Alexander. Nietzsche's Geburt der Tragödie in psychoanalytischer Beleuchtung. Imago, 1932, 17:67-80.
6474. Metz, Mary S. Existentialism and Inauthenticity in the Theater of Beckett, Ionesco and Genet. DA, 1966, 27:1377-8.
6475. Mewaldt, J. Die tragische Weltanschauung der hellenischen Hochkultur. Forsch und Fortsch, 1934, No. 14.
6476. Meyrowitz, J. The legitimization of Hippolytus. Psychoanal Rev, 1977, 64:531-538.
6477. Midgley, Graham. The Merchant of Venice: a reconsideration. Essays in Criticism, 1960, 10:119-133.
6478. Miething, Christoph. Marivaux Theater, Identitätsprobleme in der Komödie. Munich: Fink, 1975.
6479. Mihalyi, G. Beckett's Godot and the myth of alienation. Modern Drama, 1966-67, 9:277-282.
6480. Miles, John E. The Dream in Seventeenth-Century French Theatre: An Introductory Study of Dream-Sequences, Their Function and Meaning. DAI, 1974, 34:7768A-69A.
6481. Miller, Arthur. The family in modern drama. In Bogard, T., & Oliver, W. I. (eds), Modern Drama; Essays in Criticism. NY: Oxford Univ. Press, 1965, 219-233.
6482. Miller, Joyce. Theatre, communication and mental health. Mental Health & Society, 1974, 1(3-4):197-206.
6483. Miller, Robert Royce. Tragedy in Modern American Drama: The Psychological, Social, and Absurdist Conditions in Historical Perspectives. DAI, 1975, 36:3717A.
6484. Miller, R. S. Contributions to the psychopathology of everyday life. Psychoanal Rev, 1915, 121-151.
6485. Minder, Robert. Le Père et l'image de l'autorité dans la vie et la littérature allemandes: contribution à une psychanalyse nationale. Rev des Lettres Moderne, 1954, 1: 1-15.
6486. Mirek, Roman. [Characters in Shakespeare's tragedies and their personalities.] Przeglad Lekarski, 1967, 23:415-418.
6487. _____. [Dramatic chronicles of Shakespeare in psychiatric evaluation: II.] Przeglad Lekarski, 1967, 23:861-864.
6488. _____. [Eroticism in Shakespeare's comedies.] Przeglad Lekarski, 1969, 25:391-395.
6489. _____. [Personalities of characters in Shakespeare's tragedies: Troilus and Cressida, Coriolanus, Timon of Athens, Pericles, Titus Andronicus, Cymbeline, Romeo and Juliet.] Przeglad Lekarski, 1967, 23:477-480.

6490. _____. [A psychiatrist's insight into Shakespearean comedies.] Przeglad Lekarski, 1968, 24:498-502.
6491. _____. [Shakespeare's chronicles and tragedies in the light of forensic psychiatry.] Przeglad Lekarski, 1969, 25:331-333.
6492. _____. [Shakespeare's Hamlet in the light of literary research and modern psychiatry.] Przeglad Lekarski, 1966, 22:761-765.
6493. _____. [Shakespeare's Tempest: a drama of personality.] Przeglad Lekarski, 1968, 24:721-725.
6494. _____. [Sketches of the personality of figures in Shakespeare's tragedies. I. King Lear and Othello.] Przeglad Lekarski, 1966, 22:557-561.
6495. _____. Sporjrzenie psychiatry na komecie Szekspira. Przeglad Lekarski, 1968, 24:668-672.
6496. _____. [William Shakespeare: dramatist of the sick psyche.] Przeglad Lekarski, 1969, 25:445-448.
6497. Mise, Raymond J. Motivation and ritual again in Julius Caesar. Paunch, 1965, 23:45-57.
6498. Mitchell, Giles, & Wright, Eugene. Duke Ferdinand's lycanthropy as a disguise motive in Webster's The Duchess of Malfi. Lit & Psychol, 1975, 25:117-123.
6499. Mitchell, John D. Applied psychoanalysis in the drama. Amer Imago, 1957, 14:263-280.
6500. _____. The Sanskrit drama Shakuntala: a psychologic sounding board for Hindu culture. Amer Imago, 1959, 16:329-348.
6501. _____, & Schwartz, Emanuel K. A psychoanalytic approach to Kabuki: a study in culture and personality. J Psychol, 1961, 52:269-280.
6502. Mitchell, Marilyn L. William Inge. Amer Imago, 1978, 35:297-310.
6503. Mittman, Barbara G. Ambiguity and unresolved conflict in Diderot's theatre. Eighteenth-Century Studies, 1971-72, 5:270-293.
6504. Moglen, Helene S. Disguise and development: the self and society in Twelfth Night. Lit & Psychol, 1973, 23:13-20.
6505. Mollenhauer, Peter. Wahrnehmung und Wirklichkeitsbewusstsein im Hofmannsthals Reitergeschichte. German Q, 1977, 50:283-297.
6506. Möller, A. Die kunstlerische Schilderung von Geistessörungen im Drama. Psychologie und Medizin, 1929, 3:241-253.
6507. Moloney, James C., & Rockelein, Laurence. A new interpretation of Hamlet. Int J Psycho-Anal, 1949, 30:94-107.
6508. Monaco, M. Racine and the problem of suicide. PMLA, 1955, 70:441-454.
6509. Monner Sans, J. M. Sigmund Freud y le teatro contemporanée. Psiquiatrie et Criminologie, 1942, 7:611-618.
6510. Monterde, Francisco. Un Arquetipo: El Otelo de Shakespeare. Cuedernos de Bellas Artes, 1964, 24-27.
6511. Montgomerie, William. More an antique Roman than a Dane. Hibbert J, 1960, 58:67-77.

6512.   Moorad, George M.   Friedrich Hebbel's Heroes: The Con-
        flict Within the Self.   DAI, 1973, 34:1287A-88A.
6513.   Moore, Gilbert S.   The Theme of Family Disaster in the
        Tragedies of Euripides and Shakespeare.   DA, 1960, 20:
        3731.
6514.   Morcos, Gamila T.   La Psychologie dramatique des person-
        nages féminins dans le théâtre d'Henry Bataille (1896-
        1914).   Thèse, Univ. Paris, 1954.
6515.   Moreau, P.   A propos de l'inceste de Phèdre.   Rev d'His-
        toire Littéraire de France, 1934, 41:404.
6516.   Morgan, C.   The nature of dramatic illusion.   In Essays by
        Divers Hands, Vol. 2.   London: Transactions Royal Soci-
        ety Lit., 1933, 61-77.
6517.   Morgan, Ricki.   The range of emotional states in Pinter's
        Collection.   Educational Theatre J, 1978, 30:165-175.
6518.   Morgann, M.   An essay on the dramatic character of Sir John
        Falstaff.   In Smith, D. N. (ed), Shakespeare Criticism:
        A Selection.   London: Oxford Univ. Press, 1954, 171-
        172.
6519.   Morissey, LeRoy John.   The Erotic Pursuit: Changing Fa-
        shions in Eroticism in Early Eighteenth-Century English
        Comic Drama.   DA, 1965, 25:4153-54.
6520.   Morpurgo, Enrico.   I Sei Personaggi in Cerca Autore di Pir-
        andello.   Archivio Generale di Neurologie, Psichiatria e
        Psicoanalisti, 1930, 11:134-139.
6521.   Morrell, Roy.   The psychology of tragic pleasure.   In Cor-
        rigan, R. (ed), Tragedy: Vision and Form.   San Fran-
        cisco: Chandler, 1965; Essays in Criticism, 1956, 6:22-
        37.
6522.   Morris, H.   Ophelia's 'Bonny Sweet Robin.'   PMLA, 1958,
        73:601-603.
6523.   Morrison, Kristin.   Defeated sexuality in the plays and novels
        of Samuel Beckett.   Comparative Drama, 1980, 14:18-34.
6524.   _____.   Pinter, Albee, and 'The Maiden in the Shark
        Pond.'   Amer Imago, 1978, 35:259-274.
6525.   Moses, Robbie.   The Theme of Death in the Plays of Edward
        Albee.   DAI, 1975, 35:4443-44.
6526.   Mott, F. J.   Drama and the evocation of unconscious images.
        J Clinical Psychopathology & Psychotherapy, 1946, 7:783-
        793.
6527.   Mould, William.   Jocaste: mother of evil.   L'Esprit créateur,
        1968, 8:129-137.
6528.   Moureaux, José-Michel.   'L'Oedipe' de Voltaire.   Introduc-
        tion à une psycholecture.   Paris: Lettres Modernes,
        1973.
6529.   Mourgues, O. De.   Racine, or the Triumph of Relevance.
        London: Cambridge Univ. Press, 1967.
6530.   Movassaghi, Mazie B.   The Role of Women in the French
        Baroque Theater.   DAI, 1978, 39:1623A.
6531.   Mowat, Barbara A.   Images of woman in Shakespeare's
        plays.   Southern Humanities Rev, 1977, 11:145-157.
6532.   Mudford, P. G.   The artistic consistency of Browning's In a
        Balcony.   Victorian Poetry, 1969, 7:31-40.

6533.   Mueller, Carl R.   Jungian analysis.   Drama Rev, 1978, 22:
        73-86.
6534.   Muir, Kenneth.   Image and symbol in Macbeth.   Shakespeare
        Survey, 1966, 19:45-54.
6535.   _____.   The jealousy of Iago.   English Miscellany, 1951,
        2:65-83.
6536.   _____.   Madness in King Lear.   Shakespeare Survey,
        1960, 13:72-80.
6537.   _____.   Shakespeare: Hamlet.   London: Arnold, 1963.
6538.   _____.   Some Freudian interpretations of Shakespeare.
        Proceedings Leeds Philosophical Lit Society, 1952, 7:43-
        52; In The Singularity of Shakespeare, and Other Essays.
        NY: Barnes & Noble, 1977, 110-123.
6539.   Müller, J.   Virwirrung des Gefühls: der Begriff des Patho-
        logischen im Drama Goethes und Kleists mit einem Ex-
        kurs: Zur dichterischen Pathographie in Drama des 19.
        Jahrhunderts.   Berlin: Akadamie, 1974.
6540.   Müller-Freienfels, Reinhart.   Das Lebensgefühl in Arthur
        Schnitzlers Dramen.   Doctoral dissertation, Frankfurt,
        1954.
6541.   Murray, Gilbert.   Hamlet and Orestes: A Study in Tradi-
        tional Types.   NY: Oxford Univ. Press, 1914.
6542.   Mutebi, R. G.   Dramatization of the human psychology, Dhana
        (Kampala & Nairobi), 1975, 5(1):42-45.

6543.   Nakano, Yoshio.   Shakespeare's psychological techniques.
        Rising Generation, 1947, 93, No. 1.
6544.   Nakhjavani, Bahiyyih.   The Voyeur in Epyllia of the 1590's,
        'Rage of lust by gazing qualified. '   DAI, 1978, 39:298A.
6545.   Napiorkowska, Krystyna.   Language as an aspect of the
        search for identity in Harold Pinter's The Homecoming.
        Studia Anglica Posaniensia, 1976, 8:151-156.
6546.   Narkin, Anthony P.   Day-residue and Christian reference in
        Clarence's dream.   Texas Studies Lit & Language, 1967,
        9:147-150.
6547.   Nash, William A.   The Homecoming Motif in Selected Works
        by Eugene O'Neill.   DAI, 1975, 36:4116.
6548.   Natadze, R.   On the psychological nature of stage impersona-
        tion.   British J Psychol, 1962, 53:421-429.
6549.   Natanson, W.   Psychologiczne Problemy Otella.   Teatr, 11
        Aug 1956, 13-14.
6550.   Neglia, Erminio G.   La escenificación del fluir psiquico en
        teatro hispanoamericano.   Hispania, 1975, 58:884-889.
6551.   Neiditz, Minerva H.   Banishment: Separation and Loss in
        the Later Plays of Shakespeare.   DAI, 1974, 35:2235A.
6552.   _____.   Primary process mentation and the structure of
        Timon of Athens.   Hartford Studies in Lit, 1979, 11:24-
        35.
6553.   Neill, Michael.   Shakespeare's hall of mirrors: play, poli-
        tics and psychology in Richard III.   Shakespeare Studies,
        1975, 8:99-129.

6554. Nelson, Benjamin F. Actors, directors, roles, cues, meanings, identities: further thoughts on 'anomie.' Psychoanal Rev, 1964, 51:135-160.

6555. _____. Avant-garde dramatists from Ibsen to Ionesco. Psychoanal Rev, 1968, 55:505-512.

6556. _____. The Balcony and Parisian existentialism. Tulane Drama Rev, 1963, 7(3):60-79.

6557. Nelson, Cary. Prospero's island: the visionary body of The Tempest. In The Incarnate Word: Literature as Verbal Space. Urbana: Univ. Illinois Press, 1973, 53-75.

6558. Nelson, C. E. Politics and passion in Phèdre. French Rev, 1966, 39:22-35.

6559. _____. The Tragedy of Power in Racine and Shakespeare. DA, 1964, 25:2985-2986.

6560. Nelson, Donald F. To live or not to live; notes on archetypes and the absurd in Borchert's Draussen vor der Tür. German Q, 1975, 48:343-354.

6561. Nelson, I. La Sottie sans souci, essai d'interprétation homosexuelle. Paris: Champion, 1977.

6562. Nethercot, Arthur H. Madness in the plays of Eugene O'Neill. Modern Drama, 1975, 18:259-279.

6563. _____. O'Neill on Freudianism. Saturday Rev Lit, 1932, 8:759.

6564. _____. O'Neill's More Stately Mansions. Educational Theatre J, 1975, 27:161-169.

6565. _____. The psychoanalyzing of Eugene O'Neill. Modern Drama, 1960, 3:242-256; 1961, 4:357-372.

6566. _____. The schizophrenia of Bernard Shaw. Amer Scholar, 1952, 21:455-467.

6567. Neumann, H. Phaedra's death in Euripides and Racine: moral responsibility in closed and open societies. Cithara, 1966, 6(2):22-32.

6568. Neumarkt, Paul. The Amphitryon legend in Molière, Dryden, Kleist, Giradoux and Kaiser. Amer Imago, 1977, 34:357-373.

6569. _____. Hauptmann's And Pippa Dances and Victor Tausk's commentary. Amer Imago, 1973, 30:360-370.

6570. Newberry, Wilma. Echegary and Pirandello. PMLA, 1966, 81:123-129.

6571. Nicholson, Brinsley. Was Hamlet mad? Transactions of New Shakespeare Society, 1880-1886, 341-369.

6572. Nickles, Mary A. The Women in Congreve's Comedies: Characters and Caricatures. DAI, 1973, 33:6321A-22A.

6573. Nicolich, Robert N. Door, window, and balcony in L'Ecole des femmes. Romance Notes, 1971, 12:364-369.

6574. Nicoll, Allardyce. The drama of the individual. In World Drama; From Aeschylus to Anouilh. NY: Barnes & Noble, 1976 (1949), 654-673.

6575. _____. Strindberg and the play of the subconscious. In World Drama; From Aeschylus to Anouilh. NY: Barnes & Noble, 1976 (1949), 460-474.

6576. Nietsch, E. Das Menschenbild bei William Shakespeare. Psychologische Hefte der Siemens-Studien-Gesellschaft für praktische Psychologie, 1957, 12:351-354.

6577. Nilan, Mary M. Albee's The Zoo Story: alienated man and
       the nature of love. Modern Drama, 1973, 16:55-59.
6578. Nissen, I. Das psychologische Problem in Ibsens Rosmer-
       sholm. Int Zeitschrift für Individual-Psychologie, 1931,
       9:132-136.
6579. _____. Sjelelige kriser i menneskens liv. Hendrik Ibsen
       og den moderne psykologi. Oslo: Aschehoug, 1931.
6580. _____. Vildanden-Rosmersholm-Hedda Gabler. Oslo:
       Aschehoug, 1973.
6581. Nobile, C. Un paranoico omicida: Enrico IV, di Pirandello.
       Minerva Medicin, 1965, 56:183-191.
6582. Noland, Richard W. Psychoanalysis and Hamlet. Hartford
       Studies in Lit, 1974, 6:268-281.
6583. _____. The theory of the crisis of generativity in Sopho-
       cles' Oedipus the King. Hartford Studies in Lit, 1979,
       11:83-93.
6584. Nonyama, Minako. La personalidad en los dramas de Buero
       Vallejo y de Unamuno. Hispanófila, 1973, 49:69-78.
6585. Norris, Margot. Myth and neurosis in Ibsen's mature plays.
       Comparative Drama, 1976, 10:3-15.
6586. Norton, Rictor Carl. Folklore and myth in Who's Afraid of
       Virginia Woolf? Renascence, 1971, 23:159-167.
6587. Novak, Sigrid G. Images of Womanhood in the Works of Ger-
       man Female Dramatists: 1892-1918. DAI, 1974, 34:
       4276A-77A.
6588. Novikov, N. V. [Man and the ideology of consumption.]
       Voprosy Filosofii, 1968, 22(4):125-136.
6589. Novy, M. L. And you smile not, he's gagged: mutuality in
       Shakespearean comedy. Philological Q, 1976, 55:178-194.
6590. Nussbaum, Laureen Klein. The Image of Woman in the Work
       of Bertolt Brecht. DAI, 1977, 38:1426A.
6591. Nuttall, Anthony D. Two Concepts of Allegory: A Study of
       Shakespeare's The Tempest and the Logic of Allegorical
       Expression. NY: Barnes & Noble, 1967.

6592. Obermayer, August. Die Topoi und ihre psychologische Dif-
       ferenzierung in den Dramen Grillparzers. Jahrbuch der
       Grillparzer-Gesellschaft, 1970, 8:57-85.
6593. O'Connor, Patricia W. A Spanish precursor to women's lib:
       the heroine in G. Martínez Sierra's theatre. Hispania,
       1972, 55:865-875.
6594. Oczeret, Herbert. Das Hamlet-Problem und die Psycho-
       analyse. Frankfurter Zeitung, No. 65, 6 March 1914.
6595. O'Donnell, Beatrice. Synge and O'Casey Women: A Study
       in Strong-Mindedness. DAI, 1976, 37:699A-700A.
6596. Offenbacher, Emil. A contribution to the origin of Strind-
       berg's Miss Julia. Psychoanal Rev, 1944, 31:81-87.
6597. Ofrat, Gideon. The structure of ritual and mythos in the na-
       turalistic plays of August Strindberg. Theatre Research
       Int, 1979, 4:102-117.
6598. Ogdon, J. A. H. An Examination of Imagery and Libido Sym-
       bolism in Certain Literary Works. Master's thesis,
       Univ. Liverpool, 1956.

6599. Ohtski, Kenji. Analytische Würdigung von Shakespeares Hamlet. Tokyo Zeitschrift für Psychoanalyse, 1938, 6(2).

6600. Olaru, Alexandru. Shakespeare si psihiatria dramatică. Craiova, Romania: Scrisul românesc, 1976.

6601. Oldcorn, A. Pirandello o del candore? Modern Language Notes, 1976, 91:139-149.

6602. Olga, M. M. Le Confident dans la tragédie de Racine. Rev de l'Université de Laval, 1953-54, 8:59-81.

6603. Oliver, Roger W. Dreams of Passion: The Theater of Luigi Pirandello. NY: New York Univ. Press, 1979.

6604. Ollén, G. Ett Drömspel. Svensk Litteraturtidskrift, 1964, 27(1).

6605. Olson, Elder. Emotion, fiction and belief. In Tragedy and the Theory of Drama. Detroit: Wayne State Univ. Press, 1966, 127-147.

6606. O'Neill, John H. Sexuality, deviance, and moral character in the personal satire of the Restoration. Eighteenth-Century Life, 1975, 2:16-19.

6607. Onimus, Ernest. La Psychologie dans les drames de Shakespeare. Paris: 1876; Rev des deux mondes, 1876, 14: 635-657.

6608. Ophuijsen, J. H. W. Van. De psychoanalyticus ten tooneele gevoerd. Nederlandsch Tijdschrift voor Geneeskunde, 1918, 2:1118.

6609. Oppel, Horst (ed). Das moderne englische Drama. Interpretationen. Berlin: Schmidt, 1963.

6610. _____. Zur Problematik des Willenkampfes bei Shakespeare. Shakespeare Jahrbuch, 1953, 89:72-105.

6611. Orange, Linwood E. Hamlet's mad soliloquy. South Atlantic Q, 1965, 64:60-71.

6612. Orbison, Tucker. 'This distracted' globe: self in Hamlet. In Holzberger, W. G., & Waldeck, P. B. (eds), Perspectives on Hamlet. Lewisburg, Pa: Bucknell Univ. Press, 1975, 112-141.

6613. Orgel, Shelley. Iago. Amer Imago, 1968, 25:258-273.

6614. _____, & Shengold, Leonard L. The fatal gifts of Medea. Int J Psycho-Anal, 1968, 49:379-385.

6615. Oriven, G. Tartuffe reconsidered. French Rev, 1968, 41: 611-617.

6616. Orlando, Francesco. Lettura freudiana della Phèdre. Paris: Coll. Ricerca letteraria, 1971.

6617. _____. Toward a Freudian Theory of Literature with an Analysis of Racine's 'Phèdre.' Baltimore: Johns Hopkins Univ. Press, 1978; Review: Bettina L. Knapp, Nineteenth-Century French Studies, 1979-80, 8(1-2):120-122.

6618. Orley, Ray. The Separated Self: Alienation as a Major Theme in the Plays of John Osborne, Arnold Wesker, and Harold Pinter. DAI, 1977, 37:5445A.

6619. Orringer, Nelson R. Absence of color: its erotic connotations in the Divan del Tamarit. García Lorca Rev, 1975, 3:57-66.

6620. Osherson, Samuel. An Adlerian approach to Goethe's Faust. J Individual Psychol, 1965, 21:194-198.

6621. Oster, Rose-Marie G.   Do we dead awaken? Ibsen as social
      psychologist. Educational Theatre J, 1970, 22:387-396.
6622. Otsuki, Kenji. [Psychoanalytic Insight of the Poet Shake-
      speare: Analytic Appreciation of His Five Great Trage-
      dies.] Tokyo: Sozobunkasha, 1974.
6623. Ottenbacher, E.   A contribution to the origin of Strindberg's
      Miss Julie. Psychoanal Rev, 1944, 3(1):81-87.
6624. Overbeek, W. N.   Massapsychologische onderzoekingen in een
      volktheater. Mensch en Maatschappij, 1939, 15:1-21,
      129-147.
6625. Overholser, Winifred.   Shakespeare's psychiatry--and after.
      Shakespeare Q, 1959, 10:335-352.
6626. Oxenhandler, Neal.   Le Mythe de la persécution dans l'oeuvre
      de Jean Cocteau. Rev des Lettres Modernes, 1972, Nos.
      298-303, 91-107.

6627. Padel, J. H.   Analyst at Elsinore. Times Lit Supplement,
      4 June 1976, no. 3873:667.
6628. Pagnol, M.   Le Plus grand rôle de tous les temps: Hamlet.
      In Shakespeare. Paris: Hachette, 1962, 275-280.
6629. Pallerés Navarro, Mariano.   Algunos aspectos sexuales en
      tres obras de Tirso de Molina. Kentucky Romance Q,
      1972, 19:3-15.
6630. Palley, Julian.   Archetypal symbols in Bodas de sangre.
      Hispania, 1967, 50:74-79.
6631. _____.   'Si fue mi maestro un sueño': Segismundo's
      dream. Kentucky Romance Q, 1976, 23:149-162.
6632. Palmer, J. F.   Hamlet: a study of melancholia. Medical
      Magazine, 1911, 20:396-411.
6633. _____.   Jealous madness: Leontes, Othello and posthumous
      Leonatus. Medical Magazine, 1913, 22:661-665; 1914,
      23:41-48, 165-173.
6634. _____.   Lady Macbeth: a short study in certain subcon-
      scious states. Medical Magazine, 1912, 568-571.
6635. _____.   Macbeth: a study in monomania. Medical Maga-
      zine, 1910, 19:577-584.
6636. _____.   Ophelia: a short study in acute delirious mania.
      Medical Magazine, 1911, 20:396-411; 1912, 21:448-453.
6637. Palmer, Richard E.   Existentialism in T. S. Eliot's The Fam-
      ily Reunion. Modern Drama, 1962, 5:174-186.
6638. Palmieri, V. M.   [Report of a medico-legal assessment of the
      state of mind of Othello.] Annali di Neuropsichiatria e
      Psiconanalisi, 1955, 2:81-92.
6639. Palomo, Dolores J.   The Syntax of Revenge: A Structuralist
      Reading of English Revenge Drama. DAI, 1972, 33:732-A.
6640. Pam, D. S.   The murderer, the women's hope. Drama Rev,
      1975, 19:5-12.
6641. Pannenborg, W. A.   Beitrag zur Psychologie der tragischen
      Dramatiker. The Hague: Nijhoff, 1939.
6642. Paolozzi, Gabriel J.   The Psychological Struggle and the
      Scene of Persuasion in Jean Rotrou's Plays, 1628-1649.
      Doctoral dissertation, Univ. Southern California, 1951.

6643. Papenhausen, Richard W., Jr. Identity and Sexuality in Ben Jonson: A Psychoanalytic Reading of Three Comedies and a Masque. DAI, 1974, 35:1631A.

6644. Parcells, Frank H., & Segel, Nathan P. Oedipus and the prodigal son. Psychoanal Q, 1959, 28:213-227.

6645. Pargeter, Hilda. Woman Versus Man: A Study of the Relationships and Differences Between the Sexes as a Source of Tragedy in the Life and Chief Dramas of Friedrich Hebbel. Master's thesis, Birmingham Univ., 1951.

6646. Paris, Jean. Hamlet and his brothers. Theatre Annual, 1969, 25:61-79.

6647. Paris, Bernard J. Hamlet and his problems: a Horneyan analysis. Centennial Rev, 1977, 21:36-66.

6648. Parker, Alexander A. The father-son conflict in the dramas of Calderón. Forum for Modern Language Studies, 1966, 2:99-113.

6649. Parr, James E. On fate, suicide, and free will in Alarćon's El dueño de las estrellas. Hispanic Rev, 1974, 42:199-207.

6650. Partridge, Eric. Shakespeare's Bawdy: A Literary and Psychological Essay and a Comprehensive Glossary. London: Routledge & Kegan Paul, 1947, 1969; NY: Dutton, 1948, 1960.

6651. Paschall, Dorothy M. The Vocabulary of Mental Aberration in Roman Comedy and Petronius. Philadelphia: Linguistic Society of America, 1939.

6652. Pasles, Christopher. Pathological Communications in Hamlet: A Systems Analysis of Shakespeare's Tragedy. DAI, 1977, 38:811A.

6653. Passage, Charles E. E. T. A. Hoffmann's The Devil's Elixers: a flawed masterpiece. J English & Germanic Philology, 1976, 75:531-545.

6654. Patrick, Robert. Gay analysis. Drama Rev, 1978, 22:67-72.

6655. Paul, Louis. A game analysis of Albee's Who's Afraid of Virginia Woolf?: the core of grief. Lit & Psychol, 1967, 17:47-51.

6656. Paulhan, F. Racine et la maîtrisse de soir. Rev Universelle, 1926, 27:177-195.

6657. Paulissen, Mary N. Richard Steele's The Conscious Lovers: the use of the Doppelgänger. Amer Imago, 1978, 35: 419-430.

6658. Paulsen, Wolfgang. Die Funktion der Frau in den Komödien der DDR. In Die deutsche Komödie im zwanzigten Jahrhunderts. Heidelberg: Stiehm, 1976.

6659. Pauncz, Arpad. The concept of adult libido and the Lear complex. Amer J Psychotherapy, 1951, 5:187-195.

6660. _____. The Lear complex in world literature. Amer Imago, 1954, 11:51-83.

6661. _____. Der Learkomplex, die Kehrseite des Oedipuskomplexes. Zentralblatt für die gesamte Neurologie und Psychiatrie, 1932, 143:294-332.

6662. _____. Psychopathology of Shakespeare's King Lear: ex-
emplification of the Lear complex (a new interpretation).
Amer Imago, 1952, 9:57-77.

6663. Payne, Michael. Phenomenological criticism of Shakespeare.
Shakespearean Research Opportunities, 1972-74, 7-8:75-
77.

6664. _____. What's the matter with Hamlet? In Holzberger,
W. G., & Waldeck, P. B. (eds), Perspectives on Hamlet.
Lewisburg, Pa: Bucknell Univ. Press, 1975, 100-111.

6665. Pearlman, E. Shakespeare, Freud, and the two usuries, or,
money's a meddler. English Library Renaissance, 1972,
2:217-236.

6666. Peavy, Charles D. Myth, magic, and manhood in Leroi
Jones' Madheart. Studies in Black Lit, 1970, 1(2):12-20.

6667. Peck, M. W. A psychiatrist views the drama. Psychoanal
Rev, 1935, 22:306-313.

6668. Peck, Russell A. Edgar's pilgrimage: high comedy in King
Lear. Studies in English Lit, 1967, 7:219-237.

6669. Pedrini, Duilio T., & Gregory, Luria N. Hamlet's character:
the quest of literary analysis. J Amer Academy Psychoanal, 1973, 1:417-427.

6670. Peers, Edgar A. Elizabethan Drama and Its Mad Folk.
Cambridge: 1914.

6671. Pellegrino, Hélió. El mito y el complejo de edipo en la obra
Sofocles: une revaluación. Revista di Psicoanalisi, 1961,
18:123-132; Versuch einer New-Interpretierung der Ödipussage. Psyche, 1961, 15:475-485.

6672. Pérez, Carlos A. Verosimilitud psicológica de El condendo
por desconfiado. Hispanófila, 1966, No. 72, 1-21.

6673. Perret, Marion. A hair of the shrew. Hartford Studies in
Lit, 1979, 11:36-40.

6674. Perry, Ruth. Madness in Euripides, Shakespeare, and Kafka:
an examination of The Bacchae, Hamlet, King Lear and
The Castle. Psychoanal Rev, 1978, 65:253-279.

6675. Petit, Jacques (ed). Paul Claudel 8: Le Double. [Entire
issue.] Rev des Lettres Modernes, 1971, Nos. 271-275.

6676. _____. Paul Claudel: Le Double. Rev des Lettres Modernes, 1972, Nos. 310-314, 117-138.

6677. Petitt, William. The Psychology of Tragic Drama. London/
Boston: Routledge & Kegan Paul, 1975.

6678. Peyre, Henri. Shakespeare's women--a French view. Yale
French Studies, 1964, 33, 107-119.

6679. _____. The tragedy of passion: Racine's Phèdre. In
Tragic Themes in Western Literature. New Haven:
Brooks, 1955.

6680. Pfefferkorn, Eli. A touch of madness in the plays of A. B.
Yehoshua. World Lit Today, 1977, 51:198-200.

6681. Pfeifer, Sigmund. Königen Mab. Int Zeitschrift für Psychoanalyse, 1923, 9:357-368.

6682. Pfleiderer, Wolfgang. Hamlet and Ophelia. Eine psychologische Studie. Neue Shakespeare Bühne, 1908, 6:1-95.

6683. Pieterse, Cosmo. Shakespeare's blacks, Moors, black-
amoors, etc. Ba Shiru, 1973, 4(2):45-62.

6684. Pihan, Y. La Poétique du silence chez Racine. <u>Cahiers</u> <u>raciniens,</u> 1964, 16:41-55.
6685. Pilikian, H.I. Racine's <u>Phèdre</u>. <u>Drama,</u> 1975, 119:30-39.
6686. Piltch, Ziva S. From cosmology to psychology: the transformation of Acedia in the medieval morality play. <u>Centerpoint,</u> 1974, 1(1):17-23.
6687. Pinder, Donna. The normalcy of suffering and artistic survival. <u>Paunch,</u> 1974, 38:66-78.
6688. Pira, G. Eugene O'Neill, <u>Where the Cross Is Made</u>: Versuch einer Interpretation. <u>Neueren Sprachen,</u> 1960, 4: 179-182.
6689. Place, Mary Elizabeth. The Characterization of Women in the Plays of Frank Wedekind. <u>DAI,</u> 1977, 38:1427A.
6690. Plaisance, M. Censure et castration dans la dernière comédie de Lasca. In <u>Culture et Marginalités au XVIe siècle</u>. Paris: Université de Paris, 1973.
6691. Plank, Robert. Hamlet and Prospero: father figures. In <u>The Emotional Significance of Imaginary Beings</u>. Springfield, Ill: Thomas, 1968, 147-171.
6692. Plant, Richard. Gessler and Tell: psychological patterns in Schiller's <u>Wilhelm Tell</u>. <u>Modern Language Q,</u> 1958, 19: 62-70.
6693. Plard, Henri. Max Frisch, un théâtre de l'aliénation. <u>Rev</u> <u>générale Belge,</u> 1964, No. 2, 1-28.
6694. Platt, Joseph. The Maternal Theme in García Lorca's Folk Tragedies. <u>DAI,</u> 1973, 34:787A-88A.
6695. Plewa, Franz. Shakespeare und die Macht. <u>Int Zeitschrift</u> <u>für Individual-Psychologie,</u> 1936, 14:26-36.
6696. Plokker, J.H. Salome. Contribution to the psychoanalysis of a character of Oscar Wilde. <u>Nederlandsch Tijdschrift</u> <u>voor de Psychologie,</u> 1940, 7:449-462.
6697. Plummer, Scott H. Transactions, Games and Scripts in Molière's Theater: A Selective Transactional Interpretation. <u>DAI,</u> 1974, 35:2237A.
6698. Podol, Peter L. The psychological origins and the sociological dimension of the grotesque in the works of Fernando Arrabal. <u>Estreno,</u> 1976, 2(1):21-26.
6699. Poerschke, Karl. <u>Das Theaterpublikum im Lichte der Soziologie und Psychologie</u>. Emsdetten: Lechte, 1951.
6700. Politzer, Heinz. Arthur Schnitzler: the poetry of psychology. <u>Modern Language Notes,</u> 1963, 78:353-372.
6701. _____. Hugo von Hofmannsthals <u>Elektra</u>. Geburt der Tragödie aus dem Geiste der Psychopathologie. <u>Deutsche</u> <u>Vierteljahrsschrift für Literaturwissenschaft und Geistesgeschichte,</u> 1973, 47:95-119.
6702. _____. Kleists Trauerspiel vom Traum: <u>Prinz Friedrich</u> <u>von Homburg</u>. <u>Euphorion,</u> 1970, 64:200-220.
6703. _____. Oedipus und Kolonus. Versuch über eine Gemeinsamkeit von Psychoanalyse und Literaturkritik. <u>Psyche,</u> 1972, 26:489-519.
6704. Pollin, Burton R. 'Hamlet, ' a successful suicide. <u>Shakespeare Studies,</u> 1965, 1:240-260.

6705. Pomeau, René. La Surprise et le masque dans le théâtre de Marivaux. In Barber, W., et al. (eds), Studies Presented to Theodore Besterman. Edinburgh: Oliver & Boyd, 1967, 238-251.

6706. Pönitz, Karl. Shakespeare und die Psychiatrie. Therapie der Gegenwart, 1964, 103:1463-1478.

6707. Poole, A. Total disaster: Euripides' The Trojan Women. Arion, 1976, 3:257-287.

6708. Popovich, Helen. Shelf of dolls: a modern view of Ibsen's emancipated women. CEA Critic, 1977, 39(3):4-8.

6709. Porter, Thomas E. Puritan ego and Freudian unconscious. In Myth and Modern American Drama. Detroit: Wayne State Univ. Press, 1969, 26-52.

6710. Posen, Robert. A Freudian in the French theatre. H.-R. Lenormand. Lit & Psychol, 1975, 25:137-146.

6711. Post, Robert M. Fear itself: Edward Albee's A Delicate Balance. College English Assn J, 1969, 13:163-171.

6712. Postlewait, Thomas. Self-performing voices: mind, memory, and time in Beckett's drama. Twentieth Century Literature, 1978, 24:473-491.

6713. Potkay, Charles R., Jackson, Erwin D., & McTeague, James N. Whodunit? Audience reactions to the suicidal characters in Quiet Cries. Proceedings 81st Annual Convention Amer Psychol Assn, 1973, 8:445-446.

6714. Potter, P.M. Death and guilt in the works of Ödön von Harváth. German Life & Letters, 1979, 32:148-152.

6715. Potter, Vilma R. New politics, new mothers. College Language Assn J, 1972, 16:247-255.

6716. Pouillart, Raymond. Maurice Maeterlinck: subconscient et 'sadisme.' Lettres Romanes, 1973, 27:37-61.

6717. Powers, H.B. Unity in El caballero de Olmedo. Bulletin of the 'Comediantes,' 1975, 27:52-59.

6718. Poyatos, María B. 'La muralla' de Calvo-Sotelo, auto de psicología freudiana. Hispanía, 1974, 57:31-39.

6719. Praag-Chantraine, J. van. [Lope's La fianza satisfecha.] Rev Belge de Philologie et d'Histoire, 1966, 64:945-958; Actas, 1967, 2:245-252.

6720. Prat, Angel V. A Freudian character in Lope de Vega. Tulane Drama Rev, 1962, 7:44-55.

6721. Praz, Mario. John Webster and The Maid's Tragedy. English Studies, 1956, 37:255-258.

6722. Presson, Robert K. Two types of dreams in the Elizabethan drama, and their heritage: Somnium Animale and the Pricke-of-Conscience. Studies in English Lit, 1500-1900, 1967, 7:239-256.

6723. Price, George E. Shakespeare as a neuropsychiatrist. Annals Medical History, 1928, 10:159-164.

6724. Procter-Gregg, Nancy. Variation on a theme. Int J Psycho-Anal, 1953, 34:142-145; In The Yearbook of Psychoanalysis, Vol. 10. NY: IUP, 1955, 251-257.

6725. Proffer, Carl R. Pushkin and parricide: The Miserly Knight. Amer Imago, 1968, 25:347-353.

6726. Proser, Matthew N. The Heroic Image in Five Shakespeare Tragedies. Princeton: Princeton Univ. Press, 1965.

6727. Proteus, (?). [Concerning Shakespeare's sexuality.] Rassegna di Studi Sessuali, 1923, 3:342-344.

6728. Putney, Rufus. Coriolanus and his mother. Psychoanal Q, 1962, 31:364-381.

6729. Quenon, J. Anthroponymie et caractérisation dans le théâtre de Max Frisch. Rev des Langues Vivantes, 1973, 39: 526-37, 40:25-39.

6730. Quigley, Austin E. Emblematic structure and setting of David Storey's plays. Modern Drama, 1979, 22:259-276.

6731. Quijano, Margarita. La tortura de Macbeth. Cuadernos Americanos, 1964, 243-261.

6732. Rabkin, Leslie Y., & Brown, Jeffrey. Some monster in his thought: sadism and tragedy in Othello. Lit & Psychol, 1973, 23:59-67.

6733. Rabkin, N. Rabbits, ducks, and Henry V. Shakespeare Q, 1977, 28:279-296.

6734. Racamier, P. C. Hystérie et théâtre. Evolution Psychiatrique, 1952, 2:257-291.

6735. Racker, Enrique. Considérations psychanalytiques sur le Cocu Magnifique de F. Crommelynck. Rev Française de Psychanalyse, 1957, 21, No. 6, 839-855.

6736. _____. Ensayo psicoanálitico sobre la personalidad y la obra dramatica de Ricardo Wagner. Revista de Psicoanálisis, 1948, 6:32-61.

6737. _____. Sobre los celos de Otelo. Revista de Psicoanálisis, 1945, 3:1-18.

6738. Radcliff-Umstead, Douglas. Pirandello e il romanzo dell'-alienazione. Alla Botego, 1972, 10(5):24-29.

6739. Radlov, S. E. On the pure elements of the actor's art. Drama Rev, 1975, 19:117-123.

6740. Rado, Charles. Oedipus the King. Psychoanal Rev, 1956, 43:228-234.

6741. Radzinowicz, Mary A. N. Medicinable tragedy: the structure of Samson Agonistes and seventeenth-century psychopathology. In Axton, M., & Williams, R. (eds), English Drama: Forms and Development. NY: Cambridge Univ. Press, 1977, 94-122.

6742. Rahner, Rich. Ophelia in Shakespeares Hamlet. Eine psychologisch-psychiatrische Studie. Leipzig: Xenien, 1910.

6743. Rahou, J. Le Bonheur, la joie, le plaisir dans les tragédies de Racine. Thesis, Univ. Rennes, 1965.

6744. Ramachandron, T. Tennessee Williams and feminine misfits. Modern Rev, 1969, 124:169-171.

6745. Ramnoux, Clémence. Mythe, conte et tragédie: une interpretation Freudienne du Roi Lear. La Revue d'Esthétique, 1968, 21:1-25.

6746. Ramsey, Jarold. The perversion of manliness in Macbeth. Studies in English Lit, 1500-1900, 1973, 13:285-300.

6747. Ramsey, Roger. Jerry's northerly madness. Notes on Con-
       temporary Lit, 1971, 1:7-8.
6748. Rank, Otto. [An example of poetic utilization of a promise.]
       Zentralblatt für Psychoanalyse, 1911, 1:109-110.
6749. _____. Macbeth. Imago, 1917-19, 5-6:382-392.
6750. _____. Psychology and the Soul. Philadelphia: Univ.
       Pennsylvania Press, 1950, 60-70; Seelenglaute und Psy-
       chologie. Leipzig/Vienna: Deuticke, 1930.
6751. _____. Shakespeares Vaterkomplex. In Das Inzest-Motiv
       in Dichtung und Sage. Leipzig: Deuticke, 1912, 1926,
       204-233.
6752. _____. Das 'Schauspiel' in Hamlet. Ein Beitrag zur Ana-
       lyse und zum dynamischen Verstandnis der Dichtung.
       Imago, 1915, 4:41-51; In Psychoanalytische Beiträge zu
       Mythenforschung gesammelte Studien aus den Jahren 1912
       bis 1914. Leipzig: Int Psychoanalytischer Verlag, 1919,
       1922, 72-85.
6753. _____. Strindberg über den Sinn der Symptome eines
       Geisteskranken. Int Zeitschrift für Psychoanalysis, 1919,
       3:308.
6754. Rankin, Anne V. Euripides' Hippolytus. Amer Imago, 1968,
       25:333-346; Arethusa, 1974, 7:71-94.
6755. Rascovsky, Arnaoldo, & Rascovsky, Matilde W. de. Sobre
       el filicidio y su significatión en la génesis del 'acting out'
       y la conducto psicopática en Edipo. Revista de Psicoan-
       álysis, 1968, 24:717-740; Abstract in Int J Psycho-Anal,
       1968, 49:390-395.
6756. Rauhut, Franz. Il motivo psicologico in Pirandello. Veltro,
       1968, 12(1-2):99-124.
6757. Ravagnan, Luis M. [The Oedipus tragedy.] Acta Psiquiá-
       trica y Psicológica de America Latina, 1976, 22(1):5-8.
6758. Ravich, Robert A. A psychoanalytic study of Shakespeare's
       early plays. Psychoanal Q, 1964, 33:388-410.
6759. _____. Shakespeare and psychiatry. Lit & Psychol, 1964,
       14:97-105.
6760. _____. 'Such seething brains, such shaping fantasies. '
       Abbottempo, 1964, 2:28-35.
6761. Ray, Isaac. Shakespeare's delineations of insanity. Ameri-
       can J Insanity, 1872; In Contributions to Mental Pathol-
       ogy. Boston: Little, Brown, 1873, 482-534.
6762. Rea, Domenico. Pensieri in margine al romanzo; Luigi
       Compagnone, Il male oscuro; Guisseppi Berto, Psicana-
       lisi e romanzo. Nostro Tempo, 13 (138):1-7.
6763. Real, Jere. The brothel in O'Neill's Mansions. Modern
       Drama, 1970, 12:383-389.
6764. Reck, Tom S. Archetypes in Leroi Jones' Dutchman. Stud-
       ies in Black Lit, 1970, 1:66-68.
6765. Ree, K. Ibsens legeskikkelser. Samt medisinske aspekter
       av dikteren og hans dikterverk. Tidsskrift Norge Laege-
       foren, 1975, 95:1507-1511.
6766. Reed, Marian V. The Humoral Psychology of Christopher
       Marlowe's Characters. Master's thesis, West Virginia
       Univ., 1964.

6767.   Reed, Robert R., Jr. A factual interpretation of The Change-
        ling's madhouse scenes. Notes & Queries, 1950, 195:247-
        248.
6768.   _____. Hamlet, the pseudo-procrastinator. Shakespeare
        Q, 1958, 9:177-186.
6769.   _____. Richard II: portrait of a psychotic. J General
        Education, 1964, 16:55-67.
6770.   Rees, Goronwy. A case for treatment: the world of Lytton
        Strachey. Encounter, 1968, 30:71-83.
6771-   Regis, Emmanuel. La Folie dans l'art dramatique. Rev des
2.   Revues, 1902, 42.
6773.   _____. Le Personnage d'Hamlet et son Interprétation par
        Mme Sarah Bernhardt. Rev de Psychologie Clinique et
        Therapeutique, 1899, 3:336-344.
6774.   Reich, Warren W. Bestiality in the Dramas of Christian
        Dietrich Grabbe. DAI, 1971, 31:6565A-66A.
6775.   Reichert, John F. Description and interpretation in literary
        criticism. JAAC, 1969, 27:281-292.
6776.   Reid, Stephen. Desdemona's guilt. Amer Imago, 1970, 27:
        245-262.
6777.   _____. Hamlet's melancholia. Amer Imago, 1974, 31:378-
        400.
6778.   _____. 'I am misanthropos': a psychoanalytic reading of
        Shakespeare's Timon of Athens. Psychoanal Rev, 1969,
        56:442-452.
6779.   _____. In defense of Goneril and Regan. Amer Imago,
        1970, 27:277-244.
6780.   _____. Othello's jealousy. Amer Imago, 1968, 25:274-
        293.
6781.   _____. Othello's occupation: beyond the pleasure prin-
        ciple. Psychoanal Rev, 1976-77, 63:555-570.
6782.   _____. A psychoanalytic reading of Troilus and Cressida
        and Measure for Measure. Psychoanal Rev, 1970, 57:263-
        282.
6783.   _____. Teaching Oedipus Rex. College English, 1968,
        29:615-619. Reply with rejoinder: G. Geilbrun, 1968,
        30:256-260.
6784.   _____. The Winter's Tale. Amer Imago, 1970, 27:263-
        278.
6785.   Reik, Theodor. Arthur Schnitzler vor dem Anatol: Psycho-
        analytisches. Pan, 1912, 32:899-905.
6786.   _____. The Haunting Melody. NY: Farrar, Straus &
        Young, 1953, 136-145.
6787.   _____. In my mind's eye, Horatio. Complex, 1952, 7:
        15-31; In The Secret Self. NY: Farrar, Straus & Young,
        1952, 17-32.
6788.   _____. Intermezzo capricioso. In Listening with the
        Third Ear. NY: Farrar, Straus, 1949, 400-412, 423-427.
6789.   _____. 'Jessica, my child!' Amer Imago, 1951, 8:3-27;
        In The Secret Self. NY: Farrar, Straus & Young, 1952,
        35-36; In Faber, M.D. (ed), The Design Within. NY:
        Science House, 1970, 440-461.

321 Drama

6790. _____. Masochism in Modern Man. NY: Farrar & Rinehart, 1941, 234-235.
6791. _____. Oedipus und die Sphinx. Imago, 1920, 6:95.
6792. _____. Psychoanalytic experiences in life, literature, and music. In The Search Within. The Inner Experience of a Psychoanalyst. NY: Grove, 1956, 331-470.
6793. _____. Shakespeare visits a psychoanalyst. Complex, 1951, 6:34-39; In The Secret Self. NY: Farrar, Straus & Young, 1953, 11-16.
6794. _____. The three women in a man's life. Amer Imago, 1949, 6:245-259.
6795. _____. The way of all flesh. In From Thirty Years with Freud. NY: Farrar & Rinehart, 1940, 197-212.
6796. _____. Zu Freuds Deutung der Cordeliagestalt. Psychoanalytische Bewegung, 1929, 1:211.
6797. Reilly, Kevin P. Pitching the mansion and pumping the morphine: Eugene O'Neill's Long Day's Journey into Night. Gypsy Scholar, 1978, 5:22-33.
6798. Rein, David M. Orestes and Electra in Greek literature. Amer Imago, 1954, 11:33-50.
6799. Reinhard, F. Schiller als Psychotherapeut. Münchener medizinische Wochenschrift, 1928, 74:441.
6800. Reinoso, Deigo García. Notas sobre la obesidad a travès del estudio de Falstaff. Revista de Psicoanálisis, 1956, 13: 170-177.
6801. Reiss, Timothy J. Psychical distance and theatrical distancing in Sartre's drama. Yale French Studies, 1971, 46:5-16.
6802. Reitler, Rudolf. Spring Awakening by Wedekind. In Nunberg, A., & Federn, E. (eds), Minutes of the Vienna Psychoanalytic Society, Vol. 1:1906-1908. NY: IUP, 1962, 111-118.
6803. Reitz, (?). Schillers Dissertation und die neue Psychologie. Stuttgarter Neues Tagesblatt, 2 March 1934, No. 102.
6804. Relyea, Suzanne. Signs, Systems and Meanings: A Contemporary Semiotic Reading of Four Molière Plays. Middletown, Conn: Wesleyan Univ. Press, 1976.
6805. Renfrow, Jack Norman. Hamlet and the psychologists. Shakespeare Newsletter, 1963, 13(2):20.
6806. _____. Psychologists' Criticism of Hamlet. DA, 1962, 22:3671-72.
6807. Renoult, E. La Psychologie de la foule au théatre. Rev Scientifique, 1895, 4:807-809.
6808. Resenhöfft, Wilhelm. Existenzerhellung des Hexentums in Goethes Faust (Mephisots Masken, Walpurgis): Grundlinien axiomatisch-psychologischer Deutung. Bern: Lang, 1969.
6809. Reynolds, George F. Plays as literature for an audience. Univ. Colorado Study Series for Language & Lit, 1953, No. 4.
6810. Ribas, J. Carvalhal. Interpretaçao psicológica de Vestido de Noiva. Imprensa médica. 1948, 23:91-98.
6811. Ribner, Irving. Lear's madness in the nineteenth century. Shakespeare Assn Bulletin, 1947, 22:117-129.

6812. Ricaldone, M. L. Alcuni modi psicoanalitici di leggere Pirandello. Studi Novecenteschi, 1976, 5, nos. 13-14, 113-121.

6813. Ricciardelli, Rachel M. King Lear and the theory of disengagement. Gerontologist, 1973, 13:148-152.

6814. Rice, Julian C. Desdemona unpinned: universal guilt in Othello. Shakespeare Studies, 1974, 7:209-226.

6815. _____. Equus and the Jungian true symbol. Int J Symbology, 1976, 7(2):60-65.

6816. _____. Hamlet and the dream of something after death. Hartford Studies in Lit, 1974, 6:109-116.

6817. Richards, David B. Mesmerism in Die Jungfrau von Orleans. PMLA, 1976, 91:856-870.

6818. Richmond, Hugh M. Shakespeare's Sexual Comedy; A Mirror for Lovers. Indianapolis: Bobbs-Merrill, 1971.

6819. Richmond, Velma Bourgeois. Renaissance sexuality and Marlowe's women. Ball State Univ. Forum, 1975, 16(4):36-44.

6820. _____. Shakespeare's women. Midwest Q, 1978, 19:330-342.

6821. Richter, (?). Pathologie im Shakespeares dramen. Nord und Sud, 1911, 255:342-363.

6822. Ricks, Christopher. The moral and poetic structure of The Changeling. Essays in Criticism, 1960, 12:290-306.

6823. Riddel, Joseph N. A Streetcar Named Desire--Nietzsche descending. Modern Drama, 1963, 5:421-430.

6824. Riemer, Andrew. King Lear and the egocentric universe. Balcony: The Sidney Rev, 1966, 5:33-42.

6825. Riklin, Franz. Shakespeare's A Midsummer Night's Dream: ein Beitrag zum Individuations-prozess. In Wheelwright, J. B. (ed), The Reality of the Psyche; The Proceedings of the Third International Congress for Analytical Psychology. NY: Putnam, 1968, 262-292.

6826. Riley, Michael H. Ritual and the Hero in English Renaissance Tragedy. DAI, 1970, 31:2353-A.

6827. Risso, Richard David. A Study of the Psychological Structures in Four Plays by Henri De Montherlant. Doctoral dissertation, Stanford Univ., 1965.

6828. Ritter, Wolfgang. Hebbels Psychologie und dramatische Charaktergeslaltung. Marburg: Elwert, 1973.

6829. Riva, Raymond T. Beckett and Freud. Criticism, 1970, 12:120-132.

6830. Riviere, Joan. The inner world in Ibsen's The Master-Builder. In Klein, M., Heimann, P., & Mony-Kyrle, R. E. (eds), New Directions in Psychoanalysis. NY: Basic Books, 1957, 370-383; London: Tavistock, 1971.

6831. Rizza, Cécilia. La Condition de la femme et de la jeune fille dans les premières comédies de Corneille. In Leiner, W. (ed), Onze études sur l'image de la femme dans la littérature française du dix-septième siècle. Tubingen: Narr; Paris: Place, 1978, 169-193.

6832. Roberts, Patrick. The Psychology of Tragic Drama. London: Routledge & Kegan Paul, 1975.

6833. Robertson, P. L. The role of the political usurper: Macbeth and Boris Godounov. Amer Imago, 1966, 23:96-109.
6834. Robertson, W. H. Are we afraid of Virginia Woolf? Alabama J Medical Science, 1979, 16:182-183.
6835. Robinson, Charles E. The devil as doppelgänger in The Deformed Transformed: the sources and meaning of Byron's unfinished drama. Bulletin New York Public Library, 1970, 74:177-202.
6836. Robitsek, Alfred. Die Analyse von Egmont's Traum. Jahrbuch für Psychologie und Psychotherapie, 1910, 2:451-464.
6837. Roellenbleck, E. Peer Gynt als erotischen Typus sui generis. Psyche, 1969, 23:929-946.
6838. Rogers, Robert. Endopsychic drama in Othello. Shakespeare Q, 1969, 20:205-215.
6839. Rohden, G. von. Schiller und die Kriminalpsychologie. Monatschrift für Kriminalpsychologie, 1905-06, 2:81-88.
6840. Róheim, Géza. Oedipus Rex. In The Gates of the Dream. NY: IUP, 1953, 529-544; London: Bailey, 1953.
6841. _____. Teiresias and other seers. Psychoanal Rev, 1946, 33:314-334.
6842. _____. The Tragedy of Man. Samiksa, 1950, 4:102-132.
6843. Rojas, N. La patología pasional de Otelo. Medical Historia (Barcelona), 1971, 2(5):ii-xi.
6844. Roland, Alan. Pinter's homecoming: imagoes in dramatic action. Psychoanal Rev, 1974, 61:415-427.
6845. _____, & Rizzo, Gino. Psychoanalysis in search of Pirandello: Six Characters and Henry IV. Psychoanalytic Rev, 1977, 64:63-99; in Roland, A. (ed), Psychoanalysis, Creativity, and Literature. NY: Columbia Univ. Press, 1978, 323-351.
6846. Rolfs, Daniel J. Pirandello's theme of madness. Forum Italicum, 1976, 10:377-397.
6847. Röling, B. V. A. De criminologische Betekenis van Shakespeares Macbeth. Nijmegen: Dekker & Van de Vegt, 1947.
6848. Rollin, Henry J. Psychiatry and Shakespeare. Univ. Leeds Rev, 1964, 9:136-147.
6849. Rollins, Ronald G. Clerical blackness in the green garden: heroine as scapegoat in Cock-A-Doodle Dandy. James Joyce Q, 1970, 8:64-72.
6850. _____. O'Casey, O'Neill, and expressionism in Within the Gates. West Virginia Univ. Philological Papers, 1961, 13:76-81.
6851. Rollman-Branch, Hilda S. Psychical reality and the theater of fact. Amer Imago, 1969, 26:56-70.
6852. _____. Psychoanalytic reflections on Verdi's Don Carlo. Amer Imago, 1963, 20:241-255.
6853. Roman, H. Rilke's psychodramas. J English Germanic Philology, 1944, 43:402-410.
6854. Rombault, Marc. Arthur Adamov, 1908-1970. French Rev, 1971, 45:3-8.
6855. Romotsky, Sally K. R. Sex and Family in Hamlet. DAI, 1974, 34:4216A-17A.

6856. Rønning, H. Könets fånge och klassens. Ord och Bild, 1973, 82:491-499.

6857. Rosati, G. O. La resistenza e il sipario. Atti dello Psicodramma, 1977.

6858. Rose, H. Aeschylus the psychologist. Symbolae Osloenses, 1956, 32:1-26.

6859. Rose, Jacques-Léon. Oskar Kokoschka's phantasmagorical vision: the Book of Job transmogrified. Comparative Drama, 1971, 5:91-100.

6860. Rose, M. Hamlet and the shape of revenge. English Lit Renaissance, 1971, 1:132-143.

6861. Rosen, Carol. The language of cruelty in Ford's 'Tis Pity She's a Whore. Comparative Drama, 1974-75, 8:356-368.

6862. _____. Symbolic naturalism in David Storey's Home. Modern Drama, 1979, 22:277-289.

6863. Rosen, Nathan. The unconscious in Cexov's 'Van'ka' (with a note on 'Sleepy'). Slavic & East European J, 1971, 15: 441-454.

6864. Rosenbauer, Hansjürgen. Brecht und der Behaviorismus. Bad Homburg: Gehlen, 1970.

6865. Rosenberg, Harold. Missing persons. In Act and the Actor: Making the Self. NY: World, 1970, 198-204.

6866. Rosenberg, Marvin. Drama as arousal. JAAC, 1969, 27: 425-431.

6867. _____. In defense of Iago. Shakespeare Q, 1955, 6:145-148.

6868. _____. The Masks of King Lear. Berkeley: Univ. California, 1972; Review: Miriam Gilbert, Hartford Studies in Lit, 1974, 6:80-86.

6869. _____. The Masks of Macbeth. Berkeley: Univ. California Press, 1978; Review: Barbara Hodgdon, Hartford Studies in Lit, 1979, 11:72-82.

6870. _____. The Masks of Othello: The Search for Identity of Othello, Iago and Desdemona by Three Centuries of Actors and Critics. Berkeley: Univ. California Press, 1961.

6871. _____. Shakespeare's fantastic trick: Measure for Measure. Sewanee Rev, 1972, 80:51-72.

6872. _____. Shakespeare's pathos. Lit & Psychol, 1962, 12: 66-74.

6873. Rosenblatt, Jason P. Aspects of the incest problem in Hamlet. Shakespeare Q, 1978, 29:349-364.

6874. Rosenzweig, Saul. A Savoyard note on the Freudian theory of manic-depressive psychosis. Psychoanal Rev, 1944, 31:336-339.

6875. Rosner, Karl. Shakespeares Hamlet im Lichte der Neuropathologie Vortrag. Gehalten in der Gesellschaft für psychologische Forschung in München. München: Fischer, 1895.

6876. Ross, Gordon. The mad characters of Shakespeare. In Studies: Biographical and Literary. London: Simpkin, Marshall, 1897.

6877. Ross, Thomas A. A note on The Merchant of Venice. British J Medical Psychol, 1934, 14:303-311.

6878. Roswell, May. La Gonfle, Martin du Gard's unstaged farce. Romance Notes, 1973, 15:197-200.

6879. Roth, Marc Allen. Role-Playing in Historical Drama and the Changing Visions of History: A Study of Shakespeare, Schiller, Büchner, and Strindberg. DAI, 1977, 37:5806A.

6880. Rothenberg, Alan B. Infantile fantasies in Shakespearean metaphor: I. The fear of being smothered. Psychoanal Rev, 1973, 60:205-222.

6881. _____. _____. III. Photophobia, love of darkness, and 'black' complexions. Psychoanal Rev, 1977, 64:173-202.

6882. _____. _____. II. Scopophilia and fears of ocular rape and castration. Psychoanal Rev, 1973, 60:533-556.

6883. Rothenberg, Albert. Autobiographical drama: Strindberg and O'Neill. Lit & Psychol, 1967, 17:95-114.

6884. _____. The iceman changeth: toward an empirical approach to creativity. JAPA, 1969, 17:549-607.

6885. _____. Janusian thinking and creativity. In The Psychoanalytic Study of Society, Vol. 1. NY: IUP, 1976, 1-30.

6886. _____, & Shapiro, Eugene D. The defense of psychoanalysis in literature: Long Day's Journey into Night and A View from the Bridge. Comparative Drama, 1973, 7:51-67.

6887. Roux, J. L. [The theater and physicians; medicine and actors.] Union Médicale du Canada, 1959, 88:967-975.

6888. Rovatti, Piero. Per un discorso fenomenologico sul teatro. Aut Aut, 1964, No. 81, 15-54.

6889. Roy, Emil. Archetypal patterns in Fry. Comparative Drama, 1967, 1:93-104.

6890. _____. Eugene O'Neill's The Emperor Jones and The Hairy Ape as mirror plays. Comparative Drama, 1968, 2:21-31.

6891. _____. Faustus' dream of punishment. Amer Imago, 1977, 34:158-169.

6892. _____. Sexual paradox in The Changeling. Lit & Psychol, 1975, 25:124-132.

6893. _____. Tragic tension in Beyond the Horizon. Ball State Univ. Forum, 1967, 8:74-79.

6894. _____. War and manliness of Shakespeare's Troilus and Cressida. Comparative Drama, 1973, 7:107-120.

6895. Rubin, Samuel S. Hamlet: a psychoanalytic re-interpretation. Psychoanal Rev, 1971, 57:660-672.

6896. Rubinstein, Friedrich. Hamlet als Neurastheniker. Leipzig: Haacke, 1896.

6897. Rubinstein, Lothar Henry. The theme of Electra and Orestes: a contribution to the psychopathology of matricide. British J Medical Psychol, 1969, 42:99-108.

6898. Ruck, C. Euripides' mother: vegetables and the phallos in Aristophanes. Arion, n. s., 1975, 1:13-57.

6899. Rugg, E. [Lope's portrayal of fathers.] Hispanófila, 1965, 25.

6900. Ruggiero, A. William Shakespeare. M. D. Medical Newsmagazine, 1960, 173:524-536.

6901. Ruhe, Ernstpeter. Le Professeur Taranne oder Comment utiliser ses névroses. Romantisches Jahrbuch, 1976, 27:152-175.
6902. Rupp, Gordon. Luther and Mr. Osborne. Cambridge Q, 1965-66, 1:28-42.
6903. Russell, Claire, & Russell, W. M. S. Shakespeare and the Prince of Denmark. In Human Behavior: A New Approach. Boston: Little, Brown, 1961, 396-418.
6904. Rutter, George M. Slips of the tongue in mediaeval English literature. Int J Psycho-Anal, 1927, 8:405-406.

6905. Saari, Sandra E. Of madness or fame: Ibsen's Bygmester Solness. Scandinavian Studies, 1978, 50:1-18.
6906. Sacharoff, Mark. Suicide and Brutus' philosophy in Julius Caesar. J History Ideas, 1972, 33:115-122.
6907. Sachs, Hanns. The measure in Measure for Measure. Amer Imago, 1939, 1:60-81; In The Creative Unconscious. NY: Sci-Art, 1951, 72-98; In Faber, M. D. (ed), The Design Within. NY: Science House, 1970, 481-497.
6908. _____. Schillers Geisterseher. Imago, 1915, 4:69-95, 145-179; Psychoanalytic Rev, 1915, 8:87, 241, 309, 329, 647, 787, 940.
6909. _____. The Tempest. Int J Psycho-Anal, 1923, 4:43-88; Imago, 1919, 5:203-242.
6910. _____. The unconscious in Shakespeare's Tempest; analytical considerations. In The Creative Unconscious. Cambridge: Sci-Art, 1951 (1919), 243-323.
6911. Sachs, Wulf. Hamlet. In Psychoanalysis: Its Meanings and Practical Applications. London: Cassell, 1934, 197-212.
6912. Sackett, Theodore A. Creation and destruction of personality in Tristana: Galdós and Bañuel. Anales Galdosianos, 1978, Suppl:71-90.
6913. _____. [Psychological motivation in Miau.] Anales Galdosianos, 1970, 4:25-38.
6914. St. Clair, Margaret. A note on the guilt of Oedipus. Psychoanal & the Psychoanal Rev, 1961, 48:111-114.
6915. St. Leon, R. The question of guilt in Kleist's Penthesilea. Seminar, 1974, 10(1).
6916. Sale, W. The psychoanalysis of Pentheus in the Bacchae. Yale Classical Studies, 1972, 22:63-82.
6917. Salomon, H. P. Phèdre et l'inceste. Etudes Françaises, 1965, 1(2):131-135.
6918. Salter, Nancy Kay Clark. Masks and Roles: A Study of Women in Shakespeare's Drama. DAI, 1975, 36:1535A.
6919. Sandars, R. K. The irrelevance of incest to Oedipus. Agenda, 1969, 7:23-28.
6920. Sanders, Kenneth. Shakespeare's The Winter's Tale--and some notes on the analysis of a present-day Leontes. Int Rev Psycho-Anal, 1978, 5:175-178.
6921. Sandstroem, Yvonne L. Problems of identity in Hedda Gabler. Scandinavian Studies, 1979, 51:375-391.

6922. Sankovitche, T.   Folly and society in the comic theatre of
      the Pléiade.   In Folie et déraison à la Renaissance.
      Brussels: Univ. Bruxelles Press, 1976, 99-108.
6923. Santelli, C.   A Far Country ... Freud on the stage.   Ciba
      Symposium, 1963, 11:143-144.
6924. Saplala, Paz E. L.   Renaissance Psychology and the Plays of
      Thomas Middleton.   Doctoral dissertation, Univ. Minne-
      sota, 1970; DAI, 1971, 31:3519A.
6925. Sarró, Ramón.   L'Interpretation du mythe d'Oedipe chez
      Freud et chez Heidegger.   Acta Psychotherapeutica, Psy-
      chosomatica et Orthopaedogogica, 1960, 8:266-289.
6926. Sasaki, M. S.   Influence structure on Julius Caesar.   Psychol
      Reports, 1976, 39:1191-1195.
6927. Saugnieux, J.   Théologie, métaphysique et psychanalyse: ré-
      flexions sur le burlador de Sevilla.   Les Langues Néo-
      Latines, 1968, 62:27-52.
6928. Saul, Leon J.   Othello: projection in art.   JAMA, 200:39-40.
6929. Saussure, Raymond de.   Le Complex de Jocaste.   Int Zeit-
      schrift für Psychoanalyse, 1920, 6:118-122.
6930. Savin, M.   Psychanalyse de Phèdre (Fantasie).   La Table
      Ronde, 1956, 108:169-177.
6931. Saxe, Doreen.   Twentieth-Century Studies of Racine and the
      Unconscious.   DAI, 1972, 33:1741A.
6932. Saxon, Patricia Jean.   The Limits of Assertiveness: Modes
      of Female Identity in Shakespeare and the Stuart Drama-
      tists.   DAI, 1978, 38:7349A-50A.
6933. Sayce, R. A.   Le Metonymie dans l'oeuvre de Racine.   Actes
      de premier congrès international racinien.   Uzès, 1962.
6934. Scalinger, G. M.   La Psicologia a Teatre.   Naples: Fortunio,
      1896.
6935. Scanlan, Tom.   Family, Drama, and American Dreams.
      Westport, Conn: Greenwood, 1978.
6936. Schaefer, Margret.   Psychoanalysis and the marionette the-
      atre: interpretation is not depreciation.   Critical Inquiry,
      1978, 5:177-188.
6937. Schatia, Viva.   Hedda Gabler's doll's house.   Psychoanal
      Rev, 1939, 9:33-38.
6938. _____.   The Master Builder: a case of involutional psy-
      chosis.   Psychoanal Rev, 1940, 27:311-318.
6939. _____.   Peer Gynt--a study of insecurity.   Psychoanal
      Rev, 1938, 25:49-52.
6940. Schaffer, Leslie.   The durability of personal fictions: some
      comments on hysteria and the pathology of collaborative
      processes.   Rev Existential Psychol & Psychiat, 1964,
      4:233-243.
6941. Schalk, Fritz.   Melancholie im Theater von Tirso de Molina.
      In Ideen und Formen.   Frankfurt: Klostermann, 1965,
      215-238.
6942. Schechner, Richard.   In warm blood: The Bacchae.   Educa-
      tional Theatre J, 20:415-424.
6943. _____.   Who's afraid of Edward Albee?   Tulane Drama
      Rev, 1963, 7:7-10.
6944. Scheff, Thomas J.   Audience awareness and catharsis in
      drama.   Psychoanal Rev, 1976-77, 63:529-554.

6945. Scherer, B. Polonius, der Typus des Senilen: eine psychiatrische Shakespeare-studie. Anglia, 1930, 54:149-167.

6946. Schermerhorn, Karen Russell. Women in Wycherley: Their Role in His Social Criticism. DAI, 1975, 35:7879A.

6947. Schiffhort, Gerald J. The imagery of Pericles and what it tells us. Ball State Univ. Forum, 1967, 8:61-70.

6948. Schilling, G. La Terreur dans le théâtre de Racine. In Jeunesse de Racine. Paris: La Ferté-Milon, 1958, 12-16.

6949. Schlesinger, Kurt O. Thoughts on King Lear and the current generation gap. In Lindon, J. A. (ed), The Psychoanalytic Forum, Vol. 4. NY: IUP, 1972, 63-99.

6950. Schmitt, F. Krankheit und Schaffen bei Friedrich Schillers. Allgemeine Zeitschrift für Psychiatrie, 1937, 105:1-34.

6951. Schmitt, Natalie Crohn. Oedipus as an exorcism. Educational Theatre J, 1970, 22:249-255.

6952. Schoff, Francis G. Aspects of Shakespearean Criticism, 1914-1950: A Commentary Centered on British and American Criticism of Hamlet. DA, 1953, 13:230.

6953. Schlosky, Daniel Paul. Rhetorical, Psychological, and Structural Use of Paradox in Shakespeare's Love's Labour's Lost and Measure for Measure. DAI, 1978, 39:903A-04A.

6954. Schlosser, Anselm. Das Motiv der Entfremdung in der Komodie der Irrungen. Shakespeare Jahrbuch, 1965, 100-101:57-71.

6955. Schlueter, June Mayer. Genet's maids, brothel patrons, and Blacks. In Metafictional Characters in Modern Drama. NY: Columbia Univ. Press, 1979, 35-52.

6956. _____. The Theatre of the Double: The Twofold Character in Modern Self-Conscious Drama. DAI, 1977, 38:29A.

6957. Schmidbauer, Wolfgang. Psychologische und ritualistische Hermaneutik angesichts der Zauberflöte. Praxis der Kinderpsychologie und Kinderpsychiatrie, 1971, 20:146-156.

6958. Schmidt-Dengler, W. Ehre und Melancholie im Drama des Sturm und Drang. Sprachkunst, 1971, 3:11-30.

6959. Schneck, Jerome M. Anton Chekhov: psychiatrist manqué. New York State J Medicine, 1978, 78:1130-1135.

6960. Schneider, Daniel E. Play of dreams. Theatre Arts, 1949, 33:18-21.

6961. Schneider, Ernst. Mutter und Kind in den Dramen Ibsens. Zeitschrift für psychoanalytische Pädagogik, 1927-28, 2:213-225.

6962. Schneiderman, Leo. The Ramayana and the Ram Lila from a psychological standpoint. Lit East & West, 1966, 10:54-68.

6963. Schneiderman, Stuart Allen. Psychoanalysis and Hamlet. DAI, 1975, 36:2792A.

6964. _____. The saying of Hamlet. Sub-stance, 1974, 8:77-88.

6965. Schneir, Jacques. Restitution aspects of the creative process. Amer Imago, 1957, 14:211-223.

6966. Schneiter, C. Ein Traum Julius Caesars. Int Zeitschrift für Psychoanalyse, 1913, 3:557.

6967. Schoenbaum, S. Hengist, king of Kent and sexual preoccupation in Jacobean drama. Philological Q, 1950, 29:182-198.

6968. Schoff, Francis G. Hamlet and his critics. II. Elizabethan psychology. Discourse, 1962, 4:248-260.

6969. _____. _____. I. The problem and one approach. Discourse, 1961, 4:125-137.

6970. Schotz, Myra Glazer. The great unwritten story: mothers and daughters in Shakespeare. In Davidson, C. N., & Broner, E. M. (eds), The Lost Tradition. NY: Ungar, 1980, 44-54.

6971. Schero, Elliott M. A misinterpretation of Freud. College English, 1949, 10(8):476.

6972. Schreyer, J. Die psychologische Motivierung in Arnims Dramen. Halle: Niemayer, 1929; Wiesbaden: Sändig, 1970.

6973. Schröder, Cristoph von. Wille und Nervosität in Shakespeares Hamlet. Ein Versuch, Hamlets Naturell vom medicinischen Standpunkte zu beleuchten. Riga: 1893.

6974. Schroeter, James. The four fathers: symbolism in Oedipus Rex. Criticism, 1961, 3:186-200.

6975. Schücking, Levin L. Character Problems in Shakespeare's Plays. NY: Holt, 1922; Gloucester, Mass: Smith, 1919.

6976. Schutter, Dirk de, & Gillaerts, Paul. Claustrofobie voor het clausuur tijd. Dietsche Warande en Belfort, 1977, 122:127-132.

6977. Schwartz, Murray M. Between fantasy and imagination: a psychological exploration of Cymbeline. In Crews, F. (ed), Psychoanalysis and Literary Process. Cambridge, Mass: Winthrop, 1970, 219-283.

6978. _____. Leontes' jealousy in The Winter's Tale. Amer Imago, 1973, 30:250-273.

6979. _____. A Psychoanalytic Interpretation of Cymbeline and The Winter's Tale. Doctoral dissertation, Univ. California Berkeley, 1973.

6980. _____. A Thematic Introduction to Shakespeare. Saratoga Springs, NY: Empire State College Press, 1974.

6981. _____. The Winter's Tale: loss and transformation. Amer Imago, 1975, 32:145-199.

6982. Schweitzer, J. W. Racine's Andromaque: Oreste, slayer of Pyrrhus? Romance Notes, 1961, 3:37-39.

6983. Scott, Virginia. Life in art: a reading of The Seagull. Educational Theatre J, 1978, 30:357-367.

6984. Scott, William D. Shakespeare's Melancholics. London: Mills & Boon, 1962.

6985. Searles, Harold. The psychodynamics of vengefulness. In Collected Papers on Schizophrenia and Related Subjects. NY: IUP, 1965, 177-191.

6986. Sebold, R. P. El incesto, el suicidio y el primer romanticismo español. Hispanic Rev, 1973, 41:669-692.

6987. Segal, Charles Paul. Synaesthesia in Sophocles. Illinois Classical Studies, 1977, 2:88-96.

6988. Segond, J. L. Psychologie de Jean Racine. Paris: Societé d'Editions Les Belles Lettres, 1940.
6989. Sehmsdorf, Henning K. The self in isolation: a new reading of Bjørnson's Arne. Scandinavian Studies, 1973, 45:310-323.
6990. Seiden, Melvin. Malvolio reconsidered. Univ. Kansas City Rev, 1961, 28:105-114.
6991. Seidenberg, Robert. Catcher gone awry. Int J Psycho-Anal, 1970, 51:331-339.
6992. _____. For this woman's sake: notes on the 'mother' superego with the reflections on Shakespeare's Coriolanus and Sophocles' Ajax. Int J Psycho-Anal, 1963, 44:74-82.
6993. _____, & Papathomopoulos, Evangelos. Oedipus at Colonnus and the aged Sophocles. Psychoanal Q, 1960, 29: 236-239.
6994. _____, & Papathomopoulos, Evangelos. Sophocles' Ajax-- a morality for madness. Psychoanal Q, 1961, 30:404-412.
6995. Sellner, Timothy F. The Lionel-scene in Schiller's Jungfrau von Orleans: a psychoanalytic interpretation. German Q, 1977, 50:264-282.
6996. Semotán, Jiri, & Semotán, Milada. Shakespeare psychiatr. Vesmír, 1962, 42:323-324.
6997. Semple, R. H. A psychological study of Shakespeare. J Psychol Medicine, 1881, 7:193-210.
6998. Semprún Donahue, Moraima de. La sangre y la sensualidad en Lorca. García Lorca Rev, 1975, 3:45-52.
6999. Serban, A. Life in a sound. Drama Rev, 1976, 20:25-26.
7000. Seward, T. C. , & Faber, M. D. A note on Stephen Reid's essay, 'I am misanthropos': a psychoanalytic reading of Shakespeare's Timon of Athens. Psychoanal Rev, 1971, 58:617-623.
7001. Shackleton, Mitchell. Rêve et réalité chez Claudel. French Studies in Southern Africa, 1978, 7:48-67.
7002. Shainess, Natalie. Hamlet: the coup that failed. J Amer Academy Psychoanal, 1975, 3:383-403.
7003. Shakespeare, William. Hamlet: With a Psycho-Analytic Study by Ernest Jones, M. D. Drawings by F. Roberts Johnson. London: Vision Press, 1947.
7004. Shamblin, Donald G. Erotic Frustration and Its Cause in the Dramas of García Lorca. DA, 1967, 28:2263A-64A.
7005. Shank, T. Pip Simmons group. Drama Rev, 1975, 19:41-46.
7006. Shapiro, Barbara. Toward a psychoanalytic reading of Beckett's Molloy, II. Lit & Psychol, 1969, 15-30.
7007. Shapiro, Stephen A. Othello's Desdemona. Lit & Psychol, 1964, 14:56-60; In Faber, M. D. (ed), The Design Within. NY: Science House, 1970, 184-192.
7008. _____. Romeo and Juliet: reversals, contraries, transformations, and ambivalence. College English, 1964, 25:498-501.
7009. _____. 'The varying shore of the world': ambivalence in Antony and Cleopatra. Modern Language Q, 1966, 27:18-32.

7010. Shapiro, Stephen Richard. The Theme of Homosexuality in Selected Theatrical Events Produced in the United States Between 1969 and 1974. DAI, 1976, 37:1300A.

7011. Sharma, P. P. Search for self-identity in Death of a Salesman. Lit Criterion, 1974, 11(2):74-79.

7012. Sharpe, Ella Freeman. The cyclic movement in Shakespeare's plays. In Collected Papers on Psycho-Analysis. London: Hogarth, 1950, 242-243.

7013. _____. From King Lear to The Tempest. Int J Psycho-Anal, 1946, 27:19-30; In Brierly, M. (ed), Collected Papers on Psycho-analysis. London: Hogarth, 1950; NY: Anglobooks, 1952, 214-241.

7014. _____. Hamlets Ungeduld. Internationale Zeitschrift für Individual-psychologie, 1929, 7:329-339.

7015. _____. The impatience of Hamlet. Int J Psycho-Anal, 1929, 10:270-279; In Brierly, M. (ed), Collected Papers on Psycho-Analysis. London: Hogarth, 1950, 242-265; NY: Anglobooks, 1952, 203-213.

7016. _____. Psycho-analytic view of Shakespeare. In Brierly, M. (ed), Collected Papers on Psycho-Analysis. London: Hogarth, 1950; NY: Anglobooks, 1950.

7017. _____. Psychophysical problems revealed in language: an examination of metaphor. In Collected Papers on Psycho-Analysis. London: Hogarth, 1950.

7018. _____. An unfinished paper on Hamlet, Prince of Denmark. Int J Psycho-Anal, 1948, 29:98-109; In Brierly, M. (ed), Collected Papers on Psycho-Analysis. London: Hogarth, 1950; NY: Anglobooks, 1952, 242-265.

7019. Sharpe, Robert B. Irony in Drama. Chapel Hill: Univ. North Carolina Press, 1959.

7020. Shaw, W. John Lyly and breast feeding. St. Bartholomew Hospital J, 1946, 49:163-164.

7021. Shenk, Robert. The Sinners Progress: A Study of Madness in English Renaissance Drama. Salzburg: Univ. Salzburg, 1978.

7022. Sherrell, R. E. Arthur Adamov and invaded man. Modern Drama, 1965, 7:399-404.

7023. Shields, M. Sight and blindness imagery in the Oedipus Colonus. Phoenix, 1961, 15(2):63-73.

7024. Shoben, Edward Joseph, Jr. A clinical view of the tragic. Colorado Q, 1963, 11:352-363; Lit & Psychol, 1964, 14: 23-34.

7025. Short, J. P. La Peinture des passions chez Racine. Paris: Du, 1952.

7026. Shupe, Donald R. The wooing of Lady Anne: a psychological inquiry. Shakespeare Q, 1978, 29:28-36.

7027. Shuster, E. Schizophrenia and the flight from reality in golden age Spanish literature. Kentucky Foreign Language Q, 1966, 13:107-110.

7028. Sibony, Daniel. Hamlet: a writing effect. Yale French Studies, 1977, 55-56:53-93.

7029. Siemens, William L. Assault on the schizoid wasteland: René Marqués' El Apartamiento. Latin American Theatre Rev, 1974, 7:17-23.

7030. Sievers, Wieder David. An Analysis of the Influence of Freudian Psychology on American Drama, 1909-1939. Doctoral dissertation, Univ. Southern California, 1952.

7031. _____. Freud on Broadway: A History of Psychoanalysis and the American Drama. NY: Hermitage, 1955.

7032. _____. Tennessee Williams and Arthur Miller. In Hurrell, J. D. (ed), Two Modern American Tragedies. NY: Scribners, 1961, 139-145.

7033. Silhol, Robert. Magie et utopie dans La Tempete. Etudes Anglaises, 1964, 17:447-456.

7034. Silva, C. da. Hamlet e o complexo de Edipo. Jornal do Comércio, 7 May 1961.

7035. Silverberg, William V. Notes on The Iceman Cometh. Psychiatry, 1947, 10:27-29.

7036. Simon, Alfred. Le Théâtre, le mythe et la psyché. Esprit, 1965, n. s. , 33:818-823.

7037. Simon, Bennett. Mental life in Greek tragedy. In Mind and Madness in Ancient Greece; The Classical Roots of Modern Psychiatry. Ithaca: Cornell Univ. Press, 1978, 89-121.

7038. Simon, John K. Hippodrama at the psychodrome. Hudson Rev, 1975, 28:97-106.

7039. _____. Madness in Sartre: sequestration and the room. Yale French Studies, 1964, no. 30, 63-67.

7040. Simons, Richard C. The clown as a father figure. Psychoanal Rev, 1965, 52:75-91.

7041. Singer, S. Über die physiologischen Grundlagen der Shakespeareschen Psychologie. Jahrbuch der deutschen Shakespeare-Gesellschaft, 1900, 36:65-94.

7042. Singh, Ram Sewak. A psychological approach to Shakespeare. Vidya, 1965, 8:8:81-98.

7043. Sinha, K. Abhijnanasakuntalam: a psychological study. Ganganatha Jha Research Institute J, 1945, 2:243-268.

7044. Sinnot, Bethany S. The Father-Daughter Theme in Shakespeare's Plays. DAI, 1973, 34:339A.

7045. Sipahigil, Teoman. The Dramatic Use of Thought in the Structure of Othello. DAI, 1970, 31:129A.

7046. Sisson, C. J. Shakespeare's Helena and Dr. William Harvey, with a case history from Harvey's practice. Essays & Studies, 1960, 13:1-20.

7047. Sittler, Loring. The Emperor Jones--ein Individuationprozess im Sinne C. G. Jungs? Amerikastudien/American Studies, 1978, 23:118-130.

7048. Sjögren, Christine O. The status of women in several of Lessing's dramas. Studies in Eighteenth-Century Culture, 1977, 6:347-359.

7049. Skelton, Robin. J. M. Synge. Essays by Divers Hands, 1972, 37:95-107.

7050. Skene, Reg. The Cuchulian Plays of W. B. Yeats: A Study. NY: Columbia Univ. Press, 1975.

7051. Skinner, John. James M. Barrie; or the boy who wouldn't grow up. Amer Imago, 1957, 14:111-141; comment by Martin Grotjahn, 143-148.

7052. Skulsky, Harold. Revenge, honor and conscience in Hamlet.
       PMLA, 1970, 85:78-87.
7053. Slavensky, Sonia W. Suicide in the Plays of Arthur Miller:
       A View from Glory Mountain. DAI, 1973, 34:1936A.
7054. Slights, Camille. Murder, suicide and conscience: the cases
       of Brutus and Hamlet. In Brückmann, P. (ed), Familiar
       Colloquy. Ontario: Oberon Press, 1978, 113-131.
7055. Slochower, Harry. Shakespeare's Hamlet: the myth of mod-
       ern sensibility. Amer Imago, 1950, 7:197-238.
7056. _____. The Three Sisters by Anton Chekhov. In The
       Guide to Psychiatric and Psychological Literature, 1955,
       1(2).
7057. Slutsky, Jacob E. Equus and the psychopathology of passion.
       Int J Psychoanal Psychotherapy, 1976, 5:489-500.
7058. Smith, Elizabeth N. The Society of the Incomplete: The
       Psychology and Structure of Farce. DAI, 1970, 30:3958A.
7059. Smith, Gordon Ross. Authoritarian patterns in Shakespeare's
       Coriolanus. Lit & Psychol, 1959, 9:45-51; In Faber,
       M. D. (ed), The Design Within. NY: Science House,
       1970, 309-326.
7060. _____. The balance of themes in Romeo and Juliet. In
       Essays on Shakespeare. University Park: Penn State Univ.
       Press, 1965, 15-66.
7061. _____. Brutus, virtue, and will. Shakespeare Q, 1959,
       10:367-379.
7062. _____. The credibility of Shakespeare's Aaron. Lit &
       Psychol, 1960, 10:11-13; In Faber, M. D. (ed), The De-
       sign Within. NY: Science House, 1970, 35-39.
7063. _____. Good and Evil in Shakespearean Tragedy. DA,
       1957, 17:358.
7064. _____. Iago the paranoic. Amer Imago, 1959, 16:155-
       167; In Faber, M. D. (ed), The Design Within. NY: Sci-
       ence House, 1970, 170-182.
7065. _____. Negative and positive upon the psychology of Shake-
       spearean theater and audiences. College Lit, 1978, 5:94-
       100.
7066. _____. Shakespeare and Freudian interpretation. Amer
       Imago, 1959, 16:225-229.
7067. Smith, Miriam F. Psychological insights gained from litera-
       ture: analysis of King Lear. In Christian Assn for Psy-
       chological Studies, Proceedings 21st Annual Convention.
       Grand Rapids, Mich: Christian Assn for Psychological
       Studies, 1974.
7068. Smith, Raymond G. A semantic differential for theatre con-
       cepts. Speech Monographs, 1961, 28:1-8.
7069. Smith, R. J. Personal identity in Troylus and Cressida.
       English Studies in Africa, 1963, 6:7-26.
7070. Smith, Warren D. Romeo's final dream. Modern Language
       Rev, 1967, 62:579-583.
7071. Snell, Bruno. Shame and guilt: Aeschylus' Achilles. In
       Scenes from Greek Drama. Berkeley: Univ. California
       Press, 1964, 1-22.

7072. Soellner, Rolf H. Anima and Affectus: Theories of the Emo-
        tions in Sixteenth Century Grammar Schools and Their
        Reflections in the Works of Shakespeare. Doctoral dis-
        sertation, Univ. Illinois, 1954.
7073. _____. The madness of Hercules and the Elizabethans.
        Comparative Lit, 1958, 10:309-324.
7074. Sohlich, W. F. Genet's drama: rites of passage of the anti-
        hero: from alienated existence to artistic alienation.
        MLN, 1974, 89:641-653.
7075. Solomon, Rakesh H. Wall in Venice/3 women/wet shadows.
        Alan Finneran's performance landscape. Drama Rev,
        1978, 22:95-106.
7076. Somerville, Henry. Madness in Shakespearian Tragedy. Lon-
        don: Richards, 1929.
7077. Southard, G. C. The Medical Language of Aristophanes.
        Doctoral dissertation, Johns Hopkins Univ., 1970.
7078. Spanos, William V. 'Wanna go home, baby?' Sweeney Agon-
        istes as drama of the absurd. PMLA, 1970, 85:8-20.
7079. Sperber, Michael A. The 'as if' personality and Chekhov's
        'The Darling.' Psychoanal Rev, 1971, 58:14-21.
7080. Spevack, Marvin. Hamlet and imagery: the mind's eye.
        Die neueren Sprachen, 1966, 203-213.
7081. Spitzer, Leo. Le Récit de Théramène. In Linguistics and
        Literary History. Princeton: Princeton Univ. Press,
        1948.
7082. Spivack, Bernard. Falstaff and the psychomachia. Shake-
        speare Q, 1957, 8:449-459.
7083. Spotnitz, Hyman. The prophecies of Teiresias. Psychoanaly-
        sis, 1955-56, 4:37-43.
7084. _____. Talent in the playwright. Annals of Psychotherapy,
        1964, 5(1):18-22.
7085. Sproat, Kezia B. V. A Reappraisal of Shakespeare's View of
        Women. DAI, 1975, 36:3664A.
7086. Spurgeon, Carolyn F. E. Shakespeare's Imagery and What It
        Tells Us. NY: Macmillan, 1935; London: Cambridge
        Univ. Press, 1935, 1939, 1966; Excerpt in Alexander, P.
        (ed), Studies in Shakespeare. NY: Oxford Univ. Press,
        1964, 171-200.
7087- _____. Shakespeare's Iterative Imagery: I. As Under-
    8. song; II. As Touchstone, in His Work. Oxford: Oxford
        Univ. Press, 1931; London: Milford, 1931.
7089. _____. The use of imagery by Shakespeare and Bacon.
        Rev English Studies, 1933, 9:385-396.
7090. Stabler, A. P. Melancholy, ambition, and revenge in Belle-
        forest's Hamlet. Philological Q, 1966, 30:207-213.
7091. Staebler, Warren. The sexual nihilism of Iago. Sewanee
        Rev, 1975, 83:284-304.
7092. Stafford, William T. James examines Shakespeare: notes
        on the nature of genius. PMLA, 1958, 73:123-128.
7093. Stamm, Julian L. Peter Shaffer's Equus--a psychoanalytic
        exploration. Int J Psychoanal Psychotherapy, 1976, 5:
        449-461.

7094. _____. Shaw's Man and Superman. His struggle for sublimation. Amer Imago, 1965, 22:250-254.

7095. Stampfer, Judah. The Tragic Engagement. A Study of Shakespeare's Classical Tragedies. NY: Funk & Wagnalls, 1968.

7096. Stanton, Ralph G. A Midsummer Night's Dream: a structural study. Psychol Reports, 1967, 20:657-658.

7097. Stanzel, Franz K. Hamlet--psychologisches oder literarhistorisches Problem? In Muhler, R., & Fischl, J. (eds), Gestalt und Wirklichkeit. Berlin: 1967, 397-409.

7098. Stark, Karl. König Lear, eine psychiatrische Shakespeare-Studie für das gebildete Publikum. Stuttgart: Lindemann, 1871.

7099. Stark, Stanley. Suggestion regarding drama, inner creation, and role-taking (empathy), I: dramatic arts and dramatic dreaming. Perceptual Motor Skills, 1968, 26 (Suppl): 1319.

7100- Starobinski, Jean. Hamlet et Freud: Préface a la traduction
1. française de Ernest Jones, Hamlet et Oedipe. Paris: Gallimard, 1967.

7102. _____. Racine et la poésie du regard. Nouvelle Rev Française. Aug 1957, 246-263; In L'Oeil vivant. Paris: Gallimard, 1961, 69-90.

7103. Starr, Jack D. Manifestations of 'Sexuality' on the American Stage as Illustrated by Selected Plays from 1960-1969. DAI, 1975, 35:8065.

7104. States, Bert O. Chekhov's dramatic strategy. Yale Rev, 1967, 56:212-224.

7105. _____. Pinter's Homecoming: the shock of nonrecognition. Hudson Rev, 1968, 21:474-486.

7106. Stavrou, Constantine N. The neurotic heroine in Tennessee Williams. Lit & Psychol, 1955, 5(2):26-34.

7107. Stearns, Marshall Winslow. Hamlet and Freud. College English, 1949, 10:265-272; Discussion, College English, 1949, 10:475-476.

7108. Stedman, Jane W. From dame to woman: W. S. Gilbert and theatrical transvestism. In Vicinus, M. (ed), Suffer and Be Still; Women in the Victorian Age. Bloomington: Indiana Univ. Press, 1972, 30-37.

7109. Stein, Conrad. Psychanalyse appliquée, psychanalyse medicale. A propos de 'Hamlet et Oedipe' d'Ernest Jones. In La Mort d'Oedipe. Paris: Denoël, 1977.

7110. Steingesser, Richard H. Fear of the Crowd in Elizabethan Drama. DAI, 1973, 33:4365A-66A.

7111. Steinhauer, H. Eros and Psyche: a Nietzschean motif in Anglo-American literature. Modern Language Notes, 1949.

7112. Stekel, Wilhelm. Analytical comments on Ibsen's Peer Gynt. The roots of doubt. Psyche & Eros, 1920, 1:152-156.

7113. _____. A Dream Is Life and its connection with Grillparzer's neurosis. In Nunberg, H., & Federn, E. (eds), Minutes of the Vienna Psychoanalytic Society, Vol. 2: 1908-1910. NY: IUP, 1967, 2:12.

7114.   _____. On the psychopathology of Hauptmann's Griselda.
           In Nunberg, H. , & Federn, E. , (eds), Minutes of the Vi-
           enna Psychoanalytic Society, Vol. 2: 1908-1910. NY:
           IUP, 1967, 185-194.
7115.   Stenger, Edwin. Der Hamlet-Charakter. Eine psychiatrische
           Shakespeare-Studie. Berlin: Prenzlau und Biller, 1883.
7116.   Stephenson, William E. The adolescent dream-world of The
           Two Gentlemen of Verona. Shakespeare Q, 1966, 17:165-
           168.
7117.   Sterba, Richard F. The significance of theatrical perform-
           ance. Psychoanal Q, 1939, 8:335-337.
7118.   Stern, Charlotte. Actors, characters, and spectators in
           Tamayo's Un drama nuevo. Theatre J, 1979, 31:70-77.
7119.   Stern, E. S. , & Whiles, W. H. Three Ganser states and Ham-
           let. J Mental Science, 1942, 88:134-141.
7120.   Stetner, S. C. V. Baptista and his daughter. Psychoanal Rev,
           1973, 60:233-237.
7121.   _____. The bawdy bard: I. Shakespeare and the devil,
           an exploration of subliminal obscenity. Fragments, 1971,
           3:11-19.
7122.   _____, & Goodman, Oscar B. Lear's darker purpose.
           Lit & Psychol, 1968, 18:82-90.
7123.   Stevenson, G. H. Social psychiatry and Hamlet. Royal Soci-
           ety of Canada Transactions, 1949, 2:143-151.
7124.   Stewart, Bain T. The Renaissance Interpretation of Dreams
           and Their Use in Elizabethan Drama. Doctoral disserta-
           tion, Northwestern Univ. , 1942.
7125.   Stewart, Harold. Jocasta's crimes. Int J Psycho-Anal,
           1961, 42:424-430.
7126.   Stewart, John I. M. Character and Motive in Shakespeare.
           Some Recent Appraisals Examined. London: Longmans,
           1966 (1949).
7127.   _____. Shakespeare and his world: Shakespeare's char-
           acters. Listener, 1949, 42:312-316.
7128.   Stillman, Linda K. Doubling of sign and image in Roland
           Dubillard's La Maison d'os. Sub-stance, 1979, 22:85-95.
7129.   Stinson, J. J. Dualism and paradox in the puritan plays of
           David Storey. Modern Drama, 1977, 20:131-143.
7130.   Stirling, Brents. Psychology in Othello. Shakespeare Assn
           Bulletin, 1944, 19:135-144.
7131.   _____. Theme and character in Hamlet. Modern Lan-
           guage Q, 1952, 13:323-332.
7132.   Stockholder, Katherine. Fictions, phantasies, and 'reality':
           a reevaluation. Lit & Psychol, 1976, 26:17-30.
7133.   _____. Hamlet between night and day. Lit & Psychol,
           1971, 21:7-20.
7134.   _____. The other Coriolanus. PMLA, 1970, 85:228-236.
7135.   Stoll, Elmer Edgar. Freudian detective's Shakespeare.
           Modern Philology, 1950, 48:122-132.
7136.   _____. Shakespeare Studies, Historical and Comparative
           in Method. NY: Macmillan, 1927, 119-127.
7137.   _____. Source and motive in Macbeth and Othello. Rev
           English Studies, 1943, 19:25-32.

7138.   Stoller, Robert J.   Shakespearean tragedy: Coriolanus.
        Psychoanal Q, 1966, 35:263-274; In Faber, M.D. (ed),
        The Design Within.   NY: Science House, 1970, 329-339.
7139.   Stone, George W., Jr.   Garrick and Othello.   Philological Q,
        1966, 45:304-320.
7140.   Storfer, Adolf J.   Beiträge zur psychoanalytischen Bibliogra-
        phie: Plato und Freud, Musik, Asthma, Ibsen.   Psycho-
        analytische Bewegung, 1929, 1:67-73.
7141.   Stragnell, Gregory.   A psychopathological study of Ferenc
        Molnar's Liliom.   Psychoanal Rev, 1922, 9:40-49.
7142.   Strange, Sallie Minter.   Charlotte Charke: transvestite or
        conjuror?   Restoration & 18th Century Theatre Research,
        1976, 15(2):54-59.
7143.   Stroman, Ben.   Shakespeare als Shock-Therapie.   De Vlaamis
        Gids, 1964, 48:222-228.
7144.   Strong, Leonard A. G.   Shakespeare and the psychologists.   In
        Garrett, J. (ed), Talking of Shakespeare.   London: Hod-
        der & Stoughton, 1954, 187-208.
7145.   Stroud, T. A.   Hamlet and The Sea Gull.   Shakespeare Q,
        1958, 9:367-372.
7146.   Stroup, T. B.   Ritual and ceremony in the drama.   Compara-
        tive Drama, 1977, 11:139-146.
7147.   Stroupe, John H.   The masks of MacLeish's J. B.   Tennessee
        Studies in Lit, 1970, 15:75-83.
7148.   _____.   Shakespeare's Macbeth.   Explicator, 1969, 28:3.
7149.   Strout, Lilia D.   Psicomaquia y hierogamia en Las Paces de
        los Reyes y Judia de Toledo de Lope de Vega.   DAI,
        1974, 34:5205A-06A.
7150.   Stubbe, (?).   [Shakespeare and alcohol.]   Alkoholfrage, 1916,
        12:318-322.
7151.   Stümcke, H.   Sexualprobleme in der dramatischen Literatur.
        II.   Die neue Generation, 1916, 12(1, 2).
7152.   _____.   Das Sexualverbrechen in der dramatischen Dich-
        tung.   Zeitschrift für Sexualwissenschaft, 1915, 2:305-322.
7153.   Stuyver, Clara.   Ibsens dramatische Gestalten.   Psychologie
        und Symbolik.   Amsterdam: North-Holland Pub, 1952.
7154.   _____.   Psychologie en symbolik van Ibsens ouderdrama's.
        Doctoral dissertation, University Utrecht, 1942.
7155.   Styan, J. L.   Pirandellian theatre games: spectator as victim.
        Modern Drama, 1980, 23:95-111.
7156.   _____.   Psychology in the study of drama: the negative and
        the positive.   College Lit, 1978, 5:77-93.
7157.   _____.   Sight and space: the perception of Shakespeare on
        stage and screen.   Educational Theatre J, 1977, 29:18-28.
7158.   Sudhaus, Siegfried.   König Odipus Schuld.   Kiel: Lipsius und
        Fischer, 1912.
7159.   Sugnet, Charles J.   Exaltation at the close: a model for
        Shakespearean tragedy.   Modern Language Q, 1977, 38:
        323-335.
7160.   Sullivan, John J.   Stanislavski and Freud.   In Stanislavski and
        America.   NY: Hill & Wang, 1965, 188-199.
7161.   Sullivan, Patricia L.   [García Lorca's Yerma.]   Bulletin His-
        panic Studies, 1972, 49:265-275.

7162. Sullivan, Ruth Elizabeth. Big mama, big papa, and little
       sons in Ken Kesey's One Flew Over the Cuckoo's Nest.
       Lit & Psychol, 1975, 25:34-44.
7163. Sullivan, W. C. Shakespeare's Othello as a study of the mor-
       bid psychology of sex. Nineteenth Century, 1919, 85:
       1175-1180.
7164. Summer, Joseph H. The anger of Prospero. Michigan Q
       Rev, 1973, 12:116-135.
7165. Sutermeister, H. M. Schiller als Arzt. Ein Beitrag zur
       Geschichte der psychosomatischen Forschung. Bern:
       Lang, 1955.
7166. Swisher, Walter S. The symbolism of Wagner's Rheingold.
       Psychoanal Rev, 1923, 10:447-452.
7167. Symons, Norman J. The graveyard scene in Hamlet. Int J
       Psycho-Anal, 1928, 9:96-119.
7168. Sypher, Wylie. Hamlet: the existential madness. Nation,
       21 June 1946, 21.
7169. _____. The late-baroque purification: Racine. In Four
       Stages of Renaissance Style: Transformation in Art and
       Literature 1400-1700. Garden City, NY: Doubleday
       Anchor, 1955.
7170. Szafran, Willy A. [Man and theater: thoughts on the psy-
       chological reactions of the spectator.] Annales Médico-
       Psychologiques, 1976, 2:445-449.
7171. Szalita, Alberta B. Some questions for psychoanalysts and
       reflections on Ibsen's The Wild Duck. Psychoanal Rev,
       1970-71, 57:587-598.
7172. _____. [Who's Afraid of Virginia Woolf?: a psychoana-
       lytic view.] Unser Tsait, Feb 1964, 44-47.
7173. Szász, Zoltán. Freudizmus a szinpadon. Szinházi élet, 25
       Nov 1919.
7174. Szewcow, Maria. Anatolij Efros directs Chekhov's The
       Cherry Orchard and Gogol's The Marriage. Theatre Q,
       1977, 7:34-46.
7175. Szondi, Peter. Tableau and Coup de Théâtre: on the social
       psychology of Diderot's bourgeois tragedy. New Lit His-
       tory, 1980, 11:325-343; In Lektüren und Lektionen.
       Frankfurt: 1973.

7176. Tabernig, E. La mujer en la obra de Racine. Humani-
       dades, 1939, 27:259-268.
7177. Taëni, Rainer. On thin ice: Peter Handke's studies in
       alienation. Meanjin, 1977, 36:315-325.
7178. Tannenbaum, Samuel A. Hamlet and the psycho-analysts.
       Andiron Club Summons, 1928, 8:39.
7179. _____. The heart of Hamlet's mystery. J Sexology &
       Psychoanal, 1923, 1:316-323.
7180. _____. Psychoanalytic gleanings from Shakespeare.
       Psyche and Eros, 1920, 1:29-39.
7181. _____. Shakespeare and the new psychology. Dial, 1915,
       59:601-603.
7182. _____. Shakespeare Studies. NY: Author, 1930.

7183. _____. Slips of the tongue in Shakespeare. Dial, 1916, 61:89-91; Shakespeare Assn Studies, 1930, 5:63-71.

7184. _____. 'Your napkin is too little, let it alone,' a Freudian commentary. Studies in Philology, 1918, 15:73-81.

7185. _____. Über das Versprechen im Kaufmann von Venedig. H. Josef Aas, April 1912.

7186. Tarachow, Sidney. Circuses and clowns. In Psychoanalysis and the Social Sciences, Vol. 3. NY: IUP, 1951, 171-185.

7187. _____. Psychoanalytic observations on The Medium and The Telephone by Gian-Carlo Menotti. Psychoanal Rev, 1049, 36:376-384.

7188. Tarbox, Raymond. A note on M. D. Faber's essay, 'Suicide and The Ajax of Sophocles.' Psychoanal Rev, 1969, 56: 453-460.

7189. Tarrab, Gilbert. Le Happening, analyse psycho-sociologique. (Entire issue.) Rev d'Histoire du Théâtre, 1968, 20:7-102.

7190. Tausk, Victor. Ibsen the druggist. Psychoanal Q, 1934, 3: 137-141.

7191. _____. Paraphrase as commentary and critique on Gerhart Hauptmann's And Pippa Dances. Amer Imago, 1973, 30:340-359.

7192. Taylor, John Russell. British dramatists--the new arrivals: David Mercer/ after Freud and Marx. Plays & Players, 1970, 17(8):48-50.

7193. _____. Peter Shaffer. London: Longman, 1974.

7194. _____. Terence Rattigan and the sorrows of success [review article]. Drama, 1980, 135:19-22.

7195. Taylor, Michael. Realism and morality in Middleton's A Mad World, My Masters. Lit & Psychol, 1968, 18:166-178.

7196. Taylor, M. P. A father pleads for the death of his son. Int J Psycho-Analysis, 1927, 8:53-55.

7197. Taylor, Sally Thorne. Children in Shakespeare's Dramaturgy. DAI, 1975, 36:2228A-29A.

7198. Tebbe, Margaret Manzer. Contributions of William James to Speech and Theatre. DA, 1962, 13:2256.

7199. Tedesco, J. L. The white character in black drama, 1955-1970: description and rhetorical function. Communication Monographs, 1978, 45:64-74.

7200. Teller, F. Die Wechselbeziehung von psychischen Konflikt und körperlichem Leiden bei Schiller. Imago, 1921, 7: 95-126.

7201. Teplitz, Zelda. King Lear and Macbeth in relation to Shakepeare. Bulletin Philadelphia Assn Psychoanal, 1970, 20: 196-211.

7202. Terrien, Samuel. Albee's Alice. Christianity & Crisis, 1965, 25:140-143.

7203. Tharpe, Jac (ed). Tennessee Williams: A Tribute. Jackson: Univ. Press Mississippi, 1977.

7204. Theile, W. Racine. Darmstadt: Wissenschaftliche Buchgesellschaft, 1974.

7205. Thibaudet, Albert. Les Larmes de Racine. <u>Nouvelle Rev</u>
<u>Française</u>, 1932, 38:890-900.
7206. Thierry, M. Le Bonheur de Racine. <u>Rev Universelle</u>, 1935,
60:305-320.
7207. Thies, Henning. Vielnamigkeit im Kontext schizophrener Rol-
lenspiele: Pinter, <u>The Lover</u>. In <u>Namen im Kontext von</u>
<u>Dramen: Studien zur Funktionen Personennamen im eng-</u>
<u>lischen, amerikanischen und deutschen Drama.</u> Frank-
furt: Lang, 1978, 290-311.
7208. Thippavajjala, Dutta Ramesh. The Heroes of Arthur Miller.
<u>DAI</u>, 1975, 36:894.
7209. Thomov, Thomas S. Le Théâtre psychologique de Racine.
In <u>Homenaje a Arturo Marasso</u>. Bahia: Univ. Nacional
del Sur, 1972, 137-149.
7210. Thompson, Alan R. Ibsen as psychoanatomist. <u>Educational</u>
<u>Theatre J</u>, 1951, 3:34-39.
7211. Thompson, Ann. Philomel in <u>Titus Andronicus</u> and <u>Cymbeline</u>.
<u>Shakespeare Survey</u>, 1978, 31:23-32.
7212. Thompson, Judith Jarvis. Symbol, myth, and ritual in <u>The</u>
<u>Glass Menagerie</u>, The Rose Tattoo, and <u>Orpheus Descend-</u>
<u>ing</u>. In Tharpe, J. (ed), <u>Tennessee Williams: A Tribute</u>.
Hattiesburg: Univ. Mississippi Press, 1977, 697-711.
7213. Thompson, Larry. Stereotypes, 1760-1930: the black image
in early American drama. <u>Black World</u>, 1975, 24:54-69.
7214. Thorne, W. B. <u>Pericles</u> and the 'incest-fertility' opposition.
<u>Shakespeare Q</u>, 1971, 22:43-56.
7215. Thune, E. Paradox of the boy: a study of Peer Gynt's humanization. <u>Modern Drama</u>, 1976, 19:89-99.
7216. Thurman, William Richard. Anxiety in Modern American
Drama. <u>DA</u>, 1965, 25:5945.
7217. Timmons, W. M. The influence of a dramatic production
upon audience attitudes toward the play's thesis. <u>J So-</u>
<u>cial Psychology</u>, 1943, 18:305-313.
7218. _____. Some outcomes of participation in dramatics: introduction and attitude toward the play. <u>J Social Psychol</u>,
1943, 18:315-330.
7219. Tissi, Silvio. <u>Al Microscopic Psicanalitico</u>. Milan: Hoepli,
1946.
7220. Tobin, R. The too-faithful reflections: self-hatred in the
tragedies of Racine. <u>L'Esprit créateur</u>, 1968, 8(2).
7221. Toeman, Zerka. Role analysis and audience structure.
<u>Sociometry</u>, 1944, 7:205-221.
7222. Tolpin, Marian. Aeschylus' <u>Oresteia</u>: a curl in fifth-century
Athens. <u>JAMA</u>, 1969, 17:511-527.
7223. _____. Eugene Ionesco's <u>The Chairs</u> and the <u>Theater of</u>
<u>the Absurd</u>. <u>Amer Imago</u>, 1968, 25:119-139.
7224. Topsfield, L. T. Intention and ideas in <u>Flamenca</u>. <u>Medium</u>
<u>Aevum</u>, 1967, 36:119-133.
7225. Toole, William B., III. 'Iagothello': psychological action
and the theme of transformation in <u>Othello</u>. <u>South At-</u>
<u>lantic Bulletin</u>, 1976, 41(2):71-77.
7226. _____. The motif of psychic division in <u>Richard III</u>.
<u>Shakespeare Studies</u>, 1974, 27:21-32.

7227. _____. Psychological action and structure in Richard II. J General Education, 1978, 30:165-184.

7228. Tomieic, Zlatko. Otac i sin, glavni eticki problem Shakespeare ovog Hamletu. Marvlic, 1968, 1:64-71.

7229. Törnqvist, E. The illness pattern in The Master Builder. Scandinavia, 1972, 11:1-12.

7230. _____. Strindberg's The Stranger. Scandinavian Studies, 1970, 42:297-308.

7231. Touchet, Gene R. American Drama and the Emergence of Social Homophilia, 1952-1972. Doctoral dissertation, Univ. Florida, 1974.

7232. Towne, Jackson E. A psychoanalytic study of Shakespeare's Coriolanus. Psychoanal Rev, 1921, 8:84-91.

7233. Traci, Philip J. Suggestions about the bawdy in Romeo and Juliet. South Atlantic Q, 1972, 71(4):573-586.

7234. Trevelyan, H. Goethe's awareness of the unconscious and the elemental. The Gate, 1947, 1(4):34-36.

7235. Trevor-Roper, Hugh. Quel était son univers psychologique? In Pagnol, M., et al. (eds), Shakespeare. Paris: Hachette, 1962, 61-72.

7236. Troiano, James J. Pirandellism in the theatre of Roberto Arlt. Latin Amer Theater Rev, 1974, 8:37-44.

7237. Trosman, Harry. Freud and the controversy over Shakespeare authorship. JAPA, 1965, 13:475-498; Psychol Issues, 1976, 9(2-3):307-331.

7238. Trusina, K. Is there a way out? The inner world of Dürrenmatt's dramas. Communio Viatorum, 1965, 8:2-3.

7239. Tucker, Harry, Jr. Post-traumatic psychosis in Romeo und Julia auf dem Dorfe. German Life & Letters, 1972, 25: 247-251.

7240. Tübingen, Mathilde Sayler. Die Entwicklung des Symbolismus in Henrik Ibsens Gesellschaftsstuecken. Doctoral dissertation, 1937.

7241. Türck, Herman. Das psychologische Problem in der Hamlet-Tragödie. Leipzig: Hoffman, 1890.

7242. _____. Das psychologische Problem in der Hamlet-Tragödie. In Faust--Hamlet--Christus. Berlin: 1918, 201-290.

7243. Turel, A. 'King Lear.' In Bachofen-Freud: Zur Emanzipation des Mannes vom Reich d. Mütter. Bern: Huber, 1939, 61-74.

7244. Turnelle, M. Athalie and the dictators. Scrutiny, 1940, 8: 363-389.

7245. Turner, Darwin T. Dreams and hallucinations in drama of the twenties. College Language Assn J, 1960, 3:166-172.

7246. Turner, Diane E. The mythic vision in Tennessee Williams' Camino Real. In Tharpe, J. (ed), Tennessee Williams: A Tribute. Hattiesburg: Univ. Mississippi Press, 1977, 237-251.

7247. Turner, Jerry M. Statements of Feeling and Reason in the Dramas of Heinrich von Kleist. DAI, 1971, 32:2712A.

7248. Tuttle, Preston Heath. Comedy as a Reprojection of Childhood Experience: A Study of the Process by Which Emotional Content Determines Dramatic Form. DA, 1964, 24, 4316.

7249. Twitchell, James B. Shelley's metapsychological system in Act IV of Prometheus Unbound. Keats-Shelley J, 1975, 24:29-48.

7250. Tymms, R. Alternation of personality in the drama of Heinrich von Kleist and Zacharias Werner. Modern Language Rev, 1942, 37:68-70.

7251. Uchôa, Darcy de Mendonca. Edipo Rei: commentário sôbre a tragédia de Sófocles. Revista Brasilia de Psiquiátriá, 1967, 1:224-226.

7252. Uhlmann, Wilfred. Neurotische Konflikte und triebgesteurtes Sozialverhalten in den Stücken Harold Pinters. Literatur in Wissenschaft und Unterricht, 1972, 5:299-312.

7253. Ullman, Montague. A note on The Threepenny Opera. Amer J Psychol, 1959, 13:429-435.

7254. Unger, Leonard H. Deception and self-deception in Shakespeare's Henry IV. In The Man in the Name. Minneapolis: Univ. Minnesota Press, 1956, 3-17.

7255. _____. Yeats and Hamlet. Southern Rev, 1970, 6:698-709.

7256. Ure, Peter. Shakespeare and the inward self of the tragic hero. In Elizabethan and Jacobean Drama; Critical Essays. NY: Barnes & Noble, 1974, 1-21.

7257. Usimani, Renate. Friedrich Dürrenmatt as Wolfgang Schwitter. Modern Drama, 1968, 11:143-150.

7258. Vaidyanathan, T. G. The psychological interpretation of Hamlet. Osmania J English Studies, 1964, 4:67-76.

7259. Valency, M. Flight into lunacy. Theatre Arts, 1960, 44:8-11.

7260. Valgemae, Mardi. Auden's collaboration with Isherwood on The Dog Beneath the Skin. Huntington Library Q, 1967, 31:373-383.

7261. _____. Rice's The Subway. Explicator, 1967, 25:62.

7262. Van Ackere, J. E. Luigi Pirandello, of literatuur als psychodrame. Brugge: Desclée De Brouwer, 1968.

7263. Vandenbroucke, Russell. Equus: modern myth in the making. Drama & Theatre, 1975, 12:129-133.

7264. Van der Sterren, H. A. The King Oedipus of Sophocles. Int J Psycho-Anal, 1952, 33:343-350; In The Yearbook of Psychoanalysis, Vol. 9. NY: IUP, 1953, 314-327.

7265. _____. De lotgevallen van Koning Oedipus volgens de treurspelen van Sophocles. Amsterdam: Scheltema u Holkema, 1948.

7266. _____. Oedipe. Un Etude psychanalytique d'apres les tragédies de Sophocle. Paris: Presses Universitaires de France, 1976.

7267. _____. Was King Oedipus acting out? Int J Psycho-Anal, 1968, 49:394-395.

7268. Vane, George T.   The Father-Figure in Eighteenth Century
English Comedy.   DA, 1958, 19:133-134.
7269. Van Niel, P. J.   The Relapse--into death and damnation.
Educational Theatre J, 1969, 21:318-332.
7270. Varga, Laszlo, & Fye, Bonnieta.   Ghost and antic disposition: an existential and psychoanalytic interpretation of
Shakespeare's Hamlet.   Psychiat Q, 1966, 40:607-627.
7271. Various.   Homosexuality and the theatre.   Symposium.
Canadian Theatre Rev, 1976, 12:6-41.
7272. Vaughn, A.   Madness in Greek Thought and Custom.   Baltimore: 1919.
7273. Vehse, E.   Shakespeare als Protestant, Politiker, Psycholog
und Dichter.   Hamburg, 1851.
7274. Vercollier, Alain.   La Fonction des couleurs dans le théâtre
de Paul Claudel.   Claudel Studies, 1977, 4(2):12-25.
7275. Verdot, Guy.   Marcel Achard psychanalysé.   Les Nouvelles
Littéraires, 7 Nov 1963, no. 1888, 12.
7276. Verhoeff, Han.   Les Comédies de Corneille: Problématique
du genre à la lumière de la psychanalyse.   Littérature,
1978, 31:77-89.
7277. _____.   Les Comédies de Corneille.   Une Psycholecture.
Paris: Klincksieck, 1979; Review: J. H. Broome,
French Studies, 1980, 34:70-72.
7278. Versenyi, Laszlo.   Dionysus and tragedy.   Rev Metaphysics,
1962, 16(1):82-97.
7279. Vesonder, Timothy George.   Archetypal Patterns in the Plays
of Bernard Shaw.   DAI, 1976, 36:7448A-9A.
7280. Vessie, P. R.   Interpretation of Shakespeare's sex play, All's
Well That Ends Well.   Medical Record, 1937, 146:14-16.
7281. _____.   Psychiatry catches up with Shakespeare.   Medical
Record, 1936, 144:141-145.
7282. Veszy-Wagner, Lilla.   Macbeth: 'fair is foul and foul is
fair. '   Amer Imago, 1968, 25:242-257.
7283. _____.   Orestes the delinquent: the inevitability of parricide.   Amer Imago, 1961, 18:371-381.
7284. _____.   Pinero's farce The Magistrate as an anxiety
dream.   Amer Imago, 1975, 32:200-215.
7285. Victoroff, D.   Pourquoi nous applaudissons.   Rev d'aesthe-
tique, 1955, 8:79-87.
7286. Vienot, Pierre (ed).   Etudes psychomorphologiques des visages; théâtre 1947.   Paris: Galliope, 1947.
7287. Vigoroux, A.   La Pathologie mentale dans les drames de
Shakespeare.   Annales Médico-Psychologiques, 1918, 10:
152-172, 225-251.
7288. Villiers, André.   La Psychologie du comédien.   Paris:
Odette Lieutier, 1946.
7289. _____.   La Psychologie de l'art dramatique.   Paris:
Colin, 1951.
7290. Vinaver, E.   Racine et la poésie tragique.   Paris: Nizet,
1951.
7291. _____.   Racine, principes de la tragédie en marge de la
poétique d'Aristotle.   Université de Manchester, 1944.

7292. Vitelli, A. [Insanity in the tragedies of Shakespeare.] Gaz-
      zetta Internazionale di Medicina, 1922, 27:141, 152, 163.
7293. Vivier, R. Note sur les médecins et la médecine dans le
      théâtre de Molière. Bulletin de l'Académie Royale de
      Langue et de Littérature Françaises, 1964, 17(1).
7294. Vogelweith, P. Guy. Attente et intuition de la psychanalyse
      dans le théâtre de Strindberg. Scandinavia, 1973, 12(1):
      1-16.
7295. _____. Le Psychothéâtre de Strindberg: un auteur en
      quête de métamorphose. Paris: Klincksieck, 1972.
7296. Vogt, Leonard A. Sexuality in the British Drama Revival
      Since 1956. DAI, 1974, 35:3775A.
7297. Von Engeln, O. D. Shakespeare, the observer of nature.
      Scientific Monthly, 1916, 2:573-588.
7298. Von Schröder, Christoph. Wille und Nervosität in Shake-
      speares Hamlet. Ein Versuch, Hamlet Naturell vom
      medicinischen Standpunkt zu Beleuchten. Riga: 1893.
7299. Von Stockert, F. G. [Shakespeare and modern psychiatry.]
      Jahrbuch für Psychologie und Psychotherapie, 1964, 11:
      42-50.
7300. Vossler, K. Lecciones sobre Tirso de Molina. Madrid:
      Taurus, 1965.
7301. Vredenburgh, J. L. The character of the incest object: a
      study of alternation between narcissism and object choice.
      Amer Imago, 1957, 14:45-52.
7302. Vygotsky, Lev S. The Psychology of Art. Cambridge, Mass:
      M. I. T. Press, 1971 (1925), 166-196.

7303. Wadsworth, Frank W. Hamlet and the methods of literary
      analysis: a note. Amer Imago, 1962, 19:85-90.
7304. Wagner, Arthur. Permission and protection. Drama Rev,
      1969, 13:108-111.
7305. Wagner, Richard. Zum Hamlet-problem. Int Zeitschrift für
      Psychoanalyse, 1911, 1:525-527.
7306. Wainwright, J. W. A psychological study of Hamlet. Medical
      Records, 1908, 73:172-176.
7307. Wais, Kurt K. T. Erlebnis und dichtung bei Racine. Roman-
      istisches Jahrbuch, 1956, 6:110-132.
7308. Waith, E. M. Eugene O'Neill: an exercise in unmasking.
      Educational Theatre J, 1961, 13:182-191.
7309. Wakeman, Mary K. Dynamics of the tragic catharsis. Lit
      & Psychol, 1959, 4:39-41.
7310. Walder, M. Die Uneigentlichkeit des Bewusstseins. Zur
      Dramaturgie Odön von Horváths. Bonn: Bouvier, 1974.
7311. Walker, A. L. Convention in Shakespeare's description of
      emotion. Philological Q, 1938, 17:26-66.
7312. Walker, Hallam. Les Fâcheux and Molière's use of games.
      L'Esprit créateur, 1971, 11(2):21-33.
7313. Wall, John N. , Jr. Suffering and charity: similarities be-
      tween Rank's view of illness and Shakespeare's Christian
      humanism. J Otto Rank Assn, 1976, 11:29-32.

7314. Wangh, Martin. Othello: the tragedy of Iago. Psychoanal Q, 1950, 19:202-212; M. Faber, M. D. (ed), The Design Within. NY: Science House, 1970, 157-168.

7315. _____. A psychoanalytic commentary on Shakespeare's The Tragedies of King Richard the Second. Psychoanal Q, 1968, 37:212-238.

7316. _____. Underlying motivation in Pirandello's Six Characters in Search of an Author. JAPA, 1976, 24:309-328.

7317. Wardman, H. W. Sartre and the theatre of catharsis. Essays in French Lit, 1964, No. 1, 72-88.

7318. Wardropper, B. W. The unconscious mind in Calderón's El pintor de su deshonra. Hispanic Rev, 1950, 18:285-301.

7319. Warner, Elizabeth A. Work and play: some aspects of folk drama in Russia. Comparative Drama, 1978, 12:151-168.

7320. Warner, Ruth E. Decorum: Language and Evaluation of Behavior in Lyly and Shakespeare. DAI, 1977, 37:7768A.

7321. Warnken, Henry L. Iago as a projection of Othello. In Paolucci, A. (ed), Shakespeare Encomium. NY: City College Press, 1964, 1-15.

7322. Warstatt, Willi. Das Tragische. Eine psychologisch-kritische Untersuchung. Archiv für die Gesamte Psychologie, 1908, 13:1-70.

7323. Wasserman, Marlie Parker. Vivie Warren: a psychological study. In Weintraub, R. (ed), Fabian Feminist: Bernard Shaw and Women. University Park: Penn State Univ. Press, 1977, 168-173; Shaw Rev, 1972, 15:71-75.

7324. Watkins, W. B. C. The two techniques in King Lear. Rev English Studies, 1942, 18:1-26.

7325. Watson, Barbara B. The new woman and the new comedy. Shaw Rev, 1974, 17:2-16.

7326. Watson, H. M. The Theme of Death in Three Plays of Paul Claudel. DA, 1966, 27:784-5.

7327. Watson, Robert Irving. Coriolanus: an exercise in psychoanalysis. Northwestern Univ. Q, 1960, 2:41-43.

7328. Watson, Roy A. The Archetype of the Family in the Drama of Tennessee Williams. DAI, 1973, 34:1299A.

7329. Weales, Gerald. Arthur Miller. In Downer, A. S. (ed), The American Theater Today. NY: Basic Books, 1967, 85-90.

7330. Weathers, Winston. Mothers and sons: an essay on Greek tragedy. Classical J, 1951, 46:191-194, 200.

7331. _____. Winterset: the archetypal stage. In The Archetypes and the Psyche: Essays in World Literature. Tulsa, Okla: Univ. Tulsa Press, Monograph Series, No. 4, 97-102, 1968.

7332. Weber, H. -D. Kindermord als tragische Handlung. Der Deutschunterricht, 1976, 28(2):75-97.

7333. Webster, Peter D. Arrested individuation or the problem of Joseph and Hamlet. Amer Imago, 1948, 5:137, 225-245.

7334. Weigand, Hermann J. The Modern Ibsen. NY: Holt, 1925; NY: Dutton Everyman, 1960.

7335. Weigandt, W. Abnorme Charaktere in der dramatischen Literatur: Shakespeare, Goethe, Ibsen, G. Hauptmann. Hamburg: Voss, 1910.

7336. Weigard, Hermann J. Hamlet's consistent inconsistency. In Schueller, H. (ed), The Persistence of Shakespeare Idolatry. Detroit: Wayne State Univ. Press, 1964, 135-172.

7337. Weightman, John. The play as fable. Encounter, 1967, 28(2): 55-57.

7338. _____. Plays or psychodrama? Encounter, 1969, 32:62-65; In The Concept of the Avant-Garde. La Salle, Ill: Library Press, 1973, 170-175.

7339. _____. Spool, stool, drool. Encounter, 1973, 40(4):37-38.

7340. Weilgart, Wolfgang J. Shakespeare Psychognostic, Character Evolution and Transformation. Rutland, Vt: Tuttle, 1952; Tokyo: Hukuseido, 1952.

7341. Weintraub, Rodelle (ed). Fabian Feminist: Bernard Shaw and Women. University Park: Penn State Univ. Press, 1977.

7342. Weisberg, Richard. K. R. Eissler's Discourse on Hamlet. A symposium. Hamlet and ressentiment. Amer Imago, 1972, 29:318-337.

7343. Weisgram, Dianne H. Le Roi Jones' Dutchman: inter-racial ritual of sexual violence. Amer Imago, 1972, 29:215-232.

7344. Weisinger, Herbert. Iago's Iago. Univ. Kansas City Rev, 1953, 20:83-90.

7345. _____. The myth and ritual approach to Shakespearean tragedy. Centennial Rev, 1957, 1:142-166; In Grebstein, S. N. (ed), Perspectives in Contemporary Criticism. NY: Harper & Row, 1968, 322-336; In Handy, W. J., & Westbrook, M. (eds), Twentieth Century Criticism. NY: Free Press, 1974, 290-302.

7346. Weiss, Beno. Svevo's Inferiorità. Modern Fiction Studies, 1972, 18:45-51.

7347. Weissberg-Dronia, Mira. Selbstverständnis und Welterfahrung in Arthur Schnitzlers frühen Dramen. Freiburg im Breisgau, 1969.

7348. Weissman, Philip. Antigone--a preoedipal old maid. J Hillside Hospital, 1964, 13:32-42.

7349. _____. Author or analyst? New York Times, 1 Sept 1957, 1, 3 [Theatre section].

7350. _____. La Creatividad en el Teatro: Estudio Psicoanalitico. Mexico/Argentina/Spain: Siglo Veintivno, 1967.

7351. _____. Creativity in the Theater. NY: Basic Books, 1965; NY: Dell, 1965; Reviews: Edmund Pollock, Psychiatry, 1966, 29:197-199; Robert Seidenberg, Psychoanal Q, 1966, 35:143-146.

7352. _____. Development and creativity in the actor and playwright. Psychoanal Q, 1961, 30:549-567.

7353. _____. Early development of the artistic director. JAPA, 1964, 12:59-79.

7354. _____. A lively theater of lives: portraiture versus art. Modern Drama, 1959, 2:263-267.

7355. _____. Mourning Becomes Electra and The Prodigal. Modern Drama, 1960, 3:257-259.

7356. _____. Psychiatry and the theater. J Hillside Hospital, 1964, 13:100-113.
7357. _____. Psychoanalytic comments on modern theater. In The Psychoanalytic Study of Society. NY: IUP, 1962, 2:186-192.
7358. _____. Psychoanalyzing the critic. Canadian Theater Rev, 1975, 8:17-23.
7359. _____. Psychopathological characters in current drama. A study of a trio of heroines. Amer Imago, 1960, 17: 272-288.
7360. Welch, Charles A. Guilt in Selected Plays of Arthur Miller. A Phenomenological Inquiry and Creative Response. DAI, 1972, 33:1031A.
7361. Welsh, Alexander. The task of Hamlet. Yale Rev, 1980, 69:481-502.
7362. Werman, David S. Methodological problems in the psychoanalytic interpretation of literature: a review of studies on Sophocles' Antigone. JAPA, 1979, 27:451-478.
7363. Werner, Craig. Primal screams and nonsense rhymes: David Rabe's revolt. Educational Theater J, 1978, 30: 517-529.
7364. Wertham, Frederic. The matricidal impulse: critique of Freud's interpretation of Hamlet. J Criminal Psychopathology, 1941, 2:455-464; In Faber, M. D. (ed), The Design Within. NY: Science House, 1970, 113-120.
7365. _____. Medea in modern dress. In The Show of Violence. Garden City, NY: Doubleday, 1949, 211-238.
7366. West, Fred. Iago the psychopath. South Atlantic Bulletin, 1978, 43(2):27-35.
7367. West, L. J. The Othello syndrome. Contemporary Psychoanal, 1968, 4:103-110.
7368. West, Robert H. Sex and pessimism in King Lear. Shakespeare Q, 1960, 11:55-60.
7369. Wexler, Henry. Fate knocks. Int J Psycho-Anal, 1959, 40: 232-237.
7370. Weygandt, Wilhelm. Abnorme Charakters in der dramatischen Literatur. Hamburg: Voss, 1910.
7371. _____. Die abnormen Charakters bei Ibsen. Grenzfr Nerven- u Seelenlebens, 1907, 50.
7372. Wheeler, Richard P. Marriage and manhood in All's Well That Ends Well. Bucknell Rev, 1973, 21(1):103-124.
7373. _____. A Psychoanalytic Study of All's Well That Ends Well. DAI, 1971, 31:4739-A-4740-A.
7374. White, David M. Shakespeare and psychological warfare. Public Opinion Q, 1948, 12:68-72.
7375. White, Jackson E. Existential Themes in Selected Plays of Eugene O'Neill. DA, 1967, 28:1089A-90A.
7376. _____. Phèdre is not incestuous. Romance Notes, 1966, 9:89-94.
7377. White, John J. A note on Brecht and behaviourism. Forum Modern Language Studies, 1971, 7:249-258.
7378. White, J. S. George Büchner or the suffering through the father. Amer Imago, 1952, 9:365-427.

7379. White, R. S. The tragedy of Ophelia. Ariel, 1978, 9:41-53.
7380. White, Sidney Howard. What Freudian death-wish is the crown 'borrowing' in Henry IV? Ball State Teachers College Forum, 1964, 5:42-44.
7381. Whitehead, Clay C. Mozart's The Magic Flute: a paradigm for separation and initiation. Int Rev Psycho-Anal, 1978, 5:105-121.
7382. Whiteside, George. John Webster: a Freudian interpretation of his two great tragedies. In Pope, R. D. (ed), The Analysis of Literary Texts, Ypsilanti, Mich: Bilingual Press, 1980, 201-211.
7383. Whitmire, C. L. Psychoses of Shakespearean characters. Illinois Medical J, 1928, 53:64-72.
7384. Whitney, C. K. The war in Antony and Cleopatra. Lit & Psychol, 1963, 13:63-66; In Faber, M. D. (ed), The Design Within. NY: Science House, 1970, 282-286.
7385. Wickham, Harvey. Did Shakespeare murder his father? Catholic World, 1932, 134:538-546.
7386. Wigler, Stephen. If looks could kill: fathers and sons in The Revenger's Tragedy. Comparative Drama, 1975, 9:206-225.
7387. _____. The Penitent Brothel reconsidered: the place of the grotesque in Middleton's A Mad World, My Masters. Lit & Psychol, 1975, 25:17-26.
7388. _____. Thomas Middleton's A Chaste Maid in Cheapside: the delicious and the disgusting. Amer Imago, 1976, 33:197-215.
7389. Wiingaard, Jytte. Dom Juan, a reassessment in view of modern existentialism. In Johnson, R. B., Neumann, E. S., & Trail, G. T. (eds), Molière and the Commonwealth of Letters; Patrimony and Posterity. Jackson: Univ. Mississippi Press, 1975, 639-644.
7390. Wilcher, Robert. The fool and his techniques in the contemporary theatre. Theatre Research Int, 1979, 4:117-133.
7391. Wile, Ira S. Love at first sight as manifest in The Tempest. Amer J Orthopsychiat, 1938, 8:341-356.
7392. _____. The personality of King Lear as a young man. Amer J Orthopsychiat, 1935, 5:325-336.
7393. _____. Some Shakespearean characters in the light of present-day psychologies. Psychiat Q, 1942, 16:62-90.
7394. Wiles, Timothy James. Catharsis and the theatre event. DAI, 1975, 35:7928A.
7395. Wiley, Charles G. A Study of the American Woman as She Is Presented in the American Drama of the Nineteen-Twenties. DA, 1957, 17:2274.
7396. Wilkinson, Andrew M. A psychological approach to Julius Caesar. Rev English Lit, 1966, 7:65-78; In Faber, M. D. (ed), The Design Within. NY: Science House, 1970, 65-78.
7397. Willbern, David P. The Elizabethan Revenge Play: A Psychoanalytic Inquiry. DAI, 1973, 34:1261-A.
7398. _____. Paranoia, criticism, and Malvolio. Hartford Studies in Lit, 1979, 1-23.

7399. _____. Thomas Kyd's The Spanish Tragedy: inverted vengeance. Amer Imago, 1971, 28:247-267.

7400. Willeford, William. The mouse in the model. Modern Drama, 1969, 12:135-145.

7401. Williams, Edwin E. Tragedy of Destiny: Oedipus Tyrannus, Macbeth, Athalie. Cambridge: Editions XVIIᵉ siècle, 1940.

7402. Williams, Edith W. God's share: a mythic interpretation of The Chairs. Modern Drama, 1969, 12:298-307.

7403. Williams, George W. The complex Oedipus complex: Claudius, the rat. Shakespeare Newsletter, 1968, 18:12.

7404. Williams, Gordon. Acting and suffering in Hero and Leander. Trivium, 1973, 8:11-26.

7405. Williams, Gwyn. The Comedy of Errors rescued from tragedy. Rev English Lit, 1964, 5:63-71.

7406. Williams, Philip. The birth and death of Falstaff reconsidered. Shakespeare Q, 1957, 8:359-365.

7407. Williams, Roosevelt John. Modes of Alienation of the Black Writer: Problem and Solution in the Evolution of Black Drama and Contemporary Black Theatre. DAI, 1975, 35:5370A.

7408. Williamson, Marilyn L. Oedipal fantasies in Measure for Measure. Michigan Academician, 1976, 9:173-184.

7409. Wilmer, Harry A. Psychiatrist on Broadway. Amer Imago, 1955, 12:157-178.

7410. _____. Saturday's psychiatrist. Amer Imago, 1955, 12: 179-186.

7411. Wilson, Edmund. J. Dover Wilson on Falstaff. In Classics and Commercials. NY: Farrar, Straus, 1951, 162-163.

7412. _____. Morose Ben Jonson. In The Triple Thinkers. NY: Scribner's, 1948; In Barish, J.A. (ed), Ben Jonson: A Collection of Critical Essays. Englewood Cliffs, NJ: Prentice-Hall, 1963; 60-74.

7413. Wilson, Emmett, Jr. Coriolanus: the anxious bridegroom. Amer Imago, 1968, 25:224-241.

7414. Wilson, F.A.C. Swinburne and Kali: the confessional element in Atalanta in Calydon. Victorian Poetry, 1973, 11:215-228.

7415. Wilson, J. Dover. What Happens in Hamlet? Cambridge: Cambridge Univ. Press, 1951.

7416. Wilson, Robert Neal. Arthur Miller: the salesman and society. In The Writer as Seer. Chapel Hill: Univ. North Carolina, 1979, 56-71.

7417. _____. Eugene O'Neill: the web of family. In The Writer as Seer. Chapel Hill: Univ. North Carolina, 1979, 72-88.

7418-
9.   _____. Samuel Beckett: the social psychology of emptiness. J Social Issues, 1964, 20:62-70; The Writer as Seer. Chapel Hill: Univ. North Carolina Press, 1979, 134-144.

7420. Wilson, Rodger Edward. The devouring mother: analysis of Dürrenmatt's Besuch der alten Dame. German Rev, 1977, 52:274-288.

7421. Winder, M. The psychological significance of Hofmannsthal's Ariade auf Naxos. German Life & Letters, 1961, 15:100-109.

7422. Winslow, F. L. S. The psychology of Hamlet. J Psychol Medicine, 1879, 5:123-127.

7423. Winston, Florence T. The Significance of Women in the Plays of Philip Massinger. DAI, 1972, 33:2909A.

7424. Winterstein, Alfred F. R. Zur Entstehungsgeschichte der griechischen Tragödie. Imago, 1912, 8:440-505.

7425. _____. Zur Psychoanalyse des Reisens. Imago, 1912, 1:497.

7426. _____. Der Ursprung der Tragödie, ein psychoanalytischer Beitrag zur Geschichte des griechischen Theaters. Vienna: Int Psychoanalytischer Verlag, 1925.

7427. Wisdom, John O. The lust for power in Hedda Gabler. Psychoanal Rev, 1944, 31:419-437.

7428. Wismer, Lawrence Howard. Changing Concepts of Death in American Drama, 1885-1960. DA, 1964, 24:3464-65.

7429. Wit, Adriaan de. Adamov's Eurydice: a mystical initiation rite. French Rev, 1977, 50:454-459.

7430. _____. Anouilh's Euridice: a mystical initiation rite. French Rev, 1977, 50:454-459.

7431. Witham, Barry B. Anger in Equus. Modern Drama, 1979, 22:61-66.

7432. Withim, Philip M. Tragic catharsis and the resources of the ego. Psychoanal Rev, 1973, 60:497-518.

7433. Withington, R. Why put Freud into Hamlet. College English, 1949, 10:475-476.

7434. Wittels, Fritz. Tragische Motive: Das Unbewusste von Held und Helden. Berlin: Flieschel, 1911.

7435. Wohlfarth, P. Melancholie und Kurzschrift. Ein englischer Arzt, der Shakespeare beeinflusst hat. Deutscher Aerzteblätter, 1967, 64:603-607.

7436. Wolf, Ernest S. What method this madness: an inquiry into Hamlet's antic disposition. Comprehensive Psychiat, 1973, 14:189-195.

7437. Wolfenstein, Martha, and Leites, Nathan. The analysis of themes and plots. Annals Amer Academy Political Social Science, 1947.

7438. Wolff, Gustav. Der Fall Hamlet. Munich: Reinhardt, 1914.

7439. Wolff, Reinhold. Psychoanalytische Literaturkritik. Munich: 1975.

7440. Wolfinger, W. D. The seven deaths in Hamlet. Cresset, 1965, 28:7-12.

7441. Wollenberg, Robert. Shakespeare, Persönliches aus Welt und Werk. Eine psychologische Studie. Berlin: Ebering, 1939.

7442. Wolman, Benjamin B. The Antigone principle. Amer Imago, 1965, 22:186-201.

7443. Wood, Frederick T. Hamlet's madness. Notes & Queries, 1931, 160:7.

7444. Wood, James O. Shakespeare's touch of acrophobia. Topic, 1964, 7:78-82.

7445. Wood, Michael. A study of fire imagery in some plays by
       Paul Claudel. French Studies, 1965, 19(2):144-158.
7446. Wood, W. D. Hamlet, from a Psychological Point of View.
       London: Longmans, Green, 1870.
7447. Woodman, Ross G. James Reaney. In Canadian Writers.
       Toronto: New Canadian Library, 1970, 12:1-64.
7448. Woods, A. H. Syphilis in Shakespeare's tragedy of Timon of
       Athens. Amer J Psychiat, 1934, 91:95-107.
7449. Woodyard, George W. The Search for Identity: A Compara-
       tive Study in Contemporary Latin American Drama. DA,
       1967, 27:2165A-66A.
7450. Woolbert, Charles Henry. The Audience. Psychol Rev
       Monographs, 1916, No. 21. In Bertley, J. M. (ed),
       Studies in Social and General Psychology. NY: Psycho-
       logical Review Co., 1916.
7451. Wooldridge, J. B. The theme of love in Lope's El amor en-
       amorado. Bulletin of the 'Comediantes,' 1975, 27:101-
       108.
7452. Woolsey, Arthur Wallace. Illusion versus reality in some of
       the plays of Alejandro Casona. Modern Language J, 1954,
       33:80-84.
7453. Wormhoudt, Arthur. Hamlet's Mouse Trap: A Psychoanalytic
       Study of the Drama. NY: Philosophical Library, 1956.
7454. Worthen, John. Endings and beginnings: Edward Bond and
       the shock of recognition. Educational Theatre J, 1975,
       27:466-479.
7455. Worton, Michael. Obsessional theater? The role of the
       father-figure in Arthur Adamov's early plays. Nottingham
       French Studies, 1978, 17(1):71-77.
7456. Wright, Robert C. O'Neill's universalizing technique in The
       Iceman Cometh. Modern Drama, 1966, 8:1-11.
7457. Wulffen, Erich. Gerhart Hauptmanns Dramen. Berlin:
       Lichterfelde, 1911(?).
7458. _____. Kriminalpsychologie und Psychopathologie in Schil-
       lers Räubern. Halle: 1907.
7459. _____. Shakespeares grosse Verbrecher: Richard III,
       Macbeth, Othello. Berlin: Langenscheidt, 1911.
7460. _____. Shakespeares Hamlet, ein Sexualproblem. Berlin:
       Duncker, 1913.
7461. Wymer, R. Suicide and despair in the Jacobean drama.
       Master's thesis, Univ. Oxford, 1976.

7462. Xrapovickaja, G. N. Individual' naja psixologija i social'naja
       problematika v tvorcestve X. Kroga (1920-1930-e gody).
       Skandinavskij Sbornik (Tallinn), 1973, 18:202-211.

7463. Yamamoto, Tadav, et al. 'Mad scenes' in King Lear. Ang-
       lica, 1964, 5:123-142.
7464. Yamaura, Takuzo. Ophelia's mad songs--their background,
       sources and dramatic function. Essays & Studies in Eng-
       lish Language & Lit, (Japan), 1970, 56:1-42.

7465. Yankowitz, Susan. Lowell's Benito Cereno: an investigation of American innocence. Yale Theatre, 1968, 2:81-90.
7466. Yearsley, Macleod. The Sanity of Hamlet. London: Bale, Sons & Danielson, 1933.

7467. Zagel, Milton. The Family Problem in the Dramas of Friedrich Hebbel. Doctoral dissertation, Univ. Iowa, 1951.
7468. Zarlove, Jerald. Romeo and Juliet: the rites of disciplined youth. Paunch, 1965, 23:10-17.
7469. Zdenek, Joseph W. Psychical conflicts in Benavente's La malquerida. Romance Notes, 1978, 19:183-189.
7470. Zeder, Suzan Lucille. A Character Analysis of the Child Protagonist as Presented in Popular Plays for Child Audiences. DAI, 1978, 39:3236A.
7471. Zeller, James Albert. The Male-Female Configuration in Carl Sternheim's Dramas in the Context of His Social Views. DAI, 1977, 37:5865A.
7472. Zeller, Loren L. Two expressionistic interpretations of dehumanization: Rice's The Adding Machine and Muñiz's El Tintero. Essays in Lit, 1975, 2:245-255.
7473- Ziino, Giuseppe. Guglielmo Shakespeare e la scienze mod-
4.   erna. Studio medico-psicologico e guiridlico. Messina: D'Amico, 1897.
7475. Zilboorg, Gregory. Introduction to Leonid Andreyev, He Who Gets Slapped. NY: Dial, 1921; NY: Brentano's, 1922.
7476. _____. The silent tragedy of the actor. Drama, 1922, 12:247-249.
7477. _____. The theatre of the past in Soviet Russia. Drama, 1922, 12:195-196.
7478. _____. Theatre soliloquies. I. Drama, 1921, 2:225-226, 256-257.
7479. _____. _____. III. Intellectual ice cream and native drama. Drama, 1921, 2:319, 335-337.
7480. _____. _____. II. The intelligensia and the street; impressions of a travelling stranger. Drama, 1921, 2:276, 295-297.
7481. _____. _____. V. The stageless road. Drama, 1921, 2:395-396.
7482. _____. _____. VI. Chautauqua and the drama. Drama, 1921, 12:16-18, 40.
7483. _____. _____. VII. On the verge. Drama, 1922, 12:120-121.
7484. Zimmer, R. K. The emergence of the 'new' woman on the English stage. Kentucky Philological Assn Bulletin, 1975, 25-31.
7485. Ziolkowski, Theodore. An ontology of anxiety in the dramas of Schiller, Goethe and Kleist. In Sammons, J. L., & Schürer, E. (eds), Lebendige Form. Interpretationen zur deutschen Literatur. Munich: Fink, 1970, 121-146; In Frühwald, W., & Niggl, G. (eds), Sprache und Bekenntnis. Berlin: Dunsker u Humbolt, 1971.
7486. Ziomek, H. [Casona's La dama del alba.] Symposium, 1970, 24:81-85.

7487.   Zito, George V. Durkheimian suicides in Shakespeare.
        Omega: J Death & Dying, 1973, 4:293-304.
7488.   Zolotow, Maurice. To couch or not to couch.   Theatre Arts,
        1954, 38:31-32, 93-94.
7489.   Zuk, Gerold H. A note on Richard's anxiety dream.   Amer
        Imago, 1957, 14:37-39.

7490. Alexander, Franz. Fundamentals of Psychoanalysis. NY: Norton, 1948, 101.
7491. Anon. Book review. Freudian fairy tales. Nation, 1916, 103:13.
7492. Arnold, H. M. Snow White and the Seven Dwarfs. A symbolic account of human development. Perspectives in Psychiat Care, 1979, 17:218-222, 236.

7493. Baggesen, Søren. Individuation eller frelse? Kritik, 1967, 1.
7494. Balint, Alice. Die Bedeutung des Märchens für des Seelenleben des Kindes. Zeitschrift für psychoanalytische Pädagogik, 1935, 9:113-116.
7495. Barchilon, Jacques. The aesthetics of the fairy tale. In Van Baelen, J., & Rubin, D. L. (eds), La Cohérence intérieure. Etudes sur la littérature française du XVIIe siècle. Paris: Jean-Michel Place, 1977, 187-201.
7496. _____. Beauty and the Beast. From myth to fairy tale. Psychoanal & Psychoanal Rev, 1959, 46(4):19-29.
7497. Barolo, Enrico. [Social autism and Andersen's fables.] Rivista di Psicologia, 1972, 66:35-46.
7498. Beit, Hedwig von. Gegensatz und Erneurung im Märchen. Bern: Francke, 1956.
7499. _____. Symbolik des Märchens. Bern: Francke, 1952.
7500. Benedict, A. L. The psychological effect of the fairy story. New York State Medical J, 1914, 99:925-928.
7501. Bergler, Edmund. The clinical importance of Rumpelstiltskin as anti-male manifesto. Amer Imago, 1961, 18:65-70.
7502. Bethe, E. Märchen, Sage, Mythus. Leipzig: Quelle u Meyer, 1922.
7503. Bettelheim, Bruno. The importance of fairy tales. Instructor, 1970, 86:79-80.
7504. _____. Lessons for life: E. Humperdinck's Hansel and Gretel; excerpt from The Uses of Enchantment. Opera News, 1978, 43:10-14+.
7505. _____. Reflections. New Yorker, 1975, 51:50-52+.
7506. _____. The Uses of Enchantment. The Meaning and Importance of Fairy Tales. NY: Knopf, 1976; Reviews: Leslie A. Fiedler, Saturday Rev, 1976, 3(16):24-27; M. V. Hallab, Southern Rev, 1978, 14:390-394.
7507. Bilz, Josephine. Märchengeschehen und Reifungsvorgänge unter tiefenpsychologischem Gesichtspunkt. In Bühler, C.,

& Bilz, J., (eds), Das Märchen und die Phantasie des Kindes. Munich: Barth, 1958.

7508. _____. Menschliche Reifung im Sinnbild, eine psychologische Untersuchung über Wandlungmetaphern des Traums, des Wahns und des Märchens. Leipzig: Hirsel, 1943.

7509. Birrell, Gordon. The Boundless Present: Space and Time in the Literary Fairy Tales of Novalis and Tieck. Durham: Univ. North Carolina Studies in Germanic Languages & Literatures, 1979.

7510. _____. Spatial and Temporal Structure in the Märchen of Novalis and Tieck: An Approach to the Problem of Genre in Early Romanticism. Doctoral dissertation, Stanford Univ., 1968.

7511. Bittner, Guenther. Über die Symbolik weiblicher Reifung im Volksmärchen. Praxis der Kinderpsychologie und Kinderpsychiatrie, 1963, 12:210-213.

7512. Boillot, F. Les Impressions sensorielles chez La Fontaine. Paris: Presses Universitaires de France, 1929.

7513. Böklen, Ernst. Schneewittchen-Studien. In Mythologische Bibliothek. Leipzig: 1915, Vol. 7, 50-65.

7514. Bornstein, S. Das Märchen von Dornröschen in psychoanalytischer Darstellung. Imago, 1933, 19:505-517; Revista de Psicoanálisis, 1945, 3:299-313.

7515. Brachfeld, O. Über den Geschlechtswechsel in Sagen und Märchen. Zeitschrift für Sexualwissenschaft, 1929, 16: 318-323.

7516. Bradfer-Blomart, Jeanine, & Lam, Hai. [Children and fairytales.] Psychologica Belgica, 1976, 16:153-170.

7517. Brenman, M. The recall of fairy tales in normal and hypnotic states. Psychol Bulletin, 1942, 39:488-489.

7518. Briehl, Marie H. A psychoanalytic point of view on the use of fairy tales in the education of young children. Reiss-Davis Clinic Bulletin, 1976, 13(1):28-44.

7519. _____. Die Rolle des Märchens in der Kleinkinderziehung. Zeitschrift für psychoanalytische Pädagogik, 1937.

7520. Briggs, Katharine M. Symbols in fairy tales. In Davidson, H. (ed), Symbols of Power. Cambridge, Eng: Brewer; Totowa, NJ: Rowman & Littlefield, 1977, 131-155.

7521. Brill, Abraham A. Fairy tales as a determinant of dreams and neurotic symptoms. New York Medical J, 1914, 99: 561-567.

7522. Brody, Morris W. A psychoanalytical interpretation of Rapunzel: the symbolic significance of twins. Samiksa, 1954, 8:20-25.

7523. Bruce, Bertram, & Newman, Denis. Interacting plans. Cognitive Science, 1978, 2:195-233.

7524. Brun, Gudrun & Brun, Georg C. A psychological treatise on Hans Andersen's fairy tale Thumbelina. Acta Psychiatrica et Neurologica, 1946, 21:141-149.

7525. Bühler, Charlotte. Das Märchen und die Phantasie des Kindes. Berhefte zur Zeitschrift für angewandte Psychologie, 1918, 17.

7526. _____. Das Märchen und die Phantasie des Kindes. Leipzig: Barth, 1929.

7527.   Carloni, Glauco. La fiaba al lume della psicoanalisi. Ri-
        vista di Psicoanalisi, 1963, 9:169-186.
7528.   _____. I mostri delle fiabe. Atlante, 1967, (29):70-77.
7529.   Cath, Stanley H., & Cath, Claire. On the other side of Oz.
        Psychoanalytic aspects of fairy tales. In The Psycho-
        analytic Study of the Child, Vol. 33. New Haven: Yale
        Univ. Press, 1978, 621-639.
7530.   Chasseguet-Smirgel, Janine. Le Rossignol de l'empereur de
        Chine: essai psychanalytique sur le 'Faux. ' Rev Fran-
        çaise de Psychanalyse, 1969, 33:115-142.
7531.   Chukovsky, Kornei I. From two to five. Psychol Today,
        1968, 1:62-65.
7532.   _____. From Two to Five. Berkeley: Univ. California
        Press, 1963.
7533.   Coleman, Stanley M. The myth of the fairy birth. Psycho-
        anal Rev, 1939, 26:301-314.
7534.   Collier, Mary J. The psychological appeal in the Cinderella
        theme. Amer Imago, 1961, 18:399-411.
7535.   Corsini, Raymond J. The blind men and the elephant three
        ends to one tale. ETC, 1955, 12:245-247.
7536.   Crawford, Elizabeth. The wolf as condensation. Amer
        Imago, 12:307-314.

7537.   Daemmrich, Horst S. The infernal fairy tale: inversion of
        archetypal motifs in modern European literature. Mosaic,
        1972, 5(3):85-95.
7538.   Datan, N. The narcissism of the life cycle. The dialectics
        of fairy tales. Human Development, 1977, 20:191-197.
7539.   Dégh, Linda. Grimm's 'Household Tales' and its place in
        the household: the social relevance of a controversial
        classic. Western Folklore, 1979, 38:83-103.
7540.   Démoris, R. Du littéraire au littéral dans Peau d'Ane de
        Perrault. Rev des Sciences Humaines, 1977, 43:261-279.
7541.   Desmonde, William H. Jack and the Beanstalk. Amer
        Imago, 1951, 8:287-288.
7542.   DeVries, J. Over de stof der sproken en de boerden.
        Nederlands Tijdschrift voor Vokpsychologie, 1928, 33:161-
        180.
7543.   Dieckmann, Hans. Zum Aspekt des Grausamen in Märchen.
        Praxis der Kinderpsychologie und Kinderpsychiatrie.
        1967, 16(8):298-306.
7544.   _____. The favourite fairy-tale of childhood. J Analytic
        Psychol, 1971, 16:18-30.
7545.   _____. Das Lieblingsmärchen der Kindheit und seine
        Beziehung zu Neurose und Persönlichkeitsstruktur.
        Praxis der Kinderpsychologie und Kinderpsychiatrie, 1967,
        16(6):202-208.
7546.   _____. Das Lieblingsmärchen der Kindheit als thera-
        peutischer Faktor in der Analyse. Praxis der Kinder-
        psychologie und Kinderpsychiatrie, 1968, 17(8):288-292.
7547.   _____. Märchen und Träume als Helfer des Menschen.
        Stuttgart: Bonn, 1966.

7548. _____. [Typological aspects of fairy tales.] Analytische Psychologie, 1975, 6:318-335.

7549. _____. Der Wert des Märchens für die seelische Entwicklung des Kindes. Praxis der Kinderpsychologie und Kinderpsychiatrie, 1966, 15(2):50-55.

7550. Dinnerstein, Dorothy. 'The Little Mermaid' and the situation of the girl. Contemporary Psychoanal, 1967, 3:104-112.

7551. Dodd, Philip. Fairy tales, the unconscious and Strindberg's Miss Julie. Lit & Psychol, 1978, 28:145.

7552. Drory, Rina. Ali Baba and the Forty Thieves: an attempt at a model for the narrative structure of the reward-and-punishment fairy tale. In Jason, H., & Segal, D. (eds), Patterns in Oral Literature. The Hague: Mouton, 1977, 31-48.

7553. Duff, I. F. Grant. Schneewittschen. Versuch einer psychoanalytischen Deutung. Imago, 1934, 20:95-103.

7554. Dulle, Mark E. The Effect of Illustrations on Children's Interpretations of a Fairy Tale. DAI, 1979, 39(11-B), 5545.

7555. Düss, Louisa. La Méthode des fables en psychanalyse. Archives de Psychologie, 1940, 28:1-51; Zeitschrift für Kinderpsychiatrie, 1942, 9:12-24; Paris: L'Arche, 1950.

7556. Duve, Arne. Symbolikken i Hans Christian Andersen's eventyr. Oslo: Psychopress, 1967.

7557. Eckstein, Rudolf. Childhood autism, its process, as seen in a Victorian fairy tale. Amer Imago, 1978, 35:124-145.

7558. Eder, Robert. Der Schuh im Mythos, in der Symbolik, in der Sage und Legende, im Märchen und im Volksglauben. Der Forscher, 1911, No. 6, 7.

7559. Elardo, Ronald J. E. T. A. Hoffmann's Nusskacker und Mauseköning: the mouse-queen in the tragedy of the hero. Germanic Rev, 1980, 55:1-8.

7560. Epstein, Perle S. A psychiatrist looks at 'Jack and the Beanstalk. ' In Andrews, G., & Vinkenoog, S. (eds), The Book of Grass. An Anthology of Indian Hemp. NY: Grove, 1966, 177-179.

7561. Erikson, Erik H. Two American Indian tribes. In the Psychoanalytic Study of the Child, Vol. 1. NY: IUP, 1950, 337-346.

7562. Ferenczi, Sandor. [Concerning the psychology of fairy tales.] Nyugat, 1918, No. 17.

7563. Fischer, Edmund. Kindertraum und Kleinkindermärchen. Eltern u Kind, 1929, 11:73-75.

7564. Foxe, Arthur N. Terrorization of the libido and Snow White. Psychoanal Rev, 1940, 27:144-148.

7565. Franz, Marie-Louise von. Fairy tales. In Evil. Studies in Jungian Thought. Evanston, Ill: Northwestern Univ. Press, 1967.

7566. _____. An Introduction to the Interpretation of Fairy Tales. NY: Spring, 1970.

7567. Freud, Sigmund. The dream and the primal scene. In Collected Papers, Vol. 3. London: Hogarth, 1925; NY: Basic Books, 1959, 498-519.

7568. _____. The Interpretation of Dreams. NY: Basic Books, 1958, 242-244, 246, 309, 477, 501, 523, 555, 581.

7569. _____. The occurrence in dreams of material from fairy tales. In Collected Papers, Vol. 4. NY: Basic Books, 1959, 236-243; London: Hogarth, 1925; In Standard Edition, Vol. 12; In Delusion and Dream. Boston: Beacon, 1956, 134-142; Internationale Zeitschrift für Psychoanalyse, 1913, 1:147-151.

7570. Friedman, Adolph. Du und der Andere. Arbeiten zur Psycho-Hygiene, 1967, No. 11, 1-112.

7571. Friedrichs, G. Die drei mythischen Hasen und ihre Verwandten an Kirchen und anderer Gebauden und Hasen in Märchen und Sagen. Mannus, 1927, 18:339-348.

7572. Fromm, Erich. Little Red Riding Hood. In The Forgotten Language: An Introduction to the Understanding of Dreams, Fairy Tales and Myths. NY: Rinehart, 1951, 235-241; NY: Evergreen, 1959.

7573. _____. Märchen, Mythen und Träume. Konstanz/Stuttgart: Diana, 1957.

7574. Fromm-Reichman, Frieda. Sleeping Beauty. In Principles of Intensive Psychotherapy. Chicago: Univ. Chicago Press, 1960, 68-69.

7575. Galant, S. Das Sexualproblem im Lichte eines Märchens. Zeitschrift für Sexualwissenschaft, 1920, 7:22-24.

7576. Gentry, W. Doyle. Aggression in fairy tales: comparison of three cultures. Psychol Reports, 1975, 37:895-898.

7577. Girardot, N. J. Initiation and meaning in the tale of 'Snow White and the Seven Dwarfs.' J Amer Folklore, 1977, 90:274-300; 92:69-76.

7578. Goldsmith, S. The place of the fable in the character training of children. J Experimental Education, 1937, 5:343-345.

7579. Graber, Gustav H. Märchengestalten bei Jugendlichen. Schweizerischen Zeitschrift für Psychologie, 1946, 5:53-59.

7580. _____. [In the witch's house. Late comprehension of an early idée fixe.] Acta Psychotherapeutica et Psychosomatica, 1963, 11:147-153.

7581. Grammont, M. La psychologie de La Fontaine. JPNP, 1935, 32:91-98.

7582. Gregori, Ellen. Das Symbol in Märchen. Jahrbuch für Psychologie und Psychotherapie, 1955, 3:88-94.

7583. Grempel, Franz. [Anthropogenesis in fairy tales.] Zeitschrift für klinische Psychologie und Psychotherapie, 1971, 19:301-322.

7584. _____. [The maturing process in the fairy tale.] Zeitschrift für klinische Psychologie und Psychotherapie, 1971, 19:301-322.

7585. Gustin, John C. Phantasy in frigidity. Psychoanalysis, 1952, 1(2):12-26.

7586. Hagglund, Tor-Bjorn, & Hagglund, Vilja. Mourning and death in fairy tales and folklore. Psychiatria Fennica, 1976, 25-31.

7587. Handschin-Ninck, Marianne. Ältester und Jüngster im Märchen. Praxis der Kinderpsychologie und Kinderpsychiatrie, 1956, 7:167-173.

7588. Hannabuss, C. Stuart. The moral of the story; Little Red Riding Hood. Times Educational Supplement, 7 June 1974, 3080:51.

7589. Hartland, Edwin Stanley. The Science of Fairy Tales. Detroit: Singing Tree, 1968; London: Scott, 1891.

7590. Heimpel, Elizabeth. Märchen und Psychologie. Sammlung, 1953, 8:278-293.

7591. Heisig, James W. Bruno Bettelheim and the fairy tales. Children's Lit, 1977, 6:93-114.

7592. Hermans, R. La Fontaine en het vraagstuk der dierenziel. Studia Catholica, 1943, 19:161-171.

7593. Heuscher, Julius E. Cinderella, eros and psyche. Diseases Nervous System, 1963, 24:286-292.

7594. _____. A critique of some interpretations of myths and fairy tales. J Amer Folklore, 1967, 80:175-181.

7595. _____. Death in the fairy-tale. Diseases Nervous System, 1967, 28:462-468.

7596. _____. Existential crisis, death, and changing 'world-designs' in myths and fairy tales. J Existentialism, 1966, 6:45-62.

7597. _____. Humour and fairy tales: quests for wider worlds. In Chapman, A.J., & Foot, H.C. (eds), It's a Funny Thing, Humour. NY: Pergamon, 1977, 413-416.

7598. _____. J.W. Goethe's contribution to the phenomenology of thinking; based on Goethe's fairy tale. Diseases Nervous System, 1965, 26:422-427.

7599. _____. Lucifer and Eros. A commentary to the psychiatric study of fairy tales. Confinia Psychiatrica, 1964, 7:151-159.

7600. _____. The meaning of fairy tales and myths. Confinia Psychiatrica, 1968, 11:90-105.

7601. _____. Mythologic and fairy tale themes in psychotherapy. Amer J Psychotherapy, 1967, 21:655-665.

7602. _____. A Psychiatric Study of Myths and Fairy Tales; Their Origin, Meaning, and Usefulness. Springfield, Ill: Thomas, 1963, 1973; Review: A.H. Walle, J Amer Folklore, 1976, 89:102-103.

7603. Heymann, K. Märchen im Lichte der modernen Medizin. Schneewittschen. Deutsche medizinische Wochenschrift, 1929, 55:2107-2108, 2180.

7604. Hofer, Marie R. A Study of the Favorite Childhood Fairy Tales of an Adult Psychiatric Population. DAI, 1977, 37:4683-84.

7605. Hoffer, Willi. Kind und Märchen. Zeitschrift für psychoanalytische Pädagogik, 1931, 5:107-111.
7606. Huckel, Helen. One day I'll live in the castle! Cinderella
as a case history. Amer Imago, 1957, 14:303-314.
7607. Huss, Roy. Grimms' 'The Table, the Ass and the Stick':
a drama of the phallic stage. Psychoanal Rev, 1975, 62:
167-171.
7608. Hwang, I. [Fairy tales and the child's mind.] Child & Education (China), 1933, 5:260-266.

7609. Jackson, Anthony. The science of fairy tales. Folklore,
1973, 84:120-141.
7610. Jacob, G. Märchen und Traum mit besonderer Berücksichtigung des Orients. Hannover: 1923.
7611. Jaffé, Aniela. [Images and symbols from E. T. A. Hoffmann's
fairy-tale, The Golden Vessel.] In Jung, C. G., Gestaltung des Unbewussten. Zurich: Rascher, 1950.
7612. Jastrow, Joseph. Myth, custom and fairy tale. In Freud.
His Dreams and Sex Theories. NY: Pocket Books, 1948,
117-120.
7613. Jeffrey, W. D. A literary footnote to 'inhibitions, symptoms
and anxiety.' JAPA, 1977, 25:873-875.
7614. Jöckel, Bruno. Das Reifungserlebnis im Märchen. Psyche,
1948, 1:381-395.
7615. Jones, Ernest. The Life and Works of Sigmund Freud, Vol.
2. NY: Basic Books, 1956, 217, 332, 443.
7616. Jørgensen, John Christian. Methodoligischer Pluralismus:
Literaturmethodische Rotation als Zweig und als Stimulans
in der Literatur-pädagogik-veranschaulicht an Hand einer
Untersuchung des Märchens Die Nachtigall, von H. C.
Andersen. Orbis Litterarum, 1975, 30:81-108.
7617. Jung, Carl Gustav. The phenomenology of the spirit in
fairytales. In The Archetypes and the Collective Unconscious, Vol. 9. The Collected Works. London: Routledge & Kegan Paul, 1954; NY: Pantheon, 1959, 207-
254; Zurich: Rascher, 1954; In Psyche and Symbol. NY:
Anchor, 1958, 132-147.
7618. _____. On the Tale of the Otter. In Collected Works of
C. G. Jung, Vol. 18. Princeton: Princeton Univ. Press,
1976, 762-764.
7619. _____. Vorwort zu O. A. H. Schmitzs Märchen aus dem
Unbewussten. Munich: Hanser, 1932.

7620. Kallf, D. The significance of the hare in Reynard the Fox.
J Analytic Psychol, 1957, 3:183-193.
7621. Kaplan, Leo. The belief in witches and in magic; a psychoanalytic study. J Sexology & Psychoanal, 1924, 2:206-
212.
7622. Kast, Verena. [The development of the feminine in a fairy
tale.] Analytische Psychologie, 1976, 7:298-314.
7623. Katz, Leo. The Rumpelstiltskin complex. Contemporary
Psychoanal, 1974, 10:117-124.

7624.   Kielholz, Arthur.   Tierfabel und Fabeltiere.   Schweizerischen
        Zeitschrift für Psychologie, 1947, 6:249-271.
7625.   Kolbenschlag, Madonna.   Kiss Sleeping Beauty Good-Bye:
        Breaking the Spell of Feminine Myths and Models.   Garden
        City, NY: Doubleday, 1979.
7626.   Kris, Marianne.   Ein Märchenstoff in einer Kinderanalyse.
        Zeitschrift für psychoanalytische Pädagogik, 1932, 6:437-
        441.
7627.   Kuhn, H., & Schier, K. (eds).   Märchen, Mythos, Dichtung.
        Munich: Beck, 1963.

7628.   Laruccia, Victor Anthony.   Progress, Perrault, and Fairy
        Tales: Ideology and Semiotics.   DAI, 1975, 35:3655A-
        56A.
7629.   Leber, Gabrielle.   Über tiefenpsychologische Aspekte von
        Märchenmotiven.   Praxis der Kinderpsychologie und Kind-
        erpsychiatrie, 1955, 4:274-285.
7630.   Lefcowitz, Allan B., & Lefcowitz, Barbara F.   Ful sooth in
        game and pley: the fairy tale as pedagogic device.   CEA
        Critic, 1966, 28:5-7.
7631.   Lesznal, Anna.   Babonás észrevételek a mese és a tragedia
        lélektranához.   Nyugat II Halbjahr, 1918.
7632.   Leyen, Friedrich von der.   Das Märchen.   Leipzig: Quelle
        u Meyer, 1925.
7633.   _____.   Traum und Märchen.   Der Lotse, 1901, 1(2):382-
        390.
7634.   Lieberman, Marcia R.   'Some day my prince will come':
        female acculturation through the fairy tale.   College Eng-
        lish, 1972, 34:383-395.
7635.   Littner, Ner.   Adult fairy tales.   New City, 15 June 1968.
7636.   Loeffler-Delachaux, M.   Le Symbolisme des contes de fées.
        Paris: 1949.
7637.   Lorand, Sandor.   Fairy tales, Lilliputian dreams and neurosis.
        Amer J Orthopsychiat, 1937, 7:456-464.
7638.   _____.   Fairy tales and neurosis.   Psychoanal Q, 1935,
        4:234-243.
7639.   Lorenz, E.   Hänsel und Gretel.   Imago, 1931, 17:119-126.
7640.   Lüthi, Max.   Märchen.   Stuttgart: Metzler, 1962.

7641.   McCormick, Jane L.   Fairies: man's psychic mascots?
        Psychic, 1970, 2(2):40-46.
7642.   McDonald, Marjorie.   'Little Black Sambo.'   In The Psycho-
        analytic Study of the Child, Vol. 29.   New Haven: Yale
        Univ. Press, 1974, 511-528.
7643.   MacLulich, T. D.   Atwood's adult fairy tale: Levi-Strauss,
        Bettelheim, and The Edible Woman.   Essays on Canadian
        Writing, 1978, 11:111-129.
7644.   Maeder, Alphonse E.   Die Symbolik in den Legenden, Märch-
        en, Gebrauchen und Träumen.   Psychiatrisch-neurolog-
        ische Wochenschrift, 1909, 10:55-57.

7645. Mallet, Carl-Heinz. Analyse des Grimm'scher Märchens
       Der starke Hans. Praxis der Kinderpsychologie und Kind-
       erpsychiatrie, 1953, 2:53-62.
7646. _____. Die zweite und dritte Nacht im Märchen 'Das
       Gruseln.' Praxis der Kinderpsychologie und Kinderpsy-
       chiatrie, 1965, 14:216-220.
7647. Marbach, Otto, & Juer, Franziska. Eine sudslawische
       Märchen-parallele zum Urytypus der Roland-Sage. Imago,
       1926, 12:32-58.
7648. Marcus, Donald M. The Cinderella motif: fairy tale and
       defense. Amer Imago, 1963, 20:81-92.
7649. Mather, J. The unconscious significance of fairyland. Aus-
       tralasian J Psychol & Philosophy, 1933, 11:258-274; 1934,
       12:16-22.
7650. Mendelsohn, J. [Early child behavior seen in symbol pattern
       of Grimms' 'The Water Nymph. '] Analytische Psychol-
       ogie, 1977, 8(3-4):161-173.
7651. _____. Das Tiermärchen und seine Bedeutung als Aus-
       druck seelischer Entwicklungsstruktur. Praxis der Kind-
       erpsychologie und Kinderpsychiatrie, 1961, 10:8-13, 56-
       62.
7652. Meyer, Bernard C. Betty M. and the seven dwarfs: a con-
       trapuntal essay on Raynaud's disease. Amer Imago,
       1950, 7:329-341.
7653. Miller, David L. Fairy tale or myth? Science, 1976, 157-
       164.
7654. Millman, Marcia. Such a Pretty Face: Being Fat in Amer-
       ica. NY: Norton, 1980.
7655. Mintz, Thomas. Discussion of L. Veszy-Wagner, 'Little Red
       Riding Hood on the couch.' Psychoanal Forum, 1966,
       1:410-411.
7656. _____. The meaning of the rose in 'Beauty and the
       Beast.' Psychoanal Rev, 1969-70, 56:615-620.
7657. Mishler, William. H. C. Andersen's 'Tin Soldier' in a
       Freudian perspective. Scandinavian Studies, 1978, 50:
       389-395.
7658. Mitchell, Jane Tucker. A Thematic Study of Mme d'Aulnoy's
       'Contes de fées.' University, Miss: Romance Mono-
       graphs, 1978.
7659. Mott, Francis J. Mother Goose and the gastrointestinal tract.
       Psychiatric Q, 1949, 23:756-767.

7660. Niederland, William G. River symbolism. Psychoanal Q,
       1956, 25:469-504; 1957, 26:50-75.
7661. Nikiforov, A. [The erotic element in Great Russian folk
       fairy tales.] Khudozestvennie Folklor, 1929, 4-5:120-
       127.
7662. Nyborg, Eigil. Den lille Havfrue. In Schou, S. (ed),
       60'ernes danske kritik. En antologi. Copenhagen:
       Munksgaard, 1970, 36-54.

7663. Obenauer, Karl Justus. Das Märchen, Dichtung und Deutung. Frankfurt: Klostermann, 1959.

7664. O'Connell, M. F. All is not grim with the Grimm brothers. J Amer Society Psychosomatic Medicine & Dentistry, 1977, 24:21-25.

7665. Pedersen, Stefi. [The child and fairy tales.] Psykisk Hälsa, 1961, 2.

7666. Petty, Thomas A. The tragedy of Humpty Dumpty. In The Psychological Study of the Child, Vol. 8. NY: IUP, 1958, 404-412.

7667. Pickford, R. W., & Macquistan, A. S. Psychological aspects of the fantasy of Snow White and the Seven Dwarfs. Psychoanal Rev, 1942, 29:232-252.

7668. Pratt, F. From the fairy tale of science to the science of fairy tale. Pacific Spectator, 1948, 2.

7669. Propp, V. Ja. The function of the fairy tale. In Oinas, F. J., & Soudakoff, S. (eds), The Study of Russian Folklore. The Hague: Mouton, 1975, 163-168.

7670. Rank, Otto. Das Brudermärchen. In Psychoanalytische Beiträge zur Mythenforschung. Vienna: Int Psychoanalytischer Verlag, 1919, 355-380; 1922, 119-145.

7671. _____. Die Matrone von Ephesus: ein Deutungsversuch der Fabel von der treulosen Witwe. Int J Psychoanalyse, 1913, 1:50-60; In Psychoanalytische Beiträge zur Mythenforschung. Vienna: Int Psychoanalytischer Verlag, 1919, 59-71.

7672. _____. Der Sinn der Griseldafabel. Imago, 1912, 1:34-48. In Psychoanalytische Beiträge zur Mythenforschung. Vienna: Int Psychoanalytischer Verlag, 1929, 40-58.

7673. _____. Totemismus in Märchens: Grimm'schen Märchen. Imago, 1913, 2:594-596.

7674. _____, & Sachs, Hanns. Das Märchen von den zwei Brüdern. In Beutin, W. (ed), Literatur und Psychoanalyse. Munich: Nymphenburger, 1972, 182-204.

7675. Ranke, K. Betrachtung zum Wesen und zur Funktion des Märchens. Studium Generale, 1958, 11:11.

7676. Reik, Theodor. The original of the Sleeping Beauty discovered. Bulletin Menninger Clinic, 1948, 12:166-167; In The Secret Self. NY: Farrar, Straus & Young, 1952, 201-204.

7677. _____. Wie die kinder fabulieren. Imago, 1912, 1:288-289.

7678. Richardson, Maurice. Pan and company. New Statesman, 9 Nov 1962, 657-658.

7679. Riklin, Franz. Psychologie und Sexualsymbolik der Märchen. Psychiatrisch-neurologische Wochenschrift, 1907, 9:185-187, 191-192.

7680. _____. Wish Fulfillment and Symbolism in Fairy Tales. NY: Nervous & Mental Disease Monograph Series, No.

21, 1915; Psychoanal Rev, 1915, 2:102-105, 203-218, 327-340; Vienna: Heller, 1908; Sammlungen zur angewandten Seelenkunde, 1908, 2.

7681. Robinson, Vivian U. Adult Symbolism in the Literary Fairy Tales of the Late Nineteenth Century. DAI, 1971, 32: 3962A.

7682. Róheim, Géza. Dame Halle: dream and folk tales (Grimm No. 24). In Lindner, R. (ed), Explorations in Psychoanalysis. NY: Julian, 1953, 84-94.

7683. _____. Fairy tale and dream. In The Psychoanalytic Study of the Child, Vol. 8. NY: IUP, 1953, 394-403.

7684. _____. Hansel and Gretel. Bulletin Menninger Clinic, 1953, 17:90-92.

7685. _____. Masturbation fantasies. Psychiat Q, 1945, 20: 656-673.

7686. _____. A medve-és az ikrek. Ethnographia, 1914, 25: 93-97.

7687. _____. Tom, Tit, Tot. Psychoanal Rev, 1949, 36:365-369.

7688. _____. The wolf and the seven kids. Psychoanal Q, 1953, 22:253-256.

7689. Roques-von Beit, Hedwig von. Concerning the problem of transformation in the fairy tale. In Strelka, J. (ed), Perspectives in Literary Symbolism. University Park: Penn State Univ. Press, 1968, 48-71.

7690. Rosenman, Stanley. Cinderella: family pathology, identity-sculpting and mate-selection. Amer Imago, 1978, 35: 375-396.

7691. Rosenthal, Robert A. To tame a fox. Amer Imago, 1956, 13:269-306.

7692. Rowe, Karen. Feminism and fairy tales. Radcliffe Institute Working Paper, 1 March 1978, 8, 12, 19, 20.

7693. Rowley, Julius L. Rumpelstiltskin in the analytical situation. Int J Psycho-Anal, 1951, 32:190-195.

7694. Rubenstein, Ben. The meaning of the Cinderella story in the development of a little girl. Amer Imago, 1955, 12:197-205.

7695. Sale, Roger. Fairy Tales and After. From Snow White to E. B. White. Cambridge: Harvard Univ. Press, 1979.

7696. Sandford, Beryl. Cinderella. Psychoanal Forum, 1967, 2: 128-132, 141-144.

7697. Schack, May, & Møhl, Bo. Evetyrterapi-eller: Kunsten at gennemleve barndommen: En introduktion af Bruno Bettelheims The Uses of Enchantment: The Meaning and Importance of Fairy Tales. Bixen, 1978, 7(5):27-43.

7698. Scherfe, Walter. Family conflicts and emancipation in fairy tales. In Butler, F. , & Brockman, B. A. (eds), Children's Literature: The Great Excluded. Storrs, Conn: Children's Lit Assn, 1974, 77-93.

7699. Schlee, T. [Primordial structures of feminine maturation as reflected in fairy tales. Contribution to the anthropology of sexuality.] Zeitschrift klinische Psychologie Psychotherapie, 1976, 24:28-42.

7700. Schmitz, Oskar A. H. Märchen aus dem Unbewassten. Munich: Hanser, 1932.

7701. Schmotzer, F. Elementarwesen im Spiegel der Sagen und Märchen. Zeitschrift für Parapsychologie, 1934, 9:178-183.

7702. Schuman, Elliott P. A psychoanalytic study of Hansel and Gretel. J Contemporary Psychotherapy, 1972, 4:121-125.

7703. Schuurman, C. J. [The psychoanalytical and the psychosophical interpretation of fairy tales.] Folio Psychiatrica, neurologica et neurochirugica neerlandica, 1950, 53:509-518.

7704. Schwartz, Emanuel K. A psychoanalytical study of the fairy tale. Amer J Psychol, 1956, 10:740-762; In Haworth, M. R. (ed), Child Psychotherapy. NY: Basic Books, 1964, 383-395; In Riess, B. F. (ed), New Directions in Mental Health, Vol. 2. NY: Grune & Stratton, 1968.

7705. Schwartz, Murray M. Psychoanalysis in fairy land: notes on Bettelheim as interpreter. Lit & Psychol, 1977, 27:140-143.

7706. Schwarz, C. J. The witches hammer. Canadian Psychiat Assn J, 1966, 11:57-58.

7707. Secher, O. Simpson and Hans Andersen. British Medical J, 1971, 790:814.

7708. Sellschopp-Rüppell, A., & von Rad, M. Pinocchio: a psychosomatic syndrome. Psychotherapy & Psychosomatics, 1977, 28(1-4):357-360.

7709. Servadio, Emilio. Psicoanalisi dei Tre Porcellini. Circoli, 1934, 4(4).

7710. Shafii, Mohammed, & Shafii, Sharon. Symbolic expression of developmental conflicts in a Persian fairy tale. Int Rev Psycho-Anal, 1974, 1:219-225.

7711. Silberer, Herbert. Märchensymbolik. Imago, 1912, 1:176-187.

7712. Snyder, Louis L. Nationalistic aspects of the Grimm brothers' fairy tales. J Social Psychol, 1951, 33:209-223.

7713. Spiess, Karl. Das deutsche Volksmärchen. Leipzig: Aus Natur und Geisteswelt, 1917.

7714. Starbuck, E. D. Significance of the fairy tale in character education. Religious Education, 1927, 22:1004-1007.

7715. _____, Shuttleworth, Frank K., et al. A Guide to Literature for Character Training, Vol. I. Fairy Tale, Myth, and Legend. NY: Macmillan, 1928.

7716. Stein, Howard F. Peter and the Wolf, a musical tale of individuation and the imagery of new Soviet man: a psychoanalytic perspective on Russian cultural history. In The Psychoanalytic Study of Society, Vol. 7. NY: IUP, 1976, 31-64.

7717. Storfer, Adolph J. Zwei Typen der Märchenerotik. Sexualprobleme, 1912, 8:257-262.

7718. Tardieu, E. Psychologie du faible. Rev Blanche, 1895, 9.
7719. Tausch, Anne M. Einige Auswirkungen von Märcheninhalten. Psychologische Rundschau, 1967, 18(2):104-116.
7720. Taylor, Jerome. The psychology of Hans Christian Andersen's 'Little Tin Soldier.' Menninger Perspective, 1971, 2(6):13-16.
7721. Terens, Laurel F. Fairytales in Personality Assessment of Adults. DAI, 1976, 37:3099-3100.
7722. Tiberia, Vincenza. A Jungian interpretation of Goethe's alchemical allegory: The Märchen. Int J Symbology, 1975, 6(2):24-36.
7723. Tóth, Béla. [Examination of literary interest with the help of a fairy-tale drawing test in a group of children aged 6-8.] Pszichológiai Tanulmányok, 1967, No. 10, 215-219.

7724. Uspensky, Lev. How marvellous are these fairy tales. Anglo-Soviet J, 1974, 36:19-46.

7725. Veszy-Wagner, Lilla. Little Red Riding Hood on the couch. Psychoanal Forum, 1966, 1:400-408, 414-415.
7726. Vinken, P.J. Some observations on the symbolism of the broken pot in art and literature. Amer Imago, 1958, 15:149-174.
7727. Vinski-Hollinger, M. Ein psychologisch-pedagogische Betrachtung des Kindermärchens. Int Zeitschrift für Individual-Psychologie, 1933, 11:64-69.
7728. Von Franz, Marie-Louise. [The unknown visitor in fairy tales and dreams.] Analytische Psychologie, 1975, 6:437-449.

7729. Walker, Virginia, & Lunz, Mary E. Symbols, fairy tales, and school age children. Elementary School J, 1976, 77:94-100.
7730. Weiss, H.B. Three hundred years of Tom Thumb. Scientific Monthly, 1932, 32:157-166.
7731. Wheeler, H.E. The psychological case against the fairy tale. Elementary School J, 1929, 29:754-766.
7732. Wilson, Anne. Traditional Romance and Tale: How Stories Mean. Totowa, NJ: Rowman & Littlefield, 1977.
7733. Winterstein, Alfred R.F. Die Puberstätsriten der Märchen und ihre Spuren im Märchen. Imago, 1928, 14:199-274; Vienna: Int Psychoanalytischer Verlag, 1928.
7734. Wolfenstein, Martha. Jack and the Beanstalk: an American version. In Mead, M., & Wolfenstein, M. (eds), Childhood in Contemporary Cultures. Chicago: Chicago Univ. Press, 1955, 243-245.
7735. Wulffen, Erich. Das Kriminelle im deutschen Volksmärchen. Archiv für Kriminalanthropologie u Kriminalistik, 1911(?), 38.

7736. Zaunert, Paul. Traum und Märchen. Leipzig Illustratione Zeitung Märchennummer, 2 Dec 1920.

7737. Zelenin, D. M. Die religiöse Funktion der Volksmärchen. Int Archiv für Ethnographie, 1930, 31:21-31.

7738. Zillinger, G. Zur Frage der Angst und der Darstellung psychosexueller Reifungsstufen im Märchen vom Gruseln. Praxis der Kinderpsychologie und Kinderpsychiatrie, 1963, 12:33-41, 107-112, 134-143.

7739. Zipes, Jack David. Breaking the Magic Spell: Radical Theories of Folk and Fairy Tales. Austin: Univ. Texas Press, 1979.

7740. Aaros, Hans, Sørensen, Hans, & Bergaas, Asbjørn. Brikt
Jensen: Diktning eller psykologi? Edda, 1967, 54:2-60.
7741. Abel, Elizabeth. Women and schizophrenia: the fiction of
Jean Rhys. Contemporary Lit, 1979, 20:155-177.
7742. Abood, Edward. Jung's concept of individuation in Hesse's
Steppenwolf. Southern Humanities Rev, 1961, 3:1-13.
7743. Abraham, P. Créatures chez Balzac. Recherches sur la
creation intellectuelle, avec un texte inedit de Balzac.
Paris: Nouvelle Revue française, 1931.
7744. Abrahams, Roger B. Androgynes bound: Nathanael West
Miss Lonelyhearts. In Whitbread, T. B. (ed), Seven Contemporary Authors: Essays on Cozzens, Miller, West,
Golding, Heller, Albee, and Powers. Austin: Univ.
Texas Press, 1967, 49-72.
7745. Abram, Harry S. Death and denial in Conrad's The Nigger of
the 'Narcissus. ' Omega: J Death & Dying, 1976, 7:125-
135.
7746. _____. Depth psychology, science fiction, and the writings
of Stanley G. Weinbaum. Suicide, 1975, 5:93-97.
7747. _____. The psychology of physical illness as portrayed in
Thomas Mann's The Magic Mountain. Archives Internal
Medicine, 1971, 128:466-468.
7748. _____. The psychology of terminal illness as portrayed in
Solzhenitsyn's The Cancer Ward. Archives Internal Medicine, 1969, 124:758-760.
7749. Abrams, Robert E. The ambiguities of dreaming in Ellison's
Invisible Man. Amer Lit, 1978, 49:592-603.
7750. _____. 'Bartleby' and the fragile pageantry of the ego.
English Lit History, 1978, 45:488-500.
7751. Accad, Evelyne. The theme of sexual oppression in the North
African novel. In Beck, L. , & Keddie, N. (eds), Women
in the Muslim World. Cambridge: Harvard Univ. Press,
1978, 617-628.
7752. Ackermann, F. Psychologische Romane. Berliner Forsch
Stell Psychodiagnostik, 1945, No. 11.
7753. Ackermann, Jean M. Outsiders in India: How Western
Characters Are Perceived in Writings of Kamala Markandaya and R. Prawer Jhabvala. DAI, 1973, 34:1684.
7754. Ackley, Donald G. The male-female motif in Things Fall
Apart. Studies in Black Lit, 1974, 5(1):1-6.

7755. Action, H. M. Borderline psychology in recent French novels. South Atlantic Bulletin, 1942, 8(3):5.

7756. Adair, William. A Farewell to Arms: a dream book. J Narrative Techniques, 1975, 5:40-56.

7757. Adam, Ian. Character and destiny in George Eliot's fiction. Nineteenth Century Fiction, 1965, 20:127-143.

7758. Adamowski, Thomas H. Addie Bundren's solitude: the self and others. Rev Existential Psychol & Psychiat, 1977, 15:1-18.

7759. _____. Bayard Sartoris: mourning and melancholia. Lit & Psychol, 1973, 23:149-158.

7760. _____. Children of the idea: heroes and family romances in Absalom, Absalom! Mosaic, 1976, 10(1):115-131.

7761. _____. The Dickens World and Yoknapatawpha County: A Study of Character and Society in Dickens and Faulkner. DAI, 1970, 30:2995A-96A.

7762. _____. Joe Christmas: the tyranny of childhood. Novel: A Forum on Fiction, 1971, 4:240-251.

7763. _____. 'Meet Mrs. Bundren': As I Lay Dying--gentility, tact, and psychoanalysis. Univ. Toronto Q, 1980, 49: 205-227.

7764. Adams, Barbara B. Sisters under their skins: the women in the lives of Raskolnikov and Razumov. Conradiana, 1974, 6:113-124.

7765. Adams, D. J. La Femme dans les contes et les romans de Voltaire. Paris: Nizet, 1974.

7766. Adams, Laura. Existential Battles: The Growth of Norman Mailer. Athens: Ohio Univ. Press, 1976.

7767. Adams, Maurianne. Jane Eyre: woman's estate. In Diamond, A., & Edwards, L. R. (eds), The Authority of Experience. Essays in Feminist Criticism. Amherst: Univ. Massachusetts Press, 1977, 137-159.

7768. Adams, Michael Ian. Alienation in Selected Works of Three Contemporary Spanish American Authors. DAI, 1973, 33: 3628A.

7769. _____. Three Authors of Alienation: Bombal, Onetti, Carpentier. Austin: Univ. Texas Press, 1975.

7770. Adams, Robert Martin. Afterjoyce: Studies in Fiction After Ulysses. NY: Oxford Univ. Press, 1977, 65-89.

7771. Adams, Stephen D. The Homosexual Hero in Contemporary Fiction. NY: Harper & Row, 1980.

7772. Adler, Joyce. Tumatumari and the imagination of Wilson Harris. J Commonwealth Lit, 1969, 7:20-31.

7773. Adler, Ruth. The Image of Woman in the Works of Y. L. Peretz: A Socio-Psychological Study. DAI, 1976, 36: 7405A-06A.

7774. Aggeler, Geoffrey. The comic art of Anthony Burgess. Arizona Q, 1969, 25:234-251.

7775. Agrifoglio, L. Medici a medicina nell'opera di Anton Cechov. In Atti del Io. congresso nazionale, Accademia ambrosiana medici umanisti e scrittori. Rome: Art grafiche e cossidente, 1968, 45-51.

7776. Ahnebrink, Lars. The Beginnings of Naturalism in American Fiction. Cambridge: Harvard Univ. Press, 1950.

7777. Aichinger, Ingrid. E. T. A. Hoffmanns Novelle Der Sandmann und die Interpretation Sigmund Freuds. Zeitschrift für Deutsche Philologie, 1976, 95(1):113-132.
7778. Aiken, William. Hemingway's 'Ten Little Indians.' Explicator, 1969, 28:4.
7779. Aitken, David. Anthony Trollope on the 'genus girl.' Nineteenth Century Fiction, 1974, 28:417-434.
7780. Akasofu, Tetsuji. [Faulkner: A Life in His Time.] Tokyo: Tohjusha, 1977.
7781. Akin, Warren, 4th. Normal human feelings: an interpretation of Faulkner's 'Pantaloon in Black.' Studies in Short Fiction, 1978, 15:397-404.
7782. Akmakjian, H. Review: E. W. Tedlock's D. H. Lawrence and 'Sons and Lovers': Sources and Criticism. Psychoanal Rev, 1966, 53:321-322.
7783. Albanese, Carolina M. O Estreitamento da Duração Ficcional e a Expansão da Duração Psicológica em Una nuvola d'ira. Revista Letras, 1976, 25:39-49.
7784. Albaum, Elvin. La Mordida: Myth and Madness in the Novels of Malcolm Lowry. DAI, 1971, 31:6586A.
7785. Albérès, R. -M. Joyce et la naissance du monologue intérieure. In Métamorphoses du roman. Paris: Michel, 1966, 177-198, passim.
7786. _____. Métamorphoses du roman. Paris: Michel, 1966.
7787. Albers, Randal K. Female transformation: the role of women in two novels by Wright Morris. Prairie Schooner, 1979, 53:95-115.
7788. Albert, L. Joyce and the New Psychology. DA, 1958, 18: 1424-1425.
7789. Albrecht, Joyce. The Stranger and Camus' transcendental existentialism. Hartford Studies in Lit, 1972, 4(1):59-80.
7790. Albrecht, Milton C. Psychological motives in the fiction of Julien Green. J Personality, 1948, 16:278-303.
7791. Alcorn, John. Toward Freud. In The Nature Novel from Hardy to Lawrence. NY: Columbia Univ. Press, 1977, 107-112.
7792. Alden, Douglas W. Origins of the unconscious and subconscious in Proust. Modern Language Q, 1943, 4:343-357.
7793. _____. Proust and the contemporaneous notion of the subconscious. South-Central Bulletin, 1941, 1(2):5.
7794. Aldrich, Anne. Carol in a Thousand Cities. Greenwich, Conn: Fawcett, 1960.
7795. Aldrich, C. Knight. Another twist to 'The Turn of the Screw.' Modern Fiction Studies, 1967, 13:167-178.
7796. Aldridge, John W. From Vietnam to obscenity. Harpers, 1968, 236:91-97; In The Devil in the Fire. NY: Harpers Magazine Press, 1972, 169-179.
7797. _____. Gray new world. The Nation, 1955, 180:585-588.
7798. Alemán, Serafín S. El suicidio en la novela de Benito Pérez Galdós. DAI, 1973, 33:6298A.
7799. Alexander, C. The 'stink' of reality: mothers and whores in James Baldwin's fiction. Lit & Psychol, 1968, 18:9-26.

7800. Alexander, Theodor W.   Schnitzler and the inner monologue: a study in technique.   J Int Arthur Schnitzler Research Assn, 1967, 6(2):4-20.

7801. Alhadeff, Barbara.   The divided self: a Laingian interpretation of Seize the Day.   Studies in Amer Jewish Lit, 1977, 3:16-20.

7802. Alldredge, Betty Jean Edwards.   Levels of Consciousness: Women in the Stream of Consciousness Novels of Joyce, Woolf, and Faulkner.   DAI, 1976, 37:3610A.

7803. Allen, Charles A.   Katherine Anne Porter: psychology as art.   Southwest Rev, 1956, 41:223-230.

7804. _____.   Mark Twain and conscience.   In Malin, I. (ed), Psychoanalysis and American Fiction.   NY: Dutton, 1965, 131-141; Lit & Psychol, 1957, 7(2):17-21.

7805. _____.   Robert Penn Warren: the psychology of self-knowledge.   Lit & Psychol, 1958, 8(2):21-25.

7806. Allen, C. N., & Curtis, K.   A sociogrammatic study of Oedipus complex formation: D. H. Lawrence's Sons and Lovers.   Sociometry, 1939, 2:37-51.

7807. Allen, Mary Inez.   The Necessary Blankness: Women in Major American Fiction of the Sixties.   DAI, 1974, 34: 7736A.

7808. Allen, Rupert C.   An archetypal analysis of Rivas' El desengaño en un sueño.   Bulletin Hispanic Studies, 1968, 45: 201-215.

7809. _____.   Pobreza y neurosis en Misericordia de Pérez Galdós.   Hispanófila, 1968, 3:35-47.

7810. Allen, Shirley S.   Griselda's tale and the portrayal of women in the Decameron.   Philological Q, 1977, 56:1-13.

7811. _____.   Religious symbolism and psychic reality in Baldwin's Go Tell It on the Mountain.   College Language Assn J, 1975, 19:173-199.

7812. Allen, Suzanne.   Memories of a southern Catholic girlhood: Flannery O'Connor's 'A Temple of the Holy Ghost.'   Renascence, 1979, 31:83-92.

7813. Allison, George H.   The intuitive psychoanalytic perspective of Galdós Fortunata and Jacinta: a reply to the discussion by José Rallo.   Int J Psycho-Anal, 1975, 56:219-220.

7814. _____, & Ullman, Joan Connelly.   Intuitive psychoanalytic perspective of Galdós in Fortunata and Jacinta.   Int J Psycho-Anal, 1974, 55:332-343; Discussion: Rallo, J., 345-347.

7815. Allott, Miriam (ed).   Novelists on the Novel.   NY: Columbia Univ. Press, 1959.

7816. Allport, Gordon W.   Personality: a problem for science or a problem for art?   Rev de psihologia, 1938, 1:488-502.

7817. Allsup, Judith L.   Feminism in the Novels of Ellen Glasgow.   DAI, 1974, 35:1083A.

7818. Alm, Richard S.   A Study of the Assumptions Concerning Human Experience Underlying Certain Works of Fiction Written For and About Adolescents.   Doctoral dissertation, Univ. Minnesota, 1954.

7819. Almansi, Guido.   La 'Geante' di Baudelaire.   Verri, 1968, 28:58-65.

7820. _____. Il tema dell'incesto nelle opere di Svevo. Paragone, 1972, 264:47-60.

7821. Almodovar, Jean P. [Is there an 'only child syndrome'?]
Enfance, 1973, No. 3-4, 233-249.

7822. Alonso, Juan M. The Search for Identity in Alejo Carpentier's Contemporary Urban Novels: An Analysis of Los
pasos perdidos and El acoso. DA, 1968, 28:3173A.

7823. Aloyse, Sister M. The novelist as popularizer: Joyce and
'psychological' fiction. In Feehan, J. (ed), Dedalus on
Crete: Essays on the Implications of Joyce's Portrait.
Los Angeles: St. Thomas More Guild, 1956, 29-42.

7824. Alphen, Albert W. V. A Study of the Effects of Inferiority
Feelings in the Life and Works of Franz Kafka. DAI,
1970, 30-31:70-273.

7825. Alsen, Eberhard. An existential reading of Faulkner's
'Pantaloon in Black.' Studies in Short Fiction, 1977, 14:
169-178.

7826. Altamira, Rafael. La mujer en las novelas de Pérez Galdós.
Atenea, 1943, 215:145-169.

7827. Altenhöner, Friedrich. Der Traum und die Traumstruktur
im Werk Franz Kafkas. Münster: Münster Univ., 1962.

7828. Alter, Robert. Jewish dreams and nightmares. In After The
Tradition. NY: Dutton, 1969; In Malin, I. (ed), Contemporary American-Jewish Literature. Bloomington: Indiana Univ. Press, 1973, 58-77.

7829. _____. Tristam Shandy and the game of love. Amer
Scholar, 1967-68, 37:316-323.

7830. Altman, Dennis. The homosexual vision of E. M. Forster.
Meanjin Q, 1978, 37:532-540.

7831. Altus, William D. Sexual role, the short story, and the
writer. J Psychol, 1959, 47:37-40.

7832. Alvarez Villar, A. [Self-destructiveness in the novels of
Unamuno.] Arbor, 1966, 62.

7833. Alvès, José. Vidas Sécas, roman de l'absurde. In Atkinson,
D. M. (ed), Hispanic Studies in Honour of Joseph Manson.
Oxford: Dolphin, 1972, 85-98.

7834. Amadou, Anne-Lisa. The theme of water in A la recherche
du temps perdu. Modern Language Rev, 1977, 72:310-
321.

7835. Amann, J. J. Das Symbol Kafka. Eine Studie über den
Kunstler. Bern: Francke, 1974.

7836. Amenitzky, D. A. [Epilepsy in creations of F. I. Dostoevsky.]
Pamyati P. B. Gannushkina, 1934, 417-432.

7837. _____. [The psychopathic types in Brothers Karamazov.]
Problemi Psikhistrii i Psikhopatologii, 1935, 551-566.

7838. Ames, Carol. Love Triangles in Fiction: The Underlying
Fantasies. DAI, 1973, 34:717A.

7839. Ames, Van Meter. The novel: between art and science.
Kenyon Rev, 1942, 5:34-48.

7840. Ammons, Elizabeth. Fairy-tale love and The Reef. Amer
Lit, 1976, 47:615-628.

7841. _____. The heroines in Uncle Tom's Cabin. Amer Lit,
1977, 49:161-179.

7842. Amundsen, D. W. Romanticizing the ancient medical profession: the characterization of the physician in the Graeco-Roman novel. Bulletin History Medicine, 1974, 43:320-337.

7843. Anders, Günther. Kafka: Pro und Contra. Munich: Beck, 1951.

7844. _____. Reflections of my book: Kafka: Pro und Contra. Mosaic, 1970, 3:59-72.

7845. Anderson, Chester G. Baby Tuckoo: Joyce's 'features of infancy.' In Staley, T. F., & Benstock, B. (eds), Approaches to Joyce's Portrait. Pittsburgh: Univ. Pittsburgh Press, 1977, 135-168.

7846. _____. James Joyce as 'Sunny Jim': a tale of a tub. James Joyce Q, 1976, 13(3):328-349.

7847. _____. Leopold Bloom as Dr. Sigmund Freud. Mosaic, 1972, 6:23-43.

7848. Anderson, Dawn Holt. May Sarton's women. In Cornillon, S. K. (ed), Images of Women in Fiction: Feminist Perspectives. Bowling Green, Ohio: Bowling Green Univ. Popular Press, 1972, 243-250.

7849. Anderson, Halton. Steinbeck's 'Flight.' Explicator, 1969, 28:2.

7850. Anderson, Howard. Association and wit in Tristram Shandy. Philological Q, 1969, 48:27-41.

7851. Anderson, Linda R. Ideas of identity and freedom in V. S. Naipaul and Joseph Conrad. English Studies, 1978, 59: 510-517.

7852. Anderson, Reed. Señas de identidad: chronicle of rebellion. J Spanish Studies: Twentieth Century, 1974, 2:3-19.

7853. Anderson, Roger B. Crime and Punishment: psycho-myth and the making of a hero. Canadian-Amer Slavic Studies, 1977, 11:523-538.

7854. _____. Raskolnikov and the myth experience. Slavic & East European J, 1976, 20:1-17.

7855. André, Robert. Ecriture et pulsions dans le roman stendhalien. Paris: Klincksieck, 1977.

7856. _____. L'Expérience d'autrin chez Melville. Cahiers du Sud, 1962-63, 54:272-279.

7857. Andrea, O. Die Bedeutung von Krankheit und Kranksein in den Werken Thomas Manns. Deutsche Gesundheitswesen, 1964, 19:36-39.

7858. Andreas, Osborn. Joseph Conrad: A Study in Non-Conformity. NY: Philosophical Library, 1960.

7859. Andrews, L. G. The development of character in fiction. Living Age, 1905, 246.

7860. Angell, Leslie E. The umbilical cord symbol as unifying theme and pattern in Absalom, Absalom! Massachusetts Studies in English, 1968, 1:106-110.

7861. Angress, Ruth K. Kafka and Sacher-Masoch: a note on The Metamorphosis. MLN, 1970, 85:745-746.

7862. Anon. Conversation with a psychoanalyst: Janet A. Kennedy, M. D. Mystery & Detection Annual, 1972, 1:191-197.

7863. _____. Hermann Hesse über Pseudo-Psychoanalyse. Psychoanalytische Bewegung, 1931, 3:35-37.

7864. _____. Holmes as a psychiatrist. New England J Medicine, 1944, 230:155.

7865. _____. Novelists who have succumbed to the lure of psychoanalysis. Current Opinion, 1917, 63:413.

7866. _____. Procedures of Proust. Times Lit Supplement, 17 May 1973, 3767:513-515.

7867. _____. Review: F. Scott Fitzgerald's Tender Is the Night. JNMD, 1935, 82:115-117; 1979, 167:648-649.

7868. _____. Thomas Mann und die Psychoanalyse. Int Zeitschrift für Psychoanalyse, 1925, 11:247.

7869. _____. The true face of Meredith, new lives and letters: will they make us reconsider Freud's 'greatest English novelist?' Times Lit Supplement, 18 Dec 1970, 1477-1479.

7870. Anthony, Elwyn James. The madeleine and the doughnut. A study of 'screen sensations.' In The Psychoanalytic Study of the Child, Vol. 16. NY: IUP, 1961, 211-245.

7871. Antoine, Gerald. Le Mot, agent de cristallisation psychologique chez Stendhal. Neuphilologische Mitteilungen, 1965, 66:417-430.

7872. Anton, Herbert. Mythologische Erotik in Kellers 'Sieben Legenden' und im 'Senngedicht.' Berlin: Metzler, 1970.

7873. Antoniadis, Roxandra V. [The dream as design in Balzac and Faulkner.] Zagadnienia Rodzajów Literackich, 1974, 17(2):45-58.

7874. Antosh, Ruth Beharriell. Dreams and the Imagination in the Novels of J. -K. Huysmans. DAI, 1978, 39:910A.

7875. Anzieu, Didier. Contes à rebours. Paris: Bourgois, 1975.

7876. _____. Le Corps et le code dans les contes de J. L. Borges. Nouvelle Rev Psychanalyse, 1971, 3:177-210.

7877. _____. Le Discourse de l'obsessionnel dans les romans de Robbe-Grillet. Les Temps Modernes, 1965, 21:608-637.

7878. Appel, Alfred, Jr. Nabokov's dark cinema: a diptych. In Karlinsky, S., & Appel, A., Jr. (eds), The Bitter Air of Exile: Russian Writers in the West. Berkeley: Univ. California Press, 1977.

7879. _____. A Season of Dreams: The Fiction of Eudora Welty. Baton Rouge: Louisiana State Univ. Press, 1965.

7880. Appignanesi, Lisa. Femininity and the Creative Imagination: A Study of Henry James, Robert Musil and Marcel Proust. NY: Barnes & Noble, 1973.

7881. _____. Femininity and Robert Musil's Die Vollendung der Liebe. Monatshefte, 1973, 65:14-26.

7882. Aprile, Max. L'Aveugle et sa signification dans Madame Bovary. Rev d'Histoire Littéraire de la France, 1976, 76:385-392.

7883. Apter, T. E. Let's hear what the male chauvinist is saying: The Plumed Serpent. In Smith, A. (ed), Lawrence and Women. NY: Barnes & Noble, 1978, 156-177.

7884. Arakawa, Steven R. The Relationship of Father and Daughter in the Novels of Dickens. DAI, 1977, 38(6-A), 3507-08.

7885. Arango, Guillermo. La función del sueño en Las ruinas circulares de Jorge Luis Borges. Hispania, 1973, 56:249-254.

7886. Arden, E. Hawthorne's 'Case of Arthur D.' Amer Imago, 1961, 18:45-55.

7887. Arengo, Celso. Psiquiatría para San Camelo, 1936. Papeles de Son Armadans, 1970, 56:35-37.

7888. Ariail, Jacqueline Ann. An elegy for androgyny. Iowa English Bulletin: Yearbook, 1974, 24(3):13-20.

7889. Arlow, Jacob A. Pyromania and the primal scene: a psychoanalytic comment on the work of Yukio Mishima. Psychoanal Q, 1978, 47:24-51; In Coltrera, J. T. (ed), Lives, Events and Other Players: Studies in Psychobiography. NY: Aronson, 1980.

7890. Armas, F. A. de. La Celestina: an example of love melancholy. Romanic Rev, 1975, 66:288-295.

7891. Armens, Sven. Archetypes of the Family in Literature. Seattle: Univ. Washington Press, 1966; Review: Howard R. Wolf, Lit & Psychol, 1967, 17:146-148.

7892. Armstrong, Alison. Shem the penman as Glugg as the wolfman. A Wake Newsletter, 1973, n. s. 10, 51-59.

7893. Armstrong, Daniel Paul. Beyond Psychoanalysis: A Re-Examination of Conrad's Fiction in the Light of His Polish Heritage. DAI, 1976, 37:2173A-4A.

7894. Armstrong, Judith. The Novel of Adultery. NY: Barnes & Noble, 1976; Review: Cheryl L. Walker, Modern Fiction Studies, 1978-79, 24:658-660.

7895. Armstrong, Paul B. Knowing in James: a phenomenological view. Novel: A Forum on Fiction, 1978, 12:5-20.

7896. Armstrong, Robert M. Joseph Conrad. The conflict of command. In The Psychoanalytic Study of the Child, Vol. 26. NY: Quadrangle, 1971, 485-534.

7897. Armytage, W. H. G. Superman and the system. Riverside Q, 1966, 2:232-242; 1967, 3:44-51.

7898. Arner, Robert D. Sentiment and sensibility: the role of emotion and William Hill Brown's The Power of Sympathy. Studies in Amer Fiction, 1973, 1:121-132.

7899. Arnold, John. Poe's 'Lionizing': the wound and the bawdry. Lit & Psychol, 1967, 17:52-54.

7900. Arnold, St. George Tucker, Jr. Consciousness and the Unconscious in the Fiction of Eudora Welty. DAI, 1976, 36:6094A.

7901. _____. The raincloud and the garden: psychic regression as tragedy in Welty's 'A Curtain of Green.' South Atlantic Bulletin, 1979, 44:53-60.

7902. Arns, Karl. Die Bewusstslinkunst in modernen Roman. In Grundriss der Geschichte der englischen Literatur. Paderborn: Schonigh, 1941, 146-149.

7903. Aronne Amestoy, L. Cortazar la novela mandala. Buenos Aires: Garcia Cambeiro, 1972.

7904. Aronstam, Noah E. The psychoanalysis of Theophile Gautier's Clarimonde. Urologie & Cutaneous Rev, 1922, 26:420-421.

7905. Artinian, Robert W. 'Then, Venom, to Thy Work': pathological representation in Pierre et Jean. Modern Fiction
Studies, 1972, 18:225-229.

7906. Artiss, David. Key symbols in Hesse's Steppenwolf. Seminar: J Germanic Studies, 1971, 1:85-101.

7907. Arvin, Newton. Herman Melville. NY: Sloan, 1950; London:
Methuen, 1950.

7908. Asals, Frederick. The mythic dimensions of Flannery O'Connor's 'Greenleaf.' Studies in Short Fiction, 1968, 5:317-
329.

7909. Askew, Melvin W. Hawthorne, the fall, and the psychology
of maturity. Amer Lit, 1962, 34:335-343.

7910. Aspell, Joseph. Fire symbolism in A Portrait of the Artist
as a Young Man. Univ. Dayton Rev, 1968-69, 5:29-39.

7911. Aspiz, Harold. Phrenologizing the whale. Nineteenth Century
Fiction, 1968, 23:18-27.

7912. Asselineau, Roger. Introduction: Les Aventures d'Arthur
Gordon Pym. Paris: Aubier Montaign, 1973.

7913. Asivell, E. D. Reflections of a governess: image and distortion in 'The Turn of the Screw.' Nineteenth Century
Fiction, 1968, 23:49-63.

7914. Astrachan, B. M. , & Boltax, S. The cyclical disorder of
Sherlock Holmes. JAMA, 1966, 196:1094.

7915. Astrov, Vladimir. Hawthorne and Dostoevski as explorers
of the human conscience. New England Q, 1942, 15:296-
319.

7916. Atherton, James. The Books at the Wake. NY: Viking,
1960.

7917. Atkin, I. The experiment of Dr. Moreau. J Clinical Psychopathology & Psychotherapy, 1947, 8:667-671.

7918. _____. Raskolnikov: the study of a criminal. J Criminology & Psychopathology, 1943, 5:255-280.

7919. _____. Smerdyakov: a review of an amoral epileptic. J
Mental Science, 1929, 75:263-266.

7920. Atkins, Lois. Psychological symbolism of guilt and isolation
in Hawthorne. Amer Imago, 1954, 11:417-425.

7921. Atkins, S. P. J. C. Lavater and Goethe: problems of psychology and theology in The Sorrows of Young Werther.
PMLA, 1948, 63:520-576.

7922. Attebery, Louie W. The American West and the archetypal
orphan. Western Amer Lit, 1970, 5(3):205-217.

7923. Auchincloss, Louis. The Blithedale Romance: a study in
form and point of view. Nathaniel Hawthorne J, 1972,
2:53-58.

7924. _____. Swann, male chauvinist and Albertine, boy-girl.
In Life, Law and Letters. Boston: Houghton Mifflin,
1979, 97-104.

7925. Auden, W. H. A literary transference. Southern Review,
1940, 6:78-86.

7926. Auerbach, Nina. Alice and wonderland: a curious child.
Victorian Studies, 1973, 17:31-47.

7927. _____. Austen and Alcott on matriarchy: new women or
new wives. In Spilka, M. (ed), Towards a Poetics of

Fiction. Bloomington: Indiana Univ. Press, 1977, 266-286.

7928. _____. Elizabeth Gaskell's sly javelins: governing women in Cranford and Haworth. Modern Language Q, 1977, 38: 276-291.

7929. _____. The rise of the fallen woman. Nineteenth Century Fiction, 1980, 35:29-52.

7930. Auernhammer, Achim. L'Androgynie dans L'Homme sans qualitiés. L'Arc, 1978, 74:35-40.

7931. Aulagne, Louis J. Essai sur le nocturne proustien. L'Insomnie, le sommeil et les rêves dans A la Recherche du temps perdu. Psyché, 1949, 4:876-902.

7932. _____. Les fées d'A la Recherche du temps perdu. Psyché, 1952, 7:357-376, 410-434.

7933. Auser, Cortland P. John Cheever's myth of man and time: 'The Swimmer.' CEA Critic, 1967, 29:18-19.

7934. Austen, Roger. But for fate and ban: homosexual villains and victims in the military. College English, 1974, 36: 352-359.

7935-6. _____. Playing the Game: The Homosexual Novel in America. Indianapolis: Bobbs-Merrill, 1977.

7937. Austen, Zelda. Why feminist critics are angry with George Eliot. College English, 1976, 37:549-561.

7938. Austin, Garry. The relative quality of best sellers. Public Opinion Q, 1952, 16:131-132.

7939. Avery, George C. The Chinese wall: Fontane's psychograph of Effi Briest. In Weimar, K. S. (ed), Views and Reviews of Modern German Literature. Munich: Delp, 1974, 18-38.

7940. Axberger, Gunnar. Arson and fiction: a cross-disciplinary study. Psychiatry, 1973, 36:244-265.

7941. Axelsson, Arne I. Isolation and interdependence as structure in Hawthorne's four major romances. Studia Neophilologica, 1973, 45:392-402.

7942. _____. The Links in the Chain: Isolation and Interdependence in Hawthorne's Fictional Characters. Uppsala: Universitets-Biblioteket, 1974.

7943. Axthelm, P. M. The Modern Confessional Novel. New Haven: Yale Univ. Press, 1967.

7944. Aycock, Linnea. The mother/daughter relationship in the Children of Violence series. Anonymous: A Journal for the Woman Writer, 1974, 1:48-55.

7945. Ayora, Jorge. Psicologia de lo grotesque en El hombre que parecia un caballo. Explicación de Textos Literarios, 1974, 2:117-122.

7946. Azaola, José M. de. Miguel de Unamuno et l'existentialisme. La Vie Intellectuelle, 1953, 31-49.

7947. Babb, Howard S. A reading of Sherwood Anderson's 'The Man Who Became a Woman.' PMLA, 1965, 80:432-435.

7948. Babener, Liahna Klenman. The shadow's shadow: the motif
       of the double in Edgar Allan Poe's 'The Purloined Letter.'
       Mystery & Detection Annual, 1972, 1:21-32.
7949. Bacarisse, S. The realism of Galdós: some reflections on
       language and the perception of reality. Bulletin Hispanic
       Studies, 1965, 42:239-250.
7950. Bach, S., et al. A dream of the Marquis de Sade: psycho-
       analytic reflections on narcissistic trauma, decompensa-
       tion, and the reconstitution of a delusional self. JAPA,
       1972, 20:451-475.
7951. Backman, Melvin. Death and birth in Hemingway. In Mac-
       Millan, D. J. (ed), The Stoic Strain in American Litera-
       ture. Toronto: Univ. Toronto Press, 1979, 115-133.
7952. _____. Faulkner's sick heroes: Bayard Sartoris and
       Quentin Compson. Modern Fiction Studies, 1956, 2:95-
       108.
7953. Backscheider, Paula. Defoe's women: snares and prey. In
       Rosbottom, R. C. (ed), Studies in Eighteenth-Century Cul-
       ture, Vol. 5. Madison: Univ. Wisconsin Press, 1976,
       103-120.
7954. Backus, Joseph M. Henry James and psychical research:
       some new twists suggested by a recent study of 'The Turn
       of the Screw.' [Review article.] Amer Society Psychical
       Research, 1978, 72:49-60.
7955. Badami, Mary Kenny. A feminist critique of science fiction.
       Extrapolation, 1977, 18:6-19.
7956. Baden, Hans Jurgen. Literatur und Selbstmord: Casare
       Pavese, Klaus Mann, Ernest Hemingway. Stuttgart:
       Klett, 1965.
7957. Baer Bahia, Alcyon. El contendo y la defensa en la creac-
       ción artística. Revista de Psicoanálisis, 1952, 9:311-341.
7958. Baernstein, J. -A. Image, identity, and insight in The Good
       Soldier. Critique, 1966-67, 11:19-42.
7959. Baggesen, Søren. Der blicherske novelle. Copenhagen:
       Gyldendal, 1965.
7960. Bagley, Carol L. Melville's Trilogy: Symbolic Precursor of
       Freudian Personality Structure in the History of Ideas.
       DA, 1966, 66-13, 549.
7961. Baguley, David. Image et symbole: la tache rouge dans
       l'oeuvre de Zola. Cahiers Naturalistes, 1970, 40:36-41.
7962. Bailet, Michel-Henri. L'Homme de Verre. Essai d'inter-
       pretation thématique de l'échec et de la maîtrise dans le
       Décaméron. Nice: 1972.
7963. Bailis, L. A. Death in children's literature: a conceptual
       analysis. Omega, 1977-78, 8:295-303.
7964. Baines, Barbara J. Villette, a feminist novel. Victorians
       Institute J, 1976, 5:51-59.
7965. Baird, Joe L., & Grajeda, R. A Shaw story and Brooks and
       Warren. CEA Critic, 1966, 28:3-4.
7966. Baissette, Gaston. Le Roman et la médecine. In Prevost,
       J. (ed), Problèmes du roman. Brussels: Carrefour,
       1945, 304-308.
7967. Baker, Carlos. Hemingway: The Writer as Artist. Prince-
       ton: Princeton Univ. Press, 1952, 1956, 1963, 1967.

7968. Baker, Donald G. Black images: the Afro-American in popular novels, 1900-1945. J Popular Culture, 1973, 7:327-346.

7969. _____. The stratagems of Caroline Gordon; or, the art of the novel and the novelty of myth. Southern Rev, 1973, 9:523-549.

7970. Baker, Marilyn J. Against Humanism: Alienation in the Works of Elie Wiesel, Günter Grass, and Kurt Vonnegut. DAI, 1978, 38:6111A.

7971. Baker, Robert S. George Meredith and the Psychological Novel: A Study of The Ordeal of Richard Feverel, Sandra Belloni and The Egoist. DAI, 1973, 34:760A.

7972. _____. The Ordeal of Richard Feverel: a psychological approach to structure. Studies in the Novel, 1974, 6:200-217.

7973. _____. Romantic onanism in Patrick White's The Vivisector. Texas Studies in Lit & Language, 1979, 21:203-225.

7974. _____. Sir Willoughby Patterne's inner temple: psychology and 'sentimentalism' in The Egoist. Texas Studies in Lit & Language, 1975, 16:691-703.

7975. _____. Spandrell's 'Lydian Heaven': moral masochism and the centrality of Spandrell in Huxley's Point Counter Point. Criticism, 1974, 16:120-135.

7976. Baker, Sheridan. Rasselas: psychological irony and romance. Philological Q, 1966, 45:249-261.

7977. Baker, Sidney J. A linguistic law of constancy. J General Psychol, 1950, 43:47-62.

7978. Bakerman, Jane S. Patterns of guilt and isolation in five novels by 'Tucker Coe.' In Marsden, M. T. (comp), Proceedings of the 5th Annual Convention of the Popular Culture Assn. Bowling Green, Ohio: Bowling Green State Univ. Popular Press, 1975, 244-259.

7979. Bakhtin, M. M. Monologue speech of the hero, and narrative discourse in the stories of Dostoevsky--Notes from Underground. In Durgy, R. G. (ed), Fyodor Dostoevsky, Notes from Underground. NY: Crowell, 1969, 203-216; In Bakhtin's [Problems of Dostoevsky's Poetics.] Moscow: Sovetskij Pisatel', 1963, 305-318.

7980. Balakian, Nona. Three post-psychological novels. In Critical Encounters; Literary Views and Reviews. Indianapolis: Bobbs-Merrill, 1978, 95-104.

7981. Balbert, Peter. Configurations of the ego studies of Mailer, Roth, and Salinger. Studies in the Novel, 1980, 12:73-81.

7982. _____. D. H. Lawrence and the Psychology of Rhythm: The Meaning of Form in The Rainbow. The Hague: Mouton, 1974.

7983. Baldanza, Frank. Iris Murdoch and the theory of personality. Criticism, 1965, 7:176-189.

7984. _____. James Purdy's half-orphans. Centennial Rev, 1974, 18:255-272.

7985. _____. Northern gothic. Southern Rev, 1974, 10:566-582.

7986. _____. The paradoxes of patronage in Purdy. Amer Lit, 1974, 43:347-356.
7987. Baldessarim, Ross. Literary techniques and psychological effect in Hawthorne's 'The Minister's Black Veil.' Lit & Psychol, 1974, 24:115-123.
7988. Baldini Mezzalana, Bruna. Alberto Moravia e l'alienazione. Milan: Ceschina, 1971.
7989. Baldissone, Giusi. Per un'interpretazione psicoanalitica degli Ossi di seppia. Terzo Programma, 1975, 2:181-194.
7990. Bales, K. Allegory and the radical romantic ethic of The Blithedale Romance. Amer Lit, 1974, 46:41-53.
7991. Balgley, Elissa Barmack. Aspects of Duality in Camus. DAI, 1977, 38:304A.
7992. Ball, Lee, Jr. Leather-Stocking's simplicity of mind as a key to his psychological character. South Central Bulletin, 1962, 22(4):11-15.
7993. Ballew, Steven E. Faulkner's Psychology of Individualism: A Fictional Principle and Light in August. DAI, 1975, 35:6700A.
7994. Ballorain, Rolande. 'The Turn of the Screw': L'Adulte et l'enfante: Ou les deux regards. Etudes Anglaises, 1969, 22:250-258.
7995. Bandelin, C. David Copperfield: a third interesting penitent. Studies in English Lit, 1976, 16:601-611.
7996. Banerjee, Chinmoy. Tristram Shandy and the association of ideas. Texas Studies in Lit & Language, 1974, 15:693-706.
7997. Bang, C.K. Emotions and attitudes in Chrétien de Troyes' Erec et Enide and Hartmann von Aue's Erec der Wunderaere. PMLA, 1942, 57:297-326.
7998. Bannon, A. Secrets of the gay novel. One, 1961, 9:6-12.
7999. Banta, Martha. A look at Jamesian Gothicism. Yale Rev, 1967, 56, 212-224.
8000. _____. Henry James and the Occult: The Great Extension. Bloomington: Indiana Univ. Press, 1972.
8001. Barba, Sharon R. Willa Cather: A Feminist Study. DAI, 1973, 34:2605A.
8002. Barber, Patricia. Melville's self-image as a writer and the image of the writer in Pierre. Massachusetts Studies in English, 1972, 3(3):65-71.
8003. Barchilon, Jacques, & Kovel, Joel S. Huckleberry Finn: a psychoanalytic study. JAPA, 1966, 14:775-814.
8004. Barchilon, Jose. The Fall. Bulletin Philadelphia Assn Psychoanal, 1967, 17:106-111.
8005. _____. The Fall by Albert Camus: a psychoanalytic study. Int J Psycho-Anal, 1968, 49:386-389.
8006. _____. A study of Camus' mythopoeic tale The Fall with some comments about the origin of esthetic feelings. JAPA, 1971, 19:193-240; In Fitch, B. T. (ed), Albert Camus 8. Camus romancier. Paris: Minard, 1977, 204-209.
8007. Barcus, F. Earle, & Levin, Jack. Role distance in Negro and majority fiction. Journalism Q, 1966, 43:709-714.

8008. Barcus, Nancy B. Psychological determinism and freedom in Flannery O'Connor. Cithara, 1972, 12:26-33.

8009. Bardeche, Maurice. Marcel Proust Romancier. Les Sept Couleurs. Paris: 1971.

8010. Bareikis, Robert. Arthur Schnitzler's Fräulein Else: a Freudian novella? Lit & Psychol, 1969, 19:19-32.

8011. Barickman, Richard. The comedy of survival in Dickens' novels. Novel: A Forum on Fiction, 1978, 11:128-143.

8012. Barish, J. A. Veritable Saint Genet. Wisconsin Studies in Contemporary Lit, 1965, 6:267-285.

8013. Barker, Andrew W. Triumph of life in Hofmannsthal's Das Märchen der 672. Nacht. Modern Language Rev, 1979, 74:341-348.

8014. Barker, Murl G. Erotic themes in Sologub's prose. Modern Fiction Studies, 1980, 26:241-247.

8015. Barker, Warren J. The stereotyped western story. Psychoanal Q, 1955, 24:270-280.

8016. Barksdale, Richard K. Alienation and the anti-hero in recent American fiction. College Language Assn J, 1966, 10:1-10.

8017. Barlow, D. The Characters of Fontane's Novels Considered in Relation to Their Social Environment. Bachelor Litt thesis, Oxford Univ., 1953.

8018. _____. Symbolism in Fontane's Der Stechlin. German Life & Letters, 1959, 12:282-286.

8019. Barnett, Alan Wayne. Who Is Jacob? The Quest for Identity in the Writing of Virginia Woolf. DA, 1965, 26:2742.

8020. Barnett, James Harwood. Divorce and the American Divorce Novel 1859-1937. A Study in Literary Reflections of Social Influences. NY: Russell & Russell, 1968 (1939).

8021. Barnett, Louise K. Displacement of kin and the fiction of Henry James. Criticism. A Quarterly for Lit & the Arts, 1980, 22:140-155.

8022. Baron, F. Sensuality and morality in Thomas Mann's Tod in Venedig. Germanic Rev, 1970, 45:115-126.

8023. Baron, Francis Xavier. The Alienated Hero in Arthurian Romance. DAI, 1970, 30:2960A.

8024. Barr, Alan P. Cervantes' probing of reality and psychological realism in Don Quixote. Lit & Psychol, 1968, 18:111-122.

8025. Barr, Donald. Ah, Buddy: Salinger. In Balckian, N. & Simmons, C. (eds), The Creative Present. NY: Doubleday, 1963, 27-62.

8026. _____. Freud and fiction. Saturday Rev, 1956, 39:36.

8027. Barrère, J. -B. Proust et les polders de la conscience. Rev d'Histoire Littéraire de la France, 1976, 76:59-67.

8028. Barrett, William G. On the naming of Tom Sawyer. Psychoanal Q, 1955, 24:424-436.

8029. Barrucand, D. A propos des médecins et de la médecine dans Les Thibault de Roger Martin du Gard. Annales Médico-Psychologiques, 1966, 124:409-446.

8030. Bart, Bejamin F. Psyche into myth: humanity and animality in Flaubert's Saint-Julien. Kentucky Romance Q, 1973, 20:317-342.

8031. Bartel, Roland. Life and death in Eudora Welty's 'A Worn Path.' Studies in Short Fiction, 1977, 14:288-290.

8032. Bartell, James. The trauma of birth in The Death of Ivan Ilych. Psychocultural Rev, 1978, 2(2):97-117.

8033. Barton, Rebecca. Race Consciousness and the American Negro: A Study of the Correlation Between the Group Experience and the Fiction of 1900-1930. Copenhagen: Busck, 1934.

8034. Basdekis, D. Unamuno and Zola. Notes on the novel. Modern Language Notes, 1973, 88:366-374.

8035. Basler, Roy P. The interpretation of 'Ligeia.' College English, 1944; In Sex, Symbolism and Psychology. New Brunswick, NJ: Rutgers Univ. Press, 1948; Rev des Lettres Modernes, 1969, 193-198:97-112.

8036. _____. Sex, Symbolism and Psychology in Literature. New Brunswick, NJ: Rutgers Univ. Press, 1948; NY: Octagon, 1967.

8037. Bassoff, Bruce. Freedom and fatality in Robbe-Grillet's Les Gommes. Contemporary Lit, 1979, 20:434-451.

8038. _____. Little Hans and the Pederson kid. Notes on Contemporary Lit, 1978, 8:4-5.

8039. Bastos, M. L., & Molloy, S. La estrella junto a la luna: variantes de la figura materna en Pedro Páramo. MLN, 1977, 92:246-268.

8040. Battilana, Marilla. Edgar Allan Poe, nostro contemporaneo. Annali di Ca'Foscari, 1969, 8(2):1-10.

8041. Baudouin, Charles. Anatole France. Genèse d'un scepticism. Psyché, 1947, 2:1075-1082.

8042. _____. Les antithèses chez Victor Hugo. Archiv de Psychologie, 1930, 22:121-143.

8043. _____. Etudes psychanalytiques sur Victor Hugo La Médiatrice. Action et Pensée, 1943, 19.

8044. _____. La sagesse de Don Quichotte. Psyché, 1948, 3: 643-651.

8045. Baudry, Francis D. On the problem of inference in applied psychoanalysis: Flaubert's Madame Bovary. In The Psychoanalytic Study of Society, Vol. 8. New Haven: Yale Univ. Press, 1979, 331-358.

8046. Baum, Alwin L. Carroll's Alices: the semiotics of paradox. Amer Imago, 1977, 34:86-108.

8047. Baumann, Carl. Literatur und intellektueller Kitsch: Das Stendhals. Zur Sozial-neuroses der Moderne. Heidelberg: Rothe, 1964.

8048. Baumbach, Georgia A. The Psychology of Flannery O'Connor's Fictive World. DAI, 1973, 34:304A.

8049. Baumbach, J. Nightmare of a native son: Invisible Man, by Ralph Ellison. In Gibson, D. B. (ed), Five Black Writers. NY: New York Univ. Press, 1970, 73-87; Critique, 1963, 6:48-65.

8050. Bäumer, G., & Droescher, L. Von der Kindeseele. Beiträge zur Kinderpsychologie aus Dichtung und Biographie. Leipzig: Voigtländer, 1922.

8051. Baxter, Charles. A self-consuming light: Nightwood and the crisis of modernism. J Modern Lit, 1974, 3:1175-1187.

8052. Bayley, John. Dickens and the Twentieth Century. London: Gross & Pearson, 1962.

8053. Baym, Nina. Fleda Vetch and the plot of The Spoils of Poynton. PMLA, 1969, 84:102-111.

8054. _____. Hawthorne's Holgrave: the failure of the artist-hero. J English Germanic Philology, 1970, 69:584-598.

8055. _____. Hawthorne's women: the tyranny of social myths. Centennial Rev, 1971, 15:250-272.

8056. _____. The head, the heart, and the unpardonable sin. New England Q, 1967, 40:31-47.

8057. _____. The portrayal of women in American literature, 1790-1870. In Springer, M. (ed), What Manner of Woman: Essays on English and American Life and Literature. NY: New York Univ. Press, 1977, 211-234.

8058. _____. Woman's Fiction; A Guide to Novels by and About Women in America. Ithaca: Cornell Univ. Press, 1978.

8059. _____. The women of Cooper's Leatherstocking Tales. Amer Q, 1971, 23:696-709.

8060. Beach, Joseph W. The Twentieth Century Novel. Studies in Technique. NY: Appleton-Century-Crofts, 1932, 25-74.

8061. Beaman, Bruce R. Mycroft Holmes, agoraphobe. Baker Street J, 1976, 26:91-93.

8062. Beards, Richard D. Stereotyping in modern American fiction: some solitary Swedish madmen. Moderna Sprak, 1969, 63:331-337.

8063. Beardsley, Monroe C. Dostoyevsky's metaphor of the 'Underground.' J History of Ideas, 1942, 3:265-290; In Durgy, R.G. (ed), Notes from Underground. NY: Crowell, 1969, 229-260.

8064. Beatson, Peter. The Eye in the Mandala. Patrick White: A Vision of Man and God. NY: Barnes & Noble, 1976.

8065. Beattie, Munro. The many marriages of Henry James. In La France, M. (ed), Patterns of Commitment in American Literature. Toronto: Univ. Toronto Press, 1967, 93-112.

8066. Beauchamp, Andrea L.R. The Heroine of Our Common Scene: Portrayals of American Women in Four Novels by Edith Wharton and Henry James. DAI, 1976, 37:965A.

8067. Beauchamp, Gorman. Lawrence's 'The Rocking-Horse Winner.' Explicator, 1973, 31(5), Item 32.

8068. Beaujour, Michel. La Quête du délire. Les Cahiers de l'Herne, 1963, 3:279-286.

8069. Beausang, Michael. Seeds for the planting of Bloom. Mosaic, 1972, 6(1):11-22.

8070. Beck, W. Arnolphe or Monsieur de la Souche? French Rev, 1968, 42:254-261.

8071. Becker, Carol. Edgar Allan Poe: The Madness of the Method. DAI, 1976, 36:5290A.

8072. Becker, Ernest. Everyman as pervert. In Angel in Armor: A Post-Freudian Perspective on the Nature of Man. NY: Braziller, 1969, 1-38.

8073. Becker, Lucille. Henry de Montherlant and suicide. Romance Notes, 1975, 16:254-257.

385   Fiction

8074. Becker, Raymond de. The Other Face of Love. London:
       Spearman, 1967.
8075. Beckman, Richard David. A character typology for Hardy's
       novels. J English Lit History, 1963, 30:70-87.
8076. Bedick, David B. The Changing Role of Anxiety in the Novel.
       DAI, 1975, 36:3682A.
8077. Bedient, Calvin. The radicalism of Lady Chatterley's Lover.
       Hudson Rev, 1966, 19:407-416.
8078. Bednarik, Karl. The Male in Crisis. NY: Knopf, 1968.
8079. Beeck, P. v. Der psychologische Gehalt in den Romanen
       Defoes. Quakenbrück: Kelinert, 1931.
8080. Beer, Patricia. Reader, I Married Him: A Study of the
       Women Characters of Jane Austen, Charlotte Brontë,
       Elizabeth Gaskell and George Eliot. NY: Barnes & No-
       ble, 1974.
8081. Begiebing, Robert J. Norman Mailer's Why Are We in Viet-
       nam?: the rebuttal of regeneration. Amer Imago, 1980,
       37:12-37.
8082. _____. Stephen Crane's Maggie: the death of the self.
       Amer Imago, 1977, 34:50-72.
8083. Beharriell, Frederick J. Kafka, Freud, and 'Das Urteil.'
       In Durzak, M., Reichmann, E., & Weisstein, U. (eds),
       Texte und Kontexte: Studien zur deutschen und vergleich-
       enden Literaturwissenschaft. Bern: Francke, 1973, 27-
       47.
8084. _____. Psychology in the early works of Thomas Mann.
       PMLA, 1962, 77:149-155.
8085. _____. Schnitzler's Fräulein Else: 'reality' and invention.
       Modern Austrian Lit, 1977, 10:247-264.
8086. Behrens, Roy R. Lunatics, lovers, and poets: on madness
       and creativity. J Creative Behavior, 1975, 94:228-232,
       266.
8087. Beinlich, A. Zum Verhältnis von kindes- und jugendpsycho-
       logischer Forschung und dichterischer Darstellung des
       Kindes. Zeitschrift für pädagogische Psychologie, 1940,
       41:37-40.
8088. Beit-Hallalhi, Benjamin. 'The Turn of the Screw' and The
       Exorcist. Demoniacal possession and childhood purity.
       Amer Imago, 1976, 33:296-303.
8089. Beja, Morris. Bartleby and schizophrenia. Massachusetts
       Rev, 1978, 19:555-568.
8090. _____. Dividual Chaoses: case histories of multiple per-
       sonality and Finnegans Wake. James Joyce Q, 1977, 14:
       241-250.
8091. _____. Psychological Fiction. Glenview, Ill: Scott,
       Foresman, 1971.
8092. _____. Virginia Woolf, 'To the Lighthouse': A Casebook.
       London: Macmillan, 1970.
8093. _____. The wooden sword: threatener and threatened in
       the fiction of James Joyce. James Joyce Q, 1964, 2:33-
       41.
8094. Béjar Hurtado, Manuel. La personalidad en la novela de
       Ramon J. Sender. DAI, 1970, 31:4150-A.

8095. Belgion, Montgomery. God is mammon. In Human Parrot, and Other Essays. NY: Oxford Univ. Press, 1931, 117-134.

8096. Bell, Brenda J. The Figure of the Child in the Novels of George Eliot. DAI, 1975, 35:6701A.

8097. Bell, George E. The dilemma of love in Go Tell It on the Mountain. College Language Assn J, 1974, 17:397-406.

8098. Bell, Gerda. 'The child is father to the man': a brief study on Dostoevsky's knowledge of children, exemplified by his story 'A Little Hero.' New Zealand Slavonic J, 1971, 8: 32-48.

8099. Bell, J. D. Ellison's Invisible Man. Explicator, 1970, 29.

8100. Bell, Millicent. The dream of being possessed and possessing: Henry James's The Wings of the Dove. Massachusetts Rev, 1969, 10:97-114.

8101. Bell, Vereen M. Emotional matrix of David Copperfield. Studies in English Lit, 1968, 8:633-649.

8102. _____. Parents and children in Great Expectations. Victorian Newsletter, 1965, 20:177-184.

8103. Bell, William S. Proust's Nocturnal Muse. NY: Columbia Univ. Press, 1962.

8104. _____. Proust's Un Amour de Swann: A voyage to Cytherea. L'Esprit créateur, 1965, 5:26-37.

8105. Bellak, Leopold. On the psychology of detective stories and related problems. Psychoanal Rev, 1945, 32:403-407.

8106. _____. Somerset Maugham: a thematic analysis of ten stories. In White, R. W. (ed), The Study of Lives. NY: Atherton, 1966, 142-159.

8107. Bellamy, Michael O. Eros and Thanatos in William Dean Howells's 'Editha.' Amer Lit Realism 1870-1910, 1979, 12(2):283-287.

8108. Bellemin-Noël, Jean. Analectures de Jules Verne. Critique, 1970, 279-280.

8109. _____. 'Psychanalyser' le rêve de Swann. Poétique, 1971, 8:447-469.

8110. Bellman, Samuel Irving. Fathers and sons in Jewish fiction. Congress Bi-Weekly, 1967, 34:18-20.

8111. _____. The 'Jewish mother' syndrome. Congress Bi-Weekly, 1965, 32(18):3-5.

8112. _____. Man as Alien: The Isolation Theme in Thomas Hardy. DA, 1956, 16:960-961.

8113. _____. Sleep, pride, and fantasy: birth traumas and socio-biologic adaptation in the American-Jewish novel. Costerus: Essays in English & Amer Language & Lit, 1973, 8:1-12.

8114. _____. Women, children, and idiots first: the transformation psychology of Bernard Malamud. Critique, 1964-65, 7:123-138; In Field, L. A. , & Field, J. W. (eds), Bernard Malamud and the Critics. NY: New York Univ. Press, 1970, 11-28.

8115. Belson, Joel Jay. The nature and consequences of the loneliness of Huckleberry Finn. Arizona Q, 1970, 26:243-248.

8116. Bem, A. [Dramatization of delirium in Dostoevsky's The Landlady.] Collection Dostoevskii. Prague: Otto, 1929.

8117. _____. [The Gambler by Dostoevsky.] Sovremennyia Zapiski, 1925, 24:378-392.

8118. Benbow, Jerry L. Fictional Manifestations of Multiple Personality in Selected Works of Miguel de Unamuno. DAI, 1971, 31:5388A.

8119. Benert, Annette Larson. The forces of fear: Kesey's anatomy of insanity. Lex et Scientia: Int J Law & Science, 1977, 13(1-2):22-26.

8120. _____. Passion and Perception: A Jungian Reading of Henry James. DAI, 1976, 36:6095A.

8121. Benkovits, Miriam J. Some observations of woman's concept of self in the 18th century. In Fritz, P., & Morton, R. (eds), Women in the 18th Century and Other Essays. Toronto: Hakkert, 1976, 37-54.

8122. Bennett, Edwin Keppel. The psychological Novelle. In A History of the German Novelle. Cambridge: Harvard Univ. Press, 1961, 206-240.

8123. Bennett, George N. The Realism of William Dean Howells. Nashville: Vanderbilt Univ. Press, 1973.

8124. Bennett, John. The conscience of Huckleberry Finn. Philosophy, 1974, 49:123-134; 1977, 52:96-99.

8125. Bennett, Peirson S. The Motif of Seeing and the Symbol of the Eye in Herman Broch's Bergroman. DAI, 1971, 31:5388A.

8126. Bennett, Veldon J. The Role of the Female in the Works of Hermann Hesse. DAI, 1972, 33:2314A-15A.

8127. Benoit, Raymond. Hawthorne's psychology of death: 'The Minister's Black Veil.' Studies in Short Fiction, 1971, 8:553-560.

8128. Benson, Jackson J. Hemingway: The Writer's Art of Self-Defense. Minneapolis: Univ. Minnesota Press, 1969.

8129. _____. Quentin Compson: self-portrait of a young artist's emotions. Twentieth Century Lit, 1971, 17:143-159.

8130. Benson, Ruth Crego. Women in Tolstoy. The Ideal and the Erotic. Urbana: Univ. Illinois Press, 1973; DAI, 1969, 30:1519A.

8131. Benstock, Bernard. Every telling has a taling: a reading of the narrative of Finnegans Wake. Modern Fiction Studies, 1969, 15:3-25.

8132. _____. Bloom as dreamer in Finnegans Wake. PMLA, 1967, 82:90-97.

8133. Benstock, Sharl. The evasion principle: a search for survivors in Ulysses. Modern Fiction Studies, 1978, 24:159-179.

8134. Bentley, C. F. The monster in the bedroom: sexual symbolism in Bram Stoker's Dracula. Lit & Psychol, 1972, 22:27-35.

8135. Bentley, Joseph. Semantic gravitation: an essay on satire reduction. Modern Language Q, 1969, 30:3-19.

8136. Bently, Thomas J. Henry James's 'general vision of evil' in 'The Turn of the Screw.' Studies in English Lit, 1969, 9:721-735.

8137. Béranger, Jean. Analyses structurales de 'Rip Van Winkle.'
       Rev Française d'Etudes Américaines, 1978, 5:33-45.
8138. Bercovitch, Sacvan. Dramatic irony in Notes from Under-
       ground. Slavic & East European J, 1964, 8:284-291.
8139. _____. The revision of Rowland Mallet. Nineteenth Cen-
       tury Fiction, 1969, 24:210-221.
8140. Beresford, J. D. Le Déclin de l'influence de la psych-ana-
       lyse sur le roman anglais. Mercure de France, 1926,
       190:257-266.
8141. _____. Psychoanalysis and the novel. Freeman, 1920, 1:
       35-39; London Mercury, 1920, 1:426-434.
8142. Berets, Ralph. A Jungian interpretation of the dream se-
       quence in Doris Lessing's The Summer Before the Dark.
       Modern Fiction Studies, 1980, 26:117-130.
8143. Berger, Hans. Die Angst im Werk Hermann Hesses. In
       Klein, K. K., & Thurnher, E. (eds), Germantische Ab-
       handlungen. Innsbruck: Univ. Innsbruck, 1959, 271-283.
8144. Berger, Josephine M. Elizabeth Bowen's Concept of the
       Short Story: The Androgynous Mind in Literature. DAI,
       1978, 38:4174A.
8145. Bergler, Edmund. D. H. Lawrence's The Fox and the psycho-
       analytic theory on Lesbianism. JNMD, 1958, 126:488-491;
       In Moore, H. T. (ed), D. H. Lawrence Miscellany. Car-
       bondale: Southern Illinois Univ. Press, 1959, 49-55.
8146. _____. Little Dorrit and Dickens' intuitive knowledge of
       psychic masochism. Amer Imago, 1957, 14:371-388.
8147. _____. Mystery fans and the problem of 'potential mur-
       derers.' Amer J Orthopsychiat, 1945, 15:309-317.
8148. _____. A note on Herman Melville. Amer Imago, 1950,
       11:385-397.
8149. _____. Writers of half-interest. Amer Imago, 1957, 14:
       155-164.
8150. Bergotte, (?). Une Psychologie du péché. Mercure de
       France, 1924, 173:307-324.
8151. Berke, Jacqueline, & Berke, Laura. Mothers and daughters
       in Wives and Daughters: a study of Elizabeth Gaskell's
       last novel. In Davidson, C. N., & Broner, E. M. (eds),
       The Lost Tradition. NY: Ungar, 1980, 95-109.
8152. Berkvan, Doris D. La Mère et l'enfant dans les romans
       français des XIIe et XIIIe siècles. DAI, 1978, 39:3095A.
8153. Berlin, Jeffrey Bennett. The element of 'hope' in Arthur
       Schnitzler's Sterben. Seminar: J Germanic Studies,
       1974, 10(1):38-49.
8154. Berman, Jeffrey. Conrad's Lord Jim and the enigma of sub-
       limation. Amer Imago, 1976, 33:381-402.
8155. _____. Joseph Conrad: Writing as Rescue. NY: Astra,
       1977.
8156. _____. Tender Is the Night. Fitzgerald's A Psychology
       for Psychiatrists. Lit & Psychol, 1979, 29:34-48.
8157. _____. Writing as rescue: Conrad's escape from the
       heart of darkness. Lit & Psychol, 1975, 25:65-78.
8158. Bermel, A. Apollinaire's male heroine. Twentieth Century
       Lit, 1974, 20:172-182.

8159. Berna, Jacques M. Die Pubertätsrevolte in Robinson Crusoe. Almanach, 1966, 144-150.

8160. Bernabeu, Ednita P. Science fiction: a new mythos. Psychoanal Q, 1957, 26:527-535.

8161. Bernal, O. Des Fiches et des fluides dans le roman de Nathalie Sarraute. Modern Language Notes, 1973, 88:775-788.

8162. Bernard, Catherine Adelaide. Dickens and Dreams: A Study of the Dream Theories and Dream Fiction of Charles Dickens. DAI, 1977, 38:2134A.

8163. Bernard, Kenneth. Edgar Huntly: Charles Brockden Brown's unsolved murder. Library Chronicle, 1967, 33:30-53.

8164. Bernard, L. Les Odeurs dans les romans de Zola. Montpellier, 1899.

8165. Bernberg, Raymond E. Light in August: a psychological view. Mississippi Q, 1958, 11:173-176.

8166. Berne, Eric. The psychological structure of space with some remarks on Robinson Crusoe. Psychoanal Q, 1956, 25:549-567.

8167. Berner, L. Etienne Leroux: a Jungian introduction. Books Abroad, 1975, 49:255-262.

8168. Bersani, Leo. The anxious imagination. Partisan Rev, 1968, 35:49-66.

8169. _____. Balzac to Beckett: Center and Circumference in French Fiction. NY: Oxford Univ. Press, 1970.

8170. _____. The interpretation of dreams. Partisan Rev, 1965, 32:603-608; In Lucid, R. F. (ed), Norman Mailer: The Man and His Work. Boston: Little, Brown, 1971, 171-179; In Braudy, L. (ed), Norman Mailer, a Collection of Critical Essays. Englewood Cliffs, NJ: Prentice-Hall, 1972, 120-126.

8171. Berthold, Dennis. From Freud to Marx: recent directions in Hawthorne criticism. ESQ: J Amer Renaissance, 1976, 22:107-119.

8172. Bertrand, Marc. L'Amour et la sexualité dans Candide. French Rev, 1964, 37(6).

8173. Bertrand-Jennings, Chantal. L'Eros et la femme chez Zola. Paris: Klincksieck, 1977; Review: I. Finel-Honigman, French Rev, 1979, 52:490-491.

8174. Berzon, Judith R. Neither White Nor Black: The Mulatto Character in American Fiction. NY: New York Univ. Press, 1978.

8175. Bessette, Gérard. Mélie et le boeuf de Jacques Ferron. Modern Fiction Studies, 1976, 22:441-448.

8176. Beston, John B. The hero's 'fear of freedom' in Keneally. Australian Lit Studies, 1972, 5:374-387.

8177. Bethmann, Renate. Psychologische Merkmale als Kennzeichen der politisch-sozialen Klassifizierung im Wortschatz von Stendhal. Wissenschaftliche Zeitschrift der Martin-Luther Universität Halle-Wittenberg, 1970, 19(3-4):127-138.

8178. Bettelheim, Bruno. Portnoy psychoanalyzed: therapy notes found in the file of Dr. O. Spielvogel, a New York psychoanalyst. Midstream, 1969, 15(6):3-10; In Surviving and Other Essays. NY: Knopf, 1979, 387-398.

8179. Beuchut, C. Psicoanálisis y Argentina en una novela de E. Sábato. Valparaiso: Universitaria, 1970.

8180. Beutin, Wolfgang. Zum Lebensweg des 'Helden' in der mittelhochdeutschen Dichtung (Erec, Iwein, Tristan, Parzival). Bemerkungen aus psychoanalytischer Sicht. LiLi: Zeitschrift für Literaturwissenschaft und Linguistik, 1977, 26:39-57.

8181. Bewley, Marius. Hawthorne and the 'deeper psychology.' Mandrake, 1956, 2:366-373.

8182. Beysterveldt, A. van. Nueva interpretación de La Celestina. Segismundo, 1975, 21-22:87-116.

8183. Bezanker, Abraham. I. B. Singer's crises of identity. Critique: Studies in Modern Fiction, 1972, 14(2):70-88.

8184. Bhatt, Punita B. Thomas Hardy's Women: A Study of Relationships. DAI, 1972, 745A-46A.

8185. Bianchi, Ruggiero (ed). E. A. Poe, Dal gotico alla fantascienza. Turin: Turin Univ. Press, 1978.

8186. Bianco, J. El sentido del mal en la obra de Proust. Torre, 1959, 25:75-86.

8187. Bianquis, Geneviève. Le Temps dans l'oeuvre de Thomas Mann. JPNP, 1951, 44:355-370.

8188. Biasin, Gian-Paolo. Literary disease: from pathology to ontology. Modern Language Notes, 1967, 82:79-102.

8189. _____. Literary Diseases; Theme and Metaphor in the Italian Novel. Austin: Univ. Texas Press, 1975.

8190. _____. Myth and death in Cesare Pavese's the moon and the bonfires; excerpt from 'The Smile of the Gods.' In Pacifici, S. (ed), From Verismo to Experimentalism; Essays on the Modern Italian Novel. Bloomington: Indiana Univ. Press, 1970, 184-211.

8191. Bibesco, Prince A. The heartlessness of Marcel Proust. Cornhill Magazine, 1950, No. 983, 421-428.

8192. Bickerton, Derek. James Joyce and the development of the interior monologue. Essays in Criticism, 1969, 18:32-46.

8193. _____. Modes of interior monologue: a formal definition. Modern Language Q, 1967, 28:229-239.

8194. Bickman, Martin Elliott. Animatopoeia: 'Morella' as siren of the self. Poe Studies, 1975, 8:29-32.

8195. Bie, Wendy A. Mark Twain's bitter duality. Mark Twain J, 1972, 16(2):14-16.

8196. Bieber, K. Le Dédoublement de la personnalité chez H. Bosco. Modern Language Notes, 1958, 4:272-284.

8197. Bieder, J., Houillon, P., & Faidherbe, D. Réflexions sur une oeuvre de Balzac 'l'interdiction.' Annales Médico-Psychologiques, 1969, 2:559-564.

8198. Bien, Günter. Das Bild des Jugendlichten in der modernen Literatur. Deutsche Rundschau, 1964, 90(3):40-45.

8199. Bienstock, Beverly Gray. The changing image of the American Jewish mother. In Tufte, V., & Myerhoff, B. G. (eds), Changing Images of the Family. New Haven: Yale Univ. Press, 1979, 173-191.

8200.   Bierman, Joseph S.   Dracula: prolonged childhood illness, and the oral triad.   Amer Imago, 1972, 29:186-198.
8201.   Bierman, Robert.   The dreamer and the dream in Finnegans Wake.   Renascence, 1959, 11:197-200.
8202.   Bigelow, Josette M.   La Psychologie de la litote chez François Sagan.   South-Central Bulletin, 1963, 23(1):13.
8203.   Binder, Hartmut.   Kafkas Schaffensprozess, mit besonderer Berücksuchtigung des Urteils: Eine Analyse seiner Aussagan über das Schreiben mit Hilfe der Handschriften und auf Grund psychologischer Theoreme.   Euphorion, 1976, 70:129-174.
8204.   _____.   Motiv und Gestaltung bei Franz Kafka.   Bonn: Bouvier, 1966.
8205.   Biolley-Godino, M.   L'Homme-objet chez Colette.   Paris: Klincksieck, 1973.
8206.   Birbalsingh, F. M.   Mordecai Richler and the Jewish-Canadian novel.   J Commonwealth Lit, 1972, 7:72-82.
8207.   Birchby, S.   Sexual symbolism in W. H. Hodgson.   Riverside Q, 1964, 1:70-71.
8208.   Birdsall, Virginia O.   Hawthorne's fair-haired maidens: the finding light.   PMLA, 1960, 75:250-256.
8209.   Birnbaum, Milton.   Aldous Huxley's animadversions upon sexual love.   Texas Studies in Lit & Language, 1966, 8: 285-296.
8210.   Birner, Louis.   The James Bond phenomenon.   J Contemporary Psychotherapy, 1968, 1:13-18.
8211.   Bischoff, Peter.   Entfremdung und Suche in Saul Bellows Romanen.   Doctoral dissertation.   Univ. Münster, 1973.
8212.   _____.   Saul Bellows Romane: Entfremdung und Suche. Bonn: Bouvier, 1975.
8213.   Bitton, Livia E.   The Jewess as a fictional sex symbol. Bucknell Rev, 1973, 21(1):63-86.
8214.   Björk, Lennart A.   Psychological vision and social criticism in Desperate Remedies and Jude the Obscure.   In Pinion, F. B. (ed), Budmouth Essays on Thomas Hardy.   Dorchester, England: Hardy Society, 1976, 86-105.
8215.   Bjørnvig, Thorkild.   Fragment of lidenskabens psykologi.   In Albeck, G. et al. (eds), Festskrift til Jens Kruuse den 6. April 1968.   Aarhus: Universitetsforlaget, 1968, 47-54; In Brower, R., et al. (eds), I. A. Richards: Essays in His Honor.   NY: Oxford Univ. Press, 1973, 110-117.
8216.   Black, David Joseph.   Herman Hesse's Use of Dreams as a Literary Device.   DAI, 1975, 35:4501A.
8217.   Black, Michael.   The Literature of Fidelity.   NY: Barnes & Noble, 1975.
8218.   Black, Stephen A.   On reading psychoanalytically.   College English, 1977, 39:267-274.
8219.   _____.   The Scarlet Letter: death by symbols.   Paunch, 1965, 24:51-74.
8220.   Blackall, Jean Frantz.   Perspectives on Harold Frederic's Market-Place.   PMLA, 1971, 86:388-405.
8221.   Blair, Walter.   Mark Twain and Huck Finn.   The Biography of a Book.   Berkeley: Univ. California Press, 1960.

8222. Blake, J. Insight through fiction. High School J, 1950, 33: 199-201.

8223. Blake, Kathleen. Play, Gales, and Sport: The Literary Works of Lewis Carroll. Ithaca, NY: Cornell Univ. Press, 1974.

8224. _____. Sue Bridehead, the woman of the feminist movement. Studies in English Lit, 1978, 18:703.

8225. Blake, Nancy. Henry James: all around the primal scene. Rev Française d'Etudes Américaines, 1977, 3:61-69.

8226. _____. Mourning and melancholia in 'Bartleby.' Delta, 1977, 7:155-168.

8227. Blakeston, O. Sang-freud; or the thought-stream novel. Bookman, 1934, 87:36.

8228. Blanch, Robert J. Poe's imagery: an undercurrent of childhood fears. Furman Studies, 1967, 14(4):19-25.

8229. Blanchard, Lydia. Mothers and daughters in D. H. Lawrence: The Rainbow and selected shorter works. In Smith, A. (ed), Lawrence and Women. NY: Barnes & Noble, 1978, 75-100.

8230. _____. Women and fiction: the limits of criticism. [Review article.] Studies in the Novel, 1977, 9:339-354.

8231. _____. Women look at Lady Chatterley: feminine views of the novel. D. H. Lawrence Rev, 1978, 11:246-259.

8232. Blanco-Aguinaga, C. Fortunata y Jacinta. Anales Galdosianos, 1968, 3:13-24.

8233. Bleakley, Mary E. The Effect of the Sex of the Main Character in Selected Mystery, Humor, and Adventure Stories on the Interest and Comprehension of Fifth Grade Children. DAI, 1977, 38(5-A), 2542.

8234. Bleger, José. Symbiosis in The Warrior Rests. Revista de Psicoanalisis, 1962, 19:173-199.

8235. Bleich, David. Artistic form as defensive adaptation: Henry James and The Golden Bowl. Psychoanal Rev, 1971, 58: 223-244.

8236. _____. Eros and Bellamy. Amer Q, 1964, 16:445-459.

8237. _____. Utopia: The Psychology of a Cultural Fantasy. DAI, 1970, 30:4935A-36A.

8238. Bleickasten, André. The Most Splendid Failure: Faulkner's The Sound and the Fury. Bloomington: Indiana Univ. Press, 1976.

8239. _____. La Terreur et la nausée ou le langage des corps dans Sanctuaire. Sud, 1975, Nos. 14-15.

8240. Blenkner, Louis. Sin, psychology and the structure of Sir Gawain and the Green Knight. Studies in Philology, 1977, 74:354-387.

8241. Bloch, Adèle. The archetypal influences in Thomas Mann's Joseph and His Brothers. Germanic Rev, 1963, 38:151-156.

8242. _____. The mythological themes in the fictional works of Jacques Roumain. Int Fiction Rev, 1975, 2:132-137.

8243. Bloch, Alice. Sight imagery in Invisible Man. English J, 1966, 55:1019-1021, 1024.

8244. Bloch, Iwan. Ist Alfred de Musset der Verfasser von gamiani. Zeitschrift für Sexualwissenschaft, 1915-1916, 2:28-31.

8245.   Bloch, Ralph H. A Study of the Dream Motif in the Old
        French Narrative. DAI, 1970, 31:2334A.
8246.   Blom, M. A. Charlotte Brontë, feminist manquée. Bucknell
        Rev, 1973, 21(1):87-102.
8247.   Blomme, Gayle C. B. Gertrude Stein's Concepts of the Self
        and Her Literary Characters. DAI, 1973, 34:1892A.
8248.   Blondel, Charles. Marcel Proust. Héterogénéite du réel et
        généralités. Rev Philosophique, 1931, 56:5-27.
8249.   _____. Marcel Proust et l'immensité mentale. Rev Philo-
        sophique, 1931, 56:259-283.
8250.   _____. La Psychographie de Marcel Proust. Paris: Vrin,
        1932.
8251.   Blondel, Jacques. Morale, psychologie, destinée dans Le
        moulin sur la Floss. Les Langues Modernes, 1965, 59:
        342-348.
8252.   Bloom, L. Tipping and nocturnal emission. Psychoanal Rev,
        1959, 46:118.
8253.   Blotner, Joseph Leo. Mythic patterns in To the Lighthouse.
        PMLA, 1956, 71:547-562.
8254.   Blouin, E. M. Proceso de individuación y arquetipo de la Gran
        Madre en La Celestina. In Beck, M. A. et al. (eds), The
        Analysis of Hispanic Texts: Current Trends in Methodol-
        ogy. NY: Bilingual Press, 1977, 16-48.
8255.   Bluds, Peter Allan. Une Analyse psychologique de la Mar-
        quise de Merteuil et du Vicomte de Valmont dans Les
        Liaisons dangereuses de Laclos. DAI, 1976, 37:2216A.
8256.   Blue, Gladys F. The aging as portrayed in realistic fiction
        for children, 1945-1975. Gerontologist, 1978, 18:187-
        192.
8257.   Bluefarb, Sam. The head, the heart and the conflict of gen-
        erations in Chaim Potok's The Chosen. College Language
        Assn J, 1971, 14:402-409.
8258.   _____. The middle-aged man in contemporary literature:
        Bloom to Herzog. College Language Assn J, 1976, 20:1-
        13.
8259.   _____. The syncretism of Bernard Malamud. In Field,
        L. A., & Field, J. W. (eds), Bernard Malamud: A Col-
        lection of Critical Essays. Englewood Cliffs, NJ: Pren-
        tice-Hall, 1976, 72-79.
8260.   Blüher, Hans. Niels Lyhne von J. P. Jacobsen und das Prob-
        lem der Bisexualität. Imago, 1912, 1:386-400.
8261.   Blum, Ernst. Dostojewski über den Traum. Int Zeitschrift
        für Psychoanalyse, 1919, 5:307.
8262.   Blumenfeld, Walter. Don Quijote und Sancho Panza als psy-
        chologische Typen. Psychologische Rundschau, 1958, 9:
        29-52; Rev Indias, 1942, 38:338-368.
8263.   Blumenthal, Gerda. The Conquest of Dread: A Study of
        André Malraux. DA, 1955, 15:2200-2201.
8264.   Blumenthal, Warner. Father and son in the East: a new
        look at Werfel's The Forty Days of Musa Dagh. In Nel-
        son, C. (ed), Studies in Language and Literature. Rich-
        mond: Eastern Kentucky Univ. Press, 1976, 75-79.
8265.   Blumstein, Andrée Kahn. Misogyny and Idealization in the
        Courtly Romance. Bonn: Bouvier, 1977.

8266. Boafo, Y. S. Arrow of Gold: a case study of megalomania.
       Asemka: A Lit J Univ. Cape Coast, 1974, 1(2):16-24.
8267. Boak, Denis. The case of Henri Troyat. Int Fiction Rev,
       1974, 1:143-146.
8268. Boardman, Arthur. Howellsian sex. Studies in the Novel,
       1970, 2:52-60.
8269. Boardman, G. R. Greek hero and Japanese samurai: Mishi-
       ma's new aesthetic. Critique, 1970, 12:103-115.
8270. Bodenheim, Maxwell. Psychoanalysis and American fiction.
       Nation, 1922, 114:683-684.
8271. Bödeker, K. -B. Frau und Familie im erzählerischen Werk
       Franz Kafkas. Bern: Lang, 1974.
8272. Boe, John. Simenon, Apollo and Dionysus. A Jungian ap-
       proach to mysteries. In Wynn, D. (ed), Murder Ink.
       NY: Workman, 1978, 444-446.
8273. Boehm, Felix. Das Fraulein von Scuderi; psychoanalytische
       Studie über die Erzählung von E. T. A. Hoffmann. Zeit-
       schrift für Psychoanalyse, 1949, 1:29-39.
8274. Boerebach, B. M. Introduction à une étude psychologique et
       philosophique de l'oeuvre de François Mauriac. Neo-
       philologus, 1942, 27:241-275.
8275. Boesky, Dale. Correspondence with Miss Joyce Carol Oates.
       Int Rev Psycho-Anal, 1975, 2:481-486.
8276. Böhme, Hartmut. [Kafka's psychostructure.] In Flores, A.
       (ed), The Kafka Debate. New Perspectives for Our Time.
       NY: Gordian, 1977.
8277. _____. Mother Milena: on Kafka's narcissism. In
       Flores, A. (ed), The Kafka Debate: New Perspectives
       for Our Time. NY: Gordian, 1977, 80-99.
8278. _____. 'Mutter Milens': zum Narzissmus-Problem bei
       Kafka. Germanisch-Romanische Monatsschrift, 1978, 28:
       50-69.
8279. _____. Thomas Mann: Mario und der Zauberer: Posi-
       tion des Erzählers und Psychologie der Herrschaft.
       Orbis Litterarum, 1975, 30:286-316.
8280. Boisdeffre, Pierre de. Métamorphose de la littérature de
       Barrès à Malraux. Barrès--Gide--Mauriac--Bernanos--
       Montherlant--Malraux; essais psychologique littéraires,
       Vol. I. Paris: Alsatia, 1950.
8281. _____. Métamorphose de la littérature de Proust à Sartre.
       Proust--Valéry--Cocteau--Anouilh--Sartre--Camus. Es-
       sais de psychologie littéraire suivis de deux études sur la
       géneration du demi-siècle et la condition de la littéra-
       ture, Vol. II. Paris: Alsatia, 1951.
8282. Boll, Ernest. Charles Dickens in Oliver Twist. Psychoanal
       Rev, 1940, 27:133-143.
8283. _____. Social causation in the English novel of the Armis-
       tice interval. Psychiatry, 1946, 9:309-321.
8284. Bollas, Christopher. Melville's lost self: Bartleby. Amer
       Imago, 1974, 31:401-411; Psyche, 1978, 32:155-164; In
       Tennenhouse, L. (ed), The Practice of Psychoanalytic
       Criticism. Detroit: Wayne State Univ. Press, 1976,
       226-236.

8285. Bollas, Sara Flanders. The Narrow Bridge of Art: A Psy-
       choanalytic Study of Virginia Woolf's First Four Novels.
       DAI, 1976, 37:979A-80A.
8286. Bolling, Douglass. The distanced heart: artistry in E. M.
       Forster's Maurice. Modern Fiction Studies, 1974, 20:157-
       167.
8287. _____. The journey into self: Charles Williams' The
       Place of the Lion. Cresset, 1974, 37(6):14-18.
8288. _____. Structure and theme in Briefing for a Descent into
       Hell. Contemporary Lit, 1973, 14:550-564.
8289. Bolster, R. Stendhal, Balzac et le féminisme romantique.
       Paris: Minard, 1970.
8290. Bolton, H. Philip. The role of paranoia in Richard Wright's
       Native Son. Kansas Q, 1975, 7:111-124.
8291. Bomher, Noemi. Personajul feminin in romanul Fratii Jderi.
       Analele Stiintifice ale Universității Iasi, 1971, 17:73-76.
8292. Bonaparte, Marie. 'The Black Cat.' A psychoanalytic inter-
       pretation of Poe's tale. Partisan Rev, 1950, 17:834-860.
8293. _____. 'The Murders in the Rue Morgue.' Psychoanal Q,
       1935, 4:259-293.
8294. _____. Poe and the function of literature. In Phillips,
       W. (ed), Art and Psychoanalysis. Cleveland: World,
       1963, 54-88.
8295. _____. Psychoanalytic interpretations of stories by Edgar
       Allan Poe. In Ruitenbeek, H. M. (Ed), Psychoanalysis and
       Literature. NY: Dutton, 1964, 19-101.
8296. _____. 'Le Scarabee d'Or' d'Edgar Poe. Rev Française
       de Psychanalyse, 1932, 5:275-293; Revista de Psicoanáli-
       sis, 1948, 5:645-663.
8297. _____. 'Der Untergang des Hauses Usher' von Edgar Al-
       lan Poe. Psychoanalytische Bewegung, 1932, 4:421-438.
8298. Bond, David J. Recurring patterns of fantasy in the fiction
       of André Pieyre de Mandiargues. Symposium, 1975, 29:
       30-47.
8299. _____. The search for identity in the novels of Réjean
       Ducharme. Mosaic, 1976, 9(2):31-44.
8300. Bond, Martin L. Laurence Sterne's Sexual Ethic in Trisṭram
       Shandy. DAI, 1973, 33:6900A.
8301. Bondy, Francis. Italo Svevo and ripe old age. Hudson Rev,
       1967-68, 20:575-598.
8302. Bone, Robert A. The novels of James Baldwin. Tri-Quar-
       terly, 1965, 2:3-30; In Gross, S. L., & Hardy, J. E.
       (eds), Images of the Negro in American Literature. Chi-
       cago: Univ. Chicago Press, 1966, 265-288.
8303. Bone, Sandra F. Human Sexual Information, Behaviors, and
       Attitudes as Revealed in American Realistic Fiction for
       Young People, 1965-1974. DAI, 1978, 39:275A-76A.
8304. Bonheim, Helmut. Joyce's Benefictions. Berkeley: Univ.
       California Press, 1964.
8305. Bonnet, Henri. L'Ascension spirituelle de Marcel Proust,
       ses révélations psychologiques et esthétiques. Thèse,
       Paris, 1944.

8306. Bonney, William W.   Joseph Conrad and the betrayal of language.   Nineteenth Century Fiction, 1979, 34:127-153.

8307. Bonnichon, Anre.   William Styron et le second oedipe.   Etudes, 1962, 315:94-103.

8308. Bonnot, René.   Le Roman du temps.   A propos de Virginia Woolf et de James Joyce.   JPNP, 1956, 53:454-472.

8309. Bontly, Thomas J.   The Aesthetics of Discretion: Sexuality in the Fiction of Henry James.   DAI, 1967, 27:3446A-47A.

8310. Booth, Wayne C.   The Rhetoric of Fiction.   Chicago: Univ. Chicago Press, 1961.

8311. Boothby, Paula R.   Three Dimensions of the Parental Role in Selected Children's Literature 1950-1974.   DAI, 1976, 37:702A-03A.

8312. Bordaz, Robert.   Edouard Dujardin et le monologue intérieur.   Rev des Deux Mondes, 1970, 12:591-594.

8313. Bordier, Roger.   Sur le Roman contemporain: réalisme et psychologie.   Europe, 1965, 43(435-436):275-279.

8314. Bordner, Marsha.   Defoe's androgynous vision: in Moll Flanders and Roxana.   Gypsy Scholar, 1975, 2:76-93.

8315. Borel, Jacques.   Médecine et psychiatrie balzaciennes.   La Science dans le roman.   Paris: Corti, 1971.

8316. Borghigiani, Pier Antonio.   I personaggi femminili di De Maupassant.   Nuova Antologia, 1973, 517:528-540.

8317. Borie, J.   Les Fatalités du corps dans les Rougon-Macquart.   Temps Modernes, 1969, 273:1, 567-1, 591.

8318. Boring, Phyllis Z.   Adolescent friendship in two contemporary Spanish novels.   Hispanófila, 1977, 60:53-57.

8319. _____.   Maria Alice Baroso: a study in point of view.   Luso-Brazilian Rev, 1977, 14:29-39.

8320. _____.   Usmail: the Puerto Rican Joe Christmas.   College Language Assn J, 1973, 16:324-333.

8321. _____.   The world of childhood in the contemporary Spanish novel.   Kentucky Romance Q, 1976, 23:467-481.

8322. Borinsky, Alicia.   Castración y lujos: la escritura de Manuel Puig.   Revista Iberoamericana, 1975, 41:29-45.

8323. _____.   Castration artifices: notes on the writings of Manuel Puig.   Georgia Rev, 1975, 29:95-114.

8324. Born, Jürgen.   Kafka's parable, 'Before the Law.' Reflections towards a positive interpretation.   Mosaic, 1970, 3:153-162.

8325. Borst, H.   Parental attitudes in the modern novel.   Family, 1929, 10:113-115.

8326. Bort, Barry D.   The incest theme in Tom Jones.   Amer Notes & Queries, 1965, 3:83-84.

8327. Bosch, G.   El delirio y la tragedia de Alsone Quijano.   Anales del Instituto de psicologia Buenos Aires, 1938, 2:177-206.

8328. Bosch, Rafael.   La sombra y la psicopatología de Galdós.   Anales Galdosianos, 1971, 6:21-42.

8329. Böschenstein, B.   Ekstase, Mass und Askese in der deutschen Dichtung.   Bibliotheca Psychiatrica et Neurologica, 1968, 134, 189-207.

8330. Bossis, Mireille. Les Relations de parenté dans les romans de George Sand. Cahiers de l'Assn Int des Etudes Françaises, 1976, 28:297-314.

8331. Botheroyd, Paul F. Ich und Er: First and Third Person Self-Reference and Problems of Identity in Three Contemporary German-Language Novels. The Hague: Mouton, 1976.

8332. Botta, G. Thomas Wolfe o della solitudine. Naples, 1964.

8333. Boudreau, Gordon V. Of pale ushers and Gothic piles: Melville's archetectural symbology. Emerson Society Q, 1972, 67:67-82.

8334. Boulanger, J. B. A la Recherche de l'amour avec Marcel Proust. Amérique Française, No. 1, 17-25; No. 2, 25-32; No. 3, 22-31; No. 4, 24-32; No. 5, 33-41; No. 6, 41-49.

8335. Bourniquel, Camille. Balzac et l'obsession de l'infini. Esprit, 1967, 361:980-1003.

8336. Boussoulas, Nicholas I. La Peur et l'universe dans l'oeuvre d'Edgar Poe. Paris: Presses Universitaires de France, 1952.

8337. Bovet, Pierre. Victor Hugo über den Traum. Int Zeitschrift für Psychoanalyse, 1920, 6:354.

8338. Bowden, Edwin T. The Dungeon of the Heart: Human Isolation and the American Novel. NY: Macmillan, 1961.

8339. Bowen, Merlin. The Long Encounter: Self and Experience in the Writings of Herman Melville. Chicago: Univ. Chicago Press, 1960.

8340. Bowen, R. P. Balzac's interior descriptions as an element in characterization. PMLA, 1925, 40:289-301.

8341. Bowlin, Karla J. The Brother and Sister Theme in Post-Romantic Fiction. DAI, 1973, 34:1232A.

8342. Bowling, Lawrence Edward. Faulkner and the theme of isolation. Georgia Rev, 1964, 18:50-66.

8343. _____. What is the stream of consciousness technique? PMLA, 1950, 65:333-345.

8344. Bowman, Frank Paul. Melancholy in Stendhal. L'Esprit créateur, 1962, 11(1):5-13.

8345. Boxill, Anthony. 'The emasculated colonial.' Présence Africaine, 1970, No. 75, 146-149.

8346. Boyd, Wendy. Malcolm Lowry's Under the Volcano: La Despedida. Amer Imago, 1980, 37:49-64.

8347. Boyers, Robert. Attitudes toward sex in American 'high culture.' Annals Amer Academy Political Social Sciences, 1968, 376:36-52; In Pratt, J. C. (ed), Ken Kesey, One Flew Over the Cuckoo's Nest, Text and Criticism. NY: Penguin, 1977, 435-441.

8348. Boyette, Purvis Elton. Myra Breckinridge and imitative form. Modern Fiction Studies, 1971, 17:229-238.

8349. Boyle, Robert. Finnegans Wake, page 185: an explanation. James Joyce Q, 1966, 4:3-16.

8350. Boynton, Henry W. All over the lot. Bookman, 1919, 49: 729.

8351. Bozza, L.   La trilogia di Luisa Alcott.   L'educazione Nazionale, 1925, 7:15-20.
8352. Brachfeld, O.   Die Deutung eines Traumes in Rousseaus Nouvelle Heloise.   Int Zeitschrift für Individual-Psychologie, 1928, 5:374-377.
8353. Braddy, Haldeen.   Poe's flight from reality.   Texas Studies in Lit & Language, 1959, 1:394-400.
8354. Bradford, Carole A.   Alienation and the dual personality in the last three novels of Emilia Pardo Bazán.   Revista de Estudios Hispánicos, 1978, 12:399-417.
8355. Bradford, Melvin E.   Certain ladies of quality: Faulkner's view of women and the evidence of 'There Was a Queen.' Arlington Q, 1967-68, 1(2):106-139.
8356. Bradley, B. L.   Analysis of a fragment by Kafka: reflections on the theme of the barrier.   Germanic Rev, 1969, 44: 259-272.
8357. Brady, C. A.   Lunatics and selenophiles.   America, 1958, 26:448-449.
8358. Brady, Patrick.   Marcel Proust.   Boston: Twayne, 1977.
8359. Bragg, Marvin.   The psychological elements of Werther.   South Central Bulletin, 1976, 36:132-137.
8360. Brahimi, Denise.   Ecriture/Feminité/Féminisme: Refléxions sur trois romans de George Sand.   Rev des Sciences Humaines, 1977, 168:577-588.
8361. Bramer, George R.   The Quality of Love in Jane Austen's Novels.   DAI, 1966, 66-12, 141.
8362. Bramstång, M.   Flickan i badet och skalden i busken.   Svensk Litteraturtidskrift, 1972, 35(1):17-24.
8363. Brancaccio, Patrick.   Studied ambiguities: Arthur Mervyn and the problem of the unreliable narrator.   Amer Lit, 1970, 42:18-27.
8364. Brand, Alice Glarden.   Mary Wilkins Freeman: misanthropy as propaganda.   New England Q, 1977, 50:83-100.
8365. Brandabur, Edward.   A Scrupulous Meanness: A Study of Joyce's Early Work.   Urbana: Univ. Illinois Press, 1971.
8366. Brandão Lopes, R. S.   Os Condenados de Oswald de Andrade.   Minas Gerais, Suplemento Literário, 24 Sept 1977.
8367. Brandruff, W. T.   The role of order and disorder in The Long March.   English J, 1967, 56:54-59.
8368. Brandt, Thomas O.   Narcissism in Thomas Mann's Der Erwählte.   German Life & Letters, 1954, 7:233-241.
8369. Brannon, Lil.   Psychic distance in the Quentin section of The Sound and the Fury.   Publications of the Arkansas Philological Assn, 1976, 2(2):11-18.
8370. Brannon, Lilian B.   Iconology of the Child Figure in Graham Greene's Fiction.   DAI, 1978, 38:4155A.
8371. Brantley, Jill N.   'A Pattern of Experience': The Treatment of Deviance in the Post-World War II American Novel as a Test Case of the Use of Literature in the Study of Society.   DAI, 1978, 38:7407A.
8372. Brantlinger, Patricia.   Romances, novels, and psychoanalysis.   Criticism, 1975, 17:15-40.
8373. Braun, Sidney D.   Source and psychology of Sartre's Le Mur.   Criticism, 1965, 7:45-51.

8374. Brayfield, Peggy. Lawrence's 'male and female principles'
       and the symbolism of 'The Fox.' Mosaic, 1971, 4(3):41-
       51.
8375. _____. A New Feminist Approach to the Novels of Char-
       lotte Brontë. DAI, 1973, 34:1850A.
8376. Brayton, Bradford C., Jr. Richard Wright's Quest for Iden-
       tity. DAI, 1977, 38:1489A.
8377. Bredsdorff, Elias. Marx og Freud i Hans Kirks roman
       Fiskerne. In Höskuldsson, S. S. (ed), Ideas and Ideol-
       ogies. Reykjavik: Univ. Iceland Institute Literary Re-
       search, 1975, 241-261.
8378. Brée, Germaine. Jean Santeuil: an appraisal. L'Esprit
       créateur, 1965, 5:14-25.
8379. _____. The persona of the doctor in Céline's Journey to
       the End of the Night and Camus's The Plague. NY:
       Watson, 1980, 88-97.
8380. _____. Women Writers in France: Variations on a Theme.
       New Brunswick, NJ: Rutgers Univ. Press, 1973.
8381. _____, & Guiton, Margaret. An Age of Fiction: The
       French Novel from Gide to Camus. New Brunswick, NJ:
       Rutgers Univ. Press, 1958.
8382. Breiteig, B. Det erotiske i Sult. Edda, 1972, 72:329-335.
8383. Bremer, Sidney H. Invalids and actresses: Howells' duplex
       imagery for American women. Amer Lit, 1976, 47:599-
       614.
8384. _____. Woman in the Works of William Dean Howells.
       DAI, 1972, 32:4601A.
8385. Brenner, Gerry. Rabbit, Run: John Updike's criticism of
       the return to nature. Twentieth Century Lit, 1966, 12:3-
       14.
8386. Breuer, Horst. Wahnsinn im Werk Edgar Allan Poes: Lit-
       erarkritisch-psychoanalytischer Versuch. Deutsche Vier-
       teljahrsschrift für Literaturwissenschaft und Geistesgesch-
       ichtes, 1976, 50:14-43.
8387. Breugelmans, Rene. Alienation, the destiny of modern lit-
       erature? Oscar Wilde and Stefan George. Modern Lan-
       guage Rev, 1968, 2:18-28.
8388. Brewer, Derek. The interpretation of dream, folktale and
       romance with special reference to Sir Gawain and the
       Green Knight. Neuphilologische Mitteilungen, 1976, 77:
       569-581.
8389. Brian, Paul. Sexuality and the opposite sex: variations on
       a theme by Theophile Gautier and Anaïs Nin. Essays in
       Lit, 1977, 4:122-137.
8390. Brick, Allen R. George Henry Lewes' review of Wuthering
       Heights. Nineteenth Century Fiction, 1960, 14:355-359.
8391. Brienza, Susan D. Volume VII of Tristram Shandy: a dance
       of life. Univ. Dayton Rev, 1974, 10(3):59-62.
8392. Brierley, Marjorie. 'Hardy perennials' and psychoanalysis.
       Int J Psycho-Analysis, 1969, 50:447-452.
8393. Briggs, Julia. Not without but within: the psychological
       ghost story. In Night Visitors; The Rise and Fall of the
       English Ghost Story. London: Faber & Faber, 1977,
       142-164.

8394. _____. A scientific spirit: mesmerism, drugs and psychic doctors. In Night Visitors; The Rise and Fall of the English Ghost Story. London: Faber & Faber, 1977, 52-75.

8395. Brightfield, M. F. The medical profession in early Victorian England, as depicted in the novels of the period (1840-1870). Bulletin History Medicine, 1961, 35:238-256.

8396. Brill, Amy S. Remembering Mysteries: The Nineteenth-Century Detective Story as a Modern Art of Memory. DAI, 1978, 39(6-A), 3638.

8397. Brincourt, J. La Psychologie de Proust et ses contempteurs. Bulletin de la Société des Amis de Marcel Proust et des Amis de Combray, 1963, 42-55.

8398. Brink, A. W. Hermann Hesse and the Oedipal quest. Lit & Psychol, 1974, 24:66-79.

8399. Brinkley, Thomas Edwin. J. D. Salinger: A Study of His Eclecticism--Zooey as Existential Zen Therapist. DAI, 1977, 37:7127A.

8400. Brinkman, Wim. Lazarus en Oedipus. Maatstaf, 1964, 12: 428-447.

8401. Brinkmann, Horst. Zum Doppelgängermotiv bei E. A. Poe ('William Wilson') und F. D. Dostojevskij ('Dcojnik'). In Jelitte, H., & Kluge, R. D. (eds), Festschrift für Heinz Wissemann. Beiträge zur Slavistik, Vol. 2. Frankfurt: Lang, 1977.

8402. Brivic, Sheldon R. James Joyce. In Crews, F. C. (ed), Psychoanalysis and Literary Process. Cambridge, Mass: Winthrop, 1970, 118-162.

8403. _____. James Joyce from Stephen to Bloom: A Psychoanalytic Study. DAI, 1971, 31:3539A-40A.

8404. _____. Joyce in progress: a Freudian view. James Joyce Q, 1976, 13(3):306-327.

8405. _____. Time, sexuality, and identity in Joyce's Ulysses. James Joyce Q, 1969, 7:40-45.

8406. Brodhead, Richard H. The fate of Candor. In Hawthorne, Melville, and the Novel. Chicago: Univ. Chicago Press, 1976, 163-193.

8407. Brodsley, Laurel. Anaïs Nin and The Novel of the Future. Delta, 1971, 48:35-39.

8408. Brodtkorb, Paul, Jr. Ishmael's White World: A Phenomenological Reading of Moby Dick. New Haven: Yale Univ. Press, 1965.

8409. Brody, Robert. Stream-of-consciousness techniques in Cortazar's Rayuela. Symposium, 1975, 29:48-56.

8410. Brombert, Victor. An epic of immobility. Hudson Rev, 1966, 19:24-43.

8411. _____. Flaubert's Saint-Julien: the sin of existing. PMLA, 1966, 81:297-302.

8412. _____. The Novels of Flaubert: A Study of Themes and Techniques. Princeton: Princeton Univ. Press, 1966; London: Oxford Univ. Press, 1967.

8413. _____. Sartre and the existentialist novel: the intellectual as 'impossible' hero. In The Intellectual Hero. Studies

in the French Novel 1880-1955. Philadelphia: Lippincott, 1961, 181-203.
8414. Bromfield, J. G. De Lorenzino de Médicis à Lorenzaccio, étude d'un thème historique. Paris: Didier, 1972.
8415. Bronda, F. La patologia dei minatori nel Germinal di Emilio Zola. Minerva Medicine, 1966, 57:3249-3252.
8416. Brøndsted, Mogens. Vaulundur, Aladdin og Jung. Kritik, 1967, 4.
8417. Bronsen, D. Böll's women: patterns in male-female relationships. Monatshefte, 1965, 57(6).
8418. Brooks, Cleanth, & Warren, Robert Penn. Understanding Fiction. NY: Crofts, 1943.
8419. Brooks, Douglas. Moll Flanders: an interpretation. Essays in Criticism, 1969, 19:46-49.
8420. _____. Symbolic numbers, in Fielding's Joseph Andrews. In Fowler, A. (ed), Silent Poetry; Essays in Numerological Analysis. NY: Barnes & Noble, 1970, 234-260.
8421. Brooks, Ellen W. The image of woman in Lessing's The Golden Notebook. Critique: Studies in Modern Fiction, 1973, 15(1):101-109.
8422. Brooks, J. L. The character of Doña Guillermina Pacheco in Galdós novel Fortunata y Jacinta. Bulletin Hispanic Studies, 1961, 38:86-94.
8423. Brooks, Peter. Virtue-tripping: notes on Le Lys dans la vallée. Yale French Studies, 1974, 50:150-162.
8424. Brooks, Randy M. Blindfolded women carrying a torch: the nature of Conrad's female characters. Ball State Univ. Forum, 1976, 17(4):28-32.
8425. Brooks, Richard A. Rousseau's antifeminism in the Lettre a d'Alembert and Emile. In Wilyiams, C. G. S. (ed), Literature and History in the Age of Ideas; Essays on the French Enlightenment. Columbus: Ohio State Univ., 1975, 209-227.
8426. Brophy, Brigid. Detective fiction: a modern myth of violence? Hudson Rev, 1965, 18:11-30.
8427. Bross, Addison W. Joseph Conrad's Female Characters in Selected Fiction. DA, 1968, 28:2675A-76A.
8428. Broughton, Panthea Reid. Masculinity and menfolk in The Hamlet. Mississippi Q, 1969, 22:181-189.
8429. _____. Rejection of the feminine in Carson McCullers's The Ballad of the Sad Cafe. Twentieth-Century Lit, 1974, 20:34-43.
8430. Brown, Arthur W. Dickens' Props: An Analysis of Their Sexual Significance with a Chapter of Death. DA, 1967, 28:2236A-37A.
8431. _____. Sexual Analysis of Dickens' Props. NY: Emerson, 1971.
8432. Brown, Bernadine. 'The Turn of the Screw': a case of romantic displacement. Nassau Rev, 1974, 2:75-82.
8433. Brown, Daniel Russell. Swiftian scatology. Book & Bookman, 1971, 17(1):18-23.
8434. _____. The natural man in John Steinbeck's non-teleological tales. Ball State Univ. Forum, 1966, 7:47-52.

8435. Brown, Dennis. Literature and existential psychoanalysis: 'My Kinsman, Major Molineux' and 'Young Goodman Brown.' Canadian Rev Amer Studies, 1973, 4:65-73.
8436. Brown, H. Doctor François Rabelais: Pantagruel and health. Annals of Science, 1971, 27:117-134.
8437. Brown, Homer Obed. The displaced self in the novels of Daniel Defoe. Studies in Eighteenth-Century Culture, 1975, 4:69-94.
8438. Brown, Lloyd Wellesley. The business of marrying and mothering. In McMaster, J. (ed), Jane Austen's Achievement. NY: Barnes & Noble, 1976, 27-43.
8439. _____. The shape of things: sexual images and the sense of form in Doris Lessings' fiction. World Lit Written in English, 1975, 14:176-186.
8440. Brown, Martha Hursey. Images of Black Women: Family Roles in Harlem Renaissance Literature. DAI, 1976, 37: 2836A-37A.
8441. Brown, May Cameron. The language of chaos: Quentin Compson in The Sound and the Fury. Amer Lit, 1980, 51:544-553.
8442. Brown, P. L. 'The Secret Sharer' and the existential hero. Conradiana, 1971-72, 3(3):22-30.
8443. Brown, Patricia S. Creative Losers: Blacks, Children, and Women in the Novels of Joyce Cary. DAI, 1974, 34: 6627A.
8444. Brown, William Richards. Faulkner's paradox in pathology and salvation: Sanctuary, Light in August, Requiem for a Nun. Texas Studies in Lit & Language, 1967, 9:429-449.
8445. _____. William Faulkner's Use of the Material of Abnormal Psychology in Characterization. DA, 1965, 26:1036-37.
8446. Browning, Barton W. Chessmen and the Multiple Personality in the Works of Hermann Hesse. Doctoral dissertation, Wesleyan Univ., 1962.
8447. Browning, Robert M. Association and dissociation in Storm's novellen: a study of the meaning of the frame. PMLA, 1951, 66:381-405.
8448. Brownstein, Rachel Mayer. Review: Gerald Levin's Richardson the Novelist: The Psychological Patterns. Lit & Psychol, 1979, 29:60-63.
8449. Brumbaugh, Thomas B. Concerning Nathaniel Hawthorne and art as magic. Amer Imago, 1954, 11:399-405.
8450. Brumm, Ursula. Geschichte als Geschehen und Erfahrung: Eine analyse von William Faulkners Absalom, Absalom! Archiv, 1967, 204:26-50.
8451. Brunclík, J. F. M. Dostojevskij--zivot, dílo a tvorba. Nekolik strucných poznámek z hlediska psychiatrického. Casopis Lekaru Ceskych, 1974, 113:987-990.
8452. Bruneau, Jean. Existentialism and the American novel. Yale French Studies, 1948, 1:66-72.
8453. Bruner, Jerome Seymour. Identity and the modern novel. In On Knowing; Essays for the Left Hand. Cambridge: Harvard Univ. Press, 1979.

8454. Brunet, P. Le Thème du vin dans la Nouvelle Héloise. An-
       nales de la Société J. -J. Rousseau, 1975, 273-276.
8455. Brunner, John. Science fiction and the larger lunacy. In
       Nicholls, P. (ed), Science Fiction at Large. NY: Harp-
       er, 1976, 73-103.
8456. Bruss, Elizabeth W. The game of literature and some liter-
       ary games. New Lit History, 1977, 9:153-172.
8457. Bruss, Neal Howard. The Psychoanalytic Function in the
       Language of Literature: Freudian Theory, Modern Lin-
       guistics and the Tales of Edgar Allan Poe. DAI, 1975,
       35:7284A.
8458. Brunswick, Ruth M. A dream from an eleventh century
       Japanese novel. Int J Psycho-Anal, 1927, 8:402-403;
       Imago, 1928, 14:147-148.
8459. Bruyas, J. P. La Psychologie de l'adolescence dans l'oeuvre
       romanesque de Stendhal. Aix-en-Provence: Pensée Uni-
       versitaire, 1967.
8460. Bryan, J. E. Hemingway as vivisector. Univ. Rev, 1963,
       30:3-12.
8461. Bryan, James E. The psychological structure of The Catcher
       in the Rye. PMLA, 1974, 89:1065-1074; Reply by Vail,
       D., 1976, 91:120-121.
8462. _____. A reading of Salinger's 'Teddy. ' Amer Lit, 1968,
       40:352-369.
8463. Bryer, Jackson R. A psychiatrist reviews Tender Is the
       Night. Lit & Psychol, 1966, 16:198-199.
8464. Brylowski, Walter. Faulkner's Olympian Laugh. Myth in the
       Novels. Detroit: Wayne State Univ. Press, 1968.
8465. Buber, Martin. Existential guilt. [Excerpt from The Knowl-
       edge of Man.] In Smith, R. W. (ed), Guilt: Man and So-
       ciety. Garden City, NY: Doubleday Anchor, 1971, 85-
       116.
8466. Buchen, Irving H. Carson McCullers, a case of convergence.
       Bucknell Rev, 1973, 1973, 21(1):15-28.
8467. _____. Divine collusion: the art of Carson McCullers.
       Dalhousie Rev, 1974, 54:529-541.
8468. _____. Emily Brontë and the metaphysics of childhood and
       love. Nineteenth Century Fiction, 1966, 22:63-70.
8469. _____. Isaac Bashevis Singer and the eternal past. Cri-
       tique: Studies in Modern Fiction, 1966, 8:5-17.
8470. Buck, Stratton. The uses of madness. Tennessee Studies in
       Lit, 1958, 3:63-71.
8471. Buckeye, Robert. The anatomy of the psychic novel. Cri-
       tique: Studies in Modern Fiction, 1967, 9(2):35-45.
8472. Buckler, William Earl. Memory, morality, and the tragic vi-
       sion in the early novels of George Eliot. In Goodin, G.
       V. (ed), The English Novel in the Nineteenth Century; Es-
       says on the Literary Mediation of Human Values. Urbana:
       Univ. Illinois Press, 1972, 145-163.
8473. Bucknall, Barbara J. From material to spiritual food in A la
       recherche du temps perdu. L'Esprit créateur, 1971, 11:
       52-60.

8474. Budick, E. Miller. The fall of the house: a reappraisal of Poe's attitudes toward life and death. Southern Lit J, 1977, 9(2):30-50.

8475. Buell, Lawrence. The observer-hero narrative. Texas Studies in Lit & Language, 1979, 21:93-111.

8476. Bufithis, Philip Henry. The Artist's Fight for Art: The Psychiatrist Figure in the Fiction of Major Contemporary American Novelists. DAI, 1971, 32:2083A.

8477. _____. J. D. Salinger and the psychiatrist. West Virginia Univ. Bulletin: Philological Papers, 1974, 21:67-77.

8478. Buhrich, Neil, & McConaghy, Neil. Transvestite fiction. JNMD, 1976, 163:420-427.

8479. Buitenhuis, Elspeth M. Fractions of a Man: Doubles in Victorian Fiction. DAI, 1971, 32:381A.

8480. Bulhof, Francis. Agendath again. James Joyce Q, 1970, 2: 326-332.

8481. Bullock, Penelope. The mulatto in American fiction. Phylon, 1945, 6:78-82.

8482. Bullough, Vern L. 'Deviant sex' and the detective story. Mystery & Detection Annual, 1973, 2:326-330.

8483. _____. The History of Prostitution. New Hyde Park, NY: University Books, 1964, 237-250.

8484. Burchell, Samuel C. Dostoiefsky and the sense of guilt. Psychoanal Rev, 1930, 17:195-207.

8485. Burckhardt, Rainer. Die 'hartgesottene' amerikanische Detektivgeschichte und ihre gesellschaftliche Funktion. Frankfurt: Lang, 1978.

8486. Burgan, Mary Alice. Childbirth trauma in Katherine Mansfield's early stories. Modern Fiction Studies, 1978, 24: 395-412.

8487. _____. Feeling and control: a study of the proposal scenes in Jane Austen's major novels. In Goodin, G. V. (ed), The English Novel in the Nineteenth Century; Essays on the Literary Mediation of Human Values. Urbana: Univ. Illinois Press, 1972, 25-51.

8488. _____. Mr. Bennet and the failures of fatherhood in Jane Austen's novels. J English Germanic Philology, 1975, 74:536-552.

8489. Burgelin, C. Eléments psychanalytiques dans l'Enfant. In Colloque Jules Vallès. Lyon: Lyons Univ. Press, 1975, 5-24.

8490. Burgum, Edwin Berry. Ernest Hemingway and the psychology of the lost generation. In The Novel and the World's Dilemma. NY: Oxford Univ. Press, 1947, 184-204.

8491. _____. Freud and fantasy in contemporary fiction. Science & Society, 1965, 29:224-231.

8492. _____. Review: Daniel A. Weiss' Oedipus in Nottingham: D. H. Lawrence. Amer Imago, 1966, 23:180-183.

8493. _____. Review: F. C. Crews' The Sins of the Fathers: Hawthorne's Psychological Themes. Amer Imago, 1966, 23:367-374.

8494. Burke, Kenneth. Caldwell: maker of grotesques. [Excerpt from his The Philosophy of Literary Form.] In Malin,

J. (ed), Psychoanalysis and American Fiction. NY:
Dutton, 1965, 245-254.

8495. _____. Version, con-, per-, and in-. (Thoughts on
Djuna Barnes's novel, Nightwood.) In Language as Symbolic Action. Berkeley: Univ. California Press, 1966,
240-253; Southern Rev, 1966, 2:329-346.

8496. Burkhart, Charles. Charlotte Brontë. A Psychosexual Study
of Her Novels. London: Gollancz, 1973.

8497. _____. The nuns of Villette. Victorian Newsletter, 1973,
44:8-13.

8498. Burleson, Richard A. Color imagery in Great Gatsby. Fitzgerald Newsletter, 1967, 39:13-14.

8499. Burnam, T. Primitivism and masculinity in the work of
Ernest Hemingway. Modern Fiction Studies, 1955, 13:
20-24.

8500. Burness, Donald B. Womanhood in the short stories of Ama
Ata Aidoo. Studies in Black Lit, 1973, 4(2):21-24.

8501. Burns, A. The anguish of A. M. Matute. In 'Los mercad-
eres,' Hispanic Studies in Honour of Joseph Manson.
Oxford: Dolphin, 1972, 21-42.

8502. Burns, Mattie Ann. The Development of Women Characters
in the Works of William Faulkner. DAI, 1975, 35:4502A-
03A.

8503. Burns, Shannon, & Levernier, James A. Androgyny in
Stephen Crane's 'The Bride Comes to Yellow Sky.' Research Studies, 1977, 45:236-243.

8504. Burns, Stuart Le Roy. The evolution of 'Wise Blood.' Modern Fiction Studies, 1970, 16:147-162.

8505. _____. The Novels of Adolescence in America. DA,
1964, 25:2507.

8506. _____. The rapist in Frank Norris's The Octopus. Amer
Lit, 1971, 42:567-569.

8507. Burns, Wayne. Charles Reade: A Study in Victorian Authorship. NY: Bookman, 1961.

8508. _____. The critical relevance of Freudianism. Western
Rev, 1956, 301-304; Originally, Freudianism, Criticism
and Jane Eyre. Lit & Psychol, 1952, 5:4-13.

8509. _____. In death they were not divided: the moral magnificence of unmoral passion in Wuthering Heights. Hartford Studies in Lit, 1973, 5:135-159.

8510. _____. Kafka and Alex Comfort: The Penal Colony revisited. Arizona Q, 1952, 8:101-120.

8511. Burr, Bell. The physician as a character in fiction. Amer
J Insanity, 1906-07, 63:1-2.

8512. Burroughs, Franklin G., Jr. God the father and motherless
children: Light in August. Twentieth Century Lit, 1973,
19:189-202.

8513. Burstein, Janet Handler. Two locked caskets: selfhood and
otherness in the work of Isak Dinesen. Texas Studies in
Lit & Language, 1978, 20:615-632.

8514. Burton, Arthur. Existential conceptions in John Hersey's
novel: The Child Buyer. J Existential Psychol, 1961,
2:243-258.

8515. _____. Schizophrenia and existence. Psychiatry, 1960, 23:385-394.
8516. Burton, Mary E. The counter-transference of Dr. Diver. J English Lit History, 1971, 38:459-471.
8517. Burunat, Silvia. El monólogo interior como forma narrativa en la novela española (1940-1975). DAI, 1978, 39:1614A-15A.
8518. Burwell, Rose Marie. Joyce Carol Oates' first novel. Canadian Lit, 1977, 73:54-67.
8519. _____. The process of individuation as narrative structure: Joyce Carol Oates' 'Do with Me What You Will.' Critique, 1975, 17:93-106.
8520. Busch, Carolyn Lipshy. Women in the Novels of Unamuno. DA, 1966, 26:6709-10.
8521. Bush, Douglas. Sex in the modern novel. In Engaged and Disengaged. Cambridge: Harvard Univ. Press, 1966, 42-49.
8522. Bush, Lewis M. The Genesis of the American Psychological Novel. DAI, 1970, 31(1-A), 352.
8523. Buswell, Mary C. The love relationships of women in the fiction of Eudora Welty. West Virginia Univ. Philological Papers, 1961, 13:94-106.
8524. Butler, David W. Usher's hypochondriasis: mental alienation and romantic idealism in Poe's Gothic tales. Amer Lit, 1976, 48:1-12.
8525. Butler, Gerald J. The quality of emotional greatness. Paunch, 1966, No. 25, 5-17.
8526. _____. Sexual experience in D. H. Lawrence's The Rainbow. Recovering Literature, 1973, 2:1-92.
8527. Butler, Rebecca R. The Mad Preacher in Three Modern American Novels: Miss Lonelyhearts, Wise Blood, Light in August. DAI, 1978, 38:4164A-65A.
8528. Butler, Richard E. Jungian and oriental symbolism in Joseph Conrad's Victory. Conradiana, 1971-72, 3(2):36-54.
8529. Butor, Michael. Crossing the Joycean threshold. James Joyce Q, 1970, 7:160-176.
8530. _____. Thoughts on the novel: the individual and the group. Encounter, 1963, 20:17-24.
8531. Butureanu, Silvia. Psihologie si moralǎ la colette. Analele Stiintifice ale Universitatii Iasi, 1970, 16:83-97.
8532. Buvik, Per. Nana et les hommes. Cahiers Naturalistes, 1975, 49:105-124.
8533. Buxbaum, Edith. The role of detective stories in a child analysis. Psychoanal Q, 1941, 10:373-381; Zeitschrift für psychoanalytische Pädagogik, 1936, 10:113-121.
8534. Buytendijk, F. F. J. De Psychologie van de Roman, Studies over Dostojevsky. Utrecht: Spectrum, 1950, 1961.
8535. _____. Psychologie des Romans. Salzburg: Müller, 1966.
8536. Bychowski, Gustav. The archaic object and alienation. Int J Psycho-Anal, 1967, 48:384-393.
8537. _____. Marcel Proust as poet of psychoanalysis. Amer Imago, 1973, 30:26-32; Droga, 1930; Psychoanalytische Bewegung, 1932, 4:323-344.

8538.   Byrd, Max.   Detectives detected: from Sophocles to Ross
        Macdonald. Yale Rev, 1974, 64:72-83.
8539.   _____. The madhouse, the whorehouse, and the convent.
        Partisan Rev, 1977, 44(2):268-278.
8540.   _____. Visits to Bedlam. Madness and Literature in the
        Eighteenth Century. Columbia: Univ. South Carolina
        Press, 1974.

8541.   Cabaliero-Goas, M. Werther, Mischkin y Joaquin Monegro:
        Trilogia patográfica Hecha por un Psiquiatra. Barcelona:
        Apolo, 1951.
8542.   Cahill, Daniel J. Jerzy Kosinski: retreat from violence.
        Twentieth-Century Lit, 1972, 18:121-132.
8543.   Cajal, Santiago Roman y. Psicologia de Don Quijota y el
        Quijotismo. In Obras literarias completas. Madrid:
        Aguilar, 1947.
8544.   Calaf de Aguera, H. Desintegración de la personalidad en
        Tres novelitas burgueses. Cuadernos Hispano-Ameri-
        canos, 1977, 320-1:478-487.
8545.   Calder, Angus. Man, woman and male woman: Tolstoy's
        Anna and after. In Russia Discovered; Nineteenth-Century
        Fiction from Pushkin to Chekhov. NY: Barnes & Noble,
        1976, 211-236.
8546.   Calder, Jenni. Women and Marriage in Victorian Fiction.
        NY: Oxford Univ. Press, 1976; Review: H. Rosengar-
        ten, Modern Language Q, 1977, 38:381-389.
8547.   Caless, Bryn. The psychological significance of critical
        passivity in protagonist characters. J Eighteen Nineties
        Society, 1978, 9:5-9.
8548.   Calin, Vera. [The ignoring of psychology.] In Omisiunea
        Elocventa. Bucharest: Editura enciclopedica română,
        1973, 213-246.
8549.   Callan, Richard J. Animals as Mana figures in José Don-
        oso's 'Paseo' and 'Santelices.' Essays in Lit, 1975, 2:
        115-122.
8550.   _____. The archetype of psychic renewal in La Vorágine.
        Hispania, 1971, 54:470-476.
8551.   _____. La estructura arquetípica de 'La Iluvia' de Uslar
        Pietri. Cuadernos Americanos, 1974, 32(2):204-212.
8552.   _____. The function of myth and analytical psychology in
        Zona sagrada. Kentucky Romance Q, 1974, 21:261-274.
8553.   _____. The Jungian basis of Carlos Fuentes' Aura.
        Kentucky Romance Q, 1971, 18:65-75.
8554.   _____. Some parallels between O. Paz and Jung. His-
        pania, 1977, 60:916-926.
8555.   Calo, J. La Création de la femme chez Michelet. Paris:
        Nizet, 1975; DAI, 1972, 32:4556A.
8556.   Camilucci, Marcello. Psicologia, fantasia, realismo dinanzi
        al romanzo cattolico. Ulisse, 1956-57, 4:1041-1049.
8557.   Cammarata, Joan. Luis de Vargas: an oedipal figure in
        Pepita Jimenez. In Davis, L. E., & Tarán, I. (eds),
        The Analysis of Hispanic Texts. Jamaica: Bilingual
        Press, 1976, 206-225.

8558. Campbell, Findley C. Prophets of the storm: Richard Wright and the radical tradition. Phylon, 1977, 38:9-23.
8559. Campbell, Harry M. Freudianism, American romanticism, and 'Young Goodman Brown.' CEA Critic, 1971, 33(3): 3-6.
8560. Campbell, R. Du fantastique. Annales Médico-Psychologiques, 1956, 1:788-804.
8561. Campe, Joachim. Utopie und Schizophrenie: Über Jean Pauls Hesperus. In Ueding, G. (ed), Literatur ist Utopie. Frankfort: Suhrkamp, 1978, 159-188.
8562. Campo, Vera. On the personality and interpersonal relations of the Rorschach tester. British J Projective Psychol & Personality Study, 1976, 21(1):1-4.
8563. Canaday, Nicholas, Jr. Hawthorne's The Scarlet Letter. Explicator, 1970, 28.
8564. Canario, John W. The dream in 'The Tell-Tale Heart.' English Language Notes, 1970, 7:194-197.
8565. Canary, Robert H. Cabell's dark comedies. Mississippi Q, 1968, 21:83-92.
8566. Canby, Henry Seidel. Going deeper. In Definitions: Essays in Contemporary Criticism. Series 2. NY: Harcourt, 1924, 31-33.
8567. Cancalon, E. D. Fairy-Tale Structures and Motifs in 'Le Grand Meaulnes.' Bern: Lange, 1975.
8568. _____. Techniques et personnages dans les récits d'Andre Gide. Paris: Minard, 1970.
8569. Cancani, Montani L. Parallelismo letterario-patologico di Maupassant. Clinico Nuova, 1950, 10:606-608.
8570. Cannon, Emilie T. Childhood as Theme and Symbol in the Major Fiction of Ana Maria Matute. DAI, 1973, 33: 4401A.
8571. Canzoneri, Robert, & Stegner, Page (eds). Fiction and Analysis: Seven Major Themes. Glenview, Ill: Scott, Foresman, 1970.
8572. Capitanchik, Maurice. D. H. Lawrence: the sexual impasse. Books & Bookman, 1972, 18(2):28-31.
8573. Caprio, Frank S. Female Homosexuality: A Psychodynamic Study of Lesbianism. NY: Citadel, 1954; NY: Grove, 1962, Ch. 16.
8574. Carballo, Juan Rof. El erotismo en Unamuno. Revista de Occidente, 1964, 7:71-96.
8575. _____. La nebulosa de la novela. Papeles de Son Armadans, 1968, 49:229-262.
8576. Carbonnell Basset, Delfín. Don Quijote desde un punto de vista existencio-fenomenológico. Duquesne Hispanic Rev, 1963, 2:21-32.
8577. Cardona, Rodolfo (ed). Introduction to Benito Pérez Galdós La Sombra. NY: Norton, 1966, xv-xxx.
8578. Carey, Glenn O. William Faulkner on the automobile as socio-sexual symbol. CEA Critic, 1974, 36(2):15-17.
8579. Cargill, Oscar. Henry James as Freudian pioneer. Chicago Rev, 1956, 10:13-29; In Willen, G. (ed), A Casebook on Henry James's The Turn of the Screw. NY: Crowell, 1960, 223-238.

8580. _____. The Novels of Henry James. NY: Macmillan,
       1961.
8581. _____. 'The Turn of the Screw' and Alice James. PMLA,
       1963, 78:238-249; In Toward a Pluralistic Criticism.
       Carbondale: Southern Illinois Univ. Press, 1965, 95-117.
8582. Carlson, Eric. 'William Wilson': the double as primal self.
       Topic, 1976, 16:35-40.
8583. Carlson, Judith Garrett. The Dual Vision: Paradoxes, Op-
       posites, and Doubles in the Novels of Carson McCullers.
       DAI, 1977, 37:7749A.
8584. Carlton, Ann R. Patterns in Carson McCullers' Portrayal of
       Adolescence. DAI, 1972, 33:302A.
8585. Carmichael, Thomas X. Self and Society: Marriage in the
       Novels of Charles Dickens. DAI, 1977, 38(6-A), 3511-12.
8586. Carnell, Corbin Scott. The meaning of masculine and femi-
       nine in the work of C. S. Lewis. Modern British Lit,
       1977, 2:153-159.
8587. Carothers, Robert L. Herman Melville and the Search for
       the Father: An Interpretation of the Novels. DAI, 1970,
       30:4445A.
8588. _____. Melville's 'Cenci': a portrait of Pierre. Ball
       State Univ. Forum, 1969, 10(1):53-59.
8589. Carp, E. A. Rodion Raskolnikow: A Psychopathological Study.
       Amsterdam: Strengholt, 1951.
8590. Carpenter, Frederick I. The adolescent in American fiction.
       English J, 1957, 46:313-319.
8591. Carpenter, Richard C. Hawthorne's polar explorations:
       'Young Goodman Brown' and 'My Kinsman, Major Moli-
       neux. ' Nineteenth Century Fiction, 1969, 24:45-56.
8592. Carpenter, Thomas P. Abnormal psychology in twentieth-
       century novels. Lit & Psychol, 1966, 16:43-47.
8593. _____. The Material of Abnormal Psychology in Some
       Contemporary English and American Novels. DA, 1947,
       27-30.
8594. Carpi Sertori, Daniela. Per un interpretazione psicoanalitica
       di A Severed Head di Iris Murdoch. Lettore di Provin-
       cia, 1978, 33:60-70.
8595. Carrabino, Victor. Alain Robbe-Grillet and the Phenomeno-
       logical Novel. DAI, 1972, 32:5222A-23A.
8596. _____. The Phenomenological Novel of Alain Robbe-Gril-
       let. Parma: CEM, 1974.
8597. Carrere, Jean. Degeneration in the Great French Masters.
       NY: Brentano, 1922.
8598. Carrillo, Bert B. The Alienated Hero in Four Contemporary
       Spanish American Novels. DAI, 1970, 31:1264A.
8599. Carringer, Robert L. Circumscription of space and the form
       of Poe's Arthur Gordon Pym. PMLA, 1974, 89:506-516.
8600. Carroll, David. For example: psychoanalysis and fiction or
       the conflict of generation(s). Sub-stance, 1978, 21:49-67.
8601. Carroll, R. Illusion and identity: G. de Nerval and Rétif's
       Sara. Studies in Romanticism, 1976, 15:59-80.
8602. Carroll, William. Nabokov's signs and symbols. In Proffer,
       C. R. (ed), A Book of Things about Vladimir Nabokov.
       Ann Arbor, Mich: Ardis, 1974, 203-217.

8603. Carson, Barbara Harrell. Winning: Katherine Anne Porter's women. In Diamond, A., & Edwards, L. R. (eds), The Authority of Experience. Essays in Feminist Criticism. Amherst: Univ. Massachusetts Press, 1977, 239-256.

8604. Carson, Joan. Visionary experience in Wuthering Heights. Psychoanal Rev, 1975, 62:131-151.

8605. Carson, Ronald A. Comment on 'Coping with grief as bearing up and bearing down.' Suicide & Life-Threatening Behavior, 1978, 8:64-65.

8606. Carter, Duncan Albert. The Drama of Self: Role-Playing as Theme in the Novels of George Eliot. DAI, 1975, 35: 4420A.

8607. Carter, E. D., Jr. El doble en Rayuela: Retrato de un conflicto síquico. In Yates, D. A. (ed), Otros mundros otros fuegos: Fantasía y realismo mágico en Iberoamerica. East Lansing: Michigan State Univ. Press, 1975, 323-327.

8608. Carter, Nancy G. The theme of sleep in Le Roman comique. Romance Notes, 1969, 11:362-367.

8609. Carter, Thomas N. Group psychological phenomena of a political system as satirized in Animal Farm: an application of the theories of W. R. Bion. Human Relations, 1974, 27:525-546.

8610. Carter, William C. A synopsis of Proust's remarks concerning homosexuality. Proust Research Assn Newsletter, 1973, 10:22-25.

8611. Cartwright, Faith Wotton. Jonathan Swift and the psychoanalysts. Revista de la Universidad de Costa Rica, 1974, 39:47-58.

8612. Cartwright, Robert McLain. Guilt in Selected Novels of R. J. Sender. DAI, 1976, 37:2217A.

8613. Cary, Meredith. Faustus now. Hartford Studies in Lit, 1972, 4:167-173.

8614. Casares, Julio. Crítica efímera. Madrid: 1919, Vol. 2, 26-36.

8615. Caserio, Robert L. The family plot: Conrad, Joyce, Lawrence, Woolf, and Faulkner. In Plot, Story, and the Novel; From Dickens and Poe to the Modern Period. Princeton: Princeton Univ. Press, 1979, 232-279.

8616. Cash, Arthur H. The Lockean psychology of Tristram Shandy. English Lit History, 1955, 22:125-135.

8617. Cash, Joe L. The Treatment of Women Characters in the Complete Works of Joseph Conrad. DAI, 1972, 33:2925A-26A.

8618. Cashdollar, Paula M. 'My Female Friends': An Examination of Women and Women's Roles in the Writings of Jonathan Swift. DAI, 1978, 39:2950A.

8619. Casimir, Louis John, Jr. Human Emotion and the Early Novels of John Steinbeck. DA, 1966, 27:472A.

8620. Caspal, P. P. J. van. Father and son in the Lotus-eaters episode of Joyce's Ulysses. English Studies, 1979, 60: 593-602.

8621. Cassis, A. F. The dream as literary device in Graham Greene's novels. Lit & Psychol, 1974, 24:99-108.

8622. Castelli, E. (ed). L'Umanesimo e la Follia. Rome: Abete, 1971.
8623. Castello Branco, C. H. Monteiro Lobato e A Parapsicologia. São Paulo: Quatro Artes, 1973.
8624. Castelnuovo-Tedesco, Pietro. Stealing, revenge and the Monte Cristo complex. Int J Psycho-Anal, 1975, 56:231-232.
8625. Castets, Bruno. [On sadism and masochism. Apropos of the contemporary novel, The Story of O by Pauline Reage.] Evolution psychiatrique, 1969, 34:47-63.
8626. Castille, Philip. Women and myth in Faulkner's first novel. Tulane Studies in English, 1978, 23:175-186.
8627. Castle, Terry J. Amy, who knew my disease: a psychosexual pattern in Defoe's Roxana. J English Lit History, 1979, 46:81-96.
8628. Castro Klaren, S. Fragmentation and alienation in La Casa verde. Modern Language Notes, 1972, 87:286-299.
8629. Casty, Alan. 'I and It' in the stories of F. Scott Fitzgerald. Studies in Short Fiction, 1972, 9:47-58.
8630. Cata, Juanita O. The Portrait of American Indians in Children's Fictional Literature. DAI, 1977, 38(6-A), 3266-67.
8631. Cate, Hollis L. On Death and Dying in Tolstoy's 'The Death of Ivan Ilych.' Hartford Studies in Lit, 1975, 7:195-205.
8632. Catrysse, D. Diderot et la mystification. Paris: Nizet, 1971.
8633. Cattaneo, Giulio. Italo Svevo e la psicoanalisi. Belfagor, 1959, 14:454-460.
8634. Caviglia, John. A simple question of symmetry: psyche as structure in Tiempo de silencio. Hispania, 1977, 60:452-460.
8635. Cavitch, David. D. H. Lawrence and the New World. NY: Oxford Univ. Press, 1969; Review: Eugene Goodheart, Modern Fiction Studies, 1970, 16:230-234.
8636. _____. Solipsism and death in D. H. Lawrence's late works. Massachusetts Rev, 1966, 7:495-508.
8637. Cawelti, John G. The gunfighter and the hard-boiled dick: some ruminations on American fantasies of heroism. Amer Studies, 1975, 16:49-64.
8638. Ceceil, L. M. Virtuous attachment in James' The Ambassadors. Amer Q, 1967, 19:719-724.
8639. Celly, R. Répertoire des thèmes de Marcel Proust. Paris: Gallimard, 1935.
8640. Cerreta, F. Moravia's Luca Mansi and his dreams of transcendence. Italica, 1976, 53:8-28.
8641. Chabot, C. Barry. Faulkner's rescued patrimony. Rev Existential Psychol & Psychiat, 1974, 13:274-286.
8642. _____. Jane Austen's novels: the vicissitudes of desire. Amer Imago, 1957, 32:288-308.
8643. _____. Melville's The Confidence Man: a poisonous reading. Psychoanal Rev, 1976-77, 63:571-585.
8644. Chace, W. M. Review: Richard Ellmann's Consciousness of Joyce. Novel: A Forum for Fiction, 1978, 11:182-185.

8645. Chahine, S. La Dramaturgie de Victor Hugo (1816-43).
Paris: Nizet, 1971.

8646. Chaitin, Gilbert D. A Psychoanalytic Study of Stendhal's
Novels. DAI, 1970, 30:70-8351.

8647. _____. Religion as defense: the structure of The Brothers Karamazov. Lit & Psychol, 1972, 22:69-87.

8648. _____. The Unhappy Few: The Psychological Novels of
Stendhal. Bloomington: Indiana Univ. Press, 1972; Review: Eleanor B. Manheim, Hartford Studies in Lit,
1972, 4:241-244.

8649. _____. Voices of the dead: love, death and politics in
Zola's Fortune des Rougon. Lit & Psychol, 1976, 26:
131-144, 148-158.

8650. Chamberlin, Vernon A., & Weiner, Jack. Galdos' Doña Per-
fecta and Turgenev's Fathers and Sons: two interpretations of conflict between generations. PMLA, 1971, 86:
19-24.

8651. Chambers, Anthony H. A study of Tanizaki's Shōshō Shige-
moto no haha. Harvard J Asiatic Studies, 1978, 38:357-
379.

8652. Chambers, Ross. Samuel Beckett and the padded cell.
Meanjin Q, 1962, 21:457-458.

8653. Chambron, Henry. Note sur le caractère psychopathologique
de Lennie dans le roman de Steinbeck Des souris et des
hommes. Caliban (Toulouse), N. S., 1965, 1(1):87-124.

8654. Champagne, Roland A. The architectural pattern of a literary artifact: a Lacanian reading of Balzac's Jésus-
Christ en Flandre. Studies in Short Fiction, 1978, 15:
49-54.

8655. _____. A schizoanalysis of Marcel: Gilles Deleuze's
critical theories at work. Helicon, 1975, 2:39-50.

8656. Champigny, Robert. Existentialism in the modern French
novel. Thought, 1956, 31:365-384.

8657. _____. Portrait of the Symbolist Hero; an Existential
Study Based on the Work of Alain-Fournier. Bloomington: Indiana Univ. Press, 1954.

8658. _____. Suffering and death. Symposium, 1970, 24:197-
205.

8659. Chandler, Alice. 'A pair of fine eyes': Jane Austen's treatment of sex. Studies in the Novel, 1975, 7:88-103.

8660. Chandler, Simon B. Man, emotion and intellect in the Decameron. Phililogical Q, 1960, 39:400-412.

8661. Chankin, Donald O. Anonymity and Death: the Fiction of B.
Traven. University Park: Penn State Univ. Press, 1975.

8662. Chapman, Arnold. The Perdido as a type in some Spanish-
American novels. PMLA, 1955, 70:19.

8663. Chapman, Sara S. The 'Obsession of Egotism' in Henry
James's 'A Round of Visits.' Arizona Q, 1973, 29:130-
138.

8664. _____. Stalking the beast: egomania and redemptive suffering in James's 'major phase.' Colby Library Q,
1975, 11:50-66.

8665. Chardin, P. Proust lecteur de Dostoevski. Les Lettres Romanes, 1971, 25:119-152, 231-269, 333-349.

8666. Chargois, Josephine A. Two Views of Black Alienation: A
       Comparative Study of Chinua Achebe and Ralph Ellison.
       DAI, 1974, 34:7742A.
8667. Charles, C. V. Optimism and frustration in the American
       Negro. Psychoanal Rev, 1942, 29:270-299.
8668. Charles, Don C., & Charles, Linda A. Charles Dickens' old
       people. Int J Aging & Human Development, 1979-1980,
       10:231-237.
8669. Chartier, Richard. The river and the whirlpool: water
       imagery in The Ambassadors. Ball State Univ. Forum,
       1971, 12(2):70-75.
8670. Chase, Lawrence J., & Kneupper, Charles W. A literary
       analog to conflict theories: the potential for theory con-
       struction. Speech Monographs, 1974, 41:57-63.
8671. Chase, Richard. The American Novel and Its Tradition.
       Garden City, NY: Doubleday, 1957.
8672. _____. An approach to Melville. In Malin, I. (ed),
       Psychoanalysis and American Fiction. NY: Dutton, 1965,
       111-120; Partisan Rev, 1947, 14:285-294.
8673. _____. The Brontës: a centennial review. Kenyon Rev,
       1947, 7:487-506.
8674. _____. Dissent on Billy Budd. Partisan Rev, 1948, 15:
       1212-1218.
8675. _____. Finnegans Wake: an anthropological study. Amer
       Scholar, 1944, 8:418-426.
8676. _____. Herman Melville. A Critical Study. NY: Mac-
       millan, 1949.
8677. Chasseguet-Smirgel, Janine. Reflexions on the connexions
       between perversion and sadism. Int J Psycho-Anal, 1978,
       59:27-35.
8678. Chastaing, Maxine. Notes sur le style du roman. JPNP,
       1951, 44:286-302.
8679. _____. La Philosophie de Virginia Woolf. Paris:
       Presses Universitaires de France, 1951.
8680. _____. Le Roman policier 'classique.' JPNP, 1967, 64:
       313-342.
8681. _____. Roman policier et psychologie de la verité.
       JPNP, 1938, 35:210-230.
8682. _____. Virginia Woolf et la conscience réfléchissante.
       JPNP, 1938, 35:617-624.
8683. Chatfield, E. Hale. Levels of meaning in Melville's 'I and
       My Chimney.' Amer Imago, 1962, 19:163-169.
8684. Chaumeix, A. Romans psychologiques: à propos de quelques
       livres récents. Rev de deux Mondes, 1932, 8:699-709.
8685. Chavkin, Allan. Bellow's alternative to the wasteland: ro-
       mantic theme and form in Herzog. Studies in the Novel,
       1979, 11:326-337.
8686. Chemain-Degrange, Arlette. La Promotion féminine à tra-
       vers les romans africaines. Actuel Developpement, 1974,
       35-39.
8687. Chênerie, M. -C. Pour un bestiarie de Bernanos, I: la
       symbolique du cheval. Archives des Lettres Modernes,
       1972, 136 (Archives Bernanos, 3).

8688. Cherpack, C. Space, time and memory in La Nouvelle Héloïse. L'Esprit créateur, 1963, 3:167-171.
8689. Chesneau, Albert. Essai de psychocritique de Louis-Ferdinand Céline. Archives des lettres modernes, 1971, no.
129, novembre.
8690. _____. Vomir Céline. Rev des Lettres Modernes, 1974,
nos. 398-402.
8691. Chesson, Diane Marie. The Intellectual and Emotional Complex as an Expression of the Consciousness in Joyce,
Lawrence, and Woolf. DAI, 1976, 36:6081A.
8692. Childers, Helen W. American Novels about Adolescence,
1917-1953. DA, 1959, 19:2947-2948.
8693. Chinchón, Osivaldo. The Sea as a Motif in Fictional Literature of Chile. Doctoral dissertation, Univ. Virginia,
1967.
8694. Chinneswararao, G. J. Amis's Take a Girl Like You. Indian
J English Studies, 1971, 12:110-114.
8695. Chitwood, Garrett C., Jr. Love and Guilt: A Study of Suffering in Selected Medieval Works. DAI, 1971, 31:3497A-
98A.
8696. Chizh, V. Dostoevski Psikopatalog. Moscow: 1885.
8697. _____. [Dostoievsky's criminal types.] In Comptes Rendus de la 5e Session au Congrès International d'Anthropologie Criminelle. Amsterdam: DeBussey, 1902, 135-
154.
8698. Chizhevsky, Dmitri. The theme of the double in Dostoevsky.
In Wellek, R. (ed), Dostoevsky: A Collection of Critical
Essays. Englewood Cliffs, NJ: Prentice-Hall, 1962,
112-129.
8699. Choisy, Maryse. L'Anneau de Polycrate. Paris: L'Arche,
n. d.
8700. _____. Psychologie, sociologie et syntaxe des Mandarins.
Psyché, 1954, 9:522-533.
8701. Christ, Carol. Aggression and providential death in George
Eliot's fiction. Novel: A Forum on Fiction, 1976, 9:
130-140.
8702. Christman, Elizabeth A. Hell Lay About Them: Childhood
in the Work of Graham Greene. DAI, 1973, 33:6345A.
8703. Christy, Wallace M. The Shock of Recognition: A Psycho-
Literary Study of Hawthorne's Influence on Melville's
Short Fiction. DAI, 1971, 31:6543A-44A.
8704. Chronaki, Bessie. Eudora Welty's theory of place and human relationships. South Atlantic Bulletin, 1978, 43(2):
36-44.
8705. Chrzanowski, Joseph A. Alienation in the Novels of Juan
Carlos Onetti. DAI, 1972, 32:6418A-19A.
8706. _____. The double in 'Las dos Elenas.' Romance Notes,
1977, 18:6-10.
8707. _____. Psychological motivation in Borges' 'Emma
Zunz.' Lit & Psychol, 1978, 28:100-104.
8708. Chuang, Hsin-cheng. Themes of 'Dream of the Red Chamber': A Comparative Interpretation. DA, 1967, 67-3659.
8709. Church, Margaret. Dostovesky's Crime and Punishment and
Kafka's The Trial. Lit & Psychol, 1969, 19:47-55.

8710. _____. Dubliners and Vico. James Joyce Q, 1967-68, 5: 150-156.
8711. _____. Kafka and Proust: a contrast in time. Bucknell Rev, 1957, 7:107-112; In Garvin, H. R. (ed), Makers of the Twentieth-Century Novel. Lewisburg, Pa: Bucknell Univ. Press, 1977, 149-153.
8712. Ciancio, Ralph A. Faulkner's existentialist affinities. In Studies in Faulkner, Carnegie Series in English. Pittsburgh: Case Western Reserve Univ. Press, 1961.
8713. Citron, Pierre. Sur deux zones obscures de la psychologie de Balzac. In L'Année Balzacienne. Paris: Garnier, 1967, 3-27.
8714. Cixous, Hélène. Fiction and its phantoms: a reading of Freud's 'Das Unheimliche' ('The Uncanny'). New Literary History, 1976, 7:525-548.
8715. _____. Joyce, la ruse de l'écriture. Poétique, 1970, 4.
8716. _____. La Missexualité, où jouis-je? Poétique, 1976, 26:240-249.
8717. Clareson, T. D. Science fiction: the other side of realism. In SF: The Other Side of Realism. Bowling Green, Ohio: Bowling Green Univ. Press, 1971, 1-28.
8718. Clark, C. N. Love and time: the erotic imagery of Marcel Proust. Yale French Studies, 1953, 11:80-90.
8719. Clark, Mary V. Review: Jacob Wassermann's The World's Illusion. Psychoanal Rev, 1922, 9:94-97.
8720. Clark, R. T. Personality and society in Wilhelm Meister's Lehrjahre. In Jordan, G. J. (ed), Southwest Goethe Festival. Dallas: Southern Methodist Univ., 1949, 85-98.
8721. _____. Psychological framework of Goethe's Werther: his knowledge of the principles of Herder's character analysis. J English & Germanic Philology, 1974, 46:273-278.
8722. Clark, William J. Faulkner's Light in August. Explicator, 1969, 28:3.
8723. Clarke, Bruce. Miss Lonelyhearts and the detached consciousness. Paunch, 1975, 42-43:21-39.
8724. Clarke, D. C. Coconsciousness in Agudiez' Las Tardes de Thérèze Lamarck. Revista Hispánica Moderna, 1968, 34:586-595.
8725. Clarke, Delia. Raintree County: psychological symbolism, archetype, and myth. Thoth, 1970, 11(1):31-39.
8726. Clarke, Loretta M. A Critical Approach to Four Novels of Adolescence. DAI, 1971, 31:4758A.
8727. Clavering, Rose. The Conflict Between the Individual and Social Forces in Herman Melville's Works: Typee to Moby Dick. DA, 1958, 18:2137-2138.
8728. Clayton, A. J. Etapes d'un itinéraire spirituel: Albert Camus de 1937 à 1944. Paris: Minard, 1971. Archives des Lettres Moderns, No. 122, 1971.
8729. Clayton, John J. Alain Robbe-Grillet: the aesthetics of sadomasochism. Massachusetts Rev, 1977, 18:106-119.
8730. _____. Saul Bellow: In Defense of Man. Bloomington: Indiana Univ. Press, 1968.

8731- Clément, Catherine, & Pingaud, Bernard. Roman-analyse.
2.   Rev Française de Psychanalyse, 1974, 38(1):5-24.
8733. Clements, Clyde C. Symbolic patterns in You Can't Go Home
       Again. Modern Fiction Studies, 1965, 11:286-296; In
       Field, L. A. (ed), Thomas Wolfe. Three Decades of Crit-
       icism. NY: New York Univ. Press, 1968, 229-240.
8734. Cleveland, Carol L. Psychological Violence: the World of
       Flannery O'Connor. DAI, 1974, 34:5959A.
8735. Clinet, Marie-Rose. La Femme dans les romans algériens
       de langue française. Liège: Univ. Liège, 1971.
8736. Clipper, Lawrence J. Edward Waverley's night journey.
       South Atlantic Q, 1974, 73:541-553.
8737. Clive, Geoffrey. Gogol and the absurd. In The Broken
       Icon: Intuitive Existentialism in Classical Russian Fic-
       tion. NY: Macmillan, 1972, 1-29.
8738. Clupper, Beatrice B. The Male as Principal in D. H. Law-
       rence's Fiction. DAI, 1972, 32:5778A-79A.
8739. Clyman, Toby W. Women in Chekhov's Prose Works. DAI,
       1971, 32:2052A.
8740. Coale, Samuel. The quest for the elusive self: the fiction
       of Jerzy Kosinski. Critique: Studies in Modern Fiction,
       1973, 14(3):25-37.
8741. Cobb, Lawrence W. Masculine and feminine: the shape of
       the universe. Bulletin New York C. S. Lewis Society,
       1977, 8(4):1-6.
8742. Cobb, Nina Kressner. Richard Wright: exile and existential-
       ism. Phylon, 1979, 40:362-374.
8743. Cobb, W. M. Melville as humanist. J National Medical
       Assn, 1977, 69:767-768.
8744. Cochran, R. W. Circularity in The Sun Also Rises. Modern
       Fiction Studies, 1968, 14:297-306.
8745. Cockelreas, Joanne. Within the psychic bubble: the rhetoric
       of silence in modern fiction. In Tanner, W. E., et al.
       (eds), A Symposium in Rhetoric. Denton: Texas Wom-
       en's Univ. Press, 1976, 13-21.
8746. Cocks, G. A. A. Milne: sources of his creativity. Amer
       Imago, 1977, 34:313-326.
8747. Cockshut, A. O. J. Man and Woman: A Study of Love and the
       Novel, 1740-1940. NY: Oxford Univ. Press, 1978; Re-
       view: J. Halperin, Studies in the Novel, 1978, 10:363-
       367.
8748. Coddou, Marcelo. La estructura y la problemática existen-
       cial de El túnel de E. Sábato. Atenea, 1966, No. 12,
       141-168.
8749. Coffin, Tristram Potter. The Sex Kick. Eroticism in Mod-
       ern America. NY: Macmillan, 1966.
8750. Cogny, P. L'Education sentimentale de Flaubert, le monde
       en creux. Paris: Larousse, 1975.
8751. Cohan, Steven M. Gulliver's fiction. Studies in the Novel,
       1974, 6:7-16.
8752. _____. 'They are all secret': the fantasy content of Bleak
       House. Lit & Psychol, 1976, 26:79-91.

8753. Cohen, Alain. Proust and the President Schreber: a theory of primal quotation; or, for a psychoanalytics of (-desire-in) philosophy. Yale French Studies, 1975, 52:189-205.

8754. Cohen, Hubert I. 'A woeful agony which forced me to begin my tale': The Catcher in the Rye. Modern Fiction Studies, 1966-67, 12:355-366.

8755. Cohen, Mabel Blake. Review: Jo Sinclair's Wasteland. Psychiatry, 1946, 9:407-408.

8756. Cohen, Mary. 'Out of the chaos, a new kind of strength': Doris Lessing's The Golden Notebook. In Diamond, A., & Edwards, L. R. (eds), The Authority of Experience. Essays in Feminist Criticism. Amherst: Univ. Massachusetts Press, 1977, 178-193.

8757. Cohen, Richard. The inessential houses of The Great Gatsby. Hudson Rev, 1968, 2:48-57.

8758. _____. The social-Christian and Christian-social doctrines of Samuel Richardson. Hartford Studies in Lit, 1972, 4: 135-146.

8759. Cohen, Sarah Blacher. Comedy and guilt in Humboldt's Gift. Modern Fiction Studies, 1979, 25:47-57.

8760. Cohen, Sara E. The Jew in the Novels of Galdós. DAI, 1973, 34:763A-64A.

8761. Cohn, Dorrit Claire. Kafka's eternal present: narrative tense in 'Ein Landarzt' and other first-person stories. PMLA, 1968, 83:144-150.

8762. _____. Kleist's Marquise von O.... The problem of knowledge. Monatshefte, 1975, 67:129-144.

8763. _____. Narrated monologue: definition of a fictional style. Comparative Lit, 1966, 18:97-112.

8764. _____. Psyche and space in Musil's Die Vollendung der Liebe. Germanic Rev, 1974, 49:154-168.

8765. _____. Psycho-analogies: a means for rendering consciousness in fiction. In Martini, F. (ed), Probleme des Erzählens in der Weltliteratur. Stuttgart: Klett, 1971, 291-302.

8766. _____. Transparent Minds: Narrative Modes for Presenting Consciousness in Fiction. Princeton: Princeton Univ. Press, 1978.

8767. Cohn, R. G. From Chrétien to Camus: plumes and prisons. Modern Language Notes, 1965, 80:601-609.

8768. Coindreau, Maurice. Introduction to The Wild Palms. Paris: 1952.

8769. Colby, Vineta. Ut pictura poesis: the novel of domestic realism as genre. In Yesterday's Woman: Domestic Realism in the English Novel. Princeton: Princeton Univ. Press, 1974, 7-40.

8770. _____. Yesterday's Woman: Domestic Realism in the English Novel. Princeton: Princeton Univ. Press, 1974.

8771. Coldwell, Joan. Mad Shadows as psychological fiction. J Canadian Fiction, 1973, 2(4):65-67.

8772. Coleman, Stanley M. Phantom double: its psychological significance with special reference to de Maupassant and Dostoevsky. British J Medical Psychol, 1934, 14:254-273.

8773. _____. Two on a Tower: an analytical study. British J Medical Psychology, 1931, 11:55-77.

8774. Coles, Robert. Baldwin's burden. Partisan Rev, 1964, 31: 409-416.

8775. _____. Children's stories: the link to the past. In Children's Literature, Vol. 8. New Haven: Yale Univ. Press, 1980, 141-146.

8776. _____. Flannery O'Connor's South. Baton Rouge: Louisiana State Univ. Press, 1980.

8777. _____. Irony in the Mind's Life: Essays on Novels by James Agee, Elizabeth Bowen, and George Eliot. Charlottesville: Univ. Virginia Press, 1974.

8778. _____. Walker Percy: An American Search. Boston: Little, Brown, 1978.

8779. Collins, Alice K. El existencialismo de Eduardo Mallea. Doctoral dissertation, Univ. Oklahoma, 1967.

8780. Collins, Carvel. Are these mandalas. Lit & Psychol, 1953, 3:3-6.

8781. _____. A conscious literary use of Freud. Lit & Psychol, 1953, 3(3):2-4.

8782. _____. Faulkner's reputation and the contemporary novel. In Griffin, W., Jr. (ed), Literature in the Modern World. Nashville: Peabody College Bureau Publ, 1954.

8783. _____. The interior monologues of The Sound and the Fury. In Downer, A. S. (ed), English Institute Essays, 1952, 29-56; Cambridge: M. I. T. Publications in Humanities, No. 6; In Malin, I. (ed), Psychoanalysis and American Fiction. NY: Dutton, 1965, 223-243.

8784. _____. Zamyatin, Wells and the utopian literary tradition. Slavonic & East European Rev, 1965/66, 44:351-360.

8785. Collins, Helen. The nature and power of Hawthorne's women as seen through A Wonder Book and Tanglewood Tales. Nassau Rev, 1976, 3(2):16-28.

8786. Collins, H. P. Kafka's 'double figure' as a literary device. Monatshefte, 1963, 55:7-12.

8787. Collins, Joseph. Review: James Joyce's Ulysses. New York Times Book Rev, 28 May 1922; In Deming, R. (ed), James Joyce: The Critical Heritage. London: Routledge & Kegan Paul, 1970, 1, 222-226.

8788. _____. Tragedist, prophet and psychologist. North Amer Rev, 1922, 66-83.

8789. Collins, R. G. Light in August: Faulkner's stained glass triptych. Mosaic, 1973, 7:97-157.

8790. _____. Kafka's special methods of thinking. Mosaic, 1970, 3:43-57.

8791. Colum, Mary M. The psychopathic novel. Forum, 1934, 91:219-223.

8792. Comyn, Veronica. John Jasper, schizophrenic. Unisa English Studies, 1975, 13(2):1-5.

8793. Conde, David. Archetypal Patterns in Ernesto Sábato's Sobre héroes y tumbas. DAI, 1973, 33:6347A.

8794. Condon, Richard A. The broken conduit: a study of alienation in American literature. Pacific Spectator, 1954, 8: 326-332.

8795. Condray, Martha J.   Woman's One Career: Trollope's View of the Character and Proper Role of Woman.   DAI, 1970, 30:5403A.

8796. Cone, E. T.   Three ways of reading a detective story--or a Brahms intermezzo.   Georgia Rev, 1977, 31:534-574.

8797. Conely, James.   Arcana, Molloy, Malone Dies, The Unnamable: a brief comparison of forms.   Hartford Studies in Lit, 1972, 4:187-196.

8798. Conley, T.   Feminism, écriture and the closed room: the Angoisses douloureuses qui procedent d'amours.   Symposium, 1973, 27:322-332.

8799. Conquest, Robert.   Lady Chatterley's lover in the light of Dürfian psychology.   New Statesman, 1978, 18:61-70.

8800. Conroy, Peter V., Jr.   La Vision schizophrène chez Meursault.   Rev des Lettres Modernes, 1976, 479-483:129-143; In Fitch, B. T. (ed), Albert Camus 8. Camus romancier. La Peste.   Paris: Minard, 1977, 129-143.

8801. Constans, E.   Les Problèmes de la condition féminine dans l'oeuvre de Stendhal.   L'Information Littéraire, 1977, 29: 160-163.

8802. Conte, R.   Narrativa española: el realismo proscrito: J. Marse.   Insula, 1975, 346:5.

8803. Convoy, P. V.   The metaphorical web in Zola's Nana.   Univ. Toronto Q, 1978, 47:239-258.

8804. Conway, Richard H.   The Difficulty of Being a Woman: A Study of George Eliot's Heroines.   DAI, 1973, 34:722A.

8805. Cook, Reginald.   The forest of Goodman Brown's night: a reading of Hawthorne's 'Young Goodman Brown.'   New England Q, 1970, 43:473-481.

8806. Cook, Teresa A.   El femenismo en la novelistica de Emilia Pardo Bazán.   DAI, 1974, 35:2933A-34A.

8807. Cook, William K.   Isolation and Communism in Arthur Schnitzler's Early Short Stories.   Seattle: Univ. Washington Press, 1972.

8808. _____.   Isolation, flight, and resolution in Arthur Schnitzler's Die toten Schweigen.   Germanic Rev, 1975, 50:213-226.

8809. Cooke, Michael Gerard.   'Mother':   Hallucination and Death as Motifs of Escape in the Novels of Julien Green.   Washington, DC: Catholic Univ. of America Press, 1960.

8810. Cooper, David Dale.   Gertrude Stein's 'Magnificent Aspargus':   horizontal vision and unmeaning in Tender Buttons.   Modern Fiction Studies, 1974, 20:337-349.

8811. Cooper, James Glennon.   The womb of time: archetypal patterns in the novels of Jack London.   Jack London Notes, 1976, 9:16-28.

8812. _____.   The womb of time: archetypal patterns in the novels of Jack London.   Jack London Newsletter, 1976, 9:16-28; DAI, 1974, 35:2261A.

8813. Cooper, Nina.   Obsessive elements in Julien Green's short stories: early essays in style.   Studies in Short Fiction, 1973, 10:149-158.

8814. Cooperman, Stanley.   American war novels: yesterday, today, and tomorrow.   Yale Rev, 1972, 61:517-529.

8815. _____. Death and cojones: Hemingway's A Farewell to Arms. South Atlantic Q, 1964, 63:85-92.

8816. _____. John Dos Passos' Three Soldiers: aesthetics and the doom of individualism. In Klein, H. M. (ed), The First World War in Fiction. NY: Barnes & Noble, 1977, 23-31.

8817. _____. Kafka's 'A Country Doctor'--microcosm of symbolism. Univ Kansas City Rev, 1957, 24:75-80; In Manheim, L., & Manheim, E. (eds), Hidden Patterns. NY: Macmillan, 1966, 220-229.

8818. _____. Willa Cather and the bright face of death. Lit & Psychol, 1963, 13:81-87.

8819. _____. World War I and the American Novel. Baltimore: Johns Hopkins Univ. Press, 1967.

8820. _____, et al. James Joyce's Ulysses. NY: Thor, 1965.

8821. Cordesse, Gérard. De la castration dans Le Soleil se lève aussi. Caliban, 1971, 8:89-99.

8822. _____. The science-fiction of William Burroughs. Caliban, 1975, 12:33-43.

8823. Cordle, Thomas H. The role of dreams in A la Recherche du temps perdu. Romanic Rev, 1951, 260-268.

8824. Core, Deborah. 'The Closed Door': love between women in the works of D. H. Lawrence. D. H. Lawrence Rev, 1978, 11:114-131.

8825. Corino, Karl. Ödipus oder Orest? Robert Musil und die Psychoanalyse. In Durzak, M. (ed), Die deutsche Exilliteratur 1933-1945. Stuttgart: Reclam, 1973, 123-235.

8826. Corn, Mary. Homosexuality as a Joycean theme. South Central Bulletin, 1973, 33:122.

8827. Cornillon, Susan K. (ed). Images of Women in Fiction. Feminist Perspectives. Bowling Green, Ohio: Bowling Green Univ. Popular Press, 1972.

8828. Cornubert, C. Freud et Romain Rolland. Essai sur la découverte de la pensée psychanalytique par quelques écrivains français. Paris: Thèse de Médecine, 1966.

8829. Cornwell, Ethel F. Samuel Beckett: the flight from self. PMLA, 1973, 88:41-51.

8830. Coroneou, Marianthi. Suffering as Part of the Human Condition in the Fiction of Graham Greene, Albert Camus, and Nikos Kazantzakis. DAI, 1970, 30(8-A), 3454.

8831. Correa, Gustavo. El simbolismo mítico en las novelas de Pérez Galdós. Thesaurus, 1963, 18:428-444.

8832. Corrington, John W. Isolation as motif in 'A Painful Case.' James Joyce Q, 1965, 3:182-191.

8833. Corsa, Helen Storm. 'The cross-grainedness of men': the Rev. Josiah Crawley--Trollope's study of a paranoid personality. Hartford Studies in Lit, 1973, 5:160-172.

8834. _____. A fair but frozen maid: a study of Jane Austen's Emma. Lit & Psychol, 1969, 19:101-123.

8835. _____. To the Lighthouse: death, mourning and transfiguration. Lit & Psychol, 1971, 21:115-131.

8836. Cortejoso Villanueva, L. [Biology and pathology in the pages of Don Quijote de la Mancha.] Clinica y Laboratorio, 1960, 70:231-240.

8837. Corwin, Laura J.   The Concept of the Self in the Novels of
       Jane Austen.   DAI, 1971, 31:5356A-57A.
8838. Cory, Donald W.   The Homosexual in America.   NY: Green-
       berg, 1951.
8839. _____. The Lesbian in America.   NY: Citadel, 1964;
       NY: Macfadden, 1964.
8840. _____, & Le Roy, J. P.   The lesbian in literature.   Sexol-
       ogy, 1963, 30:132-135.
8841. Coskren, Robert.   'William Wilson' and the disintegration of
       self.   Studies in Short Fiction, 1975, 12:155-162.
8842. Costello, Jacqueline A., & Kloss, Robert J.   The psychologi-
       cal depths of Melville's 'The Bell-Tower.'   Emerson So-
       ciety Q, 1973, 19:254-261.
8843. Costes, Alain.   Albert Camus, ou la parole manquante.
       Etude psychanalytique.   Paris: Payot, 1974.
8844. Cotter, Michael.   Identity and compulsion: George Lam-
       ming's Natives of My Person.   New Lit Rev, 1977, 1:29-
       35.
8845. Couch, Lotte S.   Der Reigen: Schnitzler und Sigmund Freud.
       Osterreich in Geschichte und Literatur, 1972, 16:219-232.
8846. Couch, Ruth Lazelle.   Women and Thomas Hardy: A Study
       of Sex-Linked Qualities in the Characters.   DAI, 1976,
       36:6698A.
8847. Couleon, H.   L'Etrange folie de Don Quichotte; Cervantes et
       la psychiatrie.   Annales Médico-Psychologiques, 1964,
       122:555-556.
8848. Coulet, H.   [Sade's literary characteristics.]   In Le Marquis
       de Sade.   Paris: Colin, 1968.
8849. Coupe, W. A.   Der Doppelsinn des Lebens: Die Doppeldeutig-
       keit in der Novellistik Theodor Storms.   Schriften der
       Theodor-Storm-Gesellschaft, 1977, 26:9-21.
8850. Cowan, James C.   D. H. Lawrence's 'The Princess' as ironic
       romance.   Studies in Short Fiction, 1967, 4:245-251.
8851. _____. Dream work in the Quentin section of The Sound
       and the Fury.   Lit & Psychol, 1974, 24:91-98.
8852. _____. In D. H. Lawrence's The Man Who Died.   The
       function of allusions and symbols.   Amer Imago, 1960,
       17:241-253.
8853. _____. Lawrence's romantic values: studies in classic
       American literature.   Ball State Univ. Forum, 1967, 8:
       30-35.
8854. Cowan, Kathryn O.   Black/White Stereotypes in the Fiction
       of Richard Wright, James Baldwin and Ralph Ellison.
       DAI, 1972, 33:2926A.
8855. Cowley, Malcolm.   The etiology of Faulkner's art.   Southern
       Rev, 1977, 13:83-95.
8856. _____. Freud in fiction.   New Republic, 19 May 1937,
       91:51.
8857. Cox, A. J.   A question of identity.   Riverside Q, 1965, 1:88-
       110.
8858. Cox, C. B.   Intellectual masochist.   Spectator, 1967, 218:
       647-648.
8859. Cox, James M.   Remarks on the sad initiation of Huckleberry
       Finn.   Sewanee Rev, 1954, 42:389-406.

8860. _____. The Scarlet Letter: through the old manse and
the custom house. Virginia Q Rev, 1975, 51:431-447.
8861. Cox, Randolph C. Aspects of Alienation in the Novels of
Juan Goytisolo. DAI, 1972, 32:6967A.
8862. Cox, R. M. A new 'novel' by Cadalso. Hispanic Rev, 1973,
41:655-658.
8863. Crabtree, Ursula M. Facing the Bogeyman: A Comparative
Study of the Motif of the Double in the Novels of Saul
Bellow and Günter Grass. DAI, 1978, 39:1532A-33A.
8864. Crane, John K. Crossing the bar twice: post-mortem consciousness in Bierce, Hemingway, and Golding. Studies
in Short Fiction, 1969, 6:361-376.
8865. _____. Golding and Bergson: the free fall of free will.
Bulletin Rocky Mountain Modern Language Assn, 1972,
26:136-141.
8866. _____. The Psychological Experience of Time in the
Novels of Thomas Hardy. DA, 1967, 27:3834A-35A.
8867. Cranfill, Thomas, & Clark, Robert. An Anatomy of 'The
Turn of the Screw.' Austin: Univ. Texas Press, 1965.
8868. Crawford, Nelson A. Literature and the psychopath. Psychoanal Rev, 1923, 10:440-446.
8869. Creeger, George Raymond. Color Symbolism in the Works of
Herman Melville. DA, 1965, 25:6620.
8870. Creelman, M. B. Review: J. O. Love's Worlds in Consciousness: Mythopoetic Thought in the Novels of Virginia
Woolf. Contemporary Psychol, 1971, 16:232-233.
8871. Creighton, Joanne V. Unliberated women in Joyce Carol
Oates's fiction. World Lit Written in English, 1978, 17:
165-175.
8872. Cremerius, Johannes. [Robert Musil. The dilemma of a
writer of the type 'poeta doctus' according to Freud.]
Psyche, 1979, 33:723-732.
8873. Cremieux, B. La Psychologie de Marcel Proust. Revue de
Paris, Sept-Oct 1924, 838-861.
8874. Crews, Frederick C. Giovanni's garden. Amer Q, 1964,
16:402-418.
8875. _____. The logic of compulsion in 'Roger Malvin's Burial.' PMLA, 1964, 79:457-465.
8876. _____. The ruined wall: unconscious motivation in The
Scarlet Letter. New England Q, 1965, 38:312-330.
8877. _____. The Sins of the Fathers: Hawthorne's Psychological Themes. NY: Oxford Univ. Press, 1966; Review:
Robert Rogers, Lit & Psychol, 1966, 16:204-206.
8878. Cribb, T. J. Review: F. Kaplan's Dickens and Mesmerism:
The Hidden Springs of Fiction. Rev English Studies, 1977,
28:514-515.
8879. Crichfield, Grant. The romantic madman as hero: Nodier's
Michel le Charpentier. French Rev, 1978, 51:835-842.
8880. Crick, Joyce. The Impact of Theories of Psycho-Analysis
in the Later Works of Thomas Mann. Doctoral dissertation, Univ. London, 1956.
8881. _____. Psycho-analytical elements in Thomas Mann's novel Lotte in Weimar. Lit & Psychol, 1960, 10:69-75.

8882. _____. Thomas Mann and psycho-analysis: the turning
point. Lit & Psychol, 1960, 10:45-55; In Manheim, L.,
& Manheim, E. (eds), Hidden Patterns. NY: Macmillan,
1966, 171-191.

8883. Crie, Robert D. 'The Minister's Black Veil': Mr. Hooper's
symbolic fig leaf. Lit & Psychol, 1967, 17:211-218.

8884. Crivelli, Renzo S. The Enormous Room e la visione del pellegrino. Studi americani, 1975-76, 21-22:153-199.

8885. Croft, Helen. Günter Grass's Katz und Maus. Seminar,
1973, 9:253-264.

8886. Cromphout, Gustaaf Van. Blithedale and the androgyne myth:
another look at Zenobia. Emerson Society Q, 1972, 18:
141-145.

8887. Crosby, Patricia Lauer. Growth to Fulfillment: A Psychological Analysis of Six Heroines of Henry James. DAI,
1976, 3G:6096A-7A.

8888. Crosman, R. Review: Norman N. Holland's 5 Readers
Reading. Novel: A Forum on Fiction, 1976, 9:286-288.

8889. Cross, R. K. Moby-Dick and Under the Volcano: poetry
from the abyss. Modern Fiction Studies, 1974, 20:149-
156.

8890. Crossley, Roger P. A. Women in Camus. DAI, 1977,
37(10):6533-34A.

8891. Crothers, S. The Children of Dickens. NY: Scribner, 1925.

8892. Crow, Charles L. Howells and William James: 'A Case of
Metaphantasmia' solved. Amer Q, 1975, 27:169-177.

8893. Crowder, T. The rational treatment of emotion: an essay on
Jane Austen's style. Spectrum, 1961, 5:91-96.

8894. Crowley, Francis E. Epiphany in Phoenix Park: a psychoanalytic look at a Dubliner. Psychoanal Rev, 1974, 61:
63-70.

8895. _____. Henry James' The Beast in the Jungle and The
Ambassadors. Psychoanal Rev, 1975, 62:153-163.

8896. Crowley, John W. Howell's obscure hurt. J Amer Studies,
1975, 9:199-211.

8897. _____. Howells' Questionable Shapes: from psychologism
to psychic romance. Emerson Society Q, 1975, 21:169-
178.

8898. _____. The length of Howells' Shadow of a Dream. Nineteenth Century Fiction, 1972, 27:182-196.

8899. _____. The nude and the Madonna in The Damnation of
Theron Ware. Amer Lit, 1973, 45:379-389.

8900. _____. The oedipal theme in Howells' Fennel and Rue.
Studies in the Novel, 1973, 5:104-109.

8901. _____, & Crow, Charles W. Psychic and psychological
themes in Howells' 'A Sleep and a Forgetting.' ESQ: J
Amer Renaissance, 1977, 23:41-51.

8902. Cruickshank, John. Albert Camus and the Literature of Revolt. NY: Oxford Univ. Press, 1960.

8903. Cueva Tamariz, Augustin. Aspectos psicologicos del Werther
de Goethe. Rev de Medicale Legal de Colombia, 1950,
11:81-89.

8904. Culbert, Gary A. Hamlin Garland's Image of Women: An
Allegiance to Ideality. DAI, 1974, 35:2984A-85A.

8905. Culbertson, Diana, & Valley, John A.   Alberto Moravia's melancholy murderer: the conformist as personality type. Lit & Psychol, 1975, 25:79-85.

8906. _____. Personality theory in Gide: the plume of the eagle.   Hartford Studies in Lit, 1976, 8:98-115.

8907. Cubross, Jack L.   The Prostitute and the Image of Prostitution in Victorian Fiction.   DAI, 1971, 31:4708A-09A.

8908. Cunningham, A. R.   The new woman fiction of the 1890's. Victorian Studies, 1973, 17:177-186.

8909. Cunningham, Marina.   Isaac Babel: The Identity Conflict. DAI, 1977, 37:4410A.

8910. Curet, Peggy J.   The Coverdale cop-out: a study of Hawthorne's ironic view of women in The Blithedale Romance. Publications of the Arkansas Philological Society, 1976, 1(2):19-25.

8911. Curle, R.   Characters of Dostoevsky: Studies from Four Novels.   London: Heinemann, 1950, 1966.

8912. Curry, Steven Scott.   The Literature of Loss: A Study of Nineteenth-Century English and American Fiction.   DAI, 1976, 37:1529A-30A.

8913. Curtin, William M.   Willa Cather and The Varieties of Religious Experience.   Renascence, 1975, 27:115-123.

8914. Curtius, Mechthild.   Kritik der Verdinglichung in Canetti's Roman 'Die Blendung':   Eine sozialpsychologische Lituranalyse.   Bonn: Bouvier, 1973.

8915. _____. Manifestationen der Einsamkeit bei Kafka.   Zur Isolierung des Künstlers in sozialpsychologischer Sicht. Zeitschrift für Literaturwissenschaft und Linguistik, 1976, 6(21):26-44.

8916. Cushman, K.   A note on Lawrence's 'Fly in the Ointment.' English Language Notes, 1977, 15:47-51.

8917. Cutting, Rose Marie.   Defiant women: the growth of feminism in Fanny Burney's novels.   Studies in English Lit 1500-1900, 1977, 17:519-530.

8918. Cypher, James R.   The tangled sexuality of Temple Drake. Amer Imago, 1962, 19:243-252.

8919. Cyprian, Eric.   Alienation of man in the fiction of the West. Explorations (India), 1975, 2(1):21-30.

8920. Czoniczer, Elisabeth.   Quelques Antécedents de 'A la recherche du temps perdu.'   Paris: Droz, 1957.

8921. Czyba, L.   Les Avatars de l'image de la femme dans la trilogie de Jacques Vingtras.   In Colloque Jules Vallès. Lyon: Lyons Univ. Presses, 1975, 35-50.

8922. Daemmrich, Horst S.   The Devil's Elixirs: precursor of the modern psychological novel.   Papers on Language & Lit, 1970, 6:374-386.

8923. _____. Mann's portrait of the artist: archetypal patterns. Bucknell Rev, 1966, 14:27-43; In Garvin, H. R. (ed), Makers of the Twentieth-Century Novel.   Lewisburg, Pa: Bucknell Univ. Press, 1977, 166-178.

8924. _____. Fertility-sterility: a sequence of motifs in Thomas Mann's Joseph novels. Modern Language Q, 1970, 31: 461-473.

8925. Daggett, R. M. Motion and emotion in fiction (the real versus the realist). Overland Monthly, 1895, 26:614-617.

8926. Dahl, Liisa. A comment on similarities between Edouard Dujardin's monologue intérieur and James Joyce's interior monologue. Neuphilologische Mitteilungen, 1972, 73:45-54.

8927. _____. Linguistic Features of the Stream-of-Consciousness Techniques of James Joyce, Virginia Woolf, and Eugene O'Neill. Turku: Yliopisto, 1970.

8928. _____. The linguistic presentation of the interior monologue in James Joyce's Ulysses. James Joyce Q, 1969, 7:114-119.

8929. Dahl, W. Morderpsykologi og hvetepriser. En revurdering av Sandemoses En sjømann går i land. In Johansen, K., & Dahl, W. (eds), Konfrontasjoner. Essays om litteratur og politikk. Oslo: Forlaget Ny Dag, 1970, 81-101.

8930. Dahlie, Hallvard. Alienation and disintegration in Tender Is the Night. Humanities Assn Bulletin, 1971, 22(4):3-8.

8931. _____. Unconsummated relationships: isolation and rejection in Alice Munro's stories. World Lit Written in English, 1972, 11(1):43-48.

8932. Dahlin, Lois Ann. Birth Imagery in the Writings of Francis Ponge. DAI, 1977, 38:2159A.

8933. Dahrendorf, Malte. Hermann Hesses Demian and C. G. Jung. Germanisch-romanische Monatsschrift, Neue Folge, 1958, 8:81-97.

8934. Daiches, David. George Eliot's Dr. Lydgate. Proceedings Royal Society Medicine, 1971, 64:723-724.

8935. Daleski, H. M. Joseph Conrad: The Way of Dispossession. NY: Holmes & Meier, 1977.

8936. Dalma, Giovanni. Interpretazione psicoanalitica d'un episodio della Térèsa Raquin de E. Zola. Archivio Generale di Neurologie, Psichiatrie e Psicoanalisti, 1927, 8:245-256.

8937. _____. Via del Maltempo di Onofrio Fabrizi. Psicodinanismo del matricidio. Psicoanalisi, 1945, 1:70-87.

8938. Dalsimer, Katherine. From preadolescent tomboy to early adolescent girl; an analysis of Carson McCuller's The Member of the Wedding. In Psychoanalytic Study of the Child, Vol. 34. New Haven: Yale Univ. Press, 1979, 445-461.

8939. Dalton, Elizabeth Carville. Myshkin's epilepsy. Partisan Rev, 1978, 45:595-610.

8940. _____. Unconscious Structure in 'The Idiot': A Study in Literature and Psychoanalysis. Princeton: Princeton Univ. Press, 1979; DAI, 1975, 36:2888A; Review: Robert Rogers, Hartford Studies in Lit, 1980, 12:55-58.

8941. Daly, C. B. The menstruation complex in literature. Psychoanal Q, 1935, 4:307-340.

8942. Dameron, J. Lasley. Poe at mid-century: Anglo-American criticism, 1928-1960. Ball State Univ. Forum, 1967, 8(1):36-44.
8943. Dana, Richard. The stutter of eternity. A study of the themes of isolation and meaninglessness in three novels by Yukio Mishima. Critique, 1970, 12:87-102.
8944. Daniel-Rops, Henry. Une Technique nouvelle: le Monologue intérieure. Le Correspondent, 1932, No. 1664:281-305.
8945. Daniels, Marvin. Pathological vindictiveness and the vindictive character. Psychoanal Rev, 1969, 56(2):169-196.
8946. Dare, H. The quest for Durrell's Scobie. Modern Fiction Studies, 1964-65, 10:379-383.
8947. Darmon, Nicole M. S. Frauen und Erotik in Otto Flakes Romanwerk. DAI, 1976, 37:2209A.
8948. D'Arx, Paule. La Femme dans le théatre de Henry de Montherlant. Paris: Nizet, 1973; Review: Gretchen R. Besser, French Rev, 1976, 50:354-355.
8949. Dattner, Berhard. Aus Das Bildnis des Dorian Gray. Int Zeitschrift für Psychoanalyse, 1913, 3:365.
8950. _____. Psychoanalytic problems in Dostoevski's Raskolnikov. In Nunberg, H., & Federn, E. (eds), Minutes of the Vienna Psychoanalytic Society, Vol. 3: 1910-1911. NY: IUP, 1974, 180-193.
8951. Dauner, Louise. What happened in the cave? Reflection on A Passage to India. Modern Fiction Studies, 1961, 7: 258-270; In Shahane, V.A. (ed), Perspectives on E.M. Forster's 'A Passage to India.' NY: Barnes & Noble, 1968.
8952. D'Avanzo, Mario L. Reason in madness: Darl's farewell scene in As I Lay Dying. Notes on Contemporary Lit, 1979, 9:9-10.
8953. Davenport, Marguerite L. Woman in Nineteenth-Century American Fiction: Ideals and Stereotypes in the Novels of John William DeForest. DAI, 1973, 34:723A.
8954. Daviau, Donald G., & Dunkle, Harvey I. Stefan Zweig's Schachnovelle. Monatshefte, 1973, 65:370-384.
8955. David-Schwarz, H. Hesses Narziss und Goldenmund in zwei verschieden Auffassungen. Psychologische Rundschau, 1931, 3:7-13.
8956. _____. Der Typus der 'weissen' Frau im Werk Eduard von Keyserlings. Psychologische Rundschau, 1929, 1: 285-292; 1930, 1:336-340.
8957. Davidson, Cathy N. Circumsexualocution in Henry James's Daisy Miller. Arizona Q, 1976, 32:353-366.
8958. _____. Geography as psychology in the Manitoba fiction of Margaret Lawrence. Kate Chopin Newsletter, 1976, 2(2):5-10.
8959. _____. Oedipa as androgyne in Thomas Pynchon's The Crying of Lot 49. Contemporary Lit, 1977, 18:38-50.
8960. Davidson, Colleen Tighe. Beyond the Sentimental Heroine: The Feminist Character in American Novels, 1899-1937. DAI, 1976, 37:306A.
8961. Davidson, G.M. Dostoevsky and the perennial drama of man. Psychiat Q Supplement, 1963, 37:88-105.

8962. Davidson, Hugh M.   The Essai de psychologie contemporaine
      and the character of Adrien Sixte.   Modern Philology,
      1948, 46:34-48.
8963. Davidson, Joan Marie.   The Heroines in the Novels of Stend-
      hal.   DAI, 1976, 36:8092A-93A; Centerpoint, 1977, 2(2):
      58-62.
8964. Davidson, Leah.   Mid-life crisis in Thomas Mann's Death in
      Venice.   J Amer Academy Psychoanal, 1976, 4:203-214.
8965. Davies, W. M.   Meditações sôbre esoterismo em 'Grande Ser-
      tão: Veredas'.   Minas Gerais Suplemento Literário, 15
      March 1969.
8966. _____.   Mistério e Loucura n' 'A Terceira Margem do
      Rio.'   Minas Gerais Suplemento Literário, 4 Jan 1969.
8967. Davis, Barbara A.   Zeno's ontological confessions.   Twenti-
      eth Century Lit, 1972, 18:45-56.
8968. Davis, Earle.   The Flint and the Flame: The Artistry of
      Charles Dickens.   Columbia: Univ. Missouri Press, 1963.
8969. Davis, Jack L., & Davis, June H.   Poe's ethereal Ligeia.
      Bulletin Rocky Mountain Modern Language Assn, 1970,
      24:170-176.
8970. Davis, Judith.   Do men need women's liberation?   Psychia-
      try, 1974, 37:387-400.
8971. Davis, Natalie Zemon.   Women on top: symbolic sexual in-
      version and political disorder in early modern Europe.
      In Babcock, B. A. (ed), The Reversible World: Symbolic
      Inversion in Art and Society.   Ithaca: Cornell Univ.
      Press, 1978, 147-190; In Society and Culture in Early
      Modern France.   Stanford: Univ. Press, 1975, 124-
      151.
8972. Davis, Patricia C.   Chicken queen's delight: D. H. Law-
      rence's 'The Fox.'   Modern Fiction Studies, 1973-74,
      19:565-571.
8973. Davis, Robert Murray.   Hyperaesthesia with complications:
      the world of Ronald Firbank.   Rendezvous, 1968, 3(1):5-
      15.
8974. _____.   Parody, paranoia, and the dead end of language in
      The Crying of Lot 49.   Genre, 1972, 5:367-377.
8975. Davis, Sara de Saussure.   The Female Protagonist in Henry
      James's Fiction, 1870-1890.   DAI, 1975, 35:7862A-63A.
8976. Davis, William V.   Fathers and sons in the fiction of Edward
      Wallant.   Research Studies, 1972, 40:53-55.
8977. Dawson, E. W.   Lawrence's pollyanalytic esthetic for the nov-
      el.   Paunch, 1966, No. 26, 60-68.
8978. Day, Robert A.   The rebirth of Leggatt.   Lit & Psychol,
      1963, 13:74-81.
8979. Dayananda, Y. J.   The Death of Ivan Ilych: a psychological
      study On Death and Dying.   Lit & Psychol, 1972, 22:
      191-198.
8980. Deamer, Brad Alan.   Surpassing the Love of Woman: Male
      Bonding in the Fiction of Sir Walter Scott.   DAI, 1978,
      39:278A.
8981. Dean, Thomas R.   Henry James' The Ambassadors: the
      primal scene revisited.   Amer Imago, 1972, 29:233-256.

8982.   Deane, Paul.   Ayn Rand's neurotic personalities of our times.
        Rev des Langues Vivantes, 1970, 36:125-129.
8983.   _____.   The persistence of Uncle Tom: an examination of
        the image of the Negro in children's fiction series.   J
        Negro Education, 1968, 37:140-145.
8984.   Debray, Pierre.   Du roman psychologique au roman de la
        condition humaine.   Cahiers du Monde Nouveau, 1948, 3:
        63-69.
8985.   Debray-Ritzen, Pierre.   Psychologie de la littérature et de la
        création littéraire.   Paris: Retz, 1977.
8986.   Debruge, Suzanne.   L'oeuvre Hermann Hesse et la psychana-
        lyse.   Etudes Germanique, 1952, 7:252-261.
8987.   De Busscher, J.   L'Influence de la doctrine psychanalytique
        en littérature.   J de Neurologie et de Psychiatrie, 1929,
        29:619-629.
8988.   De Carlo, Andrew.   The Image of Man as Portrayed in the
        Novels of Miguel de Unamuno.   DAI, 1970, 31:3939A.
8989.   Decker, Heinz.   Der innere Monolog: zur Analyse des
        Ulysses.   Antösse, 1959, 5:127-143; Akzente, 1961, 8:
        99-125.
8990.   De Courtivron, Isabelle.   Androgyny, Misogyny, and Madness:
        Three Essays on Women in Literature.   DAI, 1974, 34:
        5905A-06A.
8991.   Deegan, Dorothy V.   The Stereotype of the Single Woman in
        American Novels.   NY: King's Crown, 1951; NY: Octa-
        gon, 1961.
8992.   De Falco, Joseph M.   The Great Good Place: a journey into
        the psyche.   Lit & Psychol, 1958, 8(2):18-20.
8993.   Deforges, Régina, & Réage, Pauline.   Confessions of O:
        Conversations with Pauline Réage.   NY: Viking, 1979;
        Paris: Pauvert, 1975.
8994.   Degnan, James P.   The reluctant Indian in Joyce's 'An En-
        counter.'   Studies in Short Fiction, 1969, 6:152-156.
8995.   De Greef, E.   Le Conte et la psychologie de l'angoisse.
        Vlaam Opvoldk Tydschifften, 1955, 35:336-353.
8996.   De Greve, Marcel.   Le Discours rabelaisien, ou la raison en
        folie.   In Folie et déraison à la Renaissance.   Brussels:
        Eds. de l'Univ. de Bruxelles, 1976, 149-159.
8997.   DeGroot, Elizabeth M.   Archetypes in the Major Novels of
        Thomas Hardy and Their Literary Application.   DA, 1967,
        28:1048A.
8998.   Dehorn, W.   Psychoanalyse und neurere Dichtung.   Germanic
        Rev, 1932, 7:245-262, 330-358.
8999.   Deinert, H.   Franz Kafka--ein Hungerkünstler.   Wirkendes
        Wort, 1963, 13:78-87.
9000.   DeJean, Joan E.   Method and madness in Cyrano de Berger-
        ac's Voyage dans la lune.   French Forum, 1977, 2:224-237.
9001.   Delacroix, E.   La Psychologie de Stendhal.   Paris: Alcan,
        1918.
9002.   Delannois, Marcel.   Le Grand Meaulnes et l'adolescence.
        Les Etudes Classiques, 1953, 23:215-227.
9003.   DeLaski, E.   The psychological attitude of Charles Dickens
        toward surnames.   Amer J Psychol, 1918, 29:337-346.

9004. Delattre, Floris. Le Roman psychologique de Virginia Woolf. Paris: Vrin, 1932, 1967.

9005. _____. Virginia Woolf et le monologue intérieur. In Feux d'automne. Paris: Didier, 1950, 225-247.

9006. Delavenay, Emile. D. H. Lawrence, the Man and His Work. London: Heinemann, 1972.

9007. _____. D. H. Lawrence and 'Sacher-Masoch.' D. H. Lawrence Rev, 1973, 6:119-148.

9008. _____. Les Trois amants de Lady Chatterley. Etudes Anglaises, 1976, 29:46-63.

9009. Deleuze, Gilles. Sacher-Masoch: An Interpretation, Together with the Entire Text of 'Venus in Furs.' London: Faber & Faber, 1971.

9010. _____. The schizophrenic and language: surface and depth in Lewis Carrol and Antonin Artaud. In Harari, J. V. (ed), Textual Strategies. Ithaca, NY: Cornell Univ. Press, 1979, 277-295.

9011. Delhez-Sarlet, C. Les Jaloux et la jalousie dans l'oeuvre romanesque de Mme de La Fayette. Rev des Sciences Humaines, 1964, 115.

9012. Dell, Floyd. Psychoanalysis and recent fiction. Psyche & Eros, 1920, 1:39-49.

9013. Delorme, C. [Family relationships in Gide's work.] Rev des Lettres Modernes, 1970, Nos. 223-7.

9014. De Madariaga, Salvador. Don Quixote. An Introductory Essay in Psychology. NY: Oxford Univ. Press, 1960.

9015. De Man, Paul. Allegory (Julie). In Allegories of Reading, Figural Language in Rousseau, Nietzsche, Rilke, and Proust. New Haven: Yale Univ. Press, 1979, 188-220.

9016. Demetrakopoulos, Stephanie A. Feminism, sex role exchanges, and other subliminal fantasies in Bram Stoker's Dracula. Frontiers: J Women Studies, 1977, 2(3):104-113.

9017. Demoreuille, Marie-Jacqueline. Enfance et adolescence dans l'oeuvre romanesque et autobiographique de Julien Green. DAI, 1971, 31:6598A-99A.

9018. Deneau, Daniel P. Bits and pieces concerning one of Robbe-Grillet's latest verbal happenings. Twentieth Century Lit, 1979, 25:37-53.

9019. _____. The brother-sister relationship in Hard Times. Dickensian, 1964, 60:173-177.

9020. Denman, C. George. Carleton's characterization of women. Carleton Newsletter, 1970, 1:10-11.

9021. Dennis, Carl. The Blithedale Romance and the problem of self-integration. Texas Studies in Lit & Language, 1973, 15:93-110.

9022. _____. Dickens' moral vision. Texas Studies in Lit & Language, 1969, 11:1237-1246.

9023. Denny, R. Reactors of the imagination. Bulletin Atomic Scientists, 1953, 9:206-210.

9024. Denton, Ramona L. Female Selfhood in Anthony Trollope's Palliser Novels. DAI, 1978, 39:3595A.

9025. De Porte, Michael V. Digression and madness in A Tale of a Tub and Tristram Shandy. Huntington Library Q, 1970, 33:43-57.

9026. _____. Nightmares and Hobbyhorses: Swift, Sterne, and Augustan Ideas of Madness. San Marino, Cal: Huntington, Library, 1974.

9027. Deredita, John. El doble en dos cuentos de Onetti. In Pupo-Walker, E. (eds), El cuento hispanoamericano ante la crítica. Madrid: Castalia, 1973, 150-164.

9028. _____. Dream and spatial form. Review, 1975, 16:19-23.

9029. De Reul, Paul. L'Oeuvre de D. H. Lawrence. Paris: 1937.

9030. Derks, P. Raabe-Studien: Beiträge zur Anwendung psychoanalytischer Interpretationsmodelle. Bonn: Bouvier, 1976.

9031. Derla, Luigi. Interpretazione dell'Ortis. Convivium, 1967, 35:536-576.

9032. DeRoach, William. The influence of William James on the composition of The American. Interpretations, 1975, 7(1):38-43.

9033. Dervin, Daniel A. Breast fantasy in Barthelme, Swift, and Philip Roth: creativity and psychoanalytic structure. Amer Imago, 1976, 33:102-122.

9034. _____. Why does Molly menstruate? A new view of psychoanalysis and creativity. Lit & Psychol, 1978, 28:125-136.

9035. Descloux, Armand. Le Docteur Antoine Thibault: Etude psychologique d'un personnage médecin dans 'Les Thibault' de Roger Martin du Guard. Paris: Editiones Universitaires, 1965.

9036. Desonay, Fernand. Le 'Grand Meaulnes' d'Alain-Fournier, essai de commentaire psychologique et littéraire. Brussels: Edit des Artistes, 1941; Brussels: La Renaissance du Livre, 1963; Paris: Nizet, 1963.

9037. Despain, Norma LaRene. Stream of Consciousness Narration in Faulkner: A Redefinition. DAI, 1976, 37:306A-7A.

9038. Dessau, Adalbert. Das Thema der Eisamkeit in den Romanen von Gabriel García Márquez. In Bahner, W. (ed), Beiträge zur französischen Aufklärung und zur spanischen Literatur. Berlin: Akademie, 1971, 517-522.

9039. Dettmering, Peter. Die Inzestproblemetik in späteren Werk Thomas Manns. Psyche, 1966, 20:440-465.

9040. _____. Das Motiv des Eindringens bei Henry James. Psyche, 1976, 30:1057-1080.

9041. _____. [Personal goal and self-destruction.] Praxis der Psychotherapie, 1976, 21:131-138.

9042. _____. Die Problematik der Suizide im Werk Thomas Manns. Psyche, 1965, 19:547-569; The theme of suicide in the works of Thomas Mann. Humanitas, 1970, 6:23-44.

9043. _____. [The psychodynamics of Heinrich von Kleist's Michael Kohlhaas.] Psyche, 1975, 29:154-169.

9044. _____. Trennungsangst und Zwillingsphantasie in Heimito von Doderers Roman Die Strudlhofstiege. Psyche, 1972, 26:549-580.

9045. Detweiler, Robert. The moment of death in modern fiction.
       Contemporary Lit, 1972, 13:269-294.
9046. _____. Patterns of rebirth in Henderson the Rain King.
       Modern Fiction Studies, 1966, 12:405-414.
9047. _____. Updike's A Month of Sundays and the language of
       the unconscious. Amer Academy of Religion J, 1979, 47:
       609-625.
9048. Deutsch, Helene. Don Quixote and Don Quixotism. Psycho-
       anal Q, 1937, 6:215-222; Ultra, 1937, 16:343-346; Imago,
       1934, 20:444-449.
9049. _____. Lord Jim and depression. In Neuroses and Char-
       acter Types. NY: IUP, 1965, 353-355; London: Hogarth,
       1965, 353-357.
9050. _____. Motherhood and sexuality. Psychoanal Q, 1933,
       2:476-488.
9051. Devlin, Albert J. Parent-Child Relationships in the Works of
       William Faulkner. DAI, 1970, 31:2910A.
9052. _____. The Reivers: readings in social psychology.
       Mississippi Q, 1972, 25:327-337.
9053. _____. Sartoris: rereading the MacCallum episode.
       Twentieth Century Lit, 1971, 17:83-90.
9054. Devlin, James E. Irving's 'Adventure of a German Student. '
       Lit & Psychol, 1979, 29:120-122.
9055. DeVoto, Bernard. Mark Twain at Work. Cambridge: Har-
       vard Univ. Press, 1942.
9056. Dew, Marjorie C. Herman Melville's Existential View of the
       Universe: Essays in Phenomenological Interpretation.
       DA, 1967, 38:672A.
9057. Diaconu, Dana. El tema de la adolescencia en la visión
       artística de Julio Cortázar. Analele Stiintifice ale Uni-
       versitatii Ias, 1976, 22:54-56.
9058. Diamond, Ruth. The archetype of death and renewal in I
       Never Promised You a Rose Garden. Perspectives in
       Psychiat Care, 1975, 8:21-24.
9059. Díaz, Janet Winecroff. A. M. Matute. NY: Twayne, 1971.
9060. _____. Techniques of alienation in recent Spanish novels.
       J Spanish Studies: Twentieth Century, 1975, 3:5-16.
9061. Dick, Bernard F. The origins of homosexual fiction. Colo-
       rado Q, 1974, 22:509-515.
9062. Dickerson, F. B. Patterns of deviance in children's litera-
       ture. J Clinical Child Psychol, 1977, 6:46-51.
9063. Dickerson, Lucia. Portrait of the artist as a Jung man.
       Kenyon Rev, 1959, 31:58-83.
9064. Dickinson, Leon. Mark the twain: the double vision of
       Samuel Clemens. Rev des Langues Vivantes, 1976, 42:
       81-91.
9065. Dickman, A. J. Time and memory in Marcel Proust's nov-
       els. Modern Language Forum, 1938, 23:12-17.
9066. Dickson, K. Spatial concentration and themes in Die Wahl-
       verwandtschaften. Forum for Modern Language Studies,
       1965, 1:159-174.
9067. Didier, Béatrice. Le Corps féminin dans Lélia. Rev d'His-
       toire Littéraire de la France, 1976, 76:634-43, 644-651.

9068. _____. Inceste et écriture chez Sade. Les Lettres Nou-
       velles, 1972, 3:150-158.
9069. Dieckhöfer, K. Die Bedeutung der Psychopathologie in cer-
       vantinischer Dichtkunst. Medecin Monatsschrift, 1975,
       29:369-371.
9070. _____. Der Lizentiat Vidriera. Ein Beitrag zur Psycho-
       pathologie künstlerischen Schaffens bei Cervantes.
       Schweizer Archiv für Neurologie und Psychiatrie, 1974,
       114:357-365.
9071. _____. Die Novelle Der eifersüchtige Estremadurer, ein
       Beispiel cervantischer Psychopathologie. Schweizer Ar-
       chiv für Neurologie und Psychiatrie, 1975, 116:149-154.
9072. Dieckmann, Hanns. [The process of individuation in Oriental
       stories-within-a-story.] Praxis der Kinderpsychologie
       und Kinderpsychiatrie, 1963, 12:41-49.
9073. Diedrick, James. Dicken's alter-ego in Bleak House: the
       importance of Lawrence Boythorn. Dickens Studies News-
       letter, 1978, 9:37-40.
9074. Dierks, Manfred. Studien zu Mythos und Psychologie bei
       Thomas Mann: An seinem Nachlass orientierte Unter-
       suchungen zum 'Tod in Venedig,' zum 'Zauberberg' und
       zur 'Joseph'-Tetralogie. Bern: Francke, 1972.
9075. Diersch, Manfred. Fräulein Else--literarische Gestaltung
       impressionistischer Weltsicht im inneren Monolog. In
       Empiriokritizismus und Impressionismus. Berlin: Rüt-
       ten & Loening, 1973, 83-115.
9076. Dietrichson, Jan W. The Image of Money in the American
       Novel of the Gilded Age. Oslo: Universtetsforlaget; NY:
       Humanities Press, 1969.
9077. Dike, Donald A. The aggressive victim in the fiction of
       Joyce Carol Oates. Greyfriar, 1974, 15:13-29.
9078. Dillingham, William B. Frank Norris. Instinct and Art.
       Boston: Houghton Mifflin, 1969.
9079. Di Lorenzo-Coscia, Madeline. Interhuman Relations in the
       Work of Albert Camus. DAI, 1977, 38(4):1433-34A.
9080. Dimeo, Steven. Psychological symbolism in three early
       tales of invisibility. Riverside Q, 1971, 5:20-27.
9081. Dimić, Ivan. La Crise psychologique dans le roman du XXe
       siècle. De Roger Martin du Gard au 'Nouveau roman.'
       Thèse, Univ. Strasbourg, 1961.
9082. _____. Roger Martin du Gard et Tolstoi, originalité de
       la psychologie des personnages de l'auteur des Thibault.
       In Jost, F. (ed), Proceedings of the IVth Congress of the
       International Comparative Literature Association, Vol. 2.
       The Hague: Mouton, 1966, 1289-1295.
9083. Diorio, Mary Ann L. G. 'Vessels of Experience': A Com-
       parative Study of Women in Selected Novels of Gustave
       Flaubert and Henry James. DAI, 1978, 38:4156A.
9084. Di Scanno, Teresa. Les Contes de fées de Mademoiselle
       Bernard ou la vérité psychologique. Annali Istituto Uni-
       verstario Orientale, Napoli, Sezione Romanza, 12:261-274.
9085. Di Stasi, Lawrence W. Aggression in Miss Lonelyhearts;
       nowhere to throw a stone. In Madden, D. (ed), Nathanael

West: The Cheaters and the Cheated. De Land, Fla: Everett/Edwards, 1973, 83-101.

9086. Ditsky, John M. The ending of The Grapes of Wrath: a further commentary. Agora: J Humanities & Social Sciences, 1973, 2:41-50.

9087. Djwa, Sandra. False gods and the true covenant: thematic continuity between Margaret Laurence and Sinclair Ross. J Canadian Fiction, 1972, 1(4):43-50.

9088. Doak, Robert Waylon. Color and Light Imagery: (I) Its Theory, and (II) Its Practice in the Novels of Joseph Conrad. DAI, 1976, 37:2892A-93A.

9089. Doane, Margaret. Guido is saved: interior and exterior monologues in Book XI of The Ring and the Book. Studies in Browning & His Circle, 1977, 5(2):53-64.

9090. Dobie, Ann B. Early stream-of-consciousness writing: Great Expectations. Nineteenth Century Fiction, 1971, 25:405-416.

9091. Dobrinsky, Joseph. The son and lover theme in Lord Jim. Cahiers Victoriens et Edouardiens, 1975, 2:161-166.

9092. Dodd, William J. Kafka and Freud: a note on In der Strafkolonie. Monatshefte, 1978, 70:129-137.

9093. Dodsworth, Martin. Women without men at Cranford. Essays in Criticism, 1963, 13.

9094. Doi, L. T. A Japanese interpretation of Erich Segal's Love Story. Psychiatry, 1972, 35:385-391.

9095. Doi, Takeo. The Psychological World of Natsume Sōseki. Cambridge: Harvard Univ. Press, 1976; Review: Sanford Goldstein, Modern Fiction Studies, 1977-78, 23:711-713.

9096. Domandi, A. K. Modern German Literature. A Library of Literary Criticism, 2 Vols. NY: Ungar, 1972.

9097. Dombrowski, T. Q. The Treatment of Family Life and Relationships in the Works of James Joyce from 'Dubliners' to 'Ulysses.' Doctoral dissertation, Univ. London, 1975.

9098. Dommergues, Pierre. L'Aliénation dans le roman américain contemporain. Paris: Union Générale d'Editions, 1976.

9099. Donaldson, Scott. Appointment with the dentist: O'Hara's naturalistic novel. Modern Fiction Studies, 1968-69, 14: 435-442.

9100. _____. The dark truth of The Piazza Tales. PMLA, 1970, 85:1082-1086.

9101. _____. Philip Roth: the meanings of Letting Go. Contemporary Lit, 1970, 11:21-35.

9102. Donno, Antonio. I modi della violenza americana in alcuni romanzi dell'ultimo ventennio. Antologia Vieussieux, 1974, 35:24-36.

9103. Donoghue, Denis. Emily Brontë: on the latitude of interpretation. Harvard English Studies, 1970, 1:105-133.

9104. _____. Joyce's psychological landscape. Studies, 1957, 46:76-90.

9105. Donohoe, Eileen Marie. Psychic Transformation Through Memory: Work and Negation in William Faulkner's Absalom, Absalom! DAI, 1978, 39:1546A-47A.

9106. Donovan, Frank Robert. The Children of Charles Dickens.
London: Frewin, 1969; Dickens and Youth. NY: Dodd,
Mead, 1968.

9107. Donovan, Robert Alan. The mind of Jane Austen. In Wein-
sheimer, J. (ed), Jane Austen Today. Athens: Univ.
Georgia Press, 1975, 109-127.

9108. _____. The Shaping Vision: Imagination in the English
Novel from DeFoe to Dickens. Ithaca: Cornell Univ.
Press, 1966.

9109. Donze, R. A. Le Comique dans l'oeuvre de Marcel Proust.
Neuchatel: Attinger, 1955.

9110. Dorner, Helen. Mind, moment, and memory: a study of
the 'stream of consciousness' novel. Unisa English Studies, 1967, 3:27-35.

9111. Doubleday, N. F. Hawthorne's Hester and feminism. PMLA,
1939.

9112. Doubrovsky, Serge. 'The nine of hearts': fragment of a
psychoreading of La Nausée. In Roland, A. (ed), Psychoanalysis, Creativity, and Literature. NY: Columbia
Univ. Press, 1978, 312-322; Boundary, 1977, 5:411-420.

9113. _____. La Place de la madeleine: écriture et fantasme
chez Proust. Paris: Mercure de France, 1974: Review:
M. R. Finn, French Rev, 1976, 50:350-351.

9114. Doughtie, Edward. Art and nature in Deliverance. Southwest
Rev, 1979, 64:167-180.

9115. Doughty, Howard M. The novels of E. M. Forster. Bookman, 1932, 75:542-549.

9116. Douglas, Ann. Studs Lonigan and the failure of history in
mass society: a study in claustrophobia. Amer Q, 1977,
29:487-505.

9117. Downing, David. Beyond convention: the dynamics of imagery and response in Hawthorne's early sense of evil.
Amer Lit, 1980, 51:463-476.

9118. Doxey, William S. Donald Barthelme's Views of My Father
Weeping: a modern view of Oedipus. Notes on Contemporary Lit, 1973, 3(2):14-15.

9119. _____. Kesey's One Flew Over the Cuckoo's Nest. Explicator, 1973, 32:4, Item 32.

9120. Doyle, Mary Ellen. The alienated protagonist of Ralph Ellison's short fiction. College Language Assn J, 1975, 19:
165-172.

9121. Drake, Constance. Josephine and emotional bankruptcy.
Fitzgerald-Hemingway Annual, 1969, 5-13.

9122. Dreistadt, Roy. A unifying psychological analysis of the
principal characters in the novel Dr. Zhivago by Boris
Pasternak. Psychology, 1972, 9(3):22-35.

9123. Drew, Elizabeth A. 'New psychology. ' In Modern Novel;
Some Aspects of Contemporary Fiction. NY: Harcourt,
1926, 75-100.

9124. Drinnon, Richard. In the American heartland: Hemingway
and death. Psychoanal Rev, 1965, 52:6-31.

9125. Dryden, Edgar A. Hawthorne's castle in the air: form and theme in The House of Seven Gables. J English Lit History, 1971, 38:294-317.

9126. Duberman, Martin. Homosexual literature. New York Times Book Rev, 10 Dec 1972, 6-7, 28-29.

9127- Dubois, Jacques. Avatars du monologue intérieur dans le
8. nouveau roman. In Matthews, J. H. (ed), Un Nouveau roman, recherches et tradition. Paris: Minard, 1964, 17-29.

9129. Duffner, J. L'Oeuvre de Marcel Proust. Etude Médico-Psychologique. Paris: Legrand, 1931.

9130. Duffy, Dennis. Memory=pain: the haunted world of Philip Child's fiction. Canadian Lit, 1980, 84:41-56.

9131. Duffy, J. M., Jr. Moral integrity and moral anarchy in Mansfield Park. J English Lit History, 1956, 23:71-91.

9132. Duffy, Mary Terese Avila. Symbolism in Esau e Jacó with emphasis on biblical implications. A tentative study. Revista de Letras, 1964, 5:98-116; Esau and Jacob. Berkeley: Univ. California Press, 1965.

9133. Dugas, L. Savoir s'ennuyer. Psychologie et vie, 1929, 3: 162-164.

9134. Dugonjic, A. Epilepsija u zivotu i literarnom opusu F. M. Dostojevskog. Neuropsihijatrija, 1975, 23:185-190.

9135. Dujardin, Edouard. Le Monologue interieur, son apparition, ses origines, sa place dans l'oeuvre de James Joyce et dans le roman contemporain. Paris: Messein, 1931.

9136. Dujardin, Marie. Edouard Dujardin et le monologue interieur. Io, 1964, 1-5.

9137. Dunaway, John M. The Metamorphoses of the Self. Lexington: Univ. Press of Kentucky, 1978.

9138. Duncan, Jennifer Ann. Self and others: the pattern of neurosis and conflict in Germinie Lacerteux. Forum Modern Language Studies, 1977, 13:204-218.

9139. Dundes, Alan. Re: Joyce--no in at the womb. Modern Fiction Studies, 1962, 8:137-147.

9140. Dunlap, Mary M. Sex and the artist in Mosquitoes. Mississippi Q, 1969, 22:190-206.

9141. Dunn, E. Myth and style in Djuna Barnes's Nightwood. Modern Fiction Studies, 1973-74, 19:545-555.

9142. Duncan, Erika. The hungry Jewish mother. In Davidson, C. N., & Broner, E. M. (eds), The Lost Tradition. NY: Ungar, 1980, 231-241.

9143. Dupuis, Michel. Eenheid en versplintering van het ik. Thema's motieven van Willem Frederik Hermanns. Hasselt: Heideland-Orbis, 1976.

9144. _____. De psycho-kritiek van Huug Kaleis en hat standpunt van de verteller roman. Enkele beschouwingen. Rev des Langues Vivantes, 1974, 40:159-166.

9145. Dupuy, Aimé. Un Personnage nouveau du roman français: l'enfant. Paris: Hachette, 1931.

9146. Durán, Gloria. La dialéctica del chacal y el Imbinche. Revista Iberoamericana, 1976, 95:251-257.

9147. Durand, Régis. Les Signes de la vérité. Rev Française d'Etudes Américaines, 1977, 3:47-59.

9148.   Dürrenmatt, Friedrich.   Der Doppelgänger.   In Gesammelte
        Hörspiele.   Zurich: 1960, 3-37.
9149.   Dussinger, John A.   Conscience and the pattern of Christian
        perfection in Clarissa.   PMLA, 1966, 81:236-245.
9150.   _____.   The Discourse of the Mind in Eighteenth-Century
        Fiction.   The Hague: Mouton, 1974.
9151.   Duthie, Elizabeth.   A fresh comparison of 'The Idiot
        Boy' and The Idiot.   Notes & Queries, 1978, 25:
        219-220.
9152-   Duus, Louise.   Neither saint nor sinner: women in late
3.   nineteenth-century fiction.   Amer Lit Realism, 1870-1910,
        1974, 7:276-278.
9154.   Dyer, Denys.   The Stories of Kleist: A Critical Study.   NY:
        Holmes & Meier, 1977.
9155.   Dyer, Joyce Ann.   Kate Chopin's Use of Natural Correlatives
        as Psychological Symbols in Her Fiction.   DAI, 1978, 38:
        6723A.

9156.   Eagelson, H.   Pedestal for statue; novels of Dorothy M.
        Richardson.   Sewanee Rev, 1934, 42:42-53.
9157.   Eales, E.   The last Proust.   Psyché, 1928, 32:92-95.
9158.   _____.   Marcel Proust as psychologist.   Psyche, 1924, 4:
        269-271.
9159.   Eans, T. R.   Henry James' The Ambassadors: the primal
        scene revisited.   Amer Imago, 1972, 29:233-256.
9160.   Earnest, Ernest.   The American Eve in Fact and Fiction,
        1775-1914.   Urbana: Univ. Illinois Press, 1974.
9161.   Eason, Shari L. B.   Ambivalent Views Toward Woman's Role
        in the Novels of Charlotte Brontë.   DAI, 1978, 38:
        6741A.
9162.   Eaton, Frank F.   Der Dichter Bruno Goetz.   Rice Univ.
        Studies, 1971, 57(4):33-37.
9163.   Eaton, M. P.   A Study of the Influence of Environment upon
        Character in the Novels of George Eliot.   Master's thesis,
        Columbia Univ., 1919.
9164.   Echaverren, Roberto.   El sueño de angustia en Tierras de la
        memoria.   MLN, 1980, 95:411-423.
9165.   Eck, Marcel.   L'Angoisse de Julien Green ou l'angoisse de
        l'ange et d'Uranus.   In L'Homme et l'angoisse.   Paris:
        Fayard, 1964, 233-247.
9166.   _____.   Approche psychanalytique de Marcel Proust (I).
        A propos de deux livres récents.   Presse Medicale, 1968,
        76:135-138.
9167.   _____.   La Gènese d'une angoisse.   Essai de psych-
        analyse de Julien Green.   La Table Ronde, 1964,
        196:130-144.
9168-   _____.   'L'Idiot de la famille.' II.   La Maladie et la per-
9.   sonalité de Flaubert selon Sartre.   A propos de l'ouvrage
        de Jean-Paul Sartre.   Nouvelle Presse Medicale, 1972,
        1:825-828.
9170.   _____.   'Marcel Proust du coté de la médicine' par Rob-

ert Soupault. Presse Médicale, 1967, 75:2847-2849.
9171. Eckstein, Rudolf, & Caruth, Elaine. From Eden to Utopia.
Amer Imago, 1965, 22:128-141.
9172. Edel, Leon. Hawthorne's symbolism and psychoanalysis. In
Manheim, L. F., & Manheim, E. (eds), Hidden Patterns.
NY: Macmillan, 1966, 93-111.
9173. _____. How to read The Sound and the Fury. In Burnshaw, S. (ed), Varieties of Literary Experience. NY:
New York Univ. Press, 1962, 241-257.
9174. _____ (ed). Introduction to The Ghostly Tales of Henry
James. New Brunswick, NJ: Rutgers Univ. Press,
1949.
9175. _____. Introduction to Henry James: A Collection of
Critical Essays. Englewood Cliffs, NJ: Prentice-Hall,
1963.
9176. _____. The madness of art. Amer J Psychiat, 1975,
132:1005-1012.
9177. _____. The Modern Psychological Novel. NY: Evergreen, 1961; NY: Grosset & Dunlap, 1964; The Psychological Novel 1900-1950. Philadelphia: Lippincott, 1955;
London: Hart & Davis, 1955.
9178. _____. Novel and camera. In Halperin, J. (ed), The
Theory of the Novel: New Essays. NY: Oxford Univ.
Press, 1974, 177-188.
9179. _____. A pre-Freudian reading of 'The Turn of the
Screw.' Nineteenth Century Fiction, 1957, 12:1-36; In
Willen, G. (ed), A Casebook on Henry James's 'The Turn
of the Screw.' NY: Crowell, 1960, 244-272.
9180. _____. Sex and the novel. New York Times Book Rev,
1 Nov 1964, 2.
9181. _____. Willa Cather and The Professor's House. In
Malin, I. (ed), Psychoanalysis and American Fiction.
NY: Dutton, 1965, 199-221; Lit & Psychol, 1954, 4(5):
69-79.
9182. Edelstein, Arnold. 'Tangle of life': levels of meaning in
The Spoils of Poynton. Hartford Studies in Lit, 1970, 2:
133-150.
9183. Edenbaum, Robert I. Dada and surrealism in the United
States: a literary instance. Arts in Society, 1968, 5:
114-125.
9184. _____. From American dream to Pavlovian nightmare.
In Madden, D. (ed), Nathanael West: The Cheaters and
the Cheated. De Land, Fla: Everett/Edwards, 1973, 201-
216.
9185. _____. The poetics of the private eye: the novels of
Dashiell Hammett. In Nevins, F. M. (ed), The Mystery
Writer's Art. Bowling Green, Ohio: Bowling Green
Univ. Popular Press, 1970, 98-121; In Madden, D. (ed),
Tough Guy Writers of the Thirties. Carbondale: Southern Illinois Univ. Press, 1968, 1979.
9186. Eder, Doris L. The idea of the double. Psychoanal Rev,
1978, 65:579-614.

9187. Edgar, Pelham. Psycho-analysis and James Joyce. In The Art of the Novel. NY: Macmillan, 1933, 301-319; NY: Russell & Russell, 1965, 301-319.

9188. Edgell, B. Dickens and child psychology. British J Educational Psychol, 1937, 7:162-171.

9189. Edinborough, Arnold. Sartre and the existential novel. Queen's Q, 1949, 56:104-112.

9190. Edinger, Edward F. Melville's 'Moby Dick': a Jungian Commentary--An American Nekyia. NY: New Directions, 1978.

9191. Edwards, D. Review: Geoffrey Thurley's Psychology of Hardy's Novels. Victorian Studies, 1978, 21:511-512.

9192. Edwards, Duane. Holden Caulfield: don't ever tell anybody anything. J English Lit History, 1977, 44:555-565.

9193. Edwards, Paul, & Ramchand, Kenneth. The art of memory: Michael Anthony's The Year in San Fernando. J Commonwealth Lit, 1969, 7:59-72.

9194. Efron, Arthur. The tale, the teller, and sexuality in Tess of the D'Urbervilles. Paunch, 1967, 28:55-80.

9195. Egan, Joseph J. The fatal suitor: early foreshadowing in Tess of the d'Urbervilles. Tennessee Studies in Lit, 1970, 15:161-164.

9196. _____. 'Markheim': a drama of moral psychology. Nineteenth Century Fiction, 1965, 20:377-384.

9197. Eggenschwiler, David. Flannery O'Connor's true and false prophets. Renascence, 1969, 21:151-163.

9198. _____. James Hogg's Confessions and the fall into division. Studies in Scottish Lit, 1971, 9(1):26-39.

9199. _____. 'Die Verwandlung,' Freud, and the chains of Odysseus. Modern Language Quarterly, 1978, 39:363-385.

9200. Egri, Peter. The function of dreams and visions in A Portrait and Death in Venice. James Joyce Q, 1967/68, 5:86-102.

9201. _____. Parallelen zurschen der Mannschen und Joyceschen Form der inneren Monologs, der Traum- und Phantasiehaftigkeit im Spiegel des Romans Lotte in Weimar. Német Filológïan Tanulmanyok, 1968, 3:131-142.

9202. _____. The place of James Joyce's interior monologue in world literature. Umana, 1971, 20(5-8):32-35.

9203. Ehrlich, Carol. Evolutionism and the Female in Selected American Novels, 1885-1900. DAI, 1974, 35:399A.

9204. Ehrlich, Richard D. Catastrophism and coition: universal and individual development in Women in Love. Texas Studies in Lit & Language, 1967, 9:117-128.

9205. Eichmann, Raymond. Holes, cavities and grottos in Zola's L'Assommoir. Publications Arkansas Philological Assn, 1975, 1(2):21-27.

9206. Eigner, Edwin Moss. The Double in the Fiction of R. L. Stevenson. DA, 1963, 24:741-742.

9207. _____. The romantic unity of Melville's Omoo. Philological Q, 1967, 46:95-108.

9208. Eirich, Susan Helen. Lire au féminin: Une Etude du discours féminin dans les romans de Duras, Woolf, et Sarraute. DAI, 1978, 39:1617A.

9209. Eisen, G. S. The suicide of Seymour Glass. <u>Suicide & Life</u>
       <u>Threatening Behavior</u>, 1980, 10:51-60.
9210. Eisinger, Chester. Saul Bellow: love and identity. <u>Accent</u>,
       1958, 18:193-199.
9211. Eisinger, Erica M. Crime and detection in the novels of
       Marguerite Duras. <u>Contemporary Lit</u>, 1974, 15:503-520.
9212. _____. Maigret and women: La mammon and la putain.
       <u>J Popular Culture</u>, 1978, 12:52-60.
9213. Ekfelt, Nils. The Narration of Dreams in the Prose Works
       of Thomas Mann and Arthur Schnitzler. A Stylistic Study.
       <u>DAI</u>, 1974, 34:6637A.
9214. Elberg, Mariam Z. Children as Portrayed by Soviet Prose
       Writers During the Period of the 'Thaw.' <u>DAI</u>, 1972, 33:
       750A.
9215. Elder, Arlene A. The 'Hindered Hand': <u>Cultural Implications</u>
       <u>of Early African-American Fiction</u>. Westport, Conn:
       Greenwood, 1978.
9216. Elkins, Charles. Isaac Asimov's 'Foundation' novels: his-
       torical materialism distorted into cyclical psycho-history.
       <u>Science-fiction Studies</u>, 1976, 3:27-36; In Olander, J. D.,
       & Greenberg, M. H. (eds), <u>Isaac Asimov</u>. NY: Tap-
       linger, 1977, 97-110.
9217. Elkins, William R. The dream world and the dream vision:
       meaning and structure in Poe's art. <u>Emporia State Re-</u>
       <u>search Studies</u>, 1968, 17:5-17.
9218. Ellem, E. W. E. M. Forster's greenwood. <u>J Modern Lit</u>,
       1976, 5:89-98.
9219. Elliott, L. W. , & Kercheville, F. M. Galdós and abnormal
       psychology. <u>Hispania</u>, 1940, 23:27-36.
9220. Elliott, S. James. Homosexuality in the crucial decade:
       three novelists' views. In Crew, L. (ed), <u>The Gay Aca-</u>
       <u>demic</u>. Palm Springs, Cal: ETC, 1978, 164-177.
9221. Ellis, Albert. Sex--the schizoid best seller. <u>Saturday Rev</u>,
       17 Mar 1951, 19.
9222. Ellis, Havelock. Concerning <u>Jude the Obscure</u>. London:
       Ulysses, 1931.
9223. _____. From <u>Rousseau to Proust</u>. Boston: Houghton,
       Mifflin, 1935.
9224. Ellis, James. The world of dreams: sexual symbolism in
       'A White Heron.' <u>Nassau Rev</u>, 1977, 3(3):3-9.
9225. Ellmann, Mary. The Bell Jar: an American girlhood. In
       Newman, C. (ed), <u>The Art of Sylvia Plath: A Symposi-</u>
       <u>um</u>. London: Faber & Faber, 1970, 221-226.
9226. Ellmann, Richard. <u>The Consciousness of Joyce</u>. NY: Ox-
       ford Univ. Press, 1977.
9227. _____. Why Molly Bloom menstruates. In Chace, W. M.
       (ed), <u>Joyce: A Collection of Critical Essays</u>. Englewood
       Cliffs, NJ: Prentice-Hall, 1974, 102-112; <u>New York Rev</u>
       <u>Books</u>, 1972, 18:25-30; In his <u>Ulysses on the Liffey</u>.
       NY: Oxford Univ. Press, 1972, 1973.
9228. Ellwood, Gracia Fay. The good guys and the bad guys.
       <u>Tolkien J</u>, 1969, 3(4):9-11.
9229. El-Meligi, A. Moneim. [Psychoregulation.] <u>Vie médicale</u>
       <u>au Canada français</u>, 1977, 6:199-203.

9230. Elovaara, Raili. The Problem of Identity in Samuel Beckett's Prose. An Approach from Philosophies of Existence. Helsinki: Suomalainen Tiedakatemia, 1976.

9231. Elrich, Gloria Chasson. Guilt and expiation in 'Roger Maloin's Burial. ' Nineteenth Century Fiction, 1972, 26:277-289.

9232. Elwin, M. The psychology of the thriller. Saturday Rev (London), 26 Aug 1933.

9233. Emery, Allan Moore. The alternatives of Melville's 'Bartleby. ' Nineteenth Century Fiction, 1975, 31:170-187.

9234. Emmett, V.J., Jr. Structural irony in D.H. Lawrence's 'The Rocking-Horse Winner. ' Connecticut Rev, 1972, 5(2):5-10.

9235. Emplaincourt, Marilyn. La Femme damnée: A Study of the Lesbian in French Literature from Diderot to Proust. DAI, 1978, 39:2316A.

9236. Empson, William. Alice in Wonderland: the child as swain. In Phillips, W. (ed), Art and Psychoanalysis. Cleveland: World, 1963; In Some Versions of Pastoral. London: Chatto & Windus, 1935; In English Pastoral Poetry. NY: Norton, 1938.

9237. Emrich, Wilhelm. Franz Kafka: A Critical Guide to His Writings. NY: Ungar, 1968 (1958).

9238. Emyr, John. Enaid Clivyfus: Golivg ar waith Kate Roberts. Denbigh, Wales: Gwasg Gee, 1976.

9239. Enderstein, Carl O. Zahnsymbolik und ihre Bedeutung in Günter Grass' Werken. Amsterdamer Beiträge zur älteren Germanistik, 1975, 4:135-155; Monatshefte, 1974, 66:5-18.

9240. Engel, Monroe. Dubliners and erotic expectation. In Brower, R.A. (ed), Twentieth-Century Literature in Retrospect. Cambridge: Harvard Univ. Press, 1971, 3-26.

9241. Engleberg, Edward. James and Arnold: conscience and consciousness in a Victorian 'Künstlerroman. ' Criticism, 1968, 10:93-114.

9242. Englander, Ann. 'The Prussian Officer'; the self divided. Sewanee Rev, 1963, 71:605-619.

9243. Engstrom, Alfred G. The man who thought himself made of glass, and certain related images. Studies in Philology, 1970, 67:390-405.

9244. Eoff, Sherman Hinkle. The formative period of Galdós' social-psychological perspective. Romanic Rev, 1950, 41:33-41.

9245. _____. Galdós in nineteenth-century perspective. Anales Galdosianos, 1966, 1:3-9.

9246. _____. A Galdosian version of picaresque psychology. Modern Language Forum, 1953, 38:5-9.

9247. _____. The Modern Spanish Novel. NY: New York Univ. Press, 1961.

9248. _____. The Novels of Pérez Galdós. St. Louis: Washington Univ. Studies, 1954.

9249. _____. The picaresque psychology of Guzman de Afarache. Hispanic Rev, 1953, 21:107-119.

9250. _____. Review: Joseph Schraibman's Dreams in the Novels of Galdós. Hispanófila, 1962, 5:51-54.

9251. _____. Tragedy of the unwanted person, in three versions: Pablos de Segovia, Pito Perez, Pascual Duarte. Hispania, 1956, 39:191-192.

9252. _____. The treatment of individual personality in Fortunata y Jacinta de Galdós. Hispanic Rev, 1949, 17:269-289.

9253. _____, & Schraibman, José. Dos novelas del absurdo: L'Etranger y Tiempo de Silencio. Papeles de Son Armadans, 1970, 56:213-241.

9254. Epstein, Edmund L. Hidden imagery in James Joyce's 'Two Gallants.' James Joyce Q, 1970, 7:369-370.

9255. _____. The Ordeal of Stephen Dedalus: The Conflict of Generations in James Joyce's 'A Portrait of the Artist as a Young Man.' Carbondale: Southern Illinois Univ. Press, 1971, 1973; DAI, 1971, 31:4766-67.

9256. Erbentrout, Edwin B. A Thousand Deaths: hyperbolic anger. Jack London Newsletter, 1971, 4(3):125-129.

9257. Eremina, L. I. Poètika psixologiceski motivirovanogo slova: Na materiale proizvedenij L. Tolstogo. Voprosy Jazykoznani ja', 1977, 5:97-109.

9258. Ermakov, J. D. Ocherki po analizu tvorchestva n. v. Gogolya. Moscow: 1924.

9259. Ermarth, Elizabeth. Maggie Tulliver's long suicide. Studies in English Lit, 1500-1900, 1974, 14:587-601.

9260. Eschholz, Paul A. Mark Twain and the language of gesture. Mark Twain J, 1973, 17(1):5-8.

9261. Eskin, Stanley G. Tristram Shandy and Oedipus Rex--reflections on comedy and tragedy. College English, 1962, 24: 271-277.

9262. Espiau de la Maëstre, A. Le Thème de la route dans l'oeuvre romanesque de Bernanos. Les Lettres Romanes, 1964, 18(1, 2).

9263. Espinosa, Gabriel. La filosofia imaginativa de Marcel Proust: psicologia estática y psicología dinámica. Revista Nacional de Cultura, 1941, 25:47-62; 26:7-19.

9264. Essex, Ruth. A Study of the Role of the Woman in Thomas Hardy's Novels. DAI, 1977, 37:5845A-46A.

9265. Estes, Nada J., & Madden, Louise P. Alcoholism in fiction: learning from the literature. Nursing Outlook, 1975, 23:517-520.

9266. Estivill Corominas, Laura. Las mujeres en las obras de D. H. Lawrence, Sons and Lovers, The Rainbow y Women in Love. Univ. Barcelona, M. A. Thesis, 1973.

9267. Estoux, Jean L. d'. Notes sur l'homosexualité dans l'oeuvre et l'exégès de Proust. In Hommage à Marcel Proust. Paris: Le Disque Vert, 1952, 105-110.

9268. Estren, Mark James. Horrors Within and Without: A Psychoanalytic Study of Edgar Allan Poe and Howard Phillips Lovecraft. DAI, 1978, 39(3-A), 1565.

9269. Ettedgui, Armand Samuel. Kafka ou le sens d'un échec. Rev Française de Psychanalyse, 1963, 27:675-682.

9270. Euzière, J. En Marge de Balzac: le mortsaufisme. Annales Médico-Psychologiques, Nov 1959.

9271. Evans, Henri. Balzac, the social pathologist. The Nineteenth Century, 1948, 144:343-354.
9272. Evans, Martha Noel. The dream sequence in Senancour's Oberman. Symposium, 1978, 32:1-14.
9273. Evans, Oliver. Anaïs Nin. Carbondale: Southern Illinois Univ. Press, 1968.
9274. _____. James' air of evil: 'The Turn of the Screw.' Partisan Rev, 1949, 16:175-187.
9275. _____. Allegory and incest in 'Rappaccini's Daughter.' Nineteenth Century Fiction, 1964, 19:185-195.
9276. Evans, Patrick. Alienation and the imagery of death: the novels of Janet Frame. Meanjin Q, 1973, 32:294-303.
9277. Evans, Robert O. Existentialism in Greene's The Quiet American. Modern Fiction Studies, 1957, 3:241-248.
9278. Evans, Timothy. Boiling the archetypal pot: Norman Mailer's American Dream. Southwest Rev, 1975, 60:159-170.
9279. Ewald, Robert James. The Jungian Archetype of the Fairy Mistress in Medieval Romance. DAI, 1978, 38:5451A.
9280. Ewbank, David R. The Role of Woman in Victorian Society: A Controversy Explored in Six Utopias, 1871-1895. DAI, 1909, 30:318A.
9281. Ewton, Ralph W., Jr. Childhood without end: Tieck's Der blonde Eckert. German Q, 1973, 46, 3.
9282. Eyzaguirre, Luis B. Patologia en La vorágine de José Eustasio Rivera. Hispania, 1973, 56:81-90.
9283. Ezergailis, Inta Miske. Günter Grass's 'fearful symmetry': dialectic, mock and real, in Katz und Maus and Die Blechtrommel. Texas Studies in Lit & Language, 1974, 16:221-235.
9284. _____. Male and Female: An Approach to Thomas Mann's Dialectic. The Hague: Nijhoff, 1975.

9285. Faber, M. D. Faulkner's The Sound and the Fury: object relations and narrative structure. Amer Imago, 1977, 24:327-350.
9286. _____. An important theme of Joyce Cary's trilogy. Discourse, 1968.
9287. _____. The painted breast: a psychological study of Melville's Pierre. Psychoanal Rev, 1979-80, 66:519-552.
9288. _____. The suicide of young Werther. Psychoanal Rev, 1973, 60:239-276.
9289. Fabre, Michel. Père et fils dans Go Tell It on the Mountain. Etudes Anglaises, 1970, 23:47-61.
9290. Faderman, Lillian. Female same-sex relationships in novels by Longfellow, Holmes, and James. New England Q, 1978, 51:309-332.
9291. _____. Lesbian magazine fiction in the early twentieth century. J Popular Culture, 1978, 11:800-817.
9292. Fagard-Hornschuh, Mechthild, & Fagard, Georges. La Nid vide: La Problématique consciente et inconsciente de Kafka. Paris: A.C.A.A., 1974.
9293. Fagin, N. B. Herman Melville and the interior monologue. Amer Lit, 1935, 6:433-434.

9294. Faguet, E. Romans psychologiques. Rev de deux Mondes, 1912, 9:906-915.

9295. Fainburg, Z. I. [Contemporary society and science fiction.] Voprosy Filosofii, 1967, 21(6):32-43.

9296. Fairbanks, Henry G. The Lasting Loneliness of Nathaniel Hawthorne: A Study of the Sources of Alienation in Modern Man. Albany, NY: Magi, 1965.

9297. Fairlie, Alison. Sentiments et sensations chez Flaubert. Cahiers de l'Association Internationale des Etudes Françaises, 1974, 26:233-249.

9298. Falconer, G. F. Assassin de Charles. In Issacharoff, M. (ed), Langages de Flaubert. Paris: Lettres Modernes-Minard, 1976, 115-141.

9299. Falk, Doris V. Poe and the power of animal magnetism. PMLA, 1969, 84:536-546.

9300. Falkenberg, Sandra. A study of female characterization in Steinbeck's fiction. Steinbeck Q, 1975, 8:50-55.

9301. Farago, V. A novel about the psychology of a revolution. New Hungarian Q, 1966, 7:76-77.

9302. Farber, Marjorie. Subjectivity in modern fiction. Kenyon Rev, 1945, 7:645-652.

9303. Farley, Pamella. Form and Function: The Image of Woman in Selected Works of Hemingway and Fitzgerald. DAI, 1974, 35:3735A.

9304. Farnell, Fred J. Eroticism as portrayed in literature. Int J Psycho-Anal, 1920, 1:396-413; In Ruitenbeek, H. M. (ed), Homosexuality and Creative Genius. NY: Astor-Honor, 1967.

9305. Farouk, Marion O. Mandeville, a Tale of the Seventeenth Century: historical novel or psychological study? In Lingner, E. et al. (eds), Essays in Honour of William Gallacher. Berlin: Humboldt Univ. Press, 1966, 111-117.

9306. Farrar, John. Sex psychology in modern fiction. Independent, 1926, 107:669-670.

9307. Farrell, Frederick, Jr., & Farrell, Edith R. The multiple murders of Thérèsa Desqueyroux. Hartford Studies in Lit, 1970, 2:195-206.

9308. Fasciati, F. Somnolence et réveil chez Andrew Gide. Cahiers de l'Association Internationale des Etudes Françaises, 1973, 25:269-283.

9309. Fassler, Joan. Children's literature and early childhood separation experiences. Young Children, 1974, 29:311-323.

9310. Fauchery, P. La Destinée féminine dans le roman européen du 18e siècle. Paris: Colin, 1972.

9311. Feal Deibe, Carlos. Oda a Salamanca. Hispanic Rev, 1971, 39:395-414.

9312. _____. Unamuno: 'El otro' y Don Juan. Madrid: Cupsa, 1976.

9313. Feaster, John. Faulkner's 'Old Man': a psychoanalytic approach. Modern Fiction Studies, 1967, 13:89-93.

9314. Feeney, Mary E. Women in the Major Fiction of George Eliot. DAI, 1974, 35:446A.

9315. Feeny, Thomas. Maternal-paternal attitudes in the fiction of Ramón Pérez de Ayala. Hispanofila, 1978, 62:77-85.

9316. _____. The Paternal Element in the Works of R. Perez de Ayala. DA, 1969, 29:4483-A.

9317. Feidelson, Charles F. Hawthorne's Scarlet Letter: a study of the meaning of meaning. Southern Humanities Rev, 1975, 9:145-157.

9318. Feinstein, Herbert. Two pairs of gloves: Mark Twain and Henry James. Amer Imago, 17:349-387.

9319. Feldman, A. Bronson. Dostoevsky and father-love exemplified by Crime and Punishment. Psychoanal Rev, 1958, 45:84-98.

9320. _____. James Joyce's 'A Painful Case' (1905). Psychoanalysis, 1957, 5:3-12.

9321. _____. A moral reformer damaged in the making. Samiksa, 1957, 11:86-92.

9322. _____. Zola and the riddle of sadism. Amer Imago, 1956, 13:415-425; In Ruitenbeek, H.M. (ed), Psychoanalysis and Literature. NY: Dutton, 1964, 272-281.

9323. Fell, Joseph P. Emotion in the Thought of Sartre. NY: Columbia Univ. Press, 1965.

9324. Felman, Shoshana. Aurélia ou 'le livre infaisable': De Foucault à Nerval. Romantisme, 1972, 3:43-55.

9325. _____. Folie et discours chez Balzac: L'Illustre Gaudissart. Littérature, 1972, No. 5, 34-44.

9326. _____. Turning the screw of interpretation. Yale French Studies, 1977, 55-56:94-207.

9327. _____. Women and madness: the critical phallacy. Diacritics, 1975, 5(4):2-10.

9328. Felstiner, John. A feminist reading of Neruda. Parnassus, 1975, 3(2):90-112.

9329. Feltman, Irene E. Study of Fiction as Source Material in Vocational Guidance. DA, 1954, 4:795.

9330. Fenichel, Robert R. A portrait of the artist as a young orphan. Lit & Psychol, 1959, 9:19-22.

9331. Fennimore, Flora. Developing the adolescent's self-concept with literature: The Loner by E. Wier. English J, 1970, 59:1272-1275+.

9332. Ferenczi, Sándor. Anatole France als Analytiker. Int Zeitschrift für Psychoanalyse, 1911, 1:461-467; Almanach, 1929, 177-186; Populäre Vorträge über Psycho-analyse, 159-168.

9333. _____. Gulliver phantasies. Int J Psycho-Anal, 1928, 9:283-300; Int Zeitschrift für Psychoanalyse, 1927, 13:379-396.

9334. _____. Mereschkovsky's Peter der Grosse und Alexei. In Contributions to Psycho-Analysis. NY: Dover, 1958, 66-67.

9335. Ferguson, Jane. Symbolic patterns in Call It Sleep. Twentieth Century Lit, 1969, 14:211-220.

9336. Ferguson, J.M., Jr. Hawthorne's 'Young Goodman Brown.' Explicator, 1969, 28:4.

9337. Ferguson, L.W. The evaluative attitudes of Jonathan Swift. Psychol Record, 1939, 3:26-44.

9338. Ferguson, M. Review: J. Armstrong's Novel of Adultery.
Victorian Studies, 1978, 21:280-282.
9339. Fernandez, Ronald. Dostoyevsky, traditional domination, and
cognitive dissonance. Social Forces, 1970, 49:299-303.
9340. _____ (ed). Social Psychology Through Literature. NY:
Wiley, 1972.
9341. Fernández de la Torriente, G. La novela de Hernández
Catá: un estudio desde la psicología. Madrid: Playor,
1976.
9342. Ferrer Bravo, Mariano. Sintomas de la patología mental que
se hallan en las obras literarias de Benito Pérez Galdós.
Barcelona: Instituto Mental de Santa Cruz, 1923.
9343. Fertig, Goldie M. The Treatment of Adolescence in Contemporary American Literature. Master's thesis, Univ.
Louisville, 1942.
9344. Feshbach, Sidney. A slow and dark birth: a study of the organization of A Portrait of the Artist as a Young Man.
James Joyce Q, 1966, 4:289-300.
9345. Festa-McCormick, Diana. Tchen and the temptation of the
flesh. Twentieth Century Lit, 1978, 24:314-323.
9346. Fetterley, Judith. A Farewell to Arms: Ernest Hemingway's
'resentful cryptogram.' In Diamond, A., & Edwards,
L. R. (eds), The Authority of Experience. Essays in
Feminist Criticism. Amherst: Univ. Massachusetts
Press, 1977, 257-273.
9347. _____. 'The Temptation to Be a Beautiful Object': double
standard and double bind in The House of Mirth. Studies
Amer Fiction, 1977, 5:199-211.
9348. Feuerlicht, Ignace. Rolle, Dienst und Opfer bei Thomas
Mann. PMLA, 1962, 77:318-327.
9349. Fialkowski, Barbara. Psychic distances in A Curtain of
Green: artistic successes and personal failures. In
Desmond, J. F. (ed), A Still Moment: Essays on the Art
of Eudora Welty. Metuchen, NJ: Scarecrow, 1978, 63-
70.
9350. Fickert, Kurt J. The Doppelgänger motif in Kafka's Blum-
feld. J Modern Lit, 1977, 6:419-423.
9351. _____. Fatal knowledge: Kafka's Ein Landarzt. Monatshefte, 1974, 66:381-386.
9352. _____. Hermann Hesse's Quest: The Evolution of the
Dichter Figure in His Work. Fredericton, N. B.: York,
1978.
9353. _____. The portrait of the artist in Hesse's 'Klein und
Wagner.' Hartford Studies in Lit, 1974, 6:180-187.
9354. Fiderer, Gerald. D. H. Lawrence's The Man Who Died.
The phallic Christ. Amer Imago, 1968, 25:91-96.
9355. _____. Masochism as literary strategy: Orwell's psychological novels. Lit & Psychol, 1970, 20:3-21.
9356. _____. A Psychoanalytic Study of the Novels of George
Orwell. DAI, 1967, 28:1074A-75A.
9357. Fiedler, Leslie A. Adolescence and maturity in the American
novel. In An End to Innocence. Boston: Beacon, 1955,
191-210.

9358. _____. Bloom or Joyce; or Jokey for Jacob. J Modern Lit, 1970, 1:19-29.

9359. _____. Boys will be boys! New Leader, 1958, 41:23-26.

9360. _____. The breakthrough: the American Jewish novelist and the fictional image of the Jew. Midstream, 1958, 4:15-35.

9361. _____. The Collected Essays of Leslie Fiedler. 2 Vols. NY: Stein & Day, 1971.

9362. _____. Come back to the raft ag'in Huck, honey. Partisan Review, 1948, 16:664-671; In The Collected Essays of Leslie Fiedler, Vol. 1. NY: Stein & Day, 1971; In An End to Innocence. Boston: Beacon, 1955, 142-151; In Scott, W. S. (ed), Five Approaches of Literary Criticism. NY: Macmillan, 1962, 303-312; In Malin, I. (ed), Psychoanalysis and American Fiction, NY: Dutton, 1965, 121-129.

9363. _____. Edgar Allan Poe and the invention of the American writer. Chicago Rev, 1959, 13:80-86.

9364. _____. The failure of love in American fiction. Bulletin Philadelphia Assn Psychoanal, 1956, 6:61-71.

9365. _____. Good good girl and good bad boy. New Leader, 1958, 41:22-25.

9366. _____. The higher sentimentality. In The Return of the Vanishing American. NY: Stein & Day, 1968; In Pratt, J. C. (ed), Ken Kesey, One Flew Over the Cuckoo's Nest, Text and Criticism. NY: Penguin, 1977, 372-381.

9367. _____. Introduction to R. Meister (ed), A Literary Guide to Seduction. NY: Stein & Day, 1963, 9-14.

9368. _____. The invention of the child. New Leader, 1958, 41:22-24.

9369. _____. Love and Death in the American Novel. NY: Stein & Day, 1957, 1966; NY: Criterion, 1960; London: Cape, 1967; NY: Delta, 1967; NY: Dell, 1969; London: Paladin, 1970.

9370. _____. Love and death in the American novel. Commentary, 1960, 29:439-447.

9371. _____. No! In Thunder. NY: Stein & Day, 1972.

9372. _____. Philip Jose Farmer's fiction. Caliban, 1975, 12: 61-64.

9373. _____. The Return of the Vanishing American. NY: Stein & Day, 1968.

9374. _____. Second thoughts on Love and Death in the American Novel: my first Gothic novel. Novel: A Forum on Fiction, 1967, 8-11.

9375. _____. Some notes on F. Scott Fitzgerald. In An End to Innocence. Boston: Beacon, 1955, 174-182; In Mizener, A. (ed), F. Scott Fitzgerald: A Collection of Critical Essays. NY: Norton, 1963.

9376. Field, Andrew. Nabokov: His Life in Art. Boston: Little, Brown, 1967.

9377. Field, L. M. Mothers in fiction. North Amer Rev, 1934, 237:250-256.

9378.   Field, Trevor. The literary significance of dreams in the
        novels of Julien Green. Modern Language Rev, 1980,
        75:291-300.
9379.   Fielding, Kenneth Joshua. Charles Dickens: A Critical In-
        troduction. Boston: Houghton Mifflin; NY: British Book
        Centre, 1979.
9380.   Figuiere, J. L'Epilepsie dans l'oeuvre de Dostoievsky.
        Thèse, Lyon, 1924.
9381.   Filer, M. Las transformaciones del yo en la obra de Julio
        Cortázar. Cuadernos Hispano-Americanos, 1970, 242:
        320-334.
9382.   Filteau, C. Le Burlesque 'aristocratique' dans Les Memoires
        du comte de Gramont d'Antoine Hamilton. XVIIe Siècle,
        1976, 110-111.
9383.   Fine, Ronald Edward. Lockwood's dreams and the key to
        Wuthering Heights. Nineteenth Century Fiction, 1969,
        24:16-30.
9384.   _____. Melville and the Rhetoric of Psychological Fic-
        tion. DA, 1966, 27:1364A.
9385.   Finholt, Richard David. American Visionary Fiction: Mad
        Metaphysics as Salvation Psychology. Port Washington,
        NY: Kennikat, 1978; DAI, 1976, 36:7420A.
9386.   Fink, Gonthier-Louis. Théologie, psychologie et sociologie
        du crime. Le conte moral de Schubert à Schiller. Re-
        cherches Germaniques, 1976, 6:55-111.
9387.   Finklestein, Bonnie B. Forster's Women--Eternal Differ-
        ences. NY: Columbia Univ. Press, 1975.
9388.   _____. Forster's women: A Room with a View. English
        Lit in Transition (1880-1920), 1973, 16:275-287.
9389.   _____. The Role of Women in the Novels of E. M. For-
        ster with Parallels to the Role of Homosexuals in
        Maurice. DAI, 1972, 33:2931A.
9390.   Finkelstein, Sidney Walter. Existentialism and Alienation in
        American Literature. NY: International, 1965; London:
        Central, 1965.
9391.   Finney, Frank F. A Critical Examination of the Transition
        from a Psychological Vision of Life to an Increasingly
        Christian Awareness of Evil in the Fiction of Thomas
        Wolfe. Doctoral dissertation, Univ. Oklahoma, 1961.
9392.   Fischer, Emeric. Le Monologue intérieur dans l'Ulysses de
        James Joyce. Rev Française, 1933, 28:445-453.
9393.   Fischer, Steven R. The Dream in the Middle High German
        Epic: Introduction to the Study of the Dream as a Literary
        Device to the Younger Contemporaries of Gottfried and
        Wolfram. Bern: Lang, 1978.
9394.   Fischer, William C., Jr. The Representation of Mental Pro-
        cession in the Early Fiction of William Dean Howells and
        Henry James. DAI, 1968, 28:4597A-98A.
9395.   Fiser, E. La Théorie du symbole littéraire de Marcel
        Proust. Paris: Corti, 1941.
9396.   Fishburn, Katherine. The nightmare repetition: the mother-
        daughter conflict in Doris Lessing's Children of Violence.

In Davidson, C. N. , & Broner, E. M. (eds), The Lost Tradition. NY: Ungar, 1980, 207-216.

9397. _____. Richard Wright's Hero: The Faces of a Rebel-Victim. Metuchen, NJ: Scarecrow, 1977.

9398. Fisher, K. A. Psychoanalysis: a dialogue. Psychoanalysis, 1953, 1:17-30.

9399. Fisher, Marvin. 'Bartleby, ' Melville's circumscribed scrivener. Southern Rev, 1974, 10:59-79.

9400. _____. Focus on Herman Melville's 'The Two Temples': the denigration of the American dream. In Madden, D. (ed), American Dreams, American Nightmares. Carbondale: Southern Illinois Univ. Press, 1970, 76-86.

9401. Fitch, Brian T. Aesthetic distance and inner space in the novels of Camus. Modern Fiction Studies, 1964, 10:279-292.

9402. _____. La Chute. In Gay-Crosier, R. (ed), Camus 1970. Quebec: Univ. Sherbrook, 1970.

9403. _____. Le Sentiment de l'aliénation dans le roman français entre 1930 et 1943, étude d'aliénation ontologique. Thèse, Univ. Strasbourg, 1962.

9404. Fitch, Robert E. La Mystique de la merde. New Republic, 1956, 135(10):17-18.

9405. Fitz, Reginald. The meaning of impotence in Hemingway and Eliot. Connecticut Rev, 1971, 4(2):16-22.

9406. Flanagan, John T. The fiction of Jessamyn West. Indiana Magazine of History, 1971, 67:299-316.

9407. Fleishman, Avram. Conrad's last novel. English Lit in Transition, 1880-1920, 1968, 12:189-194.

9408. _____. A Reading of Mansfield Park. An Essay in Critical Synthesis. Minneapolis: Univ. Minnesota Press, 1967.

9409. _____. The fictions of autobiographical fiction. Genre, 1976, 9:73-86.

9410. Fleming, Patricia J. The Integrated Self: Sexuality and the Double in Willa Cather's Fiction. DAI, 1974, 35:1653A.

9411. Fleming, Robert E. The nightmare level of The Man Who Cried I Am. Contemporary Lit, 1973, 14:186-196.

9412. Flesch-Brunningen, H. James Joyce and medicine. Ciba Symposium, 1961, 9:196-199.

9413. _____. Katherine Mansfield. Ciba Symposium, 1963, 11:129-133.

9414. Flescher, Jacqueline. The language of nonsense in Alice. Yale French Studies, 1969, 43:128-144.

9415. Fletcher, D. J. The use of colour in La Nausée. Modern Language Rev, 1968, 63:371-380.

9416. Fletcher, John. Molloy. In Friedman, M. (ed), Samuel Beckett Now: Critical Approaches to His Novels, Poetry and Plays. Chicago: Chicago Univ. Press, 1970.

9417. _____. Interpreting L'Etranger. French Rev, 1970, 43:158-167.

9418. _____. The themes of alienation and mutual incomprehension in the novels of Uwe Johnson. Int Fiction Rev, 1974, 1:81-87.

9419.   Fletcher, Marie. The fate of women in a changing South: a
        persistent theme in the fiction of Charlotte Gordon. Mis-
        sissippi Q, 1968, 21:17-28.
9420.   Fletcher, Robert Pearson. The Convention of the Double-
        Self in Nineteenth-Century English Fiction. DAI, 1976,
        37:2195A.
9421.   Flint, Allen. The saving grace of marriage in Hawthorne's
        fiction. Emerson Society Q, 1973, 19:112-116.
9422.   Flora, C. B. The passive female: her comparative image by
        class and culture in woman's magazine fiction. J Mar-
        riage & Family, 1971, 33:435-444.
9423.   Flora, Joseph M. Jacob Barnes' name: the other side of the
        ledger. English Rev, 1973, 24:14-15.
9424.   Florance, Edna C. The neurosis of Raskolnikov: a study of
        incest and murder. In Wasiolek, E. (ed), Crime and
        Punishment and the Critics. Belmont: Wadsworth, 1961,
        57-77; Archives Criminal Psychodynamics, 1955, 1:344-
        396.
9425.   Flores, Angel (ed). The Kafka Problem. NY: New Direc-
        tions, 1946.
9426.   Flower, J. A psycho-critical approach to Mauriac's Genitrix.
        In Various, Literature and Society. Studies in Nineteenth
        and Twentieth Century French Literature. Birmingham,
        Engl: Univ. Birmingham Press, 1980.
9427.   Floyd, Nathaniel M. Billy Budd: a psychological autopsy.
        Amer Imago, 1977, 34:28-49.
9428.   Flugel, J. C. Maurice Bedel's Jerome: a study of contrast-
        ing types. Psychoanal Q, 1932, 1:653-682.
9429.   Fogg, Sarah. The function of split personality in Chrétien's
        Yvain. In Zayas-Bazán, E., & Suárez, M. I. (eds), The
        27th Annual Mountain Interstate Foreign Language Confer-
        ence. Johnson City, Tenn: East Tennessee State Univ.,
        1978, 114-121.
9430.   Fontana, Ernest L. Sexual alienation in George Moore's
        'Albert Nobbs.' Int Fiction Rev, 1977, 4:183-185.
9431.   Foote, F. G. Thérapeutique de la haine. Preuves, 1965,
        No. 167, 70-73.
9432.   Ford, Jane M. The Father/Daughter/Suitor Triangle in
        Shakespeare, Dickens, James, Conrad, and Joyce. DAI,
        1976, 36:4507A.
9433.   Ford, William J. A note on Hans Castorp. Lit & Psychol,
        2(4):2-5.
9434.   Forno, Lawrence J. Challe's portrayal of women. French
        Rev, 1974, 47:865-873.
9435.   Forrey, Robert. Herman Melville and the Negro question.
        Mainstream, 1962, 15:28-29.
9436.   _____. Ken Kesey's psychopathic savior: a rejoinder.
        Modern Fiction Studies, 1975, 21:222-230.
9437.   _____. Labor's lost love. Jack London Newsletter, 1977,
        10:48-51.
9438.   _____. Male and female in London's The Sea-Wolf. Lit
        & Pscyhol, 1974, 24:135-143.
9439.   _____. Negroes in the fiction of F. Scott Fitzgerald.
        Phylon, 1967, 28:293-298.

9440. _____. Theodore Dreiser: Oedipus redivivus. <u>Modern Fiction Studies</u>, 1977, 23:341-354.

9441. _____. Three modes of sexuality in London's <u>The Little Lady of the Big House</u>. Lit & Psychol, 1976, 26:52-60.

9442. Forster, E. M. <u>Aspects of the Novel</u>. NY: Harcourt, Brace, 1927; NY: Harvest Books, 1959.

9443. Fortassier, Rose. <u>Les Mondains de 'La comédie humaine':</u> <u>Etude historique et psychologique.</u> Paris: Klincksieck, 1974.

9444. Fortunati, Vita. Una fenomenologia dell' omosessuialità: <u>The Life to Come</u> di E. M. Forster. <u>Lettore di Provincia,</u> 1976, 26:102-116.

9445. Fossum, Robert H. Poe's 'The Cask of Amontillado.' <u>Explicator</u>, 1958, 4, No. 18.

9446. _____. The summons of the past: Hawthorne's <u>Alice Doane's Appeal</u>. <u>Nineteenth Century Fiction</u>, 1968, 23:294-303.

9447. Foster, David William. Robert Arlt and the neurotic rationale. In <u>Currents in the Contemporary Argentine Novel: Arlt, Mallea, Sabato, and Cortázar</u>. Columbia: Univ. Missouri Press, 1975, 20-45.

9448. Foster, Jeannette H. An approach to fiction through the characteristics of its readers. <u>Library Q</u>, 1936, 6:124-174.

9449. _____. <u>Sex Variant Women in Literature</u>. NY: Vantage, 1956; London: Muller, 1958.

9450. Foster, John W. Separation and Return in the Fiction of Brian Moore, Michael McLaverty, and Benedict Kiely. <u>DAI,</u> 1971, 31:5399A.

9451. Foster, Ruel E. Dream as symbolic act in Faulkner. <u>Perspective</u>, 1949, 2:179-194.

9452-3. _____. <u>The Influence of Freud on the Autobiographical Novel</u>. Doctoral dissertation, Vanderbilt Univ., 1941.

9454. Foulds, G. The child's response to fictional characters and its relationship to personality traits. <u>Character & Personality</u>, 1942, 11:64-75.

9455. Fouliquié, P. Psychisme et totalité: un thème des psychologiques contemporains, illustré par une page de Saint-Exupéry. <u>L'Ecole</u>, 14 Dec 1953.

9456. Foulkes, A. P. Dream pictures in Kafka's writings. <u>Germanic Rev</u>, 1965, 40:17-30.

9457. _____. Kafka's cage image. <u>Modern Language Notes,</u> 1967, 82:462-471.

9458. Fournier, Yvonne. <u>La Psychologie du mariage chez quelques écrivains français de 1920 à 1935</u>. Thèse, Univ. Lille, 1964.

9459. Fowler, Lois J. <u>Diana of the Crossways</u>: a prophecy for feminism. In Baim, J., <u>et al.</u> (eds), <u>In Honor of Austin Wright</u>. Pittsburgh: Carnegie-Mellon Univ. Press, 1972, 30-36.

9460. Fox, Marcia Rose. The Woman Question in Selected Victorian Fiction, 1883-1900. <u>DAI</u>, 1975, 36:1495A-96A.

9461. Fox, W. H. The problem of guilt in Werfel's night <u>der Morder</u>. <u>German Life & Letters,</u> 1957, 11:25-33.

9462. Foxe, Arthur N. Poe as hypnotist. Psychoanal Rev, 1941, 28:520-525.

9463. Fox-Genovese, Elizabeth. Ambiguities of female identity: a reading of the novels of Margaret Drabble. Partisan Rev, 1979, 46:234-248.

9464. _____. Kate Chopin's awakening. Southern Studies, 1979, 18:261-290.

9465. Fradin, Joseph. Will and society in Bleak House. PMLA, 1966, 81:95-109.

9466. Fraiberg, Louis B. Durrell's dissonant quartet. In Shapiro, C. (ed), Contemporary British Novelists. Carbondale: Southern Illinois Univ. Press, 1965, 16-35.

9467. _____. The unattainable self: D. H. Lawrence's Sons and Lovers. In Shapiro, C. (ed), Twelve Original Essays on Great English Novels. Detroit: Wayne State Univ. Press, 1960, 175-201.

9468. Fraiberg, Selma. Kafka and the dream. Partisan Rev, 1956, 23:47-69. In Phillips, W. (ed), Art and Psychoanalysis. NY: Criterion, 1957, 21-53.

9469. _____. Two modern incest heroes. Partisan Rev, 1961, 28:651-661.

9470. _____. Tales of the discovery of the secret treasure. In The Psychoanalytic Study of the Child, Vol. 9. NY: IUP, 1954, 218-241.

9471. Francis, C. J. Gissing's characterization: Part III, temperament. Gissing Newsletter, 1967, 3:1-6.

9472. Francone, Carol Burr. Women in Rebellion: A Study of the Conflict Between Self-Fulfillment and Self-Sacrifice in Emma, Jane Eyre, and The Mill on the Floss. DAI, 1976, 36:4507A.

9473- Frank, Joseph. Dostoevsky: The House of the Dead.
4. Sewanee Rev, 1966, 74:779-803.

9475. _____. The masks of Stavrogin. Sewanee Rev, 1969, 77: 660-669.

9476. _____. The world of Raskolnikov. Encounter, 1967, 26: 30-35.

9477. Frank, Lawrence. Dickens' A Tale of Two Cities: the poetics of impasse. Amer Imago, 1979, 36:215-245.

9478. _____. The intelligibility of madness in Our Mutual Friend, and The Mystery of Edwin Drood. Dickens Study Annual, 1976, 5:150-195.

9479. Frank, Max. Die Farb- und Lichtsymbolik im Prosawerk Herman Melvilles. Heidelberg: Winter, 1967.

9480. Frank, Rachel. Unamuno: existentialism and the Spanish novel. Accent, 1949, 9:80-88.

9481. Franke-Heilbronn, E. Das Ende des psychologischen Romans der burgerlischen Dekadenz: James Joyce und die Aufgaben der jungen deutschen Epic. Geist der Zeit, 1938, 16:156-165.

9482. Franklin, A. W. Leontine Young and Tess of the d'Urbervilles--some thoughts on illegitimacy. British Medical J, 1966, 5490:789-799.

9483. Franklin, B. N. 'My Kinsman, Major Molineux': an inter-
       pretation. Univ. Kansas City Rev, 1955, 21:203-212.
9484. Franklin, H. Bruce. Future Perfect: American Science Fic-
       tion of the Nineteenth Century. NY: Oxford Univ. Press,
       1966.
9485. _____. Redburn's wicked end. Nineteenth Century Fic-
       tion, 1965, 20:190-194.
9486. Franklin, Phyllis. The influence of William James on Robert
       Herrick's early fiction. Amer Lit Realism, 1974, 7:395-
       402.
9487. Franklin, Rosemary. Animal magnetism in As I Lay Dying.
       Amer Q, 1966, 18:24-34.
9488. Franklin, Rosemary F. The cabin by the lake: pastoral land-
       scapes of Poe, Cooper, Hawthorne, and Thoreau. Emer-
       son Society Q, 1976, 22:59-70.
9489. Franzosa, John C., Jr. Darwin and Melville: why a tor-
       toise? Amer Imago, 1976, 33:361-380.
9490. Frappier-Mazur, Lucienne. Balzac et l'androgyne. L'Année
       Balzacienne, 1973, 253-277.
9491. _____. Balzac and the sex of genius. Renascence, 1974,
       27:23-30.
9492. _____. Le Patriarcat. In L'Expression métaphorique
       dans 'La Comédie humaine.' Paris: Klincksieck, 1976.
9493. Fraser, George Sutherland. Lawrence Durrell. A Critical
       Study. NY: Dutton, 1968.
9494. Fraser, Howard M. El universo psicodélico de Sangre pa-
       tricia. Hispanófila, 1974, 50:9-18.
9495. Fraser, Morris. The Death of Narcissus. London: Secker
       & Warburg, 1976.
9496. Frasure, Dorothy Ellen Manning. The Function of Women
       and the Theme of Love in the Novels of Georges Bernanos.
       DAI, 1976, 37(6):3671-A.
9497. Freedman, Burrill. Italo Svevo; a psychoanalytic novelist.
       Psychoanal Rev, 1931, 18:434-438.
9498. Freedman, Ralph. Romantic imagination: Hermann Hesse as
       a modern novelist. PMLA, 1958, 73:275-284.
9499. Freedman, Richard. The Conflict of the Generations in Eng-
       lish Autobiographical Fiction. DA, 1967, 67-12, 610.
9500. _____. Sufficiently decayed: gerontophobia in English lit-
       erature. In Spicker, S. F., Woodward, K. M., & Van
       Tassel, D. D. (eds), Aging and the Elderly. Atlantic High-
       lands, NJ: Humanities Press, 1978, 49-61.
9501. Freedman, William. A conversation with Henry Roth. Lit
       Rev, 1975, 18:149-157.
9502. Freel, Rugene L. A Comparative Study Between Certain Con-
       cepts and Principles of Modern Psychology and the Main
       Writings of John Steinbeck. Microfilm Abstracts, 1947,
       7:124-126.
9503. Freeman, Alma Susan. The Androgynous Ideal: A Study of
       Selected Novels by D. H. Lawrence, James Joyce, and
       Virginia Woolf. DAI, 1975, 36:877A-8A.
9504. Freemon, F. R. The Utopian medicine of H. G. Wells.
       JAMA, 1970, 212:101-102.

9505.   Freese, Peter.   Das Motiv des Doppelgängers in Truman
        Capotes 'Shut a Final Door' und E. A. Poes 'William
        Wilson.' Literatur in Wissenschaft und Unterricht, 1968,
        1:40-48.
9506.   _____. Verweisende Zeichen in William Goldings Lord of
        the Flies. Neueren Sprachen, 1972, 21:160-172.
9507.   Frémon, Jean.   L'Exhibitionnisme et sa pudeur L'Arc: Ca-
        hiers Méditerranéens, 1977, 68:41-50.
9508.   Freud, Sigmund.   The compulsion of guilt.   In Standard Edi-
        tion.   London: Hogarth; In Smith, R. W. (ed), Guilt:
        Man and Society.   Garden City, NY: Doubleday Anchor,
        1971, 63-83.
9509.   _____. Delusion and Dreams in Wilhelm Jensen's 'Gradi-
        va.' Boston: Beacon, 1956, 25-133; London: Allen &
        Unwin, 1921; In Standard Edition, Vol. 9.   London: Ho-
        garth, 1959, 3-95 (1907); Paris: Gallimard, 1931, 1949;
        Tokyo: Logos, 1929.
9510.   _____. The Interpretation of Dreams.   NY: Basic Books,
        1958, 215, 285-289, 326-327, 453-455, 469-470, 491, 535.
9511.   _____. The 'uncanny.' In Collected Papers, Vol. 4.
        NY: Basic Books, 1959, 368-407; In Standard Edition,
        Vol. 17.   London: Hogarth, 1957, 218-252 (1919).
9512.   Frey, Eugen.   Das menschlishe Gewissen nach F. M. Dosto-
        jewski und C. von Monalow und im Lichte der tiefenpsy-
        chologischen Forschung.   Schweizer Archiv für Neuro-
        logie und Psychiatrie, 1946, 57:236-269.
9513.   Fried, Lewis.   The golden brotherhood of McTeague.   Zeit-
        schrift für Anglistik und Amerikanistik, 1975, 23:36-40.
9514.   Friedman, Alan.   The stream of consciousness as a form in
        fiction.   Hudson Rev, 1964-65, 17:536-546.
9515.   Friedman, Allen W.   A 'key' to Lawrence Durrell.   Wiscon-
        sin Studies in Contemporary Lit, 1967, 8:31-42.
9516.   _____. Place and Durrell's island books.   Modern Fiction
        Studies, 1967, 13:329-341.
9517.   Friedman, Eva M.   The generation gap a century ago: the
        father-son conflict in Theodor Storm's Novellen.   Univ.
        Dayton Rev, 1974, 11(2):65-77.
9518.   Friedman, Henry J.   The masochistic character in the work
        of Edith Wharton.   Seminars in Psychiat, 1973, 5:313-
        329.
9519.   Friedman, Lawrence J.   From Gradiva to the death instinct.
        In Lindon, J. A. (ed), The Psychoanalytic Forum, Vol. 1.
        NY: IUP, 1972, 46-63.
9520.   Friedman, Maurice.   The problematic of guilt and the dialogue
        with the absurd: images of the irrational in Kafka's
        Trial.   Rev Existential Psychol & Psychiat, 1975-76, 14:
        11-25.
9521.   Friedman, Melvin J.   Jewish mothers and sons: the expense
        of chutzpah.   In Malin, I. , (ed), Contemporary American-
        Jewish Literature, Critical Essays.   Bloomington: Indi-
        ana Univ. Press, 1973, 156-174.
9522.   _____. Le Monologue intérieur dans As I Lay Dying.
        Rev des Lettres Modernes, 1959, 50-42, 331-344.

9523. _____. The schlemiel: Jew and non-Jew. Studies in Lit
Imagination, 1976, 9(1):139-153.

9524. _____. Stream of consciousness in The Portrait. In Col-
lingwood, F. (ed), Portrait: Notes. Toronto: Coles
Notes, 1970; In Morris, W. E. , & Nault, C. A. (eds),
Portraits of an Artist: A Casebook on James Joyce's A
Portrait. NY: Odyssey, 1962, 228-232; Reprinted from
Friedman's Stream of Consciousness: A Study of Literary
Method. New Haven: Yale Univ. Press, 1955, 210-243.

9525. _____. Stream of Consciousness: A Study in Literary
Method. New Haven: Yale Univ. Press, 1955.

9526. Friedman, Norman. Point of view in fiction: the development of a critical concept. PMLA, 1955, 70:1176.

9527. _____. The struggle of vermin. Ball State Univ. Forum,
1968, 9:23-32.

9528. Friedman, Paul. The nose: some psychological reflections.
Amer Imago, 1951, 8:337-350.

9529. Friedrich, K. Eine Theorie des 'Roman nouveau' (1683).
Romantisches Jahrbuch, 1963, 14.

9530. Friedrich, Reindhart H. The dream-transference in Kafka's
Ein Landarzt. Papers on Language & Lit, 1973, 9:28-34.

9531. Friedrichsmeyer, Erhard M. Aspects of myth, parody and
obscenity in Günter Grass's Die Blechtrommel and Katz
und Maus. Germanic Rev, 1965, 40:240-250.

9532. _____. The Bertram episode in Hesse's 'Glass Bead
Game. ' Germanic Rev, 1974, 49:284-297.

9533. Frierson, William Coleman. The postwar novel, 1919-1929;
impressionists and Freudians. In The English Novel in
Transition, 1885-1940. Norman: Univ. Oklahoma Press,
1942, 211-236.

9534. Fries, T. Ein romantisches Märchen: Der blonde Eckert
von Ludwig Tieck. MLN, 1973, 88:1180-1211.

9535. Friesen, Menno M. The Mask in Hawthorne's Fiction. DA,
1965, 15:5276.

9536. Fritz, Helen M. Joyce and existentialism. James Joyce
Rev, 1958, 2:13-21.

9537. Froe, Arie de. Laurence Sterne and His Novels Studied in the
Light of Modern Psychology. Groningen: Noordhoff,
1925(?)

9538. Frohock, Wilbur Merrill. Andre Malraux and the Tragic
Imagination. Stanford: Stanford Univ. Press, 1952.

9539. _____ (ed). Image and Theme: Studies in Modern French
Fiction. Cambridge: Harvard Univ. Press, 1970; Review:
J. E. Flower, Hartford Studies in Lit, 1971, 3:61-63.

9540. _____. Notes on Malraux's symbols. Romanic Rev, 1951,
42:276-281.

9541. _____. Thomas Wolfe; of time and neurosis. Southwest
Rev, 1948, 33:349-360; Reprinted as Thomas Wolfe: time
and the national neurosis. In The Novel of Violence in
America. Dallas: Southern Methodist Univ. Press, 1957,
52-68; and as Of time and neurosis. In Walser, R. (ed),
The Enigma of Thomas Wolfe. Cambridge: Harvard
Univ. Press, 1953, 222-238.

9542. Fromm, Erich. The Anatomy of Human Destructiveness.
       NY: Holt, Rinehart & Winston, 1973, 282-283.
9543. Frost, Larry Don. Behavioral Engineering in the American
       Novel, 1924-1972. DAI, 1978, 39:3578A-79A.
9544. Fry, Carol F. Fictional conventions and sexuality in Dracula.
       Victorian Newsletter, 1972, No. 42, 20-22.
9545. Fryer, Jonathan H. Sexuality in Isherwood. Twentieth-Cen-
       tury Lit, 1976, 22:343-353.
9546. Fryer, Judith. The Faces of Eve: Women in the Nineteenth
       Century American Novel. NY: Oxford Univ. Press,
       1976; Reviews: Ellen Moers, Modern Language Rev, 1979,
       74:431-434; C. Zwarg, Novel: A Forum on Fiction, 1978,
       11:176-181.
9547. _____. The temptress: Elsie Venner: the literary con-
       vention with psychological trappings. In The Faces of
       Eve; Women in the Nineteenth Century American Novel.
       New York: Oxford Univ. Press, 1976, 29-40.
9548. Fuchs, Albert. La Personnalité de Faust: Essai d'analyse
       psychologique. Bulletin de la Faculté des Lettres de
       Strasbourg, 1963, 40:499-506.
9549. Fuerst, Rudolph A. Review: Arthur Koestler's Arrival and
       Departure. Psychoanal Rev, 1946, 33:102-107.
9550. Fuller, Cynthia. The Divided Self: A Study of Modern Iden-
       tity in the Novels of Ford Madox Ford. DAI, 1971, 31:
       5360A.
9551. Fuller, Edmund. Man in Modern Fiction. NY: Random
       House, 1958.
9552. Fulmer, O. Bryan. The significance of the death of the fox
       in D. H. Lawrence's 'The Fox.' Studies in Short Fiction,
       1968, 5:275-282.
9553. Funk, Robert W. Satire and existentialism in Faulkner's
       'Red Leaves.' Mississippi Q, 1972, 25:339-348.
9554. Fürnkäs, Josef. Der Ursprung des psychologischen Romans:
       Karl Philipp Moritz' 'Anton Reiser.' Stuttgart: 1977.
9555. Furrow, Sharon. Psyche and setting: Poe's picturesque
       landscapes. Criticism, 1973, 15:16-27.
9556. Fusco, Mario. Italo Svevo e la psicanilisi. In Petronio, G.
       (ed), Il caso Svevo. Palermo: Palumbo, 1976, 59-79.
9557. Fussell, M. G. B. Billy Budd: Melville's happy ending.
       Studies in Romanticism, 1976, 15:43-57.
9558. Fusswerk-Fursay, J. La Révélation existentielle chez Dos-
       toiewski. Etude psychopathologique. Annales Médico-
       Psychologiques, 1973, 2:173-186.

9559. Gabel, Joseph. Kafka, romancier de l'aliénation. Critique,
       1953, 9:949-960.
9560. _____. Die Verdinglichung in Camus' L'Etranger. Jahr-
       buch für Psychologie und Psychotherapie, 1958, 5:123-140.
9561. Gabory, G. Essai sur Marcel Proust. Paris: Le Livre,
       1926.
9562. Gaddis, Marilyn. The Critical Reaction to Julien Green,
       1926-1956. DA, 1959, 19:1756-1757.

9563. Gaddy, Barbara E. Women in the Fictional Works of André Gide. DAI, 1968, 28:3636A.
9564. Gale, Robert L. Freudian imagery in James's fiction. Amer Imago, 1954, 11:181-190.
9565. _____. Names in James. Names, 1966, 14:83-108.
9566. Gallagher, Fergal. Further Freudian implications in William Carlos Williams' 'The Use of Force.' CEA Critic, 1972, 34(4):20-21.
9567. Gallant, Clifford J. La Mère dans l'oeuvre de François Mauriac. Kentucky Foreign Language Q, 1964, 11:79-85.
9568. Gallant, M. Le Thème de la mort chez Roger Martin du Gard. Paris: Klincksieck, 1977.
9569. Galle, Barton W. Self-Sacrifice Versus Self-Help in Selected Victorian Novels. DAI, 1977, 37(12-A), 7761.
9570. Galletti, Salvatore. Patologia del Decameron. Palermo: Flascovio, 1969.
9571. Gallo, Marta. El tiempo en 'Las Ruinas Circulares' de J. L. Borges. Revista Iberoamericana, 1970, 36:559-578.
9572. Galsworthy, John. The Creation of Character in Fiction. NY: Oxford Univ. Press, 1931.
9573. Gálvez, Manuel. La novela psicológia. In El novelista y las novelas. Buenos Aires: Emecé, 1959, Ch. 8.
9574. Gandelman, C. Proust's draft copy-books: sketches of his dreams. Amer Imago, 1977, 34:297-312.
9575. Gandesbery, Jean Johnson. Versions of Mother in the Novels of Jane Austen and George Eliot. DAI, 1976, 37:3640A-41A.
9576. Gandour, Michael. Coping with grief as 'bearing up' and 'bearing down': an exchange on James Agee's A Death in the Family. Suicide & Life-Threatening Behavior, 1978, 8:60-64.
9577. Gans, Eric Lawrence. The Discovery of Illusion: Flaubert's Early Works, 1835-1837. Berkeley: Univ. California Press, 1971.
9578. Gantt, Barbara N. The Women of Macondo: Feminine Archetypes in García Márquez Cien Años de soledad. DAI, 1977, 38:2155A.
9579. Ganz, Margaret. Review: R. M. Goldfarb's Sexual Repression and Victorian Literature. Lit & Psychol, 1971, 21:161-165.
9580. Ganzel, Dewey. Cabestro and vaquilla: the symbolic structure of The Sun Also Rises. Sewanee Rev, 1968, 76:26-48.
9581. Garber, Kathleen D. A psychological analysis of a Dostoyevsky character: Raskolnikov's struggle for survival. Perspective in Psychiat Care, 1976, 14:14-21.
9582. Garcia Reinoso, Diego. [Considerations on grief. Psychoanalytic study of some of Edgar Poe's tales.] Revista Psicoanalysis, 1961, 18:139-155.
9583. Gardiner, Judith Kegan. Wake for mother: the maternal deathbed in women's fiction. Feminist Studies, 1978, 4(2):146-165.

9584. Garfst, Betty P.   Horace Walpole and the Unconscious: An
      Experiment in Freudian Analysis.   DAI, 1968, 29(5-A):
      1511-12.
9585. Gargano, James W.   Poe's 'Ligeia':   dream and destruction.
      College English, 1962, 23:337-342.
9586. _____.   Poe's 'Morella':   a note on her name.   Amer Lit,
      1975, 47:259-264.
9587. _____.   Washington Square: a study in the growth of an
      inner self.   Studies in Short Fiction, 1976, 13:355-362.
9588. _____.   'William Wilson.'   Emerson Society Q, 1970, 60
      Suppl:18-22.
9589. Garis, Robert.   The Dickens Theatre: A Reassessment of the
      Novels.   NY: Oxford Univ. Press, 1965.
9590. Garma, Angel.   Jaqueca, seudo-oligofrenia y delirio en un
      personaje de Pérez Galdós.   Acta Neurologica Psiquia-
      triqua Argentina, 1957, 3:143-154; Ficción, 1958, 19:84-
      102.
9591. Garmon, Gerald M.   Roderick Usher: portrait of the mad-
      man as artist.   Poe Studies, 1972, 5:11-14.
9592. Garrett-Goodyear, Joan.   Stylized emotions, unrealized
      selves: expressive characterizations in Thackeray.   Vic-
      torian Studies, 1979, 22:173-192.
9593. Garrison, Joseph M., Jr.   Perception, language, and reali-
      ty in As I Lay Dying.   Arizona Q, 1976, 32:16-30.
9594. Garver, J. C.   The Children of Night: Villainy and Moral
      Insanity in Victorian Fiction.   Doctoral dissertation, Univ.
      Edinburgh, 1976.
9595. Garvin, Harry R. (ed).   Makers of the Twentieth Century
      Novel.   Lewisburg, Pa: Bucknell Univ. Press, 1977.
9596. Gasiorowska, Xenia.   Women in Soviet Fiction, 1917-1964.
      Madison: Univ. Wisconsin Press, 1968.
9597. Gassin, Jean.   Le Sadisme dans l'oeuvre de Camus.   Rev
      des Lettres Modernes, 1973, 360-365:121-144.
9598. Gates, Barbara.   Suicide and Wuthering Heights.   Victorian
      Newsletter, 1976, 50:15-19.
9599. Gatta, John, Jr.   'Busy and selfish London':   the urban figure
      in Hawthorne's 'Wakefield.'   Emerson Society Q, 1977,
      23:164-172.
9600. Gaudefroy-Demombynes, Lorraine.   La Femme dans l'oeuvre
      de Maupassant.   Paris: Mercure de France, 1943.
9601. Gaukroger, Doug.   Time structure in Catch-22.   Critique:
      Studies in Modern Fiction, 1970, 12(2):70-85.
9602. Gaull, Marilyn.   Language and identity: a study of E. E.
      Cummings' The Enormous Room.   Amer Q, 1967, 19:645-
      662.
9603. Gaultier, Jules de.   Le Bovarysme.   La Psychologie dans
      l'oeuvre de Flaubert.   Paris: Cerf, 1892.
9604. _____.   La Psychologie dans l'oeuvre de Flaubert.   Rev
      des idées, 1908, 5:40-60.
9605. Gayle, Addison, Jr.   Literature as catharsis: the novels of
      Paul Laurence Dunbar.   In Martin, J. (ed), A Singer in
      the Dawn.   NY: Dodd, Mead, 1975.

9606. Geary, Edward A. A Study of the Androgynous Figure in the Fiction of Henry James. DAI, 1971, 32:1509A.
9607. Gebstattel, Victor E. von. Anthropologie und Dichtung; Betrachtungen zum Wesenbild des Menschen bei A. Stifter. Jahrbuch für Psychologie und Psychotherapie, 1956, 4:11-23.
9608. Geha, Richard. Dostoevsky and 'The Gambler': a contribution to the psychogenesis of gambling. Psychoanal Rev, 1970, 57:95-123, 289-302.
9609. _____. Miss Lonelyhearts: a dual mission of mercy. Hartford Studies in Lit, 1971, 3:116-131.
9610. Geherin, D. J. Nothingness and beyond: Joan Didion's Play It as It Lays. Critique, 1974, 16:64-78.
9611. Geismar, Maxwell D. American Moderns. From Rebellion to Conformity. NY: Hill & Wang, 1958.
9612. _____. Frank Norris: a gulf without bottom: excerpt from Rebels and Ancestors. In Malin, I. (ed), Psychoanalysis and American Fiction. NY: Dutton, 1965, 187-198.
9613. _____. Rebels and Ancestors: The American Novel. Boston: Houghton Mifflin, 1953.
9614. _____. Writers in Crisis. Boston: Houghton Mifflin, 1942; NY: Hill & Wang, 1961; London: Secker & Warburg, 1942.
9615. Gelfant, Blanche H. The American City Novel. Norman: Univ. Oklahoma Press, 1954.
9616. _____. The forgotten reaping hook: sex in My Antonia. Amer Lit, 1971, 43:60-82.
9617. _____. Love and conversion in Mrs. Dalloway. Criticism, 1966, 8:229-245.
9618. _____. The search for identity in the novels of John Dos Passos. PMLA, 1961, 76:133-149.
9619. Gendzier, I. L. The Lawrence enigma. Amer J Psychiat, 1969, 125:1607-1609.
9620. Genil-Perrin, & Lebreuil, M. Don Quichotte paranoïaque et le bovarysme de Don Quichotte. Mercure de France, 1935, 262:45-57.
9621. Genthe, Charles V. Six, sex, sick: Seymour, some comments. Twentieth Century Lit, 1965, 10:170-171.
9622. Gerber, Helmut E. J. D. Beresford: the Freudian element. Lit & Psychol, 1956, 6(3):78-86.
9623. Gerber, Philip L. Willa Cather and the big red rock. College English, 1958, 19:152-157.
9624. Gerhardi, Gerhard C. Psychological time and revolutionary action in Le Rouge et le noir. PMLA, 1973, 88:1115-1126.
9625. _____. Romantic love and the prostitution of politics: on the structural unity of L'Education sentimentale. Studies in the Novel, 1972, 4:402-415.
9626. Gettman, R. , & Harkness, B. Morality and psychology in The Secret Sharer. In Harkness, B. (ed), Conrad's Secret Sharer and the Critics. Belmont, Cal: Wadsworth, 1962, 125-132.

9627. Ghiselin, Brewster. Automatism, intention, and autonomy in the novelist's production. Daedalus, 1963, 92:297-311.

9628. Ghurye, Charlotte W. The Writer and Society: Studies in the Fiction of Günter Grass and Heinrich Böll. Bern: Lang, 1976.

9629. Giacoman, Helmy F. La ontología de J.P. Sartre y El tunel de E. Sábato. Atenea, 1968, Nos. 421-2, 373-384.

9630. _____. La psico-metafisica del libro Nuevas Cantigas de Jaime Ferrán. Hispanófila, 1971, 42:45-55.

9631. _____. La psiconeurosis regresiva en El Señor Presidente. Cuadernos Americanos, 1970, 172:177-184.

9632. Gibbons, Kathryn G. Quentin's shadow. Lit & Psychol, 1962, 12:16-24.

9633. Gibbs, Beverly J. El túnel: portrayal of isolation. Hispania, 1965, 48:429-436.

9634. Gibson, Donald B. The Fiction of Stephen Crane. Carbondale: Southern Illinois Univ. Press, 1968; Review: Stanley Wertheim, Lit & Psychol, 1969, 19:125-128.

9635. Gibson, Lois Rauch. Attitudes Toward Childhood in Eighteenth-Century British Fiction. DAI, 1976, 36:4508A-9A.

9636. Gide, André. Octave Mirbeau: Les Vingt et un jours d'une neurasthénique. In Prétexte. Paris: Mercure de France, 1963, 115-116.

9637. Giedion-Welcher, Carola. Work in progress: a linguistic experiment by James Joyce. Transition, 1930, 29-30:174-183.

9638. Gilbert, Stuart. James Joyce. Psyché, 1948, 3:678-689.

9639. Giles, James R. Religious alienation and homosexual consciousness in City of Night and Go Tell It on the Mountain. College English, 1974, 36:369-381.

9640. Giles, Mary E. Juan Goytisolo's Juego de manos: an archetypal interpretation. Hispania, 1973, 56:1021-1029.

9641. Gill, James E. Discovery and alienation, nature and reason in Gulliver's Travels, Parts I-III. Tennessee Studies in Lit, 1978, 22:85-104.

9642. Gill, Stephen M. Antic Hay: a portraiture of psychological dislocation. Calcutta Rev, 1970, 1:513-518.

9643. Gill, Thomas H. Review: Stefan Zweig's Master Builders. Psychiatry, 1939, 2:605.

9644. Gillespie, Diane Filby. May Sinclair and the stream of consciousness: metaphors and metaphysics. English Lit in Transition, 1978, 21:134-142.

9645. Gillet, J.E. The autonomous character in Spanish and European literature. Hispanic Rev, 1956, 24:179-190.

9646. Gingell, E. The theme of fertility in Zola's Rougon-Macquart. Forum Modern Language Studies, 1977, 13:350-358.

9647. Gillibert, Jean. A propos d'un rêve de Jean Valjean. In L'Oedipe maniaque. Paris: Payot, 1978.

9648. _____. La Recherche vue par un psychanalyste: Le cas Proust. Nouvelles Littéraires, 11 June 1971.

9649. Gilman, Sander L. On the use and abuse of the history of psychiatry for literary studies. Deutsche Vierteljahrsschrift für Literaturwissenschaft und Geistesgeschichte, 1978, 52:381-399.

9650. Gilman, Stephen M. La palabra hablada en Fortunata y Jacinta. Neuva Revista de Filología Hispánica, 1961, 15: 542-560.

9651. Gimeno, A. La obra de Kafka a la luz de la fenomenología de Conrad. Revista de Psiquiatría y Psicologia Médica, 1968, 8:315-327.

9652. Gincburg, Mira. Tolstoi über den Traum. Int Zeitschrift für Psychoanalyse, 1912, 2:615.

9653. Ginsberg, Elaine. The female initiation theme in American fiction. Studies in Amer Fiction, 1975, 3:27-37.

9654. Gioli, Giovanna M. Racconto psicologico e Romance in Daisy Miller. Studi Americani, 1970, 16:231-254.

9655. Giordano, Fedora. Jack London. Cultura e Sculoa (Rome), 1978, 63-64:119-130.

9656. Giordano, Frank R., Jr. Farmer Boldwood: Hardy's portrait of a suicide. English Lit in Transition, 1978, 21: 244-253.

9657. Girard, Marie-Thérèse Vidal. Les Problèmes de la communication chez Colette: du dialogue ... au monologue intérieur. Thèse lettres, Univ. Montpellier, 1976.

9658. Girard, René. Deceit, Desire, and the Novel; Self and Other in Literary Structure. Baltimore: Johns Hopkins Univ. Press, 1965.

9659. _____. Dostoïevski: Du double à l'unité. Paris: Plon, 1963.

9660. _____. Masochism and sadism. In Deceit, Desire and the Novel; Self and Other in Literary Structure. Baltimore: Johns Hopkins Univ. Press, 1965, 176-192.

9661. _____. Narcissism: the Freudian myth demystified by Proust. In Roland, A. (ed), Psychoanalysis, Creativity, and Literature. NY: Columbia Univ. Press, 1976, 293-311.

9662. _____. Strategies of madness--Nietzsche, Wagner, and Dostoevski. In 'To Double Business Bound.' Baltimore: Johns Hopkins Univ. Press, 1978, 61-83; MLN, 1976, 91:1161-1185.

9663. Giraud, J. E. T. A. Hoffmann: Die Abenteuer der Silvesternacht. Le double visage. Recherches Germaniques, 1971, 1.

9664. Girgus, Sam B. Conscience in Connecticut: civilization and its discontents in Twain's Camelot. New England Q, 1978, 51:547-560.

9665. _____. Poe and R. D. Laing: the transcendent self. Studies in Short Fiction, 1976, 13:299-309.

9666. Gittelman, Edwin. Isaac's nominal case: In My Father's Court. In Allentuck, M. (ed), The Achievement of Isaac Bashevis Singer. Carbondale: Southern Illinois Univ. Press, 1969.

9667. Gladstein, Mimi R. The Indestructible Woman in the Works of Faulkner, Hemingway, and Steinbeck. DAI, 1974, 35: 1655A.

9668. Glaser, Frederick B.   The case of Franz Kafka.   Psychoanal
       Rev, 1964, 51:99-121.
9669. Glasgow, Janis Marilyn.   Psychological Realism in George
       Sand's Early Novels and Short Stories.   DA, 1966, 27:
       203A.
9670. Glasheen, Adaline.   Joyce and the three ages of Charles
       Stewart Parnell.   In Magalaner, M. (ed), A James Joyce
       Miscellany.   Carbondale: Southern Illinois Univ. Press,
       1959, 60-72.
9671. Glass, Terrence L.   Myths, Dreams and Reality: Cycles
       of Experience in the Novels of John Hawkes.   DAI, 1974,
       34:5171A.
9672. Glasser, William.   Moby Dick.   Sewanee Rev, 1909, 77:463-
       486.
9673. Glassman, Peter Joel.   Language and Being: Joseph Conrad
       and the Literature of Personality.   NY: Columbia Univ.
       Press, 1976; DAI, 1973, 33:5723A.
9674. Glättli, Walter.   Die Behandlung des Affekts der Furcht im
       englischen Roman des 18. Jahrhunderts.   Zurich: Juris,
       1948.
9675. Glenn, Eunice.   Fantasy in the fiction of Eudora Welty.   In
       Tate, A. (ed), A Southern Vanguard.   Englewood Cliffs,
       NJ: Prentice-Hall, 1947, 85-87; In Aldridge, J. W. (ed),
       Critiques and Essays on Modern Fiction: 1920-1951.   NY:
       Ronald, 1952, 512-514.
9676. Glick, Burton S.   A brief analysis of a short story by Dylan
       Thomas.   Amer Imago, 1957, 14:149-154.
9677. Glickfield, Charlotte W.   Some Underlying Themes in the
       Waverly Novels.   DA, 1968, 28(10-A):4127.
9678. Glicksberg, Charles I.   D. H. Lawrence and science.   Scien-
       tific Monthly, 1951, 73:99-104.
9679. _____.   The literary struggle for selfhood.   Personalist,
       1961, 42:52-60.
9680. _____.   The Self in Modern Literature.   University Park:
       Penn State Univ. Press, 1963.
9681. _____.   The Sexual Revolution in Modern American Liter-
       ature.   The Hague: Nijhoff, 1971.
9682. _____.   The theme of alienation in the American Jewish
       novel.   Reconstructionist, 1957, 23:9-12.
9683. _____.   To be or not to be: the literature of suicide.
       Queen's Q, 1960, 68:384-395.
9684. Gliserman, Martin J.   The Intersection of Biography and Fic-
       tion: A Psychological Study of Daniel Defoe and His Nov-
       els.   DAI, 1974, 34:5100.
9685. Glolus, Gordon C., & Pilliard, Richard C.   Tausk's influ-
       encing machine and Kafka's In the Penal Colony.   Amer
       Imago, 1966, 23:191-207.
9686. Glover, Edward.   On the aetiology of drug addiction.   Int J
       Psycho-Anal, 1932, 13:298-328.
9687. Glucsević, Zoran.   Patologija i stvaralacka sudbina pisca.
       Knjizevne Novine (Belgrade), 24 Dec 1966, 5.
9688. Gobert, D. L.   Merimée revisited.   Symposium, 1972, 26:
       128-146.

9689. Goddard, H. C.   A pre-Freudian reading of 'The Turn of the
       Screw.' Nineteenth Century Fiction, 1957, 12:1-36; In
       Willen, G. (ed), A Casebook of Henry James's The Turn
       of the Screw. NY: Crowell, 1960, 244-272.
9690. Godlewski, G. [Balzac or the fury of self-destruction.]
       Semaine des Hopîtaux de Paris, 1975, 51:3041-3054.
9691. Godshalk, William L.   Some sources of Durrell's Alexandria
       Quartet. Modern Fiction Studies, 1967, 13:361-374.
9692. Goff, Martyn.   The homosexual as novelist. Amigo, 1963,
       14:116-117.
9693. Going, W. T.   Faulkner's 'A Rose for Emily.' Explicator,
       1957-58, 16, No. 27.
9694. Gold, A., Jr.   It's only love: the politics of passion in God-
       win's Caleb Williams. Texas Studies in Lit & Language,
       1977, 19:135-160.
9695. Gold, Herbert.   The mystery of personality in the novel.
       Partisan Rev, 1957, 24:453-462.
9696. Goldberg, Bruce.   Skinner's behaviorist utopia. In Machan,
       T. R. (ed), The Libertarian Alternative; Essays in Social
       and Political Philosophy. Chicago: Nelson-Hall, 1974,
       94-118.
9697. Goldberger, Avriel.   Visions of a New Hero: The Heroic
       Life According to André Malraux. Paris: Minard, 1965.
9698. Golden, Herbert A.   A Study of Games Played in Ada or Ar-
       dor: A Family Chronicle by Vladimir Nabokov. DAI,
       1973, 33:5723A.
9699. Golden, Morris. Fielding's Moral Psychology. Amherst:
       Univ. Massachusetts Press, 1966.
9700. _____.   Richardson's Characters. Ann Arbor: Univ.
       Michigan Press, 1963.
9701. Goldfarb, Clare.   The question of William Dean Howells'
       racism. Ball State Univ. Forum, 1971, 12:22-30.
9702. _____.   William Dean Howells' The Minister's Charge: a
       study of psychological perception. Markham Rev, 1969,
       2:1-4.
9703. Goldfarb, Russell M. Sexual Repression and Victorian Liter-
       ature. Lewisburg: Bucknell Univ. Press, 1970.
9704. Goldgar, Harry.   Alain-Fournier and the initiation archetype.
       French Rev, 1970, 43:87-99.
9705. Goldlewski, G.   L'Univers morbide de Marcel Proust. Semi-
       nar des Hôpitaux Paris, 1972, 48:3499-3512.
9706. Goldman, Mark.   Bernard Malamud's comic vision and the
       theme of identity. Critique, 1964-65, 7:92-109; In Field,
       L. A., & Field, J. W. (eds), Bernard Malamud and the
       Critics. NY: New York Univ. Press, 1970, 51-70.
9707. Goldschläger, Alain, & Lemaire, Jacques.   Technique narra-
       tive paratoxique et psychologie des personnages dans
       L'Etranger et La Chute de Albert Camus. Neophilologus,
       1977, 61:185-193.
9708. Goldschmidt, Anthony M. E.   Alice in Wonderland psycho-
       analyzed. In Phillips, R. S. (ed), Aspects of Alice; Lewis
       Carroll's Dreamchild As Seen Through the Critics' Look-
       ing-Glasses, 1865-1971. NY: Vanguard, 1971, 279-282.

9709. Goldsmith, Arnold L. The poetry of names in The Spoils of Poynton. Names, 1966, 14:134-142.
9710. Goldstein, Bernice, & Goldstein, Sanford. Ego and 'Hapworth 16, 1924.' Renascence, 1972, 24:159-167.
9711. _____. Observations on The Sailor Who Fell from Grace with the Sea. Critique, 1970, 12:116-126.
9712. Goldstein, Melvin. A note on a perfect crime. Lit & Psychol, 1961, 11:65-67.
9713. Goldstein, M. J., Kant, H. S., & Hartman, J. J. The role of fantasy in the use of erotica. In Pornography and Sexual Deviance. A Report of the Legal and Behavioral Institute of Beverly Hills, California. Berkeley: Univ. California Press, 1973, 122-138.
9714. Goldstein, S. Review: T. Doi's Psychological World of Natsume Soseki. Modern Fiction Studies, 1977-78, 23:711-713.
9715. Golgar, H. The square root of minus one: Freud and Robert Musil's Törless. Comparative Lit Studies, 1965, 17:117-132.
9716. Gollin, Rita K. 'Dreamwork' in The Blithedale Romance. Emerson Society Q, 1973, 19:74-83.
9717. _____. Hawthorne: the writer as dreamer. Studies Amer Renaissance, 1977, 313:325.
9718. _____. Understanding fathers in American Jewish fiction. Centennial Rev, 1974, 18:273-287.
9719. Golwarz, Sergio. Jung y Ulises. In 126 ensayos de bolsillo y 126 gotas toxicas. Mexico City: Libro Mex, 1961, 128-129.
9720. Gómez Lance, Betty Rita. La actitud picaresca en la novela española del siglo XX. Mexico: Costa-Amic, 1969.
9721. Gomez Parra, S. El conductismo en la novela española contemporánea. Reseña (Madrid), 1970, 36:323-333.
9722. Gómez de Baquero, Eduardo. Novelas y novelistas. Madrid: Calleja, 1918.
9723. Gonthier, Denys Armand. El drama psicológico del 'Quijote.' Madrid: Studium, 1962.
9724. Gontier, Fernande. La Femme et le couple dans le roman de l'entre-deux guerres. (Femmes en littérature, 2). Paris: Klincksieck, 1976.
9725. _____. Les Images de la femme dans le roman français de l'entre-deux-guerres. DAI, 1973, 34:1856A.
9726. Gonzáles, Manuel J. La constante de las sensaciones olfativas en la obre de Heinrich Böll. Filología Moderna, 1973, 13:337-381.
9727. Gonzáles, Mirza N. La novela y el cuento psicológicos de Miguel de Carrión. DAI, 1974, 35:3739A-40A.
9728. González Araúzo, Angel. Patología finisecular: La suciedad doliente en la novela galdosiana. DAI, 1967, 27:3455A.
9729. González Lanuza, Eduardo. Balzac y el adulterio. Sur, 1971, 329:166-175.
9730. Gooch, Anthony. Análisis psico-semántico de un personaje de Los pazos de Ulloa y La madre naturaleza de Emilia Pardo Bazán: Julián. In En torno a Pemán. Cadiz: Excma, 1974, 443-468.

9731. Goodden, C.   Two quests for surety--a comparative inter-
       pretation of Stifter's Abdias and Kafka's Der Bau.   J Eu-
       ropean Studies, 1975, 5:341-361.
9732. Goodhand, Robert.   The psychological development in Jean
       Giradoux's Eglantine.   French Rev, 1964, 38:173-179.
9733. Goodheart, Eugene.   Freud and Lawrence.   Psychoanal Rev,
       1960-61, 4:56-64.
9734. _____.   The Utopian Vision of D. H. Lawrence.   Chicago:
       Univ. Chicago Press, 1963.
9735. Goodman, Charlotte.   Women and madness in the fiction of
       Joyce Carol Oates.   Women and Lit, 1977, 5(2):17-28.
9736. Goodman, Paul.   Kafka's Prayer.   NY: Vanguard, 1947.
9737. Goodman, Robert A.   The Image of the Jew in Argentine Lit-
       erature as Seen by Argentine Jewish Writers.   DAI, 1973,
       33:6357A.
9738. Goody, Frema Ila.   Image, Symbol, and Motif in Six Novels
       of Thomas Hardy.   DAI, 1977, 38:3481A.
9739. Goppert-Spanel, (?).   Hermann Hesses Werk als Spiegel
       seiner Seelenwicklung.   Universitas, 1951, 6:637-644,
       761-768.
9740. Gordon, Andrew.   The modern dream-vision: Freud's The
       Interpretation of Dreams and Mailer's An American
       Dream.   Lit & Psychol, 1977, 27:100-105.
9741. _____.   The Naked and the Dead: the triumph of impo-
       tence.   Lit & Psychol, 1969, 19:3-13.
9742. _____.   Pushy Jew: Leventhal in The Victim.   Modern
       Fiction Studies, 1979, 25:129-138.
9743. _____.   Why Are We in Vietnam? Deep in the bowels of
       Texas.   Lit & Psychol, 1974, 24:55-65.
9744. Gordon, David J.   Some recent novels: styles of martyrdom.
       Yale Rev, 1968, 58:112-126.
9745. _____.   The son and the father: patterns of response to
       conflict in Hemingway's fiction.   Lit & Psychol, 1966, 16:
       122-138.
9746. _____.   Washington Square: a psychological perspective.
       In Willen, G. (ed), Henry James, 'Washington Square':
       A Critical Edition.   NY: Crowell, 1970.
9747. Gordon, Jan B.   Review: Robert Kiely's Robert Louis Steven-
       son and the Fiction of Adventure.   Lit & Psychol, 1967,
       17:148-150.
9748. _____.   The Story of O and the strategy of pornography:
       cosmos and nothingness.   Western Humanities Rev, 1971,
       25:27-43.
9749. Gordon, K.   George Meredith as psychologist.   Psychol Bul-
       letin, 1938, 35:522-523.
9750. _____.   Meredith as psychologist.   J Psychol, 1939, 7:317-
       322.
9751. Gordon, K. H., Jr., et al.   The adolescent orphan in litera-
       ture. A bibliography for the study of the adolescent.
       JAPA, 1974, 22:537-541.
9752. Gordon, Lois G.   Meaning and myth in The Sound and the
       Fury and The Waste Land.   In French, Warren (ed), The
       Twenties: Fiction, Poetry, Drama.   De Land, Fla: Ever-
       ett/Edwards, 1975, 269-302.

9753.   _____. Portnoy's Complaint: coming of age in Jersey
         City. Lit & Psychol, 1969, 19:57-60.
9754.   Gordon, William Alexander. The Mind and Art of Henry
         Miller. Baton Rouge: Louisiana State Univ. Press,
         1967, 46-84; London: Cape, 1968; Henry Miller and the
         Romantic Tradition. Doctoral dissertation, Tulane Univ.,
         1963.
9755.   _____. Submission and autonomy: identity problems in
         Joyce's Portrait. Psychoanal Rev, 1974-75, 61:535-
         555.
9756.   Gorelov, A. Idei i obrazy v khudostvennom tvorchestve.
         Zvezda, 1934, 6:133-140.
9757.   Gorer, Geoffrey. The myth in Jane Austen. Amer Imago,
         1941; In Scott, W. (ed), Five Approaches to Literary
         Criticism. NY: Collier, 1962, 91-98; In Phillips, W.
         (ed), Art and Psychoanalysis. NY: Criterion, 1963, 218-
         224.
9758.   Gorjackina, M. S. Nekotorye osobennosti psixologizma Dos-
         toevskogo i Scedrina. Russkaja Literatura, 1972, 15(1):
         19-33.
9759.   Gorsky, Susan R. Old maids and new women: alternatives
         to marriage in Englishwomen's novels, 1847-1915. J
         Popular Culture, 1973, 7:68-85.
9760.   _____. The gentle doubters: image of women in English
         women's novels, 1840-1920. In Cornillon, S. K. (ed),
         Images of Women in Fiction. Bowling Green, Ohio:
         Bowling Green Univ. Popular Press, 1972, 28-54.
9761.   Gorss, Gloria Sybil. Sanity, madness and the family in Sam-
         uel Johnson's Rasselas. Psychocultural Rev, 1977, 1:
         152-160.
9762.   Görtz, Franz Josef. Günter Grass. Zur Pathogenese lines
         Markenbilds: Die Literaturkritik der Massenmedien 1959-
         1969: Eine Untersuchung mit Hilfe datenverarbeitender
         Methoden. Meisenheim: Hain, 1978.
9763.   Gose, Elliott B. Imagination Indulged: The Irrational in the
         Nineteenth-Century Novel. Montreal: McGill-Queen's
         Univ. Press, 1972.
9764.   _____. Pure exercise of imagination: archetypal sym-
         bolism in Lord Jim. PMLA, 1964, 79:137-147.
9765.   _____. Wuthering Heights: the heath and the hearth.
         Nineteenth Century Fiction, 1966, 21:1-19.
9766.   Goshgarian, Gary. Feminist values in the novels of Iris
         Murdoch. Rev des Langues Vivantes, 1974, 40:519-527.
9767.   _____. From Fable to Flesh: A Study of the Female
         Characters in the Novels of Iris Murdoch. DAI, 1973,
         33:3583A.
9768.   Gostantas, S. Dostoievski en las novelas de R. Arlt. Nueva
         Narrativa Hispanoamericana, 1973, 3(2).
9769.   Gould, Gerald L. The gate scene at Sotherton in Mansfield
         Park. Lit & Psychol, 1970, 20:75-78.
9770.   Gould, Karen L. Claude Simon's Mythic Muse. Columbia,
         SC: French Literature Publications, 1978; Review:
         Margaret W. Blades, French Rev, 1980, 53:753-754.

9771. Goulianos, Joan S. A conversation with Lawrence Durrell about art, analysis, and politics. Modern Fiction Studies, 1971, 17:159-166.

9772. Gourevitch, M. A propos d'une méconnue source Des Faux-Monnayeurs. Encéphale, 1970, 59:67-80.

9773. Gounard, J. F., & Gounard, Beverley Roberts. Richard Wright's Savage Holiday: use or abuse of psychoanalysis? College Language Assn J, 1979, 22:344-349.

9774. Goytisolo, J. La metáfora erótica, Góngora, J. Belda y Lezamia Lima. Revista Iberoamericano, 1976, 95:157-175.

9775. Graber, Gustav H. Goethes Werther. Acta Psychotherapeutica, Psychosomatica et Orthopaedagogica, 1958, 6:120-136.

9776. _____. Die schwarze Spinne; Menschheitsentwicklungen nach Jeremias Gotthelfs gleichnamiger Novelle, dargestelt unter besonderer Berucksichtigung der Rolle der Frau. Imago, 1925, 11:254-334; Vienna: Int Psychoanalytischer Verlag, 1925.

9777. Grace, Harry A. Pierre Boulle and the principle of 'functional autonomy. ' Lit & Psychol, 1961, 11:29-32.

9778. Graham, Don. Jack London's tale told by a high-grade feeb. Studies in Short Fiction, 1978, 15:429-433.

9779. _____. Psychological veracity in 'The Lost Phoebe': Dreiser's revision. Studies in Amer Fiction, 1978, 6: 100-105.

9780. Graham, Neilson. Sanity, madness and Alice. Ariel, 1973, 4(2):80-89.

9781. Graham, Victor E. The Imagery of Proust. NY: Barnes & Noble, 1966.

9782. _____. Water imagery and symbolism in Proust. Romanic Rev, 1959, 50:118-128.

9783. Grange, Kathleen M. Dr. Samuel Johnson's account of a schizophrenic illness in Rasselas (1759). Medical History, 1962, 6:162-168.

9784. _____. Samuel Johnson's accounts of certain psychoanalytic concepts. JNMD, 1962, 135:93-98.

9785. Granger, Michel. Le Bras du cannibale: aspects de la régression primitiviste dans Moby Dick. Rev Française d'Etudes Américaines, 1978, 5:47-61.

9786. Grant, Naomi M. The Role of Women in the Fiction of Ernest Hemingway. DAI, 1969, 29:4456A.

9787. Grant, Richard B. Imagery as a means of psychological revelation in Maupassant's Une Vie. Studies in Philology, 1963, 60:669-684.

9788. Grant, Vernon W. The Psychology of Sexual Emotion. NY: Longmans, Green, 1957.

9789. Grant, William E. Hawthorne's Hamlet: the archetypal structure of The Blithedale Romance. Rocky Mountain Rev of Language & Lit, 1977, 31:1-15.

9790. _____. Nathaniel Hawthorne and Empirical Psychology. DAI, 1971, 32:2686A-87A.

9791. Grassvogel, A. V. L'eccezione alla regola. MLN, 1980, 139-161.

9792. Graves, P. J. E. T. A. Hoffmanns Johannes Kreisler 'Ver-rückter Musikus'? Modern Language Q, 1969, 30(2).
9793. Gray, Eugene F. The clinical view of life: Gustave Flau-bert's Madame Bovary. In Peschel, E. R. (ed), Medicine and Literature. NY: Watson, 1980, 81-87.
9794. Gray, Francine du Plessix. The new 'older woman.' New York Times Book Rev, 15 Jan 1978, 3, 29.
9795. Grebstein, Sheldon Norman. Dreiser's Victorian vamp. Midcontinent American Studies J, 1963, 4:3-12.
9796. Green, Alfred. The mourning process in Thomas Wolfe's Of Time and the River. Bulletin New Jersey Psychoanal Society, 1968, 1:16-19.
9797. Green, Bernard A. The effects of distortion of the self: a study of the Picture of Dorian Gray. In The Annual of Psychoanalysis, Vol. VII/1979. NY: IUP, 1980.
9798. Green, Dorothy. The Young Cosima. Australian Lit Studies, 1970, 4:215-226.
9799. Green, George H. William Wilson: the 'conscience' of Edgar Allan Poe. Aberystwyth Studies, 1929, 11:1-22.
9800. Green, James L. Nightmare and Dream in John Hawkes's Novels. DAI, 1972, 33:312A.
9801. Green, M. The morality of Lolita. Kenyon Rev, 1966, 28: 352-377.
9802. Greenacre, Phyllis. Child wife as ideal: sociological con-siderations. Amer J Orthopsychiat, 1947, 17:167-171.
9803. _____. The mutual adventures of Jonathan Swift and Lem-uel Gulliver: a study in pathography. Psychoanal Q, 1955, 24:20-62.
9804. _____. The relation of the imposter to the artist. In The Psychoanalytic Study of the Child, Vol. 13. NY: IUP, 1958, 521-540.
9805. Greenberg, Alvin. The death of the psyche: a way to the self in the contemporary novel. Criticism, 1966, 8:1-18.
9806. Greenberg, Bruce L. Fitzgerald's 'figured curtain': per-sonality and history in Tender Is the Night. Fitzgerald-Hemingway Annual, 1978, 105-136.
9807. Greenberg, Martin. The Terror of Art. Kafka and Modern Literature. NY: Basic Books, 1968.
9808. Greene, G. , & Greene, C. S-M, the Last Taboo. NY: Grove, 1973.
9809. Greene, T. M. Anxiety and the search for meaning. Texas Q, 1958, 1:172-191.
9810. Greenhouse, Karen. Death--a form of life in Flannery O'Con-nor. Suicide & Life-Threatening Behavior, 1978, 8:118-128.
9811. Greening, Thomas Cartwright. Candide: an existential dream. J Existentialism, 1965, 5:413-416.
9812. _____. Existential fiction and the paradox of ethics. Antioch Rev, 1963, 23:93-107.
9813. Greenlee, James. Sartre's 'Chambre': the story of Eve. Modern Fiction Studies, 1970, 16:77-84.
9814. Greenwald, Fay T. The Young Girls in the Novels of W. D. Howells and Henry James. DAI, 1975, 35:6712A-13A.

9815.   Greenwald, Harold, & Krich, Aron.   The Prostitute in Liter-
        ature.   NY: Ballantine, 1961.
9816.   Gregg, Richard A.   Tat'jana's two dreams: the unwanted
        spouse and the demonic lover.   Slavonic & East European
        Rev, 1970, 48:492-505.
9817.   Gregor, Ian.   What kind of fiction did Hardy write?   Essays
        in Criticism, 1966, 16:290-308.
9818.   Gregory, A.   Sherwood Anderson.   Dial, 1923, 75:246.
9819.   Gregory, Thomas West.   Friendships Between Adolescent
        Males in Selected American Novels from 1945 to 1970.
        DAI, 1973, 33:6910A.
9820.   Greimas, Algirdas Julien.   Maupassant: La Semiotique du
        texte.   Paris: Seuil, 1976.
9821.   Greiner, Donald J.   The education of Robert Jordan: death
        with dignity.   Hemingway Notes, 1971, 1(2):14-20.
9822.   _____.   Ross Lockridge and the tragedy of Raintree Coun-
        ty.   Critique: Studies in Modern Fiction, 1978, 20(3):51-
        62.
9823.   Grenander, M. E.   Benito Cereno and legal oppression: a
        Szaszian interpretation.   J Libertarian Studies, 1978, 2:
        337-342.
9824.   _____.   Of graver import than history: psychiatry in fic-
        tion.   J Libertarian Studies, 1978, 2:29-44.
9825.   Grenberg, Bruce L.   Fitzgerald's 'Figured Curtains': per-
        sonality and history in Tender Is the Night.   Fitzgerald-
        Hemingway Annual, 1978, 105-136.
9826.   Gresham, Jewell H.   The Fatal Illusions: Self, Sex, Race,
        and Religion in William Faulkner's World.   DAI, 1970,
        31:5402A.
9827.   Gresset, Michel.   Psychological aspects of evil in The Sound
        and the Fury.   Mississippi Q, 1966, 19:143-153.
9828.   _____.   Le Regard et le désir chez Faulkner.   Sud, 1975,
        Nos. 14-15.
9829.   Griffin, Joseph.   Drieser's short stories and the dread of
        success.   Etudes Anglaises, 1978, 31:294-302.
9830.   Griffin, Mary N.   Coming to Manhood in America: A Study
        of Significant Initiation Novels, 1797-1970.   DAI, 1972,
        32:3951A.
9831.   Griffith, Kelley, Jr.   Weir Mitchell and the genteel romance.
        Amer Lit, 1972, 44:247-261.
9832.   Griffith, M.   A double reading of Parade's End.   Modern Fic-
        tion Studies, 1963, 9:25-38.
9833.   Griffiths, D. E., & Hobday, A. F.   The novel as a case study.
        Educational Research Bulletin, 1952, 31:19-21.
9834.   Grillo, Giuseppe.   Svevo, scrittore freudiano per gl'inglesi.
        Idea, 1963, 19:256-257.
9835.   Grilly, D. M.   A reply to Miller's 'The Habit of Sherlock
        Holmes.'   Transactions Studies College Physicians Phila-
        delphia, 1979, 5:324-327.
9836.   Grimaud, Michel Robert.   Vers une poétique psychanalytique:
        Lectures de Victor Hugo.   DAI, 1976, 37:3672A.
9837.   Grimes, Mary Loftin.   The Archetype of the Great Mother in
        the Novels of William Golding.   DAI, 1977, 37:6496A.

9838. Grimsley, Ronald R. The human problem in La Nouvelle Heloise. Modern Language Rev, 1958, 53:171-184.

9839. _____. Psychological aspects of Le Neveau de Rameau. Modern Language Q, 1955, 16:195-209.

9840. _____. Romantic emotion in Musset's Confession d'un enfant du siècle. Studies in Romanticism, 1970, 9:125-142.

9841. Grimstad, G. Is-slottet av 7. Vesaas. Edda, 1971, 71:47-50.

9842. Grinberg, Leon. Si Yo Usted: contribución al estudio de la identificación proyectiva. Revista de Psicoanálisis, 1957, 14:355-367.

9843- Grinberg, Rebeca Vaisman de. Interpretacíon psicoanalítica
4. de Las cabezas trocadas. Contribución al estudio de la patologia de la identidad. Revista di Psicoanalisi, 1966, 23:161-181.

9845. Grobe, Edwin P. Estrangement as verbal aspect in Le Symphonie pastorale. French Rev, 1970, 43:56-64.

9846. _____. The psychological structure of Camus's L'Hote. French Rev, 1966, 40:357-367.

9847. _____. Symbolic sound patterns in Nathalie Sarraute's Martereau. French Rev, 1966, 40:84-91.

9848. Grodal, Torben Kragh. Den sociale sult og den existentielle kvalme. Anal-kortprosa, 1971, 1:260-282.

9849. Groden, M. Criticism in new composition: Ulysses and The Sound and the Fury. Twentieth Century Lit, 1975, 21:265-277.

9850. Gronicka, André von. Myth plus psychology: a stylistic analysis of Death in Venice. Germanic Rev, 1956, 31:191-205; In Hatfield, H. (ed), Thomas Mann: A Collection of Critical Essays. Englewood Cliffs, NJ: Prentice-Hall, 1964, 46-61.

9851. Groos, K. Die Verwendung der Eidetik als Kunstmittel in Jack Londons Roman Martin Eden. Zeitschrift für angewandte Psychologie, 1929, 33:417-438.

9852. Gros-Louis, Dolores. Pens and needles: daughters and mothers in recent Canadian literature. Kate Chopin Newsletter, 1976-77, 2(3):8-13.

9853. Gross, Alfred W. The Transcendent Personality in the Social Novels of Heinrich Mann. DAI, 1976, 37:349A-350A.

9854. Gross, Harvey. Aschenbach and Kurtz: the cost of civilization. Centennial Rev, 1961, 6:131-143.

9855. Gross, Seymour L., & Hardy, John E. (eds). Images of the Negro in American Literature. Chicago: Univ. Chicago Press, 1966.

9856. _____, & Stewart, Randall. The Hawthorne revival. In Pearce, R. H. (ed), Hawthorne Centenary Essays. Columbus: Ohio State Univ. Press, 1964, 335-366.

9857. Gross, Theodore L. J. D. Salinger: suicide and survival in the modern world. South Atlantic Q, 1969, 68:454-462; In The Heroic Ideal in American Literature. NY: Free Press, 1971, 262-271.

9858. Grossvogel, David I. Limits of the Novel. Evolutions of a Form from Chaucer to Robbe-Grillet. Ithaca: Cornell Univ. Press, 1968.

9859. _____. Mystery and Its Fictions: from Oedipus to Agatha Christie. Baltimore: Johns Hopkins Univ. Press, 1979, 127-146.

9860. Grotine, Martin. [A psychoanalytic analysis of Alice in Wonderland.] Keshet, 1976, 70:149-154.

9861. Grotjahn, Martin. About the symbolization of Alice's adventures in Wonderland. Amer Imago, 1947, 4:32-41; In Phillips, R. S. (ed), Aspects of Alice; Lewis Carroll's Dreamchild as Seen Through the Critics' Looking-Glasses, 1865-1971. NY: Vanguard, 1971, 308-315.

9862. _____. Psychoanalytic remarks about a modern totem animal. Amer Imago, 1940, 1(1).

9863. _____. Sex and the mystery story. MAHS, 1972, 6(3): 126-140 passim.

9864. Grove, T. N. The psychological prism of Arthur Clennam in Dickens's Little Dorrit. Modern Language Rev, 1973, 68: 750-755.

9865. Groves, M. Malraux's lyricism and the death of Kyo. Modern Language Rev, 1969, 64:53-61.

9866. Grow, Lynn M. The dream scenes of Invisible Man. Wichita State Univ. Bulletin, 1974, 50(3):3-12.

9867. Grundy, Dominick E. Growing up Dickensian. Lit & Psychol, 1972, 22:99-106.

9868. Guarnero, Luisa. Stendhal e la psicologica dell'amore e delle donne. Turin: Gheroni, 1946.

9869. Gubler, D. V. A Study of Illness and Death in the Lives and Representative Works of Leo Tolstoy and Thomas Mann. Doctoral dissertation, Brigham Young Univ., 1971.

9870. Guenzel, Quentin G. The Effect of Need for Social Approval upon Group Discussion and the Perception of Persons in Fiction. DAI, 1970, 30(10-B), 4791-92.

9871. Guérard, Albert J. The brink of darkness. Amer Imago, 1947, 4:32-41.

9872. _____. Concepts of the double. In Stories of the Double. Philadelphia: Lippincott, 1967, 1-14.

9873. _____. Conrad the Novelist. Cambridge: Harvard Univ. Press, 1958.

9874. _____. Introduction to the issue, 'Perspectives on the Novel.' Daedalus, 1963, 92:197-205.

9875. _____. The misogynous vision as high art: Faulkner's Sanctuary. Southern Rev, 1976, 12:215-231; In The Triumph of the Novel. NY: Oxford Univ. Press, 1976.

9876. _____. The Triumph of the Novel: Dickens, Dostoevsky, Faulkner. NY: Oxford Univ. Press, 1976.

9877. Guignet, Jean. Deux romans existentialistes: La Nausée et L'Etranger. French Rev, 1949, 23:86-91.

9878. Guillemin, H. Hugo et le rêve. Mercure de France, 1951, 312:5-32.

9879. Guillory, Daniel L. The mystique of childhood in American literature. Tulane Studies in English, 1978, 23:229-247.

9880. Guiomar, Michel. Inconscient et imaginaire dans 'Le Grand Meaulnes.' Paris: Corti, 1964.
9881. Gulbertson, Diana, & Valley, John. Personality theory in Gide: The plume of the eagle. Hartford Studies in Lit, 1976, 8:98-115.
9882. Gullón, Ricardo. Galdós, novelista moderno. Madrid: Taurus, 1960.
9883. _____. Lo maravilloso en Galdós. Insula, 1955, 10:1, 11.
9884. _____. Una novela psicológica. Insula, 1952, 7:4.
9885. _____. [Unamuno.] Revista Hispánica Moderna, 1965, 21.
9886. Gundvaldsen, Kaare M. Franz Kafka and psychoanalysis. Univ Toronto Q, 1963, 32:266-281.
9887. Gunn, Edward. Myth and style in Djuna Barnes' Nightwood. Modern Fiction Studies, 1973, 19:545-555.
9888. Gunsteren-Viersen, Julia van. The marriage of 'he' and 'she': Virginia Woolf's androgynous theory. Dutch Q Rev Anglo-Amer Letters, 1976, 6:233-246.
9889. Gunter, G. O. The archetypal trickster figure in James Still's River of Earth. Appalachian Heritage, 1979, 7: 52-55.
9890. Gunter, R. The functioning of sentence structure in the stream-of-consciousness technique of William Faulkner's The Sound and the Fury: a study of linguistic stylistics. Mississippi Q, 1968, 22:274.
9891. Gupta, R. K. 'Bartleby': Melville's critique of reason. Indian J Amer Studies, 1974, 4:66-71.
9892. Guretzky-Cornitz, Ulrike von. Versuch einer sozialpsychologischen Interpretation des psychologischen Romans von Ludwig Tieck: 'William Lovell.' Paderborn: Author, 1977.
9893. Gutermuth, Mary. Triangular schizophrenia and the Execution of Aragon. Kentucky Romance Q, 1967, 14:379-392.
9894. Guthmann, Herbert J. The Characterization of the Psychiatrist in American Fiction, 1859-1965. DAI, 1970, 30: 4451A.
9895. Gutierrez, Donald. B. Traven's death-ship commune. Texas Q, 1977, 20:59-78.
9896. Gutiérrez-Noriega, Carlos. Cervantes y la psicología medica. Rev de Neuro-Psiquiatría, 1946, 9:107-119.
9897. _____. Contribucion de Cervantes a la psicologia y a la psiquiatría. Rev de Neuro-Psiquiatría, 1949, 7:149-190.
9898. _____. La personalidad y el character en la obra de Cervantes. San Marcos, 1947, 4:516-541.
9899. Guttmann, Allen. The Jewish Writer in America: Assimilation and the Crisis of Identity. NY: Oxford Univ. Press, 1971.
9900. Gutwirth, Marcel M. Le Narrateur et son double. Rev d'Histoire Littéraire de la France, 1971, 71(5-6):921-935.
9901. Gwiazda, Ronald Emery. The Spiral Staircase and the Blank Wall: Fantasy and Anxiety in Three Early Novels by Henry James. DAI, 1972, 35:6714A.
9902. Gwynn, Frederick L., & Blotner, Joseph L. The Fiction of J. D. Salinger. Pittsburgh: Pittsburgh Univ. Press, 1958.

9903. Gyurko, Lanin A. Alienation and the absurd in two stories by Cortázar. Kentucky Romance Q, 1974, 21:43-58.

9904. _____. The bestial and the demonic in two stories by Cortázar. Rev des Langues Vivantes, 1973, 39:112-130.

9905. _____. Borges and the theme of the double. Iberoamerikanisches Archiv, 1976, 2:193-226.

9906. _____. Cortázar fictional children: freedom and its constraints. Neophilologus, 1973, 57:24-41.

9907. _____. Destructive and ironically redemptive fantasy in Cortázar. Hispania, 1973, 56:988-999.

9908. _____. Guilt and delusion in two stories by Cortázar. Critique: Studies in Modern Fiction, 1973, 14:75-90.

9909. _____. Hallucination and nightmare in two stories by Cortázar. Modern Language Rev, 1972, 69:550-562.

9910. _____. Identity and the demonic in two narratives by Fuentes. Revista de Letras, 1974, 21:87-118.

9911. _____. The image of woman in two novels of Carlos Fuentes. Research Studies, 1975, 43:1-18.

9912. _____. Modern Hispanic American fiction. Symposium, 1971, 25:359-374.

9913. _____. Myths of Ulysses in Fuentes's Zona Sagrada. Modern Language Rev, 1974, 69:316-324.

9914. _____. The pseudo-liberated woman in Fuentes' Zona Sagrada. J Spanish Studies: Twentieth Century, 1975, 3:17-43.

9915. _____. Rivalry and the double in Borges' Guayaquil. Romance Notes, 1973, 15:37-46.

9916. _____. Self, double, and mask in Fuentes' La muerte de Artemio Cruz. Texas Studies in Lit & Language, 1974, 16:363-384.

9917. _____. Self-obsession and death in three stories by Cortázar. Research Studies, 1973, 41:234-251.

9918. _____. The stifling of identity in Las buenas consciencias. Hispania, 1976, 59:225-238.

9919. _____. Structure and theme in Fuentes' La Muerte de Artemio Cruz. Symposium, 1980, 34:29-41.

9920. Haas, Rudolf. Zum Todesmotif im Werk Hemingways. Neueren Sprache, 1959, 10:455-465.

9921. Haasse, Hella S. Zelfstandig, bijvoeglijk Zeven essays over schrijvers, schrijfsters en hun personages. Amsterdam: Querido, 1972.

9922. Habe, Hans. Tolstoi, Mauriac und die Psychoanalyse. Die Kultur, 1960, 9, No. 169.

9923. Habegger, Alfred. Austistic tyrant: Howells' self-sacrificial woman and Jamesian renunciation. Novel: Forum on Fiction, 1976, 10:27-39.

9924. Haberland, Paul M. Number symbolism: the father-daughter relationship in E. T. A. Hoffmann's 'Rat Krespel.' Language Q, 1975, 13(3-4):39-42.

9925. Haberstroh, Charles J., Jr. Melville, marriage and Mardi. Studies in the Novel, 1977, 9:247-260.

9926. _____. Redburn: the psychological pattern. Studies in Amer Fiction, 1974, 2:133-144.

9927. _____. Melville's Fathers: A Study of the Father Substitutes in Melville's Fiction. DAI, 1972, 32:4564A.

9928. Hackett, Francis. The novel and human personality. New York Times Book Rev, 15 Aug 1948.

9929. Hadas, Patricia. Spreading the difference: one way to read Gertrude Stein's Tender Buttons. Twentieth Century Lit, 1978, 24(1):57-75.

9930. Haddad, Elaine. Maximiliano Rubin. Archivium, 1957, 7: 101-114.

9931. Haddick, Vern. Fear and growth: reflections on 'The Beast in the Jungle.' J Otto Rank Assn, 1974-75, 9(2):38-42.

9932. Hafter, Monroe Z. Ironic reprise in Galdós novels. PMLA, 1961, 86:233-239.

9933. Hafter, Ronald S. Sterne's Affective Art and Eighteenth Century Psychology. Doctoral dissertation, Brandeis Univ., 1970; DAI, 1970, 31(6-A), 2877.

9934. Hagan, John. Déjà vu and the effect of timelessness in Faulkner's Absalom, Absalom! Bucknell Rev, 1963, 11(2):31-52; In Garvin, H. R. (ed), Makers of the Twentieth-Century Novel. Lewisburg: Bucknell Univ. Press, 1977, 192-207.

9935. _____. The divided mind of Anthony Trollope. Nineteenth Century Fiction, 1959, 14:1-26.

9936. _____. Patterns of character development in Tolstoy's War and Peace: Nicholas, Natasha, and Mary. PMLA, 1969, 84:235-244.

9937. _____. A reinterpretation of The Mill on the Floss. PMLA, 1972, 87:53-63.

9938. Hagood, Patricia. Lancelot and Heathcliff: Obsessive-Compulsive Traits of the Hero. DAI, 1978, 39:3563A-64A.

9939. Hagopian, John V. Hemingway: ultimate exile. Mosaic, 1975, 8(3):77-87.

9940. _____. Nihilism in Faulkner's The Sound and the Fury. Modern Fiction Studies, 1967, 13:45-55.

9941. Haig, S. The identities of Fabrice del Dongo. French Studies, 1973, 27:170-176.

9942. Hale, William H. A memorandum: from Freud to Norman Mailer, et al. Horizon, 1962, 4:55.

9943. Hales, Dell R. Dreams and the demonic in traditional Chinese short stories. In Nienhauser, W. H. (ed), Critical Essays on Chinese Literature. Hong Kong: Chinese Univ. Hong Kong, 1976, 71-88.

9944. Haley, Bruce. Mens sana in corpore sano: Victorian psychophysiology. In The Healthy Body and Victorian Culture. Cambridge: Harvard Univ. Press, 1978, 23-45.

9945. Halir, S. Psychiatrische Eindrücke bei Thomas Manns Roman der Zauberberg. Doctoral dissertation, Univ. Marburg, 1973.

9946. Hall, James. The Lunatic Giant in the Drawing Room: The British and American Novel Since 1930. Bloomington: Indiana Univ. Press, 1968.

9947. Hall, Linda B. The Cipactli monster: woman as destroyer in Carlos Fuentes. Southwest Rev, 1975, 60:246-255.
9948. Hall, Marlene La Verne. Consciousness and the Unconscious: Henry James and Jungian Psychology. DAI, 1975, 35: 6097A.
9949. Hallab, Mary C. Y. Psychoanalytic Criticism of the Life and Works of Henry James. DAI, 1971, 32:966A.
9950. Hallé, Thérèse. Le Phénomène du double chez Dostoievsky et chez Maupassant. Etudes Slaves et Est-Européens, 1957-58, 2:238-241.
9951. Halliburton, David. Edgar Allan Poe: A Phenomenological View. Princeton: Princeton Univ. Press, 1973.
9952. Hallman, Ralph J. The archetype in Peter Pan. J Analytic Psychol, 1969, 14:65-73.
9953. Halperin, John. Egoism and Self-Discovery in the Victorian Novel. NY: Lenox Hill, 1974.
9954. _____. Trollope and feminism. South Atlantic Q, 1978, 77:179-188.
9955. Halpern, Sidney. The man who forgot he crucified Jesus: an exegesis of Anatole France's Procurator of Judea. Psychoanal Rev, 1964-65, 51:597-611.
9956. Halsband, Robert. Women and literature in 18th century England. In Fritz, P. , & Morton, R. (eds), Women in the 18th Century and Other Essays. Toronto: Hakkert, 1976, 55-71.
9957. Haltresht, Michael. Disease imagery in Conrad's The Secret Agent. Lit & Psychol, 1971, 21:101-105.
9958. _____. The dread of space in Conrad's The Secret Agent. Lit & Psychol, 1972, 22:89-97.
9959. _____. Dreams as a characterization device in Hersey's 'White Lotus. ' Notes on Contemporary Lit, 1971, 1(3):4-5.
9960. Halverson, John. The shadow in Moby-Dick. Amer Q, 1963, 15:436-446.
9961. Hamblen, Abigail Ann. The best-known teenager: Huck Finn. Mark Twain J, 1967, 13(3):15-18.
9962. _____. Henry James and disease. Dalhousie Rev, 1964, 44:57-63.
9963. Hamblin, Ellen N. Adulterous Heroines in Nineteenth Century Literature: A Comparative Literature Study. DAI, 1977, 38:2761A.
9964. Hamilton, James W. Jensen's Gradiva: a further interpretation. Amer Imago, 1973, 30:380-412.
9965. Hammond, John G. Solipsism and the sexual imagination in Robert Creeley's fiction. Criticism, 1975, 16(3):59-69.
9966. Hancock, Maxine. Fire: symbolic motif in Faulkner. English Q, 1970, 3(3):19-23.
9967. Hanenkrat, F. T. An Investigation of Hawthorne's Psychology: The Themes of Evil and Love in Selected Short Stories. DAI, 1971, 32:2688A.
9968. Hankin, Cherry. Fantasy and the sense of an ending in the work of Katherine Mansfield. Modern Fiction Studies, 1978, 24:465-474.

9969. Hanney, Margaret. Notes in basic English on the 'ALP' record. Psyche, 1932, 12:86-95.

9970. Hanning, Robert W. The romance plot and the crisis of inner awareness. In The Individual in Twelfth-Century Romance. New Haven: Yale Univ. Press, 1977, 194-233.

9971. Hannum, Hunter G. Archetypal echoes in Mann's Death in Venice. Psychol Perspectives, 1974, 5:48-59.

9972. _____. Mann's Joseph novels: a journey toward individuation. Psychol Perspectives, 1975, 6:163-175.

9973. Hansen, Hans-Sievert. Narzissmus in Storms Märchen: Eine psychoanalytische Interpretation. Schriften den Theodor-Storm-Gesellschaft, 1977, 26:37-56.

9974. Hansen, Olaf. Henry Miller: der konservative avantgardist und das Obszöne. In Glaser, H. A. (ed), Wöllustige Phantasie: Sexualästhetik der Literatur. Munich: Hanser.

9975. Harada, K. The theme of incest in The Sound and the Fury and in Pierre. Amer Lit Rev, 1956, 14:1-7.

9976. Hardesty, William H., III. The femme fatale in The Idiot and The Arrow of Gold. Research Studies, 1976, 44:175-182.

9977. Hardin, James. Hermann Broch's theories on mass psychology and Der Versucher. German Q, 1974, 47:24-33.

9978. Hardin, Nancy Shields. A Sufi teaching story and Doris Lessing. Twentieth Century Lit, 1977, 23:314-326.

9979. Harding, Denys W. Psychological processes in the reading of fiction. British J Aesthetics, 1962, 2:133-147.

9980. Harding, M. Esther. Journey Into Self. NY: Longmans, Green, 1956.

9981. Hardwick, Elizabeth. Fiction chronicle. Partisan Rev, 1947, 14:427-431.

9982. Hardy, Barbara N. Women in D. H. Lawrence's work. In Spender, S. (ed), D. H. Lawrence; Novelist, Poet, Prophet. NY: Harper & Row, 1973, 90-121.

9983. Hardy, John Edward. Man in the Modern Novel. Seattle: Univ. Washington Press, 1964.

9984. Hare, A. Paul. Comparison of Bales' IPA and Parsons' AGIL category system [on the first three chapters of Lord of the Flies]. J Social Psychol, 1978, 105:309-310.

9985. Harfst, Betsy P. Horace Walpole and the Unconscious: An Experiment in Freudian Analysis. DA, 1968, 29:68-14972.

9986. Harger, Virginia A. Alienation and the Search for Self in the 'nouveau roman' of France and of Quebec. DAI, 1973, 34:3397A.

9987. Harkins, W. E. The theme of sterility in Olesha's Envy. Slavic Rev, 1966, 25:443-457.

9988. Harlow, Benjamin C. Some archetypal motifs in The Old Man and the Sea. McNeese Rev, 1966, 17:74-79.

9989. Hárnik, J. Anatole France über Seele des Kindes. Imago, 1917, 5:126-127.

9990. _____. Dostojewski: Njetotoschka Neswanowa, Bruchstuck eines Romans. Imago, 1913, 2:530-534.

9991. _____. Psychoanalytisches aus und über Goethes Wahl-
       verwandtschaften. Imago, 1912, 1:507-518.
9992. Harper, Howard M., Jr. Desperate Faith. Chapel Hill:
       Univ. North Carolina Press, 1967.
9993. _____. Fantasia and the psychodynamics of Women in
       Love. In Harper, H. M., Jr., & Edge, C. (eds), The
       Classic British Novel. Athens: Univ. Georgia Press,
       1972, 202-219.
9994. Harpprecht, Klaus. Stendhal: Psychologie, Eros, Musik.
       Merkur, 1973, 27:720-738.
9995. Harrex, S. C. A sense of identity: the novels of Kamala
       Markandaya. J Commonwealth Lit, 1971, 6:65-78.
9996. Harrington, Catherine Steta. Southern Fiction and the
       Quest for Identity. DA, 1964, 25:1210-11.
9997. Harrington, Henry R. Childhood, and the Victorian ideal
       of manliness in Tom Brown's Schooldays. Victorian
       Newsletter, 1973, 44:13-17.
9998. Harris, Charles B. George's illumination: unity in Giles
       Goat-Boy. Studies in the Novel, 1976, 8:172-184.
9999. _____. Todd Andrews, ontological insecurity and The
       Floating Opera. Critique, 1976, 18:34-50.
10,000. Harris, E. L'Approfondissement de la sensualité dans
       l'oeuvre romanesque de Colette. Paris: Nizet, 1973.
10,001. Harris, Janice H. Insight and experiment in D. H. Law-
       rence's early short fiction. Philological Q, 1976, 55:
       418-435.
10,002. _____. Our mute, inglorious mothers. Midwest Q,
       1975, 16:244-254.
10,003. _____. Sexual antagonism in D. H. Lawrence's early
       leadership fiction. Modern Language Studies, 1977,
       7(1):43-52.
10,004. Harris, Mason D., Jr. George Eliot and the Problems of
       Agnosticism: A Study of Philosophical Psychology.
       DAI, 1971, 32:1513A.
10,005. Hart, Clive. The sexual perversions of Leopold Bloom.
       In Bonnerot, L. (ed), Ulysses: Cinquant ans après.
       Paris: Didier, 1974, 131-136.
10,006. Hart, Pierre R. Psychological primitivism in Kotik Le-
       taev. Russian Lit Triquarterly, 1972, 4:319-330.
10,007. Hart, Willem Anne 't. De psychologie van Maigret. Ut-
       recht: Bruna, 1962.
10,008. Hartley, L. C. Sacred River; stream of consciousness:
       the evolution of a method. Sewanee Rev, 1931, 39:80-
       89.
10,009. Hartley, Susan R. The Later Novels of George Meredith:
       Women's Struggle for Emancipation. DAI, 1974, 34:
       6642A.
10,010. Hartman, Geoffrey H. The Fate of Reading and Other Es-
       says. Chicago: Univ. Chicago Press, 1975.
10,011. Hartocollis, P. Mysticism and violence: the case of Nikos
       Kazantzakis. Int J Psycho-Anal, 1974, 55:205-213.
10,012. Hartog, Curt. Aggression, femininity, and irony in Moll
       Flanders. Lit & Psychol, 1972, 22:121-138.

10, 013. Hartsock, Mildred E.   Henry James and The Cities of the Plain. Modern Language Q, 1968, 29:297-311.
10, 014. Hartungen, Christian von. Die Psychoanalyse in der modernen Literature: Mann, Heinrich, Die Unschuldige. Int Zeitschrift für Psychoanalyse, 1911, 1:499-501.
10, 015. Hartwick, Harry. The Foreground of American Fiction. NY: American Book, 1934.
10, 016. Harvey, C. J. D.   Maurice: E. M. Forster's 'homosexual novel.' Standpunte, 1971, 97:29-33.
10, 017. Harvey, Robert Charles. One Reader Reading: An Exploration of the Relationship Between Conscious and Unconscious Response in Reading Five Prose Fictions. DAI, 1978, 39:296A.
10, 018. Harvey, William John. Image and symbols. In The Art of George Eliot. London: Chatto & Windus, 1961, Ch. 10; NY: Oxford Univ. Press, 1962.
10, 019. Hass, Rudolf. Zum Todesmotiv im Werk Hemingways. Neueren Sprachen, 1959, 455-465.
10, 020. Hassan, Ihab Habib.   The idea of adolescence in American fiction. Amer Q, 1958, 10:312-324.
10, 021. _____. Radical Innocence: Studies in the Contemporary American Novel. Princeton: Princeton Univ. Press, 1961.
10, 022. Hatano, K. [The Psychology of Creation.] Tokyo: Ganshodo Shoten, 1938.
10, 023. Hatcher, Harlan H. Eroticism and the psychological novel. In Creating the Modern American Novel. NY: Farrar, 1935, 172-187; NY: Russell & Russell, 1965, 172-187.
10, 024. _____. The novel as an educative force. College English, 1940, 2:37-46.
10, 025. Hatfield, Henry. Death in the late works of Thomas Mann. German Rev, 1959, 34:284-288.
10, 026. Hattam, E. Hemingway's 'An Alpine Idyll.' Modern Fiction Studies, 1966, 12:261-265.
10, 027. Haule, James Mark.   The Theme of Isolation in the Fiction of Dorothy M. Richardson, Virginia Woolf, and James Joyce. DAI, 1975, 35:7905A-06A.
10, 028. Hausbrich-Kochelt, M. Analiza psychopathologicga postaci wystepujacych w powiesci Fiodora Dostojewskiego pt. 'Wspomienia z domu umarlych.' Psychiatria Polska, 1971, 5:91-95.
10, 029. Hawkes, John. The Floating Opera and Second Skin. Mosaic, 1974, 8:17-28.
10, 030. Hawkins, E. W. The stream of consciousness novel. Atlantic Monthly, 1926, Sept, 356-360.
10, 031. Haworth, Helen E. 'A milk-white lamb that bleats?' Some stereotypes of women in romantic literature. Humanities Assn Rev, 1973, 24:277-293.
10, 032. Hawthorn, Jeremy. Joseph Conrad: Language and Fictional Self-Consciousness. Lincoln: Univ. Nebraska, 1979.
10, 033. Hayes, Marie Royce. Death in the Works of Balzac, Flaubert and Zola. DAI, 1977, 37(8):5169-A.
10, 034. Hayes, Tricia.   Adolescent awakenings in the fiction of Doris Lessing. Doris Lessing Newsletter, 1979, 3:9-10.

10, 035.   Hayford, Harrison.   Melville's Freudian slip.   Amer Lit,
           1958, 30:366-368.
10, 036.   Hayles, Nancy Katherine.   The Ambivalent Ideal: The
           Concept of Androgyny in English Renaissance Literature.
           DAI, 1977, 38:2140A.
10, 037.   Hayman, David.   The empirical Molly.   In Staley, T. F.,
           & Benstock, B. (eds), Approaches to Ulysses: Ten Es-
           says. Pittsburgh: Univ. Pittsburgh Press, 1970, 103-
           135.
10, 038.   _____. From Finnegans Wake: a sentence in progress.
           PMLA, 1958, 73:136-154.
10, 039.   Hayman, Theresa Lenora D.   Alienation in the Life and
           Works of Richard Wright.   DAI, 1976, 37:2871A.
10, 040.   Haymes, Howard J.   Postwar writing and the literature of
           the women's liberation movement.   Psychiatry, 1975,
           38:328-333.
10, 041.   Hayne, Barrie Stewart.   The Divided Self: The Alter Ego
           as Theme and Device in Brockden Brown, Hawthorne
           and James.   Doctoral dissertation, Harvard Univ.,
           1964.
10, 042.   Hays, Hoffman R.   The Dangerous Sex.   NY: Putnam,
           1964.
10, 043.   Hays, Peter L.   The incest theme in Invisible Man.   West-
           ern Humanities Rev, 1969, 23:335-339.
10, 044.   _____. The Limping Hero: Grotesques in Literature.
           NY: New York Univ. Press, 1971.
10, 045.   _____. The Maimed Figure: An Ancient Archetype in
           Modern Literature.   DA, 1966, 66-1787.
10, 046.   Hayter, Aletha.   The sanitary idea and a Victorian novelist.
           History Today, 1969, 19:840-847.
10, 047.   Hayward, Susan.   Le Rôle du monologue intérieur dans les
           romans de Samuel Beckett.   Language & Style, 1974, 7:
           181-191.
10, 048.   Hazen, Lynn S.   'Vessels of Salvation': Fathers and
           Daughters in Six Dickens Novels.   DAI, 1978, 39:1587A-
           88A.
10, 049.   Headley, Susan M.   The Thematic Function of Water Im-
           agery in A la recherche du temps perdu.   DAI, 1972,
           33:2375A.
10, 050.   Heamen, Robert J.   Love, Adversity, and Achievement of
           Identity: A Study of the Young Men in the Novels of
           Charles Dickens.   DA, 1969, 30:2024A.
10, 051.   Hecht, M. B.   Uncanniness, yearning, and Franz Kafka's
           works.   Amer Imago, 1952, 9:45-55.
10, 052.   Hefter-Noeldechen, Lotte.   Kindergestalten im Amerikan-
           ischen Roman.   Berlin: 1936.
10, 053.   Heger, R.   Der österreichische Roman des 20. Jahrhun-
           derts.   Vienna: Braumüller, 1971.
10, 054.   Heider, F.   The description of the psychological environ-
           ment in the work of Marcel Proust.   Character & Per-
           sonality, 1941, 9:295-314.
10, 055.   Heilbrun, Carolyn G.   The masculine wilderness of the

American novel.   Saturday Rev, 1972, 55(5):41-44.

10, 056.   Heilman, Robert B.   Charlotte Brontë, reason and the moon.
Nineteenth Century Fiction, 1960, 14:283-302.

10, 057.   _____. The Freudian reading of 'The Turn of the Screw. '
Modern Language Notes, 1947, 62:443-445.

10, 058.   _____. Hardy's Sue Bridehead.   Nineteenth Century Fiction, 1965, 20:307-323.

10, 059.   _____. 'The Turn of the Screw' as poem.   Univ. Kansas City Rev, 1948, 14; In Scott, W. (ed), Five Approaches to Literary Criticism.   NY: Collier, 1962,
283-302.

10, 060.   Heiman, Marcel.   Rip Van Winkle: a psychoanalytic note
on the story and its author.   Amer Imago, 1959, 16:3-
47.

10, 061.   Heimer, J. W.   Patterns of betrayal in the novels of Joseph
Conrad.   Ball State Univ. Forum, 1967, 8:30-39.

10, 062.   Heinbaugh, Nan S.   The Study of Psychopathology in the
Works of Truman Capote.   DAI, 1975, 36:3043-44.

10, 063.   Heinstein, Jósef.   Egzistencializmus és freudismus Alberto
Moravia müveiben.   Filólgiai Közlöny, 1971, 17:71-
83.

10, 064.   Heiring, P. F.   The bedsteadfastness of Molly Bloom.
Modern Fiction Studies, 1969, 15:49-61.

10, 065.   Heiserman, Arthur.   The Novel Before the Novel.   Chicago:
Univ. Chicago Press, 1979.

10, 066.   _____, & Miller, James E.   J. D. Salinger: some crazy
cliffs.   Western Humanities Rev, 1956, 10:129-137.

10, 067.   Heisig, James W.   Pinocchio: archetype of the motherless
child.   In Butler, F. , & Brockman, B. A. (eds), Children's Literature: The Great Excluded.   Storrs, Conn:
Children's Lit Assn, 1974, 23-35.

10, 068.   Heldman, Elizabeth Ann.   The Dilemma of the Fragmented
Self: Psychological Allegories in the Major Tales of
Edgar Allan Poe.   DAI, 1975, 36:2206A.

10, 069.   Heller, Erich.   Man guilty and man ashamed.   I.   Man
guilty.   Reflections on The Trial.   Psychiatry, 1974,
37:10-21.

10, 070.   Heller, Peter.   The creative unconscious and the spirit: a
study of polarities in Hesse's image of the writer.   Modern Language Forum, 1954, 38:28-40.

10, 071.   _____. The masochistic rebel in German literature.
JAAC, 1953, 11:198-213.

10, 072.   Hellerman, M. Kasey.   The Coatlicue-Malinche conflict:
a mother and son identity crisis in the writings of Carlos Fuentes.   Hispania, 1974, 57:868-875.

10, 073.   Helmcke, Henry Conrad.   The Delineation of Family Relationships in the Narrative Works of Arthur Schnitzler.
Master's thesis, Duke Univ. , 1957.

10, 074.   _____. Die Familie im Romanwerk von Thomas Wolfe.
Heidelberg: Winter, 1967.

10, 075.   Helmick, Evelyn T.   Myth in the works of Willa Cather.
Midcontinent Amer Studies J, 1969, 9:63-69.

10, 076. Helms, Denise M. A note of Stephen's dream in Portrait.
          James Joyce Q, 1970, 8:151-156.
10, 077. Helson, Ravenna M. Fantasy and self-discovery. Horn-
          book, 1970, 46(2):121-134.
10, 078. _____. Heroic and tender modes in women authors of
          fantasy. J Personality, 1973, 41:493-512; In Denmark,
          F. L. (ed), Women. NY: Psychological Dimensions,
          1976, Ch. 5.
10, 079. _____. Heroic, the comic, and the tender: patterns of
          literary fantasy and their authors. J Personality, 1973,
          41:163-184.
10, 080. _____. Sex-specific patterns in creative literary fantasy.
          J Personality, 1970, 38:344-363.
10, 081. Helterman, Jeffrey. Gorgons in Mississippi: Eudora Wel-
          ty's 'Petrified Man. " Notes on Mississippi Writers,
          1974, 7:12-20.
10, 082. Hemenway, Robert. Brockden Brown's twice told insanity
          tale. Amer Lit, 1968, 40:211-215.
10, 083. _____. Enigmas of being in As I Lay Dying. Modern
          Fiction Studies, 1970, 16:133-146.
10, 084. _____. Fiction in the age of Jefferson: the early Amer-
          ican novel as intellectual document. Midcontinent Amer
          Studies J, 1968, 9:91-101.
10, 085. Hemmings, F. W. J. Balzac: An Interpretation of La Comé-
          die humaine. NY: Random House, 1967.
10, 086. _____. Fire in Zola's fiction: variations on an ele-
          mental theme. Yale French Studies, 1969, 42:26-37.
10, 087. Henderson, D. James. Exorcism, possession and the
          Dracula cult: a synopsis of object-relations psychology.
          Bulletin Menninger Clinic, 1976, 40:603-628.
10, 088. Henderson, Philip. Stephen Dedalus versus Bloom. In
          The Novel Today. London: Lane, 1936, 81-87; Folcroft,
          Pa: Folcroft, 1969, 1973.
10, 089. Hendin, Josephine. Experimental fiction. In Hoffman, D.
          (ed), Harvard Guide to Contemporary American Writing.
          Cambridge: Harvard Univ. Press, 1979.
10, 090. _____. Vulnerable men, invulnerable women; excerpt
          from Vulnerable People: a view of American fiction
          since 1945. Psychol Today, 1978, 12:21+.
10, 091. _____. The World of Flannery O'Connor. Bloomington:
          Indiana Univ. Press, 1972.
10, 092. Hendrickson, Norejane J. , Perkins, Deborah, White, Sylvia,
          & Buck, Timothy. Parent-daughter relationships in fic-
          tion. Family Coordinator, 1975, 24:257-265.
10, 093. Henel, I. Ein Hungerkünstler. Deutsche Vierteljahrschrift
          und Geistesgeschichte, 1964, 38:230-247.
10, 094. Henke, Suzette A. Joyce and Krafft-Ebing. James Joyce
          Q, 1979, 17:84-86.
10, 095. _____. Joyce's Bloom: beyond sexual possessiveness.
          Amer Imago, 1975, 32:329-334.
10, 096. _____. Joyce's Moraculous Sindbook: A Study of 'Ulys-
          ses. ' Columbus: Ohio State Univ. Press, 1978.

10,097. Henken, Leo J. Problems and digressions in the Victorian novel (1860-1900): Part XIV, psychic phenomena. Bulletin Bibliography and Dramatic Index, 1949, 19:202-205.

10,098. Henkle, Roger B. Pynchon's tapestries on the western wall. Modern Fiction Studies, 1971, 17:207-220.

10,099. Henley, Nancy M. Achievement and affiliation imagery in American fiction, 1901-1961. J Personality & Social Psychol, 1967, 7:208-210.

10,100. Hennelly, Mark M., Jr. Games and ritual in Deliverance. J Altered States of Consciousness, 1977-78, 3:337-353.

10,101. _____. Hawthorne's Opus Alchymicum: 'Ethan Brand.' Emerson Society Q, 1976, 22:96-106.

10,102. _____. Ishmael's nightmare and the American Eve. Amer Imago, 1973, 30:274-293.

10,103. _____. Oedipus and Orpheus in the maelstrom: the traumatic rebirth of the artist. Poe Studies, 1976, 9:6-11.

10,104. _____. Sibyl in the Gloom: A Study of Guilt in the Life and Novels of George Eliot. DAI, 1971, 32:920A.

10,105. _____. The time machine: a romance of the human heart. Extrapolation, 1979, 20:154-167.

10,106. Henniger, Gerd. Zur Genealogie des schwarzen Humors. Neue Deutsche Heft, 1966, 13:18-34.

10,107. Henninger, Peter. Wissenschaft und Dichtung bei Musil und Freud. MLN, 1979, 94:541-568.

10,108. Henríquez Ureña, Pedro. Pérez Galdós. Unión Hispanoamericana, 1920, 4:3.

10,109. Henry, Patrick. On the theme of homosexuality in Candide. Romance Notes, 1978, 19:44-48.

10,110. Hepburn, James G. The Art of Arnold Bennett. Bloomington: Indiana Univ. Press, 1963.

10,111. _____. Disarming and uncanny visions: Freud's 'The Uncanny' with regard to form and content in stories by Sherwood Anderson and D. H. Lawrence. Lit & Psychol, 1959, 9:9-12.

10,112. Heppenstall, Rayner. Streams of consciousness. In The Fourfold Tradition. London: Barrie & Rockliffe, 1961, 132-159.

10,113. Heraucourt, W. Die Darstellung des englischen Nationalcharakters in John Galsworthys Forsyte Sage. Marburg: Elwert, 1939.

10,114. Herbert, C. De Quincey and Dickens. Victorian Studies, 1974, 17:247-263.

10,115. Herbert, T. Walter, Jr. Homosexuality and spiritual aspiration in Moby-Dick. Canadian Rev Amer Studies, 1975, 6:50-58.

10,116. Herbert, Wray C. Conrad's psychic landscape: the mythic element in 'Karain.' Conradiana, 1976, 8:225-232.

10,117. Herlong, Ruby Padgette. A Study of Human Relationships in the Novels of Eudora Welty. DAI, 1976, 36:7422A.

10,118. Herman, Rita. Existence in Laços de Família. Luso-Brazilian Rev, 1967, 4(1):69-74.

10,119. Herndon, Jerry A. Hawthorne's dream imagery. Amer Lit, 1975, 46:538-545.

10,120. Herring, H. D. Madness in At Heaven's Gate: a metaphor of the self in Warren's fiction. Four Quarters, 1972, 21(4):56-66.

10,121. Herring, Phillip F. Experimentation with a landscape: pornotopography in Ulysses--the phallocy of imitative form. Modern Fiction Studies, 1974, 20:371-378.

10,122. Herrscher, Walter. Is sister really insane? Another look at 'Why I Live at the P. O. ' Notes on Contemporary Lit, 1975, 5:5-7.

10,123. Hertz, Neil H. Freud and The Sandman. In Harari, J. V. (ed), Textual Strategies. Ithaca, NY: Cornell Univ. Press, 1979, 296-319.

10,124. Herz, Judith Scherer. The double nature of Forster's fiction: A Room with a View and The Longest Journey. English Lit in Transition, 1978, 21:254-265.

10,125. Hesnard, Angelo Louis Marie. Le Message incompris de Kafka. Psyché, 1947, 12:1161-1173.

10,126. Hesse, Hermann. Artists and psychoanalysis. In My Belief. Essays on Life and Art. NY: Farrar, Straus & Giroux, 1974 (1918), 46-51; Almanach, 1926, 34-38; Psychoanal Rev, 1963, 50:5-10; in Sherman, M. H. (ed), Psychoanalysis in America. Springfield, Ill: Thomas, 1966.

10,127. _____. Thoughts on The Idiot of Dostoevsky. Dial, 1922, 73:199-204.

10,128. Hesse, M. Gudrun. The theme of suicide in the French-Canadian novel since 1945. Mosaic, 1972, 5(4):119-134.

10,129. Hiatt, L. R. Nabokov's Lolita: a Freudian cryptic crossword. Amer Imago, 1967, 24:360-370.

10,130. Hibbett, Howard S. Natsume Sōseki and the psychological novel. In Shively, D. H. (ed), Tradition and Modernization in Japanese Culture. Princeton: Princeton Univ. Press, 1971, 305-346.

10,131. _____. Tradition and trauma in the contemporary Japanese novel. Daedalus, 1966, 96:925-940.

10,132. Hickey, James W. Freudian criticism and Miss Lonelyhearts. In Madden, D. (ed), Nathanael West: The Cheaters and the Cheated. De Land, Fla: Everett/Edwards, 1973, 111-150.

10,133. Hicks, Eric C. Swann's dream and the world of sleep. Yale French Studies, 1965, 1:106-116.

10,134-5. Hicks, Granville (ed). The Living Novel. NY: Macmillan, 1957.

10,136. Higgins, Brian, & Parker, Hershel. The flawed grandeur of Melville's Pierre. In Pullen, F. (ed), New Perspectives on Melville. Kent, Ohio: Kent State Univ. Press, 1978, 162-196; Edinburgh: Univ. Edinburg Press, 1978, 162-196.

10,137. Hilborn, Harry W. Lo subconsciente en la psicologia de Sancho Panza. In Körner, K. -H. , & Klaus, R. (eds),

Studia Iberica. Bern: Francke, 1973, 267-280.

10,138. Hill, C. B. T. A Study of Mesmerism and the Literature of the 19th Century, with Particular Reference to Harriet Martineau. Master's thesis, Univ. Birmingham, England, 1976.

10,139. Hill, Douglas B., Jr. Faulkner's Caddy. Canadian Rev Amer Studies, 1976, 7:26-38.

10,140. Hill, J. M. Frankenstein and the physiognomy of desire. Amer Imago, 1975, 32:333-358.

10,141. Hill, John S. The dual hallucination in 'The Fall of the House of Usher.' Southwestern Rev, 1963, 48:396-402.

10,142. _____. The influence of Cesare Lombroso on Frank Norris's early fiction. Amer Lit, 1970, 42:8991.

10,143. Hiller, Catherine. Personality and Persona: The Narrators in John Updike's Fiction. DAI, 1973, 33:4416A-17A.

10,144. Hiller, Kurt. Wo bleibt der homoerotik Roman. Jahrbuch für Sexuelle Zwischenstufen, 1914, 14:328-332.

10,145. Hilliard, Raymond Francis. Role-Playing and the Development of Jane Austen's Psychological Realism. DAI, 1976, 37:2895A-96A.

10,146. Hilsbecher, Walter. Ein Gegenbild zum Fetisch 'Jugend.' Merkur, 1972, 26(285):99-101.

10,147. Hillway, Tyrus. Melville's use of two pseudo-sciences. Modern Language Notes, 1950, 64:145-150.

10,148. Himelick, Raymond. Notes on the care and feeding of nightmares: Burton, Erasmus and Sylvia Plath. Western Humanities Rev, 1974, 28:313-326.

10,149. Hindus, Maurice. The Proustian Vision. NY: Columbia Univ. Press, 1954; Toronto: Oxford Univ. Press, 1954.

10,150. Hinz, Evelyn J. Sons and Lovers: the archetypal dimensions of Lawrence's oedipal tragedy. D. H. Lawrence Rev, 1972, 5:26-53.

10,151. _____, & Teunissen, John J. The Pietà as icon in The Golden Notebook. Contemporary Lit, 1973, 14:457-470.

10,152. _____, & Teunissen, J. J. Surfacing: Margaret Atwood's Nymph Complaining. Contemporary Lit, 1979, 20:221-236.

10,153. Hinz, John P. Alice meets the Don (the story of Don Quixote and that of Alice and with the end of the dream.) South Atlantic Q, 1953, 52:253-266.

10,154. _____. A lost lady and The Professor's House. Virginia Q Rev, 1953.

10,155. _____. Restless Heir: The Boy in American Fiction. DA, 1960, 20:3727-3728.

10,156. Hirsch, Gordon D. Charles Dickens' nurse's stories. Psychoanal Rev, 1975, 62:173-179.

10,157. _____. Hero and Villain in the Novels of Charles Dickens: A Psychoanalytic Study. DAI, 1972, 32:4612A.

10,158. _____. The Laurentian double: images of D. H. Lawrence in the stories. D. H. Lawrence Rev, 1977, 10:270-276.

10,159.   . The monster was a lady: on the psychology of
          Mary Shelley's Frankenstein. Hartford Studies in Lit,
          1975, 7:116-153.

10,160.   . The mysteries in Bleak House; a psychoanalytic
          study. In Partlow, R. B. (ed), Dickens Studies Annual,
          Vol. 4. Carbondale: Southern Illinois Univ. Press,
          1975, 132-152.

10,161. Hirschbach, Frank Donald. The Arrow and the Lyre: A
          Study of the Role of Love in the Works of Thomas Mann.
          NY: Heinman, 1955.

10,162. Hirschberg, Stuart. Bloom revealed through the contents of
          his secret drawers. Notes on Contemporary Lit, 1975,
          5(5):2-3.

10,163. Hitschmann, Edward. Zur Entstehung des Kinderlichen von
          Selma Lagerlöf. Wunderbare Reise des kleinen Nils
          Holgersson mit den Wildgäusen. Almanach, 1937, 54-63.

10,164.   . Zum Werden des Romandichters. Imago, 1912,
          1:49-55.

10,165. Hoberg, Perry F. Poe: trickster-cosmologist. American
          Transcendental Q, 1975, 26:30-37; In Benton, R. P. (ed),
          Poe as Literary Cosmologer in 'Eureka. ' Hartford,
          Conn: Transcendental Books, 1975.

10,166. Hoberman, John Milton. The Psychology of the Collabora-
          tor in the Norwegian Novel. DAI, 1976, 37:323A.

10,167. Hochheimer, Wolfgang. Zur Psychologie von Goethes Wahl-
          verwandtschaften. Psyche, 1953, 7:32-54.

10,168. Hochman, Baruch. 'Another Ego': The Changing View of
          Self and Society in the Work of D. H. Lawrence. DA,
          1965, 25:7269; Los Angeles: Univ. Southern California
          Press, 1970.

10,169.   . Child and man in Philip Roth. Midstream,
          1967, 13:68-76.

10,170. Hoeber, Daniel R. The 'unkinging' of man: intellectual
          background as structural device in Sherwood Anderson's
          Poor White. South Dakota Rev, 1977, 15:45-60.

10,171. Hoekstra, Ellen Louise Jarvis. The Characterization of
          Women in the Novels of Charles Brockden Brown. DAI,
          1976, 36:8059A.

10,172. Hoerner, Dennis Roy. D. H. Lawrence's 'Carbon' and Wil-
          helm Reich's 'Core': The Bio-Psychological Basis of
          The Rainbow. DAI, 1977, 38:1379A-80A.

10,173. Hoeveler, Diane. Oedipus Agonistes' mothers and sons in
          Richard Wright's fiction. Black Amer Fiction Forum,
          1978, 12:65-68.

10,174. Hoevels, Fritz E. [A novel about a fetishist by O. Paniz-
          za.] Praxis der Psychotherapie, 1973, 18:205-213.

10,175. Hofer, Ernest H. The Realization of Conscience in the
          Later Henry James. DA, 1960, 21:197.

10,176. Hoffer, Peter Thomas. Childhood, Youth and Adolescence
          in the Works of Klaus Mann. DAI, 1975, 36:2865A.

10,177. Hoffman, Daniel Gerard. Form and Fable in American
          Fiction. NY: Oxford Univ. Press, 1961.

10,178. _____. I have been faithful to you in my fashion: the
         remarriage of Ligeia's husband. Southern Rev, 1972,
         8:89-105.
10,179. _____. Poe Poe Poe Poe Poe Poe Poe.   Garden City,
         NY: Doubleday, 1972.
10,180. Hoffman, Frederick J. Freudianism and the Literary Mind.
         Baton Rouge: Louisiana State Univ. Press, 1945, 1957;
         NY: Grove, 1961.
10,181. _____. Freudianism: A Study of Influences and Reac-
         tions, Especially as Revealed in the Fiction of James
         Joyce, D. H. Lawrence, Sherwood Anderson, and Waldo
         Frank. DA, 1943, 41:81-88.
10,182. _____. Infroyce. In Givens, S. (ed), James Joyce:
         Two Decades of Criticism. NY: Vanguard, 1948, 1963,
         390-435; In Freudianism and the Literary Mind. Baton
         Rouge: Louisiana State Univ. Press, 1945, 1957, 1967,
         116-150.
10,183. _____. Kafka's The Trial: the assailant as landscape.
         Bucknell Rev, 1960, 9:89-105; In Garvin, H. R. (ed),
         Makers of the Twentieth-Century Novel. Lewisburg:
         Bucknell Univ. Press, 1977, 154-165.
10,184. _____. The Modern Novel in America.   Chicago: Reg-
         nery, 1951.
10,185. _____. Norman Mailer and the revolt of the ego: some
         observations on recent American literature. Wisconsin
         Studies in Contemporary Lit, 1960, 1:5-12.
10,186. _____. The scene of violence: Dostoevsky and Dreiser.
         Modern Fiction Studies, 1960, 6:91-105.
10,187. Hoffman, Madelyn. This Side of Paradise. A Study in
         pathological narcissism. Lit & Psychol, 1978, 28:178-
         185.
10,188. Hoffman, Stanton DeVoren. The cities of the night: John
         Rechy's City of Night and the American literature of
         homosexuality. Chicago Rev, 1964, 17:195-206; In
         Buchen, J. (ed), The Perverse Imagination. NY: New
         York Univ. Press, 1970, 165-178.
10,189. _____. Conrad's menagerie: animal imagery and
         theme. Bucknell Rev, 1964, 12(3):59-71. In Garvin,
         H. R. (ed), Makers of the Twentieth-Century Novel.
         Lewisburg: Bucknell Univ. Press, 1977, 84-92.
10,190. Hoffman, Steven K. Individuation and character develop-
         ment in the fiction of Shirley Jackson. Hartford Studies
         in Lit, 1976, 8:190-208.
10,191. Hoffman, Nancy Y. The doctor and the detective story.
         JAMA, 1973, 224:74-77.
10,192. Hoffman, Russell. The Idea of the Unconscious in the
         Novels of Thomas Hardy. DA, 1964, 24:4190.
10,193. Hoffmann, C. G. , & Hoffmann, A. C. Re-echoes of the
         jazz age: archetypal women in the novels of 1922.
         J Modern Lit, 1979, 62-86.
10,194. Hoffmann, Charles W. The search for self, inner freedom,
         and relatedness in the novels of Max Frisch. In Heit-

ner, R. R. (ed), The Contemporary Novel in Germany: A Symposium. Austin: Univ. Texas Press, 1967, 91-113.

10, 195. Hoffmann, Gerhard. Raum und Symbol in den Kurzgeschichten Edgar Allan Poes. Jahrbuch für Amerikastudien, 1971, 16:102-127.

10, 196. Hoffmeister, Charles C. 'William Wilson' and 'The Double': a Freudian insight. Coranto, 1974, 9(2):24-27.

10, 197. Hofling, Charles K. Hemingway's The Old Man and the Sea and the male reader. Amer Imago, 1963, 20:161-173.

10, 198. _____. Notes on Camus's L'Etranger. In Smith, S. (ed), The Human Mind Revisited. Essays in Honor of Karl A. Menninger. NY: IUP, 1978, 159-204.

10, 199. _____. Thomas Hardy and the Mayor of Casterbridge. Comprehensive Psychiat, 1968, 9:428-439.

10, 200. Hoge, James O. Psychedelic stimulation and the creative imagination: the case of Ken Kesey. Southern Humanities Rev, 1972, 6:381-391.

10, 201. Hoisington, Thomas H. Dark romance in a provincial setting: Mel'nikov-Peierskijs The Krasil'nikovs. Slavic & East European J, 1978, 22:15-25.

10, 202. Hölbling, Walter. 'Dystopie der Gegenwart': science fiction und Schizophrenie in Vonneguts Slaughterhouse-Five. Arbeiten aus Anglistik und Amerikanistik, 1977, 2:39-62.

10, 203. Holderegger, Hans. Robert Walser: Eine Persönlichkeitsanalyse anhand seiner drei Berliner Romane. Berlin: Schmidt, 1973.

10, 204. Holland, Norman N. Fantasy and defense in Faulkner's 'A Rose for Emily.' Hartford Studies in Lit, 1972, 4: 1-35.

10, 205. _____. 5 Readers Reading. New Haven: Yale Univ. Press, 1975; Review: Gilbert J. Rose, Psychoanal Q, 1977, 46:341-343.

10, 206. _____. Hobbling with Horatio; or the uses of literature. Hudson Rev, 1959-60, 12:549-557.

10, 207. _____. Kafka's Metamorphosis: realism and unrealism. Modern Fiction Studies, 1958, 4:143-150; Cambridge: Publications in the Humanities No. 34, Massachusetts Institute of Technology, 1958.

10, 208-9. _____. The laughter of Laurence Sterne. Hudson Rev, 1956, 9:422-430; Cambridge: Publications in the Humanities No. 27. Massachusetts Institute of Technology, 1956.

10, 210. _____. Re-covering 'The Purloined Letter.' In Suleiman, S., & Grosman, I. (eds), The Reader in the Text: Essays on Audience and Interpretation. Princeton: Princeton Univ. Press, 1980.

10, 211. _____. Style as character: The Secret Agent. Modern Fiction Studies, 1966, 12:221-231.

10, 212. Hollenbaugh, Carol. Ruby Fisher and her demon-lover. Notes on Mississippi Writers, 1974, 7:63-68.

10, 213. Hollington, Michael Andrew. Dickens and the Double. DA, 1968, 28, 68-8114.

10, 214. Hollingsworth, Alan M. Freud, Conrad, and The Future of an Illusion. Lit & Psychol, 1955, 5(4): 78-83.

10, 215. Hollingsworth, Keith. Freud and the riddle of Mrs. Dalloway. In Wallace & Ross (eds), Studies in Honor of John Wilcox. Detroit: Wayne State Univ. Press, 1959, 239-250.

10, 216. Hollingsworth, Marian E. The Search for a Father in the Novels of Thomas Wolfe. Master's thesis, Univ. North Carolina, 1957.

10, 217. Holmberg, Hans. 'Fra det gamle Danmark.' En genetisk och analytisk studie av Karen Blixens berättelse. Kritik, 1972, 23: 74-90.

10, 218. Holmes, John Clellon. Existentialism and the novel. Chicago Rev, 1959, 13:19-26, 144, 151.

10, 219. Holmes, Theodore. Bloom, the father. Sewanee Rev, 1971, 79: 236-255.

10, 220. Holsberry, John E. Hawthorne's 'The Haunted Mind, ' the psychology of dreams, Coleridge and Keats. Texas Studies in Lit & Language, 1979, 21:307-331.

10, 221. Holsti, Keijo. [Psychological truth in Kafka's Metamorphosis.] Kirjallisuudentutkijain Seuran Vuosikirja, 1972, 26: 72-79.

10, 222. Holtan, Bernt Kristian. Kvinneportret i Dansen gjenom skuggeheimen. Norsk Litteraer Arbok, 1971, 21-43.

10, 223. Holtan, J., & Orley, I. The time-space dimension in the Lew Archer detective novels. North Dakota Q, 1972, 40:30-41.

10, 224. Ho Lung, Richard R. Life's Womb: A Jungian Archetypal Study of Five Novels by Joseph Conrad. DAI, 1975, 35:7256A.

10, 225. Hölz, Karl. Das Thema der Erinnerung bei Marcel Proust: Strukturelle Analyse der mémoire involontaire in 'A la recherche du temps perdu. ' Munich: Fink, 1972.

10, 226. Holzberg, Ruth. Beckett et Le Clézio: la chaîne sadomasochiste et le monologue du scripteur. Modern Language Studies, 1979-80, 10:60-80.

10, 227. Homans, Margaret. Repression and sublimation of nature in Wuthering Heights. PMLA, 1978, 93:9-19, 1003-1004.

10, 228. Honegger, Jürg B. Das Phänomen der Angst bei Franz Kafka. Berlin: Schmidt, 1975.

10, 229. Hoog, Armand. Psychologie du coeur et psychologie des surfaces dans le roman contemporain. Cahiers de l'Association Internationale des Etudes Françaises, 1962, 14:133-142.

10, 230. Hoops, Reinald. Der Einfluss der Psychoanalyse auf die englische Literatur. Anglistische Forschung, Heft 77. Heidelberg: Winters, 1934.

10, 231. _____. Die Weltanschauung Aldous Huxleys. English Studies, 1937, 72:73-92.

10, 232. Hope, A. D. The esthetic theory of James Joyce. Australasian J Psychol & Philosophy, 1943, 16:93-114; In

Connolly, T. E. (ed), Joyce's Portrait: Criticisms and Critiques. NY: Appleton-Century-Crofts, 1962, 183-203; London: Owen, 1964, 183-203.

10, 233. Hopkins, Robert. The function of grotesque in Humphrey Clinker. Huntington Library Q, 1969, 22:163-177.

10, 234. Hoppe, Klaus D. Psychoanalytic remarks on Schnitzler's Fraulein Else. J Int Arthur Schnitzler Research Assn, 1964, 3(1):4-8.

10, 235. Hoppe, Ralph H. The Theme of Alienation in the Novels of Theodore Dreiser. DAI, 1970, 31:389A-90A.

10, 236. Horia, Vintila. James Joyce o la novela como 'Consciencia Pura.' In Mester de novelista. Madrid: Prensa Espanola, 1972, 57-66.

10, 237. Horney, Larry J. The Emerging Woman of the Twentieth-Century: A Study of the Women in D. H. Lawrence's Novels, The Rainbow and Women in Love. DAI, 1972, 32:275A.

10, 238. Hornstra, L. 'De meiden' van Jean Genet. De Nieuwe Stem, 1967, 22(12).

10, 239. Horowitz, Renée B. Unamuno's view of women. Letras Femeninas, 1975, 1(1):56-60.

10, 240. Horton, Susan R. Desire and depression in women's fiction: the problematics and the economics of desire. Modern Fiction Studies, 1978, 24:181-195.

10, 241. Horwath, Peter. Uber den fatalismus in Clemens Brentanos Geschichte von braven Kasperl und dem schönen Annerl zur Psychologie der Novelle. German Q, 1971, 44:24-34.

10, 242. Hoskins, Robert V. The Symbol of the Severed Head in Twentieth-Century British and American Fiction. DAI, 1972, 33:756A.

10, 243. Hostie, R. Du Mythe à la religion dans la psychologie analytique de C. G. Jung. Paris: Desclée de Brouwer, 1968.

10, 244. Houghton, Donald E. Attitude and illness in James' Daisy Miller. Lit & Psychol, 1969, 19:51-60.

10, 245. _____. Whores and horses in Faulkner's 'Spotted Horses.' Midwest Q, 1970, 11:361-369.

10, 246. Houlahan, Michael O. Sexual Comedy in Tristram Shandy. DAI, 1971, 31:5363A-64A.

10, 247. Houston, John Porter. Literature and psychology: the case of Proust. L'Esprit créatur, 1965, 5:3-13.

10, 248. Houston, Neal B. Henry James's 'Maud-Evelyn': classic folie à deux. Research Studies, 1973, 41:28-41.

10, 249. Hovet, Theodore R. America's 'Lonely Country Child': the theme of separation in Sarah Orne Jewett's 'A White Heron.' Colby Library Q, 1978, 14:166-171.

10, 250. Hovey, Richard B. A Farewell to Arms: Hemingway's Liebestod II. Univ. Rev, 1967, 164-168.

10, 251. _____. Hemingway: The Inward Terrain. Seattle: Univ. Washington Press, 1968; Review: Richard W. Noland, Hartford Studies in Lit, 1969, 1:140-145.

10, 252. _____. The torrents of spring. College English, 1965, 26:406-464.

10, 253.   _____. Hemingway's 'Now I Lay Me': a psychological
            interpretation. Lit & Psychol, 1965, 15:70-78; in Ben-
            son, J.J. (ed), The Short Stories of Ernest Hemingway:
            Critical Essays. Durham: Duke Univ. Press, 1975,
            180-187.
10, 254.   _____. Love and hate in 'Rappaccini's Daughter.' Univ.
            Kansas City Rev, 1962, 29:137-145.
10, 255.   _____, & Ralph, Ruth S. Dreiser's The Genius: moti-
            vation and structure. Hartford Studies in Lit, 1970, 2:
            169-183.
10, 256.   Howard, F. S. La Fontaine on fiction writing. In The
            French Short Story, Vol. 2. Columbia: Univ. South
            Carolina, 1976, 167-172.
10, 257.   Howard, Richard. Childhood amnesia. Yale French Stud-
            ies, 1969, 43:165-169.
10, 258.   Howe, Irving. Literature on the couch. In Celebrations
            and Attacks: Thirty Years of Literary and Cultural
            Commentary. NY: Horizon, 1979, 150-154.
10, 259.   Howe, Marguerite Beede. The Art of the Self in D. H. Law-
            rence. Athens: Ohio Univ. Press, 1977.
10, 260.   _____. D. H. Lawrence as Ego Psychologist: Self and
            Being in the Novels. DAI, 1976, 37:3643A.
10, 261.   Howell, Elmo. Inversion and the 'female' principle: Wil-
            liam Faulkner's 'A Courtship.' Studies in Short Fiction,
            1967, 4:308-314.
10, 262.   Howitt, D. R. Baroja's preoccupation with clocks and his
            emphatic treatment of time in the introduction to La
            busca. In Atkinson, D. M., & Clarke, A. H. (eds), His-
            panic Studies in Honour of Joseph Manson. Oxford:
            Dolphin, 1972, 139-147.
10, 263.   Hoy, Christopher. The archetypal transformation of Mar-
            tiniano in The Man Who Killed the Deer. South Dakota
            Rev, 1976, 13(4):43-56.
10, 264.   Hoy, Nancy J. The Theme of Nostalgia for the Lost Para-
            dise of Childhood in Jean-Paul Sartre's Fiction. DAI,
            1972, 32:5791A.
10, 265.   Høystad, O. M. Skuld og skuldkjensel i S. Christiansens
            dobbeltroman Ved Golgata. Norsk Litteraer Arbok,
            197, 73-90.
10, 266.   Huas, Jeanine. Les Femmes chez Proust. Paris: Hach-
            ette, 1971.
10, 267.   Hubbard, Louise J. The Individual and the Group in French
            Literature Since 1914. Washington, DC: Catholic Univ.
            Press, 1955.
10, 268.   Hubbel, Jay B. Southern Life in Fiction. Atlanta: Univ.
            Georgia Press, 1960.
10, 269.   Hubbs, Valentine C. Metamorphosis and rebirth in Eichen-
            dorff's Marmorbild. Germanic Rev, 1977, 52:243-259.
10, 270.   Huber, R. John, & Ledbetter, Gail. Holden Caulfield,
            self-appointed catcher in the rye: some additional
            thoughts. J Individual Psychol, 1977, 33:250-256.
10, 271.   Hubert, R. R. Le Sens du voyage dans quelques contes de
            Mme d'Aulnoy. French Rev, 1973, 46:931-937.

10, 272. Hude, E. Christine.   Feminine portraiture in Born in Exile.
          Gissing Newsletter, 1972, 8(4):1-17.
10, 273. Huertas-Jourda, José.   The Existentialism of Miguel de
          Unamuno. Gainesville: Univ. Florida Press, 1963.
10, 274. Hughes, Dean T.   Romance and Psychological Realism in
          William Godwin's Novels. DAI, 1972, 33:2330A.
10, 275. Hughes, Philip Russell.   Archetypal patterns in Edgar Hunt-
          ley. Studies in the Novel, 1973, 5:176-190.
10, 276. Hughes, R. E.   The five fools in A Tale of a Tub. Lit &
          Psychol, 1961, 11:20-22.
10, 277. Huguet, Louis.   La Femme dans le destin et la création lit-
          téraire d'Alfred Döblin. Annales de l'Université d'Abid-
          jan, 1975, 8D:61-108.
10, 278. _____. Récit/Mythe/Psychanalyse: une nouvelle d'Al-
          fred Döblin: 'Bataille! Bataille!' Annales de l'Univer-
          sité d'Abidjan, 1976, 9D:207-221.
10, 279. Hull, Byron D.   Henderson the Rain King and William
          James. Criticism, 1971, 13:402-414.
10, 280. Hull, William.   Moby Dick: an interpretation. ETC, 1947,
          5:8-21.
10, 281. Hult, Sharon S.   William Faulkner's 'The Brooch':   the
          journey to the Riolama. Mississippi Q, 1974, 27:291-305.
10, 282. Humboldt, Charles.   The human essence in Soviet fiction.
          Mainstream, 1958, 11:3-32.
10, 283. Hume, Kathryn.   C. S. Lewis' trilogy: a cosmic romance.
          Modern Fiction Studies, 1974-75, 20:505-517.
10, 284. _____.   Robert Coover's fiction: the naked and the
          mythic. Novel: A Forum on Fiction, 1979, 12:127-148.
10, 285. Hume, Robert D.   Gothic versus romantic: a revaluation
          of the Gothic novel. PMLA, 1969, 84:282-290.
10, 286. Humphrey, Robert.   Creating Consciousness. A Study in
          Novelistic Techniques. Northwestern Univ. Summaries
          of Doctoral Dissertations, 1950, 18:20-24.
10, 287. _____.   Form and function of stream of consciousness
          in William Faulkner's The Sound and the Fury. Univ.
          Kansas City Rev, 1952, 19:24-40.
10, 288. _____.   Stream of consciousness. In Miller, J. E. (ed),
          Myth and Method; Modern Theories of Fiction. Lincoln:
          Univ. Nebraska Press, 1960, 63-85.
10, 289. _____.   Stream of Consciousness in the Modern Novel.
          Berkeley: Univ. California Press, 1954.
10, 290. _____.   Stream of consciousness: technique or genre?
          Philological Q, 1951, 30:434-437.
10, 291. Hunfeld, Hans.   Erinnerungsproblematik in den Neuengland-
          romanen Nathaniel Hawthornes. Doctoral dissertation,
          Univ. Kiel, 1973.
10, 292. Hungerford, Edward A.   Mrs. Woolf, Freud, and J. D.
          Beresford. Lit & Psychol, 1955, 5(3):49-51.
10, 293. Hunt, Gary Alan.   Feminism and the Modern Family:
          Howells as Domestic Realist. DAI, 1976, 37:2871A-72A.
10, 294. _____.   'A reality that can't be quite definitely spoken':
          sexuality in Their Wedding Journey. Studies in the Nov-
          el, 1977, 9:17-32.

10, 295. Hunt, George W. Updike's omega-shaped shelter: struc-
          ture and psyche in A Month of Sundays. Critique, 1978,
          19(3):47-60.
10, 296. Hunt, Jan, & Suarez, John M. The evasion of adult love
          in Fitzgerald's fiction. Centennial Rev, 1973, 17:152-
          170.
10, 297. Hunt, Morton. Sexual behavior in the 1970's. Playboy,
          1973, 20(10):84 passim.
10, 298. Hunting, C. The technique of persuasion in Orlando.
          Modern Fiction Studies, 1956, 2:17-23.
10, 299. Huntley, H. Robert. James' 'The Turn of the Screw': its
          fine machinery. Amer Imago, 1977, 34:224-237.
10, 300. Hurley, Edward T. Death and immortality: George Eliot's
          solution. Nineteenth Century Fiction, 1969, 24:222-227.
10, 301. _____. The Family as an Instrument for Theme and
          Structure in the Fiction of George Eliot. DA, 1967,
          28:677A.
10, 302. Hurley, Paul J. Young Goodman Brown's 'heart of dark-
          ness. ' Amer Lit, 1966, 37:410-419.
10, 303- Hurt, James. The primal scene as narrative model in
    4.   Ford's The Good Soldier. J Narrative Technique, 1978,
          8:200-210.
10, 305. Hussman, Lawrence E. , Jr. Dreiser's emotional power.
          Dreiser Newsletter, 1973, 4(1):12-13.
10, 306. Hutchinson, James D. Time: the fourth dimension in
          Faulkner. South Dakota Rev, 1968, 6(3):91-103.
10, 307. Hutter, Albert D. Crime and fantasy in Great Expectations.
          In Crews, F. C. (ed), Psychoanalysis and Literary Prog-
          ress. Cambridge, Mass: Winthrop, 1970, 25-65.
10, 308. _____. Dreams, transformations, and literature: the
          implications of detective fiction. Victorian Studies,
          1975, 19:181-210.
10, 309. _____. The high tower of his mind: psychoanalysis and
          the reader of Bleak House. Criticism, 1977, 14:296-
          316.
10, 310. Hutzler, Jeffrey C. Family pathology in Crime and Punish-
          ment. Amer J Psychoanal, 1978, 38:335-342.
10, 311. Hux, Samuel. So the king says--says he: historical novel/
          fictional history. Western Humanities Rev, 1979, 33:
          189-201.
10, 312. Huxley, Aldous. Do What You Will; Essays. Garden City,
          NY: Doubleday, Doran, 1929, 99-112.
10, 313. Hydak, Michael G. Door imagery in Maupassant's Bel-Ami.
          French Rev, 1976, 49:337-341.
10, 314. _____. Les Suicides d'Emma Bovary. Romanica, 1976,
          13:145-150.
10, 315. Hyman, R. J. The virtuous Princesse de Clèves. French
          Rev, 1964, 38(1).
10, 316. Hyman, Stanley Edgar. Standards: A Chronicle of Books
          for Our Time. NY: Horizon, 1966.
10, 317. Hynes, Joseph. Varieties of death wish: Evelyn Waugh's
          central theme. Criticism, 1972, 14:65-77.

10,318. Ignatius, Mary Ann. Julien Green as novelist of love. Bulletin Rocky Mountain Modern Language Assn, 1972, 26:47-51.

10,319. Ilacqua, Alma A. Amanda Starr: victim of her own false assumptions. Hartford Studies in Lit, 1976, 8:178-189.

10,320. Ilie, Paul. The structure of personality in Unamuno. In Langnas, I. A., & Sholod, B. (eds), Studies in Honor of M. J. Benardete (Essays in Hispanic and Sephardic Culture.) NY: Las Americas, 1966, 177-192.

10,321. _____. Unamuno: An Existential View of Self and Society. Madison: Univ. Wisconsin Press, 1967.

10,322. Imbert, Enrique A. Análisis de El Señor Presidente. Revista Iberoamericana, 1969, 35:53-57.

10,323. Imberty, Cl. Le Symbolisme du faucon dans la nouvelle 9 de la Ve journée du Décaméron. Rev des Etudes Italiennes, 1974, 20:147-156.

10,324. Ingelf, J. Konst och sjukdom hos Thomas Mann. Sydsven Medicinhistorie Sallsk Arsskrift, 1978, 15:65-77.

10,325. Ingham, John. The bullfighter. A study in sexual dialectic. Amer Imago, 1964, 21:95-102.

10,326. Ionescu, Rica. Paysage et psychologie dans l'oeuvre de Camus. Rev des Sciences Humaines, 1969, 34:317-330.

10,327. Irle, Gerhard. Der psychiatrische Roman. Stuttgart: Hippokrates, 1965.

10,328. Irvine, Lorna Marie. Hostility and Reconciliation: The Mother in English Canadian Fiction. DAI, 1977, 38: 1380A.

10,329. _____. A psychological journey: mothers and daughters in English-Canadian fiction. In Davidson, C. N., & Broner, E. M. (eds), The Lost Tradition. NY: Ungar, 1980, 242-252.

10,330. Irving, J. The Catcher in the Rye: an Adlerian interpretation. J Individual Psychol, 1976, 32:81-92.

10,331. Irwin, John T. Doubling and Incest/Repetition and Revenge: A Speculative Reading of Faulkner. Baltimore: Johns Hopkins Univ. Press, 1975; Reviews: Partisan Rev, 1979, 46:445-453; Salmagundi, 1977, 36:133-139; Edward Wasiolek, Novel: A Forum on Fiction, 1977, 10:182-184.

10,332. Isajiw, Olsana Olna. The Idea of Self-Realization in the Works of Anna Seghers. DAI, 1977, 38:1424A.

10,333. Isaksson, H. Lars Gyllensten's Juvenilia. In Den moderne roman og romanforskning i Norden. Oslo: Universitat forlaget, 1971, 16-30.

10,334. Iser, Wolfgang. The reality of fiction: a functionalist approach to literature. New Literary History, 1975, 7:7-38.

10,335. Islam, Shamsul. Psychological allegory in The Jungle Books. Kipling J, 1973, 40:5-8.

10,336. Israel, C. M. The fractured hero of Roth's Goodbye, Columbus. Critique, 1974, 16(2):5-11.

10,337. Issacharoff, Michael. L'Espace et la nouvelle. Paris: Corti, 1976.

10,338.   . 'Hérodias' et la symbolic combinatoire des
          Trois Contes. In Langages de Flaubert. Paris: Let-
          tres Modernes-Minard, 1976, 53-76.
10,339.   . Huysmans et la structure métaphorique du récit.
          Travaux de Linguistique et de Littérature, 1973, 11(2):
          61-70.
10,340.   Italia, Paul G.   Love and lust in James Dickey's Deliver-
          ance. Modern Fiction Studies, 1975, 21:203-213.
10,341.   Ivarsson, N. I.   Kunden bland arketyperna.   Svensk Litter-
          aturtidskrift, 1964, 27(2).
10,342.   Ivask, Ivar.   Psychologie und Geschichte in Doderers Ro-
          manwerk.   Literatur und Kritik, 1968, 24:213-217.
10,343.   Izard, C. E., et al.   Sex differences in emotional responses
          to erotic literature.   J Consulting Clinical Psychol, 1974,
          42:468.

10,344.   Jabs-Kriegsmann.   [The image of old people in German
          magazine fiction.]   Zeitschrift für Gerontologie, 1977,
          10:373-380.
10,345.   Jaccard, Roland.   Psychologie en miettes.   Monde, 4 Oct
          1977, no. 10164, 2.
10,346.   Jack, I.   Physiogomy, phrenology and characterization in
          the novels of Charlotte Brontë.   Brontë Society Trans-
          actions, 1970, 15:377-391.
10,347.   Jackson, Agnes M.   Stephen Crane's imagery of conflict in
          George's Mother.   Arizona Q, 1969, 25:313-318.
10,348.   Jackson, Elizabeth R.   The crystallization of A la recherche
          du temps perdu 1908-1909.   French Rev, 1964, 38:157-
          166.
10,349.   . L'Evolution de la mémoire involontaire dans
          l'oeuvre de Marcel Proust.   Doctorat d'Université de
          Paris, 1963; abstract in Annales de l'Université de Paris,
          1964, 34, 1:106.
10,350.   . The genesis of the involuntary memory in
          Proust's early works.   PMLA, 1961, 76:586-594.
10,351.   Jackson, H. Sheldon.   Schnitzler and the Modern Psycholog-
          ical Novel: A Study in the Form of His Fiction.   Mas-
          ter's thesis, Univ. Manchester, 1946.
10,352.   Jackson, Jocelyn E. W.   The Problem of Identity in the Es-
          says and Selected Novels of James Baldwin.   DAI, 1973,
          34:2629A.
10,353.   Jackson, Maurice.   The black experience with death: a
          brief analysis through black writings.   Omega: J Death
          & Dying, 1972, 3:203-209.
10,354.   Jackson, Naomi C.   Faulkner's women: 'demon-nun and
          angel-witch.'   Ball State Univ. Forum, 1967, 8(1):12-20.
10,355.   Jackson, Paul R.   Henry Miller's literary pregnancies.
          Lit & Psychol, 1969, 19, 35-49.
10,356.   . Review: William A. Gordon's The Mind and
          Art of Henry Miller.   Lit & Psychol, 1967, 17:143-146.
10,357.   Jackson, Richard L.   Black phobia and the white aesthetic
          in Spanish American literature.   Hispania, 1975, 58:
          467-480.

10, 358. Jackson, W. Roxana and the development of Defoe's fiction. Studies in the Novel, 1975, 7:181-194.

10, 359. Jacobs, Robert Glenn. Comrade Ossipon's favorite saint: Lombroso and Conrad. Nineteenth Century Fiction, 1968, 23:74-84.

10, 360. _____. Psychology, Setting and Impressionism in the Major Novels of Joseph Conrad. DA, 1966, 26:6022.

10, 361. Jacobsen, Margaret C. K. Women in the Novels of Defoe, Richardson and Fielding. DAI, 1975, 35:7256A.

10, 362. Jacobson, A. C. Literary genius and manic depressive insanity. Medical Record, 1912, 82:937-939.

10, 363- Jacobson, Irving F. The child as guilty witness. Lit &
4. Psychol, 1974, 24:12-23.

10, 365. Jakobovits, L. A. Evaluative reactions to exotic literature. Psychol Reports, 1965, 16:985-994.

10, 366. Jaloux, Edmond. Albert Camus, an analysis. Psyché, 1948, 3:223-232.

10, 367. _____. Julien Gracq, an analysis. Psyché, 1947, 2: 882-889.

10, 368. _____. Léon Lemonnier et le conte fantastique. Psyché, 1947, 2:1120-1130.

10, 369. _____. Thomas Wolfe: La Toile et le Roc. Psyché, 1947, 4:202-210.

10, 370. James, Henry. Review: George Eliot's Middlemarch. Galaxy, 15 Mar 1873, 425.

10, 371. Jameson, Fredric. After Armageddon: character systems in Philip K. Dick's Dr. Bloodmoney. Science-Fiction Studies, 1975, 5:31-42.

10, 372. _____. Balzac and Lacan: imaginary and symbolic in La Rabouilleuse. Social Science Information, 1977, 16(1):59-81.

10, 373. Janeway, Elizabeth. Man's World, Woman's Place: A Study in Social Mythology. NY: Morrow, 1971.

10, 374. Janney, Francis L. Childhood in English Non-Dramatic Literature from 1557-1798. Greifswald: Abel, 1925.

10, 375. Jarman, L. M. The Goncourt brothers: modernists in abnormal psychology. Bulletin Univ. New Mexico Language Series, 1939, 6, No. 3.

10, 376. Jarrell, Mackie. The handwriting of the Lilliputians. Philological Q, 1958, 37:116-119.

10, 377. Jason, Philip K. Doubles/Don Juans: Anaïs Nin and Otto Rank. Mosaic, 1978, 11(2):81-94.

10, 378. Jay, Karla. Male homosexuality and lesbians in the works of Proust and Gide. In Crew, L. (ed), The Gay Academic. Palm Springs, Cal: ETC, 1978, 216-243.

10, 379. Jayne, Edward. Pray tarry with me Young Goodman Brown. Lit & Psychol, 1979, 29:100-113.

10, 380. Jefchak, Andrew. Family struggles in Seize the Day. Studies in Short Fiction, 1974, 11:297-302.

10, 381. Jefliffe, Smith Ely, & Brink, Louise. Alcoholism and the phantasy life in Tolstoi's Redemption. New York Medical J, 1919, 109:92-97; Medical Woman's J, 1920, 27: 195-204.

10,382.   Jenkins, Lee Clinton. Faulkner, the Blacks and Women.
           Iowa City: Univ. Iowa Press, 1978.
10,383.   _____ . Faulkner, the mythic mind, and the Blacks.
           Lit & Psychol, 1977, 27:74-91.
10,384.   Jennings, L. Chantal. La Dualité de Maupassant: son at-
           titude envers la femme. Rev des Sciences Humaines,
           1970, 35:559-579.
10,385.   _____ . Les Trois visages de Nana. French Rev, 1971,
           44:117-128.
10,386.   _____ . Zola féministe? Cahiers Naturalistes, 1972,
           44:172-187; 45:1-22.
10,387.   Jennings, Lee Bryson. Ambiguous explosion: C. F. Mey-
           er's Der Schub von der Kanzel. German Q, 1970, 43:
           210-222.
10,388.   _____ . The Ludicrous Demons. Aspects of the Gro-
           tesque in German Post-Romantic Prose. Berkeley:
           Univ. California Press, 1963.
10,389.   Jensen, Brikt. Diktning eller psykologi? En studie i
           François Mauriacs roman 'Ormebolet.' Oslo: Cappe-
           len, 1963.
10,390.   Jensen, Wilhelm. Drei unveröffentlichte Briefe. Zur
           Geschichte von Freuds Gradiva-Analyse. Psychoanaly-
           tische Bewegung, 1929, 1:207-211.
10,391.   Jeremic, Ljubisa. Unutrasnj monolog kod Tolstoja i
           Dzojsa. Delo, 1966, 12:1242-1260, 1390-1406.
10,392.   Jerotić, Vladeta. Karl Gustav Jung i Herman Hese: Pojam
           individualnog process. Knjizevnost, 1970, 51:213-224.
10,393.   _____ . Psichoanalizi i Dostojevski. Savremenik (Bel-
           grade), 1970, 31:428-436.
10,394.   Jessner, L. N. Jean Pauls Titan als Bildungsroman.
           Zeitschrift für Aesthetik und allgemeine Kunstwissen-
           schaft, 1921.
10,395.   Jillson, Frederick F. The 'professional' clergyman in
           some novels by Anthony Trollope. Hartford Studies in
           Lit, 1969, 1:185-197.
10,396.   Jofen, Jean. Metamorphosis. Amer Imago, 1978, 35:347-
           356.
10,397.   Johannsen, Pauline Renee, & Nash, Lee. Alienation in
           The Great Gatsby: a socio-psychological perspective on
           the 1920's. Rocky Mountain Social Science J, 1973, 10:
           85-103.
10,398.   Johannesson, Eric O. The Novels of August Strindberg: A
           Study in Theme and Structure. Berkeley: Univ. Cali-
           fornia Press, 1969.
10,399.   _____ . The problem of identity in Strindberg's novels.
           Scandinavian Studies, 1962, 34:7-34.
10,400.   _____ . Strindberg's Taklagsöl: an early experiment in
           the psychological novel. Scandinavian Studies, 1963,
           35:223-238.
10,401.   Johansen, Hans Boll. Les Paradigmes psychologiques dans
           l'amour-passion stendhalien. Stendhal-Club, 1971, 13:
           183-200.

10, 402. Johnson, Barbara. The frame of reference: Poe, Lacan,
Derrida. In Hartman, G. H. (ed), Psychoanalysis and
the Question of the Text. Baltimore: Johns Hopkins
Univ. Press, 1978, 149-171; Yale French Studies,
1977, 55-56:457-505.

10, 403. Johnson, Bruce. Henry Green's comic symbolism. Ball
State Univ. Forum, 1965, 6:29-35.

10, 404. Johnson, C. A. Russian Gaskelliana. Rev English Lit,
1966, 7:39-51.

10, 405. Johnson, Courtney. Adam and Eve and Isabel Archer.
Renascence, 1969, 21:134-144.

10, 406. _____. Henry James' 'The Jolly Corner': a study in
integration. Amer Imago, 1967, 24:344-359.

10, 407. _____. John Marcher and the paradox of the 'Unfortun-
ate Fall.' Studies in Short Fiction, 1969, 6:121-135.

10, 408. _____. The Problem of Sex in the Writings of Henry
James. DA, 1967, 28:679A-80A.

10, 409. Johnson, Doris V. The autobiographical heroine in Anna
Karenina. Hartford Studies in Lit, 1979, 11:111-122.

10, 410. Johnson, Dorothy M. Emotion and the fiction writer.
Discourse, 1960, 3:113-118.

10, 411. Johnson, Ellwood. William James and the art of fiction.
JAAC, 1972, 30:285-296.

10, 412. Johnson, James W. The adolescent hero: a trend in modern fiction. Twentieth Century Lit, 1959, 5:3-11.

10, 413. Johnson, Lee Ann. The psychology of characterization:
James's portraits of Verena Tarrant and Olive Chancel-
lor. Studies in the Novel, 1974, 6:295-303.

10, 414. _____. Western literary realism: the California tales
of Norris and Austin. Amer Lit Realism, 1974, 7:278-
280.

10, 415. Johnson, Maurice. Remote regions of man's mind. Univ.
Kansas City Rev, 1961, 27:299-303.

10, 416. Johnson, Pamela Hansford. The sexual life in Dickens's
novels. In Slater, M. , (ed), Dickens 1970. NY: Stein
& Day, 1970, 173-194.

10, 417. Johnson, Paula. Alice among the analysts: Hartford Studies in Lit, 1972, 4:113-122.

10, 418. Johnston, Craig P. Irony and the double in short fiction
by Julio Cortázar and Severo Sarduy. J Spanish Studies: Twentieth Century, 1977, 5:11-22.

10, 419. Johnston, Kenneth G. Hemingway's 'Out of Season' and
the psychology of errors. Lit & Psychol, 1971, 21:
41-46.

10, 420. Johnstone, Douglas B. Myth and Psychology in the Novels
of John Barth. DAI, 1974, 34:5973A.

10, 421. Joiner, Lawrence D. Camus's 'The Renegade': a quest
for sexual identity. Research Studies, 1977, 45:171-
176.

10, 422. Jolas, Eugene. Inquiry into the spirit of and language of
night. Transition, 1938, 27:233-245.

10, 423. Jones, Alexander E. Mark Twain and sexuality. PMLA,
1956, 51:595-616.

10,424. _____. Point of view in 'The Turn of the Screw.'
PMLA, 1959, 74:112-122; In Willen, G. (ed), A Case-
book on Henry James's The Turn of the Screw. NY:
Crowell, 1960, 298-318.

10,425. Jones, Bartlett C. Depth psychology and literary study.
Midcontinent Amer Studies J, 1964, 5(2):50-56.

10,426. Jones, Dafydd Glyn. Rhai storïau am blentyndod. Ysgrifau Beirniadol (Wales), 1976, 9:255-273.

10,427. Jones, Dennis M. From Moralist to Psychologist to Maker
of Myth. A Study of Hawthorne's Use of Regional History. DA, 1967, 27:3011A-12A.

10,428. Jones, Ernest. Ein Beispiel von literarischer Verwer-
tungdes Versprechens. Int Zeitschrift für Psychoanalyse, 1911, 1:496-497.

10,429. _____. George Meredith über Träume. Int Zeitschrift
für Psychoanalyse, 1912, 3:54.

10,430. _____. Introduction to R. Firbank's Inclinations. Norfolk, Conn: New Directions, 1951 (1916), XII-XX; London: Duckworth, 1949-50, XII-XX.

10,431. _____. Preface to Simon O. Lesser's Fiction and the
Unconscious. Boston: Beacon, 1957.

10,432. Jones, Granville H. Henry James's Psychology of Experience: Innocence, Responsibility, and Renunciation in the
Fiction of Henry James. The Hague: Mouton, 1975;
Reviews: L. B. Holland, Nineteenth Century Fiction,
1976, 31:106-107; R. C. McLean, Modern Fiction Studies, 1976, 22:610-614; DAI, 1970, 30:5447A.

10,433. Jones, L. Window imagery: inner and outer worlds in
Alain-Fournier's Le Grand Meaulnes. Symposium, 1973,
27:333-351.

10,434. Jones, Llewellyn. Psychoanalysis and creative literature.
English J, 1934, 23:443-452.

10,435. Jones, Lucy. A propos de Lewis Carroll. Rev Française de Psychanalyse, 1950, 14:511-522.

10,436. Jones, M. V. Dostoyevsky and an aspect of Schiller's
psychology. Slavonic & East European Rev, 1974, 52:
337-354.

10,437. Jones, Peter G. Dickens' literary children. Australian
Paediatric J, 1972, 8:233-245.

10,438. _____. War and Novelists: Appraising the American
War Novel. Columbia: Univ. Missouri Press, 1976.

10,439. Jones, William M. Eudora Welty's use of myth in 'Death
of a Traveling Salesman.' J Amer Folklore, 1960, 73:
18-23.

10,440. _____. Welty's 'Petrified Man.' Explicator, 1957,
15(4), No. 21.

10,441. Joppa, Francis A. Les Types psycho-sociaux du roman
ouest-africain d'expression française: Les Colonisés
purs et les évolués. Asemka: A Lit J Univ. Cape
Coast, 1975, 3:19-33; 1976, 4:15-40.

10,442. _____. Les Types psycho-sociaux du roman ouest-africain d'expression française: Les Déracines et les
aliénés. Asemka: A Lit J Univ. Cape Coast, 1974,
1(2):25-42.

10, 443.   Jordan, Sidney.   D. H.   Lawrence's concept of the unconscious and existential thinking.   Rev Existential Psychol
& Psychiat, 1965, 5:34-43.

10, 444.   Jorgenson, Jens Peter.   Jack London's The Red One: a
Freudian approach.   Jack London Newsletter, 1975, 8:
101-103.

10, 445.   Joseph, Edward P.   Identity and Joseph Conrad.   [Ab-
stract.]   Psychoanal Q, 1962, 31:440-441.

10, 446.   Joseph, Gerhard.   Frankenstein's dream: the child as
father of the monster.   Hartford Studies in Lit, 1975,
7:97-115.

10, 447.   _____. John Barth.   Minneapolis: Univ.   Minnesota
Pamphlets on American Writers, 91, 1970.

10, 448.   Joseph, M. Evelyn.   Substance as suggestion: ambiguity
in Hawthorne.   Renascence, 1965, 17:216-220.

10, 449.   Josipovici, Gabriel (ed).   The Modern English Novel: The
Reader, the Writer and the Work.   NY: Barnes &
Noble, 1976.

10, 450.   Jost, François.   Littérature et suicide.   De Werther à
Madame Bovary.   Rev de Littérature Comparée, 1968,
42:161-198.

10, 451.   Joyce, Edward T.   Race and Sex: Opposition and Identity
in the Fiction of Carson McCullers.   DAI, 1973, 34:
3403A-04A.

10, 452.   Joyce, James K.   Philosophical and Psychological Aspects
of Carl Hauptmann's Novel.   DAI, 1972, 32:4614A-15A.

10, 453.   Joye, J. C.   J. Green et le monde de la fatalité.   Berne:
Druck, 1964; Doctoral dissertation, Univ. Berne, 1962.

10, 454.   Judson, Abe J.   Love and death in the short stories of W.
Somerset Maugham: a psychological analysis.   Psychiat
Q Supplement, 1963, 37(2):250-262.

10, 455.   Juin, H.   En Rade.   Un Dilemme.   Croquis parisiens.
Paris: Union Générale d'Editions, 1976.

10, 456.   _____ (ed).   Mademoiselle Fifi.   Paris: Gallimard.

10, 457.   _____. Les Vingt-et-un jours d'un neurasthénique.
Paris: Union Générale d'Editions, 1977.

10, 458.   Jung, Carl Gustav.   Foreword to Fierz-David: The Dream
of Poliphilo.   In Collected Works of C. G. Jung, Vol. 18.
Princeton: Princeton Univ. Press, 1976, 780-781.

10, 459.   _____. Gerard de Nerval.   In Collected Works of C. G.
Jung, Vol. 18.   Princeton: Princeton Univ. Press,
1976, 779.

10, 460.   _____. [Ulysses.]   In Deming, R. H.   (ed), James Joyce:
The Critical Heritage, 2 Vols.   Vol. 1:   1902-1927;
Vol. 2:   1928-1941.   NY: Barnes & Noble, 1970.

10, 461.   _____. Ulysses.   ein Monolog.   Eurapaische Rev, 1932,
8:547-566; In Wirklichkeit der Seele.   Zurich: Rascher,
1934, 132-169; In Realidad del Alma.   Buenos Aires,
1946; In Spring Nineteen Forty-Nine.   NY: 1949, 1-20;
In Manheim, L. F., & Manheim, E. (eds), Hidden Patterns.   NY: Macmillan, 1966, 192-219; In Problèmes de
l'âme moderne.   Paris: Buchet Chastel-Correa, 1960,
407-439; In Collected Works of C. G. Jung, Vol. 15.
NY: Pantheon, 1966, 109-134.

10,462. Junkins, Donald. Hawthorne's House of Seven Gables: a prototype of the human mind. Lit & Psychol, 1967, 17:177-192.

10,463. Just, G. Darstellung und Appell in der Blechtrommel von Günter Grass. Frankfurt: Athenäum, 1972.

10,464. Justman, Stewart. Repression and self in 'Benito Cereno.' Studies in Short Fiction, 1978, 15:301-306.

10,465. Justus, James H. The unawakening of Edna Pontellier. Southern Lit J, 1978, 10:107-122.

10,466. Jutrin, M. Le Sens du monologue intérieur dans L'Enfant de J. Valles. Rev des Langues Vivantes, 1972, 38:467-476.

10,467. Kafalenos, Emma. Philippe Sollers' Nombres: structure and sources. Contemporary Lit, 1978, 19:320-335.

10,468. Kafka, J. Tolstého kreutzerova sonáta z psychopatologic-kého hladiska. Poxnámky k psycopatológii ziarlivosti. Ceskoslovenska Psychiatrie, 1972, 68:292-297.

10,469. _____. 'Le Verdict' de Franz Kafka envisagé au point de vue psychopathologique. Encéphale, 1969, 58:481-485.

10,470. Kahane, Claire. Comic vibrations and self-construction in grotesque literature. Lit & Psychol, 1979, 29, 114-119.

10,471. Kahiluoto Rudat, Eva M. Illusión y desengaño: El feminismo barroco de María de Zayas y Sotomayor. Letras Femeninas, 1975, 1(1):27-43.

10,472. Kaiser, Helmuth. Franz Kafkas Inferno. Ein psychologische Deutung seiner Strafphasie. Vienna: Internationaler Psychoanalytischer Verlag, 1931; Imago, 1931, 17(1):41-104; In Politzer, H. (ed), Franz Kafka: Wege der Forschung. Darmstadt: Wissenschaft Buchgesellschaft, 1973, 69-142.

10,473. Kaiser, Michael. Adelbert Stifter. Eine literaturpsychologische Untersuchung seiner Erzählungen. Berlin: Bouvier, 1971.

10,474. Kalfus, Richard M. The Function of the Dream in the Works of E. T. A. Hoffmann. DAI, 1973, 34:1915A-16A.

10,475. Kallapur, S. T. Ernest Hemingway's conception of love and womanhood. Banasthali Patrika, 1972, 19:37-47.

10,476. Kallich, Martin. Swift and the archetypes of hate: A Tale of a Tub. In Pagliaro, H. E. (ed), Studies in Eighteenth Century Culture, IV. Madison: Univ. Wisconsin Press, 1975, 43-67.

10,477. Kalnins, M. D. H. Lawrence's Two Marriages and Daughters of the Vicar. Ariel, 1976, 7:32-49.

10,478. Kaminsky, Amy. The real circle of iron: mothers and children, children and mothers, in four Argentine novels. Latin Amer Lit Rev, 1976, 77-86.

10,479. Kamuf, Peggy. Inside Julie's closet. Romanic Rev, 1978, 69:296-306.

10,480. Kanes, M. The mythic structure of La Peau de changrin. Studi Francesi, 1972, 16:46-59; 1970, 14:244-256.

10,481. Kann, David J. 'Rip Van Winkle': wheels within wheels. Amer Imago, 1979, 36:178-196.

10,482. Kanzer, Mark. The Figure in the Carpet. Amer Imago, 1960, 17:339-348.

10,483. _____. The self-analytic literature of Robert Louis Stevenson. In Wilbur, G., & Muensterberg, W. (eds), Psychoanalysis and Culture. NY: IUP, 1951, 425-435; NY: Science Editions, 1967, 425-435.

10,484. _____. The vision of Father Zossina from The Brothers Karamazov. Amer Imago, 1951, 8:329-335; In Coltrera, J.T. (ed), Lives, Events, and Other Players: Studies in Psychobiography. NY: Aronson, 1980.

10,485. Kaplan, Charles. Holden and Huck: the Odysseys of youth. College English, 1956, 18:76-80.

10,486. Kaplan, Harold J. Hemingway and the passive hero. In The Passive Voice. Columbus: Ohio State Univ., 1966, 93-110.

10,487. Kaplan, Leo. Analysis of The Picture of Dorian Gray. Psyche & Eros, 1922, 3:8-21.

10,488. Kaplan, Sydney Janet. Feminine Consciousness in the Modern British Novel. Urbana: Univ. Illinois Press, 1975; DAI, 1972, 32:4165A.

10,489. _____. The limits of consciousness in the novels of Doris Lessing. In Pratt, A.V., & Dembo, L.S. (eds), Doris Lessing; Critical Studies. Madison: Univ. Wisconsin Press, 1974, 119-132; Contemporary Lit, 1973, 14:536-549.

10,490. Kappel, Lawrence. Psychic geography on Gravity's Rainbow. Contemporary Lit, 1980, 21:225-251.

10,491. Karancsy, László. Dosztojevszkij és a mai lélekábrázolás. Alföld, 1972, 23(4):47-54.

10,492. Karcher, Carolyn L. Melville and racial prejudice: a reevaluation. Southern Rev, 1976, 12:287-310.

10,493. Karl, Frederick Robert. Don Quixote as archetypal artist and Don Quixote as archetypal novel. In The Adversary Literature. NY: Farrar, Straus & Giroux, 1974, 55-67.

10,494. _____. Review: P.J. Glassman's Language and Being: Joseph Conrad and the Literature of Personality. Studies in the Novel, 1977, 9:326-332.

10,495. Karlinsky, Simon. The Sexual Labyrinth of Nikolai Gogol. Cambridge: Harvard Univ. Press, 1976; Review: John A. Koban, Modern Fiction Studies, 1977-78, 23:692-693.

10,496. Karlow, Martin Peter. 'Practical Extravagance': A Study of Hawthorne's Study of Schizophrenia as a Creative Process. DAI, 1975, 36:2822A-23A.

10,497. Karnes, Elizabeth Lueder. An Analysis of Male and Female Roles in Two Periods of Award Winning Adolescent Literature. DAI, 1976, 36:5299A.

10,498. Karpman, Benjamin. The Kreutzer Sonata; a problem in latent homosexuality and castration. Psychoanal Rev, 1938, 20-48.

10,499.   _____. Neurotic traits of Jonathan Swift as revealed by
           Gulliver's Travels. Psychoanal Rev, 1942, 29:26-54,
           165-184.
10,500.   Karpowitz, Stephen. Conscience and cannibals: an essay
           on two exemplary tales: Soul of Wood and The Pawn-
           broker. Psychoanal Rev, 1977, 64:41-62.
10,501.   _____. A psychology of the Joycean artist and aes-
           thetic. Univ. Windsor Rev, 1971, 7:56-61.
10,502.   _____. Tom Sawyer and Mark Twain: fictional women
           and real in the play of conscience with the imagination.
           Lit & Psychol, 1973, 23:5-12.
10,503.   Karrfalt, David H. Anima in Hawthorne and Haggard.
           Amer Notes & Queries, 1964, 2:152-153.
10,504.   Kasdorff, Hans. Der Todesgedanke im Werke Thomas
           Mann. Leipzig: Eichblatt, 1932.
10,505.   Kaston, C. O. Houses of fiction in What Maisie Knew.
           Criticism, 1976, 18:27-42.
10,506.   Katan, Maurits. A causerie on Henry James's "The Turn
           of the Screw." In The Psychoanalytic Study of the
           Child, Vol. 17. NY: IUP, 1962, 473-493.
10,507.   _____. The origin of 'The Turn of the Screw.' In
           The Psychoanalytic Study of the Child, Vol. 21. NY:
           IUP, 1966, 583-635.
10,508.   _____. Schnitzler's 'Das Schicksal des Freihern von
           Leisenbohg.' JAPA, 1969, 17:904-926.
10,509.   Katchadourian, H.A., & Lunde, D.T. The erotic in lit-
           erature. In Fundamentals of Human Sexuality. NY:
           Holt, Rinehart & Winston, 1972, Ch. 14.
10,510.   Katz, Alfred H. Some psychological themes in a novel of
           Christina Stead. Lit & Psychol, 1965, 15:210-215.
10,511.   Katz, Claire. Flannery O'Connor's rage of vision. Amer
           Lit, 1974, 46:54-67.
10,512.   Katz, Harvey A., Warrick, Patricia, & Greenberg, Martin
           H. Introductory Psychology Through Science Fiction.
           Chicago: Rand McNally, 1974.
10,513.   Katz, Joseph. Eroticism in American literary realism.
           Studies in Amer Fiction, 1977, 5:35-50.
10,514.   Katz, Leon. Weininger and The Making of Americans.
           Twentieth Century Lit, 1978, 24(1):8-26.
10,515.   Katz, Michael R. Dreams in Pushkin. In Riasanovsky,
           N.V., Struve, G., & Eekman, T. (eds), California
           Slavic Studies, Vol. 11. Berkeley: Univ. California
           Press, 1979, 71-103.
10,516.   Kauffman, Linda Sue. Psychic Displacement and Adapta-
           tion in the Novels of Dickens and Faulkner. DAI, 1978,
           39:3573-74A.
10,517.   Kaufmann, Walter A. (ed). Existentialism from Dostoev-
           sky to Sartre. Cleveland: Meridian, 1960.
10,518.   Kaul, A.N. Hawthorne: A Collection of Critical Essays.
           Englewood Cliffs: Prentice-Hall, 1966.
10,519.   Kavanaugh, Thomas M. Unraveling Robinson: the divided
           self in Defoe's Robinson Crusoe. Texas Studies in Lit
           & Language, 1978, 20:416-432.

10,520. Kazin, Alfred. The conquistador: or Freud in his letters. In Contemporaries. Boston: Little, Brown, 1962, 377-382.

10,521. _____. The giant killer: drink and the American writer. Commentary, 1976, 61:44-50.

10,522. _____. Hemingway, the sensuous writer. New Republic, 1977, 176 (12):21-28.

10,523. _____. The language of pundits. In Rolo, C. (ed), Psychiatry in American Life. Boston: Little, Brown 1963, 193-207; NY: Dell, 1963, 193-207; Atlantic Monthly, 1961, 208:73-78; Cornhill, 1961, 172:153-164.

10,524. _____. Melville as scripture. Partisan Rev, 1950, 17: 65-75.

10,525. _____. Psychoanalysis and contemporary literary culture. Psychoanalysis, 1958, 45(4):41-51; In Contemporaries. Boston: Little, Brown, 1962, 362-372; In Phillips, W., & Rahv, P. (eds), The Partisan Review Anthology. NY: Holt & Rinehart, 1962, 238-245; In Ruitenbeek, H. M. (ed), Psychoanalysis and Literature. NY: Dutton, 1964, 3-13.

10,526. _____. Sons, lovers and mothers. In Tedlock, E. W. (ed), D. H. Lawrence: Novelist, Poet, Prophet. NY: Harper & Row, 1973; NY: New York Univ. Press, 1965; In Twentieth Century Interpretations of 'Sons and Lovers.' Englewood Cliffs, NJ: Prentice-Hall, 1970, 74-84.

10,527. Keady, Sylvia H. Richard Wright's women characters and inequality. Black Amer Lit Forum, 1976, 10:124-128.

10,528. Keane, Susan M. Dream imagery in the novels of Bernanos. In Frohock, W. M. (ed), Image and Theme. Cambridge: Harvard Univ. Press, 1969, 11-37.

10,529. Kedesdy, Deirdre Ann Ling. Images of Women in the American Best Seller: 1870-1900. DAI, 1976, 37: 3625A-26A.

10,530. Keefe, Robert. Charlotte Brontë's World of Death. Austin: Univ. Texas Press, 1979.

10,531. Keefe, Terry. Psychiatry in the postwar fiction of Simone de Beauvoir. Lit & Psychol, 1979, 29:123-133.

10,532. Kehler, Joel R. The House of Seven Gables: house, home, and Hawthorne's psychology of habitation. Emerson Society Q, 1975, 21:142-153.

10,533. Keith, W. J. The Manticore: psychology and fictional technique. Studies in Canadian Lit, 1978, 3:133-136.

10,534. Keller, Edwin Roy, Jr. Disintegrated Man: A Study of Alienation in Selected Twentieth-Century Anti Utopian Novels. DAI, 1977, 38:2776A.

10,535. Keller, Fritz. Studien zum Phänomenon der Angst in der modernen deutschen Literatur. Winterthur: Keller, 1956.

10,536. Keller, Karin. Gesellschaft in mythischem Bann. Studien zum Roman 'Das Schloss' und anderen Werken Franz Kafkas. Wiesbaden: Athenaion, 1977.

10,537. Kellerman, Frederick. A new key to Virginia Woolf's Orlando. English Studies, 1978, 59:138-150.

10,538. Kelley, Linda M. An Analysis of the Development of the Feminine Image in Selected Novels by Machado de Assis. DAI, 1978, 39:1611A.

10,539. Kellner, Robert Scott. Sex, toads, and scorpions: a study of the psychological themes in Melville's Pierre. Arizona Q, 1975, 31:5-20.

10,540. _____. Toads and Scorpions: Women and Sex in the Writings of Herman Melville. DAI, 1977, 38:2127A.

10,541. Kellogg, Gene. Dark Prophets of Hope; Dostoevsky, Sartre, Camus, Faulkner. Chicago: Loyola Univ. Press, 1975.

10,542. Kellogg, John Felton. Aspectos de alienación en la novelística de Sebastián Juan Arbó. DAI, 1975, 36:3751A.

10,543. Kelly, Edward Hanford. Joyce's A Portrait of the Artist as a Young Man, Ch. II, Conclusion. Explicator, 1969, 27:5.

10,544. Kelly, G. Constant vicissitude of interesting passions: Ann Radcliffe's perplexed narratives. Ariel, 1979, 10: 45-64.

10,545. Kelly, H.A. Consciousness in the monologues of Ulysses. Modern Language Q, 1963, 24:3-12.

10,546. Kelly, Thomas Lee. The Quest for Self in the Early Novels of Kingsley Amis. DAI, 1975, 36:2219A-20A.

10,547. Kelvin, Norman. The divided self: William Styron's fiction from Lie Down in Darkness to The Confessions of Nat Turner. In Morris, R.K., & Malin, I. (eds), The Achievement of William Styron. Athens: Univ. Georgia Press, 1975, 208-226.

10,548. Kempton, A.P.L. Education and the child in 18th century French fiction. Studies on Voltaire & the 18th Century, 1974, 124:299-362.

10,549. _____. The theme of childhood in the 18th century French memoir novels. Studies on Voltaire & the 18th Century, 1975, 132:205-225.

10,550. Kenkel, William F. Marriage and the family in modern science fiction. J Marriage & Family, 1969, 31:6-14.

10,551. Kennedy, Alan. Christopher Isherwood's psychological makeup. In The Protean Self; Dramatic Action in Contemporary Fiction. NY: Columbia Univ. Press, 1974, 213-229.

10,552. Kennedy, Ian. Frederick Winterbourne: the good bad boy in Daisy Miller. Arizona Q, 1973, 29:139-150.

10,553. Kennedy, John Dorrance. Trollope's Widows: Beyond the Stereotypes of Maiden and Wife. DAI, 1976, 36:8075A-76A.

10,554. Kennedy, Veronica M.S. Mrs. Gamp as the Great Mother: a Dickensian use of the archetype. Victorian Newsletter, 1972, 41:1-5.

10,555. Kenner, Hugh. Dublin's Joyce. London: Chatto & Windus, 1955; Bloomington: Indiana Univ. Press, 1956.

10,556- Kenney, Blair G. Nelly Dean's witchcraft. Lit & Psychol,
7.   1968, 18:225.

10,558. Kenney, William. Doctor Sloper's double in Washington Square. Univ. Rev, 1970, 36:301-306.

10,559. Kent, George E. The black woman in Faulkner's works, with the exclusion of Dilsey. Phylon, 1974, 35:430-441; Phylon, 1975, 36:55-67.

10,560. Kenton, Edna. Henry James to the ruminant reader: 'The Turn of the Screw.' The Arts, 1924, 6:248-260; in Willen, G. (ed), A Casebook on Henry James's The Turn of the Screw. New York: Crowell, 1960, 102-114.

10,561. Kenyon, Nina N. Self-Hatred as a Basis for Criticism of American Society. DAI, 1969, 29:2713A.

10,562. Keppler, Carl Francis. The Literature of the Second Self. Tucson: Univ. Arizona Press, 1972.

10,563. Kern, Edith G. Existential Thought and Fictional Technique. Kierkegaard, Sartre, Beckett. New Haven: Yale Univ. Press, 1970.

10,564. _____. The human condition as mirrored in fictional structure. In Cadot, M., et al (eds), Actes du VIe Congrès de l'Association Internationale de Littérature Comparée. Stuttgart: Bieber, 1975, 745-748.

10,565. Kern, Jean B. The fallen woman, from the perspective of five early eighteenth-century women novelists. In Payne, H. C. (ed), Studies in Eighteenth-Century Culture, Vol. 10. Madison: Univ. Wisconsin Press, 1980.

10,566. Kerner, David. Psychodrama in Eden. Chicago Rev, 1959, 13:59-67.

10,567. Kerpneck, Harvey. Trollope's effiminate clergyman. Queen's Q, 1975, 82:191-214.

10,568. Kerscher, Rudolf. Charaktere und Charakterzeichnung in den Romanen von Julien Green. Munich: Schubert, 1962.

10,569. Kestner, Joseph A., III. The 'I' persona in the novels of Jane Austen. Studies in the Novel, 1972, 4:6-16.

10,570. _____. The Spatiality of the Novel. Detroit: Wayne State Univ. Press, 1978.

10,571. Ketchum, Anne A. Colette ou la Naissance du jour: étude d'un malentendu. Paris: Minard, 1968.

10,572. Key, M. R. Male and female friends in children's books. In Unger, R. K., & Denmark, F. L. (eds), Woman: Dependent or Independent Variable? NY: Psychological Dimensions, 1979, Ch. 5.

10,573. Keyishian, Harry. The martyrology of nymphomania: Nancy Cunnard in The Green Hat and Point Counter Point. In Marsden, M. T. (comp), Proceedings of the 6th National Convention of the Popular Culture Association. Bowling Green, Ohio: Bowling Green State Univ. Press, 1976, 292-298.

10,574. Keys, A. C. Racine's mother characters. In Adams, M. (ed), Proceedings of the Ninth Congress of the Australasian Universities' Language & Literature Association, 19-26 August 1964. Melbourne: Univ. Melbourne, 1964, 83.

10,575. Keys, Romey Thomas. Psychology of Character in Thomas Hardy and D. H. Lawrence. DAI, 1976, 37:2198A-99A.

10,576. Khan, Masud R. Suicide: the condition of consciousness. In Abbs, P. (ed), The Black Rainbow; Essays on the Present Breakdown of Culture. Totowa, NJ: Rowman & Littlefield, 1975, 63-91; London: Heinemann, 1975, 63-91.

10,577. Kharitonov, Vladimir. Tolstoy and Sterne. Soviet Lit, 1978, 8:75-83.

10,578. Kibler, L. W. Physical Love in the Twentieth-Century French Novel. DA, 1965, 26:6715-16.

10,579. Kiell, Norman. The Adolescent Through Fiction: A Psychological Approach. NY: IUP, 1959, 1964, 1970, 1974; Reviews: Helen W. Childers, Lit & Psychol, 1959, 9:55-56; Anne O. Freed, Int J Social Psychiat, 1959, 5(3):232; Eric Terdwyn, Litterair Paspoort, Dec 1959, p. 19.

10,580. _____. 'Ay there's the rub': masturbation in literature. In Marcus, I. M., & Francis, J. J. (eds), Masturbation: From Infancy to Senescence. NY: IUP, 1975, 459-491.

10,581. _____. Varieties of Sexual Experience. Psychosexuality in Literature. NY: IUP, 1976; Reviews: Strother B. Purdy, Contemporary Psychol, 1977, 22(10):748-749; Eleanor Davis, Modern Psychoanal, 1977, 2(1). Austin Silber, JAPA, 1979, 27:732-733.

10,582. _____. The very private eye of Ross Macdonald. Lit & Psychol, 1977, 27:21-34, 67-73.

10,583. Kiely, Robert. The craft of despondency--the traditional novelists. Daedalus, 1963, 92:220-237.

10,584. _____. Robert Louis Stevenson and the Fiction of Adventure. Cambridge: Harvard Univ. Press, 1964.

10,585. Kiessling, A. Die Gefühlslehre der deutschen Romantik. Beiträge dem 15 Kongress der deutschen Gesellschaft für Psychologie (Jena), 1936, 102-103.

10,586. Killoh, Ellen. Patriarchal women: a study of three novels by Janet Lewis. Southern Rev, 1974, 10:342-364.

10,587. Kimball, A. G. Savages and savagism: Brockden Browne's dramatic irony. Studies in Romanticism, 1967, 6:214-225.

10,588. Kimball, Jean. Freud, Leonardo, and Joyce: the dimensions of a childhood memory. James Joyce Q, 1980, 17:165-182.

10,589. _____. The hypostasis in Ulysses. James Joyce Q, 1973, 19:435-436.

10,590. _____. James Joyce and Otto Rank: the incest motif in Ulysses. James Joyce Q, 1976, 13(3):366-382.

10,591. Kincaid, James R. Alice's invasion of Wonderland. PMLA, 1973, 88:92-99.

10,592. _____. The education of Mr. Pickwick. Nineteenth-Century Fiction, 1969, 24:127-141.

10,593. _____. Laughter and Oliver Twist. PMLA, 1968, 83:63-70.

10,594. _____. Review: R. Langbaum's Mysteries of Identity: A Theme in Modern Literature. Virginia Q. Rev, 1978, 54:742-747.

10,595. King, C.D. Edouard Dujardin, inner monologue and the stream of consciousness. French Studies, 1953, 7:116-127.

10,596. King, Frances. Treatment of the mentally retarded character in modern American fiction. Bulletin of Bibliography, 1975, 32:106-114.

10,597. King, Graham. Garden of Zola. Emile Zola and His Novels for English Readers. NY: Barnes & Noble, 1978.

10,598. King, J. Robin. Thomas Mann's Joseph and His Brothers: religious themes and modern humanism. Thought, 1978, 53:416-432.

10,599. King, Merton P. The androgynous mind and The Waves. University Rev, 1964, 30:221-224.

10,600. _____. The Waves and the androgynous mind. Univ. Rev, 1963, 30:128-134.

10,601. King, Roma, Jr. The Janus symbol in As I Lay Dying. Univ. Kansas City Rev, 1955, 31:287-290.

10,602. Kingdon, Frank. Literature and sex. In Ellis, A., & Abarbanel, A. (eds), Sex and Today's Society, Vol. 5. NY: Ace, 1967, 174-191.

10,603. Kinkead-Weekes, Mark. Eros and metaphor: sexual relationship in the fiction of Lawrence. In Smith, A. (ed), Lawrence and Women. NY: Barnes & Noble, 1978, 101-121; Twentieth Century Studies, 1969, 1:3-19.

10,604. Kirby, David K. Two modern versions of the quest. Southern Humanities Rev, 1971, 5:387-395.

10,605. Kirchner, John H. Psychology of the scientist. Consider this: a psycholiterary study of Walden Two. Psychol Reports, 1970, 26:403-412.

10,606. Kiremidjian, David. Crime and Punishment: matricide and the woman question. Amer Imago, 1976, 33:403-433.

10,607. Kirk, Russell. Chesterton, madmen, and mad-houses. In Montgomery, J.W. (ed), Myth, Allegory, and Gospel: An Interpretation of J.R.R. Tolkien, C.S. Lewis, G.K. Chesterton, Charles Williams. Minneapolis: Bethany Fellowship, 1974, 33-51.

10,608. Kirkpatrick, Judith Ann. The Artistic Expression of the Psychological Theories of William James in the Writing of Henry James. DAI, 1975, 36:2207A.

10,609. Kirkpatrick, Smith. 'The Anointed Powerhouse.' Sewanee Rev, 1969, 77:94-108.

10,610. Kirsch, James. The enigma of Moby Dick. J Analytic Psychol, 1958, 3:131-148.

10,611. Kirschner, Nora I. Don Quijote de la Mancha: a study in classical paranoia. Annali Istituto Universitario Orientale, Sezione Romanza, 1967, 9:275-282.

10,612. Kirschner, Paul. Conrad: The Psychologist as Artist. Edinburgh: Oliver & Boyd, 1968.

10,613. Kisner, Madeleine. Color in the Worlds and Works of Poe, Hawthorne, Crane, Anderson, and Welty. DAI, 1975, 36:3714A.

10,614. Kist, E. M. A Laingian analysis of blackness in Ralph El-
         lison's Invisible Man. Studies in Black Lit, 1976, 7(7):
         10-23.
10,615. Kitayama, Riyu. Psychoanalytische Studien über den Ro-
         manschreiber, Soseki Natume. Tokyo Zeitschrift für
         Psychoanalyse, 1938, 6(2).
10,616. _____. Der Romanschreiber Soseki Natume als Neuro-
         tiker. Tokyo Zeitschrift für Psychoanalyse, 1938, 6.
10,617. Klein, James. Out of mere words: self-composition and
         A Portrait of the Artist. James Joyce Q, 1976, 13(3):
         293-305; Earlier version: Lotts, horse piss, and rotted
         straw. College English, 1973, 34:952-974.
10,618. Klein, L. C. The Portrait of the Jew in English and Ger-
         man Fiction and Drama (1830-1933). Doctoral disserta-
         tion, University College, London, 1967.
10,619. Klein, Marcus. After Alienation: American Novels in
         Mid-Century. Cleveland: World, 1964.
10,620. _____. Ralph Ellison's Invisible Man. In Gross, S. L.,
         & Hardy, J. E. (eds), Images of the Negro in American
         Literature. Chicago, Univ. Chicago Press, 1966, 249-
         264.
10,621. Klein, Viola. The Rebel Generation; a novel by Jo v.
         Amers-Küller. In The Feminine Character. NY: IUP,
         1946, 183-207.
10,622. Kleinbard, David J. D. H. Lawrence and ontological in-
         security. PMLA, 1974, 89:154-163.
10,623. _____. Laing, Lawrence and the maternal cannibal.
         Psychoanal Rev, 1971, 58:5-13.
10,624. Kleinberg, Seymour. Ambivalence: the psychology of
         sexuality in Henry James's The Portrait of a Lady.
         Markham Rev, 1969, 1(5):2-7.
10,625. Kleis, John Christopher. Passion vs. prudence: theme
         and technique in Trollope's Palliser novels. Texas
         Studies in Lit & Language, 1970, 11:1405-1414.
10,626. Klemtner, Susan S. Permanent game of excuses: deter-
         minism in Heller's Something Happened. Modern Fic-
         tion Studies, 1978-79, 24:550-556.
10,627. Kletenik, I. K. [The problem of personality in the work of
         Saint-Exupéry.] Outchonye Zapiski (Moscow), 1964,
         113-129.
10,628. Kligerman, Jack. The quest for self: James T. Far-
         rells' character Bernard Carr. Univ. Kansas City Rev,
         1962, 29:9-16.
10,629. Kliman, Bernice W. Women in Roth's fiction. Nassau
         Rev, 1978, 3(4):75-88.
10,630. Kline, T. Jefferson. Deconstructing death: Malraux's
         lapsus Lazari. Twentieth Century Lit, 1978, 24:372-
         383.
10,631. Kloss, Robert J. The function of forgetting in Joyce's
         'Clay.' Hartford Studies in Lit, 1974, 6:167-186.
10,632. _____. The gratuitous act: Gide's Lafcadio reconsid-
         ered. Psychoanal Rev, 1977, 64:111-134.

10,633. _____. The secret of Aiken's snow. Hartford Studies in Lit, 1980, 12:29-38.

10,634. _____. The symbolic structure of Eudora Welty's 'Livvie.' Notes on Mississippi Writers, 1974-75, 7:70-82.

10,635. Klotman, Phyllis R. Sin and sublimation in the novels of Samuel Richardson. College Language Assn J, 1977, 20:365-373.

10,636. Kluglein, H. Über die Romane Ina Seidels. Imago, 1926, 12:490-499.

10,637. Klussman, Paul G. Lion Feuchtwangers Roman Jud Süss: gedichtete Psychologie und prophetischer Mythos des Juden. Zeitschrift für Deutsche Philologie, 1978, 97: 87-107.

10,638. Knapp, Bettina L. Anaïs/Artaud--alchemy. Mosaic, 1978, 11(2):65-74.

10,639. _____. Céline: Man of Hate. University: Univ. Alabama Press, 1974; Review: Erika Ostrovsky, French Rev, 1975, 49:284-285.

10,640. Knapp, John V. The double life of George Bowling. Rev Existential Psychol & Psychiat, 1975-76, 14:109-125.

10,641. _____. Review: Keith M. May's Out of the Maelstrom: Psychology and the Novel in the Twentieth Century. Modern Fiction Studies, 1978-79, 24:654-658.

10,642. Knight, George Wilson. Lawrence, Joyce and Powys. Essays in Criticism, 1961, 11.

10,643. Knight, J.A. Sexual implications of money. MAHS, 1969, 3(6):29-31, 35.

10,644. Knoepflmacher, Ulrich C. Thoughts on the aggression of daughters. In Levine, G.L., & Knoepflmacher, U.C. (eds), The Endurance of Frankenstein; Essays on Mary Shelley's Novel. Berkeley: Univ. California Press, 1979, 88-119.

10,645. Knoff, William F. A psychiatrist reads Camus' The Stranger. Psychiat Opinion, 1969, 6(1):19-21, 24.

10,646. Knopf, Olga. Fiktionalismus und Psychoanalyse. Annals of Philosophy, 1922, 3:283-295.

10,647. Kobler, J.F. Hemingway's 'The Sea Change': a sympathetic view of homosexuality. Arizona Q, 1970, 26: 318-324.

10,648. Koch, S. Colette: chronicler of the erotic. Saturday Rev, 1975, 2:30-32.

10,649. Kochanek, Patricia Sharpe. In Pursuit of Proteus: A Piagetian Approach to the Structure of the Grotesque in American Fiction of the Fifties. DAI, 1973, 33:5729A-30A.

10,650. Koëlla, C.E. La Puissance du rève chez Julien Green. PMLA, 1939, 54:597-607.

10,651. Koenigsberg, Richard A. F. Scott Fitzgerald and the work of mourning. Amer Imago, 1967, 24:248-269.

10,652. Koester, R. Death by miscalculation: some notes on suicide in Fontane's prose. German Life & Letters, 1966, 20:35-37.

10,653. Koff, Robert H. The therapeutic man Friday. JAPA, 1957, 5:424-431.

10, 654. Kofman, Sarah. [The double and the devil. The uncanni-
          ness of The Sandman.] Rev Française de Psychanalyse,
          1974, 38:25-56.
10, 655. Kohlberg, Lawrence. Psychological analysis and literary
          form: a study of the double in Dostoevsky. Daedalus,
          1963, 92:345-362.
10, 656. Kohler, Dayton McCue. Time in the modern novel. Eng-
          lish J, 1948, 37:331-340; College English, 1948, 10:15-
          24.
10, 657. Kohn, G. C. An analysis of Gene Forrester in A Separate
          Peace by John Knowles. Adolescence, 1975, 10:143-
          147.
10, 658. Kohut, Heinz. Death in Venice by Thomas Mann: a story
          about the disintegration of artistic sublimation. Psy-
          choanal Q, 1957, 26:206-228; In Ornstein, P. H. (ed),
          The Search for Self. Selected Writings of Heinz Kohut:
          1950-1978. NY: IUP, 1978, 108-133; In Ruitenbeek,
          H. M. (ed), Psychoanalysis and Literature. NY: Dut-
          ton, 1964, 282-302.
10, 659. _____. Review: Frank Donald Hirschbach's The Arrow
          and the Lyre: A Study of the Role of Love in the Works
          of Thomas Mann. Psychoanal Q, 1957, 26:273-275; In
          Ornstein, P. H. (ed), The Search for Self, Vol. 1.
          NY: IUP, 1978, 255-257.
10, 660. _____. Thomas Manns Tod in Venedig: Zerfall einer
          künstlerischen Sublimierung. In Mitscherlich, A. (ed),
          Psycho-Pathographien, I: Schriftsteller und Psycho-
          analyse. Frankfurt: Suhrkamp, 1972.
10, 661. Kolb, Philip. Proust's protagonist as a 'beacon. ' L'Es-
          prit créateur, 1965, 5:38-47.
10, 662. Kolbenschlag, Madonna C. Madness and sexual mythology
          in Scott Fitzgerald. Int J Women's Studies, 1978, 1:
          263-271.
10, 663. Kolnai, Aurel. Thomas Mann, Freud und der Fortschritt.
          Volkswohl, 1929, 20:321-327.
10, 664. Kolodny, Annette. The unchanging landscape: the pastoral
          impulse in Simms' revolutionary war romances. South-
          ern Lit J, 1972, 5(1):46-67.
10, 665. Komaroff, Katherine. Not tonight, deer; Taoist story.
          Harper, 1974, 249:12.
10, 666. Kompaneets, V. V. [Psychological problems of the artist.]
          Pyccкaя Jlитepatypa, 1974, 1:46-60.
10, 667. König, R. Die naturalistische Aesthetik in Frankreich und
          ihre Auflösung. Ein Beitrag zur systemwissenschaft-
          lichen Betrachtung der Künstlerästhetik. Leipzig:
          Noske, 1931.
10, 668. Kopf, Josephine Z. Meyer Wolfsheim and Robert Cohn: a
          study of Jewish type and stereotype. Tradition, 1969,
          10(3):93-104.
10, 669. Koppel, Gene S. Sexual education and sexual values in
          Tom Jones: confusion at the core? Studies in the
          Novel, 1980, 95:627-640.
10, 670. Kordić, Radoman. Psihoanaliza i moderni roman. Delo
          (Belgrade), 1967, 13:347-360.

10,671- Korenman, Joan S.   Henry James and the murderous mind.
2.   Essays in Lit, 1977, 4:198-211.

10,673. Korg, Jacob.   The rage of Caliban.   Univ. Toronto Q,
        1967, 37:75-89.

10,674. Korges, James.   Abé and Ooka: identity and mind-body.
        Critique: Studies in Modern Fiction, 1968, 10(2):130-
        148.

10,675. Korkowski, Eugene.   The excremental vision of Barth's
        Todd Andrews.   Critique: Studies in Modern Fiction,
        1976, 18(2):51-58.

10,676. _____. Scriblerus' sinking opera.   Peri Bathous XIII.
        Lit & Psychol, 1974, 24:80-88.

10,677. Kort, Wolfgang.   Alfred Döblin: Das Bild des Menschen
        in seinen Romanen.   Bonn: Bouvier, 1970.

10,678. Korth, Virginia A.   The gifted in children's fiction.   Gifted
        Child Q, 1977, 21:246-260.

10,679. Kosinski, Mark.   Mark Twain's absurd universe and 'The
        Great Dark.'   Studies in Short Fiction, 1979, 16:335-340.

10,680. Kostelanetz, Richard C.   'The connection': heroin as ex-
        istential choice.   Texas Q, 1962, 5:159-162.

10,681. Koster, Donald B.   Poe, romance and reality.   Amer
        Transcendental Q, 1973, 19:8-13.

10,682. Kostis, Nicholas.   The Exorcism of Sex and Death in Julien
        Green's Novels.   The Hague: Mouton, 1974.

10,683. Kotchy-N'Guessan, Barthélemy.   Retour aux sources dans
        la littérature négro-africaine.   Ethnopsychologie, 1973,
        27:205-224.

10,684. Kotzin, Michael C.   Fairy tale and fiction: enchantment in
        early Conrad.   Folklore, 1980, 91:15-26.

10,685. Koura, I.   [The structure of the personality in the tale of
        Genji.]   Japanese J Applied Psychol, 1939, 5:112-159.

10,686. Koustrup, Anders.   Freud og Rifbjerg.   Meddelser fra
        Dansklaerenforeningen, 1973, 51-63.

10,687. Kovel, Joel.   On reading Madame Bovary psychoanalytically.
        Seminars in Psychiat, 1973, 5:331-345.

10,688. Kozer, José.   La desintegración de la personalidad en
        'Angústia' de Graciliano Ramos.   Revista de Cultura
        Brasileña, 1971, 31:73-79.

10,689. Kraft, M.   Studien zur Thematik von Max Frischs Roman
        'Mein Name sei Gantenbein.'   Berne: Lang & Cie, 1969.

10,690. Krakowski, Anna.   La Condition de la femme dans l'oeuvre
        d'Emile Zola.   Paris: Nizet, 1974.

10,691. Kralowski-Faygenbaum, Anna.   La Femme dans l'oeuvre
        d'Emile Zola.   Thèse, Univ. de Paris, 1962.

10,692. Kraus, A.   Beiträge zum Doppelgänger Motiv bei E. T. A.
        Hoffmann.   Rostock, 1918.

10,693. Kraus, Elisabeth.   Psychic sores in search of compassion:
        Hawkes' Death, Sleep, and the Traveller.   Critique:
        Studies in Modern Fiction, 1976, 17(3):39-52.

10,694. Kraus, Willis Keith.   A Critical Survey of the Contempo-
        rary Adolescent-Girl Problem Novel.   DAI, 1975, 35:
        7910A.

10,695. Krause, Florence P. Emasculating women in Delta Wedding. Publications Missouri Philological Assn, 1976, 1:48-57.

10,696. Krause, Sidney J. Edgar Watson Howe: our first naturalist. In Hakutani, Y., & Fried, L. (eds), American Literary Naturalism: A Reassessment. Heidelberg: Carl Winter, 1975, 37-56.

10,697. _____. Ormond: seduction in a new key. Amer Lit, 1973, 44:570-584.

10,698. Krauss, Wilhelmine. Das Doppelgängermotiv in der Romantik. Studien zum Romantischen Idealismus. Germanische Studien, Heft 99. Berlin: Emil Ebering, 1930.

10,699. Krauth, Philip L. The Necessary Coxcomb: The Theme of Egotism in the Works of Stephen Crane. DAI, 1971, 31:6014A.

10,700. Kravchenko, Maria. Dostoevsky and the Psychologists. Amsterdam: Hakkert, 1978; Review: R.B. Anderson, Slavic & E European J, 1979, 23:269-271.

10,701. Kreitzer, Neal D. The Quest for Identity in the Novels of Bernard Malamud. DAI, 1974, 35:2278A.

10,702. Krekeler, Elizabeth M. The Archetypal Dimensions of Joyce's Dedalian Novels. DAI, 1972, 33:1173A.

10,703. Krestovsky, Lydie. Le Dédoublement esthétique. Psyché, 1951, 6:308-310.

10,704. Kreutzer, Eberhard. Hugh Selby's Last Exit to Brooklyn: the psychodynamics of person and place. Amerikastudien, 1977, 22:137-151.

10,705. Kreuzer, Helmut. Boheme und Bürgertum. Neue Deutsche Heft, 1967, 14:42-60.

10,706. Krishna, S. Existentialism and the theme of alienation: a study of Albert Camus's L'Etranger. Literary Criticism, 1963, 5(4):29-31.

10,707. Kronegger, Maria Elizabeth. James Joyce and Associated Image Makers. New Haven: College & Univ. Press, 1969.

10,708. Kronhausen, Phyllis, & Kronhause, Eberhard. Erotic Fantasies. A Study of the Sexual Imagination. NY: Grove, 1969.

10,709. Krook, Dorothea. The madness of art: further reflections on the ambiguity of Henry James. Hebrew Univ. Studies in Lit, 1973, 1(1):25-38.

10,710. Krotkoff, Hertha. Themen, Motive und Symbole in Arthur Schnitzlers 'Traumnovelle.' Modern Austrian Lit, 1972, 5:70-95.

10,711. Krotz, Frederick W. Robert Musils Die Amsel, novellististische Gestaltung einer Psychose. Modern Austrian Lit, 1970, 3(1):7-38.

10,712. Krouse, Agate N. The Feminism of Doris Lessing. DAI, 1973, 34:322A.

10,713. Krueger, John P. Names and nomenclatures in science-fiction. Names, 1966, 14:203-216.

10,714. Kruppa, Joseph E. Durrell's Alexandria Quartet. The 'implosion' of the modern consciousness. Modern Fiction Studies, 1967, 13:401-416.

10,715. Krusche, D. Die kommunikative Funktion der Deformation klassischer Motive: Der Jäger Graccus. Der Deutschunterricht, 1973, 25(1):128-140.

10,716. Krutch, Joseph Wood. Five Masters: A Study in the Mutations of the Novel. Bloomington: Indiana Univ. Press, 1959; NY: Cape & Smith, 1930.

10,717. _____. Psychoanalyzing Alice. In And Even If You Do; Essays on Man, Manners and Machines. NY: Morrow, 1967, 142-145.

10,718. Kubal, David. Freud, Orwell, and the bourgeois interior. Yale Rev, 1978, 67:389-403.

10,719. Kubie, Lawrence S. The fantasy of dirt. Psychoanal Q, 1937, 6:388-425.

10,720. _____. God's Little Acre by Erskine Caldwell. Psychoanal Q, 1934, 3:328-333; Saturday Rev, 24 Nov 1934, 11.

10,721. _____. The literature of horror; an analysis of William Faulkner's Sanctuary. Saturday Rev, 21 Oct 1934, 11.

10,722. _____. William Faulkner's Sanctuary. Saturday Rev Literature, 20 Oct 1938; In Warren, R.P. (ed), Faulkner. A Collection of Critical Essays. Englewood Cliffs, NJ: Prentice-Hall, 1966, 137-146.

10,723. Kudler, Harvey. Bernard Malamud's The Natural and Other Oedipal Analogs in Baseball Fiction. DAI, 1977, 37: 5829A.

10,724. Kuepper, Karl J. Gesture and posture as elemental symbolism in Kafka's The Trial. Mosaic, 1970, 3:143-152.

10,725. Kugelmass, Harold. The Search for Identity: The Development of the Protean Model of Self in Contemporary American Fiction. DAI, 1973, 34:1285A-86A.

10,726. Kuhns, Richard F. Modernity and death: The Leopard by Giuseppe di Lampedusa. Contemporary Psychoanal, 1969, 5(2):95-119.

10,727. Kuhr, Alexander. Neurotische Aspekte bei Heidegger und Kafka. Zeitschrift für Psychosomatische Medizin, 1955, 1:217-227.

10,728. Kuitunen, M. Il motivo dell'età adoloscente in Moravia. Forum italicum, 1969, 3:79-89.

10,729. Kulenmeyer, Guenther. Studien zur Psychologie in neuen englischen Roman: Dorothey Richardson und James Joyce. Doctoral dissertation, Greifswald Univ., 1933.

10,730. Kumar, Anita S. Recurring patterns of behavior in the women characters of George Eliot. Triveni, 1971, 40(1):21-26.

10,731. Kumar, Shiv K. Bergson and the Stream of Consciousness Novel. Glasgow: Blackie, 1962; Toronto: Ryerson, 1962; NY: New York Univ. Press, 1963.

10,732. _____. Memory in Virginia Woolf and Bergson. Univ. Kansas City Rev, 1960, 26:235-239.

10,733. _____. Space-time polarity in Finnegans Wake. Modern Philology, 1957, 54:230-233.

10,734. Kumpikas, Giedré M. Male Psychology in the Novels of
Guy de Maupassant. DAI, 1974, 35:1659A.

10,735. Kunz, Don. Lost in the distance of winter: James Welch's
Winter in the Blood. Critique: Studies in Modern Fiction, 1978, 20(1):93-99.

10,736. _____. Mechanistic and totemistic symbolization in
Kesey's One Flew over the Cuckoo's Nest. Studies in
Amer Fiction, 1975, 3:65-82.

10,737. Kurfez, H. Zu Goethes Werther. Ästhetische-psychol-
ogisch Untersuchungen zur 1. and 2. Fassung. Archiv
für Geschichte der Philosophie, 1916, 22:192-202.

10,738. Kurisu, Kosei. Le Thème de l'adultère dans l'oeuvre romanesque stendhalienne des années 1829-1830. Stendhal
Club, 1975, 17:338-347.

10,739. Kushen, Betty. 'Dreams of golden domes,' manic fusion
in Virginia Woolf's Orlando. Lit & Psychol, 1979, 29:
25-33.

10,740. _____. Love's martyrs: The Scarlet Letter as secular
cross. Lit & Psychol, 1972, 22:109-120.

10,741. _____. The psychogenic imperative in the works of Virginia Woolf. Lit & Psychol, 1977, 27:52-66.

10,742. Kuttner, Alfred B. Sons and Lovers: a Freudian interpretation. Psychoanal Rev, 1916, 3:295-317.

10,743. Labor, Earl. Crane and Hemingway: anatomy of trauma.
Renascence, 1959, 11:189-196.

10,744. _____. Faulkner's The Sound and the Fury. Explicator,
1959, 4:30.

10,745. La Bossière, Camille R. Joseph Conrad and the Science
of the Unknown. Fredericton, Canada: York, 1979.

10,746. La Brie, Ross. The power of consciousness in Henry
James. Arizona Q, 1973, 29:101-114.

10,747. Labuda, A. Les Thèmes de l'adolescence dans l'oeuvre
d'Andre Gide, I: L'oeuvre juvénile. Pñ: Praca Wy-
dana, 1968.

10,748. Lacan, Jacques. The purloined letter. In Lebovici, S.,
& Widlocher, D. (eds), Psychoanalysis in France. NY:
IUP, 1979; Yale French Studies, 1972 (1966), 48:38-72.

10,749. _____. Le Séminaire sur 'La Lettre volée.' Psychanalyse, 1956, 2:1-44.

10,750. Laceiras, J. Problemas de criminologia. Criminalia.
Rev de Ciencias, 1945, 11:646-658.

10,751. La Charité, Raymond C. The drum and the owl: functional symbolism in Panurge's quest. Symposium, 1974,
28:154-165.

10,752. Lackner, Stephan. Thomas Mann, Freud und die Tiefe.
Das neue Tage-Buch, 1936, 4:1049-1051.

10,753. Lafferty, Vera. A. S. Serafimovich's forgotten novel, City
in the Steppe (1912). Canadian Slavonic Papers, 1974,
16:202-220.

10,754. Laforest, M. Les Sensations olfactives dans A Rebours de
J.K. Huysmans. In Mélanges Pierre Lambert consacrés
à Huysmans. Paris: Nizet, 1975, 231-240.

10,755. LaForgue, René. <u>La Peste</u> et la vertu. <u>Psyché</u>, 1948, 3: 406-420.

10,756. Lafue, Pierre. Nouveaux psychologues. In Prévost, J. (ed), <u>Problèmes du roman</u>. Brussels: Carrefour, 1945, 164-169.

10,757. Lagriffe, L. La Peur dans l'oeuvre de Maupassant. <u>Archivio di anthropologia criminale, psichiatria e medici legale</u>, 1913, 28:188-199.

10,758. LaGuardia, David M. Poe, 'Pym,' and initiation. <u>Emerson Society Q</u>, 1970, 6(Pt. 2 Supp):82-84.

10,759. LaGuardia, Eric. Sire de Maletroit's door. <u>Amer Imago</u>, 1958, 15:411-423.

10,760. Laguardia, Gari J. The Dialectic of Desire in Gustavo Adolfo Bécquer: A Psychoanalytic Study. <u>DAI</u>, 1976, 36:5337A-38A.

10,761. La Hood, Marvin I. Huck Finn's search for identity. <u>Mark Twain J</u>, 1967, 13(3):11-14.

10,762. Lahr-Well, Almeda Marie. The Don Juan and Feminist Myths in Unamuno: A Struggle Toward Consciousness. <u>DAI</u>, 1974, 37:2221A.

10,763. Lakshmi, Vijay. The solid and the intangible: Virginia Woolf's theory of the androgynous mind. <u>Lit Criterion</u> (Mysore), 1971, 10:28-34.

10,764. Lale, Meta, & Williams, John S. The narrator of <u>The Painted Bird</u>: a case study. <u>Renascence</u>, 1972, 24:198-206.

10,765. Lamb, Jonathan. Language and Hartleian associationism in <u>A Sentimental Journey</u>. <u>Eighteenth-Century Studies</u>, 1980, 13:285-312.

10,766. Lamdin, Lois S. Malamud's schlemiels. In Demarest, D. P., Jr., et al., (eds), <u>A Modern Miscellany</u>. Pittsburgh: Carnegie-Mellon Univ. Press, 1970, 31-42.

10,767. Lameyer, Gordon Amis. The double in Sylvia Plath's <u>The Bell Jar</u>. In Butscher, E. (ed), <u>Sylvia Plath</u>. NY: Dodd, Mead, 1977, 143-165.

10,768. Lamont, John H. Hawthorne's last novels: a study in creative failure. [Abstract.] <u>Bulletin Philadelphia Assn Psychoanal</u>, 1962, 12:38-39.

10,769. _____. Hawthorne's unfinished works. <u>Harvard Medical Alumni Bulletin</u>, 1962, Summer.

10,770. Lamonte, Rosalie Salerno. The Characterization of Woman in the Novels of Pío Baroja. <u>DAI</u>, 1975, 35:4530A-31A.

10,771. Lanapoppi, A. P. Letteratura e sublimazione: le prime novelle di Alberto Moravia. <u>Italica</u>, 1976, 53:29-56.

10,772. Landau, Elliott D., et al. (eds). <u>Child Development Through Literature</u>. Englewood Cliffs, NJ: Prentice-Hall, 1972.

10,773. Landauer, Karl. Chi mal ti vuol, mal ti sogna. Ein traum und seine Deutung im <u>Dekameron</u>. <u>Psychoanalytische Bewegung</u>, 1929, 1:76.

10,774. Landes, T. H. The function of taste in the fiction of Eudora Welty. <u>Mississippi Q</u>, 1973, 26:543-576.

10,775. Landis, Paul W. <u>The Psychological Treatment of the Historical Novel</u>. Doctoral dissertation, Univ. Illinois, 1926.

10,776. Lane, Gary. Seymour's suicide again: a new reading of J.D. Salinger's 'A Perfect Day for Bananafish.' Studies Short Fiction, 1973, 10:27-33.

10,777. Lane, Lauriat, Jr. The double in An American Tragedy. Modern Fiction Studies, 1966, 12:213-220.

10,778. Lang, Frances. Doris Lessing: madness as ideology. Off Our Backs, 1972, 10-11.

10,779. Langbaum, Robert Woodrow. The Gaiety of Vision. A Study of Isak Dinesen's Art. London: Chatto & Windus, 1964; Mulm, stråler og latter. En studie i Karen Blixens kunst. Copenhagen: Gyldendal, 1964; NY: Random House, 1965.

10,780. Langer, Kurt. Der psychische Gesundheitszustand Karl Mays: Eine psychiatrisch-tiefenpsychologische Untersuchung. Jahrbuch der Karl-May-Gesellschaft, 1978, 168-173.

10,781. Langer, Marie. Barrabas o la Persecusion por un Ideal. Revista de Psicoanálisis, 1956, 13:545-548.

10,782. _____. Viaje al centre de la terra (Juilio Verne). Una fantasía de adolescente. Revista de Psicoanálisis, 1949, 7:3-9.

10,783. Langerova, Vera Zuzana. Women Characters in the Works of Uwe Johnson. DAI, 1976, 37:2209A-10A.

10,784. Langman, F.H. Women in Love. Essays in Criticism, 1967, 17:183-205.

10,785. Langworthy, J.L. Blindness in fiction. J Applied Psychol, 1930, 14:269-286.

10,786. Lantin, Rudolf. Traum und Wirklichkeit in der Prosadichtung Arthur Schnitzlers. Cologne/Aachen: Selbstverlag, 1958.

10,787. Lape, Denis A. The Masks of Dionysus: An Application of Friedrich Nietzsche's Theory of Tragedy to the Works of Hawthorne and Melville. DAI, 1972, 32:5188A.

10,788. La Polla, Franco. Dalla fossa dei serpenti al nido di cucù. Paragone, 1975, 302:97-104.

10,789. Lapp, John C. Art and hallucination in Flaubert. French Studies, 1956, 10:322-333.

10,790. _____. The Esthetics of Negligence: La Fontaine's Contes. London: Cambridge Univ. Press, 1971.

10,791. _____. The jealous window-watcher in Zola and Proust. French Studies, 1975, 29:166-176.

10,792. _____. Proust's windows to reality. Romanic Rev, 1976, 67:38-49.

10,793. _____. The watcher betrayed and the fatal woman: some recurring patterns in Zola. PMLA, 1959, 74:276-284; In Ruitenbeek, H.M. (ed), Homosexuality and Creative Genius. NY: Obolensky, 1967, 313-330.

10,794. Lapp, S. Mario Monteforte Toledo, contemporary Guatemalan novelist. Hispania, 1961, 44:420-427.

10,795. Laroque, François, & Blake, Nancy. Bartleby l'idée fixe. Delta, 1978, 7:143-153.

10,796. _____. Mourning and melancholia in 'Bartleby.' Delta, 1978, 7:155-168.

10,797. Larsen, Golden Lavon. Archetype and Social Change in the Novels of Joyce Cary. DA, 1963, 24:299-300.

10,798. Larsen, Michael Joseph. The Concept of the 'Double' in the Works of Joseph Conrad. DAI, 1976, 37:2861A-62A.

10,799. Larson, R. C. The Dream as a Literary Device in Five Novels by Hermann Hesse: 'Unterm Rad,' 'Rosshalde,' 'Demian,' 'Steppenwulf,' 'Narziss und Goldmund.' Doctoral dissertation, Yale Univ., 1949.

10,800. Laser, Marvin. Head, heart, and will in Hawthorne's psychology. Nineteenth Century Fiction, 1955, 10:130-140.

10,801. Latham, Aaron. A farewell to machismo. New York Times Magazine, 16 Oct 1977.

10,802. Lattin, Patricia Hopkins. Childbirth and motherhood in Kate Chopin's fiction. Regionalism & the Female Imagination, 1978, 4(2):8-12.

10,803. Lauber, John. Minds bewildered and astray: the Crawfords in Mansfield Park. Studies in the Novel, 1970, 2:194-210.

10,804. Lauer, Kristin O. The Interior Monologue in The Ambassadors and The Golden Bowl. DAI, 1971, 31:6015A.

10,805. Laurence-Anderson, Judith. Changing affective life in eighteenth-century England and Samuel Richardson's Pamela. In Payne, H. C. (ed), Studies in Eighteenth-Century Culture, Vol. 10. Madison: Univ. Wisconsin Press, 1980.

10,806. Lauretis, Teresa de. Discourse and the conquest of desire in Svevo's fiction. Modern Fiction Studies, 1972, 18:91-109.

10,807. _____. Dreams as metalanguage in Svevo's Confessions of Zeno. Language & Style, 1971, 4:208-220.

10,808. Lavers, Norman. Order in The Red Badge of Courage. Univ. Rev, 1966, 287-295.

10,809. Lavine, Steven David. The degradation of erotic life: Portnoy's Complaint reconsidered. Michigan Academician, 1979, 11:357-362.

10,810. Lavrin, Janko. Dostoevsky and His Creation; A Psycho-Critical Study. London: Collins, 1920.

10,811. Lawler, D. L. An Enquiry into Oscar Wilde's Revisions of the Picture of Dorian Gray. Doctoral dissertation, Univ. Chicago, 1969.

10,812. Lawrence, D. H. Novel and the feelings. In Phoenix. NY: Viking, 1936, 755-760.

10,813. Lawson, Lewis A. Gnostic vision in Lancelot. Renascence, 1979, 32:52-64.

10,814. _____. The grotesque-comic in the Snopes trilogy. In Manheim, L., & Manheim, E. (eds), Hidden Patterns. NY: Macmillan, 1966, 243-258; Lit & Psychol, 1965, 15:107-119.

10,815. _____. Walker Percy as Martian visitor. Southern Lit J, 1976, 8:102-113.

10,816. _____. Wilkie Collins and The Moonstone. Amer Imago, 1963, 20:61-79.

10,817. Lawson, Richard H. Schnitzler's 'Das Tagebuch der Redegonda.' German Rev, 1960, 35:202-213.

517 Fiction

10,818. Lawson, Ursula D. Pathological time in E.T.A. Hoffmann's Der Sandman. Monatshefte, 1968, 60(1):51-62.
10,819. Layard, John. A Celtic Quest: Sexuality and Soul in Culh-
wch and Oliven. Zurich: Spring, 1976.
10,820. Lazere, Donald. The Unique Creation of Albert Camus.
New Haven: Yale Univ. Press, 1973.
10,821. Lázaro, Angel. España en su novelista: Galdós. Revista
Cubana, 1945, 19:42-65.
10,822. Leaska, M.A. Virginia Woolf's The Voyage Out: character
deduction and the function of ambiguity. Virginia Woolf
Q, 1973, 1:39.
10,823. Leavis, Frank Raymond. Anna Karenina: thought and significance in a great creative work. Cambridge Q, 1965-
66, 1:5-27.
10,824. _____. Thought, Words and Creativity: Art and Thought
in Lawrence. NY: Oxford Univ. Press, 1976.
10,825. Leavis, Q.D. Fiction and the Reading Public. London:
Chatto & Windus, 1939.
10,826. Lebowitz, Alan. No farewell to arms. In Engel, M. (ed),
Uses of Literature. Cambridge, Harvard Univ. Press,
1973, 187-204.
10,827. Lebowitz, Naomi. Italo Svevo. New Brunswick, NJ: Rutgers Univ. Press, 1977.
10,828. Le Breton, Maurice. Probleme du moi et technique du roman chez Virginia Woolf. JPNP, 1947, 40:20-34.
10,829. _____. Technique et psychologie chez William Faulkner.
Etudes Anglaises, 1937, 1:418-438.
10,830. _____. Temps et personne chez William Faulkner.
JPNP, 1951, 44:344-354.
10,831. Lecercle, J.L. Inconscient et création littéraire: Sur La
nouvelle Héloise. Etudes Littéraires, 1968, 1:197-204.
10,832. Lecker, Barbara. The split characters in Charles Dickens.
Studies in English Lit, 1979, 19:689-704.
10,833. Lecker, Robert A. States of mind; Henry Kreisel's novels.
Canadian Lit, 1978, 77:82-93.
10,834. LeClair, Thomas. The ascendant eye: a reading of The
Damnation of Theron Ware. Studies in Amer Fiction,
1975, 3:95-102.
10,835. _____. Case of death: the fiction of J.P. Donleavy.
Contemporary Lit, 1971, 12:329-344.
10,836. _____. Flannery O'Connor's Wise Blood: the Oedipal
theme. Mississippi Q, 1976, 29:197-205.
10,837. _____. The obsessional fiction of Stanley Elkin. Contemporary Lit, 1975, 16:146-162.
10,838. _____. The Onion Eaters and the rhetoric of Donleavy's
comedy. Twentieth-Century Fiction, 1972, 18:167-174.
10,839. _____. The unreliability of innocence: John Hawkes'
Second Skin. J Narrative Technique, 1973, 3:32-39.
10,840. Lecomte, Marcel. Note sur Kafka et le rêve. In Breton,
A. (ed), Rêve. Documents. Paris: 1938, 61-62.
10,841. Lecuyer, Maurice A. Robbe-Grillet's La Jalousie and a
parallel in the graphic arts. Hartford Studies in Lit,
1971, 3:19-38.

10,842. Ledkovsky, Marina. The interior monologue in Tolstoy's work. Mid-Hudson Language Studies, 1978, 1:113-124.

10,843. Lee, C. Nicholas. Dreams and daydreams in the early fiction of Leo N. Tolstoi. In Terras, V. (ed), American Contributions to the 7th International Congress of Slavists; Vol. 2. Literature and Folklore. The Hague: Mouton, 1973, 373-392.

10,844. Lee, Grace Farrell. The quest of Arthur Gordon Pym. Southern Lit J, 1972, 4(2):22-33.

10,845. _____. The hidden God of Isaac Bashevis Singer. Hollins Critic, 1973, 10(6):1-15.

10,846. Lee, James W. Trollope's clerical concerns: the low church clergyman. Hartford Studies in Lit, 1969, 1: 198-208.

10,847. Lee, J. N. Swift and Scatological Satire. Albuquerque: Univ. New Mexico Press, 1971.

10,848. Lee, Sonia M. The awakening of the self in the heroines of Sembène Ousmane. Critique: Studies Modern Fiction, 1975, 17(2):17-25.

10,849. _____. L'Image de la femme dans le roman francophone de l'Afrique occidentale. DAI, 1974, 35:407A.

10,850. Leeds, Barry H. Theme and technique in One Flew Over the Cuckoo's Nest. Connecticut Rev, 1974, 7(2):35-50.

10,851. Leeper, Robert W., & Madison, Peter. Lillian Smith, The Journey. In Toward Understanding Human Personalities. NY: Appleton-Century-Crofts, 1959, 164-179.

10,852. Leer, Norman. The double theme in Malamud's Assistant: Dostoevsky with irony. Mosaic, 1971, 4(3):89-102.

10,853. Lees, F. N. Identification and emotion in the novel; a feature of narrative method. British J Aesthetics, 1964, 4:109-113.

10,854. Lefay-Toury, M. -N. [Chrétien de Troyes.] Cahiers de Civilisation Médiévale, 1972, 15:93-204.

10,855. Lefcowitz, Allan B. Apologia pro Roger Prynne: a psychological study. Lit & Psychol, 1974, 24:34-43.

10,856. _____, & Lefcowitz, Barbara F. Some rents in the veil: new light on Priscilla and Zenobia in The Blithedale Romance. Nineteenth Century Fiction, 1966, 21: 263-275.

10,857. Lefcowitz, Barbara F. Dream and action in Lessing's The Summer Before the Dark. Critique, 1975, 17:107-120.

10,858. _____. The Hybris of neurosis: Malamud's Pictures of Fidelman. Lit & Psychol, 1970, 20:115-120.

10,859. Leff, Leonard J. The center of violence in Joyce Carol Oates's fiction. Notes on Modern Amer Lit, 1977, 2: item 9.

10,860. Lehan, Richard Daniel. American fiction and French literary existentialism. In Browne, R. B. , & Pizer, D. (eds), Themes and Directions in American Literature. Lafayette, Ind: Purdue Univ. Press, 1969, 186-199.

10,861. _____. Dreiser's An American Tragedy. College English, 1963; In Westbrook, M. (ed), The Modern American Novel: Essays in Criticism. NY: Random House, 1966.

10, 862. _____. Existentialism and the Modern American Novel. DA, 1959, 20:1365.

10, 863. _____. Existentialism in recent American fiction: the demonic quest. Texas Studies in Lit & Language, 1959, 1:181-202.

10, 864. Lehman, Paul Robert. The Development of a Black Psyche in the Works of John Oliver Killens. DAI, 1976, 37: 2183A-4A.

10, 865. Lehner, F. Das Pferd und der Faun. Eine Novelle von André Maurois. Psychoanalytische Bewegung, 1929, 1: 168-170.

10, 866. Leigh, David J. In Our Time: the interchapters as structural guides to a psychological pattern. Studies in Short Fiction, 1975, 12:1-8.

10, 867. Leigh, James Anthony. Reading the Text: A Study of Selected Writings of Michel Leiris, Claude Simon, Alain Robbe-Grillet, Samuel Beckett and Maurice Roche Within the Context of Contemporary Critical Theory. DAI, 1976, 37:3613A.

10, 868. Leiner, Wolfgang (comp). Onze études sur l'image de la femme dans la littérature française du dix-septième siècle. Tubingen: Narr; Paris: Place, 1978.

10, 869. Leitenberg, Barbara. The New Utopias. DAI, 1976, 36: 5282A-3A.

10, 870. Leiter, L. H. A problem in analysis: Franz Kafka's A Country Doctor. JAAC, 1958, 16:337-347.

10, 871. Leites, Nathan. Trends in affectlessness. Amer Imago, 1947, 4:89-112; In Mead, M., & Métraux, R. B. (eds), The Study of Culture at a Distance. Chicago: Univ. Chicago Press, 1953.

10, 872. _____. Trends in moral temper. Amer Imago, 1948, 5:3-37.

10, 873. Lejeune, Philippe. Ecriture et sexualité. Europe, 1971, 502-03:113-143.

10, 874. _____. [Re Marcel Proust.] Europe, 1971, Nos. 502-503.

10, 875. Lelchuk, Alan. Self, family and society in Great Expectations. Sewanee Rev, 1970, 78:407-426.

10, 876. Lemieux, R. A propos de la datation et de la distribution des lettres dans Les Liaisons dangereuses. Romance Notes, 1974, 16:109-13.

10, 877. Lemon, Charles. Sickness and health in Wuthering Heights. Brontë Society Transactions, 1963, 14, Part 73, 23-25.

10, 878. Lender, Mark Edward, & Karnchanapee, Karen R. 'Temperance tales.' Anti-liquor fiction and American attitudes toward alcoholics in the late 19th and early 20th centuries. J Studies Alcohol, 1977, 38:1347-1370.

10, 879. Lenzer, Gertrud. On masochism: a contribution to the history of a phantasy and its theory. Signs, 1975, 1: 277-324.

10, 880. Lentz, Vern B. Ford's good narrator. Studies in the Novel, 1973, 5:483-490.

10,881. Léonard, Albert. Alain-Fournier et le 'Grand Meaulnes,'
essai d'interpretation littéraire et psychologique. Paris:
Desclée de Brouwer, 1943.

10,882. Leonard, Augustin. François Mauriac ou la psychologie du
pécheur. Liege: La Pensée Catholique, 1952.

10,883. Leonard, F. M. Nana: symbol and action. Modern Fiction
Studies, 1963-64, 9:149-158.

10,884. Leonhard, Karl. [Accentuated personalities in Dostoevski.]
Psychiatria Fennica, 1974, 93-100.

10,885. Leopold, Keith. Kafka, Freud, and Ein Landarzt. German
Q, 1964, 37(2).

10,886. _____. Some problems of terminology in the analysis of
the stream of consciousness novel. J Australasian Universities Language & Lit Assn, 1960, 13:23-32.

10,887. Lepape, Pierre. Le Double, le même, et le monde dans
Bouvard et Pécuchet. Biblioteca dell'Archivum Romani-
cum, 1966, 29.

10,888. Lerenbaum, Miriam. Moll Flanders: 'A woman of her
own account.' In Diamond, A., & Edwards, L. R.
(eds), The Authority of Experience. Essays in Feminist
Criticism. Amherst: Univ. Massachusetts Press, 1977,
101-117.

10,889. Lerner, Julianna Kitty. Rabelais and Woman. DAI, 1976,
37:1595A.

10,890. Lervik, Å. H. Når kvinner dikter om kvinner. Liberalt
perspektiv, 1971, 11:44-50.

10,891. LeSage, Laurent. The French New Novel. University
Park: Penn State Univ. Press, 1969, 1962; Review:
Peter Brooks, Modern Fiction Studies, 1970, 16:255-
256.

10,892. Lesser, Simon O. The attitude of fiction. Modern Fiction
Studies, 1956, 2:47-55.

10,893. _____. Fiction and the Unconscious. Boston: Beacon,
1957.

10,894. _____. The function of form in narrative art. Psychiatry, 1955, 18:51-63.

10,895. _____. Hawthorne and Anderson: conscious and unconscious perception. [Excerpt from Fiction and the Unconscious.] In Malin, I. (ed), Psychoanalysis and American Fiction. NY: Dutton, 1965, 87-110.

10,896. _____. The image of the father: a reading of 'My
kinsman, Major Molineaux.' Partisan Rev, 1955, 22:
372-390; In Fiction and the Unconscious. Boston: Beacon, 1957; In Phillips, W. (ed), Art and Psychoanalysis.
NY: Criterion, 1957; In Scott, W. (ed), Five Approaches
to Literary Criticism. NY: Collier, 1962, 99-120.

10,897. _____. A note on Pamela. College English, 1952, 14:
13-17.

10,898. _____. The role of unconscious understanding in Flaubert and Dostoevsky. Daedalus, 1963, 92:363-382.

10,899. _____. Saint and sinner--Dostoevsky's Idiot. In Manheim, L., & Manheim, E. (eds), Hidden Patterns.
NY: Macmillan, 1966, 132-150; Modern Fiction Studies,
1958, 4:211-224.

10,900. _____. Some unconscious elements in the responses to
fiction. Lit & Psychol, 1953, 3(4):2-5.
10,901. _____. The source of guilt and the sense of guilt--Kaf-
ka's The Trial. Modern Fiction Studies, 1962, 8:44-60.
10,902. _____, & Noland, Richard W. Saint and sinner--Dos-
toevsky's Idiot--1958, 1975. Modern Fiction Studies,
1975, 21:387-404.
10,903. Lethcoe, James. Self-deception in Dostoevskij's Notes from
Underground. Slavic & East European J, 1966, 10:9-21.
10,904. _____. The structure of Robbe-Grillet's labyrinth.
French Rev, 1965, 38:497-507.
10,905. Letwin, Shirley R. Trollope on generations without gaps.
Daedalus, 1978, 107:53-70.
10,906. Leverenz, David. The Language of Puritan Feeling. An
Exploration in Literature, Psychology, and Social History. New Brunswick, NJ: Rutgers Univ. Press, 1979.
10,907. _____. Moby-Dick. In Crews, F. C. (ed), Psychoanalysis and Literary Process. Cambridge, Mass: Winthrop,
1970, 66-117.
10,908. Leverenz, Langmuir D. A Psychoanalysis of American
Literature. DAI, 1970, 31:70-13, 100.
10,909. Levi, Joseph. Hawthorne's The Scarlet Letter: a psychoanalytic interpretation. Amer Imago, 1953, 10:291-306.
10,910. Levi, P. Margot. K., an exploration of the names of Kafka's central characters. Names, 1966, 14:1-10.
10,911. Levin, Gerald. Character and fantasy in Richardson's
Sir Charles Grandison. Connecticut Rev, 1973, 7:93-99.
10,912. _____. Lovelace's dream. Lit & Psychol, 1970, 20:
121-127.
10,913. _____. Richardson, the Novelist: The Psychological
Patterns. NY: Humanities Press, 1978; Review:
Western Humanities Rev, 1979, 33:155-158; Lit & Psychol, 1979, 29:60-63.
10,914. _____. Richardson's Pamela: 'conflicting trends.'
Amer Imago, 1971, 28:319-329.
10,915. _____. The sadic heroes of C. P. Snow. Twentieth
Century Lit, 1980, 26:27-37.
10,916. _____. The symbolism of Lawrence's 'The Fox.' College Language Assn J, 1967, 11:135-141.
10,917. Levin, Harry. Apogee and aftermath of the novel. Daedalus, 1963, 92:206-219.
10,918. _____. James Joyce: A Critical Introduction. London:
Faber & Faber, 1960; Norwalk, Conn: New Directions,
1941.
10,919. _____. Life without father. In Refractions; Essays in
Comparative Literature. NY: Oxford Univ. Press,
1966, 308-320.
10,920. _____. Symbolism and Fiction. Charlottesville: Univ.
Virginia Press, 1956.
10,921. _____. Symbolism and fiction. In Contexts of Criticism. Cambridge: Harvard Univ. Press, 1957, 197.
10,922. Levin, L. Masque et identité dans Le Paysan parvenu.
Studies on Voltaire & the 18th Century, 1971, 79:177-
192.

10,923. Levine, George. The Boundaries of Fiction: Carlyle, Macauley, Newman. Princeton: Princeton Univ. Press, 1968.

10,924. _____, & Knoepflmacher, U. C. (eds). The Endurance of 'Frankenstein': Essays on Mary Shelley's Novel. Berkeley: Univ. California Press, 1979.

10,925. Levine, M. Herschel. Oedipal views of the Jew in American literature. J Psychol & Judaism, 1978, 3:102-108.

10,926. Levine, Richard A. The downward journey of purgation: notes on an imagistic leitmotif in The Narrative of Arthur Gordon Pym. Poe Newsletter, 1969, 2:29-31.

10,927. Levine, Robert T. The familiar friend: a Freudian approach to Kafka's 'The Judgment' ('Das Urteil'). Lit & Psychol, 1977, 27:164-173.

10,928. _____. My ultraviolet darling: the loss of Lolita's childhood. Modern Fiction Studies, 1979, 25:471-479.

10,929. Levine, S.J. La mal del incesto en 100 años de soledad. Revista Iberoamericana, 1971, 76-77:711-724.

10,930. LeVot, André. New modes of story-telling: dismantling contemporary fiction. In Johnson, I.D., & Johnson, C. (eds), Les Américanistes: New French Criticism on Modern American Fiction. Port Washington, NY: Kennikat, 1978, 110-129.

10,931. Levowitz-Treu, Micheline. L'Amour et la mort chez Stendhal, Métamorphoses d'un apprentissage affectif. Aran: Grand Chêne, 1978.

10,932. Levy, Karen D. Alain Fournier and the surrealist quest for unity. Romance Notes, 1978, 18:301-310.

10,933. Levy, Laurie. Outside the Bell Jar. Ohio Rev, 1973, 14:67-73.

10,934. Levy, Leo B. The Blithedale Romance: Hawthorne's voyage through chaos. Studies in Romanticism, 1968, 8:1-15.

10,935. _____. Fanshawe: Hawthorne's world of images. Studies in the Novel, 1970, 2:440-448.

10,936. _____. Henry James's confidence and the development of the idea of the unconscious. Amer Lit, 1956, 28: 347-358.

10,937. _____. The landscape modes of The Scarlet Letter. Nineteenth Century Fiction, 1969, 23:377-392.

10,938. _____. The notebook source and the 18th century context of Hawthorne's theory of romance. Nathaniel Hawthorne J, 1973, 3:120-129.

10,939. _____. Society and conscience in Huckleberry Finn. Nineteenth Century Fiction, 1964, 18:383-391.

10,940. Lévy, Maurice. Edgar Poe et la tradition 'gothique.' Caliban, 1968, 5(1):35-51.

10,941. _____. Poe and the Gothic tradition. Emerson Society Q, 1972, 66:19-29.

10,942. _____. Pym, conte fantastique? Etudes Anglaises, 1974, 27:38-44.

10,943. Levy, S.N. Proust's realistic treatment of illness. French Rev, 1942, 15:233-238, 324-329, 421-424.

10,944. Lewicki, Zbigniew. [Time in the Stream-of-Consciousness Novel: James Joyce's Ulysses and William Faulkner's The Sound and the Fury and As I Lay Dying.] Warsaw: Panstwowe Wydawnictwo Naukowe, 1975.

10,945. Lewis, Clifford L. John Steinbeck: Architect of the Unconscious. DAI, 1973, 34:781A.

10,946. Lewis, Edward William. Frame and Axis: The Control of Psychological and Formal Levels of Meaning in Mrs. Dalloway, To the Lighthouse, and The Waves. DAI, 1977, 37:7763A.

10,947. Lewis, Florence C. Isak Dinesen and feminist criticism. North Amer Rev, 1979, 264:62-72.

10,948. Lewis, Richard O. A literary-psychoanalytic interpretation of Robert Hayden's 'Market.' Negro Amer Lit Forum, 1975, 9:21-24.

10,949. Lewis, Richard W. B. Alberto Moravia: Eros and existence; excerpt from 'The picaresque saint.' In Pacifici, S. (ed), From Verismo to Experimentalism; Essays on the Modern Italian Novel. Bloomington: Indiana Univ. Press, 1970, 135-160.

10,950. Lewis, Robert W., Jr. Hemingway on Love. Austin: Univ. Texas Press, 1965.

10,951. Lewis, Stuart A. Rootlessness and alienation in the novels of Bruce Jay Friedman. College Language Assn J, 1975, 18:422-433.

10,952. Lewis, Wyndham. An analysis of the mind of James Joyce. In Time and Western Man. NY: Harcourt, Brace, 1928.

10,953. Libby, Marion V. Sex and the new woman in The Golden Notebook. Iowa Rev, 1974, 5:106-120.

10,954. Librachowa, Maria. Miedzywojenna literatura powieściowa jako źródlo materialu naukowego dla psychologa. Kwartalnik Psychologiczny, 1947, 13:24-47.

10,955. Lichtblau, Myron I. Mutism as a recurring theme in the fiction of Eduardo Mallea. Amer Hispanist, 1975, 1(3): 13-15.

10,956. Lichtenberg, Philip, & Norton, Dolores G. Honesty, trust, equality in the treatment of schizophrenia: an analysis of I Never Promised You a Rose Garden. Pennsylvania Psychiat Q, 1970, 10:33-40.

10,957. Lidoff, Joan I. The female ego: Christina Stead's heroines. New Boston Rev, 1977, 2(3):19-20.

10,958. Lieberman, H. The mysterious characters of Sherlock Holmes and Dr. Watson. Baker Street J, 1970, 20:223-230.

10,959. Lieberman, Marcia R. Sexism and the double standard in literature. In Cornillon, S.K. (ed), Images of Women in Fiction: Feminist Perspectives. Bowling Green, Ohio: Bowling Green Univ. Popular Press, 1972, 326-338.

10,960. Light, James F. Violence, dreams, and Dostoevsky: the art of Nathanael West. College English, 1958, 19:208-213.

10,961. Light, Martin. Lewis' finicky girls and faithful workers. Univ. Rev, 1963, 30:151-159.

10,962. Ligocki, Llewellyn. Poe and psychoanalytic criticism. Poe Studies, 1971, 4(2):54-55.

10,963. Lilienfeld, Jane. 'The Deceptiveness of Beauty': mother love and mother hate in To the Lighthouse. Twentieth Century Lit, 1977, 23:345-376.

10,964. _____. Reentering paradise: Cather, Colette, Woolf and their mothers. In Davidson, C. N., & Broner, E. M. (eds), The Lost Tradition. NY: Ungar, 1980, 160-175.

10,965. Lillyman, William J. The interior monologue in James Joyce and Otto Ludwig. Comparative Lit, 1971, 23:45-54.

10,966. Lincecum, Jerry B. Meredith and the Stream-of-Consciousness Novel: Two Decades of Experimentation, 1859-1879. DA, 1968, 28:4180A.

10,967. _____. A Victorian precursor of the stream-of-consciousness novel: George Meredith. South-Central Bulletin, 1971, 31:197-200.

10,968. Lind, Ilse Dusoir. Faulkner's women. In Harrington, E., & Abadie, A. J. (eds), The Maker and the Myth: Faulkner and Yoknapatawpha, 1977. Jackson: Univ. Press of Mississippi, 1978, 89-104.

10,969. Lind, Sidney E. Psychology and the Supernatural in the Writing of Henry James. Doctoral dissertation, New York Univ., 1947.

10,970. _____. 'The Turn of the Screw': the torment of critics. Centennial Rev, 1970, 14:225-240.

10,971. Lindenmeyr, A. Raskolnikov's city and the Napoleonic plan. Slavic Rev, 1976, 35:37-47.

10,972. Linder, Lyle Dean. Children in the Literary Work of Stephen Crane. DAI, 1975, 35:5413A-14A.

10,973. Linderoth, Leon Walter. The Female Characters of Ernest Hemingway. DA, 1966, 27:1060A.

10,974. Lindop, G. C. G. A Study of the Influence of Contemporary Psychological Theory on the Fiction of Thomas Hardy and George Gissing and on the Early Novels of George Moore. B. Litt. thesis, Oxford Univ., 1975.

10,975. Lindstrom, Naomi E. Madness in Arlt's fiction. Chasqui, 1975, 4(3):18-22.

10,976. Lindvåg, Anita. Psykologin i Gunnel Lindes 'Den vita stenen.' Svensklärarföreningens Årsskrift, 1973, 73:107-121.

10,977. Lins, I. [Concept of insanity according to Erasmus, Cervantes, and Augusto Comte.] Revista Paulista de Medicina, 1974, 83:182-195.

10,978. Lippe, George B. von der. The figure of E. T. A. Hoffmann as doppelgänger to Poe's Roderick Usher. MLN, 1977, 92:525-534.

10,979. Lipkin, K. M., & Daniel, R. S. The role of seduction in interpersonal relationships. MAHS, 1969, 3(6):79, 82-83, 86, 88.

10,980.   Lippit, N. M.   Tanizaki and Poe: the grotesque and the
          quest for supernal beauty.   Comparative Lit, 1977, 29:
          221-240.
10,981.   Lipsky, M.   Une Famille de Dégénérés Heredo-Alcooliques
          dans l'Oeuvre de Dostoievski Les Frères Karamazov.
          Thèse, Lyon, 1927.
10,982.   Lipton, Virginia A.   A Woman in Today's World: A Study
          of Five French Women Novelists.   DAI, 1973, 33:6918A-
          19A.
10,983.   Lisca, Peter.   Nick Carraway and the imagery of disorder.
          Twentieth Century Lit, 1967, 13:18-27.
10,984.   Lish, Terrence G.   Melville's Redburn: a study in dual-
          ism.   English Language Notes, 1967, 5:113-120.
10,985.   Lisi, L. de.   Analisi di un personaggio di Stendhal.   La
          Serpe, Revisti litterarie dell'Assazione dei medicale
          d'Italia, 1958, 8.
10,986.   Little, Sherry B.   The Relationship of the Woman Figure
          and Views of Reality in Three Works by James Joyce.
          DAI, 1971, 32:1518A-19A.
10,987.   Litz, Arthur Walton.   'A development of self':   character
          and personality in Jane Austen's fiction.   In McMaster,
          J. (ed), Jane Austen's Achievement.   NY: Barnes &
          Noble, 1976, 64-78.
10,988.   _____.   James Joyce.   NY: Twayne, 1966.
10,989.   Livingston, Leon.   Self-creation and alienation in the nov-
          els of Azorin.   J Spanish Studies: Twentieth Century,
          1973, 1:5-43.
10,990.   Llech-Walter, Colette.   Héros existenialistes dans l'oeuvre
          littéraire de J.-P. Sartre.   Perignan: Centre culturel
          esperantiste, 1960.
10,991.   Lobet, Marcel.   J.-K. Huysmans, ou le témoin écorché.
          Lyons: Vitte, 1960.
10,992.   Locklin, Gerald.   The Dream Life of Balso Snell: journey
          into the microcosm.   In Madden, D. (ed), Nathanael
          West: The Cheaters and the Cheated.   De Land, Fla:
          Everett/Edwards, 1973, 23-56.
10,993.   Lodge, David.   Family romances.   Times Lit Supplement,
          13 June 1975, 642.
10,994.   Loeblowitz-Lennard, Henry.   Some leitmotifs in Franz
          Kafka's works psychoanalytically explored.   Univ. Kan-
          sas City Rev, 1964, 13:115-118.
10,995.   Loewen, H.   Human involvement in Turgenev's and Kafka's
          country doctors.   Germano-Slavica, 1974, 3:47-54.
10,996.   Logan, John Frederick.   Psychological motifs in Melville's
          Pierre.   Minnesota Rev, 1967, 7:325-330.
10,997.   Lohmuller, Gertrude.   Die Frau im Werk vom Virginia
          Woolf.   Leipzig: Universitätsverlag von Robert Noske,
          1937.
10,998.   Lombroso, Cesare.   Emile Zola in the light of researches
          by Dr. Toulouse and recent theories of genius.   Medical
          Weekly, 1897, 5:25-29; Semana Medicina, 1897, 17:1-15.
10,999.   Long, Robert Emmet.   A note on color symbolism in The
          Great Gatsby.   Fitzgerald Newsletter, 1962, No. 17, 1-
          3.

11,000. Longen, Eugene M. Dickey's Deliverance: sex and the
         great outdoors. Southern Lit J, 1977, 9(2):137-149.
11,001. Longerbeam, Larry S. Seduction as Symbolic Action: A
         Study of the Seduction Motif in Six Victorian Novels.
         DAI, 1975, 36:2222A.
11,002. Lonie, Charles Anthony. Accumulations of Silence: Sur-
         vival Psychology in Vonnegut, Twain, and Hemingway.
         Doctoral dissertation, Univ. Minnesota, 1974.
11,003. Lopes, José Lemes. A Psiquiatria de Machado de Assis.
         Rio de Janeiro: Agir/MEC, 1974.
11,004. López Méndez, H. La medicina en el Quijote. Actas
         Luso Español Neurologia y Psiquiatria, 1971, 30:35-44.
11,005. López de Villegas, Consuelo. Matriarchs and man-eaters:
         Naipaul's fictional women. Revista/Rev Interamericana,
         1977-78, 7:605-614.
11,006. Lorch, Thomas M. The inverted structure of Balso Snell.
         Studies in Short Fiction, 1966, 4:33-41.
11,007. Lordi, R. J. Three emissaries of evil: their psychologi-
         cal relationship in Conrad's Victory. College English,
         1961, 23:136-140.
11,008. Lorenzo Rivero, L. El suicidio: una obsesión de Una-
         muno. Cuadernos Americanos, 1973, 190:227-239.
11,009. Lösel, F. Psychology, religion and myth in Arnim's Der
         tolle Invalide auf dem Fort Ratonneau. New German
         Studies, 1977, 5:75-90.
11,010. Loth, David G. The Erotic in Literature. NY: Messner,
         1961; NY: Macfadden-Bartell, 1962, 1969.
11,011. Lott, Robert E. Language and Psychology in 'Pepita Jim-
         énez. ' Urbana: Univ. Illinois Press, 1970.
11,012. Loughman, Celeste. Novels of senescence: a new na-
         turalism. Gerontologist, 1977, 17:79-84.
11,013. Loughrey, Thomas Francis. Values and Love in the Fic-
         tion of William Faulkner. DA, 1963, 23:2915.
11,014. Loughy, Robert E. William Morris' News from Nowhere:
         the novel as psychology of art. English Lit in Transi-
         tion (1800-1920), 1970, 13:1-8.
11,015. Loureiro, C. M. Graciliano Ramos e o tempo psiquico.
         Minas Gerais, Suplemento Literário, 1 May 1976.
11,016. Louria, Y. 'Dedoublement' in Dostoevsky and Camus.
         Modern Language Rev, 1961, 56:82-83.
11,017. Lourie, O. La Psychologie des romanciers Russes due
         XIX siècle. Paris: Alcan, 1905.
11,018. Love, Jean O. Orlando and its genesis: venturing and
         experimenting in art, love, and sex. In Freedman, R.
         (ed), Virginia Woolf; Revaluation and Continuity. Ber-
         keley: Univ. California Press, 1979, 188-218.
11,019. _____. Worlds in Consciousness: Mythopoetic Thought
         in the Novels of Virginia Woolf. Berkeley: Univ. Cali-
         fornia Press, 1970.
11,020. Lovett, Robert Morss. The sex life of the unmarried
         adult in English literature. In Wile, I. S. (ed), The
         Sex Life of the Unmarried Adult. NY: Garden City
         Publ, 1940, 253-277.

11,021. Lowenkron, David Henry. Jake Barnes: a student of William James in The Sun Also Rises. Texas Q, 1976, 19(1):147-156.

11,022. Lower, Richard B. On Raskolnikov's dreams in Dostoevsky's Crime and Punishment. JAPA, 1969, 17:728-742.

11,023. Lowrie, J. O. The structural significance of sensual imagery in Paul et Virginie. Romance Notes, 1971, 12: 351-356.

11,024. Lowry, E. D. Chaos and cosmos in In Our Time. Lit & Psychol, 1976, 26:108-117.

11,025. Lowtzky, Fanny. L'Angoisse de la mort et l'ídee du bien chez L. N. Tolstoi. Rev Française de Psychanalyse, 1959, 23:495-525.

11,026. Lubbock, Percy. The Craft of Fiction. NY: Cape & Smith, 1929; London: Cape, 1929.

11,027. Lucas, Nancy B. Women and Love Relationships in the Changing Fictional World of Anthony Trollope. DAI, 1974, 34:7712A.

11,028. Lucas, Peter J. Gawain's anti-feminism. Notes & Queries, 1968, 15:324-325.

11,029. Lucas, William J. The Literature of Change; Studies in the Nineteenth-Century Provincial Novel. NY: Barnes & Noble, 1977.

11,030. Luce, Stanford. Increment and excrement: Céline and the language of hate. Maledicta, 1977, 1(1):43-48.

11,031. Luchting, Wolfgang A. Literature as negative participation in life: Vargas Llosa's Los cachorros/Pichula Cuéllar. World Lit Today, 1978, 52:53-63.

11,032. _____. Sebastián Salazar Bondy's last novel. J Spanish Studies: Twentieth Century, 1973, 1:45-63.

11,033. Luck, James W. Identity and Image Development Through Black Literature. DAI, 1972, 32(12-A), 6763.

11,034. Lucow, Ben. Mature identity in Sherwood Anderson's 'The Sad Horn-Blowers.' Studies in Short Fiction, 1965, 2: 291-293.

11,035. Lukenbill, W. Bernard. Fathers in adolescent novels: some implications for sex-role reinterpretations. Library J, 1974, 99:536-540.

11,036. Lukens, Rebecca J. Inevitable ambivalence: mother and daughter in Lessing's Martha Quest. Doris Lessing Newsletter, 1978, 2:13-14.

11,037. Lundström, B. Skarpsyn och synskärpa. N agra medicinska aspekter p a James Joyce. Nordisk Medicinhistorisk Arsbok, 1973, 201-209.

11,038. Lutton, W. R. The Father's Role in Proust's A la Recherche du temps perdu. DA, 1968, 28:A4638-9.

11,039. Lutz, Hartmut. William Goldings Prosawerk: Im Lichte der Analytischen Psychologie Carl Gustav Jungs und der Psychoanalyse Sigmund Freuds. Frankfurt: Athenaion, 1975.

11,040. Lux, Josef A. Grillparzers Liebesroman. Berlin: Bong, 1911.

11,041. Lyday, L. F. Maternidad in Sábato's El túnel. Romance Notes, 1968, 10:20-26.

11, 042. Lydenberg, J. The governess turns the screw. In Willen,
          G. (ed), A Casebook on Henry James's The Turn of the
          Screw. NY: Crowell, 1960, 289-300.
11, 043. _____. Nature myth in Faulkner's 'The Bear.' Amer
          Lit, 1952, 24: 62-72.
11, 044. Lyndenberg, Robin. Against the law of gravity: female
          adolescence in Isak Dinesen's Seven Gothic Tales. Mod-
          ern Fiction Studies, 1978-79, 24: 521-532.
11, 045. Lynes, Carlos, Jr. Proust and Albertine: on the limits
          of autobiography and of psychological truth in the novel.
          JAAC, 1952, 10: 328-338.
11, 046. Lynn, Kenneth Schuyler. Adulthood in American literature.
          In Erikson, E. H. (ed), Adulthood. NY: Norton, 1978,
          237-247.
11, 047. Lyon, George Ella Hoskins. The Dilemma of the Body in
          Virginia Woolf and E. M. Forster. DAI, 1978, 39:
          873A-74A.
11, 048. Lytle, Andrew. Impressionism, the ego, and the first
          person. Daedalus, 1963, 92: 281-296.
11, 049. _____. The working novelist and the mythmaking proc-
          ess. Daedalus, 1959, 88: 326-338.
11, 050. Lytle, David J. Giovanni! My poor Giovanni! Studies in
          Short Fiction, 1972, 9: 147-156.
11, 051. _____. The case against Carwin. Nineteenth Century
          Fiction, 1971, 26: 257-269.

11, 052. McAleer, Edward C. Frank O'Connor's Oedipus trilogy.
          Hunter College Studies, 1965, No. 2, 33-40.
11, 053. McAlexander, Hubert H., Jr. History as Perception, His-
          tory as Obsession, Faulkner's Development of a Theme.
          DAI, 1974, 34: 6596A-97A.
11, 054. McAllister, Harold S. Apology for Bad Dreams: A Study
          of Characterization and the Use of Fantasy in Clarissa,
          Justine, and The Monk. DAI, 1972, 32: 6383A.
11, 055. McBride, Margaret. At four she said. James Joyce Q,
          1979, 17: 21-39.
11, 056. _____. Watchwords in Ulysses: the stylistics of sup-
          pression. J English Germanic Philology, 1978, 77: 356-
          366.
11, 057. McBridge, Charles A. Alienation from self in the short
          fiction of Leopoldo Alas' 'Clarin.' In Pincus Sigele,
          R., & Sobejano, G. (eds), Homenaje a Casalduero:
          Critica y poesia. Madrid: Gredos, 1972, 379-387.
11, 058. McCaffery, Larry. The art of metafiction: William
          Gass' Willie Master's Lonesome Wife. Critique, 1976,
          18: 21-35.
11, 059. McCall, Dan. The meaning in darkness: a response to a
          psychoanalytic study of Conrad. College English, 1968,
          29: 620-627.
11, 060. McCarroll, David L. Stephen's dream--and Bloom's.
          James Joyce Q, 1968, 6: 174-176.
11, 061. McCarthy, Harold T. Henry James: The Creative Proc-
          ess. NY: Yoseloff, 1958.

11,062. McCauley, Janie Caves. Kipling on women: a new source
         for Shaw. Shaw Rev, 1974, 17:40-44.
11,063. McCay, Mary Ann D. Women in the Novels of Charles
         Brockden Brown: A Study. DAI, 1974, 35:3692A.
11,064. McClain, W.H. E.T.A. Hoffmann as psychological realist:
         a study of Meister Floh. Monatshefte, 1955, 47:65-80.
11,065. McClintock, James I. Jack London's use of Carl Jung's
         Psychology of the Unconscious. Amer Lit, 1970, 42:
         336-347.
11,066. McCloskey, John C. What Maisie knows: a study of child-
         hood and adolescence. Amer Lit, 1965, 36:485-513.
11,067. McClure, Charlotte S. Gertrude Atherton's California
         woman: from love story to psychological drama. In
         Crow, C.L. (ed), Essays on California Writers. Bowl-
         ing Green, Ohio: Bowling Green Univ. Press, 1978,
         1-9.
11,068. McClure, John Alexander. Rudyard Kipling and Joseph
         Conrad: The Social Psychology of Imperialism. DAI,
         1976, 36:8048A.
11,069. McCole, Camille John. Freudism and the stream-of-con-
         sciousness. In Lucifer at Large. NY: Longmans,
         1937, 85-121.
11,070. _____. Sherwood Anderson, congenital Freudian.
         Catholic World, 1929, 130:129-133.
11,071. McConnell, Frank D. William Burroughs and the literature
         of addiction. In Plimpton, G., & Ardery, P. (eds),
         The American Literary Anthology, 2. NY: Random
         House, 1969, 367-381; Massachusetts Rev, 1967, 8:665-680.
11,072. McCormick, E. Allen. Poema Pictura Loquens: literary
         pictorialism and the psychology of landscape. Compara-
         tive Lit Studies, 1976, 13:196-213.
11,073. McCormick, Jane L. Psychic phenomena in literature.
         Psychic, 1972, 3(4):40-44.
11,074. McCormick, M. The first representation of the gamma al-
         coholic in the English novel. Quart J Studies Alcohol,
         1969, 30:957-980.
11,075. McCowan, P.K. The subconscious in story writing. J
         Mental Science, 1943, 89:59-63.
11,076. McCoy, Kathleen. The femininity of Moll Flanders. In
         Runte, R. (ed), Studies in Eighteenth-Century Culture 7.
         Madison: Univ. Wisconsin Press, 1978, 413-422.
11,077. McCurdy, Harold G. Literature and personality: analysis
         of the novels of D.H. Lawrence. Character & Personal-
         ity, 1940, 8:181-203.
11,078. _____. A mathematical aspect of fictional literature
         pertinent to McDougall's theory of a hierarchy of senti-
         ments. J Personality, 1948, 17:75-82.
11,079. _____. A study of the novels of Charlotte and Emily
         Brontë as an expression of their personalities. J Per-
         sonality, 1947, 16:109-152.
11,080. McCurdy, John T. Die Allmacht der Gedanken und die
         Mutterleibsphantasie in den Mythen von Hephästos und
         einen Roman von Bulwer Lytton. Imago, 1914, 3:382-
         400.

11,081. McCurry, Niki Alpert. Concepts of Childrearing and Schooling in the March Novels of Louisa May Alcott. DAI, 1977, 37:4356A.

11,082. McDaniel, Thomas R. Weber and Kafka on bureaucracy: a question of perspective. South Atlantic Q, 1979, 78: 361-375.

11,083. McDermott, John J. Symbolism and psychological realism in The Red Badge of Courage. Nineteenth Century Fiction, 1968, 23:324-331.

11,084. McDonald, Carl Brandt. Narratives of Polarities in Varieties of Psychic Experience: Studies in British and American Romanticism. DAI, 1975, 35:4535A.

11,085. MacDonald, Robert H. 'The two principles': a theory of the sexual and psychological symbolism of D. H. Lawrence's later fiction. D. H. Lawrence Rev, 1978, 11: 132-155.

11,086. Macdonald, Ross. On Crime Writing. Santa Barbara: Capra, 1973.

11,087A. _____. The writer as detective hero. In On Crime Writing. Santa Barbara: Capra, 1973, 9-24; In Lid, R. W. (ed), Essays: Classic and Contemporary. Philadelphia: Lippincott, 1967, 307-315; In Nevins, F. M. , Jr. (ed), The Mystery Writer's Art. Bowling Green, Ohio: Bowling Green Univ. Press, 1970, 295-305.

11,087. _____. A preface to The Galton Case. In On Crime Writing. Santa Barbara: Capra, 1973, 25-45; In McCormack, T. (ed), Afterwords: Novelists on Their Novels. NY: Harper & Row, 1969, 147-159.

11,088. _____. Introduction to Great Stories of Suspense. NY: Knopf, 1974, ix-xvii.

11,089- Macdonald, Susan Peck. Jane Austen and the tradition of
90. the absent mother. In Davidson, C. N. , & Broner, E. M. (eds), The Lost Tradition. NY: Ungar, 1980, 58-69.

11,091. McDonough, John J. One Day in the Life of Ivan Denisovich: a study of the structural requisites of organization. Human Relations, 1975, 28:295-328.

11,092. McDowell, Alfred B. Identity and the Past: Major Themes in the Fiction of Elizabeth Bowen. DAI, 1972, 32: 4621A.

11,093. McDowell, Frederick P. W. Psychology and theme in Brother to Dragons. PMLA, 1955, 70:565-586.

11,094. _____. Theme and artistry in Glasgow's The Sheltered Life. Texas Studies Lit Language, 1960, 1:502-516.

11,095. McDowell, M. B. Edith Wharton's ghost stories. Criticism, 1970, 12:133-152.

11,096. McFate, P. , & Golden, B. The Good Soldier: a tragedy of self-deception. Modern Fiction Studies, 1963, 9:50-60.

11,097. McGlathery, James M. The suicide motif in E. T. A. Hoffmann's 'Der Goldne Topf. ' Monatshefte, 1966, 58:115-123.

11, 098. McGowan, Marcia Phillips. Patterns of Female Experi-
          ence in Eudora Welty's Fiction. DAI, 1977, 38:788A.
11, 099. McGraw, Patricia Marie. Ideas about Children in Eight-
          eenth-Century British Fiction. DAI, 1976, 36:7441A.
11, 100. McGuire, John F. Thomas Hardy's Use of Fertility Arche-
          types in Four Novels of Character and Environment.
          DAI, 1972, 53:6936A.
11, 101. McIntyre, Allan J. Psychology and symbol: correspond-
          ences between Heart of Darkness and Death in Venice.
          Hartford Studies in Lit, 1975, 7:216-235.
11, 102. McIntyre, Clara F. Is Virginia Woolf a feminist? Per-
          sonalist, 1960, 41:176-184.
11, 103. Mack, Ruth J. A dream from an eleventh-century Japan-
          ese novel. Int J Psycho-Anal, 1927, 8:402-403.
11, 104. McKenna, Isobel. Women in Canadian literature. Canadi-
          an Lit, 1974, 62:69-78.
11, 105. Mackenzie, Manfred. A theory of Henry James's psychol-
          ogy. Yale Rev, 1974, 63:347-371.
11, 106. _____. Communities of Honor and Love in Henry
          James. Cambridge: Harvard Univ. Press, 1976.
11, 107. McKiernan, John T. The Psychology of Nathaniel Haw-
          thorne. DA, 1957, 17:3019.
11, 108. McKilligan, Kathleen M. Edouard Dujardin: 'Les Lauriers
          sont coupés' and the Interior Monologue. Hull, England:
          Univ. Hull Press, 1977.
11, 109. McKnight, Jeanne. Unlocking the Word-Hoard: Madness
          and Creativity in the Work of James Joyce. DAI, 1975,
          35:6723A-24A.
11, 110. _____. Unlocking the word-hoard: madness, identity
          and creativity in James Joyce. James Joyce Q, 1977,
          14:420-433.
11, 111. McLaughlin, Frank. The place of fiction in the develop-
          ment of values. Media and Methods, 1980, 16:18-21.
11, 112. McLean, Robert C. The deaths in Ambrose Bierce's
          'Halpin Frayser.' Papers on Language & Lit, 1974,
          10:394-402.
11, 113. _____. 'Love by the Doctor's Direction': disease and
          death in 'The Wings of the Dove.' Papers on Language
          & Lit, 1972, 8 suppl:128-148.
11, 114. McLean, Sammy. Doubling and sexual identity in stories
          by Franz Kafka. Hartford Studies in Lit, 1980, 12:1-
          17.
11, 115. McLendon, W. L. Giradoux and the split personality.
          PMLA, 1958, 73:580-581.
11, 116. MacLure, Millar. Allegories of innocence. Dalhousie
          Rev, 1960, 40:145-156.
11, 117. McMahan, Elizabeth E. The big nurse as ratchet sexism
          in Kesey's Cuckoo's Nest. CEA Critic, 1975, 37(4):
          25-27.
11, 118. _____. 'The Chrysanthemums': study of a woman's
          sexuality. Modern Fiction Studies, 1968, 14:453-458.
11, 119. _____. Sexual desire and illusion in The Bostonians.
          Modern Fiction Studies, 1979, 25:241-251.

11, 120.   McMahon, J. H.   The Imagination of Jean Genet.   New
           Haven: Yale Univ. Press, 1964.
11, 121.   McMaster, Juliet.   The equation of love and money in
           Moll Flanders.   Studies in the Novel, 1970, 2:131-144.
11, 122.   _____.   The portrait of Isabel Archer.   Amer Lit, 1973,
           45:50-66.
11, 123.   McMurray, George R.   Cambio de piel: an existential
           novel of protest.   Hispania, 1969, 52:150-154.
11, 124.   McNab, James P.   The mother in Francois Mauriac's
           Génitrix.   Hartford Studies in Lit, 1970, 2:207-213.
11, 125.   McNally, John J.   Boats and automobiles in The Great
           Gatsby: symbols of drift and death.   Hudson Rev, 1971,
           5:11-17.
11, 126.   McNamara, E.   Death in Venice: the disguised self.   Col-
           lege English, 1962, 24:233-234.
11, 127.   McNelly, Willis E.   Archetypal patterns in science fiction.
           CEA Critic, 1973, 35(4):15-19.
11, 128.   McNicholas, Mary Verity.   Fitzgerald's women in Tender
           Is the Night.   College Lit, 1977, 4:40-70.
11, 129.   MacPike, Loralee.   Environment as psychopathological
           symbolism in 'The Yellow Wallpaper.'   Amer Lit Real-
           ism, 1870-1910, 1975, 8:286-288.
11, 130.   McVicker, Cecil D.   Balzac and Otway.   Romance Notes,
           1973, 15:248-254.
11, 131.   _____.   Narcotics and excitants in the Comédie hu-
           maine.   Romance Notes, 1969, 11:291-301.
11, 132.   McWilliams, James R.   The failure of a repression.
           Thomas Mann's Tod in Venedig.   German Life & Let-
           ters, 1967, 20:233-241.
11, 133.   _____.   Thomas Mann's Die Betrogne--a study in am-
           bivalence.   College Language Assn J, 1966, 10:56-63.
11, 134.   Madariaga, Salvador de.   Don Quixote: An Introductory
           Essay in Psychology.   London: Oxford Univ. Press,
           1961.
11, 135.   Madden, David.   The paradox of the need for privacy and
           the need for understanding in Carson McCullers' The
           Heart Is a Lonely Hunter.   Lit & Psychol, 1967, 17:
           128-140.
11, 136.   _____ (ed).   Tough Guy Writers of the Thirties.   Car-
           bondale: Southern Illinois Univ. Press, 1968, 1979.
11, 137.   Madden, William A.   Wuthering Heights: the binding of
           passion.   Nineteenth-Century Fiction, 1972, 27:127-154.
11, 138.   Madeleine, Sister M.   Mauriac and Dostoevsky: psycho-
           logists of the unconscious.   Renascence, 1952, 1:7-
           14.
11, 139.   Magalaner, Marvin.   Traces of her 'self' in Katherine
           Mansfield's 'Bliss.'   Modern Fiction Studies, 1978, 24:
           413-422.
11, 140.   Maglin, Nan Bauer.   Early feminist fiction: the dilemma
           of personal life.   Prospects: Annual Amer Cultural
           Studies, 1976, 2:167-191.
11, 141.   _____.   Women in three Sinclair Lewis novels.   Massa-
           chusetts Rev, 1973, 14:783-801.

11,142. Magliola, Robert R. The magic square: polar unity in Thomas Mann's Doctor Faustus. Hartford Studies in Lit, 1974, 6:55-71.

11,143. Magnan, Jean-Marie. Incest et mélange des sangs dans l'oeuvre de William Faulkner. Sud, 1975, Nos. 14-15.

11,144. Magny, Claude-Edmonde. Les Romans: existentialisme et littérature. Poésie 46, 1946, 29:58-67.

11,145. Magretta, Joan Barbara Gorin. The Iconography of Madness: A Study in Melville and Dostoevsky. DAI, 1976, 37:1533A.

11,146. _____. Radical disunities: models of mind and madness in Pierre and The Idiot. Studies in the Novel, 1978, 10:234-250.

11,147. Maguire, Robert A. (ed). Gogol from the Twentieth Century: Eleven Essays. Princeton: Princeton Univ. Press, 1975.

11,148. Mahlendorf, Ursula R. Aesthetics, psychology and politics in Thomas Mann's Doctor Faustus. Mosaic, 1977, 11(4):1-18.

11,149. _____. Arthur Schnitzler's The Last Letter of a Litterateur: the artist as destroyer. Amer Imago, 1977, 34:238-276.

11,150. _____. E. T. A. Hoffman's The Sandman: the fictional psycho-biography of a romantic poet. Amer Imago, 1975, 32:217-239.

11,151. _____. Franz Grillparzer's The Poor Fiddler. Amer Imago, 1979, 36:118-146.

11,152. _____. Mörike's Mozart on the Way to Prague: stages and outcomes of creative experience. Amer Imago, 1976, 33:304-327.

11,153. _____. Sculptures and mother figures in Günter Grass' Tin Drum. Psychoanal Rev, 1979, 66:227-243.

11,154. Mahony, Patrick. A Hunger Artist: content and form. Amer Imago, 1978, 35:357-374.

11,155. Maier, Emanuel. The Psychology of C. G. Jung in the Works of Hermann Hesse. Doctoral dissertation, Univ. North Carolina, 1955.

11,156. Maillard, Denyse. L'Enfant américain dans le roman du middlewest. Doctoral dissertation, Univ. Paris, 1935.

11,157. Mainzer, Hubert. Thomas Manns Doktor Faustus--ein Nietzsche-Roman? Wirkendes Wort, 1971, 21:24-38.

11,158. Maldonado, Armando. Manuel Puig: The Aesthetics of Cinematic and Psychological Fiction. DAI, 1977, 38:2156A-57A.

11,159. Male, Roy R. The dual aspects of evil in 'Rappaccini's Daughter.' PMLA, 1954.

11,160. _____. Hawthorne's fancy, or the medium of The Blithedale Romance. Nathaniel Hawthorne J, 1972, 2:67-73.

11,161. _____. Review: F. C. Crews' The Sins of the Fathers. Nineteenth Century Fiction, 1966, 21:193-196.

11,162. Malek, James S. Persona, shadow, and society: a reading of Forster's 'The Other Boat.' Studies in Short Fiction, 1977, 14:21-27.

11,163.   Malin, Irving.   The authoritarian family in American fic-
          tion.   Mosaic, 1971, 4(3):153-173.
11,164.   _____ (ed).   Contemporary American-Jewish Literature;
          Critical Essays.   Bloomington: Indiana Univ. Press,
          1973.
11,165.   _____. Ken Kesey: One Flew over the Cuckoo's Nest.
          Critique, 1962, 5:81-84; In Pratt, J. C. (ed), Ken Kesey,
          One Flew over the Cuckoo's Nest, Text and Criticism.
          NY: Penguin, 1977, 429-434.
11,166.   _____. Mark Twain: the boy as artist.   Lit & Psy-
          chol, 1961, 11:78-84.
11,167.   _____. New American Gothic.   Carbondale: Southern
          Illinois Univ. Press, 1962.
11,168.   _____. Psychoanalysis and American Fiction.   NY:
          Dutton, 1965.
11,169.   _____. Sleepy oppositions.   In Isaacs, N. D., & Leit-
          er, L. H. (eds), Approaches to the Short Story.   San
          Francisco: Chandler, 1963, 56-61.
11,170.   _____. William Faulkner: An Interpretation.   Stanford:
          Stanford Univ. Press, 1957; London: Oxford Univ.
          Press, 1957; NY: Gordian, 1972.
11,171.   Malkani, M. U.   The psychological novel in Europe (break
          from tradition).   Bharat Jyoti, 31 May 1953, 4.
11,172.   Malpezzi, Frances.   A study of the female protagonist in
          Frank Waters' People of the Valley and Rudolfo Anaya's
          Bless Me, Ultima.   South Dakota Rev, 1976, 14(2):102-
          110.
11,173.   Malrieu, P.   Témoignages du romancier sur la psychologie
          ouvrière.   JPNP, 1961, 58:171-191.
11,174.   Malterre, Monique.   La Recherche de l'identité dans A
          State of Siege de Janet Frame.   Etudes Anglaises, 1972,
          25:232-244.
11,175.   Manacorda, G.   Materialismo e masochismo.   Il 'Werth-
          er, ' Foscolo e Leopardi.   Florence: La Nuova Italia,
          1973.
11,176.   Mandel, Siegfried.   Mann's Mario and the Magician, or
          who is Silvestra?   Modern Fiction Studies, 1979-80, 25:
          593-612.
11,177.   Manfredi, J. F.   The Relationship of Class-Structured
          Pathologies to the Contents of Popular Periodical Fic-
          tion 1936-1940.   Doctoral dissertation, Harvard Univ.,
          1950.
11,178.   Mangaroni, Rosella.   L'utero di Henry Miller, o della
          sostituzione.   Per la critica, 1974, 7-8:49-61.
11,179.   Manheim, Leonard F.   The absurd Miss Pamela and the
          tragic Miss Clarissa.   Nassau Rev, 1970, 2(1):1-10.
11,180.   _____. Dickens' fools and madmen.   In Partlow, R. B.,
          Jr. (ed), Dickens Studies Annual, Vol. 2.   Carbondale:
          Southern Illinois Univ. Press, 1972, 69-97.
11,181.   _____. The Dickens hero as child.   Studies in the
          Novel, 1969, 1:189-195.
11,182.   _____. Dickens' heroes, heroes and heroids.   Dickens
          Studies Annual, 1976, 5:1-22.

11, 183.   _____. The Dickens pattern--a study in psychoanalytic
              criticism. Microfilm Abstracts, 1950, 10:218-219; Ann
              Arbor: Univ. Microfilms Publ No. 1879, 1950.
11, 184.   _____. 'Floras and Doras': the women in Dickens'
              novels. Texas Studies in Lit & Language, 1965, 7:181-
              200.
11, 185.   _____. The law as 'father': an aspect of the Dickens
              pattern. Hartford Studies in Lit, 1977, 9:100-109;
              Amer Imago, 1955, 12:17-23.
11, 186.   _____. The personal history of David Copperfield: a
              study in psychoanalytic criticism. Amer Imago, 1952,
              9:21-43.
11, 187.   _____. A tale of two characters; a study in multiple
              projection. In Partlow, R. B. (ed), Dickens Studies
              Annual, Vol. 1. Carbondale: Southern Illinois Univ.
              Press, 1970, 225-237.
11, 188.   _____. A Tale of Two Cities (1859): a study in psy-
              choanalytic criticism. English Rev, 1959, 13-28.
11, 189.   _____. Thanatos: the death instinct in Dickens' later
              novels. Psychoanal Rev, 1960-61, 47(4):17-31; In Man-
              heim, L. F., & Manheim, E. (eds), Hidden Patterns:
              Studies in Psychoanalytic Literary Criticism. NY:
              Macmillan, 1966, 113-131.
11, 190.   _____, & Manheim, Eleanor B. Hidden Patterns:
              Studies in Psychoanalytic Literary Criticism. NY:
              Macmillan, 1966. Reviews: Water Sutton, Lit & Psy-
              chol, 1967, 17:57-59. Louis B. Fraiberg, Contempo-
              rary Psychol, 1968, 13:280-281.
11, 191.   Manheimer, Monica Lauritzen. The search for identity in
              Margaret Drabble's The Needle's Eye. Dutch Q Rev,
              1975, 5:24-35. [Followed by M. D.'s comments, 35-
              38.]
11, 192.   Mann, Jeanette W. Toward new archetypal forms: Boston
              Adventure. Studies in the Novel, 1976, 8:291-303.
11, 193.   Mann, John S. The theme of the double in The Call of the
              Wild. Markham Rev, 1978, 8:1-5.
11, 194.   Manning, Jeanne. Renée Vivien and the theme of the
              androgyne. Bulletin du Bibliophile, 1977, 2:151-154.
11, 195.   Manning, Stephen. A psychological interpretation of 'Sir
              Gawain and the Green Knight.' Criticism, 1964, 6:165-
              177.
11, 196.   Manning, Sylvia. Families in Dickens. In Tufte, V., &
              Myerhoff, B. G. (eds), Changing Images of the Family.
              New Haven: Yale Univ. Press, 1979, 141-153.
11, 197.   _____. Incest and the structure of Henry Esmond.
              Nineteenth Century Fiction, 1979, 34:194-213.
11, 198.   Mannoni, Octave. Fictions freudiennes. Paris: Seuil,
              1978.
11, 199.   Mansbridge, Francis. Search for self in the novels of
              Margaret Atwood. J Canadian Fiction, 1978, 22:106-
              117.
11, 200.   Manthey, Ethel V. The Sentimentally Educated Hero: A
              Comparison of Some Aspects of the Hero of Gustave

Flaubert with Two Leading Characters of Henry James.
DAI, 1977, 37(12-A):7736-37.

11, 201. Mantovani, Juanita M. The Feminine World View of Elizabeth Cleghorn Gaskell. DAI, 1974, 35:1053A.

11, 202. Maples, Robert J. B. Individuation in Nodier's La Fée aux
Miettes. Studies in Romanticism, 1968, 8:43-64.

11, 203. Maranini, L. Novembre est la première tentative d'analyse
psychologique d'un enfant artiste. In Visione e personnaggio secondo Flaubert. Padua: Liviniana, 1959.

11, 204. Marantz, Enid. The theme of alienation in the literary
works of J. -P. Sartre. Mosaic, 1968, 2:18-28.

11, 205. Marcade, Bernard. Pour une psychogéographie de l'espace
fantastique: les architectures arabesques et grotesques
chez E. A. Poe. Rev d'Esthétique, 1974, 27:41-56.

11, 206. Marcelo, J. J. A. Secrecy: a structural concept of The
Time of the Hero. World Lit Today, 1978, 52:68-70.

11, 207. March, Harold. Gide and the Hound of Heaven. Philadelphia: Univ. Pennsylvania Press, 1952.

11, 208. Marchant, Peter. The mystery of Lizaveta. Modern Language Studies, 1974, 4(2):5-13.

11, 209. Marcinowski, Jarowslaw. Drei Romane in Zählen. Int
Zeitschrift für Psychoanalyse, 1912, 2:619-638.

11, 210. Marcotte, E. The space of the novel. Partisan Rev,
1974, 41:263-272.

11, 211. Marcus, David Donald. Symbolism and mental process in
Dombey and Son. Dickens Studies Annual, 1977, 6:57-
71.

11, 212. Marcus, Mordecai. The lost dream of sex and childbirth
in 'The Chrysanthemums.' Modern Fiction Studies,
1965, 11:54-58.

11, 213. _____. Melville's Bartleby as a psychological double.
College English, 1962, 23:365-368.

11, 214. Marcus, Stephen. Appendix: Who is Fagin? In Dickens:
From Pickwick to Dombey. NY: Basic Books, 1965,
358-378.

11, 215. Marder, Herbert. The Androgynous Mind: Feminism in
the Works of Virginia Woolf. DA, 1967, 28:1440A-41A.

11, 216. _____. Beyond the lighthouse: The Years. Bucknell
Rev, 1967, 15:61-70; In Garvin, H. R. (ed), Makers of
the Twentieth-Century Novel. Lewisburg: Bucknell
Univ. Press, 1977, 62-69.

11, 217. _____. Feminism and Art: A Study of Virginia Woolf.
Chicago: Univ. Chicago Press, 1968.

11, 218. Maresco, Carol J. Gestures as meaning in Winesburg,
Ohio. College Language Assn J, 1966, 9:279-283.

11, 219. Margolies, Edward. The Art of Richard Wright. Carbondale: Southern Illinois Univ. Press, 1969.

11, 220. Marie, Jean-Noel. Le Crime comme signe de la haine de
soi: Les deséquilibres psychologiques dans l'oeuvre
romanesque de Bernanos. Rev des Lettres Modernes,
1970, 228-233:33-49.

11, 221. Marillier, L. Social psychology in contemporary French
fiction. Fortnightly Rev, 1901, 60:520-537.

11, 222. Marini, Marcelle. Territoires du feminin avec Marguerite
          Duras. Paris: Minard, 1977.
11, 223. Markle, Joyce B. Of the Farm: psychological considera-
          tions. In Fighters and Lovers. Theme in the Novels
          of John Updike. NY: New York Univ. Press, 1973,
          84-105.
11, 224. Markos, Donald W. Life against death in Henderson the
          Rain King. Modern Fiction Studies, 1971, 17:193-
          205.
11, 225. _____. Margaret Whitehead in The Confessions of Nat
          Turner. Studies in the Novel, 1972, 4:52-59.
11, 226. Marković, Vida E. The Changing Face: Disintegration of
          Personality in the Twentieth-Century British Novel, 1900-
          1950. Carbondale: Southern Illinois Univ. Press, 1970;
          London: Feffer & Simons, 1970.
11, 227. Markow, Alice Bradley. The pathology of feminine failure
          in the fiction of Doris Lessing. Critique: Studies in
          Modern Fiction, 1974, 16:88-99.
11, 228. Marks, William S., III. Advertisements for grace: Flan-
          nery O'Connor's 'A Good Man Is Hard to Find.' Stud-
          ies in Short Fiction, 1966, 4:19-27.
11, 229. _____. Melville, opium, and Billy Budd. Studies in
          Amer Fiction, 1978, 6:33-45.
11, 230. _____. The psychology of regression in D.H. Law-
          rence's 'The Blind Man.' Lit & Psychol, 1967, 17:177-
          192.
11, 231. _____. The psychology of the uncanny in Lawrence's
          'The Rocking-Horse Winner.' Modern Fiction Studies,
          1965-66, 11:381-392; In Consolo, D.P. (ed), The Rock-
          ing-Horse Winner. Columbus, Ohio: Merrill, 1969,
          71-83.
11, 232- Markson, David. Malcolm Lowry's 'Volcano.' Myth.
    3.   Symbol. Meaning. NY: Times Book, 1978.
11, 234. Marre, K.E. Colour significance in A Portrait of the Art-
          ist as a Young Man. Dutch Q Rev, 1977, 7:201-212.
11, 235. Marsden, Malcolm M. Love and threat in Katherine Anne
          Porter's fiction. Twentieth Century Fiction, 1967, 13:
          29-38.
11, 236. Marsh, John L. The psycho-sexual reading of 'The Fall
          of the House of Usher.' Poe Studies, 1972, 5:8-9.
11, 237. Marshall, Marion F. Die Bedeutung des Individuations--
          problems in Alfred Döblins Werk. DAI, 1971, 31:
          6620A.
11, 238. Marshall, Sarah L. Fathers and sons in Absalom, Ab-
          salom! Univ. Mississippi Studies English, 1967, 8:19-
          29.
11, 239. _____. Rationality and delusion in Jane Austen's Em-
          ma. Univ. Mississippi Studies in English, 1968, 9:57-
          67.
11, 240. Marshall, William H. The conclusion of Great Expecta-
          tions as the fulfillment of myth. Personalist, 1963,
          44:337-347.

11, 241.   _____. Motivation in Tess of the D'Urbervilles. Rev des Langues Vivantes, 1963, 29:224-225.

11, 242.   _____. The self, the world, and the structure of Jane Eyre. Rev de Langues Vivantes, 416-425.

11, 243.   _____. The Way of All Flesh: the dual function of Edward Overton. Studies in Language & Lit, 1963, 4:583-590.

11, 244. Marson, Eric L. Justice and the obsessed character in Michael Kohlhaas, Der Prozess, and L'Etranger. Seminar, 1966, 2(2):21-33.

11, 245.   _____, & Leopold, Keith. Kafka, Freud, and Ein Landarzt. German Q, 1964, 37:146-159.

11, 246. Martán Góngora, Helcías. Neoquijotismo y otras notas cervantinas. Norte, 1977, 275:11-13.

11, 247. Martel, M. U., & McCall, G. J. Reality-orientation and the pleasure principle: a study of American mass periodical fiction (1890-1955). In Dexter, L. A., & White, D. M. (eds), People, Society, and Mass Communications. Glencoe, Ill: Free Press, 1964, 283-334.

11, 248. Martens, W. (ed). Anton Reiser. Ein psychologischer Roman. Stuttgart: Reclam, 1972.

11, 249. Martin, Dennis M. Desire and disease: the psychological patterns of The Floating Opera. Critique: Studies in Modern Fiction, 1976, 18(2):17-33.

11, 250. Martin, J. S. Mrs. Moore: the Marabor Caves. Modern Fiction Studies, 1965-66, 11:429-433.

11, 251. Martin, Jay. Remember to remember: Henry Miller and the literary tradition. Clio, 1977, 7:75-90.

11, 252. Martin, Marjory. Fitzgerald's image of woman: anima projections in Tender Is the Night. English Studies Collection, 1976, Series 1, No. 6, 17 pp.

11, 253. Martin, Peter A. The cockroach as an identification; with reference to Kafka's Metamorphosis. Amer Imago, 1959, 16:65-71.

11, 254. Martin, Robert K. Oscar Wilde and the fairy tale: the happy prince as self-dramatization. Studies in Short Fiction, 1979, 16:74-77.

11, 255.   _____. Sexual and group relationships in 'May Day': fear and longing. Studies in Short Fiction, 1978, 15:99-101.

11, 256. Martin, Wendy. Seduced and abandoned in the New World: the image of woman in American fiction. In Gornick, V., & Moran, L. (eds), Woman in Sexist Society. NY: Basic Books, 1971, 226-239; NY: Signet, 1972.

11, 257. Martindale, Colin. Archetype and reality in 'The Fall of the House of Usher.' Poe Studies, 1972, 5:9-11.

11, 258.   _____. Transformation and transfusion of vitality in the narratives of Poe. Semiotica, 1973, 8:46-59.

11, 259. Martínez Dacosta, S. El informe sobre ciegos en E Sábato. Miami/Zaragoza: Universal, 1972.

11, 260. Martínez de Alicea, Ada Hilda. El doble en Octaedro, libro de cuentos de Cortázar. Horizontes, 1976-77, 39-40:29-31.

11, 261.   Marulli, G.   Alcuni appunti psicoanalitici sul Decamerón
           di Messer Giovanni Boccacio.   Revista de Psicopatologia
           e Neuropsichiatria, 1951, 19:57-64.
11, 262.   _____.   Sul Decamerón di Messer Giovanni Boccaccio,
           alcuni appunti psicoanalitici.   Annales Neuropsychiatri
           Psicoanalisi, 1964, 11:319-325.
11, 263.   Mashback, Frederic J.   The Child Character in Hawthorne
           and James.   DA, 1960, 21:338.
11, 264.   Maslenikov, Oleg A.   The ludicrous man-of-the-family: a
           recurrent type in Dostoevskij.   In Riasanovsky, N. V.,
           & Struve, G. (eds), California Slavic Studies, Vol. 6.
           Berkeley: Univ. California Press, 1973, 29-36.
11, 265.   Mason, M.   Why is Leopold Bloom a cuckold?   J English
           Literary History, 1977, 44:171-188.
11, 266.   Mason, Shirlene Rae.   Daniel Defoe's Paradoxical Stand on
           the Status of Women.   DAI, 1975, 35:7872A.
11, 267.   _____.   Daniel Defoe and the Status of Women.   St. Al-
           bans, Vt: Eden Women, 1978; Review: S. O. Taylor,
           18th Century Studies, 1979, 12:555-558.
11, 268.   Massey, Irving.   Escape from fiction: literature and di-
           dacticism.   Georgia Rev, 1978, 32:611-630.
11, 269.   _____.   The Gaping Pig: Aspects of Metamorphosis in
           Literature.   Berkeley: Univ. California Press, 1975.
11, 270.   Massey, Tom M.   Faulkner's Females: The Thematic
           Function of Women in the Yoknapatawpha Cycle.   DAI,
           1970, 30:3468A.
11, 271.   Masters, R. E. L.   Patterns of Incest: A Psycho-Social
           Study of Incest Based in Clinical and Historical Data.
           NY: Julian, 1963.
11, 272.   Matchand, H. L.   Sex Life in France, Including a History
           of Its Erotic Literature.   NY: Panurge, 1933.
11, 273.   Matchie, Thomas Frederick.   The Mythical Flannery O'Con-
           nor: A Psychomythic Study of A Good Man Is Hard to
           Find.   DAI, 1975, 36:277A-78A.
11, 274.   Matlaw, Ralph E.   Structure and integration in Notes from
           Underground.   PMLA, 1958, 73:101-109.
11, 275.   Matoré, Georges, & Mecz, Irene.   Le Thème de la com-
           munication dans La Recherche du temps perdu: Le volet
           et le rideau.   JPNP, 1968, 66(1):15-34.
11, 276.   Matthews, Dorothy.   The psychological journey of Bilbo
           Baggins.   In Lobdell, Jared (ed), A Tolkien Compass.
           La Salle, Ill: Open Court, 1975, 29-42.
11, 277.   Matthews, J. H.   The Inner Dream: Céline as Novelist.
           Syracuse, NY: Syracuse Univ. Press, 1978.
11, 278.   Matton, Collin G.   The Role of Women in Three of Faulk-
           ner's Families.   DAI, 1974, 35:2283A.
11, 279.   Mauerhofer, Hugo.   Der Introversion, mit spezieller Be-
           rücksichtigung des Dichters Hermann Hesse.   Doctoral
           dissertation, Univ. Bern, 1929.
11, 280.   Mauranges, J. -P.   Aliénation et châtiment chez Mark
           Twain et Heinrich Böll.   Rev des Langues Vivantes,
           1973, 29:131-136.
11, 281.   Mauriac, P.   Marcel Proust et la médecine.   Rev Hebdo-
           madaire, 1923, 23:38-57.

11, 282. Maurin, Mario. Henri de Regnier: le labyrinthe et le double. Montreal: Les Presses de l'Univ. de Montréal, 1972.

11, 283. _____. Pierre Loti et les voies du sacré. Modern Language Notes, 1966, 81:288-306.

11, 284. Maurois, André. La Psychanalyse et le roman. Psyché, 1947, 2:1040-1044.

11, 285. Mauron, Charles. Agnes. Cahiers Victoriens et Edouardiens, 1977, 4-5:17-18.

11, 286. _____. Amitié. Cahiers Victoriens et Edouardiens, 1977, 4-5:11-13.

11, 287. _____. L'Education. Cahiers Victoriens et Edouardiens, 1977, 4-5:14-16.

11, 288. _____. Le Mariage, août 1962. Cahiers Victoriens et Edouardiens, 1977, 4-5:23-26.

11, 289. _____. Note pour EMF. Cahiers Victoriens et Edouardiens, 1977, 4-5:8-10.

11, 290. _____. A propos de The Longest Journey, 'the cow is there': Le Bien-et-mal. Cahiers Victoriens et Edouardiens, 1977, 4-5:21-22.

11, 291. _____. Quelques traits de E. M. Forster. Cahiers Victoriens et Edouardiens, 1977, 4-5:5-7; Figaro Lit, 10 Jan 1959.

11, 292. _____. La Tendance orphique. Cahiers Victoriens et Edouardiens, 1977, 4-5:19-20.

11, 293. Maxwell, Richard. The abdication of masculinity in One Flew Over the Cuckoo's Nest. In Broughton, B. B. (ed), Twenty-Seven to One: A Potpourri of Humanistic Material. Ogdensburg, NY: Ryan, 1970, 203-211.

11, 294. May, Cedric R. P. Un Surnaturel humain: étude de la personnalité dans les romans de Julien Green. In Fitch, B. T. (ed), Julien Green. Paris: Minard, 1966, 75-92. (Revue des Lettres Modernes, 1966, No. 130-133, 75-92).

11, 295. May, Charles E. Literary masters and masturbators: sexuality, fantasy, and reality in Huckleberry Finn. Lit & Psychol, 1978, 28:85-92.

11, 296. _____. Myth and mystery in Steinbeck's 'The Snake': a Jungian view. Criticism, 1973, 15:322-335.

11, 297. _____. Why sister lives at the P. O. Southern Humanities Rev, 1978, 12:243-249.

11, 298. May, Judith Stinson. Family and Aggression in the Leatherstocking Series. DAI, 1976, 37:2873A-4A.

11, 299. May, Keith M. Out of the Maelstrom: Psychology and the Novel in the Twentieth Century. NY: St. Martin's, 1977.

11, 300. Mayen, Gilbert. Le Roman et la psychanalyse. In Literature and Science. Oxford: Blackwell, 1955, 72-80.

11, 301. Maynard, Reid. Red as leitmotiv in The Red Badge of Courage. Arizona Q, 1974, 30:135-141.

11, 302. Mayoux, Jean-Jacques. L'Inconscient et la vie intérieure dans le roman anglais: 1905-1940. Nancy: Centre Européen Universitaire, 1952.

11,303. Mays, Milton A. Uptown and Downtown in Henry James's America: Sexuality and the Business-Society. DA, 1966, 26:6046.

11,304. Meacham, William S. A non-fiction study in scarlet (Truman Capote's In Cold Blood). Virginia Q Rev, 1966, 42:316-319.

11,305. Mead, Margaret, & Wolfenstein, Martha. Monkey: a Chinese children's classic. In Childhood in Contemporary Cultures. Chicago: Univ. Chicago Press, 1955, 246-252.

11,306. Measham, D. C. Sentiment and sentimental psychology in Jane Austen. Renaissance & Modern Studies, 1972, 16: 61-85.

11,307. Meckier, Jerome. Burden's complaint: the disintegrated personality as theme and style in Robert Penn Warren's All the King's Men. Studies in the Novel, 1970, 2(1): 7-21.

11,308. _____. Our Ford, our Freud and the behaviorist conspiracy in Huxley's Brave New World. Thalia: Studies in Lit Humor, 1978, 1(1):35-59.

11,309. Meehan, Thomas C. Ernesto Sábato's sexual metaphysics: theme and form in El túnel. Modern Language Notes, 1968, 83:226-252.

11,310. Megay, Joyce N. Elie Rabier: an unknown source of Proust's psychology. Modern Language Q, 1978, 39:38-49.

11,311. Megna, Robert. Nathalie Sarraute: The Novelist as Social Psychologist. DAI, 1978, 39:1554A.

11,312. Mehlman, Jeffrey. Poe pourri: Lacan's 'Purloined Letter.' Semiotexte, 1975, 1(3).

11,313. _____. Revolution and Repetition: Marx/Hugo/Balzac. Berkeley: Univ. California Press, 1977.

11,314. Mein, Margaret. Proust's Challenge to Time. Manchester: Manchester Univ. Press, 1962.

11,315. _____. Le Thème de l'hérédité dans l'oeuvre de Proust. Europe, 1971, 502-03:83-99.

11,316. Meindll, Dieter. Bewusstsein als Schicksal: zu Struktur und Entwicklung von William Faulkners Generationenromanen. Stuttgart: Metzler, 1974.

11,317. Meisel, F. L. The myth of Peter Pan. In The Psychoanalytic Study of the Child, Vol. 32. New Haven: Yale Univ. Press, 1977, 545-563.

11,318. Meisel, Martin. Waverley, Freud, and topographical metaphor. Univ. Toronto Q, 1979, 48:226-244.

11,319. Meisel, Perry. Thomas Hardy: The Return of the Repressed; A Study of the Major Fiction. New Haven: Yale Univ. Press, 1972.

11,320. Meissner, W. W. A case in point. In The Annual of Psychoanalysis, Vol. 5. NY: IUP, 1977, 405-436.

11,321. Méla, Charles. Perceval. Yale French Studies, 1977, 55-56:253-279.

11,322. Melchiode, G. A. A note on Notes from Underground. Bulletin Philadelphia Assn for Psychoanal, 1966, 16:89-91.

11,323. Melczer, W. Did Don Quixote die of melancholy? In Folie et déraison à la Renaissance. Brussels: Univ. Bruxelles Press, 1976, 161-170.

11,324. Meldrum, Barbara. Fate, sex, and naturalism in Rølvaag's trilogy. In Ole Rølvaag: Artist and Cultural Leader. Northfield, Minn: St. Olaf College Press, 1975, 41-49.

11,325. _____. Images of women in Western American literature. Midwest Q, 1976, 17:252-267.

11,326. Melebeck, Paul. Time and structure in The Great Gatsby. Rev des Langues Vivantes, 1976, 42:213-224.

11,327. Melendrez, Patricia M. The archetype in Nick Joaquin's The Woman Who Had Two Navels. Saint Louis Q (Baguio City), 1968, 6:171-192.

11,328. Meligi, A. Moneim el-. [Psycho-regulation.] Vie médicale au Canada français, 1977, 6:199-203.

11,329. Melis Freda, R. Alcuni tecnicismi lessicali in un romanziere dell'800. Lingua Nostra, 1969, 30:10-15.

11,330. Melito, Ignatius Michael. Themes of Adolescence: Studies in American Fiction of Adolescence. DA, 1965, 3344.

11,331. Mellard, James M. Catch-22: Déjà vu and the labyrinth of memory. Bucknell Rev, 1968, 16:29-44.

11,332. _____. Myth and archetype in Heart of Darkness. Tennessee Studies Lit, 1968, 13:1-15.

11,333. _____. Type and archetype: Jason Compson as 'satirist.' Genre, 1971, 4:173-188.

11,334. Mellard, James M. Narrative forms in Winesburg, Ohio. PMLA, 1968, 83:1304-1312.

11,335. Melone, Thomas. Architecture du monde: Chinua Achebe et W. B. Yeats. Couch, 1970, 2:44-52.

11,336. Memmi, Germaine. Motivations inconscientes et formes dans La Verdict de Franz Kafka. Rev de l'Allemagne, 1973, 5:785-800.

11,337. Mencken, H. L. The unroofing of Winesburg. Chicago Evening Post, 20 June 1919.

11,338. Mendel, Gérard. La Révolte contre le père, une introduction à la sociopsychanalyse. Paris: Payot, 1968.

11,339. _____. Le Roman comme fiction et comme ensemble. A propos des Souvenirs du Colonel de Maumort, de Roger Martin du Gard. Rev Française de Psychanalyse, 1963, 301-320.

11,340. Mendilow, Adam A. Time and the Novel. NY: British Book Centre, 1953.

11,341. Mengel, Nanette V. Coherence in Dickens' Novels: A Study of the Relationship Between Form and Psychological Content in Pickwick Papers, Martin Chuzzlewit and Our Mutual Friend. DAI, 1974, 35:3754A-55A.

11,342. Mengeling, Marvin E. Other Voices, Other Rooms: Oedipus between the covers. Amer Imago, 1962, 19:361-374.

11,343. Menikoff, Barry. A house divided: a new reading of The Bostonians. College Language Assn J, 1977, 20:459-474.

11,344. Menkin, Gabriel A. Structure in Sherwood Anderson's Fiction. Doctoral dissertation, Univ. Pittsburgh, 1968.

11,345. Merad, G. L'Etranger de Camus vu sous an angle psychsociologique. Rev Romane, 1975, 10:51-91.

11,346. Mercier, Michel. Le Roman féminin. Paris: Presses Universitaires de France, 1976.

11,347. Merrett, Eva M. Childhood and Youth in Theodor Storm's Works. Doctoral dissertation, Johns Hopkins Univ., 1954.

11,348. Mersereau, John, Jr. Thackeray, Flaubert, Tolstoy and psychological realism. In Terras, V. (ed), American Contributions to the 8th International Congress of Slavists, Vol. 2. Columbus, Ohio: Slavica, 1978, 499-522.

11,349. Mertens, Gerald M. Hemingway's The Old Man and the Sea and Thomas Mann's The Black Swan. Lit & Psychol, 1956, 6:96-99.

11,350. Mesnyayev, G. [Themes of love and death in Bunin.] Voz, 1963, 11:59-70.

11,351. Messac, R. Le Detective novel et l'influence de la pensée scientifique. Paris: 1929.

11,352. Messick, Alan R. Tomás Rodaja: a clinical case? Romance Notes, 1970, 11:623-628.

11,353. Metcalf, Frank. The suicide of Salinger's Seymour Glass. Studies in Short Fiction, 1972, 9:243-246.

11,354. Métraux, Rhoda. A portrait of the family in German juvenile fiction. In Mead, M., & Wolfenstein, M. (eds), Childhood in Contemporary Cultures. Chicago: Univ. Chicago Press, 1955, 253-276.

11,355. Mews, Hazel. Frail Vessels: Women's Role in Women's Novels from Fanny Burney to George Eliot. London: Athlone, 1969.

11,356. Meyer, Bernard C. Death was the fate of his heroes. Columbia Univ. Forum, 1964, 7:14-19.

11,357. _____. Language and being: Joseph Conrad and the literature of personality. Lit & Psychol, 1976, 26:181-184.

11,358. Meyer, P. H. The individual and society in Rousseau's Emile. Modern Language Q, 1958, 19:99-114.

11,359. Meyers, Carolyn H. Psychotechnology in Fiction about Imaginary Societies, 1923-1962. DAI, 1969, 30:2490A-91A.

11,360. Meyers, Jeffrey. Angst and art. Critical Q, 1974, 16:370-378.

11,361. _____. D. H. Lawrence and homosexuality. In Spender, S. (ed), D. H. Lawrence. Novelist, Poet, Prophet. NY: Harper & Row, 1973, 135-158; London Magazine, 1973, 13:68-98.

11,362. _____. Homosexuality and Literature, 1890-1930. Montreal: McGill-Queens Univ. Press, 1977; London: Univ. London Press, 1977; Reviews: J. Stokes, Modern Language Rev, 1979, 74:397-399; Cheryl L. Walker, Modern Fiction Studies, 1978-79, 24:658-660.

11,363. _____. The quest for identity in Kim. Texas Studies in Lit & Language, 1970, 12:101-110.

11,364.   . 'Vacant heart and hand and eye': the homosexual theme in A Room with a View. English Lit in
Transition, 1970, 13:181-182.

11,365.   . 'The Voice of Water': Lawrence's The Virgin
and the Gypsy. English Miscellany, 1970, 21:199-207.

11,366. Meyers, Joyce. Symbol and structure in The Leopard.
Italian Q, 1965, 9:50-70.

11,367. Meyers, Sylvia H. Womanhood in Jane Austen's novels.
Novel, 1970, 3:225-232.

11,368. Meyerson, I. Quelques aspects de la personne dans le
roman. JPNP, 1951, 44:303-334.

11,369. Michael, Colette V. La Femme et le mal dans Les liaisons dangereuses de Choderlos de Laclos. DAI, 1974,
35:410A-11A.

11,370. Michael, L. The Genesis of the American Psychological
Novel. DAI, 1970, 31:352.

11,371. Michael, Wolfgang F. Thomas Mann auf dem Weg zu
Freud. Modern Language Notes, 1950, 65:166-171.

11,372. Michasiw, Barbara Lorene. The Heroines of Charles Dickens: Their Meaning and Function. DAI, 1977, 37:6505A.

11,373. Michaud, Régis. The American Novel Today: A Social and
Psychological Study. Boston: Little, Brown, 1928,
1931; Paris: 1926.

11,374. Michel, Arlette. Le Mariage chez Honoré de Balzac:
Amour et féminisme. 4 Vols. Paris: Société d'édition
'Les Belles Lettres, ' 1978.

11,375. Michel, Pierre. Philip Roth's reductive lens: from 'On
the Air' to My Life As a Man. Rev des Langues Vivantes, 1976, 42:509-519.

11,376. Mickelson, Anne Z. The family trap in The Return of the
Native. Colby Library Q, 1974, 10:463-475.

11,377.   . Vital Life Versus Sterile Denial: A Study of
Family and Sexual Relationships in the Works of Thomas
Hardy and D. H. Lawrence. DAI, 1972, 32:5191A.

11,378. Micklus, Robert. Dowell's passion in The Good Soldier.
English Lit in Transition, 1979, 22:281-292.

11,379.   . Hawthorne's Jekyll and Hyde: the Aminadat in
Aylmer. Lit & Psychol, 1979, 39:148-159.

11,380. Mignault, Louis B. Les Thèmes existentialistes dans
l'oeuvre d'Andre Malraux. DAI, 1972, 32:6990A.

11,381. Mijuskovic, B. L. Loneliness in Philosophy, Psychology,
and Literature. Atlantic Highlands, NJ: Humanities
Press, 1979.

11,382. Mileck, Joseph. Hesse and psychology. In Hermann Hesse
and His Critics. Chapel Hill: Univ. North Carolina
Press, 1958, 158-166; NY: AMS Press, 1966.

11,383. Miles, Peter. Bibliography and insanity: Smollett and
mad-business. Library (London), 1976, 31:205-222.

11,384. Miles, Robert L. A Phenomenological-Existential Analysis
of Don Quixote. DAI, 1972, 32:5239A.

11,385. Miles, Rosalind. The Fiction of Sex: Themes and Functions of Sex Difference in the Modern Novel. London:
Vision, 1974; NY: Barnes & Noble, 1975.

11,386. Miller, Carroll. Toys and slaves: the subjection of wom-
         en throughout the world in the writings of Mary Gaunt.
         South Atlantic Bulletin, 1976, 41(2):131-136.
11,387. Miller, David M. Faulkner's women. Modern Fiction
         Studies, 1967, 13:3-17.
11,388. Miller, Edmund M. Richard Mahoney's euphoria: a psy-
         chological note. Meanjin Q, 1952, 11:397-401.
11,389. Miller, Edwin Haviland. 'My Kinsman, Major Molineux':
         the playful art of Nathaniel Hawthorne. ESQ: J Amer
         Renaissance, 1978, 24:145-151.
11,390. Miller, James Arthur. The Struggle for Identity in the
         Major Works of Richard Wright. DAI, 1977, 37:5123A-
         24A.
11,391. Miller, James E., Jr. (ed). Myth and Method. Modern
         Theories of Fiction. Lincoln: Univ. Nebraska Press,
         1960.
11,392. Miller, Joseph Hills. Charles Dickens: The World of His
         Novels. Cambridge: Harvard Univ. Press, 1958.
11,393. _____. Emily Brontë. In The Disappearance of God.
         Cambridge: Harvard Univ. Press, 1963, 157-211.
11,394. Miller, Milton L. Balzac's Père Goriot. Int Zeitschrift
         für Psychoanalyse, 1937, 6:78-85.
11,395. Miller, Nancy Kipnis. Gender and Genre: An Analysis of
         Literary Femininity in the Eighteenth-Century Novel.
         DAI, 1975, 35:6674A.
11,396. Miller, W. H. The habit of Sherlock Holmes. Transac-
         tions Studies College Physicians Philadelphia, 1978, 45:
         252-257.
11,397. Miller, Walter J., & Dinnerstein, Dorothy. On Virginia
         Woolf's Orlando. Explicator, 1960, 19, No. 37.
11,398. Miller, Wayne Charles. An Armed America, Its Face in
         Fiction: A History of the American Military Novel.
         NY: New York Univ. Press, 1970.
11,399. Miller, William V. Earth-mothers, succubi, and other
         ectoplasmic spirits: the women in Sherwood Anderson's
         short stories. Mid America, 1974, 1:64-81.
11,400. Milligan, Kathleen M. 'Les Lauriers sont coupés' and the
         Interior Monologue. Hull, England: Hull Univ. Press,
         1977.
11,401. Millott, H. H. 'La Peau de Chagrin': method in madness.
         In Dargan, C., et al. (eds), Studies in Balzac's Real-
         ism. Chicago: Univ. Chicago Press, 1932, 68-89.
11,402. Millsaps, Ellen McNutt. The Family in Four Novels of
         Eudora Welty. DAI, 1976, 37:951A.
11,403. Milner, Max. Le Sens 'psychique' de Massimilla Doni et
         la conception balzacienne de l'âme. L'Année Balzaci-
         enne, 1966, 157-169.
11,404. Milton, John. Interview with Frederick Manfred. South
         Dakota Rev, 1969, 7:110-130.
11,405. Minakawa, Saburo. A Hardyan aspect: representation of
         heroines' ego. Thomas Hardy Yearbook, 1970, 1:49-52.
11,406. Mindess, Harvey. Freud on Dostoevsky. Amer Scholar,
         1967, 36:446-452.

11,407. _____. A psychologist looks at the writer. Psychol Today, 1967, 1(6):40, 55-56.

11,408. Minogue, Valerie. The imagery of childhood in Nathalie Sarraute's Portrait d'un inconnu. French Studies, 1973, 27:177-186.

11,409. Minowski, E., & Fusswerk, J. Le Problème Dostoiewski et la structure de l'épilepsie. Annales Médico-Psychologiques, 1955, 2(3):369-409.

11,410. Mintz, Jacqueline A. The myth of the Jewish mother in three Jewish, American, female writers. Centennial Rev, 1978, 22:346-355.

11,411. Miro, Emilio. Tristana o la imposibilidad de ser. Cuadernos Hispanoamericanos, 1970-71, 505-522.

11,412. Miroiu, Mihai. In the stream: James Joyce and Virginia Woolf. Analele Universitatii Bucuresti (Limbi germanice, 20), 1971, 145-157.

11,413. _____. The makers of the stream of consciousness novel. Analele Universitatii Bucuresti (Limbi germanice, 19), 1970, 137-149.

11,414. Mirza, Humayun Ali. The Influence of Hindu-Buddhist Psychology and Philosophy on J. D. Salinger's Fiction. DAI, 1976, 37:971A.

11,415. Mitchell, Breon. Hans Henny Jahnn and James Joyce: the birth of the inner monologue in the German novel. Arcadia, 1971, 6:44-71.

11,416. Mitchell, Edward B. Artists and artists: the aesthetics of Henry Miller. Texas Studies in Lit & Language, 1966, 8:103-115.

11,417. Mitchell, Giles. Incest, demonism and death in Wuthering Heights. Lit & Psychol, 1973, 23:27-36.

11,418. Mitchell, J. Stendhal: Le Rouge et le Noir. In Studies in French Literature, Vol. 22. London: Arnold, 1973.

11,419. Mitchell, Judith. Women and Wyndham Lewis. Modern Fiction Studies, 1978, 24:223-231.

11,420. Mitchell, Marilyn L. Steinbeck's strong women: feminine identity in short stories. Southwest Rev, 1976, 61:304-314.

11,421. Mitchell, Tamara K. The Irrational Element in Doris Lessing's Fiction. DAI, 1978, 38:7326A-27A.

11,422. Mitner, D. Faulkner, childhood, and the making of The Sound and the Fury. Amer Lit, 1979, 51:376-393.

11,423. Mitscherlich, Alexander. Psycho-Pathographien, I: Schriftsteller und Psychoanalyse. Frankfurt: Suhrkamp, 1972.

11,424. Mitscherlich-Nielsen, M. [Psychoanalytic comments on Franz Kafka.] Psyche (Stuttgart), 1977, 31:60-83.

11,425. Mitzman, A. Gustave Flaubert und Max Weber. Psyche, 1978, 32(5-6):441-462.

11,426. Miyoshi, Masao. The Theme of the Divided Self in Victorian Literature. DA, 1966, 27(3-A):751.

11,427. Mizzau, Marina. Il 'Rifuto della psicologia' e il mito dell' oggettivita. Aut Aut, 1960, 57:191-195.

11,428. Moan, Margaret A. Setting and structure: an approach to Hartley's The Go-Between. Criticism, 1973, 15(2):27-36.

11,429. Mochizuki, Mitsuko. Adolescent problems of the oedipal
         Stephen Dedalus. In Annual Reports of Studies, Vol. 25.
         Kyoto: Doshisha Women's College, 1974, 202-217.
11,430. _____. The unconscious process in the works of James
         Joyce. In Annual Reports of Studies, Vol. 23. Kyoto:
         Doshisha Women's College, 1972, 114-145.
11,431. _____. The unconscious process in the works of James
         Joyce (continued). In Annual Reports of Studies, Vol.
         24. Kyoto: Doshisha Women's College, 1973, 110-124.
11,432. Moers, Ellen. Bleak House: the agitating women. Dicken-
         sian, 1973, 69:13-24.
11,433. _____. Literary Women. The Great Writers. Garden
         City, NY: Doubleday, 1976.
11,434. _____. Two Dreisers. NY: Viking, 1969.
11,435. Moglen, Helene S. The double vision of Wuthering Heights:
         a clarifying view of female development. Centennial
         Rev, 1971, 15:391-405.
11,436. _____. The Philosophical Irony of Laurence Sterne.
         DA, 1966, 66-4916.
11,437. Mohrt, Michel. Les Trois obsessions de William Styron:
         le péché, le désespoir, le désir d'évasion. Arts, 1962,
         858, 3.
11,438. Moldenhauer, Joseph J. Murder as a fine art: basic con-
         nections between Poe's aesthetics, psychology, and
         moral vision. PMLA, 1968, 83:284-297.
11,439. Molley, Chester N. The Artemis-Athene and Venus Polar-
         ity in the Works of Edith Wharton: A Mythological
         Dimension with Psychological Implications. DAI, 1972,
         32:6442A.
11,440. Mollinger, Robert N. Edgar Allan Poe's 'The Oval Por-
         trait': fusion of multiple identities. Amer Imago,
         1979, 36:147-153.
11,441. Mollinger, Shermaz. The divided self in Nathaniel Haw-
         thorne and D. H. Lawrence. Psychoanal Rev, 1979,
         66(1):79-102.
11,442. Molnár, Géza von. The composition of Novalis' Die Lehr-
         linge zu Sais: a reevaluation. PMLA, 1970, 85:1002-
         1014.
11,443. Moloney, Brian. Psychoanalysis and irony in La coscienza
         di Zeno. Modern Language Rev, 1972, 67:309-318.
11,444. Monk, Donald. Colour symbolism in James Dickey's Deli-
         verance. J Amer Studies, 1977, 11:261-279.
11,445. Monk, Patricia. Psychology and myth in The Manticore.
         Studies in Canadian Lit, 1977, 2:69-81.
11,446. Monroe, Michael. Alienation in the Works of Miguel De-
         libes. DAI, 1972, 33:2927A.
11,447. Monroe, Nellie Elizabeth. The Novel and Society. Chapel
         Hill: Univ. North Carolina Press, 1941.
11,448. Montagu, M. F. Ashley. Review: Arthur Koestler's Arri-
         val and Departure. Psychiatry, 1944, 7:97.
11,449. _____. Review: Clarence P. Oberndorf's The Psychi-
         atric Novels of Oliver Wendell Holmes. Psychiatry,
         1944, 7:312.

11,450. _____. Review: Helen E. Haines' What's in a Novel. Psychiatry, 1943, 6:450.

11,451. _____. Review: Lillian Smith's Strange Fruit. Psychiatry, 1944, 7:201.

11,452. Monteiro, George. Innocence and experience: the adolescent child in the works of Mark Twain, Henry James, and Ernest Hemingway. Estudos Anglo-Americanos, 1977, 1:39-57.

11,453. Montgomery, Judith H. Pygmalion's Image: The Metamorphosis of the American Heroine. DAI, 1972, 32: 4623A-24A.

11,454. Montrelay, Michèle. 'Les Lois de l'hospitalite' en tant que lois du narcissisme: Klossowski. L'Arc, 1970, 43.

11,455. _____. A propos des romans de Pierre Klossowski: Narcissisme, Sublimation et Perversion. Recueil de comptes rendus des travaux de la section II: psychanalyse appliquée. Congrès du 30 octobre-1er novembre 1966. Paris: Publication of the Ecole Freudienne de Paris, 1966.

11,456. Moody, Michael W. Existentialism, Mexico and Artemio Cruz. Romance Notes, 1968, 10:27-31.

11,457. Mooij, Anne Louis Anton. Caractères principaux et tendances des romans psychologiques chez quelques femme-auteurs, de Mme Riccoboni à Mme de Souza (1757-1826). Groningen: de Waal, 1949.

11,458. Mooney, Stephen L. Poe's Gothic wasteland. Sewanee Rev, 1962, 69:261-283.

11,459. Moore, E. Margaret. Emma and Miss Bates: early experiences of separation and the theme of dependency in Jane Austen's novels. Studies in English Lit, 1500-1900, 1969, 9:573-585.

11,460. Moore, Harry T. Review: P. Balbert's D. H. Lawrence and the Psychology of Rhythm. Modern Language Rev, 1976, 71:907-910.

11,461. Moore, Jack B. Carson McCullers: the heart is a timeless hunter. Twentieth Century Lit, 1965, 11:76-81.

11,462. Morales, Carmen. Unamuno's concept of woman. Fu Jen Studies, 1972, 5:91-100.

11,463. Morales Galán, Carmen. El tema maternal en la concepción unamunesca de la mujer. DAI, 1971, 32:977A.

11,464. Morand, Carlos. Los adolescentes en la obra narrativa de Aldous Huxley. Santiago de Chile: Edit. Universitaria, 1963.

11,465. Moreira Andres, N. El psicoanálysis en la literatura española. Un estudio sobre Las Adelfas de los Hermanos Machado. Asclepio, 1971, 23:337-350.

11,466. Morell, Giliane. Pourquoi ris-tu, Darl?--ou le temps d'un regard. Sud, 1975, Nos. 14-15.

11,467. _____. Prisoners of the inner world: mother and daughter in 'Miss Zilphia Gant.' Mississippi Q, 1975, 28: 299-305.

11, 468. Morello-Frosch, Marta. El personaje y su doble en las ficciones de Cortázar. Revista Iberoamericana, 1968, 34:323-330.

11, 469. _____. Realidad y fantasía en la narrativa de Horacio Quiroga. Kentucky Foreign Language Q, 1964, 11:209-217.

11, 470. Moreno Villa, José. Los autores como actores. Mexico: Collegio de México, 1951.

11, 471. Morf, Gustav. The Rescue as an expression of Conrad's dual personality. Polish Rev, 1975, 20(2-3):211-216.

11, 472. _____. Der Symbolismus im Werke Joseph Conrads. Psychologische Rundschau, 1931, 2:356-361.

11, 473. Morgan, Ellen E. Alienation of the woman writer in The Golden Notebook. In Pratt, A. V., & Dembo, L. S. (eds), Doris Lessing; Critical Studies. Madison: Univ. Wisconsin Press, 1974, 54-63; Contemporary Lit, 1973, 14:471-480.

11, 474. _____. The feminist novel of androgynous fantasy. Frontiers: J Women's Studies, 1977, 2(3):40-49.

11, 475. _____. The veiled lady: the secret love of Miles Coverdale. Nathaniel Hawthorne J, 1971, 1:169-181.

11, 476. Morgan, Joyce P. The Impact of Psychoanalytical Theories on the Later Work of Thomas Mann. London: Univ. College, n. d.

11, 477. Morin, J., & Ravaud, G. Passion morbide, imagination et anomalies des conduites. Annales Médico-Psychologiques, 1957, 1:837-864.

11, 478. Morin-Gauthier, Francine. La Psychiatrie dans l'oeuvre littéraire de Guy de Maupassant. Thèse médecine. Paris: Jouve, 1944.

11, 479. Morishige, Alyce H. K. The Theme of the Self in Modern Japanese Fiction: Studies on Dazai, Mishima, Abé, and Kawabata. DAI, 1971, 31:6065A-66A.

11, 480. Morita, Shoji. Steinbeck's view of womanhood: the meaning of 'the time of waiting' in The Long Valley. Studies in Amer Lit, 1972, 8:39-52.

11, 481. Morley, Patricia A. Doppelganger's dilemma: artist and man in 'The Vivisector.' Queen's Q, 1971, 78:407-420.

11, 482. Morreale, G. Meursault's absurd act. French Rev, 1967, 40:456-462.

11, 483. Morris, Christopher D. Barth and Lacan: the world of the Moebius strip. Critique: Studies in Modern Fiction, 1975, 17(1):69-77.

11, 484. Morris, Robert K., & Malin, Irving (eds). The Achievement of William Styron. Berkeley: Univ. California Press, 1975.

11, 485. Morris, Ruth. The novel as catharsis. Psychoanal Rev, 1944, 31:88-104.

11, 486. Morris, Thomas M. Desire against Culture: Studies in the Literary and Psychohistorical Context of Lady Chatterley's Lover. DAI, 1978, 38:5463-64A.

11, 487. Morris, William E. The conversion of Scrooge: a defense of that good man's motivation. Studies in Short Fiction, 1965, 3:46-55.

11, 488. Morrison, Claudia C. Poe's 'Ligeia': an analysis. Studies in Short Fiction, 1967, 4:234-244.

11, 489. Morrison, Ian R. Emotional involvement and the failure of analysis in Adolphe. Neophilologus, 1976, 60:334-341.

11, 490. Morrison, Kristen. Lawrence, Beardsley, Wilde: The White Peacock and sexual ambiguity. Western Humanities Rev, 1976, 30:241-248.

11, 491. Morrison, Robert W. The Short Stories of Ernest Hemingway: A Search for Love and Identity. DAI, 1970, 30: 3018A-19A.

11, 492. Morriss, Margaret. The elements transcended. Canadian Lit, 1969, 42:56-71.

11, 493. Morrissette, Bruce A. The alienated 'I' in fiction. Southern Rev, 1974, 10:15-30.

11, 494. _____. Oedipus and existentialism: Les Gommes of Robbe-Grillet. Wisconsin Studies in Contemporary Lit, 1960, 1:43-74.

11, 495. _____. Les Romans de Robbe-Grillet. Paris: Minuet, 1963.

11, 496. Morrissette, Laurence. The family as fantasy system in Mauriac's Le Noeud de vipères. Rocky Mountain Rev of Language & Lit, 1977, 31:84-93.

11, 497. Morrow, Patrick D. The womb image in Vonnegut's Cat's Cradle. Notes on Contemporary Lit, 1976, 6(5):11-13.

11, 498. Mortensen, Klaus P. Sonderinger i Herman Bangs romaner. Vinten: Stjernbøger, 1973.

11, 499. Mortimer, Gail L. 'Fear death by water': the boundaries of the self in Jerzy Kosinski's The Painted Bird. Psychoanal Rev, 1976-77, 63:511-528.

11, 500. Mortimer, Ruth. Dostoevski and the dream. Modern Philology, 1956, 54:106-116.

11, 501. Mortland, Donald E. The conclusion of Sons and Lovers: a reconsideration. Studies in the Novel, 1971, 3:305-315.

11, 502. Moser, Thomas C. Towards The Good Soldier--discovery of a sexual theme. Daedalus, 1963, 92:312-325.

11, 503. _____. What is the matter with Emily Jane? Conflicting impulses in Wuthering Heights. Nineteenth Century Fiction, 1962, 17:1-19.

11, 504. Moskos, George Michael. The Individual and Individuation in Flaubert's Fiction: A Jungian Analysis. DAI, 1976, 36:6736A-38A.

11, 505- Moskowitz, Moshe. Shrub in the desert: Hebrew fiction
6. at the turn of the century. Jewish Social Studies, 1974, 36:301-315.

11, 507. Moss, Harold Gene. The surgeon's mate: Tobias Smollett and The Adventures of Roderick Random. In Peschel, E. R. (ed), Medicine and Literature. NY: Watson, 1980, 35-44.

11,508.   Moss, Howard. Dying: an introduction. New Yorker,
          1971, 47:73-75.
11,509.   _____. The Magic Lantern of Marcel Proust. NY:
          Macmillan, 1962; NY: Grosset & Dunlap, 1962.
11,510.   Moss, John G. Patterns of Isolation in English Canadian
          Fiction. DAI, 1974, 34:7770A.
11,511.   _____. Sex and Violence in the Canadian Novel: The
          Ancestral Present. Toronto: McClelland & Stewart,
          1977; Reviews: Z. Pollock, J Canadian Studies, 1979,
          14:114-121; J. Lennox, Canadian Lit, 1978, 78:65-68.
11,512.   Moss, Judith P. The body as symbol in Saul Bellow's
          Henderson the Rain King. Lit & Psychol, 1970, 20:51-
          61.
11,513.   Moss, Leonard. A key to the door image in 'The Meta-
          morphosis.' Modern Fiction Studies, 1971, 17:37-42.
11,514.   Moss, Martha N. Balzac: Sexual Polarity and the Origins
          of Character. DAI, 1975, 36:1562A.
11,515.   _____. The masks of men and women in Balzac's
          Comédie humaine. French Rev, 1976, 50:446-453.
11,516.   Moss, Robert F. Adolescence in Kipling. DAI, 1975, 35:
          6150A.
11,517.   Moss, Walter G. Why the anxious fear? Aging and death
          in the works of Turgenev. In Spicker, S. F., Wood-
          ward, K. M., & Van Tassel, D. D. (eds), Aging and the
          Elderly. Atlantic Highlands, NJ: Humanities, 1978,
          241-260.
11,518.   Mossman, E. D. Dostoevskij's early works: the more
          than rational distortion. Slavic & East European J,
          1966, 10:270-274.
11,519.   Mottram, Eric. Mississippi Faulkner's glorious mosaic of
          impotence and madness. J Amer Studies, 1968, 2:121-
          129.
11,520.   _____. Orpheus and measured forms: law, madness
          and reticence in Melville. In Pullin, F. (ed), New
          Perspectives on Melville. Kent, Ohio: Kent State Univ.
          Press, 1978, 229-254.
11,521.   Mottram, Richard Allen. Hawthorne's Men: Their Domi-
          nant Influence. DAI, 1975, 35:5419A.
11,522.   Mottram, V. H. Psycho-analysis in life and art. Univ.
          Magazine, 1915.
11,523.   Motyljowa, T. Innerer Monolog und 'Bewusstseinsstrom.'
          Kunst und Literatur, 1965, 13:603-617.
11,524.   Mouchard, Claude. Le Docteur Froid. Critique, 1976,
          32:311-316.
11,525.   Mouillaud, G. 'Le Rouge et le Noir' de Stendhal: le ro-
          man possible. Paris: Larousse, 1973.
11,526.   Mounin, Georges. Mythologies de l'adolescence dans le
          roman contemporain. In Prévost, J. (ed), Problèmes
          du Roman. Lyon: Confluences, 1943, 36-52.
11,527.   Mount, Ferdinand. Peter Handke, and alienation--fiction.
          Encounter, 1978, 50:33-37.
11,528.   Moutote, Daniel. Dostoïevski et Gide. Rev d'Histoire Lit-
          téraire de la France, 1976, 76:768-793.

11, 529. _____. L'Expression de l'égotisme dans les romans de Stendhal. Cahiers de l'Association Internationale des Etudes Françaises, 1974, 26:203-218.

11, 530. Mowrer, O. Hobart. The life and work of Edgar Allan Poe--a study in conscience-killing. In Learning Theory and Personality Dynamics: Selected Papers. NY: Ronald, 1950, 617-670.

11, 531. Moynihan, Julian. The hero's guilt, the case of Great Expectations. Essays in Criticism, 1960, 10:60-79.

11, 532. Moynihan, Robert D. Clarissa and the enlightened woman as literary heroine. J History Ideas, 1975, 36:159-166.

11, 533. Mukherjee, Asinek. The split personality of E. M. Forster. Quest (Bombay), 1968, 56:49-55.

11, 534. Muldrow, Mary T. The Psychology of Family Relationships in the Works of André Gide. Doctoral dissertation, Duke Univ., 1954.

11, 535. Muller, Charles H. Graham Greene: the melodramatic character. Unisa English Studies, 1974, 12(3):31-37.

11, 536. Muller, Gilbert H. In Our Time: Hemingway and the discontents of civilization. Renascence, 1977, 29:185-192.

11, 537. Muller, H. J. The new psychology in the old fiction. Saturday Rev, 1937, 16.

11, 538. Müller, J. Die Figur des Trinkers in der deutschen Literature seit dem Naturalismus. Psychiatrie, Neurologie und medizinische Psychologie, 1969, 21:201-211.

11, 539. Müller-Hegemann, D. Uber die Beziehungen der Psychopathologie zur Literatur. Neurologie und medizinische Psychologie, 1953.

11, 540. Mulqueen, James E. Light in August, motion, Eros and death. Notes on Mississippi Writers, 1975, 7(3):91-98.

11, 541. Munck, K. Gyllenstens roller, En studie över tematik och gestaltning i Lars Gyllenstens författarskap. Lund: Gleerup, 1974.

11, 542. Mundhenk, Rosemary K. Another World: The Mode of Fantasy in the Fiction of Selected Nineteenth-Century Writers. DAI, 1973, 33:5688A.

11, 543. Mundy, J. Women in rage: a psychological look at the helpless heroine. In Unger, R. K. , & Denmark, F. L. (eds), Woman: Dependent or Independent Variable? NY: Psychological Dimensions, 1979, Ch. 13.

11, 544. Munn, Carol. Dickens and Gissing as radical feminists. Gissing Newsletter, 1972, 8(2):1-17.

11, 545- Münzer, A. Dostojewski als Psychopathologe. Berliner
6. klinisch-therapeutische Wochenschrift, 1914, 51:1943-1945.

11, 547. Muradian, Thaddeus. The world of Updike. English J, 1965, 54:577-584.

11, 548. Murch, A. C. Eric Berne's Games and Nathalie Sarraute's Tropismes. Australian J French Studies, 1971, 8:62-83.

11, 549. Murdaugh, Elaine. Thomas Mann and the bitch goddess: rejection and reconstruction of the primal mother in

Joseph and His Brothers. Rev des Langues Vivantes, 1977, 44:395-407.

11, 550. Murphy, Earl Paulus. Thomas Pynchon's V.: A Psycho-Structural Study. DAI, 1978, 38:5464A-65A.

11, 551. Murphy, Elizabeth Jane Scott. Metaphor of Negation: The Castration Motif (A Study of the Structural Unity in the Novels and Tales of Gustave Flaubert). DAI, 1978, 39: 1623A-24A.

11, 552. Murphy, Gardner. Jack London on transmigration. Epilony. In London, J., The Star Rover. NY: Macmillan, 1963, 317-321.

11, 553. Murphy, George D. Hemingway's The Sun Also Rises. Explicator, 1969, 28:3.

11, 554. _____. Hemingway's wasteland: the controlling water symbolism of The Sun Also Rises. Hemingway Notes, 1971, 1(1):20-26.

11, 555. _____. The theme of sublimation in Anderson's Winesburg, Ohio. Modern Fiction Studies, 1968, 13:237-246.

11, 556. _____. The unconscious dimension of Tender Is the Night. Studies in the Novel, 1973, 5:314-323.

11, 557. _____, & Cherry, Carolyn L. Flannery O'Connor and the integration of personality. Flannery O'Connor Bulletin, 1978, 7:85-100.

11, 558. Murphy, Mary Janice. Dickens 'Other Women': The Mature Women in His Novels. DAI, 1976, 36:6709A-10A.

11, 559. Murray, Henry A. Bartleby and I. In Vincent, H. P. (ed), Melville Annual 1965. Kent, Ohio: Kent State Univ. Press, 1966.

11, 560. _____. In nomine diaboli. New England Q, 1951; Psychol Today, 1968, 2(4):64 passim.

11, 561. _____. Introduction to Herman Melville's Pierre, or the Ambiguities. NY: Farrar, Straus, 1949.

11, 562. Murrill, V., & Marks, William S., III. Kafka's 'The Judgement' and The Interpretation of Dreams. Germanic Rev, 1973, 48:212-228.

11, 563. Musatti, Cesare L. 'Gradiva.' Un Racconto di Wilhelm Jensen e uno Studio Analitico di Sigmund Freud con un Commento di Musatti. Turin: Boringhieri, 1961.

11, 564. _____. Svevo e la psicoanalisi. Belfagor, 1973, 28: 129-141.

11, 565. Muschg, Walter. Gotthelf. Die Geheimnisse des Erzählers. Munich: 1931.

11, 566. Musgrave, Marian E. Sexual excess and deviation as structured devices in Günter Grass's Blechtrommel and Ishmael Reed's Free-Lance Pallbearers. College Language Assn J, 1979, 10:139-166.

11, 567. Musto, David F. Sherlock Holmes and heredity. JAMA, 1966, 196:45-49.

11, 568. _____. Sherlock Holmes and Sigmund Freud: a study in cocaine. JAMA, 1968, 204:27-32; In Byck, R. (ed), Cocaine Papers by Sigmund Freud. NY: Stonehill, 1974, 355-370.

11, 569. Mutti, Giuliana. Female roles and the function of art in The Golden Notebook. Massachusetts Studies in English, 1972, 3: 78-83.

11, 570. Mužina, Matej. Reverberations of Jung's Psychological Types in the novels of Aldous Huxley. Studia Romanica et Anglica Zagrabiensia, 1972-73, 33-36:305-334.

11, 571. Myers, David. Sexual love and caritas in Thomas Mann. J English Germanic Philology, 1969, 68: 593-604.

11, 572. Myers, Sylvia H. Womanhood in Jane Austen's novels. Novel: A Forum on Fiction, 1970, 3: 225-232.

11, 573. Myers, W. F. T. Politics and personality in Felix Holt. Renaissance & Modern Studies, 1966, 10: 5-33.

11, 574. Myhren, Dagne Groven. Diktning og kulturpsykologi: En studie i Hans E. Kincks novelle: Mot ballade. Edda, 1976, 319-341.

11, 575. Nadeau, Robert L. Nightwood and the Freudian unconscious. Int Fiction Rev, 1975, 2: 159-163.

11, 576. Nagel, James. Yossarian, the old man, and the ending of Catch-22. In Critical Essays on Catch-22. Encino, Cal: Dickinson, 1974, 164-174.

11, 577. Nägele, Rainer. Theater und kein gutes: Rollenpsychologie und Theatersymbolik in Heinrich Manns Roman Der Untertan. Colloquia Germanica, 1973, 7: 28-49.

11, 578. Nakamura, K. Die psychologische Entwicklung des Grünen Heinrich in der Knabenzeit. Das deutsche Buch, No. 6, n. d.

11, 579. Nance, William L. 'The Beast in the Jungle': two versions of Oedipus. Studies in Short Fiction, 1976, 13: 433-440.

11, 580. _____. Eden, Oedipus, and rebirth in American fiction. Arizona Q, 1975, 31: 353-365.

11, 581. Napier, Elizabeth R. Aylmer as 'Scheidekünstler': the pattern of union and separation in Hawthorne's 'The Birthmark.' South Atlantic Bulletin, 1976, 41(4): 32-35.

11, 582. Naremore, James. The World Without a Self. Virginia Woolf and the Novel. New Haven: Yale Univ. Press, 1973.

11, 583. Nash, Charles Crawford. The Theme of Human Isolation in the Works of Eudora Welty. DAI, 1976, 37: 314A-15A.

11, 584. Natanson, Maurice. Being-in-reality. Philosophy & Phenomenological Research, 1959, 20: 231-237.

11, 585. Natella, A. A. Symbolic color in Borges. J Spanish Studies: Twentieth Century, 1974, 11: 38-48.

11, 586. Nathan, J. La Morale de Proust. Paris: Nizet, 1953.

11, 587. Natov, Roni L. The Strong-Minded Heroine in Mid-Victorian Fiction. DAI, 1975, 36: 3696A-97A.

11, 588. Naughton, Helen Thomas. A contemporary views Proust. L'Esprit créateur, 1965, 5: 48-55.

11, 589. Naumann, W. The individual and society in the work of Hermann Hesse. Monatshefte, 1949, 41: 33-42.

11, 590.   Navarro Tomás, Tomás.   La lengua de Galdós.   Revista
           Hispánica Moderna, 1943, 9:289-313.
11, 591.   Nayrac, Paul.   L'Angoisse de Saint-Exupéry, discours
           prononce a la séance inaugurale du congres de psychi-
           atrie et de neurologie de langue française, Strasbourg,
           21-26 juillet 1958.   Cahors, Impr. A.   Couselant, 1958,
           24p.
11, 592.   Nebeker, Helen E.   The pear tree: sexual implications in
           Katherine Mansfield's 'Bliss. '   Modern Fiction Studies,
           1972-73, 18:545-551.
11, 593.   Neesen, Peter.   Vom Louvrezirkel zum 'Prozess': Franz
           Kafka und die Psychologie Franz Brentanos.   Göppingen:
           Kümmerle, 1972.
11, 594.   Neff, Rebecca Kinnamon.   New mysticism in the writings
           of May Sinclair and T. S. Eliot.   Twentieth Century Lit,
           1980, 26:82-108.
11, 595.   Neider, Charles.   The cabalists.   In Flores, A. (ed), The
           Kafka Problem.   NY: New Directions, 1946, 398-445.
11, 596.   _____.   The Frozen Sea: A Study of Franz Kafka.
           NY: Oxford Univ. Press, 1948.
11, 597.   _____.   Kafka: His Mind and Art.   London: Routledge
           & Kegan Paul, 1949.
11, 598.   Nelson, Benjamin F.   Sartre, Genet, Freud.   Psychoanal
           Rev, 1963, 50:155-171.
11, 599.   Nelson, Carl W. , Jr.   Brown's Manichean mock-heroic:
           the ironic self in a hyperbolic world.   West Virginia
           Univ. Philological Papers, 1973, 20:26-42.
11, 600.   _____.   A method for madness: the symbolic patterns
           in Arthur Mervyn.   West Virginia Univ. Philological
           Papers, 1975, 22:29-50.
11, 601.   Nelson, Donald F.   Portrait of the Artist as Hermes: A
           Study of Myth and Psychology in Thomas Mann's 'Felix
           Krull. '   Chapel Hill: Univ. North Carolina Press, 1971.
11, 602.   _____.   Stylistic Unity and Change in Thomas Mann's
           Felix Krull: A Study of Style as the Reflection of Per-
           ception and Attitude.   DA, 1966, 27(3-A):779.
11, 603.   Nelson, Gayle.   The double standard in adolescent novels.
           English J, 1975, 64(2):53-55.
11, 604.   Nelson, Jane A.   Form and Image in the Fiction of Henry
           Miller.   Detroit: Wayne State Univ. Press, 1970; DA,
           1967, 67-15, 731.
11, 605.   Nelson, John Charles.   Love and sex in The Decameron.
           In Mahoney, E. P. (ed), Philosophy and Humanism.
           NY: Columbia Univ. Press, 1976, 339-351.
11, 606.   Nelson, John H.   The Negro Character in American Liter-
           ature.   Lawrence: Univ. Kansas Press, 1926.
11, 607.   Nelson, William (ed).   William Golding's Lord of the
           Flies: A Source Book.   NY: Odyssey, 1963.
11, 608.   Nemoianu, Virgil.   The semantics of Bramble's hypochon-
           dria: a connection between illness and style in the
           eighteenth century.   Clio, 1979, 9:39-52.
11, 609.   Nettelbeck, C. W.   The obsessional dream world of Georges
           Bernanos.   J Australasian Universities Language & Lit
           Assn, 1966, 26:242-253.

11, 610.   Neuhäuser, Rudolf.   Social reality and the hero in Dostoev-
           skij's early works: Dostoevskij and Fourier's psycho-
           logical system.   Russian Lit, 1973, 4:18-36.
11, 611.   Neumann, Dwight K.   Excremental fantasies and shame in
           Quevedo's Buscón.   Lit & Psychol, 1978, 28:186-191.
11, 612.   Neumann, Erich.   [Franz Kafka: The Judgment: a depth
           psychological interpretation.]   Analytische Psychologie,
           1974, 5:252-306.
11, 613.   _____.   Kafka's The Trial: an interpretation through
           depth psychology.   In Creative Man: Five Essays.
           Princeton: Princeton Univ. Press, 1980, 3-112.
11, 614.   Neumarkt, Paul.   Chamisso's Peter Schlemihl.   A literary
           approach in terms of analytical psychology.   Lit & Psy-
           chol, 1967, 17:120-127.
11, 615.   _____.   Kafka's A Hunger Artist: the ego in isolation.
           Amer Imago, 1970, 27:109-120.
11, 616.   Neumeister, Dorothea.   Zwischen Mythos und Psychologie:
           Zur Jubiläums-Wanderausstellung des Züricher Thomas
           Mann--Archivs.   Börsenblatt für den Deutschen Buch-
           andel, 1975, 31 (26 Sept):A295-297.
11, 617.   Neumeyer, P. F.   Franz Kafka and Jonathan Swift: a sym-
           biosis.   Dalhousie Rev, 1965, 45:60-65.
11, 618.   Neuscheler, K.   Leo Tolstoi und die Russen als Psycho-
           logen.   Zeitschrift für Menschenkunde, 1928, 4:179-187.
11, 619.   Neuse, Werner.   'Erlebte Rede' und 'inner' Monolog in
           den erzählenden Schriften Arthur Schnitzlers.   PMLA,
           1934, 49:352- .
11, 620.   Newberry, Wilma.   Ramón Pérez de Ayala's concept of the
           Doppelgänger in Belarmino y Apolonio.   Symposium,
           1980, 34:56-67.
11, 621.   Newlin, Paul A.   The Uncanny in the Supernatural Short
           Fiction of Poe, Hawthorne, and James.   DA, 1968, 28,
           68-7479.
11, 622.   _____.   'Vague shapes of the borderland':   the place of
           the uncanny in Hawthorne's gothic vision.   Emerson So-
           ciety Q, 1972, 18(2):83-96.
11, 623.   Newman, Paul B.   The Jew as existentialist.   North Amer
           Rev, 1965, 2(3):45-55.
11, 624.   Newman, Pauline.   Marcel Proust et l'existentialisme.
           Paris: Nouvelle Edit Latines, 1952.
11, 625.   Newton, Caroline.   Thomas Mann and Sigmund Freud.
           Princeton Univ. Library Chronicle, 1963, 24:135-139.
11, 626.   Newton, Olin, & Pollock, Sandy.   The application of learn-
           ing theory to the character evaluation of Dr. B. in
           Schachnovelle.   South Central Bulletin, 1969, 29:145-
           147.
11, 627.   Neyraut-Sutterman, Thérèse.   Parricide et épilepsie: a
           propos d'un article de Freud sur Dostoievski.   Rev
           Française de Psychanalyse, 1970, 34:635-652.
11, 628.   Nicolas, L. I. R. J.   Marcel Proust et la femme: essai de
           critique médico-psychologique.   Bordeaux: Cadoret,
           1931.
11, 629.   Nichols, Beverly B.   Image of social workers in fiction.
           Social Work, 1979, 24:419-420.

11, 630. Nichols, Marianna da Vinci. Women on women: the look-
          ing glass novel. Univ. Denver Q, 1976, 11(3):1-13.
11, 631. Niderst, A. 'La Princesse de Clèves, ' le roman para-
          doxal. Paris: Larousse, 1973.
11, 632. Niederland, William G. The birth of H. G. Wells's Time
          Machine. Amer Imago, 1978, 35:106-112.
11, 633. _____. The first application of psychoanalysis to a lit-
          erary work. Psychoanal Q, 1960, 29:228-235.
11, 634. Niess, R. J. Emile Zola: la femme au travail. In La
          Description: Sue, Nodier, Flaubert, Hugo, Verne,
          Zola, Alexis, Fénéon. Lille: L'Univ. de Lille III,
          1974, 40-58; Cahiers Naturalistes, 1976, 50:40-58.
11, 635. Niess, Robert J. Pierre et Jean: some symbols. French
          Rev, 1959, 32:511-519.
11, 636. Nilles, Mary. Craddock's girls: a look at some unliberated
          women. Markham Rev, 1972, 3(4):74-77.
11, 637. Nilsen, Helge Normann. Anti-Semitism and persecution
          complex: a comment on Saul Bellow's The Victim.
          English Studies, 1979, 60:183-191.
11, 638. Nin, Anaïs. The Novel of the Future. NY: Macmillan,
          1970.
11, 639. Nissman, Albert. An Investigation into the Image of the
          Teacher as Reflected in Selected American Short Stories
          Published Between 1900-1964. DA, 1966, 27(3-A):751.
11, 640. Nmolim, Charles E. Jungian archetypes and the main
          characters in Dyono's Une Vie de boy. In Jones, E. D.
          (ed), African Literature Today. No. 7: Focus on
          Criticism. A Review. NY: Africana, 1975, 117-122.
11, 641. Noakes, S. Self-reading and temporal irony in Aurélia.
          Studies in Romanticism, 1977, 16:101-119.
11, 642. Noble, David W. The analysis of alienation by 20th cen-
          tury social scientists and 19th century novelists: the
          example of Hawthorne's The Scarlet Letter. In Gorli-
          er, C. (ed), Studi e ricerche di letteratura inglese e
          americana. Milan: Cisalpino-Goliardica, 1969, 5-19.
11, 643. Noel, Daniel C. The Portent Unwound: Religious and
          Psychological Development in the Imagery of Herman
          Melville 1819-1854. DA, 1967, 28:1791A.
11, 644. _____. Tales of fictive power: dreaming and imagina-
          tion in Ronald Sukenick's postmodern fiction. Boundary
          2, 1976, 5:117-135.
11, 645. Noel-Bentley, Peter C. Review: John G. Moss's Patterns
          of Isolation. J Canadian Fiction, 1974, 3(3):116-119.
11, 646. Noffsinger, John W. Dream in The Old Curiosity Shop.
          South Atlantic Bulletin, 1977, 42(2):23-34.
11, 647. Nøjgaard, Morten. Pskologi i romanen: Om at analysere
          følelser. In Gerlach-Nielsen, M. , et al. (eds), Roman-
          teori og romananalyse. Odense: Odense Universitats-
          forlag, 1977, 79-89.
11, 648. Noland, Richard W. Lunacy and poetry: Elliott Baker's
          A Fine Madness. Critique: Studies in Modern Fiction,
          1966, 8(3):71-78.
11, 649. _____. Psychology and fiction. Hartford Studies in
          Lit, 1975, 7:26-32.

11, 650. Noma, Hiroshi. [The battle against the subconscious.] In
          Ito, S. (ed), [A Study of Joyce.] Tokyo: Eihosha,
          1955, 1965, 283-298.
11, 651. Nonaka, Ryo. Faulkner's 'stream of consciousness.'
          Studies in English Lit (Tokyo), 1959, 36:179-180.
11, 652. Norden, Ernest E. The figure of the father in the ro-
          mances of Chrétien de Troyes. South Central Bulletin,
          1978, 38:155-157.
11, 653. Normand, Jean. Conscience: its psychology. In Nathaniel
          Hawthorne: An Approach to an Analysis of Artistic Cre-
          ation. Cleveland: Case Western Reserve Univ. Press,
          1970, 212-236; In Nathaniel Hawthorne: Esquisse d'une
          analyse de la création artistique. Paris: Presses Uni-
          versitaires de France, 1964.
11, 654. Norris, Margot C. The Decentered Universe of Finnegans
          Wake: A Structuralist Analysis. Baltimore: Johns
          Hopkins Univ. Press, 1976; Review: Jay Fox, Lit &
          Psychol, 1979, 29:134-136.
11, 655. _____. The language of dream in Finnegans Wake.
          Lit & Psychol, 1974, 24:4-11.
11, 656. _____. Sadism and masochism in two Kafka stories:
          'In der Strafkolonie' und 'Ein Hungerkünstler.' MLN,
          1978, 93:430-447.
11, 657. Norris, Nancy. The Hamlet, The Town and The Mansion:
          a psychological reading of the Snopes trilogy. Mosaic,
          1973, 7:213-235.
11, 658. Norton, Charles A. The alcoholic content of A Farewell
          to Arms. Fitzgerald-Hemingway Annual, 1973, 309-
          314.
11, 659. Norton, Rictor Carl. Aesthetic Gothic horror. Yearbook
          Comparative General Lit, 1972, 21:31-40.
11, 660. _____. 'The Turn of the Screw': coincidentia opposi-
          torum. Amer Imago, 1971, 28:373-390.
11, 661. Nossen, Evon. The beast-man theme in the work of John
          Steinbeck. Ball State Univ. Forum, 1966, 7:52-64.
11, 662. Novak, Maximillian E. The extended moment: time,
          dream, history, and perspective in eighteenth-century
          fiction. In Backscheider, P.R. (ed), Probability, Time,
          and Space in Eighteenth-Century Literature. NY: AMS
          Press, 1979, 141-166.
11, 663. Novitz, David. Fiction, imagination and emotion. JAAC,
          1980, 38:279-288.
11, 664. Novotny, P. A poetic corroboration of psychoanalysis.
          Amer Imago, 1965, 22:40-46.
11, 665. Nuccitelli, Angela. A Rebours's symbol of the 'Femme-
          Fleur': a key to Des Esseintes's obsession. Symposi-
          um, 1974, 28:336-345.
11, 666. Nurmela, T. La Misogynie chez Boccace. In Tournoy,
          G. (ed), Boccaccio in Europe. Leuven Univ. Press,
          1977, 191-196.
11, 667. Nwoga, D. Ibe. Alienation in modern African fiction.
          The Muse, 1973, 5:23-27.

11, 668.   Oates, Joyce Carol.   The double vision of The Brothers
            Karamazov.   JAAC, 1968, 27:203-212.
11, 669.   _____.   Tragic vision of The Possessed.   Georgia Rev,
            1978, 32:868-393.
11, 670.   Ober, William B.   Lady Chatterley's what?   Bulletin Acad-
            emy Medicine New Jersey, 1969, 15:41-65.
11, 671.   Oberndorf, Clarence P.   The Psychiatric Novels of Oliver
            Wendell Holmes.   NY: Columbia Univ. Press, 1946;
            Westport, Conn: Greenwood Press, 1971.
11, 672.   _____.   The psychoanalytic insight of Nathaniel Haw-
            thorne.   Psychoanal Rev, 1942, 29:373-385.
11, 673.   O'Brien, Darcy.   A critique of psychoanalytic criticism,
            or what Joyce did and did not do.   James Joyce Q,
            1976, 13:275-292.
11, 674.   _____.   Joyce and sexuality.   Twentieth Century Stud-
            ies, 1969, 2:32-38.
11, 675.   _____.   Some determinants of Molly Bloom.   In Staley,
            T. F. , & Benstock, B. (eds), Approaches to Ulysses.
            Ten Essays.   Pittsburgh: Univ. Pittsburgh Press,
            1970, 137-155.
11, 676.   _____.   Some psychological determinants of Joyce's
            view of love and sex.   In Senn, F. (ed), New Light on
            Joyce from the Dublin Symposium.   Bloomington: Indi-
            ana Univ. Press, 1972, 15-27.
11, 677.   O'Brien, Justin.   Albertine the ambiguous: notes on
            Proust's transposition of sexes.   PMLA, 1950, 65:653;
            1949, 64:932-952. In Contemporary French Literature.
            New Brunswick, NJ: Rutgers Univ. Press, 1971, 85-
            114.
11, 678.   _____.   La Mémoire involontaire avant Proust.   Rev de
            Littérature Comparée, 1939, 19:19-36; Involuntary mem-
            ory before Proust. In Contemporary French Literature.
            New Brunswick, NJ: Rutgers Univ. Press, 1971, 28-
            47.
11, 679.   _____.   The Novel of Adolescence in France; The Study
            of a Literary Theme.   NY: Columbia Univ. Press,
            1937.
11, 680.   _____.   Proust confirmed by neurosurgery.   PMLA,
            1970, 85:295-297; In Contemporary French Literature.
            New Brunswick, NJ: Rutgers Univ. Press, 1971, 265-
            271.
11, 681.   _____.   Proust, Gide and the sexes III.   PMLA, 1950,
            65, 648-653.
11, 682.   Ochsborn, Judith.   Mothers and daughters in ancient Near
            Eastern literature.   In Davidson, C. N. , & Broner,
            E. M. (eds), The Lost Tradition.   NY: Ungar, 1980,
            5-14.
11, 683.   O'Connor, Lee F.   Review: Malcolm Cowley and the
            house of failure.   Lit & Psychol, 1974, 24:167-170.
11, 684.   O'Connor, Patricia W.   Eros and Thanatos in Francisco
            García Pavón's El último sábado.   J Spanish Studies:
            Twentieth Century, 1975, 3:175-185.

11, 685. O'Daniel, Therman D.   James Baldwin: an interpretive
          study. College Language Assn J, 1963, 7:37-47.
11, 686. Odumu, Ocheibi. Women talk about women: the image of
          women in the novels of Jane Austen and Emily Brontë.
          Horizon, 1973, 9:47-54.
11, 687. Ogilvie, D. M.   The Icarus complex. Psychol Today, 1968,
          2(4):31.
11, 688. Oglesby, Carl. Melville, or water consciousness and its
          madness: a fragment from a work-in-progress. In
          White, G. A. , & Newman, C. (eds), Literature in Revo-
          lution. NY: Holt, Rinehart, & Winston, 1972, 123-
          141.
11, 689. Ohmann, Richard.   Literature as sentences. College Eng-
          lish, 1966, 27.
11, 690. Øhrgaard, P.   Rifbjergs Du skall ikke vaere ked af det,
          Amalia. Kritik, 1974, 30:58-65.
11, 691. Ojemann, R. H. , & Phillips, E. B.   Fiction as a guide to
          child development. Child Development, 1932, 3:342-345.
11, 692. Ojo-Ade, Femi. Madness in the African novel: Awoonor's
          This Earth, My Brother. African Lit Today, 1979,
          10:134-152.
11, 693. O'Kell, Robert Peter. Disraeli's Coningsby: political mani-
          festo or psychological romance? Victorian Studies,
          1979, 23:57-78.
11, 694. _____.   The Psychological Romance: Disraeli's Early
          Fiction and Political Apprenticeship. DAI, 1975, 35:
          7264A.
11, 695. Olan, Levi A.   The voice of the lonesome: alienation
          from Huck Finn to Holden Caulfield. Southwest Rev,
          1963, 48:143-150.
11, 696. Oliver, Charles M. , II.   Principles of 'True Felt Emo-
          tion' in Hemingway's Novels. DAI, 1971, 31:4787A.
11, 697. Olivero, Antonio. Fyodor Dostoevsky, Psychologist and
          Teacher: A Psychologico-Philosophical Study of The
          Brothers Karamazov and Its Implications. DA, 1968,
          29 (2-A):417.
11, 698. Olney, James Leslie.   Cards of Identity and the satiric
          mode. Studies in the Novel, 1971, 3:374-389.
11, 699. Olshin, Toby A.   'Thoughtful of the main chance': Defoe
          and the cycle of anxiety. Hartford Studies in Lit, 1974,
          117-128.
11, 700. Olson, Carol Booth.   Madness in the Contemporary Amer-
          ican Novel. DAI, 1977, 38:2793A.
11, 701. _____.   Mirrors and madness: A. G. Majtabai's Mun-
          drome. Critique, 1978, 20(2):71-82.
11, 702. Olson, Susanne. Das Wunderbare und seine psychologische
          Funktion in E. T. A. Hoffmanns Die Elixiere des Teufels.
          Mitteilungen der E. T. A. Hoffmann-Gesellschaft, 1978,
          24:26-35.
11, 703. O'Neill, John P.   Workable Design: Action and Situation
          in the Fiction of Henry James.   Port Washington, NY:
          Kennikat, 1973.
11, 704. O'Neill, M. W.   The Role of Myth in the Novels of B.
          Jarnés. DA, 1969, 30:332-A.

11, 705. O'Neill, Samuel J.   Interior monologue in Al Filo de Agus.
          Hispania, 1968, 51:447-456.
11, 706. _____. Psychological-Literary Techniques in Repre-
          sentative Contemporary Novels of Mexico.   DA, 1966,
          66-3071.
11, 707. Opdahl, Keith M.   'You'll be sorry when I'm dead':   child-
          adult relations in Huck Finn.   Modern Fiction Studies,
          1979-80, 25:613-624.
11, 708. Opland, J.   In defense of Philip Roth.   Theoria, 1974, 42:
          29-42.
11, 709. Oppenheim, D. E.   Zu Schillers Novelle Der Verbrecher
          aus verlorener Ehre.   Int Zeitschrift für Individual-
          psychologie, 1928, 6:358-362.
11, 710. Orage, Alfred R.   Psycho-analysis and the mysteries.   In
          Readers and Writers (1917-1921).   London: Allen &
          Unwin, 1922, 152-155.
11, 711. Ordon, M.   Unconscious contents in Bahnivärten Thiel.
          Germanic Rev, 1951, 26:223-229.
11, 712. Ordóñez, Elizabeth.   Forms of alienation in Matute's La
          trampa.   J Spanish Studies: Twentieth Century, 1976,
          4:179-189.
11, 713. Ordway, J. A.   Psychoanalytic comments on Thomas Hardy's
          The Return of the Native.   J Maine Medical Assn, 1974,
          65:65-68.
11, 714. O'Reilly, R. F.   Ritual, myth and symbol in Gide's L'Im-
          moraliste.   Symposium, 1974, 28:346-355.
11, 715. Origlia, Dino.   Aspetti psicologico e sociali di una nuova
          litteratura: la fantascienza.   Difesa Sociale, 1954, 33:
          87-98.
11, 716. Orrok, David H.   Lenormand's Don Juan.   Lit & Psychol,
          1956, 6:87-89.
11, 717. Orsagh, Jacqueline E.   Baldwin's female characters: a
          step forward.   In O'Daniel, T. B. (ed), James Baldwin:
          A Critical Evaluation.   Washington, D. C.:   Howard
          Univ. Press, 1977, 56-68.
11, 718. Ort, Daniel.   Lawrence's Women in Love.   Explicator,
          1969, 27:38.
11, 719. Ortal, Y.   La muerte en Julián del Casal.   Papeles de
          Son Armadans, 1969, 53:317-324.
11, 720. Ortali, Hélène.   Images of women in Balzac's La Cousine
          Bette.   Nineteenth Century French Studies, 1976, 4:194-
          205.
11, 721. Ortega, José.   Alienación y agresión en Juan Goytisolo:
          'Señas de identidad' y 'Reivindicación del conde don
          Julian.'   NY: Torres, 1972.
11, 722. _____. La alienación de la soledad en En el segundo
          hemisferio de Antonio Ferres.   Cuadernos Hispano-
          Americanos, 1972, No. 260:355-363.
11, 723. _____. Andrés Hurtado: un estudio en alienación.
          Cuadernos Hispano-Americanos, 1972, 265-67:591-599.
11, 724. _____. Arturo Barea, novelista español en busca de su
          identidad.   Symposium, 1971, 25:377-391.
11, 725. _____. Estudios sobre la obra de J. Benet.   Cuadernos
          Hispano-Americanos, 1974, 284:229-258.

11, 726. Ortega, Philip D. Fables of identity: stereotype and caricature of Chicanos in Steinbeck's Tortilla Flat. J Ethnic Studies, 1973, 1(1):39-43.

11, 727. Ortega y Gasset, José. The Dehumanization of Art and Notes on the Novel. Princeton: Princeton Univ. Press, 1948.

11, 728. Orvell, Miles D. The messianic sexuality of Miss Lonelyhearts. Studies Short Fiction, 1973, 10:159-167.

11, 729. Ossip-Lourié, (?). La Psychologie des romanciers Russes du XIXᵉ Siècle. Paris: Alcan, 1912.

11, 730. Ossipow, N. Die Memoiren eines Wahnsinnigen, ein unvollendetes Werk L. N. Tolstois, zur Frage des Angstaffektes. Psychotherapie, 1913, 4(3).

11, 731. _____. Die Psychotherapie in den literarischen Werken Tolstois. Psychotherapie, 1911, 1.

11, 732. _____. Psychotherapie in Romanen von Leo Tolstoi. Psychotherapie, 1919.

11, 733. Oster, Daniel. Un Roman de l'inconscient dans la rhétorique 'schizo.' Quinzaine Littéraire, 16-30 Apr 1977, no. 254, 10.

11, 734. Oster, E. Das Verhältnis von Mutter und Kind im englischen Roman von 1700-1800. Doctoral dissertation, Bonn Univ., 1923.

11, 735. Ostrov, Leon. Marcel Proust y el psicoanálisis. La Nacción (Buenos Aires), 10 April 1960, Section 3, p. 1.

11, 736. Oswald, V. A., Jr., & Mindess, V. P. Schnitzler's Fräulein Else and the psychoanalytic theory of neuroses. Germanic Rev, 1951, 26:279-288.

11, 737. Otto, Linda M. A Study of Evil and Insanity in Tieck's Early Works. DAI, 1974, 34:4277A.

11, 738. Ottosen, Jørgen. J. P. Jacobsen's 'Mogens.' Copenhagen: Gyldendal, 1968.

11, 739. Ottosen, Leo. H. C. Branners tidlige forfatterskab. Copenhagen: Gyldendal, 1974.

11, 740. Oughourlian, Jean-Michel, & Lefort, Guy. Psychotic structure and Girard's doubles. Diacritics, 1978, 8(1): 72-74.

11, 741. Overbeck, Pat Trefzger. The women in Augie March. Texas Studies in Lit & Language, 1968, 10:471-484.

11, 742. Overton, William J. Self and society in Trollope. J English Lit History, 1978, 45:285-302.

11, 743. Oviedo, José M. Los Cachorros: fragmento de una exploración total. Revista Iberoamericana, 1970, 36:25-38.

11, 744. Owen, A. L. Psychological aspects of Spanish realism. Hispania, 1931, 14:2-7.

11, 745. Ower, John. Sociology, psychology and satire in The Apprenticeship of Duddy Kravitz. Modern Fiction Studies, 1976, 22:413-428.

11, 746. Oyarzún, Luis A. Eros en las novelas sociales de Pérez Galdos. DAI, 1973, 34:737A.

11, 747. Pace, Jean.   Flaubert's image of woman.   Southern Rev,
          1977, 13:114-130.
11, 748. Pachmuss, T.   Dostoevsky, Werfel, and Virginia Woolf:
          influences and confluences.   Comparative Lit Studies,
          1972, 9:416-428.
11, 749. _____. The technique of dream logic in the works of
          Dostoevskij.   Slavic & East European J, n. s. , 1960,
          4:221-238.
11, 750. _____. The theme of love and life in Tolstoy's The
          Death of Ivan Ilyich.   Amer Slavic Rev, 1961, 20:72-83.
11, 751. Pacifici, Sergio.   Alberto Moravia: sex, money, and love
          in the novel.   In The Modern Italian Novel: From Pea
          to Moravia.   Carbondale: Southern Illinois Univ.
          Press, 1979, 200-239.
11, 752. Pacion, S. J.   Count Leo Tolstoy: sexuality denied.
          MAHS, 1970, 4:71.
11, 753. Páez, Ramiro.   'Benito Cereno':   La historia del motín
          del barco negrero en la bahía de Arauco.   Rivista del
          Pacifico, 1967, 4:106-116.
11, 754. Page, Alex.   A dangerous day: Mrs. Dalloway discovers
          her double.   Modern Fiction Studies, 1961-1962, 7:115-
          124.
11, 755. Page, Philip.   The Princess Casamassima: suicide and
          'the penetrating imagination. '   Tennessee Studies in
          Lit, 1978, 22:162-169.
11, 756. Page, Sally R.   Faulkner's sense of the sacred.   In
          Wolfe, G. H.   (ed), Fifty Years after the Marble Faun.
          Tuscaloosa: Univ. Alabama Press, 1976.
11, 757. _____. Faulkner's Women: Characterization and Mean-
          ing.   De Land, Fla: Everett /Edwards, 1972.
11, 758. _____. [The Marble Faun.]   In Wolfe, G. H.   (ed),
          Faulkner: Fifty Years after 'The Marble Faun. '   Uni-
          versity: Univ. Alabama Press, 1976.
11, 759. _____. Women in the Works of William Faulkner.
          DAI, 1970, 31:2396A.
11, 760. Pagès, Irène M.   Le Roman de l'existence et le thème de
          la séparation dans l'oeuvre de Simone de Beauvoir.
          DAI, 1972, 32:4628A.
11, 761. Paglia, Camille Ann.   Sexual Personae: The Androgyne
          in Literature and Art.   DAI, 1977, 38:3459A.
11, 762. Pagnini, Marcello.   Il demoniaco poesco: Saggio di psi-
          coanalisi letteraria.   In Curreli, M. , & Alberto, M.
          (eds), Critical Dimensions: English, German and Com-
          parative Literature Essays.   Cuneo: SASTE, 1978,
          333-348.
11, 763. Palley, Julian.   La estructura onírica de 'El enamorado
          y la muerte. '   Cuadernos Hispano-Americanos, 1975,
          298:190-196.
11, 764. Pallister, Charles.   Fate and madness: the determinist
          vision of Darl Bundren.   Amer Lit, 1978, 49:619-633.
11, 765. Palmer, Donald D.   Unamuno, Freud and the case of Alon-
          so Quijano.   Hispania, 1971, 54:243-249.

11, 766. Palmer, William J. Abelard's fate: sexual politics in Stendhal, Faulkner and Camus. Mosaic, 1974, 7(3):29-41.

11, 767. Palms, Rosemary H. G. The Double Motif in Literature: From Origins to an Examination of Three Modern American Novels. DAI, 1972, 33:321A.

11, 768. Pancost, David W. Hawthorne's epistemology and ontology. Emerson Society Q, 1973, 19:8-13.

11, 769. Pandini, Giancarlo. Lettura 'psicologica' delle Stanze di Libero Bigiaretti. Lettore di Provincia, 1978, 31-32: 17-23.

11, 770. Pandit, M. L. The motherly women in Barrie. Jammu & Kashmir Univ. Rev, 1964, 7:40-46.

11, 771. Panek, LeRoy L. Play and games: an approach to Poe's detective tales. Poe Studies, 1977, 10:39-41.

11, 772. Pankow, Gisela. Die 'Welt des Spiegels' in zwei modernen Novellen: Ein Beitrag zur Phänomenologie des Frei-todes. Literaturwissenschaftliches Jahrbuch der Gorres-Gesellschaft, 1963, 3:345-351.

11, 773. Panshin, Alexei. Heinlein in dimension. Riverside Q, 1966, 2:35-52, 90-104, 139-209, 284-297.

11, 774. Parani, Charles. Machado de Assis and Dostoevsky. Hispania, 1966, 49:81-87.

11, 775. Paris, Bernard J. Character and Conflict in Jane Austen's Novels: A Psychological Approach. Detroit: Wayne State Univ. Press, 1979.

11, 776. _____. 'A confusion of many standards': conflicting value systems in Tess of the D'Urbervilles. Nineteenth Century Fiction, 1969, 24:57-79.

11, 777. _____. Herzog the man: an analytic view of a literary figure. Amer J Psychoanal, 1976, 36:249-260.

11, 778. _____. Horney's theory and the study of literature. Amer J Psychoanal, 1978, 38:343-353.

11, 779. _____. The inner conflicts of Maggie Tolliver: a Horneyan analysis. Centennial Rev, 1969, 13:166-199.

11, 780. _____. Notes from Underground: a Horneyan analysis. PMLA, 1973, 88:511-535.

11, 781. _____. The psychic structure of Vanity Fair. Victorian Studies, 1967, 10:389-410.

11, 782. _____. A Psychological Approach to Fiction Studies in Thackeray, Stendhal, George Eliot, Dostoevsky and Conrad. Bloomington: Indiana Univ. Press, 1974; Reviews: Norman Friedman, Sewanee Rev, 1975, 83:172-190; Richard W. Noland, Hartford Studies in Lit, 1975, 7:26-32; David H. Stewart, Western Humanities Rev, 1975, 29:95-99.

11, 783. _____. Toward a revaluation of George Eliot's The Mill on the Floss. Nineteenth Century Fiction, 1956, 11:18-31.

11, 784. _____. The two selves of Rodion Raskolnikov: a Horneyan analysis. Gradiva, 1978, 1:316-328.

11, 785. Park, M. M. Archibald Malmaison: Julian Hawthorne's contribution to gothic fiction. Extrapolation, 1974, 15: 103-116.

11, 786. Park, R. J. Strong bodies, healthful regimens, and playful recreations as viewed by utopian authors of the 16th and 17th centuries. Research Q, 1978, 49:498-511.

11, 787. Park, William. Fathers and sons--Humphrey Clinker. Lit & Psychol, 1966, 16:166-174.

11, 788. _____. Tom and Oedipus. Hartford Studies in Lit, 1975, 7:207-215.

11, 789. Parkay, Forrest W. The influence of Nietzsche's Thus Spoke Zarathustra on London's The Sea Wolf. Jack London Newsletter, 1971, 4:16-24.

11, 790. Parker, Alexander A. The psychology of the 'Picaro' in El Buscon. Modern Language Rev, 1947, 42:58-69.

11, 791. Parker, Clifford S. The Defense of the Child by French Novelists. NY: Columbia Univ. Press, 1925.

11, 792. Parker, J. M. An aspect of metaphor in the novels of Graciliano Ramos. Univ. Poitiers, Centre de Recherches Latino-Américaines, 1975, (1976), 195-209.

11, 793. Parks, A. Franklin. Yorick's sympathy for the 'little': a measure of his sentimentality in Sterne's Sentimental Journey. Lit & Psychol, 1978, 28:119-124.

11, 794. Parte, Joel. The Romance in America: Studies in Cooper, Poe, Hawthorne, Melville, and James. Middletown, Conn: Wesleyan Univ. Press, 1969.

11, 795. Pascal, Roy. The autobiographical novel and the autobiography. Essays in Criticism, 1959, 9.

11, 796. _____. The Magic Mountain and Adorno's critique of the traditional novel. In Bullivant, K. (ed), Culture and Society in the Weimar Republic. Manchester, England: Manchester Univ. Press, 1977; Totowa, NJ: Rowman & Littlefield, 1978, 1-23.

11, 797. Pasche, F. La Mort et la folie dans l'oeuvre de Balzac. In A partir de Freud. Paris: Payot, 1969.

11, 798. Pasco, Allan H. The Color Keys to 'A la recherche du temps perdu. ' Geneva: Droz, 1976.

11, 799. _____. Proust's reader and the voyage of self-discovery. Contemporary Lit, 1977, 18:20-37.

11, 800. Pasquasy, R. L'Eidetisme dans Le Grand Meaulnes. Cahiers de Pédagogie de l'Université de Liège, 1947, 7:102-109.

11, 801. Patmore, Derek. D. H. Lawrence and the Dominant Male. London: Covent Garden Press, 1970.

11, 802. Patt, Gertrud. Der Kamp zwischen Vater und Sohn im englischen Roman des 20. Jahrhunderts. Emsdetten: Lechte, 1938.

11, 803. Patten, Karl. 'Psyc-lops?': H. Rumbold, Master Barber. James Joyce Q, 1975, 13:110-111.

11, 804. Patterson, Nancy-Lou. Archetypes of the mother in the fantasies of George MacDonald. In Goodknight, G. (ed), Mythcon I: Proceedings. Los Angeles: Mythopoeic Society, 1975, 14-20.

11, 805. Patterson, Robert G. Death on the Mississippi: Mark Twain's Huckleberry Finn. Psychol Perspectives, 1976, 7:9-22.

11, 806. Patterson, Yolanda M. A. Solitude and Communication in the Works of Jean-Paul Sartre and Albert Camus. DA, 1966, 24:4154.

11, 807. Pattison, Joseph. 'The Celestial Railroad' as dream-tale. Amer Q, 1968, 20:224-237.

11, 808. _____. Point of view in Hawthorne. PMLA, 1967, 82: 363-369.

11, 809. Pattison, Robert. The Child Figure in English Literature. Athens: Univ. Georgia Press, 1978.

11, 810. Paul, Louis. A psychoanalytic reading of Hawthorne's Major Molineux. The father manqué and the protégé manqué. Amer Imago, 1961, 18:280-288.

11, 811. Pauls, Jürgen. 'Les Fleurs bleues' von Raymond Queneau: Eine Analyse des Romans unter besonderer Berücksichtigung der Symbolik. Hamburg: Romanischer Seminar der Universität Hamburg, 1973.

11, 812. Paulson, Arthur Barry. The Great Gatsby: oral aggression and splitting. Amer Imago, 1978, 35:311-330.

11, 813. Pauncz, Arpad. The Lear complex in world literature. Amer Imago, 1954, 11:51-83.

11, 814. Payk, T. R. Büchners literarische Gestalten aus psychopathologischer Sicht. Confinia Psychiatrica, 1974, 17: 101-110.

11, 815. Peace, Richard Arthur. Dostoyevsky: An Examination of the Major Novels. NY: Cambridge Univ. Press, 1971.

11, 816. _____. Gogol and psychological realism: Shinel. In Freeborn, R., Milner-Gulland, R. R., & Ward, C. A. (eds), Russian and Slavic Literature. Cambridge, Mass: Slavica, 1976, 63-91.

11, 817. _____. The logic of madness: Gogol's Zapiski sumasshedshego. Oxford Slavonic Papers, 1977, 9:28-45.

11, 818. Pear, H. T. Psychologist's and novelist's approaches to personal relations. Bulletin British Psychol Society, 1976, 20(69):3-17.

11, 819. Pearce, Roy Harvey. Robin Molineux on the analyst's couch: a note on the limits of psychoanalytic criticism. Criticism, 1959, 1:83-90; In Malin, I. (ed), Psychoanalysis and American Fiction. NY: Dutton, 1965, 309-316.

11, 820. Pearlman, E. David Copperfield dreams of drowning. Amer Imago, 1971, 28:391-403.

11, 821. Pearson, Carol. Women's fantasies and feminist Utopias. Frontiers: J Women Studies, 1977, 2(3):50-61.

11, 822. _____, & Pope, Katherine. Toward a typology of female portraits in literature. CEA Critic, 1975, 37(4): 9-13.

11, 823. Pearson, Janet Lynne. Hemingway's women. Lost Generation J, 1973, 1(1):16-19.

11, 824. Pearson, N. H. Anderson and the new Puritanism. Newberry Library Bulletin, 1948, Dec.

11, 825. Peavy, Charles D. Did you ever have a sister? Holden, Quentin and sexual innocence. Florida Q, 1968, 1:82-95.

11, 826.   _____. 'If I'd just had a mother': Faulkner's Quentin
            Compson. Lit & Psychol, 1973, 23:114-121.
11, 827.   _____. Jason Compson's paranoid pseudocommunity.
            Hartford Studies in English, 1970, 2:151-156.
11, 828.   _____. A note on the 'suicide pact' in The Sound and
            the Fury. English Language Notes, 1968, 5:207-209.
11, 829.   Peck, Ellen M. McK. Exploring the Feminine: A Study
            of Janet Lewis, Ellen Glasgow, Anaïs Nin and Virginia
            Woolf. DAI, 1974, 35:3761A.
11, 830.   Peck, H. Daniel. A World by Itself: The Pastoral Mo-
            ment in Cooper's Fiction. New Haven: Yale Univ.
            Press, 1977.
11, 831.   Peck, Susan C. George Eliot's Development As a Psycho-
            logical Novelist. DAI, 1972, 32:6997A.
11, 832.   Peckham, Morse. Discontinuity in fiction: persona, nar-
            rator, scribe. In The Triumph of Romanticism. Col-
            umbia: Univ. South Carolina Press, 1970, 318-340.
11, 833.   _____. The place of sex in the work of William Faulk-
            ner. Studies in the Twentieth Century, 1974, 14:1-20.
11, 834.   Pederson-Krag, Geraldine. Detective stories and the
            primal scene. Psychoanal Q, 1949, 18:207-214.
11, 835.   Pedrini, Lura N., & Duilio, T. Billy Budd as modern
            tragic hero. Corrective Psychiat & J Social Theory,
            1965, 11:317-322.
11, 836.   _____, & Pedrini, Duilio T. Melville's attitudes
            toward women as reflected in his novels. Psychiat Q
            Supplement, 1965, 39:231-240.
11, 837.   Pelckmans, Paul. Névrose ou sociose? Une Lecture de
            La Femme de trente ans de Balzac. Rev Romane,
            1977, 12:96-122.
11, 838.   Pendleton, Harold E. Ernest Hemingway: A Theory of
            Learning. DA, 1960, 20:3302-3303.
11, 839.   Penot, Dominique. The psychology of characters in Robbe-
            Grillet's La Jealousie. Books Abroad, 1966, 40:5-16.
11, 840.   Penton, Brian. Note on the form of the novel. London
            Aphrodite, 1929, 6:443-444.
11, 841.   Penuel, Arnold M. Galdós, Freud, and humanistic psy-
            chology. Hispania, 1972, 55:66-75.
11, 842.   Percy, Walker. The state of the novel: dying art or new
            science? Michigan Q Rev, 1977, 16:359-373.
11, 843.   Peres, A. Bernardo. Sexo e erotismo em revistas brasi-
            leiras. Paz e Terra, 1967, 1(5):113-140.
11, 844.   Pérès, J. La Rêve de la veille dans certaines parties de
            l'oeuvre de Marcel Proust. Rev Politique et Littéraire,
            1917, 65:513-517.
11, 845.   _____. Le Rêve de la veille dans le roman proustien.
            J de Psychologie, 1932, 29:105-111.
11, 846.   Pérez, Francisco Romero. Abnormal Characters in Se-
            lected Novels of Benito Pérez Galdós: Their Function
            and Purpose. DAI, 1978, 38:7367A.
11, 847.   Perez Bautista, F. L. Sociedad y medicina en la novela
            realista española. Salamanca: Univ. de Salamanca,
            1974.

11, 848.   Pérez Firmat, Gustavo.   Descent into paradiso: a study
           of heaven and homosexuality.   Hispania, 1976, 59:247-
           257.
11, 849.   Perkins, Else S.   Das Symbolisch, Mythische Element im
           Kampfe des Hans Castorp um sein Ego: Eine Studie
           aus dem Zauberberg.   Master's thesis, Univ. Utah,
           1948.
11, 850.   Perkins, M. L.   Motivation and behavior in the Neveu de
           Rameau.   In Besterman, T.   (ed), Studies on Voltaire
           and the Eighteenth Century.   Banbury, England: Vol-
           taire Foundation, 1975, 85-106.
11, 851.   _____.   The psychoanalytic Merveilleux: suspense in
           Sade's Florville et Courval.   Sub-stance, 1976, 13:107-
           119.
11, 852.   Perkins, Michael.   The Secret Record: Modern Erotic
           Literature.   NY: Morrow, 1976.
11, 853.   Perloff, Marjorie.   Cinderella becomes the wicked step-
           mother: The Portrait of a Lady as ironic fairy tale.
           Nineteenth Century Fiction, 1969, 23:413-433.
11, 854.   _____.   'A Ritual for Being Born Twice':   Sylvia Plath's
           The Bell Jar.   Contemporary Lit, 1972, 13:507-522.
11, 855.   Perrier, François.   En Guise d'extroduction: sur Charles
           Fourier.   Topique, 1970, 4-5.
11, 856.   Perry, Katherine.   Review: Mary McCarthy's The Com-
           pany She Keeps.   Psychiatry, 1942, 5:294.
11, 857.   Perry, Nick, & Wilkie, Roy.   Homo hydrogenesis: notes
           on the work of J. G. Ballard.   Riverside Q, 1970, 4:98-
           107.
11, 858.   _____.   The undivided self: J. G. Ballard's The Crystal
           World.   Riverside Q, 1973, 5:268-277.
11, 859.   Pers, Mona.   Willa Cather's Children, Studia Anglistica
           Upsaliensia, 22.   Uppsala: Univ. Uppsala, 1975.
11, 860.   Pestel, M.   L'Etrange psychose de Don Quichotte.   Essai
           sur un idéalisme engagé.   Presse Médicale, 1964, 72:
           3407-3412.
11, 861.   Peters, Eric.   Hermann Hesse.   The psychological impli-
           cations of his writings.   German Life & Letters, 1948,
           1:209-214.
11, 862.   Peters, Frederick G.   Robert Musil, Master of Hovering
           Life: A Study of the Major Fiction.   NY: Columbia
           Univ. Press, 1978.
11, 863.   Peters, Margot.   Charlotte Brontë: Style in the Novel.
           Madison: Univ. Wisconsin Press, 1973.
11, 864.   _____, & Krouse, Agate N.   Women and crime: sexism
           in Allingham, Sayers and Christie.   Southwest Rev,
           1974, 59:144-152.
11, 865.   Peters, Michael.   Aversive conditioning and alcoholism:
           a nineteenth century case report.   Canadian Psychol
           Rev, 1976, 17(1):61.
11, 866.   Petersen, John Fred.   Ernesto Sábato: Essayist and Nov-
           elist.   Doctoral dissertation, Univ. Washington, 1963.
11, 867.   _____.   Sabato's El túnel: more Freud than Sartre.
           Hispania, 1967, 50:271-276.

11,868.   Petersen, Pam. Mesmerism, popular science, and Poe.
           In Marsden, M. T. (comp), Proceedings of the Sixth
           National Convention of the Popular Culture Assn. Bowl-
           ing Green, Ohio: Bowling Green State Univ. Popular
           Press, 1976, 251-262.
11,869.   Peterson, David A. , & Eden, Donna Z.   Teenagers and
           aging: adolescent literature as an attitude source.
           Educational Gerontology, 1977, 2:311-325.
11,870.   _____, & Karmes, Elizabeth L.   Older people in ado-
           lescent literature. Gerontologist, 1976, 16:225-231.
11,871.   Peterson, M. Jeanne. The Victorian governess: status,
           incongruence in family and society. Victorian Studies,
           1970, 14:7-23.
11,872.   Peterson, S. The matrimonial theme of Defoe's Roxanna.
           PMLA, 1955, 70:167-184.
11,873.   Petesch, Donald A. Some notes on the family in Faulk-
           ner's fiction. Notes on Mississippi Writers, 1977, 10:
           11-18.
11,874.   Petiot, Henri. Une Technique nouvelle: le monologue in-
           térieur. Correspondant, 1932, 326:281-305.
11,875.   Petit, Jacques. La Fausse 'Innocence' du Chevalier Des
           Touches. Rev des Lettres Modernes, 1977, nos. 491-
           497:47-61.
11,876.   _____. Julien Green, l'homme qui venait d'ailleurs.
           Paris: Desclée, 1969.
11,877.   _____. [The mirror motif in La Peinture hollandaise.]
           Rev des Lettres Modernes, 1971, Nos. 217-275.
11,878.   _____. 'Le Rêve endormi des plaisirs fabuleux...'
           L'Inceste et l'androgyne. Rev des Lettres Modernes,
           1967, 51-64.
11,879.   Petitt, Dorothy J. The search for self-definition: the
           picture of life in the novel for adolescents. English J,
           1960, 49:616-620+.
11,880.   Petrey, Sandy. Obscenity and revolution. Diacritics,
           1973, 3(3):22-26.
11,881.   _____. Stylistics and society in La Curée. MLN,
           1974, 89:626-640.
11,882.   Petrosky, A. R. Effects of reality perception and fantasy
           in response to literature. Research in Teaching Eng-
           lish, 1976, 10:239-258.
11,883.   Petrullo, Helen B. The neurotic hero of Typee. Amer
           Imago, 1955, 12:317-323.
11,884.   Peyre, Henri. Madame Bovary. In Burnshaw, S. (ed),
           Varieties of Literary Experience. NY: New York
           Univ. Press, 1962, 331-352.
11,885.   Pfautz, H. W. The image of alcohol in popular fiction:
           1900-1904 and 1946-1950. Quart J Studies Alcohol,
           1962, 23:131-146.
11,886.   Pfeiffer, Charles Leonard. Taste and Smell in Balzac's
           Novels. Tucson: Univ. Arizona Press, 1949.
11,887.   Pflanz, Elizabeth. Sexualität und Sexualideologie des Ich-
           Erzählers in Günter Grass' Roman 'Die Blechtrommel. '
           Munich: Uni-Druck, 1976; Doctoral dissertation, Univ.
           Würzburg.

11,888.   Philbin, Alice Irene.   The Literary Femme Fatale--A So-
          cial Fiction: The Willful Female in the Deterministic
          Vision of Thomas Hardy and in the Psychological Vision
          of Henry James.   DAI, 1977, 38:2815A-16A.
11,889.   Philips, Robert.   Secret and symbol: entrances to Goyen's
          House of Breath.   Southwest Rev, 1974, 59:248-253.
11,890.   Phillips, Elizabeth.   The hocus-pocus of Lolita.   Lit &
          Psychol, 1960, 10:97-101.
11,891.   Phillips, Robert S.   Mask and symbol in Set This House on
          Fire.   In Morris, R. K., & Malin, I. (eds), The
          Achievement of William Styron.   Berkeley: Univ. Cali-
          fornia Press, 1975, 134-149.
11,892.   _____.   Painful love: Carson McCullers' parable.
          Southwest Rev, 1966, 51:80-86.
11,893.   _____.   Samuels and Samson: theme and legend in 'The
          White Rooster. '   Studies in Short Fiction, 1969, 6:331-
          333.
11,894.   _____.   William Goyen.   Boston: Twayne, 1979.
11,895.   Phillips, Roger W.   Dostoevskij's 'Underground' Narrator:
          A Study in the Psychology and Structure of Contradic-
          tion.   DAI, 1971, 31:6626A.
11,896.   Phillips, William.   Dostoevsky's underground man.   Parti-
          san Rev, 1946, 12:551-561.
11,897.   _____.   The imagery of Dreiser's novels.   PMLA,
          1963, 78:572-585.
11,898.   Phul, Ruth von.   Chamber music at the Wake.   James
          Joyce Q, 1974, 11:355-367.
11,899.   _____.   Circling the square: a study of structure.   In
          Magalaner, M. (ed), A James Joyce Miscellany: Third
          Series.   Carbondale: Southern Illinois Univ. Press,
          1962, 239-277.
11,900.   Picard, Michel.   Libertinage et tragique dans l'oeuvre de
          Roger Vailland.   Paris: Hachette, 1972.
11,901.   Pichanick, Valerie Kossew.   An abominable submission:
          Harriet Martineau's views on the role and place of
          woman.   Woman's Studies, 1977, 5:13-32.
11,902.   Pickering, Jean.   Marxism and madness: the two faces
          of Doris Lessing's myth.   Modern Fiction Studies,
          1980, 26:17-30.
11,903.   Pickup, I.   An aspect of portraiture in the novels of Bal-
          zac: psycho-physiological bridges.   In Various (eds),
          Literature and Society.   Studies in Nineteenth and Twen-
          tieth Century French Literature.   Birmingham, Engl:
          Goodman, 1980.
11,904.   Picon, Gaëtan.   Faulkner: l'angoisse et le désordre.
          Nouvelles Littéraires, 1962, 40:3.
11,905.   Pincherle, Alberto (pseud. Alberto Moravia).   Eroticism in
          literature, excerpt from 'Man As an End. '   In Hughes,
          D. A. (ed), Perspectives on Pornography.   NY: St.
          Martins, 1970, 1-3.
11,906.   Pichon Rivière, Armind A. de., & Baranger, Willy.   Ré-
          pression du deuil et intensification des mechanismes et
          des angoisses schizo-paranoïdes.   Notes sur L'Etranger

de Camus. Rev Français de Psychanalyse, 1959, 23: 409-420.

11,907. Pickar, Gertrud B. The aspect of colour in Günter Grass's Katz und Maus. German Life & Letters, 1970, 23:304-309.

11,908. Pickard, P. M. Thomas Mann's Doctor Faustus: a psychological approach. German Life & Letters, 1950, 4:90-100.

11,909. Pickens, Rupert T., & Tedder, J. D. Liberation in suicide: Meursault in the light of Dante. French Rev, 1968, 41:524-531.

11,910. Pickering, John K. J. D. Salinger: Portraits of Alienation. DAI, 1970, 30:3954A.

11,911. Pickford, R. W. Déjà vu in Proust and Tolstoy. Int J Psycho-Anal, 1944, 25:155-165.

11,912. _____. An interpretation of the fantasy of Uncle Silas. British J Medical Psychol, 1945, 20:314-321.

11,913. Pietrkiewicz, J. A Polish psychoanalytical novel of 1902. Slavic & East European J, 1951, 30:63-86.

11,914. Pilkington, John. About this madman stuff. Univ. Mississippi Studies in English, 1966, 7:65-75.

11,915. Pinsker, Sanford. The End of the Tether: Joseph Conrad's death of a sailsman. Conradiana, 1971-72, 3(2): 74-76.

11,916. _____. Joyce Carol Oates's Wonderland: a hungering for personality. Critique: Studies in Modern Fiction, 1978, 20(2):39-70.

11,917. _____. The mixed cords of David Madden's Cassandra Singing. Critique: Studies in Modern Fiction, 1973, 15(2):15-26.

11,918. _____. Suburban molesters: Joyce Carol Oates' Expensive People. Midwest Q, 1977, 19:89-103.

11,919. Pipal, Karl. Beim Lesen schöner Geschichten. Psychoanalytische Bewegung, 1932, 6:155-164, 337-346.

11,920. Piper, Ellen. Dark paradise: shades of heaven and hell in Ada. Modern Fiction Studies, 1979, 25:481-497.

11,921. Piper, Henry Dan. F. Scott Fitzgerald: A Critical Portrait. NY: Holt, Rinehart & Winston, 1965.

11,922. Piper, W. Sources and processes in the writing of fiction. Amer J Psychol, 1931, 43:188-201.

11,923. Piriou, Jean-Pierre J. Sexualité, religion et art chez Julien Green. Paris: Nizet, 1976.

11,924. _____. L'Auto-analyse et la création littéraire chez Julien Green. DAI, 1973, 34:1930A.

11,925. Piscopo, U. Le Thème de l'Italie dans Madame Bovary. Europe, 1977, 159-173.

11,926. Pitavy, François. Quentin Compson ou de regard du poète. Sud, 1975, Nos. 14-15.

11,927. Pitcher, Edward W. The physiognomical meaning of Poe's 'The Tell-Tale Heart.' Studies in Short Fiction, 1979, 16:231-233.

11,928. Pitt, Rosemary. The exploration of self in Conrad's Heart of Darkness and Woolf's The Voyage Out. Conradiana, 1978, 10:141-154.

11,929. Pitts, Rebecca E. 'The Wall': Sartre's metaphysical
trap. Hartford Studies in Lit, 1974, 6:29-54.
11,930. Pizer, Donald. The masculine-feminine ethic in Frank
Norris' popular novels. Texas Studies in Lit & Language, 1964, 6:84-91.
11,931. Pizzimenti, Grace. Two novels of Antonio Ferres: social
alienation. Modern Language Studies, 1977, 7(2):88-96.
11,932. Placer, E. L. Lo vasco en Pia Baroja. Madrid: Vasca
Elkin, 1968.
11,933. Plank, D. L. Unconscious motifs in Leonid Leonov's The
Badgers. Slavonic & East European J, 1972, 16:19-35.
11,934. Plank, Robert. Communication in science fiction. ETC,
1953, 11:16-20.
11,935. _____. The Emotional Significance of Imaginary Beings;
A Study of the Interaction Between Psychopathology, Literature, and Reality in the Modern World. Springfield,
Ill: Thomas, 1968; Review: Marvin Reznikoff, Hartford Studies in Lit, 1969, 1:63-67.
11,936. _____. Death in Venice: tragedy or mishap? Hartford
Studies in Lit, 1972, 4:95-103.
11,937. _____. The geography of utopia: psychological facts
shaping the 'ideal' location. Extrapolation, 1965, 6:39-
49.
11,938. _____. Heart transplant fiction. Hartford Studies in
Lit, 1970, 2:102-112.
11,939. _____. Imaginary voyages and toy novels. Hartford
Studies in Lit, 1974, 6:221-242.
11,940. _____. Lighter than air, but heavy as hate: an essay
in space travel. Partisan Rev, 1957, 24:106-116; In
Fiedler, L. A. (ed), The Art of the Essay. NY: Crowell, 1958.
11,941. _____. Names and roles of characters in science fiction. Names, 1961, 9:151-159.
11,942. _____. Omnipotent cannibals in Stranger in a Strange
Land. In Olander, J. D., & Greenberg, M. H. (eds),
Robert A. Heinlein. NY: Taplinger, 1978, 83-106.
11,943. _____. Orthopsychiatric observations on patterns of
literature in today's milieu: science fiction. Amer J
Orthopsychiatry, 1960, 24:799-810.
11,944. _____. Portraits of fictitious psychiatrists. Amer
Imago, 1956, 13:259-268.
11,945. _____. Quixote's mills: the man-machine encounter in
SF. Science Fiction Studies, 1973, 1:68-78. Followed
by Stanislaw Lem. Remarks occasioned by Dr. Plank's
essay, 'Quixote's mills, ' 78-83, & 'Response' by Plank,
83-84.
11,946. _____. The reproduction of psychosis in science fiction. Int Record Medicine, 1954, 167:407-421.
11,947- _____. Portraits of fictitious psychiatrists. Amer
8. Imago, 1956, 13:259-268.
11,949. _____. Science fiction. Amer J Orthopsychiat, 1960,
30:799-810.

11,950.   _____. Some psychological aspects of Lewis's trilogy.
           In Hillegas, M.R. (ed), Shadows of Imagination; The
           Fantasies of C.S. Lewis, J.R.R. Tolkien, and Charles
           Williams. Carbondale: Southern Illinois Univ. Press,
           1969, 26-40.
11,951.   _____. Ursula K. LeGuin and the decline of romantic
           love. Science Fiction Studies, 1976, 3:36-43.
11,952.   _____. Zen and the Art of Motorcycle Maintenance:
           the voyage as a quest for self-discovery. Exploration,
           1978, 5(2):33-43.
11,953.   Planz, Elizabeth. Sexualität und Sexualideologie des Ich-
           Erzählers in Günter Grass' Roman 'Die Blechtrommel. '
           Munich: Uni-Druck, 1976.
11,954.   Plater, Ormonde. The Lovingood patriarchy. Appalachian
           J, 1973, 1(2):82-93.
11,955.   Plath, D.W. Japanese psychology through Japanese litera-
           ture. Cares of careers, and careers of caretaking.
           JNMD, 1973, 157:346-357.
11,956.   Platt, Carolyn V. How feminist is Villette? Women &
           Lit, 1975, 3:16-27.
11,957.   Platzer, Hildegard. Kafka's double-figure as a literary
           device. Monatshefte, 1963, 55:7-12.
11,958.   _____. Sex, marriage, and guilt: the dilemma of
           mating in Kafka. Mosaic, 1970, 3:119-130.
11,959.   Plaut, Richard. Arthur Schnitzler als Erzähler. Doctoral
           dissertation, Univ. Basel, 1935; Basel/Frankfurt:
           Kornsand, 1935.
11,960.   Pleasant, John Ruffin, Jr. The Family Motif in Thomas
           Wolfe's Drama and Fiction. DAI, 1976, 37:2877A-78A.
11,961.   Plottke, Paul. Individual psychology in the analysis of lit-
           erature: Dr. Jekyll and Mr. Hyde. Individual Psychol
           Bulletin, 1951, 9:9-17.
11,962.   Plunkett, James T. The Quest for a Father-God in the
           Fiction of Thomas Wolfe. DAI, 1970, 3(1-A), 399.
11,963.   Podolsky, E. Wherein we set down the psychology of Don
           Juan. Medical World, 1946, 64:297-299.
11,964.   Pohl, Reinhard J.A. Die Metamorphosen des negativen
           Helden: Imagination und Mythologie im Werk von
           Robert Desnos. Hamburg: Romanisches Seminar,
           1977.
11,965.   Polanscak, A. Le Rôle du corps dans l'esthétique prous-
           tienne. Studia Romanica et Anglica Zagrabiensa, 1958,
           6:39-51.
11,966.   Politzer, Heinz. The alienated self: a key to Franz Kaf-
           ka's Castle? Michigan Q Rev, 1975, 14:398-414.
11,967.   _____. Der Fall der Frau Marquise. Beobachtungen
           zu Kafka's Die Marquis von O.... Deutsche Viertel-
           jahresschrift für Literaturwissenschaft und Geistes-
           geschichte, 1977, 51:98-128.
11,968.   _____. Franz Kafka: Parable and Paradox. Ithaca,
           NY: Cornell Univ. Press, 1962.
11,969.   Pollin, Burton. Hans Pfaall: a false variant and the
           phallic fallacy. Mississippi Q, 1978, 31:519-527.

11,970.   Pommier, Jean.   Flaubert et la naissance de l'acteur.
          JPNP, 1947, 40:185-194.
11,971.   _____.   Sensations et images chez Flaubert.   Essai
          critique psychophysiologique.   JPNP, 1949, 42:274-294.
11,972.   Pontalis, J. -B.   La Maladie de Flaubert.   In Après Freud.
          Paris: Gallimard, 1968.
11,973.   Ponting, K. G.   Rediscovering Forrest Reid.   Contemporary
          Rev, 1980, 237:34-37.
11,974.   Popov, P.   [Ego and id in the artistic creativity of Dos-
          toevsky.]   In Collection Dostoevskii.   Moscow: 1928,
          217-275.
11,975.   Pops, Martin.   The Melville Archetype.   Kent, Ohio:
          Kent State Univ. Press, 1970.
11,976.   Porcelli, Bruno.   Psicoanalisi nella Coscienza di Zeno.
          Italianistica: Rivista di Letteratura Italiana, 1978, 7:
          102-117.
11,977.   Poresky, Louise Ann.   The Elusive Self: Psyche and
          Spirit in Virginia Woolf's Novels.   DAI, 1977,
          38:2779A.
11,978.   _____.   Joe Christmas: his tragedy as victim.   Hart-
          ford Studies in Lit, 1976, 8:209-222.
11,979-   Porter, Dennis.   Sartre, Robbe-Grillet and the psychotic
    80.   hero.   Modern Fiction Studies, 1970, 16:13-26.
11,981.   Porter, Laurence M.   Autobiography versus confessional
          novel: Gide's Immoraliste and Si le grain ne meurt.
          Symposium, 1976, 30:144-159.
11,982.   _____.   The devil as double in nineteenth-century liter-
          ature: Goethe, Dostoevsky, and Flaubert.   Comparative
          Literature Studies, 1978, 15:316-335.
11,983.   _____.   The forbidden city: a psychoanalytic interpreta-
          tion of Nodier's Smarra.   Symposium, 1972, 26:331-
          348.
11,984.   _____.   The generativity crisis of Gide's Immoraliste.
          French Forum, 1977, 2:58-69.
11,985.   _____.   The Literary Dream in French Romanticism.
          A Psychoanalytical Interpretation.   Detroit: Wayne
          State Univ. Press, 1979.
11,986.   _____.   Mourning and melancholia in Nerval's Aurélia.
          Studies in Romanticism, 1976, 15:289-306.
11,987.   _____.   The narrative art of Nodier's Contes: Diderot's
          contributions to the quest for verisimilitude.   Romanic
          Rev, 1972, 63:272-283.
11,988.   _____.   The seductive Satan of Cazotte's Le Diable
          amoureux.   L'Esprit créateur, 1978, 18:3-12.
11,989.   _____.   Temptation and repression in Nodier's Trilby.
          Nineteenth-Century French Studies, 1974, 2:97-110.
11,990.   _____.   Ut somnium poesis: the conventions of French
          romantic dream-literature.   J Altered States of Con-
          sciousness, 1977-78, 3:249-259.
11,991.   Portnoy, Isadore.   The Magic Skin.   A psychoanalytic in-
          terpretation: the search for inner unity.   Amer J
          Psychoanal, 1949, 9:67-74.

11, 992. Poss, Stanley.   Manners and myths in the novels of P. H.
          Newby.   Critique, 1970, 12(1):5-19.
11, 993. Poster, Mark.   The concepts of sexual identity and the
          life-cycle in Restif de la Bretonne's utopian thought.
          Studies on Voltaire & the 18th Century, 1970, 73:241-
          271.
11, 994. Postlethwaite, Diana Lynn.   The Novelist As a Woman of
          Science: George Eliot and Contemporary Psychology.
          DAI, 1976, 37:377A-38A.
11, 995. Poston, Teresa G.   Preadolescent Needs and Problems As
          Seen in Family Life Fiction Published Between the
          Years 1965 and 1975: A Content Analysis.   DAI, 1977,
          38(4-A), 1717.
11, 996. Potvin, Janet Holm.   The Ensuance of Existentiality: A
          Study of Fire Imagery in James Joyce's 'Finnegans
          Wake. '   DAI, 1975, 35:5421A.
11, 997. Poulakis, Victoria S.   The Psychological Novels of William
          Dean Howells.   DAI, 1971, 31:5420A.
11, 998. Poulet, Georges.   L'Espace Proustien.   Paris: 1963; Re-
          view: Pierre-Henri Simon, Le Monde, 20 May 1964,
          no. 6016, 12-13.
11, 999. Pound, Edward Fox.   The Influence of Burke and the Psy-
          chological Critics on the Novels of Ann Radcliffe.   DA,
          1964, 25:1198.
12, 000. Pounds, Wayne Edward.   Paul Bowles and the Geography
          of the Inner Nature: Some Psychological Correlatives
          of Landscape.   DAI, 1977, 37:5125A.
12, 001. Powell, Grosvenor E.   Role and identity in Ralph Ellison's
          Invisible Man.   In Burrows, D. J. , et al. (eds), Private
          Dealings: Eight Modern American Writers.   Stockholm:
          Almqvist & Wiksell, 1970, 95-105.
12, 002. Power, William.   Huck Finn's father.   Univ. Kansas City
          Rev, 1962, 28:83-94.
12, 003. Praag, S. E. von.   Marcel Proust en de Karakterkunde.
          Nederlandsch Tijdschrift voor de Psychologie, 1937, 4:
          47-68.
12, 004. Pracht-Fitzell, Illse.   Peter Schlemihls wundersame Gesch-
          ichte von A. von Chamisso in psychologischer Sicht.
          Germanic Notes, 1976, 7:2-9.
12, 005. Prasad, Thakur Guru.   Lie Down in Darkness: a portrait
          of the modern phenomenon.   Indian J English Studies,
          1969, 10:71-80.
12, 006. Pratt, Annis.   Sexual imagery in To the Lighthouse: a
          new feminist approach.   Modern Fiction Studies, 1972,
          18:417-431.
12, 007. Pratt, Branwen Barley.   The role of the unconscious in
          The Eternal Husband.   Lit & Psychol, 1971, 21:29-40.
12, 008. _____ .   Sympathy for the devil: a dissenting view of
          Quilp.   Hartford Studies in Lit, 1974, 6:129-146.
12, 009. Prawer, S. S.   Robert Musil and the 'uncanny. '   Oxford
          German Studies, 1968, 3:163-182.
12, 010. Praz, Mario.   Poe and psychoanalysis.   Sewanee Rev,
          1960, 68:375-389.

12, 011. Predmore, Richard L. On interpreting Don Quixote's character. In Randall, D. B. J., & Williams, G. W. (eds), Studies in the Continental Background of Renaissance English Literature. Durham, NC: Duke Univ. Press, 1977, 186-201.

12, 012. _____. 'Young Goodman Brown': night journey into the forest. J Analytical Psychol, 1977, 22:250-257.

12, 013. Prescott, Joseph. The characterization of Leopold Bloom. Lit & Psychol, 1959, 9:3-4.

12, 014. _____. Dorothy Miller Richardson. Lit & Psychol, 1954, 4:4-5.

12, 015. _____. James Joyce's Stephen Hero. J English Germanic Philology, 1954, 53(2).

12, 016. _____. James Joyce: a study in words. PMLA, 1939, 54:304-315.

12, 017. Prévost, Jean. La Création chez Stendhal: Essai sur le métier d'écrivain et la psychologie de l'écrivain. Paris: Gallimard, 1975; Thèse Lyon. Editiones du Sagittaire, 1942.

12, 018. Price, Theodore. The Ugly Duckling: Recurrent Themes in George Eliot. DAI, 1975, 36:2854A.

12, 019. Price, W. R. The Symbolism of Voltaire's Novels. NY: A. M. S. Press, 1966.

12, 020. Prickett, Stephen. Victorian Fantasy. Bloomington: Indiana Univ. Press, 1979; Review: Eric S. Rabkin, Criticism, 1980, 22:181-183.

12, 021. Pridgeon, Charles Taylor, Jr. Insanity in American Fiction from Charles Brockden Brown to Oliver Wendell Holmes. DAI, 1970, 31:1766A-67A.

12, 022. Primeau, Marguerite A. L'Amour-passion dans l'Exil de Montherlant. French Rev, 1970, 44:322-328.

12, 023. Prior, Linda T. Theme, imagery, and structure in The Hamlet. Mississippi Q, 1969, 22:237-256.

12, 024. Pritchard, Ronald Edward. D. H. Lawrence: The Body of Darkness. Pittsburgh: Univ. Pittsburg Press, 1972.

12, 025. _____. L. P. Hartley's The Go-Between. Critical Q, 1980, 22:45-55.

12, 026. Prosky, Murray. The crisis of identity in the novels of Brian Moore. Ireland: J Irish Studies, 1971, 6(3): 106-118.

12, 027. Proudfit, Sharon L. Virginia Woolf: reluctant feminist in The Years. Criticism, 1975, 17:59-73.

12, 028. Prud'homme, Janine. L'Expression de la vie intérieure dans les romans de François Mauriac. Bulletin des Jeunes Romanistes, 1965, no. 11-12, 63-69.

12, 029. _____. François Mauriac et le cinéma: l'expression de la vie intérieure. Cahiers François Mauriac, 1978, 5:176-183.

12, 030. Pruette, Lorine. The family and the modern novel. Family, 1928, 9:46-50.

12, 031. Pryse, Marjorie. The Mark and the Knowledge: Social Stigma in Classic American Literature. Columbus: Ohio State Univ. Press, 1979.

12,032. Przemecka, Irena. [Search for identity in the American
         Negro novel.] Kwartalnik Neofilologiczny, 1975, 185-
         190.
12,033. Psichari, Henriette. Anatomie d'un chef-d'oeuvre: 'Ger-
         minal.' Paris: Mercure de France, 1964.
12,034. Puccinelli, L. Graciliano Ramos, Relações entre Ficção
         e Realidade. São Paulo: Quíron, 1975.
12,035. Pullin, Faith. Lawrence's treatment of women in Sons and
         Lovers. In Smith, A. (ed), Lawrence and Women. NY:
         Barnes & Noble, 1978, 49-74.
12,036. Pumpian-Mindlin, E. Thomas Mann's Death in Venice.
         JNMD, 1969, 149:236-239.
12,037. Puppe, Heinz W. Psychologie und Mystik in Klein und
         Wagner von Hermann Hesse. PMLA, 1963, 78:128-135.
12,038. _____. Die soziologische und psychologische Symbolik
         im Prosawerk Hermann Hesse. Doctoral dissertation,
         Univ. Innsbruck, 1959.
12,039. Purdy, Strother B. An American Tragedy and L'Etranger.
         Comparative Lit, 1967, 19.
12,040. _____. The erotic in literature. In Katchadourian,
         H. A., & Lunde, D. T. (eds), Fundamentals of Human
         Sexuality. NY: Holt, Rinehart & Winston, 1972, 354-
         388.
12,041. _____. The Hole in the Fabric: Science, Contemporary
         Literature, and Henry James. Pittsburgh: Univ. Pitts-
         burgh Press, 1970.
12,042. _____. On the psychology of erotic literature. Lit &
         Psychol, 1970, 20:23-29.
12,043. Purves, James. Edgar Allan Poe's works. Dublin Univ.
         Magazine, 1875, 86:296-306.
12,044. Pusey, William W., III. The generation gap and interper-
         sonal relationships in the novels and stories of Eduard
         von Keyserling. In Wonderley, A. W. (ed), Eduard von
         Keyserling: A Symposium. Lexington, Ky: Apra,
         1974, 29-35.
12,045. Putt, Samuel G. Henry James: A Reader's Guide. Itha-
         ca, NY: Cornell Univ. Press, 1966.
12,046. Pütz, Manfred. The Story of Identity: American Fiction
         of the Sixties. Stuttgart: Metzler, 1979.
12,047. _____. Thomas Pynchon's The Crying of Lot 49: the
         world is a tristero system. Mosaic, 1974, 7(4):125-
         137.
12,048. _____. Who am I this time?: die Romane von Kurt
         Vonnegut. Amerikastudien, 1974, 19:111-125.
12,049. Putzell, Sara Moore. Victorian Views of Man in the Nov-
         els of Charlotte Brontë and George Eliot. DAI, 1978,
         38:4851A.
12,050. Pykare, Nina Coombs. The Female Part of the Species:
         A Study of Women in Fielding. DAI, 1976, 37:991A-
         92A.

12,051. Quagliano, Anthony. Existential modes in The Moviegoer.
         Research Studies, 1977, 45:214-223.

12,052. Quellet, Réal. Les Relations humaines dans l'oeuvre de Saint-Exupéry. Thèse, Univ. Paris, 1963.

12,053. Quen, J. M., Crews, Frederick C., & Male, Roy. Frederick C. Crews' The Sins of the Fathers: an exchange. Nineteenth Century Fiction, 1967, 22:101-110.

12,054. Quigley, S. G. Pour connaître la littérature du 20ème siècle, il suffit de lire quatre auteurs: Kafka, Joyce, Faulkner et Proust ... Le reste n'est que periphrase. L'Esprit créateur, 1974, 14:64-80.

12,055. Quinn, James, & Baldessarini, Ross. Literary technique and psychological effect in Hawthorne's 'The Minister's Black Veil.' Lit & Psychol, 1974, 24:115-123.

12,056. Quinn, Patrick Frank. The French Face of Edgar Poe. Carbondale: Southern Illinois Univ. Press, 1957.

12,057. _____. Poe: 'That spectre in my path'; excerpt from The French Face of Edgar Poe. In Malin, I. (ed), Psychoanalysis and American Fiction. NY: Dutton, 1965, 61-85.

12,058. Quirk, Eugene F. Tulkinghorn's buried life: a study of character in Bleak House. J English Germanic Philology, 1973, 72:526-535.

12,059. Quirk, Thomas V. The Confidence-Man: Melville's Problem of Faith. DAI, 1977, 38:3503A.

12,060. Quist, G. Frederika Bremer och kvinnas emancipation. Opinions-historiska studier. Göteborg: Scandinavian University Books, 1969.

12,061. Quivey, James R. George Babbitt's quest for masculinity. Ball State Univ. Forum, 1969, 10(2):4-7.

12,062. Rabine, Leslie. George Sand and the myth of femininity. Women & Lit, 1976, 4(2):2-17.

12,063. Rabinovitz, Rubin. Mechanism vs organism: Anthony Burgess' A Clockwork Orange. Modern Fiction Studies, 1978-79, 34:538-541.

12,064. Rabinowitz, Nancy S. Medusa's head: myth, impotence and John Barth's Chimera. In Marsden, M. T. (comp), Proceedings of the 6th National Convention of the Popular Culture Assn. Bowling Green, Ohio: Bowling Green State Univ. Popular Press, 1976, 1125-1133.

12,065. Rabkin, Eric S. Determinism, free will, and point of view in LeGuin's The Left Hand of Darkness. Extrapolation, 1979, 20:5-19.

12,066. _____. The Fantastic in Literature. Princeton: Princeton Univ. Press, 1976.

12,067. Rabkin, Leslie Y. (ed). Psychopathology and Literature. San Francisco: Chandler, 1966.

12,068. Racelle-Latin, Danièle. Création littéraire et économie de la libido dans Voyage au bout de la nuit. In Céline: Actes du colloque international de Paris. Paris: Société d'études céliniennes, 1978, 259-280.

12,069. _____. Louis-Ferdinand Céline et la psychocritique. Rev des Langues Vivantes, 1974, 150-158.

12,070. Racker, Heinrich. Considérations psychanalytiques sur
         Le Cocu Magnifique de F. Crommelynck. Rev Fran-
         çais de Psychanalyse, 1957, 21:839-855.
12,071. Rackin, Donald. What you always wanted to know about
         Alice but were afraid to ask. Victorian Newsletter,
         1973, 44:1-5.
12,072. Rader, M. M. Dostoevsky and the demiurge. Sewanee
         Rev, 1931, 282-292.
12,073. Radford, Frederick L. Heinrich Heine, the virgin, and
         the hummingbird: Fifth Business: a novel and its sub-
         conscious. English Studies in Canada, 1978, 4:95-110.
12,074. _____. The journey towards castration: interracial
         sexual stereotypes in Ellison's Invisible Man. J Amer
         Studies, 1971, 4:227-231.
12,075. Radine, S. Quelques aspects du roman policier psycho-
         logique. Geneva: Mont-Blanc, 1960.
12,076. Radley, P. D. Goncharov's Obryo (The Abyss): boredom
         and Rajskij, or how to write a personal statement ob-
         jectively. In Baer, J. T. , & Ingham, N. W. (eds),
         Mnemozina. Studia litteraria russica. Munich: Fink,
         1974, 294-300.
12,077. Ragland, Mary E. A new look at Panurge. Hartford Stud-
         ies in Lit, 1976, 8:61-81.
12,078. _____. Rabelais and Panurge. A Psychological Ap-
         proach to Character. Amsterdam: Rodopi, 1976; At-
         lantic Highlands, NJ: Humanities Press, 1976.
12,079. Ragusa, Olga. Alberto Moravia: voyeurism and story-
         telling. In Narrative and Drama; Essays in Modern
         Italian Literature from Verga to Pasolini. The Hague:
         Mouton, 1976, 122-133; Southern Rev, 1968, 4:127-141.
12,080. Rahv, Philip. Dostoevsky in Crime and Punishment. In
         Burnshaw, S. (ed), Varieties of Literary Experience.
         NY: New York Univ. Press, 1962, 353-385.
12,081. _____. Hawthorne in analysis. In Literature and the
         Sixth Sense. Boston: Houghton, Mifflin, 1969 (1966),
         422-429.
12,082. Railton, Stephen Fredric. James Fenimore Cooper: A
         Psychological Study. DAI, 1975, 36:1509A.
12,083. Rainer, Jerome, & Rainer, Julie. Sexual Adventure in
         Marriage. NY: Simon & Schuster, 1963; NY: Messner,
         1965; London: Blond, 1965.
12,084. Rallo, José. A discussion of the paper by G. H. Allison
         and J. C. Allman on the intuitive psychoanalytic per-
         spective of Galdós in Fortunata and Jacinta. Int J
         Psycho-Anal, 1974, 55, 345-347.
12,085. Ramat, Silvio. Psicologia della forma leopardiana. Flor-
         ence: Nuova Italia, 1970.
12,086. Ramos González, A. Teoría de los pactos en la nueva
         novela americana. Cuadernos Hispano-Americanos,
         1967, 209:406-412.
12,087. Ramsdell, Elizabeth A. , & Gaier, Eugene L. Identity and
         reality reflected in adolescent fiction: the early sixties
         and the early seventies. Adolescence, 1974, 9:577-593.

12, 088. Ramsey, Roger. Current and recurrent: the Vietnam novel. Modern Fiction Studies, 1971, 17:415-431.

12, 089. Randall, Jo A. Sexual Symbolism as a Function of Repression in Jane Eyre. DAI, 1972, 32(7-B), 4225-26.

12, 090. Rank, Hugh. O'Connor's image of the priest. New England Q, 1968, 41:3-29.

12, 091. Rank, Otto. Der Doppelgänger. Eine Psychoanalytische Studie. Imago, 1914, 3. Leipzig: Int Psychoanalytischer Verlag, 1925.

12, 092. _____. Der Sinn der Griselda-Fabel. Imago, 1912, 1:34-48.

12, 093. Rao, K. S. Narayana. Love, sex, marriage and morality in Kamala Markandaya. Osman J English Studies, 1973, 10:69-77.

12, 094. Rao, V. V. B. Rama. Graham Greene and the burden of childhood. Lit Half-Yearly, 1978, 19(2):50-62.

12, 095. Rapaport, Herman. Jane Eyre and the mot tabou. MLN, 1979, 94:1093-1104.

12, 096. Raper, Julian Rowan. Glasgow's psychology of deceptions and The Sheltered Life. Southern Lit J, 1975, 8:27-38.

12, 097. _____. Invisible things: the short stories of Ellen Glasgow. Southern Lit J, 1977, 9:66-90.

12, 098. _____. The landscape of revenge: Ellen Glasgow's Barren Ground. Southern Humanities Rev, 1979, 13: 63-76.

12, 099. Raphael, Dennis, Skoczylas, Joseph, & Pengelly, S. Elizabeth. Carson McCuller's Member of the Wedding: a case study in adolescent development. Adolescence, 1980, 15(57):211-226.

12, 100. Rapping, Elayne Antler. Unfree women: feminism in Doris Lessing's novels. Women's Studies, 1975, 3:29-44.

12, 101. Rasper, H. O. Kriminalität und Perversion als Manifestation von Über-Ich-Isolierung und Liebesunfähigkeit Untersuchung der Selbstbekenntnisse im Prosawerk Jean Genets. Zeitschrift für Psychotherapie und medizinische Psychologie, 1970, 20:223-235.

12, 102. Rauzy, A. J. A propos de 'L'Immaculée Conception' d'André Breton et Paul Eduard; Contribution à l'étude des rapports du surréalisme et de la psychiatrie. Thèse, Paris, 1970, No. 530.

12, 103. Ravoux, Elisabeth. Topographie de l'adolescence dans Les Désarrois de l'éleve Törless. L'Arc, 1978, 74: 88-92.

12, 104. Ray, Laura K. The Child in the Novels of Charles Dickens. DAI, 1972, 32:7001A.

12, 105. _____. Childhood and the English novel: two English girls. Genre, 1975, 8:89-106.

12, 106. Raynaud, Jean. Science fiction et critique de l'aliénation. Rev Française d'Etudes Americaines, 1977, 3:77-92.

12, 107. Rayson, A. L. The novels of Zora Neale Hurston. Studies in Black Lit, 1975, 5:1-10.

12, 108. Rea, J. Faulkner's 'Spotted Horses.' Hartford Studies in Lit, 1970, 2:157-164.

12,109. Read, Phyllis J.   The illusion of personality: cyclical
time in Durrell's Alexandria Quartet.   Modern Fiction
Studies, 1967, 13:389-398.

12,110. Readdy, Coral Ann.   An approach to the stream of consciousness in Ulysses.   Galmahra (Brisbane), 1963, 14-
16.

12,111. Reaver, J.   Russell, & Strozier, Robert J.   Thomas Wolfe
and death.   Georgia Rev, 1962, 16:330-350; In Field,
L. A. (ed), Thomas Wolfe.   Three Decades of Criticism.
NY: New York Univ.   Press, 1968, 37-58.

12,112. Rebelsky, Freda G.   Coming of age in Davos.   An analysis
of the maturation of Hans Castorp in Thomas Mann's
The Magic Mountain.   Amer Imago, 18:413-421.

12,113. Reber, Natalie.   Studien zum Motiv des Doppelgängers bei
Dostojevskij und bei E. T. A. Hoffmann.   In Osteuro-
pastudien der Hochschulen des Landes Hessen, Reihe II,
Marburger Abhandlungen zur Geschichte und Kultur Ost-
europas, Vol. 6.   Giessen: Schmitz, 1964; Doctoral
dissertation, Univ. Bern, 1964.

12,114. Rechnitz, Robert M.   Depersonalization and the dreams in
The Red Badge of Courage.   Studies in the Novel, 1974,
6:76-87.

12,115. _____.   Perception, Identity and the Grotesque: A Study
of Three Southern Writers.   DAI, 1967, 28:2261A.

12,116. Reckley, Ralph.   The Castration of the Black Male: A
Character Analysis of Chester Himes's Protest Novels.
DAI, 1976, 36:4496A-97A.

12,117. _____.   The oedipal complex and intraracial conflict in
Chester Himes' The Third Generation.   College Language
Assn J, 1977, 21-275-281.

12,118. _____.   The use of the Doppelgänger or double in Chester Himes' Lonely Crusade.   College Language Assn J,
1977, 20:448-458.

12,119. Redding, Mary Elrich.   Call it myth: Henry Roth and
The Golden Bough.   Centennial Rev, 1974, 18:180-195.

12,120. Redfern, Walter W.   People and things in Flaubert.
French Rev, 1971, 44:79-88.

12,121. Reece, James B.   Mr. Hooper's vow.   Emerson Society
Q, 1975, 21:93-102.

12,122. Reed, Douglas.   Ballard at home.   Books & Bookmen,
1971, 10(7):10, 12.

12,123. Reed, Gail Simon.   Dr. Greenacre and Captain Gulliver:
notes on conventions of interpretation and reading.
Lit & Psychol, 1976, 26:185-190.

12,124. Reed, Kenneth T.   'This tasteless tranquility':   a Freudian
note on Johnson's Rasselas.   Lit & Psychol, 1969, 19:
61-62.

12,125. Reed, Michael D.   The power of Wuthering Heights: A
psychoanalytical examination.   Psychocultural Rev, 1977,
1(1):21-42.

12,126. Reed, Ralph.   The serpent as phallic symbol.   Psychoanal
Rev, 1922, 9:91-92.

12,127. Reeder, Roberta.   'The Black Cat' as a study in repression.   Poe Studies, 1974, 7:20-21.

12, 128.   Reedy, D. R.   Through the looking glass.   Bulletin Hispanic
           Studies, 1977, 54:125-134.
12, 129.   Regan, Nancy.   A home of one's own: women's bodies in
           recent women's fiction.   J Popular Culture, 1978, 11:
           772-788.
12, 130.   Regard, M.   Ste. -Beuve, romancier de l'égotism.   Revue
           de la Méditeranée, Jan-Apr 1960.
12, 131.   Regensteiner, Henry.   The obsessive personality in Jakob
           Wasserman's novel, Der Fall Maurizius.   Lit & Psy-
           chol, 1964, 14:106-115.
12, 132.   Reh, Albert M.   Psychologische und psychoanalytische In-
           terpretationsmethoden in der Literaturwissenschaft.   In
           Paulsen, W. (ed), Psychologie in der Literaturwissen-
           schaft.   Heidelberg: Stiehm, 1971, 34-55.
12, 133.   Rehman, R. G.   The Problems of Youth in the Early Works
           of Hermann Hesse.   Doctoral dissertation, New York
           Univ., 1951.
12, 134.   Reichbart, Richard.   Psi phenomena and Tolstoi.   J Amer
           Society for Psychical Research, 1976, 70:249-265.
12, 135.   Reid, B. L.   Smollett's healing journey.   Virginia Quart
           Rev, 1965, 41:549-570.
12, 136.   Reid, Ian.   'The woman problem' in some Australian and
           New Zealand novels.   Southern Rev; An Australian J
           Lit Studies, 1974, 7:187-204.
12, 137.   Reid, Maja D.   'Andreas Thameyers letzter Brief' and
           'Der letze Brief eines Literaten': two neglected
           Schnitzler stories.   German Q, 1972, 42:443-460.
12, 138.   Reid, Stephen.   The Beast in the Jungle and 'A Painful
           Case'; two different sufferings.   Amer Imago, 1963, 20:
           221-239.
12, 139.   _____.   Dostoeivski's Kirilov and freedom of the will.
           Hartford Studies in Lit, 1971, 3:197-208.
12, 140.   _____.   Moral passion in Portrait of a Lady and The
           Spoils of Poynton.   Modern Fiction Studies, 1966-67,
           12:24-43.
12, 141.   _____.   The oedipal pattern in Hemingway's 'The Capital
           of the World. '   Lit & Psychol, 1963, 13:37-43.
12, 142.   Reik, Theodor.   Flaubert und seine 'Versuch des heiligen
           Antonius': Ein Beitrag zue Künstler-psychologie.   Min-
           den: Bruns, 1912.
12, 143.   _____.   Freuds Studie über Dostojewski.   Imago, 1929,
           15:232-242; Almanach, 1930, 32-44.
12, 144.   _____.   Das Geschlechterverhältnis bei Schnitzler.   Die
           neue Generation, 1913, March.
12, 145.   _____.   Aus Gustave Flauberts Werken.   Int Zeitschrift
           für Psychoanalyse, 1911, 1:501-503.
12, 146.   _____.   The psychology of irony: a study based on
           Anatole France.   Complex, 1950, 1:14-26; Psyché,
           1950, 5:472-484.
12, 147.   _____.   Aus Theodor Fontane's Werken.   Int Zeitschrift
           für Psychoanalyse, 1913, 3:259.
12, 148.   Reilly, John E.   The lesser death-watch and 'The Tell-
           Tale Heart. '   Amer Transcendental Q, 1969, 2:3-9.

12,149. Reilly, John M. Richard Wright's curious thriller, Savage
         Holiday. College Language Assn J, 1977, 21:218-223.
12,150. Reilly, Robert J. Henry James and the morality of fiction.
         Amer Lit, 1967, 39:1-30.
12,151. Rein, David M. Conrad Aiken and psychoanalysis. Psy-
         choanal Rev, 1955, 42:402-411.
12,152. Reinhardt, George W. Form as consolation: thematic de-
         velopment in Ingeborg Bachmann's Malina. Symposium,
         1979, 33:41-64.
12,153. Reinoso, Diego García. Consideraciones sobre el duelo
         (estudio psicoanalitico de algunas cuentos de Edgar Poe).
         Revista di Psicoanálisi, 1961, 18:139-155.
12,154. Reiss, A. T., Jr. The social integration of queers and
         peers. Social Problems, 1961, 9:102-120; In Ruiten-
         beek, H. M. (ed), The Problem of Homosexuality in
         Modern Society. NY: Dutton, 1963, 249-278; In Gag-
         non, J. H., & Simon, W. (eds), Sexual Deviance. NY:
         Harper & Row, 1967, 197-228; In Rubington, E., &
         Weinberger, M. S. (eds), Deviance: The Interactionist
         Perspective. NY: Macmillan, 1968, 371-381.
12,155. Reiwald, Paul. Psychologie des Künstlers. Nationalzeit-
         ung, Basel, 10 Nov 1946.
12,156. Remak, H. H. H. Vinegar and water: allegory and symbol-
         ism. In Rehder, H. (ed), Literary Symbolism. Austin:
         Univ. Texas Press, 1965, 49-54.
12,157. Remenyi, Joseph. The psychology of war literature.
         Sewanee Rev, 1944, 52:137-147.
12,158. Renard, P. [The place of woman in Bernanos' work.] In
         Milner, M. (ed), Bernanos. Paris: Plon, 1972.
12,159. Reno, Christine M. Women in Voltaire's novels and
         contes. Mid-Hudson Language Studies, 1978, 1:81-96.
12,160. Resch, Y. Corps féminin, corps textuel. Essai sur le
         personnage féminin dans l'oeuvre de Colette. Paris:
         Klincksieck, 1973.
12,161. Resnik, Bramy. The Role of Women in Jakob Julius
         David's Novellen. DAI, 1972, 33:2392A-93A.
12,162. Rewak, W. J. James Agee's 'The Morning Watch': through
         darkness to light. Texas Q, 1973, 16:21-37.
12,163. Reynolds, Gordon D. Psychological Rebirth in Selected
         Works by Nathaniel Hawthorne, Stephen Crane, Henry
         James, William Faulkner, and Ralph Ellison. DAI,
         1974, 34:7719A.
12,164. Rhode, Eric. Death in twentieth-century fiction. In Toyn-
         bee, A., et al., Man's Concern with Death. NY: Mc-
         Graw-Hill, 1969, 160-176.
12,165. Rhodes, Carolyn H. Intelligence testing in Utopia. Ex-
         trapolation, 13 Dec 1971, 25-47.
12,166. Riamond, Michel. Le Monologue intérieur. In La Crise
         du Roman. Paris: Corti, 1966, 258-263, passim.
12,167. Ribble, Frederick G. The constitution of the mind and the
         concept of emotion in Fielding's Amelia. Philological
         Q, 1977, 56:104-122.
12,168. Ricard, Robert. Lo prohibido. Bulletin Hispanique, 1968,
         69:389-406.

12, 169.   . Ramon Villaamil, Rafael del Aguila, and Tor-
quemada. In Galdós et ses Romans. Paris: L'Institut
d'Etudes Hispaniques, 1961, 71-75.

12, 170.   Ricaumont, Jacques de. Sur quelques romans d'adolescence. Table Ronde, 1956, 101:131-136.

12, 171.   Rice, Julian C. Philip Roth's The Breast: cutting the
Freudian cord. Studies in Contemporary Satire, 1976,
3:9-16.

12, 172.   Richard, Claude. La Double voix dans 'The Tell-Tale
Heart.' Delta, 1975, 1:17-41.

12, 173.   Richard, J. -P. Céline et Marguerite. Critique, 1976,
32:919-335.

12, 174.   Richards, Bernard. Sources of Henry James's 'The Marriage.' Rev English Studies, 1979, 30:316-322.

12, 175.   Richards, Lewis. Sex under The Wild Palms and a moral
question. Arizona Q, 1972, 28:326-332.

12, 176.   Richards, Robert, & Richards, Chris. Feeling in The
Great Gatsby. Western Humanities Rev, 1967, 21:257-
265.

12, 177.   Richardson, Maurice. Psychoanalysis of ghost stories.
Twentieth Century, 1959, 166:419-431.

12, 178.   Richey, Clarence W. Professor Watkins' 'Sleep of Necessity': a note on the parallel between Doris Lessing's
Briefing for a Descent into Hell and the G. I. Gurdjieff-
P. D. Ouspensky system for esoteric psychology. Notes
on Contemporary Lit, 1972, 2:9-11.

12, 179.   Richmond, Arland Jerrol. The Theme of Flight in the
Works of Selected German Authors of the Twentieth
Century. DAI, 1975, 36:327A.

12, 180.   Richmond, Lee J. The maladroit, the medico, and the
magician: Saul Bellow's Seize the Day. Twentieth
Century Lit, 1973, 19:15-25.

12, 181.   Richmond, Velma Bourgeois. Sexual reversals in Thomas
Hardy and Ellen Glasgow. Southern Humanities Rev,
1979, 13:51-62.

12, 182.   Richter, Bernt. Psychogische Betrachtungen zu Thomas
Manns Novelle Mario und der Zauberer. In Wenzel,
G. (ed), Vollendung und Grösse Thomas Manns: Beit-
räge zu Werk und Personlichkeit des Dichters. Halle:
VEB, 1963, 106-117.

12, 183.   Richter, Harvena. The Inward Voyage. Princeton: Princeton Univ. Press, 1970.

12, 184.   Rico-Avelló, Carlos. Perfil psicobiográfico de La Celestina. In Criado de Val, M. (ed), 'La Celestina' y su
contorno social. Barcelona: Borrás, 1977, 155-161.

12, 185.   Ridard, M. Louis Lambert er la métapsychologie balzacienne. Paris: Foulon, 1960.

12, 186.   Riemer, S. Personality structure and Nazi fiction. Social
Forces, 1945, 24:32-36.

12, 187.   Ries, Wiebrecht. Kafka und Nietzsche. In Nietzsche
Studien. Berlin: 1973, 258-275.

12, 188.   Riesman, David. Tootle: a modern cautionary tale. In
The Lonely Crowd. New Haven: Yale Univ. Press,
1950, 107-111.

12, 189. Riffaterre, Michael. The reader's perception of the narra-
          tive. Balzac's Paix du ménage. In Valdés, M. J. , &
          Miller, J. (eds), Interpretation of Narrative. Toronto:
          Univ. Toronto Press, 1978, 28-37.
12, 190. Riggenbach, Jeff. Science fiction as will and idea: the
          world of Alfred Bester. Riverside Q, 1972, 5:168-177.
12, 191. Riggio, Thomas P. American Gothic: Poe and An Ameri-
          can Tragedy. Amer Lit, 1978, 49:515-532.
12, 192. Rigney, Barbara Hill. Madness and Sexual Politics in the
          Feminist Novel; Studies in Brontë, Woolf, Lessing and
          Atwood. Madison: Univ. Wisconsin Press, 1978, 1980;
          Review: E. Showalter, Criticism, 1979, 21:172-174.
12, 193. Rigual, Antonio R. Guilt in Selected 'Novelas contempo-
          ráneas' of Benito Pérez Galdos. DAI, 1972, 32:3962A.
12, 194. Rimmon-Kenan, Shlomith. From reproduction to produc-
          tion: the status of narration in Faulkner's Absalom,
          Absalom! Degrés, 1978, 16:1-19.
12, 195. Rinaldi, Nicholas Michael. Game-Consciousness and Game-
          Metaphor in the Work of William Faulkner. DA, 1964,
          24:4196-97.
12, 196. _____. Game imagery and game-consciousness in
          Faulkner's fiction. Twentieth Century Lit, 1964, 10:
          108-118.
12, 197. Rinehart, Nana Merete. Anthony Trollope's Treatment of
          Women, Marriage, and Sexual Morality Seen in the Con-
          text of Contemporary Debate. DAI, 1976, 37:993A.
12, 198. Ringe, Donald A. Charles Brockden Brown. In Emerson,
          E. H. (ed), Major Writers of Early American Literature.
          Madison: Univ. Wisconsin Press, 1972, 273-294.
12, 199. _____. Hawthorne's psychology of the head and heart.
          PMLA, 1950, 65:120-132.
12, 200. Rios, José Arthur. O outro lado de Henry Miller. Com-
          mentário, 1968, 10:299-304.
12, 201. Rippere, Victoria L. Ludwig Tieck's 'Der blonde Eckbert':
          a psychological reading. PMLA, 1970, 85:473-486.
12, 202. Rising, C. E. M. Forster's Maurice: a summing up.
          Texas Q, 1974, 17:84-96.
12, 203. Ritchie, L. M. Pathological realism. London Q Rev,
          1926, 145:145-152.
12, 204. Riva, Raymond T. Marcel Proust an immodest pro-
          posal. Criticism, 1968, 10:217-224.
12, 205. Rivière, Joan. The unconscious fantasy of an inner world
          reflected in examples from literature. In Klein, M. ,
          Heimann, P. , & Money-Kryle, R. (eds), New Direc-
          tions in Psycho-Analysis. The Significance of Infant
          Conflict in the Pattern of Adult Behavior. London:
          Tavistock, 1971; NY: Basic Books, 1971, 346-369.
12, 206. Rivière, Yvette. L'Aliénation dans les romans de Carson
          McCullers. Recherches Anglaises et Américaines,
          1971, 4:79-86.
12, 207. Roane, Margaret C. John Steinbeck as a spokesman for
          the mentally retarded. Wisconsin Studies in Contempo-
          rary Lit, 1964, 5:127-132.

12, 208.   Roazen, Paul. Orwell, Freud, and 1984. Virginia Q Rev, 1978, 54:675-695.

12, 209.   Robbe-Grillet, Alain. A fresh start for fiction. Evergreen Rev, 1958, 1:97-104.

12, 210.   _____. Le Realism, la psychologie et l'avenir du roman. Critique, 1956, 111-112:695-701.

12, 211.   Robert, M. Roman des origines et origines du roman. Paris: Grasset, 1972.

12, 212.   Roberts, C. H. [Thematic similarities between La Chute and The House of the Dead.] Rev des Lettres Modernes, 1972, Nos. 264-270.

12, 213.   Roberts, D. Tom Thumb and the imitation of Christ: towards a psycho-mythological interpretation of the 'hero' Oskar and his symbolic function. In Maslen, K. I. D. Proceedings and Papers of the 14th Congress of the Australasian Universities Language & Literature Association. Dunedin, New Zealand: AULLA, 1972, 160-174.

12, 214.   Roberts, Dexter M. A Psychological Interpretation of Social Philosophy in the Work of Frank Norris, American Literary Naturalist. DA, 1967, 27:4263A-64A.

12, 215.   Roberts, Dorothy Hutcherson. James Joyce's Ulysses: A Study of the Motifs of Androgyny. DAI, 1977, 38:2144A.

12, 216.   Roberts, Gemma. Temas existenciales en la novela española de postguerra. Madrid: Gredos, 1973.

12, 217.   Roberts, Heather. Mother, wife and mistress: women characters in the New Zealand novel from 1920 to 1940. Landfall, 1975, 29:233-247.

12, 218.   Roberts, James L. The individual and the community: Faulkner's Light in August. In McNeir, W., & Levy, L. B. (eds), Studies in American Literature. Baton Rouge: Louisiana State Univ. Press, 1960, 132-153.

12, 219.   Roberts, Patricia A. Archetypal Patterns in La comédie humaine: A Study of the Function and Meaning of Mythic Structures in Balzac's Literary Creation. DAI, 1973, 34:3429A.

12, 220.   Robinson, Deborah S. 'Frigidity' and the Aesthetic Vision: A Study of Karen Horney and Virginia Woolf. DAI, 1974, 35:2294A-95A.

12, 221.   Robinson, E. A. Poe's 'The Tell-Tale Heart.' Nineteenth Century Fiction, 1965, 19:369-378.

12, 222.   Robinson, Evalyne C. The Role of the Negro in William Faulkner's Public and Private Worlds. DAI, 1971, 32:2704A.

12, 223.   Robinson, James A. Psychological determinism in The Age of Innocence. Markham Rev, 1975, 5:1-5.

12, 224.   Robinson, K. E. The stream-of-consciousness technique in the structure of Joyce's Portrait. James Joyce Q, 1971, 9:63-84.

12, 225.   Robinson, M. L. Schizophrenia in fiction. British J Psychiat, 1978, 132:525.

12, 226.   Robison, Paula. Svevo: secrets of the confessional. Lit & Psychol, 1970, 20:101-114.

12, 227.   . Una Vita and the family romance. Modern Fic-
               tion Studies, 1972, 18:33-44.
12, 228. Robison, R. Time, death and the river in Dickens' novels.
               English Studies, 1972, 53:436-454.
12, 229. Robson, Vincent. The psychosocial conflict and the distor-
               tion of time: a study of Divers' disintegration in Tender
               Is the Night. Language & Lit, 1972, 1(2):55-64.
12, 230. Roby, Norman S. The Secret Self of George Meredith: A
               Study of His Heroes. DAI, 1973, 33:5690A-91A.
12, 231. Rochefort, Robert. La Culpabilité chez Kafka. Psyché,
               1948, 3:483-495.
12, 232. Rockwell, Joan. Normative attitudes of spies in fiction.
               In Rosenberg, Bernard & White, David M. (eds), Mass
               Culture Revisited. NY: Van Nostrand-Reinhold, 1971,
               325-340.
12, 233. Rodenko, Paul. Het Einde van de psychologische roman.
               Columbus, 1946, 2:17-26.
12, 234. Roditi, Edouard. De la psychologie des personnages de
               Svevo. Nouvelle Rev Française, 1974, 70-74.
12, 235. Rodrigues, Eusebio L. Reichianism in Henderson the Rain
               King. Criticism, 1973, 15:212-233.
12, 236. Rodrigues, Urbano Tavares. A evolução da ficção fran-
               cesa de André Malraux aos experiencialistas do romance
               post-psicológico. Seara Nova, 1962, 40:82-85, 93.
12, 237. Rodriguez, Alfred. An Introduction to the 'Episodios na-
               cionales' of Galdós. NY: Las Américas, 1967.
12, 238. Rodríguez Monegal, E. El mundo de José Donoso. Mundo
               Nuevo, 1967, 12:77-85.
12, 239. Roellenbleck, Ewald. Die Neurosenstruktur einer Roman-
               heldin. Zur Theorie einer neurotischen 'unio mystica.'
               Zeitschrift für Psychoanalyse, 1949, 1:39-59.
12, 240. Roellinger, Francis X. Psychical research and 'The Turn
               of the Screw.' Amer Lit, 1948-49, 20:401-412.
12, 241. Roemer, Kenneth M. Sex roles, utopia and change: the
               family in late nineteenth-century utopian literature.
               Amer Studies, 1972, 13(2):33-47.
12, 242. Rogers, Elizabeth S. Human Values and Themes in the
               Novels of Miguel Delibes. DAI, 1971, 31:6628A-29A.
12, 243. Rogers, Katharine M. The feminism of Daniel Defoe. In
               Fritz, P., & Morton, R. (eds), Woman in the 18th
               Century and Other Essays. Toronto: Hakkert, 1976,
               3-24.
12, 244.   . Inhibitions on eighteenth-century women novel-
               ists: Elizabeth Inchbald and Charlotte Smith. Eight-
               eenth Century Fiction, 1977, 11:63-78.
12, 245.   . The pressures of convention on Thackeray's
               women. Modern Language Rev, 1972, 67:257-263.
12, 246.   . Sensitive feminism vs conventional sympathy:
               Richardson and Fielding on women. Novel: A Forum
               on Fiction, 1976, 9:256-270; In Diamond, A., & Ed-
               wards, L. R. (eds), The Authority of Experience. Es-
               says in Feminist Criticism. Amherst: Univ. Massa-
               chusetts Press, 1977, 118-136.

12, 247. _____. Women in Thomas Hardy. Centennial Rev,
          1975, 19:249-258.
12, 248. Rogers, Robert. The beast in Henry James. Amer Imago,
          1956, 13:427-454.
12, 249. _____. The 'ineludible gripe' of Billy Budd. Lit &
          Psychol, 1964, 14:9-22.
12, 250. Rogers, Thomas F. 'Superfluous Men' and the Post-Stalin
          'Thaw.' The Alienated Hero in Soviet Prose During the
          Decade 1953-1963. The Hague: Mouton, 1972; DAI,
          1968, 29:910A.
12, 251. Rogg, Fay R. Aspectos psicosimbólicos del paisaje en
          Camino de perfección. Cuadernos Hispanoamericanos,
          1972, 265-67:531-536.
12, 252. Rogmann, H. El contradictorio Julián Goytisòlo. Insula,
          1976, 359:1, 12.
12, 253. Rohrberger, Mary. The daydream and the nightmare:
          surreality in Oliver Twist. Studies in the Humanities,
          1978, 6(2):21-28.
12, 254. Rom, Paul. Julian's withdrawal: François Mauriac as a
          psychologist. Individual Psychol, 1963, 1:2-4.
12, 255. _____. The notion of solidarity in the work of Albert
          Camus. J Individual Psychol, 1960, 16:146-150.
12, 256. _____. Psychiatry in modern novels. Int J Social
          Psychiat, 1965, 11:70-77.
12, 257. _____, et al. An Adlerian case of a character by Sar-
          tre. J Individual Psychol, 1965, 21:32-40.
12, 258. Romain, Y. de. L'Evolution du roman anglais. Rev
          Politique et Littéraire, 1931, 69:13-20.
12, 259. Roman, Christine M. Henry James and the surrogate
          mother. Amer Transcendental Q, 1978, 38:193-205.
12, 260. Romanofsky, Barbara R. A Study of Child Rearing Prac-
          tices in the Middle Novels of Charles Dickens. DAI,
          1978, 38:4853A.
12, 261. Romera, Antonio R. El monólógo silente en Galdos y en
          Joyce. Atenes, 1946, 257/258:373-379.
12, 262. Romero, Héctor R. La función del doppelgänger en las
          novelas de Juan Goytisolo. Kentucky Romance Q, 1977,
          24:411-418.
12, 263. Romig, Evelyn M. Women as Victims in the Novels of
          Charles Dickens and William Faulkner. DAI, 1978, 39:
          1600A.
12, 264. Rönnerstrand, T. Fagerbergs Hoknätt. En dictares
          världsbild och dess gestaltning i en roman. Gothen-
          burg: Litteraturvetenskapliga, 1976.
12, 265. Roper, David Andrew. The Theme of Aloneness in the
          Work of Hans Erich Nossack. DAI, 1977, 38:297A.
12, 266. Roper, Gordon. Robertson Davies' Fifth Business, and
          that old fantastical duke of dark corners, C. G. Jung.
          J Canadian Fiction, 1972, 1:33-39.
12, 267. Rosa, Alfred F. The psycholinguistics of Updike's 'Mu-
          seums and Women.' Modern Fiction Studies, 1974, 20:
          107-111.

12, 268.   Rosanoff, Aaron J.   A theory of personality based mainly
           on psychiatric experience.   Psychol Bulletin, 1920, 17:
           281-299.
12, 269.   Rosbottom, Ronald C.   Choderlos de Laclos.   Boston:
           Twayne, 1978.
12, 270.   _____.   Dangerous connections: a communicational ap-
           proach to Les Liaisons dangereuses.   In Free, L. R.
           (ed), Laclos: Critical Approaches to 'Les Liaisons
           dangereuses.'   Madrid: Turanzas, 1978.
12, 271.   _____.   Marivaux and the possibilities of the mémoire-
           novel.   Neophilologus, 1971, 56:43-49.
12, 272.   Rosbrow, Susan R.   Sexual Stereotyping in Magazine Fic-
           tion: A Discussion of the Romantic Myth in America.
           DAI, 1974, 35:2445.
12, 273.   Rose, Alan Henry.   Demonic Vision: Racial Fantasy and
           Southern Fiction.   Hamden, Conn: Archon, 1976.
12, 274.   _____.   The image of the Negro in the writings of Henry
           Clay Lewis.   Amer Lit, 1969, 41:255-263.
12, 275.   Rose, Charles.   Romance and the maiden archetype.   Con-
           radiana, 1974, 6:183-188.
12, 276.   Rose, E.   Psychological problems in Theodor Storm's
           Psyche.   German Q, 1943, 16:146-152.
12, 277.   Rose, Edward J.   'The queenly personality':   Walpole,
           Melville and mother.   Lit & Psychol, 1965, 216-229.
12, 278.   Rose, Ellen Cronan.   Doris Lessing's Children of Violence
           as a Bildungsroman: An Eriksonian Analysis.   DAI,
           1974, 35:3006A-07A.
12, 279.   _____.   The Eriksonian Bildunsroman: an approach
           through Doris Lessing.   Hartford Studies in Lit, 1975,
           7:1-17.
12, 280.   _____.   It's all a joke: science fiction in Kurt Vonnegut's
           The Sirens of Titan.   Lit & Psychol, 1979, 39:160-168.
12, 281.   Rose, Gilbert J.   The French Lieutenant's Woman: the
           unconscious significance of a novel to its author.
           Amer Imago, 1972, 29:165-176.
12, 282.   _____.   The orchestration of time in William Faulkner's
           Light in August.   Psychol Issues, Monograph 49, 1979,
           Ch. 11.
12, 283.   _____.   On the shores of self: Samuel Beckett's Mol-
           loy--irredentism and the creative impulse.   Psychoanal
           Rev, 1973-74, 60:587-604; Dynamische Psychiatrie,
           1974, 7(2):73-90.
12, 284.   _____.   William Faulkner's Light in August: the or-
           chestration of time in the psychology of artistic style.
           In The Psychoanalytic Study of Society, Vol. 8.   New
           Haven: Yale Univ. Press, 1979, 251-276.
12, 285.   Rose, Marilyn G.   Julien Green's heroine, the American
           child-woman.   Forum, 1961, 3:29-33.
12, 286.   Rosen, Nathan.   Chaos and Dostoevsky's women.   Kenyon
           Rev, 1958, 20:257-277.
12, 287.   Rosen, Victor H.   The relevance of 'style' to certain as-
           pects of defence and the synthetic function of the ego.
           Int J Psycho-Anal, 1961, 42:447-457.

12, 288. Rosenberg, F., & Lardies Gonzales, J. Los reflejos con-
dicionados en un cuento de Guy de Maupassant. Seminar Medecin, 1977, 150(14): 456-458.

12, 289. Rosenberg, Harold. A psychological case. In Act and the
Actor: Making the Self. NY: World, 1970, 104-125.

12, 290. Rosenberg, Rachelle A. R. The slaying of the dragon: an
archetypal study of Zola's Germinal. Symposium, 1972,
26: 349-362.

12, 291. _____. Zola's Imagery and the Archetype of the Great
Mother. DAI, 1970, 30: 3956A.

12, 292. Rosenberg, Samuel. Naked Is the Best Disguise: The
Death and Resurrection of Sherlock Holmes. Indianapolis: Bobbs-Merrill, 1974.

12, 293. _____. 'The Red-Headed League' as a Freudian parable. In Naked Is the Best Disguise. Indianapolis:
Bobbs-Merrill, 1974, 150-158; NY: Penguin, 1975.

12, 294. Rosenberg, Seymour, & Jones, Russell. A method for in-
vestigating and representing a person's implicit theory
of personality: Theodore Dreiser's view of people.
J Personality & Social Psychol, 1972, 22: 372-386.

12, 295. Rosenfield, Claire. An archetypal analysis of Conrad's
Nostromo. In Vickery, J. B. (ed), Myth and Literature.
Lincoln: Univ. Nebraska Press, 1966, 315-334; Texas
Studies in Lit & Language, 1962, 3: 510-534.

12, 296. _____. Despair and the lust for immortality. Wisconsin Studies in Contemporary Lit, 1967, 8: 174-192.

12, 297. _____. 'Men of a smaller growth': a psychological
analysis of William Golding's Lord of the Flies. Lit
& Psychol, 1961, 11: 93-101; In Nelson, W. (ed), Wil-
liam Golding's Lord of the Flies: A Source Book. NY:
Odyssey, 1963; In Manheim, L., & Manheim, E. (eds),
Hidden Patterns. NY: Macmillan, 1966, 259-274.

12, 298. _____. Paradise of Snakes. An Archetypal Analysis of
Conrad's Political Novels. Chicago: Univ. Chicago
Press, 1968.

12, 299. _____. The shadow within: the conscious and unconscious use of the double. Daedalus, 1963, 92: 326-344.

12, 300. Rosenheim, Frederick. Flight from home. Amer Imago,
1940, 1: 1-30.

12, 301. Rosenthal, Lynne Meryl. The Child Informed: Attitudes
Towards the Socialization of the Child in Nineteenth
Century English Children's Literature. DAI, 1975, 35:
6678-6679A.

12, 302. Rosenwald, George C. Art work as a force in the artist's
life: Thomas Mann's exile and Joseph and His Brothers. In Psychoanalytic Study of the Child, Vol. 33.
New Haven: Yale Univ. Press, 1978, 519-562.

12, 303. Rosenzweig, Paul Jonathan. Faulkner's motif of food in
Light in August. Amer Imago, 1980, 37: 93-112.

12, 304. _____. The Wilderness in American Fiction: A Psychoanalytic Study of a Central American Myth. DAI,
1973, 33: 5140A.

12, 305. Rosenzweig, Saul. The ghost of Henry James ... a study
in thematic apperception. Partisan Rev, 1950, 11: 436-

455; In Phillips, W. (ed), Art and Psychoanalysis. NY: Criterion, 1957, 89-111; Character & Personality, 1943, 12: 79-100.

12, 306. _____. The Jameses' stream of consciousness. Contemporary Psychol, 1958, 3: 250-257.

12, 307. Rosowsky, Ginditta. Théorie et pratique psychanalytiques dans la Coscienza di Zeno. Rev des Etudes Italiennes, 1970, 16: 49-70.

12, 308. Ross, Donald, Jr. Dreams and sexual repression in The Blithedale Romance. PMLA, 1971, 86: 1014-1017.

12, 309. Ross, Duncan M. The Indispensable Invalid: Joseph Conrad's Treatment by the Freudian Critics. DAI, 1974, 35: 471A-72A.

12, 310. Ross, Mary Beth. The 'bisexual' world of Jane Austen. Aphra, 1975, 6(1): 2-15.

12, 311. Rossi, M. M. Saggio sul pansessualismo di D. H. Lawrence. Rivista di Psicologia Normale e patologica, 1934, 30: 217-239.

12, 312. Rossky, William. As I Lay Dying: the insane world. Texas Studies in Lit & Language, 1962, 4: 87-95.

12, 313. _____. The pattern of nightmare in Sanctuary: or Miss Reba's dogs. Modern Fiction Studies, 1969, 15: 503-515.

12, 314. _____. The Reivers and Huckleberry Finn: Faulkner and Twain. Huntington Library Q, 1965, 28: 373-387.

12, 315. Rossman, Charles. Lawrence on the critics' couch: pervert or prophet. D. H. Lawrence Rev, 1970, 3: 175-185.

12, 316. Rossman, Edward S. The conflict over food in the work of J. -K. Huysmans. Nineteenth-Century French Studies, 1974, 2: 61-67.

12, 317. Roth, Mary B. Tiresias Their Muse: Studies in Sexual Stereotypes in the English Novel. DAI, 1974, 34: 6604A-05A.

12, 318. Roth, Philip. Imagining the erotic; three introductions. In Reading Myself and Others. NY: Farrar, Straus & Giroux, 1975, 191-214.

12, 319. Roth, Phyllis A. Lunatics, Lovers, and a Poet: A Study of Doubling and the Doppelgänger in the Novels of Nabokov. DAI, 1972, 33: 2950A-51A.

12, 320. _____. The psychology of the double in Nabokov's Pale Fire. Essays in Lit, 1975, 2: 209-229.

12, 321. _____. In search of aesthetic bliss: a rereading of Lolita. College Lit, 1975, 2: 28-49.

12, 322. _____. Suddenly sexual women in Bram Stoker's Dracula. Lit & Psychol, 1977, 27: 113-121.

12, 323. Rothschild, Herbert, Jr. The language of mesmerism in 'The Quarter-Deck' scene in Moby Dick. English Studies, 1972, 53: 235-238.

12, 324. Roudiez, Leon S. Une Gaîté violette (Lecture d'un roman de M. Butor). Romanic Rev, 1977, 68: 32-42.

12, 325. Roulston, Robert. The Beautiful and Damned: the alcoholic's revenge. Lit & Psychol, 1977, 27: 156-163.

12, 326. _____. Dick Diver's plunge into the Roman void: the
setting of Tender Is the Night. South Atlantic Q, 1978,
77:85-97.

12, 327. Rouquette, Michel L. [Constraint and qualification in the
Rougon-Macquart: extension of an hypothesis.] JPNP,
1972, No. 4, 407-412.

12, 328. Rovettá, Carlos. La sombra: novela primigenia de Galdós. Nosotros, 1943, 23:181-187.

12, 329. Rovit, Earl. Fathers and sons in American fiction. Yale
Rev, 1964, 53:248-257.

12, 330. _____. The ghosts in James's 'The Jolly Corner.'
Tennessee Studies in Lit, 1965, 10:65-72.

12, 331. Rovner, Marc Leslie. What William Wilson knew: Poe's
dramatization of an errant mind. Library Chronicle,
1976, 41:73-82.

12, 332. Rowe, William Woodin. Dostoevsky: Child and Man in
His Works. NY: New York Univ. Press, 1970.

12, 333. _____. Nabokov's Deceptive World. NY: New York
Univ. Press, 1971.

12, 334. Rowley, Eugene G. Individual Instinct and Societal Repression in the Works of D. H. Lawrence. DAI, 1974, 35:
3766A.

12, 335. Royer, G. [The Metamorphosis by Kafka. A study of
clinical and applied psychoanalysis.] Rivista di Psicoanalisi, 1963, 20:253-267.

12, 336. Rubenstein, Jill. The crisis of identity in Fanny Burney's
Evelina. New Rambler, 1972, 12:45-50.

12, 337. Rubenstein, Marc A. 'My Accursed Origin': the search
for the mother in Frankenstein. Studies in Romanticism, 1976, 15:165-194.

12, 338. Rubenstein, Roberta. Briefing on inner space: Doris Lessing and R. D. Laing. Psychoanal Rev, 1976, 63:83-93.

12, 339. _____. Doris Lessing's The Golden Notebook: the
meaning of its shape. Amer Imago, 1975, 32:40-58.

12, 340. _____. The Novelistic Vision of Doris Lessing. Breaking the Forms of Consciousness. Urbana: Univ. Illinois Press, 1979.

12, 341. Rubenstein, W. Franz Kafka: A Hunger Artist. Monatshefte, 1952, 44:13-19.

12, 342. Rubin, Larry. Billy Budd: what goes on behind closed
doors? Amer Imago, 1980, 37:65-67.

12, 343. _____. The homosexual motif in Willa Cather's 'Paul's
Case.' Studies in Short Fiction, 1975, 12:127-131.

12, 344. Rubin, Stephen E. Conversations with the author of I Never Promised You a Rose Garden. Psychoanal Rev,
1972, 59(2):201-215.

12, 345. Rubin, Steven J. Early short fiction of Richard Wright
reconsidered. Studies in Short Fiction, 1978, 15:405-
410.

12, 346. _____. Malamud and the theme of love and sex. Studies in Amer Jewish Lit, 1978, 4(1):19-23.

12, 347. Rudat, Wolfgang E. H. Thomas More, Hythloday, and Odysseus: an anatomy of Utopia. Amer Imago, 1980, 37:
38-48.

12,348. Ruddick, Lisa. The Seen and the Unseen: Virginia Woolf's
         'To the Lighthouse.' Cambridge: Harvard Univ. Press,
         1977; Review: Marcia Landy, Modern Fiction Studies,
         1977-78, 23:642-643.
12,349. Ruderman, Judith Gay. 'The Fox' and the 'devouring
         mother.' D.H. Lawrence Rev, 1977, 10:251-269.
12,350. _____. Lawrence's 'The Fox' and Verga's 'The She-
         Wolf': variations on the theme of the devouring mother.
         MLN, 1979, 94:153-165.
12,351. _____. The Making of The Fox: A Study of the 'De-
         vouring Mother' Figure as It Relates to D.H. Law-
         rence's Ideal of Leadership. DAI, 1976, 37:3650A.
12,352. Rüdiger, Horst. Moderne Roman und Psychoanalyse.
         Sammlung, 1951, 6:1083-1086.
12,353. Rudloff, Sandra L.M. The Woman as a Figure in the
         Works of Pierre Louÿs. DAI, 1976, 36:8100A-01A.
12,354. Rudolf, G. [Psychology of horror literature. Schizoid
         body experience on the example of Frankenstein's mon-
         ster.] Zeitschrift für Psychosomatische Medizin und
         Psychoanalyse, 1972, 18:205-219.
12,355. Rueff-Duval, Dominique. Etude de certains aspects de la
         féminité. Entretiens Psychiatriques, 1964, No. 10.
12,356. Ruehlmann, William. Saint with a Gun: The Unlawful
         American Private Eye. NY: New York Univ. Press,
         1974.
12,357. Ruf, U. Franz Kafka. Das Dilemma der Söhne. Berlin:
         Schmidt, 1975.
12,358. Rugoff, Milton A. Prudery and Passion. Sexuality in Vic-
         torian America. NY: Putnam, 1971.
12,359. Ruitenbeek, Hendrik M. (ed). The Literary Imagination:
         Psychoanalysis and the Genius of the Writer. Chicago:
         Quadrangle, 1965.
12,360. Rule, Jane V. Lesbian images. Yale Univ. Library Ga-
         zette, 1975, 50.
12,361. Rumazo, L. La presencia de sadismo en Sábato. Cuad-
         ernos Hispano-Americanos, 1972, 270:551-558.
12,362. Rümke, H.C. Over Frederik van Eeden's 'Van de koele
         meren des doods.' Amsterdam: Scheltema & Holkema,
         1964.
12,363. Russ, Joanna. Dream literature and science fiction. Ex-
         trapolation, 1969, 11:6-14.
12,364. _____. The image of women in science fiction. In
         Cornillon, S.K. (ed), Images of Women in Fiction.
         Bowling Green, Ohio: Bowling Green Univ. Popular
         Press, 1972, 79-94.
12,365. Russel, Peter. Schnitzler's Blumen: the treatment of a
         neurosis. Forum for Modern Language Studies, 1977,
         13:289-302.
12,366. Russell, Ann Z. The Image of Women in Eighteenth-Cen-
         tury English Novels. DAI, 1974, 35:1122A.
12,367. Ruthrof, H.G. A note on Henry James's psychological
         realism and the concept of brevity. Studies in Short
         Fiction, 1975, 12:369-373.

12,368. Ruthven, K. K. The savage God: Conrad and Lawrence. Critical Q, 1968, 10:39-55.
12,369. Rutt, Richard. Women in Yi dynasty through classical novels. Korea J, 1974, 14(1):41-45.
12,370. Ryals, C. de L. D. H. Lawrence's 'The Horse Dealer's Daughter.' Lit & Psychol, 1962, 12:39-43.
12,371. Ryan, J. The psychology of love in the Cuestión de amor. Hispania, 1963, 46:61-65.
12,372. Ryan, Lawrence. 'Zum letztenmal Psychologie!': Zur psychologischen Deutbarkeit der Werke Franz Kafkas. In Paulsen, W. (ed), Psychologie in der Literaturwissenschaft. Heidelberg: Stiehm, 1971, 157-173.
12,373. Rycroft, Charles. A detective story: psychoanalytic observations. Psychoanal Q, 1957, 26:229-245.
12,374. Ryder, F. G. Kafka's Findling: Oedipus manqué? Modern Language Notes, 1977, 92:509-524.
12,375. Rysan, Josef. Theodor Storm and psychic phenomena. Modern Philologie, 1955, 53:39-46.

12,376. Saagpakk, Paul F. Psychopathological Elements in British Novels from 1890-1930. DA, 1966, 27:782A-783A.
12,377. Sabatini, Arthur V. La Démence de la claustration dans Les Rougon-Macquart. DAI, 1972, 33:764A.
12,378. Sabiston, Elizabeth J. A new fable for critics: Philip Roth's The Breast. Int Fiction Rev, 1975, 2:27-34.
12,379. Saccone, Eduardo. Ancora su Svevo e la psicanalisi. MLN, 1975, 90:127-136.
12,380. _____. Commento a 'Zeno.' Bologna: Il Mulino, 1973.
12,381. _____. Malattia e psicanalisi nella Coscienza di Zeno. MLN, 1973, 88:1-42.
12,382. _____. Senilità di Italo Svevo: Dalla 'impotenza del privato' alla 'ansiosa speranza.' Modern Language Notes, 1967, 82(1):1-55.
12,383. _____. Svevo, Zeno e la psicanalisi. MLN, 1970, 85(1):67-82.
12,384. Sacharoff, Mark. Grotesque comedy in Canetti's Auto da Fe. Criticism, 1972, 14(1):99-112.
12,385. _____. Pathological, comic, and tragic elements in Kafka's 'In the Penal Colony.' Genre, 1971, 4:392-411.
12,386. Sachs, Erich. The Fall by Albert Camus: a study in Adlerian psychology. J Individual Psychol, 1972, 28:76-80.
12,387. Sachs, Hanns. Schillers Geisterscher, Parts 1, 2. Imago, 1915, 4:69-95, 145-179.
12,388. Sachs, W. Psychoanalysis: Its Meaning and Practical Application. London: Cassell, 1934.
12,389. Sack, Leopold. Die Psychoanalyse im modernen englischen Roman. Zurich: 1930.
12,390. Sackett, Sam J. Gulliver four: here we go again. Rocky Mountain MLA Bulletin, 1973, 27:212-218.
12,391. Sackville-West, Edward. Dickens and the world of child-

hood. In Inclinations. Port Washington, NY: Kennikat, 1967 (1949), 13-26.

12, 392. Sadger, Isadore. J. C. Heer Joggeli. Int Zeitschrift für
Psychoanalyse, 1911, 1: 528-529.

12, 393. Sadoff, Dianne F. Storytelling and the figure of the father
in Little Dorrit. PMLA, 1980, 95: 234-245.

12, 394. _____. Waste and Transformation: A Psychoanalytic
Study of Charles Dickens's Bleak House and Our Mutual
Friend. DAI, 1973, 34: 2653A-54A.

12, 395. Saha, Narayan. Dickens's treatment of child-psychology
--and David Copperfield. Bulletin Department English
(Calcutta), 1970-71, 6(2): 26-28.

12, 396. Saha, P. K. Conrad's Heart of Darkness. Explicator,
1969, 27: 7.

12, 397. Sahli, Janet. Le Rôle de l'enfance dans La Comédie humaine. L'Année balzacienne, 1975, 279-288.

12, 398. Said, Edward William. Joseph Conrad and the Fiction of
Autobiography. Cambridge: Harvard Univ. Press,
1966; London: Oxford Univ. Press, 1966.

12, 399. St. (Stefan Zweig?). Der Oedipus-komplex bei Werfel und
Wassermann. Psychoanalytiche Bewegung, 1931, 3: 474-
478.

12, 400. St. Armand, Barton Levi. The Dragon and Uroboros:
themes of metamorphosis in 'Arthur Gordon Pym.'
Amer Transcendental Q, 1978, 37: 57-71.

12, 401. _____. The Roots of Horror in the Fiction of H. P.
Lovecraft. Elizabethtown, NY: Dragon, 1977.

12, 402. Sakamoto, Masayuki. The discovery of one's other self--
You Can't Go Home Again reconsidered. Studies in
English Lit, 1968, 17-35.

12, 403- Salas, Eduardo J. Un enfoque psicoanalitico de las identi-
4.   caciones en Dorian Gray: La psicopatia y la perversion. Revista de Psicoanálisis, 1969, 26: 643-667.

12, 405. Salerno, Nicholas A. Catherine: theme and structure.
Amer Imago, 1961, 18: 159-166.

12, 406. Salfeld, Hans-Eduard. Die Erzähltechnik Puschkins unter
motivationspsychologischen Gesichtspunkten gesehen.
Die Welt der Slaven, 1973, 18: 308-316.

12, 407. Salgado, Maria A. El cepillo de dientes and El apartamiento: two opposing views of alienated man. Romance Notes, 1977, 17: 247-254.

12, 408. Saliba, David Robert. The nightmare in miniature:
'Ligeia.' Amer Transcendental Q, 1978, 40: 367-378.

12, 409. _____. A Psychology of Fear: The Nightmare Formula
of Edgar Allan Poe. DAI, 1978, 38: 4832A.

12, 410. Salières, François. Pathologie et littérature. Presse
Médicale, 1949, 37: 516-517.

12, 411. Sallenave, Danièle. A propos du 'monologue interieure':
lecture d'une théorie. Littérature, 1972, 5: 69-87.

12, 412. Salvesen, H. A. [Pickwick's syndrome. Why Pickwick?]
Tidskrift for den Norske Laegeforening, 1961, 81: 758-
759.

12, 413. Salzberg, Joel. Love, identity, and death: James's The Princess Casamassima reconsidered. Rocky Mountain MLA Bulletin, 1972, 26(4):127-135.

12, 414. Samet, Tom. Henry Roth's bull story: guilt and betrayal in Call It Sleep. Studies in the Novel, 1975, 7:569-583.

12, 415. Samilowitz, Hazel. James Joyce's Ulysses. Psychiat Communications, 1968, 10:21-31.

12, 416. Sampson, A. Trollope in the twentieth century. London Mercury, 1937, 35:371-377.

12, 417. Sandbank, S. Structure of paradox in Kafka. Modern Language Q, 1967, 28:462-472.

12, 418. Sandberg, Alvin. Erotic patterns in 'The Paradise of Bachelors and The Tartarus of Maids.' Lit & Psychol, 1968, 18:2-8.

12, 419. Sandberg, H. De dömdas ö--en politisk idéroman. Samlaren, 1972, 93:62-90.

12, 420. Sanders, Scott. Pynchon's paranoid history. In Levine, G., & Leverenz, D. (eds), Mindful Pleasures. Essays on Thomas Pynchon. Boston: Little, Brown, 1976. 139-159; Twentieth Century Lit, 1975, 21:177-192.

12, 421. Sands, Steven. The narcissism of Stendhal and Julien Sorel. Studies in Romanticism, 1975, 14:337-363.

12, 422. Sandstrom, Glenn. Identity diffusion: Joe Christmas and Quentin Compson. Amer Q, 1967, 19:207-223.

12, 423. Santander, Carlos. Camino de perfección de Pío Baroja: aproximacíon psicoanalitica. In En homeaje a Eleazar Huerta. Valdívia: Univ. Austral de Chile, 1965, 197-217.

12, 424. Santee, Delford L. Stendhal's Character Trios: A Study in Fragmented Personality. DAI, 1971, 31:6070A.

12, 425. Sanz Villanueva, Santos. El 'conductismo' en la novela española reciente. Cuadernos Hispano-Americanos, 1972, Nos. 263-4:593-603.

12, 426. _____. Tendencias de la novela española actual (1950-70). Madrid: Cuadernos para el diálogo, 1972.

12, 427. Saposnik, Irving. Stevenson's 'Markheim': a fictional 'Christmas sermon.' Nineteenth Century Fiction, 1966, 21:277-282.

12, 428. Sarasin, Philipp. Goethes Mignon, eine psychoanalytische Studie. Imago, 1929, 15:349-399; Vienna: Int Psychoanalytischer Verlag, 1930.

12, 429. Sardello, Robert J. An empirical-phenomenological study of fantasy, with a note on J. R. R. Tolkien and C. S. Lewis. Psychocultural Rev, 1978, 2(3):203-220.

12, 430. Sarduy, Severo. Escritos sobre un cuerpo. Buenos Aires: Sudamericana, 1969.

12, 431. _____, & Rodríguez Monegal, Emir. Por una novela novelesca y metafísica. Mundo Nuevo, 1966, 5:5-21.

12, 432. Sargent, Lyman Tower. Ambiguous legacy: the role and position of women in the English utopia. Extrapolation, 1977, 19:39-49.

12, 433. _____. Women in utopia. Comparative Lit Studies, 1973, 10:302-316.

12, 434. Sarkisian, Levon. Saroyan's Rock Wagram; a psycho-social character study. Armenian Rev, 1959, 11:61-68.
12, 435. Sarmiento, E. Estructuración y simbolismo en De sobre-
mesa de José Asunción Silva. In Actas del Tercer
Congreso Internacional de Hispanitas. Mexico: 1970,
807-814.
12, 436. Sarotte, Georges-Michel. Animalité, homérotisme et androgynie chez Jack London. Recherches Anglaises et
Américaines, 1978, 11:98-108.
12, 437. _____. Like a Brother, Like a Lover: Male Homosexuality in the American Novel and Theater from Herman Melville to James Baldwin. Garden City, NY:
Doubleday Anchor, 1978.
12, 438. Sartori, Eva Martin. Nature and Forms of Anxiety in the
Works of Pierre Choderlos de Laclos. DAI, 1975, 36:
1565A.
12, 439. Sartre, Jean-Paul. Foreword: Jean Genet's The Thief's
Journal. NY: Bantam, 1949, 1965.
12, 440. Sarvan, Charies, & Sarvan, Liebetrout. D. H. Lawrence
and Doris Lessing's The Grass Is Singing. Modern
Fiction Studies, 1978-79, 24:533-537.
12, 441. Sasaki, Miyoko. [The World of Edith Wharton: Its Fris-
son and Raison.] Tokyo: Kenkyusha, 1976.
12, 442. Satterfield, Leon. Thurber's The Secret Life of Walter
Mitty. Explicator, 1969, 27(8):57.
12, 443. Saueressig, H. Literatur und Medizin. Zu Thomas Manns
Der Zauberberg. Deutsche Medizinische Wochenschrift,
1974, 99:1780-1786.
12, 444. Saunders, Judith P. Mortal stain: literary allusion and
female sexuality in 'Mrs. Dalloway in Bond Street. '
Studies in Short Fiction, 1978, 15:139-144.
12, 445. Sautermeister, Gert. Die sozialkritische und sozialpsychologische Dimension in Franz Kafkas Die Verwandlung. Der Deutschunterricht, 1974, 26(4):99-109.
12, 446. _____. Sozialpsychologische Textanalyse: Franz Kafkas Erzählung 'Das Urteil. ' In Kimpel, D. , & Pinker-
neil, B. (eds), Methodische Praxis der Literaturwissenschaft. Kronberg: Scriptor, 1976, 1-21.
12, 447. Savage, Catharine H. Gide's criticism of symbolism.
Modern Language Rev, 1966, 61, 601-609.
12, 448. _____. L'Immoraliste: psychology and rhetoric.
Xavier Univ. Studies, 1967, 6:43-62.
12, 449. _____. The romantic Père Goriot. Studies in Romanticism, 1966, 5:104-112.
12, 450. Savage, D. S. Aldous Huxley and the dissociation of personality. Sewanee Rev, 1947, 55:537-568; In Rajan, B.
(ed), Focus Four: The Novelist as Thinker. London:
Dobson, 1948, 9-34.
12, 451. Saveson, John E. Conrad, Blackwood's, and Lombroso.
Conradiana, 1974, 6(1):57-62.
12, 452. _____. Conrad: The Later Moralist. Atlantic Highlands, NJ: Humanities Press, 1976.

12, 453.   _____. Conrad's view of primitive peoples in Lord Jim
            and The Heart of Darkness. Modern Fiction Studies,
            1970, 65:306-318.
12, 454.   _____. Contemporary psychology in The Nigger of the
            Narcissus. Studies in Short Fiction, 1970, 7:219-231.
12, 455.   _____. The intuitionist hero in Lord Jim. Conradiana,
            1972, 4(3):34-47.
12, 456.   _____. Joseph Conrad: The Making of a Moralist.
            Atlantic Highlands, NJ: Humanities Press, 1972; Re-
            view: James Walt, Conradiana, 1973, 5(3):73-75.
12, 457.   _____. Marlow's psychological vocabulary in Lord Jim.
            Texas Studies in Language & Lit, 1970, 12:457-470.
12, 458.   Sayegh, Alia. The Concept and Role of Woman in the
            Works of André Breton. DAI, 1975, 36:328A-29A.
12, 459.   Scafidel, J. R. Sexuality in Windy McPherson's Son. Twen-
            tieth Century Lit, 1977, 23:94-101.
12, 460.   Scanlan, Timothy M. Communication, separation and death
            in Rousseau's La nouvelle Héloise. DAI, 1971, 32:
            3330A.
12, 461.   Scannell, M. J. A. The Treatment of Emotion in Jane Aus-
            ten and Charlotte Brontë. Doctoral dissertation, Univ.
            Oxford, 1975.
12, 462.   Scari, Robert M. Aspectos realista-tradicionales del arte
            narrativo de Borges. Hispania, 1974, 57:899-907.
12, 463.   Schaeffer, Susan Fromberg. The editing blinks of Vladimir
            Nabokov's The Eye. Univ. Windsor Rev, 1972, 8:5-30.
12, 464.   Schafer, W. J. Irony from the underground--satiric ele-
            ments in Invisible Man. Satire Newsletter, 1969, 7:22-
            29.
12, 465.   Schaffer, Susan. The development of the double in selected
            works of Carlos Fuentes. Mester, 1977, 6:81-86.
12, 466.   Schamberger, J. Edward. Renaming Percival Brownlee in
            Faulkner's 'Bear.' College Lit, 1977, 4:92-94.
12, 467.   Schechner, Mark. Down in the mouth with Saul Bellow.
            Amer Rev, 1975, 23:40-77.
12, 468.   _____. Exposing Joyce. James Joyce Q, 1976, 13(3):
            266-273.
12, 469.   _____. Freud on Joyce. James Joyce Q, 1971, 9:280-
            296.
12, 470.   _____. James Joyce's Ulysses: A Psychoanalytic In-
            vestigation. DAI, 1972, 32:984-5.
12, 471.   _____. Joyce and psychoanalysis: two additional per-
            spectives. James Joyce Q, 1977, 14:416-419.
12, 472.   _____. Joyce in Nighttown: A Psychoanalytic Inquiry
            into Ulysses. Berkeley: Univ. California Press, 1974;
            Review by Phillip F. Herring, Modern Fiction Studies,
            1975, 21:258-264.
12, 473.   Schecter, Harold. The eye and the nerve: a psychological
            reading of James Dickey's Deliverance. In Filler, L.
            (ed), Seasoned Authors for a New Season. Bowling
            Green, Ohio: Bowling Green Univ. Popular Press,
            1980, 4-19.

12,474. _____. Kali on Main Street: the rise of the terrible mother in America. J Popular Culture, 1973, 7:251-263.

12,475. Scheer, Lieve. De Calvijn van de psychoanalyse. Dietsche Warande en Belfort, 1974, 119:49-53.

12,476. Scheible, Hartmut. Arthur Schnitzler und die Aufklärung. Munich: Fink, 1977.

12,477. Scheick, William J. Compulsion toward repetition: Sherwood Anderson's 'Death in the Woods.' Studies in Short Fiction, 1974, 11:141-146.

12,478. Scheidt, Jürgen vom. Descensus ad Inferos: Tiefenpsychologische Aspekte der Science Fiction. In Barmeyer, E. (ed), Science Fiction: Theorie und Geschichte. Munich: Fink, 1972, 133-163.

12,479. Scheuermann, Mona. From mind to society: Caleb Williams as a psychological novel. Dutch Q Rev, 1977, 7:115-127.

12,480. Schiefele, Hanns. Freuds Bedeutung für die Kunst Betrachtung Marcel Proust, James Joyce, Thomas Mann. In Reimann, F. (ed), Lebendige Psychoanalyse: die Bedeutung Sigmund Freuds für des Verstehen des Menschen. Munich: Beck, 1956; In El psicoanalisis vivente. Buenos Aires: Fabril, 1961, 167-192.

12,481. Schilder, Paul F. Psychoanalytic remarks on Alice in Wonderland and Lewis Carroll. JNMD, 1938, 87:159-168.

12,482. Schilling, G. Images et imagination de la mort dans le Voyage au bout de la nuit. L'Information Littéraire, 1971, 23:68-75.

12,483. Schlack, Beverly Ann. A Freudian look at Mrs. Dalloway. Lit & Psychol, 1973, 23:49-58.

12,484. Schlauch, Margaret. The language of James Joyce. Science & Society, 1939, 3:482-497.

12,485. Schludermann, Brigitte, & Finlay, Rosemarie. Mythical reflections of the East in Hermann Hesse. Modern Language Rev, 1969, 2:126-131.

12,486. Schmidl, Fritz. Freud and Dostoevsky. JAPA, 1965, 13:518-532.

12,487. Schmidt, C. Marcel Proust. Die Semantik der Farben in Seinem Werk 'A la recherche du temps perdu.' Bonn: Bouvier, 1977.

12,488. Schmidt, Dolores Barracano. The great American bitch. College English, 1971, 32:900-905.

12,489. Schmidt, G. Der Wahn im deutschsprachigen Schrifttum der letzten 25 Jahre, 1914-1939. Zentralblatt für die gesamte Neurologie und Psychiatrie, 1940, 97:113-143.

12,490. Schmidt, Ruth A. Woman's place in the sun: feminism in Insolación. Revista de Estudios Hispánicos, 1974, 8:69-81.

12,491. Schmidt, Willi. Schillers Frauengestalten. Int Zeitschrift für Psychoanalysis, 1913, 4:233.

12,492. Schmitz, Oskar A.H. Don Juan, Casanova und andere erotische Charaktere. Munich: Müller, 1913.

12, 493. Schmitz, Robert M. Death and Colonel Morden in Clarissa. South Atlantic Q, 1970, 69:346-353.

12, 494. _____, & Wilt, Judith. Lovelace and impotence. PMLA, 1977, 92:1005-1006.

12, 495. Schneck, Jerome M. Daniel Defoe's Moll Flanders and congenital syphilis. New York State J Medicine, 1978, 78:2104-2105.

12, 496. _____. Dostoyevsky and Freud on criminal psychopathology. Psychiat Q Supplement, 1966, 40:278-282.

12, 497. _____. Henry James, George du Maurier, and mesmerism. Int J Clinical & Experimental Hypnosis, 1978, 26(2):76-80.

12, 498. _____. Hypnagogic hallucinations. Herman Melville's Moby Dick. New York State J Medicine, 1977, 77: 2145-2147.

12, 499. _____. Hypnotic and non-hypnotic revivication with special reference to Jack London's Martin Eden. Psychiat Q, 1968, 42:504-507.

12, 500. _____. Insanity and criminality in Tobias Smollett's Roderick Random. New York State J Medicine, 1975, 75:926-928.

12, 501. _____. Karl Kahlbaum's catatonia and Herman Melville's 'Bartleby the Scrivener.' Archives General Psychiat, 1972, 27:48-51.

12, 502. _____. Legal insanity, moral insanity, and Stendhal's Le Rouge et le noir. Medical History, 1966, 10:281-290.

12, 503. _____. Moravia's modern Oedipus. Diseases Nervous System, 1968, 29:626-628.

12, 504. _____. Pseudo-malingering and Leonid Andreyev's The Dilemma. Psychiat Q, 1970, 44:49-54.

12, 505. _____. The psychopathology of Silas Marner. Amer J Psychiat, 1967, 123:1463-1464.

12, 506. _____. The psychotherapeutic statement and psychosomatic observations of Hawthorne in The Scarlet Letter. J History Behavioral Science, 1965, 1:259-261.

12, 507. _____. Sleep paralysis in F. Scott Fitzgerald's The Beautiful and the Damned. New York State J Medicine, 1971, 71:378-379.

12, 508. Schneider, C. I. Das Todesproblem bei Hermann Hesse. Marburg: Elwert, 1973.

12, 509. Schneider, Daniel John. Color-symbolism in The Great Gatsby. Univ. Rev, 1964, 31:13-18.

12, 510. _____. The divided self in the fiction of Henry James. PMLA, 1975, 90:477-460.

12, 511. _____. Symbolism in Conrad's Lord Jim: the total pattern. Modern Fiction Studies, 1966-67, 12:427-438.

12, 512. _____. The symbolism of The Sun Also Rises. Discourse, 1967, 10:334-342.

12, 513. Schneider, Ernst. Die Todes-und selbstmordphantasien Tom Sawyers. Zeitschrift für psychoanalytische Pädagogik, 1928, 3:389-400.

12, 514. Schneider, Jane Frances. The Image of Women in Selected
          Spanish Golden Age Byzantine Romances. DAI, 1978,
          39:1626A.
12, 515. Schneiderman, Leo. Folkloristic motifs in Aucassin and
          Nicolette. Connecticut Rev, 1974, 8:56-71.
12, 516. Schoenl, W. J. Abstract phraseology, Orwell, and abor-
          tion. Intellect, 1974, 103:125-127.
12, 517. Scholz, Carol K. They Share the Suffering: The Psycho-
          analyst in American Fiction Between 1920 and 1940.
          DAI, 1978, 38:6134A.
12, 518. Schönau, Walter. Thomas Bernhards 'Ereignisse' oder
          Die Wiederkehr des Verdrängten. Eine psychoanaly-
          tische Interpretation. In Bormann, A. von, et al. (eds),
          Wissen aus Erfahrungen. Werkbegriff und Interpreta-
          tion Heute. Tübingen: Niemeyer, 1976, 829-844.
12, 519. _____. Zur Wirkung der Blechtrommel von Günter
          Grass. Psyche, 1974, 28:573-599.
12, 520. Schönfelder, T. Literarische Seite: Tonio Kröger--einmal
          anders. Acta Paedopsychiatrica (Basel), 1979, 44:229-
          233.
12, 521. Schor, Naomi. Mother's day: Zola's women. Diacritics,
          1975, 5(4):11-17.
12, 522. Schorer, C. E. Hawthorne and hypnosis. Nathaniel Haw-
          thorne J, 1972, 2:239-244.
12, 523. Schorer, Mark (ed). Society and Self in the Novel. NY:
          Columbia Univ. Press, 1956.
12, 524. Schraibman, Joseph. Dreams in the Novels of Galdós.
          NY: Hispanic Institute, 1960; DA, 1959, 20:1795.
12, 525. _____. Onirología galdosiana. El Museo Canario,
          1960, 75-76:347-366; Archivo Iberamericano de Historia
          de la Medicina y Antropologia Medica, 1960, 12:273-
          287.
12, 526. _____. Los sueños en Fortunata y Jacinta. Insula,
          1960, 15:1, 12.
12, 527. _____. Tiempo de silencio y la cura psiquiatrica de un
          pueblo: España. Insula, 1977, 365:3.
12, 528. Schreiber, Annette. The myth in Charlotte Brontë. Lit &
          Psychol, 1968, 18:48-66.
12, 529. Schrero, Elliot M. The narrator's palace of thought in
          'The Sacred Fount.' Modern Philology, 1971, 68:269-
          288.
12, 530. Schroeder, Fred E. H. The development of the superego
          on the American frontier. Soundings, 1974, 57:189-
          205.
12, 531. Schroeter, James. Willa Cather and the professor's house.
          Yale Rev, 1965, 54:494-512.
12, 532. Schuber, Stephen P. From Romanticism to Realism: The
          Intrusion of Reality in Byron's Don Juan and Flaubert's
          Madame Bovary. DAI, 1977, 37:7739.
12, 533. Schuhmann, Kuno. Phrenologie und Ideologie: Frederick
          Marryats Mr. Midshipman Easy. Die Neueren Sprach-
          en, 1964, 13:567-573.

12, 534.   Schulz, Dieter. Edgar Huntley as quest romance. Amer
            Lit, 1971, 43:323-335.
12, 535.   _____. Imagination and self-improvement: the ending of
            'Roger Malvin's Burial.' Studies in Short Fiction, 1973,
            10:183-186.
12, 536.   Schulz, Max F. The aesthetics of anxiety; and, the con-
            formist heroes of Bruce Jay Friedman and Charles
            Wright. In Black Humor Fiction of the Sixties; A Plu-
            ralistic Definition of Man and His World. Athens:
            Ohio Univ. Press, 1973, 91-123.
12, 537.   _____. Leslie A. Fiedler and the hieroglyphics of life.
            Twentieth Century Lit, 1968, 14:24-34.
12, 538.   Schulze, Hedwig. Noch einmal: Leonardo da Vinci nach
            dem Roman von Mereschkowski. Int Zeitschrift für
            Psychoanalyse, 1913, 3:631.
12, 539.   Schulze, Joachim. Joseph, Gregorius und der Mythos vom
            Sonnenhelden: Zum psychologischen Hintergrund eines
            Handlungsschemas bei Thomas Mann. Jahrbuch der
            Deutschen Schiller-Gesellschaft, 1971, 15:465-496.
12, 540.   Schulze, Leonard G. Alkmene's ominous ach: on bas-
            tards, beautiful souls, and the spirit in Heinrich von
            Kleist. Studies in Romanticism, 1980, 19:249-266.
12, 541.   Schuster, Charles I. Dickens and the language of aliena-
            tion. English Language Notes, 1978, 16:117-128.
12, 542.   Schuster, E. J. Schizophrenia and the flight from reality
            in golden age Spanish literature. Kentucky Foreign
            Language Q, 1966, 13:107-108.
12, 543.   Schuster, Marilyn R. Fiction et folie dans l'oeuvre de
            Marguerite Duras. In Cagnon, M. (ed), Ethique et
            esthétique dans la littérature française du XXe siècle.
            Saratoga, Cal: Anma Libri, 1978, 123-132.
12, 544.   Schutter, Dirk de, & Gillaerts, Paul. Claustrofobie voor
            het clausuur tijd. Dietsche Warande en Belfort, 1977,
            122:127-132.
12, 545.   Schwab-Felisch, H. Melancholische Variationen. Zu Gün-
            ter Grass. 'Aus dem Tagebuch einer Schnecke.'
            Merkur, 1972, 26:1025-1030.
12, 546.   Schwartz, Armand. Création littéraire et psychologie des
            profondeurs. Paris: Scorpion, 1960.
12, 547.   Schwartz, Arthur. The American Romantics: an analysis.
            Emerson Society Q, 1964, 34:39-44.
12, 548.   Schwartz, Barry N. Jude the Obscure in the age of anxi-
            ety. Studies in English Lit, 1500-1900, 1970, 10:793-
            804.
12, 549.   Schwartz, Jerome. Scatology and eschatology in Gargan-
            tua's androgyne device. Etudes Rabelaisiennes, 1977,
            14:265-275.
12, 550.   Schwartz, Kessel. Animal symbolism in the fiction of
            Ramón Sender. In The Meaning of Existence in Con-
            temporary Hispanic Literature. Miami: Univ. Miami
            Press, 1969, 99-111.
12, 551-   _____. Homosexuality as a theme in representative con-
     2.   temporary Spanish American novels. Kentucky Romance

Q, 1975, 22:247-257.

12, 553. _____. Juan Goytisolo: ambivalent artist in search of his soul. J Spanish Studies: Twentieth Century, 1975, 3:187-197.

12, 554. _____. Juan Goytisolo, Juan sin tierra, and the anal aesthetic. Hispania, 1979, 62:9-19.

12, 555. _____. The theme of suicide in representative Spanish American novels. Hispania, 1975, 58:442-453.

12, 556. _____. The whorehouse and the whore in Spanish American fiction of the 1960s. J Interamerican Studies, 1973, 15:472-487.

12, 557. _____. Women in the novels of J. Goytisolo. Symposium, 1977, 31:357-367.

12, 558. Schwartz, Murray M. D. H. Lawrence and psychoanalysis: an introduction. D. H. Lawrence Rev, 1977, 10:215-222.

12, 559. _____. 'The Use of Force' and the dilemma of violence. Psychoanal Rev, 1972-73, 59:617-625.

12, 560. _____, & Schwartz, Albert. The Queen of Spades: a psychoanalytic interpretation. Texas Studies in Lit & Language, 1975, 17:275-288.

12, 561. Schwarz, Daniel R. Speaking of Paul Morel: voice, unity, and meaning in Sons and Lovers. Studies in the Novel, 1976, 8:225-277.

12, 562. Schwarzschild, Bettina. The forsaken: an interpretative essay on James Purdy's Malcolm. Texas Q, 1967, 10:170-177.

12, 563. Schyfter, Sara E. Rites without passage: the adolescent world of Ana Mario Moix's Julia. In Pope, R. D. (ed), The Analysis of Literary Texts. Ypsilanti, Mich: Bilingual Press, 1980, 41-50.

12, 564. Scortia, Thomas N. (ed). Strange Bedfellows: Sex and Science Fiction. NY: Random House, 1972.

12, 565. Scott, James F. D. H. Lawrence's Germania: ethnic psychology and cultural crisis in the shorter fiction. D. H. Lawrence Rev, 1977, 10:142-164.

12, 566. Scott, Marcia D. Many Ghosts to Fight: The Image of Women in British Society Between the Wars as Reflected in the Novels of English Women Authors. DAI, 1974, 35:1605A.

12, 567. Scott, Peter Dale. Vital artifice: Mary, Percy, and the psychopolitical integrity of Frankenstein. In Levine, G. L., & Knoepflmacher, U. C. (eds), The Endurance of Frankenstein; Essays on Mary Shelley's Novel. Berkeley: Univ. California Press, 1979, 172-202.

12, 568. Scott, Robert H. El túnel: the novel as psychic drama. Amer Hispanist, 1977, 2(14):13-15.

12, 569. _____. Heroic illusion and death denial in Donoso's El obsceno pájaro de la noche. Symposium, 1978, 32:133-146.

12, 570. Scouten, Kenneth. The mythological dimensions of five of Flannery O'Connor's works. Flannery O'Connor Bulletin, 1973, 2:59-72.

12,571-   Sealts, M.M.   Herman Melville's 'I and My Chimney. '
    2.   Amer Lit, 1941.
12,573.   Sears, Robert R.   Episodic and content analysis of Mark
           Twain's novels: a longitudinal study of separation
           anxiety.   In Literary Criticism and Psychology.
           Yearbook of Comparative Criticism, Vol. 7.   Uni-
           versity Park: Penn State University Press, 1976,
           199-206.
12,574.   _____, Lapidus, Deborah, & Cozzens, Christine.   Con-
           tent analysis of Mark Twain's novels and letters as a
           biographical method.   Poetics: Int for Rev Theory of
           Lit, 1978, 7(2).
12,575.   Sears, Sallie.   Notes on sexuality: The Years and Three
           Guineas.   Bulletin New York Public Library, 1977, 80:
           211-220.
12,576.   Sebald, W.G.   Thanatos: Zur motivstruktur in Kafkas
           Schloss.   Literatur und Kritik, 1972, 66-67:399-411.
12,577.   _____.   The undiscovered country: the death motif in
           Kafka's Castle.   J European Studies, 1972, 2:22-34.
12,578.   Sebilotte, L.H.   Notes sur Kafka.   Evolution Psychiatrique,
           1956, 1:339-355.
12,579.   Sebold, R.P.   Novela y autobiografía en la 'Vida' de Tor-
           res Villarroel.   Madrid: Ariel, 1975.
12,580.   Secher, Claus.   Den ideologiske moderbinding.   In Winge,
           M. (ed), Omkring Haabløse Slaegter.   Copenhagen:
           Reitzel, 1972.
12,581.   Seed, David.   Hyacinth Robinson and the politics of The
           Princess Casamassima.   Etudes Anglaises, 1977, 30:
           30-39.
12,582.   Segal, Hanna.   Delusion and artistic creativity: some re-
           flections on reading William Golding's The Spire.   In
           Lindon, J.A. (ed), The Psychoanalytic Forum, Vol. 5.
           NY: IUP, 1975, 390-430; Int Rev Psychoanal, 1974, 1:
           135-142.
12,583.   Segal, Ora.   The weak wings of pride: an interpretation
           of James's The Bench of Desolation.   Nineteenth Cen-
           tury Fiction, 1965, 20:145-154.
12,584.   Segar, Kenneth.   Determinism and character: Arthur
           Schnitzler's Traumnovelle and his unpublished critique
           of psychoanalysis.   Oxford German Studies, 1973, 8:
           114-127.
12,585.   _____.   Psychological Determinism and Moral Re-
           sponsibility in Some Narrative Works of Arthur
           Schnitzler.   Doctoral dissertation, Univ. Oxford,
           1971.
12,586.   Seiden, Melvin.   Nabokov and Dostoevsky.   Contemporary
           Lit, 1972, 13:423-444.
12,587.   _____.   Persecution and paranoia in Parade's End.
           Criticism, 1966, 8:246-262.
12,588.   _____.   Proust's Marcel and Saint Loup: inversion re-
           considered.   Contemporary Lit, 1969, 10:220-240.

12, 589. Seidenberg, Robert, & Papathomopoulos, E. Daughters who tend their fathers: a literary survey. In The Psychoanalytic Study of Society, Vol. 2. NY: IUP, 1962, 135-160.

12, 590. Seidler, Ingo. 'Das Urteil': 'Freud natürlich'? Zum Problem der Multivalenz bei Kafka. In Paulsen, W. (ed), Psychologie in der Litteraturwissenschaft. Heidelberg: Stiehm, 1971, 174-190.

12, 591. _____. 'Zauberberg' und Strafkolonie: Zum Selbstmord zwier reaktionärer Absolutisten. Germanisch-Romanische Monatschrift, 1969, 19:94-103.

12, 592. Seidlin, Oscar. Hermann Hesse: the exorcism of the demon. Symposium, 1950, 4:325-348.

12, 593. Seiple, Jo Ann Massie. Implications of the disguise: a psychological analysis of Charles Dickens' Hard Times. Papers Arkansas Philological Assn, 1978, 4(3):45-51.

12, 594. Seitz, Karl E. Das Phänomen der Angst im Werk Hermann Brochs. DAI, 1973, 33:5198A.

12, 595. Seitzman, Daniel. Salinger's 'Franny': homoerotic imagery. Amer Imago, 1965, 22:57-76.

12, 596. _____. Therapy and antitherapy in Salinger's 'Zooey.' Amer Imago, 1968, 25:140-162.

12, 597. Sellner, Timothy F. Novalis' Heinrich von Ofterdingen: Erfüllung as Individuation--An Interpretation of the Novel Based on the Psychology of C. G. Jung. DAI, 1971, 31:6632A.

12, 598. Seltzer, Leon F. Milo's culpable innocence: absurdity as moral insanity in Catch-22. Papers on Language & Lit, 1979, 15:290-310.

12, 599. _____. Narrative function vs. psychopathology: the problem of Darl in As I Lay Dying. Lit & Psychol, 1975, 25:49-64.

12, 600. _____. Opportunity of impotence: Count Mippipolous in The Sun Also Rises. Renascence, 1978, 31:3-14.

12, 601. _____. Sister Carrie and the hidden longing for love: sublimation or subterfuge. Twentieth-Century Lit, 1976, 22:192-209.

12, 602. Seizer, J. L. The psychological romance in Hawthorne's 'The Wives of the Dead.' Studies in Short Fiction, 1979, 16:311-315.

12, 603. Sémolué, Jean. Julien Green, ou l'obsession du mal. Paris: Centurion, 1964.

12, 604. Sempé, Jean-Claude. Dracula un conte psychanalytique. Etudes freudiennes, 1978, 13-14.

12, 605. Sen, Colleen T. Karol Irzykowski's Paluba: a guidebook to the future. Slavic & East European J, 1974, 17: 288-300.

12, 606. Sena, John F. Smollett's portrait of Narcissa's aunt: the genesis of an original. English Language Notes, 1977, 14:270-275.

12, 607. _____. Sterne's A Sentimental Journey. Explicator, 1970, 28.

12, 608.   Senescu, Betty C.   The Utopia Within: Some Psychological
           Aspects of Edward Bellamy's Early Writings.   DAI,
           1977, 3504-05.
12, 609.   Seng, Peter J.   The fallen idol: the immature world of
           Holden Caulfield.   College English, 1962, 23:203-
           209.
12, 610.   Sequeros Lopez, A.   La mujer en la obra de Azorin.
           Orihula: Sra Monserr, 1976.
12, 611.   Serrano Plaja, A.   Realismo 'magico' en Cervantes' 'Don
           Quijote' visto desde 'Tom Sawyer' y 'El idiota.'   Mad-
           rid: Gredos, 1967.
12, 612.   Servadio, Emilio.   Une chiave per Lolita.   Europe Let-
           teraria, 1960, 1:128-131.
12, 613.   Setschkareff, V.   Zur Interpretation von Gogols 'Nase.'
           Zeitschrift für slavische Philologie, 1951, 21:118-121.
12, 614.   Sewell, Ernestine P.   The Jungian process of individuation
           as structure in The Painted Bird.   South Central Bul-
           letin, 1978, 38:160-163.
12, 615.   Seyppel, Joachim H.   The animal theme and totemism in
           Franz Kafka.   Amer Imago, 1956, 13:69-93; Lit & Psy-
           chol, 1954, 4(4):49-65; Universitas, 1961, 4:163-172.
12, 616.   _____.   Two variations on a theme: Death in Venice
           and Across the River and Into the Trees.   Lit & Psy-
           chol, 1957, 7:8-12.
12, 617.   Shainess, Natalie.   Nymphomania and Don Juanism.   Medi-
           cal Trail Techniques Q, 1972, 19:1-6.
12, 618.   Shanane, V. A.   The Marabar Caves: fact and fiction.
           Notes & Queries, 1966, 3:36-37; 4:54-55.
12, 619.   Shapiro, Charles (ed).   Twelve Original Essays on Great
           American Novels.   Detroit: Wayne State Univ. Press,
           1958.
12, 620.   Shapiro, Stephen A.   Henry Green's Back: the presence
           of the past.   Critique, 1965, 7:87-96.
12, 621-   _____.   Joyce Cary's To Be a Pilgrim: Mr. Facing-
     2.   Both-Ways.   Texas Studies in Lit & Language, 1966,
           8:81-91.
12, 623.   Sharp, M. Corona.   The archetypal feminine: Our Mutual
           Friend.   Univ. Kansas City Rev, 1961, 27:309-311;
           1962, 28:74-80.
12, 624.   _____.   Fatherhood in Henry James.   Univ. Toronto Q,
           1966, 35:279-292.
12, 625.   Sharrock, Roger.   Singles and couples: Hemingway's A
           Farewell to Arms and Updike's Couples.   Ariel, 1973,
           4(4):21-43.
12, 626.   Shattuck, Roger.   Proust's Binoculars.   A Study of Mem-
           ory, Time, and Recognition in 'A la recherche du temps
           perdu.' London: Chatto & Windus, 1964; NY: Random
           House, 1963; NY: Vintage, 1965; Review: Victor
           Bromberg, Criticism, 1964, 6:382-383; Reviews: Roy
           Fuller, London Magazine, 1964, 4(2):94-95; Walter A.
           Strauss, MLN, 1965, 80:425-426.
12, 627.   Shaughnessy, Mary Rose.   Women and Success in Ameri-

can Society in the Works of Edna Ferber. NY: Gordon, 1976.

12, 628. Shaw, Donald Leslie. Baroja: anguish, action, and ataraxia. In The Generation of 1898 in Spain. NY:
Barnes & Noble, 1975, 95-126.

12, 629. _____. The concept of 'ataraxia' in the later novels of
Baroja. Bulletin Hispanic Studies, 1957, 34:33-34.

12, 630. Shaw, J. Thomas. Raskol'nikov's dreams. Slavic & East
European J, 1974, 17:131-145.

12, 631. Shaw, Patrick W. The excrement festival: Vonnegut's
Slaughterhouse-Five. Scholia Satyrica, 1976, 2(3):3-11.

12, 632. Shaw, Penelope Ann. Camus: A Psychocritical Study of
the Image of the Mother. DAI, 1977, 38:1441A.

12, 633. Shaw, Peter. Fathers, sons, and the ambiguities of revolution in 'My Kinsman, Major Molineux.' New England
Q, 1976, 49:559-576.

12, 634. _____. Their kinsman, Thomas Hutchinson: Hawthorne,
the Boston patriots, and his majesty's royal governor.
Early Amer Lit, 1976, 11:183-190.

12, 635. Shear, Walter. Games people play in Huckleberry Finn.
Midwest Q, 1979, 20:378-393.

12, 636. Sheehan, Bernard. The creation of Julien Green's Moïra:
autobiographical and psychological considerations.
Amer Benedictine Rev, 1973, 24:434-454.

12, 637. Sheehy, Gail. Psychological novelist as portable man:
interview. Psychol Today, 1977, 11:52-53.

12, 638. Shelby, James Townsend. Alienation in the Novels of Ana
María Matute. DAI, 1976, 37:2226A.

12, 639. Sheldon, Pamela J. Jamesian gothicism: the haunted
castle of the mind. Studies Lit Imagination, 1974, 7:
121-134.

12, 640. Shelton, Frank W. Family, community, and masculinity
in the urban novels of Richard Price. Critique, 1979,
21(1):5-15.

12, 641. _____. The family in Hemingway's Nick Adams stories.
Studies in Short Fiction, 1974, 11:303-305.

12, 642. Shengold, Leonard. Chekhov and Schreber: vicissitudes
of a certain kind of father-son relationship. Int J Psycho-Anal, 1961, 42:431-438.

12, 643. Shepard, Leslie A. The development of Gide's concept of
personality. In Garvin, H. R. (ed), Makers of the Twentieth-Century Novel. Lewisburg: Bucknell Univ. Press,
1977, 118-132; Bucknell Rev, 1969, 17(2):47-66.

12, 644. Sheppard, E. A. Henry James and 'The Turn of the Screw.'
London: Oxford Univ. Press, 1975.

12, 645. Sheppard, Richard W. The Trial/The Castle: towards an
analytical comparison. In Flores, A. (ed), The Kafka
Debate: New Perspectives for Our Time. NY: Gordian, 1977, 396-417.

12, 646. Shereikis, Robert. Selves at the center: the theme of
isolation in Dickens's Martin Chuzzlewit. Dickens Studies Newsletter, 1976, 7:38-42.

12, 647. Sherer, Raymond.   Psychological and Mythic Patterns in
          the Novels of George Moore. DAI, 1975, 35:6734A.
12, 648. Sherman, Leona F.   Ann Radcliffe and the Gothic Romance:
          A Psychoanalytic Approach. DAI, 1975, 36:1536A.
12, 649. Sherman, William David.   J. P. Donleavy: anarchic man
          as dying Dionysian. Twentieth Century Lit, 1968, 13:
          216-227.
12, 650. Sherry, Charles.   Folie à deux: Gogol and Dostoevsky.
          Texas Studies Lit & Language, 1975, 17:257-273.
12, 651. Shestov, L.   Tolstoy's Memoirs of a Madman.   Slavonic
          East European Rev, 1929, 7:465-472.
12, 652. Shields, E. F.   Death and individual values in Mrs. Dallo-
          way.   Queen's Q, 1973, 80:79-89.
12, 653. Shifts, John A.   To Him She Would Unveil Her Shy Soul's
          Nakedness: A Study of Sexual Imagery in Joyce and
          Proust. DAI, 1976, 36:7415A-16A.
12, 654. Shine, Muriel G.   Children, Childhood, and Adolescence in
          the Novels and Tales of Henry James. DAI, 1968, 29:
          273A-74A.
12, 655. _____. The Fictional Children of Henry James. Chapel
          Hill: Univ. North Carolina Press, 1969.
12, 656. Shinn, Thelma J. Wardrop.   A question of survival: an
          analysis of 'The Treacherous Years' of Henry James.
          Lit & Psychol, 1973, 23:135-148.
12, 657. _____. A Study of Women Characters in Contemporary
          American Fiction 1940-1970.   Doctoral dissertation,
          Purdue Univ. , 1972.
12, 658. _____. Women in the novels of Ann Petry.   Critique:
          Studies in Modern Fiction, 1974, 16:110-120.
12, 659. Shivers, Alfred S.   The demoniacs in Jack London.   Amer
          Book Collector, 1961, 12:11-14.
12, 660. Shoben, Edward Joseph.   For the record: the grotesque
          in fiction.   Teachers College Record, 1963, 65:257-260.
12, 661. Shoukri, Doris E. C.   The nature of being in Woolf and
          Duras.   Contemporary Lit, 1971, 12:317-328.
12, 662. Showalter, Elaine.   The Evolution of the French Novel,
          1641-1782.   Princeton: Princeton Univ. Press, 1972.
12, 663. _____. Guilt, authority, and the shadows of Little
          Dorrit.   Nineteenth Century Fiction, 1979, 34:20-40.
12, 664. _____. A Literature of Their Own.   British Women
          Novelists from Brontë to Lessing.   Princeton: Prince-
          ton Univ. Press, 1977.
12, 665. Shroeder, John W.   The mothers of Henry James.   Amer
          Lit, 1951, 22:424-431.
12, 666. Shulman, Robert.   Poe and the powers of the mind.   J
          English Lit History, 1970, 37:245-262.
12, 667. Shuman, R. Baird.   Personal isolation in the novels of
          Rosamond Lehmann.   Rev des langues Vivantes, 1960,
          24:76-80.
12, 668. Shuster, Seymour.   Dracula and surgically induced trauma
          in children.   British J Medical Psychol, 1973, 46:259-
          270.

12, 669.   Sicker, Philip. Love and Quest for Identity in the Fiction
           of Henry James. Princeton: Princeton Univ. Press,
           1980.
12, 670.   Siebenschuh, William R. The image of the child and the
           plot of Jane Eyre. Studies in the Novel, 1976, 8:304-
           317.
12, 671.   Siefert, Susan. The Dilemma of the Talented Heroine: A
           Study in Nineteenth Century Fiction. Montreal: Eden,
           1978.
12, 672.   Siegel, Mark Richard. Creative paranoia: Pynchon's ac-
           complishments in Gravity's Rainbow. DAI, 1977, 37:
           5833A-34A.
12, 673.   _____. Creative paranoia: understanding the system
           of Gravity's Rainbow. Critique, 1977, 18(3):39-54.
12, 674.   _____. Pynchon: Creative Paranoia in 'Gravity's Rain-
           bow.' Port Washington, NY: Kennikat, 1978.
12, 675.   Siemens, William Lee. Apollo's metamorphosis in Panta-
           léon y las visitadoras. In Rossman, C. R. , & Fried-
           man, A. W. (eds), Mario Vargas Llosa. Austin: Univ.
           Texas Press, 1978, 88-100.
12, 676.   _____. The devouring female in four Latin American
           novels. Essays in Lit, 1974, 1:118-129.
12, 677.   _____. Women as cosmic phenomena in Tres Tristes
           Tigres. J Spanish Studies: Twentieth Century, 1975,
           3(3).
12, 678.   Sienaert, Edgard. 'Les Lais' de Marie de France: Du
           conte merveilleux à la nouvelle psychologie. Paris:
           Champion, 1977.
12, 679.   Silber, A. A story from childhood that evoked a memory.
           Psychoanal Q, 1978, 47:284-288.
12, 680.   Silberman, Elizabeth Ann. 'A Waste of Effort': Psycho-
           logical Projection as a Primary Mode of Alienation in
           Selected Novels by Kawabata Yasunari. DAI, 1978,
           38:6125A.
12, 681.   Silver, John. A note on the Freudian reading of 'The
           Turn of the Screw.' Amer Lit, 1957, 29:207-211; In
           Willen, G. (ed), A Casebook on Henry James's 'The
           Turn of the Screw.' NY: Crowell, 1960, 239-243.
12, 682.   Silverstein, Albert. Sherlock Holmes, psychology, and
           phrenology. Baker Street J, 1972, 22(1):18-23.
12, 683.   Silverstein, Henry. The utopias of Henry James. New
           England Q, 1962, 35:468-478.
12, 684.   Silverstein, Howard. Norman Mailer: the family romance
           and the oedipal family. Amer Imago, 1977, 34:277-
           286.
12, 685.   Simmerman, Bonnie S. 'Appetite for Submission': The
           Female Role in the Novels of George Eliot. DAI, 1974,
           35:1639A.
12, 686.   Simmon, Scott. Gravity's Rainbow described. Criticism,
           1974, 16(2):54-67.
12, 687.   Simmonds, Roy S. The original manuscripts of Steinbeck's
           'The Chrysanthemums.' Steinbeck Q, 1974, 7:102-111.

12, 688.   Simmons, Donald C.   Eugene Field's 'Little Willie':   an
             excursion in bibliopaedoenuresis.   Amer Book Collector,
             1968, 18(10):35-38.
12, 689.   Simmons, Sarah T.   Attitudes de Hamilton, Marivaux,
             Crébillon fils et Laclos envers la femme d'apres leurs
             oeuvres romanesque.   DAI, 1971, 31:4795A.
12, 690.   Simon, Carol T.   A Comparative Study of Adolescents in
             Different Stages of the Same Culture As Projected in
             English and American Novels of the 18th, 19th, and
             20th Centuries.   DA, 1968, 28(10-A):4011-12.
12, 691.   Simon, Irène.   Le Roman féminin en Angleterre au XVIIIe
             siècle.   Etudes Anglaises, 1974, 27:205-213.
12, 692.   Simon, Pierre-Henri.   Psychologie proustienne de l'amour.
             Hommes et Mondes, 1950, 11:382-395.
12, 693.   Simon, R. I.   Narcolepsy and the strange malady of Silas
             Marner.   Amer J Psychiat, 1966, 123:601-602.
12, 694.   Simone, F., Felici, F., & Valerio, P.   Suicide in the
             literary work of Cesare Pavese.   Suicide & Life
             Threatening Behavior, 1977, 7:183-188.
12, 695.   Simoneaux, Katherine G.   Color imagery in Crane's Mag-
             gie: A Girl of the Streets.   College Language Assn J,
             1974, 18:91-100.
12, 696.   Simonov, Pavel.   Dostoevsky as a social scientist.   Psy-
             chol Today, 1971, 5:59-61, 102-106.
12, 697.   Simpson, Lewis P.   Mark Twain and the pathos of regen-
             eration: a second look at Geismar's Mark Twain.
             Southern Lit J, 1972, 4:93-106.
12, 698.   Sinfield, Mark.   Uncle Toby's potency: some critical and
             authorial confusions in Tristram Shandy.   Notes &
             Queries, 1978, 25:54-55.
12, 699.   Singer, Dorothy G.   Piglet, Pooh, and Piaget.   Psychol
             Today, 1972, 6:71-74, 96.
12, 700.   Singh, Satyanarian.   The psychology of heroic living in
             The Old Man and the Sea.   Osmania J English Studies,
             1973, 10:7-16.
12, 701.   Singh, V. D.   Invisible Man: the rhetoric of colour, chaos,
             and blindness.   Rajasthan Univ. Studies in English,
             1975, 8:54-61.
12, 702.   Singh, Vishnudat.   Lawrence's use of 'pecker.'   Papers
             Bibliographical Society Amer, 1970, 64:355.
12, 703.   Sinnigen, John H.   Resistance and rebellion in Tristana.
             MLN, 1976, 91:277-291.
12, 704.   Sion, Georges.   Psychologie des lettres françaises.   Rev
             des Deux Mondes, 1975, 311-314.
12, 705.   Sivert, Elaine.   Narration and exhibitionism in Le rideau
             cramoisi.   Romanic Rev, 1979, 70:146-158.
12, 706.   Sivert, Eileen.   Prosper Mérimée: isolation and fear of
             self.   Language Q, 1977, 15(3-4):53-55.
12, 707.   Sizemore, Charles W.   Anxiety in Kafka: a function of
             cognitive dissonance.   J Modern Lit, 1977, 6:380-387.
12, 708.   Sjogren, Christine O.   Cereus peruvianus in Stifter's Nach-
             sommer: illustration of a gestalt.   German Q, 1967,
             40:664-672.

12, 709.   . The enigma of Musil's Tonka. Modern Austrian
          Lit, 1977, 9:100-113.
12, 710.   . The human Gestalten and the fools in Adalbert
          Stifter's Der Nachsommer. J English & Germanic Phi-
          lology, 1971, 70:86-101.
12, 711.   . An inquiry into the psychological condition of
          the narrator in Musil's 'Tonka. ' Monatshefte, 1972,
          64:153-161.
12, 712.   . Klotilde's journey into the depths: a probe into
          a psychological landscape in Stifter's Der Nachsommer.
          Germanic Notes, 1971, 2:50-52.
12, 713.   . Mathilde and the rose in Stifter's Nachsommer.
          PMLA, 1966, 81:400-408.
12, 714.   . Wendelin and the theme of transformation in
          Thomas Mann's Wälsungblut. Comparative Lit, 1977,
          14:346-359.
12, 715. Skaggs, Peggy D. The man-instinct of possession: a per-
          sistent theme in Kate Chopin's stories. Louisiana Stud-
          ies, 1975, 14:277-285.
12, 716.   . Three tragic figures in Kate Chopin's The
          Awakening. Louisiana Studies, 1974, 13:345-364.
12, 717.   . A Woman's Place: The Search for Identity in
          Kate Chopin's Female Characters. DAI, 1973, 33:
          6325A-26A.
12, 718. Skerrett, Joseph T. The Wright interpretation: Ralph El-
          lison and the anxiety of influence. Massachusetts Rev,
          1980, 21:196-212.
12, 719. Skerry, Philip J. The Adventures of Huckleberry Finn and
          Intruder in the Dust: two conflicting myths of the Amer-
          ican experience. Ball State Univ. Forum, 1972, 13(1):
          4-13.
12, 720. Skillman, Betty Lou. The Characterization of American
          Women in Twentieth-Century American Literature for
          Children. DAI, 1976, 36:6691A-92A.
12, 721. Skinner, John. Lewis Carroll's Adventures in Wonderland.
          In Ruitenbeek, H. M. (ed), Psychoanalysis and Litera-
          ture. NY: Dutton, 1964, 226-237; Amer Imago, 1947,
          4:3-21.
12, 722. Sklepowich, Edward A. In pursuit of the lyric quarry: the
          image of the homosexual in Tennessee Williams' prose
          fiction. In Tharpe, J. (ed), Tennessee Williams; A
          Tribute. Hattiesburg: Univ. Mississippi Press, 1977,
          525-544.
12, 723. Skorburg, Mary E. An Adlerian interpretation of H. G.
          Wells' The Invisible Man. J Individual Psychol, 1975,
          31:85-96.
12, 724. Skotnicki, Irene. Die Darstellung der Entfremdung in den
          Romanen von Carson McCullers. Zeitschrift für Ang-
          listik und Amerikanistik, 1972, 20:24-45.
12, 725. Slabey, Robert M. As I Lay Dying as an existential novel.
          In Garvin, H. R. (ed), Makers of the Twentieth-Century
          Novel. Lewisburg, Pa: Bucknell Univ. Press, 1977,
          208-217; Bucknell Rev, 1963, 11(4):12-23.

12, 726.   . Faulkner's <u>Sanctuary</u>. <u>Explicator</u>, 1962, 21, No. 45.

12, 727.   . Joe Christman: Faulkner's marginal man. <u>Phylon</u>, 1960, 21.

12, 728. Slade, J. W. Escaping rationalization: options for the self in <u>Gravity's Rainbow</u>. <u>Critique</u>, 1977, 18(3):27-38.

12, 729. Slap, Laura A. Conrad Aiken's 'Silent Snow, Secret Snow': defenses against the primal scene. <u>Amer Imago</u>, 1980, 37:1-11.

12, 730. Slater, Judith. Quentin's tunnel vision: modes of perception and their stylistic realization in <u>The Sound and the Fury</u>. <u>Lit & Psychol</u>, 1977, 27:4-15.

12, 731. Sloane, David E. E. Phrenology in <u>Hard Times</u>: a source for Bitzer. <u>Dickens Studies Newsletter</u>, 1974, 5:9-12.

12, 732. Slochower, Harry, et al. (eds). <u>A Franz Kafka Miscellany</u>. NY: Twice A Year Press, 1940.

12, 733. Slochower, Harry. Freudian motifs in <u>Moby Dick</u>. <u>Complex</u>, 1950, 3:16-25.

12, 734.   . Incest in <u>The Brothers Karamazov</u>. <u>Amer Imago</u>, 1959, 16:127-145; In Ruitenbeek, H. M. (ed), <u>Psychoanalysis and Literature</u>. NY: Dutton, 1964, 303-320.

12, 735.   . A psychology of myth: Joseph the Provider. <u>Quarterly Rev Lit</u>, 1944, 2:74-77.

12, 736.   . Camus' <u>The Stranger</u>: the silent society and the ecstasy of rage. <u>Amer Imago</u>, 1969, 26:281-294.

12, 737.   . Suicides in literature: their ego function. <u>Amer Imago</u>, 1975, 32:389-416.

12, 738.   . Thomas Mann's <u>Death in Venice</u>. <u>Amer Imago</u>, 1969, 26:99-122.

12, 739.   . The uses of myth in Kafka and Mann. In Vickery, J. B. (ed), <u>Myth and Literature</u>. Lincoln: Univ. Nebraska Press, 1966, 349-355; In Romaine, S. (ed), <u>Spiritual Problems in Contemporary Literature</u>. NY: 1957, 117-126.

12, 740. Sloman, Judith. Existentialism in Pär Lagerkvist and Isaac Bashevis Singer. <u>Minnesota Rev</u>, 1965, 5:206-212.

12, 741. Slotkin, Richard. <u>Regeneration Through Violence: The Mythology of the American Frontier, 1600-1860</u>. Middletown, Conn: Wesleyan Univ. Press, 1973.

12, 742. Small, Michel. Hawthorne's <u>The Scarlet Letter</u>: Arthur Dimmesdale's manipulation of language. <u>Amer Imago</u>, 1980, 37:113-123.

12, 743. Smedman, M. Sarah. A Portrait of the Ladies: Women in Popular English Fiction, 1730-1750. <u>DAI</u>, 1976, 36:5328A.

12, 744. Smith, Allan Gardner. <u>Nineteenth-Century Psychology in Fiction of Charles Brockden Brown, Edgar Allan Poe and Nathaniel Hawthorne</u>. Doctoral dissertation, Indiana Univ., 1974.

12, 745.   . The psychological context of three tales by Poe. <u>J Amer Studies</u>, 1974, 7:279-292.

12, 746. Smith, Andrew C.   Hölderlin, Joyce and madness.   Times
          Lit Supplement, 3 Nov 1978, 1286.
12, 747. Smith, Anne (ed). Lawrence and Women.   NY: Barnes &
          Noble, 1978; Review: K. M. Hewitt, Rev English Stud-
          ies, 1979, 30:232-234.
12, 748. Smith, Anneliese H.   A pain in the ass: metaphor in John
          A. Williams' The Man Who Cried I Am.   Studies in
          Black Lit, 1972, 3(3):25-27.
12, 749. Smith, B.   Mark Twain and the mystery of identity.   Col-
          lege English, 1963, 24:425-430.
12, 750. Smith, D. J.   The mem-sahib in her books.   Lit Criterion,
          1971, 9(A):42-50.
12, 751. Smith, David J.   The Arrested Heart: Familial Love and
          Psychic Conflict in Five Mid-Victorian Novels.   DA,
          1966, 27:1839A.
12, 752. _____.   Incest patterns in two Victorian novels.   Lit &
          Psychol, 1965, 15:144-162.
12, 753. Smith, Henry Nash.   The madness of Ahab.   In Democ-
          racy and the Novel: Popular Resistance to Classic
          American Writers.   NY: Oxford Univ. Press, 1978,
          35-55; Yale Rev, 1976, 66:14-32.
12, 754. Smith, J. Harold.   The Expressed Opinions of Mark Twain
          on Heredity and Environment.   DA, 1956, 16:1142.
12, 755. Smith, James F., Jr.   From Symbol to Character: The
          Negro in American Fiction of the Twenties.   DAI, 1973,
          33:3672A-73A.
12, 756. Smith, John B.   A computational analysis of imagery in
          James Joyce's A Portrait of the Artist as a Young Man.
          In Butler, F. (ed), The Great Excluded: Critical Es-
          says on Children's Literature.   Storrs: Univ. Connecti-
          cut, 1972, 1443-1447.
12, 757. Smith, Joseph H.   Language and the genealogy of the ab-
          sent object.   In Psychiatry and the Humanities, Vol. 1,
          1970, 145-170.
12, 758. Smith, Julian.   Hemingway and the thing left out.   J Mod-
          ern Lit, 1970, 1:169-182.
12, 759. Smith, LeRoy W.   Daniel Defoe: incipient pornographer.
          Lit & Psychol, 1972, 22:165-178.
12, 760. Smith, Marcus.   The wall of blackness: a psychological
          approach to 1984.   Modern Fiction Studies, 1968, 14:
          423-433.
12, 761. Smith, Martha S.   A Study of the Realistic Treatment of
          Psychic Phenomena in Selected Fiction of William Dean
          Howells, Hamlin Garland, Henry James, Frank Norris,
          and Theodore Dreiser.   Doctoral dissertation, Univ.
          North Carolina, 1972.
12, 762. Smith, Rachel.   Sherwood Anderson: some entirely ar-
          bitrary reactions.   Sewanee Rev, 1929, 37:161-165.
12, 763. Smith, Raymond.   Review: Morris Golden's Fielding's
          Moral Psychology.   Lit & Psychol, 1947, 17:141-143.
12, 764. Smith, Ruth Elizabeth.   The Theme of Dehumanization in
          the Works of Marco Denevi.   DAI, 1977, 37:5163A.
12, 765. Smith, Samuel S.   The psychological novel.   In The Craft
          of the Critic.   NY: Crowell, 1931, 166-204.

12, 766. _____, & Isotoff, A. The abnormal from within. Dostoevsky. Psychoanal Rev, 1935, 22:361-391.

12, 767. Smith, Stan. Attitudes counterfeiting life: the irony of artifice in Sylvia Plath's The Bell Jar. Critical Q, 1975, 17:247-260.

12, 768. Smith, Susan Harris. Frankenstein: Mary Shelley's psychic divisiveness. Women & Lit, 1977, 5(2):42-53.

12, 769. Smitten, Jeffrey R. Tristram Shandy and spatial form. Ariel, 1977, 8:43-59.

12, 770. Smyer, Richard. 1984: the search for the golden country. Arizona Q, 1971, 27:41-52.

12, 771. _____. Primal Dream and Primal Crime: Orwell's Development As a Psychological Novelist. Columbia: Univ. Missouri Press, 1979.

12, 772. Smyley, Karen Marie. The African Woman: Interpretations of Senegalese Novelists Aboulaye Sadji and Ousmane Sembene. DAI, 1978, 38:4873A.

12, 773. Snapper, Johan P. Teeth on edge: the child in the modern Dutch short story. Rev National Lit, 1977, 8:137-156.

12, 774. Snider, Clifton Mark. The single self: a Jungian interpretation of Virginia Woolf's Orlando. Modern Fiction Studies, 1979, 25:263-268.

12, 775. Snodgrass, William De Witt. Crime for punishment: the tenor of part one. Hudson Rev, 1960, 13:202-253; In In Radical Pursuit. NY: Harper & Row, 1975, 141-200.

12, 776. _____. A rocking-horse: the symbol, the pattern, the way to live. Hudson Rev, 1958, 11:191-200; In In Radical Pursuit. NY: Harper & Row, 1975, 128-140.

12, 777. Snow, A. Heinrich and Mark, two medieval voyeurs. Euphorion, 1972, 66:113-127.

12, 778. Snow, C. P. Trollope: the psychological stream. In Benediks, B. S. (ed), On the Novel. London: Dent, 1971, 3-16.

12, 779. Snow, Lotus. The heat of the sun: the double in Mrs. Dalloway. Research Studies, 1973, 41:75-83.

12, 780. Snyder, Harry C. Airborne imagery in Gogol's Dead Souls. Slavic & East European J, 1979, 23:173-189.

12, 781. Sobejano, Gonzáles. Aburrimiento y erotismo en algunas novelas de Galdós. Anales Galdosianos, 1970, 4:3-11.

12, 782. _____. Forma literaria y sensibilidad social en La incógnita y Realidad de Galdós. Revista Hispánica Moderna, 1964, 30:89-107.

12, 783. _____. Galdós y el vocabulario de los amantes. Anales Galdosianos, 1966, 1:85-99.

12, 784. _____. Reflexiones sobre La Familia de Pascual Duarte. Papeles de Sou Armadans, 1968, 48:19-58.

12, 785. Sobolewska, A. Problemy motywacji i analizy psychologicznej w polskiej prozie lat 1945-1950. Pamietnik Literacki, 1977, 68(4):165-191.

12, 786. Sodowsky, Alice L. The Images of Women in the Novels of Sinclair Lewis. DAI, 1978, 38:5485A.

12, 787. Sohngen, Mary.   The experience of old age as depicted in contemporary novels. Gerontologist, 1977, 17:70-78.

12, 788. Soile, 'Sola.   The Myth of the Archetypal Hero in Two African Novelists: Chinua Achebe and James Ngugi. DAI, 1973, 34:1296A.

12, 789. Sokel, Walter H.   The ambiguity of madness: Elias Canetti's novel Die Blendung.   In Weimar, Karl S. (ed), Views and Reviews of Modern German Literature. Munich: Delp, 1974, 181-187.

12, 790. _____.   Kafka's poetics of the inner self.   Modern Austrian Lit, 1978, 11(3-4):37-58.

12, 791. _____.   Kafka und Sartres Existenzphilosophie.   Arcadia. Zeitschrift für vergleichende Literaturwissenschaft, 1970, 5:262-277.

12, 792. _____.   [Oedipal and existential meanings of The Trial.] In Kuna, F. (ed), On Kafka.   Semi-Centenary Perspectives.   London: Elek, 1976.

12, 793. Sole-Leris, A.   Psychological realism in the pastoral novel: Gil Polo's Diana Enamorada.   Bulletin Hispanic Studies, 1962, 39:43-47.

12, 794. Soleh, Arye.   [The social-psychological basis in Dostoevsky's writings.]   Ofakim, 1956, 10:295-300.

12, 795. Sollers, Philippe.   Dostoievski, Freud, la roulette.   Tel Quel, 1978, 76:9-17.

12, 796. _____.   Joyce & co.   Triquarterly, 1977, 38:107-121.

12, 797. Solomon, Eric.   The incest theme in Wuthering Heights. Nineteenth Century Fiction, 1959, 14:80-83.

12, 798. Solomon, Harry M.   Difficult beauty: Tom D'Urfey and the context of Swift's 'The Lady's Dressing Room.' Studies in English Lit, 1979, 19:431-444.

12, 799. Solomon, Jan.   The structure of Catch-22.   Critique: Studies in Modern Fiction, 1967, 9(2):46-57.

12, 800. Solomon, Margaret Claire.   The phallic tree of Finnegans Wake.   In Harmon, M. (ed), The Celtic Master.   Dublin: Dolmen, 1969, 37-43.   Abstract in Language & Lit in Hawaii, 1968, 1:45-47.

12, 801. _____.   External Geometer.   The Sexual Universe of Finnegans Wake.   Carbondale: Southern Illinois Univ. Press, 1969; DA, 1968, 29:615-16.

12, 802. Solomon, Philip H.   Céline's Death on the Installment Plan: the intoxications of delirium.   Yale French Studies, 1974, 50:191-203.

12, 803. Solotaroff, Theodore, Coles, Robert, Styron, William, & Warren, Robert Penn.   Violence in literature.   Amer Scholar, 1968, 37:482-496.

12, 804. Sommavilla, Guido.   Moravia zimbello di Freud e vice versa.   Lettura, 1971, 26:193-196.

12, 805. Sonfo, Alphamoye.   La Mère dans la littérature romanesque de la Guinée, du Mali et du Senegal.   West African J Modern Languages, 1976, 2:95-107.

12, 806. Sonstroem, David.   Fettered fancy in Hard Times.   PMLA, 1969, 84:520-529.

12, 807. Sorenson, Dale A. Structure in William Faulkner's Sartoris: the contrast between psychological and natural time. Arizona Q, 1969, 25:263-270.

12, 808. Sørensen, Villy. De djaevelske traumer. In Schou, Søren (ed), 60'ernes danske kritik. Ewantologi. Copenhagen: Munksgaard, 1970, 17-34.

12, 809. Soriano, M. Un conte à plusieurs voix. MLN, 1973, 88: 659-711.

12, 810. Sosnoski, M. K. Oskar's hungry witch. Modern Fiction Studies, 1971, 17:61-77.

12, 811. Sousa, Ronald W. The father-figure in Pedro Páramo and Páscoa feliz. Bulletin Hispanic Studies, 1977, 54:29-39.

12, 812. Sowder, William J. Faulkner and existentialism: a note on the generalissimo. Wisconsin Studies in Contemporary Lit, 1963, 4:163-171.

12, 813. _____. Lucas Beauchamp as existential hero. College English, 1963, 25:115-127.

12, 814. Spacks, Patricia Meyer. The dangerous age. Eighteenth-Century Studies, 1978, 11:417-438.

12, 815. _____. Early fiction and the frightened male. Novel: A Forum on Fiction, 1974, 8(1):5-15.

12, 816. _____. The Female Imagination. NY: Knopf, 1975.

12, 817. Spangler, George M. The Shadow of a Dream: Howells' homosexual tragedy. Amer Q, 1971, 23:110-119.

12, 818. _____. The structure of McTeague. English Studies, 1978, 59:48-56.

12, 819. _____. Suicide and social criticism: Durkheim, Dreiser, Wharton, and London. Amer Q, 1979, 31:496-516.

12, 820. Spann, M. Don't hurt the jackdaw. Germanic Rev, 1962, 37:67-78.

12, 821. Spector, Judith Ann. Sexual Dialectic in Four Novels: The Mythos of the Masculine Aesthetic. DAI, 1977, 38:2818A.

12, 822. Speir, Jerry. Ross Macdonald. NY: Ungar, 1978.

12, 823. Spencer, F. J. Crime, cricket, and Conan Doyle--more on the sporting doctor. Virginia Medical Monthly, 1969, 96:697-699.

12, 824. Spencer, John. A note on the 'steady monologuy of the interiors.' Rev English Lit, 1965, 6(2):32-41.

12, 825. Spencer, Sharon. 'Feminity' and the woman writer: Doris Lessing's The Golden Notebook and the Diary of Anaïs Nin. Women's Studies, 1973, 1:247-257.

12, 826. Sperber, Alice. Der Vorzugsschüler, Marie von Ebner-Eschenbachs Novelle. Über einen bestimmten Typus der Einstellung zum Kinde. Zeitschrift für psychoanalytische Pädagogik, 1931, 5:259-263.

12, 827. Sperber, Michael A. Camus' The Fall: the Icarus complex. Amer Imago, 1969, 26:269-280.

12, 828. _____. The daimonic: Freudian, Jungian, and existential perspectives. J Analytical Psychol, 1975, 20: 41-49.

12, 829. _____. Sensory deprivation in autoscopic illusion, and Joseph Conrad's The Secret Sharer. Psychiat Q, 1969, 43:711-718.

12, 830.   . Symptoms and structure of borderline personality organization: Camus' The Fall and Dostoevsky's Notes from Underground. Lit & Psychol, 1973, 23: 102-113.

12, 831. Sperber, Murray. 'Gazing into the glass paperweight': the structure and psychology of Orwell's 1984. Modern Fiction Studies, 1980, 26:213-226.

12, 832. Spielrein, Sabina. Das unbewusste Träumen in Kuprins Zweikampf. Imago, 1913, 2:524-525.

12, 833. Spigel, Helen T. The Sacred Image and the New Truth: A Study in Hawthorne's Women. DAI, 1970, 30:2981A.

12, 834. Spilka, Mark. David Copperfield as psychological fiction. Critical Q, 1959, 1:292-301.

12, 835.   . The death of love in The Sun Also Rises. In Shapiro, C. (ed), Twelve Original Essays on Great American Novels. Detroit: Wayne State Univ. Press, 1958.

12, 836.   . Dickens and Kafka: A Mutual Interpretation. Bloomington: Indiana Univ. Press, 1963.

12, 837.   . Erich Segal as Little Nell: or, the real meaning of Love Story. J Popular Culture, 1972, 5:782-798.

12, 838.   . Of George and Lennie and Curley's wife: sweet violence in Steinbeck's Eden. Modern Fiction Studies, 1974, 20:169-179.

12, 839.   . Kafka and Dickens: the Country Doctor. Amer Imago, 1959, 16:367-378.

12, 840.   . On Lawrence's hostility to wilful women: the Chatterley solution. In Smith, A. (ed), Lawrence and Women. NY: Barnes & Noble, 1978, 189-211.

12, 841.   . Lawrence's quarrel with tenderness. Critical Q, 1967, 9:363-384.

12, 842.   . Lawrence up-tight, or the anal phase once over. Novel: A Forum on Fiction, 1971, 4:252-267.

12, 843.   . Lessing and Lawrence: the battle of the sexes. Contemporary Lit, 1975, 16:218-240.

12, 844.   . On Lily Briscoe's borrowtd grief: a psycho-literary speculation. Criticism, 1979, 21:1-33.

12, 845.   . Little Nell revisited. Papers of the Michigan Academy of Science, Arts, and Letters, 1960, 45:427-437.

12, 846.   . The Love Ethic of D. H. Lawrence. Bloomington: Univ. Indiana Press, 1955.

12, 847.   . On Mrs. Dalloway's absent grief: a psycho-literary speculation. Contemporary Lit, 1979, 20:316-318.

12, 848.   . Playing crazy in the underground. Minnesota Rev, 1966, 6:233-243.

12, 849.   . Quentin Compson's universal grief. Contemporary Lit, 1970, 11:451-469.

12, 850.   . Review: B. J. Paris' Psychological Approach to Fiction. Novel, 1976, 9:165-170.

12, 851.   (ed). Towards a Poetics of Fiction. Bloomington: Indiana Univ. Press, 1977.

12, 852.   . Turning the Freudian screw: how not to do it.
          Lit & Psychol, 1963, 13:105-111.
12, 853. Spitz, R. A. Vagadu: une analyse dans la miroir de l'in-
          tuition de l'artiste. Rev Française de Psychanalyse,
          1934, 7:550-579.
12, 854. Spitzer, Leo. A reinterpretation of 'The Fall of the House
          of Usher.' Comparative Lit, 1952.
12, 855.   . On the significance of Don Quijote. In Nelson,
          L. (ed), Cervantes--A Collection of Critical Essays.
          Englewood Cliffs, NJ: Prentice-Hall, 1969.
12, 856. Spivey, Ted R. The reintegration of modern man: an es-
          say on James Joyce and Hermann Hesse. Studies in
          Lit Imagination, 1970, 3(2):49-64.
12, 857. Splaver, Sarah. The career novel. Personnel & Guidance
          J, 1953, 31:371-372.
12, 858. Splitter, Randolph. The 'economic' problem in Proust and
          Freud. Hartford Studies in Lit, 1979, 11:123-139.
12, 859.   . Guilt and the trappings of melodrama in Little
          Dorrit. Dickens Studies Annual, 1977, 6:119-133.
12, 860.   . Proust, Joyce and the theory of metaphor.
          Lit & Psychol, 1979, 29:4-18.
12, 861.   . Proust's Combray: the structures of animistic
          projection. Amer Imago, 1979, 36:154-177.
12, 862.   . The sane and joyful spirit. James Joyce Q,
          1976, 13(3):350-365.
12, 863. Sprague, Claire. Dream and disguise in The Blithedale
          Romance. PMLA, 1969, 84:596-597.
12, 864.   . Without contraries is no progression: Les-
          sing's The Four-Gated City. Modern Fiction Studies,
          1980, 26:99-116.
12, 865. Spranger, Eduard. Der psychologische Perspektivismus im
          Roman. Eine Skizze zur Theorie des Romans erläutert
          an Goethes Hauptwerken. Jahrbuch des freien deutschen
          Hochstifts, 1930, 70-89.
12, 866. Spreen, Otfried. Struktur des Psychologischen im Roman
          (dargestellt an Herman Hesses 'Steppenwulf.' Eine
          morphologisch-methodologische Untersuchung. Doctoral
          dissertation, Univ. Bonn, 1951.
12, 867. Squires, Paul C. Dostoevsky's master-study of the 'pro-
          test.' Scientific Monthly, 1937, 44:555-557.
12, 868.   . Dostoevsky's Raskolnikov: the criminalistic
          protest. J Criminal Law, 1937, 28:478-494.
12, 869.   . Some observations by Dostoievsky and their
          bearing on the Gestalt psychology. Australasian J
          Psychol & Philosophy, 1936, 14:295-300.
12, 870. Srivastava, Ramesh. Hemingway's 'Cat in the Rain': an
          interpretation. Lit Criticism (Mysore), 1970, 9(2):79-
          84.
12, 871. Stabb, M. S. Donoso and the new novel. Symposium,
          1976, 30:170-179.
12, 872.   . The new Murena and the new novel. Kentucky
          Romantic Q, 1975, 22:139-156.

12,873. Stacy, Paul H. Review: Mark Schechner's Joyce in Nighttown: A Psychoanalytic Inquiry into 'Ulysses.' Hartford Studies in Lit, 1975, 7:69-75.

12,874. Stafford, Jean. The psychological novel. Kenyon Rev, 1948, 10:214-227.

12,875. Staley, Thomas F., & Benstock, Bernard (eds). Approaches to Joyce's Portrait; Ten Essays. Pittsburgh: Univ. Pittsburgh Press, 1977.

12,876. Stalnaker, J. M. & Eggan, F. American novelists ranked: a psychological study. English J, 1929, 18:295-307.

12,877. Stamm, Julian L. Camus' Stranger: his act of violence. Amer Imago, 1969, 26:281-290.

12,878. Standaert, Eric. Psychografie van Franz Kafka. Nieuw Vlaams Tijdschrift, 1956, 10:166-183.

12,879. Standley, Fred L. Another Country, another time. Studies in the Novel, 1972, 4:504-512.

12,880. Stanford, Derek. C. P. Snow: the novelist as fox. Meanjin Q, 1960, 19:236-251.

12,881. Stang, Sondra J. A reading of Ford's The Good Soldier. Modern Language Q, 1969, 30:545-563.

12,882. Stanton, Robert. Daddy's girl: symbol and theme in Tender Is the Night. Modern Fiction Studies, 1958, 4: 136-142.

12,883. Stanzel, Franz K. Innerwelt--Ein Darstellungsproblem des englischen Romans. Germanisch-Romanische-Monatsschrift, 1962, 13:273-286.

12,884. Stape, John H. Dr. Jung at the site of blood: a note on Blown Figures. Studies in Canadian Lit, 1977, 2:124-126.

12,885. Stark, John. Alienation and analysis in Doctorow's The Book of Daniel. Critique: Studies in Modern Fiction, 1975, 16(3):101-110.

12,886. _____. Barbary Shore: the basis of Mailer's best work. Modern Fiction Studies, 1971, 17:403-408.

12,887. Stark, Myra C. The Home Department: The Uses of Children in the Novels of Charles Dickens. DAI, 1971, 31:6073A.

12,888. Stark, Stanley. James' mystic consciousness and Rorschach's inner creation: a suggestion on how to regard them. Psychol Reports, 1968, 23:57-58.

12,889. Starke, Catherine Juanita. Black-Portraiture in American Fiction: Stock Characters, Archetypes, and Individuals. NY: Basic Books, 1971.

12,890. _____. Negro Stock Characters, Archetypes and Individuals in American Literature. DA, 1963, 24:288.

12,891. Starobinski, Jean. Ironie et mélancholie (II): La Princesse Brambilla de E. T. A. Hoffmann. Critique, 1966, 22:438-457.

12,892. _____, Blot, J., & Silvain, P. In memoriam: P. G. Jouve. Nouvelle Rev Française, 1976, 281:37-60.

12,893. Starr, Alvin. The concept of fear in the works of Stephen Crane and Richard Wright. Studies in Black Lit, 1975, 6(2):6-10.

12, 894. Starr, H. W. 'On my knees!' In Kennedy, B. (ed), Four
Wheels to Baker Street. Fulton, Mo: The Three Students Plus, 1968, 1-3.

12, 895. Starr, William T. Water symbols in the novels of Romain
Rolland. Neophilologus, 1972, 56:146-161.

12, 896. Starzyk, L. J. Universal wish not to live in Hardy's modern novels. Nineteenth Century Fiction, 1972, 26:419-
435.

12, 897. Stasz, Clarice. Androgyny in the novels of Jack London.
Western Amer Lit, 1976, 11:121-133.

12, 898. Stauffer, Donald Barlow. Poe as phrenologist: the example of Monsieur Dupin. In Veler, R. P. (ed), Papers
on Poe. Springfield, Ohio: Chantry, 1972, 113-125.

12, 899. Stavrou, Constantine W. D. H. Lawrence's 'psychology' of
sex. Lit & Psychol, 1956, 6:90-95.

12, 900. Stedman, Jane W. Child wives of Dickens. Dickensian,
1963, 59:112-118.

12, 901. Steel, David. [The prodigal theme in Gide.] Rev d'Histoire Littéraire de la France, 1970, 70.

12, 902. Steele, Richard. Thomas Wolfe: A Study in Psychoanalytic Literary Criticism. Ardmore, Pa: Dorrance,
1977.

12, 903. Steele, R. S., & Swinney, S. V. Zane Grey, Carl Jung and
the journey of the hero. J Analytical Psychol, 1978,
23:63-89.

12, 904. Steeves, Edna L. Pre-feminism in some eighteenth-century novels. Texas Q, 1973, 16(3):48-57.

12, 905. Steig, Michael. Article-review on five Dickens studies.
Lit & Psychol, 1965, 15:230-237.

12, 906. _____. Bellow's Henderson and the limits of Freudian
criticism. Paunch, 1973, 36-37:39-46.

12, 907. _____. The central action of Old Curiosity Shop or little Nell revisited again. Lit & Psychol, 1965, 15:163-
170.

12, 908. _____. Dickens' characters and psychoanalytic criticism. Hartford Studies in Lit, 1976, 8:38-45.

12, 909. _____. Dickens' excremental vision. Victorian Studies, 1970, 13:339-354.

12, 910. _____. Erotic Themes in Dickens' Novels. DAI, 1964,
24:4704-05.

12, 911. _____. The grotesque and the aesthetic response in
Shakespeare, Dickens, and Günther Grass. Comparative Lit Studies, 1969, 6:167-181.

12, 912. _____. The iconography of David Copperfield. Hartford Studies in Lit, 1970, 2:1-18.

12, 913. _____. Iconography of sexual conflict in Dombey and
Son. In Partlow, R. B. (ed), Dickens Studies Annual,
Vol. 1. Carbondale: Southern Illinois Univ. Press,
1970, 161-167.

12, 914. _____. The intentional phallus: determining verbal
meaning in literature. JAAC, 1977, 36:51-61.

12, 915. _____. Martin Chuzzlewit: pinch and pecksniff. Studies in the Novel, 1969, 1:181-188.

12,916. _____. Phiz's marchioness. Dickens Studies, 1966, 2: 141-146.

12,917. _____. Psychological realism and fantasy in Jane Austen: Emma and Mansfield Park. Hartford Studies in Lit, 1973, 5:126-134.

12,918. _____. Re Quilp: a comment. Hartford Studies in Lit, 1974, 6:282-283.

12,919. _____. Subversive grotesque in Samuel Warren's Ten Thousand a-Year. Nineteenth Century Fiction, 1969, 24:154-168.

12,920. _____. Sue Bridehead. Novel: A Forum for Fiction, 1968, 1:260-266.

12,921. _____, & Wilson, F.A.C. Hortense versus Bucket: the ambiguity of order in Bleak House. Modern Language Q, 1972, 33:289-299.

12,922. Stein, Aaron Marc. The detective story--how and why. Princeton Univ. Library Chronicle, 1974, 36:19-46.

12,923. Stein, Barbara. Psychologische Merkmale bei Klassenbezeichnungen im Wortschatz Emile Zolas. Wissenschaftliche Zeitschrift der Martin-Luther Universität Halle-Wittenberg, 1970, 19(3-4):189-207.

12,924. Stein, Karen F. Reflections in a jagged mirror: some metaphors of madness. Aphra, 1975, 6:2-11.

12,925. Stein, Roger B. Pulled out of the bay: American fiction in the eighteenth century. Studies in Amer Fiction, 1974, 2:13-36.

12,926. Stein, William Bysshe. The Artist of the Beautiful: Narcissus and the thimble. Amer Imago, 1961, 18:35-44.

12,927. _____. Melville's 'The Confidence-Man': quicksands of the word. Amer Transcendental Q, 1974, 24:38-50.

12,928. _____. The method at the heart of madness: The Spoils of Poynton. Modern Fiction Studies, 1968, 14: 187-202.

12,929. _____. The Sacred Fount and British aestheticism: the artist as clown and pornographer. Arizona Q, 1971, 27:161-173.

12,930. Steinberg, Aaron. Faulkner and the Negro. DA, 1966, 27:1385A.

12,931. Steinberg, Abraham H. Fitzgerald's portrait of a psychiatrist. Univ. Kansas City Rev, 1955, 21:219-222; In LaHood, Marvin I. (ed), Tender Is the Night: Essays in Criticism. Bloomington: Indiana Univ. Press, 1969.

12,932. _____. Hardness, light and psychiatry in Tender Is the Night. Lit & Psychol, 1953, 3:3-8.

12,933. Steinberg, Erwin R. Freudian symbolism and communication. Lit & Psychol, 1953, 3(2):2-5.

12,934. _____. Introducing the stream-of-consciousness technique in Ulysses. Style, 1968, 2:49-58.

12,935. _____. A Kafka primer. College English, 1962, 24: 230-232.

12,936. _____. Notes on a novelist too quickly Freudened. Lit & Psychol, 1954, 4(2):23-25.

12,937. _____. The Proteus episode: signature of Stephen Dedalus. James Joyce Q, 1968, 5:187-198.

12,938. _____. The sources of the stream. In Bain, J. et al. (eds), In Honor of Austin Wright. Pittsburgh: Carnegie-Mellon Univ. Press, 1972, 87-101.

12,939. _____. '... The steady monologue of the interiors; the pardonable confusion....' James Joyce Q, 1969, 6:185-200.

12,940. _____. The Stream of Consciousness and Beyond in Ulysses. Pittsburgh: Univ. Pittsburgh Press, 1973; London: Media Directions, 1973.

12,941. _____. The stream-of-consciousness novelist: an inquiry into the relation of consciousness and language. ETC, 1960, 17:423-439.

12,942. _____. The Stream-of-Consciousness Technique in James Joyce's Ulysses. DA, 1958, 18:237-238.

12,943. _____ (ed). Stream-of-Consciousness Technique in the Modern Novel. Port Washington, NY: Kennikat, 1979.

12,944. _____. Three fragments of Kafka's 'The Hunter Graccus.' Studies in Short Fiction, 1978, 15:307-317.

12,945. Steinberger, Eva Marie. Balzac's Portrayal of Woman: A Study in the Role of Women in His Fictional Works Before 1842. DA, 1977, 38:312A-13A.

12,946. Steinhagen, Carol Therese. Plantation and Wilderness: Themes of Aggression and Regression in the Border Romances of William Gilmore Simms. DAI, 1975, 35:7270A.

12,947. Steinmetz, Joseph James. Between Zero and One: A Psychohistoric Reading of Thomas Pynchon's Major Works. DAI, 1976, 37:318A-19A.

12,948. Steinwachs, Gisela. Mythologie des Surrealismus oder die Rückverwendlung von Kultur in Natur: ein strukturale Analyse von Breton's 'Nadja.' Berlin: Luchterland, 1971.

12,949. Steisel, Marie-Georgette. Etude des couleurs dans La Jalousie. French Rev, 1965, 38:485-496.

12,950. Stekel, Wilhelm. Peculiarities of Human Behavior. Vol. II. NY: Liveright, 1958, 242 ff.

12,951. Stephens, Evelyn Delores B. The Novel of Personal Relationships: A Study of Three Contemporary British Women Novelists. DAI, 1977, 38:290A-91A.

12,952. Stepp, Walter. The ironic double in Poe's 'The Cask of Amontillado.' Studies in Short Fiction, 1976, 13:447-453.

12,953. Sterba, Editha. The school boy suicide in André Gide's novel The Counterfeiters. Amer Imago, 1951, 8:307-320; Almanach, 1930, 85-98; Zeitschrift für psychoanalytische Pädagogik, 1928-29, 3:400-409.

12,954. Sterba, Richard F. The problem of art in Freud's writings. Psychoanal Q, 1940, 9:256-268.

12,955. _____. On spiders, hanging and oral sadism. Amer Imago, 1950, 7:21-28.

12,956. _____. Remarks on Joseph Conrad's Heart of Darkness. JAPA, 1965, 13:570-583.

12,957. Stern, A. Further considerations on Alfred Adler and Ortega y Gasset. J Individual Psychol, 1971, 27:139-143.

12,958. Stern, Alf. Zauberbergpsychologie. Pester Lloyd (Budapest), 5 Jan 1936.

12,959. Stern, Erich. Thomas Mann's Zauberberg: Die Psychologie der Lungenkranken. Medizinische Klinik, 1925, 21:1592-1598.

12,960. Stern, J. P. Guilt and the feeling of guilt. In Flores, A. (ed), The Problem of 'The Judgment': Eleven Approaches to Kafka's Story. NY: Gordian, 1977, 114-132.

12,961. Stern, Madeleine B. The game's a head. Baker Street J, 1970, 20:157-165.

12,962. _____. Hungry ghosts: flux of identity in contemporary fiction. Sewanee Rev, 1935, 43:28-48.

12,963. Sternlicht, Sanford. Pincher Martin: A Freudian Crusoe. English Record, 1965, 15:2-4.

12,964. _____. The sad comedies: Graham Greene's later novels. Florida Q, 1968, 1:65-77.

12,965. Sterrenburg, Lee. Psychoanalysis and the iconography of revolution. Victorian Studies, 1975, 19:241-264.

12,966. Stevens, Cynthia C. The Imprisoned Imagination: The Family in the Fiction of Joyce Carol Oates, 1960-1970. DAI, 1974, 35:479A.

12,967. Stevenson, Catharine Barnes. The double consciousness of the narrator in Sarah Orne Jewett's fiction. Colby Library Q, 1975, 11:1-12.

12,968. Stevenson, Lionel. The Ordeal of George Meredith. NY: Scribner, 1953.

12,969. Stevick, Philip. Saki's beasts. English Lit in Transition: 1880-1920, 1966, 9:33-37.

12,970. Stewart, A. D. Fred Saberhagen: cybernetic psychologist: a study of the Berserker stories. Extrapolation, 1976, 18:42-51.

12,971. Stewart, Jack F. Existence and symbol in The Waves. Modern Fiction Studies, 1972, 18:433-447.

12,972. Stewart, Naomi. Preference for literary characters as indicators of personality characteristics. Amer Psychologist, 1947, 2:268-269.

12,973. Stewart, Walter K. Der Tod in Venedig: the path to insight. Germanic Rev, 1978, 53:50-55.

12,974. Stilman, Leon. The 'all-seeing' eye in Gogol. In Maguire, R. A. (ed), Gogol from the Twentieth Century. Princeton: Princeton Univ. Press, 1974, 376-389.

12,975. Stilwell, Robert L. Literature and utopia: B. F. Skinner's Walden Two. Western Humanities Rev, 1964, 18:331-341.

12,976. Stocker, Arnold. Ame Russe; Réalisme Psychologique des Frère Karamazov. Geneva: Editions du Mont-Blanc, 1945.

12,977. _____. L'Amour interdit. Trois anges sur la route de Sodome; étude psychologique. Geneva: Mont-Blanc, 1943.

12,978. Stockholder, Katherine. A Country Doctor: the narrator as dreamer. Amer Imago, 1978, 35:331-346.

12,979. Stoehr, Taylor. Dickens: The Dreamer's Stance. Ithaca, NY: Cornell Univ. Press, 1965.

12,980. _____. Hawthorne and Mesmerism. Huntington Library Q, 1969, 33:33-60.

12,981. _____. 'Mentalized sex' in D. H. Lawrence. Novel: A Forum on Fiction, 1975, 8:101-122.

12,982. _____. Pornography, masturbation and the novel. Salmagundi, 1967-68, 2(2):28-56.

12,983. Stoll, Elmer Edgar. Psychoanalysis in criticism: Dickens, Kipling, Joyce. In From Shakespeare to Joyce: Authors and Critics; Literature and Life. Garden City, NY: Doubleday, 1944, 339-388.

12,984. Stoll, John E. Common womb imagery in Joyce and Lawrence. Ball State Univ. Forum, 1970, 11(2):10-24.

12,985. _____. D. H. Lawrence's Sons and Lovers: self-encounter and the unknown self. Ball State Monographs, 1968, 7(11):1-48.

12,986. _____. Psychological dissociation in the Victorian novel. Lit & Psychol, 1970, 20:63-73.

12,987. _____. The Search for Integration in the Novels of D. H. Lawrence. Doctoral dissertation, Wayne State Univ., 1966.

12,988. Stollreiter-Butzon, Leonie. Über die Epilepsie des Fürsten Mychkin. Psyche, 1961, 15:517-531.

12,989. _____. [On Prince Myshkin's epilepsy. Considerations on Dostoevski's The Idiot.] Psyche, 1961, 15:517-531.

12,990. Stolte, Heinz. Mein Name sei Wadenbach: Zum Identitätsproblem bei Karl May. Jahrbuch der Karl-May-Gesellschaft, 1978, 37-59.

12,991. Stoltzfus, Ben F. Alain Robbe-Grillet and the New French Novel. Carbondale: Southern Illinois Univ. Press, 1964.

12,992. _____. Gide and Hemingway: Rebels Against God. Port Washington, NY: Kennikat, 1978.

12,993. _____. The neurotic love of Frederic Moreau. French Rev, 1958, 31:509-511.

12,994. _____. A novel of object subjectivity: Le Voyeur by Alain Robbe-Grillet. PMLA, 1962, 77:499-507.

12,995. Stone, Albert E., Jr. Henry James and childhood: 'The Turn of the Screw.' In Hague, J. A. (ed), American Character and Culture. De Land, Fla: Everett Edwards, 1964, 85-100.

12,996. _____. The Innocent Eye: Childhood in Mark Twain's Imagination. New Haven: Yale Univ. Press, 1961.

12,997. Stone, Donald D. Steinbeck, Jung, and The Winter of Our Discontent. Steinbeck Q, 1978, 11:87-96.

12,998. _____. Victorian feminism and the nineteenth-century novel. Women's Studies, 1972, 1:65-92.

12,999. Stone, Edward. A Certain Morbidness: A View of American Literature. Carbondale: Southern Illinois Univ. Press, 1969.

13,000. _____. The paving stones of Paris: psychometry from Poe to Proust. Amer Q, 1953, 121-131.

13,001. _____. Poe in and out of his time. Emerson Society Q, 1962, 29:14-17.

13,002. Stone, Elizabeth. Horatio Algers of the nightmare; J. Kosinski's characters. Psychol Today, 1977, 11:59-60.

13,003. Stone, Harry. Dickens and interior monologue. Philological Q, 1959, 38:52-65.

13,004. _____. Dickens' use of his American experiences in Martin Chuzzlewit. PMLA, 1957, 72:464-478.

13,005. Stone, Wilfred. The Cave and the Mountain: A Study of E. M. Forster. Palo Alto, Cal: Stanford Univ. Press, 1966.

13,006. _____. Forster on love and money. In Stallybrass, O. (ed), Aspects of E. M. Forster: Essays and Recollections Written for His Ninetieth Birthday January 1, 1969. London: Arnold, 1969.

13,007. _____. Overleaping class: Forster's problem in connection. Modern Language Q, 1978, 39:386-404.

13,008. Strong, Emily. Juvenile literary rape in America: a post-coital study of the writings of Dr. Seuss. Studies in Contemporary Satire, 1977, 4:34-40.

13,009. Stonys, Juozas. Psichologine analize Lorenso Sterno prozoje. Literatura, 1969, 12(3):51-69.

13,010. Storch, R. F. Metaphors of private guilt and social rebellion in Godwin's Caleb Williams. J English Lit History, 1967, 34:188-207.

13,011. Storey, Robert. Oedipus in the labyrinth: a psychoanalytic reading of Robbe-Grillet's In the Labyrinth. Lit & Psychol, 1978, 28:4-16.

13,012. Storfer, Adolf J. Thomas Mann entlarot. Psychoanalytische Bewegung, 1929, 1:174-175.

13,013. Storr, Anthony. Sexual Deviation. Baltimore: Penguin, 1964.

13,014. Storz, Gerhard. Über den 'Monologue interieur' oder die 'Erlebte Rede. ' Deutschunterricht, 1955, 7(1):41-53.

13,015. Stott, Jon C. Midsummer night's dreams: fantasy and self-realization in children's fiction. Lion & Unicorn, 1977, 1(2):25-39.

13,016. Stotz, Ingeborg Riel. Die metaphorische und psysische Bedeutung von Auge und Sehsinn bei Heinrich Böll. DAI, 1977, 37:5864A.

13,017. Stouck, David. The mirror and the lamp in Sinclair Ross's As for Me and My House. Mosaic, 1974, 7(2): 141-150.

13,018. Stowell, J. D. Some archetypes in Stifters Der Nachsommer: an attempt at restoring fictional interest. Seminar, 1970, 6:31-47.

13,019. Stragnell, Gregory. The dream in Russian literature. Psychoanal Rev, 1921, 8:225-251.

13,020. _____. A psychopathological study of Knut Hamsun's Hunger. Psychoanal Rev, 1922, 9:198-217.

13,021. Stragnell, Sylvia. Review: Rose Macaulay's Dangerous Ages. Psychoanal Rev, 1922, 9:97-99.

13,022. _____. A study in sublimation. Critical review of May Sinclair's Anne Severn and The Fieldings. Psychoanal Rev, 1923, 10:209-213.

13,023. Strandberg, V. H. Isabel Archer's identity crisis. Univ. Rev, 1968, 34:283-290.

13,024. Strauch, Carl F. Ishmael: time and personality in Moby-Dick. Studies in the Novel, 1969, 1:468-483.

13,025. Straumann, Heinrich. The psychological approach in fiction. In American Literature in the Twentieth Century. NY: Harper Torchbook, 1965, 82-99.

13,026. Straus, B. Illness, creativity and Marcel Proust. Mt. Sinai Medical J, 1979, 46:175-180.

13,027. Strauss, Sylvia. Women in 'Utopia.' South Atlantic Q, 1976, 75:115-131.

13,028. Street, James B. Kafka through Freud: totems and taboos in In der Strafkolonie. Modern Austrian Lit, 1973, 6:93-106.

13,029. Strelka, Joseph P. Hermann Hesses Rosshalde in psychoanalytischer Sicht. Acta Germanica zur Sprache und Dichtung Deutschlands, Oesterreichs und der Schweiz, 1976, 9:177-186.

13,030. Strickland, Carol A. C. The Search for the Father in Selected American Novels. DAI, 1974, 35:418A-19A.

13,031. Stroup, Herbert H. Counseling college students. Their characterization in recent fiction. Pulpit, 1961, 10:8-10.

13,032. _____. Kafka as a vocational counselor. J Counseling Psychol, 1961, 8:291-295.

13,033. Stroupe, John H. D. H. Lawrence's portrait of Ben Franklin in The Rainbow. Iowa English Yearbook, 1966, 11:64-68.

13,034. Strout, Cushing. Personality and cultural history in the novel: two American examples. New Lit History, 1970, 1:423-438.

13,035. Strozyk, F. Peter. The Figure of the Child in Selected German Novellen of the Nineteenth Century. DAI, 1974, 35:2301A.

13,036. Struc, Roman S. Madness as existence: an essay on a literary theme. Research Studies, 1970, 38:75-94.

13,037. Struelens, Jan. Oidipous, Oidipous. Nieuw Vlaams Tijdschrift, 1974, 27:995-1006.

13,038. Struve, Gleb. Monologue intérieur: the origins of the formula and the first statement of its possibilities. PMLA, 1954, 69:1101-1111.

13,039. Stubbs, John C. John Hawkes and the dream-work of The Lime Twig and Second Skin. Lit & Psychol, 1971, 21:149-160.

13,040. Styron, William. The vice that has no name. Harper's, 1968, 236:97-100.

13,041. Suárez Rendón, G. La novela de la violencia en Colombia. Bogotá: 1966.

13,042. Suderman, Elmer F. Jack Matthews and the shape of human feelings. Critique, 1979, 21(1):38-48.

13,043. Sudrann, J. Victorian compromise and modern revolution. J English Lit History, 1959, 26:425-444.
13,044. Sugarman, David W. Franz Kafka: A Psychological Study. DAI, 1976, 37:964B.
13,045. Sughé, Werner. Thomas Mann in Freud y el porvenir. Buenos Aires: Panapress, 1937, 13-18.
13,046. Suhl, Benjamin. Sartre à soixante-dix ans. French Rev, 1975, 48:1039-1042.
13,047. Suits, C. The role of the horses in 'A Voyage to the Houyhnhms.' Univ. Toronto Q, 1965, 34:118-132.
13,048. Sukenick, Lynn. Feeling and reason in Doris Lessing's fiction. Contemporary Lit, 1973, 14:515-535; In Pratt, A., & Dembo, L. S. (eds), Doris Lessing: Critical Studies. Madison: Univ. Wisconsin Press, 1974, 98-118.
13,049. _____. On women and fiction. In Diamond, A., & Edwards, L. R. (eds), The Authority of Experience. Essays in Feminist Criticism. Amherst: Univ. Massachusetts Press, 1977, 28-44.
13,050. Suleiman, S. Reading Robbe-Grillet: sadism and text in Projet pour une révolution à New York. Romanic Rev, 1977, 68:43-62.
13,051. Sullivan, J. P. The Satyricon of Petronius: A Literary Study. Bloomington: Indiana Univ. Press, 1968.
13,052. _____. The Satyricon of Petronius. Some psychoanalytical considerations. Amer Imago, 1961, 18:353-369.
13,053. Sullivan, Karen Lever. The Muse of Fiction: Fatal Women in the Novels of W. M. Thackeray, Thomas Hardy, and John Fowles. DAI, 1976, 36:7447A.
13,054. Sullivan, Mary Petrus. Moby Dick: Chapter CXXIX, 'The Cabin.' Nineteenth Century Fiction, 1965, 20:188-190.
13,055. Sullivan, Patrick W. A Study of the Adolescent as Metaphor in Four Eighteenth Century French Novels. DAI, 1971, 31:5427A.
13,056. Sullivan, R. Review: J. Moss' Sex and Violence in the Canadian Novel. Univ. Toronto Q, 1978, 47:448-451.
13,057. Sullivan, Ruth Elizabeth. The narrator in 'A Rose for Emily.' J Narrative Technique, 1971, 1:159-178.
13,058. _____. Some Variations on the Oedipal Theme in Three Pieces of Fiction: 'A Rose for Emily,' 'Three Hours after Marriage,' and 'Christabel.' DAI, 1973, 4366A-7A.
13,059. _____. William Wilson's double. Studies in Romanticism, 1976, 15:253-263.
13,060. _____, & Smith, Stewart. Narrative stance in Kate Chopin's The Awakening. Studies in Amer Fiction, 1973, 1:62-75.
13,061. Sullivan, William P. Bartleby and infantile autism: a naturalistic explanation. Bulletin West Virginia Assn College Teachers, 1976, 3(2):43-60.
13,062. Sullivan, Zohreh Tawakuli. Enchantment and the demonic in Iris Murdoch: The Flight from the Enchanter. Midwest Q, 1975, 16:276-297.

13,063. Sully, J. The child in recent English literature. Fort-
         nightly Rev, 1897, 61:218-228.
13,064. Sundquist, Eric J. Homes As Found; Authority and Geneal-
         ogy in Nineteenth-Century American Literature. Balti-
         more: Johns Hopkins Univ. Press, 1979.
13,065. _____. Incest and imitation in Cooper's Home As Found.
         Nineteenth Century Fiction, 1977, 32:261-284.
13,066. Sussman, Henry. The court as text: inversion, supplant-
         ing, and derangement in Kafka's Der Prozess. PMLA,
         1977, 92:41-55.
13,067. Sutcliffe, Emerson G. Psychological presentation in
         Reade's novels. Studies in Philology, 1941, 38:521-542.
13,068. Suttner, Christa. A note on the Droste-image and 'Das
         Spiegelbild. ' German Q, 1967, 40:623-629.
13,069. Sutton, Juliet. Thackeray's mother-in-law. Lit & Psychol,
         1965, 15:171-179.
13,070. Sutton, William A. Melville's 'Pleasure Party' and the
         art of concealment. Philological Q, 1951, 30:316-327.
13,071. Suzuki, Kenzo. [The psychological novel.] In Ara, M.,
         & Saeki, S. (eds), [An Introduction to James Joyce.]
         Tokyo: Namin-do, 1960, 1966, 162-169.
13,072. Swanson, Gayle Ruff. Henry Fielding and the Psychology
         of Womanhood. DAI, 1977, 38:291A.
13,073. Swanson, Roger M. Guilt in Selected Victorian Novels.
         DAI, 1969, 30:342A.
13,074. Swartz, Paul. Marcel Proust and the problem of time and
         self. Psychol Reports, 1978, 43:291-297.
13,075. _____. A rose for behaviorism. Psychol Reports,
         1970, 27(2):364.
13,076. Sweeney, Gerard M. Melville's smoky humor: fire-light-
         ing in Typee. Arizona Q, 1978, 34:371-376.
13,077. Swiderski, Marie Laure. La Condition de la femme fran-
         çaises au 18e siècle d'après les romans. In Fritz, P.,
         & Marton, R. (ed), Women in the 18th Century and Oth-
         er Essays. Toronto: Stevens, Hakkert, 1976, 105-125.
13,078. Swiderski, Marie Laure. L'Image de la femme dans le
         roman au début du XVIIIe siècle: Les Illustres Fran-
         çaises de Robert Challe. Studies in Voltaire & the
         Eighteenth Century, 1972, 90:1505-1518.
13,079. Symons, Julian. What they are and why we read them.
         In Mortal Consequences. A History from the Detective
         Story to the Crime Novel. NY: Schocken, 1973, 1-13;
         NY: Harper & Row, 1972, 1-13.
13,080. Sypher, Wylie. Loss of the Self in Modern Fiction and
         Art. NY: Random House, 1962.
13,081. Szafran, Willy A. Approche psychanalytique de l'obscénité
         de Céline. In Céline: Actes du colloque international
         de Paris. Paris: Société d'études céliniennes, 1978,
         281-296; Annales Médico-Psychologiques, 1977, 1:775-
         783.
13,082. _____. Louis-Ferdinand Céline: Essai psychanaly-
         tique. Brussels: Univ. de Bruxelles, 1976; Review:
         James Flagg, Modern Fiction Studies, 1977-78, 23:681-
         682.

13,083.   Szállási, A. [Chekhov and Maugham, favorite writers of
          the journal Nyugat.] Orvosi Hetilap (Budapest), 1980,
          121(4):226-229.
13,084.   Székely, Lajos. Thomas Manns Tod in Venedig. Mit An-
          merkungen über psychoanalytische und marxistische Lit-
          eraturinterpretation. Psyche, 1973, 27:614-635.
13,085.   Szczepanska, Kathryn. The Double and Double Conscious-
          ness in Dostoevsky. DAI, 1978, 39:916A-17A.
13,086.   Szépe, Helena. The problem of identity in Anna Segher's
          Transit. Orbis Litterarum, 1972, 27:145-152.
13,087.   Szövérffy, Joseph. 'Artuswelt' and 'Grawelt': shame cul-
          ture and guilt culture in Parzival. In Fletcher, H. G.
          III, & Schulte, M. B. (eds), Paradosis. NY: Fordham
          Univ. Press, 1976, 85-98.

13,088.   Tabachnick, E., & Tabachnick, N. The second birth of
          D. H. Lawrence. J Amer Academy Psychoanal, 1976,
          4:469-480.
13,089.   Tabbs, Bernard Linden. Fielding's Oedipal Fantasies: A
          Psychoanalytic Study of the Double in Tom Jones. DAI,
          1976, 37:1524A.
13,090.   Tadokoro, Nobushige. The problem of hallucinations in
          'The Turn of the Screw.' Kyushu American Lit, 1965,
          No. 8, 25-35.
13,091.   Taillieu, J. La Vie profonde de l'enfance. Brussels:
          Office de Publicité, 1944.
13,092.   Takada, Mamoru. [Fantastic story writers and dream lan-
          guage.] Bungaku, 1975, 43:763-774.
13,093.   Takaki, Ronald. Violence in the Black Imagination. NY:
          Putnam, 1972.
13,094.   Takenaka, Toyoko. [On Seymour's suicide.] Kyushu Amer
          Lit (Japan), 1970, 12:54-61.
13,095.   Takigawa, Motoo. [American Literature and Sex.] Tokyo:
          Azuma Shuppan-sha, 1968.
13,096.   Talbert, E. L. The modern novel and the response of the
          reader. J Abnormal Social Psychol, 1932, 26:409-414.
13,097.   Talon, Henri. Irony in Lord of the Flies. Essays in
          Criticism, 1968, 18:296-309.
13,098.   Tanner, Tony. Adultery in the Novel: Contract and
          Transgression. Baltimore: Johns Hopkins Univ. Press,
          1979.
13,099.   _____. City of Words: American Fiction, 1950-1970.
          NY: Harper & Row, 1971.
13,100.   Tapley, Philip Allen. The Portrayal of Women in Selected
          Short Stories by Eudora Welty. DAI, 1975, 35:5429A-
          30A.
13,101.   Tarbox, Raymond. Auditory experience in Joyce's Por-
          trait. Amer Imago, 1970, 27:301-328.
13,102.   _____. Blank hallucinations in the fiction of Poe and
          Hemingway. Amer Imago, 1967, 24:312-343.
13,103.   _____. Death in Venice: the aesthetic object as dream
          guide. Amer Imago, 1969, 26:123-144.

13,104. _____. Eudora Welty's fiction: the salvation theme. Amer Imago, 1972, 29:70-91.

13,105. _____. Exhaustion psychology and Sartre's The Age of Reason. Amer Imago, 1973, 30:80-96.

13,106. _____. Face-breast hallucinations in the fiction of Eudora Welty. Flint: Privately Printed, 1967.

13,107. Tarratt, Margaret. Cranford and 'the strict code of gentility.' Essays in Criticism, 1968, 18:152-153.

13,108. Tarshis, Jerome. Krafft-Ebing visits Dealey Plaza: the recent fiction of J.C. Ballard. Evergreen Rev, 1973, 17:137-148.

13,109. Tatar, Maria M. Mesmerism, madness, and death in E. T. A. Hoffmann's Der goldene Topf. Studies in Romanticism, 1975, 14:365-389.

13,110. _____. Psychology and poetics: J. C. Reil and Kleist's Prinz Friedrich von Homburg. Germanic Rev, 1973, 48:21-34.

13,111. _____. Spellbound: Studies on Mesmerism and Literature. Princeton: Princeton Univ. Press, 1978; Review: Nineteenth Century Fiction, 1979, 33:505-508.

13,112. Tatum, Charles M. The child point of view in Donoso's fiction. J Spanish Studies: Twentieth Century, 1973, 1:187-196.

13,113. Taube, Myron. Fanny and the lady: the treatment of sex in Fanny Hill and Lady Chatterley's Lover. Lock Haven Rev, 1974, 15, 37-40.

13,114. Taube, Otto von. Ein homosexueller Romanheld bei Balzac. Jahrbuch für Sexuelle Zwischenstufen, 1912-13, 13:179-190.

13,115. Taubenheim, Barbara Wiese. Erikson's psychosocial theory applied to adolescent fiction: a means for adolescent self-clarification. J Reading, 1979, 22:517-522.

13,116. Tavernier-Courbin, Jacqueline. Striving for power: Hemingway's neuroses. J General Education, 1978, 30:137-153.

13,117. Taylor, Archer. Gestures in an American detective story. In Estudios de Folklore. Mexico City, Mexico: 1971, 295-300.

13,118. Taylor, Chet H. The Aware Man: Studies in Self-Awareness in the Contemporary Novel. Doctoral dissertation, Univ. Oregon, 1971.

13,119. Taylor, G. Rattray. Historical and mythological aspects of homosexuality. In Marmor, J. (ed), Sexual Inversion; The Multiple Roots of Homosexuality. NY: Basic Books, 1965, 140-164.

13,120. Taylor, Gordon O. The Passages of Thought: Psychological Representation in the American Novel 1870-1900. NY: Oxford Univ. Press, 1969; DA, 1968, 29:579A-80A; Review: Frederick W. Turner, III, Hartford Studies in Lit, 1970, 2:188-191.

13,121. Taylor, Harley U. The death wish and suicide in the novels of Hermann Hesse. West Virginia Univ. Philological Papers, 1961, 13:50-65.

13,122. _____. Homoerotic elements in the novels of Hermann
         Hesse. West Virginia Univ. Philological Papers, 1967,
         16:63-71.
13,123. Taylor, Kent Hewitt. Wittgenstein and Melville: A Study
         in the Character of Meaning. DAI, 1977, 38:793A.
13,124. Taylor, Walter. Faulkner: nineteenth century notions of
         racial mixture and the twentieth-century imagination.
         South Carolina Rev, 1977, 10:57-68.
13,125. Tedlock, E. W., Jr. (ed). D. H. Lawrence and 'Sons and
         Lovers': Sources and Criticism. NY: University
         Press, 1965.
13,126. Teets, Bruce E. Conrad among the psychologists. Eng-
         lish Lit in Transition (1880-1920), 1973, 16:236-237.
13,127. _____. Conrad and guides to art as psychagogia. Con-
         radiana, 1970, 2(1):127-131.
13,128. Tefs, Wayne A. Norman N. Holland and 'A Rose for Em-
         ily': some questions concerning psychoanalytic criti-
         cism. Sphinx, 1974, 2:50-57.
13,129. Teichgraeber, Stephen E. The Treatment of Marriage in
         the Early Novels of Henry James. DA, 1967, 28:1830A.
13,130. Teillard, Ania. Anima-Animus. Psyché, 1948, 3:191-202.
13,131. Telgher, A. L'Esthétique de Marcel Proust. Rev Philo-
         sophique, 1933, 58:128-132.
13,132. Tellenbach, H. The suicide of the 'Young Werther' and
         the consequences for the circumstances of suicide of
         endogenic melancholia. Israel Annals of Psychol & Re-
         lated Disciplines, 1977, 15:16-21.
13,133. Tenenbaum, Elizabeth Brody. Concepts of the Self in the
         Modern Novel. DAI, 1972, 32:7010.
13,134. _____. The Problematic Self. Approaches to Identity
         in Stendhal, D. H. Lawrence and Malraux. Cambridge:
         Harvard Univ. Press, 1977.
13,135. Terras, Rita. The Doppelgänger in German romantic lit-
         erature. In Deguise, P., & Terras, R. (eds), Sym-
         posium on Romanticism: An Interdisciplinary Meeting.
         New London: Connecticut College, 1977, 13-20.
13,136. Terry, Phyllis C. Female Individuation in the Twentieth
         Century as Seen Through Contemporary Fiction. DAI,
         1978, 38(8-B), 3860.
13,137. Thanner, J. Symbol and function of the symbol in Theodor
         Fontane's Effi Briest. Monatshefte, 1965, 57:187-192.
13,138. Théodoridés, J. Stendhal et les hôpitaux. Hôpitaux Paris,
         1970, 66:735-743.
13,139. Therrien, Madeleine B. 'Les Liaisons dangereuses': Une
         Interpretation psychologique. Paris: Société d'ed.
         d'enseignement supérieur, 1974.
13,140. Thieme, John. Double identity in the novels of Garth St.
         Omer. Ariel: Rev Int English Lit, 1977, 8(3):81-97.
13,141. Thiher, Allen. Céline: The Novel as Delirium. New
         Brunswick, NJ: Rutgers Univ. Press, 1972.
13,142- _____. Le Feu follet: the drug addict as a tragic
    3.   hero. PMLA, 1973, 88:34-40.

13,144. Thomas, A. P.   Tragic Heroes in the Works of Miguel de Unamuno: Studies in Pathologic Disintegration. DAI, 1969, 29:4024-A.

13,145. Thomas, Barry G.   The function of the eyes in Gottfried Keller's 'Die missbrauchten Liebesbriefe.' Monatshefte, 1974, 66:46-54.

13,146. Thomas, Frank Howard III.   The Search for Identity of Faulkner's Black Characters. DAI, 1973, 33:6935A.

13,147. Thomas, Glen R.   The Freudian Approach to James's 'The Turn of the Screw': Psychoanalysis and Literary Criticism. Doctoral dissertation, Emory Univ., 1969; DAI, 1970, 31(2-A), 770.

13,148. Thomas, J. D.   The dark at the end of the tunnel: Kafka's In the Penal Colony. Studies in Short Fiction, 1966, 4:12-18.

13,149. Thomas, Leroy.   An Analysis of the Theme of Alienation in the Fictional Works of Five Contemporary Southern Writers. DAI, 1972, 33:768A.

13,150. Thomas, Peter.   Priapus in the Danse Macabre. Canadian Lit, 1974, 61:54-64.

13,151. Thomas, Richard Joyce.   Sensation and Feeling in Clarin's La Regenta. DAI, 1976, 36:5342A.

13,152. Thomas, Ruth.   The art of the portrait in the novels of Marivaux. French Rev, 1968, 42:23-31.

13,153. Thompsett, Eileen.   The theme of seduction in the 18th-century French novel: Barthe's La Jolie Femme. Forum Modern Language Studies, 1976, 12:206-216.

13,154. Thompson, Brian.   André Malraux and the artist's quest. Twentieth Century Fiction, 1978, 24:408-412.

13,155. Thompson, Currie Kerr.   The use and function of dreaming in four novels by Emilia Pardo Bazán. Historiographia Linguistica, 1976, 59:856-862.

13,156. Thompson, David J. S.   The Societal Definitions of Individualism and the Critique of Egotism as a Major Theme in American fiction. DAI, 1973, 33:4435A.

13,157. Thompson, G. R.   Dramatic irony in 'The Oval Portrait': a reconsideration of Poe's revisions. English Language Notes, 1968, 6:107-114.

13,158. _____.   The face in the pool: reflections on the Doppelgänger motif in 'The Fall of the House of Usher.' Poe Studies, 1972, 5:16-21.

13,159. _____.   Is Poe's 'Tale of the Ragged Mountains' a hoax? Studies in Short Fiction, 1959, 6:454-460.

13,160. _____.   'Proper evidences of madness': American Gothic and the interpretation of 'Ligeia.' Emerson Society Q, 1972, 66:30-49.

13,161. _____.   Reply to J. J. Moldenhauer's 'Murder as a fine art.' PMLA, 1970, 85:297-300.

13,162. Thompson, Gordon W.   Conrad's women. Nineteenth Century Fiction, 1978, 32:442-463.

13,163. Thompson, John.   Books. Harper's, Sept. 1969, 122-127.

13,164. _____.   Poor Papa. New York Rev of Books, 28 Apr.

1966, 6-7.

13,165. Thompson, Wade. Infanticide and sadism in Wuthering Heights. PMLA, 1963, 78:69-74.

13,166. Thomsen, Hans Hagedorn. Androgyneproblemet I. Kritik, 1970, 14:39-55.

13,167. _____. Androgyne problemet II. Kritik, 1970, 15:91-118.

13,168. Thomson, A.W. 'The Turn of the Screw': some points on the hallucination theory. Rev English Lit, 1965, 6(4):26-36.

13,169. Thomson, George H. Conrad's later fiction. English Lit in Transition, 1880-1920, 1969, 12:165-174.

13,170. _____. A note on the snake imagery of A Passage to India. English Lit in Transition (1880-1920), 1966, 9: 108-110.

13,171. Thoreson, Trygve Richard. Women in the Writings of Mark Twain. DAI, 1977, 37:4358A-59A.

13,172. Thornham, Susan. Lawrence and Freud. Durham Univ. J, 1977, 39:73-82.

13,173. Thornton, Hortense E. Sexism as quagmire: Nella Larsen's Quicksand. College Language Assn J, 1973, 16: 285-301.

13,174. Thornton, Lawrence. Narcissism and selflessness in The Alexandria Quartet. Deus Loci: The Lawrence Durrell Newsletter, 1978, 1(4):3-23.

13,175. Thornton, Patricia Elizabeth. The Prison of Gender: Sexual Roles in Major American Novels of the 1920's. DAI, 1977, 37:7133A-34A.

13,176. Thorslev, Peter L., Jr. Hawthorne's determinism: an analysis. Nineteenth Century Fiction, 1964, 19, 141-157.

13,177. Throne, Marilyn E. The Two Selves: Duality in Willa Cather's Protagonists and Themes. DAI, 1970, 30: 3026A-27A.

13,178. Thur, Robert. Longing for Union: The Doppelgänger in Wuthering Heights and Frankenstein. DAI, 1977, 37: 4172B.

13,179. Thurley, Geoffrey John. The Psychology of Hardy's Novels: The Nervous and the Statuesque. St. Lucia, Australia: Queensland Univ. Press, 1975.

13,180. Tibbetts, A.M. Allen Tate's The Fathers: the fatal attraction of evil. Tennessee Studies Lit, 1967, 12:155-163.

13,181. _____. Nathaniel West's The Dream Life of Balso Snell. Studies in Short Fiction, 1965, 2:105-112.

13,182. Tick, Stanley. The memorializing of Mr. Dick. Nineteenth Century Fiction, 1969, 24:142-153.

13,183. Tilley, Winthrop. The idiot boy in Mississippi: Faulkner's The Sound and the Fury. Amer J Mental Deficiency, 1955, 59:374-377.

13,184. Tilton, John W. Giles Goat-Boy: an interpretation. Bucknell Rev, 1970, 18:92-119.

13,185. Timpe, Eugene F. Ulysses and the archetypal feminine.
In Strelka, J. (ed), Perspectives in Literary Symbolism. University Park: Penn State Univ. Press, 1968,
199-213.

13,186. Tindall, William York. Forces in Modern British Literature, 1885-1946. NY: Knopf, 1947, 318-359.

13,187. _____. James Joyce. NY: Evergreen, 1960.

13,188. _____. The Literary Symbol. Bloomington: Indiana
Univ. Press, 1955.

13,189. Tinnell, Roger D. Carl Jung, Pascual Duarte, secret
stones, and the individuation process. Papers in Language & Lit, 1978, 14:91-94.

13,190. _____. La muerte de Artemio Cruz: a virtuoso study
in sensualism. MLN, 1978, 99:334-338.

13,191. Tintner, Adeline R. Isabel's carriage-image and Emma's
day dream. Modern Fiction Studies, 1976, 22:227-231.

13,192. _____. Mothers, daughters, and incest in the late novels of Edith Wharton. In Davidson, C.N., & Broner,
E.M. (eds), The Lost Tradition. NY: Ungar, 1980,
147-156.

13,193. _____. The sleeping woman: a Victorian fantasy.
Pre-Raphaelite Rev, 1978, 2(1):12-26.

13,194. Tischler, Nancy M. The Negro in Southern fiction: stereotype and archetype. Negro Amer Lit Forum, 1968,
2:3-6.

13,195. Titche, Leon L.J. The concept of the hermaphrodite
Agathe and Ulrich in Musil's novel Der Mann ohne
Eigenschaften. German Life & Letters, 1970, 23:160-
168.

13,196. _____. Into the millenium: the theme of the hermaphrodite in Robert Musil's Der Mann ohne Eigenschaften.
Oxford German Studies, 1973, 7:143-160.

13,197. Tobier, N., & Steinberg, I. 'A dreary story' by Anton
Chekhov, M.D., biography of a repression. New York
J Medicine, 1966, 1006-1011.

13,198. Tobin, Patricia Drechsel. Time and the Novel: The Ge-
nealogical Imperative. Princeton: Princeton Univ.
Press, 1979.

13,199. Todd, Janet M. Women's Friendship in Literature. The
Eighteenth-Century Novel in England and France. NY:
Columbia Univ. Press, 1980.

13,200. Todd, John, & Dewhurst, Kenneth. The double: its psychopathology and psychophysiology. JNMD, 1955, 122:
47-55.

13,201. Todd, Robert E. The Magna Mater archetype in The Scarlet Letter. New England Q, 1972, 45:421-429.

13,202. Todorov, Tzvetan. Typologie du roman policer. In Poétique de la prose. Paris: Seuil, 1971, 57-58.

13,203. Tomasi, Barbara R. The fraternal theme in Joyce's
Ulysses. Amer Imago, 1973, 30:177-191.

13,204. Toor, David. Guilt and retribution in 'Babylon Revisited.'
Fitzgerald-Hemingway Annual, 1973, 155-164.

13,205. Torrente, Nissa. Dos adolescencias argentinas en la obra
de Roberto Arlt y Ricardo Güiraldes. In Literatura de

la Emancipación Hispoamericana y Otros Ensayos.
Lima: Univ. de San Marcos, 1972, 200-205.

13, 206. Torrento, Caridad J. An analytic study of adolescent behavior (as seen through Philip Carey). Saint Louis
Univ. Research J, (Philippines), 1970, 1:694-710.

13, 207. Torres, Aldo. El adolescente en la novela chilena. Cuadernos Hispanoamericanos, 1960, No. 124, 80-93.

13, 208. Toubin, C., & Malinas, Y. Les Clés et les portes. Les
Cahiers Naturalistes, 1971, 41:15-21.

13, 209. Toulouse, E. Observation de M. Emile Zola. Rev de
Paris, 1895, 6:88-126.

13, 210. Tournadre, C. Propositions pour une psychologie sociale
de 'The Turn of the Screw.' Etudes Anglaises, 1969,
22:259-269.

13, 211. Towers, Tom H. The insomnia of Julian West. Amer
Lit, 1975, 47:52-63.

13, 212. Towne, Alfred. The myth of the western hero. Neurotica,
1950, 7:3-7.

13, 213. Towne, Jackson E. Scepticism as a Freudian 'defense-
reaction.' A psychoanalysis of Bazaroff, the hero of
Turgenev's Fathers and Sons. Psychoanal Rev, 1920,
7:159-162.

13, 214. Townsend, D. W., Jr. Phenomenology and the form of the
novel: toward an expanded critical method. Philosophy
& Phenomenological Research, 1974, 34:331-338.

13, 215. Tracy, Ann Blaisdell. Patterns of Fear in the Gothic Novel, 1790-1830. DAI, 1977, 38:3460A.

13, 216. Tracy, Bruce H. 'Walden' as a Novel: A Psychoanalytic
Reading. DAI, 1972, 33:2346A.

13, 217. Trahair, Richard C. S. A Contribution to the Psychoanalytic Study of the Modern Hero: The Case of James
Bond. Bundoora, Victoria, Canada: La Trobe Univ.,
1976.

13, 218. _____. A psychological study of the modern hero: the
case of James Bond. Australian/New Zealand J Psychiat, 1974, 8:155-165.

13, 219. Trail, George Y. The consistency of Hardy's Sue: Bridehead becomes Electra. Lit & Psychol, 1976, 26:61-68.

13, 220. Trainer, Russell. The Lolita Complex. NY: Citadel,
1966.

13, 221. Tranquez, Pierre. L'Asthénique, l'amazone et l'androgyne.
In Petit, J. (ed), Sur 'Le Chevalier des Touches.'
Paris: Minard, 1977.

13, 222. Trapp, Peter. Schund, Film und Jugendkriminalität.
Psychologische Berater gesunde praktische Lebensges-
talt, 1952, 4:460-467.

13, 223. Traschen, Isadore. Dostoyevsky's Notes from Underground. Accent, 1956, 16:255-264; In Durgy, R. G.
(ed), Notes from Underground. NY: Crowell, 1969,
217-229.

13, 224. _____. Henry Miller: the ego and I. South Atlantic
Q, 1966, 65:345-354.

13, 225. _____. The uses of myth in Death in Venice. Modern
Fiction Studies, 1965, 11:165-179.

13, 226. Travis, Leigh. D. H. Lawrence: the blood-conscious art-
          ist. Amer Imago, 1968, 25:163-190.
13, 227. Travis, Mildred J. Hawthorne's 'Egotism' and 'The Jolly
          Corner.' Emerson Society Q, 1971, 63:13-18.
13, 228. Travitsky, Betty S. The new mother of the English Ren-
          aissance: her writings on motherhood. In Davidson,
          C. N., & Broner, E. M. (eds), The Lost Tradition.
          NY: Ungar, 1980, 33-43.
13, 229. Treil, Claude. L'Indifférence dans l'oeuvre d'Albert Cam-
          us. Paris: Nizet, 1971.
13, 230. _____. L'Ironie d'Albert Camus. Procédés psychol-
          ogiques: trois aspects. Rev de l'Université Laval,
          1963, 17:687-697.
13, 231. Tremblay, N. J. Simenon's psychological 'Westerns.'
          Arizona Q, 1954, 10:217-226.
13, 232. Tremper, Ellen. Henry James's altering ego: an exam-
          ination of his psychological double in three tales.
          Texas Q, 1976, 19(3):59-75.
13, 233. Trensky, Anne T. The Cult of the Child in Minor Amer-
          ican Fiction of the Nineteenth Century. DAI, 1969, 30:
          2048A-49A.
13, 234. Trickett, Rachel. Obsessed with death. Times Lit Sup-
          plement, 24 Nov 1978, 1358.
13, 235. Trilling, Diana. The image of women in contemporary
          literature. In Lifton, R. J. (ed), The Woman in Amer-
          ica. Boston: Houghton Mifflin, 1965, 52-71; Boston:
          Beacon, 1967, 52-71.
13, 236. Trilling, Jacques. James Joyce ou l'écriture matricide.
          Etudes freudiennes, 1973, 7-8.
13, 237. _____. Un transfert littéraire. Etudes freudiennes,
          1970, 3/4:99-119.
13, 238. Tristram, Philippa. Eros and death (Lawrence, Freud
          and women), In Smith, A. (ed), Lawrence and Women.
          NY: Barnes & Noble, 1978, 136-155.
13, 239. Trouiller, D. Le Monologue intérieur dans Le Rouge et
          le Noir. Stendhal Club (Lausanne), 1969, 11:245-277.
13, 240. Trowbridge, Clinton W. Water imagery in Seize the Day.
          Critique, 1967, 9(3):62-73.
13, 241. Trowbridge, William Leigh. Myth and Dream in the Nov-
          els of William Faulkner. DAI, 1976, 36:4498A-99A.
13, 242. Truzzi, Marcello, & Morris, Scot. Sherlock Holmes as
          a social scientist. Psychol Today, 1971, 5:62-64, 85-
          87.
13, 243. Tschisch, W. von. [Turgenev as psychopathologist.]
          Voprosi Philosophii, 1899, 10:624-648, 714-793.
13, 244. Tseng, W. S. The Chinese attitude toward parental author-
          ity as expressed in Chinese children's stories. Ar-
          chives General Psychiat, 1972, 26:28-34.
13, 245. Tsukimura, Reiko. The art of fiction in the East and
          West: an observation on the technique of stream of
          consciousness in Kawabata Yasunari and James Joyce.
          In Cadot, M., et al. (eds), Actes du XVe Congres de
          l'Association Internationale de Littérature Comparée.
          Stuttgart: Bieber, 1975, 667-672.

13, 246. Tuckey, John S. Mark Twain's later dialogue: the 'me' and the machine. Amer Lit, 1970, 41:532-542.

13, 247. Tudor, Kathleen R. The Androgynous Mind in W. B. Yeats, D. H. Lawrence, Virginia Woolf and Dorothy Richardson. DAI, 1974, 35:1126A-27A.

13, 248. Tull, J. F., Jr. Alienation, psychological and metaphysical, in three 'Nivolas' of Unamuno. Humanities Assn Bulletin, 1970, 21(1):27-33.

13, 249. _____. La 'Neurastenia' de Julia en Nada menos que todo un hombre. Duquesne Hispanic Rev, 1969, 8(1):9-12.

13, 250. Turco, Lewis. American novelists as poets: the schizophrenia of mode. English Record, 1974, 25(3):23-29.

13, 251. Turner, Darwin. Sight in Invisible Man. College Language Assn J, 1970, 13:258-264.

13, 252. Turner, Gordon. The incest bond in Stead's Grain. Sphinx, 1977, 7:23-32.

13, 253. Tuttleton, James W. Aiken's 'Mr. Arcularis': psychic regression and the death instinct. Amer Imago, 1963, 20:295-314.

13, 254. _____. Combat in the erogenous zone: women in the American novel between the two World Wars. In Springer, M. (ed), What Manner of Woman: Essays on English and American Life and Literature. NY: New York Univ. Press, 1977, 271-296.

13, 255. _____. Hardy and Ellen Glasgow: Barren Ground. Mississippi Q, 1979, 32:577-590.

13, 256. Tuveson, Ernest. 'The Jolly Corner': a fable of redemption. Studies in Short Fiction, 1975, 12:271-280.

13, 257. _____. 'The Turn of the Screw': a palimpsest. Studies in English Lit, 1973, 12:783-800.

13, 258. Tvinnereim, A. Risens hjerte--en studie i S. Hoels forfatterskap. Oslo: Gyldendal, 1975.

13, 259. Twitchell, James B. Heathcliff as monomaniac. Brontë Society Transactions, 1975, 16:374-375.

13, 260. _____. Lawrence's lamias: predatory women in The Rainbow and Women in Love. Studies in the Novel, 1979, 11:23-42.

13, 261. Tými, Václav. Psychologismus jako kritérium typologie postav ve Vojne a miru. Ceskoslovenská Rusistika, 1978, 23:202-206.

13, 262. Tymms, Ralph. Doubles in Literary Psychology. Cambridge: Bowes & Bowes, 1949.

13, 263. Tyrmand, Mary E. Women and Society in the Nineteenth-Century Spanish Novel. DAI, 1974, 35:3774A.

13, 264. Tytler, Graeme D. Character Description and Physiognomy in the European Novel (1800-1860) in Relation to J. C. Lavater's Physiognomische Fragmente. Doctoral dissertation, Univ. Illinois, 1970; DAI, 1971, 31:4798-99A.

13, 265. Uchida, Ichigoro. A review of psychological studies on Edgar Allan Poe 1860-1967. In Various, Collected Es-

says by the Members of the Faculty. No. 13. Kyoritsu, Japan: Kyoritsu Women's Junior College, 1969,
120-139.

13, 266. Ueda Makoto.   Modern Japanese Writers and the Nature of
Literature.   Palo Alto, Cal: Stanford Univ. Press,
1976.

13, 267. Ueding, Gert.   Geschichte und Geschichten: Der Traum
des Gefangen im Werk Karl Mays.   Jahrbuch der Karl-
Mays-Gesellschaft, 1978, 60-86; In Gerhardt, M., &
Mattenklott, G. (eds), Kontext 2: Geschichte und Sub-
jektivität.   Munich: Bertelsmann, 1978, 109-131.

13, 268. Uitti, Karl D.   The Concept of Self in the Symbolistic Novel.   The Hague: Mouton, 1961.

13, 269. Ullman, Joan C., & Allison, George H.   Galdós as psychiatrist in Fortunata y Jacinta.   Anales Galdosianos,
1974, 9:7-36.

13, 270. Ullman, Michael Alan.   Dickens's Haunted Heroes: A
Study of the Emotional Lives of Major Characters in
Seven of Dickens's Work.   DAI, 1977, 37:6517A-18A.

13, 271. Ullmann, Stephen.   Reported speech and internal monologue
in Flaubert.   In Style in the French Novel.   Oxford:
Blackwell, 1964 (1957), 94-120.

13, 272. Ulmer, Gregory L.   Clarissa and La Nouvelle Héloïse.
Comparative Lit, 1972, 24:289-308.

13, 273. Unkeless, Elaine Rapp.   Consciousness and Androgyny in
James Joyce's Ulysses.   DAI, 1975, 35:6165A.

13, 274. _____.   Leopold Bloom as womanly man.   Modernist
Studies: Lit & Culture 1920-1940, 1976, 2(1):35-44.

13, 275. Uphaus, Robert W.   Caleb Williams: Godwin's epoch of
mind.   Studies in the Novel, 1977, 9:279-296.

13, 276. Urban, Bernd.   Franz Werfel, Freud und die Psychoanalyse: Zu unveröffentlichten Dokumenten.   Deutsche
Vierteljahrsschrift für Litteraturwissenschaft und Geistesgeschichte, 1973, 47:267-285.

13, 277. Usimani, Renate.   Twentieth-century man, the guilt-ridden
animal.   Mosaic, 1970, 3:163-178.

13, 278. Uzzell, Thomas H.   Modern innovations.   College English,
1945, 7:59-65.

13, 279. Václavik, Antonín.   Franz Kafka und seine Kunst der psychologischen Analyse.   In Reimann, P. (ed), Franz
Kafka aus Prager Sicht 1963.   Prague: Tschechoslowa-
kischen Akademie der Wissenschaften, 1965, 267-275.

13, 280. Valbuena, A.   El torno a la psicoanalisis de Don Juan.
Revista de psicologia y pedagogia, 1937, 5:170-182.

13, 281. Valeros, Jose Antonio.   On masturbation: a study of Jean
Genet's Our Lady of the Flowers.   Psychiat Q, 1968,
42:252-262.

13, 282. Vallejo Nájera, A.   La realidad clinica psiquiátrica en la
novela.   Razon y fe, 1948, 48:408-430.

13, 283. Vallés Rovira, J.   La exaltación del excremento como tema
cultural.   Papeles de son Armadans, 1969, 53:297-310.

13, 284.	Van Bark, Bella S.	The alienated person in literature.
		Amer J Psychoanal, 1961, 21:183-197.
13, 285.		.	The Sudden Guest; a critical analysis.	Amer J
		Psychoanal, 1948, 8:59-62.
13, 286.	Van de Kieft, Ruth M.	Eudora Welty.	NY: Twayne, 1962.
13, 287.	Van de Laar, E.	The Inner Structure of Wuthering Heights:
		A Study of an Imaginative Field.	The Hague:	Mouton,
		1969.
13, 288.	Van den Aardweg, G. J. M.	De neurose van Couperus.
		Nederlands Tijdschrift voor de Psychologie en haar
		Gensgebreden, 1965, 20:293-307.
13, 289.	Van der Sterren, H. A.	Ein Kindscheidsfantasie van Sir
		Arthur Conan Doyle en de Heldenbaden van Sherlock
		Holmes.	Psychologische und Neurologische Blätter,
		1946, 49:304-330.
13, 290.	Van Ghent, Dorothy.	The English Novel:	Form and Func-
		tion.	NY:	Harper, 1953, 1967; London:	Hamilton,
		1961.
13, 291.	Van Meter, Jan.	Sex and war in The Red Badge of Cour-
		age.	Genre, 1974, 7:71-90.
13, 292.	Van Tassel, Daniel E.	The search for manhood in D. H.
		Lawrence's Sons and Lovers.	Costerus, 1972, 3:197-
		210.
13, 293.	Van Tine, James.	The risks of Swiftian sanity.	Univ.
		Rev, 1966, 234-240.
13, 294.	Vanasse, André.	A propos d'une valise ou equisse psycho-
		critique de l'oeuvre de Marcel Dubé.	Livres et auteurs
		québécois, 1971, 311-322.
13, 295.	Vandenberg, Stephen C.	Great expectations, or, the future
		of psychology as seen in science fiction.	Amer Psy-
		chologist, 1956, 11:339-342.
13, 296.	Vander Beets, Richard.	Nietzsche of the north: heredity
		and race in Jack London's The Son of the Wolf.	West-
		ern Amer Lit, 1962, 2:229-233.
13, 297.	Vanderbilt, Kermit.	Literature and nature in 'The Masque
		of the Red Death.'	Nineteenth Century Fiction, 1968,
		22:379-389.
13, 298.		.	Marcia Gaylord's Electra complex:	a footnote
		to sex in Howells.	Amer Lit, 1962, 34:365-374.
13, 299.	Vanderwerff, Whitney G.	Virginia Woolf as Equilibrist:
		The Moment of Vision and the Androgynous Mind.	DAI,
		1978, 39:3606A-07A.
13, 300.	Vanderwerken, David L.	The bridge motif in The Sun Also
		Rises.	CEA Critic, 1975, 37(2):21-22.
13, 301.		.	Dos Passos' Streets of Night:	a reconsidera-
		tion.	Markham Rev, 1974, 4:61-65.
13, 302.	Vanggaard, Thorkill.	Phallós, A Symbol and Its History in
		the Male World.	NY:	IUP, 1972 (1969).
13, 303.	Vann, Barbara.	A psychological interpretation of Daisy
		Miller.	In Penninger, F. E. (ed), A Festschrift for
		Professor Marguerite Roberts.	Richmond, Va:	Univ.
		Richmond Press, 1976, 205-208.

13,304. Vargas Llosa, Mario. Literatura y suicidio: el caso de
Arguedas. El zorro de arriba y el zorro de abajo.
Revista Iberoamericana, 1980, 110-111:3-28.
13,305. Vargish, Thomas. Revenge and Wuthering Heights. Studies in the Novel, 1971, 3:7-17.
13,306. Varin, René. L'Erotisme dans la littérature étrangère de
D. H. Lawrence à H. Miller. Paris: Nord-Sud, 1951.
13,307. Various. Céline: Actes du colloque international de Paris
(27-30 juillet 1976). Paris: Société d'études céliniennes, 1978.
13,308. _____. Sexuality in Victorian Literature. [Special issue.] Victorian Newsletter, 1973, 44.
13,309. _____. [Literature and psychology: Marcel Proust.]
[Entire issue.] L'Esprit créateur, 1965, 5:3-55.
13,310. _____. What 'The Metamorphosis' means. Symposium,
1961, 15:210-227.
13,311. Vartanian, Aram. The death of Julie: a psychological
post-mortem. L'Esprit créateur, 1966, 6:77-84.
13,312. _____. Diderot and the phenomenon of the dream.
Diderot Studies, 1966, 8:217-254.
13,313. Vázques Bigi, Angel Manuel. Los conflictos psiquicos y
religiosos de 'El hermano asno.' Cuadernos Hispano-
americanos, 1968, 73:456-476; 1968, 74:120-145.
13,314. _____. Los tres planos de la creación artística de
Eduardo Barrios. Revista Iberoamericana, 1963, 29:55.
13,315. Veas Mercado, F. Monólogo interior en Macario de J.
Revulltas. Revista Canadiense de Estudios Hispánicos,
1977, 1, no. 3.
13,316. Veasey, R. [Libertinism in the 18th century French novel.] In Cruickshank, J. (ed), French Literature and
Its Background. The Eighteenth Century, Vol. 3.
London: Oxford Univ. Press, 1968, 148-162.
13,317. Vecchio, Frank. The Theme of Isolation in the Novels of
José Blancos Amor. DA, 1964, 24:4706.
13,318. Vega-Ritter, Max. Etude psychocritique de David Copperfield. In Amalric, J. -C. (ed), Studies in the Later
Dickens. Montpellier: Univ. Paul Valéry, 1974, 11-70.
13,319. Velikovsky, Immanuel. Tolstoy's Kreutzer Sonata and unconscious homosexuality. Psychoanal Rev, 1937, 24:18-
25; Imago, 1937, 23:363-370.
13,320. Vella, Michael. Djuna Barnes gains despite critics' pall.
Lost Generation J, 1976, 4(1):6-8.
13,321. Venit, James S. The Breakdown of Narrative Form and
Authority in Modern Fiction: A Study of Some Texts of
Conrad, Woolf, and Freud. DAI, 1976, 37:3655A.
13,322. Verberne, Tom. Borges, Luria and hypermnesia: a note.
Australian & New Zealand J Psychiat, 1976, 10:253-
255.
13,323. Verburg, T. Larry. Water imagery in James Dickey's
Deliverance. Notes on Contemporary Lit, 1974, 4(5):
11-13.
13,324. Verhoeff, Han. 'Adolphe' et Constant: Une étude psychocritique. Paris: Klincksieck, 1976; Review: Mary E.
Ragland, French Rev, 1976, 50:346-347.

13,325. Vernon, John E. The Garden and the Map: Schizophrenia
         in Twentieth Century Literature and Culture. Urbana:
         Univ. Illinois Press, 1973; DAI, 1970, 31:70-21, 910;
         Review: H. H. Watts. Modern Fiction Studies, 1973,
         19:664-667.
13,326. _____. Melville's 'The Bell-Tower. ' Studies in Short
         Fiction, 1970, 7:264-276.
13,327. _____. William S. Burroughs. Iowa Rev, 1972, 3:107-
         123.
13,328. Verrienti, G. Rilievi psicopatologici in tema di allucina-
         zione. Il fenomeno allucinazione analizzato da Dosto-
         jewski. I Fratelli Karamazzoff. Archivio di Psico-
         logia, Neurologia y Psichiatria, 1945, 6:226-236.
13,329. Vestdijk, S. De psychologie in de roman. De Gids, 1948,
         111(2):95-112.
13,330. Viallaneix, P. La Naissance littéraire d'Albert Camus.
         L'Information littéraire, 1971, 23:199-204.
13,331. Vialle, Louis. Sur l'esthétique du désespoir. JPNP,
         1949, 33:450-466.
13,332. Vianu, Tudor. Lirismul românesc si psihologia popoare-
         lor. Revista de Istorie si Teorie Literara, 1968, 57:
         507-509.
13,333. Vickery, John B. Finnegans Wake and sexual metamorpho-
         sis. Contemporary Lit, 1972, 13:213-242.
13,334. _____. The golden bough at Merrymount. Nineteenth
         Century Fiction, 1957, 12:203-214.
13,335. _____, & Vickery, Olga W. (eds). 'Light in August'
         and the Critical Spectrum. Belmont, Cal: Wadsworth,
         1971.
13,336. Viderman, Serge. La Plaie et le couteau: l'écriture am-
         biguë de Jean Genet. Rev Française de Psychanalyse,
         1974, 38:137-151.
13,337. Vier, Jacques. Les Maîtres du roman d'analyse psycho-
         logique avant Fromentin. In Pour l'étude du 'Dominque'
         de Fromentin. Paris: Lettres Modernes, 1958, 1-16.
13,338. Vigneron, R. Marcel Proust: creative agony. Chicago
         Rev, 1920, 12:33-51.
13,339. Villasenor Tejeda, José. La evolucion del adolescente en
         Joyce. Revista de la Facultad de Humanidades, 1959,
         1:55-59.
13,340. Villere, Maurice F. The Theme of Alienation in the Popu-
         lar Twentieth Century American Industrial and Organi-
         zational Novel. DAI, 1972, 32(10-B), 6096.
13,341. Vincenot, C. Le Reve dans Le Grand Meaulnes. Rev des
         Sciences Humaines, 1966, 122-123:265-296.
13,342. Vinchon, Jean. Un Psychiatre relit Zola. In Angell, N. ,
         et al. , Présence de Zola. Paris: Fasquelle, 1953,
         222-227.
13,343. Vineberg, Elsa. Journal d'un curé de compagne: a psy-
         choanalytic reading. MLN, 1977, 92:825-829.
13,344. _____. Marcel Proust, Nathalie Sarraute, and the psy-
         chological novel. MLN, 1975, 90:575-583.

13,345.   Vinson, Audrey L.   Miscegenation and its meaning in Go
          Down, Moses.   College Language Assn J, 1970, 14:
          143-155.

13,346.   Visser, N. W.   The novel and the concept of social net-
          work.   In Pope, R. D. (ed), The Analysis of Literary
          Texts.   Ypsilanti, Mich: Bilingual Press, 1980, 268-
          285.

13,347.   Viti, Robert Michael.   The Road to Self-Governance: A
          Study of the Themes and Imagery of Adolescence in
          Stendhal's Lucien Leuwen.   DAI, 1975, 36:3756A-57A.

13,348.   Vitoux, Pierre.   Aldous Huxley and D. H. Lawrence: an
          attempt at intellectual sympathy.   Modern Language
          Rev, 1974, 69:501-522.

13,349.   Vitti, Mario.   Family and alienation in contemporary
          Greek fiction.   In Keeley, E., & Bien, P. (eds), Mod-
          ern Greek Writers.   Princeton: Princeton Univ. Press,
          1972, 217-233.

13,350.   Vivarelli, M.   Margaret Mitchell e Via col Vento, il des-
          tino di una scrittice e di un libro.   Psiche-Roma, 1949,
          2:428-429.

13,351.   Vivas, Eliseo.   The two dimensions of reality in The
          Brothers Karamazov.   In Wellek, R. (ed), Dostoevsky:
          A Collection of Critical Essays.   Englewood Cliffs, NJ:
          Prentice-Hall, 1962, 71-89.

13,352.   Vlastos, Marion.   Doris Lessing and R. D. Laing: psycho-
          politics and prophecy.   PMLA, 1976, 91:245-258.

13,353.   Vodoz, Jules.   'La Fée aux Miettes.'   Essai sur le sub-
          conscient dans l'oeuvre de Charles Nodier.   Paris:
          Champion, 1925.

13,354.   Voelker, Joseph Craig.   James Joyce's 'Penelope':   A
          Study of the Influence of Scholastic Psychology and the
          Metaphysics of Giordano Bruno on the Character of
          Molly Bloom.   DAI, 1975, 36:3704A.

13,355.   _____.   The spirit of no-place: elements of the clas-
          sical ironic utopia in D. H. Lawrence's Lady Chatter-
          ley's Lover.   Modern Fiction Studies, 1979, 25:223-239.

13,356.   Vogel, Dan.   Cahan's Rise of David Levinsky: archetypes
          of American Jewish fiction.   Judaism, 1973, 22:278-
          287.

13,357.   Voigt, Milton.   Swift and psychoanalytic criticism.   West-
          ern Humanities Rev, 1962, 16:361-367; In Swift and the
          Twentieth Century.   Detroit: Wayne State Univ. Press,
          1969, 155-162.

13,358.   Voigtländer, Else.   Jacobsens Frau Föns.   Int Zeitschrift
          für Psychoanalyse, 1913, 3:361-362.

13,359.   Vollmershausen, Joseph.   Pavilion of Women.   A psycho-
          analytic interpretation.   Amer J Psychoanal, 1950, 10:
          53-60.

13,360.   Volpe, Edmond L.   The childhood of James' American in-
          nocents.   Modern Language Notes, 1956, 71:345-347.

13,361-   _____.   James's theory of sex in fiction.   Nineteenth
    2.   Century Fiction, 1958, 13:36-47.

13,363. Von Hänisch, I. [Depth psychological aspects of the Tarzan figure.] Analytische Psychologie, 1974, 5:122-
134.

13,364. Vondrásková, Helena. L'Image de la femme dans l'oeuvre
de Colette. In Acta Universitatis Carolinae Philologica
4 (1966). Romanistica Pragensia IV. Prague: Univ.
Karlova, 1966, 57-64.

13,365. Vooys, Signa de. The Psychological Element in the English Sociological Novel of the Nineteenth Century. Doctoral dissertation, Univ. Amsterdam, 1927.

13,366. Vopat, Carole Gottlieb. The end of The Sun Also Rises:
a new beginning. Fitzgerald-Hemingway Annual, 1972,
245-255.

13,367. Vredenburgh, Joseph. The character of the incest object:
a study of alternation between narcissism and object
choice. Amer Imago, 1957, 14:45-52.

13,368. _____. Further contributions to a study of the incest
object. Amer Imago, 1959, 16:263-268.

13,369. Vredeveld, H. Ludwig Tieck's 'Der Runenberg': an
archetypal interpretation. Germanic Rev, 1974, 49:200-
214.

13,370. Wachtler, Gundi. Der Archetypus der grossen Mutter in
Hermann Brochs Roman Der Versucher. In Durzak,
M. (ed), Hermann Broch: Perspektiven der Forschung.
Munich: Fink, 1972, 231-250.

13,371. Wadden, Anthony T. The Novel as Psychic Drama: Studies of Scott, Dickens, Eliot, and James. Doctoral dissertation, Univ. Iowa, 1970; DAI, 1971, 31:4737A.

13,372. Waddington, Miriam. Review: The Novel of the Future.
J Otto Rank Assn, 1969, 4(1):54-60.

13,373. Wade, Claire. The contributions of color and light to dif-
fering levels of reality in the novels of Joris-K. Huysmans. Symposium, 1974, 28:366-379.

13,374. Waelder, Robert. Historical fiction. JAPA, 1963, 11:
628-651.

13,375. _____. Why organic unity? College English, 1968, 30:
19-30.

13,376. Waelhens, Alphonse de. Der Roman des Existentialismus.
Universitas, 1948, 1:945-951.

13,377. Waelti-Walters, J.R. Narrative movement in J.M.G. Le
Clézio's 'Fever.' Studies in Short Fiction, 1977, 14:
247-254.

13,378. Wagatsuma, Hiroshi. Ishiwara Shintaro's early novels and
Japanese male psychology. JNMD, 1973, 157:358-369.

13,379. Wagenheim, Allan J. Square's progress: An American
Dream. Critique: Studies in Modern Fiction, 1968,
10(1):45-68.

13,380. Wagenknecht, Edward C. Eve and Henry James: Portraits
of Women and Girls in His Fiction. Norman: Univ.
Oklahoma Press, 1978.

13, 381. _____. Stream of consciousness. In Cavalcade of the English Novel. NY: Holt, 1943, 505-522.

13, 382. Wagner, C. Roland. Italo Svevo: the vocation of old age. Hartford Studies in Lit, 1970, 2:214-228.

13, 383. _____. The silence of The Stranger. Modern Fiction Studies, 1970, 16:27-40.

13, 384. Wagner, G. Five for Freedom: A Study of Feminism in Fiction. London: Allen & Unwin, 1972.

13, 385. Wagner, Geoffrey. Ford Madox Ford: the honest Edwardian. Essays in Criticism, 1967, 17:75-88.

13, 386. Wagner, Roland. The excremental and the spiritual in A Passage to India. Modern Language Q, 1970, 31:359-371.

13, 387. Waidon, H. M. The Starvation-Artist and the leopard. Germanic Rev, 1960, 35:262-269.

13, 388. Waidson, H. M. Death by water: or, the childhood of Wilhelm Meister. Modern Language Rev, 1961, 56:44-53.

13, 389. Wain, John. Poet and Doppelgänger. Listener, 1965, 73:627-629.

13, 390. Waisbren, B. A., & Walzl, F. L. Paresis and the priest. James Joyce's symbolic use of syphilis in 'The Sisters.' Annals Internal Medicine, 1974, 80:758-762.

13, 391. Wake, C. H. Flaubert's search for identity: some reflections on Un coeur simple. French Rev, 1971, 44(2):89-96.

13, 392. Walcott, William O. Notes by a Jungian analyst on the dreams in Ulysses. James Joyce Q, 1971, 9:37-48.

13, 393. _____. The paternity of James Joyce's Stephen Dedalus. J Analytic Psychol, 1965, 10:77-95.

13, 394. Walcutt, Charles Child. The fire symbolism in Moby Dick. Modern Language Notes, 1944, 59:304-310.

13, 395. _____. Man's Changing Mask: Modes and Methods of Characterization in Fiction. Minneapolis: Univ. Minnesota Press, 1966.

13, 396. Wälder, Robert. Zeno Cosini von Italo Svevo. Psychoanalytische Bewegung, 1921, 1:170-173.

13, 397. Waldhorn, Hilda K. Two Adolescents. Lit & Psychol, 1962, 12:43-51.

13, 398. Waldman, R. D. Convergence of concepts of Adler and Ortega y Gasset. J Individual Psychol, 1971, 27, 135-138.

13, 399. Waldoff, Leon. Perceiving and creating in interpretation. Hartford Studies in Lit, 1975, 7:154-169.

13, 400. Waldron, Edward E. The search for identity in Jean Toomer's Esther. College Language Assn J, 1971, 14:277-280.

13, 401. Walker, Carolyn. Transformation of self: an interview with Joyce Carol Oates. Ohio Rev, 1973, 15(1):51-61.

13, 402. Walker, Herbert. Observations on ... Dostoevsky's Notes from Underground. Amer Imago, 1962, 19:195-210.

13, 403. Walker, I. M. The legitimate sources of terror in The Fall of the House of Usher. Modern Language Rev, 1966, 61:585-592.

13, 404.   Walker, John L.   Timelessness through memory in the novels of Agustin Yáñez.   Hispania, 1974, 57:445-451.

13, 405.   Walker, Nancy.   Stages of Womanhood in Katherine Mansfield's Prelude.   DAI, 1976, 37:2206A-07A.

13, 406.   Walker, Philip.   The mirror, the window, and the eye in Zola's fiction.   Yale French Studies, 1969, 42:52-67.

13, 407.   _____.   Prophetic myths in Zola.   PMLA, 1959, 74: 444-445.

13, 408.   _____.   Zola's art of characterization in Germinal.   L'Esprit créateur, 1964, 4(2).

13, 409.   Wall, Carey.   The Sound and the Fury: the emotional center.   Midwest Q, 1970, 11:371-387.

13, 410.   Wallace, A. H.   Guy de Maupassant.   NY: Twayne, 1974.

13, 411.   Wallace, Harry Joseph.   'Lifelessness Is the Only Abnormality':   A Study of Love, Sex, Marriage, and Family in the Novels of Carson McCullers.   DAI, 1976, 37: 3630A-31A.

13, 412.   Wallace, Irving.   Self-control techniques of famous novelists.   J Applied Behavior Analysis, 1977, 10:515-525.

13, 413.   Wallach, Judith Dana L.   The Quest for Selfhood in Saul Bellow's Novels: A Jungian Interpretation.   DAI, 1975, 36:2829A.

13, 414.   Waller, G. F.   Dreaming America: Obsession and Transcendence in the Fiction of Joyce Carol Oates.   Baton Rouge: Louisiana State Univ. Press, 1979.

13, 415.   _____.   Joyce Carol Oates' Wonderland: an introduction.   Dalhousie Rev, 1974, 54:480-490.

13, 416.   Wallerstein, A.   A literary case history.   Family, 1930, 11:26-28.

13, 417.   Walsh, Thomas.   Deep similarities in 'Noon Wine.'   Mosaic, 1975, 9(1):83-92.

13, 418.   Walsh, Thomas F.   The other William Wilson.   Amer Transcendental Q, 1971, 10:17-26.

13, 419.   Walshe, M. O'C.   The Graal castle and the cave of lovers.   In Scholler, H. (ed), The Epic in Medieval Society.   Aesthetic and Moral Values.   Tübingen: Niemeyer, 1977, 257-270.

13, 420.   Walter, Donna Joanne.   Twentieth-Century Woman in the Early Novels of Doris Lessing.   DAI, 1978, 39:3608A.

13, 421.   Walter, James F.   A psychronology of lust in the Menippean tradition: Giles Goat-Boy.   Twentieth-Century Lit, 1975, 21:394-410.

13, 422.   Walton, James.   Conrad and naturalism: The Secret Agent.   Texas Studies in Lit & Language, 1967, 9:289-301.

13, 423.   Walton, L. B.   La psicología anormal en la obra de Galdos.   Boletin del Instituto Español, 1948, 4:10-13.

13, 424.   Waples, Dorothy.   Suggestions for interpreting The Marble Faun.   Amer Lit, 1941.

13, 425.   Ward, Dorothy Cox.   The Two Marys: A Study of the Women in Hermann Hesse's Fiction.   DAI, 1977, 37: 4386A.

13, 426.   Ward, J. A.   The double structure of Watch and Ward.   Texas Studies in Lit & Language, 1963, 4:613-624.

13,427. Warme, Lars G. Reflection and revelation in Michel Butor's La Modification. Int Fiction Rev, 1974, 1:88-95.

13,428. Warren, James E. Fiction is full of case histories. Clearing House, 1948, 22:259-262.

13,429. Warrick, E. Kathleen. Lotte's sexuality and her responsibility for Werther's death. Essays in Lit, 1978, 5:129-135.

13,430. Washington, Mary H. The black woman's search for identity: Zora Neale Hurston's work. Black World, 1972, 21(10):68-75.

13,431. Washington, L. M., & Washington, L. H. Several aspects of fire in Achim von Arnim's Der tolle Invalide. German Q, 1964, 37:498-505.

13,432. Wasiolek, Edward. Dostoevsky: The Major Fiction. Cambridge: Harvard Univ. Press, 1964.

13,433. _____. Dostoevsky: The Notebooks of the Possessed. Chicago: Univ. Chicago Press, 1968.

13,434. _____. Dostoevsky's notebooks for Crime and Punishment. Psychoanal Rev, 1968, 55:349-359.

13,435. _____. Raskolnikov's motives: love and murder. Amer Imago, 1974, 31:252-269.

13,436. Wasserman, Earl R. The Natural: Malamud's world Ceres. Centennial Rev, 1965, 9:438-460.

13,437. Wasserstrom, William. Heiress of All the Ages: Sex and Sentiment in the Genteel Tradition. Minneapolis: Univ. Minnesota Press, 1959.

13,438. _____. In Gertrude's closet: incest patterns in recent literature. Yale Rev, 1958, 48:245-265; In Manheim, L., & Manheim, E. (eds), Hidden Patterns. NY: Macmillan, 1966, 275-299.

13,439. _____. The origins of culture: Cooper and Freud. Amer Imago, 1960, 17:423-437; In Malin, I. (ed), Psychoanalysis and American Fiction. NY: Dutton, 1965, 47-60; In Walker, W. S. (ed), Leatherstocking and the Critics. Chicago: Scott, Foresman, 1965, 104-113.

13,440. _____. Reason and reverence in art and science. Lit & Psychol, 1962, 12:2-5.

13,441. _____. The spirit of Myrrha. Amer Imago, 1956, 13: 455-472.

13,442. Wasson, Richard. Comedy and history in The Rainbow. Modern Fiction Studies, 1967, 13:465-477.

13,443. _____. Stephen Dedalus and the imagery of sight: a psychological approach. Lit & Psychol, 1965, 15:195-209.

13,444. Waterman, Arthur. The evolution of consciousness: Conrad Aiken's novels and Ushant. Critique: Studies in Modern Fiction, 1973, 15(2):67-81.

13,445. _____. The short stories of Conrad Aiken. Studies in Short Fiction, 1979, 16:19-31.

13,446. Waters, Maureen Anne. The Role of Women in Faulkner's Yoknapatawpha. DAI, 1975, 36:332A-33A.

13,447. Waterston, George C., Jr. A Suggested Reading of a Puzzle Novel: Oedipal Themes in J. M. G. Le Clézio's First

Work, Le Procès-verbal (1963). DAI, 1978, 39:3623A-
24A.
13, 448. Watkins, Alma Taylor. Eroticism in the Novels of Filipe
(sic) Trigo. NY: Bookman, 1954.
13, 449. Watkins, Floyd C. The Confessions of Nat Turner: history and imagination. In Time and Place: Some Origins of American Fiction. Athens: Univ. Georgia
Press, 1977, 51-70.
13, 450. Watson, Charles N., Jr. Melville's Jackson: Redburn's
heroic 'double.' Emerson Society Q, 1971, 62:8-10.
13, 451. _____. Sexual conflict in The Sea Wolf: further notes
on London's reading of Kipling and Norris. Western
Amer Lit, 1976, 11:239-248.
13, 452. Watson, Fred. Allegories in 'Ragtime': balance, growth,
disintegration. Under the Sign of Pisces, 1976, 7(2):1-
5.
13, 453. Watson, G. The theme of water in Gide's early work.
Australian J French Studies, 1972, 9(2):167-179.
13, 454. Watson, Ian. Elias Canetti: the one and the many. Chicago Rev, 1969, 21:184-200.
13, 455. Watson, Jerry J. A Study of Adults' Reactions to Contemporary Junior Novels Reflecting Adolescents' Interest in
Reading about Aspects of Peer and Non-Peer Relationships. DAI, 1974, 35:3785B.
13, 456. Watson, Tommy G. Defoe's attitude toward marriage and
the position of women as revealed in Moll Flanders.
Southern Q, 1964, 3:1-8.
13, 457. Watt, Donald. The criminal-victim pattern in Huxley's
Point Counter Point. Studies in the Novel, 1970, 2:42-
51.
13, 458. _____. Hemingway's how to be. Rev Existential Psychol & Psychiat, 1977, 15:210-226.
13, 459. Watt, Ian. Conrad in the Nineteenth Century. Berkeley:
Univ. California Press, 1980.
13, 460. _____. The Rise of the Novel. Berkeley: Univ. California Press, 1956, 1962.
13, 461. Watts, C. T. Nordau and Kurtz: a footnote to the Heart
of Darkness. Notes & Queries, 1974, 21:226-227.
13, 462. Webb, Donald P. Wolmar's méthode and the function of
identity in La Nouvelle Héloïse. Romanic Rev, 1979,
70:113-118.
13, 463. Webb, Eugene. Hermine and the problem of Harry's failure in Hesse's Steppenwolf. Modern Fiction Studies,
1971, 17:115-124.
13, 464. Webb, H. W., Jr. The meaning of Ring Lardner's fiction:
a reevaluation. Amer Lit, 1960, 31:434-445.
13, 465. Webb, Igor. Marriage and sex in the novels of Ford
Madox Ford. Modern Fiction Studies, 1977-78, 23:586-
592.
13, 466. Webb, Jane Carter. The implications of control for the
human personality: Hawthorne's point of view. Tulane
Studies in English, 1974, 21:57-66.

13, 467.   Webb, Max A.   The missing father and the theme of alien-
           ation in H. G. Wells's Tono-Bungay.   English Lit in
           Transition (1880-1920),   1975, 18: 243-247.
13, 468.   Weber, Robert Wilhelm.   Die Aussage der Form.   Bei-
           hefte zum Jahrbuch für Amerikastudien, 1969, 27:1-
           104.
13, 469.   Webster, Harvey Curtis.   Ernest Hemingway: the pursuit
           of death.   Texas Q, 1964, 7:149-159.
13, 470.   Webster, Peter D.   Arrested individuation or the problem
           of Joseph K. and Hamlet.   Amer Imago, 1948, 5:225-
           245.
13, 471.   _____.   A critical examination of Franz Kafka's The
           Castle.   Amer Imago, 1951, 8:35-60.
13, 472.   _____.   'Dies Irae' in the unconscious, or the signifi-
           cance of Franz Kafka.   College English, 1950, 12:9-15;
           In Hamalian, L. (ed), Franz Kafka: A Collection of
           Criticism.   NY: McGraw-Hill, 1974, 118-125.
13, 473.   _____.   Franz Kafka's In the Penal Colony: a psycho-
           analytic interpretation.   Amer Imago, 1956, 13:399-407.
13, 474.   _____.   Franz Kafka's Metamorphosis as death and
           resurrection fantasy.   Amer Imago, 1959, 16:349-365.
13, 475.   Weeks, Lewis E., Jr.   Two types of tension: art vs.
           campcraft in Hemingway's 'Big Two-Hearted River.'
           Studies in Short Fiction, 1974, 11:433-434.
13, 476.   Wegelin, Christof.   Henry James and the treasure of con-
           sciousness.   Die neueren Sprachen, 1973, 9:484-491.
13, 477.   Wegrocki, Henry G.   Masochistic motives in the literary
           and graphic art of Bruno Schultz.   Psychoanal Rev,
           1936, 23:154-164.
13, 478.   Weinberg, Albert K.   The dream in Jean Christophe.   J
           Abnormal Psychol, 1918, 13:12-16.
13, 479.   Weinbrot, H. D.   Chastity and interpolation: two aspects
           of Joseph Andrews.   J English Germanic Philology,
           1970, 69:14-31.
13, 480.   Weiner, Seymour S.   Sincerity and variants: Paul Léau-
           taud's Petit Ami.   Symposium, 1960, 14:165-187.
13, 481.   Weinman, Heinz.   Gide ou Le paradis perdu: Essai psy-
           chanalytique sur l'imagination gidienne.   Rev des Let-
           tres Modernes, 1973, 374-79:71-84.
13, 482.   Weinreich, H.   Das Ingenium Don Quijotes.   Ein Beitrag
           zur literarischen Charakterkunde.   Münster: 1956.
13, 483.   Weir, Sybil B.   The image of women in Dreiser's fiction.
           Pacific Coast Philology, 1972, 7:65-71.
13, 484.   Weisberger, Jean.   Faulkner's monomaniacs: their in-
           debtedness to Raskolnikov.   Comparative Lit Studies,
           1968, 5:181-193.
13, 485.   Weiser, Irwin Howard.   Alternatives to the Myth of the
           Family: A Study of Parent Child Relationships in Se-
           lected Nineteenth-Century English Novels.   DAI, 1977,
           37:7147A-48A.
13, 486.   Weiss, Daniel A.   'The Blue Hotel': a psychoanalytic
           study.   In Bassan, M. (ed), Stephen Crane; A Collec-
           tion of Critical Essays.   Englewood Cliffs, NJ: Pren-
           tice-Hall, 1967, 154-164.

13,487. _____. Caliban on Prospero. A psychoanalytic study
on the novel, Seize the Day, by Saul Bellow. Amer
Imago, 1962, 19:277-306; In Malin, I. (ed), Psychoanalysis and American Fiction. NY: Dutton, 1966,
279-307; In Malin, I. (ed), Saul Bellow and His Critics.
NY: New York Univ. Press, 1967, 114-139.

13,488. _____. D. H. Lawrence's great circle: from Sons and
Lovers to Lady Chatterley. Psychoanal Rev, 1963, 50:
112-138.

13,489. _____. Oedipus in Nottingham: D. H. Lawrence. Seattle: Univ. Washington Press, 1962; Reviews: Fritz
Schmidl, Psychoanal Q, 1964, 33:286-288; Louis B.
Fraiberg, English Lit in Transition (1880-1920), 1963,
6:174-175; Eugene Goodheart, Chicago Rev, 1963, 16,
127-138; Harry T. Moore, Kenyon Rev, 1963, 25:555-
558.

13,490. _____. Oedipus in Nottinghamshire. Lit & Psychol,
1957, 7(3):33-42.

13,491. _____. The Red Badge of Courage. Psychoanal Rev,
1965, 51:597-611; 52:460-484.

13,492. Weiss, F. Of Human Bondage. Amer J Psychoanal, 1973,
33:68-76.

13,493. Weiss, Hermann F. Precarious idylls: the relationship
between father and daughter in Heinrich von Kleist's
Die Marquise von O.... MLN, 1976, 91:538-542.

13,494. Weiss, Robert O. A Study of the psychiatric elements in
Schnitzler's Flucht in die Finsternis. Germanic Rev,
1958, 33:251-275.

13,495. Weiss, Walter. Zu Adalbert Stifters Doppelbegabung. In
Rasch, W. (ed), Bildende Kunst und Literatur. Frankfurt: Klostermann, 1970, 103-120.

13,496. Weissman, Frida Shulamith. Le Monologue intérieur: A
la première, à la seconde ou à la troisième personne.
Travaux de Linguistique et de Littérature Publiés,
1976, 14(2):291-300.

13,497. _____. Le Monologue intérieur, possibilités et limites
d'un procédé littéraire. Hebrew Univ. Studies Lit,
1975, 3:196-220.

13,498. Welch, Dennis M. Image making: politics and character
development in All the King's Men. Hartford Studies
in Lit, 1976, 8:155-177.

13,499. Welch, Jack. Maidens, mothers, and grannies: Appalachian women in literature. Appalachian J, 1976, 4:
43-44.

13,500. Weldon, Roberta F. Wakefield's second journey. Studies
in Short Fiction, 1977, 14:69-74.

13,501. Welker, Robert H. Advocate for Eros: notes on D. H.
Lawrence. Amer Scholar, 1961, 30:191-202.

13,502. Wellek, René (ed). Dostoevsky: A Collection of Critical
Essays. Englewood Cliffs, NJ: Prentice-Hall, 1962.

13,503. Wellner, Klaus. Leiden an der Familie. Zur sozialpath-
ologischen Rollenanalyse im Werk Gabriele Wohmann.
Stuttgart: Klett, 1976.

13, 504.　Wells, Charles E.　The hysterical personality and the feminine character: a study of Scarlett O'Hara.　Comprehensive Psychiat, 1976, 17:353-359.

13, 505.　Wells, Glenn Lawrence, Jr.　The Role of the Female in Relation to the Artist in the Works of Joyce Cary.　DAI, 1976, 36:4521A.

13, 506.　Wells, Judith Lee.　Madness and Women: A Study of the Themes of Insanity and Anger in Modern Literature by Women.　DAI, 1977, 37:5820A.

13, 507.　Wells, Nancy.　Women in American literature.　English J, 1973, 62:1159-1161.

13, 508.　Welsh, Alexander.　A Freudian slip in The Bride of Lammermoor.　Etudes Anglaises, 1965, 18:134-136.

13, 509.　Welsh, David.　Two contemporary novels of Henryk Sienkiewicz: a reappraisal.　Slavic & East European J, 1972, 16:307-312.

13, 510.　Welz, Dieter.　Episoden der Entfremdung in Wolframs Parzival: Herzeloydentragödie und Bluttropfenszene im Verständigungsrahmen einer psychoanalytischen Sozialisationstheorie.　Acta Germanica, 1976, 9:47-110.

13, 511.　Wenger, Jared.　Character types of Scott, Balzac, Dickens, and Zola.　PMLA, 1947, 62:213-232.

13, 512.　Wenh-In Ng, Greer A.　The Figures of the Child in Victorian Novels of Protest.　DAI, 1970, 30:4419A.

13, 513.　Wentersdorf, Karl P.　Mirror-images in Great Expectations.　Nineteenth Century Fiction, 1966, 21:203-224.

13, 514.　_____.　The underground workshop of Oliver Wendell Holmes.　Amer Lit, 1963, 35:1-12.

13, 515.　Werner, W. L.　The psychology of Marcel Proust.　Sewanee Rev, 1931, 39:276-281.

13, 516.　Wertham, Fredric.　An unconscious determinant in Native Son.　J Clinical Pathology, 1944-45, 6:111-115; In Ruitenbeek, H. M. (ed), Psychoanalysis and Literature.　NY: Dutton, 1964, 321-325.

13, 517.　Wertheim, Stanley.　The conclusion of Hemingway's The Sun Also Rises.　Lit & Psychol, 1967, 17:55-56.

13, 518.　Wertime, Richard A.　Psychic vengeance in Last Exit to Brooklyn.　Lit & Psychol, 1974, 24:153-166.

13, 519.　Wesly, Margot.　Das junge Mädchen im deutschen Roman des 18. Jahrhunderts bis zum Beginn des Sturm und Drangs: Unter besonderer Berücksichtigung des gleichzeitigen französischen und englischen Romans.　Doctoral dissertation, Leipzig, 1933.

13, 520.　West, Michael.　Old cotter and the enigma of Joyce's 'The Sisters.'　Modern Philology, 1970, 67:370-372.

13, 521.　_____.　Sherwood Anderson's triumph: 'The Egg.'　Amer Q, 1968, 20:675-693.

13, 522.　West, Muriel.　Death of Miles in 'The Turn of the Screw.'　PMLA, 1964, 79:283-288.

13, 523.　_____.　Poe's 'Ligeia.'　Explicator, 1963, 22, 2, No. 15.

13, 524.　_____.　Poe's 'Ligeia' and Isaac D'Israeli.　Comparative Lit, 1964, 16:19-28.

13, 525.   West, Nathanael.   Some notes on Miss Lonelyhearts.   Con-
           tempo, 1933.
13, 526.   West, Ray B. , Jr.   Thomas Mann: moral precept as
           psychological truth.   Sewanee Rev, 1952, 60:310-317.
13, 527.   West, Rebecca.   An exponent of the new psychology.   Lit-
           erary Digest, 1922, 73:33.
13, 528.   _____.   Notes on novels.   New Statesman, 1922, 18:
           564-566.
13, 529.   West, William A.   Matt Bramble's journey to health.
           Texas Studies in Lit & Language, 1969, 11:1197-1208.
13, 530.   Westbrook, Max.   Conservative, liberal, and Western:
           three modes of American realism.   South Dakota Rev,
           1966, 4:3-19.
13, 531.   Westburg, Barry.   The Confessional Fictions of Charles
           Dickens.   DeKalb: Northern Illinois Univ. Press, 1977.
13, 532.   Westling, Louise.   Flannery O'Connor and Carson McCul-
           lers.   Flannery O'Connor Bulletin, 1979, 8:88-98.
13, 533.   _____.   Flannery O'Connor's mothers and daughters.
           Twentieth Century Lit, 1978, 24:510-527.
13, 534.   Weston, John C. , Jr.   From romance to ritual.   Fitz-
           gerald News Letter, 1959, 4:2.
13, 535.   Weston, Louise C. , & Ruggiero, Josephine A.   Male-
           female relationships in best-selling 'modern Gothic'
           novels.   Sex Roles, 1978, 4:647-655.
13, 536.   Wetzel, Frank J.   Psychology and the Utopian Individual
           in Three Novellas by Robert Musil: Die Vollendung
           einer Leibe, Tonka, und Die Amsel.   DAI, 1973,
           34(3-A), 1300.
13, 537.   Weygandt, W.   Don Quijote des Cervantes im Lichte der
           Psychopathologie.   Zeitschrift für die gesamte Neuro-
           logie und Psychiatrie, 1936, 154:159-185.
13, 538.   Wheeler, Otis B.   The five awakenings of Edna Pontellier.
           Southern Rev, 1975, 11:118-128.
13, 539.   _____.   Love among the ruins: Hawthorne's surrogate
           religion.   Southern Rev, 1974, 103:535-565.
13, 540.   Wheelock, Carter.   The Mythmaker: A Study of Motif and
           Symbol in the Short Stories of Jorge Luis Borges.
           Austin: Univ. Texas Press, 1969.
13, 541.   Whitaker, Charles Francis.   Psychological Approaches to
           the Narrative Personality in the Novels of William
           Faulkner.   DAI, 1975, 35:7276A-77A.
13, 542.   Whitcomb, Richard O.   Heinrich Böll and the mirror-
           image technique.   Univ. Dayton Rev, 1973, 10(2):41-
           46; In Proceedings: Pacific Northwest Conference on
           Foreign Languages.   Corvallis: Oregon State Univ.
           Press, 1973, 276-279.
13, 543.   White, Andrew.   Labyrinths of modern fiction.   Arcadia,
           1967, 2:288-304.
13, 544.   White, Barbara Anne.   Growing Up Female: Adolescent
           Girlhood in American Literature.   DAI, 1975, 35:
           6167A.
13, 545.   White, Gertrude M.   A Passage to India: an analysis and
           revaluation.   PMLA, 1953, 48:641-657.

13, 546. White, John O.   The Existential Absurd in Faulkner's
          Snopes Trilogy. DAI, 1971, 32:3336A.
13, 547. White, Ray Lewis.   The warmth of desire: sex in Ander-
          son's novels.   In Anderson, D. D. (ed), Sherwood And-
          erson: Dimensions of His Literary Art.   East Lansing:
          Michigan State Univ. Press, 1976, 24-40.
13, 548. Whitehead, Lee M.   Tender Is the Night and George Her-
          bert Mead: an 'actor's tragedy.' Lit & Psychol, 1965,
          15:180-191.
13, 549. Whitlock, Roger.   The psychology of consciousness in
          Daniel Deronda. Victorians Institute J, 1975, 4:17-24.
13, 550. Whitlow, Roger.   Animal and human personalities in Dick-
          ens' novels.   College Language Assn J, 1975, 19:65-74.
13, 551. _____.   Baldwin's Going to Meet the Man: racial bru-
          tality and sexual gratification.   Amer Imago, 1977, 34:
          351-356.
13, 552. _____.   The destruction/prevention of the family rela-
          tionship in Hemingway's fiction.   Lit Rev, 1976, 20:5-
          16.
13, 553. Whitt, Joseph.   The Psychological Criticism of Dostoevsky:
          1875-1951.   A Study of British American and Chief Eu-
          ropean Critics.   Doctoral Dissertation, Temple Univ.,
          1953.
13, 554. Wichmann, Brigitte.   From Sex-Role Identification Toward
          Androgyny: A Study of Major Works of Simone de
          Beauvoir, Doris Lessing and Christa Wolf.   DAI, 1978,
          39:2934A-35A.
13, 555. Wickham, Anna.   The spirit of the Lawrence women.
          Texas Q, 1966, 9:31-50.
13, 556. Widmer, Kingsley.   Lawrence as abnormal novelist.   D. H.
          Lawrence Rev, 1975, 8:220-232.
13, 557. _____.   The prophecies of passion.   Centennial Rev,
          1967, 11:82-101.
13, 558. _____.   Psychiatry and piety in Lawrence.   Studies in
          the Novel, 1977, 9:195-200.
13, 559. Wiebler, James Raymond.   The American Adolescent in
          Novels and in Social Science, 1950-1972: A Comparison
          and an Analysis.   DAI, 1973, 34:2664A-5A.
13, 560. Wiemann, Renate.   William Styron: Lie Down in Darkness.
          Zum Problem der verlorenen und wiedergewonnenen
          Unschuld im amerikanischen Roman.   Neueren Sprachen,
          1970, 19:321-332.
13, 561. Wiggins, Robert A.   Ambrose Bierce: a romantic in an
          age of realism.   Amer Lit Realism, 1971, 4(1):1-10.
13, 562. Wijsenbeek, C.   Marcel Proust.   Amer Imago, 1941, 2:
          323-346.
13, 563. Wild, Fredric M.   'A Plank in Reason':   Time, Space,
          and the Perception of the Self in the Modern Novel.
          DAI, 1973, 34:2665A.
13, 564. Wilden, Anthony G.   Death, desire and repetition in Svevo's
          Zeno.   Modern Language Notes, 1969, 84(1):98-119.
13, 565. Wilder, Amos Niven.   Mortality and contemporary litera-
          ture.   Harvard Theological Rev, 1965, 58:1-20.

13, 566. Wiley, Paul L. D. H. Lawrence. [Review article.] Con-
          temporary Lit, 1972, 13:249-254.
13, 567. Willbern, David P. Malice in paradise: isolation and
          projection in 'The Man Who Loved Islands.' D. H. Law-
          rence Rev, 1977, 10:223-241.
13, 568. Willeke, Audrone B. Socialist realism and the psychologi-
          cal novels of Alfonsas Bielauskas. J Baltic Studies,
          1977, 8:296-300.
13, 569. Willen, Gerald (ed). A Casebook on Henry James's The
          Turn of the Screw. NY: Crowell, 1960.
13, 570. Williams, David Anthony. Psychological Determinism in
          'Madame Bovary.' Hull: Hull Univ. Press, 1973.
13, 571. _____. Water imagery in Madame Bovary. Forum for
          Modern Languages, 1977, 13:70-82.
13, 572. Williams, David L. Faulkner's Women: The Myth and the
          Muse. Montreal: McGill-Queen's Univ. Press, 1977;
          DAI, 1974, 34:6610A.
13, 573. Williams, Gladys Margaret. Blind and seeing eyes in the
          novel. Obsidian, 1975, 1(2):18-26.
13, 574. Williams, Gordon. The problem of the passion in Wuther-
          ing Heights. Trivium, 1972, 7:41-53.
13, 575. Williams, Murial Brittain. Henry Fielding's Attitudes
          Toward Marriage. DA, 1964, 24:4204.
13, 576. Williams, Raymond. Modern Tragedy. Palo Alto: Stan-
          ford Univ. Press, 1966.
13, 577. Williams, Werner T. Elements in the Works of Franz
          Kafka as Analogue of His Inner Life. DAI, 1972, 32:
          5248A-49A.
13, 578. Williamson, Alan. The divided image: the quest for iden-
          tity in the works of Djuna Barnes. Critique: Studies
          in Modern Fiction, 1964, 7:58-74.
13, 579. _____. Identity and the wider Eros: a reading of Peter
          Taylor's stories. Shenandoah, 1978, 30:71-84.
13, 580. Williamson, Jack. H. G. Wells--critic of progress. The
          limits of progress--cosmic. Riverside Q, 1967, 3:96-
          116.
13, 581. _____. H. G. Wells, critic of progress. Chapter 3,
          the limits of progress: human. Riverside Q, 1968, 3:
          187-207.
13, 582. Williamson, Joan B. Suicide and adultery in the Chevalier
          de la Charette. In Mélanges de littérature: Du moyen
          âge au XXe siècle. Paris: Ecole Normale Supérieure
          de Jeune Filles, 1978, 571-587.
13, 583. Williamson, Robert Michael. Creative Fantasies, Dreams,
          Memories, and Reveries: Mark Twain's Psychological
          Tools. DAI, 1975, 36:3721A.
13, 584. Willie, K. Die Signatur der Melancholie im Werk Clemens
          Brentanos. Bern: Lang, 1970.
13, 585. Willis, Lesley H. Eyes and the imagery of sight in Pride
          and Prejudice. English Studies in Canada, 1976, 2:156-
          162.
13, 586. _____. Réalisme psychologique dans Cinq filles com-
          pliquées. J Canadian Fiction, 1975, 4:132-135.

Norman Kiell 654

13,587. Wills, Anthony A. Waverley: a psychological study. Rendezvous, 1975, 10(1):33-38.

13,588. Wills, Arthur. The doctor and the flounder: psychoanalysis and One Flew Over the Cuckoo's Nest. Studies in the Humanities, 1976, 5:19-25.

13,589. Wilmer, Harry A. Murder, you know. Psychiat Q, 1969, 43:414-447.

13,590. Wilson, C. Integrity born of hope: notes on Christopher Isherwood. Twentieth Century Lit, 1976, 22:312-331.

13,591. Wilson, Colin. Existential criticism and the work of Aldous Huxley. London Magazine, 1958, 5:46-59.

13,592. Wilson, Edmund. The ambiguity of Henry James. Hound & Horn, 1934, 7:385-406; In The Triple Thinkers. NY: Scribner, 1938, 122-164; 1948, 88-132; In Willen, G. (ed), A Casebook on Henry James's 'The Turn of the Screw.' NY: Crowell, 1960, 115-153; In Malin, I. (ed), Psychoanalysis and American Fiction. NY: Dutton, 1965, 143-186. In Schorer, M. (ed), The Story: A Critical Anthology. NY: Prentice-Hall, 1950.

13,593. _____. A Literary Chronicle: 1920-1950. Garden City, NY: Doubleday Anchor, 1956.

13,594. _____. Two neglected American novelists: I--Henry B. Fuller: the art of making it flat. New Yorker, 1970, 46:112-116, 120-122, 125-127, 131-132, 134, 137-139.

13,595. _____. Two neglected American novelists: II--Harold Frederic, the expanding upstater. New Yorker, 1970, 46:112-114, 117-119, 123-126, 129-134.

13,596. _____. Why do people read detective stories? In Classics and Commercials. NY: Farrar, Straus, 1950.

13,597. Wilson, F.A.C. Swinburne's dearest cousin: the character of Mary Gordon. Lit & Psychol, 1969, 19:89-99.

13,598. _____. Swinburne's prose heroines and Mary's femmes fatales. Victorian Poetry, 1971, 9:249-256.

13,599. Wilson, Jack H. Howells' use of George Eliot's Romola in April Hopes. PMLA, 1969, 84:1620-1627.

13,600. Wilson, James D. Incest and American romantic fiction. Studies in Lit Imagination, 1974, 7:31-50.

13,601. Wilson, Janice L. A Study of the Communication of American Human Sexuality: An Historical Grounding with an Analysis of the Literature from 1970 to 1975. DAI, 1977, 37:4708-09.

13,602. Wilson, Jean. Life and claustrophobia. Canadian Lit, 1977, 75:88-90.

13,603. Wilson, Raymond J. III. Raskolnikov's dream in Crime and Punishment. Lit & Psychol, 1976, 26:159-166.

13,604. _____. Transactional Analysis and Literature. DAI, 1974, 34:7793A.

13,605. Wilson, Robert Neal. The Writer As Social Seer. Chapel Hill: Univ. North Carolina Press, 1979.

13,606. Wilson, Robert R. The pattern of thought in Light in August. Bulletin Rocky Mountain Modern Language Assn, 1970, 24:155-161.

13,607.   Wilson, S.   Proust's A la Recherche du temps perdu as a
          document of social history.   J European Studies, 1971,
          1:213-243.
13,608.   Wilson, Stuart.   Richardson's Pamela: an interpretation.
          PMLA, 1973, 88:79-91.
13,609.   Wilt, Judith.   He could go no farther: a modest proposal
          about Lovelace and Clarissa.   PMLA, 1977, 92:19-32.
13,610.   Wiltrout, Ann E.   Women in the works of Antonio de Gue-
          vara.   Neophilologus, 1976, 60:525-533.
13,611.   Winandy, André.   Rabelais' barrel.   Yale French Studies,
          1974, 50:8-25.
13,612.   Winecoff, Janet.   Existentialism in the novels of Elena
          Soriano.   Hispania, 1964, 47:309-315.
13,613.   Wing, G.   Edwin Drood and desperate remedies: proto-
          types of detective fiction in 1870.   Studies in English
          Lit, 1973, 13:677-687.
13,614.   Winslow, J. D.   Language and destruction in Faulkner's
          'Dry September.'   College Language Assn J, 1977, 20:
          380-386.
13,615.   Winters, Warrington.   The death hug in Charles Dickens.
          Lit & Psychol, 1966, 16:109-114.
13,616.   _____.   DeQuincey and the archetypal death wish.   Lit
          & Psychol, 1964, 14:61-65.
13,617.   _____.   Dickens and the psychology of dreams.   PMLA,
          1948, 63:984-1006.
13,618.   Winterstein, Alfred R. F.   Der Sammler.   Imago, 1921,
          7, 180.
13,619.   Wisse, Ruth R.   The Schlemiel as Modern Hero.   Chicago:
          Univ. Chicago Press, 1971; DAI, 1970, 30:2983A.
13,620.   Winthrop, Henry.   Sexuality in literature.   Colorado Q,
          1973, 21:337-358.
13,621.   Witham, W. Tasker.   The Adolescent in the American
          Novel, 1920-1960.   NY: Ungar, 1964.
13,622.   Wohlfarth, P.   Der Selbstmord als psychologischer Tat-
          bestand bei Dostojewski.   Monatsschrift für Kriminal-
          psychologie und Strafrechtsreform, 1934, 25:244-255.
13,623.   _____.   [The criminal personality in the novels of Dos-
          toevsky and Conrad.]   Monatsschrift für Kriminalpsy-
          chologie, 1935, 26:346-357.
13,624.   _____.   [The psychological development of the young
          man in Dostoevsky.]   Int Zeitschrift für Individual-psy-
          chologie, 1935, 13:104-115.
13,625.   _____.   [The psychology of murder prompted by jealousy
          in Dostoevsky's The Husband.]   Archivio Generale di
          Neurologia, 1938, 19:276-287.
13,626.   Wohlgelernter, Maurice.   Mama and papa and all the com-
          plaints.   Tradition, 1969, 10:70-87.
13,627.   Wolf, Ernest S.   The disconnected self.   In Roland, A.
          (ed), Psychoanalysis, Creativity, and Literature.   NY:
          Columbia Univ. Press, 1978, 103-115.
13,628.   Wolf, Howard R.   British fathers and sons, 1773-1913:
          from filial submissiveness to creativity.   Psychoanal
          Rev, 1965, 52:53-70.

13, 629.   _____. Forms of Abandonment in Henry James. DA, 1968, 28:68-7759.

13, 630.   _____. The psychology and aesthetics of abandonment in The Ambassadors. Lit & Psychol, 1971, 21:133-147.

13, 631.   _____. Singer's children's stories and In My Father's Court: universalism and the Rankian hero. In Allentuck, M. (ed), The Achievement of Isaac Bashevis Singer. Carbondale: Southern Illinois Univ. Press, 1969, 145-158.

13, 632.   _____. What Maisie Knew: the Rankian hero. Amer Imago, 1966, 23:227-234.

13, 633.   Wolf, J. C. Science fiction and the fallacy of hope. Extrapolation, 1976, 17:151-152.

13, 634.   Wolfe, Gary K. The known and the unknown: structure and image in science fiction. In Clareson, T. D. (ed), Many Futures, Many Worlds; Theme and Form in Science Fiction. Kent, Ohio: Kent State Univ. Press, 1977, 94-110.

13, 635.   Wolf, Kary K., & Wolfe, Gary K. Metaphors of madness: popular psychological narratives. J Popular Culture, 1976, 9:895-907.

13, 636.   Wolfe, Peter. Dreamers Who Live Their Dreams: The World of Ross Macdonald's Novels. Bowling Green, Ohio: Bowling Green Univ. Press, 1977.

13, 637.   Wolfe, Robert F. The Restless Women of Edith Wharton. DAI, 1974, 35:1130A.

13, 638.   Wölfel, K. Daphnes Verwandlungen. Zu einem Kapitel in Wieland's Agathon. Jahrbuch der deutschen Schiller-Gesellschaft, 1964, 8:41-56.

13, 639.   Wolfenstein, Martha. The impact of a children's story on mothers and children. Monograph Social Research Child Development, No. 42, 11, 1946.

13, 640.   _____. Looking backward from A Clockwork Orange. In The Psychoanalytic Study of the Child, Vol. 31. New Haven: Yale Univ. Press, 1976, 535-553.

13, 641.   _____. The reality principle in story preferences of neurotics and psychotics. Character & Personality, 1944, 12.

13, 642.   Wolff, Cynthia Griffin. Kate Chopin and the fiction of limits: Désirée's baby. Southern Lit J, 1978, 10:123-133.

13, 643.   _____. Lily Bart and the beautiful death. Amer Lit, 1974, 46:16-40.

13, 644.   _____. The Psychological Fiction of Samuel Richardson. Hamden, Conn: Shoe String, 1972.

13, 645.   _____. Thanatos and Eros: Kate Chopin's The Awakening. Amer Q, 1973, 25:449-471.

13, 646.   Wolfley, Lawrence C. Repression's rainbow: the presence of Norman O. Brown in Pynchon's big novel. PMLA, 1977, 92:873-889.

13, 647.   Wolfson, Louis. Le Schizo et les langues. Les Temps modernes, 1964, No. 218.

13, 648. Wolfzettel, Friedrich.   Das romantische Motiv den steiner-
          nen Frau bei Théophile Gautier: Eine psychoanalytische
          Deutung von Arria Marcella.   Neuphilologische Mitteil-
          ungen, 1976, 77: 254-269.
13, 649. Wolkenfeld, Suzanne.   Psychological disintegration in Kaf-
          ka's A Fratricide and An Old Manuscript (psychological
          aspects of authorship).   Studies in Short Fiction, 1976,
          13: 25-29.
13, 650. _____.   Sleeping beauty retold: D. H. Lawrence's 'The
          Fox.'   Studies in Short Fiction, 1977, 14: 345-352.
13, 651. Wolpe, Hans.   Psychological ambiguity in La Nouvelle
          Héloïse.   Univ. Toronto Q, 1969, 28: 279-290.
13, 652. Wolstenholme, Susan.   Possession and personality: spirit-
          ualism in The Bostonians.   Amer Lit, 1978, 49: 580-
          591.
13, 653. Wonderley, A. Wayne.   Keyserling and feminism.   South
          Atlantic Bulletin, 1974, 39(2): 17-21.
13, 654. Wong, Timothy C.   The self and society in Tang dynasty
          love tales.   Amer Oriental Society J, 1979, 99:
          95-100.
13, 655. Wood, Barry.   Malcolm Lowry's metafiction: the biogra-
          phy of a genre [psychological aspects of authorship.]
          Contemporary Lit, 1978, 19: 1-25.
13, 656- Wood, Cynthia Nunnally.   The Mother Image in Selected
     7.   Works of Miguel de Unamuno.   DAI, 1976, 36: 4551A.
13, 658. Wood, Margery.   Norman Mailer and Nathalie Sarraute:
          a comparison of existential novels.   Minnesota Rev,
          1966, 6(1): 67-72.
13, 659. Wood, Michael.   Professors of desire.   Review: Leo
          Bersani's A Future for Astynax and Brooks' The Melo-
          dramatic Imagination.   Novel: A Forum on Fiction,
          1978, 11: 157-162.
13, 660. Woodle, Gary.   Erostrate: Sartre's paranoid.   Rev Exis-
          tential Psychol & Psychiat, 1974, 13: 30-41.
13, 661. Woodruff, S. C.   Melville and his chimney.   PMLA, 1960,
          65: 283-292; Emerson Society Q, 1959, 14: 2-6.
13, 662. Woods, Richard D.   Sangre patricia and The Doors of
          Perception.   Romance Notes, 1971, 12: 302-306.
13, 663. Woodward, J. B.   Eros and nirvana in the art of Bunin.
          Modern Language Rev, 1970, 65: 576-586.
13, 664. Woodward, Kathleen.   Passivity and passion in Little Dor-
          rit.   Dickensian, 1975, 71: 140-148.
13, 665. Woolf, Michael P.   The madman as hero in contemporary
          American fiction.   J Amer Studies, 1976, 10: 257-
          269.
13, 666. Woolf, Virginia.   Freudian fiction.   Times Lit Supplement,
          25 Mar 1920, 199.
13, 667. Wormhoudt, Arthur.   Ivanhoe and the teacher.   Amer
          Imago, 1953, 10: 39-56.
13, 668. Woronzoff, Alexander.   Andrej Belyj's Peterburg, James
          Joyce's Ulysses, and the stream-of-consciousness
          method.   Russian Language J, 1976, 107: 101-108.

13,669. Wörsching, Martha. Die rückwärts gewandte Utopie: Sozialpsychologische Anmerkungen zu Joseph Roths Roman Radetzkymarsch. Text und Kritik, 1974, 90-100.

13,670. Worth, B. S. Achievement and Affiliation Motives of Male and Female Characters in Realistic Fiction for Children, 1945-1975. DAI, 1978, 38:5917.

13,671. Worthen, John. Sanity, madness, and Women in Love. Trivium, 1975, 10:125-136.

13,672. Worthington, Mabel. The myth and Don Juan. Lit & Psychol, 1962, 12:113-124.

13,673. Wright, Celeste Turner. Elinor Wylie: the glass chimaera and the minotaur. Twentieth Century Lit, 1966, 12:15-26.

13,674. _____. Katherine Mansfield and the 'secret smile.' Lit & Psychol, 1955, 5(3):44-48.

13,675. _____. Katherine Mansfield's dog image. Lit & Psychol, 1960, 10:80-81.

13,676. _____. Katherine Mansfield's father image. Univ. California Publications, English Studies, 1955, 11:137-155.

13,677. Wright, Charles D. Melancholy Duffy and sanguine Sinico: humors in 'A Painful Case.' James Joyce Q, 1965, 3:171-181.

13,678. Wright, Nathalia. Melville and old Burton, with 'Bartleby' as an anatomy of melancholy. Tennessee Studies in Lit, 1970, 15:1-13.

13,679. _____. Mrs. Dalloway: a study in composition. College English, 1944, 5:351-355.

13,680. Wunderli-Müller, Christine B. Le Thème du mesque et les banalités dans l'oeuvre de Nathalie Sarraute. Zurich: Juris, 1971.

13,681. Wurmser, André. Je, romancier. JPNP, 1951, 44, 335-343.

13,682. Wüstenhagen, Heinz. Instinkt kontra Vernunft: Norman Mailers ideologische und aesthetische Konfusion. Zeitschrift für Anglistik und Amerikanistik, 1968, 16:362-389.

13,683. Wyatt, Bryant W. John Updike: the psychological novel in search of structure. Twentieth Century Lit, 1967, 13:89-96.

13,684. Wyatt, Frederick. Analysis of a popular novel. (Case study of a collective day-dream.) Amer Psychologist, 1947, 2:280-281.

13,685. _____. The choice of the topic in fiction: risks and rewards in comparison of André Gide's The Immoralist and Thomas Mann's Death in Venice. In Mellsart, J. (ed), Janus: Essays in Ancient and Modern Studies. Ann Arbor: Univ. Michigan, 1975, 211-241.

13,686. _____. Some comments on the use of symbols in the novel. Lit & Psychol, 1954, 4:15-23.

13,687. Wycherly, H. Alan. Hemingway's 'The Sea Change.' Amer Notes & Queries, 1969, 7:67-68.

13,688. Wylie, Harold A. Alain Robbe-Grillet: scientific humanist. Bucknell Rev, 1967, 15:1-9.

13, 689.   Wysling, Hans.   'Mythus und Psychologie' bei Thomas
           Mann.   In Dokumente und Untersuchungen.   Beiträge
           zur Thomas Mann-Forschung, Vol. 3.   Bern: Francke,
           1974; Zurich: Polygraph, 1969.
13, 690.   Wysong, Jack P.   Samuel Clemens' attitude toward the
           Negro as demonstrated in Pudd'nhead Wilson and A Con-
           necticut Yankee in King Arthur's Court.   Xavier Univ.
           Studies, 1968, 7(2):41-57.
13, 691.   Wysor, Bettie.   Lesbianism in literature.   In The Lesbian
           Myth.   NY: Random House, 1974, 190-256.
13, 692.   Wyss, Dieter.   Balzac und die Grenzen der Psychologie.
           Zeitschrift für klinische Psychologie und Psychotherapie,
           1978, 26(2):101-114.

13, 693.   Yaco, Rosemary Morris.   Suffering Women: Feminine
           Masochism in Novels by American Women.   DAI, 1975,
           36:3134B.
13, 694.   Yalom, I. D. , & Yalom, Marilyn K.   Ernest Hemingway.
           A psychiatric view.   Archives General Psychiat, 1971,
           24:485-494.
13, 695.   Yalom, Marilyn K.   Triangles and prisons: a psychologi-
           cal study of Stendhalian love.   Hartford Studies in Lit,
           1976, 8:82-97.
13, 696.   Yamanouchi, Hisaaki.   The Search for Authenticity in Mod-
           ern Japanese Literature.   Cambridge, NY: Cambridge
           Univ. Press, 1978.
13, 697.   Yáñez, Agustín.   La novela de Pérez Galdós.   Universidad
           Nacional de Colombia, 1947, 10:29-35.
13, 698.   _____.   Traza de la novela galdosiana.   Cuadernos
           Americanos, 1943, 5:222-240.
13, 699.   Yano, Shigeharu.   Psychological interpretations of Stein-
           beck's women in The Long Valley.   In Hayashi, T. ,
           Hashiguchi, T. , & Peterson, R. F. (eds), John Stein-
           beck: East and West, Steinbeck Monograph Series,
           Vol. 8.   Muncie, Indiana: Ball State Univ. Press,
           1978, 54-60.
13, 700.   Yarnes, George Ernest.   Suicide in the Narrative Works
           of Arthur Schnitzler.   Master's thesis, State Univ.
           New York Binghamton, 1970.
13, 701.   Yeazell, Ruth.   Fictional heroines and feminist critics.
           Novel: A Forum on Fiction, 1974, 8:29-38.
13, 702.   Yermakov, Ivan.   'The Nose. '   In Maguire, R. A. (ed),
           Gogol from the Twentieth Century.   Princeton: Prince-
           ton Univ. Press, 1974, 156-198.
13, 703.   Yetiv, Isaac.   Alienation in the modern novel of French
           North Africa before independence.   In Smith, R. (ed),
           Exile and Tradition; Studies in African and Caribbean
           Literature.   NY: Africana, 1976, 85-97; London:
           Longman, 1976, 85-97.
13, 704-   Yoda, A.   [Psychology of youth in Hermann Hesse's Un-
       5.   term Rad.]   Kroiku Shinri Kenkyu, 1939, 14:262-272.

13, 706. Yoder, Albert C. Oral artistry in Conrad's Heart of
          Darkness: a study of oral aggression. Conradiana,
          1970, 2(2):65-78.
13, 707. Yoder, R. A. Hawthorne and his artist. Studies in Ro-
          manticism, 1968, 7:193-206.
13, 708. Yoke, Carl B. Personality metamorphosis in Roger Ze-
          lazny's The Doors of His Face, the Lamps of His
          Mouth. Extrapolation, 1980, 21:106-121.
13, 709. York, Ruth B. V. Larbaud's Works of Imagination. DA,
          1966, 25:7281.
13, 710. Young, Glenn. Struggle and triumph in Light in August.
          Studies in the Twentieth Century, 1975, 15:33-50.
13, 711. Young, G. M. The emotions and Mr. Huxley. Life & Let-
          ters, 1934, 10:280-289.
13, 712. Young, Philip. The earlier psychologists and Poe. Amer
          Lit, 1951, 22:442-454.
13, 713. _____ . Fallen from time: the mythic Rip Van Winkle.
          In Malin, I. (ed), Psychoanalysis and American Fiction.
          NY: Dutton, 1965, 23-45.
13, 714. _____ . Three Bags Full. Essays in American Fic-
          tion. NY: Harcourt Brace Jovanovich, 1972.
13, 715. Young, Thomas B. Thematic Emphasis and Psychological
          Realism in Lawrence Durrell's Alexandria Quartet.
          DAI, 1974, 34:5214A-15A.
13, 716. Yu, Beorgcheon. The immortal twins: an aspect of Mark
          Twain. English Language & Lit (Korea Univ.), 1968,
          22:48-77.
13, 717. _____ . The still center of Hemingway's world. In
          Wagner, L. W. (ed), Ernest Hemingway; Five Decades
          of Criticism. Lansing: Michigan State Univ. Press,
          1974, 109-131.
13, 718. Yudicello, Lucio. Ernesto Sábato: el recurso de la
          melancolía. La Estafeta Literaria, 1977, 608:4-7.

13, 719. Zabel, Morton Dauwen. Conrad: the secret sharer.
          New Republic, 21 Apr 1941, 567-574.
13, 720. _____ . Introduction to Joseph Conrad's Lord Jim.
          Boston: Houghton Mifflin, 1958, V-XXXVII.
13, 721. Zac, Joel. El imposter: contribución al estudio de las
          psicopatias (psicoanálisis aplicado de las confesiones
          del estafodor Félix Krull, de Thomas Mann). Revista
          di Psicoanálisi, 1964, 21:58-75.
13, 722. Zagarell, Sandra Abelson. Charlotte Brontë from Fantasy
          to Social and Psychological Reality. DAI, 1977, 37:
          6521A.
13, 723. Zahareas, A. The tragic sense in Fortunata y Jacinta.
          Symposium, 1965, 19:38-49.
13, 724. Zak, Michele W. Feminism and the New Novel. DAI,
          1974, 34:5215A.
13, 725. _____ . The Grass Is Singing: a little novel about the
          emotions. Contemporary Lit, 1973, 14:481-490; In
          Pratt, A. , & Dembo, L. S. (eds), Doris Lessing:

Critical Studies. Madison: Univ. Wisconsin Press, 1974, 64-73.

13, 726. Zakrison, Gordon Walter. The Crisis of Identity in the Works of Max Frisch. DAI, 1976, 36:8088A.

13, 727. Zaller, R. Let us now praise James Agee. Southern Lit J, 1978, 10:144-154.

13, 728. Zambiano, Ana Laura. Greene's visions of childhood: 'The Basement Room' and The Fallen Idol. Lit/Film Q, 1974, 2:324-331.

13, 729. Zambrano, María. La mujer en la España de Galdós. Revista Cubana, 1943, 15:74-97.

13, 730. Zanger, Jules. Poe and the theme of forbidden knowledge. Amer Lit, 1978, 49:533-543.

13, 731. Zangwill, O. L. A case of paramnesia in Nathaniel Hawthorne. Character & Personality, 1945, 13:245-260.

13, 732. Zants, E. Review: K. M. McKilligan's Edouard Dujardin: 'Les Lauriers sont coupés' and the Interior Monologue. Modern Fiction Studies, 1978-79, 24:625-629.

13, 733. Zavarzadeh, Mas'ud. The Mythopoeic Reality: The Postwar American Nonfiction Novel. Urbana: Univ. Illinois Press, 1976.

13, 734. Zayed, Fernande. Actualité de Huysmans: pessimisme et psychologie 'fin-de-siècle.' In Forestier, L. (ed), Agencer un univers nouveau. L'Avant-siècle, 2. Paris: Lettres Modernes, 1976, 5-19.

13, 735. Zegger, Hrisey D. May Sinclair's Psychological Novels. DAI, 1971, 32:1537A-38A.

13, 736. Zeller, Michael. Väter und Söhne bei Thomas Mann: Der Generationsschritt als geschichtlicher Prozess. Bonn: Bouvier, 1974.

13, 737. Zelnick, Stephen. The incest theme in The Great Gatsby: an exploration of the false poetry of petty bourgeois consciousness. In Rudich, N. (ed), Weapons of Criticism: Marxism in America and the Literary Tradition. Palo Alto, Cal: Ramparts, 1976, 327-340.

13, 738. Zenke, Jürgen. Arthur Schnitzlers Fräulein Else--eine Monolognovelle? In Die deutsche Monologerzählung im 20. Jahrhundert. Cologne: Böhlau, 1976, 57-68.

13, 739. _____. Die deutsche Monologerzählung im 20. Jahrhundert. Cologne: Böhlau, 1976; Doctoral dissertation, Univ. Cologne, 1973.

13, 740. Zéphir, Jacques. La Personnalité humaine dans l'oeuvre de Marcel Proust, essai de psychologie litéraire. Paris: Minard, 1959.

13, 741. _____. Proust psychologue. Rev de l'Université Laval, 1954, 8:421-428; 1955, 10:143-148, 528-535.

13, 742. Zéraffa, Michel. Aspects structuraux de l'absurde dans la littérature contemporaine. JPNP, 1964, 61:437-456.

13, 743. _____. Claude Vallée. --La Féerie de Marcel Proust. JPNP, 1961, 58:245-246.

13, 744. _____. Thèmes psychologiques et structures romanesque dans l'oeuvre de Marcel Proust. JPNP, 1961, 58:193-216.

13, 745.   Zerbe, Evelyne A.   Veil of Shame: Role of Women in the
           Modern Fiction of North Africa and the Arab World.
           DAI, 1974, 35:2246A.
13, 746.   Ziebarth, Janet A.   Sexuality and Social Critique in the
           Novels of D. H. Lawrence, 1915-1922. DAI, 1975, 35:
           6739A-40A.
13, 747.   Ziegler, Gilette.   Mérimée et les femmes.   Europe, 1975,
           557:110-115.
13, 748.   Ziegler, Heide.   Existentielles Erleben und kurzes Erzäh-
           len. Das Komische, Tragische, Groteske und Myth-
           ische in William Faulkner's 'Short Stories. ' Amerika-
           studien, Monograph Series.   No. 45.   Stuttgart: Metz-
           ler, 1977.
13, 749.   Ziegler, Robert Earle.   Children and the Power of Imagi-
           nation: A Study of the Child in the Works of Emile
           Zola, Alphonse Daudet, Jules Renard, Pierre Loti and
           Marcel Schwob.   DAI, 1975, 35:5434A-35A.
13, 750.   Zielinski, T.   Der Rhythmus der römanischen Kunstprosa
           und seine psychologischen Grundlagen.   Archiv für die
           Gesamte Psychologie, 1906, 7:125-142.
13, 751.   Zilboorg, Gregory.   Discovery of the Oedipus complex;
           episodes from Marcel Proust.   Psychoanal Q, 1939,
           8:279-302; Revista de Psicoanálysis, 1944, 1:319-339.
13, 752.   Zimmerman, Michael.   Leopold Paula Bloom: the new
           womanly man.   Lit & Psychol, 1979, 39:176-184.
13, 753.   Zinberg, Dorothy S. , & Zinberg, Norman E.   Hans Cas-
           torp: identity crisis without reason.   Amer Imago,
           1963, 20:393-402.
13, 754.   Zinkin, L.   Death in Venice--a Jungian view.   J Analytic
           Psychol, 1977, 22:354-366.
13, 755.   Ziolkowski, Theodore.   The metaphysics of death.   In
           Dimensions of the Modern Novel.   Princeton: Prince-
           ton Univ. Press, 1969, 215-257.
13, 756.   _____ .   The telltale teeth: psychodontia to sociodontia.
           PMLA, 1976, 91:9-22.
13, 757.   Zlotnik, Jan.   The Virgin and the Dynamo: A Study of
           the Woman as Hero in the Novels of Edith Wharton,
           Ellen Glasgow and Willa Cather.   DAI, 1978, 39:878A-
           79A.
13, 758.   Zoellner, Robert H.   Conceptual ambivalence in Cooper's
           Leatherstocking.   Amer Lit, 1960, 31:397-420.
13, 759.   Zuckerman, Jerome.   The architecture of the 'Shadow
           Line. '   Conradiana, 1971-72, 3(2):87-92.
13, 760.   Zuckerman, Phyllis.   Comedy, tragedy, and madness in
           Nerval's Roman tragique.   MLN, 1974, 89:600-613.
13, 761.   Zulliger, Hans.   Der Abendteurer--Schundroman.   Zeit-
           schrift für psychoanalytische Pädagogik, 1933, 7:357-
           377.
13, 762.   _____ .   Das Bedürfnis der Jugendlichen nach Schund-
           literatur.   Schweizer Zeitschrift für Pädagogie, 1929.
13, 763.   _____ .   Schund-Phantasie und Angst-Bewältigung.   In
           Federn, P. & Meng, H. (eds), Praxis der Kinder-und
           Jugendpsychologie; Erziehung-Unterricht-Neurosenpro-
           phylaxe.   Bern: Huber, 1951, 157-169.

13, 764.   Zuluago Ospina, Alberto.   Notas sobre la novelística de la violencia en Colombia.   Cuadernos Hispanoamericanos, 1967, No. 216, 547-608.

13, 765.   Zulueta, Carmen de.   El monólogo interior de Pedro en Tiempo de silencio.   Hispanic Rev, 1977, 45:297-309.

13, 766.   Zweifel, Philip Lee.   Escape into Reality: The Role of Dreams in the Writings of Mark Twain.   DAI, 1975, 36:2831A.

13, 767.   Zwerdling, Alex.   Esther Summerson rehabilitated.   PMLA, 1973, 88:429-439.

13, 768.   Zytaruk, George J.   The phallic vision: D. H. Lawrence and V. V. Rozanov.   Comparative Lit Studies, 1967, 4: 283-297.

13, 769. Abramson, Ronald. Structure and meaning in the cinema.
In Nichols, B. (ed), Movies and Methods. Berkeley:
Univ. California Press, 1976, 558-568.

13, 770. Alfonsin, J. A. Un factor criminógeno secundario. Cinematografo y criminalidad. Revista de Psiquiatría y
Criminalia, 1938, 15:275-288.

13, 771. Alpert, Hollis. Sexual behavior in the American movie.
Saturday Rev, 1956, 39(24):9-10.

13, 772. Anast, Philip. Differential movie appeals as correlates of
attendance. Journalism Q, 1967, 44:86-90.

13, 773. Ancona, L., & Fontanesi, M. Analisi delle relazioni dina-
miche tra effetto carartico ed effetto frustrante di uno
stimolo cinematografico emotivo. Contributi dell'Istituto
di Psicologia, 1967, No. 28, 30-48.

13, 774. Andrew, James D. Realism and Reality in Cinema: The
Film Theory of André Bazin and Its Source in Recent
French Thought. DAI, 1977, 33:1711A-12A.

13, 775. Anon. Crime and the cinema in the United States. Int Rev
Educational Cinematography, 1929, 1:303-314.

13, 776. _____. The Influence of the Cinema on Children and
Adolescents: An Annotated International Bibliography.
Paris: UNESCO, 1960.

13, 777. _____. Les Problemès sociaux du cinéma: cinéma et
criminalité précoce. Rev de l'Institut du Cinéma Education, 1932, 4:73-75.

13, 778. _____. The Recreational Cinema and the Young. NY:
Columbia Univ. Press, 1938.

13, 779. _____. Social science matinees: Mount Holyoke College course entitled 'Social Psychology and Sex Roles in
Films.' Human Behavior, 1978, 7:49.

13, 780. _____. The split-screen search into troubled minds.
Life, 1968, 64:68-70.

13, 781. _____. These films delve among the shadows--the cinema is psycho-analyzed. Focus on Film, 1958, 5:8+.

13, 782. Appel, Alfred, Jr. Tristram in movielove: Lolita at the
movies. In Proffer, C. R. (ed), A Book of Things
about Vladimir Nabokov. Ann Arbor, Mich: Ardis,
1974, 123-170.

13, 783. Armes, Roy. Pasolini. Films & Filming, 1971, 17(9):55-
58.

13, 784. Arnheim, Rudolf. Art today and the film. Film Culture, 1966, 42:43-45.

13, 785. _____. Epic and dramatic film. Film Culture, 1957, 3:9-10.

13, 786. _____. Film As Art. Los Angeles: Univ. California Press, 1957, 1966; London: Faber & Faber, 1969, 1939; Berlin: Rowholt, 1932; Excerpts in Talbot, D. (ed), Film: An Anthology. NY: Simon & Schuster, 1959, 294-323.

13, 787. _____. Portrait of an artist. Film Culture, 1958, 4(3):11-13.

13, 788. Ashworth, John. Olivier, Freud, and Hamlet. Atlantic Monthly, May 1949, 30-33.

13, 789. Atkins, Thomas R. (ed). Sexuality in the Movies. Bloomington: Indiana Univ. Press, 1975.

13, 790. Atwell, L. Homosexual themes in the cinema. Tangents, 1966, 1(6):4-10; 1966, 1(4):4-9.

13, 791. Augustin, V. E. Moving picture preferences. J Delinquency, 1927, 11:206-209.

13, 792. Bach, Sheldon. Discussion of Greenberg's paper on Bergman's Wild Strawberries. Amer Imago, 1970, 27:83-89.

13, 793. Bachmann, G. Pasolini on DeSade: interview. Film Q, 1975-76, 29:39-44.

13, 794. _____. Pasolini and the Marquis de Sade. Sight & Sound, 1975-76, 45:50-54.

13, 795. Bacon, Roger. Why movies move us. Bulletin Rocky Mountain Modern Language Assn, 1972, 26:65-69.

13, 796. Bacon, S. D. A student of the problems of alcohol and alcoholism views the motion picture, The Lost Weekend. Quart J Studies Alcohol, 1945, 6:402-405.

13, 797. Bader, Alfred. Psychiatrie und kino. Schweizer Archiv für Neurologie und Psychiatrie, 1967, 99:138-139.

13, 798. Balázs, Béla. Theory of the Film. NY: Dover, 1971; London: Dobson, 1952.

13, 799. Barnett, C. A. The role of the press, radio, and motion picture and Negro morale. J Negro Education, 1943, 12:474-489.

13, 800. Bateson, G. Cultural and thematic analysis of fictional films. Transactions New York Academy Science, 1943, 5:72-78.

13, 801. Baudry, Jean-Louis. Le Dispositif: approches métapsychologiques de l'impression de réalité. In Psychanalyse et cinéma. Paris: Seuil, 1975.

13, 802. _____. Ideological effects of the basic cinematographic apparatus. Film Q, 1974-75, 28:39-47.

13, 803. Bauer, Stephen F., Balter, Leon, & Hunt, Winslow. The detective film as myth: The Maltese Falcon and Sam Spade. Amer Imago, 1978, 35:275-296.

13, 804. Bazin, André. The ontology of the photographic image. Film Q, 1960, 13(4).

13,805.   _____. Qu'est-ce que le Cinéma: I. Ontologie et Langage. Paris: Les Editions du Cerf, 1958.
13,806.   _____. What Is Cinema? Essays selected and translated by Hugh Gray, 2 Vols. Berkeley: Univ. California Press, 1967-1971.
13,807.   Beck, Bob. Creating the 'psychedelic' visual effects for
The Trip. Amer Cinemtographer, 1968, 49:176-179+.
13,808.   _____. Ghost in the family; treatment of the family
concept in movies and television. Society, 1974, 11:
78-81+.
13,809.   Becker, Henry III. The Rocking Horse Winner: film as
parable. Lit/Film Q, 1973, 1:55-63.
13,810.   Becker, Raymond de. Notes sur un cinéma homophile.
Arcadie, 1960, 74:97-100.
13,811.   Behrens, Roy R. On creativity and humor: an analysis
of Easy Street. J Creative Behavior, 1974, 8:227-238.
13,812.   Beja, Morris, Plank, Robert, & Eisenstein, Alex. Three
perspectives of a film. Extrapolation, 1968-69, 10-11;
In Clareson, T. D. (ed), Science Fiction: The Other
Side of Realism. Bowling Green, Ohio: Bowling
Green Univ. Popular Press, 1971, 263-271.
13,813.   Bellour, Raymond. Psychosis, neurosis, perversion.
Camera Obscura, 1979, 3-4.
13,814.   Belson, James I. Maps of Consciousness: Creating an
Inner Life for Character in Film and Novel. DAI,
1974, 34:4242.
13,815.   Bennett, Chester C., & Arsenian, John. The mental patient looks at The Snake Pit. Psychiat Q Supplement,
1954, 28:111-120.
13,816.   Benson, Edward, & Strom, S. H. Crystal Lee, Norma
Rae, and all their sisters; working women on film.
Film Library Q, 1979, 12(2-3):18-23.
13,817.   Berkowitz, Leonard. The effects of observing violence.
Scientific Amer, 1964, 210(2):35-41.
13,818.   _____, & Rawlings, E. Effects of film violence on inhibitions against subsequent aggression. J Abnormal
Social Psychol, 1963, 66:405-412.
13,819.   Berlin, Normand. Easy Rider: touching the tragic.
Hartford Studies in Lit, 1971, 3:12-18.
13,820.   Bier, J. P. Literatur und Film im Werke Hermann
Brochs. Rev des Langues Vivantes, 1972, 38:348-362.
13,821.   Blake, Richard A. Reality and structure in film aesthetics. Thought, 1968, 43:429-440.
13,822.   Blaustein, L. [Contributions to the psychology of the cinema spectator.] Kwartalnik Psychologiczny, 1933, 4:
192-236.
13,823.   Bloom, Samuel William. A Social Psychological Study of
Motion Picture Audience Behavior. A Case Study of
the Negro Image in Mass Communication. Doctoral
dissertation, Univ. Wisconsin, 1956.
13,824.   Bluestone, George. Time in film and fiction. JAAC,
1961, 19:311-315.
13,825.   Blumer, H. Movies and Conduct. NY: Macmillan, 1933.

13, 826. _____, & Hauser, P. M.   Movies, Delinquency, and Crime.   NY: Macmillan, 1933.

13, 827. Boese, J.   Vorstellungsbläufe am Rande des Bewusstseins, 'der psychische Film.'   Neue deutsche Forschung Abt Charakterologie, No. 13.   Berlin: Junker und Dünn- haupt, 1942.

13, 828. Bond, Kirk.   Film as literature.   Bookman, 1933, 84:188- 189.

13, 829. Bourgel, J. L.   Romantic dramas of the forties, an analy- sis.   Film Comment, 1974, 10:46-51.

13, 830. Bourguignon, Serge.   On the relationship of physical to psychological action in The Reward.   Cinema, 1965, 2(5):6-7.

13, 831. Bozzuto, J. C.   Cinematic neurosis following The Exorcist. Report of four cases.   JNMD, 1975, 161:43-48.

13, 832. Bradlow, Paul.   Two ... but not of a kind.   Film Com- ment, 1969, 3:60-61.

13, 833. Brater, Enoch.   Time and memory in Pinter's Proust screenplay.   Comparative Drama, 1979, 13:121-126.

13, 834. Braverman, Marc T., & Farley, Frank H.   Arousal and cognition: the stimulation-seeking motive and struc- tural effects in the comprehension of film.   Educational Communication & Technology J, 1978, 26:321-327.

13, 835. Brill, Abraham A.   Dr. Brill analyzes Walt Disney's masterpieces.   Photoplay, Apr. 1934.

13, 836. Brinkmann, Donald.   Zur Psychologie des Jugendfilms. Psychologe, 1953, 5:89-93.

13, 837. Britton, Andrew, et al. (eds).   The American Nightmare. Toronto: Canadian Film Institute, 1979.

13, 838. Brodbeck, Arthur J.   Placing aesthetic developments in social context: a program of value analysis.   J Social Issues, 1964, 1:8-25.

13, 839. Brody, Alan.   2001 and the paradox of the fortunate fall. Hartford Studies in Lit, 1969, 1:7-19.

13, 840. Brody, Michael.   The wonderful world of Disney: its psy- chological appeal.   Amer Imago, 1976, 33:350-360.

13, 841. Brown, Keith C.   Hemlock for the critic: a problem in evaluation.   JAAC, 1960, 18:316-318.

13, 842. Brown, Robert.   Film myth and the limits of film.   Hud- son Rev, 1951, 4:111-117.

13, 843. Brown, Walter A.   Anger arousal by a motion picture: a methodological note.   Amer J Psychiat, 1977, 134:930- 931.

13, 844. Browne, Nick.   The filmic apparatus in Bergman's Per- sona.   Psychocultural Rev, 1979, 3:111-115.

13, 845. _____.   The narrative point of view: the rhetoric of Au hazard.   Balthazar.   Film Q, 1977, 31:19-31.

13, 846. Brüel, Oluf.   Film als psycho-traumatisches Kindheitser- lebnis; Psychotherapie.   Acta Psychiatrica et Neuro- logica, 1933, 8:445-454.

13, 847. _____.   [The film as a psychotraumatic experience in childhood.]   Ugeskr Laeg, 1935, 97:305-309.

13,848. _____. A moving picture as a psychopathogenic factor: a paper on primary psychotraumatic neurosis. Character & Personality, 1938, 7:68-76.

13,849. _____. Psychic trauma through the cinema--an illustrative case. Int J Sexology, 1953, 7:61-63.

13,850. Buckle, Gerard Fort. The Mind and the Film: A Treatise on the Psychological Factors in the Film. NY: Arno, 1970 (1926).

13,851. Bullis, Roger A. An Analysis of the Interpersonal Communication of Private Detective Characters in Selected 'Mean Streets' Motion Pictures. DAI, 1978, 38(10-A), 5759-60.

13,852. Buntzen, Lynda, & Craig, Carls. Hour of the wolf: the case of Ingmar Bergman. Film Q, 1976-77, 30:23-34.

13,853. Burch, Noel. To a Distant Observer: Form and Meaning in Japanese Cinema. Berkeley: Univ. California Press, 1979.

13,854. Burke, Frank. Fellini's drive for individuation. Southwest Rev, 1979, 64:68-85.

13,855. Burzynski, Michael H., & Bayer, Dewey J. The effect of positive and negative prior information on motion picture appreciation. J Social Psychol, 1977, 101:215-218.

13,856. Butcher, Maryvonne. Mirror up to nature: national traits in movies. Commonweal, 1958, 68:513-516.

13,857. Calev, Chaim. The Stream of Consciousness in the Films of Alain Resnais. DAI, 1978, 39(4-A), 1885.

13,858. Callahan, Michael Anthony. A Critical Study of the Image of Marriage in the Contemporary Cinema. Doctoral dissertation, Univ. Southern California, 1971.

13,859. Callenbach, Ernest. Comparative anatomy of folk-myth films: Robin Hood and Antonio das Mortes. Film Q, 1964-70, 23(2):42-47.

13,860. Canestrari, Renzo. La psicologia differenziale et il cinema. Infanzia anormale, 1953, 24:284-293.

13,861. Cantor, Joanne R., Zillmann, Dolf, & Einsiedel, Edna F. Female responses to provocation after exposure to aggressive and erotic films. Communication Research, 1978, 5:395-412.

13,862. Carlisky, Mario. Psicoanalisis, teatro y cine. Buenos Aires: Paidos, 1965.

13,863. Carringer, Robert L. Rosebud, dead or alive: narrative and symbolic structure in Citizen Kane. PMLA, 1976, 91:185-193.

13,864. Carroll, Noël. Mind, medium and metaphor in Harry Smith's Heaven and Earth Magic. Film Q, 1977, 31: 37-44.

13,865. Cartwright, Rosalind D., Bernick, N., & Borowitz, G. Effect of an erotic movie on the sleep and dreams of young men. Archives General Psychiat, 1969, 20:262-271.

13,866. Casañet y Gea, M.   Peligros e inconvenientes del cinema-
         tógrafo para los niños.   Medicina, 1927, 8:1-4.
13,867. Catton, William R., Jr.   Changing cognitive structure as
         a basis for the 'sleeper effect.'   Social Forces, 1960,
         38:348-354.
13,868. Cavell, Stanley.   Knowledge as transgression: mostly a
         reading of It Happened One Night.   Daedalus, 1980,
         109:147-175.
13,869. _____. The World Viewed: Reflections on the Ontology
         of Film.   NY: Viking, 1971.
13,870. Cawelti, John G.   The Western: a look at the evolution
         of a formula.   In Adventure, Mystery, and Romance.
         Chicago: Univ. Chicago Press, 1976, 192-259.
13,871. Chaikin, Robert Andrew.   King Kong--a re-assessment.
         Psychoanal Rev, 1980, 67:271-276.
13,872. Charney, Hanna.   Images of absence in Flaubert and some
         contemporary films.   Style, 1975, 9:488-501.
13,873. Charters, W.W.   The influence of motion pictures on chil-
         dren.   Proceedings National Education Assn, 1934, 72:
         383-393.
13,874. _____. Motion Pictures and Youth.   NY: Macmillan,
         1933.
13,875. Chasseguet-Smirgel, Janine.   Entretien sur le cinéma.
         In Pour une psychanalyse de l'art et de le créativité.
         Paris: Payot, 1971.
13,876. _____. A propos de l'Année dernière à Marienbad.   In
         Entretiens sur l'Art et la psychanalyse.   Paris: 1968
         (1962).
13,877. Chodorkoff, Bernard, & Baxter, Seymour.   Secrets of a
         Soul: an early psychoanalytic film venture.   Amer
         Imago, 1974, 319-334.
13,878. Cieutat, Michel.   Le Sacre de la famille selon Hollywood:
         De l'influence des origines culturelles sur la formation
         du couple parfait (1930-1957).   Recherches Anglaises
         et Américaines, 1975, 8:209-232.
13,879. Cismaru, Alfred.   Hiroshima mon amour revisited.   Hart-
         ford Studies in Lit, 1971, 3:39-44.
13,880. Clipper, Lawrence J.   Archetypal figures in early film
         comedy.   Western Humanities Rev, 1974, 28:353-366.
13,881. Cohen, Keith.   Novel and Movies: Dynamics of Artistic
         Exchange in the Early Twentieth Century.   Doctoral
         dissertation, Princeton Univ., 1974.
13,882. Collet, Jean.   La Folie de l'homme moderne: La Vie a
         l'envers, un film d'Alain Jessua.   Signes du Temps,
         1964, n.s., no. 13, 42.
13,883. Collins, M.   A history of homosexuality in the movies.
         Drum, 1967, 27:12-21, 30-32.
13,884. Conrad, H.S., & Jones, H.E.   Psychological studies of
         motion pictures. V.   Adolescent and adult sex differ-
         ences in immediate and delayed recall.   J Social Psy-
         chology, 1931, 2:433-459.
13,885. _____. Psychological studies of motion pictures.
         Univ. California Publications in Psychol, 1930, 3.

13, 886.   Cook, Bruce R.   Science, Fiction, and Film: A Study of
           the Interaction of Science, Science Fiction, Literature,
           and the Growth of Cinema.   DAI, 1977, 37:6810A.
13, 887.   Cooper, C. D.   The reactions of sixth grade children to
           commercial motion pictures as a medium for character
           education.   J Experimental Education, 1939, 7:268-273.
13, 888.   Corliss, Richard.   Psycho therapy.   In Nobile, P. (ed),
           Favorite Movies; Critics' Choice.   NY: Macmillan,
           1973, 213-224.
13, 889.   Coulteray, George de.   Sadism in the Movies.   NY: Medi-
           cal Press, 1965.
13, 890.   Covino, Michael.   Wim Wenders: a worldwide sickness.
           Film Q, 1977-78, 31:9-19.
13, 891.   Cowart, David.   'Sacrificial ape':   King Kong and his anti-
           types in Gravity's Rainbow.   Lit & Psychol, 1978, 28:
           112-118.
13, 892.   Cox, Carole A.   Film Preference Patterns of Fourth and
           Fifth Grade Children.   DAI, 1976, 36:5017-18.
13, 893.   Cripps, Thomas.   Black Film as Genre.   Bloomington:
           Indiana Univ. Press, 1977.
13, 894.   _____.   Slow Fade to Black: The Negro in American
           Film.   NY: Oxford Univ. Press, 1977.
13, 895.   Curtis, James M.   From American Graffiti to Star Wars.
           J Popular Culture, 1980, 13:590-600.
13, 896.   Cutler, Janet K.   Eugene O'Neill on the Screen: Love,
           Hate, and the Movies.   DAI, 1977, 38:3109A.

13, 897.   Dadoun, Roger.   [Metropolis.   Mother City--mediator--
           Hitler.]   Rev Française de Psychanalyse, 1974, 38:101-
           130.
13, 898.   Dayan, D.   The tutor-code of classical cinema.   Film Q,
           1974, 28:22-31.
13, 899.   DeBecker, Raymond.   Pour eine psychanalyse du cinéma.
           Table Ronde, 1957, 109:79-89.
13, 900.   Debougnie, J.   Cinéma, grand école du soir des peuples.
           Nouvelle Rev Pédagogique, 1947, 3:159-161.
13, 901.   Debrix, Jean.   Cinema and poetry.   Yale French Studies,
           1956, 17:86-104.
13, 902.   Deer, Irving.   Strindberg's dream vision: prelude to the
           film.   Criticism, 1972, 14:253-265.
13, 903.   De Feo, G.   Les Impressions des jeunes sur les films de
           guerre.   Rev de l'Institut du cinéma Education, 1933,
           1-2:135-143, 315-319.
13, 904.   _____.   Quand et comment les jeunes fréquentent le
           cinéma.   Rev de l'Institut du cinéma Education, 1933,
           4:865-874, 944-955.
13, 905.   Degenfelder, E. P.   The four faces of Temple Drake:
           Faulkner's Sanctuary, Requiem for a Nun, and the two
           film adaptations.   Amer Q, 1976, 28:544-560.
13, 906.   Denby, David (ed).   Awake in the Dark; An Anthology of
           American Film Criticism, from 1915 to the Present.
           NY: Random House, 1977.

13,907. _____. Stolen privacy: Coppola's The Conversation.
Sight & Sound, 1974, 43:131-133.

13,908. Denis, Maurice. A propos du mythede Charlot. Psyché,
1957, 2:120-121, 367-370.

13,909. DeNitto, Dennis. Jean Cocteau's Beauty and the Beast.
Amer Imago, 1976, 33:123-154.

13,910. De Ruette, V. The cinema and child psychology. Int Rev
Educational Cinematography, 1934, 6:38-49.

13,911. _____. Cinema educatif ou cinema demoralisateur.
Rev de l'Institut du cinéma Education, 1933, 4:296-312.

13,912. Dervin, Daniel A. Creativity and collaboration in three
American movies. Amer Imago, 1977, 34:179-204.

13,913. _____. The primal scene and the technology of perception in Antonioni's Blow-up. Psychocultural Rev, 1977,
1(1):77-95.

13,914. _____. The primal scene and the technology of perception in theater and film. A historical perspective with
a look at Potemkin and Psycho. Psychoanal Rev, 1975,
62:269-304.

13,915. Deshaies, Gabriel. Les Fonctions psychologiques du cinéma. Annales Médico-Psychologiques, 1951, 1:553-573.

13,916. DeVoto, Bernard. The easy chair. Harper's, 1947, 194:
126-127.

13,917. Dominique, Claude. La Culpabilité dans le cinéma américain. Psyché, 1948, 3:603-608.

13,918. _____. A review of the Olivier Hamlet film. Psyché,
1948, 3:1179-1182.

13,919. Dowling, Ellen Condon. Review: Margaret Thorp's
America at the Movies. Psychiatry, 1940, 3:149-150.

13,920. Doyno, Victor A. 2001: years and shapes. Hartford
Studies in Lit, 1969, 1:131-132.

13,921. Durgnat, Raymond. Eros in the Cinema. London: Calder, 1966.

13,922. _____. Erotism in cinema: the dark gods--Part 1:
definitions and points of departure. Films & Filming,
1961, 8:14-16+.

13,923. _____. Erotism in cinema--Part 2: the deviationists--
Saturnalia in cans. Films & Filming, 1961, 8(2):33-
34+.

13,924. _____. Erotism in cinema--Part 8: Midnight Sun.
Films & Filming, 1962, 8(8):21-23+.

13,925. _____. Erotism in cinema--Part 6: mind and matter,
analysis of French and Italian styles--some mad love
and the sweet life. Films & Filming, 1962, 8(6):16-
18+.

13,926. _____. Erotism in cinema--Part 4: the subconscious
--from pleasure castle to libido motel. Films & Filming, 1962, 8(4):13-15+.

13,927. _____. Erotism in cinema--Part 7: symbolism--
another word for it. Films & Filming, 1962, 8(7):13-
15+.

13,928. _____. Films and Feelings. Cambridge: Massachusetts Institute of Technology, 1967; London: Faber &
Faber, 1967.

13,929.   _____. Sexual Alienation in the Cinema. London:
           Studio Vista, 1972.
13,930.   _____, et al. Obscure objects of desires. Film Com-
           ment, 1978, 16:60-64.
13,931.   Dysinger, W. S., & Ruckmick, C. A. The Emotional Re-
           sponses of Children to the Motion Picture Situation.
           NY: Macmillan, 1933.

13,932.   Eisenstein, Sergei M. Film Form. Essays in Film The-
           ory. NY: Harcourt, Brace, 1949; London: Dobson,
           1951.
13,933.   Elkin, Frederick. The psychological appeal of the Holly-
           wood Western. J Educational Sociology, 1950, 24:72-
           85.
13,934.   Elsaesser, Thomas. Screen violence: emotional struc-
           ture and ideological function in A Clockwork Orange.
           In Bigsby, C. W. E. (ed), Approaches to Popular Cul-
           ture. London: Arnold, 1976; Bowling Green, Ohio:
           Popular, 1976, 171-200.
13,935.   Epstein, Jean. Ciné-analyse ou poesie en quantité indus-
           trielle. Psyché, 1949, 4:651-657.
13,936.   Erikson, Erik Homburg. Reflections on Dr. Borg's life
           cycle. Daedalus, 1976, 105(2):1-28.
13,937.   Evans, C. Cinematography and Robbe-Grillet's Jealousy.
           In Stanford, D. E. (ed), Nine Essays in Modern Litera-
           ture. Baton Rouge: Louisiana State Univ. Press,
           1965, 117-128.
13,938.   Ewers, Hans Heinz. Der Student von Prague. In Rank,
           O., Der Doppelgänger: Psychoanalytische Studie.
           Leipzig: Int Psychoanalytischer Verlag, 1925.

13,939.   Fagan, Jim. Sex at the Cinema. London: Scripts, 1967.
13,940.   Favre, L. La musique des couleurs et le cinéma. Bul-
           letin de l'Institut général psychologique, 27:77-84.
13,941.   Fearing, Franklin. Influence of the movies on attitudes
           and behavior. Annals Amer Academy Political & So-
           cial Sciences, 1947, 254:70-79.
13,942.   _____. Psychology and the films. Hollywood Q, 1946,
           1:154-158.
13,943.   _____. The screen discovers psychiatry. Hollywood
           Q, 1946, 1:154-158.
13,944.   _____. Warrior's return: normal or neurotic. Holly-
           wood Q, 1945, 1:97-109.
13,945.   _____. A word of caution for the intelligent consumer
           of motion pictures. Quarterly of Film, Radio, Televi-
           sion, 1951, 6:129-142.
13,946.   Feldman, Silvia. Review: Joan Didion's Play It As It
           Lays. J Contemporary Psychotherapy, 1973, 5:151-
           153.
13,947.   Fell, John L. Film and the Narrative Tradition. Norman:
           Univ. Oklahoma Press, 1974.

13,948. Fenichel, Robert R. Comment on 2001 and articles in Hartford Studies in Literature on 2001. Hartford Studies in Lit, 1969, 1:133-135.

13,949. Fernandez-Zoila, Adolfo. Introduction à une étude des nevroses 'existentielles': approche psychopathologique de la thematique du film de Marcel Carné, Les Tricheurs. Evolution psychiatrique, 1960, 25:433-459.

13,950. Fervers, Carl. Zur Psychologie des Filmerlebens. Zeitschrift für experimentelle und angewandte Psychologie, 1959, 6:600-667.

13,951. Fischer, L., & Rosenbaum, J. Beyond freedom and dignity: an analysis of Jacques Tati's Playtime. Sight & Sound, 1976, 45:234-239.

13,952. Fischer, Lucy. The Lady Vanishes: women, magic and the movies. Film Q, 1979, 33:30-40.

13,953. Flik, Gotthilf. Untersuchingen über den Einfluss des Films auf kriminell gewordene Jugendliche. Psychologische Rundschau, 1954, 5:1-21.

13,954. Fodor, István. Linguistic and psychological problems of film synchronization (II). Acta Linguistica Academiae Scientiarum Hungaricae, 1969, 19:379-394.

13,955. Ford, R. Children in the Cinema. London: Allen & Unwin, 1939.

13,956-7. Forman, J. The compelling work of Harold Mayer. Film Library Q, 1976, 9(1):23-26.

13,958. Fox, M. S. The art of the movies in American life. JAAC, 1944, 3:39-52.

13,959. Fredericksen, Donald Laurence. The Aesthetic of Isolation in Film Theory: Hugo Munsterberg. NY: Arno, 1977.

13,960. Free, William J. The rape of the schoolmarm. Georgia Rev, 1971, 25:286-301.

13,961. Freimuth, Vicki S., & Jamieson, Kathleen. 'The Lottery': an empirical analysis of its impact; filmed adaptation of the story. Research in the Teaching of English, 1977, 11:235-243.

13,962. French, P. Violence in the cinema. Twentieth Century, 1964-65, 173:115-128.

13,963. Frosch, John. An ambivalent bow to Hollywood. Bulletin Amer Psychoanal Assn, 1964, 4:1-2.

13,964. Fry, Carrol L., & Stein, Jared. Isolation imagery in The Graduate: a contrast in media. Midwest Q, 1978, 19:203-214.

13,965. Fulchignoni, Enrico. Cinéma et psychologie. Reviste de Psychologie Appliqués, 1951, 1:61-72.

13,966. _____. Contributo della filmologia alla psicologia del comico. Revista di Psicologia, 1952, 48:163-164.

13,967. _____. Filmologia e psicologia infantil. Arquivos Brasleiros de Psicotécnia, 1950, 2:59-66.

13,968. _____. Sobre el valor psicológico de la imagen cinematografico. Revista de Psicologia general y aplicada, 1949, 4:11-38.

13,969. Funk, A. Film und Jugend. Eine Untersuchungen über die
         psychischen Wirkungen des Films im Leben der Jugend-
         lichen. Munich: Reinhardt, 1934.

13,970. Geduld, Harry M. (ed). Authors on Film. Bloomington:
         Univ. Indiana Press, 1979.
13,971. Gilbert, Basil. One Flew over the Cuckoo's Nest: mad-
         house or microcosm? Meanjin Q, 1976, 35:292-299.
13,972. Gill, J. M. The films of Gunvor Nelson. Film Q, 1977,
         30:28-36.
13,973. Gillibert, Jean. Lectures de films. Rev Française de
         Psychanalyse, 1974, 38:1.
13,974. Giltrow, David. Film and visual perception. Educational
         Broadcasting Int, 1978, 11:13-16.
13,975. Goldberg, Albert L. The Effect of Two Types of Sound
         Motion Pictures on Attitudes of Adults Toward Minority
         Groups. DAI, 1957, 17:295.
13,976. Goldberg, Herman G. The role of 'cutting' in the percep-
         tion of the motion picture. J Applied Psychol, 1971,
         35:70-71.
13,977. Goldman, P. , & Kasindorf, M. Jawsmania: the great
         escape. Newsweek, 1975, 86:16-17.
13,978. Goldstein, Melvin. Antonioni's Blow-Up: from crib to
         camera. Amer Imago, 1975, 32:240-263.
13,979. _____. The negative symbolic environment in Antoni-
         oni's Blow-Up. J Aesthetic Education, 1974, 8:27-42.
13,980. Goldstein, Naomi S. The Effect of Animated Cartoons on
         Hostility in Children. DA, 1957, 17:1125.
13,981. Gollub, Judith P. Nouveau roman et nouveau cinéma. DA,
         1966, 26:6712-13.
13,982. Gomery, J. Douglas. Semiology and film criticism: Chil-
         dren of Paradise. Sub-stance, 1974, 9:15-23.
13,983. Gomez, Joseph A. Peter Watkins's Edvard Munch. Film
         Q, 1976-77, 30:38-46.
13,984. Gough-Yates, Kevin. The hero. Films & Filming, 1965,
         12(3):11-16.
13,985. _____. The heroine. Films & Filming, 1966, 12(8):23-
         27; 12(9):27-32; 12(10):38-43; 12(11):45-50.
13,986. _____. Private madness and public lunacy. Films &
         Filming, 1972, 18:27-30.
13,987. Grace, Harry A. Charlie Chaplin's films and American
         culture patterns. JAAC, 1952, 10:353-363.
13,988. _____. A taxonomy of American crime film themes.
         J Social Psychol, 1955, 42:129-136.
13,989. Grau, Robert. The Theatre of Science. NY: Blom,
         1969.
13,990. Greadington, Barbara G. The Effect of Black Films on the
         Self-Esteem of Black Adolescents. DAI, 1978, 38:3774.
13,991. Greenberg, Harvey R. Dracula, erect (and otherwise):
         Dracula, Nosferatu the Vampire, Love at First Bite.
         Psychoanal Rev, 1980, 67:409-414.

13, 992. _____. Movies on Your Mind. NY: Saturday Review of Literature/Dutton, 1975.

13, 993. _____. The rags of time: Ingmar Bergman's Wild Strawberries. Amer Imago, 1970, 27:66-82.

13, 994. Greenspun, R. Floating: 3 women. Film Comment, 1977, 13:55-57.

13, 995. Gregory, John Robert. Some Psychological Aspects of Motion Picture Montage. Doctoral dissertation, Univ. Illinois, 1961.

13, 996. Grinker, Roy E., & Spiegel, John P. The returning soldier: a dissent. Hollywood Q, 1945, 1:321-328.

13, 997. Grinstein, Alexander. Miracle of Milan: some psychoanalytic notes on a movie. Amer Imago, 1953, 10:229-245.

13, 998. Grossman, M. L. Jean Vigo and the development of surrealist cinema. Symposium, 1973, 27:111-125.

13, 999. Grotjahn, Martin. Ferdinand the Bull; psychoanalytic remarks about a modern totem animal. Amer Imago, 1940, 1:33-41.

14, 000. Gundlach, Ralph H. The movies: stereotypes or realities? J Social Issues, 1947, 3:26-32.

14, 001. Gutheil, Emil A. Psychiatry on the screen. Amer J Psychol, 1959, 13:487-488.

14, 002. Guzzetti, Alfred. Christian Metz and the semiology of the cinema. J Modern Lit, 1973, 3:292-308.

14, 003. Hafeez, M. A. Psychology of films. J Education & Psychol (Baroda), 1950, 8:14-22.

14, 004. Hagenauer, Fedor, & Hamilton, James W. Straw Dogs: aggression and violence in modern film. Amer Imago, 1973, 30:221-249.

14, 005. Hamilton, James W. Cinematic neurosis: a brief case report. J Amer Academy Psychoanal, 1974, 6:569-577.

14, 006. _____. The Exorcist: some psychodynamic considerations. J Philadelphia Assn Psychoanal, 1976, 3:37-53.

14, 007. _____. Some comments about Ingmar Bergman's The Silence and its sociocultural implications. J Amer Academy Child Psychiatry, 1969, 8:367-373.

14, 008. _____. Some dynamic and genetic aspects of the 'new' American film. Bulletin Philadelphia Assn Psychoanal, 1971, 21:230-246.

14, 009. Hammond, R. M. Jensen's Gradiva: a clue to the composition of Cocteau's Orphée. Symposium, 1973, 27:126-136.

14, 010. Handel, Leo A. Hollywood Looks at Its Audience; a Report of Film Audience Research. Urbana: Univ. Illinois Press, 1950.

14, 011. Hárnik, J. Psychoanalytischer Film. Int Zeitschrift für Psychoanalyse, 1926, 12:580-581.

14, 012. Hartman, Geoffrey H. Between the acts: Jeanne Moreau's Lumière. Georgia Rev, 1977, 31:237-242.

14,013. Haskell, Molly. From Reverence to Rape: The Treatment
         of Women in the Movies. NY: Holt, Rinehart & Win-
         ston, 1974.

14,014. _____. Kesey cured: Forman's sweet insanity. In
         Peary, G., & Shatzkin, R. (eds), The Modern American
         Novel and the Movies. NY: Ungar, 1979, 266-271.

14,015. Hatfield, H. S. The talkie and its creators: a study in the
         psychology of invention. Psyche, 1929, 37:78-81.

14,016. Hegarty, J. F. Film and the Concept of a Medium: A
         Framework for Media Research and an Examination of
         Some Cultural and Psychological Correlates of Perceived
         Film Content. Doctoral dissertation, Univ. London In-
         stitute of Education, 1976.

14,017. Heisler, G. H. The effects of vicariously experiencing
         supernatural-violent events: a case study of The Exor-
         cist's impact. J Individual Psychol, 1975, 31:158-170.

14,018. Henderson, Brian. Metz: Essais I and film theory. Film
         Q, 1975, 28(3).

14,019. _____. Two types of film theory. Film Q, 1971, 24(3):
         33-42; In Nichols, B. (ed), Movies and Methods; Anthol-
         ogy. Berkeley: Univ. California Press, 1976, 388-400.

14,020. Henson, Donald E., & Rubin, H. B. Voluntary control of
         eroticism. J Applied Behavior Analysis, 1971, 4:37-44.

14,021. Herman, David. Federico Fellini. Amer Imago, 1969,
         26:251-268.

14,022. Heuyer, G., & Lebovici, S. Troubles due caractère et
         cinéma. Psyché, 1947, 2:1106-1108.

14,023. Hildebrand, H. P. 'We rob banks. ' Mental Health, 1967,
         26(4):15-17.

14,024. Hill, Derek. The face of horror. Sight & Sound, 1958-
         59, 28:6-11.

14,025. Hilleret, Maurice I. Sur le sadomachisme au cinéma.
         Hygiène Mentale, 1952, 41:6071.

14,026. Hoch, D. G. Mythic patterns in 2001: A Space Odyssey.
         J Popular Culture, 1971, 4:961-965.

14,027. Hoffmann, Frank A. Prolegomena to the study of tradi-
         tional elements in the erotic. J Amer Folklore, 1965,
         78:143-148.

14,028. Holbrook, David. Pseudo-liberators. Times Educational
         Supplement, 21 Dec 1973, 3056:11; Reply: R. Wood, 11
         Jan 1974, 3059:23.

14,029. Holland, Norman N. Aristotle for film-makers. Films in
         Review, 1958, 9:324-328.

14,030. _____. Bergman springs again. Hudson Rev, 1961, 14:
         104-111.

14,031. _____. Fellini's $8\frac{1}{2}$; Holland's '11. ' Hudson Rev, 1963,
         16:429-436.

14,032. _____. The good bad movie. Atlantic, 1959, 203(1):90-
         91; In Greene, J. E., & Bromberg, M. (eds), World-
         Wide Essays. NY: Globe, 1963, 183-187.

14,033. _____. Psychiatry in pselluloid. Atlantic, 1959, 203(2):
         105-107.

14, 034. _____. The puzzling movies: their appeal. J Society
Cinematologists, 1963, 3:17-28; J Social Issues, 1964,
20:71-96; In Smith, R. A. (ed), Aesthetics and Criticism
in Art Education. Chicago: Rand McNally, 1966, 453-
461; In White, D. M., & Averson, R. (eds), Sight, Sound,
and Society: Motion Pictures and Television in America.
Boston: Beacon, 1968, 103-114.

14, 035. _____. The Seventh Seal: the film as iconography.
Hudson Rev, 1959, 12:266-270; In Bellone, J. (ed),
Renaissance of the Film. NY: Collier, 1970, 232-240.

14, 036. _____. 2001: a psychosocial explication. Hartford
Studies in Lit, 1969, 1:20-25.

14, 037. Horányi, Ozseb. Culture and metasemiotics in film.
Semiotica, 1975, 15:265-284.

14, 038. Howard, Rolland. Homosexuality as a vehicle for masochism symbolized in the film Fireworks. Mattachine
Rev, 1961, 7(7):6-8.

14, 039. Huss, Roy. Each Other [Film rev.]. Psychoanal Rev,
1980, 67:143-146.

14, 040. Hyman, Stanley Edgar. Prince Myshkin in Hollywood. In
The Critic's Credentials. NY: Atheneum, 1978, 102-
106.

14, 041. Hyman, T. 8½ as an anatomy of melancholy. Sight &
Sound, 1974, 43:172-175.

14, 042. Ibañez Lopez, Pilar. [The film discussion, a method of
education for leisure times: application to high school
students.] Revista del Instituto de la Juventud, 1973,
No. 46, 7-49.

14, 043. Isaacs, Neil D. Fiction into Film. Nashville: Univ.
Tennessee Press, 1970.

14, 044. Iuritski, N. [The significance of the cinema to children.]
Semia i Shkala, 1948, 7:27-28.

14, 045. Jacques, Elliott. On children's film appraisal. Documentary News Letter, 1947, Aug-Sept.

14, 046. Jaehne, Karen. Istvan Szabo: dreams of memories.
Film Q, 1978, 32:30-41.

14, 047. Jameson, Richard T. John Huston's Freud. Film Comment, 1980, 16(3):50-51.

14, 048. Jarvie, Ian Charles. Hysteria and authoritarianism in the
films of Robert Aldrich. Film Culture, 1961, 22-23:
95-111.

14, 049. Jersild, Arthur T. Radio and motion pictures. Yearbook
National Society for the Study of Education, 1939, 38:
153-173.

14, 050. Jewett, Robert, & Lawrence, John S. Mythic conformity
in the cuckoo's nest. Psychocultural Rev, 1977, 1(1):
68-76.

14, 051. Johnson, William C., Jr. Literature, film, and the evolution of consciousness. JAAC, 1979, 38:29-38.

14, 052.   Jones, Dorothy B.   Quantitative analysis of motion picture
            content.   Public Opinion Q, 1942, 6:411-428.
14, 053.   Jones, H. E.   Attendance at moving pictures as related to
            intelligence and scholarship.   Parent-Teacher, Mar
            1928.
14, 054.   _____, & Conrad, H. S.   Rural preferences in motion
            pictures.   J Social Psychol, 1930, 1:419-423.
14, 055.   Jones, V.   Influence of motion pictures on moral attitudes
            of children and the permanence of the influence.   Psy-
            chol Bulletin, 1934, 31:725-726.

14, 056.   Kael, Pauline.   Peckinpah's obsession.   In Deeper into
            Movies.   Boston: Little, Brown, 1973, 393-399; New
            Yorker, 29 Jan 1972, 80-85.
14, 057.   _____.   Varieties of paranoia.   In Deeper into Movies.
            Boston: Little, Brown, 1973.
14, 058.   Kapacinskas, Thomas J.   The Exorcist and the spiritual
            problem of modern woman.   Psychol Perspectives,
            1975, 6:176-183.
14, 059.   Katz, Harvey A.   The Effects of Previous Exposure to
            Pornographic Film, Sexual Instrumentality, and Guilt on
            Male Verbal Aggression Against Women.   DAI, 1971,
            32(1-B), 562.
14, 060.   Keen, Stuart.   The great screen clowns and the develop-
            ment of world cinema.   In Chapman, A. J., & Foot,
            H. C. (eds), It's a Funny Thing, Humor.   NY: Perga-
            mon, 1977, 71-72.
14, 061.   Keilhacker, Martin.   Le Cinéma et les réactions des en-
            fants et des adolescents.   Cahiers de Pédagogie de
            l'Université de Liège, 1955, 14:67-75.
14, 062.   _____.   Kinder-und jugendpsychologische Fragen des
            Films.   Jahrbuch für Psychologie und Psychotherapie,
            1954, 2:9-20.
14, 063.   Kepner, J.   The posthumous trial of Ramon Navarro.
            Los Angeles Advocate, 1969, 3(10):5, 20-21, 23; 1969,
            3(11):1, 3, 8; 3(12):5, 36-37.
14, 064.   Kermode, Frank.   Men, women and madness.   Times Lit
            Supplement, 19 Mar 1976, 319.
14, 065.   Kindem, Gorham A.   Toward a Semiotic Theory of Visual
            Communication in the Cinema: A Reappraisal of Semi-
            otic Theories from a Cinematic Perspective and a
            Semiotic Analysis of Color Signs and Communication in
            the Color Films of Alfred Hitchcock.   DAI, 1978,
            38(9-A), 5096-97.
14, 066.   Kinder, Marsha.   The art of dreaming in Three Women
            and Providence: structures of the self.   Film Q, 1977,
            31:10-18.
14, 067.   _____.   Carlos Saura: the political development of in-
            dividual consciousness.   Film Q, 1979, 32:14-25.
14, 068.   _____.   Reflections on Jeanne Dielman.   Film Q, 1977,
            30:2-8.

14,069. _____, & Houston, Beverle. Self and Cinema. A Transformalist Perspective. Pleasantville, NY: Redgrave, 1980.

14,070. Kleitman, N. The effect of motion pictures on body temperatures. Science, 1945, 101:507-508; 1946, 102:259, 430.

14,071. Kline, T. Jefferson. Father as mirror: Bertolucci's oedipal quest and the collapse of paternity. Psychocultural Rev, 1979, 3:91-109.

14,072. _____. Orpheus transcending: Bertolucci's Last Tango in Paris. Int Rev Psycho-Anal, 1976, 3:85-95.

14,073. Kolker, Robert Phillip. The open texts of Nicolas Roeg. Sight & Sound, 1977, 46:82-84+.

14,074. _____. Orange, dogs, and ultra-violence. J Popular Film, 1972, 1:159-172.

14,075. _____, & Ousley, J. Douglas. A phenomenology of cinematic space and time. British J Aesthetics, 1973, 13:388-396.

14,076. Koriat, Asher, et al. Self-control of emotional reactions to a stressful film. J Personality, 1972, 40:601-619.

14,077. Kracauer, Siegfried. From Caligari to Hitler; A Psychological History of the German Film. Princeton: Princeton Univ. Press, 1947; Excerpts in Solomon, S. J. (ed), The Classic Cinema; Essays in Criticism. NY: Harcourt Brace Jovanovich, 1973, 43-50, 133-136. Excerpts in Talbot, D. (ed), Film: An Anthology. NY: Simon & Schuster, 1959, 449-464.

14,078. _____. Hollywood's terror films: do they reflect an American state of mind? Commentary, 1946, 2:132-134.

14,079. _____. National types as Hollywood presents them. Public Opinion Q, 1949, 13:53-72.

14,080. _____. Theory of Film. The Redemption of Physical Reality. NY: Oxford Univ. Press, 1960.

14,081. Kubie, Lawrence S. Psychiatry and the films. Hollywood Q, 1947, 2:113-117.

14,082. Lalande, Jean-Pierre. Expression de l'irrationel: Antonin Artaud, tentatives cinematographique et théâtrale. DAI, 1978, 39:3620A-21A.

14,083. Lamblin, B. Esthétique: Fonction du cinema: La poétique de l'espace. Bulletin de Psychologie, 1965, 18(21/243):1249-1257.

14,084. Landry, L. La Psychologie du cinéma. J de Psychologie, 1927, 24:134-145.

14,085. Lansbury, Coral. A cry from Bergman--a whisper of Dickens. Meanjin Q, 1973, 32:323-327.

14,086. Lanz-Stuparich, Maria. Les Adolescents et le cinéma. In Baumgarten, F. (ed), La Psychotechnique dans le monde moderne. Paris: Presses Universitaires de France, 1952, 557-561.

14,087. Last, F. W. A psychological note on a photo-play. J Abnormal Psychol, 1916, 11:344-346.

14,088.   Lawson, John H.   Film: The Creative Process.   NY: Hill & Wang, 1967.

14,089.   Lazarsfeld, Paul.   Audience research in the movie field. Annals Amer Academy Politics & Social Sciences, 1947, 254:160-168.

14,090.   Leab, Daniel J.   From Sambo to Superspade: The Black Experience in Motion Pictures.   London: Secker & Warburg, 1975.

14,091.   Lechat, Fernand.   Un film sur 'L'Enfance delinquante.' Rev Français de Psychanalyse, 1949, 13:144-148.

14,092.   Lederman, Marie Jean.   In the Realm of the Senses: a feminist perspective.   Psychocultural Rev, 1979, 3(2): 141-151.

14,093.   Leed, Jacob.   Dream--sleep and film.   Filmmakers Newsletter, 1970, 3:4-6.

14,094.   Lehman, H. C., & Witty, Paul.   The compensatory function of the movies.   J Applied Psychol, 1927, 11:33-41.

14,095.   Leites, Nathan, & Wolfenstein, Martha.   Movies: A Psychological Study.   Glencoe: Free Press, 1950.

14,096.   Lenes, Mark S., & Hart, Edward J.   The influence of pornography and violence on attitudes and guilt.   J School Health, 1975, 45:447-451.

14,097.   Leonard, N.   Theodore Dreiser and the film.   Film Heritage, 1966, 2:7-16.

14,098.   LeRoy, E.   L'Enfant et le cinéma d'aujourd'hui.   Rev Int de l'enfant, 1928, 8:704-715.

14,099.   Lesser, Simon D.   L'Avventura: a closer look.   Yale Rev, 1964, 54:41-50.

14,100.   Leventhal, Howard, & Mace, William.   The effect of laughter on evaluation of a slapstick movie.   J Personality, 1970, 38:16-30.

14,101.   Liber, B.   Minds and movies.   Medical Record, 1947, 160:238-239.

14,102.   Lichtenberg, Philip.   A Content Analysis of American Motion Pictures with Special Respect to Four Classes of Characteristics.   Doctoral dissertation, Western Reserve Univ., 1952.

14,103.   Lima, Luis Ronaldo.   Uma sociedade suicida.   Tempo Brasileiro: Revista de Cultura, 1978, 52:53-57.

14,104.   Lodge, David.   Thomas Hardy as a cinematic novelist.   In Butler, L. S. (ed), Thomas Hardy After Fifty Years. Totowa, NJ: Rowman & Littlefield, 1977, 78-89.

14,105.   Lövass, O. Ivar.   The effect of exposure to symbolic aggression on aggressive behavior.   Child Development, 1961, 32:37-44.

14,106.   Low, Barbara.   The cinema in education: some psychoanalytical considerations.   Contemporary Rev, 1925, 128:628-635.

14,107.   Lynch, F. Dennis.   Clozentropy: a new technique for analyzing audience response to film.   Speech Monographs, 1974, 41:245-252.

14,108.   Lyotard, Jean-François.   The unconscious as mise-en-scène.   In Benamou, M., & Caramello, C. (eds),

Performance in Postmodern Culture. Madison: Coda, 1977, 87-98.

14, 109. MacBean, James Roy. Sex and politics: Wilhelm Reich, world revolution, and Makavejev's WR. Film Q, 1972, 25(3):2-13.

14, 110. Maccoby, Eleanor E. , Wilson, William C. , & Burton, Roger V. Differential movie-viewing behavior of male and female viewers. J Personality, 1958, 26:259-267.

14, 111. McKintyre, Charles J. Sex, Age and Iconicity as Factors Influencing Projection on to Motion Picture Protagonists. DA, 1952-54, 16:565-570.

14, 112. Magny, Claude-Edmonde. The Age of the American Novel: The Film Aesthetic of Fiction Between the Two Wars. NY: Ungar, 1972 (1948).

14, 113. Makhdum, W. M. Some effects of the cinema situation on character. Indian J Psychol, 1938, 13:176-177.

14, 114. Malmquist, Carl P. , & Meehl, Paul E. Barabbas: a study in guilt-ridden homicide. Int Rev Psycho-Anal, 1978, 5:149-174.

14, 115. Malraux, André. Esquisse d'une psychologie du cinéma. Paris: Gallimard, 1946.

14, 116. _____. Esquisse d'une psychologie du cinéma-fragments. Formes et couleurs, 1946, 6.

14, 117. Manley, James C. Artist and audience, vampire and victim: the oral matrix of imagery in Bergman's Persona. Psychocultural Rev, 1979, 3:117-139.

14, 118. Mann, Jay, et al. Evaluating social consequences of erotic films: an experimental approach. J Social Issues, 1973, 29:113-131.

14, 119. _____. Satiation and the transient stimulus effect of erotic films. J Personality & Social Psychol, 1974, 30:729-735.

14, 120. Manvell, Roger. Psychological intensity in The Passion of Joan of Arc; excerpt from The Film and the Public. In Solomon, S. J. (ed), The Classic Cinema. NY: Harcourt Brace Jovanovich, 1973, 112-114.

14, 121. Marshall, H. Andrei Tarkovsky's The Mirror. Sight & Sound, 1976, 45:92-95.

14, 122. Mason, John Lenard. The Identity Crisis Theme in American Feature Films, 1960-1969. Doctoral dissertation, Ohio State Univ. , 1973.

14, 123. Mast, Gerald. The Comic Mind. Chicago: Univ. Chicago Press, 1979.

14, 124. _____, & Cohen, Marshall (eds). Film Theory and Criticism. Introductory Readings. NY: Oxford Univ. Press, 1979.

14, 125. Masters, William E. , & Johnson, Virginia E. Can you learn about sex from movies? Redbook, 1975, 144:68+.

14, 126. Mata, L. La ácción del cinematografo en la afectividad infantil. Archivio argentinos de Psicologia normal y Patologica, 1933-34, 1:90-91.

14,127.   Matusa, P.   Corruption and catastrophe: DePalma's
          Carrie.   Film Q, 1977, 31:32-38.
14,128.   Mellen, Joan.   Big Bad Wolves: Masculinity in the Amer-
          ican Film.   NY: Pantheon, 1977; Review: G. S. Jow-
          ett, J Amer History, 1979, 65:1200-1201.
14,129.   _____.   The moral psychology of Rohmer's tales.
          Cinema, 1971, 7:16-22.
14,130.   _____.   Sexual politics and Last Tango in Paris.   Film
          Q, 1973, 26(3):9-19.
14,131.   _____.   Women and Their Sexuality in the New Film.
          London: Davis-Poynter, 1974; NY: Horizon, 1974; NY:
          Dell, 1975.
14,132.   _____.   WR: Mysteries of the Organism.   Cineaste,
          1971-72, 5:18-21.
14,133.   Merleau-Ponty, Maurice.   The film and the new psychol-
          ogy.   Les Temps Modernes, Nov 1947, no. 26; In
          Sense and Nonsense.   Evanston, Ill: Northwestern Univ.
          Press, 1964, 48-59.
14,134.   _____.   Psychologie du cinéma.   In Sens et Non-Sens.
          Paris: Nagel, 1948.
14,135.   Metz, Christian.   Current problems of film theory: Mit-
          ry's L'Esthetique et psychologie du cinéma, Vol. II.
          In Nichols, B. (ed), Movies and Methods.   Berkeley:
          Univ. California Press, 1976, 568-578; Screen, 1973,
          14(1-2):70-81.
14,136.   _____.   Esthétique et psychologie du cinéma.   Critique,
          1965.
14,137.   _____.   Fiction film and its spectator: a metapsycho-
          logical study.   New Lit History, 1976, 8:75-105.
14,138.   _____.   Le Film de fiction et son spectateur (étude
          metapsychologique).   In Psychanalyse et cinéma.
          Paris: Seuil, 1975, 108-135.
14,139.   _____.   The imaginary signifier.   Screen, 1975, 16(2):
          14-76.
14,140.   Metzger, W.   Kind und Films.   Psychologische Praxis,
          1952, 11:18-32.
14,141.   Meyer, Timothy P.   The effects of sexually arousing and
          violent films on aggressive behavior.   J Sex Research,
          1972, 8:324-331.
14,142.   Meylau, L.   Le Film, moyen de culture.   Cahiers de
          Pedagogie de l'Universite de Liège, 1956, 15:1-11.
14,143.   Millan, Alfonso.   The use of reports of movie stories as
          a means of studying personalities during psychoanalytic
          treatment.   Psychiatric Research Reports, 1955, 2:15-
          23.
14,144.   Miller, Milton L.   The Pinter screenplay of Proust's
          Remembrance of Things Past.   Psychiat Forum, 1978,
          7(2):2-4.
14,145.   Milne, Tom.   Chabrol's schizophrenic spider.   Sight &
          Sound, 1970, 39:58-62.
14,146.   Mitchell, A. M.   Children and Movies.   Chicago: Univ.
          Chicago Press, 1929.
14,147.   _____.   The movies children like.   Survey, 1929, 63:
          213-216.

14,148. Mitry, Jean. Esthétique et psychologie du cinéma, Vols. 1&2. Paris: Editions Universitaires, 1963, 1965.

14,149. Moellenhoff, Fritz. Remarks on the popularity of Mickey Mouse. Amer Imago, 1940, 1:19-32.

14,150. Monaco, Paul. Cinema and Society: France and Germany During the Twenties. Oxford: Elsevier, 1976.

14,151. _____. The popular cinema as reflection of the group process in France, 1919-1929. History Childhood Q: J Psychohistory, 1974, 1:607-636.

14,152. Montani, Angelo, & Pietranera, Giulio. First contribution to the psychoanalysis and aesthetics of motion pictures. Psychoanal Rev, 1946, 33:177-196.

14,153. _____. [Psychoanalysis of the pure movie.] Psicoanalisi, 1946, 2:41-64.

14,154. Morin, Edgar. The Stars. NY: Grove, 1960.

14,155. Mosher, Donald L. Sex differences, sex experiences, sex guilt, and explicitly sexual films. J Social Issues, 1973, 29:95-112.

14,156. Mukarovský, Jan. An attempt at a structural analysis of a dramatic figure. In Structure, Sign, and Function. New Haven: Yale Univ. Press, 1978, 171-177.

14,157. Mukerjee, Adhir. The role of 'attention' in the motion picture. Indian J Psychol, 1953, 28:59-61.

14,158. Munsterberg, Hugo. The Film: A Psychological Study. The Silent Photoplay in 1916. NY: Dover, 1970 (1916).

14,159. _____. The Photoplay: A Psychological Study. NY: Arno, 1970 (1916).

14,160. Murray, Edward. The Cinematic Imagination: Writers and the Motion Pictures. NY: Ungar, 1972.

14,161. _____. Nine American Film Critics; A Study of Theory and Practice. NY: Ungar, 1975.

14,162. Mussatti, Cesare L. Cinema e sesso. Rivista di Psicoanalisi, 1961, 7:27-37.

14,163. Newman, Kenneth. Movies in the Seventies: some heroic types. In The Annual of Psychoanalysis, Vol. 6/1978. NY: IUP, 1979.

14,164. Nichols, Bill (ed). Movies and Methods; Anthology. Berkeley: Univ. California Press, 1976.

14,165. Nin, Anaïs. Poetics of the film. Film Culture, 1963-64, 31:12-14.

14,166. Nohl, Herman. Jugendschutz und Filmkontrolle. Sammlung, 1952, 7:165-168.

14,167. Nowell-Smith, Geoffrey. Movie and myth. Sight & Sound, 1963, 32(2):60-64.

14,168. Nudel'man, M. M. [On the relationship between images actualized by verbal description and motion pictures.] Voprosy Psikhologii, 1975, No. 4, 118-123.

14,169. Ophuijsen, J. H. W. Van. Het cabinet van Dr. Caligari. Over dood, ziel en gear. Heraldik en anale erotik.

Nederlandsch Tydschrift voor Geneeskunde, 1952, 2:
2177-2178.

14,170. Orton, W. A.   Motion pictures.   Social implications.   Encyclopedia Social Sciences, 1933, 11:65-69.

14,171. O'Toole, Lawrence.   The great ecstasy of filmmaker Herzog.   Film Comment, 1979, 15:34-39.

14,172. Panda, K. C., Das, J. K., & Kanungo, R. N.   A cross-cultural study on film preference on an Indian student
population.   J Social Psychol, 1962, 57:93-104.

14,173. _____, & Kanungo, R. N.   A study of Indian students'
attitudes towards motion pictures.   J Social Psychol,
1962, 57:23-31.

14,174. Panofsky, Erwin.   Style and medium in the motion pictures.   Critique, 1947, 1:5-28; In Denby, D. (ed),
Awake in the Dark.   NY: Random House, 1977, 30-48.

14,175. Paroissien, David H.   Dickens and the cinema.   Dickens
Studies Annual, 1978, 7:68-80.

14,176. _____.   The Life and Adventures of Nicholas Nickleby:
Alberto Cavalcanti interprets Dickens.   Hartford Studies
in Lit, 1977, 9:17-28.

14,177. Patel, A. S.   Attitudes of adolescent pupils toward cinema
films: a study.   J Education & Psychol (Baroda), 1952,
9:225-230.

14,178. Pennacchi, F.   Cinemo e adolescenza con speciale rap-
porto alle mallattie nervose e mentali.   Reviste l'Institut du cinéma Education, 1930, 2:1084-1113.

14,179. Peppard, S. Harcourt.   Children's fears and phantasies,
and the movies, radio and comics.   Child Study, 1942,
19:78-79.

14,180. Perlmutter, Ruth.   Beckett's film and Beckett and the
film.   J Modern Lit, 1977, 6:83-94.

14,181. _____.   Cinema of the grotesque.   Georgia Rev, 1979,
33:168-193.

14,182. Perry, David G., et al.   Demand awareness and participant
willingness as determinants of aggressive response to
film violence.   J Social Psychol, 1978, 105:265-275.

14,183. Perry, Ted.   The seventh art as sixth sense.   Educational
Theatre J, 1969, 21:28-35.

14,184. Peterson, R. C., & Thurstone, L. L.   The effect of a motion picture film on children's attitudes towards Germans.   J Educational Psychol, 1932, 23:241-246.

14,185. _____.   The Effect of Motion Pictures on the Social Attitudes of High School Children.   Chicago: Univ. Chicago Bookstore, 1933.

14,186. _____.   Motion Pictures and the Social Attitudes of
Children.   NY: Macmillan, 1933.

14,187. Petrie, G.   Dickens, Godard, and the film today.   Yale
Rev, 1975, 64:185-201.

14,188. Phillippon, O.   L'Influence du cinéma sur l'enfance et
l'adolescence, l'ênquete national française.   Nouvelle
Rev Pédagogique, 1952, 7:526-530.

14, 189. Phillips, Gene. The boys on the bandwagon. Take One,
          1968, 2(8):6-8.
14, 190. Piazza, François. Considération sur le Chien Andalou de
          Luis Bunuel et Salvador Dali. Psyché, 1949, 4:147-156.
14, 191. Pinschewer, Julius. Observations psychologiques sur le
          dessin animé publicitaire. In Baumgarten, F. (ed),
          La Psychotechnique dans le monde moderne. Paris:
          Presses Universitaires de France, 1952, 566-567.
14, 192. Plank, Robert. Sons and fathers, A. D. 2001. Hartford
          Studies in Lit, 1969, 1:26-33; In Clarke, A. C., Oland-
          er, J. D., & Greenberg, M. H. (eds), Tomorrow, Inc.
          NY: Taplinger, 1977, 121-149.
14, 193. Poague, Leland A. The problem of film genre: a men-
          talistic approach. Lit/Film Q, 1978, 6:152-161.
14, 194. Poffenberger, A. T. Motion pictures and crime. Scientific
          Monthly, 1921, 12:336-339.
14, 195. Ponzo, Mario. Il cinema e le imagini colletive. Archivio
          di Psicologia, Neurologia y Psichiatria, 1949, 10:389-
          405.
14, 196. Porfirio, R. G. No way out; existential motifs in the film
          noir. Sight & Sound, 1976, 45:212-217.
14, 197. Pornon, Charles. Le Rêve et le fantastique dans le ciné-
          ma français. Paris: La Nef de Paris-Editions, 1959.
14, 198. Pratt, John. Notes on commercial movie techniques.
          Int J Psycho-Anal, 1943, 24:185-188.
14, 199. Prawer, S. S. Caligari's Children. The Film As Tale of
          Horror. NY: Oxford Univ. Press, 1980.
14, 200. Preston, M. D. Children's reactions to movie horrors and
          radio crime. J Pediatrics, 1941, 19:147-168.
14, 201. Progoff, Ira. Waking dream and living myth. In Camp-
          bell, J. (ed), Myths, Dreams, and Religion. NY:
          Dutton, 1970, 176-195.
14, 202. Purcell, J. M. Tarkovsky's film Solaris (1972) a Freudian
          slip? Extrapolation, 1978, 19:126-131.
14, 203. Purdy, Strother B. [On the film.] In Katchadourian, H.
          A., & Lunde, D. T. (eds), Fundamentals of Human
          Sexuality. NY: Holt, Rinehart & Winston, 1975.

14, 204. Querido, A., et al. Psychologische bijdragen tot de film-
          problematiek. Nederlandsch Tÿdschrift voor de Psy-
          chologie, 1953, 8:6-200.
14, 205. Quigley, I. The glory and the dream: myths of the cine-
          ma. Encounter, 1975, 44:76-82.

14, 206. Rabkin, Leslie Y. The celluloid couch: psychiatrists in
          American films. Psychocultural Rev, 1979, 3:73-90.
14, 207. _____. The movies' first psychiatrist. Amer J Psy-
          chiat, 1967, 124:545-547.
14, 208. Racker, Enrique. La ventana indiscreta: Glosas psico-
          analiticas sobre una película. Revista de Psicoaná-
          lisis, 1956, 13:58-65.

14, 209. Raleigh, Henry P. Film: the revival of aesthetic symbolism. JAAC, 1973, 32:219-228.

14, 210. Ramsaye, Terry. The rise and place of the motion picture. In Schramm, W. (ed), Mass Communications.
Urbana: Univ. Illinois Press, 1960.

14, 211. Rappaport, Ernest A. From the keystone of comedy to the
last of the clowns. Psychoanal Rev, 1972, 59:333-345.

14, 212. Read, Herbert. A Coat of Many Colours. NY: Horizon,
1956.

14, 213. _____. Towards a film aesthetic. Cinema Q, 1933,
1:197-202.

14, 214. Reik, Theodor. In my mind's eye. In The Secret Self.
NY: Grove, 1960, 17-32.

14, 215. Reynolds, W. A history of homosexuality in the movies.
Drum, 1967, 27:12-21, 30-32.

14, 216. Rice, Julian C. The medium as message in Bergman's
Persona. Hartford Studies in Lit, 1977, 9:29-44.

14, 217. Richardson, Robert Dale. Literature and Film. Bloomington: Indiana Univ. Press, 1969.

14, 218. Riesman, David. The oral tradition, the written word,
and the screen. Film Culture, 1956, 2(3):1-5.

14, 219. Riesman, Evelyn. Film and fiction. Antioch Rev, 1957,
17:353-363.

14, 220. Robinson, David. Violence. Sight & Sound, 1977, 46:74-
77.

14, 221. Rogers, Robert. The psychology of the 'double' in 2001.
Hartford Studies in Lit, 1969, 1:34-36.

14, 222. Rose, Nicholas. A Psychological Study of Motion Picture
Audience Behavior. Doctoral dissertation, Univ. California, 1951.

14, 223. Rosen, Irwin C. The effect of the motion picture Gentleman's Agreement on attitudes toward Jews. J Psychol,
1948, 26:525-536.

14, 224. Rosen, Robert. Enslaved by the queen of the night: the
relationship of Ingmar Bergman to E. T. A. Hoffmann.
Film Comment, 1970, 6:26-31.

14, 225. Rosenberg, Milton J. Mr. Magoo as public dream. Q
Radio, Film, Television, 1957, 11:337-342.

14, 226. Rosenman, Martin F. Dogmatism and the movie Dr.
Strangelove. Psychol Reports, 1967, 20(3, Pt. 1),
942.

14, 227. Rosten, Leo. The intellectual and the mass media: some
rigorously random remarks. Daedalus, 1960, 89:333-
346.

14, 228. Roud, R. The redemption of despair. Film Comment,
1977, 13:23-24.

14, 229. Rubbo, Michael. Love and life in children's films. Take
One, 1967, 1(7):20-22.

14, 230. Rubenstein, Mark. King Kong: a myth for moderns.
Amer Imago, 1977, 34:1-11.

14, 231. Ruhe, Edward. Film: the 'literary' approach. Lit-Film
Q, 1973, 1:76-83.

14, 232. Sachs, David M. Media and perception in the aesthetics and psychology of movies: their relationship to psycho-analysis. Bulletin Philadelphia Assn Psychoanal, 1968, 18:172-194.

14, 233. Sachs, Hanns. Secrets of a Soul: a psychoanalytic film. Berlin: Lichtbild-Buhne, 1926.

14, 234. _____. Zur Psychologie des Films. Psychoanalytische Bewegung, 1929, 1:122-127.

14, 235. Salachas, Gilbert. Federico Fellini. Paris: Seghers, 1963.

14, 236. Salber, Wilhelm. Film und Sexualität: Untersuchungen zur Filmpsychologie. Bonn: Bouvier, 1970.

14, 237. Samuels, Charles Thomas. A Casebook on Film. NY: Van Nostrand Reinhold, 1970.

14, 238. _____. Doing violence. Amer Scholar, 1971, 40:695-700.

14, 239. _____. Mastering the Film, and Other Essays. Edited by L. Graver. Nashville: Univ. Tennessee Press, 1977.

14, 240. Sarris, Andrew. Aesthete at the movies. Commentary, 1971, 51:81-84.

14, 241. _____. The American cinema. Film Culture, 1963, 28:3-6.

14, 242. _____. The Primal Screen; Essays on Film and Related Subjects. NY: Simon & Schuster, 1973.

14, 243. _____, Stoller, James, & Greenspun, Roger. Symposium on 'cinematic style.' Film Culture, 1966, 42:89-96.

14, 244. Schaxel, Hedwig. Der Weg ins Leben. Psychoanalytische Bemerkungen zu einem russischen Film. Zeitschrift für psychoanalytische Pädagogik, 1932, 6:40-43.

14, 245. Schillaci, Anthony. Film as environment. Saturday Rev, 26 Dec 1968; In Handy, W.J., & Westbrook, M. (eds), Twentieth Century Criticism. NY: Free Press, 1974, 474-483.

14, 246. Schneider, Irving. Images of the mind: psychiatry in the commercial film. Amer J Psychiat, 1977, 134:613-620.

14, 247. _____. The psychiatric film: art, science and voyeurism. Rev Existential Psychol & Psychiat, 1966, 6:128-142.

14, 248. Schrader, Paul. Budd Boetticher: a case study in criticism. Cinema, 1970, 6(2):22-29.

14, 249. Schreiber, S. A filmed fairy tale as a screen memory. In The Psychoanalytic Study of the Child, Vol. 29. New Haven: Yale Univ. Press, 1974, 389-410.

14, 250. Schwartz, Hans J., Eckert, Jochen, & Bastine, Reiner. Die Wirkung eines aggressiven Films auf Jugendliche unter variierten äusseren Bedingungen. Zeitschrift für Entwicklungspsychologie und Pädagogische Psychologie, 1971, 3:304-315.

14, 251. Scott, E.W. Personality and movie preference. Psychol Reports, 1957, 3:17-18.

14, 252. Scott, James F.   The achievement of Ingmar Bergman.
          JAAC, 1965, 24:263-272.
14, 253. Seagoe, M. V.   The child's reaction to the movies.   J
          Juvenile Research, 1931, 15:169-180.
14, 254. Seibert, W. F., & Snow, R. E.   Cine-psychometry.   AV
          Communication Rev, 1965, 13:140-158.
14, 255. Semkow, J.   Three films on human sexuality.   Film Li-
          brary Q, 1975, 8(3):44-45.
14, 256. Shaffer, Lawrence.   Night for day, film for life.   Film Q,
          1974, 28:2-8.
14, 257. _____.   The Other.   Film Heritage, 1972-73, 8(2):13-
          18.
14, 258. _____.   Reflections on the face in film.   Film Q, 1977-
          78, 31:2-8.
14, 259. Shanks, John Arthur.   One Flew Over the Cuckoo's Nest.
          J Contemporary Psychotherapy, 1976, 8:78-79.
14, 260. Shannon, W. V.   The Godfather.   New York Times, 1 Aug
          1972, p. 33.
14, 261. Shatzkin, R.   Disaster epics: cashing in on vicarious ex-
          perience.   Society, 1975, 13:77-79.
14, 262. Sheehy, T.   Celebration: four films by James Broughton.
          Film Q, 1976, 29:2-14.
14, 263. Sicker, Albert.   [Children and motion pictures.   The in-
          fluence of films on the child's mental life.]   Schweiz-
          erischen Zeitschrift für Psychologie, 1956, No. 28,
          143 p.
14, 264. Siebanand, Paul Alciun.   The Beginnings of Gay Cinema in
          Los Angeles: The Industry and the Audience.   Doctoral
          dissertation, Univ. Southern California, 1975.
14, 265. Siegman, Aron W., & Dintzer, Leonard.   The catharsis
          of aggression and hostility.   Psychol Reports, 1977,
          41:399-410.
14, 266. Silverstein, Norman.   Movie-going for lovers of The Waste
          Land and Ulysses.   Salmagundi, 1965, 1(1):37-55.
14, 267. Skinner, John.   Censorship in films and dreams.   Amer
          Imago, 1955, 12:223-240.
14, 268. Slover, George.   Film: Blow Up: medium, message,
          mythos and make-believe.   Massachusetts Rev, 1968,
          753-770.
14, 269. Sokolov, I.   [An Analysis of the Cinema Artist.]   Moscow:
          Teakinopeihat, 1929.
14, 270. Solmi, Angelo.   Fellini.   London: Merlin, 1967.
14, 271. Solomon, Stanley J.   The Classic Cinema; Essays in Criti-
          cism.   NY: Harcourt Brace Jovanovich, 1973.
14, 272. Sontag, Susan.   Against interpretation.   Evergreen Rev,
          1964, 34:76-80.
14, 273. _____.   Film and theatre.   Tulane Drama Rev, 1966,
          11:24-37.
14, 274. Sparshott, F. E.   Basic film aesthetics.   J Aesthetic Edu-
          cation, 1971, 5(2):12-34.
14, 275. Spiegel, Alan.   Fiction and the Camera Eye: Visual Con-
          sciousness in Film and the Modern Novel.   Charlottes-
          ville: Univ. Virginia Press, 1977.

14, 276. Spiegelman, Joseph M. Ambiguity and Personality in the Perception of a Motion Picture. Doctoral dissertation, Univ. California at Los Angeles, 1952.

14, 277. Spoto, Donald M. Vertigo: the cure is worse than the dis-ease. In Solomon, S. J. (ed), The Classic Cinema. NY: Harcourt Brace Jovanovich, 1973, 266-271.

14, 278. Stacy, Paul H. Cinematic thought (commentary on 2001). Hartford Studies in Lit, 1969, 1:124-130.

14, 279. Steele, Robert. Report on a study of light variables measured as a function of time in the cinema. J Society Cinematologists, 1964, 4:37-54.

14, 280. Steene, Birgitta. Archetypal patterns in four Ingmar Bergman plays. Scandinavian Studies, 1965, 37:58-76.

14, 281. _____. Bergman's movement toward nihilism: the antiheroic stand in Secrets of Women, Brink of Life, The Seventh Seal, and the Chamber Film trilogy. In Weinstock, J. M., & Rovinsky, R. T. (eds), The Hero in Scandinavian Literature; From Peer Gynt to the Present. Austin: Univ. Texas Press, 1975, 87-105.

14, 282. _____. The isolated hero of Ingmar Bergman. Film Comment, 1965, 3:68-78.

14, 283. Stewart, G. Exhumed identity: Antonioni's Passenger to Nowhere. Sight & Sound, 1975-76, 45:36-40.

14, 284. Stoddard, G. D. What motion pictures mean to the child. Child Welfare Pamphlets No. 31. Bulletin State Univ. Iowa, 1933, No. 713.

14, 285. Sturdza, Paltin. The rebirth archetype in Robbe-Grillet's L'Immortelle. French Rev, 1975, 48:990-995.

14, 286. Stutz, Jonathan. Sex and character in Klute. Velvet Light Trap, 1972, 6:36-38.

14, 287. Sukharebsky, L. M. Group psychotherapy and the movies. In Winn, Ralph B. (ed), Psychotherapy in the Soviet Union. NY: Philosophical Library, 1961.

14, 288. Suner, August P. The third dimension in the projection of motion pictures. Amer J Psychol, 1947, 60:116-118.

14, 289. Sutermeister, H. Film und Psychohygiene. Gesundheit und Wohlfahrt, 1950, 30:249-278.

14, 290. Sutherland, Allan T. Setting up of Nighthawks. Sight & Sound, 1978-79, 48:50-52.

14, 291. Sutton, Robert, MacBean, James R., & Callenbach, Ernest. Flight power with spontaneity and humor: an interview with Dusan Makaveyev. Film Q, 1971-72, 25(2):3-9.

14, 292. Sward, Keith. Boy and girl meet neurosis. Screen Writer, 1948, 4:8-10, 24-26.

14, 293. Takase, Y. [A Study on cultural effect of moving pictures.] Japanese J Experimental Psychol, 1935, 2:251-262.

14, 294. Takenaka, T. [The cinema as an amusement of school girls.] Kyōiku Shinei Kenkyū, 1940, 15:106-129.

14, 295. Tanner, Tony. Wonder and alienation--the mystic and the moviegoer. In The Reign of Wonder; Naivety and Reality in American Literature. NY: Cambridge Univ. Press, 1965, 336-361.

14, 296. Tarantino, Michael. Tanner and Berger: the voice off-screen. Film Q, 1979, 33:32-43.

14, 297. Tarratt, Margaret. Monsters from the id. Films & Filming, 1970, 17(3):38-42.

14, 298. Taylor, Anne Robinson. The virginal male as hero in American films. Southwest Rev, 1978, 63:317-329.

14, 299. Taylor, John Russell. Cinema Eye, Cinema Ear. London: Methuen, 1964.

14, 300. Tennenbaum, E. [The role of the cinema in children's interests.] Polskie Archivium Psychologii, 1933-34, 6: 163-168.

14, 301. Thorp, M. America at the Movies. New Haven: Yale Univ. Press, 1939.

14, 302. Thurstone, L. L. Influence of motion pictures on children's attitudes. J Social Psychol, 1931, 2:291-305.

14, 303. _____. A scale of measuring attitudes toward the movies. J Educational Research, 1930, 22:93-94.

14, 304. Townsend, (?). The cinema and the child. Rev Int de l'enfant, 1929, 8:698-703.

14, 305. Trimmer, Joseph F. The Virginian: novel and films. Illinois Q, 1972, 35(2):5-18.

14, 306. Tuch, Roland. Frederick Wiseman's cinema of alienation. Film Library Q, 1978, 11(3):9-15+.

14, 307. Tyler, Parker. Screening the Sexes. Homosexuality in the Movies. NY: Holt, Rinehart & Winston.

14, 308. _____. Schizophrenic motifs in the movies: the comedic use of the retarded mental reflex. Sewanee Rev, 1946, 54:489-503.

14, 309. Ulitzsch, Ernst. Die Erotik im Film. Zeitschrift für Sexualwissenschaft, 1917, 3:431-438.

14, 310. Undank, Jack. The violence of signs. Louis Buñuel and Salvador Dali's Un Chien andalou, 1928. French Rev, 1977, 50:486-487.

14, 311. Van Wert, William F. The cinema of Marguerite Duras: sound and voice in a closed room. Film Q, 1979, 33: 22-29.

14, 312. Various. Film. [Entire issue.] Hartford Studies in Lit, 1977, 9(1).

14, 313. _____. Psychanalyse et Cinéma. Communications, 1975, 23.

14, 314. _____. [Psychanalyse et cinéma.] Communications, [Numéro spécial] 1975, no. 23.

14, 315. _____. The psychohistory of the cinema: a symposium. J Psychohistory, 1978, 5:487-508.

14, 316. Varlejs, Jana. Cine-opsis; films about mental illness. Wilson Library Bulletin, 1980, 54:328-329.

14, 317. Vaughan, D. Berlin versus Tokyo. Sight & Sound, 1977, 46:210-215.

14, 318. Vincenzo, Joe, Hendrick, Clyde, & Murray, Edward J. The relationship between religious beliefs and attending the fear-provoking religiously oriented movie: The Exorcist. Omega: J Death & Dying, 1976, 7:137-143.

14, 319. Wagenheim, Allan J. On the necessity for Hollywood. North Amer Rev, 1966, 3:28-29.

14, 320. Walker, A. Beyond the excremental cinema. Encounter, 1974, 42:47-52.

14, 321. Walker, B. The cuckoo's nest. Sight & Sound, 1975, 44: 216-217.

14, 322. Wall, W. D., & Simson, W. A. The emotional responses of adolescent groups to certain films. Part I. British J Educational Psychol, 1950, 20:153-163.

14, 323. _____. The responses of adolescent groups to certain films. Part II. British J Educational Psychol, 1951, 21:81-88.

14, 324. Warshow, Robert. The gangster as tragic hero. Partisan Rev, 1948, 15:240-244; In The Immediate Experience. Garden City, NY: Doubleday, 1962, 127-133; In Enck, J. J. (ed), Academic Discourse. NY: Appleton-Century-Crofts, 1964, 50-53; In Ross, T. J. (ed), Film and the Liberal Arts, pp. 268-273.

14, 325. _____. The Immediate Experience; Movies, Comics, Theatre and Other Aspects of Popular Culture. Garden City, NY: Doubleday, 1962.

14, 326. _____. Sadism for the masses. Partisan Rev, 1950, 17:200-202.

14, 327. Weinstein, Gene. The Apartment: Hollywood remakes its bed. Amer Q, 1962, 14:500-503.

14, 328. Wertham, Fredric. Film violence--is it necessary? Take One, 1968, 1(11):9-12.

14, 329. _____. Is so much violence in films necessary? Cine-aste, 1968, 2:4-6.

14, 330. _____. What is the effect of television and movies on sexual attitudes and behavior? MAHS, 1968, 2(3):22-23.

14, 331. Westerbeck, C. L. Beauties and the beast: Seven Beauties and Taxi Driver. Sight & Sound, 1976, 45:134-139.

14, 332. Weyl, Simon. [Charlie Chaplin and the unconscious.] Nederlandsch Tijdschrift voor Geneeskunde, 1923, 67: 1602-1604.

14, 333. Wheelock, Alan S. As ever, 'Daddy's Girl': incest motifs in Day for Night. Gypsy Scholar, 1975, 2:69-75.

14, 334. White, David Manning, & Averson, Richard. The Celluloid Weapon: Social Comment in the American Film. Boston: Beacon, 1972.

14, 335. White, Dennis L. The poetics of horror; more than meets the eye. Cinema J, 1971, 10(2):1-18.

14,336. Wiese, M. J., & Cole, S. G. A study of children's attitudes and the influence of a commercial motion picture. J Psychol, 1946, 21:151-171.

14,337. Williams, J. H. Attitudes of college students toward motion pictures. School & Society, 1933, 38:222-224.

14,338. Willis, Don. Renoir, and the illusion of detachment. Sight & Sound, 1977, 46:234-239.

14,339. _____. Yasujiro Ozu: emotion and contemplation. Sight & Sound, 1978-79, 48:44-49.

14,340. Wilner, Daniel M. Attitude as a Determinant of Perception in the Mass Media of Communication: Reactions to the Motion Picture, Home of the Brave. Doctoral dissertation, Univ. California, Berkeley, 1951.

14,341. Wilner, Nancy, & Horowitz, Mardi J. Intrusive and repetitive thought after a depressing film: a pilot study. Psychol Reports, 1975, 37:135-138.

14,342. Wilson, G. Film, perception, and point of view. MLN, 1976, 91:1026-1043.

14,343. Witty, Paul, Garfield, S., & Brink, W. Interests of high-school students in motion pictures and the radio. J Educational Psychol, 1941, 32:176-184.

14,344. Wolf, Howard R., & Spiegel, Alan. Psychoanalysis, the American film, and popular culture. Michigan Q Rev, 1971, 10(2):73-77.

14,345. Wolfenstein, Martha. The image of the child in contemporary films. In Mead, M., & Wolfenstein, M. (eds), Childhood in Contemporary Cultures. Chicago: Univ. Chicago Press, 1955, 277-293.

14,346. _____. Movie analysis in the study of culture. In Mead, M., & Métraux, R. (eds), The Study of Culture at a Distance. Chicago: Univ. Chicago Press, 1953, 267-280.

14,347. _____. Notes on an Italian film, The Tragic Hunt. In Métraux, R., & Mead, M. (eds), Themes in French Culture. Stanford: Stanford Univ. Press, 1953, 282-289.

14,348. _____, & Leites, Nathan. An analysis of themes and plots in motion pictures. Annals Amer Academy Political Social Sciences, 1947, 254, 41-48; In Schramm, W. (ed), Mass Communications. Urbana: Univ. Illinois Press, 1960, 380-391.

14,349. _____. Movie psychiatrists. Complex, 1951, 4:19-27.

14,350. _____. Movies: A Psychological Study. Glencoe, Ill: Free Press, 1950; Review: Hortense Powdermaker, Psychiatry, 1951, 14:353-355.

14,351. _____. Plot and character in selected French films: an analysis of fantasy. In Métraux, R., & Mead, M. (eds), Themes in French Culture. Stanford: Stanford Univ. Press, 1954, 89-108.

14,352. _____. Trends in French films. J Social Issues, 1955, 11:42-51.

14,353. Wollen, Peter. Cinema and semiology: some points of contact. In Nichols, B. (ed), Movies and Methods;

Anthology. Berkeley: Univ. California Press, 1976, 481-492.

14,354. _____. Signs and Meaning in the Cinema. Bloomington: Indiana Univ. Press, 1972 (1969).

14,355. Wood, Michael. America in the Movies; Or Santa Maria, It Had Slipped My Mind. NY: Basic Books, 1975.

14,356. Wood, Robin. Dyer's hand: Stars and Gays [review article]. Film Comment, 1980, 16:70-72.

14,357. _____. Ideology, genre, auteur. Film Comment, 1977, 13:46-51.

14,358. _____. Old wine, new battles: structuralism or humanism? Film Comment, 1976, 12:22-25.

14,359. _____. Responsibilities of a gay film critic; sexuality and love themes. Film Comment, 1978, 14:12-17.

14,360. _____. The return of the repressed. Film Comment, 1978, 14:24-32.

14,361. Woodbury, R. F. Children and movies. Survey, 1929, 62: 253-254.

14,362. Woodward, K. L. The exorcism frenzy. Newsweek, 11 Feb 1974, 60-66.

14,363. Worchel, Stephen. The effect of films on the importance of behavioral freedom. J Personality, 1972, 40:417-435.

14,364. Worth, Sol. Film as a non-art: an approach to the study of film. Amer Scholar, 1966, 35:322-334.

14,365. Wright, Will. Six Guns and Society: A Structural Study of the Western. Berkeley: Univ. California Press, 1975.

14,366. X, A. El cine i els somnis. Criterion, 1928, 15:442-443.

14,367. Yacowar, Maurice. Aspects of the familiar: a defense of minority group stereotyping in the popular film. Lit/Film Q, 1974, 2:129-139.

14,368. Young, James D. False identity and feeling in Raphael's Lindmann. Critique: Studies in Modern Fiction, 1971, 13(1):59-65.

14,369. Zambrano, Ana Laura. David Copperfield: novel and film. Hartford Studies in Lit, 1977, 9:1-16.

14,370. _____. Great Expectations: Dickens' style in terms of film. Hartford Studies in Lit, 1972, 4:104-112.

14,371. Zazzo, Blanka. Le Cinéma chez les adolescents. JPNP, 1957.

14,372. _____. Une enquête sur le cinéma et la lecture chez les adolescents. Enfance, 1957, Suppl 389-411.

14,373. Zilboorg, Gregory. Theatre soliloquies. IV. Art and the cinema. Drama, 1921, 2:352, 375-378.

14,374. Abrahams, Roger D. Folk drama. In Dorson, R. M.
(ed), Folklore and Folklife. Chicago: Univ. Chicago
Press, 1972, 351-362.

14,375. _____. Patterns of structure and role relationships in
the child ballad in the United States. J Amer Folklore,
1966, 79:448-462.

14,376. _____. Personal power and social restraint in the
definition of folklore. J Amer Folklore, 1971, 84:16-
30.

14,377. _____. Proverbs and proverbial expressions. In Dorson, R. M. (ed), Folklore and Folklife. Chicago: Univ.
Chicago Press, 1972, 117-127.

14,378. _____, & Dundes, Alan. Riddles. In Dorson, R. M.
(ed), Folklore and Folklife. Chicago: Univ. Chicago
Press, 1972, 129-143.

14,379. Adedeji, Joel. Folklore and Yoruba drama: Obàtálá as a
case study. In Dorson, R. M. (ed), African Folklore.
Bloomington: Indiana Univ. Press, 1972, 321-339.

14,380. Ajmal, Mohammad. The psychology of folklore. J Psychol (Lahore), 1964, 1(1):65-79.

14,381. Aldrich, M. R. Cannabis Myths and Folklore. Doctoral
dissertation, SUNY Buffalo, 1971.

14,382. Allen, Barbara. Personal experience narratives: use and
meaning in interaction. Folklore & Mythology Studies,
1978, 2:5-7.

14,383. Altman, Leon L. 'West' as a symbol of death. Psychoanal Q, 1959, 28:236-241.

14,384. Altschule, Mark David. The ideas of the Huron Indians
about the unconscious mind. In Origins of Concepts in
Human Behavior. NY: Halsted, 1977, 19-34.

14,385. Andrianova-Perete, V. [Freud's dream symbolism in the
light of Russian riddles.] Adakamija Nau XLVN a Mar-
ru, 1935, 497-505.

14,386. Ano N'guessan, Marius. La Femme dans le conte agni:
Essai d'ethno-littérature. Paris: Univ. René Descartes, 1974.

14,387. Ardener, Shirley G. Sexual insult and female militancy.
Man: J Royal Anthropological Institute, 1973, 8:422-
440.

14,388. Arewa, E. Ojo. Thirteen new tale motifs on tests, deceptions, rewards and punishments and unnatural cruelty from the East African cattle area. Southern Folklore Q, 1972, 36:61-67.

14, 389. Armstrong, Robert P. Content analysis in folkloristics. In Pool, I. de S. (ed), Trends in Content Analysis. Urbana: Univ. Illinois Press, 1959, 151-170.

14, 390. Assion, Peter. Parapsychologie, Glaube und Wissen. Zeitschrift für Volkskunde, 1976, 72:83-84.

14, 391. Azcuy, Fanny. Rasgos psico-sociologicos del folklore Afro-Cubano. Revista Mexicana de Sociologia, 1956, 18:555-562.

14, 392. Bard, Therese J. The Effects of Developmental Level, Adult Intervention, Sex and Reading Ability on Response to Four Filmed Versions of Explanatory Folk Tales. DAI, 1977, 38(3-A):1191-92.

14, 393. Barnes, Daniel R. 'Physical fact' and folklore: Hawthorne's 'Egotism; or the Bosom Serpent.' Amer Lit, 1971, 43:117-121.

14, 394. Barnouw, Victor. The analysis of folklore. In Culture and Personality. Homewood, Ill: Dorsey, 1963.

14, 395. _____. A psychological interpretation of a Chippewa origin legend. J Amer Folk-Lore, 1955, 68:73-85, 211-223, 341-355.

14, 396. Barry, Phillips. The psychopathology of ballad-singing. Folk Song Society of the North-East, 1936, 11:16-18.

14, 397. Bartlett, Frederic Charles. Psychology and the folk story. In Psychology and Primitive Culture. London: Cambridge, 1923, 57-104.

14, 398. _____. Psychology in relation to the popular story. Folklore, 1920, 31:264-293.

14, 399. _____. Some experiments on the reproduction of folk stories. Folklore, 1920, 31:30.

14, 400. Basgöz, Ilhan. Dream motif in Turkish folk stories and shamanistic initiation. Asian Folklore Studies, 1967, 26(1):1-18.

14, 401. Bauman, Richard. Differential identity and the social base of folklore. J Amer Folklore, 1971, 84:31-41; In Paredes, A., & Bauman, R. (ed), Toward New Perspectives in Folklore. Austin: Univ. Texas Press, 1971, 31-41.

14, 402. _____, Abrahams, Roger D., & Kalcik, Susan. American folklore and American studies. Amer Q, 1976, 28:360-377.

14, 403. Beck, Brenda E. F. Body imagery in the Tamil proverbs of south India. Western Folklore, 1979, 38:21-41.

14, 404. Beckwith, M. W. Folklore in America: Its Scope and Method. Poughkeepsie: Folklore Foundation, Vassar College, 1931.

14, 405. Beidelman, Thomas O. Acholi folk tales. Transition (Uganda), 1962, 3(8):5.

14, 406. _____. The filth of incest: a text and comments on Kaguru notions of sexuality, alimentation and aggression. Cahiers d'Etudes Africaines, 1972, 12:164-173.

14, 407. Ben-Amos, Dan. Folklore Genres. Austin: Univ. Texas Press, 1976.

14, 408. Berg, Charles. The Unconscious Significance of Hair.
          London: Allen & Unwin, 1951.
14, 409. Berne, Eric. The mythology of dark and fair: psychiatric
          use of folklore. J Amer Folklore, 1959, 72:1-13.
14, 410. Berry, J. W. Psychological research in the North. An-
          thropologica, 1971, 13:143-157.
14, 411. Bhattacharyya, Asutosh. The serpent as folk-deity in Ben-
          gal. Asian Folklore Studies, 1965, 24(1):1-10.
14, 412. Biderman, Sol. Literatura de cordel escatológica. O
          Estado de São Paulo, Suplemento Literário, 18 Feb
          1967, 1.
14, 413. Biehorst, John. The concept of childhood in American In-
          dian lore. Bulletin Research in Humanities, 1978, 81:
          395-405.
14, 414. Birnbaum, Mariana D. On the language of prejudice.
          Western Folklore, 1971, 30:247-268.
14, 415. Blake, C. Fred. The feelings of Chinese daughters toward
          their mothers as revealed in marriage laments. Folk-
          lore, 1979, 90:91-97.
14, 416. Bluestein, Eugene G. The Voice of the Folk; Folklore and
          American Literary Theory. Amherst: Univ. Massa-
          chusetts Press, 1972.
14, 417. Boas, Franz. The development of folk-tales and myths.
          Scientific Monthly, 1916, 3:335-343.
14, 418. Böckel, Otto. Psychologie der Volkdichtung. Leipzig:
          Teubner, 1906, 1913.
14, 419. Bogdanova, Liljana, & Bogdanova, Ana. [The dragon's
          lovers--as mentally ill; a folk belief reflected in Bul-
          garian folklore.] Izvestija na Etnografskija Institut i
          Muzej, 1972, 14:239-260.
14, 420. Boggs, R. S. [The hero in the folk tales of Spain, Ger-
          many and Russia.] Zeitschrift für Völkerpsychologie
          und Soziologie, 1931, 44:27-42.
14, 421. Bourke, J. G. Scatological Rites of All Nations. Washing-
          ton, D. C.: Lowdermilk, 1891.
14, 422. Boyer, L. Bryce. Childhood and Folklore; A Psychoanaly-
          tic Study of Apache Personality. NY: Library of Psy-
          chological Anthropology, 1979.
14, 423. _____. Folk psychiatry of the Apache of the Mescalero
          Indian Reservation. In Kiev, A. (ed), Magic, Faith
          and Healing: Studies in Primitive Psychiatry Today.
          Glencoe: Free Press, 1964, 384-419.
14, 424. _____. The man who turned into a water monster: a
          psychoanalytic contribution to folklore. In The Psycho-
          analytic Study of Society, Vol. 6. NY: IUP, 1975,
          100-133.
14, 425. _____, & Boyer, Ruth M. A combined anthropological
          and psychoanalytical contribution to folklore. Psycho-
          pathologie africaine, 1967, 3:333-372.
14, 426. _____, _____, & Hippler, Arthur E. The Alaskan
          Athabaskan potlach ceremony. Int J Psychoanal Psy-
          therapy, 1974, 3:343-365.

14,427. Brachfeld, O. Empfangnis durch das Lecken von Pulver im Volksmärchen. Zeitschrift für Sexualwissenschaft, 1930, 17:377.

14,428. Branan, Elisabeth Marie Girod. Indépendance, rêve, sommeil et solitude dans les Fables et les Contes de Jean de la Fontaine. DAI, 1976, 37:1585A-86A.

14,429. Brenner, Arthur B. The Ape: Simia qua similis. Amer Imago, 1954, 11:317-327.

14,430. Brewster, Paul G. The Incest Theme in Folksong. Helsinki: 1972.

14,431. Brink, Louise. Frazier's folklore in the Old Testament. Psychoanal Rev, 1922, 9:218-254.

14,432. _____. Frazier's Golden Bough. Psychoanal Rev, 1916, 3:43-68.

14,433. Bristowe, W. S. Spider, superstition and folklore. Transactions Connecticut Academy Arts & Sciences, 1945, 36:35-90.

14,434. Britt, S. H. , & Balcom, M. M. Jumping-rope rhymes and the social psychology of play. J Genetic Psychol, 1941, 58:289-306.

14,435. Brivic, Sheldon R. The incredible string band and Robin Williamson's 'Creation.' Hartford Studies in Lit, 1972, 4:123-134.

14,436. Brooks, G. P. The behaviorally abnormal in early Irish folklore. Papers in Psychol, 1971, 5:5-11.

14,437. Burstein, Sona R. Folklore, rumour and prejudice. Folklore, 1959, 70:361-381.

14,438. Bustamente, José Angel. [Folklore and psychiatry.] Revista de Psiquiatria Peru, 1960, 3:110-124.

14,439. _____. [Folklore in psychiatry.] Revista Archiva Neurologia Psiquitria (Cuba), 1960, 10:197-212.

14,440. Butler, G. F. Survivals of folk-lore. Alienist & Neurologist, 1911, 32:127-140.

14,441. Calame-Griaule, Geneviève. Une Affaire de famille: Reflexions sur quelques thèmes de 'cannibalisme' dans les contes africains. Nouvelle Rev Psychanalyse, 1972, 6:171-202.

14,442. Caldwell, Harry B. Ballad tragedy and the moral matrix: observations on tragic causation. New York Folklore Q, 1972, 28:209-220.

14,443. Campbell, Joseph. Folkloristic commentary. In Grimm's Fairy Tales. NY: Pantheon, 1944, 833-864.

14,444. Canal-Feijoo, B. Burla, credo, culpa en la creacíon anónima. Sociologia, etnología y psicologia en el folklore. Buenos Aires: Nova, 1951.

14,445. Cannell, M. , & Snapp, E. L. Signs, Omens, and Portents in Nebraska Folklore: Proverbial Lore in Nebraska. Univ. Nebraska Studies in Language, Lit & Criticism, 1933, No. 13.

14,446. Caramella, Santino. Demopsicologia e folklore. In Studi in onore di Carmelina Naselli. Vol. I. Catania: Univ. di Catania, 1968, 75-80.

14, 447. Carey, J. T. The ideology of autonomy in popular lyrics:
a content analysis. Psychiatry, 1969, 32:150-164.
14, 448. Caring, M'Lou. Structural parallels in dreams and narratives: developmental/sex differences in dreams and
stories of girls and boys. In Stevens, P., Jr. (ed),
Studies in the Anthropology of Play. West Point, NY:
Leisure, 1977, 155-174.
14, 449. Carneiro, Edison. Dinâmica do Folklore. Rio de Janeiro,
1950.
14, 450. Carpenter, Rhys. Folk Tale. Fiction and Saga in the
Homeric Epics. Berkeley: Univ. California Press,
1958.
14, 451. Carvalho-Neto, Paulo de. The Concept of Folklore. Coral
Gables, Fla: Univ. Miami Press, 1970.
14, 452. _____. Folklore and Psychoanalysis. Coral Gables:
Univ. Miami Press, 1972; Buenos Aires: 1956.
14, 453. _____. Folklore del Paraguay. Sistematica analitica.
Quito: Universitaria, 1961.
14, 454. _____. Folklore y Educación. Quito: Casa de la Cultura Ecuatoriapa, 1961.
14, 455. _____. Folklore y psicoanalisis. Revista de Psicologia
Normal e Patológica, 1961, 7.
14, 456. _____. La influencia del folklore en A. Machado.
Cuadernos Hispano-Americanos, 1975-76, 304-7:302-
357.
14, 457. Chavez, Angelico. The mad poet of Santa Cruz. New
Mexico Folklore Record, 1949, 3:10-17.
14, 458. Chernysheva, Tatyana. The folktale, Wells, and modern
science fiction. In Suvin, D., & Philmus, R. M. (eds),
H. G. Wells and Modern Science Fiction. Lewisburg,
Pa: Bucknell Univ. Press, 1977, 35-47.
14, 459. Child, Irvin L., Storm, Thomas, & Veroff, Joseph.
Achievement themes in folktales related to socialization
process. Ms. New Haven: Yale Univ., 1957.
14, 460. Clarke, Kenneth W. Jesse Stuart's use of folklore. In
LeMaster, J. R., & Clarke, M. W. (eds), Jesse Stuart:
Essays on His Work. Lexington: Univ. Kentucky
Press, 1977, 117-129.
14, 461. Cochran, Robert, & Cochran, Martha. Some menstrual
folklore of Mississippi. Mississippi Folklore Register,
1970, 4:108-113.
14, 462. Coffin, Tristram Potter. The Female Hero in Folklore
and Legend. NY: Seabury, 1975.
14, 463. _____. (ed). Our Living Traditions, An Introduction to
American Folklore. NY: Basic Books, 1968.
14, 464. _____. Real use and real abuse of folklore in the
writer's subconscious: F. Scott Fitzgerald. In Mid-
America Conference on Literature, History, Popular
Culture and Folklore. Lafayette, Ind: Purdue Univ.
Press, 1965, 102-112.
14, 465. Collomb, Henri. Witchcraft-anthropophagia and dyadic relationship. Psyche, 1978, 32:463-482.
14, 466. Cothran, Kay L. Anxious, dread tomorrow. Keystone
Folklore Q, 1972, 17:11-18.

14, 467.   Crawford, Nelson A.   Cats holy and profane.   Psychoanal
           Rev, 1934, 21:168-179.
14, 468.   Crook, Patricia R.   Folktales teach appreciation for human
           predicaments.   Reading Teacher, 1979, 32:449-452.
14, 469.   Crowley, Daniel J.   (ed).   African Folklore in the New
           World.   Austin: Univ. Texas Press, 1977.

14, 470.   Dalton, G. F.   Unconscious literary use of traditional mate-
           rial.   Folklore, 1974, 85:268-275.
14, 471.   Danielson, L. W.   Uses of demonic folk tradition in Selma
           Lagerlöf's Gösta Berlings saga.   Western Folklore,
           1975, 34:187-199.
14, 472.   Darlington, H. S.   The fear of false teeth.   Psychoanal
           Rev, 1944, 31:181-194.
14, 473.   Das, R. C.   Psychology of manpower management in pro-
           verbs.   Folklore (India), 1978, 224:245-253.
14, 474.   DeCaro, Rosan Jordan.   A note about folklore and litera-
           ture.   The bosom serpent revisited.   J Amer Folklore,
           1973, 86:62-65.
14, 475.   Dégh, Linda.   Folk narrative.   In Dorson, R. M.   (ed),
           Folklore and Folklife: An Introduction.   Chicago:
           Univ. Chicago Press, 1972, 53-83.
14, 476.   _____.   Symbiosis of joke and legend: a case of con-
           versational folklore.   In Folklore Today.   Bloomington:
           Indiana Univ. Press, 1976, 101-122.
14, 477.   Desmonde, William H.   The bullfight as a religious ritual.
           Amer Imago, 1952, 9:173-195.
14, 478.   Devoto, D.   [Folklore and psychology.]   Abaco, 1970, 1:11-
           44.
14, 479.   DeVries, J.   [Russian folklore research in recent years.]
           Mensch en Maatsch, 1930, 6:330-341.
14, 480.   Dorson, Richard M.   (ed).   Folklore and Folklife: An In-
           troduction.   Chicago: Univ. Chicago Press, 1972.
14, 481.   _____.   A theory for American folklore reviewed.   J
           Amer Folklore, 1969, 82:226-244.
14, 482.   Downs, Robert B.   Folk hero.   In Books That Changed the
           South.   Totowa, NJ: Littlefield, Adams, 1977, 63-73.
14, 483.   Drake, Carlos C.   Jung and his critics.   J Amer Folk-
           lore, 1967, 80:321-333.
14, 484.   _____.   Jungian psychology and its uses in folklore.
           J Amer Folklore, 1969, 82:122-131.
14, 485.   Dresser, Norine.   'The Boys in the Band is not another
           musical':   male homosexuals and their folklore.   West-
           ern Folklore, 1974, 33:205-218.
14, 486.   Dundes, Alan.   The American concept of folklore.   J
           Folklore Institute, 1966, 3:226-249.
14, 487.   _____.   On computers and folk tales.   Western Folk-
           lore, 1965, 24(1):185-189.
14, 488.   _____.   On the psychology of collecting folklore.   Ten-
           nessee Folklore Society Bulletin, 1962, 28(3):65-74.
14, 489.   _____.   Projection in folklore: a plea for psychoanaly-
           tic semiotics.   MLN, 1976, 91:1500-1533.

14, 490. _____ et al. The strategy of Turkish boys' verbal duel-
ing rhymes. J Amer Folklore, 1970, 83:325-349; Discussion, 1976, 89:87-89, 1979, 92:334-335.

14, 491. _____. A study of ethnic slurs: the Jew and the Po-
lack in the United States. J Amer Folklore, 1971, 84:
188-203.

14, 492. _____. The Study of Folklore. Englewood Cliffs, NJ:
Prentice-Hall, 1965.

14, 493. _____. The study of folklore in literature and culture:
identification and interpretation. J Amer Folklore,
1965, 78:136-142.

14, 494. _____. To love my father all: a psychoanalytic study
of the folktale source of King Lear. Southern Folklore
Q, 1976, 40:353-366.

14, 495. Durham, Philip. The cowboy and the myth. J Popular
Culture, 1967, 1:58-62.

14, 496. Eddington, Neil A. Genital superiority in Oakland Negro
folklore: a theme. Kroeber Anthropological Society
Papers, 1965, 33:99-105.

14, 497. Eggan, Dorothy. The personal use of myth in dreams.
J Amer Folklore, 1955, 68:445-453.

14, 498. Ekeh, Peter P. Benin and Thebes: elementary forms of
civilization. In The Psychoanalytic Study of Society,
Vol. 7. NY: IUP, 1976, 65-94.

14, 499. Elwell-Sutton, L. P. Family relationships in Persian folk-
literature. Folklore (London), 1976, 87:160-166.

14, 500. Emery, A. E. Lyrics, love, and logic. British Medical
J, 1979, 17(2):1280-1281.

14, 501. Errington, Shelly. Space, time, and the concept of person
in Karavar. Indonesia, 1971, 12:57-64.

14, 502. Evans, David. The singing-stammerer motif in black
tradition. Western Folklore, 1976, 35:157-160.

14, 503. Feldman, A. Bronson. Folklore light on free association.
Psychoanal Rev, 1962, 49(1):34-36.

14, 504. Ferenczi, Sándor. An anal-erotic proverb. In Further
Contributions to the Theory and Technique of Psycho-
Analysis. London: Hogarth, 1950; Int Zeitschrift für
Psychoanalyse, 1915, 3:295; Baustine zur Psycho-
analyse, 3:50.

14, 505. _____. Thalassa: a theory of genitality. Psychoanal
Q, 1933, 2:361-403; 1934, 3:1-29, 200-222.

14, 506. Fernandes, G. O Folclore Mágico do Nordeste. Rio de
Janeiro: Biblioteca de Divulgação Científica, 1938.

14, 507. Fernandez, James W. Equatorial excursions: the folklore of narcotic-inspired visions in an African religious
movement. In Dorson, R. M. (ed), African Folklore.
Bloomington: Indiana Univ. Press, 1972, 341-361.

14, 508. Ferris, William R., Jr. Racial stereotypes in white folklore. Keystone Folklore Q, 1970, 15:188-198.

14, 509. Fischer, John L. Folktales, social structure, and environment in two Polynesian outliers. J Polynesian Society, 1958, 67:11-36.

14, 510. _____. The position of men and women in Truk and Ponape. J Amer Folklore, 1956, 69:55-62.

14, 511. _____. The socio-psychological analysis of the folktale. Current Anthropology, 1963, 4:235-295.

14, 512. Fish, Lydia. Sexual folklore in Victorian England. Folklore Forum, 1975, 8:142-147.

14, 513. Fisher, Stephen L. Folk culture or folk tale: prevailing assumptions about the Appalachian personality. In Williamson, J.W. (ed), An Appalachian Symposium. Boone, N.C.: Appalachian State Univ. Press, 1977, 14-25.

14, 514. Flandrin, Jean-Louis. [Old and modern commonplace sayings about the child in the family.] Perspectives Psychiatriques, 1976, No. 55, 13-27.

14, 515. Flom, G.T. Noa words in North Sea regions; a chapter in folklore and linguistics. J Amer Folklore, 1925, 38:400-418.

14, 516. Frazer, James George. Folk-Lore in the Old Testament. NY: Tudor, 1923.

14, 517. Freehof, Solomon W. Three psychiatric stories from rabbinic lore. Psychoanal Rev, 1942, 29:185-187.

14, 518. Freeman, Derek. Thunder, blood, and the nicknaming of God's creatures. Psychoanal Q, 1968, 38:353-399.

14, 519. Frenzel, H. John Millington Synge's Work as a Contribution to Irish Folk-Lore and to the Psychology of Primitive Tribes. Düren: Danielewski, 1932.

14, 520. Freud, Sigmund. The execretory functions in psychoanalysis and folklore. In Collected Papers, Vol. 5. NY: Basic Books, 1959 (1913), 88-91.

14, 521. _____. Preface to John G. Bourke's Scatological Rites of All Nations. Washington, DC: 1891.

14, 522. _____, & Oppenheim, D.E. Dreams in Folklore. NY: IUP, 1958.

14, 523. Friedl, Erika. Women in contemporary Persian folktales. In Beck, L., & Keddie, N.R. (eds), Women in the Muslim World. Cambridge: Harvard Univ. Press, 1978, 629-650.

14, 524. Friedman, Adele C. Love, sex, and marriage in traditional French society: documentary evidence of folksongs. French Rev, 1978, 52:242-254.

14, 525. Frye, Northrop. Spiritus Mundi; Essays on Literature, Myth, and Society. Bloomington: Indiana Univ. Press, 1976.

14, 526. Gaignebet, Claude. Une coutume de folklore juridique dans l'oeuvre de Rabelais. Arts et Traditions Populaires, 1970, 18:183-194.

14, 527. Gardner, Howard. The structural analysis of protocols and myths: a comparison of the methods of Jean

Piaget and Claude Lévi-Strauss. Semiotica, 1972, 5:31-57.

14, 528. Garrison, Vivian E., & Arensberg, Conrad M. The evil eye: envy or risk of seizure? Paranoia or patronal dependency? In Maloney, C. (ed), The Evil Eye. NY: Columbia Univ. Press, 1976, 286-328.

14, 529. Georges, Robert A. Feedback and responses in storytelling. Western Folklore, 1979, 38:104-110.

14, 530. _____, & Dundes, Alan. Toward a structural definition of the riddle. J Amer Folklore, 1963, 76:111-118.

14, 531. Gifford, Edward S. The Evil Eye: Studies in the Folk-lore of Vision. NY: Macmillan, 1958.

14, 532. Gleason, Philip. Our new age of romanticism. America, 1967, 116(7):372-375.

14, 533. Glendinning, Robert J. Archetypal structure of Hymisqvioä. Folklore, 1980, 91:92-110.

14, 534. Gloyne, Howard F. Tarantism: mass hysterical reaction to spider bite in the Middle Ages. Amer Imago, 1950, 7:29-42.

14, 535. Goja, Hermann. The alteration of folk songs by frequent singing: a contribution to the psychology of folk poetry. In The Psychoanalytic Study of Society, Vol. 3. NY: IUP, 1964, 111-170; Imago, 1920, 6:132-241.

14, 536. Goldenweiser, Alexander A. Folk-psychology. Psychol Bulletin, 1912, 9:373-380.

14, 537. Goodman, Paul. Introduction to Jablow, Alta, Yes & No. The Intimate Folklore of Africa. NY: Horizon, 1961.

14, 538. Gorfain, Phyllis, & Glazier, Jack. Sexual symbolism, origins, and the ogre in Mbeere, Kenya. J Amer Folklore, 1978, 91:925-946.

14, 539. Görög-Karady, Veronika. Préférence parentale et inégalité raciale: étude d'un thème ideologique dans la littérature orale africaine. Research African Lit, 1977, 8:54-82.

14, 540. Greene, Sarah. From amnesia to illegitimacy: the soap opera as contemporary folklore. In Abernethy, F. E. (ed), Observations and Reflections on Texas Folklore. Austin, Texas: Encino Press, 1972, 79-90.

14, 541. Gunda, Béla. Sex and semiotics. J Amer Folklore, 1973, 86:143-151.

14, 542. Hampton, Bill R. On identification and Negro tricksters. Southern Folklore Q, 1967, 31:55-65.

14, 543. Hand, Wayland D. American Folk Legend, A Symposium. Berkeley: Univ. California Press, 1971.

14, 544. _____. Curative practice in folk tales. Fabula, 1967, 13:264-269.

14, 545. _____. The curing of blindness in folk tales. In Volksüberlieferung. Göttingen: Schwartz, 1968, 81-87.

14, 546. _____. Hangmen, the gallows, and the dead man's hand in American folk medicine. In Mandel, J., & Rosenberg, B. A. (eds), Medieval Literature and Folklore Studies. New Brunswick, NJ: Rutgers Univ. Studies, 1970, 323-329.

14, 547. Hannett, Frances. The haunting lyric. The personal and social significance of American popular song. Psychoanal Q, 1964, 33:226-269.

14, 548. Hansen, William F. The structural study of myth, or Oedipus at the Sorbonne. Folklore Forum, 1972, 5:70-71.

14, 549. Hart, Henry H. The eye in symbol and symptom. Psychoanal Rev, 1949, 36:1-21; In The Yearbook of Psychoanalysis, Vol. 6. NY: IUP, 1950, 256-275.

14, 550. Hawkes, Bess Lomax. Folksongs and functions: some thoughts on the American lullaby. J Amer Folklore, 1974, 87:140-148.

14, 551. Heise, Karl. Der Kuckuck und die Meise im Volksmunde und dem Volksglauben der Braunschweiger. Imago, 1924, 10:340-342.

14, 552. Helbig, Alethea K. Manabozho: trickster, guide, and alter ego. Michigan Academician, 1975, 7:357-371.

14, 553. Heller, Hugo. On the history of the devil. In Nunberg, H., & Federn, E. (eds), Minutes of the Vienna Psychoanalytic Society, Vol. 2: 1908-1910. NY: IUP, 1967, 117-124.

14, 554. Hellwig, Albert. Hexenglaube und Sympathiekuren. Artzliche Sachver-ständigenzeitung, 1916, 22:145-148.

14, 555. Hennigh, Lawrence. Control of incest in Eskimo folktales. J Amer Folklore, 1966, 79:356-369.

14, 556. Herzog, Edgar. Psyche und Tod: Wandlungen des Todesbildes im Mythos und in den Träumen heutiger Menschen. Zürich: Rascher, 1960.

14, 557. Hippler, Arthur E. Popular art styles in Mariachi festivals. Amer Imago, 1969, 26:167-181.

14, 558. _____, Boyer, L. Bryce, & Boyer, Ruth M. The psychocultural significance of the Alaska Athabascan potlatch ceremony. In The Psychoanalytic Study of Society, Vol. 6. NY: IUP, 1975, 204-234.

14, 559. Hoffmann, Fernand. We are what we speak: the psychology of the Luxemburger seen through the evolution of his dialect, speech habits, proverbs and saying. Lore & Language, 1974, 2(1):5-14.

14, 560. Holzapfel, Otto. Zur Phänomenologie des Ringbrauchtums. Zeitschrift für Volkskunde, 1968, 64:32-51.

14, 561. Horner, George R. Folklore as a psychological projective system. Conch: Biafran J, 1971, 3:3-13.

14, 562. Horton, Donald. The dialogue of courtship in popular songs. Amer J Sociology, 1957, 62:569-579.

14, 563. Huckenbeck, Herbert. Probleme ethnopsychologischer Forschung. In Foltin, H. F. et al. (eds), Kontakte und Grenzen: Probleme der Volks-, Kulture- und Sozialforschung. Göttingen: Schwartz, 1969, 35-48.

14, 564. Hudson, Wilson M. Freud's myth of the primal horde. In A Good Tale and a Bonnie Tune. Dallas: Southern Methodist Univ. Press, 1964, 72-100.

14, 565. Hufford, David J. Psychology, psychoanalysis, and folklore. Southern Folklore Q, 1974, 38:187-197.

14, 566. Hunt, W. On bullfighting. Amer Imago, 1955, 12:343-353.

14, 567.   Hurvits, Nathan.   Jews and Jewishness in the street rhymes of American children.   Jewish Social Studies, 1954, 16: 135-150.

14, 568.   Hymes, Dell H.   The contribution of folklore to sociolinguistic research.   J Amer Folklore, 1971, 84:42-50; In Paredes, A., & Bauman, R. (eds), Toward New Perspectives in Folklore.   Austin: Univ. Texas Press, 42-50.

14, 569.   Inman, W. S.   Styes, barley and wedding rings.   British J Medical Psychol, 1946, 20:331-338; In The Yearbook of Psychoanalysis, Vol. 3.   NY: IUP, 1947, 297-308.

14, 570.   Ireland, Tom, & Stovall, Jim.   Phenomenology and folklore.   In Cashion, G. (ed), Conceptual Problems in Contemporary Folklore Study.   Bloomington, Ind: Folklore Forum, 1973(?), 75-81.

14, 571.   Ishida, Eiichiro.   The mother-son complex in East Asiatic religion and folklore.   In Die Wiener Schule der Völkerkunde.   Festschrift zum 25 jährigen Bestand.   Vienna: 1955, 411-419.

14, 572.   Iyeki, Jean-François.   Essai sur la psychologie du Bonto.   Kinasha: Office National de la Recherche, 1970.

14, 573.   Jackson, Bruce.   Circus and street: psychological aspects of the black toast.   J Amer Folklore, 1972, 85:123-139.

14, 574.   Jageland, A. van.   De angst in de Volkspsychologie.   Volkskunde, 1968, 69:110-115.

14, 575.   Jarett, Dennis.   The singer and the bluesman: formulation of personality in the lyrics of the blues.   Southern Folklore Q, 1978, 42:31-37.

14, 576.   Johnson, G. B.   Double meaning in the popular negro blues.   J Abnormal Social Psychol, 22:12-30.

14, 577.   Johnson, Robbie Davis.   Folklore and women: a social interactional analysis of the folklore of a Texas madam.   J Amer Folklore, 1973, 86:211-224.

14, 578.   Jones, Ernest.   Nightmare, Witches, and Devils.   NY: Norton, 1931.

14, 579.   _____.   Psychoanalysis and folk lore.   Scientia, 1934, 55:209-220.

14, 580.   _____.   The symbolic significance of salt in folklore and superstition.   In Essays in Applied Psycho-Analysis.   London: Hogarth, 1928; NY: IUP, 1964.

14, 581.   Kabronsky, V. (ed).   [Uncensored Russian Limericks.]   NY: Russica, 1978.

14, 582.   Kakar, Sudhir.   Aggression in Indian society: an analysis of folk-tales.   Indian J Psychol, 1974, 49:119-126.

14, 583.   Kamen-Kaye, D. J.   A bug and a bonfire.   J Ethnopharmacology, 1979, 1:103-110.

14, 584.   Kanner, Leo.   Folklore of the Teeth.   NY: Macmillan, 1928.

14, 585. _____. The tooth as a folkloristic symbol. Psychoanal Rev, 1928, 15:37-52.

14, 586. Karefa-Smart, John A. M. Doctors, development, and demons in Africa. In Olson, A. M. (ed), Disguises of the Demonic; Contemporary Perspectives on the Power of Evil. NY: Association Press, 1975, 150-156.

14, 587. Kelchner, G. D. Dreams in Old Norse Literature and Their Affinities to Folk-Lore. London: Cambridge Univ. Press, 1935.

14, 588. Kenagy, S. G. Sexual symbolism in the language of the air force pilot: a psychoanalytic approach to folk speech. Western Folklore, 1978, 37:89-101.

14, 589. Ketner, Kenneth L. Superstitions pigeons, hydrophobia, and conventional wisdom. Western Folklore, 1971, 30: 1-17.

14, 590. Keyser, Samuel Jay, & Prince, Alan. Folk etymology in Sigmund Freud, Christian Morgenstern, and Wallace Stevens. Critical Inquiry, 1979-80, 6:65-78.

14, 591. Kiev, Ari. Curanderismo: Mexican-American Folk Psychiatry. NY: Free Press, 1968; Review: L. B. Boyer, Psychoanal Q, 1969, 38:329-332.

14, 592. _____ (ed). Magic, Faith and Healing: Studies in Primitive Psychiatry Today. Glencoe, Ill: Free Press, 1964.

14, 593. Klein, V. Der ungarische Hexenglaube. Zeitschrift für Ethnologie, 1935, 66:374-402.

14, 594. Klymasz, Robert B. Ukrainian incest ballads from Western Canada. Canadian Folk Music J, 1973, 1:35-37.

14, 595. Koch, Adelaide. Consideraçoes psychanalyticas sobre symbols e contos populares. Revista de Neurologie e Psychiatria de São Paulo, 1940, 6:7-18.

14, 596. Korten, David C. The life game: survival strategies in Ethiopian folktales. J Cross-Cultural Psychol, 1971, 2:209-224.

14, 597. Kostov, Kiril. Ein Inzestmotiv in Volkserzählungen der Zigeuner Bulgariens. Balkansko Ezikoznanie, 1975, 18(3):71-74.

14, 598. Kracke, Waud H. Dreaming in Kagwahiv: dream beliefs and their psychic uses in an Amazonian Indian culture. In The Psychoanalytic Study of Society, Vol. 8. New Haven: Yale Univ. Press, 1979, 119-174.

14, 599. Krauss, Friedrich S. Erotische Sprichworter bei den russischen Juden. Sexualprobleme, 1908, 5:452-466.

14, 600. _____. Folkloristisches von der Mutterschaft. Munich: Lange, 1912.

14, 601. Krestovsky, Lydie. Thèmes migrateurs: de l'epopée égyptienne au folklore russe. Psyché, 1949, 4:1017-1025.

14, 602. Krige, Eileen J. Girls' puberty songs and their relation to fertility, health, morality and religion among the Zulu. Africa (London): 1968, 38:173-198.

14, 603. Kurikawa, H. [The Psychology of Folk-Tales and Nursery Tales.] Tokyo: Tôen-Syobo, 1936.

14,604. La Barre, Weston. Aymara folklore and folk temperament. J Folklore Institute, 1965, 2:25-30.

14,605. _____. Aymara: history and worldview. J Amer Folklore, 1966, 79:130-144.

14,606. _____. Folklore and psychology. J Amer Folklore,
1948, 61:382-390.

14,607. _____. The influence of Freud on anthropology. Amer
Imago, 1958, 15:275-328.

14,608. _____. The psychopathology of drinking songs. Psychiatry, 1939, 2:203-212.

14,609. Laiblin, Wilhelm. Die Symbolik der Erlössung und Wied-
ergeburt im deutschen Volksmärchen. Zentralblatt für
Psychotherapie u ihre Grenzgebiete, 1943.

14,610. Latynin, B. A. [The cosmic tree and the tree of life in
the folklore and art of Eastern Europe.] Izvetsia Akadamie ist mat Kultur, 1933, No. 69.

14,611. Laubscher, B. J. F. Sex, Custom and Psychopathology. A
Study of South African Pagan Natives. London: Routledge & Kegan Paul, 1937.

14,612. Layard, John. The incest taboo and the virgin archetype.
Eranos Jahrbuch, 1945, 12:253-307.

14,613. _____. The Virgin Archetype. Zurich: Spring, 1972.

14,614. Lebo, Dell. Psychology in gypsy lore. J Education &
Psychol, (Baroch) 1957, 15:136-145.

14,615. Lee, Sonia M. The image of the woman in the African
folktale from the sub-Saharan Francophone area. Yale
French Studies, 1976, 53:19-28.

14,616. Legman, Gershon. The Horn Book: Studies in Erotic
Folklore and Bibliography. NY: University Books,
1964. Review: Alex Comfort; Folklore, 1964, 75:281-
282.

14,617. Legnaro, Aldo. [Going against common sense.] Kölner
Zeitschrift für Soziologie und Sozialpsychologie, 1974,
26:630-636.

14,618. LeGoff, J., & LeRoy Ladurie, E. Mélusine maternelle
et defrícheuse. Annales. Economies--Sociétés--Civili-
sations, 1971, 26:587-622.

14,619. Lessa, William A. Oedipus-type tales in Oceania. J
Amer Folklore, 1956, 69:63-73.

14,620. Levine, Lawrence W. Slave songs and slave consciousness: an exploration in neglected sources. In Hareven,
T. K. (ed), Anonymous Americans; Explorations in Nineteenth-Century Social History. Englewood Cliffs, NJ:
Prentice-Hall, 1971, 99-130.

14,621. Lewis, Mary Ellen B. The feminists have done it: applied folklore. J Amer Folklore, 1974, 87:85-87.

14,622. Luck, R. Gudrun, die bruderliebende Schwester, Ein
Beitrag zur Wesenkunde germanischen Menschentums.
Zeitschrift für Menschenkunde, 1937, 13:3.

14,623. Lugn, Pehr. Die magische Bedeutung der weiblichen
Kopfbedeckung im schwedischen Volksglauben. Mitteilungen der Anthropologie Gesellschaft in Wien, 1920, 50:
81-106.

14, 624. Luomala, Katharine. Numskull claps and tales: their structure and function in Oceanic asymmetrical joking relationships. J Amer Folklore, 1966, 79:157-194.

14, 625. Lüthi, Max. Es war einmal--Vom Vesen des Volkmärchens. Göttingen: Vandenhoeck & Ruprecht, 1962.

14, 626. _____. Volksmärchen und Volkssage. Bern: Francke, 1961.

14, 627. Lynn, Kenneth Schuyler. Violence in American literature and folklore. In Visions of America. Westport, Conn: Greenwood, 1973, 189-205.

14, 628. McClelland, David C., Davis, William, Wanner, Eric, & Kalin, Rudolf. A cross-cultural study of folk-tale content and drinking. Sociometry, 1966, 29:308-331.

14, 629. _____, & Friedman, G. A. A cross-cultural study of the relationship between child-training practices and achievement motivation appearing in folk tales. In Swanson, G. E., et al. (eds), Readings in Social Psychology, NY: Holt, 1952, 243-249.

14, 630. McCullen, Joseph T., Jr. Ancient rites for the dead and Hawthorne's Roger Malvin's Burial. Southern Folklore Q, 1966, 30:313-322.

14, 631. McDowell, John Holmes. Children's Riddling. Bloomington: Indiana Univ. Press, 1979.

14, 632. Maday, Bela C. The ethnologist and mental health. Ethnologia Europaea: Rev Int d'Ethnologie Européenne, 1970, 4:33-38.

14, 633. Maloney, Clarence (ed). The Evil Eye. NY: Columbia Univ. Press, 1976.

14, 634. Mandel'shtam, Osip E. Literary Moscow: birth of the fabula. In Selected Essays, Austin: Univ. Texas Press, 1977.

14, 635. Mann, John. Concerning Dundes' criticisms of Mann's analysis of German folktales. Amer Anthropologist, 1964, 66:644-645.

14, 636. _____. The Folktale as a Reflector of the Individual and Social Structure. Doctoral dissertation, Columbia Univ., 1958.

14, 637. Maranda, Elli Köngäs. Theory and practice of riddle analysis. J Amer Folklore, 1971, 84:51-61; In Paredes, A., & Bauman, R. (eds), Toward New Perspectives in Folklore. Austin: Univ. Texas Press, 1972, 51-61.

14, 638. Marett, Robert R. Psychology and Folklore. London: Methuen, 1920; Atlantic Highlands, NJ: Humanities Press, 1971; Detroit: Gale, 1974.

14, 639. Mars, Louis P. La Psychopathologie du Vaudou. Psyché, 1948, 3:1064-1088.

14, 640. _____. The story of zombi in Haiti. Man, 1945, 45: 38-40.

14, 641. _____, & Devereux, George. Haitian Voodoo and the ritualization of the nightmare. Psychoanal Rev, 1951, 38:334-342.

14, 642. Martin, C. B., & Long, E. M., Jr. Sex during the men-
          strual period. MAHS, 1969, 3(6):37, 40, 43, 46, 49.
14, 643. Meletinsky, Eleazar. Marriage: its function and position
          in the structure of folktales. In Maranda, P. (ed),
          Soviet Structural Folkloristics, I. The Hague: Mouton,
          1974, 61-72.
14, 644. Mendelsohn, J. Die Bedeutung der Volksmärchens für das
          seelische Wachstun des Kindes. Praxis der Kinderpsy-
          chologie und Kinderpsychiatrie, 1958, 7.
14, 645. Michelet, Jules. Satanism and Witchcraft: A Study in
          Medieval Superstition. NY: Walden, 1939.
14, 646. Mieder, Wolfgang. The use of proverbs in psychological
          testing. J Folklore Institute, 1978, 15:45-55.
14, 647. Mitropol'skaja, Nina. Problema varianta i psixologija ust-
          nogo tvorcestva v uslovijax lokal'noj fol'klornoj tradicii.
          Literatura, 1974, 16(2):7-28.
14, 648. Mogk, Eugen. Das Ei im Volksbrauch und Volksglauben.
          Zeitschrift des Vereines für Volkskunde, 1915, 215-223.
14, 649. Moldenhauer, Joseph J. The rhetorical function of pro-
          verbs in Walden. J Amer Folklore, 1967, 80:151-159.
14, 650. Money, John, & Hosta, G. Negro folklore of male preg-
          nancy. J Sexual Research, 1968, 4:34-50.
14, 651. Money-Kyrle, Roger. Superstition and Society. London:
          Hogarth, 1939.
14, 652. Müller, Erwin. Psychologie des deutschen Volkmärchens.
          Munich: Kösel & Pustet, 1928.
14, 653. Mukerji, Chandra. Bullshitting: road lore among hitch-
          hikers. Social Problems, 1978, 25:241-252.
14, 654. Mundal, Else. Fylgjemotiva i norrøn litteratur. Oslo:
          Universitätforlaget, 1974.
14, 655. Munroe, Ruth H., & Munroe, Robert L. Population densi-
          ty and movement in folktales. J Social Psychol, 1973,
          91:339-340.
14, 656. Murase, Anne E. Personality and lore. Western Folk-
          lore, 1975, 34:171-185.

14, 657. Nagy, Gregory John. Six studies of sacral vocabulary re-
          lating to the fireplace. Harvard Studies in Classical
          Philology, 1974, 78:71-106.
14, 658. Neto, P. de Carvalho. Folklore y psicoanálysis. [Re-
          view.] Amer Anthropologist, 1957, 59:1134-1135.
14, 659. Neumann, Erich. The Origins and History of Conscious-
          ness. NY: Pantheon, 1954; London: Routledge &
          Kegan Paul, 1954.
14, 660. Noel, Thomas. Theories of the Fable in the Eighteenth
          Century. NY: Columbia Univ Press, 1975.
14, 661. Noy, Dov. Family confrontation and conflict in Jewish
          magic folk tales. In Noy, D., & Ben-Ami, I. (eds),
          Folklore Research Center Studies: Vol. I. Jerusalem:
          Magnes, 1970, 201-208.

14, 662. Oaks, Priscilla. 'Roll, Jenny Jenkins, Roll': little girls and maidens in American folksongs--an analysis of sexual attitudes. In Kirkpatrick, M. (ed), Women's Sexual Development. Explorations of Inner Space. NY: Plenum, 1980.

14, 663. Oba, C. [Aetiological myth and folklore about animals.] Japanese J Psychol, 1929, 4:67-82.

14, 664. Okezie, Joyce Ann. The Role of Quoting Behavior as Manifested in the Use of Proverbs in Igbo Society. DAI, 1978, 38:5635A.

14, 665. Opie, Iona, & Opie, Peter. Lore and Language of Schoolchildren. London: Oxford Univ. Press, 1959.

14, 666. Oring, Elliott. Whalemen and their songs: a study of folklore and culture. New York Folklore Q, 1971, 27: 130-152.

14, 667. Ottenheimer, Harriet J. Catharsis, communication, and evocation: alternative views of the sociopsychological functions of blues singing. Ethnomusicology, 1979, 23: 75-86.

14, 668. Owen, A. R. G. Brownie, incubus and poltergeist. Int J Parapsychol, 1964, 6:455-472.

14, 669. Owen, Morfydd E. Meddygon Myddfai: a preliminary survey of some medieval medical writing in Welsh. Studia Celtica, 1976, 10-11:210-233.

14, 670. Parmée, D. 'Cric? crack!': Fables of LaFontaine in Haitian Creole: a literary ethol-socio-linguistic curiosity. Nottingham French Studies, 1976, 15:12-16.

14, 671. Patai, Raphael. Exorcism and xenoglossia among the Safed Kabbalists. J Amer Folklore, 1978, 91:823-833.

14, 672. Paton, W. R. Folk-medicine, nursery-lore, etc., from the Aegean Island. Folk-Lore, 1907, 18:329-331.

14, 673. Patrick, Michael D. The Role of Folklore in the Study of Gerontology. Rolla: Univ. Missouri, n. d.

14, 674. Paulme, Denise. La Mère dévorante: Essai sur la morphologie des contes africains. Paris: Gallimard, 1976.

14, 675. _____. Oral literature and social behavior in Black Africa. In Skinner, E. P. (ed), Peoples and Cultures of Africa. Garden City, NY: Doubleday, 1973, 525-542.

14, 676. p'Bitek, Okot. Acholi folk tales. Transition (Uganda), 1962, 2(6-7):21-24; 1963, 3(10):5-6.

14, 677. Penrith, S. Punishment and reward: an analysis of plot structure in the Xhosa folktale. Limi (Pretoria), 1978, 6(1-2):12-30.

14, 678. Perkins, Richard. The dreams of Flóamanna saga. Saga-Book, 1976, 19:191-238.

14, 679. Perrotti, Nicola. La coda del diavolo. Psiche, 1949, 2: 455-456.

14, 680. Petzoldt, Leander. AT 470. Friends in life and death: Zur Psychologie und Geschichte einer Wundererzählung. Rheinisches Jahrbuch für Volkskunde, 1969, 19:101-161.

14, 681. Pina, L. de. Le Folklore medical africain. Scientia, 1940, 67:193-204.

14, 682. Pomorska-Jakobson, Krystyna. Observations on Ukrainian erotic folk songs. Minutes Seminar Ukrainian Studies, 1973-74, 4:73-74.

14, 683. Propp, V. Ya. [Notes on the origin of the fantastical folk tales.] Sovetsk etnografie, 1934, 1-2:128-151.

14, 684. Pulner, I. [Ceremonies and beliefs of the Jews in connection with pregnancy, women in confinement and newborn children.] Ethnografiichnii Visnik, 1929, 8:100-114.

14, 685. Raglan, FitzRoy R. S. Myth and ritual. J Amer Folklore, 1955, 68:454-461.

14, 686. Ramos, Arthur. Estudos de Folk-lore. Rio de Janeiro: Livraria da Casa do Estudante do Brasil, 1952.

14, 687. _____. O Folklore Negro de Brasil; demo Psychologia e Psychanalyse. Rio de Janeiro: Civilização Brasileira, 1935.

14, 688. Ramoux, Clémens. La Rivalité du pere et du fils dans la légende irlandaise. Psyché, 1947, 2:1357-1373.

14, 689. Ramsay, J. W. The wife who goes out like a man, comes back as a hero: the art of two Oregon Indian narratives. PMLA, 1977, 92:9-18.

14, 690. Randle, Martha C. Psychological types from Iroquois folktales. Amer J Folklore, 1952, 65:13-21.

14, 691. Reaver, J. Russell. From reality to fantasy, opening-closing formulas in the structures of American tall tales. Southern Folklore Q, 1972, 36:369-382.

14, 692. Reik, Theodor. The Symbolism of Fire, Earth, and Water. [A tape.] NY: J. Norton, 1952, Catalogue No. 29068.

14, 693. Rennick, Robert M. Obscene names and naming in folk tradition. Names, 1968, 16:207-229.

14, 694. Renwick, R. deV. Two Yorkshire poets: a comparative study. Southern Folklore Q, 1976, 40:239-281.

14, 695. Rhoads, Ellen. Little Orphan Annie and Lévi-Strauss; the myth and the method. J Amer Folklore, 1973, 86:345-357.

14, 696. Richmond, Winthrop E. Narrative folk poetry. In Dorson, R. M. (ed), Folklore and Folklife. Chicago: Univ. Chicago Press, 1972, 85-98.

14, 697. Roache, L. E. Psychophysical attributes of the Ogboni Edan. African Arts, 1971, 4(2):48-53, 80.

14, 698. Robinson, Charles Frederick. Some psychological elements in famous superstitions. J Religions, Psychol & Education, 1905, 1:248-267.

14, 699. Rockland, L. H. 'What kind of a fool am I?' A study of popular songs in the analysis of a male hysteric. Psychiatry, 1970, 33:516-525.

14, 700. Róheim, Géza. The bear in the haunted mill. Amer Imago, 1948, 5:70-82.

14, 701. _____. Children's games and rhymes in Duan (Normamby Island). Amer Anthropologist, 1943, 45:99-119.

14, 702. _____. Hungarian shamanism. In Psychoanalysis and the Social Sciences, Vol. 3. NY: IUP, 1951, 131-169.

14, 703. _____. The language of birds. Amer Imago, 1953, 10: 3-14.

14, 704. _____. Magic and theft in European folk-lore. J Psychopathology, 1940, 2: 54-61.

14, 705. _____. Psychoanalysis and the folktale. Int J Psycho-Anal, 1922, 3:180-186.

14, 706. _____. [Psychoanalysis, anthropology and folklore.] Szébszó, 1937, 1:202-211.

14, 707. _____. [Psychoanalysis, criticism, and Hungarian folk-lore.] Szádadunk, 1928, 3:572-577.

14, 708. _____. Die Sedna-Saga. Imago, 1924, 10:159-177.

14, 709. _____. Skt. Nikolaus im Volksbrauch und Volksglauban. Pester Lloyd, 1919, 12:7-9.

14, 710. _____. The song of the sirens. Psychoanal Q, 1948, 17:18-44.

14, 711. _____. The story of the light that disappeared. Samiksa, 1947, 1: 51-85.

14, 712. _____. [Survivals of Shamanistic cure in a nursery rhyme.] Ethnographia, 1912, 23:360-362.

14, 713. _____. Wedding ceremonies in European folklore. Samiksa, 1954, 8:137-173.

14, 714. Rolleston, J. D. The folk-lore of alcoholism. British J Inebriety, 1942, 39:30-36.

14, 715. _____. Ophthalmic folk-lore. British J Ophthalmology, 1942, 26:481-502.

14, 716. Rudolph, Ebermut. Cui bono? Anmerkungen zum Streit um die sog[enannte] 'parapsychologische Volkskunde.' Zeitschrift für Volkskunde, 1976, 72:74-80.

14, 717. Sal y Rosas, Federico. El mal de corazón (Sonko-Nanay) del folklore psiquiatrico del Peru. Acta Psiquiátrica y Psicológica de America Latina, 1967, 13:31-38.

14, 718. Samter, Ernst. Geburt, Hochzeit, und Tod. Beitrag zur vergleichenden Folkskunde. Leipzig: Teubner, 1911.

14, 719. Sanchez, R. J., & Jocovella, B. Las Supersticiones. Contribucion a la Metodologia de la Investigacion Folklorica. Buenos Aires: 1939.

14, 720. Savard, Rémi. La Faim et la mort dans la littérature orale montagnaise. Anthropologica, 1977, 19:15-26.

14, 721. Schiebe, Karl E., & Sarbin, Theodore R. Towards a theoretical conceptualization of superstition. British J Philosophy Science, 1966, 40(3):143-158.

14, 722. Schmaier, M. D., & Dundes, Alan. Parallel paths. J Amer Folklore, 1961, 74:142-145.

14, 723. Schmidt, H. Das Ethos in den Erzählungen arabischer Bauern in Palästina. Archiv für die gesamte Psychologie, 1932, 86:211-220.

14, 724. Schnier, Jacques. The symbol of the ship in art, myth and dreams. Psychoanal Rev, 1951, 38:53-65.

14, 725.   Schwartz, Alvin.   Children, humor, and folklore.   In
           Heins, P. (ed), Crosscurrents of Criticism.   Horn
           Book Essays, 1968-1977.   Boston: Horn, 1977, 205-
           216.
14, 726.   Segalen, Martine.   Le Mariage et la femme dans les pro-
           verbes du sud de la France.   Annales du Midi, 1975,
           87:265-288.
14, 727.   _____.   Le Mariage, l'amour et les femmes dans les
           proverbes populaires français.   Ethnologie Française,
           1975, 5:119-162.
14, 728.   Seguin, Carlos A.   [Ethno-psychiatry and folklore psychi-
           atry.]   Revista Interamericana de Psicologia, 1972, 6:
           75-80.
14, 729.   _____.   [Towards a Latin American psychiatry.]   Acta
           Psiquiatrica y Psicológica de América Latina, 1972,
           18:413-419.
14, 730.   Senior, Michael.   The Phaedra complex: Amour Courtois
           in Malory's 'Morte D'Arthur.'   Folklore, 1971, 80:36-
           59.
14, 731.   Sereno, Renzo.   Some observations on the Santa Claus
           custom.   Psychiatry, 1951, 14:375-386.
14, 732.   Shrut, Samuel D.   Coping with the 'evil eye' or early rab-
           binical attempts at psychotherapy.   Amer Imago, 1960,
           17:201-213.
14, 733.   Simpson, J.   The function of folklore in Jane Eyre and
           Wuthering Heights.   Folklore, 1974, 85:47-61.
14, 734.   Siyavusgil, S. E.   [Folklore and psychology.]   Istambul
           Univ. Yayinlav, No. 10, 216-217.
14, 735.   Skeels, Dell R.   Guingamor and Guerrehés: psychological
           symbolism in a medieval romance.   J Amer Folklore,
           1966, 79:52-83.
14, 736.   _____.   Two psychological patterns underlying the
           morphologies of Propp and Dundes.   Southern Folklore
           Q, 1967, 31:244-261.
14, 737.   Skynner, A. C. Robin.   The relationship of psychotherapy
           to sacred tradition.   In Needleman, J., & Lewis, D.
           (eds), On the Way to Self-Knowledge.   NY: Knopf,
           1976, 204-205.
14, 738.   Speck, F. G.   Montagnais and Naskapi tales from the
           Labrador peninsula.   J Amer Folklore, 1925, 38:1-32.
14, 739.   Spielberg, Joseph.   Humor in a Mexican American Palo-
           milla: some historical, social and psychological im-
           plications.   Revista Chicano-Riqueña, 1974, 2(3):41-50.
14, 740.   Spitz, Sheryl A.   Social and psychological themes in East
           Slavic folk lullabies.   Slavic & East European J, 1979,
           23:14-24.
14, 741.   Stahl, William Harrison.   Moon madness.   Annals Medical
           History, 1937, 9:248-263.
14, 742.   Stanley, Gordon, et al.   Some characteristics of charis-
           matic experience: glossolalia in Australia.   J Science
           Study Religion, 1978, 17:269-278.
14, 743.   Steckert, Ellen.   Two Voices of Tradition: The Influence
           of Personality and Collecting Environment upon the

Songs of Two Traditional Folksingers. DA, 1966, 26: 7251-52.

14, 744. Stein, Howard F. Envy and the evil eyes among Slovak-Americans: an essay in the psychological ontogeny of belief and ritual. Ethos, 1974, 2:15-46; In Maloney, C. (ed), The Evil Eye. NY: Columbia Univ. Press, 1976, 193-222.

14, 745. Steiner, Fritz. Taboo. Baltimore: Penguin, 1967.

14, 746. Stekert, Ellen J. Focus for conflict: Southern mountain medical beliefs in Detroit. J Amer Folklore, 1970, 83:115-147.

14, 747. Steward, Julian Haynes. The ceremonial buffoon of the American Indian. In Evolution and Ecology; Essays on Social Transformation. Urbana: Univ. Illinois Press, 1977, 347-365.

14, 748. Story, W. L. The folklore of adolescence: autograph books. Southern Folklore Q, 1953, 17:207-212.

14, 749. Stuckey, Sterling. Through the prism of folklore: the black ethos in slavery. Massachusetts Rev, 1968, 9: 417-437; In Lane, A. J. (ed), The Debate over Slavery. Urbana: Univ. Illinois Press, 1971, 245-268.

14, 750. Sutton-Smith, Brian. Psychology of childlore: the triviality barrier. Western Folklore, 1970, 29:1-8.

14, 751. Tanner, Jeri. The teeth in folklore. Western Folklore, 1968, 27:97-105.

14, 752. Tarachow, Sidney. Folk tales and folkways. In The Annual Survey of Psychoanalysis, Vol. 1. NY: IUP, 1950, 321-325.

14, 753. Tchoungui, Pierre. Ethnic survivals and the modern shift: literary imagology and ethno-psychology; Cameroon as reflected by its writers. Diogenes, 1972, 80:102-149.

14, 754. Thompson, S. Literature for the unlettered. In Stallknecht, N. P. , & Frenz, H. (eds), Comparative Literature: Method and Perspective. Carbondale: Southern Illinois Univ. Press, 1961, 1971, 201-217.

14, 755. Thompson, Stith. The Folktale. Berkeley: Univ. California Press, 1977; NY: Dryden, 1946.

14, 756. _____. Motif-Index of Folk Literature. Bloomington: Indiana University Studies 1932-1936, 6 Vols.

14, 757. Tissot, Georges. Identité et symbole: nous et les Amérindiens. Studies in Religion, 1972, 2:11-35.

14, 758. Toelken, Barre. The Dynamics of Folklore. Boston: Houghton, Mifflin, 1979.

14, 759. _____. Riddles wisely expounded. Western Folklore, 1966, 25:1-16.

14, 760. Turner, Victor Witter. African ritual and Western literature: is a comparative symbology possible? In Fletcher, A. J. S. (ed), The Literature of Fact. NY: Columbia Univ. Press, 1976, 45-81.

14, 761. Turville-Petre, G. Dreams in Icelandic tradition. Folklore, 1958, 69:93-111.

715   Folklore

14, 762. Tybnikov, N. A. [Psychological characteristics of memory
          in folklore data.] Sovetskaya pedagogisk, 1940, 2:64-
          70.

14, 763. Upadhyaya, Hari S. The Joint Family Structure and Fam-
          ilial Relationship Patterns in the Bhojpuri Folksongs.
          DAI, 1976, 28:4557A.
14, 764. _____. Mother-daughter relationship patterns in the
          Hindu joint family: a study based upon the analysis of
          the Bhojpuri folksongs in India. Folklore, 1968, 79:
          217-226.

14, 765. Van der Ven, D. J. [Folklore as a science in the Nether-
          lands.] Mensch en Maatsch, 1930, 6:457-475.
14, 766. Van Gennep, A. Folklore et psychologie. J de Psychol-
          ogie, 1926, 23:773-775.
14, 767. Van Haver, Jozef. Nederlandse Incantatieliteratuur.
          Ghent: Koninklijke Vlaamse Academie voor Taal-en
          Letterkunde, 1964.
14, 768. Veith, Ilza. The supernatural in Far Eastern concepts of
          mental disease. Bulletin History Medicine, 1963, 37:
          139-155.
14, 769. Veszy-Wagner, Lilla. Serf Balazs: a 'boy without the
          dike'; a stage before the solution of the Oedipal con-
          flict. Amer Imago, 1958, 15:181-194.

14, 770. Walsh, Maurice N. A psychoanalytic interpretation of a
          primitive dramatic ritual. J Hillside Hospital, 1962,
          11:3-20.
14, 771. Walton, David A. Folklore as compensation: a content
          analysis of the Negro animal tale. Ohio Folklore,
          1974, 1-11.
14, 772. Weiss, H. B. Oneirocritica Americana. Bulletin New
          York Public Library, 1944, 4-8:519-541.
14, 773. Wenk, W. Das Volksmärchen als Bildungsgut. Ein Beit-
          rag zur grundsatzlichen Beurteilung des Volksmärchens
          als Bildungsgut an Hand einer Untersuchung von Grimms
          Kinder und Hausmarchen. Langesalza: Beyer, 1929.
14, 774. Westermarck, E. On the study of popular sayings. Na-
          ture, 1928, 122:701-703.
14, 775. White, Robert B., Jr. The imagery of sexual repression
          in Season of Fear. North Carolina Folklore, 1971, 19:
          80-84.
14, 776. Willoughby, R. R. Ghosts of the sophisticated. J Social
          Psychol, 1934, 5:508-515.
14, 777. Wimmer, Wolf. Parapsychologie, Aberglaube und Ver-
          brechen. Zeitschrift für Volkskunde, 1975, 71:181-201.
14, 778. _____. Zu Rudolphs parapsychologischer Volkskunde.
          Zeitschrift für Volkskunde, 1976, 72:81-83.
14, 779. Wolf Eric R. The Virgin of Guadalupe, a Mexican national
          symbol. J Amer Folklore, 1958, 71:34-39.

14, 780. Wright, George O. Projection and displacement: a cross-cultural study of folktale aggression. J Abnormal & Social Psychol, 1954, 49:523-528; Doctoral dissertation, Howard Univ., 1952.

14, 781. Wundt, Wilhelm. Elements of Folk Psychology. NY: Macmillan, 1916 (1912).

14, 782. _____. Völkerpsychologie: Eine Untersuchung der Entwicklungsgesetze von Sprache, Mythus und Sitte. Leipzig: Englelmann, 1905.

14, 783. Yanga, Tshimpaka. Inside the proverbs: a sociolinguistic approach. African Languages/Langues Africaines, 1977, 3:130-157.

14, 784. Yen, Alsace. Thematic patterns in Japanese folktales: a search for meanings. Asian Folklore Studies, 1974, 33(2):1-36.

14, 785. Zaleskie, Z. L. La Psychologie du voyage et la vocation de comparatiste. North Carolina Folklore, 1965, 13(1-2):108-116.

14, 786. Zammit-Maempel, G. The evil eye and protective cattle horns in Malta. Folklore, 1968, 79:1-16.

14, 787. Zeckel, Adolf. The totemistic significance of the Unicorn. In Psychoanalysis and Culture. NY: IUP, 1951, 344-360.

14, 788. Zelenin, D. K. [Religio-magic function of the folk story.] Sbornik Statei S. F. Oldenburgu Akadamie Nauk, 1934, 215-240.

14, 789. Abadi, Mauricio. Dioniso-Estudio psicoanalitico del mito y culto dionisíacoe. Revista de Psicoanálysis, 1955, 12:18-39.

14, 790. _____. Renacimento de Edipo: La Vida del Hombre en la Dialéctica del Adentro y del Afuera. Buenos Aires: Editorial Nova, 1960.

14, 791. Abou Zeid, A. La psychanalyse des myths. Egyptian J Psychol, 1946, 2:233-251.

14, 792. Abraham, Karl. Dreams and myths: a study in folk psychology. In Clinical Papers and Essays on Psychoanalysis. NY: Basic Books, 1955, 153-209; London: Hogarth, 1955 (1909); Rêve et mythe. In Oeuvres complete, Vol. I. Paris: Payot, 1965; NY: Nervous & Mental Disease Monograph Series No. 15, 1913; Traum und Mythus. Schriften zür angewandten Seelenkunden, 1909, 4.

14, 793. _____. The spider as a dream symbol. In Selected Papers. London: Hogarth, 1927, 326-332.

14, 794. _____. Zwei Beiträge zur Symbolforschung. Imago, 1923, 1:122-126.

14, 795. Albouy, P. La Création mythologique chez Victor Hugo. Paris: Corti, 1963.

14, 796. Almansi, Renato J. Applied psychoanalysis. II. Religion, mythology, and folklore. In Annual Survey Psychoanal, Vol. 4. NY: IUP, 1953, 340-355.

14, 797. _____. Applied psychoanalysis. Religion, mythology and folklore. In Annual Survey Psychoanal, Vol. 5. NY: IUP, 1954, 5:438-457.

14, 798. _____. Ego-psychological implications of a religious symbol: a cultural and experimental study, Vol. 3. In The Psychoanalytic Study of Society, 1964, 39-70.

14, 799. _____. Religion, mythology, and folklore. In Annual Survey of Psychoanal, Vol. 6. NY: IUP, 1955, 397-418.

14, 800. Altschule, Mark D. The incestuous hippopotamus. In Roots of Modern Psychiatry. NY: Grune & Stratton, 1965.

14, 801. Ammon, G. Von Ödipus zu Laios. Selecta, 1971, 13: 2261-2262.

14, 802. Anon. Superfecundation in mythology, history and poetry. New England J Medicine, 1979, 300:49-50.

14, 803.   Ansbacher, Heinz.   More on the Laius complex.   J Indi-
           vidual Psychol, 1973, 29:88-91.
14, 804.   Ansell, C.   Dybbuks and their divines.   Psychoanal Rev,
           1970, 57:657-659.
14, 805.   Anson, John.   The female transvestite in early monasti-
           cism: the origin and development of a motif.   Viator,
           1974, 5:1-32.
14, 806.   Anzieu, Didier.   Freud et la mythologie.   Nouvelle Rev de
           Psychanalyse, 1970, 1.
14, 807.   _____.   Oedipe avant le complexe, ou de l'interpréta-
           tion psychanalytique des mythes.   Les temps modernes,
           1966, 22:675-715.
14, 808.   Arlow, Jacob A.   Ego psychology and the study of mythol-
           ogy.   JAPA, 1961, 9:371-393.
14, 809.   _____.   The Madonna's conception through the eye.   In
           Muentserberger, W., & Axelrad, S. (eds), The Psycho-
           analytic Study of Society, Vol. 3.   NY: IUP, 1964,
           13-25.
14, 810.   Astier, Colette.   Le Mythe d'Oedipe.   Paris: Colin, 1974.
14, 811.   Atkins, N.   The Oedipus myth, adolescence and the suc-
           cession of generations.   JAPA, 1970, 18:868-875.

14, 812.   Bachofen, Johann J.   Entwicklung des Oedipusmythus.   In
           Schroeter, M. (ed), Der Mythus von Orient und Occi-
           dent: Eine Metaphysik der alten Welt.   Munich: 1926,
           259-271.
14, 813.   Bailey, P.   Hero myths according to Freud.   New Repub-
           lic, 1915, 2:160-161.
14, 814.   Balint, M.   Eros and Aphrodite.   Int J Psycho-Anal, 1938,
           19:199-213.
14, 815.   Bally, G.   Das Inzestmotiv: die Überwindung der Ver-
           gänglichkeit im Mythus.   Psyche, 1947, 1:206-221.
14, 816.   Balter, Leon.   The mother as source of power.   A psy-
           choanalytic study of three Greek myths.   Psychoanal Q,
           1969, 38:217-274.
14, 817.   Barfield, Owen.   Dream, myth, and philosophical double
           vision.   In Campbell, J. (ed), Myths, Dreams, and
           Religion.   NY: Dutton, 1970, 211-224.
14, 818.   Barnes, Francis F.   The myth of the seal ancestor.   Psy-
           choanal Rev, 1953, 40:150-156.
14, 819.   Barnett, B.   The oracle of Trophonius.   British J Psy-
           chiat, 1968, 114:650-651.
14, 820.   Barnouw, Victor.   Wisconsin Chippewa Myths and Tales.
           Madison: Univ. Wisconsin Press, 1977, 1979.
14, 821.   _____.   A psychoanalytic interpretation of a Chippewa
           origin legend.   J Amer Folklore, 1955, 68:73-85, 211-
           223, 341-355.
14, 822.   Barthes, Roland.   Mythologies.   London: Cape, 1972; NY:
           Hill & Wang, 1972.
14, 823.   Bastian, A.   Zur Mythologie und Psychologie der Nigritier
           in Guinea.   Berlin: Reimer, 1895.
14, 824.   Bastide, Roger.   Transmission de Légende de groups so-
           ciaux.   Psyché, 1949, 4:746-756.

14, 825.   Baumann, H. Afrikanische Wild-und Buschgeister. Zeit-
           schrift für Ethnologie, 1939, 70:208-239.
14, 826.   _____. Das doppelte Geschlect: ethnologische Studien
           zur Bisexualität in Ritus und Mythos. Berlin: Reimer,
           1955.
14, 827.   Beck, Jane C. 'Dream messages' from the dead. J Folk-
           lore Institute, 1973, 10:173-186.
14, 828.   Becker, Michael. The Narcissus myth in Ovid. Amer J
           Psychoanal, 1977, 37:259-261.
14, 829.   Beit-Hallahmi, Benjamin, et al. Twinship in mythology
           and science: ambivalence, differentiation, and the
           magical bond. Comprehensive Psychiat, 1974, 15:345-
           353.
14, 830.   Benedict, Laura Watson. A Study of Bagobo Ceremonial,
           Magic and Myth. Annals New York Academy Science,
           1916, 25:1-308.
14, 831.   Benedict, Ruth. Myth. Encyclopedia Social Sciences,
           1933, 11:178-181.
14, 832.   Bennett, Benjamin. Nietzsche's idea of myth: The Birth
           of Tragedy from the spirit of eighteenth-century aes-
           thetics. PMLA, 1979, 94:420-433.
14, 833.   Berg, William. Pandora: pathology of a creation myth.
           Fabula, 1976, 17:1-25.
14, 834.   Bergin, Thomas Goddard, & Harold, Max (eds). The New
           Science of Giambattista Vico. Revised Translation of
           the Third Edition (1744). Ithaca: Cornell Univ. Press,
           1968.
14, 835.   Bergmann, Martin S. The impact of ego psychology on
           the study of the myth. Amer Imago, 1966, 23:257-264.
14, 836.   _____. Recall and distortion of legendary material in
           the course of psychoanalysis. In Lindner, R. (ed),
           Explorations in Psychoanalysis. NY: Messner, 1953,
           71-83.
14, 837.   Bertin, Gerald A. The Oedipus complex in Tristan et
           Iseult. Kentucky Foreign Language Q, 1958, 5:60-65.
14, 838.   Bianchi, I. Die dunkle Herkunft; zum Oedipus-Problem;
           Oedipus Shicksal. Wendepunkt, 1945, 22:103-119.
14, 839.   Bidney, David. The concept of myth and the problem of
           psychocultural evolution. Amer Anthropologist, 1950,
           52:15-26.
14, 840.   _____. Myth, symbolism, and truth. In Vickery, J. B.
           Myth and Literature; Contemporary Theory and Prac-
           tice. Lincoln: Univ. Nebraska Press, 1966, 3-13.
14, 841.   _____. Vico's new science of myth. In Tagliacozzo,
           G. , & White, H. V. (eds), Giambattista Vico, an Inter-
           national Symposium. Baltimore: Johns Hopkins Univ.
           Press, 1969, 259-277.
14, 842.   Blomeyer, Rudolf. [Oedipus, Freud, and anti-authoritari-
           anism.] Analytische Psychologie, 1977, 8:41-51.
14, 843.   Blümner, Hugo. Das Märchen von Amor und Psyche in
           der deutsche Dichtkunst. Neue Jahrbücher für das
           klassische Altertum, Geschichte und deutsche Literatur
           und für Pädagogik, 1903, 11:648-673.

14, 844. Boas, Franz. Mythology and folklore. In General Anthropology. NY: Heath, 1938, 609-626.
14, 845. Bois-Reymind, Fanny de. Der unsterbliche Ödipus.
Psyche, 1956, 9:627-633.
14, 846. Bonaparte, Marie. La Faute d'Orphée à l'envers. Rev
Française de Psychanalyse, 1953, 17:221-228.
14, 847. _____. The legend of the unfathomable waters. Amer
Imago, 1946, 4:20-31; In The Yearbook of Psychoanalysis, Vol. 3. NY: IUP, 1947, 281-290.
14, 848. Borkenau, Franz. Zwei Abhandlungen zur griechischen
Mythologie. Psyche, 1957, 11:1-27.
14, 849. Boyer, L. Bryce. An example of legend distortion from
the Apaches of the Mescalero Indian Reservation. J
Amer Folklore, 1964, 77:118-42.
14, 850. _____. Stone as a symbol in Apache mythology. Amer
Imago, 1965, 22:14-39.
14, 851. Brandon, S. G. F. The deification of time. Studium Generale, 1970, 23:485-497.
14, 852. Brès, Y. Oedipe ou Freud? Rev philosophique de la
France, 1973, 163:35-52.
14, 853. Brill, Abraham. Psychoanalytic Psychiatry. NY: Vintage, 1959.
14, 854. Brink, Louise. Women Characters in Richard Wagner.
NY: Nervous and Mental Disease Publishing, 1924.
14, 855. Brocher, Henri. Le Mythe du héros et la mentalité primitive. Paris: Alcan, 1932.
14, 856. Brock-Utney, A. Eine Studie zur Psychologie der Mythen-
Phantasie. In Various, Festskrift til Anathon Aall.
Oslo: Aschehoug, 1937, 230-256.
14, 857. Broos, Karl. Zur Psychologie des Mythos. Int Monatsschrift für Wissenschaft Kunst und Technik, July 1914.
14, 858. Brown, Calvin Smith. Faulkner's universality. In Harrington, E. , & Abadie, A. J. (eds), The Maker and the
Myth. Jackson: Univ. Mississippi Press, 1977, 146-
169.
14, 859. Bruner, Jerome S. Myth and identity. In Murray, Henry
A. (ed), Myth and Mythmaking. NY: Braziller, 1960;
Daedalus, 1959, 8:349-358.
14, 860. Bugard, P. L'Interpretation psychanalytique du mythe
d'Orphee et son application au symbolisme musical.
Rev Française de Psychanalyse, 1934, 7:320-371.
14, 861. Buis, C. Oedipus, Dionysus and Eros. Psychiatrie,
Neurologie, Neurochirgurie, 1964, 67:427-438.
14, 862. Bulliet, G. Venus Castina. Famous Female Impersonators, Celestial and Human. NY: Covici, Friede, 1928.
14, 863. Bullough, Vern L. Homosexuality as submissive behavior:
example from mythology. J Sex Research, 1973, 9:283-
288.
14, 864. Bunker, Henry A. The feast of Tantalus. Psychoanal Q,
1952, 21:355-372.
14, 865. _____. Mother-murder in myth and legend: a psychoanalytic note. Psychoanal Q, 1944, 13:198-207.
14, 866. _____. Narcissus: a psychoanalytic note. In Psychoanalysis and the Social Sciences, NY: 1951, 159-162.

14, 867. _____. Tantalus: a pre-oedipal figure of myth. Psychoanal Q, 1953, 22:159-173.
14, 868. _____, & Lewin, Bertram D. A psychoanalytic notation
of the root GN, KN, CN. In Psychoanalysis and Culture. NY: IUP, 1951, 363-367.
14, 869. Burrows, David J., et al. Myths and Motifs in Literature. NY: Free Press, 1973.
14, 870. Burridge, K. O. L. Lévi-Strauss and myth. In Leach, E.
(ed), The Structural Study of Myth and Totemism. NY:
Tavistock.
14, 871. Bushnell, J. La Virgen de Guadalupe as surrogate mother. Amer Anthropologist, 1958, 60:261-265.
14, 872. Bychowski, Gustav. A brief visit to India: observations
and psychoanalytic implications. Amer Imago, 1968,
25:59-76.
14, 873. _____. Review: A. DeGroot's Saint Nicholas: A Psychoanalytic Study of His History and Myth. Amer
Imago, 1966, 23:277-278.

14, 874. Caillois, Roger. Man and the Sacred. Glencoe, Ill:
Free Press, 1959.
14, 875. Caldwell, Richard S. The blindness of Oedipus. Int Rev
Psychoanal, 1974, 1:207-218.
14, 876. _____. Hephaestus: a psychological study. Helios,
1978, 6(1):43-59.
14, 877. Calogeras, Roy C. Lévi-Strauss and Freud: their 'structural' approaches to myths. Amer Imago, 1973, 30:
57-79.
14, 878. Campbell, Joseph. Bios and mythos: prolegomena to a
science of mythology. In Wilbur, G. B., & Muensterberger, W. (eds), Psychoanalysis and Culture. NY:
IUP, 1951; NY: Science Editions, 1967, 329-343.
14, 879. _____. Creative Mythology. NY: Viking, 1969.
14, 880. _____. The Hero with a Thousand Faces. NY: Pantheon, 1949; NY: Meridian, 1959; Frankfurt: Fischer,
1953; Princeton: Princeton Univ. Press, 1968.
14, 881. _____. The historical development of mythology. Daedalus, 1959, 88:232-254; In Murray, H. A. (ed), Myth
and Mythmaking. NY: Viking, 1959.
14, 882. _____ (ed). Man and Transformation. NY: Pantheon,
1964.
14, 883. _____. The Masks of God: Primitive Mythology. NY:
Viking, 1959.
14, 884. _____. The Mythic Image. Princeton: Bollingen,
1975; Review: David Beres, Psychoanal Q, 1978, 47:
134-136.
14, 885. _____ (ed). Myths, Dreams, and Religion. NY: Dutton, 1970.
14, 886. _____. Occidental Mythology. NY: Viking, 1964.
14, 887. Candland, Douglas K. Speaking words and doing deeds.
Amer Psychol, 1980, 35:191-198.
14, 888. Cantarella, Raffaele. Psychoanalytische Elemente in der
griechischen Tragödie. Almanach, 1936, 128-149.

14, 889.   Carlisky, Mario.   Edipo y las enigmas de la Esfringe.
            Buenos Aires: Nova, 1952.
14, 890.   _____. Oedipus, beyond complex. Psychoanal Rev,
            1967, 54:296-302.
14, 891.   Carloni, Glauco, & Nobili, D. [Filicide: II.   Filicide in
            myth and art.] Revista Sperimentale di Freniatria e
            Medicina Legale delle Alienazione Mentali, 1972, 96:
            1337-1380.
14, 892.   Carroll, David.   Freud and the myth of the origin.   New
            Lit History, 1975, 6:513-528.
14, 893.   Carroll, Michael P.   Lévi-Strauss on the Oedipus myth:
            a reconsideration. Amer Anthropologist, 1978, 80:805-
            814.
14, 894.   Cassirer, Ernst.   Essay on Man.   New Haven: Yale Univ.
            Press, 1944.
14, 895.   _____. Language and Myth. NY: Harper, 1946.
14, 896.   _____. The Philosophy of Symbolic Forms.   New Hav-
            en: Yale Univ. Press, 1955.
14, 897.   Castiglioni, A.   Adventures of the Mind.   Knopf, 1946.
14, 898.   Chambers, Ross.   A theatre of dilemma and myth.   Mean-
            jin Q, 1966, 25:306-317.
14, 899.   Chase, Richard.   Myth revisited.   Partisan Rev, 1950, 17:
            885-891.
14, 900.   _____. Notes on the study of myth. Partisan Rev,
            1946, 12:338-346.   In Handy, W. J., & Westbrook, M.
            (eds), Twentieth Century Criticism.   NY: Free Press,
            1974, 244-251.
14, 901.   _____. Quest for Myth.   Baton Rouge: Louisiana State
            Univ. Press, 1949.
14, 902.   Cheney, C. O.   The psychology of mythology.   Psychiat Q,
            1927, 1:198-209.
14, 903.   Chodoff, Paul.   Discussion of J. W. Fernandez.   'Filial
            piety and power: psychosocial dynamics in the legends
            of Shaka and Sundiata.' In Masserman, J. H. (ed),
            Science and Psychoanalysis, Vol. 14.   NY: Grune &
            Stratton, 1969, 60-63.
14, 904.   Choisy, Maryse.   Autour de Tristan et Yseult.   Psyché,
            1953, 8:324-349.
14, 905.   _____. Le Complex de Phaéton. Psyché, 1950, 5:770-
            776.
14, 906.   _____. Descente aux enfers. Psyché, 1952, 7:1-5.
14, 907.   _____. Mythes d'hier et d'aujourd'hui. Psyché, 1950,
            5:290-303.
14, 908.   _____. Symboles et mythes. Psyché, 1947, 2:646-660.
14, 909.   Christoffel, H.   Dulce estne tempus in agorum cultu con-
            sumere? Schweizerischen Zeitschrift für Psychologie,
            1944, 3:30-36.
14, 910.   Cinquemani, A. M.   Henry Reynolds' Mythomyste's and the
            continuity of ancient modes of allegories in seven-
            teenth century England. PMLA, 1970, 85, 1041-1049.
14, 911.   Clancier-Gravelat, Anne.   Oedipe et création littéraire.
            Rev Française de Psychanalyse, 1967, 31:891-895.

14,912. Clemen, C. Die Anwendung der Psychoanalyse auf Myth-
         ologie und Religionsgeschichte. Archiv für die Gesamte
         Psychologie, 1928, 71:1-128; Leipzig: Akademie Ver-
         lags, 1928.
14,913. _____. Mythologie, Religionsgeschichte und Psycho-
         analyse. In Prinzhorn, H. (ed), Auswerkung der Psy-
         choanalyse in Wissenschaft und Leben. Leipzig: Der
         Neue Geist Verlag, 1928, 172-195.
14,914. Clements, M. Mythology and psychological presupposition.
         Educational Theory, 1964, 14:224-228.
14,915. Coleman, Stanley M. The myth of the fairy birth. Psy-
         choanal Rev, 1939, 26:301-314.
14,916. Consoli, Silla. [The myth of the siren: I. Variations,
         underlying fantasies, and psychopathological implica-
         tions.] Evolution Psychiatrique, 1974, 39:63-89.
14,917. Coriat, Isadore H. A note on the Medusa symbolism.
         Amer Imago, 1941, 2:281-285.
14,918. Costa, E., & Alborghetti, M. [Myth and symbols in the
         evolution of the mind.] Rivista Sperimentale di Frenia-
         tria e Medicina Legale delle Alienazioni Mentali, 1974,
         98:785-806.
14,919. Courville, Cyril Brian. Craniocerebral injuries as found
         in myths, legends, and folk tales of the ancient world.
         Bulletin Los Angeles Neurological Society, 1960, 25:
         193-210.
14,920. _____. Epilepsy in mythology, legend, and folk tale.
         Bulletin Los Angeles Neurological Society, 1951, 16:
         213-224.
14,921. _____. Injuries of the Skull and Brain as Described in
         the Myths, Legends and Folk-Tales of the Various Peo-
         ples of the World. NY: Vantage, 1967.
14,922. Covello, Lucio. [The sin of Narcissus.] Evolution Psy-
         chiatrique, 1976, 4:451-459.
14,923. Cox, Howard L. The place of mythology in the study of
         culture. Amer Imago, 1948, 5:83-94.

14,924. Dalma, Juan. Nota sobre el complejo de Layo (el padre
         frente al hijo). La Prensa Médico Argentina, 1953,
         40, 1806-1809.
14,925. _____. Reflexiones sobre el concepto edípico. Revista
         de Psicquiatria y Psicologia Médica de Europa y Amér-
         ica Latinas, 1955, 2:53-61.
14,926. Daly, C.D. Hindu-Mythologie und Kastrations-Complex.
         Imago, 1927, 13:145-198; Vienna: Int Psychoanalytisch-
         er Verlag, 1927.
14,927. Danzel, Theodor Wilhelm. Die psychologischen Grund-
         lagen der Mythologie. In Festschrift Meinhof. Ham-
         burg: Augustin, 1927, 495-501; Archiv der Religion-
         wissenschaften, 1922, 21:430-439.
14,928. D'Aquili, Eugene G. Neurobiological bases of myth and
         concepts of deity. Zygon, 1978, 13:257-275.

14,929. Dardel, E.   Magic, mythe et historie.   JPNP, 1950, 43:
         193-229.

14,930. De, Ranajitkumar.   On certain excerpts from the Abor
         mythology.   Indian J Psychol, 1951, 26:37-44.

14,931. de la Cuadra, José L.   [The proportio sesquitertia in psy-
         chology and natural science.]   Analytische Psychologie,
         1977, 8(2):77-129.

14,932. Delcourt, Marie.   Hermaphrodite, Myths and Rites of the
         Bisexual Figure in Classical Antiquity.   London: Studio
         Books, 1956.

14,933. Depuydt-Berte, Raymonde.   [From Moses to Saturn: a
         myth of the Freud-Jung period (1906-1914).]   Rev de
         Psychologie et des Sciences de l'Education, 1975, 10:
         345-366.

14,934. Desmonde, William H.   The bull fight as a religious ritu-
         al.   Amer Imago, 1952, 9:173-195.

14,935. _____.   The Eleusinian mysteries.   J Hillside Hospital,
         1952, 1:204-218.

14,936. _____.   Magic, Myth, and Money.   Glencoe, Ill: Free
         Press, 1962.

14,937. Deutsch, Helene.   Bisexuality and immortality in the Diony-
         sus myth.   [Abstract.]   Psychoanal Q, 1968, 37:321-
         322.

14,938. _____.   A Psychoanalytic Study of the Myth of Dionysus
         and Apollo.   Two Variants of the Son-Mother Relation-
         ship.   NY: IUP, 1969.

14,939. Devereux, George.   The awarding of a penis as compen-
         sation for rape: a demonstration of the clinical rele-
         vance of the psycho-analytic study of cultural data.   Int
         J Psycho-Anal, 1957, 38:398-401.

14,940. _____.   Considerations psychanalytiques sur la divina-
         tion, particulièrement en Grèce.   In Caquot, A., &
         Leibovici, M. (eds), La Divination, Vol. 2.   Paris:
         1968, 449-471.

14,941. _____.   Dreams in Greek Tragedy: An Ethno-Psycho-
         Analytic Study.   Berkeley: Univ. California Press,
         1976.

14,942. _____.   The Enetian horses of Hippolytos.   Antiquité
         Classique, 1964, 33:375-383.

14,943. _____.   Homer's wild she-mules.   J Hellenic Studies,
         1965, 85:29-32.

14,944. _____.   La naissance d'Aphrodite.   In Pouillon, J., &
         Maranda, P. (eds), Mélanges Claude Lévi-Strauss, Vol.
         2.   The Hague: Mouton, 1969, 1229-1252.

14,945. _____.   Observation and belief in Aischylos' accounts
         of dreams.   Psychotherapy & Psychosomatics, 1967,
         15:114-134; In Philippopoulos, G. S. (ed), Dynamics in
         Psychiatry.   Basel/NY: Karger, 1968, 30-50.

14,946. _____.   The oedipal situation and its consequences in
         the epics of ancient India.   Samiksa, 1951, 5:5-13.

14,947. _____.   The psychosomatic miracle of Iolaos.   A hy-
         pothesis.   Psychotherapy & Psychosomatics, 1971, 26:
         167-195.

14,948. _____. Retaliatory homosexual triumph over the father: a further contribution to the counter-oedipal sources of the Oedipus complex. Int J Psycho-Anal, 1960, 41:157-161.

14,949. _____. Sociopolitical functions of the Oedipus myth in early Greece. Psychoanal Q, 1963, 32:205-214.

14,950. _____. Why Oedipus killed Laius. Int J Psycho-Anal, 1953, 34:132-141.

14,951. DeWolf, M. J. Comments on Freud and Kronos. Psychoanal Q, 1972, 41:420-423.

14,952. Di Gaetani, John Louis. Comic uses of myth. Richard Wagner and James Joyce. In Richard Wagner and the Modern British Novel. Rutherford, NJ: Fairleigh Dickinson Univ. Press, 1978, 130-157.

14,953. Dimock, Edward C. Manasa, goddess of snakes. In Kitagawa, J. M., & Long, C. H. (eds), Myths and Symbols. Chicago: Univ. Chicago Press, 1969, 217-226.

14,954. Dodds, Eric R. The Greeks and the Irrational. Berkeley: Univ. California Press, 1951; Boston: Beacon, 1957.

14,955. Dorson, Richard M. Theories of myth and the folklorist. Daedalus, 1959, 88:280-290.

14,956. Douglas, W. W. The meaning of 'myth' in modern criticism. Modern Philology, 1953, 50:232-242.

14,957. Dournes, Jacques. L'Inceste préferentiel: étude de mythologie. Homme, 1971, 11(4):5-19.

14,958. Dowling, Allan. In the Beginning Was the Myth. NY: Vantage, 1968.

14,959. Downing, Christine. Sigmund Freud and the Greek mythological tradition. Amer Academy of Religion J, 1975, 43:3-14.

14,960. Dracoulidès, N. N. La Généalogie des Atrides et l'aventure d'Oreste; introduction à l'étude du complexe d'Oreste. Psyché, 1952, 7:805-817; 1953, 8:32-34.

14,961. Dube, S. C. Myths, religion and ritual of the Kamars. Eastern Anthropology, 1947, 1:27-42.

14,962. DuBois-Reymond, Fanny. Der unsterbliche Oedipus. Psyché, 1956, 9:627-633.

14,963. Ducey, Charles P. The Shaman's dream journey: psychoanalytic and structural complementarity in myth interpretation. In The Psychoanalytic Study of Society, Vol. 8. New Haven: Yale Univ. Press, 1979, 71-118.

14,964. Dundes, Alan. Earth-diver: creation of the mythopoeic male. Amer Anthropologist, 1962, 64:1032-1051.

14,965. _____. The father, the son, and the Holy Grail. Lit & Psychol, 1962, 12:101-112.

14,966. _____. On the psychology of legend. In Hand, W. D. (ed), UCLA Conference on American Folk Legend, 1969. American Folk Legend; a Symposium. Berkeley: Univ. California Press, 1971, 21-36.

14,967. DuPlessis, R. Psyche, or wholeness. Massachusetts Rev, 1979, 20:77-96.

14,968. Dutt, K. Guru. The significance of myth. Aryan Path, 1972, 43(4):160-163.

14,969. Edmunds, Lowell, & Ingber, Richard. Psychoanalytic writings on the Oedipus legend; a bibliography. Amer Imago, 1977, 34:374-386.

14,970. Edsman, C. M. Ignis divinus. Le Feu comme moyen de rajeunissement et d'immortalité: contes, légendes, mythes et rites. Lund, Sweden: Gleerup, 1949.

14,971. Eggan, Dorothy. The personal use of myth in dreams. J Amer Folklore, 1955, 68:445-453.

14,972. Ehrentheil, Otto F. A case of premature ejaculation in Greek mythology. J Sex Research, 1974, 10:128-131.

14,973. Ehrenwald, J. Hippocrates' Kairos and the existential shift. Amer J Psychoanal, 1969, 29:89-93.

14,974. Ehrenzweig, Anton. The origin of the scientific and heroic urge (the guilt of Prometheus). Int J Psycho-Anal, 1949, 30:108-123.

14,975. Eisenstein, Samuel. Otto Rank: The Myth of the Birth of the Hero. In Alexander, F., et al. (eds), Psycho-analytic Pioneers. NY: Basic Books, 1966, 36-50.

14,976. Ekeh, Peter P. Benin and Thebes: elementary forms of civilization. In The Psychoanalytic Study of Society, Vol. 7. NY: IUP, 1976, 65-93.

14,977. Eliade, Mircea. Myth and Reality. NY: Harper & Row, 1968; London: Allen & Unwin, 1964.

14,978. _____. The Myth of the Eternal Return. NY: Pantheon, 1954.

14,979. _____. Myths, Dreams, and Mysteries. NY: Harper & Row, 1967, 1961.

14,980. Eliot, Alexander. The permanence of pagan myth. Texas Q, 1967, 10:71-94; In The Creatures of Arcadia. Indianapolis: Bobbs Merrill, 1967.

14,981. Elwin, V. The vagina dentata legend. British J Medical Psychol, 1943, 19:439-453.

14,982. Emrich, Wilhelm. Symbolinterpretation und Mythenforschung. In Protest und Verheissung. Frankfurt: 1960, 67-94.

14,983. Engelman, Suzanne R. The phoenix, dragon and sphinx: a glimpse at cultural metaphors. Int J Symbology, 1971, 7:94-105.

14,984. Engle, Bernice S. The Amazons in ancient Greece. Psychoanal Q, 1942, 11:512-554.

14,985. _____. Attis: a study of castration. Psychoanal Rev, 1936, 23:363-372.

14,986. _____. Lemnos, island of women. Psychoanal Rev, 1945, 32:353-358.

14,987. _____. Melampus and Freud. Psychoanal Q, 1942, 11:83-86; Revista de Psicoanálysis, 1945, 2:439-442.

14,988. Erlenmeyer, E. H. Note on Freud's hypothesis regarding taming of fire. Int J Psycho-Anal, 1932, 13:411-413.

14,989. Farber, Ada. Segmentation of the mother: women in Greek myth. Psychoanal Rev, 1975, 62:29-47.

14,990. Farnell, L. R. The value and methods of mythologic study. Proceedings British Academy, 1919-20, 9:37-51.

14, 991. Feder, Lillian. Ancient Myth in Modern Poetry. Prince-
          ton: Princeton Univ. Press, 1972.
14, 992. Federn, Paul. Märchen-Mythus-Urgeschichte. In Federn,
          P., & Meng, H. (eds), Das psychoanalytische Volks-
          buch. Bern: Huber, 1926, 499-517; 1928, 2:243-262;
          Bern: Huber, 1939, 636-653.
14, 993. Feldman, Harold. How we create 'fathers' and make them
          'sons.' Amer Imago, 1955, 12:71-86.
14, 994. Feldman, T. Gorgo and the origins of fear. Arion, 1965,
          4:484-494.
14, 995. Ferenczi, Sándor. Bridge symbolism and the Don Juan
          legend. In Further Contributions to the Theory and
          Technique of Psychoanalysis. NY: Basic Books, 1952,
          356-358; Int Zeitschrift für Psychoanalyse, 1922.
14, 996. _____. Symbolic representation of the pleasure and
          reality principle in the Oedipus myth. In Sex and Psy-
          choanalysis, Vol. 1. NY: Basic Books, 1958, 253-
          269; Imago, 1912, 1:276-284; In Populäre Vorträge über
          Psychoanalyse. Leipzig: 1922, 142-153; Psyche, 1972,
          26:520-529; In Contributions to Psycho-Analysis. Bos-
          ton: 1916, 214-227; In Further Contributions to the
          Theory and Techniques of Psychoanalysis. NY: Basic
          Books, 1952, 253-269.
14, 997. _____. The symbolism of the head of Medusa. In
          Further Contributions to the Theory and Technique of
          Psychoanalysis. NY: Basic Books, 1952, 360; Int Zeit-
          schrift für Psychoanalyse, 9:69; Bausteine zur Psycho-
          analyse, 3:54.
14, 998. Fergusson, Francis. 'Myth' and the literary scruple.
          Sewanee Rev, 1956, 64:171-185; In The Human Image
          in Dramatic Literature. Gloucester, Mass: Smith,
          1957; Garden City, NY: Doubleday Anchor, 1957; In
          Grebstein, S. N. (ed), Perspectives in Contemporary
          Criticism. NY: Harper & Row, 1968, 337-344.
14, 999. _____. Oedipus according to Freud, Sophocles, and
          Cocteau. In Literary Landmarks; Essays on the Theory
          and Practice of Literature. New Brunswick, NJ: Rut-
          gers Univ. Press, 1975, 101-113.
15, 000. Fernandez, James W. Filial piety and power: psychoso-
          cial dynamics in the legends of Shaka and Sundiata. In
          Masserman, J. H. (ed), Science and Psychoanalysis,
          Vol. 14. NY: Grune & Stratton, 1969, 47-60.
15, 001. Ferris, William R., Jr. Myth and the psychological
          school: fact or fantasy. New York Folklore Q, 1974,
          30:254-266.
15, 002. Fervel, J. Réflexions sur la circoncision. Psyché, 1952,
          7:98-102.
15, 003. Fiedler, Leslie A. Greek mythologies. Encounter, 1968,
          30:41-55.
15, 004. Figes, Eva. Patriarchal Attitudes. NY: Stein & Day,
          1970, 42-48.
15, 005. Fingarette, Herbert. Orestes: paradigm hero and central
          motif of contemporary ego psychology. Psychoanal Rev,
          1963, 50:437-461.

15,006. Fischer, F. N. Mythe en Sage. Groot-Nederland, May 1920.

15,007. Fischer, John L. A Ponapean Oedipus tale: structural and sociopsychological analysis. J Amer Folklore, 1966, 79:109-129.

15,008. _____, & Swartz, Marc J. Socio-psychological aspects of some Trukese and Ponapean love songs. J Amer Folklore, 1960, 73:218-224.

15,009. Fogelson, Raymond D. Psychological theories of windigo 'psychosis' and a preliminary application of a models approach. In Spiro, M. E. (ed), Context and Meaning in Cultural Anthropology. NY: Free Press, 1965, 74-99.

15,010. Fontana, A. E., et al. [Oedipus and the time accepted.] Acta Psiquiatrica y Psicologica de America Latina, 1974, 20:284-292.

15,011. Fontenrose, Joseph. The Ritual Theory of Myth. Berkeley: Univ. California Press, 1966.

15,012. Fraiberg, Louis, & Fraiberg, Selma. Hallowe'en ritual and myth in a children's holiday. Amer Imago, 1950, 7:289-328.

15,013. Francq, H. -G. Les Malheurs d'Oedipe: étude comparée de l'Oedipe de Corneille, Voltaire, Sophocle, Sénèque, Gide, Cocteau. Rev de l'Université Laval, 1965, 20: 211-224, 458-480, 560-569, 657-675.

15,014. Frank, Gerda. The theme of incest in the myth of Osiris. In The Annual of Psychoanalysis, Vol. 4. NY: IUP, 1976, 447-478.

15,015. Franklin, H. Bruce. The Wake of the Gods: Melville's Mythology. Stanford: Stanford Univ. Press, 1963.

15,016. Franz, Marie-Louise von. Alchemical Active Imagination. Irving, Texas: Univ. Dallas Press, 1979.

15,017. Frazer, James George. Myths of the Origin of Fire. NY: Macmillan, 1930.

15,018. _____. The New Golden Bough. Garden City, NY: Doubleday, 1961; The Golden Bough. A Study in Magic and Religion. NY: Macmillan, 1922, 1950, 1963, 1978.

15,019. Fredericks, Sigmund Casey. Revivals of ancient mythologies in current science fiction and fantasy. In Clareson, T. D. (ed), Many Futures, Many Worlds; Theme and Form in Science Fiction. Kent, Ohio: Kent State Ohio Press, 1977, 50-65.

15,020. Freilich, Morris. Myth, method, and madness. Current Anthropology, 1975, 16:207-226.

15,021. Freud, Sigmund. The acquisition of fire. Psychoanal Q, 1932, 1:210-215; Int J Psycho-Anal, 1932, 13:405-410.

15,022. _____. Civilization and Its Discontents. In Standard Edition, Vol. 21. London: Hogarth, 1935 (1930).

15,023. _____. The Interpretation of Dreams. NY: Basic Books, 1958, 256, 345, 351, 357, 398, 400-401, 619.

15,024. _____. Medusa's head. In Collected Papers, Vol. 5. NY: Basic Books, 1959, 105-106. In Standard Edition, Vol. 18. London: Hogarth: 1957, 273-274; Int J Psycho-Anal, 1941, 22:69-70.

15, 025.   . A mythological parallel to a visual obsession. In Collected Papers, Vol. 4. NY: Basic Books, 1959, 345-346; In Standard Edition, Vol. 14; In Obras Completas, Vol. 18. Buenos Aires: 163-167.

15, 026.   . The Problem of Lay-Analysis. NY: Brentano's, 1927.

15, 027.   . The theme of the three caskets. In Collected Papers, Vol. 4. NY: Basic Books, 1959, 244-256; In Standard Edition, Vol. 12. London: Hogarth, 1958, (1913), 290-301; NY: Basic Books, 1958, 290-301.

15, 028.   . Totem and Taboo. London: Kegan Paul, 1950; NY: New Republic, 1927. In Standard Edition, Vol. 13. London: Hogarth, 1955, (1913), 1-161.

15, 029. Freund, Philip. The meaning of myth to modern man. J Otto Rank Assn, 1967, 2(2):52-53; 54-69.

15, 030.   . Myths of Creation. NY: Washington Square Press, 1965.

15, 031. Friedman, Joel, & Gassel, Sylvia. Odysseus: the return of the primal father. Psychoanal Q, 1952, 21:215-223.

15, 032. Friedman, John Block. Orpheus in the Middle Ages. Cambridge: Harvard Univ. Press, 1970.

15, 033. Friedrich, Paul, & Redfield, James. Speech as a personality symbol: the case of Achilles. Language, 1978, 54:263-288.

15, 034. Fromm, Erich. The Oedipus complex and the Oedipus myth. In Anshen, R. N. (ed), The Family: Its Function and Destiny. NY: Harper, 1949, 334-358.

15, 035. Frye, Northrop. Fables of Identity: Studies in Poetic Mythology. NY: Harcourt, Brace & World, 1963, 1961.

15, 036.   . Literature and myth. In Thorpe, J. (ed), Relations of Literary Study. NY: Modern Language Assn, 1967, 27-56.

15, 037.   . Myth, fiction, and displacement. Daedalus, 1961, 90:587-605; In Fables of Identity. NY: Harcourt, Brace & World, 1963, 1961; In Handy, W. J., & Westbrook, M. (eds), Twentieth Century Criticism. NY: Free Press, 1974, 156-169.

15, 038.   . Mythos and logos. Yearbook Comparative & General Lit, 1969, No. 18, 5-18.

15, 039.   , Knights, L. C., et al. Myth and Symbol: Critical Approaches and Applications. Lincoln: Univ. Nebraska Press, 1963.

15, 040. Galdston, Iago. Sophocles contra Freud: a reassessment of the Oedipus complex. Bulletin New York Academy Medicine, 1954, 30:803-817.

15, 041. Garma, Angel. Oedipus was not the son of Laius and Jocasta. Int J Psychoanal Psychotherapy, 1978-79, 7: 316-325.

15, 042. Gay, Volney P. Scatology and eschatology in a North American Indian myth. South Carolina Rev, 1978, 7: 387-393.

15,043.   Geha, Richard.   For the love of Medusa.   A psychoanalytic
          glimpse into gynecocide.   Psychoanal Rev, 1975, 62:49-
          77.

15,044.   Georgiadès, G.   Le Rêve de Pénélope.   Psyché, 1949, 4:
          740-745.

15,045.   Gerhardt, Mia I.   Old Men of the Sea.   Amsterdam: Polak
          & van Gennep, 1967.

15,046.   Gernet, Louis.   La Notion mythique de la valeur en Grèce.
          JPNP, 1948, 41:415-462.

15,047.   Gesemann, G.   Sociologische und psychologische Zusam-
          mengänge in der Sagenforschung.   Zeitschrift für Völk-
          erpsychologie und Soziologie, 1928, 4:19-43.

15,048.   Gillibert, Jean.   L'Oedipe maniaque.   Paris: Payot, 1978.

15,049.   Gingerich, Willard P.   From Dream to Memory: A Psy-
          cho-Historical Introduction to Nahuatl Myth and Moral
          Philosophy.   DAI, 1978, 38:4861A.

15,050.   Girard, René.   Symétrie et dissymétrie dans le mythe
          d'Oedipe.   Critique, 1968, 249.

15,051.   Glendenning, Robert J.   The dreams in Sturia Poroārson's
          'Islendinga Saga' and literary consciousness in 13th
          century Iceland.   Arv: J Scandinavian Folklore, 1973-
          74, 29-30:128-148.

15,052.   Glenn, Jules (NMI).   Psychoanalytic writings on classical
          mythology and religion, 1909-1960.   Classical World,
          1976, 70:225-247.

15,053.   Glenn, Justin.   Polyphemus myth: its origin and inter-
          pretation.   Greece & Rome.   New Surveys in the Clas-
          sics, 1978, 25:141-155.

15,054.   Golden, Lester M.   Freud's Oedipus: its mytho-dramatic
          basis.   Amer Imago, 1967, 24:271-280.

15,055.   Goldfrank, Esther S.   Isleta variants: a study in flexibil-
          ity.   J Amer Folklore, 1926, 39:70-78.

15,056.   _____.   'Old Man' and the father image in Blood (Black-
          foot) society.   In Psychoanalysis and Culture.   NY:
          IUP, 1951, 132-141.

15,057.   Gordon, Pierre.   Les Origines de Rome, valeur historique
          de la légende.   Psyché, 1949, 4:983-1002.

15,058.   Gotz, Berndt.   Jungfräuliche Göttinnen und Gottesmutter.
          Zeitschrift für Sexualwissenschaft, 1931, 18:298-314.

15,059.   Gould, Thomas.   The innocence of Oedipus and the nature
          of tragedy.   Massachusetts Rev, 1969, 10:281-300.

15,060.   Graber, Gustave H.   Der Sohn-Komplex der Vater.   Der
          Psychologe, 1952, 250-258.

15,061.   _____.   Zeugung, Geburt und Tod.   Werden und Verge-
          hen im Mythus und in der Vorstellung des Kindes.
          Zurich: Rascher, 1934.

15,062.   Grambo, Ronald.   Guilt and punishment in Norwegian leg-
          ends.   Fabula, 1970, 11:253-270.

15,063.   Graves, Robert.   Jungian mythology.   Hudson Rev, 1952,
          5:245-257.

15,064.   _____.   The Oedipus myth.   Atlantic Monthly, 1955,
          195:56-59.

15,065.   _____.   The White Goddess.   A Historical Grammar of
          Poetic Myth.   NY: Vintage, 1958.

15, 066.   _____, & Patai, Renato.   Some Hebrew myths and leg-
            ends.   Encounter, 1963, 20(2):3-18, 20(3):12-18.
15, 067.   Green, André.   Le Discours vivant.   Vendôme: Presses
            Universitaires de France, 1973.
15, 068.   _____. La Magie d'Hephaïstos.   Critique, 1971, 293.
15, 069.   _____. Oedipe: mythe et vérité.   Arc, 1968, 38:15-
            26.
15, 070.   _____. Un Oeil en trop: le complexe d'Oedipe dans
            la tragédie.   Paris: Minuit, 1969.
15, 071.   _____. Orestes and Oedipus.   Int Rev Psycho-Anal,
            1975, 2:355-364.
15, 072.   Green, R.   Transsexualism: mythological, historical and
            cross-cultural aspects.   In Benjamin, H. (ed), The
            Transsexual Phenomenon.   NY: Julian, 1966, 173-186.
15, 073.   Gresseth, Gerald K.   Linguistics and myth theory.   West-
            ern Folklore, 1969, 28:153-162.
15, 074.   Griaule, Marcel.   Descente du troisième verbe chez les
            Dogons du Sudan.   Psyché, 1947, 2:1333-1347.
15, 075.   Grinstein, Alexander.   The boy and the dyke.   Int J Psy-
            cho-Anal, 1953, 34:265-270.
15, 076.   Groos, Karl.   Zur Psychologie des Mythos.   Int Monats-
            schrift für Wissenschaft Kunst und Technik, 1914, 8:
            1243-1259.
15, 077.   Günter, Heinrich.   Psychologie der Legende; Studien zu
            einer wissenschaftlichen Heiligengeschichte.   Freiburg:
            Herder, 1949.
15, 078.   Guthrie, Thomas C.   Oedipus myth in ancient Greece.
            Psychiat Q, 1955, 29:543-544.

15, 079.   Hacker, F. J.   The reality of myth.   Int J Psycho-Analy-
            sis, 1964, 45:438-443.
15, 080.   Haffter, Carl.   Animagestalten in der germanische Myth-
            ologie.   Psyche, 1951, 5:555-559.
15, 081.   Haimowitz, Morris L., & Haimowitz, Natalie R.   The
            evil eye: fear of success.   In Human Development.
            NY: Crowell, 1960, 742-754.
15, 082.   Hall, Larry Joe.   The Development of Myth in Post-World
            War II American Novels.   Doctoral dissertation, North
            Texas State Univ., 1974.
15, 083.   Hallowell, A. Irving.   Myth, culture and personality.
            Amer Anthropologist, 1947, 49:544-556.
15, 084.   Hankoff, L. D.   The hero as madman.   J History Behavior-
            al Sciences, 1975, 11:315-333.
15, 085.   Harding, M. Esther.   Woman's Mysteries Ancient and
            Modern.   A Psychological Interpretation of the Feminine
            Principle as Portrayed in Myth, Story, and Dreams.
            NY: Harper & Row, 1976; NY: Pantheon, 1955.
15, 086.   Harris, H. E.   Pandora.   Psychiatric Communications,
            1969, 10:19-21.
15, 087.   Hassall, James C.   The serpent as symbol.   Psychoanal
            Rev, 1919, 6:296-305.
15, 088.   Hassan, Ihab Habib.   Towards a method in myth.   J Amer
            Folklore, 1952, 65:205-215.

15,089.   Hausmann, Raoul.   Le Mythe d'Oedipe selon Bachofen.
          Psyché, 1947, 2:681-691.
15,090.   Hellerman, M. Kasey.   Coatlicue-Malinche conflict: a
          mother and son identity crisis in the writings of Carlos
          Fuentes.   Hispania, 1974, 57:868-875.
15,091.   Hellpach, W.   Ethnomythe und Magethos.   Zeitschrift für
          Menschenkunde, 1934, 10, No. 1.
15,092.   Henderson, Joseph L.   Ancient myths and modern man.
          In Jung, C. G., et al. (eds), Man and His Symbols.
          NY: Doubleday, 1964, 104-157.
15,093.   _____, & Oakes, M.   The Wisdom of the Serpent: The
          Myths of Death, Rebirth and Resurrection.   NY: Bra-
          ziller, 1963.
15,094.   Hen-li, Yin.   A behavioristic study of the creation myth.
          Bulletin Institute Ethnology (Taipei), 1962, 14:129-172.
15,095.   Herd, E. W.   Myth criticism: limitations and possibilities.
          Mosaic, 1969, 2:69-77.
15,096.   Hermann, F.   [The animal as creator.   Comparative
          mythology.] Studium Generale, 1967, 20:129-138.
15,097.   Hermann, Imre.   The giant mother, the phallic mother,
          obscenity.   Psychoanal Rev, 1949, 36:302-306.
15,098.   Herskovitz, Melville, & Herskovitz, Frances.   Sibling
          rivalry, the Oedipus complex, and myth.   J Amer
          Folklore, 1958, 71:1-15; In Dahomean Narrative: A
          Cross-Cultural Analysis.   Evanston: Northwestern
          Univ. Press, 1966, 85-95.
15,099.   Herzog, Edgar.   Psyche and Death: Archaic Myths and
          Modern Dreams in Analytic Psychology.   NY: Putnam,
          1967.
15,100.   Hill, T. D.   Narcissus, Pygmalion, and the castration of
          Saturn: two mythographical themes in the Roman de la
          Rose.   Studies in Philology, 1974, 71:404-426.
15,101.   Hillman, James (ed).   Puer Papers.   Irving, Texas: Univ.
          Dallas Press, 1980.
15,102.   Hoop, Johannes H. van der.   [The meaning of The Golem.]
          Die Nieuwe Gids, 7 July 1918.
15,103.   Hopper, Stanley Romaine.   Myth, dream, and imagination.
          In Campbell, J. (ed), Myths, Dreams, and Religion.
          NY: Dutton, 1970, 111-137.
15,104.   Horia, Vintilă.   The forest as mandala.   In Kitagawa,
          J. M. (ed), Myths and Symbols.   Chicago: Univ. Chi-
          cago Press, 1969, 387-395.
15,105.   Horton, Andrew S.   The Oedipus Tyrannus Theme in West-
          ern Literature.   DAI, 1974, 34:7707A.
15,106.   Hough, J. N.   Jupiter, Amphitryon, and the cuckoo.   Clas-
          sical Philology, 1970, 65:95-96.
15,107.   Howard, Stephen.   Oedipus of Thebes: the myth and its
          other meanings.   Amer J Psychoanal, 1976, 36:147-
          154.
15,108.   Huckel, Helen.   The tragic guilt of Prometheus.   Amer
          Imago, 1955, 12:325-336.
15,109.   Hudson, Wilson M.   Jung on myth and the mythic.   In
          Hudson, W. M., & Maxwell, A. (eds), The Sunny

Slopes of Long Ago. Dallas: Southern Methodist Univ. Press, 1966, 181-197.

15, 110. Hughes, Richard E. The Lively Image: Four Myths in Literature. Cambridge, Mass: Winthrop, 1975.

15, 111. Hurwitz, Siegmund. [Ahasver, the eternal wanderer: historical and psychological aspects.] Analytische Psychologie, 1975, 6:450-471.

15, 112. _____. Psychological aspects in early Hasidic literature. In Hillman, J. (ed), Studies in Jungian Thought: Timeless Documents of the Soul. Evanston, Ill: Northwestern Univ. Press, 1968, 151-239.

15, 113. Hyman, Stanley Edgar. The ritual view of myth and mythic. In Vickery, J. B. (ed), Myth and Literature. Lincoln: Univ. Nebraska Press, 1966, 47-58.

15, 114. Hymes, Dell H. The 'wife' who 'goes out' like a man: reinterpretation of Clackamas Chinook myth. Ha-Sifrut Lit: Theory-Poetics-Hebrew & Comparative Lit, 1975, 20:28-43; In Kristeva, J., et al., Essays in Semiotics. The Hague: Mouton, 1971, 296-326; In Maranda, P., & Köngäs, E. (eds), Structural Analysis of Oral Tradition. Philadelphia: Univ. Pennsylvania Press, 1971, 49-80.

15, 115. Isaac-Edersheim, E. Der Ewige Jude. Int Zeitschrift für Psychoanalyse, 1941, 26:286-315.

15, 116. _____. Messias, Golem, Ahasver: Drei mythische Gestalten des Judentums. Int Zeitschrift für Psychoanalyse, 1941, 26:179-213.

15, 117. Isler, Gotthilf. Zur psychologischen Deutung von Volkerzählungen. Fabula, 1973, 14:141-155.

15, 118. Issacharoff, Ammon. Hippolytus as an alternative to Oedipus: a study in triangular relationships. Psychotherapy & Psychosomatics, 1967, 15:32.

15, 119. Izeddin, A. Eine mohammedanische Legend. Imago, 1932, 18:189-213.

15, 120. Jacobs, Melville. Psychological inferences from a Chinook myth. J Amer Folklore, 1952, 65:121-137.

15, 121. Jacoby, Mario. [Authority and revolt: the myth of patricide.] Analytische Psychologie, 1975, 6:524-540.

15, 122. Jacques, Henri-Paul. Mythologie et psychanalyse. Le Châtiment des Danaides. Montreal: Leméac, 1969.

15, 123. Jadot, Lucie. [The myth of the hero according to Jung.] Rev de Psychologie et des Sciences de l'Education, 1975, 10:249-294.

15, 124. James, E. O. The nature and function of myth. Folk-Lore, 1957, 68:474-482.

15, 125. Jenichen, Richard. Über den alptraum in der sächsischen Sagenwelt. Int Zeitschrift für Psychoanalyse, 1914, 4:481-485.

15, 126. Jennings, Lee Bryson. Treasure and the quest for the
          self in Wagner, Grillparzer, and Hebbel. In Wetzels,
          W. D. (ed), Myth and Reason; A Symposium. Austin:
          Univ. Texas Press, 1973, 71-100.

15, 127. Jewett, Robert, & Lawrence, John Shelton. The American
          Monomyth. Garden City, NY: Doubleday, 1977.

15, 128. Jones, Ernest. The Madonna's conception through the
          ear. In Essays on Applied Psycho-Analysis, Vol. 2.
          NY: IUP, 1964 (1914), 266-357.

15, 129. Jones, Katherine. King Mark disguised as himself. Amer
          Imago, 1959, 16:115-125.

15, 130. Jung, Carl Gustav. Archetypes of the collective uncon-
          scious. In Handy, W. J., & Westbrook, M. (eds),
          Twentieth Century Criticism. NY: Free Press, 1974,
          205-232; extracted from The Collected Works of C. G.
          Jung, Vol. 9. Princeton: Princeton Univ. Press,
          1959, 1969.

15, 131. _____. Essays on a Science of Mythology; the Myth of
          the Divine Child and the Mysteries of Eleusis. NY:
          Pantheon, 1949; Zurich: Rascher; Amsterdam: Panthe-
          on, 1941.

15, 132. _____. On the psychology of the trickster figure. In
          Collected Works of C. G. Jung, Vol. 9. Princeton:
          Princeton Univ. Press, 1968, 255-272.

15, 133. _____. Psychology of the Unconscious. NY: Dodd,
          Mead, 1916.

15, 134. _____. The spirit in man, art and literature. Fore-
          word to Schmid-Guisan: Day and Night. In Collected
          Works of C. G. Jung, Vol. 18. Princeton: Princeton
          Univ. Press, 1976, 759-761.

15, 135. _____. Wandlungen und Symbole der Libido. Beiträge
          zur Entwichlungageschichte des Denkens. Leipzig:
          Deuticke, 1938.

15, 136. _____, & Kerényi, Karl. Essays on a Science of
          Mythology. Princeton: Princeton Univ. Press, 1969;
          Einführung in das wesen der Mythologie. Zurich: 1951.

15, 137. Jung, Emma, & Franz, Marie-Louise von. The Grail
          Legend. NY: Putnam, 1971; Zurich: Jung Institute,
          1968.

15, 138. Kabascik, Joan. The Epic of Gilgamesh and Life Stage
          Development Theory. DAI, 1975, 36:1393.

15, 139. Kahler, Erich. The persistence of myth. In Out of the
          Labyrinth. NY: Braziller, 1967.

15, 140. Kanzer, Mark. Oedipus: history, legends, plays, com-
          plexes. Int J Psychoanal Psychotherapy, 1978-79,
          7:326-332.

15, 141. Kaplan, Bert. Psychological themes in Zuni mythology
          and Zuni TAT's. In The Psychoanalytic Study of Soci-
          ety, Vol. 2. NY: IUP, 1962, 2:255-262.

15, 142. Kaplan, Leo. The Baalshem legend. Psyche & Eros,
          1921, 2:173-183.

15, 143. Karlson, Karl J. Psychoanalysis and Mythology. Doctoral
          dissertation, Clark Univ. , 1912.
15, 144. _____. Psychoanalysis and mythology. J Religion &
          Psychol, 1914, 7:137-213.
15, 145. Karpman, Ben. The psychopathology of exhibitionism.
          Psychoanal Rev, 1926, 13:63-97.
15, 146. Kausen, Rudolph. Laius complex and mother-child symbi-
          osis. J Individual Psychol, 1972, 28:33-37.
15, 147. _____. Von Freud zu Laios. Selecta, 1971, 13:773.
15, 148. Kayton, Lawrence. The relationship of the vampire legend
          to schizophrenia. J Youth & Adolescence, 1972, 1:303-
          314.
15, 149. Keewaydinoquay. The legend of Miskwedo. J Psychedelic
          Drugs, 1979, 11:29-31.
15, 150. Kellett, E. E. The Story of Myths. NY: Harcourt, Brace,
          1927.
15, 151. Kelley, D. M. Mania and the moon. Psychoanal Rev,
          1942, 29:406-426.
15, 152. Kelman, Harold. Kairos: The auspicious movement.
          Amer J Psychoanal, 1969, 29:59-83.
15, 153. Kentsmith, D. K. 'The Rape of the Lock' revisited. Psy-
          chiat Q, 1973, 47:571-585.
15, 154. Kerényi, Karl. Goddesses of Sun and Moon. Irving,
          Texas: Univ. Dallas Press, 1979.
15, 155. _____. Mnemosyne--Lesmosyne: on the springs of
          'memory' and 'forgetting. ' Spring, 1977, 1:120-130.
15, 156. _____. Romandichtung und Mythologie. Zurich: Rhein,
          1945.
15, 157. _____. Prometheus: Archetypal Image of Human Ex-
          istence. NY: Bollingen, 1963.
15, 158. _____. Zum Porträt des Oedipus. Neue Zürcher Zeit-
          ung, 6 May 1956.
15, 159. Kerner, D. Till Eulenspiegel. Ein Beitrag zur Psycho-
          pathologie. Aerzteblalt Rheinland-Pfalz, 1965, 18:111-
          116 passim.
15, 160. Kido, M. Interpretation of Japanese myth. Japanese J
          Psychol, 1929, 4:45-64.
15, 161. Kielholz, Arthur. Der zerstuckelte Osiris. Ein krimino-
          logischer Beitrag zu seinem mythus. Schweizerischen
          Zeitschrift für Psychologie, 1943, 1:241-257.
15, 162. Kimball, Arthur Samuel. Merlin's miscreation and the
          repetition compulsion in Malory's Morte D'Arthur.
          Lit & Psychol, 1975, 25:27-33.
15, 163. Kinsler, Arthur W. Korean fertility cult for children in
          Shaman ritual and myth. Korea J, 1977, 17(2):27-34.
15, 164. Kirchhoff, Frederick A. A science against science: Rus-
          kin's floral mythology. In Knoepflmacher, U. C. , &
          Tennyson, G. B. (eds), Nature and the Victorian Imagi-
          nation. Berkeley: Univ. California Press, 1977, 246-
          258.
15, 165. Kirk, G. S. Myth, Its Meaning and Functions in Ancient
          and Other Cultures. Berkeley: Univ. California Press,
          1970; Cambridge, Engl: Cambridge Univ. Press, 1972.

15, 166. Kirste, H. [The four faces of Eros in antiquity. A con-
          tribution to ancient psychology.] Annales de l'Institut
          Pasteur, 1966, 111:2241-2243.

15, 167. Kitagawa, Joseph Mitsuo, & Long, Charles H. (eds).
          Myths and Symbols: Studies in Honor of Mircea Eliade.
          Chicago: Univ. Chicago Press, 1969.

15, 168. Kluckhohn, Clyde. Myths and rituals: a general theory.
          Harvard Theological Rev, 1942, 35:45-79.

15, 169. _____. Recurrent themes in myths and mythmaking.
          Daedalus, 1959, 88:268-279; In Murray, H. A. (ed),
          Myth and Mythmaking. NY: Braziller, 1960; Boston:
          Beacon, 1968, 46-60; In Ohmann, R. M. (ed), The Mak-
          ing of Myth. NY: Putnam, 1962, 61-63.

15, 170. Kluger-Schärf, Rivkah. [Some psychological aspects of the
          Gilgamesh epic.] Analytische Psychologie, 1975, 6:
          386-427.

15, 171. Knapp, Bettina L. The Golem and ecstatic mysticism. J
          Altered States of Consciousness, 1977-78, 3:355-369.

15, 172. _____. The Prometheus Syndrome. NY: Whitston,
          1979; Review: Ann Demaitre, French Rev, 1980, 53:
          928-929.

15, 173. Kocker, Robert P. Toward a definition of myth in litera-
          ture. Thoth, 1965, 5:3-21.

15, 174. Koopmann, Helmut. Mythus und Psychologie. In Die Ent-
          wicklung des 'intellektualen' Romans bei Thomas Mann.
          Bonn: 1962, 147-168.

15, 175. Kouretas, Demetrios, et al. L'Homosexualité du père
          d'Oedipe et ses conséquences. Annales Médicales
          Athens, 1963, 2:5-6.

15, 176. _____. The Oedipus myth: how and why Sophocles
          constructed the myth for the stage and how and why it
          was interpreted by Freud. Akadimaiki Iatriki, 1961,
          257; abstract in Psychoanal Q, 1963, 32:142-143.

15, 177. _____. Psychanalyse et mythologie: la névrose sexu-
          elle des Danaïdes. Rev Française de Psychanalyse,
          1957, 21:597-602.

15, 178. Krauss, Friedrich S. Die Ödipussage in südslawischer
          Volksüberlieferung. Imago, 1935, 21:358-367.

15, 179. Kreichgauer, P. B. Die Kpalltore am Rande der Erde in
          der altmexikanischen Mythologie. Anthropologist, 1916,
          12-13:272.

15, 180. Kris, Ernst, & Kurz, Otto. Legend, Myth, and Magic in
          the Image of the Artist: A Historical Experiment.
          New Haven: Yale Univ. Press, 1979; Review: Hanna
          Charney, Psychoanal Rev, 1980, 67:283-284.

15, 181. Kroeber, A. L. Seven Mohave Myths. Berkeley: Univ.
          California Press, 1948.

15, 182. Kuiper, Pieter C. Comment on papers by Drs. Orgel and
          Shengold. 'The fatal gifts of Medea.' Int J Psycho-
          Anal, 1968, 49:383-385.

15, 183. Kursh, Charlotte Olmsted. Children of Capricorn: Pan
          and the mermaid. Bucknell Rev, 1966, 14:14-25.

15, 184. _____. Heracles and the centaur. Psychoanal Rev,
          1968, 55:387-399.

15, 185. LaBarre, Weston. They Shall Take Up Serpents. Minne-
          apolis: Univ. Minnesota Press, 1962.
15, 186. Laiblin, Wilhelm. Märchenforschung und Tiefenpsychol-
          ogie. Darmstadt: Wiss, 1969.
15, 187. Lancaster, Elizabeth. Sex and complex: Oedipus or
          Kronos? Man, 1932, 32:151-152.
15, 188. Landy, Marcia. Summary of lecture by Northrop Frye on
          'The revelation of Eve. ' Seventeenth Century News,
          1968, 26:33.
15, 189. Langbaum, Robert Woodrow. Browning and the question
          of myth. Philological Q, 1966, 71:575-584.
15, 190. Langer, Marie. Le 'mythe de l'enfant roti. ' Rev Fran-
          çaise de Psychanalyse, 1950, 7:389-401.
15, 191. Langer, Susanne K. Philosophy in a New Key. Cam-
          bridge: Harvard Univ. Press, 1967.
15, 192. Lantis, Margaret. Nunivak Eskimo personality as re-
          vealed in the mythology. Anthropological Papers, Univ.
          Alaska, 1953, 2:109-174.
15, 193. Larue, Herald A. Ancient Myth and Modern Man. Engle-
          wood Cliffs, NJ: Prentice-Hall, 1975.
15, 194. Lasky, Melvin J. The Prometheans: on the imagery of
          fire and resolution. Encounter, 1968, 31:22-32.
15, 195. Laszlo, Violet S. de (ed). Psyche and Symbol. A Selec-
          tion from the Writings of C. G. Jung. Garden City,
          NY: Doubleday, 1958.
15, 196. Latif, Israil. Psychoanalytic interpretation of certain
          myths. Indian J Psychol, 1947, 22:98-99.
15, 197. Lazarsfeld, Sofie. Did Oedipus have an Oedipus complex?
          Amer J Orthopsychiatry, 1944, 14:226-229.
15, 198. Leach, Edmund Ronald. Lévi-Strauss in the Garden of
          Eden: an examination of some recent developments in
          the analysis of myth. In Hayes, E. N., & Hayes, T.
          (eds), Claude Lévi-Strauss: The Anthropologist as
          Hero. Cambridge: Massachusetts Institute Technology
          Press, 1970, 47-60; Transactions New York Academy
          Science, 1961, Series 2, 386-396.
15, 199. _____ (ed). The Structural Study of Myth and Totem-
          ism. London: Tavistock, 1967.
15, 200. Leal, Louis. Myth and social realism in Miguel Angel
          Asturias. Comparative Lit Studies, 1968, 5:237-247.
15, 201. Lederer, Wolfgang. The bottomless lake, and the bottom-
          less pit. In The Fear of Women. NY: Grune &
          Stratton, 1968, 233-237.
15, 202. _____. Historical consequences of father-son hostility.
          Psychoanal Rev, 1967, 54:248-276.
15, 203. _____. Oedipus and the serpent. Psychoanal Rev,
          1964-65, 51:619-644.
15, 204. Leeuwe, J. de. [Myth analysis in unselected subjects.]
          Psychiatrische en Neurologische Bladen, 1939, 43:333-
          354.
15, 205. _____. [Some connections between mythical expressions
          and psychic processes.] Mensch en Maatsch, 1939,
          15:259-281.

15, 206. Legrand, Gérard. Sur Oedipe: Anatomie de la mythologie. Paris: 1972.

15, 207. Le Guen, Claude. L'Oedipe originaire. Paris: 1974.

15, 208. Le Maitre, H. Les Mythes antiques en France. Mosaic, 1939, 2:25-41.

15, 209. Lessa, William. Oedipus-type tales in Oceania. J Amer Folklore, 1956, 69:63-73.

15, 210. Lesser, Simon O. Our feelings about man-made creatures, imaginary and real. Comments on the golem and the robot. Lit & Psychol, 1965, 15:28-31.

15, 211. Lestavel, Jean. Le Vent et les mythes. Psyché, 1954, 9:259-266.

15, 212. Leuba, John H. Batrachomomyachie. Document pour la défense et illustration du thème oedipien. Rev Française de Psychanalyse, 1948, 12:55-79.

15, 213. _____. Les Grands mystiques chrétien, l'hysterie et la neurasthenie. J de Psychologie, 1925, 22:236-251.

15, 214. Levin, A. J. The Oedipus myth in history and psychiatry: a new interpretation. Psychiatry, 1948, 11:283-299.

15, 215. Levin, Harry. Some meanings of myth. Daedalus, 1959, 88:223-231; In Murray, H. A. (ed), Myth and Mythmaking. NY: Braziller, 1960.

15, 216. Lévi-Strauss, Claude. Myth and Meaning. NY: Schocken, 1978.

15, 217. _____. The Raw and the Cooked: Introduction to a Science of Mythology. NY: Harper & Row, 1970.

15, 218. _____. A structural analysis of myth. In Structural Anthropology. NY: Basic Books, 1963, 203-207.

15, 219. _____. The structural study of myth. J Amer Folklore, 1955, 28:428-444; In Gras, V. W. (ed), European Literary Theory and Practice. NY: Delta, 1973.

15, 220. Lévy Bruhl, Lucien. Le Temps et l'espace du monde mythique. Scientia, 1935, 57:139-149.

15, 221. Lewis, Nolan D. C. Some theriomorphic symbolisms and mechanisms in ancient literature and dreams. I: Cat, dog and horse dreams. Psychoanal Rev, 1963, 50:536-556.

15, 222. Lewy, Ernst. Historical charismatic leaders and mythical heroes. J Psychohistory, 1979, 6:377-392.

15, 223. Liberman, David. Autismo transferencial. Narcissismo: El mito de Eco y Narcisso. Revista de Psicoanálisis, 1958, 15:369-385.

15, 224. Lickorish, John R. Adler and Achilles. Individual Psychologist, 1973, 10(2):10-17.

15, 225. Lidz, Theodore, & Rothenberg, A. Dionysus reborn. Psychiatry, 1968, 31:116-125.

15, 226. Limentani, A. Problemi di ambivalenza, riparazio e situazioni edipiche: Il mito d'Orfeo. Rivista di Psicoanalisi, 1966, 12:253-267.

15, 227. Lindzey, Gardner. Some remarks concerning incest, the incest taboo, and psychoanalytic theory. Amer Psychologist, 1967, 22:1051-1059.

15, 228. Link, Margaret S. The Pollen Path. A Collection of
          Navaho Myths, Retold by Margaret Schevill Link, with
          a Psychological Commentary by Joseph J. Henderson.
          Stanford, Cal: Stanford Univ. Press, 1956.
15, 229. Little, R. B. Oral aggression in spider legends. Amer
          Imago, 1966, 23:169-179.
15, 230. Lixfeld, Hannjost. Tiefenpsychologische Sagendeutung und
          volksundliche Erzählforschung: Zur Untersuchung der
          'Sennenpuppensage' durch Gotthilf Isler. Fabula, 1973,
          14:124-137.
15, 231. Locke, Norman. A myth of ancient Egypt. Amer Imago,
          1961, 18:105-128.
15, 232. Lorenz, Emil F. Das Titanen-Motiv in der allgemeinen
          Mythologie. Imago, 1913, 2:22-72.
15, 233. Lowenfeld, Henry. The decline in belief in the devil.
          The consequence for group psychology. Psychoanal Q,
          1969, 38:455-462.
15, 234. Lowrié, Anton. The Jewish god and the Greek hero.
          Amer Imago, 1948, 5:152-166.
15, 235. Lublinski, I. Eine weiters mythische Urschicht vor dem
          Mythos. Zeitschrift für Völkerpsychologie und Soziol-
          ogie, 1930, 6:35-64.
15, 236. Luiz Vianna Guedes, Fernando. [A psychoanalytic re-
          flection on the Rio Grande legend of 'The Little Black
          Boy of the Pasture. '] Revista Brasileira de Psicoaná-
          lise, 1976, 10:395-406.
15, 237. Luquet, G. H. Le Rire dans les légendes océaniennes.
          J de Psychologie, 1930, 27:268-288.

15, 238. McConnell, U. S. The symbol in legend. Psyche, 1933,
          13:94-137.
15, 239. MacKay, D. E. The Double Invitation in the Legend of
          Don Juan. Palo Alto, Cal: Stanford Univ. Press,
          1943.
15, 240. McLuhan, Marshall. [The teeth as a symbol, according
          to the myth of Cadmos.] Dentale Cadmos, 1969, 37:
          1735-1736.
15, 241. MacWatters, M. R. C. A birth of the hero myth from
          Kashmir. Int J Psycho-Anal, 1921, 2:416-419.
15, 242. Malinowski, Bronislaw. Myth in Primitive Psychology.
          London: Kegan Paul & Trench, 1926; NY: Norton,
          1926.
15, 243. _____. _____. In Magic, Science, and Religion,
          and Other Essays. Boston: Beacon, 1948, 78-79.
15, 244. _____. _____. In Dawson, W. R. (ed), Frazer Lec-
          tures, 1922-1932. NY: Macmillan, 1932, 66-119.
15, 245. _____. The role of myth in life. Psyche, 1926, 24:
          29-39.
15, 246. Maranda, R. Computers in the bush: tools for the auto-
          matic analysis of myths. In Helm, J. (ed), Essays on
          the Verbal and Visual Arts. Seattle: Univ. Washington
          Press, 1967.

15, 247.   Marcus, Ned N.   Prometheus reconsidered: sublimation and vicissitudes of the symbolic ego.   Psychoanal Rev, 1967, 54:83-106.

15, 248.   Margolis, Marvin, & Parker, Philip.   The stork fable-- some psychodynamic considerations.   JAPA, 1972, 20: 494-511.

15, 249.   Marshak, M. D.   A psychological approach to mythology.   Didaskalos, 1968, 2:3.

15, 250.   Masson, J. M.   Fratricide among the monkeys: psycho- analytic observations on an episode in the Vālmikirā- māyanam.   Amer Oriental Society J, 1975, 95:672- 678.

15, 251.   Matthews, Honor.   The Hard Journey: The Myth of Man's Rebirth.   London: Chatto & Windus, 1968.

15, 252.   May, Rollo.   The daemonic love and death.   Psychol To- day, 1968, 1:16-25.

15, 253.   _____.   The meaning of the Oedipus myth.   Rev Exis- tential Psychol Psychiat, 1961, 1:44-52.

15, 254.   _____.   Values, myths, and symbols.   Amer J Psychi- at, 1975, 132:703-706.

15, 255.   Mazzatta, Giuseppe.   Canzoniere and the language of the self.   Studies in Philology, 1978, 75:271-296.

15, 256-   Medlicott, R. W.   Leda and the swan--an analysis of the
7.   theme in myth and art.   Australian/New Zealand J Psychiat, 1970, 4:15-23.

15, 258.   Métraux, Alfred.   Twin heroes in South American mythol- ogy.   J Amer Folklore, 1946, 59:114-123.

15, 259.   Meunier, Mario.   La Légende et le mythe d'Oedipe.   Psy- ché, 1947, 2:669-676.

15, 260.   Miller, Arthur A.   An interpretation of the symbolism of Medusa.   Amer Imago, 1958, 15:389-399.

15, 261.   Miller, David L.   Orestes: myth and dream as catharsis.   In Campbell, J. (ed), Myth, Dreams, and Religion.   NY: Dutton, 1970, 26-47.

15, 262.   Minder, Robert.   Mythes et complexes agressifs dans l'Allemagne moderne.   Psyché, 1948, 3:783-794.

15, 263.   Miskimin, Alice.   Britomart's crocodile and the legends of chastity.   J English Germanic Philology, 1978, 77: 17-36.

15, 264.   Mitchell, Roger E.   The Oedipus myth and complex in Oceania, with special reference to Truk.   Asian Folk- lore Studies, 1968, 27:131-146.

15, 265.   Moloney, James Clark.   Carnal myths involving the sun.   Amer Imago, 1963, 20:93-104.

15, 266.   _____.   Mother, God and superego.   JAPA, 1954, 2: 120-151.

15, 267.   _____.   Oedipus Rex, Cu Chulain, Khepri and the ass.   Psychoanal Rev, 1967, 54:201-247.

15, 268.   _____.   The origin of the rejected and crippled hero myths.   Amer Imago, 1959, 16:271-328.

15, 269.   _____.   The psychosomatic aspects of myths.   Amer Imago, 1961, 18:57-64.

15, 270. Moon, Sheila. A Magic Dwells: A Poetic and Psychologi-
          cal Study of the Navaho Emergence Myth. Middletown,
          Conn: Wesleyan Univ. Press, 1970.
15, 271. Moser, Dietz-Rüdiger. Die Tannhäuser-Legende. Berlin:
          de Gruyter, 1977.
15, 272. Muensterberger, Werner. Remarks on the function of
          mythology. In The Psychoanalytic Study of Society,
          Vol. 3. NY: IUP, 1964, 94-97.
15, 273. Mühlher, Robert. Dichtung und Krise: Mythos und Psychol-
          ogie in der Dichtung des 19. und 20. Jahrhunderts.
          Vienna: 1951.
15, 274. Mullahy, Patrick. Oedipus Myth and Complex, a Review
          of Psychoanalytic Theory. NY: Hermitage, 1948; NY:
          Evergreen, 1958; Reviews: Mabel Blake Cohen, Psy-
          chiatry, 1949, 12:91-92; Clara Thompson, Psychiatry,
          1949, 12:92-93.
15, 275. Muller, Armand. Petite incursion dans la mythologie
          grecque. Acta Psychotherapeutica, Psychosomatica et
          Orthopaedagogica, 1957, 5:74-87.
15, 276. Munden, Kenneth J. A contribution to the psychological
          understanding of the origin of the cowboy and his myth.
          Amer Imago, 1958, 15:103-148.
15, 277. Murray, Henry A. American Icarus. In Burton, A., &
          Harris, R.W. (eds), Clinical Studies of Personality,
          Vol. 2. NY: Harper, 1955, 615-641.
15, 278. _____. Introduction to the issue, 'Myth and Mythmak-
          ing.' Daedalus, 1959, 88:211-222.
15, 279. _____ (ed). Myth and Mythmaking. NY: Braziller,
          1960; Boston: Beacon, 1968.
15, 280. Musil, Robert. Der bedrohte Oedipus. Der Querschnitt,
          1931, 11:685-686.

15, 281. Nagarajan, S. A note on myth and ritual in The Serpent
          and the Rope. J Commonwealth Lit, 1972, 7(1):45-48.
15, 282. Nandris, Grigore. The historical Dracula: the theme of
          his legend in the western and eastern literatures of
          Europe. Comparative Lit Studies, 1966, 3:367-396.
15, 283. Nash, H. Judgment of the humanness-animality of mytho-
          logical hybrid (part-human, part-animal) figures. J
          Social Psychol, 1974, 92:91-102.
15, 284. Neumann, Erich. Amor and Psyche: the Psychic Develop-
          ment of the Feminine, a Commentary on the Tale of
          Apuleius. NY: Pantheon, 1956.
15, 285. _____. The Origins and History of Consciousness, 2
          Vols. NY: Harper Torchbooks, 1962.
15, 286. Newman, Lawrence E., & Stroller, Robert J. Spider
          symbolism and bisexuality. JAPA, 1969, 17:862-872.
15, 287. Niederland, William G. River symbolism. Psychoanal
          Q, 1956, 25:469-504.
15, 288. Noble, P. The role of fairy mythology in La Mort de Roi
          Artur. Sprachforum, 1971, 45:480-483.

15, 289. Oba, C. Aetiological myth and folklore about animals. Japanese J Psychol, 1929, 4, No. 2.

15, 290. Ober, William B. Elias Lönnrot, M. D. (1802-1884). The Kalevala. New York State J Medicine, 1969, 69:1227-1235.

15, 291. O'Flaherty, Wendy D. Asceticism and sexuality in the mythology of Siva, Part I. History of Religions, 1969, 8(3):300-337.

15, 292. Ohmann, Richard (ed). The Making of Myth. NY: Putnam, 1962.

15, 293. Okpewho, Isidore. Poetry and pattern: structural analysis of an Ijo creation myth. J Amer Folklore, 1979, 92:302-325.

15, 294. Opler, Morris E. The Lipan Apache death complex and its extensions. Southwestern J Anthropology, 1945, 1: 133-141.

15, 295. Ortigues, Marie-Cécile. Oedipe africain. Paris: 1966.

15, 296. Osmun, G. F. Changes of sex in Greek and Roman mythology. Classical Bulletin, 1978, 54:75-79.

15, 297. Pagés Larraya, F. [Reminiscence and quiliasme in San Ignacio de Mojos.] Acta Psiquiatrica y Psicologica de America Latina, 1974, 20:352-366.

15, 298. Parin, Paul. Zur Bedeutung von Mythus, Ritual und Brauch für die vergleichende Psychiatrie. Bibl Psychiatrie Neurologie, 1967, 133:179-196; In Petrilowitsch, N. (ed), Beiträge zur Vergleichenden Psychiatrie. Basel: Karger, 1967.

15, 299. Patel, R. M. Understanding the culture through mythological stories. Amer J Psychoanal, 1960, 20:83-85.

15, 300. Payne, Sylvia M. The myth of the barnacle goose. Int J Psycho-Anal, 1929, 10:218-227.

15, 301. Pearson, Gerald H. J. A note on the medusa; a speculative attempt to explain a ritual. Bulletin Philadelphia Assn Psychoanal, 1967, 17:1-9.

15, 302. Peradotto, J. Myth and psychology. In Classical Mythology: An Annotated Bibliographical Survey. Urbana: Univ. Illinois, 1973, 26-33.

15, 303. Perry, John Weir. Lord of the Four Quarters: Myths of the Royal Father. NY: Braziller, 1966.

15, 304. _____. Roots of Renewal in Myth and Madness. San Francisco: Jossey-Bass, 1977.

15, 305. Petrus, Earl P. The Golem: significance of the legend. Psychoanal Rev, 1966, 53:63-68.

15, 306. Piatigorsky, A. M. Some general remarks on mythology from a psychologist's point of view. Semiotica, 1974, 10:221-231.

15, 307. Pivnicki, D. Mythos and psychiatry. Confinia Psychiatrica, 1974, 17:177-183.

15, 308. Plank, Robert. The Golem and the robot. Lit & Psych, 1965, 15:12-28.

15, 309. _____. Golems und Roboter. Forum, 1965, 12:510-515.

15,310. Pohorilles, N. E. Die Psychologie des Mythos. Sonntags-
         beil Nr. 5 zur Vossischen Zeitschrift, 2 Feb 1913.
15,311. Politzer, Heinz. Hatte Odipus einen Odipus-Komplex? In
         Paulsen, W. (ed), Psychologie in der Litteraturwissen-
         schaft. Heidelberg: Stiehm, 1971, 115-139.
15,312. Pones, Hermann. Psychoanalyse und Dichtung. In Beutin,
         W. (ed), Literatur und Psychoanalyse. Munich: 1972,
         100-136; In Urban, B. (ed), Psychoanalyse und Litera-
         turwissenschaft. Tübingen: 1973.
15,313. Posinsky, S. H. The death of Maui. JAPA, 1957, 5:485-
         489.
15,314. _____ . Oedipal gods and moral man. Amer Imago,
         1962, 19:101-125.
15,315. Pötscher, Walter. Oedipus. In Jahrbüch für Psychologie,
         Psychotherapie und medizinische Anthropologie, 1970,
         18:36-?.
15,316. _____ . Die Oidipus-Gestalt. Eranos: Acta Philo-
         logica Suecana, 1973, 71:12-44.
15,317. Powers, R. Myth and memory. In Mosak, H. H. (ed),
         Alfred Adler: His Influence on Psychology Today.
         Park Ridge, NJ: Noyes, 1974, 271-290.
15,318. Prado Huante, Hector. La invidia de la matriz (la gene-
         sis en la mitologia Japanesa). Cuadernos de Psico-
         análisis, 1965, 1:357-341.
15,319. Pratt, Dallas. The Don Juan myth. Amer Imago, 1960,
         17:321.

15,320. Rabant, Claude. Le Mythe à l'avenir (re) commence.
         Esprit, 1971, 4.
15,321. Rachewiltz, B. de, et al. [Twins in myth.] Acta Gene-
         ticae Medicae et Gemellologiae, 1976, 25:17-19.
15,322. Radin, Paul. The Trickster. A Study in American Indian
         Mythology, with Commentaries by Karl Kerényi and
         Carl G. Jung. NY: Philosophical Library, 1956; Lon-
         don: Routledge & Paul, 1955.
15,323. _____ . Winnebago Hero Cycles: A Study of Aboriginal
         Literature. Baltimore: Waverly, 1948.
15,324. Raglan, Fitz Roy R. S. The Hero; A Study in Tradition,
         Myth, and Drama. London: Methuen, 1936; NY: Ox-
         ford Univ. Press, 1937; London: Watts, 1949; NY:
         British Book Centre, 1949; NY: Vintage, 1956.
15,325. _____ . Jocasta's Crime: An Anthropological Study.
         London: Methuen, 1933; NY: Dutton, 1933.
15,326. Rahv, Philip. The myth and the powerhouse. Partisan
         Rev, 1953, 20:635-648.
15,327. Ramnoux, Clémence. La carnage des héros. Psyché,
         1950, 5:880-903.
15,328. _____ . Experience sur la transmission des legendes.
         Psyché, 1948, 3:310-323.
15,329. _____ . La Mort du héros. Psyché, 1948, 3:1020-
         1040; 1952, 7:46-52.
15,330. _____ . Naissances divines et héroiques. Psyché, 1948,
         3:1343-1353.

15, 331. Rank, Otto. Daphnis und Chloë. Int Zeitschrift für Psychoanalyse, 1919, 5:307.
15, 332. _____. Don Juan. Une Etude sur le double. Paris:
Denoël et Steele, 1932, 9-163.
15, 333. _____. Don Juan und Leporello. In Almanach. Leip-
zig/Vienna/Zurich: Int Psychoanalytischer Verlag,
1927, 172-180.
15, 334. _____. Das Inzest-Motiv in Dichtung und Sage: Grun-
züge einer Psychologie des dichterischen Schaffen.
Leipzig: Deuticke, 1912, 1926.
15, 335. _____. Die Lohengrinsage; ein Beitrag zu ihrer Motivgestaltung und Deutung. Sammlungen zur angewandten
Seelenkunde 13. Leipzig: Deuticke, 1911.
15, 336. _____. Die Matrone von Ephesus. Zeitschrift, 1913,
1:50-60.
15, 337. _____. The myth of the birth of the hero: a psychological interpretation of mythology. In Nunberg, H.,
& Federn, E. (eds), Minutes of the Vienna Psychoanalytic Society, Vol. 2: 1908-1910. NY: Nervous &
Mental Disease Publishing, 1914; NY: Brunner, 1952;
NY: IUP, 1967, 65-72; Sammlungen zur angewandten
Seelenkunde, 1910, 5; Leipzig: Deuticke, 1909, 1922.
15, 338. _____. Mythologie. Jahrbuch der Psychoanalyse,
1914, 6:367-373.
15, 339. _____. Mythologie und Psychoanalyse. Psychoanalytische Beiträge zur Mythenforschung, 1919:1-20; 1922:
1-19 (1913).
15, 340. _____. Mythus und Märchen. Psychoanalytische Beiträge zur Mythenforschung, 1919: 381-420; 1922: 146-
184 (1914).
15, 341. _____. Psychoanalytische Beiträge zur Mythenforschung;
gesammelte Studien aus den Jahren 1912 bis 1914. Vienna: Int Psychoanalytischer Verlag, 1919, 1922.
15, 342. _____. Zum nachträglichen Gehorsam. Int Zeitschrift
für Psychoanalyse, 1911, 1:576-580. Under title:
Nachträglicher Gehorsam als Sagenmotiv. Psychoanalytische Beiträge zur Mythenforschung, 1919: 157-163.
Under title: Mennekin-Piss und Dukaten-Scheisser.
Psychoanalytische Beiträge zur Mythenforschung, 1922,
107-118.
15, 343. Rappaport, Ernest A. Notes on blindness and omnisci-
ence: from Oedipus to Hitler. Psychoanal Rev, 1976,
63:281-290.
15, 344. Read, Herbert. Myth, dream and poem. transition,
1938, 27:176-192.
15, 345. Reboul, Jean. L'Oeuil, le mythe et la psychanalyse.
Psyché, 1949, 4:958-972.
15, 346. Reddy, P. C. Chenceetha and her divine bridegroom.
Eastern Anthropologist, 1948, 1:10-20.
15, 347. Rees, C. Some seventeenth-century versions of the judgment of Paris. Notes & Queries, 1977, 24:197-200.
15, 348. Reik, Theodor. Dogma and Compulsion; Psychoanalytic
Studies of Religion and Myths. NY: IUP, 1951.

15, 349.   _____. Mythology. Int J Psycho-Anal, 1921, 2:101-
              105.

15, 350.   _____. Oedipus and the Sphinx. In Compulsion and
              Doubt. NY: IUP, 1952; Imago, 1920, 4:95-131; British
              J Psychol, 1921, 1:181-194.

15, 351.   _____. Psychoanalyse und Mythos. Zeitschrift für
              psychoanalytische Pädagogik, 1926, 1:175-177.

15, 352.   _____. Psychoanalese (Scherzo). In Listening with the
              Third Ear. NY: Farrar Straus, 1949, 458-463.

15, 353.   Renz, Barbara. Geschwäntze Götter und Gottähnliche
              Wesen. Zeitschrift für Sexualwissenschaft, 1927, 14:
              270-273.

15, 354.   Retterstol, N. [Psychiatric aspects of persons mentioned
              in sagas of the Norwegian kings.] Tidsskrift Norske
              Laegeforening, 1962, 82:1219-1222.

15, 355.   Ricklin, Franz. Oedipus und Psychoanalyse. Wissen und
              Leben, 1912, 10:545-554.

15, 356.   Ricoeur, Paul. Fatherhood: from phantasm to symbol.
              In The Conflict of Interpretations. Evanston, Ill:
              Northwestern Univ. Press, 1974, 468-497; In Le Conflit
              des interprétations: Essais d'herméneutique. Paris:
              1969, 458-486.

15, 357.   Rieff, Philip. A modern mythmaker. In Murray, H. A.
              (ed), Myth and Mythmaking. NY: Braziller, 1960.

15, 358.   Righter, William. Myth and interpretation. New Lit His-
              tory, 1972-3, 3:319-344.

15, 359.   _____. Myth and Literature. London: Routledge &
              Kegan Paul, 1975.

15, 360.   Ringgren, Helmer. Dieu, le temps et le destin dans les
              épopées Parsanes. JPNP, 1956, 53:407-423.

15, 361.   Robbins, Lewis L. A contribution to the psychological
              understanding of the character of Don Juan. Bulletin
              Menninger Clinic, 1956, 20:166-180.

15, 362.   Robinson, C. F. Some psychological elements in famous
              superstitions. Amer J Religion, Psychol & Education,
              1905, 1:248-267.

15, 363.   Rogers, Robert. Prometheus as a scapegoat. Lit & Psy-
              chol, 1961, 11:6-11.

15, 364.   Róheim, Géza. Animism, Magic and the Divine King.
              NY: IUP, 1930.

15, 365.   _____. The anthropological evidence and the Oedipus
              complex. Psychoanal Q, 1952, 21:537-542.

15, 366.   _____. Aphrodite, or the woman with a penis. Psy-
              choanal Q, 1945, 14:350-390.

15, 367.   _____. Charon and the obolos. Psychiat Q Supplement,
              1946, 20:160-196.

15, 368.   _____. [Dragons and dragon killers.] Ethnographia,
              1911, 22:128-142, 193-209.

15, 369.   _____. The dragon and the hero. Amer Imago, 1(2):
              40-58; 1(3):61-94.

15, 370.   _____. The Eternal Ones of the Dream; A Psychoanaly-
              tic Interpretation of Australian Myth and Ritual. NY:
              IUP, 1945.

15, 371. _____. The evil eye. Amer Imago, 1952, 9:351-363;
In Yearbook of Psychoanalysis, Vol. 9. NY: IUP,
1953, 283-291.
15, 372. _____. Fire in the dragon. Amer Imago, 1950, 7:163-
172.
15, 373. _____. The Gates of the Dream. NY: IUP, 1952.
15, 374. _____. Héros phalliques et symboles maternels dans
la mythologie australienne. Paris: Gallimard, 1970;
The Eternal Ones of the Dream. NY: IUP, 1945.
15, 375. _____. Myth and folktale. In Vickery, J. B. (ed),
Myth and Literature. Lincoln: Univ. Nebraska Press,
1966, 25-32.
15, 376. _____. Magic and Schizophrenia. Bloomington: Indiana Univ. Press, 1962.
15, 377. _____. Metamorphosis. Amer Imago, 1948, 5:167-172.
15, 378. _____. Mondmythologie und Mondreligion. Imago, 1927,
13:442-537; Leipzig: Int Psychoanalytischer Verlag,
1927.
15, 379. _____. Myth and folk-tale. Amer Imago, 1941, 2:266-
279; In Phillips, W. (ed), Art and Psychoanalysis.
NY: Criterion, 1957, 333-345.
15, 380. _____. Myth and Schizophrenia. NY: IUP, 1955.
15, 381. _____. Mythology of Arnhem Land. Amer Imago,
1951, 8:181-187.
15, 382. _____. The Origin and Function of Culture. NY: Nervous & Mental Disease Monographs, 1943.
15, 383. _____. The panic of the gods. Psychoanal Q, 1952,
21:92-106.
15, 384. _____. Die Psychoanalyse primitiver Kulturen. Imago,
1932, 1:297-563.
15, 385. _____. The Riddle of the Sphinx, or Human Origins.
London: Hogarth, 1934.
15, 386. _____. Saint Agatha and the Tuesday woman. Int J
Psycho-Anal, 1946, 27:119-127.
15, 387. _____. Teiresias and other seers. Psychoanal Rev,
1946, 38:314-344.
15, 388. _____. The thread of life. Psychoanal Q, 1948, 17:
471-486.
15, 389. _____. Die wilde Jagd. Imago, 1926, 12:465-477.
15, 390. _____. Zwei gruppen von Igelsagen. Zeitschrift des
Vereines für Volkskunde, 1913, 23:404-414.
15, 391. Rooth, Anna Birgitta. The creation myths of the North
American Indians. Anthropos, 1957, 52:497-508.
15, 392. Rosolato, Guy. Perspective de la mort dans la tragédie.
In Essais sur le symbolisme. Paris: Gallimard,
1969.
15, 393. Rossi, Romolo. [Seneca and Nero: mastermind and execution of a matricide: a psychoanalytic viewpoint.]
Archivio di Psicologia, Neurologia e Psichatria, 1975,
36:363-377.
15, 394. Roth, N. Early electromedicine and the Frankenstein
myth. Medical Instrument, 1978, 12(4):248.
15, 395. Roychoudhury, Arun K. Sita myth of the Ramayana.
Samiksa, 1954, 8:235-243.

15, 396.   Ruben, Herbert E.   Some meanings of the 'belly button'
           to children.   Bulletin Philadelphia Assn Psychoanal,
           1955, 4:98-100.
15, 397.   Rubenstein, Richard L.   Dreams, psychoanalysis, and
           Jewish legend.   In The Religious Imagination.   Indiana-
           polis: Bobbs-Merrill, 1968, 22-42.
15, 398.   _____.   The significance of castration anxiety in Rab-
           binic mythology.   Psychoanal Rev, 1963, 50:289-312.
15, 399.   Rudwin, M. J.   The Devil in Legend and Literature.   Chi-
           cago: Open Court, 1931.
15, 400.   _____.   Les Ecrivains diabolique de France.   Paris:
           Figuiere, 1937.
15, 401.   _____.   Die Teufelszehnen im geistlichen Drama des
           deutschen Mittelalters.   Baltimore: Johns Hopkins
           Press, 1914.
15, 402.   Ruthven, K. K.   Myth.   London: Methuen, 1976.
15, 403.   Rysan, Josef.   Symbols and mythological behavior.   Psy-
           chiat Research Reports, 1961, 14:34-48.

15, 404.   Sadoff, R. L.   On the nature of crying and weeping.   Psy-
           chiat Q, 1966, 40:490-503.
15, 405.   Safouan, Moustapha.   Etudes sur l'Oedipe.   Paris: Seuil,
           1974.
15, 406.   Sarnoff, Charles A.   Mythic symbols in two precolumbian
           myths.   Amer Imago, 1969, 26:3-20.
15, 407.   Sarró, Ramon.   The interpretation of the Oedipus myth
           according to Freud and Heidegger.   J Existential Psy-
           chiat, 1960-61, 4:478-500; Medical Clinica (Barcelona),
           1958, 31:153-157; Acta Psychotherapeutica et Psycho-
           somatica, 1960, 8:266-289.
15, 408.   Saussere, R. de.   Le Complex de Jocaste.   Int Zeitschrift
           für Psychoanalyse, 1920, 6:118-122.
15, 409.   Schach, Paul.   Some observations on the generation-gap
           theme in the Icelandic sagas.   In Scholler, H. (ed),
           The Epic in Medieval Society: Aesthetic and Moral
           Values.   Tübingen: Niemeyer, 1977, 361-381.
15, 410.   _____.   Symbolic dreams of future renown in Old Ice-
           landic literature.   Mosaic, 1971, 4(4):51-73.
15, 411.   Schapiro, Meyer.   The Myth of Oedipus.   NY: Dürlacher-
           Askew, 1944; Instead, 1948-49.
15, 412.   Scheiner, Peter W.   Ödipus-Stoff und Ödipus Motive in der
           deutschen Literatur.   Doctoral dissertation, Univ. Vi-
           enna, 1964.
15, 413.   Schirrer, Julius.   Das Archaion.   Die Frage nach dem
           Geist.   Psyche, 1948, 2:284-294.
15, 414.   _____.   Gedanken zur Herakles-Mythe.   Zeitschrift für
           psychosomatische Medizin, 1956-57, 3:291-304.
15, 415.   _____.   Die classische Oedipus-Sage.   Zeitschrift für
           psychosomatische Medizin und Psychoanalyse, 1956-57,
           3:45-58.
15, 416.   Schmidbauer, Wolfgang.   Mythos und Psychologie.   Studium
           Generale, 1969, 22:890-912.

15, 417. _____. Mythos und Psychologie: Methodische Probleme, aufgezeigt an der Oedipus-Sage. Munich, 1970.

15, 418. Schneck, Jerome M. Aesculapius, Hippolytus, and the
legend of Phaedra. JAMA, 1963, 184:223-225.

15, 419. _____. Freud and Kronos. Amer J Psychiat, 1968,
125:692-693.

15, 420. Schneiderman, Leo. The cult of Osiris in relation to
primitive initiation rites. Psychoanal Rev, 1965, 52:
38-50.

15, 421. _____. The death of Apsyrtus. Psychoanal Rev, 1967,
54:159-176.

15, 422. _____. A theory of repression in the light of archaic
religion. Psychoanal Rev, 1966, 53:56-68.

15, 423. Schnier, Jacques. Dragon lady. Amer Imago, 1947, 4(3):
77-98; In Yearbook of Psychoanalysis, Vol. 4. NY:
IUP, 1948, 312-329.

15, 424. _____. Morphology of a symbol: the octopus. Amer
Imago, 1956, 13:3-31.

15, 425. Schouten, J. The Rod and Serpent of Asklepios. Symbol
of Medicine. Amsterdam: Elsevier, 1967.

15, 426. Schroeder, J. A. [The Story of Amor and Psyche in the
Light of Psychoanalysis.] Baarn: Hollandia-Drukkery,
1917.

15, 427. Schumann, Hans-Joachinson von. Phänomenologische und
psychoanalytische Untersuchung der Homerischen
Träume. Ein Beitrag zur Klärung der umstrittenen
Blindheit des Dichters. Psychotherapy & Psychosomatics, 1955, 3:205-219.

15, 428. _____. Träume der Blinden vom Standpunkt der Phänomenologie; Tiefenpsychologie, Mythologie und Kunst;
ein Beitrag zur Klärung der bewussten und unbewussten
Problematik der Blinden. Psychologische Praxis, 1959,
25:1-152.

15, 429. Schwarzbaum, Haim. Jewish and Moslem sources of a
Falasha creation myth. In Patai, R., Utley, F. L., &
Noy, D. (eds), Studies in Biblical and Jewish Folklore.
Bloomington: Indiana Univ. Press, 1960.

15, 430. Sebeok, Thomas A. (ed). Myth: A Symposium. Bloomington: Indiana Univ. Press, 1955.

15, 431. Secretan, Philibert. Oedipe comme mythe interdisciplin-
aire. Cahiers Internationaux de Symbolisme, 1966, 12:
73-84.

15, 432. Sehmsdorf, Henning K. The archetypal hero in Nordic
myth and legend. Proceedings Pacific Northwest Conference on Foreign Languages, 1977, 28(1):99-103.

15, 433. _____. Archetypal structures in Scandinavian mythology.
In Wonderley, A. W. (ed), Facets of Scandinavian Literature. Lexington, Ky: APRA, 1974, 53-66.

15, 434. Seidenberg, Robert. Psychosexual aspects of Hymen.
Psychoanal Q, 1951, 20:472-474.

15, 435. Sereno, Renzo. Some observations on the Santa Claus
custom. Psychiatry, 1951, 14:387-396.

15, 436. Servadio, Emilio. Die Angst vor dem bösen Blick.
Imago, 1936, 22:396-408.

15, 437. _____. La Fée dans l'enfance et dans le myth. Psyché, 1947, 2:1319-1332; Circoli, 1937, 6:111-112.
15, 438. _____. Note sur la tête de la Méduse. Psyché, 1948,
3:73-75.
15, 439. Seyler, Clarence A. Slips of the tongue in the Norse
sagas. Int J Psycho-Anal, 1956, 36:134-135.
15, 440. Sidler, Nikolaus. Zur Universalität des Inzestitabu.
Stuttgart: 1971.
15, 441. Silberer, Herbert. Phantasy und Mythos. Jahrbuch der
Psychoanalyse, 1910, 2:541-622.
15, 442. _____. Das Zerstückelungsmotiv in Mythos. Imago,
1914, 3:502-523.
15, 443. Simenauer, Erich. The miraculous birth of Hambageu,
hero-god of the Sonjo. Tanganyika Notes & Records,
1955, 38:23-30.
15, 444. Singer, Irving. Erotic transformations in the legend of
Dido and Aeneas. MLN, 1975, 90:767-783.
15, 445. Skeels, Dell R. Eros and Thanatos in Nez Perce river
mythology. Amer Imago, 1964, 21:103-110.
15, 446. _____. Grizzly-Bear Woman in Nez Perce Indian
mythology. Northwest Folklore, 1968, 3:1-9.
15, 447. Slater, A. S. From rhetoric and structure to psychology
in Hrafnkels saga Freysgooa. Scandinavian Studies,
1968, 40:36-50.
15, 448. Slater, Philip E. The Glory of Hera. Greek Mythology
and the Greek Family. Boston: Beacon, 1968.
15, 449. Slochower, Harry. Mythopoesis: Mythic Patterns in the
Literary Classics. Detroit: Wayne State Univ. Press,
1970; Reviews: Simon O. Lesser, Psychoanal Q, 1973,
42:152; John E. Gedo, Amer Imago, 1970, 27:329-337;
Rebecca Patterson, Lit & Psychol, 1973, 23:37-44.
15, 450. _____. Oedipus: Fromm or Freud. Complex, 1952,
8:52-64.
15, 451. _____. Psychoanalytic distinction between myth and
mythopoesis. JAPA, 1970, 18:150-164.
15, 452. Slote, Bernice (ed). Myth and Symbol. Lincoln: Univ.
Nebraska Press, 1963.
15, 453. Smith, Catherine F. The invention of sex in myth and
literature. In McCune, M. W., Orbison, T., & Withim, P. M. (eds), The Binding of Proteus; Perspectives
on Myth and the Literary Process. Lewisburg, Pa:
Bucknell Univ. Press, 1980, 252-262.
15, 454. Solari, Swayne E. La psicologia deferencial de los sexos
en la escuela bioantropológica contemporánea y en la
mitologia griega. Revista de psicologia, 1959, 1:7-45.
15, 455. Solomon, Maynard, et al. (eds). Myth, Creativity, Psychoanalysis; Essays in Honor of Harry Slochower. Detroit: Wayne State Univ. Press, 1979.
15, 456. Soulé, Michel. Contribution à la compréhénsion de l'imaginaire des parents: a propos de l'adoption ou le roman
de Polybe et Mérope. Rev Française de Psychanalyse,
1968, 32:419-464.

15, 457. Speiser, F. Die Frau als Erfinderin von Kultgeraten in
          Melanesien. Schweizerischen Zeitschrift für Psychol-
          ogie, 1944, 3:46-54.
15, 458. Sperling, Melitta. Spider phobias and spider fantasies:
          a clinical contribution to the study of symbol and symp-
          tom choice. JAPA, 1971, 19:472-498.
15, 459. Spiegel, Rose. Reflections on depression and melancholy:
          from myth to psychoanalysis. J Amer Academy Psy-
          choanal, 1976, 4:279-300.
15, 460. Spiegelman, J. Marvin. The Tree: Tales in Psycho-
          Mythology. Los Angeles: Phoenix, 1974.
15, 461. Spielmeyer, R. The epic of Gilgamesh; resolution of con-
          cepts of evil and death in ancient Babylonia. New
          York State J Medicine, 1979, 79:1618-1621.
15, 462. Spiro, Melford E. Ghosts, Ifaluk and teleological func-
          tionalism. Amer Anthropologist, 1952, 54:497-503.
15, 463. _____. The Oedipus complex in Burma. JNMD, 1973,
          157:389-395.
15, 464. Spotnitz, Hyman. The prophecies of Teiresias. Psycho-
          anal & Psychoanal Rev, 1955-56, 3:37-43.
15, 465. _____, & Resnikoff, Philip. The myths of Narcissus.
          Psychoanal Rev, 1954, 41:173-181.
15, 466. Sproul, Barbara C. Primal Myths: Creating the World.
          NY: Harper & Row, 1979.
15, 467. Starr, Omega Means. A search for the identity of Yamm
          'Prince Sea' of the Canaanite Baal and Anath cycle.
          Folklore, 1973, 84:224-237.
15, 468. Steele, Thomas S. Zen and the art: the identity of the
          Erlkönig. Ariel, 1979, 10:83-93.
15, 469. Stein, Conrad. La Mort d'Oedipe. Paris: Denoël, 1978.
15, 470. _____. Notes sur la mort d'Oedipe. Rev Français de
          Psychanalyse, 1959, 23:735-756.
15, 471. Stein, Murray. Hephaistos: a pattern of introversion.
          Spring, 1973, 35-51.
15, 472. _____. Hera: bound and unbound. Spring, 1977, 105-
          119.
15, 473. Stein, Robert M. The Oedipus myth and the incest arche-
          type. In Spectrum Psychologie. Zurich: Rascher,
          1965.
15, 474. Steiner, Grundy. The graphic analogue from myth in
          Greek romance. Illinois Studies in Language & Lit,
          1969, 58:123-137.
15, 475. Stephens, W. N. The Oedipus Complex: Cross-Cultural
          Evidence. NY: Free Press, 1962.
15, 476. Sterba, Richard F. Kilroy was here. Amer Imago, 1948,
          5:173-181.
15, 477. Stern, Max M. Ego psychology, myth and rite. In The
          Psychoanalytic Study of Society, Vol. 3. NY: IUP,
          1964, 71-93.
15, 478. Stewart, H. Jocasta's crimes. Int J Psycho-Anal, 1961,
          42:424-430.
15, 479. Stock, B. Myth and Science in the 12th Century. Prince-
          ton: Princeton Univ. Press, 1972.

15,480. Stolorow, Robert D.   Narcissus revisited. Amer J Psy-
          choanal, 1975, 35:286.
15,481. Strange, William C.   The proper marriage of allegory and
          myth in Nerval's Horus.   Modern Language Q, 1967,
          317-328.
15,482. Streatfeild, D. [The riddle of the Sphinx.] Analytische
          Psychologie, 1977, 8:216-237.
15,483. Sullivan, Harry S.   Sleep, dreams and myths.   In The
          Interpersonal Theory of Psychiatry.   NY: Norton,
          1953, 329-343.
15,484. Sulloway, Frank J.   The myth of the hero in the psycho-
          analytic movement.   In Freud, Biologist of the Mind.
          Beyond the Psychoanalytic Legend.   NY: Basic Books,
          1979, 445-495.
15,485. Sutton, T. C., & Sutton, M.   Science fiction as mythology.
          Western Folklore, 1969, 28:230-237.
15,486. Sutton, Walter.   Psychological and myth criticism.   In
          Modern American Criticism.   Englewood Cliffs, NJ:
          Prentice-Hall, 1963, 175-219.
15,487. Szwed, John F., & Abrahams, Roger D.   After the myth:
          studying Afro-American cultural patterns in the planta-
          tion literature.   In Crowley, D. J. (ed), African Folk-
          lore in the New World.   Austin: Univ. Texas Press,
          1977, 65-86.

15,488. Tagliacozzo, Giorgio, & White, Hayden W. (eds).   Giam-
          battista Vico, an International Symposium.   Baltimore:
          Johns Hopkins Univ. Press, 1969.
15,489. Tarachow, Sidney.   Applied Psychoanalysis.   Mythology.
          In Annual Survey of Psychoanalysis, Vol. 1.   NY:
          IUP, 1950, 317-321.
15,490. _____.   Applied psychoanalysis.   IV.   Mythology and
          folklore.   In Annual Survey of Psychoanalysis, Vol. 2.
          NY: IUP, 1951, 553-567.
15,491. _____.   Applied psychoanalysis.   II.   Religion and
          mythology.   In Annual Survey of Psychoanalysis, Vol.
          3.   NY: IUP, 1952, 494-511.
15,492. _____.   Introductory remarks, panel on mythology and
          ego psychology.   In The Psychoanalytic Study of Soci-
          ety, Vol. 3.   NY: IUP, 1964, 9-12.
15,493. _____.   Mythology and ego psychology.   In The Psycho-
          analytic Study of Society, Vol. 3.   NY: IUP, 1964,
          9-12.
15,494. Tegethoff, Ernst.   Studien zum Märchentypus von Amor
          und Psyche.   Bonn: Schroeder, 1922.
15,495. Thass-Thienemann, Theodore.   Oedipus and the Sphinx:
          the linguistic approach to unconscious fantasies.
          Psychoanal Rev, 1957, 44:10-33.
15,496. This, Bernard. [Birth and smiling.] Rev de Médecine
          Psychosomatique et de Psychologie Médicale, 1976, 18:
          105-119.
15,497. _____.   Inceste, adultère, écriture.   Esprit, 1971, 644-
          677.

15, 498. Tourney, Garfield. Freud and the Greeks: a study of the
          influence of classical Greek mythology and philosophy
          upon the development of Freudian thought. J History
          Behavioral Sciences, 1965, 1:67-85.
15, 499. _____, & Plazak, Dean J. Evil eye in myth and schizo-
          phrenia. Psychiat Q, 1954, 28:478-495.
15, 500. Turner, Terence S. Oedipus: time and structure in nar-
          rative form. In Spencer, Robert F. (ed), Forms of
          Symbolic Action. Seattle: Univ. Washington Press,
          1969, 26-67.
15, 501. Twitchell, James. The vampire myth. Amer Imago,
          1980, 37:83-92.

15, 502. Ullman, Montague. The social roots of the dream. Amer
          J Psychoanal, 1960, 20:180-189.
15, 503. Usandivaras, R. J. [A myth as a model for the group:
          the Argonauts' voyage.] Acta Psiquiatrica Psicologica
          America Latina, 1977, 23:12-22.

15, 504. Valbuena, A. El torno a la psicoanalisis de Don Juan.
          Revista de Psicologia y Pedagogia, 1937, 5:170-180.
15, 505. Van Teslaar, James S. The death of Pan: a classical
          instance of a verbal misinterpretation. Psychoanal Rev,
          1921, 8:180-183.
15, 506. Velikovsky, Immanuel. Oedipus and Akhnaton. Myth and
          History. Garden City, NY: Doubleday, 1960.
15, 507. Verble, Margaret. Emotional distance in the narration of
          legends. J Amer Folklore, 1975, 88:296-299.
15, 508. Vernant, Jean-Pierre. Oedipe sans complexe. In Ver-
          nant, J. P., & Nacquet, V. (eds), Mythe et tragédie en
          Grèce ancienne. Paris: Maspéro, 1972, 77-98; Bul-
          letin de Psychologie, 1978, 31:12-17.
15, 509. _____. Prométhée et la fonction technique. JPNP,
          1952, 45:419-429.
15, 510. Veszy-Wagner, Lilla. The bearded man. Amer Imago,
          1963, 20:133-147.
15, 511. _____. The corpse in the car: a minor myth creation.
          Amer Imago, 1972, 29:53-69.
15, 512. _____. An Irish legend as proof of Freud's theory of
          joint parricide. Int J Psycho-Anal, 1957, 38:117-120.
15, 513. _____. Serf Balázs: a 'boy without the dike' a stage
          before the solution of the Oedipal conflict. Amer
          Imago, 1958, 15:181-193.
15, 514. _____. The symbolism of the bird. Amer Imago,
          1973, 30:97-112.
15, 515. Vickery, John B. The Golden Bough: impact and arche-
          type. Virginia Q Rev, 1963, 39:37-57.
15, 516. _____ (ed). Myth and Literature. Contemporary The-
          ory and Practice. Lincoln: Univ. Nebraska Press,
          1969.
15, 517. Vivas, Eliseo. Myth: some philosophical problems.
          Southern Rev, 1970, 6:89-103.

15, 518. Von Franz, Marie-Louise. Le Cri de Merlin: Jung's
          myth. Psychol Perspectives, 1975, 6: 22-36.

15, 519. Waldmann, H. [Dionysus and insanity. A phenomenologi-
          cal study.] Confinia Psychiatria, 1970, 13:199-222.
15, 520. Walker, H. Myth in Giono's Le Chant du Monde. Sym-
          posium, 1961, 15:139-146.
15, 521. Wangh, Martin. Day residue in dream and myth. JAPA,
          1954, 2:446-452.
15, 522. Wayne, R. Prometheus and Christ. In Psychoanalysis
          and the Social Sciences, Vol. 3. NY: IUP, 1951, 201-
          219.
15, 523. Weigert-Vowinckel, Edith. The cult and mythology of the
          Magna Mater from the standpoint of psychoanalysis.
          Psychiatry, 1938, 1:347-378.
15, 524. Weisinger, Herbert. The Agony and the Triumph: Papers
          on the Use and Abuse of Myth. East Lansing: Michi-
          gan State Univ. Press, 1964.
15, 525. Wels-Schon, Grete. Von der Mutter der Pallas Athene.
          Psyche, 1954, 7: 627-632.
15, 526. Werman, David S., & Rhoads, John M. The Faust legend
          seen in the light of an analytic case. JAPA, 1976, 24:
          101-121.
15, 527. Wesselski, A. Der Gott ausser Funktion. Archiv Ori-
          entální, 1929, 1:300-311.
15, 528. West, Michael. Problems of identity in the Narcissus
          myth. Folklore & Mythology Studies, 1978, 2:8-10.
15, 529. Westerman Holstijn, A. J. Klassicke mysteriën en psycho-
          analyse. Nederlandsch Tijdschrift voor de Psychologie,
          1955, 10:335-354.
15, 530. Weston, Jessie. From Ritual to Romance. Garden City,
          NY: Doubleday Anchor, 1957.
15, 531. Wheelwright, Philip Ellis. The Burning Fountain. A Study
          in the Language of Symbolism. Bloomington: Indiana
          Univ. Press, 1954, 1968.
15, 532. _____. Poetry, myth and reality. In Goldberg, G. J.,
          & Goldberg, N. (eds), The Modern Critical Spectrum.
          Englewood Cliffs, NJ: Prentice-Hall, 1962, 306-320;
          In Handy, W. J., & Westbrook, M. (eds), Twentieth
          Century Criticism. NY: Macmillan, 1974, 252-266.
15, 533. White, John J. Mythology in the Modern Novel. A Study
          of Prefigurative Techniques. Princeton: Princeton
          Univ. Press, 1971.
15, 534. _____. Myths and patterns in the modern novel. Mo-
          saic, 1969, 2:42-55.
15, 535. Wieseler, Friedrich. Narkissos. Göttingen: 1856.
15, 536. Winters, D. New source for Lancelot's madness. Studies
          in Philology, 1934, 31:379-384.
15, 537. Winterstein, Alfred R. F. Die Nausikaaepisode in der
          Odyssee. Imago, 1920, 6:349-383.
15, 538. Wittels, Fritz. Myth and paranoia. In Freud and His
          Time. NY: Grosset & Dunlap, 1931, 81-122.

15, 539. _____. Tragische Motive oder das Unbewusste in Held und Heldin. Berlin: Fleischel, 1911.

15, 540. Wolf, Michel J. de. Comments on Freud and Kronos. Psychoanal Q, 1972, 41:420-423.

15, 541. Wolfenden, J. H. Baron Munchausen as an expert witness. Bulletin History Medicine, 1970, 44:474-476.

15, 542. Woltmann, A. G. The riddle of the Amazon. Psychoanal Rev, 1971, 58:135-148.

15, 543. Wundt, Wilhelm. Völkerpsychologie. Eine Untersuchung der Entwicklungsgesetze von Sprache, Mythus und Sitte. Leipzig: Engelmann, 1905.

15, 544. Wyschogrod, Edith. Sons without fathers: a study in identity and culture. J Amer Academy Psychoanal, 1978, 6:249-262.

15, 545. Wyss, Dieter, et al. [Narcissus--anthropological psychopathology of a communication disorder.] Zeitschrift Klinische Psychologie Psychotherapie, 1976, 24:358-367.

15, 546. _____. [Oedipus--anthropology of enlightenment and interpretation.] Zeitschrift Klinische Psychologie Psychotherapie, 1977, 25:43-51.

15, 547. Yampey, Nasim. [The meaning and function of two South American myths.] Acta Psiquiatrica Psicologica América Latina, 1977, 23:172-183.

15, 548. Zaehner, R. Sexual symbolism in the Svetāśvatara Upanishad. In Kitagawa, J. M. (ed), Myths and Symbols. Chicago: Univ. Chicago Press, 1969, 209-215.

15, 549. Zander, W. Das Schicksal des Wanderers in der Mythologie. In Schelkopf, A., & Elbardt, S. (eds), Aspekte der Psychoanalyse. Göttingen: Vandenhoek & Ruprecht, 1969, 155-170.

15, 550. Zeckel, Adolf. The totemistic significance of the Unicorn. In Psychoanalysis and Culture. NY: IUP, 1951, 344-360.

15, 551. Zeldenrust, E. L. K. Über die anthropologische Interpretation des Ödipus-Mythos. Nervenarzt, 1963, 34:359-365.

15, 552. Ziner, Feenie. The ghost of Lady Guinevere. Amer J Psychoanal, 1978, 38:169-178.

15, 553. Ziolkowski, Theodore. Hesse, myth, and reason: methodological prolegomena. In Wetzels, W. D. (ed), Myth and Reason; A Symposium. Austin: Univ. Texas Press, 1973, 127-155.

15, 554. _____. Some features of religious figuralism in twentieth-century literature. In Miner, E. R. (ed), Literary Uses of Typology. Princeton: Princeton Univ. Press, 1977, 345-369.

15, 555. Abadi, Mauricio. Dante e la Divina Commedia. Rivista
          di Psicoanalisi, 1962, 8:195-213.
15, 556. _____. Dante y la Divina Comedia. Introducción a su
          estudio psicoanalitico. Rivista di Psicoanalisi, 1961,
          18:96-117.
15, 557. Abenheimer, Karl M., & Halliday, J. L. The Treatise of
          the Two Married Women and the Widow. Psychoanal
          Rev, 1944, 31:233-252.
15, 558. Abraham, Karl. Eine Traumanalyse bei Ovid. Int Zeit-
          schrift für Psychoanalysis, 1911, 2:159-160.
15, 559. Abraham, Nicolas. [Time, rhythm and the unconscious.
          Considerations for psychoanalytic esthetics.] Rev Fran-
          çaise Psychanalyse, 1972, 36:557-583.
15, 560. Abrams, Meyer H. The Milk of Paradise: The Effect of
          Opium Visions on the Works of DeQuincey, Crabbe,
          Francis Thompson, and Coleridge. Cambridge: Har-
          vard Univ. Press, 1934.
15, 561. _____. Unconscious expectations in the reading of po-
          etry. J English Lit History, 1942, 9:235-244.
15, 562. Abrams, Robert E. An early precursor of 'The Sleepers':
          Whitman's 'The Last of the Sacred Army.' Walt Whit-
          man Rev, 1976, 22:122-125.
15, 563. _____. The function of dreams and dream-logic in
          Whitman's poetry. Texas Studies in Lit & Language,
          1975, 17:599-616.
15, 564. Ackerman, Stephen Joseph, Jr. Moral Architecture:
          Pope's Personal Psychology. DAI, 1976, 36:5309A.
15, 565. Adams, George R. Sex and clergy in Chaucer's 'General
          Prologue.' Lit & Psychol, 1968, 18:215-222.
15, 566. Adams, Hazard. Blake and Yeats: the Contrary Vision.
          London: Russell & Russell, 1968.
15, 567. Adams, Richard Perrill. The archetypal pattern of death
          and rebirth in Milton's 'Lycidas.' In Vickery, J. B.
          (ed), Myth and Literature. Lincoln: Univ. Nebraska
          Press, 1966, 187-191.
15, 568. Adlard, John. The colour-research of the poets of the
          'Nineties. J Francis Thompson Society, 1974, 4-5:12-
          16.
15, 569. Adler, Alfred. Yvain der Löwenritter. Int Zeitschrift für
          Individual-Psychologie, 1935, 13:185-189.

15, 570. Adolf, Helen. Mysticism and the growth of personality: a study in Dante's Vita nuova. In Sola-Salé, J. M., et al. (eds), Studies in Honor of Tatiana Fotitch. Washington, DC: Catholic Univ. of America Press, 1973, 165-176.

15, 571. _____. Personality in medieval poetry and fiction. Deutsche Vierteljahrsschrift für Literaturwissenschaft und Geistesgeschichte, 1970, 44:9-19.

15, 572. _____. Wrestling with the angel: Rilke's 'Gazing Eye' (Der Schauende) and the archetype. In Strelka, J. (ed), Perspectives in Literary Symbolism. University Park: Penn State Univ. Press, 1968, 29-39.

15, 573. A. E. (G. W. Russell). Song and Its Fountains. NY: Macmillan, 1932.

15, 574. Aers, David. William Blake and the dialects of sex. J English Lit History, 1977, 44:500-514.

15, 575. Agosti, S. Il Testo Poetico. Teoria e pratiche d'analisi. Milan: Rizzoli, 1972.

15, 576. Ahluwalia, Harsharan Singh. The private self and the public self in Whitman's 'Lilacs.' Walt Whitman Rev, 1977, 23:166-174.

15, 577. Aigrisse, Gilberte. [Actualization of the archetype of the androgyne in a poem of Roger Bodart.] Rev de Psychologie et des Sciences de l'Education, 1975, 10:295-314.

15, 578. Aiken, Conrad. Disintegration in modern poetry. Dial, 1924, 76:535-540.

15, 579. Aitken, B. Day-dreams in the Spanish ballads. Psyche, 1928, 9:44-55.

15, 580. Aleksić, Branko. Gran maestro d'amore Francesco Petrarka: Ispitivanje njegove psihologije ljubavi i osvrt na neka tumačenja. Knjizevna Kritika, 1976, 7(5):44-66.

15, 581. Alexander, Franz. The psychoanalyst looks at contemporary art. In Lindner, R. (ed), Explorations in Psychoanalysis. NY: Messner, 1953, 139-154.

15, 582. Ali, Raza. The 'decadent' view of life and Dowson's poetry. Thoth, 1972-73, 13(1):19-32.

15, 583. Allen, Frank. Sex and the dreaming egotist: a reading of 'Love among the Ruins.' Browning Society Notes, 1975, 5(1):8-14.

15, 584. Allen, Gay Wilson. A note on comparing Whitman and Nietzsche. Walt Whitman Rev, 1965, 11:74-75.

15, 585. Allen, James Lovic. The road to Byzantium: archetypal criticism and Yeats. JAAC, 1973, 32:53-64.

15, 586. Allen, Rupert C. J. R. Jiménez and the world tree. Revista Hispánica Moderna, 1969 (1972), 306-322.

15, 587. _____. Un poema existencialista de Antonio Machado. Duquesne Hispanic Rev, 1963, 2:1-71.

15, 588. _____. The Symbolic World of Federico García Lorca. Albuquerque: Univ. New Mexico Press, 1972.

15, 589. Allison, Eileen. Robert Frost's Poetic Treatment of Human Relationships. DAI, 1971, 31:4148A-49A.

15, 590. Alper, B. S.   Mysticism of William Blake; a psychological
          re-examination.   Poet Lore, 1938, 44:344-350.
15, 591. Alvarez, Alfred.   Convictions of excellence.   New States-
          man, 2 Feb 1962, 163-164.
15, 592. _____.   Sylvia Plath.   In Newman, C. (ed), The Art
          of Sylvia Plath.   Bloomington: Indiana Univ. Press,
          1970, 56-88.
15, 593. Amanuddin, Syed.   Love and sex in Indo-English poetry.
          Creative Moment, 1974, 3(1):15-26.
15, 594. Amusco, A.   El motivo erótico en Espadas como labios de
          V. Aleixandre.   Insula, 1976, 313:167-179.
15, 595. Amyot, Gerald F.   Contrasting visions of death in the po-
          etry of Poe and Whitman.   Walt Whitman Rev, 1973,
          19:103-111.
15, 596. Andia, Ernesto D.   Diagnosis de la poesia y su arquetipo.
          Buenos Aires: Editorial 'El Ateneo, ' 1951.
15, 597. Andreas-Salomé, Lou.   Des Dichters Erleben.   Neue Rund-
          schau, March 1919.
15, 598. Andreasen, Nancy J. C.   Donne's Devotions and the psychol-
          ogy of assent.   Modern Phililogy, 1965, 62:207-216.
15, 599. Andrews, Linda L.   'I Am the Poet of the Woman the
          Same as the Man':   Whitman's view of women as de-
          picted in 'Song of Myself. '   Ball State Univ. Forum,
          1975, 16(4):68-76.
15, 600. Andronika, J. L.   A Comparative Study of Ovid's Treatment
          of Erotic Themes in the Different Genres of His Poetry.
          DAI, 1972, 32:6948A.
15, 601. Angus, Douglas.   The theme of love and guilt in Coler-
          idge's three major poems.   J English Germanic Philol-
          ogy, 1960, 59:655-668.
15, 602. Anon.   On the 'Four Quartets' of T. S. Eliot.   London:
          British Book Centre, 1954.
15, 603. _____.   Der Frauenfuss in der Dichtung.   Zukunft, 23
          March 1912.
15, 604. _____.   Sexualsymbolik in der Lyrik.   Zeitschrift für
          Psychoanalyse, 1913, 1:518-519.
15, 605. _____.   Symbolik in einem chinesischen Gedicht.   Int
          Zeitschrift für Psychoanalyse, 1913, 3:468.
15, 606. Anshutz, H. L. , & Cummings, D. W.   Blake's 'The Sick
          Rose. '   Explicator, 1970, 29.
15, 607. Anthéaume, A. , & Dromard, G.   Poésie et folie: essai
          de psychologie et de critique.   Paris: 1908.
15, 608. Antonius, Brother (William Everson).   Robinson Jeffers:
          Fragments of an Older Fury.   Berkeley, Cal: Oyez,
          1968.
15, 609. Apollonio, Carla.   La crisis existenziale dell'uomo con-
          temporaneo nelle prime poesie di Thomas Stearns Eliot
          ed Eugenio Montale.   Otto/Novecento, 1977, 1:77-96.
15, 610. Appleyard, J. A.   Coleridge's Philosophy of Literature:
          The Development of a Concept of Poetry, 1791-1819.
          Cambridge: Harvard Univ. Press, 1965.
15, 611. Aprile, Giuseppe.   Dante: Inferní dentro e fuori.   Paler-
          mo: Vespro, 1977.

15, 612.   Aring, Charles D.   Perception as a moral test.   JNMD,
            1968, 144:539-545.
15, 613.   Arkans, Norman.   Visions and experience in Hardy's
            dream poems.   Modern Language Q, 1980, 41:54-72.
15, 614.   Armstrong, I. A.   Coleridge on Imagination.   NY: Har-
            court, Brace, 1935.
15, 615.   Armstrong, Isobel (ed).   Browning and Victorian poetry
            of sexual love.   In Robert Browning.   Athens: Ohio
            Univ. Press, 1975, 267-298.
15, 616.   _____.   The role and the treatment of emotion in Vic-
            torian criticism of poetry.   Victorian Periodicals News-
            letter, 1977, 10:3-16.
15, 617.   Armytage, W. H.   Thomas Beddoes, 1760-1808.   British
            Medical J, 1960, 182:1358-1359.
15, 618.   Arner, Robert D.   Mythology and the maypole of merry-
            mount: some notes on Thomas Morton's 'Rise Oedipus.'
            Early Amer Lit, 1971, 6:156-164.
15, 619.   Arnheim, R. , Auden, W. H. , Shapiro, K. , & Stauffer, D.
            A.   Poets at Work.   NY: Harcourt, Brace, 1948.
15, 620.   Aronoff, Marcia.   Dream and non-dream in Dante's The
            Vita Nuova.   Cithara, 1976, 16:18-32.
15, 621.   Aspiz, Harold.   'The Body Electric':   science, sex, and
            metaphor.   Walt Whitman Rev, 1978, 24:137-142.
15, 622.   _____.   Educating the Kosmos: 'There Was a Child
            Went Forth. '   Amer Q, 1966, 18:655-666.
15, 623.   _____.   A reading of Whitman's 'Faces. '   Walt Whit-
            man Rev, 1973, 19:37-48.
15, 624.   _____.   'Unfolded out of the folds' in 'Unfolding the
            folds. '   Walt Whitman Rev, 1966, 12:81-87.
15, 625.   Asselineau, Roger.   L'Evolution de Walt Whitman après
            la première édition des Feuilles d'Herbe.   Paris:
            Didier, 1954.
15, 626.   _____.   The Evolution of Walt Whitman.   The Creation
            of a Book.   Vol. 2.   Cambridge: Harvard Univ.
            Press, 1960.
15, 627.   _____.   Le Thème de la mort dans l'oeuvre de Walt
            Whitman.   Lettre Modernes, 1954, 10:32-48.
15, 628.   _____.   'Passage to India. '   Calamus, 1978, 16:11-14.
15, 629.   _____.   Whitman Agonistes.   Walt Whitman Newsletter,
            1957, 3:3-5.
15, 630.   Atkins, Adelheid M.   Crisis Behavior in German Expres-
            sionism: The Poetry of Georg Trakl.   DAI, 1971, 32:
            1463A.
15, 631.   Atkinson, Michael.   Robert Bly's 'Sleepers Joining Hands':
            shadow and self.   Iowa Rev, 1976, 7(4):135-153.
15, 632.   Auden, W. H.   In memory of Sigmund Freud.   In The Col-
            lected Poetry of W. H. Auden.   NY: Knopf, 1945.
15, 633.   Audry, Collette.   La Genèse d'un poème.   Psyché, 1947,
            2:890-903.

15, 634.   Bachi, A.   Dante prima della mirable visione.   'Men che
            dramma. '   Il Ponte, 1966, 22:2.

15, 635. Bachler, Karl. Männer, Mächte und Dämonen. Psycho-
          logische Berater gesunde praktische Lebensgestalt, 1952,
          4:290-294.
15, 636. Bacon, L. Analytic psychology and poetry. In Die kultur-
          elle Bedeutung der komplexen Psychologie. Berlin:
          Springer, 1935, 365-369.
15, 637. Bailliet, Thereisa S. Frauen im Werk Eichendorffs: Ver-
          körperungen heidnischen und christlichen Geistes.
          Bonn: Bouvier, 1972.
15, 638. Bairamov, A. S. [The psychological aspect of the creativ-
          ity of Azerbaidzhan poet and thinker Imadeddin Nasimi.]
          Voprosy Psikhologii, 1976, No. 1, 156-160.
15, 639. Baird, Julian. Swinburne, Sade, and Blake: the pleasure-
          pain paradox. Victorian Poetry, 1971, 9:49-75.
15, 640. Baker, Carlos. The father-son succession in Aeschylus'
          Prometheia and Shelley's Prometheus Unbound. In Shel-
          ley's Major Poetry: The Fabric of a Vision. Prince-
          ton: Princeton Univ. Press, 1948, 281-283.
15, 641. Baker, James Volant. The Sacred River: Coleridge's
          Theory of the Imagination. Louisiana: Louisiana State
          Univ. Press, 1957; Oxford: Oxford Univ. Press, 1958.
15, 642. Balakian, Nona. Realists of the interior: women poets of
          today. In Critical Encounters. Indianapolis: Bobbs-
          Merrill, 1978, 156-158.
15, 643. Balandier, G. Le Poète et le magicien: deux attitudes de
          rupture. Psyché, 1948, 3:1365-1371.
15, 644. Balázs, Mary Elizabeth Webber. Walt Whitman and Wil-
          liam James: Stirrers of the Long Silent American
          Mind. DA, 1966, 27:764A-765A.
15, 645. Bald, M. A. The psychology of Shelley. Contemporary
          Rev, 1927, 131:359-366.
15, 646. Baldridge, Marie. Some psychological patterns in the po-
          etry of T. S. Eliot. Psychoanalysis, 1954, 3:19-47.
15, 647. Bambrey, Thomas Edward. The Development of Byron's
          Narrative Personality. DAI, 1977, 38:2800A-01A.
15, 648. Barberi Squarotti, G. L''ambiguita' della 'Vita Nuova. '
          In Psicoanalisi e strutturalismo di fronte a Dante.
          Vol. III: Incontro con le altre opere. Florence:
          Olschki, 1972, 7-55.
15, 649. Baron, Frances Xavier. Children and violence in Chaucer's
          Canterbury Tales. J Psychohistory, 1979, 7(1):77-103.
15, 650. _____. Mother and son in Sir Perceval of Galles. Pa-
          pers on Language & Lit, 1972, 8:3-14.
15, 651. Baron, Frank, Dick, Ernst S. , & Maurer, Warren R.
          (eds), Rilke: The Alchemy of Alienation. Lawrence,
          Kans: Regents, 1980.
15, 652. Barron, David B. 'Endymion': the quest for beauty.
          Amer Imago, 1963, 20:27-47.
15, 653. _____. A study in symbolism. Psychoanal Rev, 1947,
          34:395-431.
15, 654. Barron, Frank. The dream of art and poetry. Psychol
          Today, 1968, 2:18-23.
15, 655. Barschi, Jack. The Sexual Imagery in Robinson Jeffers'
          Narrative Poetry. DAI, 1969, 30:2519A.

15, 656. Bartholomae, Eleanor Ann. The Dynamics of Conflict: A Psychoanalytic-Literary Study of the Life and Poetry of George Herbert. DAI, 1976, 37:979A.

15, 657. Baruch, Elaine H. Marvell's 'Nymph': a study of feminine consciousness. Etudes Anglaises, 1978, 31:152-160.

15, 658. Basler, Roy P. Psychological pattern in the Love Song of J. Alfred Prufrock. In Knickerbocker, W. S. (ed), Twentieth Century English. NY: Philosophical Library, 1946, 384-400.

15, 659. _____. Sex, Symbolism, and Psychology in Literature. New Brunswick: Rutgers Univ. Press, 1948.

15, 660. _____. The taste of it: observations on current erotic poetry. Mosaic, 1973, 6:93-105.

15, 661. _____. Tennyson the psychologist; the failure of his contemporaries to understand Maud. South Atlantic Q, 1944, 43:143-159.

15, 662. Bass, Eban. Frost's poetry of fear. Amer Lit, 1972, 43:603-615.

15, 663. Bassermann, Dieter. Der späte Rilke. Munich: Leibnitz, 1947.

15, 664. Bassim, Tamara. La Femme dans l'oeuvre de Baudelaire. Boudy: La Baconnière, 1974.

15, 665. Baudouin, Charles. Esquisse d'un psychanalyse de l'Enéide. Psyché, 1952, 7:6-23.

15, 666. _____. Gérard de Nerval ou le nouvel Orphée. Psyché, 1947, 2:8-14.

15, 667. _____. The laws of imagery and of poetic symbols. J Sexology & Psychoanal, 1923, 1:59-72.

15, 668. _____. Psychoanalysis and Aesthetics. NY: Dodd, Mead, 1924; Paris: 1929.

15, 669. _____. Le Voile de la danse, poème. Geneva: Cailler, 1945.

15, 670. Baudoux, Luce. L'Inconscient concerté syntaxe et lexique dans l'oeuvre de Mallarmé. Rev de Esthétique, 1964, 17:105-119.

15, 671. _____. Inconscient freudien et structures formelle de la poésie. Rev Philosophique de Louvain, 1963, 61:435-466.

15, 672. Bayley, John. Keats and sex. In The Uses of Division; Unity and Disharmony in Literature. NY: Viking, 1976, 130-145.

15, 673. _____. The poem as personality, illustrated by the poetry of Peter Levi. Agenda, 1968, 6(2):62-65.

15, 674. Baym, Nina Zippin. The erotic motif in Melville's 'Clarel.' Texas Studies in Lit & Language, 1974, 16:315-328.

15, 675. _____. God, father, and lover in Emily Dickinson's poetry. In Elliot, E. (ed), Puritan Influences in American Literature. Urbana: Univ. Illinois Press, 1979, 193-209.

15, 676. Bays, Gwendolyn M. The orphic vision of Nerval, Baudelaire, and Rimbaud. Comparative Lit, 1967, 1:17-26.

15,677. _____. Rimbaud, father of Surrealism? Yale French
          Studies, 1964, 31.
15,678. Beach, Joseph Warren. Obsessive Images: Symbolism in
          Poetry of the 1930's and 1940's. Minneapolis: Univ.
          Minnesota Press, 1960.
15,679. _____. Poetry as release of emotion. In Romantic
          View of Poetry. Minneapolis: Univ. Minnesota Press,
          1944, 87-109.
15,680. Beamish-Thiriet, Françoise M. The Myth of Woman in
          Baudelaire and Blok. DAI, 1974, 34:4187A.
15,681. Beauchamp, Gorman. Wordsworth's archetypal resolution.
          Concerning Poetry, 1974, 7:13-19.
15,682. Beauregard, David N. Venus and Adonis: Shakespeare's
          representation of the passions. Shakespeare Studies,
          1975, 8:83-98.
15,683. Beck, Michael. William Blake and psychobiological inte-
          gration. Psychoanal Rev, 1979, 66:245-251.
15,684. Beckman, Sabina. Color symbolism in Troilus and Cri-
          seyde. College Language Assn J, 1976, 20:68-74.
15,685. Begley, Carl E., & Lebo, Dell. Dylan Thomas' 'If I
          Were Tickled by the Rub of Love': a psychoanalytic
          interpretation. Psychology, 1968, 5:68-75.
15,686. _____. A two factor theory of psychoanalytic symbol-
          ism: in prose and verse. Int J Symbology, 1971, 2(2):
          1-6.
15,687. Béguin, Albert. L'Ame romantique et la rêve: Essai sur
          le romantisme allemand et la poésie française, 2 Vols.
          Marseilles: 1937; Paris: 1946.
15,688. Behn, Siegfried. Die Dichtung als eine Quelle der Psychol-
          ogie. Psychologische Beiträge, 1954, 1:554-582.
15,689. Behr-Pinnow, C. v. Die Vererbung bei den Dichtern. Ar-
          chiv der Julius Klaus-Stiftung für Verebungsforschung,
          Sozialanthropologie und Rassenhygiene, 1935, 10:237-
          312.
15,690. Beidler, Peter G. Art and scatology in the Miller's Tale.
          Chaucer Rev, 1977, 12:90-102.
15,691. Belasco, Simon. The psychoacoustic interpretation of
          vowel color preferences in French rime. Phonetica,
          1959, 3:167-182.
15,692. Belaval, Yvon. Poésie et psychanalyse. In Poèmes d'au-
          jourd'hui. Paris: Gallimard, 1964, 39-59.
15,693. Beliaeva, L. I. [On the interrelation of meaning and
          rhythm in the process of reading verses.] Voprosi
          Psikhologii, 1958, 4:70-84.
15,694. Bell, Barbara Currier. 'Lycidas' and the stages of grief.
          Lit & Psychol, 1975, 25:166-174.
15,695. Bellemin-Noël, Jean. Le Narcissisme des 'Narcisses.'
          Littérature, 1972, 6:33-55.
15,696. Belmont, David E. Telemachus and Nausicaa: a study of
          youth. Classical J, 1967, 63:1-9.
15,697. Belmore, Herbert W. Sexual elements in Rilke's poetry.
          German Life & Letters, 1966, 19:252-261.

15, 698. Beltrán, Juan R. El complejo psicológico de Lope de Vega. Anales del Instituto de psicologia, 1941, 3:81-93.

15, 699. Bem, Jeanne. Psychanalyse et poétique baudelairienne. Poétique, 1976, 25:31-35.

15, 700. Benamou, Michel. The structures of Wallace Steven's imagination. Mundus Artium, 1967, 1:73-84.

15, 701. Benítez, F. Tensión poética en Yerma de García Lorca. Explicación de textos literatura, 1975, 4:39-45.

15, 702. Benítez Vinueza, Leopoldo. Jorge Carrera Andrade: El sensualismo poético. Revista Nacional de Cultura, 1963, 25:156-157.

15, 703. Benoit, Raymond. The mind's return: Whitman, Teilhard, and Jung. Virginia Q Rev, 1967, 13:21-28.

15, 704. Bequette, Michael Kenneth. Dante Gabriel Rossetti: the synthesis of picture and poem. Hartford Studies in Lit, 1972, 4:216-227.

15, 705. Beres, David. A dream, a vision, and a poem: a psychoanalytical study of the origins of the 'Rime of the Ancient Mariner.' Int J Psycho-Anal, 1951, 32:97-116; In The Yearbook of Psychoanalysis, Vol. 8. NY: IUP, 1952, 306-343.

15, 706. Berger, Harry, Jr. The Spenserian dynamics. Studies in English Lit 1500-1900, 1968, 111:1-18.

15, 707. Bergler, Edmund. 'Jemanden ablehnen--Jemanden bejahen.' Imago, 1937, 23:289-303.

15, 708. _____, & Garma, Angelo. A great poet's opinion of the development of the conscience. In Bergler, Edmund, The Battle of the Conscience. Washington, DC: Institute of Medicine, 1948, 39-57.

15, 709. Bergsten, S. Jaget och världen, Kosmiska analogier i svensk 1900-talslyrik. Uppsala: Almqvist & Wiksell, 1971.

15, 710. Bernfeld, Siegfried. Vom dichterischen Schaffen der Jugend, Neue Beiträge zur Jugendforschung. Leipzig: Int Psychoanalytischer Verlag, 1924.

15, 711. Bernstein, Gene M. Keats' 'Ode on a Grecian Urn': individuation and the Mandala. Massachusetts Studies in English, 1973, 4:24-30.

15, 712. Berry, D. Apollinaire and the Tantalus complex. Australian J French Studies, 1972, 9, No. 1, 55-79.

15, 713. Berry, David C., Jr. Orphic and Narcissistic Themes in the Poetry and Criticism of James Dickey, 1951-1970. DAI, 1974, 34:5058A.

15, 714. Berryman, John Despondency and madness: on Lowell's 'Skunk Hour.' In The Freedom of the Poet. NY: Farrar, Straus, 1976, 316-322.

15, 715. Bersani, Leo. Baudelaire and Freud. Berkeley: Univ. California Press, 1977; Review: Comparative Lit, 1979, 31:176-177.

15, 716. Bertocchi, D. Segni e simboli in Purgatorio XXIX. In Pcicoanalisi e structuralismo di fronte a Dante. Vol. II. Lettura della 'Commedias.' Florence: Olschki, 1972, 251-267.

15, 717. Béttica-Giovannini, R.   La vittoria riportata contro la
          schiztosomiasi in Cina nel distretto dello Yukiang, in
          due poesie di Mao Tsé-Toung. Medicina Secoli, 1973,
          10:45-64.
15, 718. Beyette, Kent.   Wordsworth's medical muse: Erasmus
          Darwin and psychology in 'Strange Fits of Passion Have
          I Known. ' Lit & Psychol, 1973, 23:93-101.
15, 719. Bezanson, W.   Melville's Clarel: the complex passion.
          J English Lit History, 1954, 21:146-159.
15, 720. Bickman, Martin Elliott.   Kora in heaven: love and death
          in the poetry of Emily Dickinson.   Emily Dickinson
          Bulletin, 1977, 32:79-104.
15, 721. _____. Occult traditions and American romanticism:
          a Jungian perspective. In Frank, L. (ed), Literature
          and the Occult: Essays in Comparative Literature.
          Arlington: Univ. Texas Press, 1977, 1-11, 54-64.
15, 722. _____. Voyages of the Mind's Return: A Jungian Study
          of Poe, Emerson, Whitman, and Dickinson. DAI, 1975,
          36:266A.
15, 723. Birnbaum, Ferdinand.   Inferno, Purgatorio, Paradiso.
          Int Zeitschrift für Individual-Psychologie, 1948, 17:97-
          108.
15, 724. Bishop, Michael.   Eyes and seeing in the poetry of Pierre
          Reverdy. In Cardinal, R. (ed), Sensibility and Crea-
          tion; Studies in Twentieth-Century French Poetry. NY:
          Barnes & Noble, 1977, 57-71.
15, 725. Bishop, Nadean H.   The Mother Archetype in Arnold's
          Merope and Swinburne's Atalanta in Calydon. DAI,
          1973, 33:6862A-63A.
15, 726. Bisi, Nora Rascovsky de.   Rilke y el problema de la
          muerte. Revista de Psicoanálisis, 1963, 20:237-252.
15, 727. Black, Stephen A.   Journeys into chaos: a psychoanalytic
          study of Whitman, his literary processes and his po-
          ems. Lit & Psychol, 1974, 24:47-54.
15, 728. _____. Radical utterances from the soul's abysms:
          towards a new sense of Whitman. PMLA, 1973, 88:
          100-111.
15, 729. _____. Whitman and psychoanalytic criticism: a re-
          sponse to Arthur Golden. Lit & Psychol, 1970, 20:79-
          81.
15, 730. _____. Whitman and the failure of mysticism: identity
          and identification in 'Song of Myself. ' Walt Whitman
          Rev, 1969, 15:223-230.
15, 731. _____. Whitman's Journey into Chaos: A Psychoanaly-
          tic Study of the Poetic Process. Princeton: Princeton
          Univ. Press, 1975; Reviews: Maurice Kramer, Lit &
          Psychol, 1976, 26:124-130; E. Fred Carlisle, J English
          & Germanic Philology, 1977, 76:271-273; Stephen A.
          Weissman, Psychoanal Q, 1978, 47:142-144.
15, 732. Blackmur, R. P.   Conrad Aiken. New Republic, 22 Jan
          1930, 61:255-256.
15, 733. Blackwood, R. T.   William James and Walt Whitman.
          Walt Whitman Rev, 1975, 21:78-79.

15,734.   Blake, Kathleen.   Toward a utopian psychology: the qual-
          ity of life in Milton's Eden.   North Dakota Q, 1978,
          46(2):29-37.
15,735.   Bland, Edward.   Racial bias and Negro poetry.   Poetry,
          1944, 63:328-333.
15,736.   Blanton, Smiley.   The Healing Power of Poetry.   NY:
          Crowell, 1960.
15,737.   Blasing, Mutlu.   'The Sleepers': the problem of the self
          in Whitman.   Walt Whitman Rev, 1975, 21:111-119.
15,738.   Bleich, David.   The determination of literary value.   Lit
          & Psychol, 1967, 17:19-30.
15,739.   Blessing, Richard Allen.   The shape of the psyche: vision
          and technique in the late poems of Sylvia Plath.   In
          Lane, G. (ed), Sylvia Plath; New Views on the Poetry.
          Baltimore: Johns Hopkins Univ. Press, 1979, 57-73.
15,740.   Bliss, Hilde S., & Bliss, Donald T.   Coleridge's Kubla
          Khan.   Amer Imago, 1949, 6:261-273.
15,741.   Bloch, Adèle.   Kazantsakis and the image of Christ.   Lit
          & Psychol, 1965, 15:2-11.
15,742.   Block, Sandra Jean.   The Archetypal Feminine in the Po-
          etry of Denise Levertov.   DAI, 1978, 39:2936A.
15,743.   Bloom, Harold.   The Anxiety of Influence: A Theory of
          Poetry.   London: Oxford Univ. Press, 1975, 1973;
          Reviews: John Bayley, Modern Language Rev, 1973,
          748-754; Alvin H. Rosenfeld, Southern Rev, 1975, 11:
          444-451.
15,744.   _____.   [Work in progress.]   Coleridge: the anxiety of
          influence.   Diacritics, 1972, 2(1):36-41.
15,745.   _____.   Coleridge: the anxiety of influence.   In Hart-
          man, G. H. (ed), New Perspectives on Coleridge and
          Wordsworth.   NY: Columbia Univ. Press, 1972, 247-
          268.
15,746.   _____.   Death and the native strain in American poetry.
          In Mack, A. (ed), Death in American Experience.   NY:
          Schocken, 1973, 83-96.
15,747.   _____.   Poetry and Repression.   Revisionism from
          Blake to Stevens.   New Haven: Yale Univ. Press,
          1976; Reviews: K. Tololyan, English Language Notes,
          1978, 15:229-237; R. Pinsky, Modern Philology, 1979,
          76:300-303; R. D. Sheats, Keats-Shelley J, 1978, 27:138-
          144.
15,748.   _____.   Shelley's Mythmaking.   New Haven: Yale Univ.
          Press, 1959.
15,749.   _____.   Yeats.   NY: Oxford Univ. Press, 1970.
15,750.   Bloom, Robert.   Poetry's Auden.   J Modern Lit, 1970,
          1(1):119-122.
15,751.   Bly, Robert.   Developing the underneath.   Amer Poetry
          Rev, 1973, 2(6):44-45.
15,752.   Bodkin, Maud.   Archetypal Patterns in Poetry.   Psycho-
          logical Studies in Imagination.   NY: Oxford Univ.
          Press, 1934; NY: Vintage, 1958.
15,753.   _____.   Archetypal patterns in tragic poetry.   British
          J Psychol, 1930, 21:183-202.

15, 754.   . Studies of Type Images in Poetry, Religion and
                Philosophy. NY: Oxford Univ. Press, 1951.
15, 755.   . A study of 'The Ancient Mariner' and of the re-
                birth archetype. [Excerpt from Archetypal Patterns in
                Poetry.] In Goldberg, G. J., & Goldberg, N. M. (eds),
                The Modern Critical Spectrum. Englewood Cliffs, NJ:
                Prentice-Hall, 1962, 275-305.
15, 756.   . Truth in poetry. Philosophy, 1935, 10:467-472.
15, 757. Böckel, O. Psychologie der Volksdichtung. Leipzig:
                Teubner, 1906.
15, 758. Bogardus, Emory S. Social distance in poetry. Sociology
                & Social Research, 1951, 36:40-47.
15, 759. Bogner, Delmar. The sexual side of Meredith's poetry.
                Victorian Poetry, 1970, 8:110-119.
15, 760. Boney, Elaine E. Existentialist Thought in the Work of
                Rainer Maria Rilke. DA, 1959, 19:1750-1751.
15, 761. Bonner, Arnold F. Tennyson's Narrative Treatment of
                Married Love. DAI, 1977, 38(6-A), 3510.
15, 762. Bonnet, Marguerite. Lautréamont et Michelet. Rev d'His-
                toire Littéraire de la France, 1964, 64(4).
15, 763. Bonuzzi, L., & Carletti, G. F. Considerzioni intorno alla
                communicazione simbolica. Nota in margine ad una
                rappresentazione 'spaziale' dell'inferno e del Paradiso
                di Dante. Acta Medica Historica Patav, 1967-68, 14:
                61-72.
15, 764. Boon, Jean-Pierre. Baudelaire, Correspondances et le
                magnétisme animal. PMLA, 1971, 86:406-410.
15, 765. Bopp, Léon. La Psychologie des 'Fleur du Mal.' Vol. I.
                Geneva: Droz, 1963; Reviews: Alison Fairlie, French
                Studies, 1964, 18(4):395-397; Antoine Fongaro, Studi
                Francesi, 1965, 9(25).
15, 766.   .   . Vol 2: L'Espace abstrait-Poids,
                consistances et mouvements--Les végétaux et les ani-
                maux. Geneva: Droz, 1964; Review: Alison Fairlie,
                French Studies, 1966, 20(2):202-204.
15, 767.   .   . Vol 3. La Pensée poétique. Gen-
                eva: Droz, 1966.
15, 768.   .   . Vol. 4: L'Homme. Paris: Ro-
                manes et françaises, 1969.
15, 769. Borges, Jorge Luis. The dream of Coleridge. In Other
                Inquisitions, 1937-1952. Austin: Univ. Texas Press,
                1967, 14-17.
15, 770. Borgese, G. A. Wrath of Dante: the eighth canto of The
                Inferno. Speculum, 1938, 13:183-193.
15, 771. Borroff, Marie. William Carlos Williams: the diagnostic
                eye. In Peschel, E. R. (ed), Medicine and Literature.
                NY: Watson, 1980, 56-65.
15, 772. Bostetter, E. E. Shelley and the mutinous flesh. Texas
                Studies in Lit & Language, 1959.
15, 773. Boughner, D. C. The psychology of memory in Spenser's
                Faerie Queene. PMLA, 1932, 47:89-96.
15, 774. Boulenger, (?). Poésie et démence. J de Neurologie et
                de Psichiatrie, 1910, 15:221-229.

15, 775. Bour, Pierre. [From neologism to poetry.] Evolution Psychiatrique, 1972, 37:327-330.
15, 776. Bourgeois, Louis. Verlaine et l'angoisse. Europe, 1974, 545-46:60-68.
15, 777. Bowen, Zack. Goldenhair: Joyce's archetypal female. Lit & Psychol, 1967, 17:219-228.
15, 778. Bowers, Fredson. Arthur Hugh Clough: the modern mind. Studies in English Lit, 1966, 6:708-716.
15, 779. Boyer, Thomas. Brahms as Count Peter of Provence: a psychosexual interpretation of the Magelone poetry. Musical Q, 1980, 66:262-286.
15, 780. Boyers, Robert. Sexton's Live or Die. In McClatchy, J. D. (ed), Anne Sexton: The Artist and Her Critics. Bloomington, Ind: Indiana Univ. Press, 1978.
15, 781. Boyette, Purvis Elton. Milton and the Sacred Fire: Sex Symbolism in 'Paradise Lost.' DAI, 1967, 27:3420A.
15, 782. _____. _____. In Rothstein, E. (ed), Literary Monographs, Vol. 5. Madison: Univ. Wisconsin Press, 1973, p. 63-138.
15, 783. _____. Shakespeare's sonnets: homosexuality and the critics. Tulane Studies in English, 1975, 21:35-46.
15, 784. _____. Something more about the erotic motive in Paradise Lost. Tulane Studies in English, 1967, 15: 19-30.
15, 785. Bradley, Edward M. Ovid Heroides V: reality and illusion. Classical J, 1969, 64:158-162.
15, 786. Bradley, Edward Sculley. The controlling sexual imagery in Whitman's 'Song of Myself.' In Deakin, M., & Lisca, P. (eds), From Irving to Steinbeck. Gainesville: Univ. Florida Press, 1972, 45-54.
15, 787. Braendlin, Hans Peter. Convention and Individuation in German Baroque Imagery: Psycho-Religious Night and Light Metaphors in the Poetry of Opits, Dach, and Gryphius. DAI, 1976, 37:2208A.
15, 788. Braet, H. Fonction et importance du songe dans la chanson de geste. Moyen Age, 1971, 77:405-416.
15, 789. Brandi, C. Psicoanalisi e poesia: Baudelaire, Mallarmé, Lautréamout. L'Immagine, 1948, 2.
15, 790. Brandt-Pedersen, Finn. Den psykosomatiske poesi. In Brostrøm, T. (ed), Labyrint og Arabesk. Copenhagen: Gyldendal, 1967, 80-93.
15, 791. Brelich, A. The place of dreams in the religious world concept of the Greeks. In Grunebaum, G. E. von, & Callois, R. (eds), The Dream and Human Societies. Berkeley: Univ. California Press, 1966, 293-301.
15, 792. Bremond, H. Le Romantisme et le dogme de l'inspiration poétique. Psychologie et vie, 1930, 4:158-163.
15, 793. Breugelmans, René. Novalis' Gewissen and the relevance of the basic Jungian concepts to the understanding of his work and world-view. Proceedings Pacific Northwest Conference on Foreign Languages, 1977, 28(1):17-21.
15, 794. Brezzi, P. Le strutture della Respublica Christiana. In Psicoanalisi e structuralismo di fronte a Dante. Vol.

III: <u>Incontro con le altre opere.</u> Florence: Olschki, 1972, 175-193.

15, 795. Brient, Michel. L'Aliénation poétique. <u>Arts Lettres,</u> 1946, 6:334-339.

15, 796. Briggs, H. E. Keats's conscious and unconscious reactions to criticism of 'Endymion.' <u>PMLA,</u> 1945, 60:1106-1129.

15, 797. Brill, Abraham A. Poetry as an oral outlet. <u>Psychoanal Rev,</u> 1931, 18:357-378; <u>Imago,</u> 1933, 19:145-167.

15, 798. Brill, Lesley W. Chastity as ideal sexuality in the third book of <u>The Faerie Queen.</u> <u>Studies in English Lit,</u> 1971, 11:15-26.

15, 799. Brink, Louise, & Jelliffe, Smith E. The role of animals in the unconscious, with some remarks on theriomorphic symbolism as seen in Ovid. <u>Psychoanal Rev,</u> 1917, 4: 253-271.

15, 800. Britton, J. W. Evidence of improvement in poetic judgment. <u>British J Psychol,</u> 1954, 45:196-208.

15, 801. Broe, Mary Lynn. A subtle psychic bond: the mother figure in Sylvia Plath's poetry. In Davidson, C. N. , & Broner, E. M. (eds), <u>The Lost Tradition.</u> NY: Ungar, 1980, 207-216.

15, 802. Brombert, Victor. Lyrisme et dépersonnalisation: L'exemple de Baudelaire (<u>Spleen</u>-LXXV). <u>Romantisme,</u> 1973, 6: 29-37.

15, 803. Brooks, Cleanth. The case of Miss Arabella Fermor. In <u>The Well-Wrought Urn.</u> NY: Harvest, 1947, 80-104.

15, 804. Broome, Peter. Henri Michaux and failure in mescaline. <u>Australian J French Studies,</u> 1964, 1:188-220.

15, 805. Brown, Diane S. The Theme of Childhood in Nineteenth-Century French Poetry. <u>DAI,</u> 1973, 34:2610A.

15, 806. Brown, Emerson, Jr. Chaucer, the Merchant, and their tales; getting beyond old controversies. <u>Chaucer Rev,</u> 1978, 13:141-156.

15, 807. Brown, Eric D. Archetypes of Transformation: A Jungian Analysis of Chaucer's 'Wife of Bath's Tale' and 'Clerk's Tale. ' <u>DAI,</u> 1973, 33:5672A.

15, 808. _____. Symbols of transformation: a specific archetypal examination of the 'Wife of Bath's Tale. ' <u>Chaucer Rev,</u> 1978, 12:202-217.

15, 809. _____. Transformation and the 'Wife of Bath's Tale': a Jungian discussion. <u>Chaucer Rev,</u> 1976, 10:303-315.

15, 810. Brown, Nathaniel Hapgood. <u>Sexuality and Feminism in Shelley.</u> Cambridge: Harvard Univ. Press, 1979; Review: Anne K. Mellor, <u>Criticism,</u> 1980, 22:178-181.

15, 811. _____. <u>Shelley's Theory of Erotic Love.</u> <u>DA,</u> 1964, 24:4676.

15, 812. Brown, P. D. G. Oskar Panizza's first and last books: a study in late nineteenth-century poetry. <u>Germanic Rev,</u> 1973, 48:269-287.

15, 813. Brown, P. L. R. Psychological aspects of some Yeatsian concepts. <u>Mosaic,</u> 1977, 11(1):21-35.

15, 814. Brown, Russell E. Time of day in early expressionist poetry. <u>PMLA,</u> 1969, 84:20-28.

15, 815.   Brown, W.   Temporal and accentual rhythm.   Psychol
           Rev, 1911, 18:336-346.
15, 816.   _____.   Time in English verse rhythm.   Archiv de Psy-
           chologie, 1908, 1:10; Columbia Contributions to Philos-
           ophy & Psychol, 1908.
15, 817.   Bruce, H. A.   Mr. Sludge the Medium.   J Amer Society
           Psychical Research, 1945, 39:128-143.
15, 818.   Bruns, A.   Entfremdung und Antizipation in J. E. Volds
           Lyrik.   Skandinavistik, 1973, 3:125-139.
15, 819.   Bruns, Gerald L.   Poetry as reality; the Orpheus myth
           and its modern counterparts.   In Modern Poetry and
           the Idea of Language; A Critical and Historical Study.
           New Haven: Yale Univ. Press, 1974, 206-231.
15, 820.   Buck, L. A., et al.   Creative potential in schizophrenia.
           Psychiatry, 1977, 40:146-162.
15, 821.   Bugyi, B.   [The pathography of Janus Pannonius as re-
           flected in his poetry.]   Therapie Hungarica, 1974, 22:
           90-93.
15, 822.   Bullough, Geoffrey.   Mirror of Minds--Changing Psycho-
           logical Beliefs in English Poetry.   London: Univ. Lon-
           don Press, 1962.
15, 823.   Bunker, Henry A.   Tantalus: a pre-oedipal figure of
           myth.   Psychoanal Q, 1953, 22:159-173.
15, 824.   Burke, Kenneth.   Freud--and the analysis of poetry.
           Amer J Sociology, 1939, 45:391-417; In The Philosophy
           of Literary Form.   NY: Knopf, 1941; NY: Vintage,
           1957; in Phillips, W. (ed), Art and Psychoanalysis.
           Cleveland: Meridian, 1963; in Ruitenbeek, H. M. (ed),
           Psychoanalysis and Literature.   NY: Dutton, 1964,
           114-141.
15, 825.   _____.   Policy made personal: Whitman's verse and
           prose--salient traits.   In Hindus, M. (ed), Leaves of
           Grass: One Hundred Years After.   Palo Alto, Cal:
           Stanford Univ. Press, 1955, 74-108.
15, 826.   Burmeister, Klaus D.   Studies in the Erotic Motif in Early
           Minnesang.   DAI, 1971, 32:2051A.
15, 827.   Burnett, Anne.   Desire and memory (Sappho frag 94).
           Classical Philology, 1979, 74:16-27.
15, 828.   Burnett, David Graham.   The thematic function of sexual
           identity in T. Gautier's Comédie de la mort.   Notting-
           ham French Studies, 1977, 16(1).
15, 829.   _____.   The theme of ocean exploration in the poetry
           of Théophile Gautier.   Explorations, 1977, 4(2):31-38.
15, 830.   Busemann, A.   Über lyrische Produktivität und Lebensab-
           lauf.   Zeitschrift für angewandte Psychologie, 1926,
           26:177-201.
15, 831.   Bush, Douglas.   Science and English Poetry.   NY: Oxford
           Univ. Press, 1968.
15, 832.   Bychowski, Gustav.   Walt Whitman; a study in sublimation.
           In Psychoanalysis and the Social Sciences, Vol. 3.
           NY: IUP, 1951, 223-261.

15, 833. Cady, Joseph. Not happy in the capital: homosexuality in the Calamus poems. Amer Studies, 1978, 19:5-22.

15, 834. Calhoun, Thomas O. On John Milton's A Mask at Ludlow. Milton Studies, 1974, 6:165-179.

15, 835. Cambon, Fernand. La Fileuse: Remarques psychanalytiques sur le motif de la 'fileuse' et du 'filage' dans quelques poèmes et contes allemands. Littérature, 1976, 23:56-74.

15, 836. Cambon, G. Il poeta come testimone corale. Italica, 1965, 42(2).

15, 837. Cameron, Kenneth W. Emily Dickinson and Hesperian depression. Amer Transcendental Q, 1972, 14:184-185.

15, 838. Cameron, S. The sense against calamity: ideas of self in three poems by Wallace Stevens. J English Lit History, 1976, 43:584-603.

15, 839. Campbell, K. T. S. 'The Phoenix and the Turtle' as a signpost of Shakespeare's development. British J Aesthetics, 1970, 10:169-179.

15, 840. Campbell, Paul W. An Experimental Study of the Retention and Comprehension of Poetry Resulting from Silent Reading and from Oral Interpretation. DA, 1960, 20:3426.

15, 841. Cane, Melville. Threshold to creation. Univ. Kansas City Rev, 1952, 19:3-6.

15, 842. Carballa, Juan Rof. Medicina y estética en Gottfried Benn. In Peitz, W. (ed), Denken in Widersprüchen: Korrelarien zur Gottfried-Benn-Forschung. Freiburg: Becksman, 1972, 300-324.

15, 843. Cardinal, Roger. André Breton: the surrealist sensibility. Modern Language Rev, 1968, 1:112-126.

15, 844. _____ (ed). Sensibility and Creation; Studies in Twentieth-Century French Poetry. NY: Barnes & Noble, 1977.

15, 845. Carmody, F. J. The Evolution of Apollinaire's Poetics 1901-1914. Berkeley: Univ. California Press, 1964.

15, 846. Carnicelli, D. D. Beauty's rose: Shakespeare and Adler on love and marriage. In Mosak, H. H. (ed), Alfred Adler: His Influence on Psychology Today. Park Ridge, NJ: Noyes, 1974, 291-302.

15, 847. Carpenter, Edward, & Barnefield, George. The Psychology of the Poet Shelley. London: Allen & Unwin, 1925; NY: Dutton, 1925.

15, 848. Carpenter, Frederic I. 'Post Mortem': 'The Poet Is Dead.' Western Amer Lit, 1977, 12:3-10.

15, 849. Carruth, H. Act of love: poetry and personality. Sewanee Rev, 1976, 84:305-313.

15, 850. Carter, Steve. The metaphor of assimilation and 'Rise O Days from Your Fathomless Deeps.' Walt Whitman Rev, 1978, 24:155-161.

15, 851. Cartwright, Faith Wotton. Psychological projection in the Rime of the Ancient Mariner. Revista de la Universidad de Costa Rica, 1974, 39:37-45.

15, 852. Casagrande, G. Purgatorio, Canto XXVIII. In Psicoanalisi e structuralismo di fronte a Dante. Vol. II: Lettura della 'Commedia.' Florence: Olschki, 1972, 139-
143.

15, 853. Casanova, A. Mon come allargarsi di spazi politici. In
Psicoanalisi e structuralismo di fronte a Dante. Vol.
III: Incontro con le altre opere. Florence: Olschki,
1972, 151-174.

15, 854. Catel, Jean. Emily Dickinson: Essai d'analyse psychologique. Rev Anglo-Américaine, 1925, 2:394-405.

15, 855. _____. Walt Whitman: La Naissance du poète. Paris:
Rieder, 1929.

15, 856. Caudwell, Christopher. Illusion and Reality: A Study of
the Sources of Poetry. NY: International, 1937.

15, 857. Cavanagh, Michael. Fathers and daughters: a reading of
Ransom's 'Janet Waking.' Notes on Modern Amer Lit,
1979, 3:Item 15.

15, 858. Caws, Mary Ann. Robert Desnos and the flasks of night.
Yale French Studies, 1974, 50:108-119.

15, 859. Cervantes, Alfonso. Emotion, feeling and language in
Cienfuegos' poetry. Mester, 1976, 6:24-31.

15, 860. Chabot, C. Barry. The 'melancholy dualism' of Robert
Frost. Rev Existential Psychol & Psychiat, 1974, 13:
42-56.

15, 861. Chaitin, Gilbert D. Psychoanalysis and literary interpretation. Lit & Psychol, 1977, 27:174-182.

15, 862. Chaliff, Cynthia. The bees, the flowers, and Emily Dickinson. Research Studies, 1974, 42:93-103.

15, 863. _____. The psychology of economics in Emily Dickinson. Lit & Psychol, 1968, 18:93-100.

15, 864. Chambers, A. B. Three notes on Eve's dream in Paradise
Lost. Philological Q, 1967, 46:186-193.

15, 865. Chambers, Ross. 'La Femme aux yeux bandés.' Claudel
et le masque de la cécité. Rev des Lettres Modernes,
1974, nos. 391-397.

15, 866. Chari, V. K. Poetic emotions and poetic semantics.
JAAC, 1976, 34:287-299.

15, 867. _____. Structure of Whitman's catalogue poems. Walt
Whitman Rev, 1972, 18:3-17.

15, 868. Charity, A. Dante and the aesthetes. Towards an existential interpretation of the Divine Comedy. Blackfri-
ars, 1963, 44.

15, 869. Charney, Hanna. Le Scepticisme de Valéry. Paris:
Didier, 1969.

15, 870. Charters, Ann. I Maximus: Charles Olson as mytholo-
gist. Modern Poetry Studies, 1971, 2:49-60.

15, 871. Chasse, Charles. Les Themes de la sterilité et la vir-
ginité chez Mallarmé. Rev des Sciences Humaines,
1953, 70:171-181.

15, 872. Chatfield, E. Hale. Neurosis and poetry: a myth of madness? Univ. Rev, 1966, 32:163-167.

15, 873. Chatham, James R. Gestures, facial expressions and sig-
nals in the Poema del Cid. Revista de Estudios Hispánicos, 1972, 6:455-471.

15, 874. Chatman, Seymour. Auden's 'The Questioner Who Sits Sly.' Explicator, 1969, 28:3.

15, 875. Chaussivert, J. S. Le Sens haschischin de l'Invitation au Voyage. J Australasian Universities Modern Language Assn, 1976, 45:27-35.

15, 876. Chavez, E. A. Sor Juana. Ensayo de psicología. Mexico: 1970, 1931.

15, 877. Chavis, Geraldine G. Dreams as Motif in John Keats' Works. DAI, 1974, 34:6631A.

15, 878. Chayes, Irene C. 'Kubla Khan' and the creative process. Studies in Romanticism, 1966, 6:1-21.

15, 879. Chernenko, Alexandra. The birth of a new spiritual awareness. Canadian Slavonic Papers, 1974, 16:73-98.

15, 880. Cherniss, Michael D. The narrator asleep and awake in Chaucer's Book of the Duchess. Papers on Language & Lit, 1972, 8:115-126.

15, 881. Cherry, Charles L. Whitman and language. Walt Whitman Rev, 1968, 14:56-58.

15, 882. Chessick, Richard D. The sense of reality, time, and creative inspiration. Amer Imago, 1957, 14:317-331.

15, 883. Cholst, Sheldon. The Only Baby: Poems and Notes on Psychiatric Theory. NY: Whittier, 1958.

15, 884. Chouinard, Timothy. Eliot's 'oeuvre,' Bradley's 'finite centres,' and Jung's anima concepts. J Analytical Psychol, 1971, 16(1):48-68.

15, 885. Christensen, F. Creative sensibility in Wordsworth. J English Germanic Philology, 1946, 45:361-368.

15, 886. Christiansen, Erik M. Zur Psychologie primitiver Lyrik. Archiv für die gesamte Psychologie, 1964, 116:230-247.

15, 887. Christina, John L. The Psychology of Love in the Cancionero de Baena. DAI, 1972, 32:4557A.

15, 888. Ciardi, John. Freud and modern poetry. Saturday Rev, 1956, 39:8.

15, 889. Ciotti, A. Fra Dolcino, Dante e i commentatori trecenteschi della Commedia. In Psicoanalisi e structuralismo di fronte a Dante. Vol. I: Premesse. Florence: Olschki, 1972, 429-442.

15, 890. Clancier-Gravelat, Anne. Ebauche d'une étude psychocritique de l'oeuvre de Guillaume Apollinaire. Rev des Lettre Modernes, 1972, 327-330:8-39.

15, 891. Clark, John R. Dryden's 'Mac Flecknoe,' 48. Explicator, 1971, 29:Item 56.

15, 892. Clarke, John Covell. The Psychology of Blake's Visionary Mythopoeia. Doctoral dissertation, Western Reserve Univ., 1964.

15, 893. Clément, Catherine B. Michelet et Freud: De la sorcière à l'hysterique. Europe, 1973, 535-36:111-117.

15, 894. Clendenning, John. Emerson's 'Days': a psychoanalytic study. Amer Transcendental Q, 1975, 25:6-11.

15, 895. Cluysenaar, Anne. Post-culture: pre-culture? In Schmidt, M., & Lindop, G. (eds), British Poetry Since 1960. Cheadle: Carcanet Press, 1972, 213-232.

15, 896. Coburn, K. Coleridge and Wordsworth and 'the supernatural.' Univ. Toronto Q, 1956, 25.

15, 897. Cody, John. Emily Dickinson's Vesuvian face. Amer
          Imago, 1967, 24:161-180.
15, 898. Coggins, K., Hensley, R., & Mull, H. K. Introversion
          and the appreciation of literature. Amer J Psychol,
          1942, 55:560-561.
15, 899. Cohen, Edward H. The text of 'Apparition': a purview of
          the Henley-Stevenson friendship. Studies in Scottish
          Lit, 1973, 11:66-81.
15, 900. Cohen, Joseph. Owen Agonistes. English Lit in Transi-
          tion, 1965, 8:253-268.
15, 901. Cohen, Maurice. Chaucer's Prioress and her tale. A
          study of anal character and anti-semitism. Psychoanal
          Q, 1962, 31:232-249.
15, 902. Cohn, Hans W. Else Lasker-Schüler: The Broken World.
          NY: Cambridge Univ. Press, 1974.
15, 903. Cohn, R. G. Mallarmé's windows. Yale French Studies,
          1976, 54:23-31.
15, 904. Coimbra Martins, A. Un Poète des couleurs: Gomes Le-
          al. In Various, Regards sur la génération portugaise
          de 1870. Paris: Fundação Calouste Gulbenkian, 1971,
          101-188.
15, 905. Colby, Vineta. Browning's Saul: the exorcism of romantic
          melancholy. Victorian Poetry, 1978, 16:88-99.
15, 906. Collier, G., & Kuiken, D. A phenomenological study of
          the experience of poetry. J Phenomenological Psychol,
          1977, 7:209-225.
15, 907. Collins, Martha. The self-conscious poet: the case of
          William Collins. J English Lit History, 1975, 42:362-
          377.
15, 908. Collins, Michael J. The rhetorical double in modern Brit-
          ish poetry. Modern British Lit, 1977, 2:176-181.
15, 909. Columbus, Robert R., & Claudette, Kemper. 'Sordello'
          and the speaker: a problem in identity. Victorian Po-
          etry, 1964, 2:251-267.
15, 910. Colussi, D. L. Roethke's 'The Gentle.' Explicator, 1969,
          27:9.
15, 911. Combs, Robert L. Hart Crane and the Psychology of Ro-
          manticism. DAI, 1972, 32:5779A.
15, 912. _____. Vision of the Voyage: Hart Crane and the Psy-
          chology of Romanticism. Memphis, Tenn: Memphis
          State Univ. Press, 1978; Review: Amer Lit, 1979, 51:
          285-287.
15, 913. Concha, V. G. de la. Primera etapa de un 'novisimo':
          P. Gimferrer: Arde el amor. Papeles de Son Arma-
          dans, 1972, 64:45-61.
15, 914. Cook, David A. The content and meaning of Swinburne's
          'Anactoria.' Victorian Poetry, 1971, 9:77-93.
15, 915. Cook, Harry James. The individualization of a poet: the
          process of becoming in Whitman's 'The Sleepers.'
          Walt Whitman Rev, 1975, 21:101-110.
15, 916. Cook, James Wyatt. Augustinian neurosis and the therapy
          of orthodoxy. Universitas, 1964, 2:51-62.

15, 917. Cooley, Peter. Autism, autoeroticism, auto-da-fe: the
          tragic poetry of Sylvia Plath. Hollins Critic, 1973, 10:
          1-15.

15, 918. Cooper, David Dale. The Paradox of Spirit and Instinct:
          A Comparative Examination of the Psychologies of C. G.
          Jung and Sigmund Freud. DAI, 1978, 38:7330A-31A.

15, 919. _____. The poet as elaborator: analytical psychology
          as a critical paradigm. Critical Inquiry, 1979-80, 6:51-
          64.

15, 920. Cooper, Douglas W. Tennyson's Idylls: A Mythography
          of the Self. DA, 1967, 67:2886.

15, 921. Cope, J. Girolamo Preti's aesthetic allegory: a marinis-
          tic poem on violence in love and art. Modern Language
          Notes, 1962, 90-94.

15, 922. Copley, F. O. Emotional conflict and its significance in the
          Lesbia-poems of Catullus. Amer J Philology, 1949, 70:
          22-40.

15, 923. Cornioley, Hans. Sexualsymbolik in der Frommen Helene
          von Wilhelm Busch. Psychoanalytische Bewegung, 1929,
          1:154-160.

15, 924. Cornwell, John. Coleridge: Poet and Revolutionary. Lon-
          don: Allen Lane, 1973.

15, 925. Corrigan, Matthew. Chaucer's failure with woman: the
          inadequacy of Criseyde. Western Humanities Rev, 1969,
          23:107-120.

15, 926. _____. A phenomenological glance at a few lines of
          Roethke. Modern Poetry Series, 1971, 2:165-174.

15, 927. Corsa, Helen Storm. Dreams in Troilus and Criseyde.
          Amer Imago, 1970, 27:53-65.

15, 928. _____. Is this a mannes herte? Lit & Psychol, 1966,
          16:184-191.

15, 929. Cottrell, Robert D. Belleau's descriptions of the female
          bosom in La Bergerie. Studies in Philology, 1978, 75:
          391-402.

15, 930. Cowan, James C. The theory of relativity and The Bridge.
          Hartford Studies in Lit, 1971, 3:108-115.

15, 931. Cowan, Lyn. Masochism. Studies on the relations be-
          tween poetry, archetypal psychology and Jungian imagin-
          ation. In Various, Spring 1979. An Annual of Arche-
          typal Psychology and Jungian Thought. Irving, Texas:
          Univ. Dallas Press, 1980.

15, 932. Coxe, Louis Osborne. Edwin Arlington Robinson: The
          Life of Poetry. NY: Pegasus, 1969; Review: Ells-
          worth Barnard, Hartford Studies in Lit, 1971, 3:154-
          156.

15, 933. Crane, A. R. Psychology and poetry. Australasian J Psy-
          chol & Philosophy, 1951, 29:21-35.

15, 934. Crichton-Miller, Hugh. William Sharp and the Immortal
          Hour. British J Medical Psychol, 1925, 5:35-44.

15, 935. Cuatrecasas, Juan. Psicología y poesía. Cuadernos
          Americanos, 1966, 83-100.

15, 936. Cummings, D. W. , & Herum, John. Metrical boundaries
          and rhythm-phrases. Modern Language Q, 1967, 28:
          405-412.

15,937. Cunningham, Donald H. Emily Dickinson's 'I Heard a Fly
        Buzz. ' Amer Notes & Queries, 1968, 6:150-151.
15,938. Cunningham, J. S. Pope: The Rape of the Lock. London:
        Arnold, 1961.
15,939. Curran, L. C. Rape and rape victims in 'Metamorphoses. '
        Arethusa, 1978, 11:213-241.

15,940. Dale, Kathleen A. Extensions: beyond resemblance and
        the pleasure principle in Wallace Stevens' supreme fic-
        tion. Boundary 12, 1975, 4:255-273.
15,941. Dalla Volta, Amedeo. Un poeta intimista; contributo allo
        studio dei tipi di orientamento psicologico. Archivio
        di Psicologia, Neurologia y Psichiatria, 1946, 7:241-302.
15,942. Danelius, Gerhard. Ovid's Metamorphoses: the great
        poem of neurotic suffering. In Kirsch, H. (ed), The
        Well-Tended Tree. NY: Putnam, 1971, 351-362.
15,943. D'Angelo, G. Presencia de la maternidad en la poesía de
        G. Mistral. Thesaurus, 1967, 22:221-250.
15,944. Darling, Susan. Psychosexual Aspects of the Poetry of
        Dante Gabriel Rossetti. DAI, 1976, 37:328A-29A.
15,945. Das, J. P. , Rath, R. , & Das, Rhea S. Understanding
        versus suggestion in the judgment of literary passages.
        J Abnormal Social Psychol, 1955, 51:624-628.
15,946. Dattner, Bernhard. Die Stadt als Mutter. Int Zeitschrift
        für Psychoanalyse, 1914, 2:59.
15,947. Davis, Donald M. The technique of guilt by association in
        Paradise Lost. South Atlantic Bulletin, 1972, 37(1):29-
        34.
15,948. Davis, Robert Gorham. A note of 'The Use of Force' and
        Freud's 'The Dream of Irma's Injection. ' William Car-
        los Williams Newsletter, 1976, 2(1):9-10.
15,949. Davis, Robin R. The honey machine: imagery patterns in
        Ariel. New Laurel Rev, 1972, 1(2):23-31.
15,950. De Gaultier, J. Rythmies et effectivité. La Poésie
        comme rythme de reprise. Psychologie et vie, 1930,
        4:74-77.
15,951. De Groot, A. W. Le Mètre et le rhythme du vers. J de
        Psychologie, 1933, 30:326-332.
15,952. de J. Hart, Robert A. Poetry and psychic experience.
        Light, 1971, 91:3486:141-147.
15,953. De Leo, Phyllis C. Sex, Art, and Death: Dominant
        Themes in the Poetry of Winfield Townley Scott.
        DAI, 1978, 38:6722A.
15,954. DeMichelis, Eurialo. Scienza e poesia. Ponte, 1960, 16:
        67-75.
15,955. DeSalvo, Leta P. The Arrested Syllable: A Study of the
        Death Poetry of Emily Dickinson. DA, 1966, 27:1916A.
15,956. DeVries, Louis P. The Nature of Poetic Literature.
        Seattle: Univ. Washington Press, 1930.
15,957. Del Re, Gabrielle. Sensibilita Fisiologica e mito in John
        Keats. English Miscellany, 1971, 22:155-172.
15,958. Decker, Susan D. 'Love's mansion': sexuality in Yeats's
        poetry. Modern British Lit, 1979, 4:17-32.

15,959. Delacroix, H. L'Invention et le génie. In Dumas, G.,
         Nouveau Traité de Psychologie, Vol. 6. Paris: Al-
         can, 1939, 447-539.
15,960. Delattre, Floris. Deux essais sur la psychologie sociale
         de l'Angleterre. 1: Les poètes Anglais et la guerre.
         Paris: Gamber, 1931.
15,961. Della Vedova, R. Dinamica lacaniana del 'corps morcele':
         ipotesi per una lettura d'Inferno' XXVIII. In Psicoana-
         lisi e structuralismo di fronte a Dante. Vol. II: Let-
         tura della 'Commedia.' Florence: Olschki, 1972, 119-
         133.
15,962. _____, & Silvotti, M. T. Inferno. I in Guido da Pisa.
         In Psicoanalisi e structuralismo di fronte a Dante. Vol.
         III: Incontro con le altre opere. Florence: Olschki,
         1972, 331-370.
15,963. _____, & Silvotti, M. T. Inferno. I nelle tre redazioni
         del 'Commentarium di Pietro Alighieri.' In Psicoana-
         lisi e structuralismo di fronte a Dante. Vol. I: Pre-
         messe. Florence: Olschki, 1972, 49-93.
15,964. Dembo, L. S. Hart Crane's early poetry. Univ. Kansas
         City Rev, 1961.
15,965. Dereau, D. P. Pope's iv'ry gate: The Dunciad. Modern
         Language Notes, 1959, 74:208-211.
15,966. Derrida, Jacques. Les Sources de Valéry: Qual, Quelle.
         MLN, 1972, 87(4):563-599.
15,967. Deschamps, Robert. L'Ogre de Jacques Chessex: La Po-
         ésie au service de la psychanalyse. Présence Franco-
         phone: Rev Littéraire, 1978, 16:153-161.
15,968. Dettmering, Peter. [A world of fantasmagorical objects.
         Samuel Taylor Coleridge, 'The Rime of the Ancient
         Mariner.'] Psyche (Stuttgart), 1979, 33:229-244.
15,969. _____. Heinrich von Kleist: Zur Psychodynamik in
         seiner Dichtung. Munich: Nymphenburger, 1975.
15,970. Devereux, George. A counteroedipal episode in Homer's
         Iliad. Bulletin Philadelphia Assn Psychoanal, 1955, 4:
         90-97.
15,971. _____. The exploitation of ambiguity in Pindar's O. 3.
         27. Rheinisches Museum für Philologie, 1966, 109:289-
         298.
15,972. _____. Penelope's character. Psychoanal Q, 1957, 26:
         378-386.
15,973. _____. The nature of Sappho's seizure as evidence of
         her inversion. Classical Q, 1970, 20:17-31.
15,974. Di Cyan, E. Poetry and Creativeness with notes on the
         role of psychedelic drugs. Perspectives in Biology &
         Medicine, 1971, 14:639-650.
15,975. Di Donato, Robert. The Function of Trance and Dream in
         the Poetry of Annette von Droste-Hülshoff. DAI, 1978,
         38:4814A.
15,976. Diamond, Arlyn. Chaucer's women and women's Chaucer.
         In Diamond, A., & Edwards, L. R. (eds), The Authority
         of Experience: Essays in Feminist Criticism. Amherst:
         Univ. Massachusetts Press, 1977, 60-83.

15,977. Dichler, G. Experimentalphonteische Untersuchungen über den Einschläger im deutschen Vers. Archiv für die gesamte Psychologie, 1928, 64:374-382.

15,978. Dickstein, Morris. The price of experience: Blake's reading of Freud. In Smith, J. H. (ed), The Literary Freud. New Haven: Yale Univ. Press, 1980, 67-111.

15,979. Dieckmann, Liselotte. Symbols of isolation in some late nineteenth-century poets. In Hofacker, E. , & Dieckmann, L. (eds), Studies in Germanic Languages and Literature. St. Louis, Mo: Washington Univ. Press, 1963, 133-148.

15,980. Diederichs-Maurer, Anna Katharina. Le Thème de l'angoisse chez Verlaine. Düsseldorf/Cologne: Diederichs, 1971.

15,981. Diggory, Terence. Armored women, naked men; Dickinson, Whitman, and their successors. In Gilbert, S. M. , & Gutar, S. (eds), Shakespeare's Sisters. Bloomington: Indiana Univ. Press, 1979, 135-150.

15,982. Dillingham, William B. 'Neither believer nor infidel': themes of Melville's poetry. Personalist, 1965, 46, 501-516.

15,983. Dillon, David. Toward passionate utterance: an interview with W. D. Snodgrass. Southwest Rev, 1975, 60:278-290.

15,984. Diotti, A. Dante visto attraverso la Respublica Christicolarum di Pierre Dubois. In Psicoanalisi i structuralismo di fronte a Dante. Vol. I: Premesse. Florence: Olschki, 1972, 95-128.

15,985. Dobbs, Jeannine. Not Another Poetess: A Study of Female Experience in Modern American Poetry. DAI, 1973, 34:2555A.

15,986. _____. 'Viciousness in the kitchen': Sylvia Plath's domestic poetry. Modern Language Studies, 1978, 7:11-25.

15,987. Dodsworth, Martin. Patterns of morbidity: repetition in Tennyson's poetry. In Armstrong, I. (ed), The Major Victorian Poets: Reconsiderations. Lincoln: Univ. Nebraska Press, 1969, 7-34.

15,988. Doggett, Frank. Stevens on the genesis of a poem. Contemporary Lit, 1975, 16:463-477.

15,989. Doherty, Joseph F. Whitman's 'Poem of the Mind. ' Semiotica, 1975, 14:345-363.

15,990. Donaldson, Scott. The alien pity: a study of character in E. A. Robinson's poetry. Amer Lit, 1966, 38:219-229.

15,991. Dorsten, J. A. van. Arts of memory and poetry. English Studies, 1967, 48:419-425.

15,992. Downey, June E. Emotional poetry and the preference judgment. Psychol Rev, 1915, 22:259-278.

15,993. _____. The Imaginal Reaction to Poetry. The Affective and the Aesthetic Judgment. Bulletin No. 2. Univ. Wyoming Department Psychology, 1912.

15,994. Dracoulidès, N. N. Investigation psychanalytique de la vie et de l'oeuvre du poète Palamas. Proïa, 11-12 April 1943.

15,995.   _____. Mobiles psychologiques du déclin de la poésie
            lyrique. Nea Estia, 15 Aug 1930.
15,996. Dragonetti, Roger. The double play of Arnaut Daniel's
            Sestina and Dante's Divina Commedia. Yale French
            Studies, 1977, 55-56:227-252.
15,997.   _____. Le Style suave dans le Banquet et dans la Di-
            vinia Commedia. In Psicoanalisi e structuralismo di
            fronte a Dante. Vol. III: Incontro con le altre opere.
            Florence: Olschki, 1972, 87-110.
15,998. Draper, Anita B. The artistic contribution of the weird
            seizures to 'The Princess.' Victorian Poetry, 1979,
            17:180-191.
15,999. Drew, Elizabeth A. T. S. Eliot: The Design of His Po-
            etry. NY: Scribner, 1949; London: Eyre, 1950.
16,000. Drew, Philip. Another view of 'Fifine at the Fair.' Es-
            says in Criticism, 1967, 17:244-255.
16,001. DuBois, William R. Walt Whitman's Poetry: A Record
            of Crises in Identity. DAI, 1971, 31:6599A-600A.
16,002. Duchene, François. The Case of the Helmeted Airman:
            A Study of W. H. Auden's Poetry. Totowa, NJ: Row-
            man & Littlefield, 1972.
16,003. Dunham, Larry J. The Pleasure-Pain Motif in the Poetry
            of John Keats. DAI, 1973, 34:1275A-76A.
16,004. Durán, Manuel. Liberty and eroticism in the poetry of
            Octavio Paz. Books Abroad, 1963, 27(4).
16,005. Durand, Marguerite. Perception de durée dans les phrases
            rythmees. JPNP, 1946, 39:305-321.
16,006. Durham, Lorraine. The death-rebirth motif in Eliot's
            Waste Land. Appalachian State Teachers College Fac-
            ulty Publications, 1959-60, 15-22.
16,007. Durr, Robert Allen. Poetic Vision and the Psychedelic
            Experience. Syracuse: Syracuse Univ. Press, 1970.
16,008. Durrant, Geoffrey. Zeno's arrow: time and motion in
            two of Wordsworth's Lucy poems. Mosaic, 1969, 2:10-
            24.
16,009. Duthil, R. La Comprehension de la poesie. Psychologie
            et Vie, 1930, 4:12-14.

16,010. Eastman, Max. The poet's mind. North Amer Rev, 1908,
            187:417-425.
16,011. Eberhart, Richard. Will and psyche in poetry. In Allen,
            D. C. (ed), The Moment in Poetry. Baltimore: Johns
            Hopkins Univ. Press, 1962, 48-72.
16,012. Edelson, Marshall. Language and Interpretation in Psycho-
            analysis. New Haven: Yale Univ. Press, 1975.
16,013.   _____. Two questions about psychoanalysis and poetry.
            In Smith, J. H. (ed), The Literary Freud. New Haven:
            Yale Univ. Press, 1980, 113-118.
16,014. Eder, Doris L. Freud and H. D. Book Forum, 1975, 1:
            365-369.
16,015.   _____. The meaning of Wallace Stevens' two themes.
            Critical Q, 1969, 11:181-190.

16,016. Edgar, Irving I. The psychological sources of poetic creative expression and Tennyson's 'In Memoriam.' In
Essays in English Literature and History. NY: Philosophical Library, 1972, 1-14.

16,017. Edwards, Thomas R. Imagination and Power: A Study of
Poetry on Public Themes. NY: Oxford Univ. Press,
1971.

16,018. Eggenschwiler, David L. Psychological complexity in
'Porphyria's Lover.' Victorian Poetry, 1970, 8:39-40.

16,019. _____. Sexual parody in 'The Triumph of Life.' Concerning Poetry, 1972, 5(2):28-36.

16,020. _____. Wordsworth's discordia discors. Studies in
Romanticism, 1969, 8:78-94.

16,021. Eglinton, John. Personality in poetry. Dublin Magazine,
1956, 31:1-5.

16,022. Ehrlich, Victor. Milton's early poetry: its Christian humanism. Amer Imago, 1975, 32:77-112.

16,023. Eigeldinger, M. Baudelaire et le rêve maîtrisé. Romantisme, 1977, 15:34-44.

16,024. Eilwanger, W. [The Fidget and the Wild Hunter. Psychology of the unkempt Peter.] Psyche, 1973, 27:636-642.

16,025. Eiseley, Loren. Darwin, Coleridge, and the theory of unconscious creation. Daedalus, 1965.

16,026. Elledge, W. Paul. Byron and the Dynamics of Metaphor.
Nashville, Tenn: Vanderbilt Univ. Press, 1968.

16,027. _____. Byron's hungry sinner: the quest motif in Don
Juan. J English Germanic Philology, 1970, 69:1-13.

16,028. _____. Fountains within: motivation in Coleridge's
'Dejection: An Ode.' Papers in Language & Lit, 1971,
7:304-308.

16,029. _____. Whitman's 'Lilacs' as romantic narrative.
Virginia Q Rev, 1966, 12:59-67.

16,030. Elliott, Phillip L. Tennyson's 'In Memoriam.' Explicator,
1970, 28.

16,031. Ellis, David Alfred. Wordsworth's Poetry of Relationship:
A Study of Ambivalence, Guilt, and the Poetic Personality. DAI, 1978, 38:5494A.

16,032. Embry, Thomas J. Sensuality and chastity in 'L'allegro'
and 'Il penseroso.' J English Germanic Philology,
1978, 77:504-529.

16,033. Emde-Boas, Conrad van. The connection between Shakespeare's sonnets and his "transvesti-double" plays.
Int J Sexology, 1950, 4:67-72.

16,034. Ende, Stuart A. Keats and the Sublime. New Haven:
Yale Univ. Press, 1976.

16,035. _____. The melancholy of the descent of poets: Harold
Bloom's The Anxiety of Influence: A Theory of Poetry.
Boundary, 1974, 2:608-615.

16,036. Endres, Rolf. Understanding the lifestyle of medieval literary character. J Individual Psychol, 1974, 30:251-
264.

16,037. Enscoe, Gerald Eugene. Ambivalence in 'Kubla Khan': the
cavern and the dome. Bucknell Rev, 1964, 12(1):29-36.

16,038.   . Eros and the Romantics: Sexual Love As a
                Theme in Coleridge, Shelley and Keats. Studies in
                English Literature, Vol. 45. The Hague: Mouton,
                1967; Atlantic Highlands, NJ: Humanities Press, 1967;
                DA, 1963, 24:296-297.
16,039.   Erlich, Avi. Ambivalence in John Donne's 'Forbidding
                Mourning.' Amer Imago, 1979, 36:357-372.
16,040.   Erskine, John. The kinds of poetry. J Philosophy, Psy-
                chol & Scientific Methods, 1912, 9:617-627.
16,041.   Es, J. van. Le Thème de la femme dans la poésie de
                Lépold Sédar Senghor. Levende Talen, 1969, 261:570-
                576.
16,042.   Espmark, K. Livsdyrkaren A. Lundkvist. Studier i hans
                lyrik till och med 'Vit man.' Stockholm: Bonniers,
                1964.
16,043.   Evans, R. O. Remarks on Sappho's 'Phainetai Moi.'
                Studium Generale, 1969, 10:1016-1025.
16,044.   Eyler, Audrey S. An explication of poem 354. Emily
                Dickinson Bulletin, 1976, 29:40-43.
16,045.   Eysenck, H. J. Some factors in the appreciation of poetry,
                and their relation to temperamental qualities. Char-
                acter & Personality, 1940, 9:160-167.

16,046.   Faas, Egbert. Formen der Bewusstseindarstellung in der
                dramatischen Lyrik Pounds und Eliots. Germanisch-
                Romanische-Monatsschrift, 1968, 18:172-191.
16,047.   . Poesie als Psychogramm: Die dramatisch-
                monologische Verdichtung im viktorianischen Zeitalter.
                Munich: Fink, 1974.
16,048.   Faderman, Lillian. Emily Dickinson's homoerotic poetry.
                Higginson J, 1978, 18:19-27.
16,049.   Fagg, Helga B. The Problem of Anxiety in Rainer Maria
                Rilke's The Notebooks of Malte Laurids Brigge. DAI,
                1971, 31:6546A.
16,050.   Faguet, E. Voltaire poète psychologue. Rev des Cours
                Conferences, May 1901.
16,051.   Faimberg, Haydée. 'The Snark Was a Boojum.' Int Rev
                Psycho-Anal, 1977, 4:243-249.
16,052.   Fairchild, A. H. R. The Psychology of the Creative Imag-
                ination in Poetry, with Special Reference to Shake-
                speare, Wordsworth, and Milton. Doctoral disserta-
                tion, Yale Univ., 1904.
16,053.   Faris, Paul. Eroticism in Emily Dickinson's 'Wild
                Nights!' New England Q, 1967, 40:269-274.
16,054.   Faucher, Eugene. Instincts and poetry. Diogenes, 1968,
                63:48-69.
16,055.   Favati, G. Paradiso XXVII: San Pietro in Dante. In
                Psicoanalisi e structuralismo di fronte a Dante. Vol.
                II. Lettura della 'Commedia.' Florence: Olschki,
                1972, 327-354.
16,056.   . Sul testo della Mon. di Dante: proposta di nu-
                ove lezioni. In Psicoanalisi e structuralismo di fronte

a Dante. Vol. I: Premesse. Florence: Olschki, 1972, 3-42.

16, 057. Favre-Dive, A. Eluard et l'enfant. Rev des Sciences Humaines, 1971, fasc. 142, 36:237-260.

16, 058. Fechner, J. -U. Der Antipetrarkismus. Studien zur Liebessatire in barocker Lyrik. Heidelberg: Winter, 1966.

16, 059. Feder, Lillian. The voice from Hades in the poetry of Ezra Pound. Michigan Q Rev, 1971, 10:167-186.

16, 060. Fein, Richard J. Whitman and the emancipated self. Centennial Rev, 1976, 20:36-49.

16, 061. Feinberg, Susan G. Whitman's 'Out of the Cradle Endlessly Rocking. ' Explicator, 1978, 37(1):35-36.

16, 062. Feit, Joanne. 'Another Way to See': Dickinson and Her English Romantic Precursors. DAI, 1975, 35:4514A.

16, 063. Feldman, A. Bronson. The confessions of William Shakespeare. Amer Imago, 1953, 10:113-166.

16, 064. Ferdiere, Gaston. Intérêt psychologique et psychopathologique des comptines et formulettes de l'enfance. Evolution Psychiatrique, 1947, 3:45-63.

16, 065. _____. Prêchimoni-prochimora-ou le prêtre dans les comptines. Psyché, 1947, 2:560-567.

16, 066. Ferenczi, Sándor. Goethe on the reality value of the poet's fantasy. In Final Contributions to the Problems and Methods of Psychoanalysis. NY: Basic Books, 1955, 324; Int Zeitschrift für Psychoanalyse, 1912, 2: 679; Baustine zur Psychoanalyse, 3:41.

16, 067. Ferguson, F. Coleridge and the deluded reader: 'The Rime of the Ancient Mariner. ' Georgia Rev, 1977, 31: 617-635.

16, 068. Ferlazzo, Paul J. Sex for Whitman--the body mystic. Calamus: Walt Whitman Q: Int (Tokyo), 1974, 9:29-40.

16, 069. Ficke, Arthur Davison. A note on the poetry of sex. In Calverton, V. F. , et al. (eds), Sex in Civilization. NY: Macauley, 1929, 666-667.

16, 070. Fiedler, Leslie A. Archetype and signature. The relationship of poet and poem. In No! in Thunder. Boston: Beacon, 1960, 309-328; Sewanee Rev, 1952.

16, 071. _____. Images of Walt Whitman. In An End to Innocence. Boston: Beacon, 1952, 152-173.

16, 073. Firchow, P. E. Private faces in public places: Auden's 'The Orators. ' PMLA, 1977, 92:253-272.

16, 074. Fischer, Steven R. Dreams as a Literary Device in the Middle High German Precourtly, Courtly, and Heroic Epics. DAI, 1974, 34:7188A-89A.

16, 075. Fisher, Stephanie A. Circean Fatal Women in Milton's Poetry: Milton's Concept of the Renaissance Woman. DAI, 1971, 32:2639A.

16, 076. Fitchem, Patricia Ileen. Language Experiment and Dreams in the Poetry of Robert Desnos. DAI, 1977, 37(8): 5168-69-A.

16, 077. Fitzgerald, V. The influence of poetry on mood. Bulletin Randolph-Macon Women's College, 1922, 8:28-38.

16, 078. Fletcher, Ian. Swinburne. Writers & Their Work, No. 228, 1973, 1-66.

16, 079. Flint, F. Cudworth. Metaphor in contemporary poetry. Symposium, 1930.

16, 080. Flores Arroyuelo, Francisco J. El signo poético (fenomenología, psicología y ciencia literaria). In Homenaje al Prof. Muñoz Cortés. Murcia: Univ. de Murcia, 1977, 165-179.

16, 081. Flory, Wendy Stallard. Fathers and daughters: Coleridge and 'Christabel. ' Women & Lit, 1975, 3(1):5-15.

16, 082. Flourney, Henri. Poetry and memories of childhood. Int J Psycho-Anal, 1950, 31:103-107; Rev Française de Psychanalyse, 1949, 13:342-350.

16, 083. Fodor, A. Asherah of Ugarit. Amer Imago, 1952, 9:128-146.

16, 084. Foley, John M. Beowulf and the psychohistory of Anglo-Saxon culture. Amer Imago, 1977, 34:133-154.

16, 085. Folly, (?). Etude psychologique de l'inspiration poétique considerée comme le persistance d'un état imaginatif infantile. Belge de Neurologie et de Psychiatrie, 1933, 33:123-126.

16, 086. Forbes, Jill. Two flagellation poems by Swinburne. Notes & Queries, 1975, 22:443-445.

16, 087. Forrest, David V. E. E. Cummings and thoughts that lie too deep for tears. Of defenses in poetry. Psychiatry, 1980, 43:13-42.

16, 088. _____. Poiesis and the language of schizophrenia. Psychiatry, 1965, 28:1-18.

16, 089. Forrey, Robert. Whitman and the Freudians. Mainstream, 1961, 14(1):45-52.

16, 090. Forstner, Lorne J. Coleridge's 'The Ancient Mariner' and the case for justifiable 'mythocide': argument on psychological, epistemological and formal grounds. Criticism, 1976, 18:211-229.

16, 091. Foster, David William. Love and death in an early Spanish ballad. Papers in Language & Lit, 1972, 8:127-134.

16, 092. Foster, Genevieve W. Archetypal imagery of T. S. Eliot. PMLA, 1945, 60:567-585.

16, 093. Foster, John W. The poetry of Margaret Atwood. Canadian Lit, 1977, 74:5-20.

16, 094. Foster, M. H. Poetry and emotive meaning. J Philosophy, 1950, 47:657-660.

16, 095. Foster, Steven. Bergson's 'Intuition' and Whitman's 'Song of Myself. ' Texas Studies in Lit & Language, 1964, 6:385-387.

16, 096. _____. Eidetic imagery and imagiste perception. JAAC, 1969, 28:133-145.

16, 097. _____. The Gestalt configurations of Wallace Stevens. Modern Language Q, 1967, 28:60-76.

16, 098. Fox, Jeffrey R. Swift's 'scatological' poems: the hidden norm. Thoth, 1975, 15(3):3-13.

16, 099. Fox, Steven J. Art and Personality: Browning, Pater, Wilde and Yeats. DAI, 1972, 33:751A.

16,100.   Frank, Bernhard.   Homosexual love in four poems by
          Rilke.   In Crew, L.   (ed), The Gay Academic.   Palm
          Springs, Cal: ETC, 1978, 244-251.

16,101.   _____.   The Wiles of Words: Ambiguity in Emily Dick-
          inson's Poetry.   DA, 1966, 27:1784A.

16,102.   Frankenberg, Lloyd.   Pleasure Dome: On Reading Modern
          Poetry.   Boston: Houghton Mifflin, 1949; Review:
          Philip A. Holman, Jr., Psychiatry, 1951, 14:117.

16,103.   Franklin, Rosemary F.   Literary model for Frost's sui-
          cide attempt in the Dismal Swamp.   Amer Lit, 1979,
          50:645-646.

16,104.   Freedman, William.   T. S. Eliot's 'Gerontion' and the
          primal scene.   Amer Imago, 1979, 36:373-386.

16,105.   French, A. L.   The psychopathology of Donne's Holy Son-
          nets.   Critical Rev, 1970, 13:111-124.

16,106.   Frese, Dolores Warwick.   The homoerotic underside in
          Chaucer's Miller's Tale and Reeve's Tale.   Michigan
          Academician, 1977, 10:143-150.

16,107.   Fretet, Jean.   L'Aliénation poétique: Rimbaud, Mallar-
          mé, Proust.   Paris: Janin, 1946.

16,108.   Freud, Sigmund.   The relation of the poet to daydreaming.
          In Collected Papers, Vol. 4, London: Hogarth, 1925,
          1950; NY: Basic Books, 1959, 173-183.   In Standard
          Edition, Vol. 9; In Obras Completas, 18:51-64.

16,109.   Friedman, Donald M.   The mind in the poem: Wyatt's
          'They Flee from Me.'   Studies in English Lit, 1967,
          7:1-13.

16,110.   Friedman, P.   The bridge: a study in symbolism.   Psy-
          choanal Q, 1952, 21:51.

16,111.   Friedman, Susan S.   Mythology, Psychoanalysis, and the
          Occult in the Late Poetry of H. D.   DAI, 1974, 34:
          6638A.

16,112.   _____.   Who buried H. D. ?   A poet, her critics, and
          her place in 'the literary tradition.'   College English,
          1975, 36:801-814.

16,113.   Friedmann, Hugo.   Eduard Mörike.   Int Zeitschrift für
          Psychoanalyse, 1911, 1:486-493.

16,114.   Fritsch, A.   Zur psychologischen Charakteristik des Kunst-
          und des Volksliedes.   Archiv für die gesamte Psychol-
          ogie, 1941, 108:372-411.

16,115.   Frost, Cheryl.   Illusion and reality: psychological truth in
          Chaucer's portrait of January.   LiNQ (James Cook
          Univ., North Queensland), 1976, 5(1):37-45.

16,116.   Fulbright, James S.   William Blake and the Emancipation
          of Women.   DAI, 1979, 34:7132A.

16,117.   Furbank, P. N.   New poetry.   Listener, 1965, 73:379.

16,118.   Furtado, Diego.   Verlaine, o poeta visto por un psiquia-
          tra.   Lisbon: Livaria Luso-Espanhola, 1947.

16,119.   Gabriel, André.   Poésie et subconscient à l'époque baroque
          en France.   DAI, 1977, 38:825A-26A.

16,120.   Gabriel, P.   Poetry--the child's heritage.   Child & Fam-
          ily, 1966, 5:29.

16,121. Galand, René. Baudelaire's psychology of play. French Rev, 1971, 44:12-19.

16,122. Gangewere, R. J. Theodore Roethke: the future of a reputation. Carnegie Series in English, 1970, 11:65-73.

16,123. Ganidel, G. Esquisse d'une étude sur le langage de Baudelaire. Evolution Psychiatrique, 1956, 1:133-140.

16,124. Garber, Fredrick. Wordsworth at the universal dance. Studies in Romanticism, 1969, 8:168-182.

16,125. Gatti-Taylor, Marisa. The child as an archetypal image in the poetry of Victor Hugo. Michigan Academician, 1978, 10:249-263.

16,126. Gebser, Jean. Über das Wesen des Dichterischen. Schweizerischen Zeitschrift für Psychologie, 1944, 3: 216-231.

16,127. Geeze, Charlyne. La mujer en la poesía de Dámaso Alonso. Cuadernos Hispanoamericanos, 1973, 280-282:255-262.

16,128. Gelpi, Albert. Emily Dickinson and the Deerslayer: the dilemma of the woman poet in America. San Jose Studies, 1977, 3:80-95.

16,129. _____. The Tenth Muse: The Psyche of the American Poet. Cambridge: Harvard Univ. Press, 1975; Review: C. B. Chabot, Books Abroad, 1976, 50:662-663.

16,130. Genet, Jacqueline. William Butler Yeats: Les Fondments et l'évolution de la création poétique: Essai de psychologie littéraire. Lille: Univ. de Lille, 1976.

16,131. George, Diana Hume. Blake and Freud. Ithaca, NY: Cornell Univ. Press, 1980.

16,132. _____. Malignant fires and the chain of jealousy: Blake's treatment of Oedipal conflict. Hartford Studies in Lit, 1979, 11:197-211.

16,133. Georgiades, G. A. Le Rêve de Pénélope. Psyché, 1949, 4:740-745.

16,134. Gerenday, Lynn de. The problem of self-reflective love in Book III of The Faerie Queen. Lit & Psychol, 1976, 26:37-48.

16,135. Gershman, Herbert S. Existentialism and post-war poetry. Kentucky Foreign Language Q, 1958, 5:115-122.

16,136. Gesell, Arnold. Genius, giftedness and growth. In The March of Medicine. NY: Columbia Univ. Press, 1943, 100-140.

16,137. Gibbons, Kathryn Gibbs. The art of H. D. Mississippi Q, 1962, 15:152-160.

16,138. Gibbons, R. F. Ocean's Poem: A Study of Marine Symbolism in Leaves of Grass. DA, 1959, 19:2344-2345.

16,139. Gibson, I. K. Lorca's Balada triste: children's songs and the theme of sexual disharmony in Libro de poemas. Bulletin Hispanic Studies, 1969, 46:21-38.

16,140. Gilbert, Sandra M. Fine, white flying myth: confessions of a Plath addict. Massachusetts Rev, 1978, 19:585-603.

16,141. _____, & Gubar, Susan (eds). Shakespeare's Sisters: Feminist Essays on Women Poets. Bloomington: Indiana Univ. Press, 1979.

16,142. Gillibert, Jean. A propos d'un poème d'Arthur Rimbaud: 'Memoire.' In L'Oedipe maniaque. Paris: Payot, 1978.

16,143. Gilman, Ernest B. Marvell's perspectives of the mind. In The Curious Perspective; Literary and Pictorial Wit of the Seventeenth Century. New Haven: Yale Univ. Press, 1978, 204-231.

16,144. Gilmore, Thomas B., Jr. The comedy of Swift's scatological poems. PMLA, 1976, 91:33-43.

16,145. _____. Freud and Swift: a psychological reading of 'Strephon and Chloe.' Pennsylvania Language & Lit, 1978, 14:147-151.

16,146. _____. Swift's scatological poems. PMLA, 1976, 91: 466-467.

16,147. Ginestier, Paul. Homo faber and poetry. In Grebstein, S. N. (ed), Perspectives in Contemporary Criticism. NY: Harper & Row, 1968, 357-369; In The Poet and the Machine. Durham: Univ. North Carolina Press.

16,148. _____. The Poet and the Machine. Durham: Univ. North Carolina Press, 1961.

16,149. Gitzen, J. Floating on solitude: the poetry of Robert Bly. Modern Poetry Studies, 1976, 7:231-241.

16,150. Giusto, J.-P. Explication de Mèmoire. In Petitfils, P. (ed), Etudes rimbaudiennes 3. Paris: Les Lettres Moderne, 1972, 45-52.

16,151. Givler, R. C. The psycho-physiological effect of the elements of speech in relation to poetry. Psychol Bulletin, 1915, 19:1-132.

16,152. Glaus, A. Über Depersonalisation, nihilistiche Wahnideen, Spiegelbilder, Doppelgäng und Golem im Werke von Droste-Hülshoff. Monatschrift für Psychiatrie und Neurologie, 1953, 125:398-416.

16,153. Glenn, Jerry. Nightmares, dreams and intellectualization in the poetry of Paul Celan. World Lit Today, 1977, 51:522-525.

16,154. Glickman, Robert J. Guillermo Valencia: a psycho-philosophical evaluation. Revista de Letras, 1974, 6:62-73.

16,155. Glicksberg, Charles I. The lost self in modern literature. Personalist, 1962, 43:527-538.

16,156. _____. Poetry and Freudian aesthetic. Univ. Toronto Q, 1948, 17:121-129.

16,157. Godlewski, G. [Baudelaire, the unusual.] Semaine des Hôpitaux de Paris, 1976, 52(44):2553-2568.

16,158. _____. Musset l'immature. Seminar Hôpitaux Paris, 1977, 53(44):2573-2575.

16,159. Goffin, Robert. Emily Dickinson. New Hungarian Q, 1964, 5(15):181-186.

16,160. _____. L'Hermétisme freudien de Mallarmé. Empreintes, 1948, 5:31-41.

16,161. Gohin, Yves. De la psychocritique à une psycholecture. Dans la nuit de Michaux. In Université de Paris VII. Recherches en sciences des texte. Grenoble: Presses Universitaires de Grenoble, 1977, 115-123.

16,162. Goja, Hermann. Das Zersingen der Volklieder. Ein Beit-
         rag zur Psychologie der Volksdichtung. Imago, 1920,
         6:132-240.
16,163. Golden, Morris. In Search of Stability: The Poetry of
         William Cowper. NY: Twayne, 1960.
16,164. _____. Sterility and eminence in the poetry of Charles
         Churchill. J English Germanic Philology, 1967, 66:
         333-346.
16,165. Goldfarb, Russell M. Sexual meaning in 'The Last Ride
         Together.' Victorian Poetry, 1965, 3:255-261.
16,166. Goldin, Frederick. The Mirror of Narcissus in the Court-
         ly Love Lyric. Ithaca, NY: Cornell Univ. Press,
         1967.
16,167. Goldman, Arnold. Yeats, spiritualism, and psychical re-
         search. In Harper, G. M. (ed), Yeats and the Occult.
         Toronto: Macmillan, 1975, 108-129.
16,168. Golub, Ellen. Untying goblin apron strings: a psycho-
         analytic reading of 'Goblin Markel.' Lit & Psychol,
         1975, 25:158-165.
16,169. Gömöri, G. Attila József and the poetry of the conscious
         mind. Books Abroad, 1974, 48:58-63.
16,170. Gonzáles, José E. La individualidad psicológica y moral
         de Martín Fierro en la primera parte del poema. Sin
         Nombre, 1972, 3(2):5-20.
16,171. Goodwin, J. The 'why' of nursery rhymes. J Amer Med-
         ical Women's Assn, 1978, 33:66-73.
16,172. Gordon, Jan B. 'A Portrait of Jenny': Rossetti's aes-
         thetics of communion. Hartford Studies in Lit, 1969,
         1:89-106.
16,173. _____. 'Who is Sylvia?' The art of Sylvia Plath.
         Modern Poetry Studies, 1970, 1:6-34.
16,174. Gordon, Kate. Homer on imagination. J General Psychol,
         1940, 23:401-413.
16,175. _____. Theory of imagination in the Iliad and Odyssey.
         Psychol Bulletin, 1940, 37:590.
16,176. Goth, Maja. The myth of Narcissus in the works of Rilke
         and Valéry. Wisconsin Studies in Contemporary Lit,
         1965-66, 6-7:12-20.
16,177. Götlind, Erik. The appreciation of poetry: a proposal of
         certain empirical inquiries. JAAC, 1957, 15:322-330.
16,178. Gourevitch, M. L'Angoisse et le poète. Perspectives in
         Psychiatry, 1976, 14:94-96.
16,179. Graf, Oskar M. Der psychoanalysierte Rilke. Aufbau,
         29 April 1955.
16,180. Graham, Theodora R. Woman as Character and Symbol
         in the Work of William Carlos Williams. DAI, 1974,
         35:2267A-68A.
16,181. Grammont, M. Comment Victor Hugo compose un poème.
         L'intuition. JPNP, 1936, 33:545-569.
16,182. Graucob, K. Kindliches und jugendliches Seelenleben in
         deutscher Dichtung. Erfurt: Stenger, 1936.
16,183. Graves, Robert. On English Poetry; Being an Irregular
         Approach to the Psychology of This Art, from Evidence

Mainly Subjective. NY: Knopf, 1922, 26, 39, 84-85, 117.

16,184. Gray, Ed. Effeminacy in male poets. Amer Notes & Queries, 1965, 3:136.

16,185. Gray, J. M. Tennyson's Doppelganger: 'Balin and Balan.' Lincoln: Tennyson Society, 1971.

16,186. Green, Jesse D. Williams' Kora in Hell: the opening of the poem as 'Field of action.' Contemporary Lit, 1972, 13:295-314.

16,187. Green, Martin Burgess. The Labyrinth of Shakespeare's Sonnets: An Examination of Sexual Elements in Shakespeare's Language. London: Skilton, 1974; NY: Humanities, 1974.

16,188. Green, Paul. The relevance of surrealism with some Canadian perspectives. Modern Language Rev, 1969, 2:59-70.

16,189. Green, Rosemary M. The Treasure Chest of the Mind: Uses of Memory in Sidney, Shakespeare, and Renaissance Lyric Poetry. DAI, 1976, 37:1563A.

16,190. Greenacre, Phyllis. The imposter. Psychoanal Q, 1958, 27:359-382.

16,191. Greenberg, Herbert. Quest for the Necessary: W. H. Auden and the Dilemma of Divided Consciousness. Cambridge: Harvard Univ. Press, 1968.

16,192. Greene, Donald. On Swift's 'scatological' poems. Sewanee Rev, 1967, 75:672-689.

16,193. _____, Schakel, Peter J., & Gilmore, Thomas B., Jr. Swift's scatological poems. PMLA, 1976, 91:464-467.

16,194. Greene, Donald Joseph. From accidie tonneurosis: the Castle of Indolence revisited. In Novak, M. E. (ed), English Literature in the Age of Disguise. Los Angeles: Univ. California Press, 1977, 131-156.

16,195. Greene, Robert W. Pierre Reverdy, poet of nausea. PMLA, 1970, 85:48-55.

16,196. Greenspan, Cory R. Charles Olson: language, time, and person. Boundary, 1973-74, 1-2:340-357.

16,197. Greenway, Geri D. Patterns of Rebirth Imagery in the Poetry of Clemens Brentano. DAI, 1970, 31:2876A.

16,198. Gregory, Hossag K. Cowper's love of subhuman nature: a psychoanalytic approach. Philological Q, 1967, 46:42-57.

16,199. Gregory, J. C. Dreams, revelation, mysticism, and poetry. Fortnightly Rev, 1953, 180:338-343.

16,200. Greiner, Walter. Deutsche Einflüsse auf die Dichtungstheorie von Samuel Taylor Coleridge. Neueren Sprachen, 1960, 2:57-65.

16,201. Gretton, Francis. Images of Color in the Poetry of William Blake. DAI, 1974, 35:3740A.

16,202. Grexnev, V. A. O psixologiceskix principax 'Knjagini Ligovskoj' M. Ju. Lermontova. Russkaja Literatura, 1975, 18:36-46.

16,203. Griffith, Clark. Emily and 'Him': a modern approach to Emily Dickinson's love poetry. Iowa English Yearbook, 1961, 6:13-22.

16, 204.   _____. The Long Shadow: Emily Dickinson's Tragic
            Poetry. Princeton: Princeton Univ. Press, 1964.
16, 205.   _____. Sex and death: the significance of Whitman's
            Calamus themes. Phililogical Q, 1960, 39:18-38.
16, 206.   Griska, Joseph M., Jr. Wordsworth's mood disturbance:
            a psychoanalytic approach to three poems. Lit & Psy-
            chol, 1974, 24:144-152.
16, 207.   Grotjahn, Martin. Otto Rank on Homer and two unknown
            letters from Freud to Rank in 1916. J Otto Rank Assn,
            1969, 4(1):75-78.
16, 208.   Gruber, Loren C. The Wanderer and Arcite: isolation
            and the continuity of the English elegiac mode. Pro-
            ceedings Society for New Language Study, 1972, 1(1):1-
            10.
16, 209.   Grunes, Dennis. John Donne's 'The Good-Morrow.' Amer
            Imago, 1976, 33:261-265.
16, 210.   Grunfeld, Frederic V. Shockingly mad, madder than ever,
            quite mad. Horizon, 1972, 14:106-119.
16, 211.   Guder, G. Annette von Droste-Hülshoff's conception of
            herself as poet. German Life & Letters, 1957, 11:13-
            24.
16, 212.   Guest, Ann M. Imagery of color and light in Scott's nar-
            rative poems. Studies in English Lit, 1972, 12:705-
            720.
16, 213.   Guidubaldi, E. Dalla selva oscura alla candida rosa: psi-
            coanalisi di un diario di guarigione freudjunghianamente
            ricostruibile. In Lectura Dantis Mystica: Il poema
            sacro alla luce delle conquiste psicologiche odierne.
            Florence: Olschki, 1969, 317-372.
16, 214.   _____. Dante europeo. Vol. III. Poema sacro come
            esperienza mistica. Florence: Olschki, 1968.
16, 215.   _____. Per una fenomenologia della visione dantesca.
            Annali dell'Istituto di Studi Danteschi, 1967, 1, 137p.
16, 216.   Gunn, Douglas G. Factors in the appreciation of poetry.
            British J Educational Psychol, 1951, 21:96-104.
16, 217.   Gunter, Garland O. Archetypal Patterns in the Poetry of
            Tennsyon, 1823-1850. DA, 1967, 27:3010A.
16, 218.   Günther, Hans R. G. Persönlichkeit und Geschichte. Augs-
            burg: Beyschlag, 1947.
16, 219.   Guttry, Lottie L. Walt Whitman and the woman reader.
            Walt Whitman Rev, 1976, 22:102-110.

16, 220.   Hack, Arthur. The Psychological Pattern of Shelley's
            'Prometheus Unbound.' DAI, 1967, 28:1078A.
16, 221.   Hacklander, Friedrich. Zur Psychologie des Dichters.
            Zeitschrift für psychoanalytische Pädagogik, 1926-27,
            1:300-304.
16, 222.   Hadden, R. E. Dr. Robert Bridges and his Testament of
            Beauty. Irish J Medical Science, 1961, 426:233-240.
16, 223.   Haenni, Carol H. The Associative Mind of Emily Dickin-
            son: Color Imagery, Fascicle Unity, and Psychological
            Continuity. DAI, 1978, 39(6-A), 3579.

16, 224. Hagenbüchle-Imfeld, Helen. The Black Goddess: A Study of the Archetypal Feminine in the Poetry of Randall Jarrell. Bern: Francke, 1974.

16, 225. Hagopian, John V. Chaucer as psychologist in Troilus and Criseyde. Lit & Psychol, 1955, 5:5-11.

16, 226. _____. Contemporary science and the poets reconsidered. Science, 1954, 190:951-955.

16, 227. _____. A psychological approach to Shelley's poetry. Amer Imago, 1955, 12:25-45; In Ruitenbeek, H. M. (ed), Homosexuality and Creative Genius. NY: Obolensky, 1967, 293-310.

16, 228. Hahn, Claire. Yeats studies and the parameters of psychoanalytic criticism. Lit & Psychol, 1974, 24:171-176.

16, 229. Hahn, Otto. La Littérature et la drogue. Temps Modernes, 1964, 20:1010-1013.

16, 230. Haldar, Rangin. The working of an unconscious wish in the creation of poetry and drama. Indian J Psychol, 1931, 12:188-205.

16, 231. Hall, Calvin S. Attitudes toward life and death in poetry. Psychoanal Rev, 1965, 52:67-83.

16, 232. Halverson, John. Chaucer's Pardoner and the progress of criticism. Chaucer Rev, 1970, 4:184-202.

16, 233. _____. Prufrock, Freud, and others. Sewanee Rev, 1968, 76:571-588.

16, 234. Hamecher, Peter. Der männliche Eros im Werke Stefan George. Jahrbuch für Sexuelle Zwischenstufen, 1914, 14:10-23.

16, 235. Hamilton, James W. Object loss, dreaming and creativity: the poetry of John Keats. In The Psychoanalytic Study of the Child, Vol. 24. NY: IUP, 488-531.

16, 236. Hamilton, M. P. Death and old age in the Pardoner's Tale. Studies in Philology, 1939, 36:571-576.

16, 237. Hamm, V. M. Chaucer: heigh ymaginacioun. Modern Language Notes, 1954, 69:394-395.

16, 238. Hammond, M. A note concerning rhythm tests in poetry and in music. J Applied Psychol, 1931, 15:90-91.

16, 239. Hanna, Ralph. Cresseid's dream and Henryson's Testament. In Rowland, B. (ed), Chaucer and Middle English Studies. Kent, Ohio: Kent State Univ. Press, 1975, 288-297.

16, 240. Hanson, R. Galen. Anxiety as human predicament: Whitman's 'Calamus' No. 9. Walt Whitman Rev, 1975, 21:73-75.

16, 241. Hanson, Thomas B. Physiognomy and characterization in the Miller's Tale. Neuphilologische Mitteilungen, 1971, 72:477-482.

16, 242. Hardesty, William H. Rossetti's lusty women. Cimarron Rev, 1976, 35:20-24.

16, 243. Harding, Denys W. Practice at liking: a study in experimental aesthetics. Bulletin British Psychol Society, 1968, 21:3-10.

16, 244. Harding, Eugene J. A possible pun in Keats's 'Ode to a Nightingale.' Keats-Shelley J, 1975, 24:15-17.

16, 245.   Harding, R. E. M.   An Anatomy of Inspiration; with an Ap-
            pendix on the Birth of a Poem by R. M. B. Nicholls.
            Cambridge: Heffer, 1942.
16, 246.   Hardy, Barbara N.   The Advantage of Lyric; Essays on
            Feeling in Poetry.   Bloomington: Indiana Univ. Press,
            1977.
16, 247.   Hark, Ina Rae.   Edward Lear: eccentricity and Victorian
            angst.   Victorian Poetry, 1978, 16:112-122.
16, 248.   Harris, Derek R.   Luis Cernuda: A Study of the Poetry.
            London: Támesis, 1973.
16, 249.   _____.   The Poetry of Luis Cernuda.   Doctoral dis-
            sertation, Hull Univ. , 1968.
16, 250.   Harris, Marion.   Nature and materialism: fundamentals
            in Whitman's epistemology.   Walt Whitman Rev, 1963,
            9:85-88.
16, 251.   Harris, Wendell V.   Freud, form and flights by night.
            Reply and rejoinder to N. N. Holland's "Psychological
            Depths and 'Dover Beach. '"   Victorian Studies, 1966,
            10:70-82.
16, 252.   Harrison, Antony H.   The aesthetics of androgyny in Swin-
            burne's early poetry.   Tennessee Studies in Lit, 1978,
            23:87-99.
16, 253.   Hart, Edward L.   'Christopher must slay the dragon. '
            Lit & Psychol, 1967, 17:115-119.
16, 254.   Hartley, C. L.   The Spirit of Walt Whitman--A Psycho-
            logical Study in Blank Verse.   Manchester, England:
            1908.
16, 255.   Hartman, Geoffrey H.   Diction and defense in Wordsworth.
            In Smith, J. H. (ed), The Literary Freud.   New Haven:
            Yale Univ. Press, 1980, 205-215.
16, 256.   _____.   (ed).   New Perspectives on Coleridge and Words-
            worth.   Selected Papers from the English Institute.
            NY: Columbia Univ. Press, 1972.
16, 257.   _____.   Spectral symbolism and the authorial self: an
            approach to Keats's 'Hyperion. '   Essays in Criticism,
            1974, 24:1-19.
16, 258.   _____.   The touching compulsion: Wordsworth and the
            problem of literary representation.   Georgia Rev, 1977,
            31:345-361.
16, 259.   Hartog, Curt.   Psychic resolution in Gray's 'Elegy. '   Lit
            & Psychol, 1975, 25:5-16.
16, 260.   Hartsook, John H.   Béquer and the creative imagination.
            Hispanic Rev, 1967, 35:252-269.
16, 261.   Harwood, Britton J.   The Wife of Bath and the dream of
            innocence.   Modern Language Q, 1972, 33:257-273.
16, 262.   Haskell, Ann S.   The Doppelgängers in Chaucer's Troilus.
            Neuphilologische Mitteilungen, 1971, 72:723-734.
16, 263.   _____.   The portrayal of women by Chaucer and his
            age.   In Springer, M. (ed), What Manner of Woman:
            Essays on English and American Life and Literature.
            NY: New York Univ. Press, 1978, 1-14.
16, 264.   Hassler, Donald M.   Belief and death in Wordsworth's
            'Peter Bell. '   Bulletin New York Public Library, 1974,
            77:251-257.

16, 265.   Hastings, Marshall D.   Androgynous Imagery in Nineteenth
           Century French Poetry.   DAI, 1974, 34:7756A.
16, 266.   Hatcher, Elizabeth R.   Chaucer and the psychology of fear:
           Troilus in Book V.   J English Lit History, 1973, 40:
           307-324.
16, 267.   Hauge, Ingvar.   Freud, Marx eller Kristus.   En linje i
           W. H. Audens diktning.   Samtiden (Oslo), 1955, 64:335-
           345.
16, 268.   Haule, J.   E. E. Cummings as comic poet: the economy
           of the expenditure of Freud.   Lit & Psychol, 1975, 25:
           175-180.
16, 269.   Havard, R. G.   Image and persona in Rosalía de Castro's
           En las orillas del Sar.   Hispanic Rev, 1974, 42:393-
           411.
16, 270.   Havens, Raymond Dexter.   The Mind of a Poet; A Study of
           Wordsworth's Thought with Particular Reference to 'The
           Prelude.'   Baltimore: Johns Hopkins Univ. Press,
           1941.
16, 271.   Haworth, Helen E.   Virtuous romantics--indecency, indeli-
           cacy, pornography and obscenity in romantic poetry.
           Papers in Language & Lit, 1974, 10:287-306.
16, 272.   Hécaen, H.   Henri Michaux: Connaissance par les gouf-
           fres.   JPNP, 1964, 61:115.
16, 273.   Heckel, H.   Das Don Juan-Problem in der neueren Dich-
           tung.   Stuttgart: Metzlersche, 1915.
16, 274.   Heckhausen, Heinz, & Maurer, Karl.   Über psychologische
           und literarische Analyse poetischer Texte.   Poetica,
           1967, 1:253-283.
16, 275.   Hedetoft, Ulf.   Robert Lowell: alienated consciousness/
           consciousness of alienation: the split ideology.   Lan-
           guage & Lit, 1974, 2(4):8-17.
16, 276.   Heimann, J.   Die Heilung der Elisabeth Browning in ihren
           Sonetten.   Imago, 1935, 21:227-254.
16, 277.   Heitmann, Klaus.   Tiefenpsychologische Beiträge zur
           Deutung der Vita Nuova.   Deutsches Dante Jahrbuch,
           1974-75, 49-50:7-35.
16, 278.   Heldreth, Leonard G.   Dream Images and Symbols in
           Wordsworth's Poetry.   DAI, 1974, 34:7705A-06A.
16, 279.   Helms, Randel.   Blake at Felpham: a study in the psy-
           chology of vision.   Lit & Psychol, 1972, 22:57-66.
16, 280.   Henderson, Archibald.   Robert Frost's 'Out, Out'--?
           Amer Imago, 1977, 34:12-27.
16, 281.   Henderson, J. L.   Stages of psychological development ex-
           emplified in the poetical works of T. S. Eliot.   J An-
           alytic Psychol, 1956, 1:133-144; 1957, 2:33-49.
16, 282.   Heninger, S. K.   A Jungian reading of Kubla Khan.   JAAC,
           1960, 18:358-367.
16, 283.   Henry, Freeman G.   Les Fleurs du Mal and the exotic:
           the escapist psychology of a visionary poet.   Nine-
           teenth-Century French Studies, 1979-80, 8(1-2):62-75.
16, 284.   Hensel, Gerhard.   Das Optische bei Wordsworth.   Ein
           Beitrag zur Psychologie des dichterischen Schaffens.
           Archiv für die gesamte Psychologie, 1930, 76:83-192.

16, 285. Hermann, Imré. Benvenuto Cellinis dichterische Periode.
          Imago, 1924, 10:418-423.
16, 286. Hershenson, David B. Vocational development theory be-
          fore 1400. J History Behavioral Sciences, 1974, 10:
          170-179.
16, 287. Herzog, U. Robert Walsers Poetik. Literatur und sozi-
          ale Entpremdung. Tübingen: Niemeyer, 1974.
16, 288. Hesketh, Phoebe. Poetry and the unconscious mind. Con-
          temporary Rev, 1959, 196:180-182.
16, 289. Hess, Gertrud. [King Stag: the Eros problem in modern
          poetry.] Analytische Psychologie, 1975, 6:472-481.
16, 290. Hess, M. W. The universal particular situation in sculp-
          ture and poetry. Monist, 1934, 44:255-261.
16, 291. Hesse, Hermann. Hermann Hesse über Psychoanalyse.
          [Abstract of Neue Rundschau article.] Psychoanaly-
          tische Bewegung, 1931, 3:35-37.
16, 292. _____. Notizen zum Thema Dichtung und Kritik. Neue
          Rundschau, Dec 1930.
16, 293. Hevner, K. An experimental study of the affective value
          of sounds in poetry. Amer J Psychol, 1937, 49:419-
          434.
16, 294. Higgins, J. The conflict of personality in C. Vallejo's
          Poemas humanos. Bulletin of Hispanic Studies, 1966,
          43:47-55.
16, 295. Higgs, Robert F. Emily Dickinson's 'Test of Trouble'.
          In Burton, T. G. (ed), Essays in Memory of Christine
          Burleson in Language and Literature. Johnson City:
          East Tennessee State Univ., 1969, 129-137.
16, 296. Hildebrand, W. H. Shelley's early vision poems. Studies
          in Romanticism, 1969, 8:198-215.
16, 297. Hill, B. Father and son. Thomas Beddoes and Thomas
          Lovell Beddoes. Practitioner, 1960, 184:513-518.
16, 298. Hill, J. C. Poetry and the unconscious. British J Medi-
          cal Psychol, 1924, 4:125-133.
16, 299. Hill, J. M. 'The Book of the Duchess,' melancholy, and
          that eight-year sickness. Chaucer Rev, 1974, 9:35-50.
16, 300. Hines, Thomas J. The Later Poetry of Wallace Stevens:
          Phenomenological Parallels with Husserl and Heidegger.
          Lewisburg, Pa: Bucknell Univ. Press, 1976.
16, 301. Hinrichson, Otto. Bemerkungen über die schöpferische
          Kraft des Unbewussten. Psychiatrisch-neurologische
          Wochenschrift, 1939, 41:28-32.
16, 302. _____. Psychopathie und Dichtung. Psychiatrisch-
          neurologische Wochenschrift, 1931, 33:516-518, 530-
          532.
16, 303. _____. Sexualität und Dichtung. Wiesbaden: Berg-
          mann, 1912; Grenzfragen des Nerven- und Seelenlebens,
          85.
16, 304. _____. Ein weitere Beitrag zur Psychologie des Dich-
          ters. Grenzfragen des Nerven- und Seelenslebens,
          1913 (?).
16, 305. _____. Zur Psychologie und Psychopathologie des Dich-
          ters. Wiesbaden: Bergmann, 1911.

16, 306. Hinterleithner, W. [Shicksal analysis of a poetic creative process.] Psyche, 1960, 14:442-470.

16, 307. Hirschberg, Stuart. An encounter with the irrational in Ted Hughes's 'Pike.' Concerning Poetry, 1976, 9(1): 63-64.

16, 308. Hirsh, John C. The imagery of dedication in Robert Lowell's 'For the Union Dead.' J Amer Studies, 1972, 6: 201-205.

16, 309. Hitschmann, Edward. Ein Dichter und sein Vater. Imago, 1916, 4:337-345.

16, 310. _____. Gottfried Keller. Psychoanalytische Behauptungen und Vermutungen über sein Wesen und sein Werk. Imago, 1915-16, 4:223-247.

16, 311. _____. Zum Tagträumen der Dichter. Imago, 1923, 9:499-502.

16, 312. Hobbs, John N. Love and time in Rossetti's 'The Secret Stream.' Victorian Poetry, 1971, 9:395-404.

16, 313. Hobson, Alan. Symbols of Transformation in Poetry. London: Guild of Pastoral Psychology, 1963.

16, 314. Hoche, A. Die Geisteskranken in der Dichtung. Munich: Lehmann, 1939.

16, 315. Hoeveler, Diane Long. The Erotic Apocalypse: The Androgynous Ideal in Blake and Shelley. DAI, 1977, 37:6498A.

16, 316. Hoffman, Daniel Gerard. Barbarous Knowledge. Myth in the Poetry of Yeats, Graves and Muir. NY: Oxford Univ. Press, 1967.

16, 317. _____. Edwin Muir: the story and the fable. Yale Rev, 1966, 55:403-426.

16, 318. _____. Poetry. In Harvard Guide to Contemporary American Writers. Cambridge: Harvard Univ. Press, 1979.

16, 319. _____. Significant wounds: the early poetry of Robert Graves. Shenandoah, 1966, 17:21-40.

16, 320. Hoffman, Frederick J. From surrealism to 'The Apocalypse': a development in twentieth century irrationalism. J English Lit History, 1948, 15:147-165.

16, 321. Holberg, Stanley M. Rossetti and the trance. Victorian Poetry, 1970, 8:299-314.

16, 322. Holbrook, David. Dylan Thomas and Poetic Dissociation. Carbondale: Southern Illinois Univ. Press, 1964.

16, 323. _____. R. D. Laing and the death circuit. Encounter, 1968, 31(2):35-45.

16, 324. _____. Sylvia Plath: Poetry and Existence. London: Athlone, 1976; Atlantic Highlands, NJ: Humanities Press, 1976; Review: E. R. Davey, J European Studies, 1978, 8:53-54.

16, 325. _____. The 200-inch distorting mirror. New Society, 11 July 1968, 57-58.

16, 326. Holland, Norman N. Freud and form: facts about fiction. Victorian Studies, 1966, 10:76-82.

16, 327. _____. Literary interpretation and three phases of psychoanalysis. In Roland, A. (ed), Psychoanalysis, Cre-

ativity, and Literature: A French-American Inquiry.
NY: Columbia Univ. Press, 1978, 233-247; Critical
Inquiry, 1976, 3:221-233; Comunità, 1978, 179:218-234.
16,328. _____. Literary value: a psychoanalytic approach.
Lit & Psychol, 1964, 14:43-55.
16,329. _____. Meaning as transformation: 'The Wife of Bath's
Tale.' College English, 1967, 28:279-290.
16,330. _____. Poems in Persons: An Introduction to the Psychoanalysis of Literature. NY: Norton, 1973, 1975;
Review: E. Wolf, JAPA, 1975, 23:675-676.
16,331. _____. Psychological depths and 'Dover Beach.' Victorian Studies, 1965, 9:5-28; In Grebstein, S.N. (ed),
Perspectives in Contemporary Criticism. NY: Harper
& Row, 1968, 248-267.
16,332. Hollis, James R. Convergent patterns in Yeats and Jung.
Psychol Perspectives, 1973, 4:60-68.
16,333. Holloway, John. Conrad Aiken, folk-poet. Art International, 1971, 15(8):80-84, 87.
16,334. Holmes, Doris. Holmes' 'Herself.' Explicator, 1970, 28.
16,335. Holmes, S.W. Browning's Sordello in the light of Jung's
theory of types. PMLA, 1941, 56:758-796.
16,336. Holstein, Michael E. Coleridge's 'Christabel' as psychodrama: five perspectives on the intruder. Wordsworth
Circle, 1976, 7:119-128.
16,337. _____. Poet, Hero, and Persona: A Study of the Personal and Poetic Identities of John Keats. DAI, 1973,
33:3586A.
16,338. Holtsmark, Erling B. Spiritual rebirth of the hero: Odyssey 5. Classical J, 1966, 61:206-210.
16,339. Holub, A. Beziehungen zwischen Auge und Dichtung. Int
Zeitschrift für Individual-Psychologie, 1931, 6:448-455.
16,340. Hoog, Armand. Poésie et psychanalyse. La Nef, 1946,
21:122-125.
16,341. Hoover, Suzanne R. Coleridge, Humphrey Davy, and some
early experiments with a consciousness-altering drug.
Bulletin Research in the Humanities, 1978, 81:9-27.
16,342. Hopwood, V.G. Dream, magic, and poetry. JAAC, 1951,
10:152-159.
16,343. _____. Interpretation of dream and poetry. Univ.
Toronto Q, 1952, 21:128-139.
16,344. Hotch, Ripley. The dilemma of an obedient son: Pope's
Epistle to Dr. Arbuthnot. Essays in Lit, 1974, 1:37-
45.
16,345. Hough, Graham. Poetry and the anima. Spring, 1973,
85-96.
16,346. House, Elizabeth Balkman. Robert Frost on Women and
Marriage. DAI, 1976, 36:7422A.
16,347. Houwens Post, H. [Sá-Carneiro.] Ocidente, 1973, 84:
161-168.
16,348. Hovey, Richard B. Tennyson's 'Locksley Hall': a re-interpretation. Univ. Houston Q, 1963, 4:24-30.
16,349. Howard, Donald R. Literature and sexuality: Book III of
Chaucer's Troilus. Massachusetts Rev, 1967, 8:442-
456.

16, 350. Howells, T. H., & Johnson, A. A.   A study of metre-sense in poetry.   J Applied Psychol, 1931, 15:539-544.

16, 351. Hoyle, James F.   'Kubla Khan' as an elated experience. Lit & Psychol, 1966, 16:27-39.

16, 352. _____.   Sylvia Plath: a poetry of suicidal mania.   Lit & Psychol, 1968, 18:187-204.

16, 353. Huber, M.   Clemens Brentano.   Die Chronika des fahrenden Schülers.   Bern: Francke, 1976.

16, 354. Hubler, Edward.   The unromantic lady.   In The Sense of Shakespeare's Sonnets.   Princeton: Princeton Univ. Press, 1952, Ch. 2.

16, 355. Hughes, Felicity A.   Psychological allegory in The Faerie Queene III, xi-xii.   Rev English Studies, 1978, 29:129-146.

16, 356. Hughes, Richard E.   Browning's Childe Roland and the broken taboo.   Lit & Psychol, 1959, 9(2):18-19.

16, 357. _____.   Metaphysical poetry as event.   Hartford Studies in Lit, 1971, 3:191-196.

16, 358. Huit, C.   La Psychologie de Dante.   Annales de Philosophie Chrétienne, 1901, 44:45-46.

16, 359. Hull, Gloria T.   Women in Byron's Poetry: A Biographical and Critical Study.   DAI, 1972, 33:2894A.

16, 360. Hulseberg, Richard A.   The Validation of the Self in Wordsworth and Keats.   DAI, 1972, 32:5791A.

16, 361. Hume, Robert D.   The development of Blake's psychology: the quest for an understanding of man's position in the world.   Rev des Langues Vivantes, 1969, 35:240-258.

16, 362. Humphries, R.   The dreams of Aeneas.   Int Zeitschrift für Individual-Psychologie, 1927, 5:344-347.

16, 363. Hundt, Joachim.   Der Traumglaube bei Homer.   Griefswald: 1935.

16, 364. Hunt, John D.   The symbolist vision of 'In Memoriam.' Victorian Poetry, 1970, 8:187-198.

16, 365. Hunt, Russell A.   Whitman's poetics and the unity of 'Calamus.'   Amer Lit, 1975, 46:482-494.

16, 366. Hunter, G. K.   Review: E. Le Comte's Milton and Sex. Sewanee Rev, 1978, 86:414-421.

16, 367. Hunter, W. B.   Eve's demonic dream in Paradise Lost; the poet's conception in terms of contemporary dream and demon lore.   J English Lit History, 1946, 13:255-265.

16, 368. Hunting, Claudine.   Quelques aspects de la femme dans l'oeuvre poétique de Mallarmé.   Claudel Studies, 1976, 3(1):48-63.

16, 369. Huntley, John F.   Body sickness and social sickness in Milton's figure of Satan.   Lit & Psychol, 1968, 18:101-110.

16, 370. Hurry, David.   William Carlos Williams' Paterson and Freud's Interpretation of Dreams.   Lit & Psychol, 1978, 28:170-177.

16, 371. Hyde, William J.   Hardy's spider webs.   Victorian Poetry, 1970, 8:265-268.

16, 372. Hyman, Stanley Edgar.   Poetry and Criticism: Four Revolutions in Literary Taste.   NY: Atheneum, 1961.

16,373. _____. 'The Rape of the Lock.' Hudson Rev, 1960,
13:406-412.

16,374. Hynes, Samuel. The squaring of human sorrow. Times
Lit Supplement, 13 Oct 1978, No. 3993:1137.

16,375. Hytier, Jean. L'Activité poétique et l'activité esthétique
dans la poésie. J de Psychologie, 1926, 23:160-182.

16,376. _____. The Poetics of Paul Valéry. Garden City,
NY: Doubleday Anchor, 1966; La Poétique de Valéry.
Paris: Colin, 1953.

16,377. Ilie, Paul. Espronceda and the romantic grotesque. Studies in Romanticism, 1972, 11:94-112.

16,378. Irwin, John T. Figurations of the writer's death: Freud
and Hart Crane. In Smith, J. H. (ed), The Literary
Freud. New Haven: Yale Univ. Press, 1980, 217-260.

16,379. Istituto Dantesco Europeo. Psicoanalisi e structuralismo
di fronte a Dante: della lettura profetica medievale agli
odierni strumenti critici. Vol. I. Premesse. Vol. II.
Lettura della 'Commedia.' Vol. III. Incontro con le
altre opere. Florence: Olschki, 1972.

16,380. Iwakura, Tomahide. Psychosexuale Analyse von Shake-
spears 'Sonnetten.' Tokyo Zeitschrift für Psychoanalyse, 1938, 6(2).

16,381. Jackaman, Rob. Man and mandala: symbol as structure
in a poem by Dylan Thomas. Ariel: Rev Int English
Lit, 1976, 7(4):22-33.

16,382. Jackson, E. The quantitative measurement of assonance
and alliteration in Swinburne. Amer J Psychol, 1942,
55:115-123.

16,383. Jacob, Cary F. The psychology of poetic talent. J Abnormal Psychol, 1922, 17:231-253.

16,384. Jacobs, Edward C. Further reflections on 'La Belle Dame
Sans Merci' as anima archetype. J Altered States of
Consciousness, 1978-79, 4:291-296.

16,385. Jacobs, Willis D. Williams' 'Between Walls.' Explicator,
1970, 28.

16,386. _____. Williams' 'Great Mullen.' Explicator, 1970,
28.

16,387. _____. Williams' 'To Awaken an Old Lady.' Explicator, 1970, 29.

16,388. Jacobson, Sibyl C. Arnold's father-son poems. Concerning Poetry, 1976, 9(1):47-56.

16,389. Jacomuzzi, A. Il palinsesto della retorica e altri studi
danteschi. In Psicoanalisi e structuralismo di fronte a
Dante. Vol. II. Lettura della 'Commedia.' Florence:
Olschki, 1972, 41-63.

16,390. Jacquier-Roux, B. J. -L. Le Thème de l'eau dans 'Les
Fleurs du Mal.' Paris: La Pensée Universelle, 1973.

16,391. Jamati, Georges. Le Langage poetique. JPNP, 1951, 44:
269-279.

16, 392. James, David G. Skepticism and Poetry. An Essay on
the Poetic Imagination. NY: Barnes & Noble, 1960
(1937).

16, 393. James, Max H. The child image and attitude in the poetry
of George Herbert. Christianity & Lit, 1976, 26(1):9-
19.

16, 394. Jarcho, S. Amy Lowell and the death of John Keats.
Clio Medica, 1977, 12:91-95.

16, 395. Jarrell, Randall. Freud to Paul: the stages of Auden's
ideology. Partisan Rev, 1945, 12:437-457; In The Third
Book of Criticism. NY: Farrar, Straus & Giroux,
1979, 153-190.

16, 396. Jayne, Edward. Up against the 'Mending Wall': the psychoanalysis of a poem by Frost. College English, 1973,
34:934-952.

16, 397. Jayne, Richard. Rilke and the problem of poetic inward-
ness. In Baron, F., Dick, E. S., & Maurer, W. R.
(eds), Rilke: The Alchemy of Alienation. Lawrence,
Kans: Regents, 1980, 191-222.

16, 398. _____. The Symbolism of Space and Motion in the
Works of Rainer Maria Rilke. Frankfurt: Athenäum,
1972.

16, 399. Jean, Marcel, & Meizei, Arpad. Maldoror. Paris:
Pavois, 1947.

16, 400. Jean, Raymond. L'Erotique de Guillaume Apollinaire.
Cahiers du Sud, 1966, 53, No. 386, 13-21.

16, 401. Jeffrey, Lloyd N. Browning as psychologist: three notes.
College English, 1956, 17:345-347.

16, 402. _____. A Freudian reading of Keats's 'Ode to Psyche.'
Psychoanal Rev, 1968, 55:289-306; In Feldman, M. J.,
et al., (eds), Fears Related to Death and Suicide. NY:
Mss Information Corp., 1974, 173-190.

16, 403. Jennings, M. Chaucer's Troilus and the ruby. Notes &
Queries, 1976, 23:533-537.

16, 404. Jerman, B. R. Browning's witless Duke. PMLA, 1957,
72:488-493.

16, 405. Jentsch, Ernst. Das Pathologische bei Otto Ludwig. Wiesbaden: Bergmann, 1913; Grenzfragen des Nerven- und
Seelenlebens, 1913, 90.

16, 406. Jespersen, Otto. Cause psychologique de quelques phénom-
ènes de métrique germanique. J de Psychologie, 1933,
30:333-338.

16, 407. Johnson, Diane L. A Closer Reading of Earth: Sexual
Mysticism in the Poetry of George Meredith. DA, 1969,
30:1529A.

16, 408. Johnson, John. 'Prufrock' as mimetic portrait: a psychological reading. Gypsy Scholar, 1976, 3:96-110.

16, 409. Johnson, Wendell Stacy. Auden, Hopkins, and the poetry
of reticence. Twentieth Century Lit, 1974, 20:165-171.

16, 410. _____. Sex and Marriage in Victorian Poetry. Ithaca,
NY: Cornell Univ. Press, 1975; Review: M. Monta-
brut, English Studies, 1979, 60:330-332.

16, 411. Johnston, Arthur Cyrus. Narcissism and D. G. Rossetti's
The House of Life. DAI, 1978, 38:6143A.

16,412.   Jones, D.   Sidney's erotic pen: an interpretation of one
           of the Arcadia poems.   J English & Germanic Philol-
           ogy, 1974, 73:32-47.
16,413.   Jones, D. P.   Walt Whitman's Perception of Time.   DA,
           1967, 27:3050A.
16,414.   Jones, Joyce Marie Meeks.   Jungian Psychology in Liter-
           ary Analysis: A Demonstration Using T. S.   Eliot's Po-
           etry.   Washington, DC: University Press of America,
           1980; DAI, 1976, 36:6084A.
16,415.   Jones, Katherine.   A note on Milton's 'Lycidas.'   Amer
           Imago, 1962, 19:141-155.
16,416.   Jordan, Francis X.   Archetypal Patterns in the Poetry of
           D. H.   Lawrence, DAI, 1976, 37:2197A-98A.
16,417.   Jordan, Jim.   How I came to write 'Sonnets to My Psy-
           chiatrist,' why they are not confessional, and why the
           image in the mirror is not always my own.   Windless
           Orchard, 1976, 26:28-31.
16,418.   Jourdan, Bernard.   The Disinteriorized Self: Aspects and
           Extensions of the Idea of Family in Wordsworth.   DAI,
           1976, 36:4511A.
16,419.   Jouve, Pierre Jean.   The unconscious: spirituality-catas-
           trophe.   Poetry (London), 1941, 1:112-114.
16,420.   Jung, Carl Gustav.   On the relation of analytical psychol-
           ogy to poetic art.   British J Psychol, 1923, 3:213-231;
           In Contributions to Analytical Psychology.   NY: Har-
           court, Brace, 1928, 225-249.
16,421.   _____.   Psychology and poetry.   Transition, 1930, 19-
           20:23-45.
16,422.   _____.   Schiller's ideas on type problems.   In Collected
           Works of C. G.   Jung, Vol. 6.   Princeton: Princeton
           Univ. Press, 1971, 67-135.
16,423.   _____.   The type problem in poetry.   Carl Spitteler:
           Prometheus and Epimetheus.   In Collected Works of
           C. G.   Jung, Vol. 6.   Princeton: Princeton Univ.
           Press, 1971, 166-273.
16,424.   _____.   Ulysses--a monologue.   Nimbus, 1953, 2:7-20.
16,425.   Jung, Gustav.   Der Erotiker Heinrich Heine.   Zeitschrift
           für Sexualwissenschaft, 1924, 11:113-127.
16,426.   _____.   Das erotische Element in Kunst und Dichtung.
           Zeitschrift für Sexualwissenschaft, 1924, 11:277-288,
           297-301.

16,427.   Kahn, Coppélia.   Self and Eros in Venus and Adonis.
           Centennial Rev, 1976, 20:351-371.
16,428.   Kahn, S. J.   Psychology in Coleridge's poetry.   JAAC,
           1951, 9:208-226.
16,429.   Kalk, Marjorie Sondheim.   The social and psychological
           significance of Palazzeschi's Opere giovanili.   DAI,
           1976, 36:6736A-37A.
16,430.   Kammer, Jeanne Henry.   Repression, Compression and
           Power: Six Women Poets in America, 1860-1960.
           DAI, 1976, 37:2182A.

16, 431. Kandela, A. A. Tennyson's Idea of Woman in Relation to
          Contemporary and Eastern Influences. Doctoral dis-
          sertation, Univ. Dundee, 1975.

16, 432. Kaplan, Abraham, & Kris, Ernst. Esthetic and ambiguity.
          Philosophical & Phenomenological Research, 1948, 8:
          415-435.

16, 433. Kaplan, Fred. Conclusion. In Miracles of Rare Device:
          The Poet's Sense of Self in Nineteenth-Century Poetry.
          Detroit: Wayne State Univ. Press, 1972, 156-168.

16, 434. _____. Dickens and Mesmerism: The Hidden Springs
          of Fiction. Princeton: Princeton Univ. Press, 1975.
          Review: Nineteenth Century Fiction, 1979, 33: 505-508.

16, 435. Karpman, Ben. A modern Gulliver: a study in coprophilia.
          Psychoanal Rev, 1949, 36: 162-185.

16, 436. Kart, Lawrence. Richard Cory: artist without an art.
          Colby Library Q, 1975, 11: 160-161.

16, 437. Kartiganer, Donald M. Process and product: a study of
          modern literary form. Massachusetts Rev, 1971, 12:
          297-328, 799-816.

16, 438. Kastor, Frank S. Milton's tempter: a genesis of a sub-
          portrait in Paradise Lost. Huntington Library Q, 1970,
          33: 373-385.

16, 439. Katz, Gerda R. The theme of motherhood in Yerma and
          La tía Tula. Language Q, 1977, 15(3-4): 15-18.

16, 440. Kaufmann, H. Goethe's Gedicht au Frau von Stein vom
          14. April 1776. Weimarer Beiträge, 1964, 10: 359-371.

16, 441. Kauvar, Gerald B. The psychological structure of English
          romantic poetry. Psychoanal Rev, 1977, 64: 21-40.

16, 442. Kavka, Jerome. Richard Cory's suicide: a psychoanalyst's
          view. Colby Library Q, 1975, 11: 150-159.

16, 443. _____. The suicide of Richard Cory: an explication of
          the poem by Edwin Arlington Robinson. In The Annual
          of Psychoanalysis, Vol. 4. NY: IUP, 1976, 479-500.

16, 444. Keach, William. Elizabethan Erotic Narratives: Irony
          and Pathos in the Ovidian Poetry of Shakespeare, Mar-
          lowe, and Their Contemporaries. New Brunswick, NJ:
          Rutgers Univ. Press, 1977.

16, 445. Keith, A. L. Virgil as a master of psychology. Psycho-
          anal Rev, 1922, 9: 436-439.

16, 446. Kelley, Theresa M. Deluge and buried treasure in Words-
          worth's 'Arab Dream.' Notes & Queries, 1980, 27: 70-
          71.

16, 447. Kellog, Alfred L. Amatory psychology and amatory frus-
          tration in the interpretation of the Book of the Duchess.
          In Chaucer, Langland, Arthur: Essays in Middle Eng-
          lish Literature. New Brunswick, NJ: Rutgers Univ.
          Press, 1972, 59-107.

16, 448. Kelly, Michael J. Coleridge and dream phenomenology.
          Massachusetts Studies in English, 1967, 1: 1-7.

16, 449. Keogh, J. G. Marvell's 'To His Coy Mistress.' Explica-
          tor, 1969, 28: 2.

16, 450. _____. Shakespeare's Sonnet LXXIII. Explicator, 1969,
          28: 1.

16, 451. Kernberger, Katherine Anne. 'A Lovely and a Fearful
          Thing': Byron's Sexual Politics in Don Juan. DAI,
          1977, 38:2810A.
16, 452. Kerner, D. El medico-poeta Gottfried Benn. Folia Hu-
          manitas (Barcelona), 1970, 8:831-847.
16, 453. Kessler, Edward. Crane's 'Black Tambourine.' Explica-
          tor, 1970, 29.
16, 454. Khanna, Lee Cullen. Images of women in Thomas More's
          poetry. In Moore, M. J. (ed), Quincentennial Essays
          on St. Thomas More. Boone, North Carolina: Albion,
          1978, 78-88.
16, 455. Kidder, R. M. Twin obsessions: the poetry and paintings
          of E. E. Cummings. Georgia Rev, 1978, 32:342-368.
16, 456. Kiehl, James M. On Howard Nemerov. Salmagundi, 1973,
          22-23:234-257.
16, 457. Kimble, Mark W. The Scatological Poetry of Swift and
          Pope: Intention and Technique. DAI, 1971, 31:4722A.
16, 458. Kincaid, James R. Antithetical criticism, Harold Bloom,
          and Victorian poetry. Victorian Poetry, 1976, 14:365-
          382.
16, 459. Kinney, Thomas L. The popular meaning of Chaucer's
          'Physician's Tale.' Lit & Psychol, 1978, 28:76-84.
16, 460. Kirchner, Jane. The Function of the Persona in the Po-
          etry of Byron. Salzburg: Univ. Salzburg, 1973.
16, 461. Kirschbaumer, L. Poetry in schizophrenia and other psy-
          choses. JNMD, 1940, 91:141-156.
16, 462. [No entry. For Kwinn, see 16,498]
16, 463. Klages, L. Vom Wesen des Rhythmus, Kampen auf Sylt.
          Berlin: Kampman, 1934.
16, 464. Kleinschmidt, H. J. Death of Elpenor. J Hillside Hospital,
          1956, 3:4-7.
16, 465. Kloss, Robert J. Chaucer's The Merchant's Tale: tender
          youth and stooping age. Amer Imago, 1974, 31:65-79.
16, 466. Knapp, Bettina L. Gérard de Nerval the mnemonic poet.
          Le Point noir. Symposium, 1979, 33:331-344.
16, 467. Knapp, James F. Delmore Schwartz: poet of the orphic
          journey. Sewanee Rev, 1970, 78:506-516.
16, 468. _____. Eliot's 'Prufrock' and the form of modern po-
          etry. Arizona Q, 1974, 30:5-14.
16, 469. Knapp-Tepperberg, Eva-Maria. Baudelaire: 'A une pas-
          sante.' Psychoanalytische Bemerkungen zu einer Text-
          variante. Germanisch-romanische Monatsschrift, N. F.,
          24:182-192.
16, 470. Knapton, Antoinette. Mythe et psychologie chez Marie de
          France dans 'Guigemar.' Chapel Hill: Univ. North
          Carolina Studies in Romance Languages & Literature,
          1976; DAI, 1971, 32:2464A.
16, 471. Knight, George Wilson. The Mutual Flame; on Shake-
          speare's Sonnets and the Phoenix and the Turtle. NY:
          Macmillan, 1955; London: Methuen, 1955.
16, 472. _____. Mysticism and masturbation: an introduction to
          the lyrics of John Cowper Powys. In Neglected Powers;

Essays on Nineteenth and Twentieth Century Literature.
NY: Barnes & Noble, 1971, 156-196.

16,473. Knights, L. C. Poetry and things hard for thought. Times
Lit Supplement, 29 Feb 1980, no. 4014, 239-241.

16,474. Koch, K. Wishes, Lies, and Dreams: Teaching Children
to Write Poetry. NY: Chelsea, 1970.

16,475. Kohler, Dorothea B. Vaudeville Act with Doppelgänger.
DAI, 1970, 30:3011A-12A.

16,476. Kohlhepp, B. Horatius Flaccus und die Psychiatrie. Bay-
erische Aerzteblätter, 1972, 27:39-394.

16,477. Kohli, Devindra. Intelligence of heart: women in Yeats's
poetry. Indian J English Studies, 1967, 8:83-105.

16,478. Kolinsky, Muriel. 'Me Tarzan you Jane?': Whitman's
attitudes toward women from a women's liberation point
of view. Walt Whitman Rev, 1977, 23:155-165.

16,479. Kostis, Nicholas. Sexuality and the poetic mission in
Apollinaire's 'Les Sept épées.' Symposium, 1977, 31:
17-42.

16,480. Kostyleff, Nicolas. Enquête sur le mécanisme de l'inspiration poétique. Le Grande Revue, 1912, 9:25, 10:10.

16,481. _____. Le Mécanisme d'un génie poétique. JPNP,
July-Oct 1912.

16,482. Koyama, K. [Religious consciousness of antique Japanese
as manifested in poems of Kokin-Shû.] Japanese J
Psychol, 1930, 5:19-40.

16,483. Kraetzer, Arthur F. (ed). Psychoanalytic notes. In
Baudelaire, C., The Flowers of Evil. NY: Smith,
1950.

16,484. Krebs, Edgar. Das Unbewusste in den Dichtungen Conrad
Ferdinand Meyers. Psychoanalytische Bewegung, 1930,
2:325-338.

16,485. Krejcik, N. Experimentalphonetische Untersuchungen über
einige wichtige Formen des Vierschlägers im deutschen
Vers. Archiv für die gesamte Psychologie, 1928, 64:
453-462.

16,486. Kries, J. V. Goethe als Psycholog. Tübingen: Mohr,
1924.

16,487. Krijgers Janzen, E. ['Deja vu' and 'depersonalisatie.'
Two poems by Achterberg. A confrontation with clinical phenomenology.] Nederlands Tijdschrift Psychologie, 1966, 21:136-147.

16,488. Krippendorf, Ilse. Rainer Maria Rilke, Psyche und Werk
II. Die Dichtung als Spiegel der Personlichkeit. Zeitschrift für Psychotherapie und medizinische Psychologie, 1952, 2:110-122.

16,489. Kučera, Otakar. The mechanism of regression in the poetry of Baudelaire and his followers. Int J Psycho-
Anal, 1950, 31:98-102.

16,490. _____. [The nature, the mechanisms and the function
of creative art.] Sborník Psychoanaltických Prací,
1947, 2:101-157.

16,491. _____. [The origin of a 'poet maudit': Ducasse-
Lautreamont.] Sborník Psychoanalytických Prací, 1948,
3:125-142.

16,492. Kuhn, Reinhard C. The hermeneutics of silence: Michaux
         and mescaline. Yale French Studies, 1974, 50:130-141.
16,493. Kung, T. [Nature of 400 Drugs in Verses, with Vernacular
         Interpretations.] Peking: Jen min wei sheng ch'u pan
         she, 1972.
16,494. Kuplis, Aija. The Image of Woman in Bertolt Brecht's
         Poetry. DAI, 1976, 37:3661A-62A.
16,495. Kuppuswamy, B. Identity crisis in Rama according to
         Yogavasishta. J Psychol Researches, 1977, 21:158-165.
16,496. Kurz, Paul Konrad. Identity and society: the world of
         Max Frisch. In On Modern German Literature, Vol. 2.
         University: University Alabama Press, 1970-71, 104-
         154.
16,497. _____. The individual's awareness of self and world
         as manifested in German lyric poetry since 1945. In
         On Modern German Literature, Vol. 3. University:
         University Alabama Press, 1973, 65-73.
16,498. Kwinn, David. Meredith's psychological insight in 'Modern
         Love' XXIII. Victorian Poetry, 1969, 7:151-153.
16,499. Kyritz, Heinz-Georg. Das Unbewusste im Dichtungserleb-
         nis Agnes Miegels. German Q, 1971, 44:58-68.

16,500. LaBarre, Weston. The psychopathology of drinking songs:
         a study of the content of the 'normal' unconscious.
         Psychiatry, 1939, 2:203-212.
16,501. LaBelle, J. Theodore Roethke's 'The Lost Son': from
         archetypes to literary history. Modern Language Q,
         1976, 37:179-195.
16,502. La Rue, R. Whitman's sea: large enough for Moby
         Dick. Walt Whitman Rev, 1966, 12:51-59.
16,503. Lackey, Allen D. Chaucer's Troilus and Criseyde, IV.
         295-301. Explicator, 1973, 32:Item 5.
16,504. Ladimer, Bethany. Madness and the irrational in the work
         of André Breton: a feminist perspective. Feminist
         Studies, 1980, 6(1):175-195.
16,505. Lalli, Biancamaria Tedeschini. Emily Dickinson, Pros-
         pettive Critiche. Florence: Le Monnier, 1963.
16,506. Lalo, Charles. L'Analyse esthétique d'un oeuvre d'art;
         essai sur les structures et la supra-structure de la
         poésie. JPNP, 1946, 39:259-282.
16,507. Lanati, Barbara. Emily Dickinson: La mia lettera al
         mondo. In Emily Dickinson: Poesie. Rome: Savelli,
         1976.
16,508. Lancashire, Ian. Sexual innuendo in the Reeve's Tale.
         Chaucer Rev, 1972, 6:159-170.
16,509. Land, Stephen K. Coleridge, Freud, and the 'Tribe of
         Asra.' Lit & Psychol, 1972, 22:49-50.
16,510. Landy, Marcia. Kinship and the role of women in Para-
         dise Lost. Milton Studies, 1972, 4:3-18.
16,511. _____. Language and mourning in 'Lycidas.' Amer
         Imago, 1973, 30:294-312.
16,512. Lane, Gary M. I Am: A Study of E. E. Cummings'
         Poems. Lawrence: Univ. Kansas Press, 1976.

16, 513. _____. Sylvia Plath's The Hanging Man: a further
note. Contemporary Poetry, 1975, 2:40-43.

16, 514. Langbaum, Robert Woodrow.   The new nature poetry.
Amer Scholar, 1959, 28:323-340.

16, 515. _____. The Poetry of Experience: The Dramatic Monologue in Modern Literary Tradition.   NY: Random
House, 1957.

16, 516. Lange, S.   Haiku in psychiatric nursing education.   Nursing
Outlook, 1964, 12:52-53.

16, 517. Langer, Susanne.   'Expressive language' and the expressive function of poetry.   In Werner, H. (ed), On Expressive Language.   Worcester: Clark Univ.   Press,
1959, 3-9.

16, 518. Langner, E.   Form-und Farbbeachtung und psychophysische
Konsstitution bei zeitgenössischen Dichtern.   Würzburg:
Stürtz, 1936.

16, 519. Lanham, Richard A.   Chaucer's 'Clerk's Tale':   the poem
not the myth.   Lit & Psychol, 1966, 16:157-165.

16, 520. Lapp, John C.   Mémoire: art et hallucination chez Rimbaud.   Cahiers de l'Association Internationale des
Etudes Françaises, 1971, 23:163-175.

16, 521. Larsen, Finn Stein.   Et forestillingsmønster i Per Langes
lyric.   Aarhus: Universitetsforlaget, 1964.

16, 522. Larson, Charles R.   Coleridge's 'Ancient Mariner' and the
Skinner Box.   CEA Critic, 1974, 37:21-22.

16, 523. Lasser, Michael I.   Sex and sentimentality in Whitman's
poetry.   Emerson Society Q, 1966, No. 43, 94-97.

16, 524. Laulan, R.   [A strange case of perversion of emotivity.
The obsession of the scaffold in Villiers de l'Isle-
Adams.]   Le Presse Médicale, 1959, 67:2325-2326,
2362-2363.

16, 525. Laurent, E.   La Poésie décadente devant la science psychiatrique.   Paris: Malone, 1897.

16, 526. Laurila, K. S.   Die psychoanalytische Auffassung von der
Dichtung.   Helicon, 1940, 3:159-165.

16, 527. Lavers, A.   The world as icon: on Sylvia Plath's themes.
In Newman, C. (ed), The Art of Sylvia Plath.   Bloomington: Indiana Univ.   Press, 1970, 100-135.

16, 528. Lavers, Norman.   Freud, 'The Clerk's Tale, ' and literary
criticism.   College English, 1964, 26:180-187.

16, 529. Lawson, Mildred.   Creative and sexual energy in Blake's
Milton.   Amer Notes & Queries, 1977, 15:68-70.

16, 530. Leaf, C.   Creative highlights in the life of Shaul Tchnerichovsky.   Hebrew Medical J, 1964, 1:238-239.

16, 531. Leavis, Frank Raymond.   'Thought' and emotional quality.
Notes in the analysis of poetry.   Scrutiny, 1945, 13:53-
71.

16, 532. Leavy, Stanley A.   John Keats's psychology of creative
imagination.   Psychoanal Q, 1970, 39(2):173-197.

16, 533. Le Comte, Edward S.   Milton and Sex.   NY: Columbia
Univ. Press, 1978.

16, 534. _____. Yet Once More: Verbal and Psychological Patterns in Milton.   NY: Columbia Univ. Press, 1953.

16, 535. Lee, Harry B. Poetry production as a supplemental emer-
          gency defense against anxiety. Psychoanal Q, 1938, 7:
          232-242.
16, 536. Lefcowitz, Barbara F. Omnipotence of thought and the
          poetic imagination: Blake, Coleridge, and Rilke.
          Psychoanal Rev, 1972, 59:417-432.
16, 537. _____. The Shaping Flame: Self, Nature, and Madness
          in the Poetry of Christopher Smart and William Blake.
          DAI, 1971, 31:4125A-26A.
16, 538. Leggett, B. J. The poetry of insight: persona and point
          of view in Housman. Victorian Poetry, 1976, 14:325-
          329.
16, 539. Lehmann, Herbert. A conversation between Freud and
          Rilke. Psychoanal Q, 1967, 35:423-427.
16, 540. Lehnert, Herbert. Alienation and transformation: Rilke's
          poem 'Der Schwan.' In Baron, F., Dick, E. S., &
          Maurer, W. R. (eds), Rilke: The Alchemy of Aliena-
          tion. Lawrence, Kans: Regents, 1980, 95-112.
16, 541. Lemaire, J. Jean Meschinot, précurseur de Maurice
          Scève? Studi Francesi, 1976, 58:72-76.
16, 542. Lemly, J. Masks and self-portraits in Jonson's late po-
          etry. J English Lit History, 1977, 44:248-266.
16, 543. Lensing, George S. Dickinson's 'I Started Early--Took
          My Dog.' Explicator, 1972, 31:Item 30.
16, 544. _____, & Moran, Ronald. Four Poets and the Emotive
          Imagination: Robert Blye, James Wright, Louis Simp-
          son, and William Stafford. Baton Rouge: Louisiana
          State Univ. Press, 1976.
16, 545. Lento, Takako U. The deathwish and the self in contem-
          porary American poetry. Kyushu Amer Lit (Japan),
          1978, 19:17-27.
16, 546. Leonhardt, Wilhelm. Liebe und Erotik in den Uranfängen
          der deutschen Dichtkunst. Dresden: Kraut, 1910.
16, 547. Leopold, K. B. The effect of creative work on aesthetic
          appreciation: an experiment in the teaching of poetry.
          British J Educational Psychol, 1933, 3:42-64.
16, 548. Lerner, Arthur. Psychoanalytically Oriented Criticism of
          Three American Poets: Poe, Whitman and Aiken.
          Teaneck, NJ: Fairleigh Dickinson Univ. Press, 1970;
          DAI, 1968, 28:1229A.
16, 549. Lerner, Laurence. Sex in Arcadia. In The Uses of Nos-
          talgia; Studies in Pastoral Poetry. NY: Schocken,
          1972, 81-104.
16, 550. Lervik, A. H. Ole Bulls dikt Ordene. Edda, 1973, 73:
          129-137.
16, 551. Lesser, Simon O. The Odyssey: the hidden dreams.
          Minnesota Rev, 1967, 4:293-303.
16, 552. _____. 'Sailing to Byzantium'--another voyage, another
          reading. College English, 1966, 28:291-310.
16, 553. Levi Bianchini, Marco. Die psychoanalytische Traumthe-
          orie in einem Distischon aus dem dritten nachchrist-
          lichen Jahrhundert. Int Zeitschrift für Psychoanalyse,
          1940, 25:409-417.

16, 554. Levin, Gerald. Swinburne's 'End of the World' fantasy. Lit & Psychol, 1974, 24:109-114.

16, 555. Levin, Harry. Clinical demonstrations on four poets. Saturday Rev Lit, 1949, 32, 15.

16, 556. Levine, Bernard. A psychopoetic analysis of Yeats's 'Leda and the Swan.' Bucknell Rev, 1969, 17:85-111.

16, 557. Levy, Lynne H. Piers Plowman and the Concept of Poverty. DAI, 1977, 37(12-A), 7740.

16, 558. Lévy-Volensi, J. L'Inspiration poétique et la psychopathologie. Hygiène Mentale, 1935, 30:21-42.

16, 559. Lewalski, Barbara K. Milton on women--yet once more. Milton Studies, 1974, 6:3-20.

16, 560. Lewis, Aubrey. The psychology of Shakespeare. In The State of Psychiatry. NY: Science House, 1967, 295-298.

16, 561. Lewis, B. R. Creative Poetry. Stanford, Cal: Stanford Univ. Press, 1931.

16, 562. Lewis, Dorothy O., & Lewis, Melvin. The psychoanalytic model of a dream used as poetic form: Valéry and Freud. Psychoanal Rev, 1976, 63:459-469.

16, 563. Leynardi, (?). La Psicologia dell'arte vella Divina Commedia. Turin: 1894.

16, 564. Libby, A. God's lioness and the priest of Sycorax: Plath and Hughes. Contemporary Lit, 1974, 15:386-405.

16, 565. _____. Roethke, water father. Amer Lit, 1974, 46: 267-288.

16, 566. Lima, Robert. Coitus interruptus: sexual transsubstantiation in the works of Jorge Luis Borges. Modern Fiction Studies, 1973, 19:407-418.

16, 567. Lindbäck, Eeland. [The poetry of Fröding in relation to contemporary social problems.] Edda, 1933, 18-57.

16, 568. Lindberg, Brita. The theme of death in Emily Dickinson's poetry. Studia Neophilologica, 1962, 34:269-281.

16, 569. Linde, B. J. D. van der. Zum Thema 'Die Träume der Dichter.' Int Zeitschrift für Psychoanalyse, 1913, 3: 465-466.

16, 570. Link, Franz. Identität und Identifizierung in Whitmans 'Song of Myself.' In Studien zur englischen und amerikanischen Sprache und Literatur. Neumünster: Wachholtz, 1974, 486-506.

16, 571. Lobel, R. Les Poètes de l'Afrique noire. Outremer, 1929, 1:366-374.

16, 572. Lobet, Marcel. Valéry psychanalysé. Rev Générale Belge, 1964, 100(9):135-137.

16, 573. Lodge, Ann. Satan's symbolic syndrome. Psychoanal Rev, 1956, 43:411-422.

16, 574. Logan, John. John Logan on poets and poetry today. Voyages, 1971-1972, 4(3-4), 17-24.

16, 575. Long, Charles H. The Quest Dialectic: The Jungian and Kierkegaarden Quest for Unity in W. H. Auden's 'The Quest,' New Year Letter, and For the Time Being. DAI, 1974, 34:5187A.

16, 576. Loriga, V. Sanguineti e l'avanguardia. Elsinore (Rome), 1964, 1(6).

16, 577. Lowell, Amy. Poetry and Poets. Boston: Houghton Mifflin, 1930.

16, 578. _____. To a gentleman who wanted to see the first drafts of my poem in the interest of psychological research into the workings of the creative mind. In Ballads for Sale. Boston: Houghton Mifflin, 1927.

16, 579. Lowes, John Livingston. The Road to Xanadu. Boston: Houghton Mifflin, 1927.

16, 580. Loya, Arieh. Poetry as a social document: the social position of the Arab woman as reflected in the poetry of Nizar Qabbani. Int J Middle East Studies, 1975, 6: 481-494.

16, 581. Lozynsky, Artem. S. Weir Mitchell on Whitman: an unpublished letter. Amer Notes & Queries, 1975, 13:120-121.

16, 582. _____. Walt Whitman on marriage. Notes & Queries, 1975, 22:120-121.

16, 583. Lucas, F. L. The Greatest Problem and Other Essays. NY: Macmillan, 1961.

16, 584. Lucie-Smith, Edward. Between suicide and revolution: the poet as role-player. Saturday Rev, 19 Apr 1975, 14-18.

16, 585. Luck, Georg. The woman's role in Latin love poetry. In Galinsky, G. K. (ed), Perspectives of Roman Poetry. Austin: Univ. Texas Press, 1974, 15-31.

16, 586. Luengo, Anthony E. Magic and illusion in 'The Franklin's Tale. ' J English Germanic Philology, 1978, 77:1-16.

16, 587. Lugiato, L. I personaggi della 'Divina Commedia' visti da un alienista. Parte I-II. Rome: Tip Ospedalia Psichiatria Provinca di Milano, 1932.

16, 588. Lujan, Lawrence J. A Psychology for Critics: Some Suggested Applications of Structural Principles Derived from Gestalt Psychology to an Understanding of Literature, Especially of English Romantic Poetry and Criticism. DAI, 1978, 39:900A.

16, 589. Luke, David. 'How is it that you live, and what is it that you do?': the question of old age in English romantic poetry. In Spicker, S. F. et al. (eds), Aging and the Elderly. Atlantic Highlands, NJ: Humanities Press, 1978, 221-240.

16, 590. Lungarini, E. Il segno in Dante: ipotesi sul primo libro del DVE. In Psicoanalisi e structuralismo di fronte a Dante. Vol. III: Incontro con le altre opere. Florence: Olschki, 1972, 79-86.

16, 591. Lupton, Mary Jane. A Psychoanalytic Study of the Poetry of Samuel Taylor Coleridge. DAI, 1909, 30:1530A-31A.

16, 592. _____. 'The Rime of the Ancient Mariner': the agony of thirst. Amer Imago, 1970, 27:141-159.

16, 593. Lussy, F. de. ['La Jeune parque.'] Rev des Lettres Modernes, 1977.

16, 594. Lynch, David. Yeats's Final Questions: A Psychological Study. DAI, 1974, 34:4270A.

16, 595. Lyon, Judson S. Romantic psychology and the inner senses: Coleridge. PMLA, 1966, 81:246-260.

16, 596. McAlpine, Monica E. The Pardoner's homosexuality and how it matters. PMLA, 1980, 95:8-22.

16, 597. MacCallum, H. R. Emotion and pattern in aesthetic experience. Monist, 1930, 40:53-72.

16, 598. McCanles, Michael. Love and power in the poetry of Sir Thomas Wyatt. Modern Language Q, 1968, 29:145-160.

16, 599. McCann, Janet. 'Prologues to What Is Possible': Wallace Stevens and Jung. Ball State Univ. Forum, 1976, 17: 46-50.

16, 600. McCarthy, Kevin M. 'Sameness' versus 'saneness' in Poe's 'Morella.' Amer Notes & Queries, 1973, 11:149-150.

16, 601. McClave, Heather. Situations of the Mind: Studies of Center and Periphery in Dickinson Stevens Ammons and Plath. DAI, 1975, 36:3715A.

16, 602. Maccoby, H. Z. A commentary on Burt Norton. Notes & Queries, 1968, 15:50-57.

16, 603. McCurdy, Harold H. The history of dream theory. Psychol Rev, 1946, 53:225-233.

16, 604. _____. La Belle Dans Sans Merci. Character & Personality, 1944, 13:166-177.

16, 605. Macdermott, M. M. Vowel sounds in poetry: their music and tone-colour. Psychol Monographs, 1940, No. 13.

16, 606. McDowell, Frederick P. W. Psychology and theme in Brother to the Dragons. PMLA, 1955, 70:565-586.

16, 607. McFadden, George. 'Life Studies': Robert Lowell's comic breakthrough. PMLA, 1975, 90:96-106.

16, 608. McGann, Jerome J. The significance of biographical context: two poems by Lord Byron. In Martz, L. L., & Williams, A. L. (eds), The Author in His Work. New Haven: Yale Univ. Press, 1978, 347-364.

16, 609. McGuire, Mary Ann C. A metaphorical pattern in Emily Dickinson. Amer Transcendental Q, 1976, 29(2):83-85.

16, 610. McHaney, Thomas L. Robinson Jeffers' 'Tamar' and The Sound and the Fury. Mississippi Q, 1969, 22:261-263.

16, 611. McHughes, Janet E. L. A Phenomenological Analysis of Literary Time in the Poetry of James Dickey. DAI, 1972, 33:2942A.

16, 612. McIntyre, Allan J. Romantic transcendence and the robot in Heinrich von Kleist and E. T. A. Hoffmann. Germanic Rev, 1979, 54:29-34.

16, 613. McLaughlin, Elizabeth. 'The Extasie'--deceptive or authentic? Bucknell Rev, 1970, 18:55-78.

16, 614. McLeod, James R. Bibliographic notes on the creative process and sources of Roethke's The Lost Son. Northwest Rev, 1971, 11:97-111.

16, 615. McManmon, John J. Phalli non erecti, feminae non fecundatae, et entia neutra. Antigonish Rev, 1971, 2(2): 63-72.

16, 616. McNab, C. (De Masirevich, C.). On the Four Quartets of T. S. Eliot. NY: Barnes & Noble, 1965, 1953.

16, 617. McShane, F. The new poetry. Amer Scholar, 1967-68, 37:642-646.

16, 618. Magliola, Robert R. Phenomenological Criticism: Its
Theory and Methodology, with Practical Applications to
the Poetry of Hart Crane and Charles Baudelaire.
DAI, 1971, 34:4127A-28A.

16, 619. Magnuson, Paul A. The Problems of Personal Identity
and Guilt in Coleridge's Poetry. DAI, 1970, 30:3466A-
67A.

16, 620. Mahoney, Patrick J. Ben Jonson's 'best piece of poetrie.'
Amer Imago, 1980, 37:69-82.

16, 621. _____. Shakespeare's sonnet number 20: its symbolic
gestalt. Amer Imago, 1979, 31:69-79.

16, 622. Mais, M. Troilus: a medieval psychoanalysis. Annuale
Mediaeviale, 1970, 11:81-88.

16, 623. Majdiak, Daniel, & Wilkie, Brian. Blake and Freud: poetry and depth psychology. J Aesthetic Education,
1972, 6:87-98.

16, 624. Major, Erich. Die Grundkrafte des dichterischen Schaffens. Leipzig: Klinckhardt und Biermann, 1913 (?).

16, 625. Major, Minor W. A new interpretation of Whitman's Calamus poems. Walt Whitman Rev, 1967, 13:51-54.

16, 626. Malkoff, Karl. Escape from the Self; a Study in Contemporary American Poets and Poetics. NY: Columbia
Univ. Press, 1977; Review: Sewanee Rev, 1979, 87:
308-313.

16, 627. _____. Theodore Roethke: An Introduction to the Poetry. NY: Columbia Univ. Press, 1966.

16, 628. Malmud, R. S. Poetry and the emotions, (1) a dilemma
for critics, (2) experimental verification. J Abnormal
Social Psychol, 1928, 22:443-472.

16, 629. _____. The poetry of promise. J Educational Psychol,
1930, 21:527-544.

16, 630. Malpique, Cruz. Psicologia barroca do poeta Mário de
Sá-Carneiro e una breve referência a Fernando Pessoa.
Boletin da Biblioteque Pública Municipale de Matosinhos,
1963, 10:9-43.

16, 631. Mandel, Barrett J. Artistry and psychology in William
Cowper's Memoir. Texas Studies in Lit & Language,
1970, 12:431-442.

16, 632. Mann, John S. Dream in Emily Dickinson's poetry.
Dickinson Studies, 1978, 34:19-26.

16, 633. Manning, Peter J. Byron and His Fictions. Detroit:
Wayne State Univ. Press, 1978.

16, 634. Mannoni, Octave. Poesia e psicoanalisi. Il Verri, 1968,
28:20-43; Poésie et psychanalyse. Psychanalyse, 1957,
3:139-163.

16, 635. Marcel, Jean, & Mezei, Arpad. Le Rêve dans les chants
de Maldoror. Arts et Lettres, 1948, 11:56-59.

16, 636. Marcovitz, Eli. Bemoaning the lost dream: Coleridge's
'Kubla Khan' and addiction. Int J Psycho-Anal, 1964,
45:411-425.

16, 637. Marcus, Mordecai. On Emily Dickinson's 'Not with a
club the heart is broken.' Explicator, 1962, 20(7),
No. 54.

16, 638. _____. Psychoanalytic approaches to Frost's 'Mending Wall. ' In Gibbs, K. (ed), Studies in the Poetry of Robert Frost. Boston: Hall, 1979.

16, 639. _____. The whole pattern of Robert Frost's 'Two Witches': contrasting psychosexual modes. Lit & Psychol, 1976, 26:69-78.

16, 640. Margitic, M. R. Paysages et sexualité chez Laforgue. Romantisme, 1977, 15:82-91.

16, 641. Marin, L. Purgatorio, Canto IX. In Psicoanalisi e structuralismo di fronte a Dante. Vol. II: Lettura della 'Commedia. ' Florence: Olschki, 1972, 1-73.

16, 642. Marsden, Dora. Lingual psychology. Egoist, 1916, 3:95-102.

16, 643. Marsh, Florence G. Wordsworth's 'Ode': obstinate questionings. Studies in Romanticism, 1966, 5:219-243.

16, 644. Marshall, George, Jr. 'Evelyn Hope's Lover. ' Victorian Poetry, 1966, 4:32-34.

16, 645. Marshall, William H. Byron's Parisina and the function of psychoanalytic criticism. Personalist, 1961, 42:213-223.

16, 646. Martin, D. R. Attitudes of an age group to poetry. British J Educational Psychol, 1947, 17:51-52.

16, 647. Martin, Elizabeth P. Psychological Landscape in Fourteenth Century Poetry and Painting. DAI, 1973, 33: 6877A.

16, 648. Martin, H. Névrose et poésie. Et publicacion par Pères Comp de Jésus, 1898, 74:145-167, 338-361.

16, 649. Martin, Robert K. Conversion and identity: the 'Calamus' poems. Walt Whitman Rev, 1979, 25:59-66.

16, 650. _____. The Homosexual Tradition in American Poetry. Austin: Univ. Texas Press, 1979; Review: John M. Clum, Amer Lit, 1980, 52:323-324.

16, 651. _____. Whitman's 'The Sleepers, ' 33-35. Explicator, 1974, 33, Item 13.

16, 652. _____. Whitman's 'Song of Myself': homosexual dream and vision. Partisan Rev, 1975, 42:80-96.

16, 653. Martin, W. Freud and imagism. Notes & Queries, 1961, 407-471, 474.

16, 654. Martindale, Colin. The evolution of English poetry. Poetics: Int Rev for Theory of Lit, 1978, 7(2).

16, 655. _____. Father's absence, psychopathology, and poetic eminence. Psychol Reports, 1972, 31:843-847.

16, 656. _____. Romantic Progression: The Psychology of Literary History. NY: Halsted/Wilet, 1975.

16, 657. [No entry. For Mais, see 16, 622]

16, 658. Maslenikov, Oleg A. The Frenzied Poets: Andrey Biely and the Russian Symbolists. Westport, Conn: Greenwood, 1968.

16, 659. Masson, Bernard. Musset et son double: Lecture de Lorenzaccio. Paris: Minard, 1978.

16, 660. _____. Relire les 'Nuits': Musset sous la lumière de Jung. Rev d'Histoire Littéraire de la France, 1976, 76(2):192-210.

16, 661. Mathewson, Jeanne T. For love and not for hate: the value of virginity in Chaucer's Physician's Tale. Annuale Mediaevale, 1973, 14:35-42.

16, 662. Mattfield, Mary S. Wilbur's 'The Puritans.' Explicator, 1970, 28.

16, 663. Mauron, Charles. Introduction a la psychanalyse de Mallarmé. L'Aliénation poétique. Temps Modernes, 1948, 36:455-478.

16, 664. _____. Introduction to the Psychoanalysis of Mallarmé. Berkeley: Univ. California Press, 1963; Neuchâtel: Baconnière, 1968, 1950; Reviews: Austin, L. J., Modern Language Rev, 1965, 453-455; Reck, R. D., South-Central Bulletin, 1965, 25(3):43-44; Robert Jouanny, Studi Francesi, 1964, 8:311-314.

16, 665. May, Rollo. Creativity and encounter. In Ruitenbeek, H. M. (ed), The Creative Imagination. Chicago: Quadrangle, 1965, 283-291; Amer J Psychoanal, 1964, 24: 39-45.

16, 666. Mayoral, M. Un recuerdo from La flor. Insula, 1969, 275-276(1):12-13.

16, 667. Mazzariol, Ferruccio. La personalitá poetica di Nicola Lisi. Studium, 1972, 68:296-309.

16, 668. Mazzaro, Jerome. John Berryman and the Yeatsian mask. Rev Existential Psychol & Psychiat, 1973, 12:141-162.

16, 669. _____. Theodore Roethke and the failures of language. Modern Poetry Studies, 1970, 1:73-96.

16, 670. _____. Ventures into evening: self-parody in the poetry of John Logan. Salmagundi, 1968, 2(4):78-95.

16, 671. _____. William Carlos Williams: The Later Poems. Ithaca, NY: Cornell Univ. Press, 1973.

16, 672. Mecke, Gunter. [The Ligurinus-shock: a narcissistic puberty crisis and its return in a fifty-year old man.] Psyche, 1975, 29:421-444.

16, 673. Meerwein, Fritz. Über Ursprung, Inhalt und Form banalet Gedichte Schizophrener. Schweizer Archiv für Neurologie und Psychiatrie, 1950, 66:261-318.

16, 674. Mehlman, Jeffrey. Baudelaire with Freud: theory and pain. Diacritics, 1974, 4:7-13.

16, 675. _____. On tear-work: L'art de Valéry. Yale French Studies, 1975, 52:152-173.

16, 676. Mehnert, Henning. Alfred de Mussets Lorenzaccio und die psychologische Motivation des Dandy-Dichters. Romanisches Jahrbuch, 1975, 26:122-126.

16, 677. Mehrotra, R. R. Wordsworth and the psychology of childhood. Criticism and Research, 1964, 84-91.

16, 678. Meiners, R. K. On modern poetry, poetic consciousness, and the madness of poets. In Sugarman, S. (ed), Evolution of Consciousness: Studies in Polarity. Middletown, Conn: Wesleyan Univ. Press, 1976, 106-120.

16, 679. Meinert, Monica. Der soziale und psychologische Hintergrund zur Entstehung des frühen deutschen Minnesangs. Acta Germanica, 1969, 4:3-15.

16, 680. Meissner, William. The rise of the angel: life through death in the poetry of Sylvia Plath. Massachusetts Studies in English, 1971, 3(2):34-39.

16, 681. Melchiori, Barbara. Browning's Don Juan. Essays in Criticism, 1966, 16:416-439.

16, 682. _____. Browning's Poetry of Reticence. NY: Barnes & Noble, 1968.

16, 683. Mellor, Anne Kostelanetz. Physiognomy, phrenology, and Blake's visionary heads. In Essick, R. N., & Pearce, D. R. (eds), Blake in His Time. Bloomington: Indiana Univ. Press, 1978, 53-74.

16, 684. Meltzer, François. On Rimbaud's 'Voyelles.' Modern Philology, 1979, 76:344-354.

16, 685. Mendel, Sydney. Dissociation of sensibility. Dalhousie Rev, 1971, 51:218-227.

16, 686. Meneghini, L. C. [Creativity and poetry: a psychoanalytic approximation.] Revista Brasileira de Psicánalise, 1977, 11:171-204.

16, 687. Menemencioglu, Melahat. L'Automatisme psychique dans le poème hermétique. Cahiers de l'Association Internationale des Etudes Françaises, 1963, 15:141-149.

16, 688. Merewether, John A. 'The Burning Chain'--The Paradoxical Nature of Love and Women in Byron's Poetry. DAI, 1971, 32:2699A.

16, 689. Merquior, José Guilherme. Psicoanálisis y Literatura. (Una Interpretación de la Poesía de João Cabral de Melo Neto.) Revista de Cultura Brasileña, 1976, 41: 5-19.

16, 690. Merriman, James D. The poet as heroic thief: Tennyson's 'The Hesperides' reexamined. Victorian Newsletter, 1969, No. 35:1-5.

16, 691. Mersch, Arnold. Themes of Loneliness and Isolation in the Poetry of Robert Frost. DAI, 1970, 30:3470A.

16, 692. Messer, Richard. Jeffers' inhumanism: a vision of the self. In Crow, C. L. (ed), California Writers. Bowling Green, Ohio: Bowling Green Univ. Press, 1978, 11-19.

16, 693. Mester, Ludwig. Die Seele in der Bewegung. Sammlung, 1953, 8:238-252.

16, 694. Metcalf, John T. Psychological studies of literary form. Psychol Bulletin, 1938, 35:337-357.

16, 695. Mettra, Paul. Un Pessimisme irrémédiable. Nouvelles Littéraires, 1971, 29:8.

16, 696. Meyer, Adolf F. Träumen, Denken und Dichten. Gegenwart (Heidelberg), 9 Mar 1912.

16, 697. Meyers, Jeffrey. The personality of Belinda's baron: Pope's The Rape of the Lock. Amer Imago, 1969, 26: 71-77.

16, 698. _____. Yeats' 'Blood and the Moon.' Explicator, 1972, 30:Item 50.

16, 699. Meyers, Joyce. 'Childe Roland to the Dark Tower Came': a nightmare confrontation with death. Victorian Poetry, 1970, 8:335-339.

16, 700.   Meyers, Robert.   Ode: intimations of immortality from
           recollections of early childhood.   Explicator, 1969, 28.
16, 701.   Michaels, Leonard.   Byron's 'Cain. '   PMLA, 1969, 84: 71-
           78.
16, 702.   Mickel, Emanuel John.   Baudelaire's changing view of the
           artificial paradises.   Romance Notes, 1971, 12: 318-325.
16, 703.   Mileck, Joseph.   Wolfgang Borchert: 'Draussen vor der
           Tur': a young poet's struggle with guilt and despair.
           Monatshefte, 1959, 51: 328-336.
16, 704.   Miles, Josephine.   The Vocabulary of Poetry; Three Stud-
           ies.   Berkeley: Univ. California Press, 1946.
16, 705.   Miller, Edwin Haviland.   'The Sleepers, ' in Miller, E. H.
           (ed), A Century of Whitman Criticism.   Bloomington:
           Indiana Univ. Press, 1969.
16, 706.   _____. Walt Whitman's poetry.   Amer Lit Scholarship,
           1968, 52-53.
16, 707.   _____. Walt Whitman's Poetry: A Psychological Jour-
           ney.   Boston: Houghton Mifflin, 1968; NY: New York
           Univ. Press, 1969; Reviews: Arthur Golden, Lit &
           Psych, 1969, 19: 61-65 & 1970, 20: 83-92; Hershel Park-
           er, Modern Language Q, 1975, 33: 54-66.
16, 708.   Miller, F. Dewolfe.   Emily Dickinson: self-portrait in the
           third person.   New England Q, 1973, 46: 119-124.
16, 709.   Miller, James E. , Jr.   Four cosmic poets.   Univ. Kansas
           City Rev, 1957, 23: 312-320.
16, 710.   _____. Walt Whitman's omnisexual vision.   In Bruc-
           coli, M. J. (ed), The Chief Glory of Every People: Es-
           says on Classic American Writers.   Carbondale: South-
           ern Illinois Univ. Press, 1973, 231-259, 283-285.
16, 711.   Miller, Lewis Holmes.   William James, Robert Frost, and
           'The Black Cottage. '   In Tharpe, J. (ed), Frost: Cen-
           tennial Essays III.   Jackson: Univ. Press Mississippi,
           1978, 368-381.
16, 712.   Miller, R. Baxter.   'No Crystal Stair': unity, archetype,
           and symbol in Langston Hughes's poems on women.
           Negro Amer Lit Forum, 1975, 9: 109-114.
16, 713.   Miller, Ralph N.   Associationist psychology and Stedman's
           theory of poetry.   Markham Rev, 1976, 5: 65-71.
16, 714.   Miller, Tracey R.   The boy, the bird and the sea: an
           archetypal reading of 'Out of the Cradle. '   Walt Whit-
           man Rev, 1973, 19: 93-103.
16, 715.   Millhauser, Milton.   A plurality of after-worlds: Isaac
           Taylor and Alfred Tennyson.   Hartford Studies in Lit,
           1969, 1: 37-49.
16, 716.   Mills, Ralph J. , Jr.   Creations Very Self: On the Per-
           sonal Element in Recent American Poetry.   Fort Worth:
           Texas Christian Univ. Press, 1969.
16, 717.   _____. _____.   In Cry of the Human; Essays on
           Contemporary American Poetry.   Urbana: Univ. Illi-
           nois Press, 1975, 1-47.
16, 718.   _____. Donald Hall's poetry.   Iowa Rev, 1971, 2: 82-
           123.
16, 719.   _____. Poems of the deep mind.   Tennessee Poetry J,
           197, 4(2): 16-25.

16, 720.   Mills, William.   The Stillness in Moving Things: The
            World of Howard Nemerov.   Memphis, Tenn: Memphis
            State Univ. Press, 1975.
16, 721.   Milne, Fred.   'Pantisocracy': a reflection of Coleridge's
            opium use?   English Language Notes, 1972, 9:177-182.
16, 722.   Minaty, W.   Ernst Stadler und die erotische Motivik in
            seiner 'Aufbruch-Dichtung.'   Sprachkunst, 1974, 5:33-
            48.
16, 723.   Minot, Walter S.   Millay's 'ungrafted tree': the problem
            of the artist as woman.   New England Q, 1975, 48:260-
            269.
16, 724.   Mintz, Thomas.   The psychology of a nursery rhyme.
            Amer Imago, 1966, 23:22-47.
16, 725.   Mirek, Roman.   [Psychiatric problems in Shakespeare's
            sonnets.]   Przeglad Lekarski, 1968, 24:885-886; 1970,
            26:344-347.
16, 726.   Mirmina, Emilia.   Esame psicologico della poesi di Pas-
            coli.   Iniziative, 1962, 11(4):34-36.
16, 727.   Mishael, I.   Shaul Tchnerichovsky among his brethren.
            Hebrew Medical J, 1964, 1:239-242.
16, 728.   Mitchell, Robert L.   From heart to spleen: the lyrics of
            pathology in nineteenth-century French poetry.   In
            Peschel, E.R. (ed), Medicine and Literature.   NY:
            Watson, 1980, 153-159.
16, 729.   Mivata, Bosi.   Über den Nihilismus des Dichters Bashio.
            Zeitschrift für Psychoanalyse (Tokyo), 1938, 6.
16, 730.   Mizejewski, Linda.   Images of woman in Wallace Stevens.
            Thoth, 1973-74, 14(1):13-21.
16, 731.   Modiano, Raimonda.   Coleridge's views on touch and other
            senses.   Bulletin of Research in the Humanities, 1978,
            81:28-41.
16, 732.   Molinari, R.   Il commento dantesco di Giovanni da Serra-
            valle.   In Psicoanalisi e structuralismo di fronte a
            Dante.   In Vol. I: Premesse.   Florence: Olschki,
            1972, 503-528.
16, 733.   Mollinger, Robert N.   The hero as poetic image.   Psychol
            Perspectives, 1974, 5(1):60-66.
16, 734.   _____.   Psychic images and poetic technique in Dom
            Moraes' poetry.   World Lit Written in English, 1975,
            14:357-370.
16, 735.   _____.   A symbolic complex: images of death and
            daddy in the poetry of Sylvia Plath.   Descant, 1975,
            19(2):44-52.
16, 736.   Moncel, Christian.   Exposé de poétique.   De quelques
            phénomènes psychologiques: description et théorie ex-
            périmentale.   Riorges: Moncel, 1977.
16, 737.   Monrad, M.J.   Über den psychologischen Ursprung der
            Poesie und Kunst.   Archiv für dem systematische Phi-
            losophie, 1895, 1:347-362.
16, 738.   Montanari, F.   Poesia e teologia nella Commedia di Dante.
            In Premesse, Vol. 1.   Florence: Olschki, 405-410.
16, 739.   Montgomery, Marion.   The Reflective Journey Toward Or-
            der; Essays on Dante, Wordsworth, Eliot, and Others.
            Athens: Univ. Georgia Press, 1973, 265-282.

16, 740.   Moore, Merrill.   A brief 'psychoanalysis' of The Noise
           That Time Makes.   Lit & Psychol, 1953, 3(5):7-8.
16, 741.   _____.   Concerning the creative process in literature.
           In Hoch, P. H., & Ziebin, J. (eds), Experimental Psy-
           chopathology.   NY: Grune & Stratton, 1957, 120-128.
16, 742.   _____.   Notes on a limerick.   Amer Imago, 1956, 13:
           147-148.
16, 743.   Moore, Robert N., Jr.   Aggression in the Poetry of
           James Dickey.   DAI, 1974, 34:5195A.
16, 744.   Moore, Thomas V.   The Hound of Heaven.   Psychoanal
           Rev, 1918, 5:345-366.
16, 745.   Morales, Rafael.   Vincente Aleixandre en su verso y en
           su prosa.   La Estafeta Literaria, 1969, No. 420, 8-10.
16, 746.   Moran, Ronald, & Lensing, George.   The emotive imagina-
           tion: a new departure in American poetry.   Southern
           Rev, 1967, 3:51-67.
16, 747.   Morel, Jean-Pierre.   Aurélia, Gradiva X: Psychanalyse
           et poésie dans Les Vases communicants.   Rev de Lit-
           térature Comparée, 1972, 46:68-89.
16, 748.   _____.   Breton and Freud.   Diacritics, 1972, 2(2):18-
           26.
16, 749.   Morey, Frederick L.   The four fundamental archetypes in
           mythology, as exemplified in Emily Dickinson's poems.
           Emily Dickinson Bulletin, 1973, 24:196-206.
16, 750.   _____.   Jungian Dickinson.   Emily Dickinson Bulletin,
           1975, 27:4-72.
16, 751.   Morgan, Kathleen Eiluned.   The analysis of guilt: poetry
           of W. H. Auden.   In Christian Themes in Contemporary
           Poets.   Chester Springs, Pa: Dufour, 1965, 92-122.
16, 752.   Morrill, P. H.   Psychological Aspects of the Poetry of Ed-
           ward Arlington Robinson.   Doctoral dissertation, North-
           western Univ., 1956.
16, 753.   Morris, David B.   The kinship of madness in Pope's Dun-
           ciad.   Philological Q, 1972, 51:813-831.
16, 754.   Morrow, Patrick.   Denise Levertov's 'The Five Day Rain.'
           Notes on Contemporary Lit, 1972, 2(1):4-6.
16, 755.   Mortari, I.   Da Jacopo della Lana all'Anonimo Fiorentino.
           In Psicoanalisi e structuralismo di fronte a Dante.
           Vol. I.   Premesse.   Florence: Olschki, 1972, 471-501.
16, 756.   Moskowitz, Moshe.   Bialik's Scroll of Five: the poet as
           sacrificer.   Amer Imago, 1976, 33:216-229.
16, 757.   Motola, Gabriel.   'The Waste Land': symbolism and
           structure.   Lit & Psychol, 1968, 18:205-214.
16, 758.   Moustakes, Clark E.   Loneliness.   Englewood Cliffs, NJ:
           Prentice-Hall, 1961, passim.
16, 759.   Moutote, Daniel.   L'Egotisme de Valéry.   Rev d'Histoire
           Littéraire de la France, 1978, 78:759-780.
16, 760.   _____.   [Theme of egotism in Valéry.]   Rev des Let-
           tres Modernes, 1974, Nos. 413-416.
16, 761.   Muchnic, Helen.   Poetry of loss.   In Russian Writers.
           NY: Random House, 1971, 100-113.
16, 762.   Mudford, P. G.   Sweeney among the nightingales.   Essays
           in Criticism, 1969, 19:285-291.

16, 763. Mudge, Jean McClure. Emily Dickinson and the Image of Home. Amherst: Univ. Massachusetts Press, 1975.

16, 764. Mudrick, Marvin. Cocteau's poem of childhood. Spectrum, 1957, 1(3):25-33.

16, 765. Mueller, William R. Psychoanalysis and poet: a note. Psychoanalysis, 1957, 5:55-66.

16, 766. Muggigrosso, R. M. Whitman and the adolescent mind. English J, 1968, 57:982-984.

16, 767. Muller, Armand. L'Art et la psychanalyse. Rev Française de Psychanalyse, 1953, 17:297-319.

16, 768. Müller-Freienfels, Richard. Psychologische Poetik. Aus Natur und Geisteswelt. Leipzig: Teubner, 1913.

16, 769. Mullican, James S. Dickinson's 'Water Makes Many Beds.' Explicator, 1968, 27:23.

16, 770. Mundinger, Gerhard H. The Acoustic and Optic Phenomena in the Poetic Works of Gottfried Keller. Doctoral dissertation, Univ. Wisconsin, 1951.

16, 771. Münter-Halle, F. Psychoanalyse und Dichtung. Int Zeitschrift für Psychoanalyse, 1913, 3:446-449.

16, 772. Murphy, B. W. Creation and destruction: notes on Dylan Thomas. British J Medical Psychol, 1968, 41:149-167.

16, 773. Murphy, J. The primitive character of poetic genius. Man, 1942, 37-41.

16, 774. Murphy, Michael W. Violent imagery in the poetry of Gerard Manley Hopkins. Victorian Poetry, 1969, 7:1-16.

16, 775. Murray, F. W. La imagen arquetípica en la poesía de R. López Veldarde. Chapel Hill, NC: Hispanófila, 1972.

16, 776- Murray, Henry A. Conrad Aiken: poet of creative dis-
7.   solution. Perspectives, U. S. A., 1953, No. 5, 27-36; Wake, 1952, 11:95-106.

16, 778. Murry, J. Middleton. Studies in Keats. London: Oxford Univ. Press, 1930.

16, 779. Murtaugh, Daniel M. Women and Geoffrey Chaucer. J English Lit History, 1971, 38:473-492.

16, 780. Muschg, Walter. Dichtung als archaisches Erbe. Imago, 1933, 19:99-112; Almanach, 1934, 117-138.

16, 781. Musial, Thomas J. The two heroes, two bards and two worlds of The Odyssey. Sewanee Rev, 1968, 76:106-116.

16, 782. Myers, Karen M. Female Archetypes in Selected Longer Poems of Shelley. DAI, 1978, 38:4850A-51A.

16, 783. Näcke, P. Zur homosexuellen Lyrik. Archiv für Kriminalanthropologie und Kriminalistik, 1902, 10.

16, 784. Nash, Charles Crawford. Women and the female principle in the works of William Carlos Williams. Publications Missouri Philological Assn, 1978, 3:91-100.

16, 785. Nef, W. Die Lyrik als besondere Dichtungsgattung. Ein Beitrag zur psychologischen Grundlegung der Aesthetik. Zurich: 1899.

16, 786. Nelson, Cary. Suffered-encircling shapes of mind: in-
          habited space in Williams. J Modern Lit, 1970, 1:549-
          564.
16, 787. Nelson, Charles Alan. Patterns of Water Imagery in Walt
          Whitman's Leaves of Grass. DAI, 1975, 35:4444A-45A.
16, 788. Nethercot, Arthur H. The Road to Tryermaine; A Study
          of the History, Background, and Purposes of Coleridge's
          Christabel. Chicago: Univ. Chicago Press, 1939;
          Cambridge: Cambridge Univ. Press, 1940.
16, 789. Neumann, Annemarie. Digest of Rank's articles on Hom-
          er. J Otto Rank Assn, 1969, 4(1):79-80.
16, 790. Neuss, Paula. Double meanings: I. Double entendre in
          The Miller's Tale. Essays in Criticism, 1974, 24:325-
          340.
16, 791. Neumarkt, Paul. Hartmann von Aue: the psychologism of
          a medieval poet. Amer Imago, 1973, 30:157-176.
16, 792. Newman, C. Candor is the only wile: the art of Sylvia
          Plath. Triquarterly, 1967, 7:39-64.
16, 793. _____ (ed). The Art of Sylvia Plath. Bloomington:
          Indiana Univ. Press, 1970.
16, 794. Newman, Francis X. House of Fame, 7-12. English Lan-
          guage Notes, 1968, 6(1):5-12.
16, 795. Newman, Israel. The physiology of consciousness and its
          relation to poetry. Poetry, 1948, 72:96-102, 162-166.
16, 796. Newton, Nancy. Myth and Self in the Poetry of Antonio
          Machado. DAI, 1973, 33:3661A.
16, 797. Nicholes, Eleanor L. The Shadowed Mind: The Influence
          of the Schizophrenic Process on the Process of the Po-
          etry of John Clare. Doctoral dissertation, New York
          Univ., 1950.
16, 798. Niederland, William S. The symbolic river-sister equa-
          tion in poetry and folklore. J Hillside Hospital, 1957,
          6:91-99.
16, 799. Niedermann, Julius. Der Dichter als Analytiker. Int
          Zeitschrift für Psychoanalyse, 1913, 4:102-103.
16, 800. Nigro, D. Death and suicide in modern lyrics. Suicide,
          1975, 5:232-245.
16, 801. Nims, J. The poetry of Sylvia Plath: a technical analy-
          sis. In Newman, C. (ed), The Art of Sylvia Plath.
          Bloomington: Indiana Univ. Press, 1970, 136-152.
16, 802. Nissen, T. Die Physiologie und Psychologie der Furcht
          in der Odyssee. Archiv für die gesamte Psychologie,
          1925, 52:177-194.
16, 803. Nist, John. The art of Chaucer: pathedy. Tennessee
          Studies in Lit, 1966, 11:1-10.
16, 804. Nitchie, George W. Human Values in the Poetry of Robert
          Frost. Durham: Duke Univ. Press, 1960.
16, 805. Noferi, A. Il Canzoniere del Petrarch: scrittura del
          desiderio e desiderio della scrittura. Paragone, 1974,
          296:3-24.
16, 806. Noland, Richard W. Psychoanalysis and Yeats. Hartford
          Studies in Lit, 1975, 7:33-47.

16, 807. Nollendorfs, Valters.   The rite of life: a theme and its
          variations in the poetry of Soviet Latvia.   Mosaic,
          1973, 6(4):199-208.
16, 808. Noonan, Paula E.   The nature of dream experience in
          Keats's narrative poetry.   Gypsy Scholar, 1976, 3:84-
          95.
16, 809. Norman, Sylvia.   Twentieth-century theories on Shelley.
          Texas Studies in Lit Language, 1967, 9:223-237.
16, 810. Norton, G. P.   Contrapasso and archetypal metamorphoses
          in the seventh bolgia of Dante's Inferno.   Symposium,
          1971, 25:162-170.
16, 811. Noval, Martin.   The Unconscious in Freud and Breton.
          DAI, 1974, 34:6703.

16, 812. Oates, Joyce Carol.   When they all are sleeping.   Modern
          Poetry Studies, 1973, 4:341-344.
16, 813. Obermüller, K.   Zur Melancholie in der barocken Lyrik.
          Bonn: Bouvier, 1974.
16, 814. O'Connor, William V., & Stone, Edward (eds).   A Case-
          book on Ezra Pound.   NY: Crowell, 1959.
16, 815. Odier, Charles.   A literary portrayal of ambivalence.
          Int J Psycho-Anal, 1923, 4:321-322.
16, 816. Ogilvie, John T.   From woods to stars: a pattern of
          imagery in Robert Frost's poetry.   South Atlantic Q,
          1959, 58:64-76.
16, 817. O'Hear, Michael F.   The Constant Dream: Coleridge's
          Vision of Woman and Love.   DAI, 1971, 31:4174A-75A.
16, 818. O'Keefe, Mary Ellen.   John Donne's Preoccupation with
          Death: The Public and Private Voices.   DAI, 1977,
          38:2143A.
16, 819. Okerlund, Arlene N.   Spenser's wanton maidens: reader
          psychology and the bower of bliss.   PMLA, 1973, 88:
          62-68.
16, 820. Olney, James Leslie.   'A powerful emblem': the towers
          of Yeats and Jung.   South Atlantic Q, 1973, 72:494-
          515.
16, 821. _____.   The Rhizome and the Flower.   The Perennial
          Philosophy--Yeats and Jung.   Berkeley: Univ. Califor-
          nia Press, 1980.
16, 822. _____.   W. B. Yeats' daimonic memory.   Sewanee Rev,
          1977, 85:583-603.
16, 823. Olson, Paul R.   Circle of Paradox: Time and Essence in
          the Poetry of Juan Ramón Jimenez.   Baltimore: Johns
          Hopkins Univ. Press, 1967.
16, 824. O'Neal, Cothburn M.   The syndrome of masochism in
          Chaucer's Pardoner: synopsis of the Pardoner.   In
          Shockley, M. (ed), 1967 Proceedings of the Conference
          of College Teachers of English of Texas, Vol. 32.
          Lubbock: Texas Technicological College, 1967, 18-23.
16, 825. O'Neill, Y. V.   A speculation concerning the grain in
          Chaucer's 'Prioress's Tale. '   Medical History, 1968,
          12:185-190.

16, 826. Onimus, J. Pour lire 'Répétitions' de P. Eluard. L'In-
          formation Littéraire, 1973, 1:18-25.
16, 827. Ossipoff, N. [The double Petersburg poem by Dostoevsky.]
          In Collection Dostoevskii. Prague: Otto, 1929, 39-63.
16, 828. Oster, G. D. Guillaume Apollinaire. Paris: Seghers,
          1975.
16, 829. Ostriker, Alicia. Body language: imagery of the body in
          women's poetry. In Michaels, L., & Ricks, C. (eds),
          The State of the Language. San Francisco: Univ.
          California Press, 1980, 247-263.
16, 830. Ostwald, Hans. Erotische Volkslieder aus Deutschland.
          Berlin: Verlag d Diskussion, 1913 (?).
16, 831. O'Sullivan, Maurice J. The mask of allusion in Robert
          Hayden's 'The Diver.' College Language Assn J, 1973,
          17:85-92.
16, 832. Owens, R. J. Intellect, music and emotion: a note on
          George Eliot's verse. George Eliot Fellowship Rev,
          1976, 7:15-17.
16, 833. Ower, John. Erotic mythology in the poetry of Tennessee
          Williams. In Tharpe, J. (ed), Tennessee Williams: A
          Tribute. Hattiesburg: Univ. Mississippi Press, 1977,
          609-623.
16, 834. Oxenhandler, Neal. Concealed emotions in the poetry of
          Max Jacob. Dada/Surrealism, 1975, 5:53-57.
16, 835. _____. The quest for pure consciousness in Husserl
          and Mallarmé. In Hardison, O. B. (ed), The Quest for
          Imagination; Essays in Twentieth-Century Aesthetic
          Criticism. Cleveland: Case Western Reserve Univ.
          Press, 1971, 149-166.
16, 836. Oyamada, Gibun. [Poe's World: From Poetry to the Uni-
          verse.] Tokyo: Schichosha, 1969.

16, 837. Pace, George B. Physiognomy and Chaucer's Summoner
          and Alisoun. Traditio, 1962, 18:289-317.
16, 838. Paden, W. D. Tennyson in Egypt. A Study of the Imagery
          in His Earlier Work. Lawrence: Univ. Kansas Publi-
          cations, 1942.
16, 839. Pagari, David Lee. Existentialism and the homosexual
          poet. One Institute Q, 1963, 6(3-4):46-57.
16, 840. Pagliaro, A. Il proemio del Poema sacro. In Lectura
          Dantis Mystica: Il poema sacro alla luce delle con-
          quiste psicologiche odierne. Florence: Olschki, 1969,
          3-28.
16, 841. _____. Proemio e prologo della Divina Commedia. In
          Lettura Classensi, Vol. 2. Ravenna: Longo, 1966(?),
          113-148.
16, 842. Pagnini, Marcello. Emily Dickinson, 'I never told the
          buried gold.' Un esempio di semiosi pluriisotopica.
          Strumenti Critici, 1976, 29:57-86.
16, 843. Pailthorpe, G. W. Primary processes of the infantile mind
          demonstrated through the analysis of a prose-poem.
          Int J Psycho-Anal, 1941, 22:44-59.

16, 844.   Palley, Julian.   Las secretas galerías de Antonio Machado.
           Cuadernos Americanos, 1975, 34:210-216.
16, 845.   Palomo, Dolores J.   The fate of the Wife of Bath's 'bad
           husbands.'   Chaucer Rev, 1975, 9(4):303-319.
16, 846.   Paolazzi, C.   Purgatorio, Canto I.   In Psicoanalisi e
           structuralismo di fronte a Dante, Vol. II.   Lettura
           della 'Commedia.'   Florence: Olschki, 1972.
16, 847.   Paolucci, Anne.   Women in the politic love ethic the Divine
           Comedy and the Faerie Queene.   Dante Studies, 1972,
           90:139-153.
16, 848.   Parent, M., & Parent, P.   [Themes of water and wind in
           Paul Valéry.]   Rev des Lettres Modernes, 1974, Nos.
           413-416.
16, 849.   Parkinson, Thomas.   The loneliness of the poet.   In Har-
           tog, J., Audy, J.R., & Cohen, Y.A. (eds), The Ana-
           tomy of Loneliness.   NY: IUP, 1980.
16, 850.   Parsons, James.   Myths, emotions, and the great audi-
           ence.   Poetry, 1950, 77:52-55.
16, 851.   Patrick, Catherine.   Creative thought in poets.   Archives
           of Psychol, 1935, 26:1-74; Psychol Bulletin, 1935, 32:
           572-573.
16, 852.   _____.   How responses to good and poor poetry differ.
           J Psychol, 1939, 8:253-283.
16, 853.   _____.   Whole and part relationships in creative thought.
           Amer J Psychol, 1944, 54:128-131.
16, 854.   Patterson, Rebecca.   The cardinal points symbolism of
           Emily Dickinson.   Midwest Q, 1973, 14:293-317, 15:31-
           48.
16, 855.   _____.   Emily Dickinson's palette.   Midwest Q, 1964,
           5:271-292; 6:97-117.
16, 856.   Paul, Sherman.   Hart's Bridge.   Urbana: Univ. Illinois
           Press, 1972.
16, 857.   Pavletti, L.   L'esegesi umanistica di Benvenuto da Imola.
           In Psicoanalisi e structuralismo di fronte a Dante.   Vol.
           I: Premesse.   Florence: Olschki, 1972, 445-470.
16, 858.   Pearce, Roy Harvey.   The Continuity of American Poetry.
           Princeton: Princeton Univ. Press, 1961.
16, 859.   Pearlman, E.   The psychological basis of the Clerk's Tale.
           Chaucer Rev, 1977, 11:248-257.
16, 860.   Pease, Donald.   The bridge: emotional dynamics of an
           epic of consciousness.   In French, W.G. (ed), The
           Twenties; Fiction, Poetry, Drama.   De Land, Fla:
           Everett/Edwards, 1975, 387-403.
16, 861.   Peck, John.   Perpetuae H.D.   Parnassus, 1975, 3(2):42-
           74.
16, 862.   Peck, Russell A.   Sovereignty and the two worlds of 'The
           Franklin's Tale.'   Chaucer Rev, 1967, 1:253-271.
16, 863.   Pederson-Krag, Geraldine.   The genesis of a sonnet.   In
           Psychoanalysis and the Social Sciences, Vol. 3.   NY:
           IUP, 1951, 263-276.
16, 864.   _____.   O Poesy! for thee I hold my pen.   In Wilbur,
           G., & Muensterberger, W. (eds), Psychoanalysis and
           Culture.   NY: IUP, 1951, 445-457; NY: Science Edi-
           tions, 1967, 436-454.

16, 865. Pedrini, Lura N., & Pedrini, Duilio T. Serpent imagery and symbolism in the major English romantic poets: Blake, Wordsworth, Coleridge, Byron, Shelley, Keats. Psychiat Q Supplement, 1960, 34:189-244; 1961, 35:36-99.

16, 866. Pelckmans, Paul. Salomé, une figure de l'anima. Essai de psycholecture du poeme 'Salomé.' Rev des Langues Vivantes, 1976, no. 1.

16, 867. Pennar, Meirion. Syniad 'Y Caredd Digerydd' ym marddoniseth Gymraeg yr Oesoedd Canol. Ysgrifau Beirniadol (Wales), 1976, 9:33-40.

16, 868. Peres, J. Anticipations des principes de la psychanalyse dans l'oeuvre d'un poète français, Jules Laforgue. JPNP, 1922, 19:921-927.

16, 869. Perlmutter, Elizabeth F. Hide and seek: Emily Dickinson's use of the existential sentence. Language & Style, 1977, 10:109-119.

16, 870. Perloff, Marjorie. Angst and animism in the poetry of Sylvia Plath. J Modern Lit, 1970, 1:57-74.

16, 871. Peschel, Enid Rhodes. Arthur Rimbaud: the aesthetics of intoxication. Yale French Studies, 1974, 50:65-80.

16, 872. _____. Flux and Reflux: Ambivalence in the Poems of Arthur Rimbaud. Geneva: Droz, 1977.

16, 873. Peterson, Carl A. Rossetti's A Last Confession as dramatic monologue. Victorian Poetry, 1973, 11:127-142.

16, 874. Petrie, Neil H. Psychic Disintegration in the Early Poetry of Tennyson. DAI, 1970, 30:70-5966.

16, 875. Pfeiffer, Ernst. Rilke psychoanalytisch: zu einer Kritik. Sammlung, 1959, 14:333-336.

16, 876. Philip, B. R. The effect of general and of specific labelling on judgmental scales. Canadian J Psychol, 1951, 5:18-28.

16, 877. Phillips, J. E. Walt Whitman, Philosopher, Psychologist, Prophet. NY: Phillips, 1953.

16, 878. Phillips, Robert. The Confessional Poets. Carbondale: Southern Illinois Univ. Press, 1973.

16, 879. _____. The dark funnel: a reading of Sylvia Plath. Modern Poetry Studies, 1972, 3:49-74; In The Confessional Poets. Carbondale: Southern Illinois Univ. Press, 1973, 6-14, 128-152.

16, 880. _____. Arrest for the unattainable: John Logan's anonymous lovers. Modern Poetry Studies, 1979, 9:178-186.

16, 881. Pickford, R. W. Rossetti's Sudden Light as an experience of déjà vu. British J Medical Psychol, 1942, 19:192-200.

16, 882. Pittfield, R. L. Chaucer's nervous depression. JMND, 1935, 82:30-32.

16, 883. Pittman, Philip McM. The strumpet and the snake. Rossetti's treatment of sex as original sin. Victorian Poetry, 1974, 12:45-54.

16, 884. Plank, Robert. Denial in interpreting a poem and in psychotherapy. Acta Psychotherapeutica, Psychosomatica et Orthopaedagogica, 1960, 8:365-377.

16, 885. Plotkin, Frederick. Natural fact and poetic insight. Hartford Studies in Lit, 1969, 1:71-82.

16, 886. Plunkett, P. M. Meredith's 'Modern Love, I. ' Explicator, 1970, 28.

16, 887. Poilvet Le Guenn, Jean. La Grande oeuvre architecturale d'un poète inspiré: étude critique, analytique et psychologique de l'épopée spiritualiste chrétienne des Cavaliers de Dieu de Wilfrid Lucas. Hautes-Alpes: Louis-Jean, 1961.

16, 888. Poleksić, J. L. [Analysis of some etho-psychiatric data of Njegos poetry.] Srpski Arhiv Celokupno Lekaritvo, 1976, 104:583-588.

16, 889. Politzer, Heinz. 'Cherubin. ' In Hüttner, J. , & Schindler, O. G. , (eds), Grillparzer-Forum Forchtenstein. Berlin: Böhlau: 1970.

16, 890. Pollak, Ellen. Rereading the Rape of the Lock: Pope and the paradox of female power. In Payne, H. C. (ed), Studies in Eighteenth-Century Culture, Vol. 10. Madison: Univ. Wisconsin Press, 1980.

16, 891. Pongs, Hermann. L'Image poétique et l'inconscient. J de Psychologie, 1933, 30:120-163.

16, 892. _____. Psychoanalyse und Dichtung. Euphorion, 1933, 34:38-72; In Beutin, W. (ed), Literatur und Psychoanalyse. Munich: Nymphenburger, 1972, 100-136.

16, 893. Porter, Laurence M. Artistic self-consciousness in Rimbaud's poetry. In Mitchell, R. L. (ed), Pre-text/Text/Context: Essays on Nineteenth-Century French Literature. Columbus: Ohio State Univ. Press, 1980.

16, 894. Porter, Peter. Poetry and madness. Southerly, 1976, 36:385-405.

16, 895. Poss, Stanley. Low skies, some clearing, local frost. New England Q, 1968, 41:438-442.

16, 896. Pottle, F. A. Wordsworth and Freud. Bulletin General Theology, 1948, 34.

16, 897. Powers, Richard Gid. Cummings' 'I Will Be. ' Explicator, 1970, 28(6):54.

16, 898. Pradines, Maurice. L'Antinomie de la raison scientifique: imagination et intuition. JPNP, 1949, 42:5-26.

16, 899. Prasad, Veena Ravi. Color-scheme in the poetry of Wallace Stevens. Indian J Amer Studies, 1976, 5(1-2):1-9.

16, 900. Pratt, Robert A. Some Latin sources of the Nonnes Preest on dreams. Speculum, 1977, 52:538-570.

16, 901. _____. Three old French sources of Nonnes Preestes Tale. Speculum, 1972, 47:422-444, 648-668.

16, 902. Predmore, M. P. The nostalgia for paradise and the dilemma of solipsism in the early poetry of Antonio Machado. Revista Hispánica Moderna, 1975, 38:30-52.

16, 903. Preger, J. W. A note on William Blake's lyrics. Int J Psycho-Anal, 1920, 1:196-199.

16, 904. Prescott, Frederic C. The Poetic Mind. NY: Macmillan, 1926.

16, 905. _____. Poetry and dreams. J Abnormal Psychol, 1912, 7:17-46, 104-43.

16,906. _____. Poetry and Myth. Port Washington, NY: Kennikat, 1967.

16,907. Prescott, J. F. The extensive medical writings of soldier-poet John McCrae. Canadian Medical Assn J, 1980, 122:110, 113-114.

16,908. Preston, Kerrison. Blake and Rossetti. London: Moring, 1944.

16,909. Price, John. Phedon's fury: some psychoanalytic notes on The Faerie Queen II, Canto IV. Lit & Psychol, 1976, 26:167-171.

16,910. _____. Wordsworth's 'Lucy.' Amer Imago, 1974, 31.

16,911. Prins, S. A. Gespräch über Psychoanalyse zwischen Frau, Dichter und Arzt. Celle: Kampmann, 1926; Heidelberg: Kampmann, 1927.

16,912. Profizi, J. Charles Baudelaire: Etude psychanalytique d'après 'Les Fleurs du Mal.' Paris: l'Athanor, 1974.

16,913. Proppe, Katherine Muller. Reason, Sensuality and John Skelton: Patristic Psychology and Literary Attitudes in the Late Medieval Period. DAI, 1975, 35:5358A-59A.

16,914. Protze, H. Der Baum als totemistisches Symbol in der Dichtung. Imago, 1917, 5:58-62.

16,915. Prudhomme, S. Qu'est-ce que la poésie? Rev de Deux Mondes, 1897, 143:597-605.

16,916. Przyluski, J. Le Rythme et l'improvisation poetique. JPNP, 1934, 31:801-808.

16,917. Pulley, Honor M. Note on Freud and Blake. Int J Psycho-Anal, 1925, 6:51-52.

16,918. Purekevich, Renate. Gottfried Benn, Arzt und Dichter. Zum Integralen seiner Persönlichkeit und zum Medizinisch-Naturwissenschaftlichen in seinem Werk. DAI, 1972, 1178A.

16,919. Putnam, B. I, my ego, and my identity. Perspectives in Psychiat Care, 1975, 13:176.

16,920. Pyne-Timothy, Helen. Perceptions of the black woman in the work of Claude McKay. College Language Assn J, 1975, 19:152-164.

16,921. Quaghebeur, Marc. Une Pathographie méconnue d'Arthur Rimbaud. Rev des Lettres Modernes, 1973, 370-73: 163-173.

16,922. Quill, Katherine M. The Poetry of Christina Rossetti: A Study in the Creative Imagination. DAI, 1977, 38: 3520A.

16,923. Quilligan, M. Words and sex: the language of allegory in the De planctu naturae, the Roman de la Rose, and Book II of The Faerie Queene. Allegorica, 1977, 2: 195-216.

16,924. Quinn, M. Bernetta. The Metamorphic Tradition in Modern Poetry. NY: Gordian, 1967.

16,925. _____. Paterson: landscape and dream. J Modern Lit, 1970, 1:523-548.

16,926. _____. Randall Jarrell: landscapes of life and 'Life.'
Shenandoah, 1969, 20:49-78.

16,927. Raben, J. Content analysis and the study of poetry. In
Gerbner, G., et al. (eds), The Analysis of Communication Content. NY: Wiley, 1969, 175-186.

16,928. Radcliff-Umstead, Douglas. Cainism and Gerard de Nerval.
Philological Q, 1966, 45:395-408.

16,929. Rader, Ralph W. Tennyson's 'Maud': The Biographical
Genius. Berkeley: Univ. California Press, 1963.

16,930. Radner, Susan G. Love and lover in Browning's 'Evelyn
Hope.' Lit & Psychol, 1966, 16:115-116.

16,931. Raleigh, John H. A new reading of 'Lycidas.' Prairie
Schooner, 1968-69, 42:303-318.

16,932. Ramond, Michèle. Romance de la lune, lune: naissance
et signification du thème gitan. Imprévue, 1977, 135-
167.

16,933. _____. Sujet psychique et sujet narrateur. Romance
de la lune, lune. In Sujet et sujet parlant dans le
texte. Toulouse: Le Mirail Univ. Presse, 1977, 63-
71.

16,934. Ramsey, J. Wordsworth and the childhood of language.
Criticism, 1976, 18:243-255.

16,935. Rands, Alma Clare. Thomas Brown's theories of association and perception as they relate to his theories of
poetry. JAAC, 1970, 28:473-483.

16,936. Rank, Otto. Ein Beispiel von poetischer Verwertung des
Versprechens. Int Zeitschrift für Psychoanalyse, 1910,
1:109-110.

16,937. _____. Die Don Juan Gestalt. Ein Beitrag zum Ver-
ständnis der sozialen Funktion der Dichtkunst. Imago,
1922, 8:142-196; Leipzig: Int Psychoanalytischer Verlag, 1924.

16,938. _____. The Don Juan Legend. Princeton: Princeton
Univ. Press, 1975.

16,939. _____. Don Juan und Leporello. Almanach, 1927, 172-
180.

16,940. _____. Der Doppelgänger; eine psychoanalytische Studie.
Imago, 1914, 3:97-164; In Psychoanalytische Beiträge
zur Mythenforschung. Leipzig: Int Psychoanalytische
Verlag, 1919, 267-354.

16,941. _____. Die "Geburts-Rettungsphantasie" in Traum und
Dichtung. Int Zeitschrift für Psychoanalyse, 1914, 2:43-
49.

16,942. _____. Ein gedichteter Traum. Int Zeitschrift für
Psychoanalyse, 1915, 3:231-235.

16,943. _____. Homer: psychologische Beiträge zur Entstehungsgeschichte des Volkepos. Imago, 1917, 3:133-169.

16,944. _____. Die Nackheit in Sage und Dichtung. Imago,
1913, 2:267-301, 409-446; In Psychoanalytische Beiträge
zur Mythenforschung. Leipzig: Int Psychoanalytischer
Verlag, 1919, 177-266; Psychoanal Rev, 1923, 10.

16,945. _____. 'Um Städte werben.' Int Zeitschrift für Psychoanalyse, 1914, 2:50-58; In Psychoanalytische Beiträge
zur Mythenforschung. Leipzig: Int Psychoanalytischer
Verlag, 1919, 164-176.

16,946. Ranson, John Crowe. The psychologist looks at poetry.
Virginia Q Rev, 1935, 11:575-592; In The World's Body.
NY: Scribner, 1938.

16,947. Rascovsky De Bisi, Nora. Rilke y el problema de la
muerte. Revista di Psicanálisi, 1963, 20:237-252.

16,948. Rashbook, R. F. Keats, Oberon and Freud. Notes &
Queries, 1951, 196:34-39.

16,949. Ray, David. The lightning of Randall Jarrell. Prairie
Schooner, 1961, 35:45-52.

16,950. Read, Herbert. The creative experience in poetry. In
The Forms of Things Unknown: Essays Toward an
Aesthetic Philosophy. NY: Horizon, 1960; In Grebstein, S. N. (ed), Perspectives in Contemporary Criticism. NY: Harper & Row, 1968, 284-293.

16,951. _____. Wordsworth. NY: Hillary, 1960.

16,952. Reece, James B. Poe's 'Dream-Land' and the imagery of
opium dreams. Poe Studies, 1975, 8:24.

16,953. Reed, Gail H. V. Chaucer's Women: Commitment and
Submission. DAI, 1974, 34:4215A-16A.

16,954. Reed, Michael D. Morris' 'Rapunzel' as an oedipal fantasy. Amer Imago, 1973, 30:313-322.

16,955. Rees, Garnet. Guillaume Apollonaïre and the search for
identity. In Beaumont, E. M., Cocking, J. M., &
Cruickshank, J. (eds), Order and Adventure in Post-
Romantic French Poetry. NY: Barnes & Noble, 1973,
162-175; Oxford: Blackwell, 1973, 162-175.

16,956. Rees, Richard D., & Pedersen, Dahrl M. A factorial
determination of points of view in poetic evaluation and
their relation to various determinants. Psychol Reports, 1965, 16:31-39.

16,957. Rehm, Walther. Der Todesgedanke in der deutschen Dichtung vom Mittelalter bis zur Romantik. Halle: 1928.

16,958. Reichertz, Ronald. Roethke's 'Where Knock Is Open Wide.'
Explicator, 1967, 26:34.

16,959. Reicke, Ilse. Das Dichten in psychologischer Betrachten.
Zeitschrift für Aesthetik und allgemeine Kunstwissenschaft, 1915, 10:290-345.

16,960. Reid, Stephen. The Iliad: Agamemnon's dream. Amer
Imago, 1973, 30:33-56.

16,961. _____. Keats's depressive poetry. Psychoanal Rev,
1971, 58:395-418.

16,962. Reik, Theodor. Dichtung und Psychoanalyse. Pan, 1912,
3(1).

16,963. _____. Der Weg allen Fleisches. Psychoanalytische
Bewegung, 1930, 2:123-132.

16,964. _____. Zum Inzestkomplex: Aus Dichtern. Int Zeitschrift für Psychoanalyse, 1914, 2:194-195.

16,965. Rein, David M. Poe's dreams. London Magazine, 1962,
2:42-58.

16, 966.   Reinartz, Kay F.   Walt Whitman and feminism.   Walt
          Whitman Rev, 1973, 19:127-137.
16, 967.   Reinhard, E.   Der Ausdruck von Lust und Unlust in der
          Lyrik.   Archiv für die gesamte Psychologie, 1908, 12:
          481-545.
16, 968.   Reiss, Edmund.   The symbolic surface of the Canterbury
          Tales: the Monk's Portrait.   Chaucer Rev, 1968, 2:
          254-272.
16, 969.   _____.   Whitman's debt to animal magnetism.   PMLA,
          1963, 78:80-88.
16, 970.   Reitman, F.   Lear's nonsense.   J Clinical Psychopathol-
          ogy & Psychotherapy, 1946, 7:671-678.
16, 971.   Remmers, H. H. , & Hadley, J. E.   Curricular material
          and measuring devices for teaching appreciation of po-
          etry.   Bulletin Purdue Univ. , 1936, 37:227-237.
16, 972.   Renou, Louis.   Art et le religion dans la poétique sans-
          krite: le 'jeu de mots' et ses implications.   JPNP,
          1951, 44:280-285.
16, 973.   Revard, Stella.   Yeats, Mallarmé, and the archetypal
          feminine.   Papers on Language & Lit, 1972, 8(Suppl):
          112-127.
16, 974.   Reynolds, Jerry D.   Attitude Change by the Stimulus of the
          Oral Interpretation of Poetic Literature.   DA, 1967,
          27(11-A):3967.
16, 975.   Ricca, M.   Psicologia infantile della Divina Commedia.
          Messina: Alicò e Zuccaro, 1922.
16, 976.   Ricci, François.   Le Thème maternel chez Rimbaud: Es-
          quisse d'une psychocritique.   In Reflexions et recherches
          de nouvelle critique.   Paris: Les Belles Lettres, 1969,
          143-155.
16, 977.   Rich, Adrienne Cecile.   When we dead awaken: writing as
          re-vision.   College English, 1973, 34:18-30.
16, 978.   Rich, N. B.   New perspective on the companion poems of
          Robert Browning.   Victorian Newsletter, 1969, No. 36,
          5-9.
16, 979.   Richards, Bertrand F.   Jarrell's 'Seele im Raum. '   Ex-
          plicator, 1974, 33:Item 22.
16, 980.   Richards, Ivor Armstrong.   Science and Poetry.   NY:
          Norton, 1926.
16, 981.   Richmond, Hugh M.   Psychoanalytic approach to Lovelace.
          Lit & Psychol, 1964, 14:125-127.
16, 982.   Riddel, Joseph N.   H. D. and the poetics of 'spiritual real-
          ism. '   Contemporary Lit, 1969, 10:447-473.
16, 983.   Ridgeway, Jacqueline.   The necessity of form to the poetry
          of Louise Bogan.   Women's Studies, 1977, 5:137-149.
16, 984.   Ries, Lawrence R.   Wolf Masks; Violence in Contemporary
          Poetry.   Port Washington, NY: Kennikat, 1977.
16, 985.   Rinaker, Clarissa.   Some unconscious factors in the sonnet
          as a poetic form.   Int J Psycho-Anal, 1931, 12:167-187.
16, 986.   Rizzo, E. M.   [The written language of a paranoid schizo-
          phrenic.   Phenomenologic existential interpretation and
          relations with poetic surrealism.]   Giornale de Psichi-
          atria di Neuropatologia, 1961, 89:105-143.

16, 987.   Robert, Karl.   Oedipus.   Geschichte eines poetischen
            Stoffes im griechischen Albertum.   Berlin: Weidmann,
            1915.
16, 988.   Roberts, Donald R.   The death wish of John Donne.
            PMLA, 1947, 62:958-976.
16, 989.   Roberts, Helene E.   The dream world of Dante Gabriel
            Rossetti.   Victorian Studies, 1974, 17:371-393.
16, 990.   Robertson, Duncan.   Auden's 'The Wanderer. '   Explicator,
            1970, 28.
16, 991.   Robinson, David.   The romantic quest in Poe and Emer-
            son: 'Ulalume' and 'The Sphinx. '   Amer Transcendental
            Q, 1975, 26, Suppl: 26-30.
16, 992.   Robinson, Jeffrey.   Celebration: the lyric poetry of Mel-
            ville Cane.   Amer Scholar, 1969, 38:286-296.
16, 993.   Robinson, Virginia P.   References to Homer in Art and
            Artist.   J Otto Rank Assn, 1969, 4(1):81-85.
16, 994.   Robitsek, Alfred.   Bemerkungen zu einem Gedicht Lilien-
            crons.   Imago, 1925, 11:352-353.
16, 995.   Roche, T. P. , Jr.   Review: M. Green's Labyrinth of
            Shakespeare's Sonnets: An Examination of Sexual Ele-
            ments in Shakespeare's Languages.   Shakespeare Q,
            1978, 29:439-449.
16, 996.   Rodino, Richard H.   Blasphemy or blessing?   Swift's
            scatological poems.   Papers in Language & Lit, 1978,
            14:152-170.
16, 997.   Rodriguez, Katharine Ball.   La Présence de la femme dans
            la vie et dans l'oeuvre poétique de Guillaume Apollin-
            aire.   DAI, 1977, 38(5):2836-A.
16, 998.   Roesler, M. C.   The Sea and Death in Walt Whitman's
            Leaves of Grass.   DA, 1963, 24:1606.
16, 999.   Rogers, Robert.   A gathering of roses.   Hartford Studies
            in Lit, 1973, 5:61-76.
17, 000.   Rogers, Robert.   Keats's strenuous tongue: a study of
            'Ode on Melancholy. '   Lit & Psychol, 1967, 17:2-12;
            discussed by Aileen Ward, The psychoanalytic theory
            of poetic form: a comment, p. 33-35.
17, 001.   Rolfs, Daniel J.   Dante and the problem of suicide.   Mich-
            igan Academician, 1974, 6:367-376.
17, 002.   _____.   Dante, Petrarch, Boccaccio and the problem of
            suicide.   Romanic Rev, 1976, 67:200-225.
17, 003.   _____.   Sleep, dreams and insomnia in the Orlando
            Furioso.   Italica, 1976, 53:453-474.
17, 004.   Roller, Bert.   Children in American Poetry, 1610-1900.
            Nashville: Peabody College for Teachers, 1930.
17, 005.   Rollin, H. R.   Childe Harolde: father to Lord Byron.
            British Medical J, 1974, 2:714-716.
17, 006.   Rom, Paul.   A misquotation by Adler.   Lit & Psychol,
            1965, 15:191-193.
17, 007.   Romig, Evelyn M.   An achievement of H. D. and Theodore
            Roethke: psychoanalysis and the poetics of teaching.
            Lit & Psychol, 1978, 28:105-111.
17, 008.   Roomsliter, P. C. , et al.   Perception and English poetic
            meter.   PMLA, 1973, 88:200-208.

17, 009. Rose, Edward J. Blake and the double: the spectre as Doppelgänger. Colby Library Q, 1977, 13:127-139.

17, 010. Rose, Edgar S. The anatomy of imagination. College English, 1967, 27:346-354.

17, 011. Rosenblatt, Jon. Sylvia Plath: The Poetry of Initiation. Chapel Hill: Univ. North Carolina Press, 1979.

17, 012. Rosenfeld, Alvin H. The eagle and the axe: a study of Whitman's 'Song of the Broad Axe.' Amer Imago, 1968, 25:354-370.

17, 013. Rossiter, A. P. Poetry as Gagagram; an inquiry into meaning. Psyche, 1935, 15:174-187.

17, 014. Rossky, William. Imagination in the English Renaissance: psychological and poetic. Studies in Renaissance, 1958, 5:49-73.

17, 015. Rosteutscher, Joachim. Hölderlin: Der Künder der grossen Natur. Bern u Munich: Francke, 1962.

17, 016. Rothenberg, Alan B. The oral rape fantasy and rejection of mother in the imagery of Shakespeare's Venus and Adonis. Psychoanal Q, 1971, 40:447-468.

17, 017. Rothenberg, Albert. Inspiration, insight, and the creative process in poetry. College English, 1970, 32:172-183.

17, 018. Rottenbiller, Henry. Metaphorik der psychogenen Kausalität in der Dichtung Heinrich von Kleist. DAI, 1971, 32:1527A.

17, 019. Rowland, Beryl. A cake-making image in Troilus and Cressida. Shakespeare Q, 1970, 21:191-194.

17, 020. _____. Chaucer as a pawn in 'The Book of the Duchess.' Notes & Queries, 1967, 6:1.

17, 021. _____. Chaucer's mistake: 'The Book of the Duchess.' Notes & Queries, 1966, 4:99-100.

17, 022. _____. Chaucer's 'The Wife of Bath's Prologue,' D. 389. Explicator, 1965, 24:2.

17, 023. _____. New light on the 'Physician's Tale.' J English Lit History, 1973, 40:165-178.

17, 024. Rudat, Wolfgang E. H. The Canterbury Tales: anxiety release and wish fulfillment. Amer Imago, 1978, 35:407-418.

17, 025. Runnels, James A. Mother, Wife, and Lover: Symbolic Women in the Works of W. B. Yeats. DAI, 1973, 34:336A.

17, 026. Rusch, Frederik L. Of eidólons and orgone. Walt Whitman Rev, 1967, 13:11-15.

17, 027. Russel, F. T. A poet's portrayal of emotion. Psychol Rev, 1921, 28:222-238.

17, 028. Russo, J., & Simon, Bennett. Homeric psychology and the oral epic tradition. J History Ideas, 1968, 29:485-498; In Simon, Bennett, Mind and Madness in Ancient Greece. The Classical Roots of Modern Psychiatry. Ithaca, NY: Cornell Univ. Press, 1978, 78-156.

17, 029. Ryals, Clyde de L. The 'fatal woman' symbol in Tennyson. PMLA, 1959, 74:438-443.

17,030.   Sachs, Arieh.   Sexual dialectic in the early poetry of Dylan Thomas.   Southern Rev, 1964, 1(2):43-47.

17,031.   Sachs, Hanns.   Baudelaire, der Verfluchte.   Almanach, 1932, 191-194.

17,032.   _____.   Gemeinsame Tagtraum und Dichtung.   Almanach, 1926, 44-53.

17,033.   _____.   Psychoanalyse und Dichtung.   Das psychoanalytische Volksbuch, 1926, 456-467; 1928, 2:195-207; 1939, 595-603.

17,034.   Sadoff, Dianne F.   Imaginative transformation in William Morris' 'Rapunzel.'   Victorian Poetry, 1974, 12:153-164.

17,035.   Sagara, M.   On Mr. Watanabe's Nihon Shika Keishiki Ron. A study of Japanese verse form.   Japanese J Psychol, 1929, 4:109-118.

17,036.   _____.   On verse-form of "dodoïtau."   Japanese J Psychol, 1929, 4:365-382.

17,037.   _____.   Some literatures on "5-7 Chō."   Japanese J Psychol, 1930, 5, No. 1.

17,038.   St. Armand, Barton Levi.   Poe's emblematic raven: a pictorial approach.   Emerson Society Q, 1976, 22:191-210.

17,039.   _____.   The power of sympathy in the poetry of Robinson and Frost: the 'inside' vs. the 'outside' narrative.   Amer Q, 1967, 19:564-574.

17,040.   Sait, J. E.   Tennyson's Treatment of Personality: An Interpretive Guide.   Doctoral dissertation, Univ. London, 1975.

17,041.   Sakuma, K.   On rhythms of poetry.   Japanese J Psychol, 1928, 3:1-44.

17,042.   Salamon, Lynda B.   'Double, Double': perception in the poetry of Sylvia Plath.   Spirit: A Magazine of Poetry, 1970, 37(2):34-39.

17,043.   Salinger, Herman.   Helping Heinrich Heine explain his archetypal 'Night Journey' poem.   Lit & Psychol, 1963, 13:30-36.

17,044.   Salsano, F.   Dante come senso lirico.   In Psicoanalisi e strutturalismo di fronte a Dante.   Vol. I: Premesse. Florence: Olschki, 1972, 411-422.

17,045.   Sanderrindtorff, E.   Zur Psychologie des Dichtkindes.   Zeitschrift für pädagogische Psychologie, 1931, 32:98-109.

17,046.   Sands, Donald B.   Non-comic, non-tragic wife: Chaucer's Dame Alys as sociopath.   Chaucer Rev, 1978, 12:171-182.

17,047.   Sanguineti, E.   Il realismo di Dante.   Florence: Sansoni, 1965.

17,048.   Santa Cruz, Luis.   A poesia negra no Brasil.   Cadernos Brasileiros, 1962, 4(4):46-65.

17,049.   Sanzo, Eileen.   Blake and the Great Mother archetype.   Nassau Rev, 1978, 3(4):105-116.

17, 050. Sapegno, Natalino. Il monde culturale e psicologico del
          Petrarca. In Prolemi dell'Umanesimo. Rome: Ateneo,
          1972.
17, 051. Sarotte, Georges-Michel. Comme un frère, comme un
          amant, l'homosexualité masculine dans le roman et le
          théâtre américains de Herman Melville à James Bald-
          win. Paris: Flammarion, 1976.
17, 052. Sartre, Jean-Paul. Baudelaire. London: Hamilton, 1964
          (1949).
17, 053. Sautter, Diana. Dylan Thomas and archetypal domination.
          Amer Imago, 1974, 31:335-359.
17, 054. Scalabrino, G. Borsani. Il misticismo naturale visto at-
          traverso i mandala orientali già accostati a Dante da
          R. Guardini. In Lectura Dantis Mystica: Il poema
          sacro alla luce delle conquiste psicologiche odierne.
          Florence: Olschki, 1969, 31-55.
17, 055. Scazzoso, P. Tonalità bizantina del Paradiso. In Psico-
          analisi e structuralismo di fronte a Dante. Vol. II.
          Lettura della 'Commedia.' Florence: Olschki, 1972,
          271-283.
17, 056. Schakel, Peter J. Swift's remedy for love: the scatologi-
          cal poems. Papers in Language & Lit, 1978, 14:137-
          147.
17, 057. _____. Swift's scatological poems. PMLA, 1976, 91:
          465-566.
17, 058. Schapiro, Barbara. Shelley's 'Alastor' and Whitman's
          'Out of the Cradle': the ambivalent mother. Amer
          Imago, 1979, 36:245-259.
17, 059. Schechter, Harold. The return of Demeter: the poetry
          of Daniela Gioseffi. Psychocultural Rev, 1977, 1(4):
          452-458.
17, 060. Scherrer, E. Psychologie der Lyrik und des Gefühls.
          Ein Beitrag zum Leib-Seele-Problem. Zurich: 1925.
17, 061. Schlosstein, Sallie Elizabeth. Byron: The Inverted Role
          of the Female in His Poetry. DAI, 1975, 35:5424A-
          25A.
17, 062. Schmeling, K. Perioden der Pubertät und der Poesie.
          Zeitschrift für Sexualwissenschaft, 1931, 17:438-442.
17, 063. Schmidt, H.D. Die vergleichende Tier-Mensch-Deutung
          bei Rainer Maria Rilke in psychologischer Licht.
          Schweizerischen Zeitschrift für Psychologie, 1959, 18:
          104-111.
17, 064. Schneck, Jerome M. Robert Browning and mesmerism.
          Bulletin Medical Library Assn, 1956, 44:443-451.
17, 065. Schneider, H. Hölderline Hälfte des Lebens. Monats-
          schrifte für Psychiatrie und Neurologie, 1946, 111:292-
          301.
17, 066. Schneider, K. Der Dichter in der Psychopathologie.
          Cologne: Rheinlandverlag, 1922.
17, 067. Schneider, Pierre-Bernard, Junod, L., & Hermann, P.
          Note sur la méthodologie de la compréhension psychol-
          ogique et psychopathologique d'un texte poétique.
          Schweizer Archiv für Neurologie und Psychiatrie, 1967,
          99:171-176.

17,068. Schöne, Walter. Walt Whitman und seine Phalluspoesie. Sexual-Problemen von Marcuse, Mar/Apr/May 1911.

17,069. Schramm, W. L. The melodies of verse. Science, 1935, 82:61-62.

17,070. Schramm, W. von. Die Bedeutung der Traume und Traumdichtungen im Werk und Leben Jean Pauls. Jean-Paul Blätter, 1927, 2:17-24.

17,071. Shreck, Alfred. Analyse des Entstehens eines lyrischen Gedichtes. Zeitschrift für Psychotherapie und medizinischen Psychologie, 1952, 2:149-152.

17,072. Schroeder, Fred E. H. Obscenity and its function in the poetry of E. E. Cummings. Sewanee Rev, 1965, 78: 469-478.

17,073. Schuchard, Ronald. 'Our mad poetics to confute': the personal voice of T. S. Eliot's early poetry and criticism. Orbis Litterarum, 1976, 31:208-223.

17,074. Schulman, Grace. Rich's 'Diving Into the Wreck.' Amer Poetry Rev, 1973, 2(5):11.

17,075. Schultze-Naumberg, B. Die Vererbung der dichterischen Begabung. Zeitschrift für Rassenkunde, 1939, 10:176-189.

17,076. Schulze, F. W. 'Vita brevis-ars longa' als Emotions-Ursache und Motiv-Mitte in Keats Dichtung. In Müller-Schwefe, G., & Tuzinski, K. (eds), Literatur-Kultur-Gesellschaft in England und Amerika: Aspekte und Forschungsbeiträge. Frankfurt: Diesterweg, 1966, 320-336.

17,077. Schumann, H-J von. Phänomenologische und psychoanalytische Untersuchung der Homerischen Träume. Acta Psychotherapeutica, Psychosomatica et Orthopaedagogica, 1955, 3:205-219.

17,078. Schwaber, Paul. Stays against Confusion: The Poems of John Clare. DA, 1966, 66-12, 591.

17,079. Schwartz, Delmore. The cunning and the craft of the unconscious and the preconscious. [Review article.] Poetry, 1959, 94:203-205.

17,080. Schwartz, Kessel. The Isakower phenomenon and the dream screen in the early poetry of Vicente Aleixandre. Revista de Letras, 1974, 6:210-218.

17,081. _____. Sea, love, and death in the poetry of Aleixandre. Hispania, 1967, 50:219-228; In The Meaning of Existence in Contemporary Literature. Miami: Univ. Miami Press, 1969, 37-51.

17,082. Schwartz, Murray M. Critic, define thyself. In Hartman, G. H. (ed), Psychoanalysis and the Question of the Text. Baltimore: Johns Hopkins Univ. Press, 1978, 1-17.

17,083. _____, & Bollas, Christopher. The absence at the center: Sylvia Plath and suicide. In Lane, G. (ed), Sylvia Plath; New Views on the Poetry. Baltimore: Johns Hopkins Univ. Press, 1979, 179-202; Criticism, 1976, 18:147-172.

17,084. Scigaj, Leonard M. Myth and Psychology in the Poetry of Ted Hughes. DAI, 1978, 38:4819A-20A.

17, 085. Scripture, E. W.   Ein Einblick in den unbewussten Vers-
          mechanismus.   Zeitschrift für Psychologie, 1927, 102:
          307-309.

17, 086. _____. Experimentelle Untersuchungen uber die Matrik
          Beowulf.   Zeitschrift für Psychologie, 1927, 102:307-
          309.

17, 087. _____. The nature of verse.   British J Psychol, 1921,
          11:225-235.

17, 088. _____. Die neue Metrik.   Archiv für die gesamte Psy-
          chologie, 1928, 64:463-474.

17, 089. _____. Die Versform des Anfangsmonologs in Goethes
          Faust.   Zeitschrift für Psychologie, 1927, 104:109-112.

17, 090. Seashore, H. G.   A review of Shramm's 'Approaches to a
          Science of English Verse.'   Univ. Iowa Studies Psychol
          Music, 1936, 4:377-379.

17, 091. Seeger, Raymond J.   Scientist and poet.   Amer Scientist,
          1959, 47:350-360.

17, 092. Seferis, George.   Cavafy and Eliot--a comparison.   In On
          the Greek Style: Selected Essays in Poetry and Hellen-
          ism.   Boston: Little, Brown, 1966.

17, 093. Segond, (?).   L'Oeuvre et la pensée de Charles Baudelaire,
          contribution a une psychologie de l'angoisse.   Paris:
          Montaigne et Aubier, 1949.

17, 094. Seiden, Morton I.   Patterns of belief: myth in the poetry
          of William Butler Yeats.   Amer Imago, 1948, 5:259-
          300.

17, 095. _____. A psychoanalytic essay on William Butler
          Yeats.   Accent, 1946, 3:178-190.

17, 096. Semi, F.   Interpretazioni dantesche.   [Special No.]   Ateneo
          Veneto, 1965.

17, 097. Semprún Donahue, Moraima de.   Cristo en Lorca.   Expli-
          cación de textos literatura, 1975, 4:23-34.

17, 098. _____. Una franca interpretación de 'Poemas del lago
          Edem Mills' de García Lorca.   García Lorca Rev,
          1975, 79-90.

17, 099. _____. ['Romance sonámbulo.']   Cuadernos Ameri-
          canos, 1974, 194:257-260.

17, 100. Sen, Sunil Kanti.   The dating and unconscious meaning of
          Milton's 'On his blindness.'   Bulletin Department Eng-
          lish (Calcutta), 1969-70, 5(1):20-22.

17, 101. Sena, John F.   Samuel Garth and the dispensary: the
          project and the poem.   In Peschel, E. R. (ed), Medi-
          cine and Literature.   NY: Watson, 1980, 28-34.

17, 102. Serrano Poncela, Segundo.   John Donne o la sensualidad.
          Insula (Madrid), 1966, 21:1, 12.

17, 103. Servadio, Emilio.   I complessi di Dante.   Le Ore, 1966,
          14:2.

17, 104. _____. Psicoanalisis della creazione poetica.   Meridi-
          ano di Roma, 1937, 5(7&14).

17, 105. Seth, G.   Psychological aspects of contemporary poetry.
          British J Psychol, 1937, 27:425-435.

17, 106. Sewell, Elizabeth.   The Orphic Voice.   Poetry and Natural
          History.   NY: Columbia Univ. Press, 1960.

17,107. Seyppel, Joachim H. A renaissance of German poetry:
         Gottfried Benn. Modern Language Forum, 1954, 39:
         115-125.
17,108. Shahane, V. A. Aspects of Walt Whitman's symbolism.
         Lit Criticism (Mysore), 1962, 5:72-78.
17,109. Shakel, Peter J. Swift's 'Verses Wrote in a Lady's Ivory
         Table Book.' Explicator, 1970, 28.
17,110. Shakir, Evelyn. Books, death and immortality: a study of
         Book V of The Prelude. Studies in Romanticism, 1969,
         8:156-167.
17,111. Shands, H. C. Malinowski's mirror: Emily Dickinson as
         Narcissus. Contemporary Psychoanal, 1976, 12:300-
         334.
17,112. Shapiro, Karl. Myths, emotions, and the great audience.
         Poetry, 1950, 75:52-56.
17,113. _____. Poets and psychologists. Poetry, 1952, 80:
         166-184.
17,114. Sharma, S. P. A Study of Themes. Self, Love, War and
         Death in Relationship to Form in the Poetry of Walt
         Whitman. DA, 1964, 24:4703-4704.
17,115. Sharpe, Ella Freeman. Dream Analysis. London: Ho-
         garth, 1961, Ch. 1.
17,116. Shawcross, John T. Form and content in Milton's Latin
         elegies. Huntington Library Q, 1970, 33:331-350.
17,117. Sheed, Wilfred. A. Alvares: The Savage God. In The
         Good Word and Other Words. NY: Dutton, 1978, 68-
         72.
17,118. Sheehan, D. The control of feeling: a rhetorical analysis
         of Inferno XIII. Italica, 1974, 51:193-206.
17,119. Shengold, Leonard. A discussion of the paper by Bennett
         Simon on 'The Hero as an Only Child : An Unconscious
         Fantasy Structuring Homer's Odyssey. ' Int J Psycho-
         Anal, 1974, 55:563-565.
17,120. Shepler, Frederic J. Beyond dreams. Diacritics, 1975,
         5:20-26.
17,121. Sherbo, Arthur. The 'mad' poet and the sane biographer.
         In Shepard, D. (ed), English Symposium Papers, I.
         Fredonia, NY: SUNY College, 1970, 29-45.
17,122. Sherman, Dean. Robinson's Battle after War. Explicator,
         1969, 27(8):63.
17,123. Sherwood, Terry G. Conversion psychology in John
         Donne's 'Good Friday' poem. Harvard Theological Rev,
         1979, 72:101-122.
17,124. Shideler, Ross. A functional theory of literature applied
         to poems by Valéry and Ekelof. Psychocultural Rev,
         1978, 2(3).
17,125. _____. Glassclear eye of dreams in twentieth-century
         Swedish poetry. World Lit Today, 1977, 51:530-534.
17,126. Shimizu, H. A study of Whitman's imagery. Walt Whit-
         man Rev, 1959, 5:26-28.
17,127. Shinn, Thelma J. The art of a verse novelist approach-
         ing Robinson's late narratives through James's The Art
         of the Novel. Colby Library Q, 1976, 12:91-100.

17, 128. Shumaker, Wayne. Unpremeditated Verse: Feeling and
          Perception in Paradise Lost. Princeton: Princeton
          Univ. Press, 1967.
17, 129. Shurr, William H. The Mystery of Iniquity: Melville as
          Poet, 1857-1891. Lexington: Univ. Kentucky Press,
          1973.
17, 130. Siemoneit, Regina P. A Piagetian investigation of the
          genesis of Goethe's views of God and man as reflected
          in four poems. In Zayas-Bazán, E. , & Suárez, M. L.
          (eds), The 27th Annual Mountain Interstate Foreign Lan-
          guage Conference. Johnson City, Tenn: East Tennes-
          see State Univ. , 1978, 84-95.
17, 131. Silver, Carole G. 'The Defence of Guenevere': a further
          interpretation. Studies English Lit, 1969, 9:695-702.
17, 132. Silvia, D. S. Chaucer's Canterbury Tales, D. 44 a-f.
          Explicator, 1970, 28.
17, 133. Silz, W. Heine's syraesthesia. PMLA, 1942, 57:469-488.
17, 134. _____. Otto Ludwig and the process of poetic creation.
          PMLA, 1945, 60:860-878.
17, 135. Simenauer, Erich. Ein archaisches Befruchtungssymbol in
          der Dichtung Rilkes. Schweizerischen Zeitschrift für
          Psychologie, 1954, 13:259-270.
17, 136. _____. 'Pregnancy envy' in Rainer Maria Rilke. Amer
          Imago, 1954, 11:235-248.
17, 137. _____. Der Traum bei Rilke. Bern: Haupt, 1976;
          Reviews: B. Blume, MLN, 1978, 93:530-531; R. Ex-
          ner, World Lit Today, 1978, 52:103.
17, 138. _____. [Rainer Maria Rilke from a psychoanalytic
          viewpoint.] Psyche, 1976, 30:1081-1112.
17, 139. _____. Rilkes Darstellung der Dinge im Lichte der
          'Metapsychologie' Freuds. Schweizerischen Zeitschrift
          für Psychologie, 1949, 8:277-294.
17, 140. _____. R. M. Rilke's dreams and his conception of
          dreams. In Baron, F. , Dick, E. S. , & Maurer, W. R.
          (eds), Rilke: The Alchemy of Alienation. Lawrence,
          Kans: Regents, 1980, 243-262.
17, 141. Simon, Bennett. The hero as an only child: an uncon-
          scious fantasy structuring Homer's Odyssey. Int J
          Psycho-Anal, 1974, 55:555-562; Rejoinder to L. Shen-
          gold, Int J Psycho-Anal, 1975, 56:377.
17, 142. _____. Mental life in the Homeric Epics. In Mind and
          Madness in Ancient Greece; The Classical Roots of
          Modern Psychiatry. Ithaca, NY: Cornell Univ. Press,
          1978, 53-77.
17, 143. _____, & Weiner, H. Models of mind and mental ill-
          ness in ancient Greece: I. The Homeric model of
          mind. J History Behavioral Sciences, 1966, 2:303-314;
          In Simon, Bennett, Mind and Madness in Ancient
          Greece. The Classical Roots of Modern Psychiatry.
          Ithaca, NY: Cornell Univ. Press, 1978, 53-77.
17, 144. Simpson, D. Keats's lady, metaphor, and the rhetoric
          of neurosis. Studies in Romanticism, 1976, 15:265-288.
17, 145. Simpson, Lewis P. A note on Allen Tate. Southern Rev,
          1979, 15:519-520.

17,146. Simpson, Michael A. Death and modern poetry. In Feifel, H. (ed), New Meanings of Death. NY: McGraw-
Hill, 1977, 313-333.
17,147. Sims, James H. Death in Poe's poetry: variations on a
theme. Costerus: Essays in English & Amer Lan-
guage & Lit, 1973, 9:159-180.
17,148. Sinfield, Alan. Double meanings: II. Sexual puns in
Astrophil and Stella. Essays in Criticism, 1974, 24:
341-355.
17,149. Singer, Jerome K. The Unholy Bible: A Psychological
Interpretation of William Blake. NY: Putnam, 1970.
17,150. Siomopoulos, G. Poetry as affective communication.
Psychoanal Q, 1977, 46:499-513.
17,151. Skinner, B. F. The alliteration in Shakespeare's sonnets:
a study in literary behavior. Psychol Record, 1939,
3:186-192.
17,152. _____. Reflections on meaning and structure. In
Brower, R., Vendler, H., & Hollander, J. (eds), I.A.
Richards; Essays in His Honor. NY: Oxford, 1973,
199-209.
17,153. Slater, E. The colour imagery of poets. Schweizer Archiv Neurologie und Psychiatrie, 1963, 91:303-308.
17,154. Slaughter, William. Eating poetry. Chicago Rev, 1974,
25(4):124-128.
17,155. Sloane, Eugene N. Coleridge's Kubla Khan: the living
catacombs of the mind. Amer Imago, 1972, 29:97-122.
17,156. Smidt, Kristian. Poetry and Belief in the Work of T. S.
Eliot. Atlantic Highlands, NJ: Humanities Press,
1961 (1949).
17,157. Smith, A. Helen. Water imagery in Leaves of Grass.
Walt Whitman Rev, 1971, 17:82-92.
17,158. Smith, B. H. Sorrow's mysteries: Keats' 'Ode on Melancholy.' Studies English Lit, 1966, 6:679-691.
17,159. Smith, Gordon Ross. Mannerist frivolity and Shakespeare's Venus and Adonis. Hartford Studies in Lit,
1971, 3:1-11.
17,160. _____. A note on Shakespeare's Sonnet 143. Amer
Imago, 1957, 14:33-36.
17,161. Smith, Hammet W. Karl Jay Shapiro: a poet of human
relations. College Language Assn J, 1958, 1:97-100.
17,162. Smith, R. B. Sexual ambivalence in Tennyson. CEA
Critic, 1965, 27(1):8-9; 28:(1)12.
17,163. Smith, Susan Harris. Paul Eluard's 'Yves Tanguy': an
analysis. Dada/Surrealism, 1975, 5:49-52.
17,164. Smyser, J. W. Wordsworth's dream of poetry and science:
The Prelude V. PMLA, 1956, 71:269-275.
17,165. Snider, Clifton Mark. The Struggle for the Self: A Jungian Interpretation of Swinburne's 'Tristram of Lyon-
esse.' DAI, 1976, 36:6716A-17A.
17,166. Sohngen, Mary, & Smith, Robert J. Images of old age
in poetry. Gerontologist, 1978, 18:181-186.
17,167. Soldati, Joseph A. The functions of color in poetry.
Essays in Lit, 1977, 4:49-58.

17, 168.   Sonnenfeld, A.   Eros and poetry: Mallarmé's disappearing
            visions.   In Beaumont, A. E. , Cocking, J. M. , &
            Cruickshank, J. (eds), Order and Adventure in Post-
            Romantic French Poetry.   Oxford: Blackwell, 1973,
            89-98.
17, 169.   Souriau, Paul.   La Rêverie esthétique.   Essai sur la psy-
            chologie du poète.   Paris: 1906.
17, 170.   Spatz, Jonas.   Love and death in Tennyson's 'Maud. '
            Texas Studies in Lit & Language, 1974, 16:503-510.
17, 171.   _____. The mystery of Eros: sexual initiation in
            Coleridge's 'Christabel. '   PMLA, 1975, 90:107-116.
17, 172.   Spearing, Anthony C.   Medieval Dream-Poetry.   Cam-
            bridge: Cambridge Univ. Press, 1976.
17, 173.   Spender, Stephen.   The making of a poem.   Partisan Rev,
            1946, 13:294-308.
17, 174.   Speroni, C.   Dante's prophetic morning-dreams.   Studies
            in Philology, 1948, 45:50-59; In Clements, R. J. (ed),
            American Critical Essays on The Divine Comedy.   NY:
            New York Univ. Press, 1967, 182-192.
17, 175.   Sperry, Stuart M. , Jr.   Byron and the meaning of 'Man-
            fred. '   Criticism, 1974, 16:189-202.
17, 176.   _____. Keats and the chemistry of poetic creation.
            PMLA, 1970, 85:268-277.
17, 177.   _____. Romance as wish-fulfillment: Keats's The Eve
            of St. Agnes.   Studies in Romanticism, 1971, 10:27-43.
17, 178.   Spivey, Ted R.   Archetypal symbols in the major poetry
            of T. S. Eliot and Conrad Aiken.   Int J Symbology,
            1971, 2(3):16-26.
17, 179.   Splitter, Randolph.   Pound's dream of the Gods: a baker's
            half-dozen of the Cantos.   Sou'wester, 30 Oct 1970, 81-
            99.
17, 180.   Spoerl, Howard D.   The Status and Mission of Poetry.
            North Montpelier, Vt: Driftwood Press, 1948.
17, 181.   Spranger, E.   Wis erfasst man einen Nationalcharakter?
            Erzeihung, 1939, 15:41-62.
17, 182.   Spratt, P.   Eliot and Freud.   Lit Half-Yearly, 1960, 1:55-
            68.
17, 183.   Stai, A.   Diktning og psykoanalyse.   Edda, 1935, 22:1-18.
17, 184.   Stallman, Robert L.   'Rapunzel' unravelled.   Victorian Po-
            etry, 1969, 7:221-232.
17, 185.   Stalloni, Y.   Verlaine, poète de l'eau?   Europe, 1974,
            52, nos. 545-6:108-114.
17, 186.   Stamelman, Richard Howard.   The Drama of Self in Guil-
            laume Apollinaire's 'Alcools. '   Chapel Hill: Univ.
            North Carolina Press, 1976.
17, 187.   Standberg, Victor.   Hart Crane and William James: the
            psychology of mysticism.   McNeese Rev, 1975-76, 22:
            14-25.
17, 188.   Stanford, Donald E.   Foster Damon's dream frontiers.
            Southern Rev, 1971, 7(1):xv-xx.
17, 189.   Stange, G. R.   The Victorian city and the frightened poets.
            Victorian Studies, 1968, 11:627-640.

17,190. Stanford, Donald E.   Edward Arlington Robinson's 'The
         Wandering Jew. ' Tulane Studies in English, 1978, 23:
         95-107.
17,191. Starobinski, Jean.   André Chénier and the allegory of po-
         etry.   In Kroeber, K. , & Walling, W. (eds), Images
         of Romanticism; Verbal and Visual Affinities.   New
         Haven: Yale Univ. Press, 1978, 39-60.
17,192. Stäuble, Michèle (ed).   Etudes baudelairiennes VI-VII:
         Charles Baudelaire: Un Mangeur d'opium.   Boudry:
         Baconnière, 1976.
17,193. Stavrou, Constantine N.   Whitman and Nietzsche: A Com-
         parative Study of Their Thought.   Chapel Hill: Univ.
         North Carolina Press, 1964.
17,194. Steadman, John M.   'The Pardoner's Tale': old age and
         contemptus mundi.   In Nature into Myth; Medieval and
         Renaissance Moral Symbols.   Pittsburgh: Duquesne
         Univ. Press, 1979, 104-114.
17,195. Stearns, M.W.   A note on Chaucer's use of Aristotelian
         psychology.   Studies in Philology, 1946, 43:15-21.
17,196. Steig, Michael.   Donne's divine rapist: unconscious fan-
         tasy in Holy Sonnet XIV.   Hartford Studies in Lit, 1972,
         4:52-58.
17,197. Stein, William Bysshe.   Melville's poetry: its symbols
         and individuation.   Lit & Psychol, 1957, 7(2):21-26.
17,198. _____. The Poetry of Melville's Late Years: Time,
         History, Myth, and Religion.   Albany: State Univ. of
         New York Press, 1970.
17,199. Steinmetz, J. -L. Ici, maintenant, les Illuminations. Lit-
         térature, 1973, 11:22-45.
17,200. Stekel, Wilhelm.   Der Dichter über infantile Träumen.
         Int Zeitschrift für Psychoanalyse, 1912-13, 3:52.
17,201. _____. Ein erotisches gedicht von Mozart. Int Zeit-
         schrift für Psychoanalyse, 1913, 3:556.
17,202. _____. Poetry and neurosis. Contributions to the psy-
         chology of the artist and of artistic creative ability.
         Psychoanal Rev, 1923, 10:73-96, 190-208, 316-328,
         457-466; 1924, 11:48-60. Wiesbaden: Bergmann, 1909.
17,203. _____. Die Psychoanalyse in der modernen Lyrik.
         Int Zeitschrift für Psychoanalyse, 1912-13, 3:259.
17,204. _____. Die Träume der Dichter. Eine vergleichende
         Untersuchung der unbewussten Triebkräfte bei Dichtern,
         Neurotiken und Verbrechern. Bousteine zur Psychol-
         ogie des Künstlers und des Kunstwerkes. Wiesbaden:
         Bergmann, 1912.
17,205. Stemplinger, F.   Friedrich Hölderlin, eine psychiatrische
         Studie zu Benedikt Luchmullers Hölderlin-Epos Brand
         im Tempel.   Allgemeine Zeitschrift für Psychiatrie,
         1932, 97:517-521.
17,206. Stephenson, William.   Applications of communication the-
         ory: interpretation of Keats' 'Ode on a Grecian Urn. '
         Psychol Record, 1972, 22:177-192.
17,207. Stepto, Michele Leiss.   Mothers and fathers in Blake's
         'Songs of Innocence. ' Yale Rev, 1978, 67:357-370.

17, 208.   Sterba, Richard F.   Bemerkungen zum dicterischen Aus-
           druck des modernen Naturgefühls. Imago, 1928, 14:
           322-333.

17, 209.   _____.   Über zwei Verse von Schiller. Imago, 1935,
           21:112-114; Almanach, 1936, 150-154.

17, 210.   Sterzinger, O. Die Grunde des Gefallens und Missfallens
           am poetischen Bilde. Archiv für die gesamte Psychol-
           ogie, 1913, 29:16-91.

17, 211.   Stetson, R. H.   Rhythm and rhyme. Psychol Monographs,
           1903, 4:413-466.

17, 212.   Stevens, James R.   The Poetry of Rosalía de Castro: A
           Psychological and Philological Interpretation of Its
           Imagery. DAI, 1971, 32:1532A.

17, 213.   Stevens, Wallace.   The irrational element in poetry; ex-
           cerpt from 'Opus posthumous.' In Gibbons, R. (ed),
           The Poets Work. Boston: Houghton Mifflin, 1979, 48-
           58.

17, 214.   Stewart, John.   John Crowe Ransom. Shenandoah, 1963,
           14(3):33-48.

17, 215.   Sticca, Sandro.   Existential anguish in the poetry of Reyes
           Carbonell. Duquesne Hispanic Rev, 1972, 11(2-3):1-22.

17, 216.   Stilwell, Robert L.   The multiplying entities: D. H. Law-
           rence and five other poets. Sewanee Rev, 1968, 76:
           530-533.

17, 217.   Stitt, G. G.   The Psychology of Reform: Augustine and the
           Poetic of George Herbert.   Master's thesis, Univ.
           Edinburgh, 1975.

17, 218.   Stocker, Arnold.   L'Âme chez les poetes.   Paris: Spes,
           1940.

17, 219.   _____.   La Prière du Grand Will--Etude psychologique
           de quelques sonnets de Shakespeare.   In Des Hommes
           qui Racontent leur Ame.   St. Maurice, Switzerland:
           Editions St. Augustin, 1943, 189-284.

17, 220.   Stoll, Elmer E.   Poetry and the passions; an aftermath.
           PMLA, 1940, 55:979-992.

17, 221.   _____.   Poetry and the passions again.   J English Ger-
           manic Philology, 1941, 40:509-525.

17, 222.   Stone, Carole.   Three mother-daughter poems: the strug-
           gle for separation. Contemporary Psychoanal, 1975,
           11:227-239.

17, 223.   Storch, Rudolph F.   Metaphors of private guilt and social
           rebellion in Godwin's 'Caleb Williams.' J English Lit
           History, 1967, 37:18-30.

17, 224.   Stovall, F.   Desire and Restraint in Shelley. Durham:
           Duke Univ. Press, 1931.

17, 225.   Strickland, E.   Metamorphoses of the muse in romantic
           poesis: Christabel. J English Lit History, 1977, 44:
           641-658.

17, 226.   Strohmayer, Wilhelm.   Über Pubertätskrisen und die Be-
           deutung des Kindheitserlebnisses.   Zwei Dichterbeiträge
           zur Kinderforschung. Zeitschrift für Kinderforschung,
           1922, 27:113-130.

17, 227.   Strong, Margaret K.   A new reading of Tennyson's The
           Lotos Eaters. Psychoanal Rev, 1921, 8:184-186.

17, 228. Stroud, J. B. Learning curves for poetry. Amer J Psy-
          chol, 1931, 43:684-686.
17, 229. Stroud, Joanne Herbert. Archetypal Symbols in the Poetry
          of W. B. Yeats. DAI, 1976, 37:302A.
17, 230. Stumberg, D. A study of poetic talent. J Experimental
          Psychol, 1928, 11:219-234.
17, 231. Stybel, A. J. Meeting Shaul Tchnerichovsky. Hebrew
          Medical J, 1964, 1:299-233.
17, 232. Sullivan, R. C. Poems on autism: beyond research data.
          J Austism Child Schizophrenia, 1977, 7:397-407.
17, 233. Sullivan, Ruth Elizabeth. Backward to Byzantium. Lit &
          Psychol, 1967, 17:13-18.
17, 234. Sullivan, Zohreh Tawakuli. Memory and the meditative
          structure in T. S. Eliot's early poetry. Renascence,
          1977, 29:97-105.
17, 235. Sundell, Michael S. The theme of self-realization in
          'Frost at Midnight.' Studies in Romanticism, 1967, 7:
          34-39.
17, 236. Sundquist, Eric J. In country heaven: Dylan Thomas and
          Rilke. Comparative Lit, 1979, 31:63-78.
17, 237. Sus, Oleg. Nová koncepce psychologie literárního tvoření
          a 'psychopoetika.' Slovenská Literatúra (Bratislava),
          1966, 13:32-53.
17, 238. Suther, Marshall. The Dark Night of Samuel Taylor Col-
          eridge. NY: Columbia Univ. Press, 1960.
17, 239. _____. Visions of Xanadu. NY: Columbia Univ.
          Press, 1965.
17, 240. Swan, Jim. History, pastoral and desire: Andrew Mar-
          vell's mower poem. Int Rev Psycho-Anal, 1976, 3:193-
          202.
17, 241. Swisher, W. S. A psychoanalysis of Browning's 'Pauline.'
          Psychoanal Rev, 1920, 7:115-134.

17, 242. Takahashi, Yushiro. [Study of Keats--Evolution of Ego
          and Idealism.] Tokyo: Hokuseido, 1973.
17, 243. Takahasi, Tetsu. [Poetic works which mask psychoses.]
          Zeitschrift für Psychoanalyse (Tokyo), 1939, 7, Nos.
          9-10.
17, 244. Takatsuki, R. English translation of Hsin Hsin Ming.
          Acta psychologica (Keijo, Japan), 1939, 3:55-60.
17, 245. Tanner, James T. F. Walt Whitman and William James.
          Calamus (Tokyo), 1970, 2:6-23.
17, 246. Tarozzi, Bianca. La nascita del mostro. Per la critica,
          1974, 7-8:75-86.
17, 247. _____. Sogno e incubo americano (o di Robert Lowell).
          Per la critica, 1973, 3:43-51.
17, 248. Tate, Allen. Tension in poetry. Southern Rev, 1938,
          4(1):101-115.
17, 249. Taylor, D. Patterns in Hardy's poetry. J English Lit
          History, 1975, 42:258-275.
17, 250. Taylor, Eugene C. Shelley as mythmaker. J Abnormal
          Psychol, 1919, 14:64-90.

17, 251. Taylor, Marisa G. The Theme of Childhood Recollections
          in the Poetry of Victor Hugo. DAI, 1974, 34:7248A.
17, 252. Taylor, William E. Personality, poetry, and priorities.
          Humanities in the South, 1974, 39:1-2, 5-6.
17, 253. Tefs, Wayne A. The Agitated Heart: Frost's Psychologi-
          cal Theme. DAI, 1978, 39:2933A-34A.
17, 254. Tennyson, Charles. The dream in Tennyson's poetry.
          Virginia Q Rev, 1964, 40:228-248.
17, 255. Thaddeus, Janice Farrar. Insanity and Poetry: William
          Collins, William Cowper, and Christopher Smart. DA,
          1965, 26:2731-32.
17, 256. Thale, Jerome. Sydney Dobell's Roman: the poet's ex-
          perience and his work. Amer Imago, 1955, 12:87-113.
17, 257. Thompson, Phyllis J. Archetypal Elements in the Faerie
          Queene. DA, 1966, 65-14, 398.
17, 258. Thompson, Susan. Boundaries of the Self: Poetry by
          Frost, Roethke, and Berryman, Considered in the Light
          of the Language of Schizophrenia. DAI, 1975, 35:
          5430A-31A.
17, 259. Thornbury, Charles W. The significance of dreams in
          The Dream Songs. Lit & Psychol, 1975, 25:93-107.
17, 260. Thundyil, Zacharias. Circumstance, circumference, and
          center: immanence and transcendence in Emily Dickin-
          son's poems of extreme situations. Hartford Studies in
          Lit, 1971, 3:73-92.
17, 261. Thurley, Geoffrey John. The poetry of breakdown: Robert
          Lowell and Anne Sexton. In The American Moment;
          American Poetry in the Mid-Century. NY: St. Martins,
          1978, 70-90.
17, 262. _____. Rexroth and Patchen: alternatives to break-
          down. In The American Moment; American Poetry in
          the Mid-Century. NY: St. Martins, 1978, 159-171.
17, 263. Tillinghast, Richard. Worlds of their own. Southern Rev,
          1909, 5:582-583.
17, 264. Tobin, Frank. Concupiscentia and courtly love. Romance
          Notes, 1972, 14:387-393.
17, 265. Todd, John Emerson. Emily Dickinson's Use of the Per-
          sona. DA, 1965, 26:3309-10.
17, 266. _____. The persona in Emily Dickinson's love poems.
          Michigan Academician, 1969, 1:197-207.
17, 267. Todd, Robert E. The magna mater archetype in 'The
          Pardoner's Tale.' Lit & Psychol, 1965, 15:32-40.
17, 268. Todorov, Tzvetan. Théories de la poésie. Poétique,
          1976, 28:385-389.
17, 269. Tonelli, L. La psicologia del Petrarca. Bilychnis, 1930,
          19:341-353.
17, 270. Tóth, L. Deux poèmes d'inspiration narcissique. Schweiz-
          erischen Zeitschrift für Psychologie, 1943, 2:42-49.
17, 271. Trachtenberg, Alan. Whitman's romance of the body: a
          note on 'This Compost.' In Peschel, E. R. (ed), Medi-
          cine and Literature. NY: Watson, 1980, 189-199.
17, 272. Trail, George W. The psychological dynamics of D. H.
          Lawrence's 'Snake.' Amer Imago, 1979, 36:345-356.

17, 273. Travi, E. Emblematismo dantesco: l'acqua. Annali dell' Istituto di Studi Danteschi, 1967, 1, 112 p.

17, 274. Treichler, R. Die seelische Erkrankung Friedrich Hölder-lins in ihren Beziehungen zu seinem dichterischen Schaffen. Zentralblatt für die gesamte Neurologie und Psychiatrie, 1936, 155:40-144.

17, 275. Trimpi, Helen P. The theme of loss in the earlier poems of Catherine Davis and Edgar Bowers. Southern Rev, 1973, 9:595-616.

17, 276. Triplett, N., & Sanford, E. C. Studies of rhythm and meter. Amer J Psychol, 1901, 12:361-387.

17, 277. Tripp, Raymond P., Jr. Chaucer's psychologizing of Ver-gil's Dido. Bulletin Rocky Mountain Modern Language Assn, 1970, 24:51-59.

17, 278. Trovato, Mario. Due elementi di filosofia psicologica dantesca: l'anima e l'intelligenza. Forum Italicum, 1970, 4:185-201.

17, 279. Tsanoff, Radoslav A. On the psychology of poetic con-struction. Amer J Psychol, 1914, 25:528-537.

17, 280. Tsur, Reuven. Emotion, emotional qualities, and poetry. Psychocultural Rev, 1978, 2(3):165-180.

17, 281. Tuerk, Richard. Sadakichi Hartmann's 'How Poe wrote the Raven': a biochemical explanation. Markham Rev, 1973, 3:81-85.

17, 282. Turnell, Martin. Tristan Corbière: the resurrection of a poet. Southern Rev, 1977, 13:518-553.

17, 283. Turner, Myron. Disguised passion and the psychology of suicide in Sidney's Old Arcadia. Papers in Language & Lit, 1979, 15:17-37.

17, 284. _____. Distance and astonishment in the old Arcadia: a study of Sidney's psychology. Texas Studies in Lit & Language, 1978, 20:303-329.

17, 285. Tuttle, Robert Clifford. The Identity of Walt Whitman: Motive, Theme, and Form in Leaves of Grass. DA, 1965, 26:2763.

17, 286. Twitchell, James B. 'Desire and loathing strangely mixed': the dream work of Christabel. Psychoanal Rev, 1974, 61:33-44.

17, 287. _____. Levels of consciousness in Keats' 'Endymion.' J Altered States of Consciousness, 1977-78, 3:309-323.

17, 288. _____. The Romantic Psychodrama: An Interpretation of 'The Rime of the Ancient Mariner, ' 'Manfred' and 'Prometheus Unbound, ' Act IV. DAI, 1972, 32:5204A-05A.

17, 289. _____. The supernatural structure of Byron's 'Man-fred. ' Studies in English Lit, 1975, 15:601-614.

17, 290. Tytell, John. Sexual imagery in the secular and sacred poems of Richard Crashaw. Lit & Psychol, 1971, 21: 21-27.

17, 291. Ullman, B. L. Psychological foreshadowing in the satires of Horace and Juvenal. Amer J Philology, 1950, 71: 408-416.

17, 292. Ungaretti, John R. Pederasty, heroism, and the family in classical Greece. J Homosexuality, 1978, 3:291-300.

17, 293. Untermeyer, Louis. Conrad Aiken: our best known unread poet. Saturday Rev, 25 Nov 1967, 28-29, 76-77.

17, 294. Uroff, Margaret D. Sylvia Plath on motherhood. Midwest Q, 1973, 15:70-90.

17, 295. _____. Sylvia Plath's women. Concerning Poetry, 1974, 7(1):45-56.

17, 296. Ustick, M. Repression: the poetry of Alden Nowlan. Canadian Lit, 1974, 60:43-50.

17, 297. Valency, Maurice. In Praise of Love. NY: Macmillan, 1961.

17, 298. Valentine, C. W. The function of images in the appreciation of poetry. British J Psychol, 1923-24, 14:164-191.

17, 299. Valori, P. Dante e la teologia della storia. In Psicoanalisi e strutturalismo di fronte a Dante. Vol. I: Premesse. Florence: Olschki, 1972, 423-427.

17, 300. Van Emde Boas, Conrad. The connection between Shakespeare's sonnets and his double travesty plays. Int J Sexology, 1950, 4:67-72.

17, 301. _____. Shakespeares Sonneten en Hun Verband met de Travesti-Double Spelen: een medisch-psychologische Studie. Amsterdam: Wereldbibliotheek, 1951.

17, 302. Vance, R. W. A reading of 'The Sleepers.' Walt Whitman Rev, 1972, 18:17-28.

17, 303. Various. A symposium on women in Swift's poems: Vanessa, Stella, Lady Acheson, and Celia. Papers on Language & Lit, 1978, 14(2):115-151.

17, 304. _____. Lectura Dantis Mystica: Il poema sacro alla luce delle conquiste psicologiche odierne. Florence: Olschki, 1969.

17, 305. _____. Poetry criticism. [Special Issue.] Agenda, 1976, 14(3).

17, 306. _____. Le maschere del dio prestigiatore: il poema sacro come organico susseguirsi delle più suffragate 'costanti d'inconscio.' Florence: Olschki, 1969.

17, 307. Vazzana, S. La struttura psicologica dell'opera pascoliana. Rome: Ciranna, 1974.

17, 308. Vermeule, Emily. Aspects of Death in Early Greek Art and Poetry. Berkeley: Univ. California Press, 1979.

17, 309. Verschuer, V. von. Die homosexuellen in Dantes Gottlicher Komodie. Jahrbüch für Sexuellen Zwischenschaffen, 1906, 8:351-364.

17, 310. Verstseg-Solleveld, C. M. Das Wiegenlied. Imago, 1937, 23:304-329.

17, 311. Verstraete, B. C. Ovid on homosexuality. Echos du Monde Classique, 1975, 19:79-83.

17, 312. Vertue, H. St. H. Morbid significance of modern verse. Guy's Hospital Gazette, 1949, 63:277-281.

17,313. Veszy-Wagner, Lilla. Mistress Pókai--a contribution to the theory of obsessive doubts. Amer Imago, 1960, 17:111-131.

17,314. Vidrine, Donald R. The Theme of Sterility in the Poetry of Mallarmé: Its Development and Evolution. DA, 1968, 29:618A-19A.

17,315. Vieth, David M. The mystery of personal identity: Swift's verses on his own death. In Martz, L. L., & Williams, A. L. (eds), The Author and His Work. New Haven: Yale Univ. Press, 1978, 245-262.

17,316. Vikis-Freibergs, Vaira. Echoes of the dainas and the search for identity in contemporary Latvian poetry. J Baltic Studies, 1975, 6:17-29.

17,317. Villar, Arturo del. La muerte, obsesión y tema total de Juan Ramón Jiménez. Arbor, 1975, 355-56:91-109.

17,318. Vincent, Sybil Korff. Flat-breasted miracles: realistic treatment of the woman's problem in the poetry of Edwin Arlington Robinson. Markham Rev, 1976, 6:14-15.

17,319. Viola, I. Premessa ad una lettura psicologica del Purgatorio. In Lectura Dantis Mystica: Il poema sacro alla luce delle conquiste psicologiche odierne. Florence: Olschki, 1969, 426-443.

17,320. Vitoux, Pierre. Jupiter's fatal child in 'Prometheus Unbound.' Criticism, 1968, 10:115-125.

17,321. Vlach, R. L'Exil et le poète; essai sur la psychologie de l'exil dans l'oeuvre d'Adam Mickiewicz. Amer Slavic Rev, 1960, 19:614-617.

17,322. Vodoz, J. Roland. Un Symbole. Paris: Champion, 1920.

17,323. Vogel, Lucy. Masks and doubles in Blok's early poetry. Russian Language J, 1976, 105:60-76.

17,324. Volkan, Vamik D. Five poems by Negro youngsters who faced a sudden desegregation. Psychiat Q, 1963, 607-617.

17,325. Vol'kenshtein, M. [Poetry as a complex informational system.] Nauka i Zhizn', 1970, 37:72-78.

17,326. Von Molnár, G. The composition of Novalis' Die Lehrlinge zu Sacs: a reevaluation. PMLA, 1970, 85:1002-1014.

17,327. Waddington, Miriam. Form in poetry. J Otto Rank Assn, 1968, 3(1):40-51.

17,328. Waddington, R. Melancholy against melancholy: Samson Agonistes as Renaissance tragedy. In Wittreich, J. A., Jr. (ed), Calm of Mind; Tercentenary Essays on 'Paradise Regained' and 'Samson Agonistes.' Cleveland: Case Western Reserve Univ. Press, 1971, 259-287.

17,329. Waggoner, Hyatt H. Science and the poetry of Robinson Jeffers. Amer Lit, 1940, 10:275-288.

17,330. Wailes, S. L. Theme and structure in Ulrich Füetrer's 'Poytislier.' MLN, 1977, 92:577-582.

17,331. Wain, John. The prophet Ezra v. 'The Egotistical Sublime.' Encounter, 1969, 33:63-70.

17, 332. Wais, K. K. T.   Das Vater-Sohn-Motiv in der Dichtung
1880-1930.   Leipzig: de Gruyter, 1931.
17, 333. Walcutt, Charles Child.   Yeats' 'Among the School Children, ' stanza V.   Explicator, 1968, 26(9): 72.
17, 334. Waldoff, Leon.   The father-son conflict in Prometheus Unbound.   The psychology of a vision.   Psychoanal Rev,
1975, 62: 79-96.
17, 335. _____.   The Mythic Basis of Three Major Poems of the
Romantic Period.   DA, 28: 68-17, 854.
17, 336. _____.   The quest for father and identity in 'The Rime
of the Ancient Mariner. '   Psychoanal Rev, 1971, 58:
439-453.
17, 337. _____.   Wordsworth's healing power: basic trust in
'Tinturn Abbey. '   Hartford Studies in Lit, 1972, 4:147-
166.
17, 338. Walker, Cheryl L.   The Women's Tradition in American
Poetry.   DAI, 1974, 34: 4294A-95A.
17, 339. Walker, Steven F.   Mallarmé's symbolist ecologue: the
'Faune' as pastoral.   PMLA, 1978, 93:106-117.
17, 340. Wall, Richard J. , & Fitzgerald, Roger.   Yeats and Jung:
an ideological comparison.   Lit & Psychol, 1963, 13:
44-52.
17, 341. Walsh, William.   The Use of Imagination: Educational
Thought and the Literary Mind.   London: Chatto &
Windus, 1959.
17, 342. Walsh, William P.   Sexual discovery and Renaissance
morality in Marlowe's 'Hero and Leander. '   Studies in
English Lit, 1500-1900, 1972, 12:33-54.
17, 343. Walzer, P. O.   Fragments d'esthétique.   Australian J
French Studies, 1971, 8(2): 230-242.
17, 344. _____.   The physiology of sex.   Yale French Studies,
1970, 44: 215-230.
17, 345. Wang, Veronica C.   The Theme of Isolation in Matthew
Arnold's Poetry.   DA, 1968, 28:3653A.
17, 346. Ward, Aileen.   The psychoanalytic theory of poetic form:
a content analysis.   Lit & Psychol, 1967, 17:30-37;
with comments, 1967, 17:37-46.
17, 347. Ward, Arthur Douglas.   Death and Eroticism in the Poetry
of Keats and Tennyson.   DAI, 1976, 37:344A-45A.
17, 348. Ware, J. Garth.   Coleridge's great poems reflecting the
mother image.   Amer Imago, 1961, 18:331-352.
17, 349. Warner, Anne Bradford.   Literary Tradition and Psychoanalytic Technique in Berryman's Dream Songs.   DAI,
1977, 38:3505A-06A.
17, 350. Warner, I. R.   Subjective time and space in Alberti's
Baladas y canciones de la Quinta del Mayor Loco.
Bulletin Hispanic Studies, 1973, 50:374-384.
17, 351. Warner, Janet.   D. G. Rossetti: love, death and art.
Hartford Studies in Lit, 1972, 4:228-240.
17, 352. Warren, Robert Penn.   Introduction: Rime of the Ancient
Mariner.   NY: Reynal, 1946.
17, 353. Wasserman, Earl R.   The limits of allusion in 'The Rape
of the Lock. '   J English Germanic Philology, 1966,
65:428-437.

17, 354. Wasserstrom, William. Cagey John: Berryman as medicine man. Centennial Rev, 1968, 12:334-354.
17, 355. Watson, David S. The Man of Law's Tale: Loss and Separation in the Canterbury Tales. DAI, 1971, 31: 4737A-38A.
17, 356. Waxler, Robert Phillip. William Blake: The Sexual Dynamics of His Early Illuminated Works. DAI, 1976, 37: 995A-96A.
17, 357. Weaver, B. Wordsworth Prelude: the poetic function of memory. Studies in Philology, 1937, 34:552-563.
17, 358. Webb, J. H. An Essay on the Influence of Poetry on the Mind. London: Hastings, 1839.
17, 359. Weber, J.-P. Genèse de l'oeuvre poétique. Paris: Gallimard, 1960.
17, 360. Webster, Brenda S. Dream and the Dreamer in the Works of W. B. Yeats. DA, 1968, 28:4192A.
17, 361. _____. Yeats; A Psychoanalytic Study. Stanford, Cal: Stanford Univ. Press, 1973; Review: P. Keane, New Republic, 1974, 170:24-26.
17, 362. _____. Yeats' 'The Shadowy Waters': oral motifs and identity in the drafts. Amer Imago, 1971, 28:3-16.
17, 363. Webster, Peter D. A critical fantasy or fugue. Amer Imago, 1949, 6:297-309.
17, 364. Weidhorn, Manfred. The anxiety dream in literature from Homer to Milton. Studies in Philology, 1967, 64:65-82.
17, 365. _____. Dreams and guilt. Harvard Theological Rev, 1965, 58:69-90.
17, 366. _____. The literary debate on the dream problem. Milton Q, 1971, 5(2):27-34.
17, 367. Weightman, John. Mallarmé and the language obsession. Encounter, 1978, 51:96-109.
17, 368. Weinberg, Albert K. Nephew and maternal uncle: a motive of early literature in the light of Freudian psychology. Psychoanal Rev, 1918, 5:381-397.
17, 369. Weiner, S. Ronald. The chord of self: Tennyson's 'Maud.' Lit & Psychol, 1966, 16:175-183.
17, 370. Weisberg, Robert. Randall Jarrell: the integrity of his poetry. Centennial Rev, 1973, 17:237-255.
17, 371. Weisblatt, S. The creativity of Sylvia Plath's Ariel period: toward origins and meanings. In The Annual of Psychoanalysis, Vol. 5. NY: IUP, 1977, 379-404.
17, 372. Weiskel, Thomas. Romantic Sublime: Studies in the Structure and Psychology of Transcendence. Baltimore: Johns Hopkins Univ. Press, 1976; Reviews: Carl Woodring, Keats-Shelley J, 1978, 27:133-135; J. B. Barth, English Language Notes, 1978, 15:219-222.
17, 373. Weiss, Jeri L. The Feminine Assertion: Women in the World of William Carlos Williams. DAI, 1973, 34: 344A.
17, 374. Weiss, Karl. On the psychogenesis of refrain and rhyme. In Nunberg, H., & Federn, E. (eds), Minutes of the Vienna Psychoanalytic Society, Vol. 4: 1912-1918. NY: IUP, 1975, 163-166.

17, 375.   . Rhyme and refrain. A contribution to the psychogenesis of the poetic means of expression. Imago,
1933, 19:2(6).

17, 376.   Weissman, Hope Phyllis. Antifeminism and Chaucer's
characterization of women. In Econonou, G. D. (ed),
Geoffrey Chaucer. NY: McGraw-Hill, 1975, 93-110.

17, 377.   Weissman, Judith. Vision, madness, and morality: poetry
and the theory of the bicameral mind. Georgia Rev,
1979, 33:118-148.

17, 378.   Welch, Dennis M. William Blake's 'Apocalypse': A Theo-
Psychological Interpretation. DAI, 1972, 33:736A.

17, 379.   Wellek, René. Review: Josephine Miles' Wordsworth and
the Vocabulary of Emotion. Modern Language Notes,
1943, 58:641-645.

17, 380.   Wells, F. L. Frau Wirtin and associates; a note on alien
corn. Amer Imago, 1951, 8:93-97.

17, 381.   . Hölderlin: greatest of 'schizophrenics.' J Abnormal Social Psychol, 1946, 41:199-200.

17, 382.   Wells, Henry W. Poet and psychiatrist. Merrill Moore,
M. D. JNMD, 1955, 122:595-602; Hopkins Rev, 1952,
6(1).

17, 383.   Wells, Larry D. Annette von Droste-Hülshoff's Johannes
Niemand: much ado about nobody. Germanic Rev,
1977, 52:109-121.

17, 384.   Weltner, Peter. The antinomic vision of Lyly's Endymion.
English Lit Renaissance, 1973, 3:5-29.

17, 385.   Wenger, C. N. Browning's dramatic monologues. College
English, 1941, 3:225-239.

17, 386.   Wentersdorf, Karl P. Chaucer's 'Merchant's Tale' and its
Irish analogues. Studies in Philology, 1966, 63:604-
629.

17, 387.   Westbrook, Perry Dickie. Abandonment and desertion in
the poetry of Robert Frost. In Frost: Centennial Essays II. Jackson: Univ. Mississippi Press, 1976, 291-
304.

17, 388.   Westler, Max Jay. The Sexual Orchard: A Study of Masculine and Feminine Relationships in the Early Poetry
of William Carlos Williams. DAI, 1975, 35:7927A.

17, 389.   Whalley, George. The Poetic Process. London: Routledge & Kegan Paul, 1953.

17, 390.   Wheeler, Richard P. Poetry and fantasy in Shakespeare's
sonnets 88-96. Lit & Psychol, 1972, 22:151-162.

17, 391.   . Yeats' 'Second Coming': what rough beast?
Amer Imago, 1974, 31:233-251.

17, 392.   White, Georgiana Donase. The Theme of Guilt in the Poetry and Plays of T. S. Eliot. DAI, 1976, 37:2906A.

17, 393.   White, W. Suicide and the poet: A. E. Housman. Today's Japan: Orient/West, 1960, 5:41-46.

17, 394.   White, William M. The dynamics of Whitman's poetry.
Sewanee Rev, 1972, 80:347-360.

17, 395.   Whitely, P. L., & McGeoch, J. A. The curve of retention
for poetry. J Educational Psychol, 1928, 19:471-479.

17, 396. Whiteside, George. A Freudian dream analysis of 'Sweeney Among the Nightingales.' Yeats Eliot Rev, 1978, 5:14-17.

17, 397. _____. T. S. Eliot's 'Dans le Restaurant.' Amer Imago, 1976, 33:155-173.

17, 398. Whiting, Charles G. Sexual imagery in La Jeune Parque and Charmes. PMLA, 1971, 36:940-945.

17, 399. Wickert, Max A. Form and Archetype in William Morris. DA, 1966, 66-1123.

17, 400. Wiesmann, Peter. Kirke und Odysseus. Versuch einer Deutung. Schweizerischen Zeitschrift für Psychologie, 1945, 4:124-136.

17, 401. Wijsen, Louk M. P. T. Cognition and synthetic text: an interpretation of Eichendorff's 'Waldgespräch.' Lit & Psychol, 1979, 39:185-192.

17, 402. Wilbur, Robert Hunter. The art of poetry IX: Conrad Aiken--an interview. Paris Rev, 1968, 11:97-124.

17, 403. Wilding, Michael. Allusion and innuendo in MacFlecknoe. Essays in Criticism, 1969, 19:355-370.

17, 404. Williams, A. Hyatt. Keats' 'La Belle Dame Sans Merci': the bad-breast mother. Amer Imago, 1966, 23:63-81.

17, 405. Williams, Miller. Color as symbol and the two-way metaphor in the poetry of John Crowe Ransom. Mississippi Q, 1969, 22:29-37.

17, 406. Williamson, Alan. The network and the community. Amer Poetry Rev, 1974, 3(1):19-21.

17, 407. Williamson, George. A Reader's Guide to T. S. Eliot. NY: Farrar, Straus, 1966, 57-70.

17, 408. Wilner, Eleanor. The poetics of Emily Dickinson. J English Lit History, 1971, 38:126-154.

17, 409. Wilson, F. A. C. Yeats's 'A Bronze Head': a Freudian investigation. Lit & Psychol, 1972, 22:5-12.

17, 410. Wilson, Harry B. Psychological Projection in Six Romantic Poems. DAI, 1976, 37:3631A.

17, 411. Wilson, James D. Beatrice Cenci and Shelley's vision of moral responsibility. Ariel, 1978, 9:75-89.

17, 412. Wilson, R. J. George Herbert's 'A Parodie': its double meaning. Amer Imago, 1977, 34:155-157.

17, 413. Wilson, Robert F., Jr. The fecal vision in 'MacFlecknoe.' Satire Newsletter, 1970, 8:1-4.

17, 414. Wilson, Robert N. Aesthetic symbolism. Amer Imago, 1955, 12:275-292.

17, 415. _____. Man Made Plain: The Poet in Contemporary Society. Cleveland: Allen, 1959.

17, 416. _____. The poet in American society. In The Arts in Society. Englewood Cliffs, NJ: Prentice-Hall, 1964, 1-34.

17, 417. _____. Poetic creativity, process and personality. Psychiatry, 1954, 17:163-176.

17, 418. Wimsatt, William K., Jr. The Verbal Icon. Studies in the Meaning of Poetry. NY: Noonday Press, 1954.

17, 419. Winterstein, Alfred R. F. La Géante. Int Zeitschrift für Psychoanalyse, 1912, 2:224.

17, 420. _____. Die Nausikaäepisode in der Odyssee. Imago, 1920, 6:349-384.

17, 421. _____. Psychoanalyse und Dichtung. Psychoanalytische Bewegung, 1933, 5:373-375.

17, 422. Winzie, George B., Jr. The Songs of Bilitis: a voyage in lesbianism. Archives Criminal Psychodynamics, 1957, 2:530-540.

17, 423. Witcutt, W. P. Blake: A Psychological Study. London: Hollis & Caster, 1946; Toronto: McClelland & Stewart, 1946.

17, 424. _____. The structure of psyche. A psychological examination of the poetry of William Blake. Wind & Rain, 1945, 3:14-21.

17, 425. Wittels, Fritz. Alles um Liebe; eine Urweltdichtung. Berlin: Fleischel, 1912.

17, 426. Wolf, Howard R. E. A. Robinson and the integration of the self. In Mazzaro, J. (ed), Modern American Poetry: Essays in Criticism. NY: McKay, 1970, 40-59.

17, 427. Wolf, M. Existential psychology and a romantic poem. Psychiat Q, 1968, 42[Suppl]:297-302.

17, 428. Wolfenstein, Martha. Analysis of a juvenile poem. In The Psychoanalytic Study of the Child, Vol. 11. NY: IUP, 1956, 450-470.

17, 429. Wolff, G. Psychiatrie und Dichtung. Wiesbaden: 1903.

17, 430. Womack, Judy. The American woman in 'Song of Myself.' Walt Whitman Rev, 1973, 19:67-72.

17, 431. Wood, Ann Douglas. Mrs. Sigourney and the sensibility of the inner space. New England Q, 1972, 45:163-181.

17, 432. Woodman, Leonora. 'A Giant on the Horizon': Wallace Stevens and the 'Idea of Man.' Texas Studies in Lit & Language, 1974, 15:759-786.

17, 433. Woodman, Ross. Shaman, poet, and failed initiate: reflections on romanticism and Jungian psychology. Studies in Romanticism, 1980, 19:51-82.

17, 434. Woodring, Carl. Christabel of Cumberland. Rev English Lit, 1966, 7:43-53.

17, 435. Woodward, Kathleen M. Master songs of mediation: the late poems of Eliot, Pound, Stevens, and Williams. In Spicker, S. F., et al. (eds), Aging and the Elderly. Atlantic Highlands, NJ: Humanities Press, 1978, 181-202.

17, 436. Woolley, Mary Lynn. Wordsworth's symbolic Vale as it functions in 'The Prelude.' Studies in Romanticism, 1968, 7:176-189.

17, 437. Wordsworth, Jonathan. Double meanings: III. 'What is it, that has been done?' The central problem of Maud. Essays in Criticism, 1974, 24:356-362.

17, 438. Wormhoudt, Arthur. Cold pastoral. Amer Imago, 1951, 8:275-285.

17, 439. _____. The Demon Lover; A Psychoanalytic Approach to Literature. NY: Exposition, 1949.

17, 440. _____. The five layer structure of sublimation and literary analysis. Amer Imago, 1956, 13:205-219.

17,441. _____. The Muse at Length. A Psychoanalytical Study
of the Odyssey. Boston: Christopher, 1953.
17,442. _____. A psychoanalytic interpretation of The Love
Song of J. Alfred Prufrock. Perspective, 1949, 2:109-
117.
17,443. _____. The unconscious identification of words and
milk. Amer Imago, 1949, 6:57-68.
17,444. Worthington, Mabel P. Byron's Don Juan: certain psychological aspects. Lit & Psychol, 1957, 7(4):50-55.
17,445. _____. Comment on 'Kubla Khan' as an elated experience. Lit & Psychol, 1966, 16:40-42.
17,446. _____. Gilbert and Sullivan songs in the works of
James Joyce. Hartford Studies in Lit, 1969, 1:209-218.
17,447. Wunnenberg, Wulf. [Contemporary mythical figures.]
Praxis der Psychotherapie, 1975, 20:266-276.
17,448. Wylder, Edith. The speaker of Emily Dickinson's 'My
Life Had Stood--A Loaded Gun.' Rocky Mt Modern
Language Assn Bulletin, 1969, 23:3-8.

17,449. Yang, Kuo-Shu, & Tzuo, Huan-Yuan. The functional relationships between the pleasantness value and the char-
acter-number of the Chinese classical poem. Acta
Psychologica Taiwanica, 1961, 3:125-131.
17,450. Yoeli, M. The life and poetry of Shaul Tchnerichovsky.
Hebrew Medical J, 1964, 1:243-249.
17,451. Yost, George, Jr. An identification in Keats' 'Ode to
Psyche.' Philological Q, 1957, 36:496-500.
17,452. Young, H. McClure. The Sonnets of Shakespeare; A Psychosexual Analysis. Columbia, Mo: Author, 1937.
17,453. Young, Gloria L. 'The fountain of all forms': poetry and
the unconscious in Emerson and Howard Nemerov. In
DeMott, R. J., & Marovitz, S. E. (eds), Artful Thunder;
Versions of the Romantic Tradition in American Literature. Kent: Kent State Univ. Press, 1975, 241-267.
17,454. Young, J. R. Medicus magnus. J History Medicine & Al-
lied Sciences, 1980, 35:40-57.

17,455. Zeck, Gregory R. Hart Crane's 'The Wine Menagerie':
the logic of metaphor. Amer Imago, 1979, 36:197-214.
17,456. Zillig, M. Zur Psychologie des dichterisch schaffenden
Kindes. Ein Beitrag zur Wissenschaftlichen Personlichkeitsforschung. Zeitschrift für Psychologie, 1929, 112:
302-324.
17,457. Zimmerman, Michael. The pursuit of pleasure and the
uses of death: Wallace Stevens' 'Sunday Morning.'
Univ. Rev, 1966, 93-100.
17,458. Zweig, Paul. The new Surrealism. Salmagundi, 1973,
22-23:269-284.
17,459. _____. The Sonnets of Shakespeare. In The Heresy
of Self-Love: A Study of Subversive Individualism. NY:
Harper & Row, 1968, 100-108.

SCRIPTURES

17, 460. Ahrens, Hans. Die Bibel im Spiegel deutsches Geistesle-
bens. Das Kain- und Abel- Motiv. In Deutsche Bibel-
Archiv Hamburg Jahresberich 1949-50, 1950, 1-6.
17, 461. Albright, William F. Yahweh and the Gods of Canaan.
Garden City, NY: Doubleday, 1968.
17, 462. Alcorn, D. E. New Testament psychology. British J Medical Psychol, 1937, 16:270-280.
17, 463. Allwohn, A. Die Ehe des Propheten Hosea in psychoanalytischer Beleuchtung. Giessen: Töpelmann, 1926.
17, 464. Almansi, Renato J. A further contribution to the psychoanalytic interpretation of the Menorah. J Hillside Hospital, 1954, 3:3-18.
17, 465. _____. A psychoanalytic interpretation of the Menorah.
J Hillside Hospital, 1953, 2:80-95.
17, 466. Anderson, Felix A. Psychopathological glimpse of some
Biblical characters. Psychoanal Rev, 1927, 14:56-70.
17, 467. Anon. Moisés, ultima revelação de Freud. Imprensa
médica, 1942, 18:143-145.
17, 468. Arlow, Jacob A. The consecration of the prophet. Psychoanal Q, 1951, 20:374-397.
17, 469. Armstrong, Richard G. The Bible and sexuality. In
Wynn, J. C. (ed), Sexual Ethics and Christian Responsibility. NY: Association Press, 1970, 199-206.
17, 470. Asher, Charles W. The divine and human in Jesus Christ.
Psychol Perspectives, 1976, 7:168-181.

17, 471. Bach, Marcus. Psychic elements in Buddhism. Fate,
1967, 20(1):85-91.
17, 472. Bahnsen, Greg L. Homosexuality: A Biblical View.
Grand Rapids, Mich: Baker Book House, 1978.
17, 473. Bakan, David. Freud and the Zohar. Commentary, 1960,
29:65-66.
17, 474. _____. Sigmund Freud and the Jewish Mystical Tradition. NY: Van Nostrand, 1958.
17, 475. Barag, G. G. The mother in the religious concepts of Judaism. Amer Imago, 1946, 4:32-53.
17, 476. Bareau, André. The superhuman personality of Buddha and
its symbolism in the Mahāparinirvānasūtra of the Dhar-
maguptaka. In Kitagawa, J. M., & Long, C. H. (eds),
Myths and Symbols. Chicago: Univ. Chicago Press,
1969, 9-21.

849

17, 477.   Baron, Salo Wittmayer.   Moses and Monotheism: a review
           of Freud.   In Ancient and Medieval Jewish History.
           New Brunswick, NJ: Rutgers Univ.   Press, 1972, 3-9;
           Amer J Sociology, 1939, 45:471-477.
17, 478.   Batteau, John M.   Sexual differences: a cultural conven-
           tion?   Christianity Today, 1977, 21:8-10.
17, 479.   Beck, S. J.   Abraham's ordeal.   Psychoanal Rev, 1963,
           50:175-189.
17, 480.   Beg, Moazziz Ali.   The theory of personality in the Bha-
           gavad Gita--a study in transpersonal psychology.
           Psychologia.   Int J Psychol in the Orient, 1970, 13(1):
           12-17.
17, 481.   Beirnaert, Louis.   Introduction to the reading of Freud's
           texts on religion.   In Wolman, B. B.   (ed), Psychoanaly-
           sis and Catholicism.   NY: Gardner, 1976, 19-30.
17, 482.   Beiswanger, G. W.   The character value of the Old Testa-
           ment stories.   Univ. Iowa Studies: Studies in Char-
           acter, 1930, 3(3).
17, 483.   Bellak, Leopold.   A note about Adam's apple.   Psychoanal
           Rev, 1942, 29:300-302.
17, 484.   Bennett, Boyce M.   Vision and audition in biblical prophecy.
           Parapsychol Rev, 1978, 9:1-12.
17, 485.   Benno, Jacob.   The childhood and youth of Moses.   In
           Essays in Honor of the Very Rev. Dr. J. H. Hertz.
           London: Goldston, 1942.
17, 486.   Berguer, Georges.   Some Aspects of the Life of Jesus
           from the Psychological and Psychoanalytical Point of
           View.   NY: Harcourt, Brace, 1923.
17, 487.   Berkley-Hill, Owen.   A short study of the life and char-
           acter of Mohammed.   Int J Psycho-Anal, 1921, 2:31-53.
17, 488.   Bigger, Stephen F.   Family laws of Leviticus 18 in their
           setting.   J Biblical Lit, 1979, 98:187-203.
17, 489.   Binet-Sanglé, Charles.   Le Prophète Elie.   Archivio di
           Anthropologia Criminale, Psichiatria e Medicale Legale,
           1904, 19:161-209.
17, 490.   _____.   Le Prophète Elisée.   Archivio di Anthropologia
           Criminale, Psichiatria e medicale Legale, 1905, 20:136-
           141.
17, 491.   _____.   Les Prophètes Juifs; étude de psychologie mor-
           bide (des origines à Elie).   Paris: Dujarri, 1905.
17, 492.   _____.   Le Prophète Samuel.   Annales Médico-Psychol-
           ogiques, 1903, 19:204-212.
17, 493.   Bird, Phyllis.   Images of women in the Old Testament.
           In Ruether, R. R. (ed), Religion and Sexism.   NY:
           Simon & Schuster, 1974, 41-88.
17, 494.   Bitton, Livia E.   Biblical names of literary Jewesses.
           Names, 1973, 21:103-109.
17, 495.   Blumenthal, Erik.   Individual psychology and Baha'i.   In
           Mosak, H. H. (ed), Alfred Adler: His Influence on
           Psychology Today.   Park Ridge, NJ: Noyes, 1974,
           228-237.
17, 496.   Bonaparte, Marie.   Eros, Saul de Tarsus et Freud.   Rev
           Française de Psychanalyse, 1957, 21:23-33.

17, 497.   Booth, A. Peter.   Abraham and Agememnon: a compara-
           tive study of myth.   Humanities Assn Bulletin, 1974,
           25:290-297.
17, 498.   Bose, Girindrashekhar.   The Gita--a psychological study.
           Probashi, Oct 1931.
17, 499.   Brandt, Lewis W.   Freud and Schiller.   Psychoanal Rev,
           1959, 46(4):97-101.
17, 500.   Brenner, Arthur B.   The covenant with Abraham.   Psy-
           choanal Rev, 1952, 39:34-52.
17, 501.   _____.   The great mother goddess: puberty initiation
           rites and the covenant of Abraham.   Psychoanal Rev,
           1950, 37:320-340.
17, 502.   _____.   Onan, the levirate marriage, and the genealogy
           of the Messiah.   JAPA, 1962, 10:701-721.
17, 503.   Brewster, Paul G.   Sex in the Scriptures.   Tennessee
           Folklore Society Bulletin, 1962, 28:48-51.
17, 504.   Brim, Charles J.   Job's illness: pellagra.   In Sorsby, A.
           (ed), Tenements of Clay.   London: Friedmann, 1974,
           23-28; Archives Dermatology & Syphilology, 1942, 46:
           371-376.
17, 505.   Brody, Matthew.   Phylogenesis of sexual morality.   Psy-
           chiatric exegesis on Onan and Samson.   New York State
           J Medicine, 1968, 68:2510-2514.
17, 506.   Burke, Kenneth.   On the first three chapters of Genesis.
           In May, R. (ed), Symbolism in Religion and Literature.
           NY: Braziller, 1960, 118-151.
17, 507.   Bychowski, Gustav.   The ego and the introjects: origins
           of religious experience.   In Psychoanalysis and the So-
           cial Sciences, Vol. 5.   NY: IUP, 1958, 246-279.

17, 508.   Captain, Philip A.   The effect of positive reinforcement
           on comprehension, attitudes, and rate of Bible reading
           in adolescents.   J Psychol & Theology, 1975, 3:49-55.
17, 509.   Carlson, David E.   Jesus' style of relating: the search
           for a biblical view of counseling.   J Psychol & Theol-
           ogy, 1976, 4:181-192.
17, 510.   Carmichael, Calum M.   Ceremonial crux: removing a
           man's sandal as a female gesture of contempt.   J Bib-
           lical Lit, 1977, 96:321-336.
17, 511.   Carr, B.   Biblical and theological basis for the struggle
           for human rights.   Ecumenical Rev, 1975, 27:117-123.
17, 512.   Cerling, Charles E.   Some thoughts on a biblical view of
           anger: a response.   J Psychol & Theology, 1974, 2:
           266-268.
17, 513.   Cesarman, Fernando C.   'Ecocide' in the myth of the
           Deluge.   Cuadernos de Psicoanálisis, 1971, 6:3-9.
17, 514.   Charny, Israel W.   And Abraham went to slay Isaac: a
           parable of killer, victim, and bystander in the family
           of man.   J Ecumenical Studies, 1973, 10:304-310.
17, 515.   Chaudhuri, Arun K. B.   A psychoanalytic study of the Hin-
           du Mother Goddess (Kali) concept.   Amer Imago, 1956,
           13:123-146.

17, 516.   Choisy, Maryse.   Quelques reflexions sur une psychologie
            de Cain.   Psyché, 1953, 8:89-95.
17, 517.   Churgin, G. A.   Erich Fromm al ha-Tanah.   Bitzaron,
            1975, 66(3):101-106.
17, 518.   Cole, D. T.   A personality sketch of Cain, the son of
            Adam.   J Psychol & Theology, 1978, 6:37-39.
17, 519.   Cole, William G.   Sex and Love in the Bible.   London:
            Hodder & Stoughton, 1960, 342-372; NY: Association
            Press, 1960, 342-372.
17, 520.   Coriat, Isadore H.   Dreams and the Samson myth.   Int
            Zeitschrift für Psychoanalyse, 1914, 2:460-462.
17, 521.   Corrêa, Paulo D.   O onanismo, um tema biblico: coitus
            interruptus.   Revista brazileira de médeca, 1950, 7:
            263-269.
17, 522.   Craddock, Fred.   How does the New Testament deal with
            the issue of homosexuality?   Encounter, 1979, 40:197-
            208.
17, 523.   Craig, Robert P. , & Middleton, Carl.   Sexuality and reli-
            gious education.   Religious Education, 1977, 72:595-605.
17, 524.   Cronbach, Abraham.   New studies in the psychology of
            Judaism.   Hebrew Union College Annual, 1946, 19:206-
            273.
17, 525.   _____.   The psychoanalytic study of Judaism.   In
            Hebrew Union College Annual, Vol. 9.   Philadelphia:
            Jewish Publication Society, 1932, 605-731.
17, 526.   _____.   The psychology of religion.   A bibliographical
            survey.   Psychol Bulletin, 1928, 25:701-719.

17, 527.   Darroch, Jane.   An interpretation of the personality of
            Jesus.   British J Medical Psychol, 1947, 21:75-79.
17, 528.   De Oliveira, Walderedo.   El simbolismo de la Torre de
            Babel; la confusión de lenguas y la disociacion es-
            quizofrenica.   Revista de Psicoanálisis, 1951, 8:359-
            391.
17, 529.   Desmonde, William H.   The murder of Moses.   Amer
            Imago, 1950, 7:351-367.
17, 530.   Dolto, Françoise.   L'Evangile au risque de la psychana-
            lyse.   Paris: Delarge, 1978.
17, 531.   Dreifuss, Gustav.   The binding of Isaac: Genesis 22--The
            Akedah.   J Analytical Psychol, 1975, 20:50-56.
17, 532.   _____.   The figure of Satan and Abraham: in the leg-
            ends on Genesis 22, the Akedah.   J Analytical Psychol,
            1972, 17:166-178.
17, 533.   _____.   Isaac, the sacrifical lamb.   J Analytical Psy-
            chol, 1971, 16:69-78.

17, 534.   Eckstein, Rudolf.   The Tower of Babel in psychology and
            in psychiatry.   Amer Imago, 1950, 7:77-141.
17, 535.   Ehrenwald, Jan.   Scriptural demonology and the healing
            miracles of the Bible.   In From Medicine Man to Freud.
            NY: Dell 1956, 103-113.

17, 536. Eliade, Mircea. Symbolism indien de l'abolition du temps.
          JPNP, 1952, 45:430-438.
17, 537. Ellis, Albert, & Sagarin, Edward. Potiphar's wife. In
          A Study of the Oversexed Woman. NY: Gilbert, 1964,
          38-42.
17, 538. Epstein, Louis M. Marriage Laws in the Bible and the
          Talmud. Cambridge: Harvard Univ. Press, 1942;
          Oxford: Oxford Univ. Press, 1944; Review: James E.
          Hughes, Psychiatry, 1943, 6:253.
17, 539. Evans-Wentz, Walter (ed). The Tibetan Book of the Dead.
          NY: Galaxy, 1960.

17, 540. Fagan, Joen. It ain't necessarily so. Transactional An-
          alytical J, 1976, 6:156-158.
17, 541. Farbridge, Maurice H. Studies in Biblical and Semitic
          Symbolism. London: Kegan Paul, 1923; NY: Dutton,
          1923.
17, 542. Feldman, Arthur A. The Davidic dynasty and the Davidic
          messiah. Amer Imago, 1960, 17:163-178.
17, 543. _____. Freud's Moses and Monotheism and the three
          stages of Israelitish religion. Psychoanal Rev, 1944,
          31:361-418.
17, 544. Feldman, Sandor S. Patterns in obedience and disobedi-
          ence. Amer Imago, 1969, 21-36.
17, 545. _____. The sin of Reuben, first-born son of Jacob.
          In Psychoanalysis and the Social Sciences, Vol. 4.
          NY: IUP, 1955, 282-287.
17, 546. Fiedler, Leslie A. Master of dreams. Partisan Rev,
          1967, 34:339-358.
17, 547. Fingert, Hyman H. Psychoanalytic study of the minor
          prophet, Jonah. Psychoanal Rev, 1954, 41:55-65.
17, 548. Fodor, A. The fall of man in the Book of Genesis.
          Amer Imago, 1954, 11:203-231.
17, 549. _____. Was Moses an Egyptian? In Psychoanalysis
          and the Social Sciences, Vol. 3. NY: IUP, 1951,
          189-200.
17, 550. Fortes, Meyer. Oedipus and Job in West African Religion.
          Cambridge: Cambridge Univ. Press, 1959.
17, 551. Fortune, R. F. The symbolism of the serpent. Int J
          Psycho-Anal, 1926, 7:237-243.
17, 552. Foxe, A. N. Pilate. J Criminology & Psychopathology,
          1943, 5:281-287.
17, 553. Frank-Kameneckii, J. S. [The province of woman in Bibli-
          cal eschatology.] Sbornik statei S. F. Oldenburgu Aka-
          damie Nauk, 1934, 535-548.
17, 554. Freedman, A. M. Drugs and sexual behavior. MAHS,
          1967, 1(3):25-27, 30-31.
17, 555. Freemantle, Anne. The Oedipal legend in Christian hagi-
          ology. Psychoanal Q, 1950, 19:408-409.
17, 556. Freud, Sigmund. The Interpretation of Dreams. NY:
          Basic Books, 1958, 69-70, 97, 334, 380-381, 458.

17, 557. _____. The Moses of Michelangelo. In Collected Papers, Vol. 4. London: Hogarth, 1925; NY: Basic Books, 1959, 257-287; In Standard Edition, Vol. 13. London: Hogarth, 1957, 211-236 (1914); Rev Française de Psychanalyse, 1927, 1:120-147.

17, 558. _____. Moses and Monotheism. NY: Knopf, 1939; In Standard Edition, Vol. 23, London: Hogarth, 1964, 3-137 (1939); Budapest: Bibliotheca, 1946; Milan: Pepe Dizz, 1953; Paris: Gallimard, 1948; Amsterdam: Breughel-Uitgever, 1947; Review: William V. Silverberg, Psychiatry, 1939, 2:417-420.

17, 559. _____. Wenn Moses ein Ägypter war. Imago, 1937, 23:387-419; Moses an Egyptian. Int J Psycho-Anal, 1938, 19:291-298.

17, 560. Fromm, Erich. You Shall Be As Gods: A Radical Interpretation of the Old Testament and Its Tradition. Greenwich, Conn: Fawcett, 1966; London: Cape, 1977.

17, 561. Frye, Northrop. History and myth in the Bible. In Fletcher, A. J. S. (ed), The Literature of Fact. NY: Columbia Univ. Press, 1976, 1-19.

17, 562. Gangel, Kenneth D. Toward a biblical theology of marriage and family: IV. Epistles and revelation. J Psychol & Theology, 1977, 5:318-331.

17, 563. Garnot, Jean Sainte Fare. Les Fonctions, les pouvoirs, et la nature du nom propre dans l'ancienne Egypte d'aprés les Textes des Pyramides. JPNP, 1948, 41: 463-472.

17, 564. Gelberman, J. H. , & Kobak, D. The Psalms as psychological and allegorical poems. In Leedy, J. J. (ed), Poetry Therapy. Philadelphia: Lippincott, 1969, 133-141.

17, 565. Gerber, Israel J. The Psychology of the Suffering Mind. NY: Jonathan David, 1951.

17, 566. Goitein, Lionel. Green pastures: Psalm XXIII. Amer Imago, 1956, 13:409-414.

17, 567. _____. The importance of the Book of Job for analytic thought. Amer Imago, 1954, 11:407-415.

17, 568. Goldman, Norman S. Rabbinic theology and the unconscious. J Religion & Health, 1978, 17:144-150.

17, 569. Goleman, Daniel. The Buddha on meditation and states of consciousness. In Tart, C. T. (ed), Transpersonal Psychologies. NY: Harper & Row, 1975, 203-230.

17, 570. Gonen, Jay Y. The men said, 'Let us make God in our image, after our likeness.' Lit & Psychol, 1971, 21: 69-79.

17, 571. Granek, M. [The madman concept and its implications in the Talmudic literature and its exegesis.] Annales Médico-Psychologiques, 1976, 1(1):17-36.

17, 572. Graves, Robert, & Patai, Raphael. Hebrew Myths: The Book of Genesis. Garden City, NY: Doubleday, 1964; NY: McGraw-Hill, 1966.

17, 573. Greenwald, Anthony G. Does the Good Samaritan parable increase helping? A comment on Darley and Batson's no-effect conclusion. J Personality & Social Psychol, 1975, 32:578-583.

17, 574. Gressot, Michel. Le Mythe dogmatique et le système moral des Manichéens. Rev Française de Psychanalyse, 1953, 17:398-427.

17, 575. Grimm, R. R. Die Paradiesesche. Eine erotische Utopie des Mittelalters. In Hundsnurscher, F., & Müller, V. (eds), Getempert und gemischet. Göppingen: Kümmerle, 1972, 1-25.

17, 576. Grinberg, L. Rivalry and envy between Joseph and his brothers. Samiksa, 1963, 17:150-171.

17, 577. Grollman, Earl A. Judaism in Sigmund Freud's World. NY: Appleton-Century-Crofts, 1965.

17, 578. _____. Some sights and insights of history, psychology and psychoanalysis concerning the father-god, and mother-goddess concepts of Judaism and Christianity. Amer Imago, 1963, 20:187-209.

17, 579. Gubitz, Myron B. Amalek: the eternal adversary. Psychol Perspectives, 1977, 8:34-58.

17, 580. Guirdham, Arthur. Christ and Freud. NY: Macmillan, 1959.

17, 581. Gutheil, Emil A. Traumdeutung im Talmud. Psychoanalytische Praxis, 1933, 3:89-91.

17, 582. Gutierrez, Donald. A 'new heaven and an old earth': D. H. Lawrence's Apocalypse and the Book of Revelation. Rev Existential Psychol & Psychiat, 1977, 15:61-85.

17, 583. Guze, H. Psychosocial adjustment of transsexuals: an evaluation and theoretical formulation. In Green, R., & Money, J. (eds) Transsexualism and Sex Reassignment. Baltimore: Johns Hopkins Univ. Press, 1969, 171-181.

17, 584. Haeberle, Erwin J. Historical roots of sexual repression. In Gochros, H. L., & Gochros, J. S. (eds), The Sexually Oppressed. NY: Association Press, 1977, 3-27.

17, 585. Halder, Aruna. The Buddhist conception of personality based on Abhidharmakosa of Vasubandhu. Samiksa, 1967, 21(2):55-66.

17, 586. Hall, G. Stanley. Jesus, the Christ, in the Light of Psychology, 2 Vols. NY: Doubleday, Page, 1917.

17, 587. Halverson, John. Religion and psychosocial development in Sinhalese Buddhism. J Asian Studies, 1978, 37:221-232.

17, 588. Hammes, John A. Atheistic humanistic and Christian humanistic perspectives on the human condition. J Psychol & Theology, 1975, 3:36-41.

17, 589. Hasofer, A. M. Studies in the history of probability and statistics. xvi. Random mechanisms in talmudic literature. Biometrika, 1967, 54:316-321.

17, 590. Hauptman, Judith. Images of women in the Talmud. In Ruether, R. R. (ed), Religion and Sexism; Images of Woman in the Jewish and Christian Traditions. NY: Simon & Schuster, 1974, 184-212.

17, 591. Heidel, Alexander (ed). The Gilgamesh Epic and Old Testament Parallels. Chicago: Univ. Chicago Press, 1946.

17, 592. Henn, Thomas Rice. Imagery. In The Bible As Literature. NY: Oxford Univ. Press, 1970, 63-79.

17, 593. Hofling, Charles K. Notes on Raychaudhuri's 'Jesus Christ and Sree Krishna.' Amer Imago, 1958, 15:213-226.

17, 594. Hower, John T. The misunderstanding and mishandling of anger. J Psychol & Theology, 1974, 2:269-275.

17, 595. Hughes, Richard E. Szondi's theory of the Cain complex. Amer Imago, 1979, 36:260-274.

17, 596. Irwin, Joyce. Use of Hebrews 11:11 as embryological proof-text. Harvard Theological Rev, 1978, 71:312-316.

17, 597. Jacobson, Evelyn Margaret. The Depiction of Human Love Relationships in Early Middle High German Versions of Genesis. DAI, 1977, 38:1424A-25A.

17, 598. Johnson, Paul E. Jesus as psychologist. Pastoral Psychol, 1951, 2:17-21.

17, 599. Joines, Karen R. Serpent Symbolism in the Old Testament: A Linguistic Archaeological, and Literary Study. Haddonfield, NJ: Haddonfield House, 1974.

17, 600. Jones, Ernest. The birth and death of Moses. Int J Psycho-Anal, 1958, 39:1-4.

17, 601. _____. A psycho-analytic study of the Holy Ghost. In Essays in Applied Psycho-Analysis. London: Hogarth, 1923, 415-430; London: Hogarth, 1951, 2:358-373; Imago, 1923, 9:58-72; Archivio Generale di Neurologie, Psichiatria e Psicoanalisti, 1922, 3:117-126.

17, 602. _____. Review: Sigmund Freud's Moses and Monotheism. Int J Psycho-Anal, 1940, 21:230-240; Int Zeitschrift für Psychoanalyse, 1940, 25:418-430.

17, 603. Jung, Carl Gustav. Aion: Researches into the Phenomenology of the Self. NY: Pantheon, 1959.

17, 604. _____. Answer to Job. NY: Meridian, 1959.

17, 605. _____. Concerning rebirth. 2. The psychology of rebirth. In Collected Works of C. G. Jung, Vol. 9. Princeton: Princeton Univ. Press, 1968, 120-122, 128, 135-147.

17, 606. _____. Modern Man in Search of a Soul. NY: Harcourt Brace, 1933; London: Paul, Trench, Trubner, 1933. In Collected Works. NY: Pantheon, 1953-61.

17, 607. _____. Psychological aspects of the mother archetype. In Collected Works of C. G. Jung, Vol. 9. Princeton: Princeton Univ. Press, 1968, 98-100.

17, 608.   Kahn, Jack. Job's Illness: Loss, Grief and Imagination.
           A Psychological Interpretation. Oxford/NY: Pergamon,
           1975.
17, 609.   Kara, Ashok. The ego dilemma and the Buddhist experience
           of enlightenment. J Religion & Health, 1979, 18:144-
           159.
17, 610.   _____. Psychology of Buddhism. Honesdale, Pa:
           Himalayan International Institute, 1980.
17, 611.   Katz, Joseph. The Joseph dreams anew. Psychoanal Rev,
           1963, 50:252-278.
17, 612.   Kee, Howard Clark. The linguistic background of 'shame'
           in the New Testament. In Black, M., & Smalley, W. A.
           (eds), On Language, Culture, and Religion. The Hague:
           Mouton, 1974, 133-147.
17, 613.   Kinkel, Johann. Wissenschaftliche Lehren in alten Reli-
           gions-und Bibelglauben und den sogenannten. Volks-
           weisheiten (Sprechen). Lozi Gedanke, 1927, 8:1-22.
17, 614.   Klein, Joel. Psychology Encounters Judaism. NY: Phi-
           losophical Library, 1979.
17, 615.   Kluger, Rivkah Schärf. Satan in the Old Testament.
           Evanston, Ill: Northwestern Univ. Press, 1967.
17, 616.   König, Eduard. Die Sexualität im Hohen Lied und ihre
           Grenze. Zeitschrift für Sexualwissenschaft, 1922, 9:1-
           4.

17, 617.   Langer, Georg. Die Erotik der Kabbala. Prague: Flesch,
           1923.
17, 618.   Lauer, C. Das Wesen des Traumen in der Beurteilung
           der talmudischen und rabbinischen Literatur. Int Zeit-
           schrift für Psychoanalyse, 1913, 1:459-469.
17, 619.   Laughlin, Henry P. King David's anger. Psychoanal Q,
           1954, 23:87-95.
17, 620.   Lazarsfeld, R. Mythos und Komplex. Int Zeitschrift für
           Individual-Psychologie, 1930, 8:261-263.
17, 621.   Leach, Edmund Ronald. Pulleyar and the Lord Buddha:
           an aspect of religious syncretism in Ceylon. Psycho-
           anal & Psychoanal Rev, 1962, 49(2):81-102.
17, 622.   Leschnitzer, Adolf F. Faust and Moses. Amer Imago,
           1949, 6:229-243.
17, 623.   Levin, A. J. Oedipus and Samson, the rejected hero-child.
           Int J Psycho-Anal, 1957, 38:105-116.
17, 624.   Levin, Max. Psychoanalytic interpretation of two state-
           ments from the Talmud. Int J Psycho-Anal, 1930, 11:
           94-95.
17, 625.   Levin, Sidney. Saul's illness. Central African J Medi-
           cine, 1965, 11:301-302.
17, 626.   Levy, Ludwig. Die Sexualsymbolik der Bibel und des Tal-
           mud. Zeitschrift für Sexualwissenschaft, 1914, 1:274-
           279, 318-326.
17, 627.   _____. Ist das Kainszeichen die Beschneidung? Ein
           kritischer Beitrag zur Bibelexegese. Imago, 1919, 5:
           290-293.

17, 628. _____. Die Kastration in der Bibel. Imago, 1920, 6: 393-397.

17, 629. _____. Die Sexualsymbolik des Ackerbaus in Bibel und Talmud. Zeitschrift für Sexualwissenschaft, 1916, 2: 437-444.

17, 630. _____. Sexualsymbolik in der biblischen Paradies-geschichte. Imago, 1917, 3:16-30.

17, 631. _____. Sexualsymbolik in der Samsonsage. Zeitschrift für Sexualwissenschaft, 1916, 3:256-271.

17, 632. Lodzer, Itzik. Psychedelics and Kabbalah. Response, 1968, 2(1); In Sleeper, J. A., & Mintz, A. L. (eds), The New Jews. NY: Vintage, 1972, 176-192.

17, 633. Lorenz, Emil F. Die Traüme des Pharao, des Mundschen-ken und des Bäckers. Psychoanalytische Bewegung, 1930, 2:33-45.

17, 634. Lowenfeld, Henry. Freud's Moses and Bismarck. In Psychoanalysis and the Social Sciences, Vol. 2. NY: IUP, 1950, 277-290.

17, 635. Ludowyk-Gyömröi, Edith. A note on the interpretation of 'Pastdati' in early Buddhist texts. Univ. Ceylon Rev, 1943, 1:74-82.

17, 636. _____. The valuation of Saddhā in early Buddhist texts. Univ. Ceylon Rev, 1947, 5:32-50.

17, 637. Lustig, Eric. On the origin of Judaism: a psychoanalytic approach. In The Psychoanalytic Study of Society, Vol. 7. New Haven: Yale Univ. Press, 1976, 359-367.

17, 638. Lynch, Thomas H. Corroboration of Jungian psychology in the biblical story of Abraham. Psychotherapy: The-ory, Research & Practice, 1971, 8:315-318.

17, 639. McLean, Helen Vincent. A few comments on Moses and Monotheism. Psychoanal Q, 1940, 9:207-213; Tokyo J Psychoanal, 1967, 25(2):4.

17, 640. Marbach, Otto. Das Fest der Midinetten. Imago, 1930, 16:502-530.

17, 641. March, Hans. Die Psychotherapie Jesu. Schwerin, Meck-lenberg: Bahn, 1929.

17, 642. Margetts, E. L. The concept of levels of consciousness in the Upanishads. Canadian Medical Assn J, 1951, 65: 391.

17, 643. Marmura, Michael E. God and His creation: two medi-eval Islamic views. In Savory, R. M. (ed), Introduction to Islamic Civilisation. NY: Cambridge Univ. Press, 1976, 46-53.

17, 644. Matthews, Marjorie S. Issue and Answers in the Book of Job and Joban Issues and Answers in Three Twentieth Century Writers: Carl Jung, Robert Frost, and Archi-bald MacLeish. DAI, 1977, 37(12-A), 7800.

17, 645. May, Rollo (ed). Symbolism in Religion and Literature. NY: Braziller, 1960.

17, 646. Meng, Heinrich. War Buddha schizophrenen? Psyche, 1962, 16:374-377.

17,647. Meredith, Charles P. A Comparative Examination of Anxiety, Guilt, Prejudice and Loneliness in Selected Scriptural and Psychological Writings. DAI, 1973, 33(10-A), 5496-97.

17,648. Meyer, Donald B. The Bible versus psychology. In The Positive Thinkers. Garden City, NY: Doubleday, 1965, 290-295.

17,649. Meyer, Stephen G. The Psalms and personal counseling. J Psychol & Theology, 1974, 2:26-30.

17,650. Monchy, S. J. R. de. Adam--Cain--Oedipus. Amer Imago, 1962, 19:3-17.

17,651. More, Joseph. The prophet Jonah. Amer Imago, 1970, 27:3-11.

17,652. Morgan, Douglas Neil. Love: Plato, the Bible and Freud. Englewood Cliffs, NJ: Prentice-Hall, 1964.

17,653. Mukherjee, K. C. Sex in Tantras. J Abnormal Social Psychol, 1926, 21:65-74.

17,654. Murray, H. G. Psychoanalysts catch Job. Christian Century, 1929, 46:514-515.

17,655. Murry, John Middleton. Sigmund Freud's Moses and Monotheism. In Poets, Critics, Mystics; A Selection of Criticism Written Between 1919 and 1955. Carbondale: Southern Illinois Univ. Press, 1970, 117-123.

17,656. Naftalin, Moses. Footnote to the genesis of Moses. Psychoanal Q, 1958, 27:403-405.

17,657. Nelson, Benjamin N. The quest for certitude and the books of Scripture, nature, and conscience. In Gingerich, O. (ed), The Nature of Scientific Discovery. Washington, DC: Smithsonian Institute Press, 1975, 355-372.

17,658. Neuman, R. P. What was the sin of Onan? The problem of masturbation in patriarchal culture. Psychocultural Rev, 1979, 3(1):59-72.

17,659. Newell, H. Whitman. An interpretation of the Hindu worship of Siva linga. Bulletin Philadelphia Assn Psychoanal, 1955, 4:82-86.

17,660. Oates, Wayne E. The diagnostic use of the Bible. Pastoral Psychol, 1950, 1(9):43-46.

17,661. Oehlschlegel, L. Regarding Freud's book on Moses; a religio-psychoanalytical study. Psychoanal Rev, 1943, 30:67-76.

17,662. Ong, Walter J. La Dame et l'enjeu. Psyché, 1953, 8:156-171.

17,663. Owens, Claire Myers. Zen Buddhism. In Tart, C. T. (ed), Transpersonal Psychologies. NY: Harper & Row, 1975, 153-202.

17,664. Papin, Edwin Ross. Sex, Symbolism, and the Bible. NY: Vantage, 1972.

17, 665. Parcells, Frank H., & Segel, Nathan P. Oedipus and the prodigal son. Psychoanal Q, 1959, 28:213-227.

17, 666. Parrinder, Edward Geoffrey. Sex in the World's Religions. NY: Oxford Univ. Press, 1980.

17, 667. Patai, Raphael. Sex and Family in the Bible and Middle East. Garden City, NY: Doubleday, 1959.

17, 668. _____, Utley, Francis L., & Noy, Dov. Studies in Biblical and Jewish Folklore. Indiana Univ. Folklore Series No. 13. Bloomington: Univ. Indiana Press, 1960.

17, 669. Pederson, John E. Some thoughts on a biblical view of anger. J Psychol & Theology, 1974, 2:210-215.

17, 670. Peto, Andrew. The demonic mother imago in Jewish religion. In Psychoanalysis and the Social Sciences, Vol. 5. NY: IUP, 1958, 280-287.

17, 671. Piper, Otto A. Sex in Biblical perspective. In Wynn, J. C. (ed), Sexual Ethics and Christian Responsibility; Some Divergent Views. NY: Association Press, 1970, 97-111.

17, 672. Polheim, Rudolf W. Die geschichtlichen Bücher des Alten Testamentes psycho-pathologisch betrachtet, Teil I und Teil II. Zeitschrift für psychosomatische Medizin und Psychoanalyse, 1962, 8:141-44, 213-222.

17, 673. Porter, J. R. Samson's riddle: Judges 14:14, 18. J Theological Studies, 1962, 13:106-109.

17, 674. Preuss, Julius. Mental disorders in the Bible and Talmud. Israel Annals of Psychiat, 1975, 13:221-238.

17, 675. Priest, John Franklin. Myth and dream in Hebrew scripture. In Campbell, J. (ed), Myths, Dreams, and Religion. NY: Dutton, 1970, 48-67.

17, 676. Rank, Otto. The incest of Amnon and Tamar. [Excerpt from Das Inzest-Motiv in Dichtung und Sage.] Tulane Drama Rev, 1962, 7:38-43.

17, 677. Rapaport, David. L'Arbre de la science. Psyché, 1957, 11:347-358.

17, 678. Raychaudhuri, Arun Kumar. Jesus Christ and Sree Krisna: a psychoanalytic study. Amer Imago, 1957, 14: 389-405.

17, 679. [No entry. For Reik, see 17, 684]

17, 680. Reich, Wilhelm. The Murder of Christ. The Emotional Plague of Mankind. NY: Farrar, Straus & Giroux, 1966.

17, 681. Reid, Stephen. Moses and Monotheism: guilt and the murder of the primal father. Amer Imago, 1972, 29: 11-34.

17, 682. Reider, Norman. Medieval Oedipal legends about Judas. Psychoanal Q, 1960, 515-527.

17, 683. Reik, Theodor. A booth away from the house. Psychoanal Rev, 1963, 50:167-186.

17, 684. _____. The Creation of Woman. A Psychoanalytic Inquiry into the Myth of Eve. NY: Braziller, 1960.
17, 685. _____. Dogma and Compulsion. NY: IUP, 1951.
17, 686. _____. Der Eigene und der Fremde Gott, zur Psychoanalyse der religiösen Entwicklung. Leipzig: Int Psychoanalytischer Verlag, 1923; Amer Imago, 1968, 25:3-15.
17, 687. _____. Ein psychoanalytischer Beitrag zu Bibelerk-
klärung. Imago, 1917, 5:31-42.
17, 688. _____. Mystery on the Mountain. The Drama of the
Sinai Revelation. NY: Harper, 1959.
17, 689. _____. Myth and Guilt. NY: Braziller, 1957.
17, 690. _____. Pagan Rites in Judaism. NY: Farrar, Straus,
1964.
17, 691. _____. Ritual: Psychoanalytic Studies. NY: IUP,
1958, 305-361; London: Hogarth, 1931; Review: Will,
Otto J., Jr., Psychiatry, 1947, 10:443-445.
17, 692. Resch, Andreas. Der Traum im Heilsplan Gottes: Deutung und Bedeutung des Traums im Alten Testament.
Freiburg: Herder, 1964.
17, 693. Reuther, R. What do the Synoptics say? The sexuality of
Jesus. Christianity & Crisis, 1978, 38:134-137.
17, 694. Reynierse, James H. Behavior therapy and Job's recovery.
J Psychol and Theology, 1975, 3:187-194.
17, 695. _____. A behavioristic analysis of the Book of Job.
J Psychol & Theology, 1975, 3(2):75-81.
17, 696. Riklin, Franz. Betrachtung zur christlichen Passions-
geschichte. Wissen und Leben, 1913, 6:13.
17, 697. Roazen, Paul. Religion: realism and utopianism: a hero
in history. In Freud: Political and Social Thought.
NY: Knopf, 1968, 167-192.
17, 698. Roback, Abraham A. Freudian psychology and Jewish com-
mentators of the Bible. Jewish Forum, 1918, 1:528-
533.
17, 699. Roberts, W. H. A psychological study of the growing Jesus.
Open Court, 1931, 45:243-255.
17, 700. Rochat, O. Evangile et psychanalyse. Action et Pensée,
1942, 18.
17, 701. Roellenfleck, Ewald. Magna Mater im Alten Testament-
eine psychoanalytische Untersuchung. Darmstadt: Clas-
sen und Roether, 1949.
17, 702. Róheim, Géza. [Adam's dream.] NYUGAT, 1913.
17, 703. _____. The covenant of Abraham. Int J Psycho-Anal,
1939, 20:452-459.
17, 704. _____. The garden of Eden. Psychoanal Rev, 1940,
27:1-26, 177-199.
17, 705. _____. The passage of the Red Sea. Man, 1923, 23:
152-155.
17, 706. _____. Zur Psychologie der Bundesriten. Imago, 1920,
6:397-399.
17, 707. _____. Some aspects of semitic monotheism. In Psychoanalysis and the Social Sciences, Vol. 4. NY: IUP,
1965, 169-178.

17, 708. Rosenfeld, Eva M. The pan-headed Moses--a parallel.
Int J Psycho-Anal, 1951, 32:83-93; Rev Française de
Psychanalyse, 1951, 15:425-444.

17, 709. Rosenzweig, Efraim M. Some notes, historical and psy-
choanalytical, on the people of Israel and the land of
Israel with special reference to Deuteronomy. Amer
Imago, 1940, 1:50-64.

17, 710. Rubenstein, Richard L. The Religious Imagination. A
Study in Psychoanalysis and Jewish Theology. Indianapolis: Bobbs-Merrill, 1968; Review: Richard W. Noland, Hartford Studies in Lit, 1970, 2:70-74.

17, 711. Ruether, Rosemary R. (ed). Religion and Sexism; Images
of Woman in the Jewish and Christian Traditions. NY:
Simon & Schuster, 1974.

17, 712. Saintyves, P. Essais de folklore biblique. Paris: Libraire Critique, 1923.

17, 713. Sapp, Stephen. Sexuality, the Bible, and Science. Philadelphia: Fortress, 1977.

17, 714. Sarma, R. N. New light on dream psychology. J Oriental
Research, 1928, 251-265.

17, 715. Sastry, N. S. N. Symbolism in Hindu gods. Indian J Psychol, 1944, 19:190-193.

17, 716. Satyanand, D. Dynamic Psychology of the Gita of Hindu-
ism. New Delhi: Oxford Univ. Press, 1972.

17, 717. Schendler, David. Judas, Oedipus and various saints.
Psychoanalysis, 1954, 2:41-46.

17, 718. Schindler, Walter. Depth psychology and dream interpretation in the Bible. Int J Sexology, 1954, 8:77-82.

17, 719. Schlossman, Howard H. God the Father and His sons.
Amer Imago, 1972, 29:35-52.

17, 720. Schnaper, Nathan. The Talmud: psychiatric relevancies
in Hebrew tradition. In Sipe, A. W. R. (ed), Hope:
Psychiatry's Commitment. NY: Brunner/Mazel, 1970,
185-202; J Religion & Health, 1967, 6:171-187.

17, 721. Schneidau, H. N. In praise of alienation: the Bible and
western culture. Georgia Rev, 1974, 28:705-746.

17, 722. Schnier, Jacques. The Tibetan Lamaist ritual: Chöd.
Int J Psycho-Anal, 1957, 38:402-407.

17, 723. Schroeder, Theodore. Mathias the prophet. J Religion &
Psychol, 1913, 6:59-65.

17, 724. Schweitzer, Albert. The Psychiatric Study of Jesus. Boston: Beacon, 1958.

17, 725. Shengold, Leonard. Freud and Joseph. In Kanzer, M.
(ed), The Unconscious Today: Essays in Memory of
Max Schur. NY: IUP, 1971, 473-494.

17, 726. _____. A parapraxis of Freud in relation to Karl Abraham. Discussion by Mark Kanzer. Amer Imago,
1972, 29:123-159; 160-164.

17, 727. Shoham, S. Giora. The Isaac syndrome. Amer Imago,
1976, 33:329-349.

17, 728. _____. The Mark of Cain. NY: Oceana, 1970.

17, 729. Sims, Bennett Jones. Sex and homosexuality: Protestant
          Episcopal Church statement. Christianity Today, 1978,
          22:23-30.
17, 730. Singer, Richard E. Job's Encounter. NY: Bookman,
          1963; Review: Harry Slochower, Amer Imago, 1964,
          21:185-186.
17, 731. Slap, Joseph W. The genesis of Moses. Psychoanal Q,
          1958, 27:400-402.
17, 732. Slochower, Harry. The Hebrew memory of a chosen God.
          The Book of Job. In Mythopoesis. Mythic Patterns in
          the Literary Classics. Detroit: Wayne State Univ.
          Press, 1970, 47-66.
17, 733. Snell, James H. A Study of the Relationship between the
          Teachings of Jesus in the Book of Matthew and Exis-
          tential Psychology as Represented by Rollo May. DAI,
          1978, 39(4-B), 1939.
17, 734. Solek, M. Z. [Biblical stories on psychological back-
          ground.] Haninuh (Israel), 1954-55, 27:333-337.
17, 735. Sorsby, Arnold. Noah: an albino. In Sorsby, A. (ed),
          Tenements of Clay. London: Friedmann, 1974, 15-22.
17, 736. Sparkman, Collys F. Satan and his ancestors from a
          psychological standpoint. J Religion & Psychol, 1912,
          5:52-86, 163-194.
17, 737. Spector, Samuel I. Old age and the sages. Int J Aging
          & Human Development, 1973, 4:199-209.
17, 738. Spero, Moshe Ha Levi. Anticipation of dream psychology
          in the Talmud. J History Behavioral Sciences, 1975,
          11:374-380.
17, 739. _____. Anxiety and religious growth: a Talmudic
          perspective. J Religion & Health, 1978, 16:52-59.
17, 740. _____. Samson and Masada: altruistic suicides re-
          considered. Psychoanal Rev, 1978, 65:631-639.
17, 741. Spiegel, Shalom. The Last Trial. NY: Pantheon, 1967.
17, 742. Spitz, H.-J. Die Metaphorik des geistigen Schriftsinns.
          Ein Beitrag zur allegorischen Bibelauslegung des ersten
          Christlichen Jahrtausands. Munich: Fink, 1972.
17, 743. Stein, Calvert. Psychotherapy in the Bible. J Amer
          Academy Psychiat & Neurology, 1976, 1:67-70.
17, 744. Stein, Franz. Die Bedeutung der Namen in der Bibel.
          Psychoanalytische Bewegung, 1927-28, 2:92-93.
17, 745. Stocker, Arnold. L'Amour interdit: trois anges sur la
          route de Sodome. Geneva: Mont-Blanc, 1943.
17, 746. Stone, Maurice L. The Bibliotherapeutic Effect of Bible
          Reading upon Manifest Anxiety. DAI, 1970, 33(4-A),
          1530.
17, 747. Suhr, Elmer G. Krishna and Mithra as messiahs. Folk-
          lore, 1966, 77:205-221.
17, 748. Szondi, L. Thanatos and Cain. Amer Imago, 1964, 21:
          52-63.

17, 749. Tarachow, Sidney. Judas, the beloved executioner.
          Psychoanal Q, 1960, 29:528-554. In Coltrera, J. T.

(ed), Lives, Events and Other Players: Studies in Psychobiography. NY: Aronson, 1980.

17, 750. Tennessen, Herman. A masterpiece of existential blasphemy: The Book of Job. Humanities Assn Bulletin, 1973, 24:157-164.

17, 751. Teslaar, James S. Van. The theogony of 'El.' A biblical instance of purposive condensation. Psyche & Eros, 1920, 1:114-117.

17, 752. Theodoropoulos, Jane. 'Adam's rib.' Psychoanal Rev, 1967, 54(3):150-152.

17, 753. Tournier, Paul. A Doctor's Casebook in the Light of the Bible. NY: Harper, 1960.

17, 754. Trevett, Laurence D. Origin of the creation myth: a hypothesis. JAPA, 1957, 5:461-468.

17, 755. Trilling, Jacques. Freud, Abraham et le Pharaou. Etudes freudiennes, 1969, 1-2.

17, 756. Uleyn, Arnold. [A psychoanalytic reading of the Gospel according to Mark.] Gedrag: Tijdschrift voor Psychologie, 1977, 5:166-181.

17, 757. Velikovsky, Immanuel. Psychoanalytische Ahnungen in der Traumdeutungskunst der alten Hebräer nach den Traktät Brachoth. Psychoanalytische Bewegung, 1933, 5: 66-69.

17, 758. Versteeg-Solleweld, C. M. Das Märchen vom Marienkind. Imago, 1937, 23:115-125.

17, 759. Victorius, Käte. Der Moses des Michelangelo von Sigmund Freud. Psyche, 1956, 10:1-10.

17, 760. Vorwall, H. Die Sexualität in Alten Testament. Zeitschrift für Sexualwissenschaft, 1928, 15:127-132.

17, 761. Vowinkel, E. W. The cult and mythology of the Magna Mater from the standpoint of psychoanalysis. Psychiatry, 1938, 1:347-378.

17, 762. Walker, Daniel Pickering. Esoteric symbolism. In Kirkwood, G. M. (ed), Poetry and Poetics from Ancient Greece to the Renaissance. Ithaca: Cornell Univ. Press, 1975, 218-232.

17, 763. Walker, Larry L. 'Love' in the Old Testament: some lexical observations. In Hawthorne, G. F. (ed), Current Issues in Biblical and Patristic Interpretation. Grand Rapids, Mich: Eerdmans, 1975, 277-288.

17, 764. Wasson, R. G., & Ingalls, D. H. The soma of the Rig Veda: what was it? J Amer Oriental Society, 1971, 91:169-187.

17, 765. Watkins, John G. Concerning Freud's paper on The Moses of Michelangelo. Amer Imago, 1951, 8:61-63.

17, 766. Wayne, Robert. Prometheus and Christ. In Psychoanalysis and the Social Sciences, Vol. 3. NY: IUP, 1951, 201-219.

17, 767. Wehr, G. [The task of depth psychological Bible inter-
          pretation.] Analytische Psychologie, 1974, 5(1):48-54.
17, 768. Weidhorn, Manfred. Eve's dream and the literary tradi-
          tion. Tennessee Studies in Lit, 1967, 12:39-50.
17, 769. Weigert-Vowinckel, E. The cult and mythology of the
          Magna Mater from the standpoint of psychoanalysis.
          Psychiatry, 1938, 1:348-353.
17, 770. Weininger, O. O. The Psychology of Judaism. Albuquer-
          que, NM: American Institute for Psychological Re-
          search, 1980.
17, 771. Weiss, Samuel A. The Biblical story of Ruth: analytic
          implications of the Hebrew Masoretic text. Amer
          Imago, 1959, 16:195-209.
17, 772. Wellisch, Erich. Isaac and Oedipus. A Study in Biblical
          Psychology of the Sacrifice of Isaac, The Akedah. Lon-
          don: Routledge, Kegan Paul, 1954; NY: Humanities
          Press, 1955.
17, 773. Westman, H. The Springs of Creativity. NY: Atheneum,
          1961.
17, 774. Wilder, Amos Niven. Myth and dream in Christian scrip-
          ture. In Campbell, J. (ed), Myths, Dreams, and Reli-
          gion. NY: Dutton, 1970, 68-90.
17, 775. Williams, Cyril G. Ecstaticism in Hebrew prophecy and
          Christian glossolalia. Studies in Religion, 1973, 3:320-
          338.
17, 776. Wise, Carroll A. Psychiatry and the Bible. NY: Harper,
          1956.
17, 777. Wittels, Fritz. Psychoanalysis and history: the Niebelungs
          and the Bible. Psychoanal Q, 1946, 15:88-103; In
          Yearbook for Psychoanalysis, Vol. 1. NY: IUP, 1947,
          267-279; Revista de Psicoanálisis, 1946, 4:48-63.
17, 778. Wolff, Werner. Changing Concepts of the Bible: A Psy-
          chological Analysis of Its Words, Symbols and Beliefs.
          NY: Hermitage, 1951.
17, 779. Wolman, Benjamin B. Why did Jesus die on the cross?
          In Psychoanalysis and Catholicism. NY: Gardner,
          1976, 115-142.
17, 780. Wood, R. W. Homosexual behavior in the Bible. One In-
          stitute Q, 1962, 5:10-19.
17, 781. Woods, Ralph Louis (ed). The World of Dreams; An Anth-
          ology. NY: Random House, 1947.
17, 782. Wulff, M. An appreciation of Freud's Moses and Monothe-
          ism. In Max Eitingon in Memoriam. Jerusalem: Is-
          rael Psychoanalytic Society, 1951, 124-142.

17, 783. Young, R. D. Sex, the Bible and modern man. J School
          Health, 1970, 40:527-531.

17, 784. Zabriskie, Colleen. A psychological analysis of biblical
          interpretations pertaining to women. J Psychol & The-
          ology, 1976, 4:304-312.

17, 785.   Zeligs, Dorothy F.   Abraham and monotheism.   Amer
           Imago, 1954, 11:293-316.
17, 786.   _____.   Abraham and the covenant of the pieces.
           Amer Imago, 1961, 18:173-186.
17, 787.   _____.   A character study of Samuel.   Amer Imago,
           1955, 12:355-386.
17, 788.   _____.   The family romance of Moses.   Amer Imago,
           1966, 23:110-131.
17, 789.   _____.   Moses and Pharaoh: a psychoanalytic study of
           their encounter.   Amer Imago, 1973, 30:192-220.
17, 790.   _____.   Moses encounters the daemonic aspect of God.
           Amer Imago, 1970, 27:370-391.
17, 791.   _____.   Moses in Midian: the burning bush.   Amer
           Imago, 1969, 26:379-400.
17, 792.   _____.   The mother in Hebraic monotheism.   In The
           Psychoanalytic Study of Society, Vol. 1.   NY: IUP,
           1960, 287-311.
17, 793.   _____.   The personality of Joseph.   Amer Imago, 1955,
           12:47-69.
17, 794.   _____.   Psychoanalysis and the Bible: A Study in Depth
           of Seven Leaders.   NY: Bloch, 1974.
17, 795.   _____.   A psychoanalytic note on the function of the
           Bible.   Amer Imago, 1957, 14:57-60.
17, 796.   _____.   Psychological factors in the teaching of Bible
           stories.   Jewish Education, 1951, 22(3):24-28.
17, 797.   _____.   Saul, the tragic king.   Part I & II.   Amer
           Imago, 1957, 14:61-85, 165-189.
17, 798.   _____.   Solomon: man and myth.   Psychoanal Rev,
           1961, 48(1):77-103, 48(2):91-110.
17, 799.   _____.   A study of King David.   Amer Imago, 1960,
           17:179-200.
17, 800.   _____.   Two episodes in the life of Jacob.   Amer
           Imago, 1953, 10:181-203.
17, 801.   Zimmerman, Frank.   The book of Ecclesiastes in the light
           of some psychoanalytic observations.   Amer Imago,
           1948, 5:301-305.

17, 802. Abrams, R. H. A study in rote memory and the Lord's Prayer. School & Society, 1935, 42:863-864.

17, 803. Anast, Philip. Similarity between self and fictional character choice. Psychol Record, 1966, 16:535-539.

17, 804. Ansari, Anwar. A study of social and political group differences in literary appreciation. Manas, 1964, 11:21-29.

17, 805. Ashby, Marylee Stull, & Wittmaier, Bruce C. Attitude changes in children after exposure to stories about women in traditional or nontraditional occupations. J Educational Psychol, 1978, 70:945-949.

17, 806. Asheim, Lester. Portrait of the book reader as depicted in current research. In Schramm, W. (ed), Mass Communications. Urbana: Univ. Illinois Press, 1960.

17, 807. Ausubel, David P., & Schwartz, F. G. The effects of a generalizing-particularizing dimension of cognitive style on the retention of prose material. J General Psychol, 1972, 87:55-58.

17, 808. Bachtold, L. M., et al. Personality characteristics of creative women. Perceptual Motor Skills, 1973, 36:311-319.

17, 809. Bailey, Matilda. Sociopsychological considerations in literature. Proceedings Annual Reading Institute, 1964, 3:89-95.

17, 810. Barnum, Phyllis W. Discrimination against the aged in young children's literature. Elementary School J, 1977, 77:301-306.

17, 811. Baruch, Dorothy. An experiment in comparing responses to two types of poetry, rhymed and unrhymed, in nursery school, kindergarten, and first grade. J Educational Psychol, 1936, 27:591-602.

17, 812. Bass, B. M. Famous sayings test: general manual. Psychol Reports, Monograph Suppl 6, 1958, 4:479-497.

17, 813. Baumgarten, Franziska. A proverb test for attitude measurement. Personnel Psychol, 1952, 5:249-261.

17, 814. Beaugrande, Robert de, & Miller, Genevieve W. Processing models for childrens' story comprehension. Poetics, 1980, 9:181-202.

17, 815. Beck, Samuel J. The Rorschach Test: Exemplified in Classics of Drama and Fiction. NY: Stratton Medical Book, 1976.

17, 816. Beechick, Ruth A. Children's Understanding of Parables: A Developmental Study. DAI, 1974, 34:7578.

17, 817. Bellon, Elner C. A Content Analysis of Children's Books Set in the South. DAI, 1974, 34:6936-37.

17, 818. Beshai, James. Content analysis of Arabic stories. Proceedings Annual Convention Amer Psychol Assn, 1972, 7:297-298.

17, 819. _____. Content analysis of Egyptian stories. J Social Psychol, 1972, 87:197-203.

17, 820. Beyard-Tyler, Karen. Adolescent Reading Preferences for Type of Theme and Sex of Protagonist. DAI, 1978, 39(3-A), 1459.

17, 821. Bhatt, L. S. Measurement of ability to judge poetry. Education & Psychol (Delhi), 1955, 2(2):15-22.

17, 822. Black, John B., & Bower, Gordon H. Story understanding as problem-solving. Poetics, 1980, 9:223-250.

17, 823. Blatt, Gloria T. Violence in Children's Literature: A Content Analysis of a Select Sampling of Children's Literature and a Study of Children's Responses to Literary Episodes Depicting Violence. DAI, 1972, 33:2316A.

17, 824. Bliss, William D. Birth order of creative writers. J Individual Psychol, 1970, 26:200-202.

17, 825. Bloomer, Richard H. Characteristics of portrayal and conflict and children's attraction to book. Psychol Reports, 1968, 23:99-106.

17, 826. Blount, N. S. The effect of selected junior novels and selected adult novels on student attitudes toward the 'ideal' novel. J Educational Research, 1965, 59:179-182.

17, 827. Bodem, Maruerite M. The role of fiction in children's reading. Elementary English, 1975, 52:470-471+.

17, 828. Boder, D. P. The adjective-verb quotient: a contribution to the psychology of language. Psychol Record, 1940, 3:310-343.

17, 829. Brabner, George, Jr. A link between the arts and sciences? B. F. Skinner's concept of contingencies of reinforcement. Psychol Record, 1979, 29:57-64.

17, 830. Brown, G. I. Literature in the elementary schools; literature and psychological process. Rev Educational Research, 1964, 34:192-193.

17, 831. Brown, Garth H. Development of story in children's reading and writing. Theory into Practice, 1977, 16:357-362.

17, 832. Buck, G. Figures of speech: a psychological study. In Scott, F. N. (ed), Contribution to Rhetorical Theory. Ann Arbor: Univ. Michigan Press, 1895, 1-27.

17, 833. Buirski, P., & Kramer, E. Literature as a projection of the author's personality. J Projective Techniques, 1970, 34:27-30.

17, 834. Burch, M. C. Determination of a content of the course in literature of a suitable difficulty for junior and senior high school students. Genetic Psychol Monographs, 1928, 4:165-332.

17, 835. Butsch, Richard J. Person Perception in Scientific and Medieval World Views: A Comparative Study of Fantasy Literature. DAI, 1975, 36:2519.

17, 836. Carlsen, G. Robert. Literature in the secondary school. Rev Educational Research, 1961, 31:173-178.

17, 837. Carroll, H. A. A method of measuring prose appreciation. English J, 1932, 22:184-189.

17, 838. _____. A preliminary report on a study of the interrelationships of certain appreciations. J Educational Psychol, 1932, 23:505-510.

17, 839. _____. A standardized test of prose appreciation for junior high school pupils. J Educational Psychol, 1932, 23:604-606.

17, 840. Castello, D., et al. [Musical theatre as a psychopedagogic instrument. New experiences on relationship of musical theatre and lower grade middle schools.] Minerva Pediatrica, 1974, 26:49-58.

17, 841. Cattell, James McK. A statistical study of eminent men. Popular Science Monthly, 1903, 62:359-377.

17, 842. Charlesworth, Roberta A. The Process of Reading Poetry: Implications for Curriculum. DAI, 1979, 39(7-A), 4012-13.

17, 843. Choppin, Bruce H., & Purves, Alan C. A comparison of open-ended and multiple-choice items dealing with literary understanding. Research in the Teaching of English, 1969, 3:15-24.

17, 844. Cooper, Charles R. Empirical studies of responses to literature: review and suggestions. J Aesthetic Education, 1976, 10:77-93.

17, 845. _____. The measuring of appreciation of literature: a review of attempts. Research in the Teaching of English, 1971, 5:5-23.

17, 846. _____. Preferred Modes of Literary Response: The Characteristics of High School Juniors in Relation to the Consistency of Their Reactions to Three Dissimilar Short Stories. DAI, 1969, 1680A.

17, 847. Connor, Jane M., & Serbin, Lisa A. Children's responses to stories with male and female characters. Sex Roles, 1978, 4:637-645.

17, 848. Crosby, F., Simons, L., & Kane, V. Sexism and racism in children's books: a quantitative analysis of temporal trends. Catalog of Selected Documents in Psychology, 1977, 7:71-72, MS. 1523.

17, 849. Crouse, J. H. Retroactive interference in reading prose materials. J Educational Psychol, 1971, 62:39-41.

17, 850. Dahl, Lüsa. The attributive sentence structure in the stream-of-consciousness technique with special reference to the interior monologue used by Virginia Woolf, James Joyce, and Eugene O'Neill. Neuphilologische Mitteilungen, 1967, 68:440-454.

17, 851.   Das, J. P. , Rath, R. , & Das, Rhea S.   Understanding
           versus suggestion in the judgment of literary passages.
           J Abnorm Social Psychol, 1955, 51:624-628.
17, 852.   Davis, James S.   The Responses of Secondary School Stu-
           dents to Passages of Contemporary Fiction Focusing on
           Violent Incidents.   DAI, 1974, 35:717-718.
17, 853.   Decharms, R. , & Moeller, G. H.   Values expressed in
           children's readers: 1800-1950.   J Abnormal Social
           Psychol, 1962, 64:136-142.
17, 854.   Delia, Jesse G.   Attitude toward the disclosure of self-
           attributions and the complexity of interpersonal con-
           structs.   Speech Monographs, 1974, 41:119-126.
17, 855.   Dennis, Wayne.   Creative productivity between the ages
           of 20 and 80 years.   J Gerontology, 1966, 21:1-8.
17, 856.   Dillon, George L.   Discourse processing and the nature of
           the literary narrative.   Poetics, 1980, 9:163-180.
17, 857.   Dilworth, Collett B.   Visualization and the Experience of
           Poetry: A Study of Selective Variables in Reader Re-
           sponse.   DAI, 1975, 35:4978.
17, 858.   Dimmit, M.   The constriction and evaluation of a scale to
           measure audience attitude toward any play.   Bulletin
           Purdue Univ. , 1936, 37:275-282.
17, 859.   Downey, June E.   The psychology of figures of speech.
           Amer J Psychol, 1919, 30:103-115.
17, 860.   Dudek, S. Z.   Regression and creativity: a comparison of
           the Rorschach records of successful vs. unsuccessful
           painters and writers.   JNMD, 1968, 147:535-546.
17, 861.   Duffy, Gerald G.   The construction and validation of an
           instrument to measure poetry writing performance.
           Educational & Psychol Measurement, 1968, 28:1233-
           1236.
17, 862.   Duncan, Melba Hurd.   The clinical use of fiction and biog-
           raphy featuring stuttering.   J Speech & Hearing, 1949,
           14:139-142.
17, 863.   Durost, Walter N.   Issues in the measurement of litera-
           ture acquaintance at the secondary-school level.   J Edu-
           cational Psychology, 1952, 43:31-44.

17, 864.   Early, Margaret, & Odland, Norine.   Literature in the
           elementary and secondary schools.   Rev Educational
           Research, 1967, 37:178-185.
17, 865.   Ebersole, Peter.   Impact of literary works upon college
           students.   Psychol Reports, 1974, 34:1127-1130.
17, 866.   Elkind, David.   Ethnicity and reading: three avoidable
           dangers.   In The Child and Society.   NY: Oxford Univ.
           Press, 1979, 41-47.
17, 867.   Ellis, James I.   Adolescent awareness of stability and
           change in literature.   Educational Rev, 1977, 29:241-253.
17, 868.   Ellis, Katherine.   A New Approach to the Interpretation
           of Stories as Projective Documents.   DA, 1950, 100.
17, 869.   Eppel, E. M.   A new test of poetry discrimination.   Brit-
           ish J Educational Psychol, 1950, 20:111-116.

17, 870.   Evans, John L.   Two Aspects of Literary Appreciation Among High School Students.   Judgment of Prose Quality and Emotional Responses to Literature, and Selected Aspects of Their Reading Interests.   DAI, 1969, 30(2-A), 617.

17, 871.   Farmer, George L.   Majority and Minority Americans: An Analysis of Best Selling American Fiction from 1926-1966.   DA, 1968, 28(11-A):4457-58.
17, 872.   Favat, F. Andre.   Child and Tale: An Hypothesis on the Origins of Interest.   DAI, 1971, 32(5-A), 2480.
17, 873.   Flesch, Rudolf F.   Estimating the comprehension difficulty of magazine articles.   J General Psychol, 1943, 28:63-80.
17, 874.   Floyd, Charles K.   The Development of a Children's Bedtime Story Based on Progressive Relaxation Suggestions and the Investigation of Its Sleep-Inducing Effects.   DAI, 1969, 30(5-B), 2398-99.
17, 875.   Forehand, G. A.   The problems of measuring response to literature.   Clearing House, 1966, 40:369-375.
17, 876.   Fox, C.   The method of testing literary appreciation.   British J Psychol, 1938, 29:1-11.
17, 877.   Fraad, Harriet.   Sex-Role Stereotyping and Male-Female Character Distribution in Popular, Prestigious, and Sex-Role Defining Children's Literature from 1959 to 1972.   DAI, 1976, 36:5295-96.
17, 878.   Frasher, Ramona S., & Frasher, James M.   The influence of story characters' roles on comprehension.   Reading Teacher, 1978, 32:160-164.
17, 879.   Funkhouser, Linda, & O'Connell, Daniel C.   Temporal aspects of poetry readings by authors and adults.   Bulletin Psychonomic Society, 1978, 12:390-392.

17, 880.   Gamst, Glenn, & Freund, Joel S.   Effects of subject-generated stories on recall.   Bulletin Psychonomic Society, 1978, 12:185-188.
17, 881.   Gardner, Howard, & Gardner, J.   Children's literary skills.   J Experimental Education, 1971, 39:42-46.
17, 882.   _____, & Lohman, William.   Children's sensitivity to literary styles.   Merrill-Palmer Q, 1975, 21:113-126.
17, 883.   Gordon, Kate.   A dissected-story test.   Psychol Bulletin, 1913, 14:66.
17, 884.   Gorham, D. R.   A proverb test for clinical and experimental use.   Psychol Reports, Monograph Suppl 1, 1956, 2:1-12.
17, 885.   Griffith, Helen.   Time patterns in prose.   A study in prose rhythms based upon voice records.   Psychol Monographs, 1929, 39:1-82.
17, 886.   Groff, Patrick.   How do children read biography about adults?   Reading Teacher, 1971, 24:609-615+.

17, 887.   Guise, Carolyn, and Penprase, Teresa. Psychological
            literature: human behavior in the English class.
            English J, 1974, 63:72-75.

17, 888.   Halász, László. [Approval and activation level in poetic
            experience.] Magyar Pszichológiai Szemle, 1966, 23:
            398-408.
17, 889.   _____. [Examination of the gift for writing by means
            of experimental themes.] Pszichológiai Tanulmányok,
            1965, 8:421-435.
17, 890.   _____. [Experimental research into the effect mechan-
            ism of literary works.] Pszichológiai Tanulmányok,
            1968, No. 11, 411-427.
17, 891.   _____. [Methodological problem in the psychological
            study of literary creativity and receptivity.] Pszicho-
            lógiai Tanulmányok, 1970, 12:319-333.
17, 892.   _____. [Psychological study of processes in the per-
            ception of a serialized literary work.] Bulletin de
            Psychologie, 1976-77, 30:774-780.
17, 893.   Harary, Frank. Structural study of 'A Severed Head. '
            Psychol Reports, 1961, 19:473-474.
17, 894.   Hardy-Brown, Karen. Formal operations and the issue of
            generalizability: the analysis of poetry by college stu-
            dents. Human Development, 1979, 22:127-136.
17, 895.   Harms, Jeanne. McLain. Children's responses to fan-
            tasy in literature. Language Arts, 1975, 52:942-946.
17, 896.   Hartley, H. W. Tests of the interpretative reading of po-
            etry for teachers of English. Teachers College Contri-
            bution to Education, 1930, No. 433.
17, 897.   Heidler, J. B., & Lehman, H. C. Chronological age and
            productivity. English J, 1937, 26:294-304.
17, 898.   Helson, Ravenna M. The creative spectrum of authors of
            fantasy. J Personality, 1977, 45:310-326.
17, 899.   _____. Creativity in women. In Sherman, J. A., &
            Denmark, F. L. (eds), The Psychology of Women: Fu-
            ture Directions in Research. NY: Psychological Di-
            mensions, 1977, Ch. 8.
17, 900.   _____. Experiences of authors in writing fantasy: two
            relationships between creative process and product. J
            Altered States of Consciousness, 1977-78, 3:235-248.
17, 901.   _____. The heroic, the comic, and the tender: pat-
            terns of literary fantasy and their authors. J Personal-
            ity, 1973, 41:163-184.
17, 902.   _____. The imaginative process in children's literature:
            quantitative analysis. Poetics: Int Rev for Theory of
            Lit, 1978, 7(2).
17, 903.   _____. Psychological dimensions and patterns in writ-
            ings of critics. J Personality, 1978, 46:348-301.
17, 904.   Herrell, James M. Sex difference in emotional responses
            to 'erotic literature. ' J Consulting & Clinical Psychol,
            1975, 43:921.

17,905. Hillman, Judith Stevinson. Analysis of male and female roles in two periods of children's literature. J Educational Research, 1974, 68:84-88.

17,906. Hochholzer, H. Lehrling und Schifttum. Zeitschrift für pädagogische Psychologie, 1930, 31:319-353.

17,907. Holdsworth, Janet N. Vicarious experience of reading a book in changing nursing students' attitudes. Nursing Research, 1968, 17:135-139.

17,908. Hopkins, Ronald H. Familiarity and difficulty of author-title materials for use in studies of long-term memory. Bulletin Psychonomic Society, 1978, 2:77-79.

17,909. Huber, M. B. The influence of intelligence upon children's reading interests. Teachers College Contributions to Education, No. 312, 1928.

17,910. Huck, Charlotte S. Literature as the content of reading. Theory into Practice, 1977, 16:363-371.

17,911. Hurst, A. S., & McKay, J. Experiments on time relations of poetical metres. Univ. Toronto Studies, Psychol Series, 1900, 1:155-175.

17,912. Jennings, Sally A. The effects of sex stereotyping in children's stories on preference and recall. Child Development, 1975, 46:220-223.

17,913. Jusczyk, Peter W. Rhymes and reasons: some aspects of the child's appreciation of poetic form. Developmental Psychol, 1977, 13:599-607.

17,914. Kammann, Richard. Verbal complexity and preference in poetry. J Verbal Learning & Verbal Behavior, 1966, 5:536-540.

17,915. Karl, Herbert. The approach to literature through cognitive processes. English J, 1968, 57:181-187.

17,916. Katura, H. [The great resemblance between 7-5 syllable-meter in Japanese versification and Chinese 7-word poetry.] Japanese J Psychol, 1940, 15:72-74.

17,917. _____. [On the historical shift of 5-7 syllable meter into 7-5 one in Japanese versification.] Japanese J Psychol, 1939, 14:315-318.

17,918. Kaufmann, F. W., & Taylor, W. S. Literature as adjustment. J Abnormal Social Psychol, 1936, 31:229-334.

17,919. Kingston, A. J., & Lovelace, T. L. First graders' perception of stereotyped story characters. Reading Improvement, 1979, 16:66-70.

17,920. Koblinsky, Sally Gentry, et al. Sex role stereotypes and children's memory for story content. Child Development, 1978, 49:452-458.

17,921. _____. Sex role stereotypes and children's memory for story content. Child Development, 1978, 49:452-458.

17,922. Koeller, Shirley. The effect of listening to excerpts from
         children's stories about Mexican-Americans on the atti-
         tudes of sixth graders. J Educational Research, 1977,
         70:329-334.

17,923. Koen, F., Becker, A., & Young, R. The psychological
         reality of the paragraph. J Verbal Learning & Verbal
         Behavior, 1969, 8:49-53.

17,924. Koenig, Fredrick, & Edmonds, Dale. Cognitive complex-
         ity and affective value of literary stimuli. Perceptual
         Motor Skills, 1972, 35:947-948.

17,925. Kozlowski, Lynn T. Effects of distorted auditory and of
         rhyming cues on retrieval of tip-of-the-tongue words
         by poets and nonpoets. Memory & Cognition, 1977,
         5:477-481.

17,926. Kroh, E. Eidetiker unter deutschen Dichtern. Zeitschrift
         für Psychologie, 1920, 85:118-162.

17,927. Kudszus, Winfried G. [Literature and schizophrenia. Re-
         search trends and research tasks.] Confinia Psychia-
         trica, 1979, 22(3):160-175.

17,928. Kuethe, James L. Perpetuation of specific schemata in
         literature for children. Psychol Reports, 1966, 18:433-
         434.

17,929. Lawson, James H. The Development of a Poetry Test for
         Grades Eleven and Twelve. DAI, 1969, 30(2-A), 495-
         496.

17,930. LePere, Jean M. Literature in the elementary school.
         Rev Educational Research, 1961, 31:179-187.

17,931. Lehman, Harvey C., & Heidler, Joseph B. Chronological
         age vs. quality of literary output. Amer J Psychol,
         1949, 62:75-89.

17,932. Leinweber, B. Empirisch-psychologische Beiträge zur
         Typologie des dichtenschen Schaffens. Langenzala:
         Beyer, 1929.

17,933. Lindauer, Martin S., & Arcamore, Amelia. Concept
         formation and the identification of poetic style. Psy-
         chol Reports, 1974, 35:207-210.

17,934. Lipsky, A. Rhythm as a distinguishing characteristic of
         prose style. Archiv de Psychologie, 1907, No. 4, 1-
         44.

17,935. London, Ivan D. Revenge of heaven: a brief methodologi-
         cal account. Psychol Reports, 1974, 34:1023-1030.

17,936. Lucena, José. [Intellectual productivity in senescent
         Brazilian writers: significance for mental health.]
         Jornal Brasileiro de Psiquiatria, 1974, 23:291-312.

17,937. Mabie, E. C. The responses of theatre audiences; experi-
         mental studies. Speech Monographs, 1952, 19:235-243.

17,938. Mackintosh, H. K. A critical study of children's choices
         of poetry. Univ. Iowa Studies: Studies in Education,
         1932, 7.

17,939. Madison, John P. An Analysis of Values and Social Action in Multi-Racial Children's Literature. DAI, 1973, 34(1-A), 516.

17,940. Maier, Norman R. F., Julius, M., & Thurber, J. Studies in creativity: individual differences in the storing and utilization of information. Amer J Psychol, 1967, 80: 492-519.

17,941. Mandler, Jean M., & De Forest, Marsha. Is there more than one way to recall a story? Child Development, 1979, 50:886-889.

17,942. Marshall, Gail. Make way for children. Elementary School J, 1975, 75:480-484.

17,943. Martindale, Colin. An experimental simulation of literary change. J Personality & Social Psychol, 1973, 25:319-326.

17,944. Mauer, Ruth A. Young children's responses to a physically disabled storybook hero. Exceptional Children, 1979, 45:326-330.

17,945. Merriam, Sharan B. Coping with Male Mid-Life: A Systematic Analysis Using Literature as a Data Source. DAI, 1978, 39(5-A), 2690-91.

17,946. Michael, William B., Rosenthal, Bernard G., & DeCamp, Michael A. An experimental investigation of prestige-suggestion for two types of literary material. J Psychol, 1949, 28:303-323.

17,947. Milgrim, Sally A. A Comparison of the Effect of Classics and Contemporary Literary Works on High-School Students' Declared Attitudes Towards Certain Moral Values. DA, 1968, 28(10-A):3899.

17,948. Miller, E. O. A study of the pre-school child's picture and story books by the battery of tests method. J Applied Psychol, 1929, 13:592-599.

17,949. Miller, G. R., & Coleman, E. B. A set of thirty-six prose passages calibrated for complexity. J Verbal Learning & Verbal Behavior, 1967, 6:851-854.

17,950. Miller, L. L., et al. Marijuana: effects on storage and retrieval of prose material. Psychopharmacology, 1977, 51:311-316.

17,951. Mills, David H. The relationship of abstraction to selected personality and intellectual variables. Psychology, 1965, 2(4):10-15.

17,952. Mills, John A., & Kessel, Frank S. Retroactive inhibition of descriptive prose. Psychol Reports, 1965, 17:917-918.

17,953. Minister, Kristina A. The Perception of Literature by Silent Readers and Oral Interpreters: A Theory and an Exploratory Experimental Study. DAI, 1978, 38(9-A), 5124-25.

17,954. Mosher, Donald L., & Greenberg, Irene. Females' affective responses to reading erotic literature. J Consulting Clinical Psychol, 1969, 33:472-477.

17,955. Munro, Robert W. The Effect of Selected Literary Material on Behaviorally Maladjusted Adolescents. DAI, 1971, 32(2-A), 811-812.

17, 956. Neisser, Ulric, & Hupcey, John A. A Sherlockian experiment. Cognition: Int J Cognitive Psychol, 1974-75, 3:307-311.

17, 957. Norton, R. The homosexual literary tradition: course outline and objectives. College English, 1974, 35:674-684.

17, 958. Olson, Miles C. A study of physiological responses to film, video, audio and print. Int J Instructional Media, 1978, 5:87-93.

17, 959. Osborn, Mary S. Regional-Psychological Story for Children Ages Eight to Twelve: An Evolution of Some Critical Insights. DAI, 1973, 33(8-A), 4249.

17, 960. Paisley, W. J. Identifying the unknown communicator in painting, literature, and music: the significance of minor encoding habits. J Communications, 1964, 14: 219-237.

17, 961. Peltola, Bette J. A Study of the Indicated Literary Choices and Measured Literary Knowledge of Fourth and Sixth Grade Boys and Girls. DA, 1966, 27(3-A), 609.

17, 962. Penney, James F. Using literary works to illustrate psychology in everyday life. Junior College J, 1959, 30: 157.

17, 963. Peters, William H., & Blues, Ann G. Teacher intellectual disposition as it relates to student openness in written response to literature. Research in the Teaching of English, 1978, 12:127-136.

17, 964. Petrosky, Anthony R. Genetic epistemology and psychoanalytic ego psychology: clinical support for the study of responses to literature. Research in the Teaching of English, 1977, 11:28-38.

17, 965. _____. Individual and Group Responses of Fourteen-and Fifteen-year-olds to Short Stories, Poems, Novels, and Thematic Apperception Tests: Case Studies Based on Piagetian Genetic Epistemology and Freudian Psychoanalytic Ego-Psychology. DAI, 1975, 35:852A.

17, 966. Pine, F. Thematic drive content and creativity. J Personality, 1959, 27:136-151.

17, 967. Pomeranz, Regina Esther. The Search for Self in the Adolescent Protagonist in the Contemporary American Novel: A Method of Approach for the College Teacher of Literature. DA, 1966, 27(3-A), 780.

17, 968. Pooley, R. C. Measuring the appreciation of literature. English J, 1935, 24:627-633.

17, 969. Posen, Robert. Social scientific study of literature: a psycholinguistic approach. Psycho-Lingua, 1975, 5:19-28.

17, 970. Potter, Beverly A. Sex of the protagonist in children's storybooks: effect on self-concept. J Instructional Psychol, 1978, 5:6-14.

17,971. Purves, Alan C. Using the IEA data bank for research in reading and response to literature. Research in the Teaching of English, 1978, 12:289-296.

17,972. _____, & Beach, Richards (eds). Literature and the Reader: Research in Response to Literature, Reading Interests, and the Teaching of Literature. Urbana, Ill: National Council Teachers English, 1972.

17,973. Rakes, Thomas A., et al. Reader preference as related to female aggressiveness and stereotyped character role. Reading Improvement, 1977, 14:30-35.

17,974. Razik, T. A. Psychometric measurement of creativity. In Mooney, R. L., & Razik, T. A. (eds), Explorations in Creativity. NY: Harper & Row, 1967, 301-309.

17,975. Rhodes, James M. The Dynamics of Creativity: An Interpretation of the Literature on Creativity with a Proposed Procedure for Objective Research. DA, 1957, 17:96.

17,976. Rigg, M. G. Measuring the ability to judge poetry. Proceedings Oklahoma Academy Science, 1939, 19:157-158.

17,977. _____. The relationship between discrimination in music and discrimination in poetry. J Educational Psychol, 1937, 28:149-152.

17,978. _____. Rigg Poetry Test, Forms C and D. Stillwater: School of Education Oklahoma A & M College, 1937.

17,979. Riley, William Patrick. Encounter Criticism: Identity Development Through Prose Fiction. DAI, 1975, 36: 2202A-03A.

17,980. Ross, Campbell. A comparative study of the responses made by grade 11 Vancouver students to Canadian and New Zealand poems. Research in the Teaching of English, 1978, 12:297-306.

17,981. Rozhina, L. N. [Some conditions that arouse interest in the subjective experiences and thoughts of literary heroes in young schoolchildren.] Voprosy Psikhologii, 1966, No. 2, 139-146.

17,982. Sakaguchi, Masahiko. [A psychological study of the sentences of the old Japanese poetical works of Mannyō, Kokin and Shinkokin.] Japanese J Psychol, 1952, 22: 167-174.

17,983. Schlager, Norma M. Developmental Factors Influencing Children's Responses to Literature. DAI, 1975, 35: 5136-37.

17,984. Schneyer, J. Wesley. The effects of reading on children's attitudes. Reading Teacher, 1969, 23:49+.

17,985. Scott, Kathryn P., & Feldman-Summers, Shirley. Children's reactions to textbook stories in which females are portrayed in traditionally male roles. J Educational Psychol, 1979, 71:396-402.

17,986. Sebeok, Thomas A., & Zeps, V. J. Computer research in psycholinguistics: towards an analysis of poetic language. Behavior Science, 1961, 6:365-369.

17,987. Segal, Stanley J. The Role of Personality Factors in Vo-
         cational Choice: A Study of Accountants and Creative
         Writers. DA, 1954, 14:714-715.

17,988. Seibert, Warren F. The motion picture as a psychological
         testing medium: a look at cine-psychometrics. View-
         points, 1970, 46:91-102.

17,989. Shafer, Robert E. The reading of literature. J of Read-
         ing, 1965, 8:345-349.

17,990. Shedd, Patricia T. The Relationship Between Attitude of
         the Reader Towards Women's Changing Role and Re-
         sponse to Literature Which Illuminates Women's Role.
         DAI, 1977, 38(6-A), 3404.

17,991. Sherwin, Joseph S. Social and Psychological Assumptions
         About Human Behavior in Selected Literary Works: An
         Analysis of the Literature at Present Required Reading
         in a Selected Secondary School and the Implications of
         the Analysis for the Improvement of Instruction in Lit-
         erature. DA, 1955, 15:245-246.

17,992. Shirley, Fehl L. Case studies of the influence of reading
         on adolescents. Research in the Teaching of English,
         1969, 3:30-41.

17,993. _____. The influence of reading on concepts, attitudes,
         and behavior. J Reading, 1969, 12:369-372+.

17,994. Shrodes, Caroline. Bibliotherapy: an application of psy-
         choanalytic theory. Amer Imago, 1960, 17:311-319.

17,995. Simonton, Dean K. Age and literary creativity: a cross-
         cultural and transhistorical survey. J Cross-Cultural
         Psychol, 1975, 6:259-277.

17,996. Skinner, B. F. A quantitative estimate of certain types of
         sound-patterning in poetry. Amer J Psychol, 1941,
         54:64-79.

17,997. Smith, J. R. Analytic study of the factors involved in
         learning to appreciate literature. Indiana Univ. School
         of Education Bulletin, 1933, 10:47-69.

17,998. Snyder, E. D. Hypnotic Poetry: A Study of Trance-Induc-
         ing Technique in Certain Poems and Its Literary Signifi-
         cance. Philadelphia: Univ. Pennsylvania Press, 1930.

17,999. Sola Pool, Ithiel de (ed). Trends in Content Analysis.
         Urbana: Univ. Illinois Press, 1959.

18,000. Speer, R. K. Measurement of appreciation in poetry,
         prose, and arts, and studies in appreciation. Teach-
         ers College Contribution to Education, 1929.

18,001. Squire, James. The Responses of Adolescents While Read-
         ing Four Short Stories. Champaign, Ill: National Coun-
         cil of Teachers of English, 1964.

18,002. Stark, Stanley. Historiography and the Rorschach frame-
         work: 'literary skill' vs 'literary qualities. ' Percep-
         tual Motor Skills, 1968, 26:Suppl:1108+.

18,003. Telford, W. H. , Jr. , & Synnott, C. S. Use of the semantic
         differential with poetic forms. Psychol Record, 1972,
         22:369-373.

18, 004.   Tengarrinha, José. A novela e o leitor português. Lisbon: Prelo, 1973.
18, 005.   Thayer, Lee O., & Pronko, Nicholas Henry. Some psychological factors in the reading of fiction. J Genetic Psychol, 1958, 93:113-117.
18, 006.   Tibbets, Sylvia L. Research in sexism: some studies of children's reading material revisited. Educational Research Q, 1979, 4:34-39.
18, 007.   Tóth, Bela. [Favorite tales and pieces of reading in the initial period of learning to read.] Pszichológiai Tanulmányok, 1966, 9:277-294.
18, 008.   _____. [Interest--psychological features of the disposition for reading poems in childhood.] Pszichológiai Tanulmányok, 1965, 8:243-257.
18, 009.   Tressin, D. Toward understanding; stories that illustrate problems of adjustment faced by young people. English J, 1966, 55:1170-1174.

18, 010.   Vergara, Allys Dwyer. A critical study of a group of college women's responses to poetry. Teachers College Contributions to Education, 1946, No. 923.
18, 011.   Vriese, Jack W. An Experimental Study of Occupation and Its Influence on Audience Response in the Theatre. Ann Arbor, Mich: University Microfilm No. 4995, 1953.

18, 012.   Wainer, Howard, & Berg, William. Dimensions of de Maupassant: a multidimensional analysis of students' perception of literature. Amer Educational Research J, 1972, 9:485-491.
18, 013.   _____, & Schofer, Peter. Measuring the effect of a liberal arts education on the perception of poetry. Amer Educational Research J, 1977, 14:125-135.
18, 014.   Washburne, Vera Z. Literature in teaching psychology. Junior College J, 1948, 19:125-129.
18, 015.   Weisgerber, C. A. Accuracy in judging emotional expressions as related to understanding of literature. J Social Psychol, 1957, 46:253-258.
18, 016.   Weissman, Alan. The English Romantics and modern psychology. Centerpoint, 1975-76, 1(4):9-16.
18, 017.   Wells, Elizabeth J. A statistical analysis of the prose style of Ernest Hemingway: 'Big Two-Hearted River. ' In Benson, J. J. (ed), The Short Stories of Ernest Hemingway: Critical Essays. Durham: Duke Univ. Press, 1975, 129-135.
18, 018.   Wells, F. L. A statistical study of literary merit. Archives of Psychol, 1907, 17(7).
18, 019.   Wells, R. E. A study of tastes in humorous literature among pupils of junior and senior high schools. J Educational Research, 1934, 28:81-91.

18,020. Whitehill, Buell, Jr., & Hochman, F.J. A study of audience reaction to a stereotype character. Educational Theatre J, 1952, 4:139-142.

18,021. Williams, C.B. A note on the statistical analysis of sentence-length as a criterion of literary style. Biometrika, 1940, 31:356-361.

18,022. Williams, E.D., Winter, L., & Woods, J.J. Tests of literary appreciation. British J Educational Psychol, 1938, 8:265-284.

18,023. Wilson, James R. Responses of College Freshmen to Three Novels. Urbana, Ill: National Council of Teachers of English, 1966.

18,024. Wilson, Robert W. The poet and the projective test. JAAC, 1958, 16:319-327.

18,025. Winkeljohann, Rosemary, & Gallant, Ruth. Queries; should we use children's classics that offer stereotypic images of sex roles? Language Arts, 1980, 57:446-450.

18,026. Winkler, Barbara. [Effects of context on judgments of an aversive soliloquy: an experimental study.] Zeitschrift für experimentelle und angewandte Psychologie, 1978, 25:671-680.

18,027. Wunderlich, Elaine. Black Americans in children's books. Reading Teacher, 1974, 28:282-285.

18,028. Yule, G.U. The Statistical Study of Literary Vocabulary. Cambridge: Cambridge Univ. Press, 1944.

18,029. Zhabitskaya, L.G. [Psychological investigation of criteria of literary development.] Voprosy Psikhologii, 1972, No. 5, 89-100.

18,030. Zimet, Sara Goodman. The rationale for inclusion of aggression themes in elementary reading textbooks. Psychol in the Schools, 1970, 7:232-237.

18,031. Zimmerman, Peggy. Retention in threatening and nonthreatening stories by kindergarten children. Graduate Research in Education, 1968, 4:81-91.

18,032. Zipf, George K. The repetition of words, time-perspective and semantic balance. J General Psychol, 1945, 32:127-148.

18,033. Abrams, Allan S. Poetry therapy in the psychiatric hospital. In Lerner, A. (ed), Poetry in the Therapeutic Experience. NY: Pergamon, 1978, 63-71.

18,034. Alston, Edwin Frederick. Bibliotherapy and psychotherapy. Library Trends, 1962, 2:159-176; Japanese-American Forum, 1963, 7:34-47.

18,035. Anand, Santokh S. Health, disease, and poetry. J Post-Graduate Medicine, 1970, 105-119.

18,036. _____. The use of poetry in psychotherapy. Psychol Studies, 1975, 20:31-41.

18,037. Anderson, Catherine J. Poetry therapy in psychiatric nursing. Libri (Copenhagen), 1975, 25:133-137.

18,038. Anderson, Walt (ed). Therapy and the Arts: Tools of Consciousness. NY: Harper, 1977.

18,039. Andree, O. Die Wirkung von Literatur und Dichtung auf Patienten in einer rationalen Psychotherapie. Psychiatrie, Neurologie und medizinische Psychiatrie, 1969, 21:152-156.

18,040. Andrews, Miriam. Poetry programs in mental hospitals. Perspectives in Psychiatric Care, 1975, 13(1):17-18.

18,041. Angel, Ernest. Where-to, therapy and theatre? Council News, Council Psychoanal Psychotherapists, 1969, Jan:1-2.

18,042. Anon. Troubled psyches: therapy without mystery. Times Lit Supplement, 1971, 10:215-221.

18,043. Ansell, Charles. Psychoanalysis and poetry. In Lerner, A. (ed), Poetry in the Therapeutic Experience. NY: Pergamon, 1978, 12-23.

18,044. Appel, K. E. Psychiatric therapy; explanatory or poetic therapy, interpretive therapy and bibliotherapy. In Hunt, J. McV. (ed), Personality and the Behavior Disorders, Vol. 2. NY: Ronald, 1944, 1128-1133.

18,045. Armistead, J. M. Tragicomic design of Lucius Junius Brutus: madness as providential therapy. Papers in Language & Lit, 1979, 15:38-51.

18,046. Aron, Raymond. Reflections after the psychodrama. Encounter, 1968, 31(6):64-70.

18,047. Askew, Melvin W. Literature and the psychotherapist. Psychoanalysis, 1958, 45:102-112.

18,048. Atwood, George E. The impact of Sybil on a patient with multiple personality. Amer J Psychoanal, 1978, 38:277-279.

18, 049. Bagchi, Amelendu. The Sanskritist's approach to the mental health theory of Freud. Indian J Psychol, 1954, 29: 61-74.

18, 050. Baldwin, Neil. The therapeutic implications of poetry writing: a methodology. J Psychedelic Drugs, 1976, 8: 307-312.

18, 051. Barron, Jules. Poetry and therapeutic communication: nature and meaning of poetry. Psychotherapy: Theory, Research & Practice, 1974, 11: 87-92.

18, 052. Barsky, M., et al. The use of creative drama in a children's group. Int J Group Psychotherapy, 1976, 26: 105-114.

18, 053. Bentley, Eric Russell. Theatre and therapy. In Theatre of War. NY: Viking, 1972, 385-401.

18, 054. Berger, Milton Miles. Poetry as therapy--and therapy as poetry. In Leedy, J.J. (ed), Poetry Therapy. Philadelphia: Lippincott, 1969, 75-87.

18, 055. Berry, Franklin M. Approaching poetry therapy from a scientific orientation. In Lerner, A. (ed), Poetry in the Therapeutic Experience. NY: Pergamon, 1978, 127-142.

18, 056. _____. Contemporary bibliotherapy: systematizing the field. In Rubin, R.J. (ed), Bibliotherapy Sourcebook. Phoenix, Ariz: Oryx, 1978, 185-190.

18, 057. Birnbaum, Henrik. The sublimation of grief: poems by two mourning fathers. In Erlich, V., et al. (eds), For Wiktor Weintraub. The Hague: Mouton, 1975, 85-98.

18, 058. Bishop, Jay. Creativity, art and play therapy. Canadian Counselor, 1978, 12: 138-146.

18, 059. Blaicher, Günther. Freie Zeit--Langeweile-Literatur: Studien zur therapeutischen Funktion der englischen Prosaliteratur im 18. Jahrhundert. Berlin: de Gruyter, 1977.

18, 060. Blanton, Smiley. The Healing Power of Poetry. NY: Crowell, 1960.

18, 061. _____. The use of poetry in individual psychotherapy. In Leedy, J.J. (ed), Poetry Therapy. Philadelphia: Lippincott, 1969, 171-179.

18, 062. Blumberg, M.L. Creative dramatics: an outlet for mental handicaps. J Rehabilitation, 1976, 42: 17-20.

18, 063. Borgna, E. [Poetic experience of a schizophrenic patient.] Rivista Sperimentale di Freniatria, 1971, 95: 844-857.

18, 064. Brand, Alice Glarden. Therapy in Writing. Lexington, Mass: Heath, 1980.

18, 065. Brand, Howard. Hawthorne on the therapeutic role. J Abnormal Social Psychol, 1952, 47: 856-868.

18, 066. Bridges, William E. Transcendentalism and psychotherapy: another look at Emerson. Amer Lit, 1969-70, 41: 157-177.

18, 067. _____. Walt Whitman today. California English J, 1969, 5: 31-37.

18,068. Brodsky, Paul. Guiding fiction and mental hygiene. In
         Mosek, H. H. (ed), Alfred Adler: His Influence on
         Psychology Today. Park Ridge, NJ: Noyes, 1973,
         135-141.
18,069. Brookes, Jayne M. Producing Marat/Sade: theater in a
         psychiatric hospital. Hospital & Community Psychiat,
         1975, 26:429-435.
18,070. Brothers, Wellington R. The Therapeutic Function of Cre-
         ativity in the Life and Works of Hermann Hesse. Doc-
         toral dissertation, Harvard Univ., 1967.
18,071. Brown, David H. Poetry As a Counseling Tool: The Re-
         lationship Between Response to Emotion Oriented Poetry
         and Emotions, Interests, and Personal Needs. DAI,
         1978, 38(8-A), 4575.
18,072. Buck, Lucien A., & Kramer, Aaron. Poetry as a means
         of group facilitation. J Humanistic Psychol, 1974, 14:
         57-72.
18,073. Burke, Kenneth. Thoughts on the poets' corner. In
         Leedy, J. J. (ed), Poetry Therapy. Philadelphia: Lip-
         pincott, 1969, 104-112.

18,074. Card, P. Poetry as a bridge to the lost. RN, 1964, 32:
         46-49.
18,075. Cardinal, Roger. Image and word in schizophrenic crea-
         tion. Forum Modern Language Studies, 1973, 9:103-
         120; In Higgins, I. (ed), Literature and the Plastic
         Arts, 1880-1930. NY: Barnes & Noble, 1974, 103-
         120.
18,076. Carp, E. A. [Sartre and the fundamentals of modern so-
         ciotherapy.] Psychotherapy & Psychosomatics, 1969,
         17:119-125.
18,077. Chase, Janet. Poetry therapy. Human Behavior, 1973,
         25.
18,078. Chetkow, B. H. Community theatre: another tool for
         achieving social change in poverty neighborhoods.
         Mental Health Society, 1978, 5:101-109.
18,079. Clancy, Mary, & Lauer, Roger. Zen telegrams: a
         warm-up technique for poetry therapy groups. In
         Lerner, A. (ed), Poetry in the Therapeutic Experience.
         NY: Pergamon, 1978, 97-107.
18,080. Coché, E., et al. Therapeutic effects of problem-solving
         training and play-reading groups. J Clinical Psychol,
         1977, 33:820-827.
18,081. Combecker, Hans. Dichtung als psychotherapeutische
         Selbsthilfe: zu zwei amerikanischen 'confessional
         poems.' Neueren Sprachen, 1971, 20:545-550.
18,082. Coogan, J. P. Apollo and Psyche: poetry as therapy.
         Smith Kline & French Psychiat Reporter, 1966, 20-23.
18,083. Crootof, Charles. Poetry therapy for psychoneurotics in
         a mental health center. In Leedy, J. J. (ed), Poetry
         Therapy. Philadelphia: Lippincott, 1969, 38-51.

18,084. _____, Harari, C., Harrower, Molly, & Parker, Rolland S. Symposium: Poetry as therapy and therapist as poet. J Clinical Issues in Psychol, 1970, 1:34-38.

18,085. Dars, E., et al. [Auto-activation in scenic expression.] Encephale, 1973, 62:345-347.

18,086. Davis, Martha S. Poetry Group Therapy Versus Interpersonal Group Therapy: Comparison of Treatment Effectiveness with Depressed Women. DAI, 1979, 39(11-B), 5543.

18,087. De Wispelaere, Paul. Literatuur als therapie: Michel Leiris. De Vlaame Gids, 1965, 49:553-575.

18,088. Devereux, George. The psychotherapy scene in Euripides' Bacchae. J Hellenistic Studies, 1970, 90:35-48.

18,089. Dewane, Claudia M. Humor in therapy. Social Work, 1978, 23:508-510.

18,090. Diatkine, René, & Gillibert, Jean. Psychodrame et théâtre. Esprit, n.s., 1965, no. 338, 931-942.

18,091. Dieckmann, Hans. [Favorite fables.] Praxis der Psychotherapie, 1974, 19(1):26-37.

18,092. Diener, Gottfried. Relation of the delusionary process in Goethe's Lila to analytic psychology and to psychodrama. Group Psychotherapy & Psychodrama, 1971, 24:5-13.

18,093. Domash, Leanne. The therapeutic use of writing in the service of the ego. J Amer Academy Psychoanal, 1976, 4:261-269.

18,094. D'Orsi, R., et al. [Psychoanalytic considerations on poetic production of psychoneurotic patients.] Ospedale Psichiatrico, 1971, 39:275-296.

18,095. Dracoulidès, N. N. Aristophanes and psychotherapy. Société Française d'Histoire de la Médecine, 22 Oct 1965.

18,096. Draper, John W. Humoral therapy in Shakespeare's plays. Bulletin History Medicine, 1961, 35:317-325.

18,097. Dugas, L. La Première manière de Barrès; la psychothérapie et le culte du moi. Rev Politique et Littéraire, 1928, 66:741-747.

18,098. Eckstein, Rudolf. The Orpheus and Eurydice theme in psychotherapy. Bulletin Menninger Clinic, 1966, 30: 207-224; Cuadernos de Psicoanálisis, 1966, 2(3-4):71-86.

18,099. Edgar, Ken[neth]. The epiphany of the self via poetry therapy. In Lerner, A. (ed), Poetry in the Therapy Experience. NY: Pergamon, 1978, 24-40.

18,100. _____. A case of poetry therapy. Psychotherapy: Theory, Research & Practice, 1979, 16:104-106.

18,101. _____, & Hazley, Richard. A curriculum proposal for training poetry therapist. In Leedy, J. J. (ed), Poetry Therapy. Philadelphia: Lippincott, 1969, 260-268.

18, 102. _____, Hazley, Richard, & Levit, Herbert. Poetry
          therapy with hospitalized schizophrenics. In Leedy,
          J. J. (ed), Poetry Therapy. Philadelphia: Lippincott,
          1969, 29-37.
18, 103. _____, & Hazley, Richard. Validation of poetry ther-
          apy as a group therapy technique. In Leedy, J. J. (ed),
          Poetry Therapy. Philadelphia: Lippincott, 1969, 113-
          123.
18, 104. Edwards, Beverly Sigler. The therapeutic value of read-
          ing. Elementary English, 1972, 49:213-218.
18, 105. Ehrenwald, J. Freud versus Jung--the mythophobic ver-
          sus the mythophilic temper in psychotherapy. Israel
          Annals Psychiat, 1968, 6:115-125.
18, 106. [No entry. For Eckstein, see 18, 098]
18, 107. England, Martha W. A heritage of sanity: the transac-
          tional therapy of Dr. Eric Berne and Dr. Samuel John-
          son. Bulletin New York Public Library, 1974, 77:161-
          188.
18, 108. Enquist, Per Olov. [Does poetry have a therapeutic func-
          tion?] Vär lösen: Kristen Kulturtidskrift, 1965, 56:
          69-71.
18, 109. Entralgo, Pedro L. The Therapy of the Word in Classical
          Antiquity. New Haven: Yale Univ. Press, 1970.
18, 110. Erickson, C. R., et al. Poetry as subtle therapy. Hos-
          pital Community Psychiat, 1972, 23:56-57.

18, 111. Faguet, Robert A. A long time ago in a galaxy far, far
          away.... Amer J Psychoanal, 1978, 38:359-360.
18, 112. Falk, Florence. Cosmic mass. Drama Rev, 1976, 20(1):
          90-98.
18, 113. Fédida, P. Temps et negation. La Création dans la cure
          psychoanalytique. Psychanalyse à l'université, 1977,
          2(7).
18, 114. Feldshuh, David. Zen and the actor. Drama Rev, 1976,
          20(1):79-89.
18, 115. Fleischl, Maria F. Poetry therapy. Int Mental Health
          Research Newsletter, 1968, 10(2).
18, 116. Forrest, David V. The patient's sense of the poem. In
          Leedy, J. J. (ed), Poetry Therapy. Philadelphia:
          Lippincott, 1969, 231-259.
18, 117. Friedman, Neil. James Baldwin and psychotherapy.
          Psychotherapy, 1966, 3:177-183.
18, 118. Friedrich, Gerhard. Akutagawa: existential images and
          psychodramas. Satire Newsletter, 1967, 4:105-107.

18, 119. Gahm, T. C. 'The play's the thing': rehab center stage.
          Rehabilitation Record, 1973, 14:20-21.
18, 120. Gardner, Richard A. Dramatized storytelling in child psy-
          chotherapy. Acta Paedopsychiatrica, 1975, 4:110-
          116.

18, 121.   . Mutual storytelling as a technique in child psychotherapy and psychoanalysis. Science & Psychoanal,
1969, 14:123-136.

18, 122.   Gettis, Alan.   Psychotherapy and the fat lady.   J Religion
& Health, 1978, 17:127-129.

18, 123.   Ghiselin, Brewster.   Art and psychiatry: characterization
as therapy, therapy as characterization.   Michigan Q
Rev, 1977, 16:12-22.

18, 124.   Ginn, Ildri L.   Catharsis: its occurrence in Aristotle,
psychodrama and psychoanalysis.   Group Psychotherapy
& Psychodrama, 1973, 26:7-22.

18, 125.   Goines, Leonard.   The blues as black therapy.   Black
World, 1973, 23(1):28-40.

18, 126.   Gold, Susanne.   Literature and madness; literature group
for former mental patients.   Theory into Practice,
1976, 15:326-331.

18, 127.   Golden, Leon.   Epic, tragedy, and catharsis.   Classical
Philology, 1976, 71:77-85.

18, 128.   Goldfield, M. D., & Lauer, Roger M.   The use of creative
writing in groups of young drug abusers.   New Physician, 1971, 449-457.

18, 129.   Graff, Gerald E.   Mythotherapy and modern poetics.
Tri-Quarterly, 1968, 11:76-90.

18, 130.   Graham, E. Ellis, & Whitmore, Lillian E.   The use of
drama for diagnosis and therapy.   J Colorado-Wyoming
Academy Science, 1954, 4:57-58.

18, 131.   Grassi, B.   [Further contribution to the study of poetic
compositions by mental patients: the aridity in psychopathology.]   Rassegna di Neuropsichiatria, 1961, 15:
355-362.

18, 132.   . [On the subject of poetic compositions of mental patients.]   Rassegna di Neuropsichiatria, 1964, 18:
233-244.

18, 133.   Graziano, Frank.   Poetry-writing therapy and schizophrenia: a poet's point of view.   Lit & Psychol, 1979,
29:49-59.

18, 134.   Greenberg, S. A.   AFTLI and/or poetry therapy.   In
Leedy, J. J. (ed), Poetry Therapy.   Philadelphia: Lippincott, 1969, 212-222.

18, 135.   Greene, George.   Elizabeth Bowen: imagination as therapy.   Perspective, 1965, 14:42-52.

18, 136.   Greening, Thomas Cartwright.   The uses of autobiography.
In Anderson, W. (ed), Therapy and the Arts: Tools
of Consciousness.   NY: Harper & Row, 1977, 90-112.

18, 137.   Greenwald, Harold.   Poetry as communication in psychotherapy.   In Leedy, J. J. (ed), Poetry Therapy.   Philadelphia: Lippincott, 1969, 142-154.

18, 138.   Greifer, Eli.   Poetry therapy.   Brooklyn Psychologist, 1964.
18, 139.   . Principles of Poetry Therapy.   NY: Poetry
Therapy Center, 1963.

18, 140.   Guillaumin, J.   [The real and the super-real: the poetic
treatment of reality in treatment and elsewhere.]   Rev
Française de Psychanalyse, 1971, 35:883-919.

18, 141.   Haines, William H.   Pornography.   J Social Therapy, 1956,
           2: 27-36.
18, 142.   Halprin, Ann.   Community art as life process.   Drama
           Rev, 1973, 17(3): 64-80.
18, 143.   Hamilton, James W.   Gender rejection as a reaction to
           early sexual trauma and its partial expression in verse.
           British J Medical Psychol, 1968, 41: 405-410.
18, 144.   Hammer, Emanuel F.   Interpretations couched in the po-
           etic style.   Int J Psychoanal Psychotherapy, 1978-79,
           7: 240-253.
18, 145.   Harrower, Molly.   Poems emerging from the therapeutic
           experience.   JNMD, 1969, 149: 213-223.
18, 146.   _____.   The therapy of poetry.   Current Psychiat
           Therapies, 1974, 14: 97-105.
18, 147.   _____.   The Therapy of Poetry.   Springfield, Ill:
           Thomas, 1972.
18, 148.   _____.   Variations on the theme.   Artist as therapist,
           therapist as artist.   Voices, 1975-76.
18, 149.   Hartman, Esther A.   Imaginative Literature as a Projec-
           tive Technique: A Study in Bibliotherapy.   DA, 1950-
           51, 26: 15-17.
18, 150.   Hatfield, Louis Duana.   As the Twig Is Bent; Therapeutic
           Values in the Use of Drama and the Dramatic in the
           Church.   NY: Vantage, 1965.
18, 151.   Hayakawa, S. I.   Metamessages and self-discovery.   In
           Leedy, J. J. (ed), Poetry Therapy.   Philadelphia: Lip-
           pincott, 1969, 269-272.
18, 152.   Heniger, Owen E.   Poetry therapy in private practice: an
           Odyssey into the healing power of poetry.   In Lerner,
           A. (ed), Poetry in the Therapeutic Experience.   NY:
           Pergamon, 1978, 56-62.
18, 153.   Heuscher, Julius E.   Inauthenticity, flight from freedom,
           despair.   Amer J Psychoanal, 1976, 36: 331-337.
18, 154.   Hindman, James.   Developmental approaches to theatre.
           Drama Rev, 1976, 20: 75-78.
18, 155.   Hitchings, W. D.   Poetry, a way to fuller awareness.   In
           Leedy, J. J. (ed), Poetry Therapy.   Philadelphia: Lip-
           pincott, 1969, 124-132.
18, 156.   Hobson, Robert F.   Imagination and amplification in psy-
           chotherapy.   J Analytical Psychol, 1971, 16(1): 79-105.
18, 157.   Hoffman, Frederick J.   La Thérapeutique du néant: Les
           romans de William Styron.   Rev des Lettres Modernes,
           1967, 33-56.
18, 158.   Huntoon, Mary.   The creative arts as therapy.   In Ruiten-
           beek, H. M. (ed), The Creative Imagination.   Chicago:
           Quadrangle, 1965, 251-259.

18, 159.   Jean, Norma, & Déak, Frantisek.   Anna Halprin's theatre
           and therapy workshop.   Drama Rev, 1976, 20(1): 50-54.
18, 160.   Johansson, Majken.   [Literature as psychotherapy.]   Vår
           lösen: Kristen Kulturtiskrift, 1965, 56: 104-105.

18,161. Johnson, D., et al. Increasing hospital-community contact through a theater program in a psychiatric hospital. Hospital Community Psychiat, 1975, 26:435-438.

18,162. Johnston, Nancy. Group reading as a treatment tool with geriatrics. Amer J Occupational Therapy, 1965, 19: 192-195.

18,163. Jones, R. E. The double door. In Leedy, J. J. (ed), Poetry Therapy. Philadelphia: Lippincott, 1969, 223-230.

18,164. _____. Treatment of a psychotic patient by poetry therapy. In Leedy, J. J. (ed), Poetry Therapy. Philadelphia: Lippincott, 1969, 19-28.

18,165. Jorgensen, Paul A. Hamlet's therapy. Huntington Library Q, 1964, 27:239-258.

18,166. Kahn, J. H. 'Do not interpretations belong to God?' The validity of interpretations in psychotherapy and in literature. British J Medical Psychol, 1975, 48:227-236.

18,167. Kankeleit, Otto. Die schopferische Macht des Unbewussten, ihre Auswirkungen in der Kunst und in der modernen Psychotherapie. Berlin: de Gruyter, 1933.

18,168. Kanters, Robert. Trois stations de psychothérapie. Rev de Paris, 1963, 1:133-143.

18,169. Kantor, Robert E., & Hoffman, Lynn. Brechtian theater as a model for conjoint family therapy. Family Process, 1966, 5:218-229.

18,170. Kaufman, F. W., & Taylor, W. S. Literature as adjustment. J Abnormal & Social Psychol, 1936, 31:229-234.

18,171. Kelly, George A. Social understanding and social therapy in Schiller and Hegel. Studies in Burke & His Time, 1972, 13:2203-2228.

18,172. Keyes, Margaret F. Dante and the tasks of individuation. Art Psychotherapy, 1977, 4:159-165.

18,173. Kienle, G. Das Märchen in der Psychotherapie. Zeitschrift für Psychotherapie und medizinische Psychologie, 1959.

18,174. Killinger, Barbara E. The Place of Humour in Adult Psychotherapy. DAI, 1978, 38(7-B), 3400.

18,175. Kinsman, Robert S. Folly, melancholy, and madness: a study in shifting styles of medical analysis and treatment. In The Darker Vision of the Renaissance; Beyond the Fields of Reason. Berkeley: Univ. California Press, 1974, 273-320.

18,176. Kliphuis, M. A. R. Creative process therapy: preliminary observations. Art Psychotherapy, 1973, 1:177-179.

18,177. Knoff, William F. Depression: a historical overview. Amer J Psychoanal, 1975, 35:41-46.

18,178. Kobak, Dorothy. Poetry therapy in a '600' school and in a counseling center. In Leedy, J. J. (ed), Poetry Therapy. Philadelphia: Lippincott, 1969, 180-187.

18,179. _____, & Nisenson, E. Poetry therapy; a way to solve emotional problems. Instructor, 1971, 81:75.

18,180. Kohler, F. Ein Beitrag zum Problem der Ichspaltung,
         dargestelt an Beispielen in der Literatur. Zentralblatt
         für Psychotherapie, 1937, 10:82-103.
18,181. Kolyszko, P. Psychosis. A poem written at the moment
         psychosis was burning out. Confinia Psychiat, 1976,
         19:65-67.
18,182. Kopp, Sheldon. The Wizard of Oz behind the couch. Psy-
         chol Today, 1970, 3(10):70-73, 84.
18,183. Kouretas, Demetrios. The oracle of Trophonius: a kind
         of shock treatment associated with sensory deprivation
         in ancient Greece. British J Psychiat, 1967, 113:1441-
         1446.
18,184. Kramer, Aaron. The use of poetry in a private mental
         hospital. In Leedy, J. J. (ed), Poetry Therapy. Phi-
         ladelphia: Lippincott, 1969, 200-212.
18,185. _____ et al. Poetic creativity in deaf children. Amer
         Annals Deaf, 1976, 121:31-37.
18,186. Kremer-Marietti, Angèle. Drôles de drames. Nouvelles
         Littéraires, 10 Sept 1964, no. 1932.

18,187. La Charité, Raymond C. Rabelais: the book as therapy.
         In Peschel, E. R. (ed), Medicine and Literature. NY:
         Watson, 1980, 11-17.
18,188. Láin Entralgo, Pedro. The Therapy of the Word in Clas-
         sical Antiquity. New Haven: Yale Univ. Press, 1970.
18,189. Lange, Jean. Mental illness and writers' motif. Men-
         ninger Perspective, 1972, 25-28.
18,190. Lauer, Roger M. Abuses of poetry therapy. In Lerner,
         A. (ed), Poetry in the Therapeutic Experience. NY:
         Pergamon, 1978, 72-80.
18,191. _____. Creative writing as a therapeutic tool. Hos-
         pital & Community Psychiat, 1972, 23:55-56.
18,192. _____, & Goldfield, M. Creative writing in group
         therapy. Psychotherapy Theory Research & Practice,
         1970, 7:248-252.
18,193. Lawlor, Justus G. Poetry therapy? Psychiatry, 1972,
         35:227-237.
18,194. Lazarsfeld, Sofie. Fiction and related media as acceler-
         ators of therapy. In Mosak, H. H. (ed), Alfred Adler:
         His Influence on Psychology Today. Park Ridge, NJ:
         Noyes, 1973, 124-134.
18,195. _____. The use of fiction in psychotherapy. Amer J
         Psychotherapy, 1949, 3:26-33.
18,196. Leedy, Jack J. Poetry and medicine. MD Medical News-
         magazine, 1964, 8:144.
18,197. _____. Poetry the Healer. Philadelphia: Lippincott,
         1973; Review: Robert N. Ross, Psychotherapy: The-
         ory, Research & Practice, 1975, 12:255-257.
18,198. _____. Poetry Therapy, a New Ancillary Therapy in
         Psychiatry. NY: Poetry Therapy Center, 1966.
18,199. _____ (ed). Poetry Therapy: The Use of Poetry in the
         Treatment of Emotional Disorders. Philadelphia: Lip-

pincott, 1969; Review: Schloss, Gilbert A. , & Grundy, Dominck E. , Lit & Psychol, 1971, 21:51-55.

18, 200. _____. Principles of poetry therapy. In Poetry Therapy. Philadelphia: Lippincott, 1969, 67-74.

18, 201. _____. Some principles of poetry therapy. Brooklyn Psychologist, 1964, Sept.

18, 202. _____. The value of poetry therapy. Amer J Psychiat, 1970, 126:1183-1184.

18, 203. _____, & Rapp, Elaine. Poetry therapy and some links to art therapy. Art Psychotherapy, 1973, 1(2):145-151.

18, 204. Lehmann, Günther K. Erfahrung mit dem Stegreifmärchenspiel im Rahmen der klinischen Psychotherapie. Psychiatrie, Neurologie und medizinische Psychologie, 1968, 20(10):374-380.

18, 205. Leito Lobo, Fabio. Invenção do en reenstruturação de unego feminino acompanhada na produção poetica de una paciente. Revista di Psicoanálisi, 1961, 18:71-84.

18, 206. Lerner, Arthur. Poetry as therapy. APA Monitor, 1975, Sept-Oct.

18, 207. _____ (ed). Poetry in the Therapeutic Experience. NY: Pergamon, 1978.

18, 208. _____. Poetry therapy. Amer J Nursing, 1973, 73: 1336-1338.

18, 209. _____. Poetry therapy: a healing art. Study of English, 1974, 22-27.

18, 210. _____. Poetry therapy and semantics. ETC, 1976, 33: 417-422.

18, 211. Lessner, Johanna W. The poem as catalyst in group counseling. Personnel & Guidance J, 1974, 53:33-38.

18, 212. Leys, Duncan. Literature in healing. Library Assn Record, 1964, 66:161-166.

18, 213. Lippke, Richard L. Is purgation therapeutic? Players, 1975, 50:31-33.

18, 214. Liss, Edward. Creative therapy. In Ruitenbeek, H. M. (ed), The Creative Imagination. Chicago: Quadrangle, 1965, 261-265.

18, 215. Loeb, Roger C. Machines, mops, and medicaments: therapy in the cuckoo's nest. Lex et Scientia: Int J Law & Science, 1977, 13:38-41.

18, 216. Luber, Raymond F. Evaluation of poetic mood with the semantic differential. Psychol Reports, 1976, 39:499-502.

18, 217. _____. Poetry therapy helps patients express feelings. Hospital Community Psychiat, 1973, 24:387.

18, 218. _____. Recurrent spontaneous themes in group poetry therapy. J Amer Academy Psychoanal, 1978, 6:369-379.

18, 219. Lutz, G. M. Poetry as therapy. Educational Forum, 1970, 34:215-218.

18, 220. Manocchio, Tony, & Petitt, William. Families Under Stress: A Psychological Interpretation. London/Boston: Routledge & Kegan Paul, 1975.

18, 221. Marcuse, M.   Erlebnis--Reproduction und Abreaktion
          durch literarische Gestaltung in der Autokatharsis.
          Zentralblatt für Psychotherapie, 1932, 5:211-217.
18, 222. Margolis, Gary F.   The Use of Poems in Counseling The-
          ory and Practice.   DAI, 1972, 32:3693.
18, 223. Marlin, William.   A portrait through poetry and drawing.
          Amer J Art Therapy, 1974, 13:237-249.
18, 224. Mazzonis, Emiliana.   [The film Marat-Sade: on attempted
          therapy with psychodrama.]   Minerva Medica, 1967, 58:
          1586.
18, 225. Mazzu, N.   Poetry: a therapeutic tool in the early stages
          of alcoholism treatment.   J Studies on Alcohol, 1979,
          40:123-128.
18, 226. Menninger, William C.   Bibliotherapy.   Bulletin Menninger
          Clinic, 1937, 1:263-273.
18, 227. Merloo, Joost A. M.   The universal language of rhythm.
          In Leedy, J. J. (ed), Poetry Therapy.   Philadelphia:
          Lippincott, 1969, 52-66.
18, 228. Millard, David A.   Literature and the therapeutic imagina-
          tion.   British J Social Work, 1977, 7(2):173-184.
18, 229. Miller, Arlyn H.   The spontaneous use of poetry in an
          adolescent girls' group.   Int J Group Psychotherapy,
          1973, 23:223-227.
18, 230. Miller, David K.   Poetry therapy with psychotic patients.
          J Contemporary Psychotherapy, 1978, 9:135-138.
18, 231. Miller, J.   Theatre, communication and mental health.
          Mental Health & Society, 1974, 1:197-206.
18, 232. Miller, L.   Theatre and community: The Tent of Joseph.
          Mental Health & Society, 1976, 3:240-245.
18, 233. Miller, R. J.   Student theatre as a means of promoting
          communication, self-development and creativity.   Men-
          tal Health & Society, 1976, 3:233-239.
18, 234. Mintz, N. L.   Creative processes and products: applica-
          tions to the expressive movement in education and psy-
          chotherapy.   Confinia Psychiatrica, 1973, 16:80-90.
18, 235. Moreno, J. L.   Comments on Goethe and psychodrama.
          Group Psychotherapy and Psychodrama, 1971, 24:14-16.
18, 236. _____. Das Stegreif-Theater.   Berlin: Kiepenheuer,
          1923.
18, 237. Morrison, Morris R.   Poetry therapy with disturbed ado-
          lescents.   In Leedy, J. J. (ed), Poetry Therapy.   Phi-
          ladelphia: Lippincott, 1969, 88-103.   In Golubchick,
          L. H., & Persky, B., (eds), Urban, Social and Educa-
          tional Issues.   Dubuque, Iowa: Kendall-Hunt, 1974,
          169-176.
18, 238. _____. The use of poetry in the treatment of emo-
          tional dysfunction.   Art Psychotherapy, 1978, 5:93-98.
18, 239. Morrison, Theresa.   A new way with poetry.   J Rehabili-
          tation, 1974, 40:28-31.
18, 240. Morton, Carlos.   Nuyorican theatre.   Drama Rev, 1976,
          20(1):43-49.
18, 241. Moss, A. E.   Hamlet and role-construct theory.   British J
          Medical Psychol, 1974, 47:253-264.

18, 242. _____. Shakespeare and role-construct therapy. British J Medical Psychol, 1974, 47:235-252.

18, 243. Müller, Christian, & Bader, A. The cinema and the mental patient: a new form of group therapy. Current Psychiat Therapies, 1968, 8:169-172.

18, 244. Murphy, D. C. The therapeutic value of children's literature. Nursing Forum, 1972, 11:141-164.

18, 245. Murphy, J. M. The therapeutic use of poetry. Current Psychiat Therapies, 1978, 18:65-71.

18, 246. Nemiah, J. C. The art of deep thinking: reflections on poetry and psychotherapy. Seminars in Psychiat, 1973, 5:301-311.

18, 247. Noszlopi, L. Note on the dream from the point of view of the psycho- and sociodrama. Int J Sociometry & Sociatry, 1963, 3(3-4).

18, 248. Novey, Riva. The artistic communication and the recipient. Death in Venice as an integral part of a psychoanalysis. Psychoanal Q, 1964, 32:25-52.

18, 249. Novey, Samuel. Why some patients conduct actual investigations of their biographies. JAPA, 1966, 14:376-387.

18, 250. Nydes, Jules. Creativity and psychotherapy. Psychoanal Rev, 1962, 49:29-33.

18, 251. Oberndorf, Clarence P. Psychoanalysis in literature and its therapeutic value. In Roheim, G. (ed), Psychoanalysis and the Social Sciences, Vol. 1. NY: IUP, 1947, 297-310; in Ruitenbeek, H. M. (ed), Psychoanalysis and Literature. NY: Dutton, 1964, 102-113.

18, 252. O'Hearne, Lillian P. The use of fairytales in redecision. Transactional Analysis J, 1974, 4(4):32-35.

18, 253. Olsen, Henry D. Bibliotherapy to help children solve problems. Elementary School J, 1975, 75:422-429.

18, 254. Orsia, Benedetto, & De Maio, Domenico. Considerazioni psicopatolgische a proposito di un talento poetico attuelizzatosi nel corso di crisi dissociative. Archivio Psicologia, Neurologia e Psichiatria, 1965, 26:279-314.

18, 255. Padel, J. H. 'That the thought of hearts can mend': an introduction to Shakespeare's Sonnets for psychotherapists and others. Times Lit Supplement, 19 Dec 1975, 1519-1521.

18, 256. Parisi, Peter Elliot. Therapeutic Relations and Aesthetic Unities. DAI, 1975, 35:6676A.

18, 257. Parker, Lois J. Classical and Existential Comparative Uses of Myth and Modern Literature: A Study of Counseling Persons in Boundary Situations. DAI, 1978, 39(6-A), 3380-81.

18, 258. Parker, Rolland S. Poetry as a therapeutic art. In Leedy, J. J. (ed), Poetry Therapy. Philadelphia: Lippincott, 1969, 155-170.

18, 259. Parsons, Virgil. Contact vs. contract: the process of
          taming. J Psychiat Nursing & Mental Health Services,
          1972, 10(3):18-20.
18, 260. Pearson, L. The Use of Written Communications in Psy-
          chotherapy. Springfield, Ill: Thomas, 1965.
18, 261. Pierce, C. M. Greek poetry and modern psychotherapy.
          Amer J Psychother, 1963, 17:631-640.
18, 262. Pietropinto, Anthony. Monsters of the mind: nonsense
          poetry and art psychotherapy. Art Psychotherapy,
          1975, 2:45-54.
18, 263. _____. Poetry therapy in groups. Current Psychiat
          Therapies, 1975, 15:221-232.
18, 264. Plank, Robert. The Emotional Significance of Imaginary
          Beings: A Study of the Interaction Between Psycho-
          therapy, Literature, and Reality in the Modern World.
          Springfield, Ill: Thomas, 1968.
18, 265. Powell, J. W. , et al. Group reading and group therapy.
          Psychiatry, 1952, 213-256.
18, 266. Putzel, Judith. Toward Alternative Theories of Poetry
          Therapy. Doctoral dissertation, Univ. Massachusetts,
          1975.

18, 267. Radŏsevič, Z. Psychiatry and bibliotherapy. Amer Hos-
          pital Library Q, 1964, 4:14.
18, 268. Ramon, E. , et al. A new approach to creative psycho-
          therapy by integration of folk legends, drama and clay
          modelling. Confinia Psychiatrica, 1978, 21:33-39.
18, 269. Rance, C. , et al. Poetry as a group project. Amer J
          Occupational Therapy, 1973, 27:252-255.
18, 270. Reider, N. , Olinger, Davida, & Lyle, Jeanetta. Amateur
          dramatics as a therapeutic agent in the psychiatric
          hospital. Bulletin Menninger Clinic, 1939, 3:20-26.
18, 271. Reiter, Sherry. The future of poetry therapy. Art Psy-
          chotherapy, 1978, 5:13-14.
18, 272. _____. Poetry therapy. Art Psychotherapy, 1978, 5:
          13-14.
18, 273. Robinson, S. , & Mowbray, J. Why poetry? In Leedy,
          J. J. (ed), Poetry Therapy. Philadelphia: Lippincott,
          1969, 188-199.
18, 274. Roggeman, Willy. Hans Carossa: de autobiographie als
          therapie. Nieuw Vlaams Tydschrift, 1958, 12:1210-
          1217, 1316-1324.
18, 275. Rom, Paul. Goethe on psychotherapy. J Individual Psy-
          chol, 1963, 19:182-184.
18, 276. Rongione, Louis A. The psychological aspects of science
          fiction can contribute much to bibliotherapy. Catholic
          Library World, 1964, 36:96-99.
18, 277. Rose, Gilbert J. King Lear and the use of humor in
          treatment. JAPA, 1969, 17:927-940.
18, 278. Ross, Deborah L. Poetry Therapy Versus Traditional
          Supportive Therapy: A Comparison of Group Process.
          DAI, 1977, 38(3-B), 1417-18.

18, 279. Ross, Robert N. Parsing concepts: a discovery technique for poetry therapy. In Lerner, A. (ed), Poetry in the Therapeutic Experience. NY: Pergamon, 1978, 41-55.

18, 280. Rothenberg, Albert. Poetic process and psychotherapy. Psychiatry, 1972, 35:238-254.

18, 281. _____. Poetry and psychotherapy: kinships and contrasts. In Leedy, J. (ed), Poetry the Healer. Philadelphia: Lippincott, 1973, 91-126.

18, 282. _____. Poetry in therapy, therapy in poetry. Sciences, 1972, 12:30-31.

18, 283. Rubin, Alec. Primal theatre. Drama Rev, 1976, 20(1): 55-63.

18, 284. Rubin, R. J. (ed). Bibliotherapy Sourcebook. Phoenix, Ariz: Oryx, 1978.

18, 285. Rule, Janice. The actor's identity crises: postanalytic reflections of an actress. Int J Psychoanal Psychotherapy, 1973, 2:51-76.

18, 286. Russell, Peter. Schnitzler's Blumen. The treatment of a neurosis. Forum for Modern Language Studies, 1977, 13:289-302.

18, 287. Ryan, B. J. Teaching self-expression through the use of poetic imagery. Perspectives in Psychiatric Care. 1967, 5:189-191.

18, 288. Ryan, Paul Ryder. Theatre as prison therapy. Drama Rev, 1976, 20(1):31-42.

18, 289. Sarotte, Georges M. Tennessee Williams: theater as psychotherapy. In Like a Brother, Like a Lover. NY: Anchor, 1978, 107-120; In Comme un frere, comme un amant. Paris: Flammarion, 1976.

18, 290. Sauber, S. R. Prior structure versus ambiguity as a therapeutic variable. Int J Social Psychiat, 1973, 9:66-72.

18, 291. Schaar, K. A storefront poet. APA Monitor, 1979, 10(9/10):7.

18, 292. Schattner, Gertrud, & Courtnay, Richard (eds). Drama in Therapy, 2 Vols. Drama in Therapy for Children, Vol. I; Drama in Therapy for Adults, Vol. II. NY: Drama Book, 1980.

18, 293. Schauffler, R. H. The Poetry Cure. NY: Dodd, 1927.

18, 294. Schimel, John L. The function of wit and humor in psychoanalysis. J Amer Academy Psychoanal, 1978, 6: 369-379.

18, 295. Schloss, Gilbert A. Psycho-Poetry: A New Approach to Self-Awareness Through Poetry Therapy. NY: Grosset & Dunlap, 1976.

18, 296. _____, & Grundy, Dominick E. Action techniques in psychopoetry. In Lerner, A. (ed), Poetry in the Therapeutic Experience. NY: Pergamon, 1978, 81-96.

18, 297. _____. Poetry therapy. Lit & Psychol, 1971, 21:51-55.

18, 298. Schmidbauer, Wolfgang. Tell about what you keep quiet. Literature and psychoanalysis. Therapie der Gegenwart, 1970, 109:1699-1700 passim.

18, 299. Schuller, Arthur B. On the psychotherapeutic process and the destruction of the therapist: contributions by Hermann Hesse. Int Rev Psycho-Anal, 1976, 3(2):181-192.
18, 300. Schwarz, G. S. Marquis de Sade, a pioneer of psychodrama? Pirquet Bulletin Clinical Medicine, 1967, 14(3):4-6.
18, 301. Sclabassi, S. H. Literature as a therapeutic tool: a review of the literature on bibliotherapy. Amer J Psychotherapy, 1973, 27:70-77.
18, 302. Segal, Dov. Limits in the therapeutic effect of the act of creation. The case of the Jewish poet Heinrich Heine. Confinia Psychiatrica, 1978, 21:183-186.
18, 303. Seguin, Carlos A. What folklore psychotherapy can teach us. Psychotherapy & Psychosomatics, 1974, 24:293-302.
18, 304. Shaw, H. L. Hypnosis and drama: a note on a novel use of self-hypnosis. Int J Clinical Experimental Hypnosis, 1978, 26:154-157.
18, 305. Shrodes, Caroline. Bibliotherapy: an application of psychoanalytic theory. Amer Imago, 1960, 17:311-319.
18, 306. _____. The dynamics of reading: implications for bibliotherapy. ETC, 1961, 18:21-33.
18, 307. Silverman, Hirsch L. Psychological implications of poetry therapy. Society & Culture, 1973, 4:215-228.
18, 308. Simmer, Bill. Robert Wilson and therapy. Drama Rev, 1976, 20(1):99-110.
18, 309. Simon, Bennett. The epic as therapy. In Mind and Madness in Ancient Greece. Ithaca: Cornell Univ. Press, 1978, 78-88.
18, 310. _____. Tragedy and therapy. In Mind and Madness in Ancient Greece; The Classical Roots of Modern Psychiatry. Ithaca: Cornell Univ. Press, 1978, 122-154.
18, 311. Solomon, Joan. Poetry therapy. Sciences, 1972, 20-25.
18, 312. Solow, Lee H. Reflections of Psychotherapy and the Psychotherapist in the Cinematic Eye: A Historical/Phenomenological Perspective. DAI, 1979, 39(7-B), 3540-41.
18, 313. Spice, Wilma H. A Jungian View of Tolkien's Gandalf: An Investigation of Enabling and Exploitative Power in Counseling and Psychotherapy from the Viewpoint of Analytical Psychology. DAI, 1976, 37:1417B.
18, 314. Squarzina, Luigi. Total theatre: cruelty, exorcism, psycho-drama. Modern Language Rev, 1968, 1:95-107.
18, 315. Stainbrook, Edward. Poetry and behavior in the psychotherapeutic experience. In Lerner, A. (ed), Poetry in the Therapeutic Experience. NY: Pergamon, 1978, 1-11.
18, 316. Steffens, Elizabeth. Using literature in group therapy. Hospital & Community Psychiat, 1970, 21:227.
18, 317. Stege, John Joseph. Communication Therapy, Paradox, and Change in The Merchant of Venice, Measure for Measure, and The Tempest. DAI, 1975, 35:6112A.

18, 318.   Stern, A. M.   Emile Zola; the influence of medical theories
           on French naturalism.   Applied Therapeutics, 1965, 7:
           323-331.
18, 319.   Stierlin, Helm.   Liberation and self-destruction in the cre-
           ative process.   In Smith, J. H. (ed), Psychiatry and the
           Humanities, Vol. 1.   New Haven: Yale Univ. Press,
           1976, 51-72.
18, 320.   Strulle, Arlene de.   Sexual fantasy theatre.   Drama Rev,
           1970, 20(1):64-74.
18, 321.   Sughi, Cesare.   Psicodramma, sociodramma, tecnica te-
           atrale.   Verri, 1968, 28:87-95.
18, 322.   Swede, George.   Poetry therapy.   Old Nun Magazine,
           1975, 1:51-53.

18, 323.   Tarrab, Gilbert.   Psychodrame et happening.   Rev d'His-
           toire du Théâtre, 1968, 20:70-94.
18, 324.   Tate, Candace.   Byron's Don Juan: myth as psychodrama.
           Keats-Shelley J, 1980, 29:131-150.
18, 325.   Tatham, Campbell.   Mythotherapy and postmodern fictions:
           magic is afoot.   In Benamou, M. , & Caramello, C.
           (eds), Performance in Postmodern Culture.   Madison:
           Univ. Wisconsin Press, 1977, 137-157.
18, 326.   Teichmann, Max.   Danton's Death: an early psychodrama.
           Komos, 1973, 3:21-23.
18, 327.   Thompson, Denys.   The uses of poetry.   In The Uses of
           Poetry.   NY: Cambridge Univ. Press, 1978, 194-225.
18, 328.   Timm, Charlotte Palmer.   Reading guidance in adjustment.
           Wilson Library Bulletin, 1959, 34:146-148.
18, 329.   Tyler, Parker.   An American theater motif: the psycho-
           drama.   Amer Q, 1963, 15:140-151.
18, 330.   Tyszkiewicz, M.   [Poetic creativity in chronically ill
           schizophrenics.]   Psychiatria Polska, 1973, 7:409-413.

18, 331.   Various.   Theatre and therapy.   [Entire issue.]   Drama
           Rev, 1976, 20(1):3-110.
18, 332.   Vest, W. E.   William Shakespeare, therapeutist.   Southern
           Medical J, 1944, 31:457-464; Transactions Amer Thera-
           peutic Society, 1943, 43:18-29.
18, 333.   Victor, George.   Interpretations couched in mythical
           imagery.   Int J Psychoanal Psychotherapy, 1978-79,
           7:225-239.
18, 334.   Villapecellin, Alvaro.   [The fables of Düss as exploratory
           instruments of psychological problems.]   Revista de
           Psicologia General y Aplicada, 1972, 27:509-522.
18, 335.   Völker, Ludwig.   Muse Melancholie--Therapeutikum Po-
           esie--Studien zum Melancholie--Problem in der deutsch-
           en Lyrik von Hölty bis Benn.   Munich: Fink, 1978.

18, 336.   Wagner, Arthur.   Transactional analysis and acting.
           Tulane Drama Rev, 1967, 11:81-88.

18,337.   Waldoff, Leon.   Prufrock's defenses and our response.
          Amer Imago, 1969, 26:182-193.
18,338.   Watts, U. N.   Effects of therapy on the creativity of a
          writer.   Amer J Orthopsychiat, 1962, 32:186-192.
18,339.   Weblin, J. E.   The patient's dilemma: who is an 'author-
          ity'?   Australian/New Zealand J Psychiat, 1973, 7:192.
18,340.   Wethered, Audrey G.   Drama and Movement in Therapy.
          London: Macdonald & Evans, 1973.
18,341.   _____.   Movement and Drama in Therapy.   Boston:
          Plays, 1973.
18,342.   Widroe, Harvey, & Davidson, Joan.   The use of directed
          writing in psychotherapy.   Bulletin Menninger Clinic,
          1961, 25:110-119.
18,343.   Williams, Juanita.   The Effectiveness of Poetry in Facili-
          tating Openness.   DAI, 1979, 39(9-B), 4603.
18,344.   Wispelacre, Paul de.   Literatuur als therapie en mythe:
          Michel Leiris.   De Vlaamse Gids, 1965, 49:553-575.
18,345.   Wolf, N.   [Short stories and poems of young drug ad-
          dicts.]   Bibliotheca Psychiatrica, 1976, 154:85-92.
18,346.   Wolman, Benjamin B.   Poetry and psychotherapy.   Voices:
          The Art & Science of Psychotherapy, 1970, 6:56-59.

18,347.   Ziolko, H. U.   [An undisguised case history in an example
          of contemporary literature.   Psychoanalytic reflections
          on K. Struck's The Mother.]   Zeitschrift Psychosoma-
          tische Medizin und Psychoanalyse, 1979, 25:84-93.
18,348.   Zoellner, Robert.   Talk-write: a behavioral pedagogy for
          composition.   College English, 1969, 30:267-320.

18, 349. Abraham, Karl. Dreikäsehoch; zur Psychoanalyse des
          Wortwitzes. Imago, 1918, 5:294-295.
18, 350. Abrahams, Roger D. , & Dundes, Alan. On elephantasy
          and elephanticide. Psychoanal Rev, 1969, 56:225-241.
18, 351. Adams, V. The anatomy of a joke. New York Times,
          28 Aug 1979, Section C, 1-3.
18, 352. Adler, Alfred. Zusammenhänge zwischen Neurose und
          Witz. Int Zeitschrift für Individual-Psychologie, 1927,
          5:12-19.
18, 353. Ahlman, E. Till komikens psykogenes. Tidskrift for
          psykology och pedagogiska forskning, 1929, 1:70-79.
18, 354. Alexander, Lloyd. No laughter in heaven. Hornbook,
          1970, 46:11-19.
18, 355. Allport, Gordon W. , & Postman, Leo J. The basic psy-
          chology of humor. In Newcomb, T. M. , & Hartley,
          E. L. (eds), Readings in Social Psychology. NY: Holt,
          1947, 547-558.
18, 356. Alter, Robert. Jewish humor and the domestication of
          myth. In Defenses of the Imagination. Jewish Writers
          and Modern Historical Crisis. Philadelphia: Jewish
          Publication Society, 1977, 155-167; In Levin, H. (ed),
          Veins of Humor, Harvard English Studies, No. 3.
          Cambridge, Harvard Univ. Press, 1972, 255-267.
18, 357. Anderson, Don. Comic modes in modern American fic-
          tion. Southern Rev (Adelaide), 1975, 8:152-165.
18, 358. Anderson, Phillip Bruce. The Genius of Nonsense: A
          Study of the Later Eighteenth-Century English Farce.
          DAI, 1976, 37:978A.
18, 359. Andrus, T. C. A study of laugh patterns in the theatre.
          Speech Monographs, 1946, 13:114.
18, 360. Annal, Charles William. Black Humor in Selected Works
          of Donne, Jonson, Shakespeare and Burton. DAI,
          1977, 37:5840A.
18, 361. Appelberg, B. [The Theory of the Comic in the 17th and
          18th Century.] Helsingfors: Söderstrom, 1944.
18, 362. Arieti, Silvano. New views on the psychology and psycho-
          pathology of wit and the comic. Psychiatry, 1950, 13:
          43-62.
18, 363. Aristides (Pseud). Jokes and their relation to the con-
          scious. Amer Scholar, 1978, 47:302+.

18, 364. Aschkenasy, Nehama. The Fool as Modern Hero: A Study of Clowning, Folly, and the Ludic Element in Some Modern Works. DAI, 1978, 38:7311A-12A.

18, 365. Austin, James C. Gold dust, dust bowl and gopher prairie. Rev Française d'Etudes Américaines, 1977, 4:31-37.

18, 366. Autrand, Michel. L'Humour de Jules Renard. Paris: Klincksieck, 1978.

18, 367. Bacon, Deborah. The Meaning of Nonsense: A Psychoanalytic Approach to Lewis Carroll. Doctoral dissertation, Columbia Univ., 1950.

18, 368. Baghbaw, Hafizullah. The Content and Concept of Humor in Magadi Theater. DAI, 1977, 37:7895.

18, 369. Baldensperger, Fernand. Les Definitions de l'humor. In Etudes d'Histoire Litteraire. Paris: 1907.

18, 370. Barchilon, Jacques. Pleasure, mockery and creative integration. Int J Psycho-Anal, 1973, 54:19-34.

18, 371. Barnes, Linda Horvay. The Dialectics of Black Humor: Process and Product: A Reorientation Toward Contemporary American and German Black Humor Fiction. European University Papers, Series 18, Vol. 15. Bern: Lang, 1978.

18, 372. Barrett, Robert Michael. The Assault of Laughter: Black Humor as a Contemporary American Fictional Form. DAI, 1977, 38:259A.

18, 373. Barrick, Mac E. Racial riddles and the Polish joke. Keystone Folklore Q, 1970, 15:3-15.

18, 374. Bawdon, H. H. The comic as illustrating the summation-irradiation theory of pleasure-pain. Psychol Rev, 1910, 17:336-346.

18, 375. Ben-Amos, Dan. The 'myth' of Jewish humor. Western Folklore, 1973, 32:112-131.

18, 376. Bénard, Charles. La Théorie du comique dans l'esthétique allemande. Rev philosophique, 1880, 10.

18, 377. Benstock, Benjamin. Ironic Alchemy: A Study of Language, Humor and Significance in James Joyce's Finnegans Wake. Kentucky Microcards, Series A; Modern Languages Series, No. 138. Lexington: Univ. Kentucky Press, 1963; DA, 1958, 17:1795.

18, 378. _____. Joyce--Again's Wake: An Analysis of 'Finnegans Wake.' Seattle: Univ. Washington Press, 1965.

18, 379. Bentley, Joseph. Satire and the rhetoric of sadism. Centennial Rev, 1967, 11:387-404.

18, 380. Berger, Arthur. Anatomy of the joke. J Communication, 1976, 26:113-115.

18, 381. Bergeret, J. [Toward a metapsychology of humor.] Rev Française de Psychanalyse, 1973, 37:539-567.

18, 382. Bergler, Edmund. Anxiety, 'feet of clay,' and comedy. Amer Imago, 1949, 6:97-109.

18, 383. _____. A clinical contribution to the psychogenesis of humor. Psychoanal Rev, 1937, 24:34-53.

18,384.   . The dislike for satire at length; an addition to the theory of wit. Psychiat Q Supplement, 1952, 26: 190-201.

18,385.   . Laughter and the Sense of Humor. NY: Grune & Stratton, 1956.

18,386. Bergson, Henri. Laughter. An Essay on the Meaning of the Comic. London: Macmillan, 1911, 1935; Paris: Alcon, 1900, 1930.

18,387.   . Laughter. In Sypher, W. (ed), Comedy. Garden City, NY: Doubleday, 1956, 59-190.

18,388.   . Le Rire. Rev de Paris, 1900, 7:512-545, 759-791.

18,389. Berkoben, Lawrence D. Coleridge on wit. Humanities Assn Bulletin, 1964, 15:24-30.

18,390. Bettersworth, John K. The humor of the old Southwest: yesterday and today. Mississippi Q, 1964, 17:87-94.

18,391. Bier, Jesse. Sick humor and the function of comedy. Humanist, 1979, 39:45-49.

18,392. Bischoff, Joan. With Manic Laughter: The Secular Apocalypse in American Novels of the 1960's. DAI, 1975, 36:2818A.

18,393. Bishop, Michael. Laughter and the smile in Stendhal. Modern Language Rev, 1975, 70:50-70.

18,394. Bouissac, Paul. A semiotic approach to nonsense: clowns and limericks. In Sebeok, T.A. (ed), Sight, Sound, and Sense. Bloomington: Indiana Univ. Press, 1977, 244-263.

18,395. Breme, Frederick J. Humor and Its Relationship to Needs. DAI, 1976, 37:1981.

18,396. Brennan, Joseph J. The Comic in the Plays of Eugene O'Neill: The Use of Characterization Situation, and Language in Relation to Henri Bergson's Theory of Comedy. DAI, 1974, 35:1088A.

18,397. Brill, Abraham A. Freud's theory of wit. J Abnormal Psychol, 1911, 6:279-316.

18,398.   . Introduction to Mendelsohn, S.F., Here Is a Good One. NY: Bloch, 1947.

18,399.   . Introduction to Mendelsohn, S.F., The Jew Laughs. Philadelphia: Jewish Publication Society, 1935.

18,400.   . The mechanism of wit and humor in normal and psychopathic states. Psychiat Q, 1940, 14:731-749.

18,401. Brinkmann, D. Beitrag zur sprachpsychologischen Analyse des Witzes. Schweizerischen Zeitschrift für Psychologie, 1944, 3:138-141.

18,402. Brooks, Van Wyck. Mark Twain's humor. Dial, 1920, 68:275-291.

18,403.   . Mark Twain's satire. Dial, 1920, 68:424-443.

18,404. Brown, Waln K. Cognitive ambiguity and the 'pretended obscene riddle.' Kentucky Folklore Record, 1973, 18: 89-101.

18,405. Brumbaugh, F., & Wilson, F.J. Children's laughter. J Genetic Psychol, 1940, 51:3-29.

18,406. Brunvand, Jan Harold. Some thoughts on the ethnic riddle jokes. Indiana Folklore, 1970, 3:128-142.

18,407. _____. The study of contemporary folklore: jokes. Fabula, 1972, 13:1-19.

18,408. Bryant, Jennings, & Meyer, Timothy P. A developmental analysis of children's favorite jokes. In Chapman, A. J., & Foot, H. C. (eds), It's a Funny Thing, Humour. Oxford: Pergamon, 1977, 223.

18,409. Bungert, Hans. William Faulkner und die humoristische Tradition des amerikanischen Südens. Heidelberg: Carl Winter, 1971.

18,410. Burns, Thomas A., & Burns, Inger H. Doing the Wash: An Expressive Culture and Personality Study of a Joke and Its Tellers. Norwood, Pa: Norwood, 1976; Review: Western Folklore, 1979, 38:122-126.

18,411. Butturff, Douglas R. Laughter and discovered aggression in Sir Gawain and the Green Knight. Lit & Psychol, 1972, 22:139-147.

18,412. Cantor, Joanne R. What is funny to whom? The role of gender. J Communication, 1976, 26:164-172.

18,413. Carlson, Constance H. Wit and irony in Hawthorne's The House of Seven Gables. In Sprague, R. S. (ed), A Handful of Spice. Orono: Univ. Maine Press, 1968, 159-168.

18,414. Cattell, R. B., & Luborsky, L. B. Measured response to humor as an indicator of personality structure. I. Analysis of humor. Amer Psychologist, 1946, 1:257-258.

18,415. Cawelti, John C. The sanity of Mad. In Brack, O. M., Jr., (ed), American Humor. Scottsdale, Ariz: Arete, 1977, 171-178.

18,416. Cecil, C. D. Delicate and indelicate puns in Restoration comedy. Modern Language Rev, 1966, 61:572-578.

18,417. Chapiro, M. L'Illusion comique. Paris: Presses Universitaires de France, 1940.

18,418. Chapman, Antony J., & Foot, Hugh C. (eds). It's a Funny Thing, Humour. International Conference on Humour & Laughter Held in Cardiff, 1976. Oxford NY: Pergamon, 1977.

18,419. _____, & Gadfield, Nicholas J. Is sexual humor sexist? J Communication, 1976, 26:141-153.

18,420. Chiaromonte, Nicola. Pirandello and humor. In Chiaromonte, M. (ed), The Worm of Consciousness. NY: Harcourt Brace Jovanovich, 1976, 80-93.

18,421. Chickering, Howell D., Jr. Robert Frost, romantic humorist. Lit & Psychol, 1966, 16:139-150.

18,422. Clark, John R. Bowl games: satire in the toilet. Modern Language Studies, 1974, 4(2):43-58.

18,423. Cohen, Hennig. A comic mode of the romantic imagination: Poe, Hawthorne, Melville. In Rubin, L. (ed), The Comic Imagination in American Literature. New Brunswick, NJ: Rutgers Univ. Press, 1973, 85-99.

18,424.   Cohen, Sarah Blacher. Comic Relief: Humor in Contem-
           porary American Literature. Urbana: Univ. Illinois
           Press, 1978.
18,425.   _____. Sex: Saul Bellow's hedonistic joke. Studies in
           Amer Fiction, 1974, 2:223-229.
18,426.   Coleridge, Samuel Taylor. On wit and humor. Lecture
           IX. In Raysor, T. M. (ed), Miscellaneous Criticism.
           Cambridge: Harvard Univ. Press, 1936.
18,427.   Coley, William B. The background of Fielding's laughter.
           J English Lit History, 1959, 26:229-252.
18,428.   Couradaveaux, Victor. Le Rire dans la vie et dans l'art.
           Paris: 1875.
18,429.   Couturier, Maurice. Nabokov's laughter. Rev Fran-
           çaises d'Etudes Américaines, 1977, 4:115-122.
18,430.   Covino, William A. Lugubrious drollery: humor and
           horror in Conrad's fiction. Modern Fiction Studies,
           1977, 23:217-225.
18,431.   Cox, James M. Humor and America: the southwestern
           bear hunt, Mrs. Stowe, and Mark Twain. Sewanee
           Rev, 1975, 83:573-601.
18,432.   _____. Mark Twain: The Fate of Humor. Princeton:
           Princeton Univ. Press, 1966.
18,433.   _____. Toward vernacular humor. Virginia Q Rev,
           1970, 46:311-330.
18,434.   Craig, Martha. The secret wit of Spenser's language.
           In Alpers, P. J. (ed), Edmund Spenser. Baltimore:
           Penguin, 1969.
18,435.   Crossley, Brian. Spenser's bawdy: a note on The Fairy
           Queen 2:6. Papers on Language & Lit, 1973, 9:314-
           319.

18,436.   Daiches, David. Misunderstanding as humour: an aspect
           of the English comic tradition. In More Literary Es-
           says. Chicago: Univ. Chicago Press, 1968, 19-41.
18,437.   Dance, Daryl C. Wit and Humor in Black American Lit-
           erature. DAI, 1972, 32:4558A-59A.
18,438.   Daniels, R. Balfour. The wit and humor of Samuel But-
           ler (1835-1902). North Dakota Q, 1965, 33:44-49.
18,439.   Davies, Leland J. Attitudes toward old age and aging as
           shown by humor. Gerontologist, 1977, 17:220-226.
18,440.   Delay, Jean, Pichot, P., Guilbert, M., & Perse, J. Un
           test d'appréciation de l'humour--application dans la
           paranoia. Rev de Psychologie Appliqués, 1954, 4:297-
           316.
18,441.   Dentan, Michel. Humour et création littéraire dans
           l'oeuvre de Kafka. Geneva: Droz, 1961.
18,442.   Devereux, George. Mohave Indian verbal and motor
           profanity. In Psychoanalysis and the Social Sciences,
           Vol. 3. NY: IUP, 1951, 99-127.
18,443.   Dhar, B. Chesterton's conception of humour. Modern
           Rev, 1970, No. 759, 186-189.
18,444.   Dick, Ernst S. Structures of humor in Dürrenmatt's
           savage comedy. In White, K. S. (ed), Savage Comedy:

Structures of Humor. Amsterdam: Rodopi, 1978, 25-27.

18, 445. Diot, Rolande. S. J. Perelman et la Dementia Precox school of humor: autopsie du Perelmontage. Rev Française d'Etudes Américaines, 1977, 4:91-102.

18, 446. Diserens, C. M., & Bonifield, M. Humor and the ludicrous. Psychol Bulletin, 1930, 27:108-111.

18, 447. Dollard, J. The dozens: dialectic of insult. Amer Imago, 1939, 1:3-25.

18, 448. Dooley, Lucile. A note on humor. Psychoanal Rev, 1934, 21:49-58.

18, 449. _____. The relation of humor to masochism. Psychoanal Rev, 1941, 28:37-46.

18, 450. Douglas, Mary. The social control of cognition: some factors in joke perception. Man, 1968, 3:361-376.

18, 451. Doyle, C. C. Title-author jokes, now and long ago. J Amer Folklore, 1973, 86:52-54.

18, 452. Draper, John W. Theory of the comic in eighteenth-century England. J English Germanic Philology, 1938, 37:207-223.

18, 453. Dresser, John W. Two Studies on the Social Function of Joking As an Outlet for Aggression. DA, 1967, 28(2-A), 778-779.

18, 454. Dresser, Norine. The metamorphosis of the humor of the black man. New York Folk Q, 1970, 26:216-228.

18, 455. Dugas, L. La Fonction psychologique du rire. Rev philosophique, 1906, 62.

18, 456. _____. Psychologie du rire. Paris: 1910.

18, 457. Dundes, Alan. Jokes and covert language attitudes: the curious case of the wide-mouth frog. Language in Society, 1977, 6:141-147.

18, 458. Dunn, Richard J. 'Inverse sublimity': Carlyle's theory of humor. Univ. Toronto Q, 1970, 40:41-57.

18, 459. Dusenberg, Robert. Hawthorne's merry company: the anatomy of laughter in the tales and short stories. PMLA, 1967, 82, 285-288.

18, 460. Eastman, Max. Enjoyment of Laughter. NY: Simon & Schuster, 1936.

18, 461. _____. The Sense of Humor. New York: Scribner, 1921.

18, 462. _____. Wit and nonsense: Freud's mistake. Yale Rev, 1936, 26:71-87.

18, 463. Ede, Lisa Susan. The Nonsense Literature of Edward Lear and Lewis Carroll. DAI, 1976, 36:5314A.

18, 464. Egner, F. Humor und Witz unter strikturpsychologischen Gesichtpunkt. Archiv für die Gesamte Psychologie, 1932, 84:330-371.

18, 465. Eidelberg, Ludwig. A contribution to the study of wit. Psychoanal Rev, 1945, 32:33-61; In Studies in Psychoanalysis. NY: Nervous & Mental Disease Monograph Series, 1948, 174-202.

18,466. Enck, John Jacob, Forter, Elizabeth T., & Whitley, Alvin (eds). The Comic in Theory and Practice. NY: Appleton-Century-Crofts, 1960.
18,467. Erskine, John. Humor. Century, 1928, 11:421-426.
18,468. Escarpit, Robert. Réévaluation de l'humour. Rev Française d'Etudes Américaines, 1977, 4:17-22.
18,469. Esselbrugge, K. Die Struktur des Humors bei Gottfried Keller. Jahrbuch für Charakterologie, 1929, 6:177-213.
18,470. Eysenck, H. J. The appreciation of humour: an experimental and theoretical study. British J Psychol, 1942, 32:295-309.
18,471. _____. An experimental analysis of five tests of 'appreciation of humor.' Educational & Psychological Measurements, 1943, 3:191-214.

18,472. Fabritius, Rudolph. Komik und Humor in William Saroyans Erzählung 'The Pomegranate Trees.' Die Neueren Sprache, 1966, 15:372-377.
18,473. Feldman, Sandor S. A supplement to Freud's theory of wit. Psychoanal Rev, 1941, 28:201-217.
18,474. Ferenczi, Sándor. The psychoanalysis of wit and the comical. In Further Contributions to the Theory and Technique of Psycho-Analysis. London: Hogarth, 1926, 332-344; Populäre Vorträge über Psychoanalyse, 89-102.
18,475. Fine, Gary A. Obscene joking across cultures. J Communication, 1976, 26:134-140.
18,476. Fisher, S. T. Kipling's hysterical laughter. Notes & Queries, 1978, 25:333.
18,477. Flugel, J. C. Humor and laughter. In Lindzey, G., (ed), Handbook of Social Psychology, Vol. 2. Cambridge, Mass: Addison Wesley, 1954, 709-734.
18,478. Frank, Ernst. Bibelwitz. Die Gegenwart, 1912, No. 1.
18,479. Frank, Roberta. Some uses of paronomasia in Old English scriptural verse. Speculum, 1972, 47:207-226.
18,480. Frankel, Esther B. An Experimental Study of Psychoanalytic Theories of Humor. DA, 1953, 13:1257-1258.
18,481. Franz, T. R. The Bases of Humor in Three Novels of Unamuno. DAI, 1970, 31:2913-A.
18,482. Freud, Sigmund. Humour. In Collected Papers, Vol. 5. London: Hogarth, 1950, 1959, 215-221; In Standard Edition, Vol. 21; In Gesammelte Schriften, Vol. 11, 1928, 402-408; Int J Psycho-Anal, 1928, 9:1-6; Almanach, 1928, 9-16; Imago, 1928, 14:1-6.
18,483. _____. The Interpretation of Dreams. NY: Basic Books, 1958, 62-63, 340-341, 345-346, 407-409.
18,484. _____. Jokes and Their Relation to the Unconscious. NY: Norton, 1961; London: Routledge & Kegan Paul, 1960; London: Fisher & Unwin, 1917; In Standard Edition, Vol. 8. London: Hogarth, 1953-61.
18,485. Froeschels, Emil. Philosophy in Wit. NY: Philosophical Library, 1948.

18, 486.   Frohock, Wilbur Merrill.   The edge of laughter: some
           modern fiction and the grotesque.   In Levin, H. (ed),
           Veins of Humor.   Cambridge: Harvard Univ. Press,
           1972, 243-254.
18, 487.   Fry, William F., Jr.   Sweet Madness: A Study of Humor.
           Mountain View, Cal: Pacific Books, 1963; Review:
           Philip Weissman, Psychoanal Q, 1964, 33:600-601.

18, 488.   Ganz, Margaret.   The vulnerable ego: Dickens' humor in
           decline.   In Partlow, R. B. (ed), Dickens Studies An-
           nual, Vol. 1.   Carbondale: Southern Illinois Univ.
           Press, 1975, 23-40.
18, 489.   Garth, T. R.   The psychology of riddle solutions.   J Edu-
           cational Psychol, 1920, 11:16-33.
18, 490.   Gaultier, Paul.   Le Rire et la caricature.   Paris: 1906.
18, 491.   Gelus, Marjorie.   Laughter and joking in the works of
           Heinrich von Kleist.   German Q, 1977, 50:452-473.
18, 492.   Gessel, Michael.   Katherine Anne Porter: the low comedy
           of sex.   In Brack, O. M., Jr. (ed), American Humor.
           Scottsdale, Ariz: Arete, 1977, 139-152.
18, 493.   Gindin, James.   Well beyond laughter: directions from
           fifties' comic fiction.   Studies in the Novel, 1971, 3:
           357-364.
18, 494.   Girard, René.   Perilous balance: a comic hypothesis.   In
           'To Double Business Bound'; Essays on Literature,
           Mimesis, and Anthropology.   Baltimore: Johns Hopkins
           Press, 1978, 121-135.
18, 495.   Goldsmith, Lisa A.   Adaptive regression, humor, and
           suicide.   J Consulting & Clinical Psychol, 1979, 47:628-
           630.
18, 496.   Goldstein, J. H., & McGhee, P. E. (eds).   The Psychology
           of Humor.   NY: Academic Press, 1972.
18, 497.   Goldstein, Jeffrey H.   Theoretical notes on humor.   J
           Communication, 1976, 26:104-112.
18, 498.   _____, & McGhee, Paul E. (eds).   The Psychology of
           Humor: Theoretical Perspectives and Empirical Issues.
           NY: Academic Press, 1972.
18, 499.   _____, McGhee, Paul E., Smith, Jean R., Chapman,
           Anthony J., & Foot, Hugh C.   Humour, laughter and
           comedy: a bibliography of empirical and nonempirical
           analyses in the English language.   In Chapman, A. J.,
           & Foot, H. C. (eds), It's a Funny Thing, Humour.   Ox-
           ford: Pergamon, 1977, 469-504.
18, 500.   Gombrich, E. H., & Kris, Ernst.   The principles of cari-
           cature.   British J Medical Psychol, 1938, 17:319-392;
           In Psychoanalytic Explorations of Art.   NY: IUP, 1952
           (193), 189-203.
18, 501.   Goodchilds, J. D.   On being witty: causes, correlates,
           and consequences.   In Goldstein, J. H., & McGhee,
           P. E. (eds), The Psychology of Humor.   NY: Academic
           Press, 1972, 173-193.
18, 502.   Goodman, Paul.   Comic plots.   In The Structure of Litera-
           ture.   Chicago: Univ. Chicago Press, 1954.

18, 503. Granfield, A. J., & Giles, H.   Towards an analysis of
          humor through symbolism.   Int J Symbology, 1975, 6:
          17-23.
18, 504. Grebstein, Sheldon Norman.   The comic anatomy of Port-
          noy's complaint.   In Cohen, S. B. (ed), Comic Relief.
          Urbana: Univ. Illinois Press, 1978, 152-171.
18, 505. Greenberg, Andrea.   Form and function of the ethnic joke.
          Keystone Folklore Q, 1972, 17:144-161.
18, 506. Greig, John Y. T.   Freud's theory of wit.   British J Medi-
          cal Psychol, 1923, 3:51-58.
18, 507. _____. The Psychology of Laughter and Comedy.   NY:
          Dodd, 1923; NY: Cooper Square, 1969.
18, 508. Greiner, Donald J.   Comic Terror: The Novels of John
          Hawkes.   Memphis: Memphis State Univ. Press, 1973.
18, 509. _____. Djuna Barnes' Nightwood and the origins of
          black humor.   Critique: Studies in Modern Fiction,
          1975, 17(1):41-54.
18, 510. Grotjahn, Martin.   Beyond Laughter; Humor and the Sub-
          conscious.   NY: McGraw-Hill, 1957, 1966.
18, 511. _____. Jewish jokes and their relation to masochism.
          In Mendel, W. H. (ed), A Celebration of Humor.   Los
          Angeles: Mara, 1970.
18, 512. _____. Sexuality and humor: don't laugh! Psychol To-
          day, 1972, 6(2):50-53.
18, 513. Grziwok, Rudolf, & Scodel, Alvin.   Some psychological
          correlates of humor preferences.   J Consulting Psychol,
          1956, 20-42.
18, 514. Gunter, Peter A.   Nietzschean laughter.   Sewanee Rev,
          1968, 76:493-506.
18, 515. Gurewitch, Morton.   Comedy: The Irrational Vision.
          Ithaca, NY: Cornell Univ. Press, 1975.
18, 516. Gutierrez-Noriega, Carlos.   Significado y transcendencia
          del humorismo en Cervantes.   San Marcos, 1948, 4:
          43-69.

18, 517. Haberland, Paul M.   The Development of Comic Theory in
          Germany During the 18th Century.   Göppingen: Küm-
          merle, 1971.
18, 518. Hall, Ernest Jackson.   The Satirical Element in the Amer-
          ican Novel.   Doctoral dissertation, Univ. Pennsylvania,
          1922.
18, 519. Hall, H. G.   Molière, satirist of 17th-century French
          medicine: fact and fantasy.   Proceedings Royal Society
          Medicine, 1977, 70:425-431.
18, 520. Hamill, Ralph C.   The role of the risqué story.   J Ab-
          normal Social Psychol, 1921, 16:269.
18, 521. Hansen, Arlene J.   Entropy and transformation: two types
          of American humor.   Amer Scholar, 1974, 43:405-421.
18, 522. Hansen, J.   The homosexual joke.   Tangents, 1966, 1:26-
          30.
18, 523. Harms, E.   The development of humor.   J Abnormal So-
          cial Psychol, 1943, 38:351-369.

18, 524. Hárnik, J.   Zum infantilen Charakter des Witzes.   Int
　　　　　 Zeitschrift für Psychoanalyse, 1912-13, 3:167.
18, 525. Hasley, Louis.   Humor in literature: a definition.   CEA
　　　　　 Critic, 1970, 32(5):10-11.
18, 526. Hassel, R. Chris, Jr.   Armado's sexual puns.   Language
　　　　　 Q, 1971, 9(3-4):7-8, 42.
18, 527. Hauck, Richard Boyd.   A Cheerful Nihilism: Confidence
　　　　　 and 'The Absurd' in American Humorous Fiction.
　　　　　 Bloomington: Indiana Univ. Press, 1971.
18, 528. Hecker, E.   Die Physiologie und Psychologie des Lachens
　　　　　 und des Komischen.   Berlin: 1873.
18, 529. Heim, A.   An experiment on humour.   British J Psychol,
　　　　　 1936, 27:148-161.
18, 530. Hellyar, R. H.   The meaning of the comic.   Psyche, 1927,
　　　　　 30:78-99.
18, 531. Hershinow, Sheldon J.   Schlemiel humor in the contempo-
　　　　　 rary American novel.   In Marsden, M. T. (comp),
　　　　　 Proceeding of the Fifth National Convention of the Popu-
　　　　　 lar Culture Assn.   Bowling Green, Ohio: Bowling
　　　　　 Green State Univ. Popular Press, 1975, 615-628.
18, 532. Hewitt, J. W.   Humor in Homer and in Vergil.   Classical
　　　　　 Weekly, 1929, 22:177-181.
18, 533. Heymans, G.   Zur Psychologie der Komik.   Zeitschrift
　　　　　 für Psychologie, 1899, 20:164-173.
18, 534. Hill, Hamlin.   Black humor: its cause and cure.   Colora-
　　　　　 do Q, 1968, 17:57-64.
18, 535. _____.   Modern American humor: the Janus laugh.
　　　　　 College English, 1963, 25:170-176.
18, 536. Hill, W. W.   Navaho humor.   General Series in Anthropol-
　　　　　 ogy, 1943, No. 9.
18, 537. Hilty, Peter.   Kingsley Amis and mid-century humor.
　　　　　 Discourse, 1960, 3:26-28, 37-45.
18, 538. Hitschmann, Edward.   Zur Psychologie des jüdischen
　　　　　 Witzes.   Psychoanalytische Bewegung, 1930, 2:580-586.
18, 539. Hoffman, Helen B.   The Relationship between Defensive
　　　　　 Style, Hostility Arousal, Humor Preference and Humor
　　　　　 Production.   DAI, 1976, 36:6382-83.
18, 540. Holman, Clarence Hugh.   Detached laughter in the South.
　　　　　 In Cohen, S. B. (ed), Comic Relief.   Urbana: Univ.
　　　　　 Illinois Press, 1978, 87-104; In Holman, C. H., Win-
　　　　　 dows on the World; Essays on American Social Fiction.
　　　　　 Knoxville: Univ. Tennessee Press, 1979, 27-47.
18, 541. Hong, Howard V.   The comic, satire, irony, and humor:
　　　　　 Kierkegaardian reflections.   In French, P. A., et al.
　　　　　 (eds), Midwest Studies in Philosophy.   Morris: Univ.
　　　　　 Minnesota Press, 1976, 98-105.
18, 542. Hooker, E. N.   Humour in the age of Pope.   Huntington
　　　　　 Library Q, 1948, 11:361-386.
18, 543. Horvay, Linda Rosemarie.   The Dialectics of Black Humor:
　　　　　 Process and Product.   DAI, 1977, 37:6476A-77A.
18, 544. Hunt, Leigh.   Wit and Humour.   London: 1910.
18, 545. Hunt, Sandra Ann.   The Black Humor Novel in American
　　　　　 Literature.   DAI, 1977, 38:3483A.

18, 546.   Jacobs, Melville.   Humor and social structure in an oral
           literature.   In Diamond, S.   (ed), Culture in History.
           NY: Columbia Univ.   Press, 1960, 181-189.
18, 547.   Janoff, Bruce L.   Beyond Satire: Black Humor in the
           Novels of John Barth and Joseph Heller.   DAI, 1972,
           33:1728A.
18, 548.   _____.   Black humor: beyond satire.   Ohio Rev, 1972,
           14(1):5-20.
18, 549.   _____.   Black humor, existentialism, and absurdity:
           a generic confusion.   Arizona Q, 1974, 30:293-304.
18, 550.   Janus, Samuel S.   The great comedians: personality and
           other factors.   Amer J Psychoanal, 1975, 35:169-174.
18, 551.   _____, Bess, Barbara E., & Janus, Beth R.   The
           great comediennes: personality and other factors.
           Amer J Psychoanal, 1978, 38:367-372.
18, 552.   Jekels, Ludwig.   On the psychology of comedy.   In Se-
           lected Papers.   London: Imago, 1952, 97-104.
18, 553.   Johnson, John.   Tears and laughter: the tragic novels of
           J. P. Donleavy.   Michigan Academician, 1976, 9:15-24.
18, 554.   Johnson, Ragnar.   Two realms and a joke: bisociation
           theories of joking.   Semiotica, 1976, 16:195-221.
18, 555.   Jones, Victor H.   Laughter in Hawthorne's fiction.   Col-
           lege Lit, 1978, 57-61.
18, 556.   Juleus, Nels.   Humor: the hidden barrier.   Etc., 1976,
           33:289-291.
18, 557.   Jünger, F. G.   Über das Komische.   Berlin: Widerstands,
           1936.

18, 558.   Kahane, Claire.   Comic variations and self-construction
           in grotesque literature.   Lit & Psychol, 1979, 29:114-
           119.
18, 559.   Kallen, Horace M.   The aesthetic principle in comedy.
           Amer J Psychol, 1911, 22.
18, 560.   Kambouropoulous, P.   Individual differences in the sense
           of humor.   J Abnormal Social Psychol, 1926, 37:268-
           278.
18, 561.   Kanzer, Mark.   Gogol: a study of wit and paranoia.
           JAPA, 1955, 3:110-125.
18, 562.   Kaplan, Elizabeth W.   Sources and Functions of Visual
           Humor in Rabelais' First Four Books.   DAI, 1974, 34:
           4266A-67A.
18, 563.   Kelling, G. W.   An empirical investigation of Freud's the-
           ory of jokes.   Psychoanal Rev, 1971, 58:473-485.
18, 564.   Kellogg, Thelma.   Early American Social Satire.   Doc-
           toral dissertation, Radcliffe College, 1929.
18, 565.   Kenny, Douglas T.   The contingency of humor apprecia-
           tion on the stimulus-confirmation of joke-ending ex-
           pectation.   J Abnormal Social Psychol, 1955, 51:644-
           648.
18, 566.   Keough, William Richard.   Violence and American Humor.
           DAI, 1976, 37:2182A-83A.

18, 567. Ketterer, David. Take-off to cosmic irony: science-fiction humor and the absurd. In Cohen, S. B. (ed), Comic Relief; Humor in Contemporary American Literature. Urbana: Univ. Illinois Press, 1978, 70-86.

18, 568. Kiely, Robert. The comic masks of Edgar Allan Poe. Umanesimo, 1967, 1(5):31-41.

18, 569. Kincaid, James R. Dickens and the Rhetoric of Laughter. NY: Oxford Univ. Press, 1971.

18, 570. Kintanar, Thelma B. The Significance of the Comic in James Joyce's Ulysses. DA, 1968, 29:1541.

18, 571. Kitch, John Charles. Dark Laughter: A Study of the Pessimistic Tradition in American Humor. DA, 1965, 25:6595.

18, 572. Kline, George Louis. Philosophical puns. In Walton, C., & Anton, J. P. (eds), Philosophy and the Civilizing Arts. Athens: Ohio Univ. Press, 1975, 213-235.

18, 573. Kline, Linus W. The psychology of humor. Amer J Psychol, 1907, 18:421-441.

18, 574. Kline, Paul. The psychoanalytic theory of humor and laughter. In Chapman, A. J., & Foot, H. C. (eds), It's a Funny Thing, Humour. NY: Pergamon, 1977, 7-12.

18, 575. Knox, Edmund Valpy. The Mechanism of Satire. Cambridge, England: Cambridge Univ. Press, 1951.

18, 576. Koch, Manfred. Konstitutionelle Varianten des Sinnes für Komik. Zeitschrift für Psychotherapie und medizinische Psychologie, 1955, 5:203-214.

18, 577. Koegler, Ronald R. In defense of the pun. Amer Imago, 1959, 16:231-235.

18, 578. Koestler, Arthur. The Act of Creation. A Study of the Conscious and Unconscious Processes of Humor, Scientific Discovery and Art. NY: Macmillan, 1964.

18, 579. _____. Part I. The comic. In Insight and Outlook. NY: Macmillan, 1949, 3-110.

18, 580. _____. Humour and wit. In Janus; A Summing Up. NY: Random House, 1978, 109-130.

18, 581. _____. Other theories of the comic: Bergson and Freud. In Insight and Outlook. NY: Macmillan, 1949, 417-430.

18, 582. Kollarits, Jenö. Zur Psychologie des Spasses, des Spassmachers und über scherzende Neurastheniker. JPNP, 1915, 21:224-232.

18, 583. Korsmeyer, C. The hidden joke: generic uses of masculine terminology. In Vettereling-Braggin, M., et al. (eds), Feminism and Philosophy. Totowa, NJ: Rowland & Littlefield, 1977, 138-153.

18, 584. Kosztolányi, A. [On the structure of jokes.] Psychol Studies Univ. Budapest, 1939, 3:128-137.

18, 585. Krause, David. The principle of comic disintegration. James Joyce Q, 1970, 8(1):3-12.

18, 586. Kravitz, Seth. London jokes and ethnic stereotypes. Western Folklore, 1977, 36:275-301.

18, 587.   Kris, Ernst.   Ego development and the comic.   Int J Psy-
           cho-Anal, 1938, 19:77-90; Revista de Psicoanálisis,
           1951, 8:518-530; In Psychoanalytic Explorations in Art.
           NY: IUP, 1952, Ch. 8.
18, 588.   _____.   Laughter as an expressive process.   In Psy-
           choanalytic Explorations in Art.   NY: IUP, 1952
           (1939), 217-239.
18, 589.   _____.   The psychology of caricature.   Int J Psycho-
           Anal, 1936, 17:285-303; In Psychoanalytic Explorations
           in Art.   NY: IUP, 1952, 173-188; Imago, 1934, 20:
           450-466.
18, 590.   _____, & Gombrich, E.   The principles of caricature.
           British J Medical Psychol, 1938, 17:319-342.
18, 591.   Krishna Menon, V. K.   A Theory of Laughter: With Spe-
           cial Relation to Comedy and Tragedy.   London: Allen
           & Unwin, 1931.

18, 592.   La Fave, Lawrence, & Mannell, Roger.   Ethnic humour
           as a function of reference groups and identification
           classes.   In Lancy, D. F., & Tindall, B. A. (eds),
           The Anthropological Study of Play: Problems and Pros-
           pects.   Cornwall, NY: Leisure, 1976, 217-229.
18, 593.   Lamblin, M.   Le Rire de H. Bergson--'Hippiás Majeur'
           de Platon.   Bulletin de Psychologie, 1967, 20(23-24),
           1382-1394.
18, 594.   Landis, C., & Ross, J. W. H.   Humor and its relation to
           other personality traits.   J Social Psychol, 1933, 4:
           156-175.
18, 595.   Le Clair, Thomas.   Death and black humor.   Critique:
           Studies in Modern Fiction, 1975, 17(1):5-40.
18, 596.   Leacock, Stephen Butler.   Humor and Humanity: An In-
           troduction to the Study of Humor.   NY: Holt, 1938;
           Toronto: Nelson, 1937.
18, 597.   _____.   The psychology of American humor.   McGill
           Univ. Magazine, 1907, 6:55-75.
18, 598.   Leak, Gary K.   Effects of hostility arousal and aggressive
           humor on catharsis and humor preference.   J Personal-
           ity & Social Psychol, 1974, 30:736-740.
18, 599.   Lee, Joan Cook, & Griffith, R. M.   Forgetting of jokes:
           a function of repression.   J Individual Psychol, 1963,
           19:213-215.
18, 600.   Legman, Gershon.   No laughing matter.   Neurotica, 1952,
           9:49-64.
18, 601.   _____.   No Laughing Matter: Rationale of the Dirty
           Joke.   NY: Breaking Point, 1975.
18, 602.   _____.   The Rationale of the Dirty Joke: An Analysis
           of Sexual Humor.   NY: Grove, 1968; London: Hart-
           Davis, MacGibbon, 1978; Review: R. G. Collins, Mo-
           saic, 1970, 3:148-155.
18, 603.   _____.   Toward a motif-index of erotic humor.   J
           Amer Folklore, 1962, 75:227-248.

18, 604. Leventhal, Howard, & Cupchik, Gerald C. A process
          model of humor judgment. J Communication, 1976,
          26:190-204.
18, 605. Lévêque, Charles. Le Rire, le comique, et le risible
          dans l'esprit et dans l'art. Rev des deux mondes,
          1863, 47.
18, 606. Levin, Harry (ed). Veins of Humor. Cambridge: Har-
          vard Univ. Press, 1972.
18, 607. Levine, Jacob. Responses to humor. Scientific American,
          1956, 194(2):31-35.
18, 608. _____, & Redlich, Frederick C. Failure to understand
          humor. Psychoanal Q, 1955, 24:560-572.
18, 609. _____, & _____. Intellectual and emotional factors
          in the appreciation of humor. J General Psychol, 1960,
          62:25-35.
18, 610. Levowitz, Herbert J. Smiles and laughter: some neuro-
          logic, developmental, and psychodynamic considerations.
          New York Library Forum, 1978, 1:109-116.
18, 611. Lewis, Paul. Laughing at fear: two versions of the mock
          gothic. Studies in Short Fiction, 1978, 15:411-414.
18, 612. Limón, José E. Agringado joking in Texas Mexican soci-
          ety: folklore and differential identity. New Scholar,
          1977, 6:33-50.
18, 613. Lipps, Theodor. Komik und Humor. Berlin: 1898.
18, 614. Litman, R. A. Grave Humor. Los Angeles: Mara, 1970.
18, 615. Little, Matthew. As I Lay Dying and 'dementia praecox'
          humor. Studies in Amer Humor, 1975, 2:61-70.
18, 616. Loftis, J. Comedy and Society from Congreve to Fielding.
          Stanford, Cal: Stanford Univ. Press, 1959.

18, 617. MacCary, W. Thomas. The significance of a comic pat-
          tern in Plautus and Beaumarchais. Modern Language
          Notes, 1973, 88:1262-1287.
18, 618. McDonald, Walter R. Look back in horror: the functional
          comedy of Catch-22. CEA Critic, 1973, 35(2):18-21.
18, 619. McDougall, William. A new theory of laughter. Psyche,
          1922, 2:292-303.
18, 620. McQuade, Raymond Francis. Wit and Humor in the Novels
          of Thomas Hardy. DAI, 1977, 37:5144A-45A.
18, 621. McWhinney, Norman N. Sex, Time and Laughter. (A
          New Theory of the Comic). DA, 1968, 29:875A.
18, 622. Marino, Vincent. Creating Conscience Through Black
          Humor: A Study of Kurt Vonnegut's Novels. DAI,
          1978, 39:2941A.
18, 623. Marshall, William H. Le Rire chez Apollinaire. Roman-
          ica, 1975, 12:93-101.
18, 624. Martin, Bruce K. Poe's 'Hop-Frog' and the retreat from
          comedy. Studies in Short Fiction, 1973, 10:288-290.
18, 625. Martin, Lillien J. Psychology of aesthetics: experimental
          prospecting in the field of the comic. Amer J Psychol,
          1905, 16.

18,626. Mathewson, L. Bergson's theory of the comic in the light
         of English comedy. Univ. Nebraska Studies in Lan-
         guage, Lit & Criticism, 1920, No. 5.
18,627. Mauron, Charles. Psychocritique du genre comique.
         Paris: Corti, 1964; Review: Pierre-Henri Simon, Le
         Monde, 20 May 1964, no. 6016, 12-13.
18,628. Mehlman, Jeffrey. How to read Freud on jokes: the
         critic as Schadchen. New Lit History, 1975, 6:439-461.
18,629. Mélinaud, C. Pourquoi rit-on? Etude sur la cause psy-
         chologique du rire. Rev des deux mondes, 1895.
18,630. Mellard, James M. Jason Compson: humor, hostility and
         the rhetoric of aggression. Southern Humanities Rev,
         1969, 3:259-267.
18,631. Menahem, Samuel F. The Effect of Role Playing on the
         Creation of Humor. DAI, 1976, 37:956.
18,632. Mendel, Werner M. Humor as an index of emotional
         means. J Biological Psychol, 1971, 13(2):53-61.
18,633. Meyer, Russell Joseph. Tudor Laughter: A Preliminary
         Study for a Theory of Humor. DAI, 1977, 37:6504A-
         05A.
18,634. Michael, I. Lloyd. A Particular Kind of Joking: Nathan-
         ael West and Burlesque. DAI, 1973, 33:5188A-89A.
18,635. Milburn, Daniel Judson. The psychology of wit. In The
         Age of Wit, 1650-1750. NY: Macmillan, 1966, 77-119.
18,636. Miller, David. Achelous and the butterfly: toward an
         archetypal psychology of humour. Spring, 1973, 1-23.
18,637. Miller, E. K. Symbol, license and poetic localization in
         British humorous monologues. Southern Folklore Q,
         1976, 40:31-38.
18,638. Miller, Edward K. The use of stereotypes in inter-ethnic
         joking as a means of communication. Folklore Annual
         Univ. Folklore Assn, 1977, 7-8:28-42.
18,639. Mindess, Harvey. If Hamlet had had a sense of humor.
         In Chapman, A. J., & Foot, H. C. (eds), It's a Funny
         Thing, Humour. NY: Pergamon, 1977, 3-5.
18,640. Mintz, Lawrence E. Jewish humor: a continuum of
         sources, motives, and functions. American Humor,
         1977, 4(1):4-5.
18,641. Mishler, William. A reading of Hjalmar Bergman's story.
         'Konstapel Wiliam. ' Scandinavica, 1971, 10:33-41.
18,642. Mitchell, Carol A. Sexual perspective in the appreciation
         and interpretation of jokes. Western Folklore, 1977,
         36:303-329.
18,643. Monson, Dianne L. Children's Responses to Humorous
         Situations in Literature. DA, 1967, 27(8-A):2448-49.
18,644. Moore, H. K. Psychological Anecdotes and Stories. Mil-
         waukee: Editions Unlimited, 1955.
18,645. Moore, Jack B. Black humor in an early American short
         story. Early Amer Lit Newsletter, 1966, 1(2):7-8.
18,646. Morris, Harry. John Donne's terrifying pun. Papers on
         Language & Lit, 1973, 9:128-137.
18,647. Morton, Murry K. A paradise of parodies. Satire News-
         letter, 1971, 9(1):33-42.

18, 648. Moses, Joseph.   Comic compulsion.   Sewanee Rev, 1978,
          86:84-100.
18, 649. Muir, Kenneth.   The uncomic pun.   In The Singularity of
          Shakespeare, and Other Essays.   NY: Barnes & Noble,
          1977, 20-37.
18, 650. Mukherji, N.   The psychology of laughter.   Indian J Psy-
          chol, 1935, 10:95-110.
18, 651. Müller-Braunschweig, Carl.   Sigmund Freud über den
          humor.   Zeitschrift für Sexualwissenschaft, 1927, 14:
          310.
18, 652. Müller-Suur, Hemmo.   Max und Moritz unmoralisch?
          Der Humor von Wilhelm Busch und die Kindliche Psyche.
          Criançaportugesa, 1952-53, 12:207-213.
18, 653. Murray, Henry A.   The psychology of humor.   J Abnor-
          mal Social Psychol, 1934, 29:66-81.
18, 654. Musurillo, H.   Dream symbolism in Petronina frag. 30.
          Classical Philology, 1958, 53:108-110.

18, 655. Nagel, James.   Catch-22 and angry humor: a study of the
          normative values of satire.   Studies in Amer Humor,
          1974, 1:99-105.
18, 656. Nguyen, A.   Le rire et la derision.   Evolution psychia-
          trique, 1955, 1:67-118.
18, 657. Numasawa, Koj.   Black humor: an American aspect.
          Studies in English Lit, 1968, 44:177-193.

18, 658. Oberndorf, Clarence P.   Kidding--a form of humor.   Int
          J Psycho-Anal, 1932, 13:479-480.
18, 659. Obeyesekere, Ranjini, & Obeyesekere, Gananath.   Psycho-
          logical release: comic ritual dramas in Sri Lanka.
          Drama Rev, 1976, 20:5-19.
18, 660. O'Connell, Walter E.   The adaptive function of wit and
          humor.   J Abnormal Social Psychol, 1960, 60:263-270.
18, 661. _____.   Creativity in humor.   Social Psychol, 1969,
          78:237-241.
18, 662. _____.   Freudian humour: the eupsychia of everyday
          life.   In Chapman, A.J., & Foot, H.C. (eds), Humour
          and Laughter.   London: Wiley, 1976.
18, 663. _____.   Multidimensional investigation of Freudian
          humor.   Psychiat Q, 1964, 38:97-108.
18, 664. _____.   Resignation, humor and wit.   Psychoanal Rev,
          1964, 51:49-56.
18, 665. _____.   A Study of the Adaptive Functions of Wit and
          Humor.   DA, 1958, 19:1126.
18, 666. _____, & Peterson, Penny.   Humor and repression.
          J Existential Psychiat, 1964, 4:309-315.
18, 667. O'Mahony, Michael, Palmer, Robert, & King, Jennifer.
          The art of revue: further emphases for the psychology
          of humour.   In Chapman, A.J., & Foot, H.C. (eds),
          It's a Funny Thing, Humour.   Oxford: Pergamon, 1977,
          73-84.

18, 668.   Omwake, L.   Factors influencing the sense of humor.   J
           Social Psychol, 1939, 10:95-114.
18, 669.   _____.   A study of sense of humor: its relation to sex,
           age, and personal characteristics.   J Applied Psychol,
           1937, 21:688-704.
18, 670.   Onís, Federico de.   El humorismo de Galdós.   Revista
           Hispánica Moderna, 1943, 9:289-313.
18, 671.   Oring, Elliott.   Review: Gershon Legman's Rationale of
           the Dirty Joke: An Analysis of Sexual Humor.   Western
           Folklore, 1977, 36:365-371.

18, 672.   Param, Charles.   Humor and Manuel Rojas.   In Kraft,
           W. C. (ed), Proceedings: Pacific Northwest Conference
           on Foreign Languages, Vol. 25, Part 1.   Corvallis:
           Oregon State Univ. Press, 1974, 177-183.
18, 673.   Park, Rose R.   An Investigation of Riddles of Children,
           Ages Five-Fourteen, Using Piaget-Derived Definitions.
           DAI, 1972, 33(3-A), 905-906.
18, 674.   _____.   A study of children's riddles using Piaget-de-
           rived definitions.   J Genetic Psychol, 1977, 130:57-67.
18, 675.   Perl, R. E.   The influence of a social factor upon the ap-
           preciation of humor.   Amer J Psychol, 1933, 45:308-
           312.
18, 676.   _____.   A review of experiments on humor.   Psychol
           Bulletin, 1933, 30:752-763.
18, 677.   Perlis, Mildred E.   The social functions of marriage wit.
           Marriage & Family Living, 1954, 16:49-50.
18, 678.   Peters, U. H.   [Word play and schizophrenic language dis-
           order--what constitutes the difference?]   Confinia Psy-
           chiatrica, 1979, 22:58-64.
18, 679.   Piccoli, G. A.   Il Comico, l'umore e la Fantasia.   Turn:
           Bocea, n. d.
18, 680.   Pickle, Charles DeWitt.   Nikolaj Gogol and Black Humor.
           DAI, 1975, 35:5420A.
18, 681.   Piddington, R.   The Psychology of Laughter.   A Study in
           Social Adaptation.   London: Figurehead, 1933.
18, 682.   Pini, L. G.   Come si rideva in antico.   Burle, strava-
           ganze, facezie die Toscani d'altri tempe.   Milan:
           Hoepli, 1932.
18, 683.   Pinsker, Sanford.   Guilt as comic idea: Franz Kafka and
           the postures of American-Jewish writing.   J Modern
           Lit, 1977, 6:466-471.
18, 684.   _____.   The Schlemiel as Metaphor: Studies in the
           Yiddish and American Jewish Novel.   Carbondale:
           Southern Illinois Univ. Press, 1971; DAI, 1968, 28:
           3679A-80A.
18, 685.   _____.   The schlemiel in Yiddish and American litera-
           ture.   Chicago Jewish Forum, 1967, 25:191-195.
18, 686.   Pisani, Assunta Sarnacchiaro.   The Raging Impotence:
           Humor in the Novels of Dostoevsky, Faulkner, and
           Beckett.   DAI, 1977, 38(1):248-249-A.
18, 687.   Plass, Paul.   Freud and Plato on Sophistic joking.   Psy-
           choanal Rev, 1972, 59:347-360.

18, 688. Pocius, Gerald L. Frank William, Newfoundland joke-teller Part 4: the social and psychological aspects of Frank's performances and the content of his notebooks. Lore & Language, 1978, 2(9):6-25.

18, 689. Poulet, Georges. Molière. [Excerpt from Studies in Human Time.] In Grebstein, S. N. (ed), Perspectives in Contemporary Criticism. NY: Harper & Row, 1968, (1950), 293-298.

18, 690. Prentice, Norman, & Fathman, Robert E. Joking riddles: a developmental index of children's humor. Proceedings Annual Convention Amer Psychol Assn, 1972, 7: 119-120.

18, 691. Prerost, Frank J. Reduction of aggression as a function of related content in humor. Psychol Reports, 1976, 38:771-777.

18, 692. _____, & Brewer, Robert E. Humor content preferences and the relief of experimentally aroused aggression. J Social Psychol, 1977, 103:225-231.

18, 693. Racamier, P. C. [Between humor and madness.] Rev Française de Psychanalyse, 1973, 37:655-668.

18, 694. Rackin, Donald. Laughing and grief: what's so funny about Alice in Wonderland? In Guiliano, E. (ed), Lewis Carroll Observed. NY: Potter, 1976, 1-18.

18, 695. Raeithel, Gert. Amerikanischer Humor--eine soziale Funktion. Merkur, 1970, 24:644-659.

18, 696. Railliet, G. Comportement à l'égard des disgraciés de la nature. Bulletin du Comité du Folklore Champenois, 1961-1965, Nos. 76-80, 41-45.

18, 697. Raley, A. L. A psychometric study of humor. Année Psychologique, 1946, 1:265.

18, 698. Rapp, Albert. The dawn of humor. Classical J, 1948, 43:275-280.

18, 699. _____. The Origins of Wit and Humor. NY: Dutton, 1951.

18, 700. _____. A phylogenetic theory of wit and humor. J Social Psychol, 1949, 30:81-96.

18, 701. Raynaud, Jean. Des Mécanismes du jeu de mots. Rev Françaises d'Etudes Américaines, 1977, 4:23-30.

18, 702. Reich, Annie. The structure of the grotesque-comic sublimation. In The Yearbook of Psychoanalysis, Vol. 6. NY: IUP, 1950, 200-209; Bulletin Menninger Clinic, 1949, 13:160-171.

18, 703. Reik, Theodor. Freud and Jewish wit. Psychoanalysis, 1954, 2(3):12-20.

18, 704. _____. Grenzland des Witzes. Psychoanalytische Bewegung, 1932, 4:289-322.

18, 705. _____. Das Kind im Manne. Imago, 1937, 23:14-23.

18, 706. _____. Künstlerisches Schaffen und Witzarbeit. Imago, 1929, 15:200-231.

18, 707. _____. Lust und Lied im Witz; Sechs psychoanalytische Studien. Vienna: Int Psychoanalytischer Verlag, 1929, 1930.

18, 708. _____. Psychoanalysis and wit. In Listening with the
          Third Ear. NY: Farrar, Straus, 1949, 249-257.
18, 709. _____. Über den zynischen Witz. Almanach, 1930,
          204-224.
18, 710. _____. Vom Wesen des judischen Witzes. Almanach,
          1937, 71-81.
18, 711. _____. Der Witz als Bestätigung der analen Sexualthe-
          orie. Int Zeitschrift für Psychoanalyse, 1912, 2:417-
          418.
18, 712. _____. Zur Psychoanalyse des judischen Witzer.
          Imago, 1929, 15:63-88.
18, 713. _____. Die zweifache Überraschung. Psychoanalytische
          Bewegung, 1929, 1:212-227; Abstract: Psychoanal Rev,
          1933, 20:227.
18, 714. Rhoades, John Douglas. Language Use in Joke Character-
          izations: A Study of Language Stereotypes in Kenya.
          DAI, 1977, 37:7188A.
18, 715. Rice, Joseph Allen. Flash of Darkness: Black Humor in
          the Contemporary American Novel. Doctoral disserta-
          tion, Florida State Univ., 1967.
18, 716. Richman, Joseph. The foolishness and wisdom of age:
          attitudes toward the elderly as reflected in jokes.
          Gerontologist, 1977, 17:210-219.
18, 717. Roback, Abraham A. Humor in Jewish folklore. Chicago
          Jewish Forum, 1948, 6:167-173.
18, 718. Rose, Alan Henry. Blackness in the fantastic world of
          old Southwestern humor. In Demonic Vision; Racial
          Fantasy and Southern Fiction. Hamden, Conn: Archon,
          1976, 19-38.
18, 719. Ross, Stephen M. Jason Compson and Sut Lovingood:
          Southwestern humor as stream of consciousness. Stud-
          ies in the Novel, 1976, 8:278-290.
18, 720. Rossi, M. M. Sulla natura psicologica del comico. Re-
          vista psicologici, 1926, 22:22-32.
18, 721. Rosten, Leo. The mischief of language. Saturday Rev,
          1972, 55(11):29-31.
18, 722. Rourke, Constance. American Humor. A Study of the
          National Character. Garden City, NY: Doubleday,
          1953.
18, 723. _____. Examining the roots of American humor.
          Amer Scholar, 1935, 4:245-252, 254.
18, 724. Rovit, Earl. Humor and the humanization of art. Cen-
          tennial Rev, 1965, 9:135-152.
18, 725. Rowe, W. Woodin. Observations on black humor in Gogol
          and Nabokov. Slavic & East European J, 1975, 18:392-
          399.
18, 726. Roy, Bruno. L'Humour érotique au XVe siècle. In
          L'Erotisme au Moyen Age. Montreal: Aurore, 1977,
          165-171.
18, 727. Roy, Dennis-Prudent. Dissertation médico-chirurgicale
          sur le rire, considéré comme phénomène sémiologique.
          Paris: 1812.

18, 728.   Rubin, Louis D. , Jr. (ed). The Comic Imagination in
            American Literature. New Brunswick, NJ: Rutgers
            Univ. Press, 1973.
18, 729.   _____. The great American joke. South Atlantic Q,
            1973, 72:82-94.
18, 730.   Ruggiers, Paul G. (ed). Versions of Medieval Comedy.
            Norman: Univ. Oklahoma Press, 1977.
18, 731.   Rullmann, Wilhelm. Wit und Humor. Berlin: Fleischel,
            1912 (?).
18, 732.   Russell, Olga Wester. Humor in Pascal. An Examination
            of the Comic Humor of the French Philosopher Pascal.
            North Quincey, Mass: Christopher, 1977.

18, 733.   Sakumo, Makoto. Laughter As a Weapon: Fielding's
            Fundamental Theory of Creation. Tokyo: Seijo Univ.
            Press, 1975.
18, 734.   Schauer, Otto. Uber das Wesen der Komik. Archiv für
            gesamte Psychologie, 1910, 18.
18, 735.   Schiller, P. v. A configurational theory of puzzles and
            jokes. J General Psychol, 1938, 18:217-234.
18, 736.   _____. Der Witz und das Komische. Beiträge dem 15
            Kongress der deutschen Gesellschaft für Psychologie,
            Jena, 1936, 89-92.
18, 737.   Schilling, E. N. The Comic Spirit: Boccaccio to Thomas
            Mann. Detroit: Wayne State Univ. Press, 1965.
18, 738.   Schmidt, H. E. , & Williams, D. I. The evolution of the-
            ories of humour. J Behavioural Science, 1971, 1(3):
            95-106.
18, 739.   Scholes, Robert E. Comedy and grotesquerie. In Fabu-
            lation and Metafiction. Urbana: Univ. Illinois Press,
            1979, 139-192.
18, 740.   Schone, Annemarie. Das 'Grausame' im deutschen und
            englischen literarischen Kinderhumor. Psychologische
            Beiträge, 1957, 3:108-125.
18, 741.   Schulman, Robert. The serious functions of Melville's
            phallic jokes. Amer Lit, 1961, 33:179-194.
18, 742.   Schulz, Max F. Black Humor Fiction of the Sixties.
            Athens: Ohio Univ. Press, 1973.
18, 743.   _____. Pop, op, and black humor: the aesthetics of
            anxiety. College English, 1968, 30:230-240.
18, 744.   _____. Toward a definition of black humor; excerpt
            from 'Black Humor Fiction of the Sixties. ' In Cohen,
            S. B. (ed), Comic Relief. Urbana: Univ. Illinois
            Press, 1978, 14-27; Southern Rev, 1973, 9:117-134.
18, 745.   _____. The unconfirmed thesis: Kurt Vonnegut, black
            humor, and contemporary art. Critique: Studies in
            Modern Fiction, 1971, 12(3):5-28.
18, 746.   Schwartz, Steven. The effects of arousal on appreciation
            for varying degrees of sex-relevant humor. J Experi-
            mental Research in Personality, 1972, 6:241-247.
18, 747.   _____. The Effects of Sexual Arousal, Sex Guilt and
            Expectancy for Censure in Appreciation for Varying

Degrees of Sex Relevant Humor. DAI, 1972, 32(8-B), 4869-70.

18, 748. Servadio, Emilio. Il motto di spirito. Rivista Italiana di Psicoanalisi, 1933, 2:256-274.

18, 749. Sheed, Wilfred. The wit of George S. Kaufman and Dorothy Parker. In The Good Word and Other Words. NY: Dutton, 1978, 159-163.

18, 750. Sherer, Ray L. Laughter in Our Mutual Friend. Texas Studies in Lit & Language, 1971, 13:509-521.

18, 751. Shulman, Max. American humor: its cause and cure. Yale Rev, 1961, 51:119-124.

18, 752. [No entry. For Schulman, see 18, 741]

18, 753. Simon, John K. What are you laughing at, Darl? Madness and humor in As I Lay Dying. College English, 1963, 25:104-110.

18, 754. Simon, Richard K. Freud's concepts of comedy and suffering. Psychoanal Rev, 1977, 64:391-407.

18, 755. Skaggs, Merrill Maguire. The uses of enchantment in frontier humor and The Robber Bridegroom. Studies in Amer Humor, 1976, 3:96-102.

18, 756. Skeels, Dell. The function of humor in three Nez Perce Indian myths. Amer Imago, 1954, 11:249-261.

18, 757. Slap, J. W. On sarcasm. Psychoanal Q, 1966, 35:98-108.

18, 758. Slater, Maya. Humour in the Works of Proust. London: Oxford Univ. Press, 1979.

18, 759. Smith, W. Comedy and the comic experience. Psychol Bulletin, 1910, 7:84-87.

18, 760. Stern, J. P. War and the comic muse: The Good Soldier Schweik and Catch-22. Comparative Lit, 1968, 20:193-216.

18, 761. Stevens, Phillips, Jr. Bachama joking categories: toward new perspectives in the study of joking relationships. J Anthropological Research, 1978, 34:47-71.

18, 762. Stirrup, Barbara E. Techniques of rape: variety of wit in Ovid's Metamorphoses. Greece & Rome, 1977, 24: 170-184.

18, 763. Stora, Judith. Paroles de shlemil; l'humour juif dans la littérature américaine. Rev Française d'Etudes Américaines, 1977, 4:81-90.

18, 764. Strongin, Carol Diane. The Anguished Laughter of Shakespeare, Chekhov, and Beckett: An Exploration of Their Tragicomic Drama. DAI, 1976, 37:302A.

18, 765. Styan, J. I. The Dark Comedy: The Development of Modern Comic Tragedy. Cambridge, Eng: Cambridge Univ. Press, 1962.

18, 766. Summo, Anthony J. Humor in review. J Social Therapy, 1958, 4:201-208.

18, 767. Süss, Wilhelm. Das Problem des Komischen im Altertum. Neue Jahrbuch für klassische Altertum, 1920, 23(1-2).

18, 768. Swabey, Marie Collins. The comic as nonsense, sadism, or incongruity. J Philosophy, 1958, 55:819-833.

18, 769. _____. Comic Laughter. A Philosophical Essay. New Haven: Yale Univ. Press, 1961.

18, 770. Swan, Jim. Giving new depth to the surface. Psycho-
          analysis, literature, and society. Psychoanal Rev,
          1975, 62:5-28.

18, 771. Tarachow, Sidney. Applied psychoanalysis. V. Comedy,
          wit and humor. Annual Survey Psychoanal, 1951, 2:
          568-572.
18, 772. _____. Remarks on the comic process and beauty.
          Psychoanal Q, 1949, 18:215-226.
18, 773. Taylor, Archer. The anecdote: a neglected genre. In
          Mandel, J. , & Rosenberg, B. A. (eds), Medieval Liter-
          ature and Folklore Studies. New Brunswick, NJ: Rut-
          gers Univ. Press, 1971, 223-228.
18, 774. Tharp, Mel. A social study of mountain folk humor.
          Tennessee Folklore Society Bulletin, 1977, 43:186-187.
18, 775. Thomas, W. K. Satiric catharsis. Univ. Windsor Rev,
          1968, 3(2):33-44.
18, 776. Tibbetts, Sylvia L. What's so funny? Humor in chil-
          dren's literature. California J Educational Research,
          1973, 24:42-46.
18, 777. Tilton, John W. Cosmic Satire in the Contemporary Novel.
          Lewisburg, Pa: Bucknell Univ. Press, 1977.
18, 778. Torrance, Robert M. The Comic Hero. Cambridge:
          Harvard Univ. Press, 1978.
18, 779. Toth, Emily. Dorothy Parker, Erica Jong, and new
          feminist humor. Regionalism & the Female Imagina-
          tion, 1977-78, 3(2-3):70-85.
18, 780. Trangott, John. The rake's progress from court to come-
          dy: a study in comic form. Studies in English Lit,
          1966, 6:381-407.
18, 781. Treadwell, Y. Bibliography of empirical studies of wit
          and humor. Psychol Reports, 1967, 20(3, P&2), 1079-
          1083.
18, 782. Trieber, J. Marshall. The scornful grin: a study of
          Poesque humor. Poe Studies, 1971, 4:32-34.

18, 783. Varisco, Raymond. Campaign jokes--Goldwater and John-
          son. Tennessee Folklore Society Bulletin, 1965, 31(4):
          108-112.
18, 784. Vereecken, J. L. T. Over woordspelingen. Nederlandsch
          Tydschrift voor de Psychologie, 1962, 7:389-399.
18, 785. Visser, H. L. A. Humor's weldaad. Mensch en Maatsch,
          1935, 11:1-16.
18, 786. Vorhees, Richard J. The new comedy. Canadian Forum,
          1957, 37:37-39.
18, 787. Vorpahl, Ben M. Such Stuff as Dreams Are Made On:
          History, Myth and the Comic Vision of Mark Twain
          and William Faulkner. DA, 1967, 28:698A.

18, 788. Waldmeir, Joseph J. Two novelists of the absurd; Heller and Kesey. Wisconsin Studies in Contemporary Lit, 1964, 5:192-204; In Pratt, J. C. (ed), Ken Kesey. One Flew Over the Cuckoo's Nest, Text and Criticism. NY: Penguin, 1977, 401-418.

18, 789. Wallace, Ronald H. The Last Laugh, Form and Affirmation in the Contemporary American Novel. Columbia: Univ. Missouri Press, 1979.

18, 790. Walsh, Maurice N. Some character aspects of the satirist (Pietro Aretino). Amer Imago, 1961, 18:235-262.

18, 791. Watson, Donald G. The dark comedy of the Henry VI plays. Thalia: Studies in Lit Humor, 1978, 1(2):11-21.

18, 792. Waxler, Myer. The Role of Ambiguity and Ambiguity Tolerance in the Appreciation of Humor. DAI, 1976, 37:3056-3057.

18, 793. Weber, Samuel. The divaricator: remarks on Freud's Witz. Glyph, 1977, 1:1-27.

18, 794. _____. Sideshow; or remarks on a canny moment. MLN, 1973, 88:1102-1133.

18, 795. Wechssler, E. Über den Witz. Heidelberg, 1914.

18, 796. Weiss, Justin L. An Experimental Study of the Psychodynamics of Humor. DA, 1955, 15:873.

18, 797- Welsford, E. The Fool: His Social and Literary History.
8. London: Faber, 1935; NY: Farrar, 1936.

18, 799. West, Michael. Scatology and eschatology: the heroic dimensions of Thoreau's wordplay. PMLA, 1974, 89: 1043-1064.

18, 800. Wheeler, Otis B. Some uses of folk humor by Faulkner. Mississippi Q, 1964, 17:107-122.

18, 801. White, E. B. Some remarks on humor. In Essays of E. B. White. NY: Harper, 1977, 243-249.

18, 802. White, Kenneth S., et al., (ed). Savage Comedy: Structures of Humor. Amsterdam: Rodopi, 1978; Atlantic Highlands, NJ: Humanities Press, 1978.

18, 803. Wieck, David T. Funny things. JAAC, 1966, 25:437-447.

18, 804. Willeford, William. The Fool and His Scepter. Evanston, Ill: Northwestern Univ. Press, 1969.

18, 805. Williamson, Elizabeth. Criticism on American humor: an annotated checklist. Amer Humor: An Interdisciplinary Newsletter, 1978, 5(1):15-43.

18, 806. Wincelberg, Shimon. A deadly serious lunacy. In Kostelanetz, R. (ed), On Contemporary Literature. NY: Avon, 1964, 388-391.

18, 807. Winick, Charles. A content analysis of orally communicated jokes. Amer Imago, 1963, 20:271-291.

18, 808. _____. The social contexts of humor. J Communication, 1976, 26:124-128.

18, 809. Winterstein, Alfred R. F. Contributions to the problem of humor. Psychoanal Q, 1934, 3:303-316; Psychoanalytische Bewegung, 1932, 4:513-525.

18, 810. Wisse, Ruth R. The Schlemiel as Modern Hero. Chicago: Chicago Univ. Press, 1980.

18, 811. Wolfenstein, Martha. Children's Humor--A Psychological Analysis. Glencoe, Ill: Free Press, 1954.

18,812.   . Children's understanding of jokes. In The Psy-
          choanalytic Study of the Child, Vol. 8. NY: IUP,
          1953, 162-176.
18,813. Wolff, H. A., Smith, C. E., & Murray, H. A. The psychol-
          ogy of humor. J Abnormal Social Psychol, 1934, 28:
          341-365.
18,814. Wright, J. A History of Caricature and Grotesque in Lit-
          erature and Art. London: Chatto & Windus, 1875.

18,815. Yalisove, Daniel. The effect of riddle structure on chil-
          dren's comprehension of riddles. Developmental Psy-
          chol, 1978, 14:173-180.

18,816. Zants, E. The comic structure of A la recherche du
          temps perdu. French Rev, 1974, 47(6):144-150.
18,817. Zemach, Shlomo. A theory of laughter. JAAC, 1959, 17:
          311-329.
18,818. Zijderveld, Anton C. Jokes and their relation to social
          reality. Social Research, 1968, 35:286-311.
18,819. Zumwalt, Rosemary. Plain and fancy: a content analysis
          of children's jokes dealing with adult sexuality. West-
          ern Folklore, 1976, 35:258-267.
18,820. Zwerling, Israel. The favorite joke in diagnostic and
          therapeutic interview. Psychoanal Q, 1955, 24:104-114.

18, 821.   Abbott, Sidney, & Love, B.   Sappho Was a Right-On Woman: A Liberated View of Lesbianism.   NY: Stein & Day, 1972.
18, 822.   Abram, Harry S.   Conan Doyle looks at medicine.   Medical Times, 1971, 99:106-108.
18, 823.   Accardo, P.   Letter: bedtime stories.   Amer J Disturbed Child, 1976, 130:1037.
18, 824.   Achard Arrosa, Laura.   Psychoanalytic study of the actor and his character.   Revista Uruguaya de Psicoanalisis, 1961-62, 4:389-416.
18, 825.   Aird, C., & McIntosh, R. A.   Shakespeare's Richard III and the Ellis-Van Creveld syndrome.   Practitioner, 1978, 220:656-662.
18, 826.   Albarracín Teulón, A.   La medicina en la obra de Lope de Vega.   Boletin de la Sociedad Española de Historia de la Medicina, 1962, 2(3).
18, 827.   Albeaux-Fernet, M. (ed).   Endocrinologie et littérature, trois textes de Georges Duhamel, Andre Maurois, Marcel Jouhandeau.   Paris: Masson, 1972.
18, 828.   Ali-Shammem, A., & Mehrotra, Ramesh C.   Language style: an individual way of feeling.   Psycho-Lingua, 1978, 48:55-60.
18, 829.   Alter, Maria P.   The Concept of Physician in the Writings of Hans Carossa and Arthur Schnitzler.   Bern: Lang, 1971; DA, 1961, 27(6):1991.
18, 830.   Amundsen, Darrel W.   Images of physicians in classical times.   J Popular Culture, 1977, 11:643-655.
18, 831.   Anderson, Lorin.   Freud, Nietzsche.   Salmagundi, 1980, 47-48:3-29.
18, 832.   Anon.   [Drink and sobriety in Shakespeare's dramas.]   Alkoholfrage, 1936, 32:153-154.
18, 833.   _____.   Honorato de Balzac y el mundo de la medicina.   Prensa Medicina Argentina, 1972, 59:200-203.
18, 834.   _____.   Lexical paradox.   M. D. Medical Newsmagazine, 1959, 3:129-132.
18, 835.   Antoniolo, Roland.   La Médecine dans la vie et l'oeuvre de François Rabelais.   Geneva: Droz, 1976.
18, 836.   _____.   Rabelais et la médecine.   Geneva: Droz, 1976.
18, 837.   Aries, Phillippe.   Centuries of Childhood.   A Social History of Family Life.   NY: Vintage, 1965.

18,838.   Arieti, Silvano.   Creativity.   The Magic Synthesis.   NY:
           Basic Books, 1976.
18,839.   _____, & Arieti, J.   Love Can Be Found.   NY: Har-
           court Brace Jovanovich, 1977.
18,840.   Arkin, A. M.   A short note on Empedocles and Freud.
           Amer Imago, 1949, 6:197-203.
18,841.   Asch, Solomon.   On the use of the metaphor in the de-
           scription of persons.   In Werner, H., (eds), On Ex-
           pressive Language.   Worcester, Mass: Clark Univ.
           Press, 1955, 29-38.
18,842.   Austin, Avel.   Ulysses and the Human Body.   DA, 1966,
           27:1778.
18,843.   Aziza, Claude, Oliviéri, Claude, & Sctrick, Robert.   Dic-
           tionnaire des symboles et des thèmes littéraires.
           Paris: Nathan, 1978.

18,844.   Baier, Lee.   An early instance of 'daydreams.'   Notes
           & Queries, 1970, 17(11):409.
18,845.   Bailey, J. O.   Heredity as villain in the poetry and fiction
           of Thomas Hardy.   Thomas Hardy Yearbook, 1970,
           1:9-19.
18,846.   Bailey, Richard Weld.   Computer-assisted poetry: the
           writing machine is for everybody.   In Mitchell, J. L.
           (ed), Computers in the Humanities.   Minneapolis: Univ.
           Minnesota Press, 1974, 283-295.
18,847.   Baker, Sidney J.   The sexual symbolism of language.
           Int J Sexology, 1948, 2:13-18.
18,848.   Ballorain, Rolande.   Le Nouveau féminisme Américain.
           Paris: Denoël, 1972.
18,849.   Bantock, G. H.   Literature and the social sciences.   Criti-
           cal Q, 1975, 17:99-127.
18,850.   Bär, Eugen.   Archetypes and ideas: Jung and Kant.
           Philosophy Today, 1976, 20:114-123.
18,851.   _____.   Psychoanalysis and semiotics.   Semiotica,
           1976, 10:369-387.
18,852.   Baranova, F., et al.   [The external appearance of chil-
           dren's books.]   Psikhologiya, 1932, 4:7-22.
18,853.   Barbéris, P.   Balzac et le mal du siècle.   Contribution
           à une physiologie du monde moderne, Vol. 1, 1799-
           1829.   Une Expérience de l'absurde: aliénations et
           prises de conscience, Vol. 2, 1830-1833.   De la prise
           de conscience à l'expression.   Paris: Gallimard,
           1970.
18,854.   Barilli, Renato.   Psicoanalisi, antropoanalisi, estetica.
           Verri, 1968, 28:66-78.
18,855.   Barkan, L.   Elementated Man: Studies in the Metaphor
           of the Human Body.   Doctoral dissertation, Yale Univ.,
           1971.
18,856.   Barker, Andrew W.   Heimito von Doderer and the 'sci-
           ence' of physiognomy.   New German Critique, 1977,
           5:91-109.

18, 857. Barker-Benfield, G. J. The Horrors of the Half-Known
          Life. Male Attitudes Toward Women and Sexuality in
          Nineteenth-Century America. NY: Harper & Row,
          1976.

18, 858. Barrett, Edwin B., Jr. Little Dorritt and the diseases of
          modern life. Nineteenth Century Fiction, 1970, 25:199-
          215.

18, 859. Bartsch, W. [Simulation and self-mutilation in history and
          medicine.] Medizinische Monatsschrift, 1960, 14:190-
          194.

18, 860. Bataillon, M. La Profession médicale et son langage de-
          vant la littérature: Problèmes espagnols du XVIe si-
          ècle. In Le Réel dans la littérature et dans la langue.
          Paris: Klincksieck, 1967, 23-39.

18, 861. Bates, H. R. Sherlock Holmes and syphillis. Canadian
          Medical Assn J, 1975, 113(9):815.

18, 862. Baudelaire, Charles. Artificial Paradise; On Hashish and
          Wine as Means of Expanding Individuality. NY: Herder
          & Herder, 1971; Les Paradis Artificiels. In Oeuvres
          Complètes, Vol. 4. Paris: Conard, 1923-1966 (1860);
          Les Paradis Artificels. Paris: Gallimard, 1977.

18, 863. Baudoin, Charles. Tolstoi: The Teacher. London: Ke-
          gan Paul; NY: Dutton, 1923; Paris: Delachaux et
          Niestlé, 1921.

18, 864. Baylen, Joseph O. Mark Twain, W. T. Stead and 'The
          Tell-Tale Hands.' Amer Q, 1964, 16:606-612.

18, 865. Bazin, Nancy Topping. The concept of androgyny: a
          working bibliography. Women's Studies, 1974, 2:217-
          235.

18, 866. Beardsley, Elizabeth Jane. Referential genderization. In
          Gould, C. C., & Wartofsky, M. W. (eds), Women and
          Philosophy; Toward a Theory of Liberation. NY:
          Putnam, 1976, 285-293.

18, 867. Beatty, W. K. Some medical aspects of Rudyard Kipling.
          Practitioner, 1975, 215:532-542.

18, 868. Beaty, N. L. The Craft of Dying: A Study in the Literary
          Tradition of the Arts Moriendi in England. New Haven:
          Yale Univ. Press, 1970.

18, 869. Beauvoir, Simone de. The Coming of Age. NY: Putnam,
          1972; London: Weidenfeld & Nicolson, 1972; Paris:
          Gallimard, 1970.

18, 870. Beech, Harold Reginald. The symptomatic treatment of
          writer's cramp. In Eysenck, H. J. (ed), Behaviour
          Therapy and the Neuroses. NY: Pergamon, 1960,
          349-372.

18, 871. Beerman, H. Sherlock Holmes and forensic pathology.
          Transactions Studies College Physicians Philadelphia,
          1978, 45:243-248.

18, 872. Beermann, Maria. L'Enfant dans la littérature française
          à la fin du XIXe et au commencement du XXe siècle.
          Münster: Aschendorffs, 1928.

18, 873. Béhar, Henri. L'Univers médical de Proust. Paris:
          Gallimard, 1971.

18, 874. Beharriell, Frederick J. Schnitzler's Vienna, 1966. J Arthur Schnitzler Research Assn, 1967, 6(1):4-13.

18, 875. Beidler, Philip D. Truth-telling and literary values in the Vietnam novel. South Atlantic Q, 1979, 78:141-156.

18, 876. Bell, Marilynn P. Using the Black Female Autobiography to Teach Freshman College English. DAI, 1977, 38(6-A), 3441-42.

18, 877. Benesch, H. Friedrich Schillers Dissertation zum psychophysischen Grundproblem. Wissenschaftliche Zeitschrift der Universität Jena, 1954-55, 4(1):107-113.

18, 878. _____. Friedrich Schillers psychologische Ansichten. In Wellek, A. (ed), Bericht über den 21. Kongress der deutschen Gesellschaft für Psychologie. Göttingen: 1957, 124-128.

18, 879. Bennett, S., & Simon, B. Mind and Madness in Ancient Greece: The Classical Roots of Modern Psychology. Ithaca, NY: Cornell Univ. Press, 1978.

18, 880. Bentham, Jeremy. Offences against one's self: paederasty: I. J Homosexuality, 1978 [1785], 3:389-405.

18, 881. Berelson, B., & Salter, P. J. Majority and minority Americans: an analysis of magazine fiction. Public Opinion Q, 1946, 10:168-190.

18, 882. Beresford, T. P. Poetry and medicine. Pharos, 1979, 42(4):8-10.

18, 883. Berger, I. Semantic clues to societal disorder: impediments to creativity. ETC, 1974, 31:129-147.

18, 884. Bergeron, David M. Sickness in Romeo and Juliet. College Language Assn J, 1977, 20:356-364.

18, 885. Bergler, Edmund. Does 'writer's block' exist? Amer Imago, 1950, 7:43-54.

18, 886. _____. The double yardstick in judging a writer's talent. Amer Imago, 1954, 11:335-338.

18, 887. _____. On obscene words. Psychoanal Q, 1936, 5: 226-248.

18, 888. _____. Das Plagiat: Deskription und Versuch einer Psychogenese einiger Spezialformen. Psychoanalytische Bewegung, 1932, 4:393-420.

18, 889. Berndt, Ronald M. An anthropologist looks at literature. Meanjin Q, 1957, 16:153-161.

18, 890. Bernfeld, Siegfried. Das Kind braucht keinen Schutz von Schund! Es schützt sich selbst. Literarische Welt, 1927, No. 29; Reply by Peterson, J. Zeitschrift für psychoanalytische Pädagogik, 1926-27, 1:313-315.

18, 891. Berthiaume, A. De quelques analogies dans les récits de voyage de Jacques Cartier. Cahiers de l'Association Int des Etudes Françaises, 1975, 27:13-26.

18, 892. Bertman, Sandra, & Krant, J. To know of suffering and the teaching of empathy. Social Science & Medicine, 1977, 11:639-644.

18, 893. Beutin, Wolfgang. Psychoanalytische Kategorien bei der Untersuchung mittelhochdeutscher Texte. In Richter, D. (ed), Literatur im Feudalismus. Stuttgart: Metzler, 1975, 261-296.

18,894.　Bever, Thomas Gordon.　The psychology of language and structuralist investigations of nativism.　In Harman, G. (ed), On Noam Chomsky; Critical Essays.　NY: Doubleday Anchor, 1974, 146-164.

18,895.　Biasin, G.　Literary diseases: from pathology to ontology. MLN, 1967, 82:79-102.

18,896.　＿＿＿＿.　Literary Diseases.　Theme and Metaphor in the Italian Novel.　Austin:　Univ.　Texas Press, 1975.

18,897.　Billow, Richard M.　Metaphor:　a review of the psychological literature.　Psychol Bulletin, 1977, 84:81-92.

18,898.　Binet, Léon, & Vallery-Radot, Pierre.　Médecine et littérature.　Prestige de la médecine.　Paris: Expansion Scientifique Française, 1965.

18,899.　Black, Max.　Aldous Huxley, Literature and Science. [Review article.]　Scientific Amer, 1964, 210:141-144.

18,900.　Blakar, Rolv Mikkel.　Språk er makt.　Oslo:　Pax, 1973.

18,901.　Blake, J. B.　Literary style in American medical writing. A historical view.　JAMA, 1971, 16:77-80.

18,902.　Bleich, David, Kintgen, Eugene R., Smith, Bruce, & Vargyai, Sandor J.　The psychological study of language and literature:　a selected and annotated bibliography.　Style, 1978, 12:113-210.

18,903.　Bodansky, O.　Physicians who abandoned medicine for literature:　John Keats, Arthur Conan Doyle, Arthur Schnitzler and Somerset Maugham.　Proceedings Virchow-Pirquet Medical Society, 1978, 32:13-20.

18,904.　Bogenstätter, W.　Uber Schillers medizinische Dissertation 'Versuch über den Zusammenhang der tierischen Natur des Menschen mit seiner geistigen' 1780.　Doctoral dissertation, Univ. Munich, 1955.

18,905.　Borroff, Marie.　Creativity, poetic language, and the computer.　Yale Rev, 1972, 60:481-513.

18,906.　Boswell, John.　Christianity, Social Tolerance, and Homosexuality.　Gay People in Western Europe from the Beginnings of a Christian Era to the Fourteenth Century. Chicago:　Univ. Chicago Press, 1980.

18,907.　Bowles, E. (ed).　Computers in Humanistic Research: Readings and Perspectives.　Englewood Cliffs, NJ: Prentice-Hall, 1967.

18,908.　Boyer, Paul, & Nissenbaum, Stephen.　Salem Possessed: The Social Origins of Witchcraft.　Cambridge:　Harvard Univ. Press, 1974.

18,909.　Brandenburg, D.　Medizininsches in Tausendundeiner Nacht. Ein literaturgeschtlicher Beitrag zur islamischen Heilkunde.　Stuttgart:　Fink, 1973.

18,910.　Brandt, Peter Aage.　Lingvistik og pskoanalyse.　Papir, 1975, 1(4):39-56.

18,911.　Brill, Abraham A.　The writer and his outlets.　In Frederick J. G. (eds), The Psychology of Writing Success.　NY: Business Bourse, 1933, 27-45.

18,912.　Bronda, F.　Letterati contro medici.　In Atti del Io. congresso nazionale, Accademia ambrosiana medici umanisti e scrittori.　Rome:　Arti grafiche e cossidente, 1968, 111-117.

18,913. Bronowski, Jacob. The creative process. In A Sense of the Future; Essays in Natural Philosophy. Cambridge: M. I. T. Press, 1977, 6-15; In Rosalansky, J. D. (ed), Creativity. NY: Fleet Academic, 1971, 1-16.

18,914. _____. The Visionary Eye: Essays in the Arts, Literature, and Science. Cambridge: M. I. T. Press, 1978.

18,915. Brown, H. Science and the Human Comedy. Natural Philosophy in French Literature from Rabelais to Maupertuis. Toronto: Univ. Toronto Press, 1976.

18,916. Brown, Ivor. The bard and the body. Medical World, 1959, 91:60-64.

18,917. Brown, J. L. Review: J. W. V. Goethe's Theory of Colours. Contemporary Psychol, 1971, 16:696-697.

18,918. Brown, Lloyd Wellesley. Black entitles: names as symbols in Afro-American literature. Studies in Black Lit, 1970, 1(1):16-44.

18,919. Bruck, F. Schiller und die Medizin. Münchener medizinische Wochenschrift, 1934, 81:1547ff.

18,920. Brun, Rudolf. Psychoanalytische Behandlung und Heilung eines Schreibkrampfes verbunden mit Steifigkeit und Paraesthesien in den Armen. Acta Psychotherapeutica, Psychosomatica et Orthopaedagogica, 1964, 12:382-390.

18,921. Brunner, Theodore F. Marijuana in ancient Greece and Rome? The literary evidence. Bulletin History Medicine, 1973, 47:344-355.

18,922. Bry, Ilse, & Afflerbach, Lois. Links between the humanities and the literature of the human sciences. Wilson Library Bulletin, 1968, 42:510-525.

18,923. Bryan, A. I. The psychology of the reader. Library J, 1939, 64:7-12.

18,924. Bryant, Margaret M., & Aiken, Janet R. Psychology of English. NY: Columbia Univ. Press, 1940.

18,925. Bucy, P. C. 'The proper study of mankind is man.' Alexander Pope (1688-1744). Surgical Neurology, 1979, 11(1):80.

18,926. Bunker, Henry A. A dream of an inhibited writer. Psychoanal Q, 1953, 22:519-524.

18,927. Burger, Gérard M. Le Thème de l'obscenité dans la littérature française des douzième et treizième siècles. DAI, 1974, 34:4189A.

18,928. Burnyeat, J. P. Mental health insights in literature. Mental Hygiene, 1966, 50:184-185; Mental Hygiene, 1967, 51:32-33.

18,929. Burress, Lee A., III. Thoreau on ether and psychedelic drugs. Notes & Queries, 1974, 12:99-100.

18,930. Burton, Dwight L. The relationship of literary appreciation to certain measurable factors. J Educational Psychol, 1952, 43:436-439.

18,931. Burtt, H. E., Beck, H. C., & Campbell, E. Legibility of backbone titles. J Applied Psychol, 1928, 12:217-227.

18,932. Calvet, Jean. L'Enfant dans la littérature française, 2 Vols. Paris: Lanore, 1947.

18,933.   Camden, Carroll. The mind's construction in the face.
          In Renaissance Studies in Honor of Hardin Craig. Palo
          Alto, Cal: Stanford Univ. Press, 1941, 208-220; Phi-
          lological Q, 1941, 20:400-412.
18,934.   Cameron, Alex J. The Image of the Physician in the
          American Novel 1859 to 1925. DAI, 1973, 33:6342A.
18,935.   Cameron, Eleanor. Into something rich and strange: of
          dreams, art, and the unconscious. Library of Con-
          gress Q, 1978, 35:92-107.
18,936.   Camus, Albert. Philosophy and fiction. In The Myth of
          Sisyphus. NY: Knopf, 1955, 93-103.
18,937.   Carroll, H. A. Appreciation of literature and abstract in-
          telligence. J Educational Psychol, 1934, 25:54-57.
18,938.   _____. Influence of the sex factor upon appreciation of
          literature. School & Society, 1933, 37:468-472.
18,939.   Carroll, John B. (ed). Language, Thought, and Reality.
          Selected Writings of Benjamin Lee Whorf. NY: Wiley,
          1956; Englewood Cliffs, NJ: Prentice-Hall, 1964; Re-
          view: Oscar Legault, Psychiatry, 1958, 21:319-320.
18,940.   Carsley, J. D. The interests of children in books. Brit-
          ish J Educational Psychol, 1957, 27:13-23.
18,941.   Carter, Angela. The Sadeian Woman and the Ideology of
          Pornography. NY: Pantheon, 1979.
18,942.   Castellanos, A., et al. Scientific applications of science
          fiction according to general system theory. Acta Car-
          diologica (Brussels), 1979, 34:279-281.
18,943.   Ceccio, J. Medicine in Literature. NY: Longman, 1978.
18,944.   Chafe, W. L. Language and consciousness. Language,
          1974, 50:111-133.
18,945.   Chakraborty, S. C. Physiognomy in Robert Browning.
          Panjab Univ. Research Bulletin, 1972, 3(2):31-70.
18,946.   Chandler, A., & Barnhart, Edward N. Bibliography of
          Experimental Esthetics and the Psychology of Art.
          Berkeley: Univ. California Press, 1937.
18,947.   Chandler, Simon B. Shakespeare and sleep. Bulletin His-
          tory Medicine, 1955, 29:255-260.
18,948.   Chasseguet-Smirgel, Janine (ed). Female Sexuality: New
          Psychoanalytic Views. Ann Arbor: Univ. Michigan
          Press, 1970.
18,949.   Chenoweth, Lawrence. The search for the self in the
          twentieth century. In The American Dream of Success.
          North Scituate, Mass: Duxbury, 1974.
18,950.   Child Study Association of America. Insights. A Selec-
          tion of Creative Literature About Childhood. NY:
          Aronson, 1973.
18,951.   Christopher, Georgia. Homeopathic physic and natural
          renovation in Samson Agonistes. J English Lit History,
          1970, 37:361-373.
18,952.   Cline, Clarence Lee. Qualifications of the medical prac-
          titioners of Middlemarch. In Ryals, C. de L. (ed),
          Nineteenth Century Literary Perspectives. Durham,
          N. C.: Duke University Press, 1974, 271-281.
18,953.   Cohen, Gillian. The psychology of reading. New Lit His-
          tory, 1972, 4:75-90.

18,954. Cohen, Hennig. Wordplay on personal names in the writings of Herman Melville. Tennessee Studies in Lit, 1963, 8:85-97.

18,955. Cohen, John. The natural history of swearing. ETC, 1961, 18:275-281.

18,956. Cole, J. Preston. The Problematic Self in Kierkegaard and Freud. New Haven: Yale Univ. Press, 1971.

18,957. Collier, Mary J., & Gaier, Eugene L. The childhood story preferences of adolescent Finnish girls. Amer Imago, 1961, 18:187-204.

18,958. _____. The hero in the preferred childhood stories of college men. Amer Imago, 1959, 16:177-194.

18,959. _____. The preferred childhood stories of college women. Amer Imago, 1958, 15:401-410.

18,960. Condrau, Gion. Psychotherapie eines Schreibkrampfes. Zeitschrift für psychosomatische Medizin und Psychoanalyse, 1961, 7:255-267.

18,961. Conway, Jill. Stereotypes of femininity in a theory of sexual evolution. Victorian Studies, 1970, 14:47-62.

18,962. Cooper, David Dale. The Paradox of Spirit and Instinct: A Comparative Examination of the Psychology of Carl Gustav Jung and Sigmund Freud. DAI, 1978, 38:7330A-31A.

18,963. Cooper, Helen, et al. (eds). 1978 bibliography of literature in English by and about women: 600-1976. Women & Lit, 1979, 7(entire issue).

18,964. Corti, Maria. An Introduction to Literary Semiotics. Bloomington: Indiana Univ. Press, 1978.

18,965. Cory, Donald W., & Masters, R. E. L. Violation of Taboo: Incest in the Great Literature of the Past and Present. NY: Julian, 1963.

18,966. Cott, Nancy F. Passionlessness: an interpretation of Victorian sexual ideology, 1790-1850. In Cott, N. F., & Pleck, E. H. (eds), A Heritage of Her Own. NY: Simon & Schuster, 1979, 162-181.

18,967. Coveney, Peter. Poor Monkey. The Child in Literature. London: Rockliff, 1957.

18,968. Craig, George. Reading: who is doing what to whom? In Josipovici, G. (ed), The Modern English Novel: The Reader, the Writer and the Work. NY: Barnes & Noble, 1976, 15-36.

18,969. Crew, Louie, & Norton, Rictor. Checklist of resources. College English, 1974, 36:401-404.

18,970. Crisp, A. H., & Moldofsky, H. A psychosomatic study of writer's cramp. British J Psychiat, 1965, 111:841-858.

18,971. _____. Therapy of writers cramp. In Masserman, J. H. (ed), Current Psychiatric Therapies, Vol. 7. NY: Grune & Stratton, 1961-69, 69-72.

18,972. Crompton, Louis. Jeremy Bentham's essay on 'Paederasty.' J Homosexuality, 1978, 4:91-107.

18,973. Culler, J. Saussure. London: Harvester/Fontana, 1976.

18,974. Curti, Merle. Human Nature in American Thought: A History. Madison: Univ. Wisconsin Press, 1980.

18,975. Damon, G., & Stuart, L. The Lesbian in Literature: A Bibliography. San Francisco: Daughters of Bilitis, 1967.

18,976. Damourette, Jacques, & Pichon, E. La Grammaire en tant que mode d'exploration de l'inconscient. Evolution Psychiatrique, 1925, 1:237-257.

18,977. Danto, Arthur C. Freudian explanations and the language of the unconscious. In Smith, J. H. (ed), Psychoanalysis and Language. New Haven: Yale Univ. Press, 1978, 325-353.

18,978. Darnton, R. Mesmerism and the End of the Enlightenment in France. Cambridge: Harvard Univ. Press, 1969.

18,979. Dattner, Bernhard. Aphorismen von Gabriele Reuter. Int Zeitschrift für Psychoanalyse, 1912, 2:472-473.

18,980. David, Michel. La lingua della psicanalisi nella cultura italiana. Lingua Nostra, 1964, 25:79-87.

18,981. David-Peyre, Y. Le Personnage du médecin et la relation médecin-malade dans la littérature ibérique, XVIe et XVIIe siècle. Doctoral dissertation, Univ. Paris, 1971.

18,982. Day, B. Sexual Life Between Blacks and Whites. NY: World, 1972.

18,983. DeBakey, L. The fictional physician-scientist of nineteenth-century America: Herman Melville. Southern Medical J, 1968, 61:55-63.

18,984. _____. _____.: Nathaniel Hawthorne. Anesthesia & Analgesia, 1968, 47:108-118.

18,985. _____. _____.: scientific milieu. Anesthesia & Analgesia, 1967, 46:725-733; Southern Medical J, 1966, 59:1455-1463.

18,986. DeFord, M. A. The psychology of mystery story writing. Writer, 1964, 77:12-14.

18,987. De La Mare, A. C. The Handwriting of Italian Humanists, Vol. 1. Florence: Olschki, 1974.

18,988. Delaney, J., Lupton, M. J., & Totti, E. The Curse: A Cultural History of Menstruation. NY: Dutton, 1976.

18,989. De Mause, Lloyd. The History of Childhood. NY: Harper & Row, 1974.

18,990. Dempsey, Peter J. The Psychology of Sartre. Oxford: Blackwell, 1950.

18,991. Deneve, Albert. Emblem of the Human Spirit: Arthur Schnitzler's Der Geist im Wort und der Geist in der Tat. DAI, 1976, 36:8084A.

18,992. Derrida, Jacques. Of Grammatology. Baltimore: Johns Hopkins Univ. Press, 1976.

18,993. Dettelbach, Cynthia Golomb. In the Driver's Seat: The Automobile in American Literature and Popular Culture. Westport, Conn: Greenwood, 1976.

18,994. Dewhurst, Kenneth, & Reeves, Nigel. Friedrich Schiller --Medicine, Psychology and Literature. With the First English Edition of His Complete Medical and Psychological Writings. Berkeley: Univ. California Press, 1978.

18,995. Di Almeida, A., Jr. [Drunkenness in the theatre of Shakespeare.] Revista da Faculdade de Direito da Universidade de São Paulo, 1939, 35:97-164.

18,996. Dobson, J. Doctors in literature. Library Assn Record, 1969, 71:269-274.

18,997. Doggart, J. Dickens and the doctors--a centenary causerie. Practitioner, 1970, 204:449-453.

18,998. Dos Passos, John. Some remarks on science by a litterateur. Conditioned Reflex, 1968, 3:143-144.

18,999. Dowden, E. Elizabethan psychology. Atlantic Monthly, 1907, 100:388-399.

19,000. Dreiser, Theodore. Moods: Philosophical and Emotional, Cadenced and Declaimed. NY: Simon & Schuster, 1935.

19,001. Drolet, A. [The physician in the French-Canadian novel.] Union Médicale du Canada, 1960, 89:493-499.

19,002. Duda, G. Krankeiten und Tod. Ein Mediziner untersucht Leben und Tod Friedrich Schillers. Der Quell, 1959, 11:994-1002, 1031-1037.

19,003. Dudley, F.A. The impact of science on literature. Science, 1952, 115:412-415.

19,004. Duffy, Philip Howlett. The Theory and Practice of Medicine in Elizabethan England as Illustrated by Certain Dramatic Texts. Cambridge: Harvard Univ. Press, 1914.

19,005. Dufrenne, Mikel. The Phenomenology of Aesthetic Experience. Evanston, Ill: Northwestern Univ. Press, 1973.

19,006. Dumortier, J. Le Vocabulaire médical d'Eschyle et les écrits hippocratiques. Paris: Les Belles Lettres, 1975.

19,007. Ebin, David. The Drug Experience. First-Person Accounts of Addicts, Writers, Scientists, and Others. NY: Grove, 1961.

19,008. Eco, Umberto. A Theory of Semiotics. Bloomington: Indiana Univ. Press, 1976.

19,009. Eder, Montague D. Symbol-metaphor. Int J Psycho-Anal, 1930, 11:40-47.

19,010. Einhorn, Jürgen W. Spiritalis Unicornis. Das Einhorn als Bedeutungsträger in Literatur und Kunst des Mittelalters. Munich: Fink, 1976.

19,011. Ekstein, Rudolf. Psychoanalytic precursors in Greek antiquity. Bulletin Menninger Clinic, 1975, 39:246-247.

19,012. Eliasberg, Wladimir G. Psychiatric viewpoints on indecency, obscenity, and pornography in literature and the arts. Amer J Psychotherapy, 1962, 16:477-483.

19,013. Elkes, Joel. Language and the human psyche. In Musès, C., & Young, A.M. (eds), Consciousness and Reality. The Human Pivot Point. NY: Outerbridge & Lazard/Dutton, 1972, 258-277.

19,014. Ellinwood, Everett H. Perception of faces: disorders in organic and psychopathological states. Psychiat Q, 1969, 43:622-646.

19,015. Ellis, Joseph. Habits of mind and an American enlightenment. Amer Q, 1976, 28:150-164.

19,016. Elovaara, Raili. The Problem of Identity in Samuel Beckett's Prose: An Approach from Philosophies of Existence. Helsinki: Soumalainen Tiedeakatemia, 1976.

19,017. Elton, William (ed). Aesthetics and Language. NY:
Philosophical Library, 1954.

19,018. Enachescu, Constantin. Le 'Roman schizophrénique': a
propos de la création littéraire et artistique des malades schizophrènes. Annales Médico-Psychologiques,
1968, 1:177-202.

19,019. Engelhardt, Dietrich v. Medizin und Literatur in der
Neuzeit: Perspektive und Aspekte. Deutsche Vierteljahrsschrift für Literaturwissenschaft und Geistesgeschichte, 1978, 52:351-380.

19,020. Engle, Harrison. Hidden cameras and human behavior:
an interview with Allen Funt. Film Comment, 1965,
3:42-53.

19,021. Erdt, Terrence. The Calvinist psychology of the heart
and the 'sense' of Jonathan Edwards. Early Amer Lit,
1978, 13:165-180.

19,022. Erickson, Milton H. A special inquiry with Aldous Huxley
into the nature and character of various states of consciousness. Amer J Clinical Hypnosis, 1965, 8:14-33.

19,023. Esslin, Martin. Freud's Vienna. In Miller, J. (ed),
Freud: The Man, His World, His Influence. Boston:
Little, Brown, 1972, 41-54.

19,024. Eykman, Christoph. Phänomenologie der Interpretation.
Bern: Francke, 1977.

19,025. Fagan, F. Alcohol and the writer. JAMA, 1973, 225:
992-993.

19,026. Farb, Peter. Word Play. In What Happens When People
Talk. NY: Knopf, 1974.

19,027. Feasy, L. Children's appreciation of poems. British J
Psychol, 1927, 18:51-67.

19,028. Fellner, Carl H. Paperback psychiatry. J Medical Education, 1969, 44:585-588.

19,029. Felong, Michael. Morte de Moriarty: a pathological inquiry into the medical peculiarities of Professor James
Moriarty. Baker Street J, 1974, 24(2):89-93.

19,030. Feltes, N. N. Phrenology: from Lewes to George Eliot.
Studies in the Lit Imagination, 1968, 1(1):13-22.

19,031. Felton, Gary. On the literary use of color names: a
psychosymbolic approach. Names, 1966, 14:123-124.

19,032. Ferenczi, Sandor. On obscene words. In Contributions to
Psychoanalysis. NY: Basic Books, 1950 (1911), 132-
153.

19,033. Fichtner, B., & Brecht, M. Psychiatrie zur Zeit Hölder-
lins. Tübingen: 1972.

19,034. Fisher, Benjamin Franklin. The Very Spirit of Cordiality:
The Literary Uses of Alcohol and Alcoholism in the

Tales of Edgar Allan Poe. Baltimore: Univ. Baltimore Press, 1978.

19,035. Fite, Warner. Psycho-analysis and sex psychology. Nation, 1916, 103:127-129.

19,036. Fizer, John. Psychologism and Psychoaesthetics: A Historical and Critical View of Their Relations. Atlantic Highlands, NJ: Humanities, 1980.

19,037. Fodor, Nandor. Psychopathology and problems of oral libido in the use of language. Amer Imago, 1956, 13: 347-381.

19,038. Ford, Nick A. Literature as an aid to social development. Teachers College Record, 1957, 58:377-381.

19,039. Forrester, J. M. George Eliot and physiology. Proceedings Royal Society Medicine, 1971, 64:724-726.

19,040. Foster, G. R. Emerson on mental health. J Abnormal Social Psychol, 1943, 38:377-383.

19,041. Fox, Stella. Lesbian Love in Literature. NY: Avon, 1962.

19,042. Francis, K. H. Some popular scientific myths in Rabelais: a possible source. In Ireson, J. C., McFarlane, I. D., & Rees, G. (eds), Studies in French Literature. Manchester, England: Manchester Univ. Press, 1968, 121-134; NY: Barnes & Noble, 1968, 121-134.

19,043. Francoeur, Louis. Le Monologue intérieur narratif (sa syntax, sa sémantique et sa pragmatique). Etudes littéraires, 1976, 341-365.

19,044. Frässdorf, W. Die psychologischen Anschauungen Jean-Jacques Rousseau. Pädagogisches Magazin, 1929, 1214:1-248.

19,045. Freeman, Gillian. The Undergrowth of Literature. NY: Delta, 1970.

19,046. Freitag, Gunter. Die literarischen Interresen von Schulern und Schulerimen einer hoheren Lehranstalt. Psychologische Beiträge, 1953, 1:264-311.

19,047. Freud, Sigmund. Ansprache im Frankfurter Goethe-Haus. Int Zeitschrift für Individual-Psychologie, 1930, 5:421-426.

19,048. _____. The antithetical meaning of primal words. In Standard Edition, Vol. 11. London: Hogarth, 1959.

19,049. Frey, T. P. [The medical views of August Strindberg.] Lakartidningen, 1980, 77:231-236.

19,050. Friedlander, Kate. Children's books and their function in latency and pre-puberty. Amer Imago, 1942, 3:129-150. Int Zeitschrift für Psychoanalyse, 1941, 26:232-251.

19,051. Friedlander, W. J. Mark Twain, social critic, and his image of the doctor. Annals Internal Medicine, 1972, 77:1007-1010.

19,052. Friedman, J. J. Psychology of the audience in relation to the architecture of the theatre. Psychoanal Q, 1953, 22:561-570.

19,053. Fritz, Paul, & Morton, Richard (eds). Women in the 18th Century and Other Essays. Toronto: Stevens, Hakkert, 1976.

19, 054.   Fugate, Joe K.   The Psychological Basis of Herders' Aesthetics.   The Hague: Mouton, 1966.
19, 055.   Fulcher, J. Rodney.   Puritans and the passions: the faculty psychology in American Puritanism.   J History Behaviour Sciences, 1973, 9:123-139.
19, 056.   Furst, Daniel C., III.   Sterne and Physick: Images of Health and Disease in Tristram Shandy.   DAI, 1974, 35:3738A.

19, 057.   Garber, Marjorie Beth.   The healer in Shakespeare.   In Peschel, E. R. (ed), Medicine and Literature.   NY: Watson, 1980, 103-112.
19, 058.   Garde, Noel I.   The Homosexual in Literature: A Chronological Bibliography Circa 700 B. C. -1958.   NY: Village Press, 1959.
19, 059.   Gardner, Howard.   Senses, symbols, operations: an organization of artistry.   In Perkins, D., & Leondar, B. (eds), The Arts and Cognition.   Baltimore: Johns Hopkins Univ. Press, 1977, 88-117.
19, 060.   Gardner, William.   The psychology of Plato.   Canadian Psychiat Assn J,   1968, 13:463-464.
19, 061.   Gaskell, E.   Dickens and medicosocial reform.   JAMA, 1971, 16:111-116.
19, 062.   Gass, William H.   Fiction and the Figures of Life.   NY: Knopf, 1971; NY: Random Vintage, 1972.
19, 063.   Gathorne-Hardy, Jonathan.   The Unnatural History of the Nanny.   NY: Dial, 1973.
19, 064.   Gaubert, S.   Proust: la médecine et les médecins.   Profession et création.   In Roman et société.   Paris: Colin, 1973, 84-98.
19, 065.   Gay, Peter.   Freud, Jews and Other Germans: Masters and Victims in Modernist Culture.   NY: Oxford Univ. Press, 1978.
19, 066.   Gaylin, Willard Marvin.   Feelings; Our Vital Signs.   NY: Harper & Row, 1979; NY: Ballantine, 1980.
19, 067.   Geizer, I. N.   [Medicine in the life and creative works of A. P. Chekhov.]   Klinischeskia Meditsina, 1960, 41:3-10.
19, 068.   Gerhardi, Gerhard C.   Zola's biological vision of politics: revolutionary figures in La Fortune des Rougon and Le Ventre de Paris.   Nineteenth-Century French Studies, 1974, 2:164-180.
19, 069.   Gibbons, Reginald (ed).   The Poets' Work.   29 Masters of 20th Century Poetry on the Origins and Practice of Their Art.   Boston: Houghton Mifflin, 1979.
19, 070.   Gillespie, J. D.   Medical notes about Shakespeare and his times.   Edinburgh Medical J, 1875, 20:1061-1082.
19, 071.   Ginsberg, Mitchell.   Nietzschean psychiatry.   In Solomon, R. C. (ed), Nietzsche: A Collection of Critical Essays.   Garden City, NY: Anchor, 1973, 293-315.
19, 072.   Gioanola, E.   L'uomo dei topazi.   Saggio psicanalitico su C. C. Gadda.   Genoa: Il Melangolo, 1977.
19, 073.   Girard, René.   The plague in literature and myth.   Texas Studies in Lit & Language, 1974, 15:833-850.

19,074. Glenn, Jules. Tooth symbolism in Herodotus. Psychoanal Rev, 1978, 65:471-473.

19,075. Glicksberg, Charles I. Literature and Religion: A Study in Conflict. Dallas: Southwest Methodist Univ. Press, 1960.

19,076. _____. Literature and science: a study in conflict. Scientific Monthly, 1944, 59:467-472.

19,077. _____. Literature and the meaning of life. South Atlantic Q, 1956, 55:153-162.

19,078. Gold, Milton. Freud's news on art. Psychoanal Rev, 1961, 48:111-115.

19,079. Goldberg, J. The understanding of sickness in Donne's Devotions. Renaissance Q, 1971, 24:507-517.

19,080. Goldbladt, Hermann. Shakespeare als Physionomiker. Psychologie und Medizin, 1930, 4:83-110.

19,081. Goldman, L. A dermatologist excoriates bits of world literature and even smaller bits of music. Amer Medical Assn Archives Dermatology, 1960, 82:551-564.

19,082. Goldman, Maureen. American Women and the Puritan Heritage: Anne Hutchinson to Harriet Beecher Stowe. DAI, 1975, 36:1503A-4A.

19,083. Goldwert, Marvin. The search for the lost father-figure in Spanish-American history: a Freudian view. Americas, 1978, 34:533-536.

19,084. Goll, A. Criminal types in Shakespeare. J Criminal Law & Criminology, 1939, 30:22-51.

19,085. Gombrich, Ernst H. Freud's aesthetics. Encounter, 1966, 26(1):30-40.

19,086. Goodin, George (ed). The English Novel in the Nineteenth Century: Essays on the Literary Mediation of Human Values. Urbana: Univ. Illinois Press, 1972.

19,087. Goodman, Paul. On a writer's block. Complex, 1952, 7:42-50.

19,088. Gordon, Caroline. How to Read a Novel. NY: Viking, 1957.

19,089. Gore, Neil Stanley. Psychological Functions of Metaphor. DAI, 1977, 38:2861B.

19,090. Gorman, W., & Heller, L. G. The psychological significance of words. Psychoanal Rev, 1964, 51(1):5-14.

19,091. Gornick, Vivian, & Moran, Barbara K. (eds). Woman in Sexist Society. Studies in Power and Powerlessness. NY: Basic Books, 1971; NY: National American Library, 1972.

19,092. Gourevitch, D., & Gourevitch, M. Eugene Hugo et le Docteur Esquirol. Perspectives in Psychiat, 1978, 16(65):57-71.

19,093. Gowan, John Curtis. France, Art and Creativity. Buffalo: Creative Education Foundation, 1975.

19,094. Grace, A. G. The reading interests of adults. J Educational Research, 1929, 19:265-275.

19,095. Graham, Robert J. Concepts of Women in American Literature. Doctoral dissertation, Univ. Pennsylvania, 1973.

19,096.   Grande, E.   Presencia de medicos en el teatro argentino.
          Archiva Historia Medica Argentina, 1973, 3:7-12.
19,097.   Granjel, Luis.   El médico galdosiano.   In Baroja y otra
          figuras del '98.   Madrid: Guadarrana, 1960, 247-272;
          Archivo Ibero-Americano de Historia de la Medicina y
          Antropologia Médica, 1954, 6:163-176.
19,098.   Gras, Vernon W. (ed).   European Literary Theory and
          Practice: From Existential Phenomenology to Structur-
          alism.   NY: Delta, 1973.
19,099.   Greco, E.   [Medical knowledge of the Elizabethan period
          in Shakespeare.]   Policlinico, 1961, 68:120-123.
19,100.   Green, Martin.   Transatlantic Patterns: Cultural Com-
          parisons of England with America.   NY: Basic Books,
          1977.
19,101.   Green, Mary Jean.   A moral image of modern man: the
          doctor in the work of Martin du Gard.   In Peschel,
          E.R. (ed), Medicine and Literature.   NY: Watson,
          1980, 98-102.
19,102.   Greene, Maxine.   Curriculum and consciousness.   Teach-
          ers College Record, 1971, 73:253-269.
19,103.   _____.   Literature, existentialism, and education.   In
          Denton, D.E. (ed), Existentialism and Phenomenology
          in Education: Collected Essays.   NY: Teachers Col-
          lege Press, 1974, 63-86.
19,104.   Greet, T.Y., Edge, Charles E., & Munro, John M. (eds).
          The Worlds of Fiction: Stories in Context.   Boston:
          Houghton Mifflin, 1964.
19,105.   Greimas, A-J., & Courtes, J.   The cognitive dimension
          of narrative discourse.   New Lit History, 1976, 7:433-
          448.
19,106.   Griffith, G.W.   Jonathan Swift's Relation to Science.   Doc-
          toral dissertation, Vanderbilt Univ., 1970.
19,107.   Grinspoon, Leonard.   Marihuana Reconsidered.   Cam-
          bridge: Harvard Univ. Press, 1971, 55-116.
19,108.   Gropp, F.   Zur Aesthetik und statistichen Beschreibung
          des Prosarythmus.   Fortschritte der Psychologie und
          ihrer Andwendung, 1917, 4:43-79.
19,109.   Guest-Gornall, R.   Samuel Taylor Coleridge and the doc-
          tors.   Medical History, 1973, 17:327-342.
19,110.   Guillaume, Paul.   A propos d'une parabole.   JPNP, 1950,
          43:546-554.
19,111.   Gulick, J.   Literature unit in human relations.   English
          J, 1952, 41:348-351.
19,112.   Gustin, John C.   Psychology of the actor.   Psychoanaly-
          sis, 1955-56, 4:29-36.

19,113.   Hagstrum, Jean H.   Sex and Sensibility.   Ideal and Erotic
          Love from Milton to Mozart.   Chicago: Univ. Chicago
          Press, 1979.
19,114.   Hail, H.G.   Moliere, satirist of seventeenth-century
          French medicine: fact and fantasy.   Proceedings Royal
          Society Medicine, 1977, 70:425-431.

19,115. Hale, Nathan G., Jr. Freud and the Americans: The
         Beginnings of Psychoanalysis in the United States, 1876-
         1917, Vol. 1. NY: Oxford Univ. Press, 1971.
19,116. Hall, Calvin S. Slang and dream symbols. Psychoanal
         Rev, 1964, 51:38-48.
19,117. Haller, John S., & Haller, R. M. The Physician and
         Sexuality in Victorian Literature. Urbana: Univ. Illi-
         nois Press, 1974.
19,118. Halliday, Frank E. Five Arts. London: Duckworth,
         1946; Toronto: Nelson, 1946.
19,119. Hamilton, M. P. Latin and English passages on dreams.
         Studies in Philology, 1936, 33:1-9.
19,120. Hammer, Emanuel F. Creativity. NY: Random, 1961.
19,121. Hanak, Miroslav John. Dostoevsky's metaphysics in the
         light of Nietzsche's psychology. New Zealand Slavonic
         J, 1972, 9:20-37.
19,122. Hanson, T. B. Stylized Man: The Poetic Use of Physiog-
         nomy in Chaucer's Canterbury Tales. Doctoral dis-
         sertation, Univ. Wisconsin, 1970.
19,123. Harris, D. F. Shakespeare's perception of the functional
         importance of the brain. Medical Life, 1927, 34:15-
         21.
19,124. Harrison, F. The Dark Angel: Aspects of Victorian Sex-
         uality. NY: Universe Books, 1978.
19,125. Hart, Donald C. The Literature of Drug Experience in
         French and English: An Historical, Critical, and Bib-
         liographical Study. DAI, 1973, 34:2562A.
19,126. Hart, James D. The Popular Book: A History of Amer-
         ica's Literary Taste. NY: Oxford Univ. Press, 1950.
19,127. Hartley, H. W. Developing personality through books.
         English J, 1951, 40:198-204.
19,128. Hartman, G., & Shumaker, A. (eds). Creative Expres-
         sion; The Development of Children in Art, Music, Lit-
         erature and Dramatics. NY: Day, 1932.
19,129. Hartman, Geoffrey H. The reading process: a phenom-
         enological approach. In Cohen, R. (ed), New Direc-
         tions in Literary History. Baltimore: Johns Hopkins
         Univ. Press, 1974, 125-145.
19,130. Hartogs, Renato. Four-Letter Word Games. The Psy-
         chology of Obscenity. NY: Evans, 1967.
19,131. Harvey, J. The content characteristics of best-selling
         novels. Public Opinion Q, 1953, 17:91-114.
19,132. Hastings, James C. Carlos Castaneda: Don Juan's
         Teachings and Humanistic Psychology. DAI, 1978, 39:
         279A.
19,133. Havelock, Eric Alfred. The psychology of rhythmic mem-
         orization. In The Greek Concept of Justice. Cam-
         bridge: Harvard Univ. Press, 1978.
19,134. Hayman, D. The broken cranium: headwounds in Zola,
         Rilke, Céline: a study in contrasting modes. Com-
         parative Lit Studies, 1972, 9:207-233.
19,135. Hazard, Paul. Books, Children and Men. Boston: Horn,
         1948.

19,136.   Heidegger, Martin. Poetry, Language, Thought. NY:
           Harper & Row, 1971.
19,137.   Heilbrun, Carolyn G. Reinventing Motherhood. NY: Nor-
           ton, 1979.
19,138.   Heitner, Robert R. Goethe's ailing women. MLN, 1980,
           95:497-515.
19,139.   Helson, Ravenna. Through the pages of children's books.
           Psychol Today, 1973, 7(6):107-117, passim.
19,140.   Hendley, W. Clark. Dear Abby, Miss Lonelyhearts, and
           the eighteenth century: the origins of the newspaper
           advice column. J Popular Culture, 1977, 11:345-352.
19,141.   Henry, William E. Art and cultural symbolism: a psy-
           chological study of greeting cards. JAAC, 1947, 6:36-
           44.
19,142.   Herzberg, L. Mann on mountain sickness. Lancet, 1977,
           1(8005):258-259.
19,143.   Hiatt, May P. The sexology of style. Language & Style,
           1976, 9:98-108.
19,144.   Hickey, Mary V. The Early Adolescent's Reactions to the
           Literary and Cultural Portrayal of Women. DAI, 1974,
           35:3077.
19,145.   Hingley, Ronald. Russian Writers and Soviet Society 1917-
           1978. NY: Random House, 1979.
19,146.   Hirn, Y. The Origins of Art: A Psychological and Soci-
           ological Inquiry. London: 1900.
19,147.   Hirsch, E. J., Jr. The psychologic basis of readability.
           In The Philosophy of Communication. Chicago: Univ.
           Chicago Press, 1977.
19,148.   Hirschfeld, Magnus. Numa Praetorius. Bibliographie
           der homosexuellen Belletristik. Jahrbuch für Sexuelle
           Zwischenstufen, 1-20 passim.
19,149.   Hoare, John E. The Psychology of Playwriting, Audience,
           Writer, Play. NY: Dramatists Play Service, 1949.
19,150.   Hoffman, N. Y. The doctor and the detective story.
           JAMA, 1973, 224:74-77.
19,151.   Hofling, Charles K. The place of great literature in the
           teaching of psychiatry. Bulletin Menninger Clinic,
           1966, 30:368-373.
19,152.   Holland, Norman N. Indexing Psychological Abstracts us-
           ing ternary-coded letter fields. Indecks Newsletter,
           1975, 2:4-7.
19,153.   _____. Pornography and the mechanisms of defense.
           In Technical Report of the Commission on Obscenity
           and Pornography: Preliminary Studies. Washington,
           DC: Supt. of Documents, 1971, 1:115-129.
19,154.   _____. A touching of literary and psychiatric educa-
           tion. Seminars in Psychiat, 1973, 5:287-299.
19,155.   _____. What can a concept of identity add to psycho-
           linguistics? In Smith, J. H. (ed), Psychoanalysis and
           Language. New Haven: Yale Univ. Press, 1978, 171-
           234.
19,156.   Hollander, Edwin P. Popular literature in the undergrad-
           uate social psychology course. Amer Psychologist,
           1956, 11:95-96.

19,157. Hoomes, Eleanor W. Sexism in High School Literary Anthologies. DAI, 1979, 39:4022-23A.

19,158. Horowitz, Louise K. Love and Language. A Study of the Classical French Moralist Writers. Columbus: Ohio State Univ. Press, 1977.

19,159. Hudson, Liam. Language, truth, and psychology. In Michaels, L., & Ricks, C. (eds), The State of Language. San Francisco: Univ. California Press, 1980, 449-457.

19,160. Hughes, Douglas A. (ed). Perspectives on Pornography. NY: St. Martin, 1970.

19,161. Hungerford, Edward. Poe and phrenology. Amer Lit, 1930, 2:209-231.

19,162. _____. Walt Whitman and his chart of bumps. Amer Lit, 1931, 3.

19,163. Hunt, Morton M. The Affair. A Portrait of Extramarital Love in Contemporary America. NY: World, 1969; NY: New American Library, 1973.

19,164. _____. The Natural History of Love. NY: Knopf, 1959.

19,165. _____. The Young Person's Guide to Love. NY: Farrar, Straus & Giroux, 1976.

19,166. Huxley, Aldous. Culture and the individual. In Andrews, B., & Vinkenoog, S. (eds), The Book of Grass. An Anthology of Indian Hemp. NY: Grove, 1966, 192-201.

19,167. _____. The Doors of Perception, and Heaven and Hell. NY: Harper & Row, 1954.

19,168. Hynes, Samuel. Phenomenology. Novel: A Forum for Fiction, 1969, 2:179-183.

19,169. Idema, W. Diseases and doctors, drugs and cures. A very preliminary list of passages of medical interest in a number of traditional Chinese novels and related plays. Chinese Science, 1977, 2:37-63.

19,170. Irrig, Madeline. Developing character through reading. Wilson Library Bulletin, 1959, 33:571-573.

19,171. Isenberg, Arnold. Critical communication. Philosophical Rev, 1949, 58:330-344.

19,172. Iser, Wolfgang. The reading process: a phenomenological approach. In The Implied Reader; Patterns of Communication in Prose Fiction from Bunyan to Beckett. Baltimore: Johns Hopkins Univ. Press, 1974, 274-294.

19,173. Jackson, Murray. Jung's 'archetype': clarity or confusion? J Mental Science, 1960, 33:83-94.

19,174. _____. Jung's 'archetypes' and psychiatry. J Mental Science, 1960, 106:1518-1526.

19,175. _____. Jung's later work. The archetype. J Mental Science, 1962, 35:199-204.

19,176. Jacobs, Robert Louis. A Freudian view of The Ring. Music Rev, 1965, 26:201-219.

19,177. Jacobson, A. C.   Tuberculosis and the creative mind.
         Medical Library & Historical J, 1907, 5:225-249.
19,178. _____. Tuberculosis and genius; with particular refer-
         ence to Francis Thompson. In Recent Studies of Tub-
         erculosis. St. Louis: Interstate Medical Journal Co.,
         1914, 131-138.
19,179. Jahoda, Marie. The Impact of Literature: A Psychologi-
         cal Discussion of Some Assumptions in the Censorship
         Debate. NY: Research Center for Human Relations,
         New York Univ., 1954.
19,180. Jarcho, S.   Cicero's essay 'On Old Age.' Bulletin New
         York Academy Medicine, 1971, 47:1440-1445.
19,181. Jáuregui, María Francisca de.   Estudio grafológico sobre
         Rubén Darío. Cuadernos Hispanoamericanos, 1967,
         71:624-628.
19,182. Jespersen, Otto. Language: Its Nature, Development and
         Origin. London: Allen & Unwin, 1922.
19,183. Jimenez-Hernandes, Adolfo.   Los materiales literarios y
         el desarrollo psicologico del niño. Pedagogia (Rio
         Piedras), 1955, 3(2):7-33.
19,184. Jiménez Herrero, J.   La medicina y los médicos en el
         teatro de Casona. Boletin del Instituto de Estudios
         Asturianos, 1968, 22:319-351.
19,185. Johnson, Wendell Stacy. Living in Sin; The Victorian
         Sexual Revolution. Chicago: Nelson-Hall, 1979.
19,186. Jones, Peter G. Philosophy and the Novel; Philosophical
         Aspects of Middlemarch, Anna Karenina, The Brothers
         Karamazov, A la recherche du temps perdu, and the
         Methods of Criticism. NY: Oxford Univ. Press, 1975.
19,187. Jordan, John E.   Racial prejudice and word symbolism.
         J Social Psychol, 1975, 95:291-292.
19,188. Josse, G.   Les Corrélations de l'art de la folie: a pro-
         pos des romans d'une paraphrene. Encéphale, 1967,
         56(Suppl), 24-30.
19,189. Jousse, Marcel. Les Lois psycho-physiologiques du style
         oral vivant et leur utilisation philologique. L'Ethno-
         graphie, bulletin semestriel, 1931, n. s. 23, 23-40.
19,190. _____. Mimetisme humain et psychologie de la lecture.
         Paris: Geuthner, 1935.
19,191. _____. Mimetisme humain et style manuel. Paris:
         Geuthner, 1936.

19,192. Kain, Richard M.   James Joyce and the game of lan-
         guage. Studies in Lit Imagination, 1970, 3(2):19-25.
19,193. Kaluza, Irena. The Functioning of Sentence Structure in
         the Stream-of-Consciousness Technique of William
         Faulkner's The Sound and the Fury: A Study in Lin-
         guistic Stylistics. Krakow, U. J., 1967.
19,194. Kamber, Richard.   A Study of the Relationship Between
         Philosophy and Literature. DAI, 1975, 36:938A.
19,195. Kaplan, Abraham.   Obscenity as an esthetic category.
         Law & Contemporary Problems, 1955, 20:544-559.

19, 196. _____, & Kris, Ernst. Esthetic ambiguity. Philosophy & Phenomenology Rev, 1948, 8:415-485.

19, 197. Kaplan, Bernard. Some psychological methods for the investigation of expressive language. In Werner, Heinz (ed), On Expressive Language. Worcester, Mass: Clark Univ. Press, 1955, 11-18.

19, 198. Kaplan, Donald M. On stage fright. Drama Rev, 1969, 14(1): 60-83.

19, 199. _____. Theatre architecture: a derivation of the primal cavity. Tulane Drama Rev, 1968, 12:105-116.

19, 200. Kaplan, Fred. 'The Mesmeric Mania': the early Victorians and animal magnetism. J History Ideas, 1974, 35:691-702.

19, 201. Kaplan, Harold. Beyond society: the idea of community in classic American writing. Social Research, 1975, 42:204-229.

19, 202. Karlen, Arno. Sexuality and Homosexuality. A New View. NY: Norton, 1971.

19, 203. Karpas, M. J. Socrates in the light of modern psychopathology. J Abnormal Psychol, 1915, 10:185-200.

19, 204. Karpinskaya, N. [Literary material in the training of the very young.] Doshkol'noe Vospitanie, 1968, 41:23-27.

19, 205. Kaufman, M. Ralph. The Greeks had some words for it. Early Greek concepts of mind and 'insanity.' Psychiat Q, 1966, 40:1-33.

19, 206. Kaufmann, Walter. Nietzsche als der erste grosse Psychologe. Nietzsche Studien, 1978, 7:261-287.

19, 207. _____. Tragedy and Philosophy. Garden City, NY: Doubleday, 1968.

19, 208. Keenan, E. The doctor and literature. Minnesota Medicine, 1966, 49:408 passim.

19, 209. Kelley, D. M. Note on the symbol interpretation of the word crap in coprophilia. Psychoanal Rev, 1950, 37: 71-72.

19, 210. Kelly, H. A. Love and Marriage in the Age of Chaucer. Ithaca, NY: Cornell Univ. Press, 1975.

19, 211. Kennedy, Alan. Meanings and Signs in Fiction. NY: St. Martin's, 1979.

19, 212. Kenny, Anthony. Mental health in Plato's Republic. In The Anatomy of the Soul; Historical Essays in the Philosophy of Mind. NY: Barnes & Noble, 1973, 1-27.

19, 213. Kerkhoff, A. H. La Médecine dans Homère, une bibliographie. Janus, 1975, 62:43-49.

19, 214. Kern, Stephen. Explosive intimacy; psychodynamics of the Victorian family. In De Mause, L. (ed), The New Psychohistory. NY: Psychohistory Press, 1975, 29-53.

19, 215. Kerner, D. Der Arzt-Dichter Anton Chekhov. Über den siebzig Jahrestag seiner Tod, 14-15 Juli 1964. Deutsche Medizin J, 1965, 16:372-378.

19, 216. _____. Der Arzt-Dichter Hans Carossa. Medizinische Welt, 1968, 9:588-593.

19, 217. Kerner, F. François Rabelais, médico-poeta. Folia Humanitas (Barcelona), 1967, 5:265-282.

19, 218. Kerr, Howard. Mediums and Spirit-Rappers, and Roaring Radicals: Spiritualism in American Literature. Urbana: Univ. Illinois Press, 1972.

19, 219. Kerr, W. A., & Remmers, H. H. The cultural value of 100 representative American magazines. School & Society, 1941, 54:476-480.

19, 220. Kessler, J. The censorship of art and the art of censorship. Lit Rev, 1969, 12:409-431.

19, 221. Kiefer, M. American Children Through Their Books, 1700-1835. Philadelphia: Univ. Pennsylvania Press, 1948.

19, 222. Kiell, Norman (ed). Psychoanalysis, Psychology and Literature: A Bibliography. Madison: Univ. Wisconsin Press, 1963.

19, 223. Kiken, K. [Literary taste of primary school children.] Psychologia Wychowawcza, 1938-39, 11:66-83.

19, 224. King, L. S. Style analysis: Carlyle. JAMA, 1968, 204: 449-450.

19, 225. _____. Style analysis: Samuel Johnson. JAMA, 1968, 203:41-42.

19, 226. King, Richard H. The Party of Eros: Radical Social Thought and the Realm of Freedom. Durham: Univ. North Carolina Press, 1972; NY: Dell, 1973.

19, 227. Kingston, Albert J., & Lovelace, Terry. Sexism and reading: a critical review of the literature. Reading Research Q, 1977-78, 13:133-161.

19, 228. Kintgen, Eugene R. Psycholinguistics and literature. College English, 1978, 39:755-769.

19, 229. Kircher, Clara J. Behavior Patterns in Children's Books: A Bibliography. Washington, DC: Catholic Univ. America Press, 1966.

19, 230. Kirkendall, Lester A. Semantics and sexual communication. ETC: Rev General Semantics, 1966, 23:235-244.

19, 231. Kirsner, R. J. The Schizoid World of Jean-Paul Sartre and R. D. Laing. St. Lucia: Univ. Queensland Press, 1976.

19, 232. Klein, M. La Faculté de médecine de Strasbourg au temps de Goethe. Rev d'Allemagne, 1971, 3:98-122.

19, 233. Knight, Everett W. Literature Considered as Philosophy. London: Routledge & Kegan Paul, 1957.

19, 234. Knight, Richard P., & Wright, Thomas. Sexual Symbolism: A History of Phallic Worship. NY: Matrix, 1966.

19, 235. Knoff, W. Depression: a historical overview. Amer J Psychoanal, 1975, 35:41-46.

19, 236. Koffka, K. The art of the actor as a psychological problem. Amer Scholar, 1942, 11:315-326.

19, 237. Kohlhepp, B. Horatius Flaccus und die Psychiatrie. Bayerisches Aerzteblatt, 1972, 27:390-394.

19, 238. Kornexl, E. Begriff und Einschätzung der Gesundheit des Körpers in der griechischen Literatur von ihren Anfängen bis zum Hellenisimus. Innsbruck: Wagner, 1970.

19, 239. Krapp, George P.   The psychology of dialect writing.
          Bookman, 1926, 63:522-527.
19, 240. Krippner, Stanley.   The effects of psychedelic experience
          on language functioning.   In Aaronson, B. S., & Os-
          mond, H. (eds), Psychedelics: The Uses and Implica-
          tions of Hallucinogenic Drugs.   NY: Anchor Books,
          1970, 214-238.
19, 241. Kubusch, H. H.   Leib und Seele.   Eine Studie auf der
          Grundlage inschriftlicher Grabepigramme der Griechen.
          Doctoral dissertation, Erlangen-Nürnberg, 1973.
19, 242. Kuhns, R.   Structure and Experience: Essays on the Af-
          finity Between Philosophy and Literature.   NY: Basic
          Books, 1971.
19, 243. Kurth, R. T., et al.   Oliver Wendell Holmes, M. D. (1809-
          1894); medical and literary knowledge intertwined.
          New York State J Medicine, 1980, 1:121-124.

19, 244. La Casce, Steward.   Swift on medical extremism.   J His-
          tory Ideas, 1970, 31:599-606.
19, 245. Laing, R. D., & Cooper, D. G.   Reason and Violence: A
          Decade of Sartre's Philosophy 1950-1960.   London:
          Tavistock, 1964.
19, 246. Lakoff, Robin T.   Language and interpretation in psycho-
          analysis; review article.   Language, 1978, 54:377-394.
19, 247- Landau, Elliott D., Epstein, Sherrie L., & Stone, Ann P.
      8. (eds).   The Exceptional Child Through Literature.
          Englewood Cliffs, NJ: Prentice-Hall, 1978.
19, 249. Lapati, Americo D.   Skinner and the nature of psychology.
          New Scholasticism, 1976, 50:376-379.
19, 250. Laskowsky, Henry J.   The rhetoric of sex.   Colorado Q,
          1974, 23:149-157.
19, 251. Laverty, C. D.   Science and Pseudo-Science in the Writ-
          ings of Edgar Allan Poe.   Doctoral dissertation, Duke
          Univ., 1951.
19, 252. Lawson, Richard H.   Poets and physicians in Arthur
          Schnitzler's 'The Bachelor's Death' and 'An Author's
          Last Letter.'   In Peschel, E. R. (ed), Medicine and
          Literature.   NY: Watson, 1980, 48-55.
19, 253. Le Unes, Arnold.   Psychological thrillers revisited: a
          tentative list of 'master thrillers.'   Amer Psychol,
          1974, 29:211-213.
19, 254. Leary, Timothy.   The Politics of Ecstasy.   NY: Putnam,
          1968.
19, 255. Lee, Bill, & Lee, Lynn.   An analysis of Thoreau's hand-
          writing.   Thoreau Society Bulletin, 1970, No. 113, 4-5.
19, 256. Lee, Irving J.   A Study of Emotional Appeal in Rhetorical
          Theory, with Special Reference to Invention, Arrange-
          ment, and Style.   Summaries of doctoral dissertations,
          Northwestern Univ., 1939, 7:36-40.
19, 257. Lee, Virgil J., Jr.   The Face in Shakespeare: A Study
          of Facial Gesture and Attitude as Aspects of Dramatic
          Energeia.   DAI, 1970, 30:4416A.

19, 258.   Lehman, H. C.   The chronological ages of greatest pro-
            ductivity: chemists, inventors, poets, et altera.   Psy-
            chol Bulletin, 1935, 32:676.
19, 259.   Lehnhoff, Wilhelm.   Spiele und Streiche aus den Kindheit-
            stagen der Dichter und Meister.   Leipzig: Brandstet-
            ter, 1913.
19, 260.   Lenneberg, Eric Heinz.   The neurology of language.   In
            Bloomfield, M. W., & Haugen, E. I. (eds), Language As
            a Human Problem.   NY: Norton, 1975, 101-119.
19, 261.   Levi, Albert William.   Literature, Philosophy and Imagi-
            nation.   Bloomington: Indiana Univ. Press, 1962.
19, 262.   _____.   The uses of the humanities in personal life.
            J Aesthetic Education, 1976, 10:5-17.
19, 263.   Levitas, G. B. (ed).   The World of Psychology, 2 Vols.
            NY: Braziller, 1963, 1965.
19, 264.   Levy, F.   [Contribution to the psychodynamic study of
            doctor-patient relationship.]   Psychologie Médicale,
            1973, 5:345-357.
19, 265.   Levy, H.   Iowa theater lab's Moby Dick.   Drama Rev,
            1975, 19:63-67.
19, 266.   Lewin, B. D.   The train ride--a study of one of Freud's
            figures of speech.   Psychoanal Q, 1970, 39:71-89.
19, 267.   Lewis, Clarence Irving.   Four-letter words.   In Selected
            Literary Essays.   NY: Cambridge Univ. Press, 1969,
            169-174.
19, 268.   Lewis, Felice F.   Literature and the Obscenity Question:
            Trends in Fiction Involved in Obscenity Litigation in
            the United States, 1821-1870, and Literary Implications
            of Judicial Decisions.   DAI, 1974, 35:1015A.
19, 269.   Leytham, G. W. H.   Literary statistics.   Bulletin British
            Psychol Society, 1959, 37:14-17.
19, 270.   Lidderdale, Jane, & Nicholson, Mary.   Mr. Joyce's
            dreadful eye attack.   James Joyce Q, 1970, 7:186-190.
19, 271.   Likhenshtein, E. I.   [Medical themes in the works of L.
            N. Tolstoi.]   Klinischeskia Meditsina, 1960, 38:141-
            148.
19, 272.   Lind, Katherine W.   The social psychology of children's
            reading.   Amer J Sociology, 1936, 41:454-469.
19, 273.   Lindauer, Martin S.   Duration aspects of time related
            words.   Perceptual & Motor Skills, 1969, 9:100-101.
19, 274.   _____.   The nature and use of the cliché.   J General
            Psychol, 1968, 78:133-143.
19, 275.   Lindner, M.   Die Medizin im Leben Schillers.   Zahn-
            ärztliche Mitteilungen, 1955, 9:289-291.
19, 276.   Line, W. H.   Shakespeare's doctors.   Midland Medical J,
            1906, 5:86-88.
19, 277.   Lippmann, Walter.   Preface to Politics.   NY: Holt, 1913.
19, 278.   Lipton, Lawrence.   The Erotic Revolution.   Los Angeles:
            Sherbourne, 1965.
19, 279.   Loeb, Edwin.   The function of proverbs in the intellectual
            development of primitive peoples.   Scientific Monthly,
            1952, 74:100-104.
19, 280.   Logan, John Frederick.   The age of intoxication.   Yale
            French Studies, 1974, 50:81-95.

19, 281. López Méndez, H. La medicina en el Quijota. Madrid: Quevedo, 1969.

19, 282. Lopez Piñero, J. M. La medicina y la enfermedad en la España de Galdos. Cuadernos Hispanoamerica, 1971, 250:1-14.

19, 283. Loria, L. Medicina e poesia nella vita di Friedrich Schiller. Pagine di storia della medicina, 1959, 3(6): 18-22.

19, 284. Lottan, Sara. The ability of children to distinguish between the 'make believe' and the 'real' in children's literature. Hachinuch: J Educational Thought, 1967, No. 1, 25-33.

19, 285. Louros, N. C. Molière and medicine. Int Surgery, 1978, 63(5): 71-74.

19, 286. Louttit, C. M. An historical note on the application of psychology. J Applied Psychol, 1934, 18:304-305.

19, 287. Low, Marie E. D. Self in Triplicate: The Doctor in the Nineteenth-Century British Novel. DAI, 1973, 34: 2638A.

19, 288. Low, Peter. The physiological idiom in the poetry of Supervielle. J Australasian Univs. Language & Lit Assn, 1976, 46:266-275.

19, 289. Lowbury, E. Pandora's box. Thoughts on health and illness in poetic literature. Annual Rev College Surgeons England, 1973, 53:355-369.

19, 290. Lucey, P. Great literature: a resource for comprehending behavior. Amer J Nursing, 1965, 65:126-128.

19, 291. Lundström, Bengt. [Visual and visionary power: some medical aspects of the case of James Joyce.] Nordisk Medicin historisk Arsbok, 1973, 1-9.

19, 292. Lyons, J. B. James Joyce and Medicine. NY: Oxford Univ. Press, 1973.

19, 293. Lyons, John B. Anatomy in James Joyce's Ulysses. Practitioner, 1972, 209:374-379.

19, 294. McCormick, Jane L. Ghosts in literature. Psychic, 1973, 4(3):44-48.

19, 295. McGlynn, Paul D. Graffiti and slogans: flushing the id. J Popular Culture, 1972, 6:351-356.

19, 296. McHenry, Lawrence C., J. Medical case notes on Samuel Johnson in the Heberden Manuscripts. New Rambler, 1964, 15:11-15.

19, 297. McKellar, Peter. Imagination and Thinking: A Psychological Analysis. NY: Basic Books, 1957.

19, 298. _____. Three aspects of the psychology of originality in human thinking. British J Aesthetics, 1963, 3:129-147.

19, 299. McKenzie, Leon. Analysis of Bildungsroman literature as a research modality in adult education: an inquiry. Adult Education, 1975, 25:209-216.

19, 300. McLeod, A. M. Physiology and medicine in a Greek novel: Achilles Tatius' Leucippe and Clitophon. J Hellenistic Studies, 1969, 89:97-105.

19,301. McMillan, Dougald. transition. The History of a Liter-
         ary Era 1927-1938. NY: Braziller, 1975.
19,302. Madden, J. S. Melancholy in medicine and literature:
         some historical considerations. British J Medical
         Psychol, 1966, 39:125-130.
19,303. Mahony, Patrick J. Freud As a Writer. NY: Interna-
         tional Universities Press, 1980.
19,304. Malfetti, James L., & Eidlitz, E. M. (eds). Perspectives
         on Sexuality. NY: Holt, Rinehart & Winston, 1971.
19,305. Mandrou, R. Magistrats et sorciers en France au 17e
         siecle. Une analyse de psychologie historique. Paris:
         Plon, 1968.
19,306. Mann, Thomas. Freud und die Zukunft. In Adel des
         Geistes. Stockholm: 1945; Freud and the future. In
         Baumer, F. L. (ed), Intellectual Movements in Modern
         European History. NY: Macmillan, 1965, 128-135;
         In Essays of Three Decades. NY: Knopf, 1937, 1947;
         Daedalus, 1959, 88:374-378.
19,307. _____. Freud's position in the history of modern
         thought. Criterion, 1933, 12:549-570; In Past Masters
         and Other Papers. NY: Knopf, 1933; London: Secker,
         1933.
19,308. Mannion, R. A. The scalpel and the pen. François Rabe-
         lais, 1483-1553. Priest, doctor, humanist philosoph-
         er. J Indiana State Medical Assn, 1978, 71:1004-1007.
19,309. _____. The scalpel and the pen. Tobias George
         Smollett, 1721-1771. J Indiana State Medical Assn,
         1978, 71:706-709.
19,310. Mardershtein, I. G. [The Reflection of Physiological The-
         ory of the Brain in Literary Writings.] Tashkent,
         USSR: State Medical Publishing House, 1962.
19,311. Marinescu, E. R. [What girls read.] Anale de Psiholo-
         gie, 1938, 5:102-134.
19,312. Maritain, Jacques. Creative Intuition in Art and Poetry.
         NY: Pantheon, 1960.
19,313. Marks, E. Simone de Beauvoir; Encounters with Death.
         New Brunswick, NJ: Rutgers Univ. Press, 1973.
19,314. Marotti, Arthur F. The purgations of Middleton's The
         Family of Love. Papers on Language & Lit, 1971,
         7:80-84.
19,315. Martin, J. P. Neurology in fiction: 'The Turn of the
         Screw.' British Medical J, 1973, 4:717-721.
19,316. Martin, Wendy. The American Sisterhood; Writings of
         the Feminist Movement from Colonial Times to the
         Present. NY: Harper & Row, 1972.
19,317. Massey, Irwin. The contribution of neurology to the
         scepticism of Alfred de Vigny. J History Medicine,
         July 1954.
19,318. Masters, R. E. L. Forbidden Sexual Behavior and Moral-
         ity. NY: Lancer, 1962.
19,319. _____. Sex, ecstacy and psychedelics. In Robinson,
         F., & Lehrman, N. (eds), Sex American Style.
         Chicago: Playboy Press, 1971, 144-180.

19,320.   _____, & Houston, J.   The Varieties of Psychedelic
           Experience.   NY: Holt, Rinehart & Winston, 1966;
           NY: Dell, 1967.

19,321.   Matson, Elson L.   A Study of Years of Formal Education
           As a Factor in Audience Response to Ideational Con-
           tent and Treatment in Plays.   Ann Arbor, Mich: Uni-
           versity Microfilm No. 4975, 1953.

19,322.   Matthews, F. H.   The Americanization of Sigmund Freud:
           adaptations of psychoanalysis before 1917.   J Amer
           Studies, 1967, 1:39-62.

19,323.   Maxwell, Desmond E. S.   American Fiction: The Intellect-
           ual Background.   NY: Columbia Univ. Press, 1963.

19,324.   May, Robert.   Sex and Fantasy.   Patterns of Male and
           Female.   NY: Norton, 1980.

19,325.   Meagher, John C.   Vanity, Lear's feather, and the path-
           ology of editorial annotation.   In Leech, C., & Marge-
           son, J. M. R.   (eds), World Shakespeare Congress.
           Toronto: Univ. Toronto Press, 1972, 244-259.

19,326.   Medawar, Peter B.   Science and literature.   Encounter,
           1969, 32(1):15-23.

19,327.   Mertz, D. P., & Burger, F.   Zur Darstellung der Gicht
           in Geschichte, Satire und Malerie.   Fortschritt Medi-
           zin, 1978, 96:1257-1260.

19,328.   Mette, Alexander.   Medizin und Morphologie in Büchners
           Schaffen.   Sinn und Form, 1963, 15:747-755.

19,329.   _____.   Die physiologischen Dissertationen Friedrich
           Schillers im Blickfeld der heutigen Medizin.   Zeit-
           schrift für Geschichte der Naturwissenschaften, Tech-
           nik und Medizin, 1960, 1:35-49.

19,330.   _____.   Schillers physiologische Schriften in ihrer
           Beziehung zur heutigen Hirnphysiologie.   Aufbau, 1955,
           11:898-904.

19,331.   Meve, E. B.   L. N. Tolstoi i A. P. Chekhov o G. A. Zak-
           harine.   Klinische Medizin (Moskow), 1979, 57(5):107-
           109.

19,332.   Mew, Peter.   Projection and expression.   British J Aes-
           thetics, 1972, 12:354-358.

19,333.   Michelson, Peter.   The Aesthetics of Pornography.   NY:
           Heider, 1971.

19,334.   Mickel, Emanuel John.   The Artificial Paradises in French
           Literature.   The Influence of Opium and Hashish on
           the Literature of French Romanticism and Les Fleurs
           du Mal.   Durham: Univ. North Carolina Press,
           1969.

19,335.   _____.   The Influence of Opium and Hashish on French
           Literature in the First Half of the Nineteenth Century.
           DA, 1966, 27:184.

19,336.   Miège, Denise.   Littérature erotique feminine.   Vol. 2:
           Du XIXe siècle à nos jours.   Paris: Civilisation nou-
           velle, 1973.

19,337.   Milic, Louis T.   Winged words: varieties of computer
           application to literature.   Computer & the Humanities,
           1967, 2:24-31.

19,338.   Miller, Donald S., & Davis, E.H.   Shakespeare and
          orthopedics.   Surgery Gynecology Obstetrics, 1969,
          128:358-366.
19,339.   Miller, Henry.   The rise of schizophrenia.   New English
          Weekly, 1936, 10:69-70.
19,340.   Miller, Jonathan (ed).   Freud: The Man, His World, His
          Influence.   Boston: Little, Brown, 1972.
19,341.   Millett, Kate.   Sexual Politics.   Garden City, NY: Dou-
          bleday, 1970; NY: Avon, 1971; Review: Meredith
          Tax, Ramparts, 1970, 9(5):50-58.
19,342.   Millhauser, Milton.   Science, literature, and the image
          of man.   Humanist, 1963, 23:85-88.
19,343.   Minor, Nata.   Capitales de non-lieu: Vienne, Freud,
          Schnitzler.   Critique, 1975, 339-340.
19,344.   Missreigler, Anton.   Uber das Verlieben in Autoren.
          Fortschritte der Sexualwissenschaft und Psychoanalyse,
          1926, 2:513-518.
19,345.   Mitchell, John D.   Applied psychoanalysis in the director-
          actor relationship.   Amer Imago, 1956, 13:223-339.
19,346.   Mitchell, S.   Sentiment and suffering: women's recrea-
          tional reading in the 1860s.   Victorian Studies, 1977,
          21:29-45.
19,347.   Mizzau, Marina.   Semantica e psicoanalisi.   Verri, 1968,
          28:79-86.
19,348.   Mogilnicki, R.L.   The Educational Implications of Some
          Writings on the Development of the Affective Domain
          in Children.   DA, 1969, 29(11-A):3919.
19,349.   Monahan, John.   John Stuart Mill on the liberty of the
          mentally ill: a historical note.   Amer J Psychiat,
          1977, 134:1428-1429.
19,350.   Mondor, H.   Les Médecins consultants dans Proust.
          Formes et Couleurs, 1943, 3.
19,351.   Monod-Cassidy, Hélène.   Le Mesmérisme: Opinions
          contemporaines.   Studies in Voltaire & the Eighteenth
          Century, 1972, 89:1077-1087.
19,352.   Montaigne, Michel E. de.   Of drunkenness.   In Complete
          Works.   NY: Arts, 1953, 244-251.
19,353.   Moody, Stanley E.   Experimental Study of the Concentra-
          tions of Audience Interest in Ten Theatre Productions.
          DA, 1956, 16:2557.
19,354.   Moore, John R.   Defoe's project for lie-detection.   Amer
          J Psychol, 1955, 68:672.
19,355.   Moorman, L.J.   Tuberculosis and Genius.   Chicago:
          Univ. Chicago Press, 1940.
19,356.   Morawski, Stefan.   Art and obscenity.   JAAC, 1967, 26:
          193-207.
19,357.   Morgan, George Allen.   What Nietzsche Means.   NY:
          Harper & Row, 1965.
19,358.   Morgan, Michael J.   Molyneux's Question: Vision, Touch
          and the Philosophy of Perception.   London: Cambridge
          Univ. Press, 1977.
19,359.   Morgan, W.L., & Leahy, A.M.   The cultural content of
          general interest magazines.   J Educational Psychol,
          1934, 25:530-536.

19, 360.   Morris, Phyllis Sutton.   Sartre's Concept of a Person:
           An Analytic Approach.   Amherst: Univ. Massachu-
           setts Press, 1975.
19, 361.   Morton, Frederic.   A Nervous Splendor.   Vienna, 1888-
           1889.   Boston: Atlantic-Little, Brown, 1979.
19, 362.   Motley, Michael T.   An analysis of Spoonerisms as psy-
           cholinguistic phenomena.   Speech Monographs, 1973,
           40: 66-71.
19, 363.   Mukárovský, Jan.   Structure, Sign, and Function.   New
           Haven: Yale Univ. Press, 1978.
19, 364.   Mullen, F. G., Jr.   Estimation of the universality of
           Freudian and Jungian sexual symbols.   Perceptual &
           Motor Skills, 1968, 26: 1041-1042.
19, 365.   Muller, Herbert J.   Science and Criticism.   NY: Brazil-
           ler, 1956, 130-172.
19, 366.   Müller, O.   Friedrich Schillers Doctordissertation.   Ein
           psychiatrischer Beitrag zu seiner Säkularfeier.   All-
           gemeine Zeitschrift für Psychiatrie und psychische-
           gerichtliche Medizin, 1859, 16: 751-766.
19, 367.   Murray, T. J.   Dr. Samuel Johnson's movement disorder.
           British Medical J, 1979, 1: 1610-1614.

19, 368.   Naevestad, Marie.   The Colors of Rage and Love.   Oslo:
           Universitetsforlaget, 1979.
19, 369.   Nardelli, Robert R.   Some aspects of creative reading.
           J Educational Research, 1957, 50: 495-508.
19, 370.   Neaman, Judith S.   Suggestions of the Devil, the Origins
           of Madness.   Garden City, NY: Anchor, 1975.
19, 371.   Nethersole, Reingard.   Poets, poetry and philosophy:
           some thoughts on Heidegger's influence upon German
           literature and literary criticism since the war.   Eng-
           lish Studies in Africa, 1978, 21: 99-106.
19, 372.   Newton, Esther.   Mother Camp: Female Impersonators
           in America.   Englewood Cliffs, NJ: Prentice-Hall,
           1972.
19, 373.   Newton, William.   Hardy and the naturalists: their use
           of physiology.   Modern Philology, 1951, 49: 28-41.
19, 374.   Nichol, B. P.   Some beginning writings on Gertrude
           Stein's theories of personality.   Open Letter (Toronto),
           1972, 2d Series, No. 2: 41-47.
19, 375.   Niederland, William G.   Clinical aspects of creativity.
           Amer Imago, 1967, 24: 6-34.
19, 376.   Nixon, H. K.   Psychology for the Writer.   NY: Harper,
           1928.
19, 377.   Nobel, D.   George Henry Lewes, George Eliot and the
           physiological society.   J Physiology (London), 1976,
           263: 45P-54P.
19, 378.   Nobile, Philip (ed).   The New Eroticism; Theories,
           Vogues and Canons.   NY: Random House, 1971.
19, 379.   Noland, Richard W.   Developmental psychology and the
           arts.   Massachusetts Rev, 1975, 16: 357-368.
19, 380.   Nordentoft, Kresten.   Kierkegaard's psykologi.   Copen-
           hagen: Gad, 1972.

19,381.   Norris, C.   William Empson and the Philosophy of Liter-
          ary Criticism.   Atlantic Highlands, NJ: Humanities
          Press, 1978; Review: R. Fuller, Encounter, 1979,
          53:41-42.
19,382.   Norris, C. B.   The Image of Physicians in Modern Amer-
          ican Literature.   Doctoral dissertation, Univ. Mary-
          land, 1969.
19,383.   Norton, Rictor Carl.   The homosexual literary tradition:
          course outline and objectives.   College English, 1974,
          35:674-692.

19,384.   Oberhelman, Steve.   Popular dream-interpretation in an-
          cient Greece and Freudian psychoanalysis.   J Popular
          Culture, 1977, 11:683-695.
19,385.   O'Dell, Scott.   An adventure with memory and words.
          Psychol Today, 1968, 1(8):40-43.
19,386.   O'Driscoll, Robert.   Yeats on personality: three unpub-
          lished lectures.   In O'Driscoll, R., & Reynolds, L.
          (eds), Yeats and the Theatre.   NY: Maclean-Hunter,
          1975, 4-59.
19,387.   Ormsby-Lennon, Hugh.   Radical physicians and conserva-
          tive poets in Restoration England: Dryden among the
          doctors.   Studies in Eighteenth-Century Culture, 1978,
          7:389-411.
19,388.   Osborn, M. L.   The source of Shakespeare's medical
          knowledge.   Rivista Storia Medicina, 1976, 20:180-186.
19,389.   Oscoy de Ortiz, S.   El poeta Manuel Acuna en la escuela
          de medicina.   Boletin Societe Mexicana Historia Filo-
          sofia Medicina, 1978, 4(22):13-19.
19,390.   Osgood, Charles R., Suci, G. J., & Tannenbaum, P. H.
          The Measurement of Meaning.   Urbana: Univ. Illinois
          Press, 1957.

19,391.   Panara, R. F.   The deaf writer in America from Colonial
          times to 1970.   I-II.   Amer Annals of the Deaf, 1970,
          115:509-513, 673-679.
19,392.   Partridge, Burgo.   A History of Orgies.   NY: Crown,
          1960; NY: Avon, 1960.
19,393.   Paul, Sherman.   Toward a general semantics literary
          theory.   ETC, 1947, 4:31-37.
19,394.   Payne, William M.   American literary criticism and the
          doctrine of evolution.   Int Monthly, 1900, 2.
19,395.   Pearsall, Ronald.   The Worm in the Bud: The World of
          Victorian Sexuality.   NY: Macmillan, 1969.
19,396.   Peller, Lili E.   Daydreams and children's favorite books.
          In The Psychoanalytic Study of the Child, Vol. 14.
          NY: IUP, 1959, 414-433.
19,397.   Peraza de Ayala, Trino.   La psiquiatria española en el
          siglo XIX.   Madrid: Consejo Superior de Investiga-
          ciones Cientificas, 1947.
19,398.   Perceau, Louis.   Bibliographie du roman érotique au XIX
          siècle.   2 Vols.   Paris: Fourdrinier, 1930.

19, 399. Perris, Noel. Dr. Bowdler's Legacy; a History of Expurgated Books in England and America. NY: Atheneum, 1969.

19, 400. Peschel, Enid Rhodes (ed). Medicine and Literature. New Haven, Conn: Watson, 1980.

19, 401. Peterson, Audrey C. Brain fever in 19th century literature: fact and fiction. Victorian Studies, 1976, 19: 445-464.

19, 402. Peyre, Henri. The doctor as man of letters. In Peschel, E. R. (ed), Medicine and Literature. NY: Watson, 1980, 39-47.

19, 403. Philipson, Morris. Outline of a Jungian Aesthetics. Evanston, Ill: Northwestern Univ. Press, 1963.

19, 404. Pickard, P. M. I Could a Tale Unfold: Violence, Horror and Sensationalism in Stories for Children. London: Tavistock, 1961. Atlantic Highlands, NJ: Humanities, 1961.

19, 405. Pilon, A. Barbara. Non-stereotyped literature for today's bright girls. Gifted Child Q, 1977, 21:234-238.

19, 406. Pitcher, Evelyn G., & Prelinger, Ernst. Children Tell Stories. An Analysis of Fantasy. NY: IUP, 1963, 1973.

19, 407. Pizer, Donald. Evolutionary ideas in late nineteenth-century English and American literary criticism. JAAC, 1961, 19:305-310.

19, 408. _____. The problem of philosophy in the novel. Bucknell Rev, 1970, 18:53-62.

19, 409. Plank, Robert. Spontaneous projection of meaningful forms. J Projective Techniques, 1957, 21:142-147.

19, 410. Plaut, Paul. Psychologie der produktiven Persönlichkeit. Stuttgart: 1929.

19, 411. Plutchik, Robert. Language for the emotions. Psychol Today, 1980, 13:68-69+.

19, 412. Pollin, Burton. Nicholson's lost portrait of William Godwin: a study in phrenology. Keats-Shelley J, 1967, 16:51-60.

19, 413. Pollock, Thomas C. The Nature of Literature: Its Relation to Science, Language, and Human Experience. Princeton: Princeton Univ. Press, 1942.

19, 414. Pomeranz, Herman. Medicine in the Shakespearean Plays and Dickens's Doctors. NY: Powell, 1936.

19, 415. Porter, Laurence M. Syphilis as muse in Thomas Mann's Doctor Faustus. In Peschel, E. R. (ed), Medicine and Literature. New Haven, Conn: Watson, 1980, 147-152.

19, 416. Porterfield, A. L. Mirror Mirror: On Seeing Yourself in Books. Dallas: Texas Christian Univ. Press, 1957.

19, 417. Potestà, P. [Edgar Allan Poe epistemologist.] Medicina nei Secoli, 1978, 5:281-287.

19, 418. Poulet, Georges. Phenomenology of reading. New Lit History, 1969, 1:53-68.

19, 419. Powdermaker, Hortense. An anthropologist looks at the movies. Annals Amer Academy Political Social Sciences, 1947, 254:8-87.

19, 420. _____. Hollywood, the Dream Factory; An Anthropologist Looks at the Movie Makers. Boston: Little,
Brown, 1950.

19, 421. Prätorius, Numa. Bibliographie der Homosexualität. II:
Belletristik. Jahrbuch für Sexuelle Zwischenstufen,
1908, 9.

19, 422. Primiero, M. L'igiene e la cultura fisica nei poemi
omerici. Rivista Storia Medica, 1973, 17:25-30.

19, 423. Pufe, B. Medizingeschichtliche Elemente in Epigrammen
der Anthologia Graeca. Doctoral dissertation, Er-
langen-Nürnberg, 1978.

19, 424. Pyle, Wilma J. Sexism in children's literature. Theory
and Practice, 1976, 15:116-119.

19, 425. Quaytman, Wilfred. Ego factors in psychotherapist's
writing block. J Contemporary Psychotherapy, 1973,
5:135-139.

19, 426. Rajadurai, E. B. Shakespeare and the Renaissance Sciences: An Annotated Bibliography. Doctoral dissertation, Kent State Univ., 1970.

19, 427. Ramzy, I. From Aristotle to Freud. Bulletin Menninger
Clinic, 1956, 20:112-123.

19, 428. Rasmussen, E. The physician in Norwegian literature.
Tidskrift for den Norske Laegeforening, 1961, 81:701-
705.

19, 429. Raushenbush, Esther. Literature for Individual Education. NY: Columbia Univ. Press, 1942.

19, 430. Read, John. Science, literature, and human thought. J
Chemical Education, 1960, 37:110-117.

19, 431. Reade, Brian (ed). Sexual Heretics--Male Sexuality in
English Literature from 1850 to 1900. NY: Coward-
McCann, 1970; London: Routledge & Kegan Paul,
1970.

19, 432. Reedy, D. R. Signs and symbols of doctors in the Diente
del Parnaso. Hispania, 1964, 47:705-710.

19, 433. Reggy, Mae Alice. Self-Concept and Race: Basis for
Reactions to a Short Story? DAI, 1976, 37:3488-89.

19, 434. _____. Self-identity through literature. College English, 1973, 35:307-311.

19, 435. Regula, M., & Jernej, J. Grammatica italiana descrit-
tiva su basi storiche e psicologiche. Bern: Francke,
1965.

19, 436. Reichart, R. R., & Laslett, H. R. A study of the value
of high-school literature courses. J Educational Psychol, 1939, 30:421-439.

19, 437. Reisner, Robert. Erotic messages on lavatory walls.
Sexology, 1969, 35:601-603.

19, 438. _____. Graffiti: Two Thousand Years of Wall Writing.
NY: Cowles, 1972.

19, 439. _____. Show Me the Good Parts: The Reader's Guide
to Sex in Literature. NY: Citadel, 1964.

19,440. Reiss, Edmund. Whitman's debt to animal magnetism. PMLA, 1963, 78:80-88.

19,441. Reitz, --. Schillers Dissertation und die neue Psychologie. Stuttgarter Neues Tagesblatt, no. 102, 2 Mar 1934.

19,442. Ribon, J. F. Dostoievsky: prophète ou antéchrist. Evolution Psychiatrique, 1972, 37:205-223.

19,443. Richards, Bernard. Mercury and syphilis: word-play in Sedley and Congreve. Notes & Queries, 1978, 25:32-34.

19,444. Richet, C. Le Langage et l'intelligence. Rev de deux Mondes, 1925, 25:555-572.

19,445. Rickman, J. On quotations. Int J Psycho-Anal, 1929, 10:242-248.

19,446. Ricoeur, Paul. Freud and Philosophy. New Haven: Yale Univ. Press, 1970.

19,447. _____. Image and language in psychoanalysis. In Smith, J. H. (ed), Psychoanalysis and Language. New Haven: Yale Univ. Press, 1978, 293-324.

19,448. Riesman, David. The Oral Tradition. The Written Word, and the Screen Image. Yellow Springs, Ohio: Antioch Press, 1956.

19,449. Riley, Mark. Purpose and unity of Plutarch's De genio Socratis. Greek Roman & Byzantine Studies, 1977, 18:257-273.

19,450. Roback, Abraham A. Curiosities of Yiddish Literature. Cambridge, Mass: Sci-Art, 1933.

19,451. Robbins, C. W. Sartre and the moral life. Philosophy, 1977. 52:409-424.

19,452. Robin, P. A. The Old Physiology in English Literature. London: 1911.

19,453. Rocchietta, S. [Two centuries of English songs with medico-pharmaceutical themes.] Minerva Medica, 1979, 70:2839-2843.

19,454. Roddey, Gloria J. The Metaphor of Counsel: A Shift from Objective Realism to Psychological Subjectivism in the Conceptual Cosmology of Puritanism. DAI, 1970, 31:367A-68A.

19,455. Rodgers, B. The Queens' Vernacular. A Gay Lexicon. San Francisco: Straight Arrow Books, 1972.

19,456. Rof Carballo, Juan. Medicina y actividad creadora. Madrid: Revista de Occidente, 1964.

19,457. Rogers, J. F. Genius and health. Scientific Monthly, 1926, 23:509-518.

19,458. Rohovit, D. Dean. Metaphor and mind. Amer Imago, 1960, 17:289-309.

19,459. Rosenberg, B. G., & Sutton-Smith, B. Sex and Identity. NY: Holt, Rinehart & Winston, 1972.

19,460. Rosenham, Mollie Schwartz. Images of male and female in children's readers. In Atkinson, D., et al. (eds), Women in Russia. Palo Alto, Cal: Stanford Univ. Press, 1977, 293-305.

19,461. Ross, S. D. Literature and Philosophy: An Analysis of the Philosophical Novel. NY: Appleton-Century-Crofts, 1969.

19,462.   Rothenberg, Alan B. , & Hausman, C.R.   The Creativity
          Question.   Durham, North Carolina: Duke Univ. Press,
          1976.
19,463.   Rougemont, Denis de.   Love in the Western World.   NY:
          Harcourt Brace, 1940; London: Faber, 1940; NY:
          Pantheon, 1956.
19,464.   Rousseau, George S.   Doctors and Medicine in the Novels
          of Tobias Smollett.   DA, 1967, 27:2160A.
19,465.   _____.   Science and the discovery of the imagination in
          enlightened England.   Eighteenth Century Studies, 1969,
          3:108-134.
19,466.   Rovit, Earl.   American literary ego: an essay in psycho-
          history.   Southern Rev, 1978, 14:409-427.
19,467.   Royce, Joseph R. (ed).   Psychology and the Symbol: An
          Interdisciplinary Symposium.   NY: Random House,
          1965.
19,468.   Rowen, M.J.   Doctors and Robert Louis Stevenson.   J
          Medical Society New Jersey, 1978, 75:482-483.
19,469.   Rubinstein, B.B.   On metaphor and related phenomena.
          Psychoanal & Contemporary Science, 1972, 1:70-108.
19,470.   Ruthrof, H.G.   Reading works of literary art.   J Aesthetic
          Education, 1974, 8(4):75-90.

19,471.   Sagarin, Edward.   The Anatomy of Dirty Words.   NY:
          Stuart, 1962.
19,472.   Sagebiel, R.W.   Medicine in the life and letters of Samuel
          Johnson.   I.   The status of medicine in the 18th cen-
          tury.   Ohio Medical J, 1961, 57:382-384.
19,473.   _____.   Medicine in the life and letters of Samuel John-
          son.   II,   Dr. Johnson's personal ailments.   Ohio Medi-
          cal J, 1961, 57:520-522.
19,474.   Said, Edward William.   Beginnings: Intention and Method.
          NY: Basic Books, 1975.
19,475.   Salm, Peter.   The Poem As Plant: A Biological View of
          Goethe's Faust.   Cleveland: Case Western Reserve
          Press, 1971.
19,476.   Sams, Henry W.   Malinowski and the novel; or, cultural
          anthropology versus mere fiction.   J General Education,
          1974, 26:125-138.
19,477.   Sánchez Granjel, Luis.   Médicos novelistas y novelistas
          médicos.   Salamanca: Real Academia de Medecina,
          1973.
19,478.   _____.   La personalidad médica de Pío Baroja.   Medi-
          cal History (Barcelona), 1973, 20:8-26.
19,479.   Sancho de San Román, R.   El quéhacer médico en la obra
          de Tirso de Molina.   Bolétin de la Sociedad Española
          de Historia de la Medicina, 1962, 2(4).
19,480.   Sanders, Jacquelyn.   Psychological significance of chil-
          dren's literature.   Library Q, 1967, 37:15-22.
19,481.   Sanguiliano, Iris.   Moon-gazing and the creative process:
          an encounter with writers.   Psychotherapy: Theory,
          Research & Practice, 1971, 8:307-309.

19,482. Sano, Katsuo. College students' attitudes toward literature. Japanese J Psychol, 1950, 20(3):27-32.

19,483. Santiago, Luciano P.R. The lyrical expression of adolescent conflict in the Beatles' songs. Adolescence, 1969,
4:199-210.

19,484. Santucci, Luigi. Das Kind--Sein Mythos und sein Märchen.
Hanover: Schroedel, 1964.

19,485. Sartre, Jean-Paul. Imagination: A Psychological Critique.
Ann Arbor: Univ. Michigan Press, 1962.

19,486. Saueressig, Heinz. Literatur und Medizin: Zu Thomas
Manns Roman Der Zauberberg. Deutsche Medizinische
Wochenschrift, 1974, 99:1780-1786.

19,487. _____. Die medizinische Region des Zauberberg. In
Rothe, W. (ed), Die deutsche Literatur in der Weimarer
Republik. Stuttgart: Reclam, 1974, 141-155.

19,488. Scanlon, Leone. Essays on the Effect of Feminism and
Socialism upon the Literature of 1880-1914. DAI, 1974,
34:4218A.

19,489. Scarborough, John. Roman Medicine. Ithaca, NY: Cornell Univ. Press, 1969.

19,490. Scarlett, E.P. Some hoaxes in medical history and literature. Archives Internal Medicine, 1964, 113:291-296.

19,491. Schaechter, Mordkhe. Max Weinreich's translation of
Freud. In For Max Weinreich on His Seventieth Birthday: Studies in Jewish Languages, Literature and Society. The Hague: Mouton, 1964, 306-319.

19,492. Schechner, Mark. James Joyce and psychoanalysis: a
selected checklist. James Joyce Q, 1976, 13:383-384.

19,493. Scher, Steven P., et al. (comps). A bibliography on the
relations of literature and the other arts, 1973. Hartford Studies in Lit, 1974, 6:87-107.

19,494. Schick, Alfred. The pluralism of psychiatry in Vienna.
Psychoanal Rev, 1978, 65:14-37.

19,495. _____. The Vienna of Sigmund Freud. Psychoanal
Rev, 1968-69, 55:529-551.

19,496. Schmidt, Peter. Gesundheit und Krankheit in romantischer
Medizin und Erzählkunst. Jahrbuch des freien deutschen
Hochstifts, 1966, 197-228.

19,497. Schorske, Carl E. Fin-de-Siecle. Vienna Politics-Culture.
NY: Knopf, 1979.

19,498. _____. Politics and the psyche in fin de siecle Vienna:
Schnitzler and Hofmannsthal. Amer Historical Rev,
1961, 66:930-946.

19,499. Schroeder, Theodore Albert. Legal Obscenity and Sexual
Psychology. NY: 1908.

19,500. Schubert, Delwyn G. The relationship between reading
ability and literary appreciation. California J Educational Research, 1953, 4:201-202.

19,501. Schwaber, Paul. Scientific art: The Interpretation of
Dreams. In The Psychoanalytic Study of the Child,
Vol. 31. New Haven: Yale Univ. Press, 1976, 515-
533.

19,502. Schwartz, R.B. Samuel Johnson and the New Science.
Madison: Univ. Madison Press, 1971.

19, 503. Schwyzer, Hans-Rudolf. The intellect in Plotinus and the archetype of C. G. Jung. In Mansfield, J. , & de Rijk, L. M. (eds), Kephalaion. Atlantic Highlands, NJ: Humanities Press, 1975, 214-222.

19, 504. Scott, Colin A. Sex and art. Amer J Psychol, 1896, 7.

19, 505. Scott, Donald F. Epilepsy in literature. In About Epilepsy. NY: IUP, 1969, Ch. 12.

19, 506. Screech, M. A. Medicine and literature: aspects of Rabelais and Montaigne. In Sharratt, P. (ed), French Renaissance Studies 1540-70: Humanism and the Encyclopedia. Edinburgh: Edinburgh Univ. Press, 1976, 156-169.

19, 507. Sebeok, Thomas A. (ed). Style in Language. NY: Wiley, 1960.

19, 508. Sechrist, Frank K. The Psychology of Unconventional Language. Worcester, Mass: 1913.

19, 509. Sederberg, Peter C. , & Sederberg, Nancy B. Transmitting the nontransmissible: the function of literature in the pursuit of social knowledge. Philosophy & Phenomenological Research, 1975, 36:173-196.

19, 510. Segal, Charles Paul. Humanism and classical literature: modern problems and perspectives. Classical J, 1971, 67:29-37.

19, 511. Segers, Rien T. Studies in Semiotics: The Evaluation of Literary Texts. Lisse: Ridder, 1978.

19, 512. Segre, Cesare. I segni e la critica: Fra strutturalismo e semiologia. Turin: Einaudi, 1969.

19, 513. _____. Semiotics and Literary Criticism. The Hague: Mouton, 1973.

19, 514. Seidel, George J. The unconscious and creativity. In The Crisis of Creativity. Notre Dame, Indiana: Univ. Notre Dame Press, 1966, 51-122.

19, 515. Sena, John Francis. The English Maladay: The Idea of Melancholy from 1700 to 1760. Doctoral dissertation, Princeton Univ. , 1967.

19, 516. _____. Swift, the Yahoos and 'The English Malady. ' Papers on Language & Lit, 1971, 7:300-303.

19, 517. Servadio, Emilio. Psicologia dell'attore. In Conferenze dell'Associoazione Culturale Italiana, No. 4. Turin: A. C. I. , 1960-61, 55-69.

19, 518. Seskin, Jane, & Ziegler, B. Older Women/Younger Men. Garden City, NY: Doubleday Anchor, 1979.

19, 519. Sewell, Elizabeth. First reports from an experimental college. J Applied Behavioral Science, 1968, 4:351-359.

19, 520. _____. Science and literature. Commonweal, 1966, 84:218-221, 448-449.

19, 521. Shaffer, Elinor S. Studies in Coleridge's Aesthetics. DAI, 1967, 28:1409A.

19, 522. Sharma, Arvind. Mescaline and Hindu mystical experience. Studies in Religion/Sciences Religieuses, 1975, 5:171-176.

19, 523. Sharp, Donald B. (ed). Commentaries on Obscenity. Metuchen: Scarecrow, 1970.

19, 524.   Sheed, Wilfred.   The case for dirty linen.   Commonweal,
            1964, 80:448-449.
19, 525.   Sheridan, N.   Doctors and literature.   British Medical J,
            1978, 2:1779-1780.
19, 526.   Sherman, Murray H.   Psychoanalysis and Old Vienna:
            Freud, Reik, Schnitzler, Kraus.   NY: Human Sci-
            ences Press, 1978.
19, 527.   _____.   Psychoanalysis in America: Historical Per-
            spectives.   Springfield, Ill: Thomas, 1966.
19, 528.   Shoemaker, F.   Aesthetic Experience and the Humanities:
            Modern Ideas of Aesthetic Experience in the Reading of
            World Literature.   NY: Columbia Univ. Press, 1943.
19, 529.   Shoenberg, P. J.   A dialogue with Mandeville.   Brit J Psy-
            chiat, 1976, 129:120-124.
19, 530.   Shopper, M.   The use of children's literature and toys in
            the teaching of child development to medical students
            in the preclinical years.   J Amer Academy Child Psy-
            chiat, 1969, 8:1-15.
19, 531.   Shumaker, Wayne.   English Autobiography.   Its Emer-
            gence, Materials, and Form.   Berkeley: Univ. Cali-
            fornia Press, 1954.
19, 532.   _____.   Literature and the Irrational: A Study in An-
            thropological Backgrounds.   Englewood Cliffs, NJ:
            Prentice-Hall, 1960.
19, 533.   Shuttleworth, Frank K.   A critical study of two lists of
            best books for children.   Genetic Psychol, Monographs,
            1932, 11:247-319.
19, 534.   Siegel, C.   Die Bilder und Gleichnisse bei Schopenhauer.
            Zur Psychologie der philosophischen und literarischen
            Form.   Zeitschrift für angewandte Psychologie, 1927,
            29:41-73.
19, 535.   Silberger, Julius.   Using literary materials to teach psy-
            chiatry.   Seminars in Psychiat, 1973, 5:275-285.
19, 536.   Simili, A.   Alessandro Manzoni nel pensiero di un medico.
            Per il centenario della morte.   Minerva Medica, 1973,
            64:4065-4071.
19, 537.   Simpson, R. R.   Shakespeare and Medicine.   London: Liv-
            ingstone, 1959.
19, 538.   Singer, Jerome L.   Vico's insight and the scientific study
            of the stream of consciousness.   In Tagliacozzo, G.,
            et al. (eds), Conference on Vico and Contemporary
            Thought, New York, 1976.   Atlantic Highlands, NJ:
            Humanities Press, 1980, 57-68.
19, 539.   Sirota, S.   Teaching literature through creative drama--
            an aid in the development of balanced expression.
            Mental Health & Society, 1978, 4:55-60.
19, 540.   Sisk, John P.   The promise of dirty words.   Amer Schol-
            ar, 1975, 44:385-404.
19, 541.   Sisson, Charles Jasper.   Shakespeare's Helena and Dr.
            William Harvey.   Essays & Studies, 1960, 13:1-20.
19, 542.   Slochower, Harry.   Applied psychoanalysis as a science
            and as an art.   In Psychoanalysis As an Art and a
            Science; a Symposium by Otto Rank and Others.   De-
            troit: Wayne State Univ. Press, 1968, 165-174.

19, 543.   Smith, Carolyn F.   Religious symbolism and the uncon-
           scious psyche in the 'Four Waters' of Sta. Teresa.
           Revista de Estudios Hispánicos, 9:391-402.
19, 544.   Smith, Henry Nash.   The morals of power: business en-
           terprise as a theme in mid-nineteenth-century American
           fiction.   In Schulz, M. (ed), Essays in American and
           English Literature.   Athens: Ohio Univ. Press, 1967,
           90-107.
19, 545.   Smith, H. Rossiter.   Medicine and poetry.   Notes & Quer-
           ies, 1952, 197:423-425.
19, 546.   Smith, Joseph H., & Parloff, Gloria H. (eds).   Psychoan-
           alysis and Language.   New Haven: Yale Univ. Press,
           1978.
19, 547.   Sobel, Dava.   For stage fright, a remedy proposed.   Sci-
           ence Times.   New York Times, 20 Nov 1979, Section
           C 1, 2.
19, 548.   Sohngen, M.   The writer as an old woman.   Gerontologist,
           1975, 15:493-498.
19, 549.   Solomon, David (ed).   The Marijuana Papers.   Philadelphia:
           Bobbs-Merrill, 1966; NY: Signet, 1968, 145-266.
19, 550.   Sontag, Susan.   Illness as Metaphor.   NY: Farrar, Straus
           & Giroux, 1978; NY: Vintage, 1978; New York Rev of
           Books; Vol. 24, Nos. 21 & 22 (26 Jan 1978); 25, No. 1
           (9 Feb 1978); 25, No. 2 (23 Feb) 1978.
19, 551.   Sorenson, Robert C., & Sorenson, Theodore C.   A pro-
           posal for the use of content analysis evidence in literary
           infringement cases.   Social Forces, 1955, 33:262-267.
19, 552.   Soupault, Robert.   Marcel Proust du côté de la médecine.
           Paris: Plon, 1967.
19, 553.   Spanos, William V. (ed).   Martin Heidegger and the Ques-
           tion of Literature; Toward a Post-Modern Literary Her-
           meneutics.   Bloomington: Indiana Univ. Press, 1980.
19, 554.   Spradin, W.W.   Drama as an adjunct to teaching human
           behavior.   J Medical Education, 1966, 41:377-380.
19, 555.   Springmann, R.R.   On the use of the seventh Hebrew letter
           as a phallic symbol.   Psychiat Q, 1969, 43:472-476.
19, 556.   Sprott, Samuel Ernest.   The English Debate on Suicide from
           Donne to Hume.   LaSalle, Ill: Open Court, 1961.
19, 557.   Stambolian, George, & Marks, Elaine.   Homosexualities
           and French Literature: Cultural Contexts/Critical Texts.
           Ithaca, NY: Cornell Univ. Press, 1979.
19, 558.   Starbuck, E.D., et al.   A Guide to Books for Character.
           Vol. II.   Fiction.   NY: Macmillan, 1930.
19, 559.   Starch, D.   The 100 greatest books selected by 100 quali-
           fied persons.   J Applied Psychol, 1942, 26:257-267.
19, 560.   Steig, Michael.   George Cruikshank and the grotesque: a
           psychodynamic approach.   In Patten, R.L. (ed), George
           Cruikshank: A Revaluation.   Princeton: Princeton
           Univ. Library, 1973-74, 189-211.
19, 561.   Stein, Morris I., & Heinze, Shirley J.   Creativity and the
           Individual.   Summaries of Selected Literature in Psy-
           chology and Psychiatry.   Glencoe, Ill: Free Press,
           1960.

19, 562. Steiner, George. Language and Silence. Essays on Language, Literature and the Inhuman. NY: Atheneum, 1967.

19, 563. _____. Whorf, Chomsky, and the student of literature. In On Difficulty and Other Essays. NY: Oxford Univ. Press, 1978, 137-163; In Wimsatt, W. K. (ed), Literary Criticism: Idea and Act. Berkeley: Univ. California Press, 1974, 242-262.

19, 564. Stern, Alfred. Sartre: His Philosophy and Psychoanalysis. NY: Liberal Arts Press, 1953.

19, 565. Stern, Karl. The Flight from Woman. NY: Farrar, Straus & Giroux, 1965; London: Allen & Unwin, 1966; NY: Noonday, 1965.

19, 566. Stern, Madeleine B. Heads and Headlines: The Phrenological Fowlers. Norman: Univ. Oklahoma Press, 1971.

19, 567. Stockholder, Fred E. A Schopenhauerian reading of Heartbreak House. Shaw Rev, 1976, 19:22-43.

19, 568. Stoehr, Taylor. Hawthorne's Mad Scientists: Pseudoscience and Social Science in Nineteenth-Century Life and Letters. Hamden, Conn: Shoe String, 1978.

19, 569. _____. Physionomy and phrenology in Hawthorne. Huntington Library Q, 1974, 37:355-400.

19, 570. Stone, Alan A., & Stone, Sue S. (eds). The Abnormal Personality Through Literature. Englewood Cliffs, NJ: Prentice-Hall, 1966.

19, 571. Stone, Leo. On the principal obscene word of the English language. Int J Psycho-Anal, 1954, 35:30-56.

19, 572. Stone, Philip J., Dunphy, Dexter C., Smith, Marshall S., & Ogilvie, Daniel M. The General Inquirer: A Computer Approach to Content Analysis. Cambridge: M.I.T. Press, 1966.

19, 573. Stooke, David Edward. The Portrait of the Physician in Selected Prose Fiction of Nineteenth-Century American Authors. DAI, 1977, 37:5130A.

19, 574. Strachey, John. Some unconscious factors in reading. Int J Psycho-Anal, 1930, 11.

19, 575. Strainchamps, Ethel. Our sexist language. In Gornick, V., & Moran, B. K. (eds), Woman in Sexist Society; Studies in Power and Powerlessness. NY: Basic Books, 1971, 240-250.

19, 576. Strandness, Theodore Benson, et al. Language, Form and Idea. NY: McGraw-Hill, 1964.

19, 577. Strout, Cushing. The pluralistic identity of William James: a psycho-historical reading of The Varieties of Religious Experience. Amer Q, 1971, 23:135-152.

19, 578. Strug, Cordell. Seraph, snake, and saint: the subconscious mind in James' Varieties. J Amer Academy Religion, 1974, 42:505-515.

19, 579. Stuchlik, J. [Language neomorphisms in the so-called poetic tongue.] Annales Médico-Psychologiques, 1963, 121:1-11.

19, 580.   Svendsen, Kester, & Mintz, Samuel I.   Relations of liter-
           ature and science.   Selected bibliography for 1953.
           Symposium, 1954, 8:208-213.
19, 581.   Sward, Barbara, & Harris, Dale B.   The reading ease,
           human interest value, and thematic content of St. Nicho-
           las Magazine; a study of children's literature.   J Edu-
           cational Psychology, 1951, 42:153-165.
19, 582.   Sweiger, Jill D.   Conceptions of Children in American
           Juvenile Periodicals: 1830-1870.   DAI, 1977, 37:(12-A)
           7928.
19, 583.   Symonds, John Addington.   A Problem in Modern Ethics:
           Being an Inquiry into the Phenomenon of Sexual Inver-
           sion.   London: 1896.
19, 584.   Szekely, S.   [The problem of tuberculosis in Csehov's
           works.]   Orvosi Hetilap, 1960, 101:853-858.
19, 585.   Szwejcerowa, A.   Molier o medycynie i o lekarzach.   Ar-
           chives History Medicine (Warsaw), 1977, 40:9-16.

19, 586.   Tabori, Paul.   Taken in Adultery.   A Short History of
           Woman's Infidelity Throughout the Ages.   Its Rewards
           and Its Punishments.   NY: Pyramid, 1962.
19, 587.   Taft, Ronald.   A psychological assessment of professional
           actors and related professions.   Genetic Psychol Mono-
           graphs, 1961, 64:309-383.
19, 588.   Takamizu, R.   [Tolstoy's observations on marriage.]
           Zeitschrift für Psychoanalyse (Tokyo), 1939, 7, Nos.
           11-12.
19, 589.   Tannenbaum, Maria Anita G.   Attitudes on Illicit Love in
           Literature from Pagan Latinity to the Christian Middle
           Ages.   DAI, 1977, 37:5806A-07A.
19, 590.   Taschereau, Yves.   Le Portuna: La Médecine dans l'oeu-
           vre de Jacques Ferron.   Montreal: L'Aurore, 1975.
19, 591.   Taylor, Velma L.   An Analysis of Fictional Short Stories
           Found in Current Magazines Read Most Often by Indiana
           High School Students with Reference to Treatment of
           American Social Classes.   Doctoral dissertation, Univ.
           Indiana, 1953.
19, 592.   Tellez Carrasco, P. J.   Las drogas en la literatura.   In
           Int Congress of History Medicine, 24th, Budapest, 1974.
           Acta Budapest, 1976, 1081-1090.
19, 593.   Terman, Louis M., & Lima, Margaret.   Children's Read-
           ing.   NY: Appleton, 1925.
19, 594.   Testenoir, Marie-Louise.   Freud et Vienne en 1900.
           Critique (Paris), 1975, 31:819-836.
19, 595.   Thass-Thienemann, Theodore.   The Subconscious Lan-
           guage.   NY: Washington Square Press, 1967; Review:
           Robert J. Kloss, Lit & Psychol, 1968, 18:233-238.
19, 596.   Theobald, David W.   The imagination and what philosophers
           have to say.   Diogenes, 1966, No. 57, 54-63.
19, 597.   Théordidès, J.   Stendhal du coté de la science.   Aran,
           Switzerland: Grande chene, 1972.

19,598.   Thoenelt, Klaus.   Heinrich Manns Psychologie des Fasch-
           ismus.   Monatshefte, 1971, 63:220-234.
19,599.   Thompson, J. S.   The case against Noam Chomsky and
           B. F. Skinner.   Lit & Ideology, 1972, 11:49-60.
19,600.   Tietze, Thomas R.   The return of Oscar Wilde?   A study
           in automatic writing.   Psychic, 1971, 3(3):26-29.
19,601.   Torgersen, J. H.   [Shakespeare and his physician son-in-
           law (John Hall) in Stratford.]   Tidsskrift för den Norske
           Laegeförening, 1964, 84:1605-1608.
19,602.   Tourney, Garfield.   Empedocles and Freud, Heraclitus and
           Jung.   Bulletin History Medicine, 1956, 30:109-123.
19,603.   Tozzer, Alfred M.   Biography and biology.   Amer Anthro-
           pologist, 1933, 35:418-432.
19,604.   Trautmann, Joanne, & Pollard, Carol (eds).   Literature
           and Medicine: Topics, Titles and Notes.   Hershey,
           Pa: Hershey Medical Center, 1976.
19,605.   Trosman, Harry, & Simmons, Roger D.   The Freud li-
           brary.   JAPA, 1973, 21:646-687.
19,606.   Trotter, W. D., et al.   The stutterer as a character in
           contemporary literature: a bibliography.   J Speech
           Hearing Disorders, 1976, 41:553-554.
19,607.   Tsuchida, K.   Reply to Mr. Kido's critique on my 'Philo-
           sophical study of Japanese literature.'   Japanese J
           Psychol, 1929, 4, No. 1.
19,608.   Twersky, Jacob.   Blindness in Literature.   NY: Ameri-
           can Foundation for the Blind, 1954.
19,609.   Tynan, K.   Dirty books can stay.   In Nobile, P. (ed),
           The New Eroticism.   NY: Random House, 1971.

19,610.   Uitti, Karl D.   Context in language and literature.   Ro-
           mance Philology, 1965, 18:300-315.
19,611.   Ungern Sternberg, I.   Racine reflété par son écriture.
           Paris: Société de graphologie, 1912.
19,612.   Uroff, Margaret D.   The doctors in 'Rappaccini's Daught-
           er.'   Nineteenth Century Fiction, 1972, 27:61-70.
19,613.   Ussery, Huling E.   Chaucer's Physician.   Medicine and
           Literature in 14th Century England.   New Orleans:
           Tulane Univ. Press, 1971.

19,614.   Valesio, Paolo.   The language of madness in the Renais-
           sance.   Yearbook Italian Studies, 1971, 199-234.
19,615.   Various.   Special issue on psychology and style.   Lan-
           guage & Style, 1977, 10(4).
19,616.   Vartaman, Aram.   La Mettrie, Diderot and sexology in
           the Enlightenment.   In Macary, J. (ed), Essays on the
           Age of Enlightenment.   Geneva: Droz, 1977, 347-367.
19,617.   Vash, P. D.   Creative literature for doctors.   New Eng-
           land J Medicine, 1970, 283:1524.
19,618.   Verso, M. L.   The literary doctor.   Victorian History J,
           1976, 47:6-22.
19,619.   Vicari, E. P.   Learning and Imagination in Robert Burton.
           Doctoral dissertation, Univ. Toronto, 1969.

19, 620.   Vicinus, Martha (ed). Suffer and Be Still: Women in the
           Victorian Age. Bloomington: Indiana Univ. Press,
           1972.
19, 621.   Vienot, Pierre (ed). Etudes psychomorphologiques de vis-
           ages; théâtre 1947. Paris: Galliope, 1947.
19, 622.   Vincent, Jewell W. Some influences of Sigmund Freud on
           the 1920's in the United States. Southern Q, 1964, 2:
           138-149.
19, 623.   Virtanen, Reino. Claude Bernard and the history of ideas.
           In Visscher, M. B. , & Grande, F. (eds), Claude Ber-
           nard and Experimental Medicine. Cambridge, Mass:
           Schenkman, 1967.
19, 624.   Vivas, Eliseo. The legacy of Sigmund Freud: philosophi-
           cal. Kenyon Rev, 1940, 2:173-185.
19, 625.   Von der Mühlen, Horst. [A suicidal dialogue.] Zeitschrift
           für klinische Psychologie und Psychotherapie, 1973, 21:
           46-53.
19, 626.   Vuyk, R. Adventure books before and after puberty. Ned-
           erlandsch Tijdschrift voor de Psychologie, 1961, 16:1-
           8.

19, 627.   Waggoner, H. H. Science in the thought of Mark Twain.
           Amer Lit, 1937.
19, 628.   Wagner, Linda Welshimer. The dominance of heredity in
           the characterizations of Henry James. South Dakota
           Rev, 1965, 2:69-77.
19, 629.   Waldrop, Bernard Keith. Aesthetic Uses of Obscenity in
           Literature. DA, 1965, 25:7250.
19, 630.   Walker, L. V. The psychology of sight translation. Clas-
           sical J, 1925, 20:486-488.
19, 631.   Walshe-Brennan, K. S. Psychodynamics of pornography.
           Nursing Mirror, 1976, 142:58-60.
19, 632.   Warnock, Mary. The nature of the mental image: phe-
           nomenology, Sartre and Wittgenstein. In Imagination.
           Berkeley: Univ. California Press, 1976, 131-195.
19, 633.   Warren, Neil. Freudians and Laingians. Encounter,
           1978, 50:56-63.
19, 634.   Washburn, M. F. , Hatt, E. , & Holt, E. B. Affective sen-
           sitiveness in poets and scientific students. Amer J
           Psychol, 1923, 34:105-106.
19, 635.   Wecter, Dixon. Burke's theory concerning words, images,
           and emotion. PMLA, 1940, 55:167-181.
19, 636.   _____. The Hero in America: A Chronicle of Hero
           Worship. NY: Scribner's, 1941.
19, 637.   Weil-Malherbe, Rosanne. Le Temps chronique est une
           réalité physiologique. French Rev, 1971, 44:508-512.
19, 638.   Weinrich, Harald. Eine List der sprachlichen Vernunft.
           Deutsche Akademie für Sprach und Dichtung, 1977, 87-
           92.
19, 639.   Weintraub, Stanley. Medicine and the biographer's art.
           In Peschel, E. R. (ed), Medicine and Literature. NY:
           Watson, 1980, 128-139.

19,640. Weisberger, Charles A.   Accuracy in judging emotional
         expressions as related to understanding of literature.
         J Social Psychol, 1957, 46:253-258.
19,641. Weisman, A. D., & Kastenbaum, R.   The Psychological
         Autopsy.   Community Mental Health J, Monograph No.
         4.   NY: Behavior Publications, 1973.
19,642. Weismann, Donald L.   Language and Visual Form: The
         Personal Record of a Dual Creative Process.   Austin:
         Univ. Texas Press, 1968.
19,643. Weitz, Morris.   Hamlet and the Philosophy of Literary
         Criticism.   Chicago: Univ. Chicago Press, 1964.
19,644. _____. Philosophy in Literature.   Detroit: Wayne
         State Univ. Press, 1963.
19,645. Wellek, Albert.   Der Sprachgeist als Doppelempfinder.   In
         Witz. Lyrik. Sprache.   Beiträge zur Literatur- und
         Sprachtheorie.   Berne: Francke, 1970, 147-150.
19,646. Wellek, René.   Literary criticism and philosophy.   Scrut-
         iny, 1937, 5:375-383; In Bentley, E. (ed), The Impor-
         tance of Scrutiny.   NY: Stewart, 1948, 23-30.
19,647. Werner, Heinz.   On Expressive Language; Papers Pre-
         sented at the Clark University Conference on Expres-
         sive Language Behavior.   Worcester, Mass: Clark
         Univ. Press, 1955.
19,648. Wertham, Frederic.   Dark Legend: A Study in Murder.
         NY: Duell, Sloan & Pearce, 1941.
19,649. West, Michael.   Walden's dirty language: Thoreau and
         Walter Whiter's geocentric etymological theories.
         Harvard Library Bulletin, 1974, 22:117-128.
19,650. Westbrook, Perry D.   Free Will and Determinism in
         American Literature.   Teaneck, NJ: Fairleigh Dickin-
         son Univ. Press, 1979.
19,651. Whyte, Lancelot L.   The Unconscious Before Freud.   NY:
         Basic Books, 1960; Garden City: Doubleday Anchor,
         1962.
19,652. Widmann, R. L.   Trends in computer applications to liter-
         ature.   Computers & the Humanities, 1975, 9:231-235.
19,653. Wilkins, Kay S.   Some aspects of the irrational in 18th
         century France.   In Besterman, T. (ed), Studies on
         Voltaire and the Eighteenth Century.   Banbury, Eng-
         land: Voltaire Foundation, 1975, 107-201.
19,654. Will, Frederic.   Palamas, Lorca, and the question of
         tropes in literature.   In Literature Inside Out.   Aus-
         tin: Univ. Texas Press, 1964, 54-70.
19,655. Willey, Jack R.   The Médico as a Literary Personage in
         the Works of Benito Pérez Gáldos.   DAI, 1970, 30:
         3482A.
19,656. Williams, C. B.   Statistics as an aid to literary studies.
         Science News, 1952, 24:99-106.
19,657. Williams, Don, & Ashby, W. Allen.   City path: following
         in the heart of Don Juan.   Psychoanal Rev, 1978, 65:
         327-344.
19,658. Wilson, D. G.   Imagination and insight.   Proceedings Royal
         Society Medicine, 1971, 64:811-818.

19,659.   Wilson, F. T.   Reading interests of young children.   J
          Genetic Psychol, 1941, 58:363-389.
19,660.   _____.   Stories that are liked by young people.   J
          Genetic Psychol, 1943, 63:55-69.
19,661.   _____.   Young children's favorite stories and charac-
          ters, and their reasons for liking them.   J Genetic
          Psychol, 1943, 63:157-164.
19,662.   Wilson, H.   Milton's reaction to his blindness.   Medical
          History, 1960, 4:186-195.
19,663.   Wilson, Robert A.   Playboy's Book of Forbidden Words.
          Chicago: Playboy Press, 1973.
19,664.   Wisbey, R. A.   (ed).   The Computer in Literary and Lin-
          guistic Research: Papers from a Cambridge Symposi-
          um.   NY: Cambridge Univ. Press, 1972.
19,665.   Wishy, Bernard W.   Images of the American Child in the
          Nineteenth Century.   DA, 1959, 19:2331-2332.
19,666.   Witty, Paul, Coomer, A., & McBean, D.   Children's
          choices of favorite books: a study conducted in the
          elementary schools.   J Educational Psychol, 1946, 37:
          266-278.
19,667.   Wood, Austin B.   Psychodynamics through literature.
          Amer Psychologist, 1955, 10:32-33; Lit & Psychol,
          1954, 4(1):5-7.
19,668.   Wright, Kenneth J. T.   Metaphor and symptom: a study of
          integration and its failure.   Int Rev Psycho-Anal, 1976,
          3:97-108.

19,669.   Young, K.   The psychology of hymns.   J Abnormal Social
          Psychol, 1926, 20:391-406.
19,670.   Young, Philip.   Revolutionary Ladies.   NY: Knopf, 1977.
19,671.   Young, Wayland.   The excluded words.   Evergreen Rev,
          1964, 8:28-32, 90.

19,672.   Zborowski, Mark.   The place of book-learning in tradi-
          tional Jewish culture.   Harvard Educational Rev, 1949,
          19:87-109; In Mead, M., & Wolfenstein, M. (eds),
          Childhood in Contemporary Cultures.   Chicago: Univ.
          Chicago Press, 1955, 118-141.
19,673.   Zeman, F. D.   Life's later years: medical history of old
          age (in Roman literature).   J Mt. Sinai Hospital, 1945,
          11:300-307.
19,674.   Zola, Emile.   The Experimental Novel and Other Essays.
          NY: 1893 (1880).